The Blackwell Companion to Philosophy

SECOND EDITION

Edited by

NICHOLAS BUNNIN

and

E. P. TSUI-JAMES

Blackwell
Publishing

First edition published 1996
Reprinted 1996 (twice), 1998, 1999, 2002

Second edition published 2003

350 Main Street, Malden, MA 02148-5018, USA
108 Cowley Road, Oxford OX4 1JF, UK
550 Swanston Street, Carlton South, Victoria 3053, Australia
Kurfürstendamm 57, 10707 Berlin, Germany

Library of Congress Cataloging-in-Publication Data

The Blackwell companion to philosophy / edited by Nicholas Bunnin and
E. P. Tsui-James. — 2nd ed.
  p. cm. — (Blackwell companions to philosophy)
  Includes bibliographical references and index.
  ISBN 0–631–21907–2 — ISBN 0–631–21908–0 (pbk.)
  1. Philosophy. I. Bunnin, Nicholas. II. Tsui-James, E. P. III. Series.
B21 .B56 2003
100—dc21
                                                            2002023053

A catalogue record for this title is available from the British Library.

Set in 10 on 12½ pt Photina
by SNP Best-set Typesetter Ltd, Hong Kong
Printed and bound in the United Kingdom by T. J. International, Padstow, Cornwall

For further information on
Blackwell Publishing, visit our website:
http://www.blackwellpublishing.com

For Antonia and Oliver Bunnin and Jamie Perry

Contents

Preface to the Second Edition

We thank readers for their gratifying response to the first edition of the Companion. The second edition provides new chapters on Philosophy of Biology; Bioethics, Genethics and Medical Ethics; Environmental Ethics; Business Ethics; Ethnicity, Culture and Philosophy; Plato and Aristotle; Francis Bacon; Nietzsche; Husserl and Heidegger; and Sartre, Foucault and Derrida. There are significant revisions or extensions to chapters on Metaphysics, Philosophy of Language, Philosophy of Mind, Political and Social Philosophy, Philosophy of Religion, Philosophy and Feminism, and Hobbes. The discussion of Descartes, Spinoza and Leibniz is now divided between two chapters, and in a new section Malebranche is considered along with Descartes in the first of these. A longer chapter on Medieval Philosophy replaces the chapter by C. F. J. Martin, who was unavailable to extend his work. We welcome our new contributors and hope that readers will continue to be challenged and delighted by the Companion as a whole.

Nicholas Bunnin
E. P. Tsui-James

Preface to the First Edition

This Companion complements the *Blackwell Companions to Philosophy* series by presenting a new overview of philosophy prepared by thirty-five leading British and American philosophers. Introductory essays by John Searle and Bernard Williams, which assess the changes that have shaped the subject in recent decades, are followed by chapters exploring central problems and debates in the principal subdisciplines of philosophy and in specialized fields, chapters concerning the work of great historical figures and chapters discussing newly developing fields within philosophy. Throughout the course of its chapters, the Companion examines the views of many of the most widely influential figures of contemporary philosophy.

Although wide-ranging, the Companion is not exhaustive, and emphasis is placed on developments in Anglo-American philosophy in the latter part of the twentieth century. A premise underlying the Companion is that major participants in philosophical debate can provide accounts of their own fields that are stimulating, accessible, stylish and authoritative.

In its primary use, the Companion is an innovative textbook for introductory courses in philosophy. Teachers can use the broad coverage to select chapters in a flexible way to support a variety of courses based on contemporary problems or the historical development of the subject. Specialist chapters can be used selectively to augment standard introductory topics or to prepare students individually for term papers or essays. Chapters include initial summaries, boxed features, cross-references, suggestions for further reading, references and discussion questions. In addition, terms are marked for a common glossary. These features and the problem-setting nature of the discussions encourage students to see the subject as a whole and to gain confidence that explorations within philosophy can lead to unexpected and rewarding insights. In this aspect, the Companion reflects the contributors' experience of small group teaching, in which arguments and perspectives are rigorously tested and in which no solution is imposed.

In its secondary use, the Companion will accompany students throughout their undergraduate careers and will also serve the general reader wishing to understand the central concepts and debates within philosophy or its constituent disciplines. Students are unlikely to read the whole volume in their first year of study, but those continuing with philosophy will find their appreciation of the work deepening over time as they gain insight into the topics of the more advanced chapters. The Companion will help them to formulate questions and to see connections between what they have already studied and new terrain.

In its final use, the Companion bears a special relationship to the *Blackwell Companions to Philosophy* series. Many readers will wish to read the integrated discussions of the chapters of the present Companion for orientation before turning to the detailed, alphabetically arranged articles of the volumes in the Companion series. Although conceived as a separate volume, the Companion to Philosophy will serve as a useful guide to the other excellent Companions in what amounts to a comprehensive encyclopedia of philosophy.

The general reader might begin with the introductory essays and turn to chapters on Epistemology, Metaphysics, Ethics and Political and Social Philosophy, or to historical chapters from Ancient Greek Philosophy to Hume. Cross-references and special interests will lead readers to other chapters.

Cross-references in the text are marked in small capitals followed by a chapter number or page numbers in parentheses: ETHICS (chapter 6) or PROBABILITY (pp. 308–11). We have used our judgement in marking terms appearing many times in the text for cross-references, and hope that we have supplied guidance without distracting readers. The Companion also provides a glossary of 210 terms and a comprehensive index. Both appear at the end of the volume, and readers are advised to use them regularly for help in reading the chapters. When an author does not refer to a book by its first edition, a recent publication is cited in the text, and the original date of publication (or in some cases of composition) will appear in square brackets in the references.

As editors, we are fully aware of our good fortune in attracting superb contributors. The complexity of their insights and the clarity of their presentations are the chief attractions of the Companion. We appreciate their care in making the difficult not only accessible but delightful as well. We also wish to thank the Departments of Philosophy at the University of Essex and the University of Hong Kong for their support throughout the preparation of this volume. We are especially grateful to Laurence Goldstein, Tim Moore and Frank Cioffi for their comments and advice. A version of the Companion is published in Chinese by the Shandong Academy of Social Sciences, and we appreciate the friendly co-operation of our Chinese co-editors.

Our cover illustration, R. B. Kitaj's philosophically resonant *If Not, Not*, is a work by an American artist working in London during the period that provides the main focus of our volume.

Nicholas Bunnin
E. P. Tsui-James

Notes on Contributors

David Archard is Reader in Moral Philosophy and Director of the Centre for Ethics, Philosophy and Public Affairs at the University of St Andrews. He is the author of *Sexual Consent* (1998) and co-editor of *The Moral and Political Status of Children: New Essays* (2002).

Thomas Baldwin is Professor of Philosophy at the University of York. He previously taught at the University of Cambridge (where he was Fellow of Clare College) and at Makerere University. He has published *G. E. Moore* (1990) and *Contemporary Philosophy: Philosophy in English since 1945* (2001) in addition to many articles on issues in metaphysics and the philosophy of language.

David Bell is Professor of Philosophy at the University of Sheffield. He is the author of works on Frege, Husserl and Kant. His interests include the foundations of arithmetic, solipsism and the nature and origins of the analytic tradition.

Rebecca Bennett is Lecturer in Bioethics at the Centre for Social Ethics and Policy, School of Law, University of Manchester. She edited (with Charles Erin) *HIV and AIDS: Testing, Screening and Confidentiality* (1999).

Robert Bernasconi is Moss Professor of Philosophy at the University of Memphis. He is the author of *The Question of Language in Heidegger's History of Being* (1985) and *Heidegger in Question* (1993) as well as numerous articles on Hegel and on twentieth-century European philosophy. He has edited collections of essays on Derrida and on Levinas and most recently *Race* (2001).

Simon Blackburn is Professor of Philosophy at the University of Cambridge. A former editor of the journal *Mind*, he has written *Ruling Passions* (1998), *Spreading the Word* (1984), *Essays in Quasi Realism* (1993) and *The Oxford Dictionary of Philosophy* (1994). His current work concerns problems of realism and its alternatives as they have emerged in historical and contemporary work.

Lesley Brown is Tutorial Fellow in Philosophy, Somerville College, University of Oxford. She has written on Plato, especially his metaphysics and epistemology, and on ancient philosophy of language.

Nicholas Bunnin is Director of the Philosophy Project at the Institute for Chinese Studies, University of Oxford and previously taught at the University of Glasgow and the University of Essex. He compiled (with Jiyuan Yu) the *Dictionary of Western Philosophy: English–Chinese* (2001) and edited (with Chung-ying Cheng) *Contemporary Chinese Philosophy* (2002). His main interests are in metaphysics, the philosophy of mind and political philosophy.

Taylor Carman is Assistant Professor of Philosophy at Barnard College, Columbia University. He is co-editor of *The Cambridge Companion to Merleau-Ponty* (forthcoming) and the author of *Heidegger's Analytic: Interpretation, Discourse, and Authenticity in 'Being and Time'* (forthcoming), and of other articles on Husserl, Heidegger, and Merleau-Ponty.

David E. Cooper is Professor of Philosophy at the University of Durham and Director of the Durham Institute of Comparative Ethics. His books include *Metaphor* (1986), *Existentialism: A Reconstruction* (2nd revd edn 2000), *World Philosophies: An Historical Introduction* (2nd revd edn 2002) and *The Measure of Things: Humanism, Humility and Mystery* (2002).

Martin Davies is Professor of Philosophy in the Research School of Social Sciences, Australian National University. He was formerly Wilde Reader in Mental Philosophy at the University of Oxford. He has published widely in the areas of philosophy of language, mind and psychology.

Georges Enderle is Arthur and Mary O'Neil Professor of International Business Ethics at the University of Notre Dame. His books include *Business Students Focus on Ethics* (1993), translated into Portuguese (1997) and Chinese (2001).

Charles A. Erin is Senior Lecturer in Applied Philosophy and Fellow of the Institute of Medicine, Law and Bioethics at the University of Manchester. He has written widely on topics in bioethics and edited (with Rebecca Bennett) *HIV and AIDS: Testing, Screening and Confidentiality* (1999).

Richard Francks is Director of Undergraduate Studies in Philosophy at the University of Leeds. His main interests are in epistemology, the history of philosophy and the philosophy of history.

Miranda Fricker is Lecturer in Philosophy at Birkbeck College, University of London and was previously Lecturer in Philosophy and British Academy Postdoctoral Fellow at Heythrop College, University of London. She has published articles in epistemology, ethics and social philosophy, and edited (with Jennifer Hornsby) *The Cambridge Companion to Feminism in Philosophy* (2000). Her current work focuses on the idea of an ethics of epistemic practice.

Sebastian Gardner is Reader in Philosophy at University College, London. He is the author of *Irrationality and the Philosophy of Psychoanalysis* (1993) and *Kant and the Critique of Pure Reason* (1999). His interests lie in aesthetics, psychoanalysis and the history of philosophy.

Stephen Gaukroger is Professor of History of Philosophy and History of Science at the University of Sydney. He is the author of *Explanatory Structures* (1978), *Cartesian Logic* (1989), *Descartes: An Intellectual Biography* (1995), *Francis Bacon and the Transformation of Early Modern Philosophy* (2000) and *Descartes' System of Natural Philosophy* (2001). He has also edited four collections of essays and published translations of Descartes and Arnaud.

Jorge J. E. Gracia is a State University of New York Distinguished Professor and holds the Samuel F. Capon Chair in the Department of Philosophy, State University of New York, University at Buffalo. He has written widely on medieval philosophy, metaphysics, philosophical historiography, philosophy of language and philosophy in Latin America. His books include *Introduction to the Problem of Individuation in the Early Middle Ages* (2nd revd edn 1988), *Individuality: An Essay on the Foundations of Metaphysics* (1988), *Philosophy and Its History: Issues in Philosophical Historiography* (1992), *A Theory of Textuality: The Logic and Epistemology* (1995), *Texts: Ontological Status, Identity, Author, Audience* (1996) and *Metaphysics and Its Task: The Search for the Categorical Foundation of Knowledge* (1999).

A. C. Grayling is Reader in Philosophy at Birkbeck College, London, and Supernumerary Fellow at St Anne's College, Oxford. Among his books are *An Introduction to Philosophical Logic* (3rd edn 1992), *The Refutation of Scepticism* (1985), *Berkeley: The Central Arguments* (1986), *Wittgenstein* (1988), *Russell* (1993), *Moral Values* (1998), *The Quarrel of the Age* (2000) and *The Meaning of Things* (2001). He has edited *Philosophy: A Guide Through the Subject* (1995) and *Philosophy: Further Through the Subject* (1998).

Jean Grimshaw taught Philosophy and Women's Studies at the University of the West of England, Bristol. She is the author of *Feminist Philosophers: Women's Perspectives on Philosophical Traditions* (1986) and a number of articles, mainly on feminism and philosophy. She has edited (with Jane Arthurs) *Women's Bodies: Discipline and Transgression* (1999).

Gary Gutting is Professor of Philosophy at the University of Notre Dame. He is the author of *Religious Belief and Religious Skepticism* (1982), *Michel Foucault's Archaeology of Knowledge* (1989) and *French Philosophy in the Twentieth Century* (2001).

Susan Haack formerly Professor of Philosophy at the University of Warwick, currently Professor of Philosophy at the University of Miami, is the author of *Deviant Logic* (1974), *Philosophy of Logic* (1978), *Evidence and Inquiry: Towards Reconstruction in Epistemology* (1993) and *Manifesto of a Passionate Moderate: Unfashionable Essays* (1998). Her main areas of interest are the philosophy of logic and language, epistemology and metaphysics and pragmatism. She is a past President of the Charles Peirce Society.

John Haldane is Professor of Philosophy and formerly Director of the Centre for Philosophy and Public Affairs at the University of St Andrews. He has published widely in the philosophy of mind, the philosophy of value and the history of philosophy. He is co-author with J. J. C. Smart of *Atheism and Theism* (1996) in the Blackwell Great Debates in Philosophy series.

John Harris is Sir David Alliance Professor of Bioethics, Institute of Medicine, Law and Bioethics, University of Manchester. He is a member of the United Kingdom Human Genetics Commission and of the Ethics Committee of the British Medical Association. He was a Founder Director of the International Association of Bioethics and a founder member of the Board of the journal *Bioethics*. Among his books are *The Value of Life* (1985) and *Clones, Genes and Immortality* (1998) (a revised edition of *Wonderwoman and Superman*, 1992), and he is editor of *Bioethics* (2001) in the Oxford Readings in Philosophy series.

Ross Harrison teaches philosophy at the University of Cambridge, where he is also a Fellow of King's College. Among his publications are *Bentham* (1983), *Democracy* (1993) and (as editor and contributor) *Henry Sidgwick* (2001).

Martin Hollis was Professor of Philosophy at the University of East Anglia, Norwich. He specialized in the philosophy of social science, especially in topics to do with rationality. Among his books are *Models of Man* (1977), *The Cunning of Reason* (1987), *The Philosophy of Social Science* (1994), *Reason in Action* (1995), *Trust Within Reason* (1998) and *Pluralism and Liberal Neutrality* (1999). The last two volumes were published after his untimely death in 1998.

Søren Holm is Professor of Clinical Bioethics at the University of Manchester. He is the author of *Ethical Problems of Clinical Practice: The Ethical Reasoning of Health Care Professionals* (1997) and has edited (with Inez de Beaufort and Medard Hilhorst) *In the Eye of the Beholder: Ethics and Medical Change of Appearance* (1996) and (with John Harris) *The Future Of Human Reproduction: Ethics, Choice and Regulation* (1998).

Michael Inwood is Tutorial Fellow in Philosophy at Trinity College, Oxford. He has published several books on Hegel. His other interests include ancient philosophy and Heidegger. He is especially interested in the interconnections between Greek and German philosophy.

Peter Jones was Professor of Philosophy and Director of the Institute for Advanced Studies in the Humanities at the University of Edinburgh. He is the author of numerous works, including *Hume's Sentiments* (1982).

Robin Le Poidevin is Professor of Metaphysics at the University of Leeds, where he was Head of the School of Philosophy 1988–2001. He is the author of *Change, Cause and Contradiction: A Defence of the Tenseless Theory of Time* (1991) and *Arguing for Atheism: An Introduction to the Philosophy of Religion* (1996) and has edited *Questions of Time and Tense* (1998) and (with Murray MacBeath) *The Philosophy of Time* (1993).

William G. Lycan is William Rand Kenan, Jr Professor of Philosophy at the University of North Carolina. He has published a number of books, including *Consciousness* (1987), *Judgement and Justification* (1988) and *Consciousness and Experience* (1996). He is the editor of *Mind and Cognition* (1990). His interests are in the philosophy of mind, the philosophy of language and epistemology.

A. W. Moore is Tutorial Fellow in Philosophy at St Hugh's College, Oxford. He is the author of *The Infinite* (2nd edn 2001) and *Points of View* (1997). He has also edited two collections of essays: *Meaning and Reference* (1993) and *Infinity* (1993).

Richard Norman is Professor of Moral Philosophy at the University of Kent. His publications include *The Moral Philosophers* (1983), *Free and Equal* (1987) and *Ethics, Killing and War* (1995).

David Papineau is Professor of Philosophy of Science at King's College, London. He has published widely in epistemology, the philosophy of mind and the philosophy of science. His books include *Reality and Representation* (1987), *Philosophical Naturalism* (1993), *Introducing Consciousness* (2000) and *Thinking About Consciousness* (2002).

David Pears is Emeritus Professor of Philosophy at the University of Oxford. His most recent publications are *The False Prison: A Study in the Development of Wittgenstein's Philosophy* (2 vols, 1987 and 1988) and *Hume's System: An Examination of Book I of the Treatise* (1991). His other interests include entomology and the visual arts.

Leon Pompa was Professor of Philosophy at the University of Birmingham. His research interests include the history of philosophy and the philosophy of history. He has published a number of articles on the problems of fact, value and narrative in history and on Descartes, Vico, Kant, Hegel, Marx, Collingwood and Wittgenstein. He co-edited with W. H. Dray *Substance and Form in History: Essays in Philosophy of History* (1981), was editor and translator of *Vico: A Study of the 'New Science'* (2nd edn 1990) and is the author of *Human Nature and Historical Knowledge: Hume, Hegel and Vico* (1990).

Howard Robinson is Professor of Philosophy, Central European University, Budapest. He was previously Soros Professor of Philosophy at the Eötvös Loránd University, Budapest and Reader in Philosophy at the University of Liverpool. His main interests are in the philosophy of mind and in idealism. He is the author of *Matter and Sense* (1982) and *Perception* (1994), and co-author (with John Foster) of *Essays on Berkeley* (1985). He edited *Objections to Physicalism* (1991) and is currently editing Berkeley's *Principles* and *Three Dialogues* for Oxford University Press's World Classics series.

Holmes Rolston, III is University Distinguished Professor and Professor of Philosophy at Colorado State University. He has written seven books, most recently *Genes, Genesis and God* (1999), *Philosophy Gone Wild* (1986), *Environmental Ethics* (1988), *Science and Religion: A Critical Survey* (1987) and *Conserving Natural Value* (1994). He gave the Gifford Lectures, University of Edinburgh, 1997–8, has lectured on seven continents, is featured in Joy A. Palmer's (ed.) *Fifty Key Thinkers on the Environment* and is past and founding president of the International Society for Environmental Ethics.

George MacDonald Ross is Senior Lecturer in the Department of Philosophy at the University of Leeds and Director of the Philosophical and Religious Studies Subject Centre of the Learning and Teaching Support Network. He has written extensively on Leibniz and other seventeenth- and eighteenth-century philosophers, and is the author of *Leibniz* (1984).

R. M. Sainsbury is Stebbing Professor of Philosophy at King's College, London and was editor of the journal *Mind* for several years until 2000. He has published *Russell* (1979), *Paradoxes* (1995) and *Logical Forms* (2000). His main interests are in philosophical logic and the philosophy of language.

John R. Searle is Mills Professor of Mind and Language at the University of California where he has been a faculty member since 1959. Before that, he was a lecturer at Christ Church, Oxford, and he received all his university degrees from Oxford. Most of his work is in the philosophy of mind, the philosophy of language, and social philosophy. His most recently published books are *Rationality in Action* (2001) and *Mind, Language and Society* (1998). He is the author of several other important books, including *Speech Acts: An Essay in the Philosophy of Language* (1969), *Expression and Meaning: Studies in the Theory of Speech Acts* (1985), *Intentionality* (1983), *Minds, Brains and Science, the 1984 Reith Lectures* (1989), *The Rediscovery of Mind* (1992) and *The Construction of Social Reality* (1995).

N. E. Simmonds is a Fellow of Corpus Christi College, Cambridge where he lectures in law. His interests include the philosophy of law and political philosophy. He has published *The Decline of Judicial Reason* (1984), *Central Issues in Jurisprudence* (1986) and numerous articles on the philosophy of law.

John Skorupski is Professor of Moral Philosophy at the University of St Andrews. He is the author of *John Stuart Mill* (1989) and *English-Language Philosophy 1750–1945* (1993). His most recent book is *Ethical Explorations* (1999).

Elliott Sober is Hans Reichenbach Professor and Henry Vilas Research Professor at the University of Wisconsin, Madison and Centennial Professor at the London School of Economics. He is the author of *The Nature of Selection* (1984), *Reconstructing the Past* (1988), *Philosophy of Biology* (1993) and (with David S. Wilson) *Unto Others: Evolution and Psychology of Unselfish Behaviour* (1988).

Tom Sorell is Professor of Philosophy at the University of Essex. He is the author of *Hobbes* (1986), *Descartes* (1987), *Moral Theory and Capital Punishment* (1987), *Scientism* (1991), (with John Hendry) *Business Ethics* (1994) and *Moral Theory and Anomaly* (2000). He is the editor of *The Rise of Modern Philosophy* (1993), *The Cambridge Companion to Hobbes* (1995), *Health Care, Ethics, and Insurance* (1998), *Descartes* (1999), and (with John Rogers) *Hobbes and History* (2000).

Charles Taliaferro is Professor of Philosophy at St Olaf College, Northfield, Minnesota and the author of *Consciousness and the Mind of God* (1994), *Contemporary Philosophy of Religion* (1999) and the co-editor of *A Companion to Philosophy of Religion* (1998).

Mary Tiles is Professor of Philosophy at the University of Hawaii at Manoa. Her interests include the history and philosophy of mathematics, science and technology and their interactions with culture (European and Chinese). She has published *Living in a Technological Culture* (with Hans Oberdiek) (1995), *An Introduction to Historical Epistemology* (with James Tiles) (1993), *Mathematics and the Image of Reason* (1991) and *Bachelard: Science and Objectivity* (1984).

Eric P. Tsui-James studied as a postgraduate at Oriel College, Oxford. He taught philosophy at St Hilda's College, Oxford, for two years before moving to the University of Hong Kong in 1990. He has published work on the metaphysics of mathematics, but his research interests now centre around the work of William James, especially the nineteenth-century psychological and physiological contexts of his radical empiricism.

Robert Wardy teaches philosophy and classics at St Catharine's College, Cambridge. He has published in the fields of ancient Greek philosophy and rhetoric, Latin literature, the philosophy of language and Chinese philosophy.

Bernard Williams is Monroe Deutsch Professor of Philosophy, University of California, Berkeley, and was White's Professor of Moral Philosophy and a Fellow of Corpus Christi College, Oxford. His works include *Morality* (1972), *Problems of the Self* (1973), *Descartes: The Project of Pure Enquiry* (1978), *Moral Luck* (1981), *Ethics and the Limits of Philosophy* (1985), *Shame and Necessity* (1993) and *Making Sense of Humanity* (1995).

R. S. Woolhouse is Professor of Philosophy at the University of York. He is the author of *Locke's Philosophy of Science and Knowledge* (1971), *Locke* (1983), *The Empiricists* (1988) and *Descartes, Spinoza, Leibniz: The Concept of Substance in Seventeenth-Century Philosophy* (1993).

Contemporary Philosophy in the United States

JOHN R. SEARLE

Philosophy as an academic discipline in America has considerably fewer practitioners than do several other subjects in the humanities and the social sciences, such as sociology, history, English, or economics; but it still shows enormous diversity. This variety is made manifest in the original research published by professional philosophers, whose differing points of view are expressed in the large number of books published each year, as well as in the many professional philosophy journals. There are over two thousand colleges and universities in the United States, of which nearly all have philosophy departments, and the number of professional philosophers is correspondingly large.

Because of this diversity, any generalizations about the discipline as a whole, which I am about to make, are bound to be misleading. The subject is too vast and complex to be describable in a single essay. Furthermore, anyone who is an active participant in the current controversies, as I am, necessarily has a perspective conditioned by his or her own interests, commitments and convictions. It would be impossible for me to give an 'objective' account. I am not therefore in what follows trying to give a neutral or disinterested account of the contemporary philosophical scene; rather I am trying to say what in the current developments seems to me important.

In spite of its enormous variety, there are certain central themes in contemporary American philosophy. The dominant mode of philosophizing in the United States is called 'analytic philosophy'. Without exception, the best philosophy departments in the United States are dominated by analytic philosophy, and among the leading philosophers in the United States, all but a tiny handful would be classified as analytic philosophers. Practitioners of types of philosophizing that are not in the analytic tradition – such as phenomenology, classical pragmatism, existentialism, or Marxism – feel it necessary to define their position in relation to analytic philosophy. Indeed, analytic philosophy is the dominant mode of philosophizing not only in the United States, but throughout the entire English-speaking world, including Great Britain, Canada, Australia and New Zealand. It is also the dominant mode of philosophizing in Scandinavia, and it is also becoming more widespread in Germany, France, Italy and throughout Latin America. I personally have found that I can go to all of these parts of the world and lecture on subjects in contemporary analytic philosophy before audiences who are both knowledgeable and well trained in the techniques of the discipline.

1 Analytic Philosophy

What, then, is analytic philosophy? The simplest way to describe it is to say that it is primarily concerned with the analysis of meaning. In order to explain this enterprise and its significance, we need first to say a little bit about its history. Though the United States now leads the world in analytic philosophy, the origins of this mode of philosophizing lie in Europe. Specifically, analytic philosophy is based on the work of Gottlob Frege, Ludwig Wittgenstein, Bertrand Russell and G. E. Moore, as well as the work done by the logical positivists of the Vienna Circle in the 1920s and 1930s. Going further back in history, one can also see analytic philosophy as a natural descendant of the empiricism of the great British philosophers Locke, Berkeley and Hume, and of the transcendental philosophy of Kant. In the works of philosophers as far back as Plato and Aristotle, one can see many of the themes and presuppositions of the methods of analytic philosophy. We can best summarize the origins of modern analytic philosophy by saying that it arose when the empiricist tradition in epistemology, together with the foundationalist enterprise of Kant, were tied to the methods of logical analysis and the philosophical theories invented by Gottlob Frege in the late nineteenth century. In the course of his work on the foundations of mathematics, Frege invented symbolic logic in its modern form and developed a comprehensive and profound philosophy of language. Though many of the details of his views on language and mathematics have been superseded, Frege's work is crucial for at least two reasons. Firstly, by inventing modern logic, specifically the predicate calculus, he gave us a primary tool of philosophical analysis; and, secondly, he made the philosophy of language central to the entire philosophical enterprise. From the point of view of analytic philosophy, Frege's work is the greatest single philosophical achievement of the nineteenth century. Fregean techniques of logical analysis were later augmented by the ordinary language analysis inspired by the work of Moore and Wittgenstein and are best exemplified by the school of linguistic philosophy that flourished in Oxford in the l950s. In short, analytic philosophy attempts to combine certain traditional philosophical themes with modern techniques.

Analytic philosophy has never been fixed or stable, because it is intrinsically self-critical and its practitioners are always challenging their own presuppositions and conclusions. However, it is possible to locate a central period in analytic philosophy – the period comprising, roughly speaking, the logical positivist phase immediately prior to the 1939–45 war and the postwar phase of linguistic analysis. Both the prehistory and the subsequent history of analytic philosophy can be defined by the main doctrines of that central period.

In the central period, analytic philosophy was defined by a belief in two linguistic distinctions, combined with a research programme. The two distinctions are, firstly, that between analytic and synthetic propositions, and, secondly, that between descriptive and evaluative utterances. The research programme is the traditional philosophical research programme of attempting to find foundations for such philosophically problematic phenomena as language, knowledge, meaning, truth, mathematics and so on.

One way to see the development of analytic philosophy over the past thirty years is to regard it as the gradual rejection of these two distinctions, and a corresponding rejection of foundationalism as the crucial enterprise of philosophy. However, in the central period, these two distinctions served not only to identify the main beliefs of analytic philosophy, but, for those who accepted them and the research programme, they defined the nature of philosophy itself.

1.1 Analytic versus synthetic

The distinction between analytic and synthetic propositions was supposed to be the distinction between those propositions that are true or false as a matter of definition or of the meanings of the terms contained in them (the analytic propositions) and those that are true or false as a matter of fact in the world and not solely in virtue of the meanings of the words (the synthetic propositions). Examples of analytic truths would be such propositions as 'Triangles are three-sided plane figures', 'All bachelors are unmarried', 'Women are female', '2 + 2 = 4' and so on. In each of these, the truth of the proposition is entirely determined by its meaning; they are true by the definitions of the words that they contain. Such propositions can be known to be true or false *a priori*, and in each case they express necessary truths. Indeed, it was a characteristic feature of the analytic philosophy of this central period that terms such as 'analytic', 'necessary', '*a priori*' and 'tautological' were taken to be co-extensive. Contrasted with these were synthetic propositions, which, if they were true, were true as a matter of empirical fact and not as a matter of definition alone. Thus, propositions such as 'There are more women than men in the United States', 'Bachelors tend to die earlier than married men' and 'Bodies attract each other according to the inverse square law' are all said to be synthetic propositions, and, if they are true, they express *a posteriori* empirical truths about the real world that are independent of language. Such empirical truths, according to this view, are never necessary; rather, they are contingent. For philosophers holding these views, the terms '*a posteriori*', 'synthetic', 'contingent' and 'empirical' were taken to be more or less co-extensive.

It was a basic assumption behind the logical positivist movement that all meaningful propositions were either analytic or empirical, as defined by the conceptions that I have just stated. The positivists wished to build a sharp boundary between meaningful propositions of science and everyday life on the one hand, and nonsensical propositions of metaphysics and theology on the other. They claimed that all meaningful propositions are either analytic or synthetic: disciplines such as logic and mathematics fall within the analytic camp; the empirical sciences and much of common sense fall within the synthetic camp. Propositions that were neither analytic nor empirical propositions, and which were therefore in principle not verifiable, were said to be nonsensical or meaningless. The slogan of the positivists was called the verification principle, and, in a simple form, it can be stated as follows: all meaningful propositions are either analytic or synthetic, and those which are synthetic are empirically verifiable. This slogan was sometimes shortened to an even simpler battle cry: the meaning of a proposition is just its method of verification.

3

1.2 The distinction between evaluative utterances and descriptive utterances

Another distinction, equally important in the positivist scheme of things, is the distinction between those utterances that express propositions that can be literally either true or false and those utterances that are used not to express truths or falsehoods, but rather, to give vent to our feelings and emotions. An example of a descriptive statement would be, 'The incidence of crimes of theft has increased in the past ten years'. An instance of the evaluative class would be 'Theft is wrong'. The positivists claimed that many utterances that had the form of meaningful propositions were used not to state propositions that were verifiable either analytically or synthetically, but to express emotions and feelings. Propositions of ethics look as if they are cognitively meaningful, but they are not; they have only 'emotive' or 'evaluative' meaning. The propositions of science, mathematics, logic and much of common sense fall in the descriptive class; the utterances of aesthetics, ethics and much of religion fall in the evaluative class. It is important to note that on this conception evaluative propositions are not, strictly speaking, either true or false, since they are not verifiable as either analytic or empirical. The two distinctions are crucially related in that all of the statements that fall on one side or the other of the analytic–synthetic distinction also fall within the descriptive class of the descriptive–evaluative distinction.

The importance that these two distinctions had for defining both the character of the philosophical enterprise and the relationships between language and reality is hard to exaggerate. One radical consequence of the distinction between descriptive and evaluative propositions was that certain traditional areas of philosophy, such as ethics, aesthetics and political philosophy, were virtually abolished as realms of cognitive meaningfulness. Propositions in these areas were, for the most part, regarded as nonsensical expressions of feelings and emotions, because they are not utterances that can be, strictly speaking, either true or false. Since the aim of philosophers is to state the truth, and since evaluative utterances cannot be either true or false, it cannot be one of the aims of philosophy to make any evaluative utterances. Philosophers might analyse the meaning of evaluative terms, and they might examine the logical relationships among these terms, but philosophers, *qua* philosophers, can make no first-order evaluations in aesthetics, ethics or politics, as these first-order evaluations are not, strictly speaking, meaningful. They may have a sort of secondary, derivative meaning, called 'emotive meaning', but they lack scientifically acceptable cognitive meaning.

If the task of philosophy is to state the truth and not to provide evaluations, what then is the subject matter of philosophy? Since the methods of philosophers are not those of empirical science – since their methods are *a priori* rather than *a posteriori* – it cannot be their aim to state empirical truths about the world. Such propositions are the propositions of the special sciences. The aim of philosophers, therefore, is to state analytic truths concerning logical relations among the concepts of our language. In this period of philosophy, the task of philosophy was taken to be the task of conceptual analysis. Indeed, for most philosophers who accepted this view, philosophy and conceptual analysis were the same. Where traditional philosophers had taken their task to be the discussion of the nature of the good, the true, the beautiful and the just, the positivist and post-positivist analytic philosophers took their task to be the analysis of the meaning of concepts such as 'goodness', 'truth', 'beauty' and 'justice'. Ideally the analysis of these and other philosophically interesting concepts, such as 'knowledge', 'certainty' and 'cause', should give necessary and sufficient conditions for the application of these concepts. They saw this as being the legitimate heir of the traditional philosophical enterprise, but an heir purged of the metaphysical nonsense and confusion that had discredited the traditional enterprise.

If we combine the assumption that philosophy is essentially a conceptual, analytic enterprise with the assumption that its task is foundational – that is, its task is to provide secure foundations for such things as knowledge – then the consequence for the positivists is that philosophical analysis tends in large part to be reductive. That is, the aim of the analysis is to show, for example, how empirical knowledge is based on, and ultimately reducible to, the data of our experience, to so-called sense data. (This view is called 'phenomenalism'.) Similarly, statements about the mind are based on, and therefore ultimately reducible to, statements about external behaviour (behaviourism). Necessary truth is similarly based on conventions of language as expressed in definitions (conventionalism); and mathematics is based on logic, especially set theory (logicism). In each case, the more philosophically puzzling phenomenon is shown to have a secure foundation in some less puzzling phenomenon, and indeed, the ideal of such analysis was to show that the puzzling phenomena could be entirely reduced to less puzzling phenomena. 'Phenomenalism' supposedly gave science a secure foundation because science could be shown to be founded on the data of our senses. Since the form of the reduction was analytic or definitional, it had the consequence that statements about empirical reality could be translated into statements about sense data. Similarly, according to behaviourism, statements about mental phenomena could be translated into statements about behaviour.

Within the camp of analytic philosophers who thought the aim of philosophy was conceptual analysis, there were two broad streams. One stream thought ordinary language was in general quite adequate, both as a tool and as a subject matter of philosophical analysis. The other stream thought of ordinary language as hopelessly inadequate for philosophical purposes, and irretrievably confused. The philosophers of this latter stream thought that we should use the tools of modern mathematical logic both for analysing traditional philosophical problems and, more importantly, for creating a logically perfect language, for scientific and philosophical purposes, in which certain traditional confusions could not even arise. There was never a rigid distinction between these two streams, but there were certainly two broad trends: one which emphasized ordinary language philosophy and one which emphasized symbolic logic. Both streams, however, accepted the central view that the aim of philosophy was conceptual analysis, and that in consequence philosophy was fundamentally different from any other discipline; they thought that it was a second-order discipline analysing the logical structure of language in general, but not dealing with first-order truths about the world. Philosophy was universal in subject matter precisely because it had no special subject matter other than the discourse of all other disciplines and the discourse of common sense.

A further consequence of this conception was that philosophy became essentially a linguistic or conceptual enterprise. For that reason, the philosophy of language was

5

absolutely central to the philosophical task. In a sense, the philosophy of language was not only 'first philosophy'; all of philosophy became a form of philosophy of language. Philosophy was simply the logical investigation of the structure of language as it was used in the various sciences and in common life.

2 The Rejection of These Two Distinctions and the Rejection of Foundationalism

Work done in the 1950s and 1960s led to the overcoming of these two distinctions; and with the rejection of these two distinctions came a new conception of analytic philosophy – a conception that emerged in the 1970s and 1980s and which is still being developed. The rejection of these two distinctions and of the foundationalist research programme led to an enormous upheaval in the conception of the philosophical enterprise and in the practice of analytic philosophers. The most obvious problem with traditional analytic philosophy was that the reductionist enterprise failed. In every case, the attempts to provide reductionist analyses of the sort proposed by the phenomenalists and behaviourists were unsuccessful, and by 1960 the lack of success was obvious. A series of important theoretical developments also took place at this time, but for the sake of simplicity I shall concentrate on only five of these: Quine's rejection of the analytic–synthetic distinction, Austin's theory of speech acts, Wittgenstein's criticism of foundationalism, Rawls's work in political philosophy and the changes in the philosophy of science due to Kuhn and others.

2.1 Quine's attack on the analytic–synthetic distinction

Perhaps the most important criticism of the analytic–synthetic distinction was made by W. V. O. Quine in a famous article entitled 'Two dogmas of empiricism' (Quine 1953). In this article, Quine claimed that no adequate, non-circular definition of analyticity had ever been given. Any attempt to define analyticity had always been made using notions that were in the same family as analyticity, such as synonymy and definition, and consequently, the attempts to define analyticity were invariably circular. However, an even more important objection that emerged in Quine's article was this: the notion of an analytic proposition is supposed to be a notion of a proposition that is immune to revision, that is irrefutable. Quine claimed that there were no propositions that were immune to revision, that any proposition could be revised in the face of recalcitrant evidence, and that any proposition could be held in the face of recalcitrant evidence, provided that one was willing to make adjustments in other propositions originally held to be true. Quine argued that we should think of the language of science as being like a complex network that was impinged upon by empirical verification only at the edges. Recalcitrant experiences at the edges of science can produce changes anywhere along the line, but the changes are not forced on us by purely logical considerations; rather, we make various pragmatic or practical adjustments in the network of our sentences or beliefs to accommodate the ongoing character of our experiences. Language, on this view, is not atomistic. It does not consist of a set of propositions, each of which can be assessed in isolation. Rather, it consists of a holistic network, and, in this network, propositions as groups confront experience; propositions individually are not simply assessed as true or false. (This holism of scientific discourse was influenced by the French philosopher of science, Duhem, and the view is frequently referred to as 'the Duhem–Quine thesis'.)

Most philosophers today accept some version or other of Quine's rejection of the analytic–synthetic distinction. Not everybody agrees with his actual argument (I, for one, do not), but now there is general scepticism about our ability to make a strict distinction between those propositions that are true by definition and those that are true as a matter of fact. The rejection of the analytic–synthetic distinction has profound consequences for analytic philosophy, as we shall see in more detail later.

At this point it is important to state that if there is no well-defined class of analytic propositions, then the philosopher's propositions cannot themselves be clearly identified as analytic. The results of philosophical analysis cannot be sharply distinguished from the results of scientific investigation. On the positivist picture, philosophy was not one among other sciences; rather, it stood outside the frame of scientific discourse and analysed the logical relations between, on the one hand, that discourse and its vocabulary and, on the other, experience and reality. Philosophers, so to speak, analysed the relation between language and reality, but only from the side. If we accept Quine's rejection of the analytic–synthetic distinction, then philosophy is not something that can be clearly demarcated from the special sciences. It is, rather, adjacent to, and overlaps with, other disciplines. Although philosophy is more general than other disciplines, its propositions do not have any special logical status or special logical priority with regard to the other disciplines.

2.2 Austin's theory of speech acts

The British philosopher J. L. Austin was suspicious of both the distinction between analytic and synthetic propositions, and the distinction between evaluative and descriptive utterances. During the 1950s he developed an alternative conception of language (Austin 1962). His first observation was that there is a class of utterances that are obviously perfectly meaningful, but which do not even set out to be either true or false. A man who says, for example, 'I promise to come and see you' or a qualified authority who says to a couple, 'I pronounce you man and wife' is neither reporting on nor describing a promise or a marriage respectively. Such utterances should be thought not as cases of describing or stating, but rather as doing, as acting. Austin baptized these utterances 'performatives' and contrasted them with 'constatives'. The distinction between constatives and performatives was supposed to contain three features: constatives, but not performatives, could be true or false; performatives, on the other hand, though they could not be true or false, could be felicitous or infelicitous, depending on whether or not they were correctly, completely and successfully performed; and finally, performatives were supposed to be actions, doings or performances, as opposed to mere sayings or statings. But, as Austin himself saw, the distinctions so drawn did not work. Many so-called performatives turned out to be capable of being true or false; for example, warnings could be either true or false. And statements, as well as performatives, could be infelicitous. For example, if one made a statement for which one had insufficient evidence, one would have made an infelicitous statement. And finally, stating is as much performing an action as promising or ordering or apologizing. The abandonment of the performative–constative distinction led Austin to a general theory of speech acts. Communicative utterances in general are actions of a type he called 'illocutionary acts'.

One great merit of Austin's theory of speech acts is that it enabled subsequent philosophers to construe the philosophy of language as a branch of the philosophy of action. Since speech acts are as much actions as any other actions, the philosophical analysis of language is part of the general analysis of human behaviour. And since intentional human behaviour is an expression of mental phenomena, it turns out that the philosophy of language and the philosophy of action are really just different aspects of one larger area, namely, the philosophy of mind. On this view, the philosophy of language is not 'first philosophy'; it is a branch of the philosophy of mind. Though Austin did not live to carry out the research programme implicit in his initial discoveries, subsequent work, including my own, has carried this research further.

By treating speaking as a species of intentional action we can give a new sense to a lot of old questions. For example, the old question, 'How many kinds of utterances are there?' is too vague to be answered. But if we ask 'How many kinds of illocutionary acts are there?', we can give a precise answer, since the question asks, 'How many possible ways are there for speakers to relate propositional contents to reality in the performance of actions that express illocutionary intentions?' An analysis of the structure of those intentions reveals five basic types of illocutionary act: we tell people how things are (Assertives), we try to get them to do things (Directives), we commit ourselves to doing things (Commissives), we express our feelings and attitudes (Expressives) and we bring about changes in the world through our utterances, so that the world is changed to match the propositional content of the utterance (Declarations). (For details see Searle 1979 and 1983.)

2.3   Wittgenstein's rejection of foundationalism

The single most influential analytic philosopher of the twentieth century, and indeed, the philosopher whom most analytic philosophers would regard as the greatest philosopher of the century, is Ludwig Wittgenstein.

Wittgenstein published only one short book during his lifetime, which represents his early work, but with the posthumous publication of his *Philosophical Investigations* in 1953, a series of his later writings began to become available. Now, we have a sizeable corpus of the work he did in the last twenty years of his life. Through painstaking analysis of the use of language, particularly through analysis of psychological concepts, Wittgenstein attempted to undermine the idea that philosophy is a foundational enterprise. He asserted, on the contrary, that philosophy is a purely descriptive enterprise, that the task of philosophy is neither to reform language nor to try to place the various uses of language on a secure foundation. Rather, philosophical problems are removed by having a correct understanding of how language actually functions.

A key notion in Wittgenstein's conception of language is the notion of a language game. We should think of the words in language as being like the pieces in a game. They are not to be understood by looking for some associated idea in the mind, or by following some procedure of verification, or even by looking at the object for which they stand.

Rather, we should think of words in terms of their use, and referring to objects in the world is only one of many uses that words have. The meaning of a word is given by its use, and the family of uses that a group of words has constitutes a language game. Examples include the language game we play in describing our own sensations, or the language game we play in identifying the causes of events. This conception of language leads Wittgenstein to the rejection of the conception that the task of philosophical analysis is reductionist or foundationalist. That is, Wittgenstein rejects the idea that language games either have or need a foundation in something else, and he rejects the idea that certain language games can be reduced to certain other kinds of language games. The effect, Wittgenstein says, of philosophical analysis is not to alter our existing linguistic practices or to challenge their validity; it is simply to describe them. Language neither has nor needs a foundation in the traditional sense.

I said that Wittgenstein was the single most influential philosopher in the analytic tradition, but there is a sense in which it seems to me he has still not been properly understood, nor had his lessons been fully assimilated by analytic philosophers. I will have more to say about his influence later.

2.4   Rawls's theory of justice

The conception of moral philosophy in the positivist and post-positivist phases of analytic philosophy was extremely narrow. Strictly speaking, according to the positivists, moral utterances could not be either true or false, so there was nothing that the philosopher could say, *qua* philosopher, by way of making moral judgements. The task for the moral philosopher was to analyse moral discourse, to analyse the meaning and use of moral terms such as 'good', 'ought', 'right', 'obligation', etc. It is important to see that this conception of moral philosophy was a strict logical consequence of the acceptance of the distinction between evaluative and descriptive utterances. For if evaluative utterances cannot be either true or false, and if first-order moral discourse consists in evaluative utterances, and if the task of the philosopher is to state the truth, it follows that the philosopher, *qua* philosopher, cannot make any first-order moral judgements. As a philosopher, all he or she can do is the second-order task of analysing moral concepts.

Some philosophers of the positivist and post-positivist periods rejected this narrow conception of moral philosophy, and there were a series of attacks mounted on the distinction between evaluative and descriptive utterances, including some attacks by myself in the mid-1960s (Searle 1964). It remained, however, for John Rawls to reopen the traditional conception of political and moral philosophy with the publication of his book *A Theory of Justice* in 1971. For the purposes of the present discussion, the important thing about Rawls's work was not that he refuted the traditional dichotomy of descriptive and evaluative utterances, but that he simply ignored it and proceeded to develop a theory of political institutions of a sort that has a long philosophical tradition and which the positivists thought they had overcome. Rawls, in effect, revived the social contract theory, which had long been assumed to be completely defunct; but he did it by an ingenious device: he did not attempt, as some traditional theorists had done, to show that there might have been an original social contract, nor did he try to show that the participation of individuals in society involved a tacit contract. Rather, he used the following thought experiment as an analytic tool: think of the sort of society that rational beings would agree to if they did not know what sort of position they themselves would occupy in that society. If we imagine rational beings, hidden behind a veil of ignorance, who are asked to select and agree on forms of social institutions that would be fair for all, then we can develop criteria for appraising social institutions on purely rational grounds.

The importance of Rawls for our present discussion is not whether he succeeded in developing new foundations for political theory, but the fact that his work gave rise to a renewed interest in political philosophy, which was soon accompanied by a renewed interest in the traditional questions of moral philosophy. Moral and political philosophy had been confined to a very small realm by the positivist philosophers, and for that reason seemed sterile and uninteresting. Very little work was done in that area, but since the 1970s it has grown enormously, and is now a flourishing branch of analytic philosophy.

2.5   Post-positivist philosophy of science

Throughout the positivist period the model of empirical knowledge was provided by the physical sciences, and the general conception was that the empirical sciences proceeded by the gradual but cumulative growth of empirical knowledge through the systematic application of scientific method. There were different versions of scientific method, according to the philosophers of that period, but they all shared the idea that scientific, empirical propositions are essentially 'testable'. Initially a proposition was thought testable if it could be confirmed, but the most influential version of this idea is Popper's claim that empirical propositions are testable if they are falsifiable in principle. That is, in order for a proposition to tell us how the world is as opposed to how it might be or might have been, there must be some conceivable state of affairs that would render that proposition false. Propositions of science are, strictly speaking, never verifiable – they simply survive repeated attempts at falsification. Science is in this sense fallible, but it is at the same time rational and cumulative.

This picture of the history of science was very dramatically challenged in Thomas Kuhn's book *The Structure of Scientific Revolutions* (1962). According to Kuhn, the history of science shows not a gradual and steady accumulation of knowledge but periodic revolutionary overthrows of previous conceptions of reality. The shift from Aristotelian physics to Newtonian physics, and the shift from Newtonian physics to relativistic physics are both illustrations of how one 'paradigm' is replaced by another. When the burden of puzzling cases within one paradigm becomes unbearable, a new paradigm emerges, which provides not just a new set of truths but a whole new way of looking at the subject matter. 'Normal sciences' always proceed by puzzle-solving within a paradigm, but revolutionary breakthroughs, rather than puzzle-solving within a paradigm, are matters of overthrowing one paradigm and replacing it with another.

Just as Kuhn challenged the picture of science as essentially a matter of a steady accumulation of knowledge, so Paul Feyerabend challenged the conception of there being a unitary rational 'scientific method' (Feyerabend 1975). Feyerabend tried to show that the history of science reveals not a single rational method but rather a series of opportunistic, chaotic, desperate (and sometimes even dishonest) attempts to cope with immediate problems. The lesson that Feyerabend draws from this is that we should abandon the constraining idea of there being such a thing as a single, rational method that applies everywhere in science; rather, we should adopt an 'anarchistic' view, according to which 'anything goes'. Reactions to Kuhn and Feyerabend, not surprisingly, differ enormously among analytic philosophers. Kuhn sometimes seems to be arguing that there is not any such thing as the real world existing independently of our scientific theories, which it is the aim of our scientific theories to represent. Kuhn, in short, seems to be denying realism. Most philosophers do not take this denial of realism at all seriously. Even if Kuhn were right about the structure of scientific revolutions, this in no way shows that there is no independent reality that science is investigating. Again, most philosophers would accept Feyerabend's recognition of a variety of methods used in the history of science, but very few people take seriously the idea that there are no rational constraints on investigation whatever. Nonetheless, the effect of these authors has been important in at least the following respect. The positivists' conception of science as a steady accumulation of factual knowledge, and of the task of the philosopher as the conceptual analysis of scientific method, has given way to an attitude to science that is at once more sceptical and more activist. It is more sceptical in the sense that few philosophers are looking for the one single method that pervades every enterprise called 'science', but it is more activist in the sense that philosophy of science interacts more directly with scientific results. For example, recent philosophical discussions about quantum mechanics, or about the significance of Bell's theorem within quantum mechanics, reveal that it is now impossible to say exactly where the problem in physics ends and the problem in philosophy begins. There is a steady interaction and collaboration between philosophy and science on such philosophically puzzling questions.

3   Some Recent Developments

The results of the changes that I have just outlined are to make analytic philosophy on the one hand a more interesting discipline, but on the other hand a much less well-defined research project. In the way that the verification principle formed the core ideology of the logical positivists and in the way that the conceptual analysis formed the core research project of the post-positivistic analytic philosopher, there is now no ideological point of reference that is commonly agreed upon; nor is there a universally accepted research programme. For example, conceptual analysis thirty years ago was taken to be the heart of analytic philosophy, but now many philosophers would deny that it is the central element in the philosophical enterprise. Some philosophers, indeed, would say that the traditional enterprise of attempting to find logically necessary and sufficient conditions for the applicability of a concept is misconceived in principle. They think the possibility of such an enterprise has been refuted by Quine's refutation of the analytic–synthetic distinction, as well as Wittgenstein's observation that many philosophically puzzling concepts have not a central core or essence of meaning, but a variety of different uses united only by a 'family resemblance'. Many other philosophers would say that conceptual analysis is still an essential part of the philosophical enterprise, as indeed it has been since the time of Plato's dialogues, but it is no longer seen to be the whole of the enterprise. Philosophy is now, I believe, a much more interesting subject than it was a generation ago because it is no longer seen as something separate from, and sealed off from, other disciplines. In particular, philosophy is now seen by most analytic philosophers as being adjacent to and overlapping with the sciences. My own view, which I feel is fairly widely shared, is that words like 'philosophy' and 'science' are in many respects misleading, if they are taken to imply the existence of mutually exclusive forms of knowledge. Rather, it seems to me that there is just knowledge and truth, and that in intellectual enterprises we are primarily aiming at knowledge and truth. These may come in a variety of forms, whether in history, mathematics, physics, psychology, literary criticism or philosophy. Philosophy tends to be more general than other subjects, more synoptic in its vision, more conceptually or logically oriented than other disciplines, but it is not a discipline that is hermetically sealed off from other subjects. The result is that many areas of investigation which were largely ignored by analytic philosophers a generation ago have now become thriving branches of philosophy, including cognitive science, the philosophy of biology and the philosophy of economics. In what follows, I will confine my discussion to five major areas of philosophical research: cognitive science, the causal theory of reference, intentionalistic theories of meaning, truth-conditional theories of meaning, and Wittgenstein's conception of language and mind and his response to scepticism.

3.1 Philosophy and cognitive science

Nowhere is the new period of collaboration between philosophy and other disciplines more evident than in the new subject of cognitive science. Cognitive science from its very beginnings has been 'interdisciplinary' in character, and is in effect the joint property of psychology, linguistics, philosophy, computer science and anthropology. There is, therefore, a great variety of different research projects within cognitive science, but the central area of cognitive science, its hardcore ideology, rests on the assumption that the mind is best viewed as analogous to a digital computer. The basic idea behind cognitive science is that recent developments in computer science and artificial intelligence have enormous importance for our conception of human beings. The basic inspiration for cognitive science went something like this: human beings do information processing. Computers are designed precisely to do information processing. Therefore one way to study human cognition – perhaps the best way to study it – is to study it as a matter of computational information processing. Some cognitive scientists think that the computer is just a metaphor for the human mind; others think that the human mind is literally a computer program. But it is fair to say that without the computational model there would not have been a cognitive science as we now understand it.

This conception of human cognition was ideally suited to the twentieth-century analytic tradition in philosophy of mind because of the analytic tradition's resolute materialism. It was anti-mentalistic and anti-dualistic. The failure of logical behaviourism led not to a revival of dualism but to more sophisticated versions of materialism. I will now briefly summarize some of the recent developments in materialistic philosophies of mind that led to the computational theory of the mind.

The logical behaviourists' thesis was subject to many objections, the most important being the objection that it ignores internal mental phenomena. In science and common sense it seems more natural to think of human behaviour as being caused by internal mental states rather than to think of the mental states as simply consisting of the behaviour. This weakness in behaviourism was corrected by the materialist identity thesis, sometimes called 'physicalism'. According to the physicalist identity theory, mental states are identical with states of the brain. We do not know in detail what these identities are, but the progress of the neurosciences makes it seem overwhelmingly probable that every mental state will be discovered to be identical with some brain state. In the early version of the identity thesis it was supposed that every type of mental state would be discovered to be identical with some type of physical state, but after some debate this began to seem more and more implausible. There is no reason to suppose that only systems with neurons like ours can have mental states; indeed, there is no reason to suppose that two human beings who have the same belief must therefore be in the same neurophysiological state. So, 'type–type identity theory' naturally gave way to 'token–token identity theory'. The token identity theorists claimed that every particular mental state is identical with some particular neurophysiological state, even if there is no type correlation between types of mental states and types of physical states. But that only leaves open the question, 'What is it that two different neurophysiological states have in common if they are both the same mental state?' To many analytic philosophers it seemed obvious that the answer to our question must be that two neurophysiological states are the same type of mental state if they serve the same function in the overall ecology of the organism. Mental states on this view can be defined in terms of their causal relations to input stimuli, to other mental states, and to external behaviour. This view is called 'functionalism' and it is a natural development from token–token identity theory.

However, the functionalist has to answer a further obvious question: 'What is it about the states that gives them the causal relations that they do have?' If mental states are defined in terms of their causal relations, then what is it about the structure of different neurophysiological configurations that can give them the same causal relations? It is at precisely this point that the tradition of materialism in analytic philosophy converges with the tradition of artificial intelligence. The computer provides an obvious answer to the question that I have just posed. The distinction between the software and the hardware, the program and the physical system that implements the program, provides a model for how functionally equivalent elements at a higher level can be realized in or implemented by different physical systems at a lower level. Just as one and the same program can be implemented by quite different physical hardware systems, so one and the same set of mental processes can be implemented in different neurophysiological or other forms of hardware implementations. Indeed, on the most extreme version of this view, the mind is to the brain as the program is to the hardware. This sort of functionalism came to be called 'computer functionalism' or 'Turing machine functionalism', and it coincides with the strong version of 'artificial intelligence' (Strong AI), the version that says having a mind just is having a certain sort of program.

I have refuted Strong AI in a series of articles (Searle 1980a, 1980b). The basic idea of that refutation can be stated quite simply. Minds cannot be equivalent to programs because programs are defined purely formally or syntactically and minds have mental contents. The easiest way to see the force of the refutation is to see that a system, say oneself, could learn to manipulate the formal symbols for understanding a natural

13

language without actually understanding that language. I might have a program that enables me to answer questions in Chinese simply by matching incoming symbols with the appropriate processing and output symbols, but nonetheless I still would not thereby understand Chinese. However, though the project of computer functionalism is almost certainly a failure, the results of the enterprise are in many respects quite useful. Important things can be learned about the mind by pursuing the computer metaphor, and the research effort has not necessarily been wasted. The most exciting recent development has been to think of mental processes not on the model of the conventional serial digital computer, but rather to think of brain processes on the model of parallel distributed processing computers. The most exciting recent development, in my view, in cognitive science has been the development of such 'neural net models' for human cognition.

In concluding this section, I want to point out that in my view the chief weakness of analytical philosophy of mind, a weakness it shares with the past 300 years in the philosophy of mind, has been its assumption that there is somehow an inconsistency between mentalism and materialism. Analytic philosophers, along with the rest of the Cartesian tradition, have characteristically assumed that 'mental' implies 'non-material' or 'immaterial' and that 'material' or 'physical' implies 'non-mental'. But if one reflects on how the brain works, it seems that both of these assumptions are obviously false. What that shows is that our whole vocabulary, our whole terminology of the mental and physical, needs wholesale revision.

3.2   The causal theory of reference

A central question in analytic philosophy of language, since Frege (and indeed in philosophy since the time of Plato), has been: How does language relate to the world? How do words hook on to things? In answering this question, the analytic tradition had characteristically found a connection between the notion of reference and the notion of truth. An expression, such as a proper name, refers to or stands for or designates an object because associated with that name is some descriptive content, some concept of the object in question, and the object in question satisfies or fits that descriptive content. The expression refers to the object only because the description is true of the object. This is the standard reading of Frege's famous distinction between sense and reference, between Sinn and Bedeutung. Expressions refer to objects in virtue of their sense and the sense provides a description, a 'mode of presentation', of the object in question. Something analogously applies with general terms: general terms are true of an object because each general term has associated with it a cluster of features, and the term will be true of the object if the object in question has those features.

In the 1970s this conception of the relation between language and reality was attacked by a number of philosophers, most prominently Donnellan (1970), Kripke (1972) and Putnam (1975). A variety of arguments were mounted against the traditional conception of meaning and reference, but the common thread running through these arguments was that the descriptive content associated with a word provided neither necessary nor sufficient conditions for its application. A speaker might refer to an object even though the associated description that he or she had was not true of that object; a speaker might have a description that was satisfied by an object even though that was not the object to which he or she was referring. The most famous version of this argument was Putnam's 'twin earth' example. Imagine a planet in a distant galaxy exactly like ours in every respect except that on this planet what they call 'water' has a different chemical composition. It is not composed of H_2O but has an extremely complicated formula that we will abbreviate as 'XYZ'. Prior to 1750, prior to the time that anyone knew the chemical composition of water, the people on twin earth had in their minds exactly the same concept of water as the people on earth. Nonetheless our word 'water' does not refer to the stuff on twin earth. Our word 'water', whether or not we knew it in 1750, refers to H_2O; and this is a matter of objective causal relations in the world which are independent of the ideas that people have in their heads. Meanings on this view are not concepts in people's heads, but objective relations in the world. Well, if associated ideas are not sufficient for meaning, what is? The answer given by the three authors I have mentioned is that there must be some sort of causal connection between the use of the word and the object or type of entity in the world that it applies to. Thus, if I use the word 'Socrates', it refers to a certain Greek philosopher only because there is a causal chain connecting that philosopher and my current use of the word. The word 'water' is not defined by any checklist of features; rather, 'water' refers to whatever stuff in the world was causally related to certain original uses of the word 'water', and these uses subsequently came to be accepted in the community and were then passed down through a causal chain of communication.

There is a very natural way of connecting the computer functionalist conception of the mind with the causal theory of reference. If the mind were a computer program, and if meaning were a matter of causal connections to the world, then the way the mind acquires meanings is for the system that implements the computer program to be involved in causal interactions with the world.

3.3   Intentionalistic theories of meaning

Much of the best work in speech act theory done after the publication of Austin's *How to Do Things with Words* in 1962, and my *Speech Acts* in 1969, attempted to combine the insights of Paul Grice's account of meaning with the framework provided by the theory of speech acts. In a series of articles beginning in the late 1950s (Grice 1957, 1968), Grice had argued that there is a close connection between the speaker's intentions in the performance of an utterance and the meaning of that utterance. In his original formulation of this view, Grice analysed the speaker's meaning in terms of the intention to produce an effect on the hearer by means of getting the hearer to recognize the intention to produce that very effect. Thus, for example, according to Grice, if a speaker intends to tell a hearer that it is raining, then in the speaker's utterance of the sentence, 'It is raining', the speaker's meaning will consist of his or her intention to produce in the hearer the belief that it is raining by means of getting the hearer to recognize his or her intention to produce that very belief. Subsequent work by Grice altered the details of this account, but the general principle remained the same: meaning is a matter of a self-referential intention to produce an effect on a hearer by getting the hearer to recognize the intention to produce that effect. Grice combined this analysis of meaning with an analysis of certain principles of conversational cooperation. In conversation, people accept certain tacit principles, which Grice calls

'Maxims of Conversation' – they accept the principles that the speaker's remarks will be truthful and sincere (the maxim of quality), that they will be relevant to the conversational purposes at hand (the maxim of relation), that the speaker will be clear (the maxim of manner) and that the speaker will say neither more nor less than is necessary for the purposes of the conversation (the maxim of quantity).

There has been a great deal of controversy about the details of Grice's analysis of meaning, but the basic idea that there is a close connection between meaning and intention has been accepted and has proved immensely useful in analysing the structure of certain typical speech act phenomena. My own view is that Grice confuses that part of meaning which has to do with representing certain states of affairs and certain illocutionary modes, and that part of meaning that has to do with communicating those representations to a hearer. Grice, in short, confuses communication with representation. However, the combination of an intentionalistic account of meaning, together with rational principles of co-operation, is immensely fruitful in analysing such problems as those of 'indirect speech acts' and figurative uses of language such as metaphors. So, for example, in an indirect speech act, a speaker will characteristically mean something more than what he or she actually says. To take a simple example, in a dinner table situation a speaker who says 'Can you pass the salt?' would usually not just be asking a question about the salt-passing abilities of the hearer; he or she would be requesting the hearer to pass the salt. Now the puzzle is this: how is it that speakers and hearers communicate so effortlessly when there is a big gulf between what the speaker means and what he or she actually says? In the case of metaphor, a similar question arises: how does the speaker communicate so effortlessly his or her metaphorical meaning when the literal meaning of the sentence uttered does not encode that metaphorical meaning? A great deal of progress has been made on these and other problems using the apparatus that Grice contributed to the theory of speech acts.

One of the marks of progress in philosophy is that the results of philosophical analysis tend to be appropriated by other disciplines, and this has certainly happened with speech act theory. Speech act theory is now a thriving branch of the discipline of linguistics, and the works of Austin and Grice, as well as my own, are as well known among linguists as they are among philosophers.

3.4   Truth-conditional theories of meaning

Philosophers such as Quine and his former student, Donald Davidson, have always felt that intentionalistic theories of meaning of the sort proposed by Grice and Searle were philosophically inadequate, because the intentionalistic notions seemed as puzzling as the notion of meaning itself and because they could necessarily involve linguistic meaning in their ultimate analyses. So Quine and Davidson attempted to give accounts of meaning that did not employ the usual apparatus of intentionality. The most influential version of this attempt is Davidson's project of analysing meaning in terms of truth conditions. The basic idea is that one knows the meaning of a sentence if one knows under what conditions it is true or false. Thus, one knows the meaning of the German sentence 'Schnee ist weiss' if one knows that it is true if and only if snow is white. Now since a theory of meaning for a language should be able to state the meaning of each of the sentences of the language, and since the meanings of the sentences of the language are given by truth conditions, and since truth conditions can be specified independently of the intentionalistic apparatus, it seems to Davidson that a theory of truth (that is, a theory of the truth conditions of the sentences) of a language would provide a theory of meaning for that language.

In order to carry out the project of explaining meaning in terms of truth, Davidson employs the apparatus of Tarski's semantic definition of truth, a definition that Tarski had worked out in the 1930s. Tarski points out that it is a condition of adequacy on any account of truth that for any sentence s and any language L, the account must have the consequence that

s is true in L if and only if p,

where for s can be substituted the structural description of any sentence whatever, for L, the name of the language of which s is a part, and for p, the sentence itself or a translation of it. Thus, for example, in English, the sentence 'Snow is white' is true if and only if snow is white. This condition is usually called 'convention T' and the corresponding sentences are called 'T-sentences'.

Now Davidson notes that convention T employs the fact that the sentence named by s has the same meaning as the sentence expressed by p, and thus Tarski is using the notion of meaning in order to define the notion of truth. Davidson proposes to turn this procedure around by taking the notion of truth for granted, by taking it as a primitive, and using it to explain meaning.

Here is how it works. Davidson hopes to get a theory of meaning for a speaker of a language that would be sufficient to interpret any of the speaker's utterances by getting a theory that would provide a set of axioms which would entail all true T-sentences for that speaker's language. Thus, if the speaker speaks German, and we use English as a meta-language in which to state the theory of the speaker's language, Davidson claims we would have an adequate theory of the speaker's language if we could get a set of axioms which would entail a true T-sentence stated in English for any sentence that the speaker uttered in German. Thus, for example, our theory of meaning should contain axioms which entail that the speaker's utterance 'Schnee ist weiss' is true in the speaker's language if and only if snow is white. Davidson further claims that we could make this into an empirical theory of the speaker's language by proceeding to associate the speaker's utterances with the circumstances in which we had empirical evidence for supposing that the speaker held those utterances to be true. Thus, if we hear the speaker utter the sentence 'Es regnet', we might look around and note that it was raining in the vicinity, and we might then form the hypothesis that the speaker holds true the sentence 'Es regnet' when it is raining in his or her immediate vicinity. This would provide the sort of empirical data on which we would begin to construct a theory of truth for the speaker's language.

It is important to note that we are to think of this as a thought experiment and not as an actual procedure that we have to employ when we try to learn German, for example. The idea is to cash out the notion of meaning in terms of truth conditions, and then cash out the notion of truth conditions in terms of a truth theory for a language, which is a theory that would entail all the true T-sentences of the language. The empirical basis on which the whole system rests is that of the evidence we could get concerning the conditions under which a speaker holds a sentence to be true. If the project could in principle be carried out, then we would have given an account of meaning which employed only one intentionalistic notion, the notion of 'holding true' a sentence.

Over the past twenty years there has been quite an extensive literature on the nature of this project and how it might be applied to several difficult and puzzling sorts of sentences – for example, indexical sentences, sentences about mental states or modal sentences. Enthusiasm for this project seems to have waned somewhat in recent years.

In my view, the central weakness of Davidson's enterprise is as follows: any theory of meaning must explain not only what a speaker represents by his or her utterances, but also how he or she represents them, under what mental aspects the speaker represents truth conditions. For this reason, a theory of meaning cannot just correlate a speaker's utterance with states of affairs in the world; it must explain what is going on in the speaker's head which enables the speaker to represent those states of affairs under certain aspects with the utterances that the speaker makes. Thus, for example, suppose that snow is composed of H_2O molecules in crystalline form, and suppose the colour white consists of light wave emissions of all wavelengths, then the sentence 'Schnee ist weiss' is true if and only if H_2O molecules in crystalline form emit light of all wavelengths. Now this second T-sentence is just as empirically substantiated as the earlier example, 'Schnee ist weiss' is true if and only if snow is white. Indeed, it is a matter of scientific necessity that the state of affairs described by the former is identical with the state of affairs described by the latter. But the former example simply does not give the speaker's meaning. The speaker might hold true the sentence 'Schnee ist weiss' under these and only these conditions and not know the slightest thing about H_2O molecules and wavelengths of light. The T-sentence gives the truth conditions, but the specification of the truth conditions does not necessarily give the meaning of the sentence, because the specification does not yet tell us how the speaker represents those truth conditions. Does he or she represent them under the aspect of snow being white, or what is the same fact in the world, does he or she represent them under the aspect of frozen H_2O crystals emitting light of all wavelengths? Any theory that cannot give that information is not a theory of meaning.

There are various attempts to meet these sorts of objections, but, in my view, they are not successful. In the end, all truth definitional accounts of meaning, like the behaviourist accounts which preceded them, end up with a certain 'indeterminacy' of meaning. They cannot account in objective terms for all of the subjective details of meaning, and both Davidson and Quine have acknowledged that their views result in indeterminacy.

3.5 Wittgenstein's legacy

Wittgenstein's work covers such a vast range of topics, from aesthetics to mathematics, and covers these topics with so much depth and insight, that it continues to be a source of ideas and inspiration for analytic philosophers and is likely to continue to be so for many years to come. I will mention only three areas.

3.5.1 Philosophical psychology

One of Wittgenstein's main areas of research was that of psychological concepts such as belief, hope, fear, desire, want, expect and sensation concepts such as pain and seeing. Perhaps his single most controversial claim in this area is that concerning a private language. He claims that it would be logically impossible for there to be a language that was private in the sense that its words could only be understood by the speaker because they referred to the speaker's private inner sensations and had no external definition. Such a language would be absurd, he said, because for the application of such words there would be no distinction between what seemed right to the speaker and what really was right. But unless we can make a distinction between what seems right and what really is right, we cannot speak of right or wrong at all, and hence we cannot speak of using a language at all. 'An inner process', says Wittgenstein (1953), 'stands in need of outward criteria'. Wittgenstein is here attacking the entire Cartesian tradition, according to which there is a realm of inner private objects, our inner mental phenomena, and the meanings of the words that stand for these entities are entirely defined by private ostensive definitions. No other single claim of Wittgenstein's has aroused as much controversy as the 'private language argument'. It continues to be a source of fascination to contemporary philosophers, and many volumes have been written about Wittgenstein's analysis of psychological concepts.

3.5.2 Following a rule

Wittgenstein is part of a long tradition that emphasizes the distinction between the modes of explanation of the natural sciences and the modes of explanation of human behaviour and human cultural and psychological phenomena generally. His analysis of this problem chiefly deals with the phenomenon of human behaviour which is influenced or determined by mental contents, and, most importantly, by the phenomena of human beings following a rule. What is it for a human being to follow a rule? Wittgenstein's analysis of this stresses the difference between the way that rules guide human behaviour and the way that natural phenomena are results of causes. Wittgenstein throughout emphasizes the difference between causes and reasons, and he also emphasizes the roles of interpretation and rule following. On the most extreme interpretation of Wittgenstein's remarks about following a rule, he is the proponent of a certain type of scepticism. According to one view of Wittgenstein, he is arguing that rules do not determine their own application, that anything can be interpreted to accord with a rule, and consequently that anything can be interpreted to conflict with a rule. If taken to its extreme, this argument would have the consequence that, logically speaking, rules do not constrain human behaviour at all. And if that is right, then mental contents, such as knowledge of meanings of words or principles of action or even beliefs and desires, do not constrain human behaviour, because they are everywhere subject to an indefinite range of different interpretations. Wittgenstein's solution to this scepticism is to propose that interpretation comes to an end when we simply accept the cultural practices of the community in which we are imbedded. Interpretation comes to an end, and we just act on a rule. Acting on a rule is a practice, and it is one that we are brought up to perform in our culture. The sceptical implications of Wittgenstein's account of rule following are resolved by an appeal to a naturalistic solution: we are simply the sort of beings who follow culturally and biologically conditioned practices.

This interpretation of Wittgenstein is largely due to Saul Kripke (1982) and it has aroused considerable controversy. My own view is that Kripke has misinterpreted Wittgenstein in certain crucial respects, but whether or not his interpretation is correct, it has been a source of continuing discussion in contemporary philosophy.

3.5.3   Philosophical scepticism

Important work on philosophical scepticism has been continued by philosophers who are inspired or provoked by Wittgenstein, notably Thomson Clarke and Barry Stroud. These philosophers point out that a really serious analysis of our use of epistemic discourse shows that the problem of scepticism cannot be simply overcome by the usual analytic philosopher's methods of pointing out that the sceptic raises the demand for justification beyond that which is logically appropriate. Clarke and Stroud claim that the problem of scepticism goes deeper than this solution will allow. Following Wittgenstein in investigating the depth grammar of language, they find that any solution to the sceptic's predicament – that is, any justification for our claims to have knowledge about the world – rests on a much deeper understanding of the difference between ordinary or plain discourse and philosophical discourse. Work in this line of research is continuing at present.

4   Overall Assessment

I have not attempted to survey all of the main areas of activity in contemporary analytic philosophy. Most importantly, I have left out contemporary work in ethics. Perhaps of comparable importance, I have had nothing to say about purely technical work in logic. There is, furthermore, a thriving branch of analytic philosophy called 'action theory', which should be mentioned at least in passing. The general aim of analytic action theory is to analyse the structure of human actions in terms of the causal relations between such mental states as beliefs, desires and intentions, and the bodily movements which are in some sense constitutive of the actions. Finally, it is worth calling attention to the fact that among analytic philosophers there has been a great revival of interest in the history of philosophy. Traditional analytic philosophers thought of the history of philosophy as mostly the history of mistakes. Some of the history of the subject could be useful for doing real philosophy; but the overall conception was that the history of philosophy had no more special relevance to philosophy than the history of mathematics to mathematics, or the history of chemistry to chemistry. This attitude has changed recently, and there is now a feeling of the historical continuity of analytic philosophy with traditional philosophy in a way that contrasts sharply with the original view of analytic philosophers, who thought that they marked a radical, or indeed, revolutionary break with the philosophical tradition.

It is too early to provide an assessment of the contribution that will be made by work done in philosophy at the present time, or even in the past few decades. My own view is that the philosophy of mind and social philosophy will become ever more central to the entire philosophical enterprise. The idea that the study of language could replace the study of mind is itself being transformed into the idea that the study of language is really a branch of the philosophy of mind. Within the philosophy of mind, perhaps the key notion requiring analysis is that of intentionality – that property of the mind by which it is directed at or about or of objects and states of affairs in the world independent of itself. Most of the work done by analytic philosophers in the philosophy of mind has tended to cluster around the traditional mind–body problem. My own view is that we need to overthrow this problem: in its traditional version, it was based on the assumption that mental properties and physical properties were somehow different from each other, and that therefore, there was some special problem not like other problems in biology as to how they could both be characteristics of the human person. Once we see that so-called mental properties really are just higher-level physical properties of certain biological systems, I believe this problem can be dissolved. Once it is dissolved, however, we are still left with the task of analysing what is the central problem in the philosophy of language and in cognitive science, as well as the philosophy of mind, namely, the way that human representational capacities relate the human organism to the world. What are called 'language', 'mind', 'thinking', 'speaking' and 'depicting' are just different aspects of this mode of relating to reality.

I believe that the causal theory of reference will be seen to be a failure once it is recognized that all representations must occur under some aspect or other, and that the extensionality of causal relations is inadequate to capture the aspectual character of reference. The only kind of causation that could be adequate to the task of reference is intentional causation or mental causation, but the causal theory of reference cannot concede that ultimately reference is achieved by some mental device, since the whole approach behind the causal theory was to try to eliminate the traditional mentalism of theories of reference and meaning in favour of objective causal relations in the world. My prediction is that the causal theory of reference, though it is at present by far the most influential theory of reference, will prove to be a failure for these reasons.

Perhaps the single most disquieting feature of analytic philosophy in the fifty-year period that I have been discussing is that it has passed from being a revolutionary minority point of view held in the face of traditionalist objections to becoming itself the conventional, establishment point of view. Analytic philosophy has become not only dominant but intellectually respectable, and, like all successful revolutionary movements, it has lost some of its vitality in virtue of its very success. Given its constant demand for rationality, intelligence, clarity, rigour and self-criticism, it is unlikely that it can succeed indefinitely, simply because these demands are too great a cost for many people to pay. The urge to treat philosophy as a discipline that satisfies emotional rather than intellectual needs is always a threat to the insistence on rationality and intelligence. However, in the history of philosophy, I do not believe we have seen anything to equal the history of analytic philosophy for its rigour, clarity, intelligence and, above all, its intellectual content. There is a sense in which it seems to me that we have been living through one of the great eras in philosophy.

References

Austin, J. L. 1962: *How to do Things with Words*. Oxford: Clarendon Press.
Donnellan, K. 1970: Proper Names and Identifying Descriptions. *Synthèse*, 21, 335–58.
Feyerabend, P. 1975: *Against Method*. London: Humanities Press.
Grice, H. P. 1957: Meaning. *Philosophical Review*, 66.

—— 1968: Utterer's Meaning, Sentence-Meaning, and Word-Meaning. *Foundations of Language*, 4, 1–18.

Kripke, S. 1972: Naming and Necessity. In G. Harman and D. Davidson (eds) *Semantics of Natural Language*, Dordrecht: Reidel.

—— 1982: *Wittgenstein on Rules and Private Language*. Cambridge, MA: Harvard University Press.

Kuhn, T. 1962: *The Structure of Scientific Revolutions*. Chicago: University of Chicago Press.

Putnam, H. 1975: The Meaning of 'Meaning'. In his *Philosophical Papers, Vol. 2: Mind, Language and Reality*, Cambridge: Cambridge University Press.

Quine, W. V. O. 1953: Two Dogmas of Empiricism. In his *From a Logical Point of View*, Cambridge, MA: Harvard University Press.

Rawls, J. 1971: *A Theory of Justice*. Cambridge, MA: Harvard University Press.

Searle, J. R. 1964: How to Derive 'Ought' from 'Is'. *Philosophical Review*, 73.

—— 1969: *Speech Acts: An Essay in the Philosophy of Language*. Cambridge: Cambridge University Press.

—— 1979: *Expression and Meaning*. Cambridge: Cambridge University Press.

—— 1980a: Minds, Brains and Programs. *Behavioral and Brain Sciences*, 3, 417–24.

—— 1980b: Intrinsic Intentionality. *Behavioral and Brain Sciences*, 3, 450–6.

—— 1983: *Intentionality: An Essay in the Philosophy of Mind*. Cambridge: Cambridge University Press.

Wittgenstein, L. 1953: *Philosophical Investigations* (translated by G. E. M. Anscombe). Oxford: Blackwell.

Contemporary Philosophy: A Second Look

BERNARD WILLIAMS

1 The Identity of Analytical Philosophy

Given the title of John Searle's essay, this second introduction might have been expected to complement the first geographically, by dealing with present philosophical developments in places other than the United States, but this is not in fact what it will try to do. Philosophy in the United States, in other English-speaking parts of the world, and in many other countries as well, is now very largely the same. In these places, there is one philosophical culture, and inasmuch as it contains different approaches, and some of the philosophy that is done within that culture is distinct from 'analytical' philosophy, that itself is not a matter of geographical region.

It is true that 'analytical' philosophy, the style of philosophy described in Searle's essay and overwhelmingly represented in this volume, is often professionally distinguished (in job advertisements, for instance) from 'continental' philosophy, and this does represent, in a clumsy way, something which until recently was true: that the ways in which philosophy was done in France, Germany and other countries of continental Europe were typically different from the 'analytical' style. To a much more limited extent, that remains so. (Chapters 40–2 describe the situation in continental Europe.) However, it is absurd to mark philosophical differences with these two labels. Apart from involving a strange cross-classification – rather as though one divided cars into front-wheel drive and Japanese – the labels are seriously misleading, in helping one to forget that the origins of analytical philosophy itself lay in continental Europe (notably so, when its founding father is taken to be Frege and its greatest representative Wittgenstein), and that the interests of 'continental' philosophy are not confined to the European continent.

Moreover, it is not simply a matter of labelling. It is not that the distinction in itself is unproblematical, and only needs more aptly chosen titles to represent it. The distinctions involved are obscure, and the titles serve to conceal this fact. The term 'continental' serves to discourage thought about the possible contrasts to analytical philosophy, and so about the identity of analytical philosophy itself. At the same time, the vague geographical resonance of the term does carry a message, that analytical philosophy is familiar as opposed to exotic, and perhaps – if some older stereotypes are in play – that it is responsible as opposed to frivolous. This is indeed what many analytical philosophers believe about it, and they believe it not so much in contrast to activities going on in some remote continent, but, in many cases, as opposed to work done in their local departments of literature. It is not true that work in other styles does not exist in the heartlands of analytical philosophy; it merely does not exist in departments of philosophy. The distinctions involved are not geographical but professional, and what is at issue is the identity of philosophy as a discipline.

In particular, what is at issue is the identity of philosophy as a subject that can sustain ongoing, cumulative, research. If it can do this, it can make a claim which the humanities do not always find it easy to make, except to the extent that they are branches of history: that there is something to be found out within their disciplines, that they can add to knowledge. It has been part of the attraction of analytical philosophy that, without the procedures of the experimental or theoretical sciences and with a more human subject matter, it can claim to achieve results which command, if not agreement, at least objective discussion, and which represent intellectual progress. It has achievements that are not arbitrarily personal, and they compare favourably to those of the social sciences (at least if one leaves aside the quite peculiar case of economics).

I do not think that these claims are empty. I think that the achievements of analytical philosophy are remarkable, and I agree with Searle that the subject is in various ways more interesting than it was forty years ago. Its virtues are indeed virtues. I think it is hard to be in good faith a teacher of philosophy unless you believe that there is something worth doing that you, in virtue of your experience, can do and which you can help other people to do. I think that the virtues of good philosophy are to a considerable extent workmanlike. Quite certainly, no philosophy which is to be worthwhile should lose the sense that there is something to be got right, that it is answerable to argument and that it is in the business of telling the truth.

These things, I believe, are represented by the best of what is called analytical philosophy, and to that extent I am committed to it. My own work has largely been in its style. Yet, having now worked in it for a long time, and having, like Searle, seen it change, I am a great deal more puzzled about it than I once was; in particular, I am puzzled about the ways in which it must understand itself if it is to have those virtues, and also about the costs of sustaining those virtues. There is one understanding of these virtues which is certainly widespread among analytical philosophers, and which directly serves the promise of ongoing research: that these are indeed the virtues of a science. Some philosophers who are impressed by this conception of what they are doing ritualize it into the forms of presentation familiar from the sciences. Sometimes this is mere scientism, but in other cases it signals the fact that their branch of philosophy is near neighbour to some science, such as quantum mechanics or cognitive science.

But the virtues of workmanlike truthfulness which analytical philosophy typically cultivates are much more important than any attempt to make philosophy look like a science. With many other branches of philosophy there is no plausible version of sharing a party wall with science, and yet these virtues are still regarded as virtues. In fact, even in the case of the more scientific areas of philosophy, it is obvious enough that these virtues are not recommended only because they are possessed by its scientific neighbours: they are taken to be intellectual virtues, good in the same way for philosophy and for science.

24

But how far can philosophy cultivate just these virtues and remain true to other aspects of the legacy of the subject, to aims that it has pursued in the past? The sciences aim to make claims that can and should be conveyed in ways that are minimally expressive; they are not meant to convey feeling, or to display much literary imagination, or to speak (at least overtly) in a persuasive mode. But if we think in particular of moral or political philosophy, is this ambition actually true to the traditions of the subject, even as those are embodied in the historical canon of analytical philosophy itself? Is it true to a tradition that contains Plato, Hobbes, Hume, Kant and (come to that) John Stuart Mill? Is it in fact true to any great figure of that tradition, except perhaps Aristotle? And if we are to take him as our model, we are left with many questions to consider – whether, for instance, the affectless treatises that we possess do represent his voice; if so, whether the tone does not represent a quite special view of ethical life; and whether we should not weigh rather soberly the fact that the closest previous imitation of Aristotle was to be found in a movement called scholasticism.

Particularly in moral and political philosophy, but not only there, there is a question of what the procedures typical of analytical philosophy mean. There are many virtuous and valuable things that they make possible, and at the same time there are resources of philosophy in the past that they seemingly exclude, and it is important not to assume that this balance is simply given to us, above all by an unquestionable and transparent interpretation of the ideals of intellectual responsibility. I do not want to suggest that the adoption of the analytical style is a mere abdication, a cowardly refusal to adopt a more imaginative and committed manner which (critics sometimes suggest) is obviously to hand. Still less is it simply a matter of scientistic camouflage. It is a feature of our time that the resources of philosophical writing typically available to analytical philosophy should present themselves so strongly as the responsible way of going on, the most convincing expression of a philosopher's claim on people's attention. But that is an historical fact, and we should try to understand it as such. I do not think that I adequately understand it, and, for that reason, I would not like to predict what other possibilities there may prove to be for a philosophy that preserves the merits of analytical philosophy.

In the rest of this essay, I shall try to give an outline of some principal concerns of analytical moral and political philosophy. This will supplement the account that John Searle has given of the state of the art in other areas, but I hope also that in describing some of what analytical philosophy has recently done for these subjects, it may encourage readers to ask what new things it might be able to do.

2   Meta-ethics

Philosophical studies have often been understood, in the analytical tradition but not only there, as being *higher-order*, in the sense that natural science, for instance, will study natural phenomena, while the philosophy of science will study, from some particular points of view, the operations of science. Some of moral philosophy (or, as I shall also call it, ethics) is certainly a higher-order study. It discusses such things as the nature of moral judgements, and asks whether they express genuine beliefs, whether they can be objectively true, and so forth. Such higher-order questions are the concern of meta-ethics. At one time (thirty to fifty years ago) it was widely thought in analytical philosophy that ethics consisted only of meta-ethics. A powerful source of this conception was the belief in a firm distinction between fact and value, to which Searle has referred. However, the idea of ethics as simply meta-ethics does not follow directly from the distinction between fact and value, and those who used the distinction to support that idea needed two further assumptions.

One was that philosophy itself should be in the business of 'fact' (which, for the purposes of the distinction, included theory) and not of value. This was connected with a certain conception of philosophy, important to the identity of analytical philosophy, in which it is taken to derive its authority from its theoretical stance as an abstract intellectual enquiry. Some earlier philosophers, such as G. E. Moore, had indeed believed in the distinction between fact and value, but had supposed that philosophers, in one way or another, could have quite a lot to say substantively about values. The journey from the fact–value distinction to a view of ethics as only meta-ethics involved the assumption that this was impossible or inappropriate.

The second assumption involved in the journey was that meta-ethics itself could be value-neutral, that the study of the nature of ethical thought did not commit one to any substantive moral conclusions. A yet further assumption, which was not necessary to the journey but did often accompany it, was that meta-ethics should be linguistic in style, and its subject should be 'the language of morals'. This latter idea has now almost entirely disappeared, as the purely linguistic conception of philosophical study has more generally retreated. Beyond that, however, there are now more doubts about the extent to which meta-ethics can be value-neutral, and, in addition, philosophers simply feel freer in making their own ethical commitments clear. Meta-ethics remains a part of ethics, but most writings in philosophical ethics now will declare substantive moral positions, either in close association with some meta-ethical outlook or in a more free-standing manner.

Recent meta-ethical discussions have carried on the traditional interest in the objectivity of ethics. In this connection, 'moral judgements' are often grouped together and compared with everyday statements of fact or with scientific statements. Some theories claim that moral judgements lack some desirable property that factual statements can attain, such as objectivity or truth, while other theories claim that they can have this property. These debates, particularly those conducted under the influence of positivism, have tended to assimilate two different issues. One concerns the prospects of *rational agreement* in ethical matters. The other concerns the *semantic status* of moral judgements: whether they are, typically, statements at all (as opposed, for instance, to prescriptions), and whether they aim at truth.

Objectivity is best understood in terms of the first kind of question. There clearly are substantive and systematic disagreements about ethical questions, both between different societies or cultures, and within one society (particularly when, as now, the culture of one society may be highly pluralist). Some of these disagreements may turn out to be due to misunderstanding or bad interpretation and dissolve when local practices are better understood, but this is not true of all of them. Since ancient times it has been suggested that these disagreements have a status different from disagreements about facts or about the explanation of natural phenomena. With the latter, if the parties understand the question at issue, they see how after further enquiry they may end up in one of several positions: they may come to rational agreement on one answer or another, they may recognize that such evidence as they can obtain underdetermines the answer and leaves them with intelligible room for continued disagreement, or they may advance in understanding to a point at which they see that the question in its original form cannot be answered, for instance because it was based on a false presupposition.

By contrast, it is suggested that we can understand an ethical dispute perfectly well, and yet it be clear that it need not come out in any of these ways. Disagreeing about an ethical matter, the parties may radically disagree about the kinds of considerations that would settle the question, and the suggestion is that at the end of the line there may be no rational way of arriving at agreement. This is the suggestion that ethical claims lack objectivity. Some theories have associated this position with a view about the semantic status of moral utterances. Emotivism, a theory closely associated with positivism, held that moral utterances were merely expressions of emotion, not far removed from expletives, and it took this, reasonably enough, not to be an objectivist theory. In this case, the semantic account and the denial of objectivity went closely together. However, it is a mistake to think that the two issues are in general simply related to one another.

A clear illustration of this is Kant's theory. Kant supposed that moral statements, or at any rate the most basic of them, were actually prescriptions, and he understood the fundamental principle of morality to be an imperative. However, when the issue is expressed in terms of rational agreement or disagreement, Kant is quite certainly an objectivist: the Categorical Imperative, together in some cases with empirical information, determines for any rational agent what morality requires, and all rational agents are in a position to agree on it. Another example of objectivity which is at least non-committal about the semantics involved comes from virtue theory. Aristotle believed that experienced and discriminating agents who had been properly brought up would reach rational agreement in action, feeling, judgement and interpretation. He believed, moreover, that this possibility was grounded in the best development and expression of human nature, and that views about what counted as the best human development could themselves command rational agreement. This certainly offers a kind of objectivity, but it does not particularly emphasize agreement in belief; no doubt some agreement in belief will matter, but so equally will agreement in feeling and in practical decision.

However, even if objectivity need not imply rational agreement in belief, it may be argued that the converse holds: that a theory which represents moral judgements as basically expressing beliefs must be committed to objectivity. Beliefs, this argument goes, are true or false. If moral judgements express beliefs, then some of them are true and there is such a thing as truth in morality. So if people disagree about what to believe, someone must be wrong. This certainly sounds as though there must be objectivity. The difficulty with this argument is that it seems to be too easy to agree that moral judgements admit of truth or falsehood. They are certainly called 'true' and 'false', as even the emotivists had to concede, and the claim that nevertheless they are not really true or false needs some deciphering. Emotivism itself offered a semantic analysis in terms of which such judgements turn out not really to be statements, which certainly gives some content to the claim that they are not really true or false. However, such analyses run into difficulty precisely because the air of being a statement that surrounds moral judgements is not merely superficial – they behave syntactically just as other kinds of statements do.

An alternative is to argue that moral judgements can indeed be true or false, but that nothing interesting follows from this. On some theories of truth, sometimes called 'redundancy' theories, to claim that 'P' is true is to do no more than to assert that P. Any theory of truth must accept the equivalence '"P" is true if and only if P'; the peculiarity of redundancy theories is to claim that this is all there is to the nature of truth. If this is correct, then the truth or falsehood of moral judgements will follow simply from their taking a statemental form, which allows them to be asserted or denied. Objectivity will then either be understood as something that necessarily goes along with truth and falsehood, in which case, on the redundancy theory, it will be no more interesting or substantive than truth; or it will be more interesting and substantive – implying for instance the possibility of rational agreement – in which case, on the redundancy view, it will not follow just from the fact that moral judgements can be true or false.

It is widely, though not universally, agreed that an adequate theory of truth needs to go beyond the redundancy view, but it is disputed how far it needs to go. Some argue that if one takes seriously the claim that a given proposition is true, then this does imply the idea that there could be convergence in belief on the proposition under favourable circumstances. This approach brings the idea of truth itself nearer to that of objectivity as that has been introduced here. Others hold that a properly 'minimalist' theory of truth need not bring in such a strong condition.

If objectivism and the mere truth of moral statements have often been assimilated to one another, *realism*, equally, is often assimilated to one or both of them. Yet we should expect realism, if it is an issue at all, to be a further issue. Elsewhere in philosophy, for instance in the philosophy of mathematics or the philosophy of science, it can be agreed that statements of a certain kind (about numbers, or about subatomic particles) are capable of truth, and also that they can command rational agreement, and yet it is thought by many philosophers that this does not answer the question whether those statements should be interpreted *realistically*, where this means (very roughly indeed) that the statements are taken to refer to objects that exist independently of our thoughts about them. Even if it is not easy to give a determinate sense to such questions, at any rate one would not expect realism to follow trivially from the claim that moral statements can be true or false.

Some philosophers, influenced by the late John Mackie and in the line of Hume, deny realism by claiming that the moral properties of people, actions and so forth, are not 'in the world' but are 'projected' on to it from our feelings and reactions. According to the most familiar version of this view, secondary qualities such as colours are also projected on to the world, and this raises the question whether the metaphor has not mislocated the most significant issues about moral properties. The theory implies that ethical outlooks are 'perspectival' or related to human experience in ways in which physical theory (at least) is not, but this does not take us very far: it will not tell us anything very distinctive about ethical realism to know only that ethical concepts are perspectival in a sense in which colour concepts, or perhaps psychological concepts, are also perspectival. An anti-realism that gives moral properties much the same status as colours will probably satisfy many moral realists. We need to ask how far the moral concepts and outlooks of various human groups can intelligibly differ while the rest of their ways of describing the world, in particular their psychological concepts for describing people's behaviour, remain the same. Again, how far can their psychological concepts themselves intelligibly vary, and how should we understand those variations?

In considering such questions, it is helpful to abandon a very limiting assumption which has been made up to this point in the discussion, namely, that all 'moral judgements' are essentially of the same kind and stand in the same relation to such matters as truth and objectivity. In considering moral disagreement, philosophers have concentrated on cases in which the parties express themselves in terms of the 'thin' ethical concepts such as 'good', 'right' and 'ought'. The parties share the same moral and other concepts, and disagree about whether a given judgement should be asserted or denied: they disagree, for instance, about whether capital punishment is wrong. To represent disagreement in this way may seem to isolate in a helpful way its moral focus. But a lot of moral discussion – to differing degrees in different societies – is conducted in terms of 'thick' concepts, such as 'brutality' or 'betrayal' or 'sentimentality', and it is a mistake to suppose that such concepts are merely convenient devices for associating a bunch of empirical considerations with a thin ethical concept. It has been increasingly accepted in recent discussions that the application of such concepts is guided by their evaluative point, and that one cannot understand them without grasping that point. (This does not mean that anyone who understands such a concept must have adopted it as his or her own, but it does mean that he or she needs to have imaginatively identified, as an ethnographer does, with those who use it.) At the same time, however, such concepts apply to some empirical states of affairs and not to others, and there is room for truth, objectivity and knowledge to be displayed in their application.

If this is correct, then it may be more helpful to consider ethical disagreement, not at the ultimate cutting edge of the practical judgements about what ought or ought not to happen, but further back, in the network of more substantive and thicker concepts that back up such judgements. Such concepts will typically serve more purposes than expressing bare 'moral judgements'. They may play a role, for instance, in a scheme of psychological explanation. The question will then become, rather, why and to what extent different cultures differ in their ethical concepts, and, more broadly, in the frameworks of understanding that go with such concepts. Seen in this light, meta-ethical questions move further away from being questions in the philosophy of language or the theory of justification or epistemology, and become more like questions in the theory of cultural understanding. Indeed they may become directly questions of cultural understanding. The most basic question about objectivity may turn out to be the question of the extent to which different human societies share an underlying determinate framework of ethical concepts. By turning in such a direction, philosophical discussion becomes more empirical and historical, more richly related to other disciplines, and more illuminating. At the same time, it means that philosophers have to know about more things, or people in other disciplines have to take on issues in philosophy. To that extent, philosophy tends to lose a distinctive subject matter and its identity becomes blurred.

3   Ethical Theory

I have already said that analytical philosophers are happier than they once were to recognize that what they say in moral philosophy is likely to have a substantive ethical content, and that even meta-ethics is likely to have some such consequences. There is a problem, however, about how this is related to the authority of philosophy. If philosophers are going to offer moral opinions – within their subject, that is to say, and not simply as anyone offers moral opinions – they need to have some professional claim to attention. They are not, as philosophers, necessarily gifted with unusual insight or imagination, and they may not have a significantly wide experience or knowledge of the world. Their claim to attention rests on their capacity for drawing distinctions, seeing the consequences of assumptions, and so forth: in general, on their ability to develop and control a theoretical structure. If the authority of philosophy lies in its status as a theoretical subject, the philosopher's special contribution to substantive ethical issues is likely to be found in a theoretical approach to them. One of the most common enterprises in moral philosophy at present is the development of various ethical theories.

The aim of ethical theory is to cast the content of an ethical outlook into a theoretical form. An ethical theory must contain some meta-ethics, since it takes one view rather than another of what the structure and the central concepts of ethical thought must be, though it need not have an opinion on every meta-ethical issue. It is committed to putting forward in a theoretical form a substantive ethical outlook. In doing this, ethical theories are to different degrees revisionary. Some start with a supposedly undeniable basis for ethics, and reject everyday moral conclusions that conflict with it. (It is a good question why the basis should be regarded as undeniable if it has such consequences.) Others, less dogmatically, consider the moral conclusions that would be delivered by conflicting outlooks, and decide which outlook makes the most coherent systematic sense of those conclusions that we (that is to say, the author and those readers who agree with him or her) find most convincing. Unsystematized but carefully considered judgements about what we would think it right to do in a certain situation, or would be prepared to say in approval or criticism of people and their actions, are often called in the context of such a method 'moral intuitions'. (The term 'intuition' has a purely methodological force: it means only that these judgements seem to us, after consideration, pre-theoretically convincing, not that they are derived from a faculty of intuiting moral truths.) A preferred method is to seek what John Rawls has called a 'reflective equilibrium' between theory and intuitions, modifying the theory to accommodate robust intuitions, and discarding some intuitions which clash with the theory, particularly if one can see how they might be the product of prejudice or confusion.

Moral theories are standardly presented as falling into three basic types, centring respectively on *consequences*, *rights* and *virtues*. The first are unsurprisingly called 'consequentialist', and the last 'virtue theories'. The second are often called 'deontological', which means that they are centred on duty or obligation, but this is a cross-classification, since consequentialist theories also give prominence to an obligation, that of bringing about the best consequences. (In the case of the most familiar and popular consequentialist theory, utilitarianism, the value of the consequences is expressed in terms of welfare or preference-satisfaction.) In terms of obligations, the difference is rather that pure consequentialist theories present only one basic obligation, while the second type of theory has many. A more distinctive mark of difference is to be found in the idea of a *right*: the second type of theory grounds many of an agent's obligations in the rights of others to expect certain behaviour from that agent, a kind of consideration that utilitarians and other consequentialists regard as being at best derivative, and at worst totally spurious.

Another way of understanding the division into three is in terms of what each theory sees as most basically bearing ethical value. For the first type of theory, it is *good states of affairs*, and right action is understood as action tending to bring about good states of affairs. For the second type, it is *right action*; sometimes what makes an action right is a fact about its consequences, but often it is not – its rightness is determined rather by respect for others' rights, or by other obligations that the agent may have. Virtue theory, finally, puts most emphasis on the idea of a *good person*, someone who could be described also as an ethically admirable person. This is an important emphasis, and the notion of a virtue is important in ethics. However, once the types of theory are distinguished in this way, it is hard to see them as all in the same line of business. Consequentialist and rights theories aim to systematize our principles or rules of action in ways that will, supposedly, help us to see what to do or recommend in particular cases. A theory of the virtues can hardly do that: the theory itself, after all, is going to say that what you basically need in order to do and recommend the right things are virtues, not a theory about virtues. Moreover, virtuous people do not think always, or usually, about the virtues. They think about such things as good consequences or people's rights, and this makes it clear that 'virtue theory' cannot be on the same level as the other two types of theory.

4   Morality, Politics and Analytical Philosophy

Among moral concepts, that of rights is closest to law and also to politics, and philosophical discussions of them often cross those boundaries. Given these relations, it is not surprising that the kind of theory most often constructed to articulate the idea of moral rights is contractualist, invoking the idea of an agreement that might be rationally arrived at by parties in some hypothetical situation in which they were required to make rules by which they could live together. The inspiration of contractualist theories goes back, in particular, to Kant. Kant's own construction relies on some ideas that are not shared by many modern theorists, in particular that a commitment to the basic principle of morality (the so-called 'Categorical Imperative') is presupposed by the very activity of a rational agent. It also involves a very obscure doctrine of freedom. The modern theories inspired by Kantian ideas are less committed than Kant was to showing that morality is ultimate rationality, and they allow also more empirical material into the construction than Kant did.

The leading example of such a theory is that of John Rawls. His model of a set of contracting parties reaching an agreement behind 'a veil of ignorance' has had an immense influence on thinking about morality. It was designed for a purpose in political philosophy, of constructing a theory of social justice. In Rawls's theory, the veil of ignorance is introduced to disguise from each contractor his own particular advantages and disadvantages and his own eventual position in the society that is being designed. The political theory that uses this thought experiment is liberal, giving a high priority to liberty and at the same time emphasizing redistribution of resources in the interests of the disadvantaged. It is significant that when Rawls first produced his theory he saw it in universalist terms, as offering a construction of social justice which would apply to any society that met the conditions (very roughly) of being able to think about social ideals and having the resources to implement them. Now, however, he has moved in the direction of seeing the theory of justice as one that expresses the aspirations of a particular social formation, the modern pluralist state.

Much recent political philosophy has centred on this liberal project, of defining terms of just coexistence for people living in a pluralist society. One interpretation of that aim is to look for terms of coexistence that will not presuppose a common conception of the good. On such an account, citizens can understand themselves as sharing a social existence although they have as individuals, or as members of communities less extensive than the state, varying conceptions of a good life. Rawls has interpreted his own purpose in those terms; it is expressed, for instance, in the fact that the parties in the original position were supposed to make their decision on (broadly) self-interested grounds, and not in the light of any antecedent conception of what a good society would be. The values that they were taken to have were expressed only in the list of 'primary goods' in terms of which they made their choice, a list which made it clear already that they set a high value on liberty, for instance, and did not assess everything in terms of utility.

In fact, Rawls's aim of making his theory as independent as possible from substantial claims about the good does put it under some strain. At least in the first version of the theory, the basic conception of justice included a large-scale commitment to economic redistribution, and while this made it very welcome to many liberals (particularly in the American sense of that word), it laid it open to the criticism from others more inclined to libertarianism, such as Robert Nozick, that the theory incorporated not only rightful terms of coexistence but a substantial and distinctive conception of social justice as economic equality. In the later versions of Rawls's theory, this conception is less prominent, but even more weight than before is laid on the idea that coexistence in a liberal pluralist society is not 'a mere *modus vivendi*' but a condition that calls on important moral powers of toleration and respect for autonomy. This emphasis does seem to express a distinctive conception of the good, of a Kantian kind, to a point at which it looks as though the condition of pluralism is not simply a contingency of modern life, but an important vehicle of ethical self-expression.

Others, such as Ronald Dworkin, have pursued liberal theory, and in pluralist terms, while accepting a commitment to a distinctive conception of the good. Others, again, have claimed to reject liberal pluralism altogether and have turned in what is sometimes called a 'communitarian' direction. It is hard to tell in some cases where writers of this tendency stand in relation to the politics of liberalism. While a few, notably Alasdair MacIntyre, despairing of the whole enterprise, try only to diagnose our condition and store some ethical goods for a better time, others seem to share in the liberal undertaking but prefer, in opposition to Rawls's Kantianism, a more Hegelian type of discourse to express it.

It is a rather odd feature of communitarian theories, at least if they take a traditionalist turn, that they recommend a politics that does not sit very easily with the existence of such theories themselves, except perhaps as a kind of interim measure. They seek a politics in which people's relations are formed by shared understandings which to a considerable extent must be unspoken and taken for granted, and the exchange of abstract political theories plays no obvious role in this conception of social life. (Hegel, many of whose concerns are re-enacted in these debates, thought he had an answer to this, in his conception of a society that could ultimately reconcile abstract understanding and concrete practice, but few current disputants are happy to pay the price of admission to the Hegelian system.)

The liberals, on the other hand, have a conception of modern political life which at least coherently embraces the existence of their own theories, since they understand the modern state as a formation in which authority is peculiarly vested in discursive argument, rather than in traditional or charismatic leadership. It is true that many political philosophers in the analytical tradition (unlike Rawls himself, and also unlike Habermas, who comes from a sociological tradition) do not see the role of their theories in these terms, but rather as advancing trans-historical views about the demands of a just political order. But even if liberals do not always recognize the point themselves, the role of theory in liberal political philosophy can be given a special justification in terms of current political reality. Liberals coherently believe that the project of political theory makes sense, because they are committed to thinking that in our circumstances it makes sense to engage in a political activity of explaining the basic principles of democratic government in such terms.

In this respect, moral philosophy is in an altogether worse situation. It typically lacks an account of why the project of articulating moral theories makes any sense at all. As many writers have pointed out, it bears little relation to the psychology of people's ethical lives, and inasmuch as it claims that turning morality into a theory makes it more rational, there is a pressing question of what concept of rationality is being invoked. To a limited extent, there may be an answer to that question, inasmuch as some ethical questions, such as those raised by medical ethics, are public questions, closely tied to politics and the law. In those cases, we need a public discourse to legitimate some answers, since it is a public issue what should be permitted, and mere appeals to ethical or professional authority will no longer do. But it would be a mistake to suppose that in such cases we are presented with a pure concept of moral rationality which we then apply to our historical circumstances. Rather, what counts as a rational way of discussing such questions is influenced by the historical circumstances, and above all by the need to give a discursive justification, in something like a legal style, for procedures which increasingly are adopted in a public domain and can be challenged in it.

Moreover, many important ethical issues are not of this kind at all. Morality has always been connected not only with law and politics, but also with the meaning of an individual's life and his or her relations to other people. In these connections, the authority of theory over the moral life remains quite opaque. Certainly, it will not do to rely on the inference: philosophy must have something to say about the moral life; the most responsible form of philosophy is analytical philosophy; what analytical philosophy is best at is theory; so philosophy's contribution to the moral life is theory.

In rejecting this uninviting argument, some will want to attack the second premise. However, it may be more constructive, and offer more of a challenge to thinking about what one wants of philosophy, if one reconsiders the third premise, that what analytical philosophy does best is theory. Analytical philosophy's own virtues, such as its unfanatical truthfulness, could encourage it in ethics to remind us of detail rather than bludgeon us with theory.

Truthfulness in personal life, and even in politics, is not necessarily opposed to the exercise of the imagination. It is relevant here that an imaginative truthfulness is a virtue in the arts. Writers in moral philosophy sometimes urge us to extend our ethical understanding by turning to imaginative literature, in particular the novel. To the extent that this is good advice, it is not because novels are convenient sources of psychological information, still less because some of them are morally edifying. It is because imaginative writing can powerfully evoke the strength of ethical considerations in giving sense to someone's life or to a passage of it, and, equally, present the possible complexity, ambivalence and ultimate insecurity of those considerations. Good literature stands against the isolation of moral considerations from the psychological and social forces that both empower and threaten them. But this isolation of moral considerations from the rest of experience is an illusion very much fostered by moral philosophy itself; indeed, without that illusion some forms of moral philosophy could not exist at all. So there are lessons here not just for philosophy's use of other writing, but for philosophical writing itself. The truthfulness that it properly seeks involves imaginative honesty and not just argumentative accuracy.

Analytical philosophy, or some recognizable descendant of it, should be able to make a richer contribution to ethics than has often been the case up to now. If it is to do so, it will need to hold on to two truths which it tends to forget (not only in ethics, but most damagingly there): that philosophy cannot be too pure, and must merge with other kinds of understanding; and that being soberly truthful does not exclude, but may actually demand, the imagination.

PART I

AREAS OF PHILOSOPHY

1

Epistemology

A. C. GRAYLING

For most of the modern period of philosophy, from Descartes to the present, epistemology has been the central philosophical discipline. It raises questions about the scope and limits of knowledge, its sources and justification, and it deals with sceptical arguments concerning our claims to knowledge and justified belief. This chapter firstly considers difficulties facing attempts to define knowledge and, secondly, explores influential responses to the challenge of scepticism. Epistemology is closely related to METAPHYSICS (chapter 2), which is the philosophical account of what kinds of entities there are. Epistemological questions are also crucial to most of the other areas of philosophy examined in this volume, from ETHICS (chapter 6) to PHILOSOPHY OF SCIENCE (chapter 9) and PHILOSOPHY OF MATHEMATICS (chapter 11) to PHILOSOPHY OF HISTORY (chapter 14). Chapters on individuals or groups of philosophers from DESCARTES (see chapter 26) to KANT (chapter 32) discuss classical epistemology, while several chapters about more recent philosophers also follow epistemological themes.

Introduction

Epistemology, which is also called the theory of knowledge, is the branch of philosophy concerned with enquiry into the nature, sources and validity of knowledge. Among the chief questions it attempts to answer are: What is knowledge? How do we get it? Can our means of getting it be defended against sceptical challenge? These questions are implicitly as old as philosophy, although their first explicit treatment is to be found in PLATO (c.427–347 BC) (see chapter 23), in particular in his *Theaetetus*. But it is primarily in the modern era, from the seventeenth century onwards – as a result of the work of DESCARTES (1596–1650) (chapter 26) and LOCKE (1632–1704) (chapter 29) in association with the rise of modern science – that epistemology has occupied centre-stage in philosophy.

One obvious step towards answering epistemology's first question is to attempt a definition. The standard preliminary definition has it that knowledge is *justified true belief*. This definition looks plausible because, at the very least, it seems that to know something one must believe it, that the belief must be true, and that one's reason for believing it must be satisfactory in the light of some criterion – for one could not be said to know something if one's reasons for believing it were arbitrary or haphazard. So each of the three parts of the definition appears to express a necessary condition for knowledge, and the claim is that, taken together, they are sufficient.

There are, however, serious difficulties with this idea, particularly about the nature of the justification required for true belief to amount to knowledge. Competing proposals have been offered to meet the difficulties, either by adding further conditions or by finding a better statement of the definition as it stands. The first part of the following discussion considers these proposals.

In parallel with the debate about how to define knowledge is another about how knowledge is acquired. In the history of epistemology there have been two chief schools of thought about what constitutes the chief means to knowledge. One is the 'rationalist' school (see chapters 26 and 27), which holds that reason plays this role. The other is the 'empiricist' (see chapters 29, 30 and 31), which holds that it is experience, principally the use of the senses aided when necessary by scientific instruments, which does so.

The paradigm of knowledge for rationalists is mathematics and logic, where necessary truths are arrived at by intuition and rational inference. Questions about the nature of reason, the justification of inference, and the nature of truth, especially necessary truth, accordingly press to be answered.

The empiricists' paradigm is natural science, where observation and experiment are crucial to enquiry. The history of science in the modern era lends support to empiricism's case; but precisely for that reason philosophical questions about perception, observation, evidence and experiment have acquired great importance.

But for both traditions in epistemology the central concern is whether we can trust the routes to knowledge they respectively nominate. Sceptical arguments suggest that we cannot simply assume them to be trustworthy; indeed, they suggest that work is required to show that they are. The effort to respond to scepticism therefore provides a sharp way of understanding what is crucial in epistemology. Section 2 below is accordingly concerned with an analysis of scepticism and some responses to it.

There are other debates in epistemology about, among other things, memory, judgement, introspection, reasoning, the 'a priori–a posteriori' distinction, scientific method and the methodological differences, if any, between the natural and the social sciences; however, the questions considered here are basic to them all.

1   Knowledge

1.1   Defining knowledge

There are different ways in which one might be said to have knowledge. One can know people or places, in the sense of being acquainted with them. That is what is meant when one says, 'My father knew Lloyd George'. One can know how to do something, in the sense of having an ability or skill. That is what is meant when one says, 'I know how to play chess'. And one can know that something is the case, as when one says, 'I know that Everest is the highest mountain'. This last is sometimes called 'propositional knowledge', and it is the kind epistemologists most wish to understand.

The definition of knowledge already mentioned – knowledge as justified true belief – is intended to be an analysis of knowledge in the propositional sense. The definition is arrived at by asking what conditions have to be satisfied if we are correctly to describe someone as knowing something. In giving the definition we state what we hope are the necessary and sufficient conditions for the truth of the claim 'S knows that p', where 'S' is the epistemic subject – the putative knower – and 'p' a proposition.

The definition carries an air of plausibility, at least as applied to empirical knowledge, because it seems to meet the minimum we can be expected to need from so consequential a concept. It seems right to expect that if S knows that p, then p must at least be true. It seems right to expect that S must not merely wonder whether or hope that p is the case, but must have a positive epistemic attitude to it: S must believe that it is true. And if S believes some true proposition while having no grounds, or incorrect grounds, or merely arbitrary or fanciful grounds, for doing so, we would not say that S knows p; which means that S must have grounds for believing p which in some sense properly justify doing so.

Of these proposed conditions for knowledge, it is the third that gives most trouble. The reason is simply illustrated by counter-examples. These take the form of cases in which S believes a true proposition for what are in fact the wrong reasons, although they are from his or her own point of view persuasive. For instance, suppose S has two friends, T and U. The latter is travelling abroad, but S has no idea where. As for T, S saw him buying and thereafter driving about in a Rolls Royce, and therefore believes that he owns one. Now, from any proposition p one can validly infer the disjunction 'p or q'. So S has grounds for believing 'T owns a Rolls or U is in Paris', even though, *ex hypothesi*, he has no idea of U's location. But suppose T in fact does not own the Rolls – he bought it for someone else, on whose behalf he also drives it. And further suppose that U is indeed, by chance, in Paris. Then S believes, with justification, a true proposition: but we should not want to call his belief knowledge.

Examples like this are strained, but they do their work; they show that more needs to be said about justification before we can claim to have an adequate account of knowledge.

1.2   Justification

A preliminary question concerns whether having justification for believing some p entails p's truth, for, if so, counter-examples of the kind just mentioned get no purchase and we need not seek ways of blocking them. There is indeed a view, called 'infallibilism', which offers just such a resource. It states that if it is true that S knows p, then S cannot be mistaken in believing p, and therefore his justification for believing p guarantees its truth. The claim is, in short, that one cannot be justified in believing a false proposition.

This view is rejected by 'fallibilists', who claim that one can indeed have justification for believing some p although it is false. Their counter to infallibilism turns on identifying a mistake in its supporting argument. The mistake is that whereas the truth of 'S knows that p' indeed rules out the possibility that S is in error, this is far from saying that S is so placed that he cannot possibly be wrong about p. It is right to say: (1) '*it is impossible* for S to be wrong about p if he knows p', but it is not invariably right to say

(2) 'if S knows *p*, then *it is impossible* for him to be wrong about *p*'. The mistake turns on thinking that the correct wide scope reading (1) of 'it is impossible' licenses the narrow scope reading (2) which constitutes infallibilism.

An infallibilist account makes the definition of knowledge look simple: S knows *p* if his belief in it is infallibly justified. But this definition renders the notion of knowledge too restrictive, for it says that S can justifiably believe *p* only when the possibility of *p*'s falsity is excluded. Yet it appears to be a commonplace of epistemic experience that one can have the very best evidence for believing something and yet be wrong (as the account of scepticism given below is at pains to show), which is to say that fallibilism seems the only account of justification adequate to the facts of epistemic life. We need therefore to see whether fallibilist theories of justification can give us an adequate account of knowledge.

The problem for fallibilist accounts is precisely the one illustrated by the Rolls Royce example above, and others similar to it (so-called 'Gettier examples', introduced in Gettier 1963), namely, that one's justification for believing *p* does not connect with the truth of *p* in the right way, and perhaps not at all. What is required is an account that will suitably connect S's justification both with his belief that *p* and with *p*'s truth.

What is needed is a clear picture of 'justified belief'. If one can identify what justifies a belief, one has gone all or most of the way to saying what justification is; and en route one will have displayed the right connection between justification, on the one hand, and belief and truth on the other. In this connection there are several standard species of theory.

Foundationalism

One class of theories of justification employs the metaphor of an edifice. Most of our ordinary beliefs require support from others; we justify a given belief by appealing to another or others on which it rests. But if the chain of justifying beliefs were to regress without terminating in a belief that is in some way independently secure, thereby providing a foundation for the others, we would seem to lack justification for any belief in the chain. It appears necessary therefore that there should be beliefs which do not need justification, or which are in some way self-justifying, to serve as an epistemic underpinning.

On this view a justified belief is one which either is, or is supported by, a foundational belief. The next steps therefore are to make clear the notion of a 'foundation' and to explain how foundational beliefs 'support' non-foundational ones. Some way of understanding foundationalism without reliance on constructional metaphors is needed.

It is not enough barely to state that a foundational belief is a belief that requires no justification, for there must be a reason why this is the case. What makes a belief independent or self-standing in the required way? It is standardly claimed that such beliefs justify themselves, or are self-evident, or are indefeasible or incorrigible. These are not the same things. A belief might be self-justifying without being self-evident (it might take hard work to see that it justifies itself). Indefeasibility means that no further evidence or other, competing, beliefs, can render a given belief insecure. Yet this is a property that the belief might have independently of whether or not it is self-justifying. And so on. But what these characterizations are intended to convey is the idea that a certain immunity from doubt, error or revision attaches to the beliefs in question.

It might even be unnecessary or mistaken to think that it is *belief* that provides the foundations for the edifice of knowledge: some other state might do so. Perceptual states have been offered as candidates, because they appear to be suitably incorrigible – if one seems to see a red patch, say, then one cannot be wrong that one seems to see a red patch. And it appears plausible to say that one's belief that *p* needs no further justification or foundation than that things appear to one as *p* describes them to be.

These suggestions bristle with difficulties. Examples of self-evident or self-justifying beliefs tend to be drawn from logic and mathematics – they are of the '*x* is *x*' or 'one plus one equals two' variety, which critics are quick to point out give little help in grounding contingent beliefs. Perceptual states likewise turn out to be unlikely candidates for foundations, on the grounds that perception involves the application of beliefs which themselves stand in need of justification – among them beliefs about the nature of things and the laws they obey. What is most robustly contested is the 'myth of the given', the idea that there are firm, primitive and original data which experience supplies to our minds, antecedent to and untainted by judgement, furnishing the wherewithal to secure the rest of our beliefs.

There is a difficulty also about how justification is transmitted from foundational beliefs to dependent beliefs. It is too strong a claim to say that the latter are deducible from them. Most if not all contingent beliefs are not entailed by the beliefs that support them; the evidence I have that I am now sitting at my desk is about as strong as empirical evidence can be, yet given the standard sceptical considerations (such as, for example, the possibility that I am now dreaming) it does not entail that I am sitting here.

If the relation is not a deductive one, what is it? Other candidate relations – inductive or criterial – are by their nature defeasible, and therefore, unless somehow supplemented, insufficient to the task of transmitting justification from the foundations to other beliefs. The supplementation would have to consist of guarantees that the circumstances that defeat non-deductive justification do not in fact obtain. But if such guarantees – understood, to avoid circularity, as not being part of the putative foundations themselves – were available to protect non-deductive grounds, then appeal to a notion of foundations looks simply otiose.

1.3   Coherence

Dissatisfaction with foundationalism has led some epistemologists to prefer saying that a belief is justified if it coheres with those in an already accepted set. The immediate task is to specify what coherence is, and to find a way of dealing in a non-circular way with the problem of how the already accepted beliefs came to be so.

Hard on the heels of this task comes a number of questions. Is coherence a negative criterion (that is, a belief lacks justification if it fails to cohere with the set) or a positive one (that is, a belief is justified when it coheres with the set)? And is it to be understood strongly (by which coherence is sufficient for justification) or weakly (by which coherence is one among other justifying features)?

The concept of coherence has its theoretical basis in the notion of a system, understood as a set whose elements stand in mutual relations of both consistency and (some kind of) interdependence. Consistency is of course a minimum requirement, and goes without saying. Dependence is more difficult to specify suitably. It would be far too strong – for it would give rise to assertive redundancy – to require that dependence means mutual entailment among beliefs (this is what some have required, citing geometry as the closest example). A more diffuse notion has it that a set of beliefs is coherent if any one of them follows from all the rest, and if no subset of them is logically independent of the remainder. But this is vague, and anyway seems to require that the set be known to be complete before one can judge whether a given belief coheres with it.

A remedy might be to say that a belief coheres with an antecedent set if it can be inferred from it, or from some significant subset within it, as being the best explanation in the case. To this someone might object that not all justifications take the form of explanations. An alternative might be to say that a belief is justified if it survives comparison with competitors for acceptance among the antecedent set. But here an objector might ask how this can be sufficient, since by itself this does not show why the belief merits acceptance over equally cohering rivals. Indeed, any theory of justification has to ensure as much for candidate beliefs, so there is nothing about the proposal that distinctively supports the coherence theory. And these thoughts leave unexamined the question of the 'antecedent set' and its justification, which cannot be a matter of coherence, for with what is it to cohere in its turn?

1.4 Internalism and externalism

Both the foundationalist and coherence theories are sometimes described as 'internalist' because they describe justification as consisting in internal relations among beliefs, either – as in the former case – from a vertical relation of support between supposedly basic beliefs and others dependent upon them, or – as in the latter – from the mutual support of beliefs in an appropriately understood system.

Generally characterized, internalist theories assert or assume that a belief cannot be justified for an epistemic subject S unless S has access to what provides the justification, either in fact or in principle. These theories generally involve the stronger 'in fact' requirement because S's being justified in believing p is standardly cashed in terms of his having reasons for taking p to be true, where *having reasons* is to be understood in an occurrent sense.

Here an objection immediately suggests itself. Any S has only finite access to what might justify or undermine his beliefs, and that access is confined to his particular viewpoint. It seems that full justification for his beliefs would rarely be available, because his experience would be restricted to what is nearby in space and time, and he would be entitled to hold only those beliefs which his limited experience licensed.

A related objection is that internalism seems inconsistent with the fact that many people appear to have knowledge despite not being sophisticated enough to recognize that thus-and-so is a reason for believing p – that is the case, for example, with children.

A more general objection still is that relations between beliefs, whether of the foundationalist or coherence type, might obtain without the beliefs in question being true of anything beyond themselves. One could imagine a coherent fairy tale, say, which in no point corresponds to some external reality, but in which beliefs are justified nevertheless by their mutual relations.

This uneasy reflection prompts the thought that there should be a constraint on theories of justification, in the form of a demand that there should be some suitable connection between belief possession and external factors – that is, something other than the beliefs and their mutual relations – which determines their epistemic value. This accordingly prompts the idea of an alternative: externalism.

1.5 Reliability, causality and truth-tracking

Externalism is the view that what makes S justified in believing p might not be anything to which S has cognitive access. It might be that the facts in the world are as S believes them to be, and that indeed they caused S to believe them to be so by stimulating his or her sensory receptors in the right kind of way. S need not be aware that this is how his or her belief was formed. So S could be justified in believing p without it.

One main kind of externalist theory is reliabilism, the thesis – or cluster of theses – having it that a belief is justified if it is reliably connected with the truth. According to one influential variant, the connection in question is supplied by reliable belief-forming *processes*, ones which have a high success rate in producing true beliefs. An example of a reliable process might be normal perception in normal conditions.

Much apparent plausibility attaches to theories based on the notion of external linkage, especially of causal linkage, between a belief and what it is about. An example of such a theory is Alvin Goldman's (1986) account of knowledge as 'appropriately caused true belief', where 'appropriate causation' takes a number of forms, sharing the property that they are processes which are both 'globally' and 'locally' reliable – the former meaning that the process has a high success rate in producing true beliefs, the latter that the process would not have produced the belief in question in some 'relevant counterfactual situation' where the belief is false. Goldman's view is accordingly a paradigm of a reliabilist theory.

An elegant second-cousin of this view is offered by Robert Nozick (1981). To the conditions

(1) p is true

and

(2)   S believes p

Nozick adds

(3)   if p were not true, S would not believe p

and

(4)   if p were true, S would believe it.

Conditions (3) and (4) are intended to block Gettier-type counter-examples to the justified true belief analysis by annexing S's belief that p firmly to p's truth. S's belief that p is connected to the world (to the situation described by p) by a relation Nozick calls 'tracking': S's belief *tracks* the truth that p. He adds refinements in an attempt to deflect the counter-examples that philosophers are always ingenious and fertile at devising.

If these theories seem plausible it is because they accord with our pre-theoretical views. But as one can readily see, there are plenty of things to object to in them, and a copious literature does so. Their most serious flaw, however, is that they are question-begging. They do not address the question of how S is to be confident that a given belief is justified; instead they help themselves to two weighty realist assumptions, one about the domain over which belief ranges and the other about how the domain and S are connected, so that they can assert that S is justified in believing a given p even if what justifies him lies outside his own epistemic competence. Whatever else one thinks of these suggestions, they do not enlighten S, and therefore do not engage the same problem that internalist theories address.

But worst of all – so an austere critic might say – the large assumptions to which these theories help themselves are precisely those that epistemology should be examining. Externalist and causal theories, in whatever guise and combination, are better done by empirical psychology where the standard assumptions about the external world and S's connections with it are premised. Philosophy, surely, is where these premises themselves come in for scrutiny.

1.6 Knowledge, belief and justification again

Consider this argument: 'If anyone knows some p, then he or she can be certain that p. But no one can be certain of anything. Therefore no one knows anything.' This argument (advanced in this form by Unger 1975) is instructive. It repeats Descartes's mistake of thinking that the psychological state of feeling certain – which someone can be in with respect to falsehoods, such as the fact that I can feel *certain* that Arkle will win the Derby next week, and be wrong – is what we are seeking in epistemology. But it also exemplifies the tendency in discussions of *knowledge* as such to make the definition of knowledge so highly restrictive that little or nothing passes muster. Should one care if a suggested definition of knowledge is such that, as the argument just quoted tells us, no one can know anything? Just so long as one has many well-justified beliefs which work well in practice, can one not be quite content to know nothing? For my part, I think one can.

This suggests that in so far as the points sketched in preceding paragraphs have interest, it is in connection with the *justification of beliefs* and not the *definition of knowledge* that they do so. Justification is an important matter, not least because in the areas of application in epistemology where the really serious interest should lie – in questions about the Philosophy of science (chapter 9), the Philosophy of history (chapter 14) or the concepts of evidence and proof in Law (see chapter 13) – justification is the crucial problem. That is where epistemologists should be getting down to work. By comparison, efforts to define 'knowledge' are trivial and occupy too much effort in epistemology. The disagreeable propensity of the debate generated by Gettier's counter-examples – anticipated beautifully in Russell's review of James (Russell 1910: 95) – to proceed on a chessboard of '-isms', as exemplified above, is a symptom.

The general problem with justification is that the procedures we adopt, across all walks of epistemic life, appear highly permeable to difficulties posed by scepticism. The problem of justification is therefore in large part the problem of scepticism; which is precisely why discussion of scepticism is central to epistemology.

2 Scepticism

Introduction

The study and employment of sceptical arguments might in one sense be said to define epistemology. A chief epistemological aim is to determine how we can be sure that our means to knowledge (here 'knowledge' does duty for 'justified belief') are satisfactory. A sharp way to show what is required is to look carefully at sceptical challenges to our epistemic efforts, challenges which suggest ways in which they can go awry. If we are able not just to identify but to meet these challenges, a primary epistemological aim will have been realized.

Scepticism is often described as the thesis that nothing is – or, more strongly, can be – known. But this is a bad characterization, because if we know nothing, then we do not know that we know nothing, and so the claim is trivially self-defeating. It is more telling to characterize scepticism in the way just suggested. It is a challenge directed against knowledge claims, with the form and nature of the challenge varying according to the field of epistemic activity in question. In general, scepticism takes the form of a request for the justification of those knowledge claims, together with a statement of the reasons motivating that request. Standardly, the reasons are that certain considerations suggest that the proposed justification might be insufficient. To conceive of scepticism like this is to see it as being more philosophically troubling and important than if it is described as a positive thesis asserting our ignorance or incapacity for knowledge.

2.1 Early scepticism

Some among the thinkers of antiquity – Pyrrho of Elis (*c*.360–*c*.270 BC) and his school, and Plato's successors in his Academy – expressed disappointment at the fact that centuries of enquiry by their philosophical predecessors seemed to have borne little fruit either in cosmology or ethics (this latter was broadly construed to include politics). Their disappointment prompted them to sceptical views. The Pyrrhonians argued that because enquiry is arduous and interminable, one should give up trying to judge what is true and false or right and wrong; for only thus will we achieve peace of mind.

A less radical form of scepticism overtook Plato's successors in the Academy. They agreed with Pyrrho that certainty must elude us, but they tempered their view by accepting that the practical demands of life must be met. They did not think it a workable option to 'suspend judgement' as Pyrrho recommended, and therefore argued that we should accept those propositions or theories which are more PROBABLE (pp. 308–11) than their competitors. The views of these thinkers, known as Academic sceptics, are recorded in the work of Sextus Empiricus (*c*.150–*c*.225).

In the later Renaissance – or, which is the same thing, in early modern times – with religious certainties under attack and new ideas abroad, some of the sceptical arguments of the Academics and Pyrrhonians acquired a special significance, notably as a result of the use to which René Descartes put them in showing that they are powerful tools for investigating the nature and sources of knowledge.

In Descartes's day the same person could be both astronomer and astrologer, chemist and alchemist, or physician and magician. It was hard to disentangle knowledge from nonsense; it was even harder to disentangle those methods of enquiry which might yield genuine knowledge from those that could only deepen ignorance. So there was an urgent need for some sharp, clean epistemological theorizing. In his *Meditations* (1986) Descartes accordingly identified epistemology as an essential preliminary to physics and mathematics, and attempted to establish the grounds of certainty as a propaedeutic to science. Descartes's first step in that task was to adapt and apply some of the traditional arguments of scepticism. (I shall comment on his use of scepticism again later.)

The Anatomy of Scepticism

Sceptical arguments exploit certain contingent facts about our ways of acquiring, testing, remembering and reasoning about our beliefs. Any problem that infects the acquisition and employment of beliefs about a given subject matter, and in particular any problem that infects our confidence that we hold those beliefs justifiably, threatens our hold on that subject matter.

The contingent facts in question relate to the nature of perception, the normal human vulnerability to error and the existence of states of mind – for example, dreaming and delusion – which can be subjectively indistinguishable from those that we normally take to be appropriate for acquiring justified beliefs. By appealing to these considerations the sceptic aims to show that there are significant questions to be answered about the degree of confidence that we are entitled to repose in our standard epistemic practices.

Sceptical considerations pose problems for epistemologists of both the rationalist and the empiricist camps. This division into competing schools of thought about knowledge is rough but useful, giving a shorthand way of marking the difference between those who hold that reason is the chief means to knowledge, and those who accord that role to experience. Rationalists emphasize reason because in their view the objects of knowledge are propositions that are eternally, immutably and necessarily true – the examples they offer are the propositions of mathematics and logic – and these, they say, can only be acquired by reasoning. Empiricists hold that substantive and genuine knowledge of the world can only be learned through experience, by means of the senses and their extension via such instruments as telescopes and microscopes. The rationalist need not deny that empirical awareness is an important, even an ineliminable, aid to reason, nor need the empiricist deny that reason is an important, even an ineliminable, aid to experience; but both will insist that the chief means to knowledge is respectively one or the other.

The refinements of debate about these matters merit detailed examination for which this is not the place. For present purposes, the point to note is that scepticism is a problem for both schools of thought. For both, possibilities of error and delusion pose a challenge. For the empiricist in particular, to these must be added distinctive problems about perception.

2.2 Error, delusion and dreams

One characteristic pattern of sceptical argument is drawn from a set of considerations about error, delusions and dreams. Consider the error argument first. We are fallible creatures; we sometimes make mistakes. If, however, we are ever to be able to claim to know (that is, at least to be justified in believing) some proposition *p*, we must be able to exclude the possibility that at the time of claiming to know *p* we are in error. But since we typically, or at least frequently, are not aware of our errors as we make them, and might therefore unwittingly be in error as we claim to know *p*, we are not justified in making that claim.

The same applies when a person is the subject of a delusion, illusion or hallucination. Sometimes people undergoing one or other of these states do not know that they are doing so, and take themselves to be having veridical experiences. Clearly, although they think they are in a state which lends itself to their being justified in claiming to know *p*, they are not in such a state. Therefore they are not justified in claiming to know *p*. So in order for anyone to claim knowledge of some *p*, they must be able to exclude the possibility that they are the subject of such states.

This pattern of argument is at its most familiar in the argument from dreaming employed by Descartes. One way of setting it out is as follows. When I sleep I sometimes dream, and when I dream I sometimes – indeed, often – do not know that I am dreaming. So I can have experiences that appear to be veridical waking experiences on the basis of which I take myself to be justified in claiming to know such and such. But because I am dreaming, I do not in fact know such and such; I merely dream that I do. Might I not be dreaming now? If I cannot exclude the possibility that I am now, at this moment, dreaming, I am unable to claim knowledge of the things I at this moment take myself to know. For example, it seems to me that I am sitting at a desk next to a window admitting a view of trees and lawns. But because I might be dreaming that this is so, I cannot claim to know it.

In these arguments the possibility of error, delusion or dreaming acts as what might be called a 'defeater' to knowledge claims. The pattern is: if one knows *p*, then nothing is acting to subvert one's justification to claim knowledge of *p*. But one can seem to oneself fully entitled to claim to know some *p*, and in fact lack that entitlement, as the foregoing considerations show. So our claims to knowledge are in need of better grounds than we standardly take ourselves to have. We must find a way of defeating the defeaters.

2.3 Perception

Both rationalist and empiricist views about the sources of knowledge are threatened by the arguments just sketched. Arguments that pose particular problems for empiricism are suggested by the nature and limitations of perception, the best current account of which tells us something like the following story.

Light reflects from the surfaces of objects in the physical environment and passes into the eyes, where it irritates the cells of the retinas in such a way as to trigger impulses in the optic nerves. The optic nerves convey these impulses to the region of the cerebral cortex that processes visual data, where they stimulate certain sorts of activity. As a result, in ways still mysterious to science and philosophy, coloured 'motion pictures' arise in the subject's consciousness, representing the world outside his or her head. This remarkable transaction is repeated *mutatis mutandis* in the other sensory modalities of hearing, smell, taste and touch, giving rise to perceptions of harmonies and melodies, perfumes and piquancies, smoothness, softness, warmth – and so forth.

This model can be used to furnish another sceptical application of the defeater argument. The complex causal story thus told is one which – so the sceptic can point out – might be interrupted in problematic ways at any point along its length. The experiences which we say result from the interaction of our senses and the world might occur in us for other reasons. They might occur when, as noted above, we dream, hallucinate or suffer delusions; or, to be fanciful, they might be produced in us by a god, or by a scientist who has connected our brains to a computer. From the point of view of the experiencing subject, there might be no way of telling the difference. So, says the sceptic, unless we find means of excluding these possibilities, we are not entitled to claim knowledge of what we standardly take ourselves to know.

2.4   Perceptual relativities

These same considerations about perception can prompt sceptical challenge by a different route. A little reflection of the kind taught us by Locke, BERKELEY (1685–1753) (chapter 30) and other earlier contributors to the debate shows that some of these properties we seem to perceive in objects are not 'in the objects themselves' but are in fact creatures of the perceptual relation. The qualities of objects – their colour, taste, smell, sound and texture – vary according to the condition of the perceiver or the conditions under which they are perceived. The standard examples are legion: grass is green in daylight, black at night; tepid water feels warm to a cold hand, cool to a hot hand; objects look large from close by, small from far away; and so on.

These perceptual relativities are cited by the sceptic to raise questions not just about whether perception is a trustworthy source of information about the world, but whether the world can be said to exist independently of perception at all. For what if the properties by whose means we detect the presence of objects cannot be described apart from their being objects of perception? Consider the old conundrum whether a sound is made by the tree that falls in the forest when no sentient being is present to hear it do so. The answer, on a standard theory of perception current in contemporary science, is that the tree falls in complete silence. For if there is no ear to hear, there is no sound; there are only at best the conditions – vibrating airwaves – which would cause sound to be heard if there were normally functioning eardrums, aural nerves and the rest to be stimulated by them.

These considerations suggest a sceptical picture in which perceivers are in something like the following predicament. Imagine a man wearing a visorless helmet which so encloses his head that he cannot see, hear, taste or smell anything outside it. Imagine that a camera, a microphone and other sensors are affixed to the top of the helmet, transmitting pictures and other information to its interior. And suppose finally that it is impossible for the wearer to remove the helmet to compare this information with whatever is outside, so that he cannot check whether it faithfully represents the exterior world. Somehow the wearer has to rely on the intrinsic character of the information available inside the helmet to judge its reliability. He knows that the information sometimes comes from sources other than the exterior world, as in dreams and delusions; he has deduced that the equipment affixed to the helmet works upon the incoming data and changes it, for example adding colours, scents and sounds to its picture of what intrinsically has none of these properties (at very least, in those forms); he knows that his beliefs about what lies outside the helmet rest on the inferences he draws from the information available inside it, and that his inferences are only as good as his fallible, error-prone capacities allow them to be. Given all this, asks the sceptic, have we not a job of work to do to justify our claims to knowledge?

2.5   Methodological and problematic scepticism

Before considering these arguments and canvassing some ways of responding to them, it is important to note two things. One is that sceptical arguments are not best dealt with by attempts at piecemeal – that is, one-by-one – refutation. The second is that there is a vitally important distinction to be drawn between two ways in which scepticism can be employed in epistemology. It is important to note these matters because otherwise the prima facie implausibility of most sceptical arguments will mislead us into underestimating their significance. I take each point in turn.

Attempted refutation of sceptical arguments piecemeal is, arguably, futile for two good reasons. As suggested at the outset, sceptical arguments are at their strongest not when they seek to prove that we are ignorant about some subject matter but when they ask us to justify our knowledge claims. A challenge to justify is not a claim or a theory, and cannot be refuted; it can only be accepted or ignored. Since the sceptic offers reasons why justification is needed, the response might be to inspect those reasons to see whether the challenge needs to be met. This indeed is one good response to scepticism. Where the reasons are cogent, the next good response is to try to meet the challenge thus posed.

The second reason is that sceptical arguments taken together have the joint effect of showing that there is work to be done if we are to get a satisfactory account of knowledge – and scepticism indicates what is needed. If one could refute, or show to be ungrounded, one or another individual sceptical argument, others would be left in place still demanding that such an account be sought.

These points can be illustrated by considering Gilbert Ryle's (1900–76) attempt to refute the argument from error by using a 'polar concept' argument. There cannot be counterfeit coins, Ryle observed, unless there are genuine ones, nor crooked paths unless there are straight paths, nor tall men unless there are short men. Many concepts come in such polarities, a feature of which is that one cannot grasp either pole unless one grasps its opposite at the same time. Now, 'error' and 'getting it right' are conceptual polarities. If one understands the concept of error, one understands the concept of getting it right. But to understand this latter concept is to be able to apply it. So our very grasp of the concept of error implies that we sometimes get things right.

Ryle obviously assumed that the error sceptic is claiming that, for all we know, we might always be in error. Accordingly his argument – that if we understand the concept of error, we must sometimes get things right – is aimed at refuting the intelligibility of claiming that we might always be wrong. But of course the error sceptic is not claiming this. He or she is simply asking how, given that we sometimes make mistakes, we can rule out the possibility of being in error on any given occasion of judgement – say, at this present moment.

But the sceptic need not concede the more general claims that Ryle makes, namely, that for any conceptual polarity, both poles must be understood, and – further and even more tendentiously – to understand a concept is to know how to apply it, and for it to be applicable is for it actually to be applied (or to have been applied). This last move is question-begging enough, but so is the claim about conceptual polarities itself. For the sceptic can readily cite cases of conceptual polarities – 'perfect–imperfect', 'mortal–immortal', 'FINITE–INFINITE' (chapter 11) – where it is by no means clear that the more exotic poles apply to anything, or even that we really understand them. After all, taking a term and attaching a negative prefix to it does not guarantee that we have thereby grasped an intelligible concept.

These comments suggest that sceptical arguments, even if singly they appear implausible, jointly invite a serious response; which is what, in large measure, epistemology seeks to offer. But there is still the matter of the distinction between methodological and problematic scepticism to be explained, and here a brief recapitulation of Descartes's use of sceptical arguments will be helpful.

Descartes's Method of Doubt

Descartes's aim was to find a basis for knowledge, which he did by looking for a starting point about which he could be certain. To find certainty he needed to rule out anything that could be doubted, however absurd that doubt, for only in this way would we be left with what is truly indubitable. In the first *Meditation* he embarks on this task by borrowing some sceptical arguments from the ancients. First he cites the fact that we can be misled in perception. But this is not a thoroughgoing enough scepticism, for even if we misperceive there is still much that we can know. So he next considers the possibility that on any occasion of claiming to know something, one might be dreaming. This sceptical thought catches more in its net, but is still insufficient, for even in dreams we can know such things as, for example, mathematical truths. So, to get as sweeping a consideration as possible, Descartes introduces the 'evil demon' idea. Here the supposition is that with respect to everything about which one could possibly be misled, an evil demon is indeed misleading one. Famously, what such a being cannot mislead one about is *cogito ergo sum* – when one thinks 'I exist', this proposition is true.

It is essential to note that Descartes's use of these arguments is *purely methodological*. The rest of the *Meditations* is devoted to showing that we know a great deal, because the fact (as Descartes unsuccessfully tries to prove) that there is a good DEITY (see chapter 15) guarantees that, just so long as we use our faculties responsibly, whatever is perceived with clearness and distinctness to be true will indeed be true. This is because a good deity, unlike an evil one, would not wish us to embrace ignorance. Descartes was by no means a sceptic, nor did he think that sceptical arguments, least of all the one employed as a device to set aside as many beliefs as possible, were persuasive. The 'method of doubt' is merely a tool.

Descartes' successors, however, were far more impressed by the sceptical arguments he employed than his answer to them. For the tradition of epistemological thinking after his time, these and allied sceptical arguments were not mere methodological devices, but serious problems requiring solution. Hence the distinction I draw here between *methodological* and *problematic* scepticism.

It is clear that there are sceptical considerations that have merely methodological utility, and are not genuinely problematic, because they do not represent a stable and cogent challenge to our ordinary epistemological standards. Descartes's 'evil demon' is a case in point. Since the hypothesis that there is such a thing is as arbitrary and groundless as a hypothesis can get, it does not merit being taken seriously otherwise than as a ploy to make a point. But sceptical considerations about perception, error, delusion and dreams raise more interesting and troubling general issues, and accordingly merit examination.

Among the many things worth noting about Descartes's discussion are the following two. Firstly, as hinted earlier, his quest for certainty is arguably misconceived. Certainty is a psychological state one can be in independently of whether or not one believes truly. The falsity of a belief is no bar to one's feeling certain that it is otherwise. Descartes sought to specify ways of recognizing which of our beliefs are true, but he led himself into talk of certainty because – and this is the second point – he assumed that epistemology's task is to provide one with a way of knowing, from one's own subjective viewpoint, when one possesses knowledge. Accordingly, he starts with the private data of a single consciousness and attempts to move outside it, seeking guarantees for the process en route. Nearly all of Descartes's successors in epistemology, up to and including RUSSELL (1872–1970) (chapter 37) and Ayer (1910–89), accepted this perspective on their task. In this respect at least they are all therefore Cartesians. It is largely for this reason, as we shall see hinted below, that they found it hard to meet scepticism's challenge.

2.6 *Some responses to scepticism*

The sceptical challenge tells us that we suffer an epistemic plight, namely, that we can have the best possible evidence for believing some *p*, and yet be wrong. Stated succinctly and formally, scepticism is the observation that there is nothing contradictory in the conjunction of statements *s* embodying our best grounds for a given belief *p* with the falsity of *p*.

An informative representation of scepticism thus summarized is as follows. Sceptical arguments open a gap between, on the one hand, the grounds a putative knower has for some knowledge claim, and, on the other hand, the claim itself. Responses to scepticism generally take the form of attempts either to bridge this gap or to close it. The standard perceptual model, in which beliefs are formed by sensory interaction with the world, postulates a causal bridge across the gap; but that bridge is vulnerable to sceptical sabotage, so the causal story at least needs support. Descartes, as noted, identified the epistemological task as the need to specify a guarantee – call it X – which, added to our subjective grounds for belief, protects them against scepticism and thus elevates belief into knowledge. His candidate for X was the goodness of a deity; rejecting this candidate (while continuing to accept his view of the epistemological task) obliges us to find an alternative. If an X cannot be found to support a bridge across the sceptical gap, the option is to try closing it – or more accurately, to show that there is no gap at all. Both the quest for X and the closing of the gap have constituted major epistemological endeavours against scepticism in modern philosophy. Some of these endeavours, in brief, are as follows.

Descartes's immediate successors were, as mentioned, unpersuaded by his attempt to bridge the gap by invoking a good divinity to serve as X. LOCKE (chapter 29), without much fanfare, employed a weaker version of the Cartesian expedient by saying that we can ignore sceptical threats to the causal story because 'the light that is set up in us shines bright enough for all our purposes'. From Locke's point of view it does not matter whether the inner light is set up by God or nature; the point is that there is something – X, the inner light which could be, perhaps, reason, empirical intuition or native trust in the reliability of the senses – that gives us grounds for accepting our ordinary knowledge-acquiring means as adequate.

Others, not content with such unsatisfactory moves, look for X elsewhere, and claim to find it in some version of foundationalism, the thought – sketched above – that our epistemic system has a basis in special beliefs that are in some way self-justifying or self-evident and which, in conjunction with the evidence we ordinarily employ in making knowledge claims, secures them against scepticism. As we saw earlier, a chief ground for rejecting such theories is alleged to be that none of them identifies satisfactory candidates for 'foundations'. But one stimulating way of making something like a foundationalist case is offered by Kant, whose attempt prompted others.

2.7   Transcendental arguments

KANT (1724–1804) (chapter 32) regarded failure to refute scepticism as a 'scandal' to philosophy, and offered his *Critique of Pure Reason* (1929) as a solution. His thesis is that our minds are so constituted that they impose a framework of interpretative concepts upon our sensory input, among them those of the objectivity and causal interconnectedness of what we perceive. Application of these concepts transforms mere passive receipt of sensory data into EXPERIENCE (pp. 726–33) properly so called. Our faculties are such that when raw data comes under the interpreting activity of our concepts, they have already had spatial and temporal form conferred on them by the nature of our sensory capacities; all our experience, considered as relating to what is outside us, is experience of a spatially structured world, and all our experience, considered as relating to its received character in our minds, is of a temporally structured world. Upon the spatio-temporal data thus brought before our minds we impose the categories, that is, the concepts that make experience possible by giving it its determinate character. And here is Kant's point: if the sceptic asks us to justify our claims to knowledge, we do so by setting out these facts about how experience is constituted.

Kant claimed HUME (1711–76) (chapter 31) as his inspiration for these ideas, because Hume had argued that although we cannot refute scepticism – reason was not, he claimed, up to the task – we should not be troubled, for human nature is so constituted that we simply cannot help having the beliefs that scepticism challenges us to justify. Those beliefs include, for example, that there is an external world, that causal relations hold between events in the world, that inductive reasoning is reliable, and so forth. From this hint Kant elaborated his theory that the concepts that the sceptic asks us to justify are constitutive features of our capacity to have any experience at all.

The strategy, if not the details, of Kant's attack upon scepticism has prompted interest in more recent philosophy. The argument he employs is a transcendental argument, briefly characterizable as one which says that because A is a necessary condition for B, and, because B is the case, A must be the case also. An example of such an argument in action against scepticism is as follows.

A typical sceptical challenge concerns belief in the unperceived continued existence of objects. What justifies our holding this belief and premising so much upon it? The transcendental arguer answers that because we take ourselves to occupy a single unified world of spatio-temporal objects, and because on this view spatio-temporal objects have to exist unperceived in order to constitute the realm as single and unified, a belief in their unperceived continued existence is a condition of our thinking both about the world and our experience of it in this way. Since we do indeed think this way, the belief that the sceptic asks us to justify is thereby justified. A contemporary thinker who makes notable use of this style of argument is P. F. Strawson (b. 1919).

2.8   Idealism and phenomenalism

There is, in parallel to these Kantian ways of responding to the sceptical challenge, another approach, which denies the existence of a scepticism-generating gap. The chief figures in this camp are Berkeley and, more recently, the phenomenalists, who – allowing for differences among them, and for the fact that the two latter held these views only for part of their careers – include MILL (1806–73) (chapter 35), Russell and Ayer.

In Berkeley's view, scepticism arises from thinking that behind or beyond our sensory experiences there lies a *material* world. The word 'material' means 'made of matter', and 'matter' is a technical philosophical term supposed to denote an empirically undetectable substance believed by Berkeley's philosophical predecessors to underpin the sensorily detectable properties of things, such as their colours, shapes and textures. Berkeley rejected the concept of matter thus understood – it is a common misreading of him to take it that he thereby denied the existence of physical objects; he did no such thing – arguing that because physical objects are collections of sensible qualities, and because sensible qualities are ideas, and because ideas can only exist if perceived, the existence of objects therefore consists in their being perceived; if not by finite minds such as our own, then everywhere and at all times by an infinite mind. (We may note that Berkeley thought that his refutation of scepticism was at the same time a powerful new argument for the existence of God.)

Berkeley's habit of saying that things exist 'in the mind' has led uncritical readers to suppose he means that objects exist only in one's head, which is what a subjective idealist or solipsist might try to hold. Berkeley's idealism, whether or not it is otherwise defensible, is at least not quite so unstable a view. His 'in the mind' should be read as meaning 'with essential reference to experience or thought'.

For present purposes, the point is that Berkeley sought to rebut scepticism by denying the existence of a gap between experience and reality, on the grounds that experience and reality are the same thing. (He had a theory of how, despite this, we can nevertheless imagine, dream and make mistakes.) The phenomenalists, with one very important difference, argued likewise. Their view, briefly stated, is that all our beliefs about the world are derived from what appears to us in experience. When we analyse appearances – the 'phenomena' – we see that they are built out of the basic data of sense: the smallest visible colour patches in our visual fields, the least sounds in our auditory fields. Out of these sense-data we 'logically construct' the chairs and tables, rocks and mountains constituting the familiar furniture of the everyday world.

An alternative but equivalent way of putting this point, the phenomenalists claim, is to say that statements about physical objects are merely convenient shorthand for longer and more complicated statements about how things seem to us in the usual employment of our sensory capacities. And to say that objects continue to exist unperceived is to say – in Mill's phrase – that they are 'permanent possibilities of sensation', meaning that one would experience them if certain conditions were fulfilled.

Berkeley holds that things remain in existence when not perceived by finite minds because they are perceived by a deity. The phenomenalists argue that what it means to say that things exist unperceived is to say that certain counterfactual conditionals are true, namely, those asserting that the things in question would be perceived if some perceiver were suitably placed with respect to them. These conditionals are notoriously problematic, because it is not clear how to understand them. What, in particular, makes them true when they are (or seem quite obviously to be) true? The usual answers, in terms of possible worlds, laws, ideal regularities and similar exotica, do little to help. It is not clear that much of an advance is made over Berkeley's ubiquitous deity by substituting barely true counterfactuals in its place. Berkeley's view has the modest attraction that everything in the world is actual – anything that exists is perceived – whereas in the phenomenalist's universe most of what exists does so as a possibility rather than an actuality, namely, as a possibility of perception.

One thing is clear, at least: that one does not get phenomenalism simply by subtracting the theology from Berkeley's theory. One has to do that and then, in the resulting metaphysical gap, substitute a commitment to the existence of barely true counterfactuals, with an accompanying commitment to the existence of possibilia. Both Berkeley's theory and phenomenalism thus exact high prices for closing the sceptical gap.

2.9 Sceptical epistemology versus anti-Cartesianism

Some epistemologists do not attempt to refute scepticism for the good reason that they think it true or at least irrefutable. Their views might be summarized as stating that scepticism is the inevitable result of epistemological reflection, so we should accept either that we are only ever going to have imperfectly justified beliefs, always subject to revision in the light of experience, or that we have to recognize that scepticism, despite being irrefutable, is not a practical option, and therefore we have to live as most people anyway do, namely, by simply ignoring it.

Some commentators on Hume interpret him as taking this latter view of the matter, and accordingly call it the 'Humean' response to scepticism. In Stroud (1984) and Strawson (1985), something like the Humean view is taken.

Others in the recent debate are more combative, among them DEWEY (1859–1952) (see chapter 36) and WITTGENSTEIN (1889–1951) (chapter 39). Despite substantial differences in other respects, these two thinkers hold an interesting view in common, which is that scepticism results from accepting the Cartesian starting-point among the private data of individual consciousness. If instead, they say, we begin with the public world – with considerations relating to facts about the essentially public character of human thought and language – a different picture emerges.

Dewey argued that the Cartesian model makes the epistemic subject a merely passive recipient of experiences, like someone sitting in the dark of a cinema watching the screen; but, he pointed out, ours is in fact a participant perspective – we are actors in the world, and our acquisition of knowledge is the result of our doings there.

Wittgenstein contested the very coherence of the Cartesian approach by arguing that PRIVATE LANGUAGE (pp. 817–20) is impossible. A private language in Wittgenstein's sense is one that is logically available only to one speaker, which is what a Cartesian subject would need in order to begin discoursing about his private inner experience. His argument is this: language is a rule-governed activity, and one only succeeds in speaking a language if one follows the rules for the use of its expressions. But a solitary would-be language-user would not be able to tell the difference between actually following the rules and merely believing that he is doing so; so the language he speaks cannot be logically private to himself; it must be shareable with others. Indeed, Wittgenstein argues that language can only be acquired in a public setting (he likens language-learning to the training of animals; to learn a language is to imitate the linguistic behaviour of one's teachers), which similarly weighs against the idea that the Cartesian project is even in principle possible.

The anti-sceptical possibilities of the private language argument seem not to have been wholly apparent to Wittgenstein himself. In draft notes on scepticism and knowledge written in the last months of his life – later published under the title *On Certainty* (1969) – he offers a response to scepticism, which marks a return to a more traditional approach, not unlike that offered by Hume and Kant. It is that there are some things we have to accept in order to get on with our ordinary ways of thinking and speaking. Such propositions as that there is an external world, or that the world came into existence a long time ago, are simply not open to doubt; it is not an option for us to question them. Nor therefore, says Wittgenstein, can we say that we know them, because knowledge and doubt are intimately related, in that there can only be knowledge where there can be doubt, and vice versa.

The propositions we cannot doubt constitute the 'scaffolding' of our ordinary thought and talk, or – Wittgenstein varies his metaphors – they are like the bed and banks of a river, down which the stream of ordinary discourse flows. In this sense the beliefs that scepticism attempts to challenge are not open to negotiation; which, says Wittgenstein, disposes of scepticism.

These thoughts are as suggestive as they are in the philosophies of Hume and Kant; but one of the problems with Wittgenstein's way of putting them is that he uses foundationalist concepts in describing the relation of 'grammatical' propositions to ordinary ones, but repudiates foundationalism as such, and seems to allow a version of relativism by doing so – the river's bed and banks, he says, might in time be worn away. But relativism is just scepticism in disguise – it is, indeed, arguably the most powerful and troubling form of scepticism, for it is the view that knowledge and truth are relative to a point of view, a time, a place, a cultural or cognitive setting: and knowledge and truth thus understood are not knowledge and truth.

Concluding Remarks

There is much one would like to insist upon in trying correctly to describe the work that needs to be done in epistemology, for that is the necessary preliminary to making what progress we can. Here I shall simply underline a couple of remarks already made above.

Firstly, debates over the definition of 'knowledge' seem to me to be a side-show. The justification of claims in the natural sciences, the social sciences (not least history) and law is where the real work cries out to be done in epistemology. And this comment applies only to the empirical case: what of the epistemological questions that press in ETHICS (chapter 6) and the PHILOSOPHY OF MATHEMATICS (chapter 11)? There can be no guarantee – and indeed it is unlikely – that high generalities about justification and knowledge will apply univocally across all these fields. 'Justification' is a dummy concept that needs to be cashed out in terms particular to particular fields; so much should be obvious from the fact that unrestrictedly general accounts of justification prove hopelessly vulnerable to counter-example.

Secondly, little in current literature about scepticism makes one confident that its nature is properly understood. Scepticism defines one of the central problems in epistemology, namely, the need to show how justification of belief is possible. This is done by meeting the challenge to show that sceptical considerations do not after all defeat our best epistemic endeavours in this or that specified field. Implicit in this characterization are two important claims: firstly, that scepticism is best understood as a *challenge*, not as a *claim* that we do or can know nothing; and secondly, that the best way to respond to scepticism is not by attempting to refute it on an argument-by-argument basis, but by showing how we come by justification for what we believe. Somehow these two points, which were obvious to our predecessors, seem to have been lost to sight.

Further Reading

General

Some useful texts are R. Nozick (1981); J. Dancy and E. Sosa (1992); B. Williams (1978); K. Lehrer (1974); L. BonJour (1985); P. F. Strawson (1985); and G. Pappas and M. Swain (1978).

The classic texts in epistemology include Plato's *Meno* and *Theaetetus*, Descartes's *Meditations*, Locke's *Essay Concerning Human Understanding*, Berkeley's *Principles of Human Knowledge* and *Three Dialogues Between Hylas and Philonous*, Hume's *Treatise of Human Nature* and *Enquiry Concerning Human Understanding*, and Kant's *Critique of Pure Reason*. One of the best short elementary books remains Russell's *The Problems of Philosophy* (1912, much reprinted).

Knowledge

The debate about knowledge and justification commands a large literature, of which the following are good examples: W. Alston (1983); L. BonJour (1985); A. Brueckner (1988); R. Chisholm (1977); J. Dancy (1985); F. Dretske (1971); R. Feldman (1985); E. Gettier (1963); A. Goldman (1979, 1980, 1986); G. Harman (1973, 1984); K. Lehrer (1974); P. Moser (1985); R. Nozick (1981); J. Pollock (1979, 1984, 1986); R. Shope (1983); E. Sosa (1981).

Scepticism

The best general introduction to sceptical arguments remains Bertrand Russell's *The Problems of Philosophy*, but it is essential to see the arguments in a classic setting, and for this one must read René Descartes's *Meditations on First Philosophy* (translated by J. Cottingham, 1986), especially the *First Meditation*. Useful discussions of sceptical arguments and the sense-datum theory are to be found in A. J. Ayer (1956) and J. L. Austin (1961), although one should also look at Ayer's reply (1967). For discussion of perception see J. Dancy (1988); T. Crane (1992); R. Swartz (1965); F. Jackson (1977); and M. Perkins (1983).

For an attempt at being sceptical see P. Unger (1975). For responses to scepticism influenced by Kant see P. F. Strawson (1959, 1985) and A. C. Grayling (1985). Allied lines of thought occur in G. E. Moore (1959) and L. Wittgenstein (1969). More recent discussions are B. Stroud (1984) and M. Williams (1991). Scepticism, foundationalism and coherence theories of knowledge are discussed in K. Lehrer (1974) and in useful papers collected by G. S. Pappas and M. Swain (1978) and M. Clay and K. Lehrer (1989). For a discussion of the views variously taken by Dewey and Wittgenstein see R. Rorty (1979). A textbook which surveys the field and provides a useful bibliography is J. Dancy (1985). For the history of scepticism see M. Burnyeat (1983) and R. Popkin (1979).

References

Classical texts

Berkeley, G. 1995 [1710]: *The Principles of Human Knowledge* (edited by H. Robinson). Published with *Three Dialogues*. Oxford: Oxford University Press.
——1995 [1713]: *Three Dialogues Between Hylas and Philonous* (edited by H. Robinson). Published with *The Principles of Human Knowledge*. Oxford: Oxford University Press.
Descartes, R. 1986 [1641]: *Meditations on First Philosophy* (translated by J. Cottingham). Cambridge: Cambridge University Press.
Hume, D. 1978 [1739–40]: *A Treatise of Human Nature* (edited by P. H. Nidditch). Oxford: Clarendon Press.
——1975 [1748]: *Enquiry Concerning Human Understanding* (edited by P. H. Nidditch). Oxford: Clarendon Press.
Kant, I. 1929 [1781 and 1787]: *Critique of Pure Reason* (1st edn 1781, 2nd edn 1787) (translated by N. K. Smith). London: Macmillan.
Locke, J. 1975 [1690]: *An Essay Concerning Human Understanding* (edited by P. H. Nidditch). Oxford: Clarendon Press.
Plato 1961: *Meno* and *Theaetetus*. In *The Collected Dialogues of Plato* (edited by E. Hamilton and H. Cairns). Princeton, NJ: Princeton University Press.

Other writings

Alston, W. 1983: What is Wrong with Immediate Knowledge? *Synthèse*, 55.

Austin, J. L. 1961: *Sense and Sensibilia*. Oxford: Oxford University Press.

Ayer, A. J. 1956: *The Problem of Knowledge*. London: Macmillan.

—— 1967: Has Austin Refuted the Sense-Datum Theory? *Synthèse*, 17.

BonJour, L. 1985: *The Structure of Empirical Knowledge*. Cambridge, MA: Harvard University Press.

Brueckner, A. 1988: Problems with Internalist Coherentism. *Philosophical Studies*, 54.

Burnyeat, M. (ed.) 1983: *The Sceptical Tradition*. Berkeley: University of California Press.

Chisholm, R. 1977: *Theory of Knowledge*. Englewood Cliffs, NJ: Prentice-Hall.

Clay, M. and Lehrer, K. (eds) 1989: *Knowledge and Scepticism*. Boulder, CO: Westview Press.

Crane, T. (ed.) 1992: *The Contents of Experience*. Cambridge: Cambridge University Press.

Dancy, J. 1985: *Introduction to Contemporary Epistemology*. Oxford: Blackwell.

—— (ed.) 1988: *Perceptual Knowledge*. Oxford: Oxford University Press.

Dancy, J. and Sosa, E. (eds) 1992: *A Companion to Epistemology*. Oxford: Blackwell.

Dretske, F. 1971: Conclusive Reasons. *Australasian Journal of Philosophy*, 49.

Feldman, R. 1985: Reliability and Justification. *The Monist*, 68.

Gettier, E. 1963: Is Justified True Belief Knowledge? *Analysis*, 23.

Goldman, A. 1979: What is Justified Belief? In G. Pappas (ed.) *Justification and Knowledge*. Dordrecht: Reidel.

—— 1980: The Internalist Conception of Justification. In *Midwest Studies in Philosophy* 5, ed. P. A. French et al. Minneapolis: University of Minnesota Press.

—— 1986: *Epistemology and Cognition*. Cambridge, MA: Harvard University Press.

Grayling, A. C. 1985: *The Refutation of Scepticism*. London: Duckworth.

Harman, G. 1973: *Thought*. Princeton, NJ: Princeton University Press.

—— 1984: Positive versus Negative Undermining in Belief Revision. *Noûs*, 18.

Jackson, F. 1977: *Perception*. Cambridge: Cambridge University Press.

Lehrer, K. 1974: *Knowledge*. Oxford: Clarendon Press.

Moore, G. E. 1959: *Philosophical Papers*. London: Allen and Unwin.

Moser, P. 1985: *Empirical Justification*. Dordrecht: Reidel.

Nozick, R. 1981: *Philosophical Explanations*. Cambridge, MA: Harvard University Press.

Pappas, G. and Swain, M. (eds) 1978: *Knowledge and Justification*. Ithaca, NY: Cornell University Press.

Perkins, M. 1983: *Sensing the World*. Indianapolis: Hackett Publishing.

Pollock, J. 1979: A Plethora of Epistemological Theories. In G. Pappas (ed.) *Justification and Knowledge*. Dordrecht: Reidel.

—— 1984: Reliability and Justified Belief. *Canadian Journal of Philosophy*, 14.

—— 1986: *Contemporary Theories of Knowledge*. Totowa, NJ: Rowman and Littlefield.

Popkin, R. 1979: *The History of Scepticism*. Berkeley: University of California Press.

Rorty, R. 1979: *Philosophy and the Mirror of Nature*. Princeton, NJ: Princeton University Press.

Russell, B. 1910: *Philosophical Essays*. New York: Longman, Green.

—— 1912: *The Problems of Philosophy*. London: Oxford University Press.

Shope, R. 1983: *The Analysis of Knowing*. Princeton, NJ: Princeton University Press.

Sosa, E. 1981: The Raft and the Pyramid: Coherence versus Foundations in the Theory of Knowledge. In *Midwest Studies in Philosophy* 5, ed. P. A. French et al. Minneapolis: University of Minnesota Press.

Strawson, P. F. 1959: *Individuals*. London: Methuen.

—— 1985: *Scepticism and Naturalism: Some Varieties*. London: Methuen.

Stroud, B. 1984: *The Significance of Philosophical Scepticism*. Oxford: Clarendon Press.

Swartz, R. (ed.) 1965: *Perceiving, Sensing and Knowing*. Berkeley: University of California Press.

Unger, P. 1975: *Ignorance*. Oxford: Clarendon Press.

Williams, B. 1978: *Descartes: The Project of Pure Enquiry*. Harmondsworth: Penguin Books.

Williams, M. 1991: *Unnatural Doubts*. Oxford: Blackwell.

Wittgenstein. L. 1969: *On Certainty*. Oxford: Blackwell.

Discussion Questions

1 How important is it to have a definition of knowledge?

2 If a proposition is false, can one be justified in believing it?

3 Why do 'Gettier examples' raise difficulties for a fallibilist account of knowledge?

4 Could states other than beliefs provide the foundations of knowledge?

5 If there are foundational beliefs, how are they related to dependent beliefs?

6 Is a belief justified if it coheres with an already accepted set of beliefs? Do we have an adequate account of the notion of coherence?

7 Does justification consist in internal relations among beliefs?

8 Can a belief be justified for someone who does not have cognitive access to what justifies the belief?

9 Is knowledge 'appropriately caused true belief'?

10 Does the notion of 'tracking' help to explain how beliefs are justified?

11 If there is no certainty, can there be knowledge?

12 Should we seek a single account of justified belief or different accounts tailored to the different areas in which epistemological questions may be asked?

13 What role does scepticism play in philosophy?

14 How can we disentangle those methods of enquiry that might yield genuine knowledge from those that can only deepen our ignorance?

15 Our knowledge claims are sometimes in error without our knowing it. Does this undermine justification for any such claims?

16 Could you be dreaming now?

17 Could the experiences I take to be of the world have some other origin, without my being able to tell that this is so?

18 Can the properties by which we detect the presence of objects be described apart from their being objects of perception?

19 Are we like the man in a visorless helmet who cannot check the information transmitted to him to see whether it faithfully represents the external world?

20 Can sceptical arguments that are singly implausible jointly require a serious response?

21 What is the importance of distinguishing methodological and problematic scepticism?

22 Can epistemology provide a way of knowing from a first-person subjective viewpoint? Is there any other viewpoint available?

23 If scepticism opens a gap between the grounds for a knowledge claim and the claim itself, is it better to bridge the gap or to close it?

24 Could the possibility of our having experience be unintelligible to us unless we held a certain belief, and yet that belief be false?

25 Are experience and reality the same thing?

26 Can we accept the role of counterfactuals in a phenomenalist account of physical objects?

27   What follows from beginning our account of knowledge with the public world rather than with the private data of individual consciousness?

28   Does the 'private language argument' show that the Cartesian project is impossible?

29   If there are propositions that are simply not open to doubt, how can we identify them? How are they related to propositions that we can doubt?

2

Metaphysics

SIMON BLACKBURN

With a section on Time by Robin Le Poidevin

Metaphysics is the exploration of the most general features of the world. We conceive of the world about us in various highly general ways. It is orderly, and structured in space and time; it contains matter and minds, things and properties of things, necessity, events, causation, creation, change, values, facts and states of affairs. Metaphysics seeks to understand these features of the world better. It aims at a large-scale investigation of the way things hang together. Within this broad description there are two conceptions of the subject. Metaphysicians may think of themselves as investigating the facts, or discovering the broad structures of reality. Or, they may see the enterprise as more self-reflective, gaining an understanding of how we represent the facts to ourselves: how our 'conceptual scheme' or perhaps any possible conceptual scheme, structures our own thought about reality. Once this description is completed, it may be that everything possible has been done, for we have no alternative but to continue to think from within the conceptual scheme whose features we have mapped.

1 Metaphysics and its Doubters

An influential distinction in the self-image of metaphysics is due to Strawson (1959). Metaphysics may be a purely descriptive enterprise. Or, it may be that there is reason for revision; the ways we think about things do not hang together, and some categories are more trustworthy than others. Revisionary metaphysics then seeks to change our ways of thought in directions it finds necessary. The distinction between revisionary and descriptive metaphysics is not sharp, for it is out of the descriptions that the need for revision allegedly arises, and in fact the metaphysicians Strawson cites as revisionary – PLATO (c.427–347) (chapter 23), DESCARTES (1596–1650) (chapter 26), BERKELEY (1685–1753) (chapter 30) – believed themselves to be discovering no more than things that are implications of our necessary ways of thinking. Revisionary metaphysics is frequently associated with ambitious, and sometimes wild, philosophical speculation; descriptive metaphysics is intellectually more conservative. But metaphysics characteristically has a practical dimension; since Plato it has been concerned to promote views about the nature of human beings, their relations with nature, or GOD (chapter 15), or with the larger SOCIAL WHOLES (p. 383) of which they are a part. Here it may be that descriptive metaphysics is ethically and politically more radical, for a preferred description of human life may have far-reaching implications, and indeed it is not possible for any serious ETHICS (chapter 6) or POLITICAL PHILOSOPHY (chapter 8) to be entirely silent about metaphysics. And radical views may have conservative implications, as when postmodernist views of the relative and contingent nature of all our judgements lead to failures of conviction, and the retreat of the intellectual into social and political inertia (Rorty 1989).

Sometimes these themes have been presented as general topics of Being, and some authors give the impression that metaphysics is the science of Being. This is, however, misleading, for there may be nothing or little to be said about Being as such, even if there is a lot to say about the kinds of things that exist, and the categories under which they fall. And in fact the study of Being rapidly turns into the study of things in these categories, and of the relationship with them that characterizes particular thinkers at particular times. But what is right in the idea that metaphysics is the science of Being is that the most abstract study in this abstract discipline concerns the broad nature of reality, and the possibility of its objective representation.

What motivates the study of metaphysics? Centrally, problems arise when we cannot see how things hang together. We suffer from disquiet with the plurality of different kinds of things that exist, or with the mixture of elements that we want to keep together. Paradigmatic metaphysical problems arise when broad areas of our commitments clash, as for instance when we think of ourselves as complex natural organisms on the one hand, or as conscious purposive or even free agents on the other, or when we think of TIME (pp. 82–5) as flowing on the one hand, but recognize that it makes no sense to ask how fast it flows, on the other. Consider the list of minds, physical things, abstract objects, values, events, processes, dispositions, necessities, states of affairs, properties, facts and other basic categories that we seem to recognize. We need a story about how they relate to each other: are some of them equivalent to others? Are some made up of others? Are some of them redundant, or others suspicious in other ways? And just as notably, we need a story about how we relate to them. How do we know about them, and why are they important to us? Such vague disquiet is typically focused by the discovery of paradox and inconsistency, apparently showing that our conceptions are inadequate. Among the earliest examples of philosophical argument in the Western tradition are the paradoxes of motion of Zeno of Elea (fifth century BC), purporting to show that everyday thought about the flow of time and motion in space involves contradiction. What we all naturally believe cannot possibly be true. The moral Zeno wanted us to draw from this discovery is not quite clear, but the paradox served until the nineteenth century as a spur to philosophers and mathematicians to find a better way of conceptualizing change in time.

It seems that such topics should permit of some disciplined, intelligent, investigation. But it is controversial how such an investigation should be conducted. If metaphysics purports to tell us what things exist, or even just how to think about what things exist, then it seems to be trespassing on the domain of the PHYSICAL SCIENCES (chapter 9), and it is unclear how a philosophical study can have anything significant to add to their results. The question is whether there is anything left for philosophy to do, once fundamental science has told us what it enables us to know about these topics. The view that there is something further, and that by some process of rational thought we can obtain reliable views about the nature of space, time, mind, causation and the rest is often described as belief in a 'first philosophy', or philosophy as a discipline with its own methods and results, and the very possibility of such a first philosophy has been a constant object of doubt. Metaphysics is thus preoccupied with its own possibility. It is not unique among philosophical topics in this. But whereas we believe in our hearts, as it were, that there must be such a subject as ethics, or that there must be interesting things to be said within the THEORY OF MEANING (see chapter 3) or even mind, there is no such presumption that there could be a disciplined method for achieving results when the topics are the abstract categories I listed.

Consider as an example the problem of relating MIND AND MATTER (see chapter 5). Among the first philosophical thoughts many people have are ones about their own conscious lives, and the gap there seems to be between that consciousness and the similar lives of others, and the mystery of that consciousness arising at all in the world as we otherwise understand it to be. The fact of consciousness seems undeniable, but it also seems mysterious how it can exist in a physical world of the kind to which we know ourselves to belong. We can think of this as a problem of relating a puzzling or *exotic* fact or kind of entity to a relatively domestic or *familiar* class of facts or entities. By this I mean that we may begin by being happy with some kinds of fact, made to obtain by some kinds of thing, such as the facts of physical nature, or facts about the patterns into which events fall. We feel we understand facts of this sort. We understand what makes them obtain, and how we know them to be true. This class is that of the familiar (homely) aspects of the world: ones that do not puzzle us unduly. But then we realize that we have other beliefs as well; ones which on the face of it relate to different kinds of fact, and posit different kinds of thing. In this case minds are posited, but we shall shortly meet other examples. We may not be able to understand how mind is even possible in a physical universe (how minds can relate to bodies; how they can make physical things happen). Then the main motive to metaphysical inquiry is to put the exotic class into some sort of intelligible relation to the familiar class. An intelligible relation will mean that we understand how both classes of facts exist, and how the world is constituted so that each of them obtains, how our everyday thoughts about their relationship can be true.

If we think of it this way, we can see three main points at which choice is possible in metaphysics. First, there is the question of the authority of the familiar class. At a particular period of time some starting points may seem natural. We may be at home, for example, with the results and concepts of the physical sciences (and in fact the conviction that the world is fundamentally nothing but a physical world is certainly the most common view among contemporary Western philosophers). If so, these results and concepts give us our class of familiar facts, and the task is that of relating more exotic subjects to them. But to other philosophers there may be something wrong-headed or arbitrary or prejudiced about choosing just one privileged familiar class. Perhaps, for example, when we understand how complex and strange are the facts and states of affairs posited by contemporary physics, we will lose any confidence that others are more exotic by comparison. Even deciding what facts and states of affairs belong to

63

physics occupies a great deal of PHILOSOPHY OF SCIENCE (chapter 9): does physical theory, for example, postulate real PROBABILITIES AND CHANCES (pp. 308–11), and if so how are we to think of their existence? What justifies our tendency to take science as an objective description of independent reality, as opposed to seeing it as an INSTRUMENT (pp. 294–5) for prediction and control of empirical fact (and how is this distinction to be drawn)? But even when a privileged class has been identified and doubts about its nature and the source of its privilege satisfactorily settled, there will be a second question of what counts as a satisfactory fit between the exotic and the familiar. What kinds of relationship should put worries about mind or values or abstract objects to rest, if we wish to see our world as fundamentally the world as described by physics? What accommodations should we be looking for? Thirdly, and finally, there will be different attitudes to the exotic class. If it seems sufficiently exotic, so that its objects and facts seem only dimly related to those of the familiar class, a radical response will be eliminativism, or the suggestion that it is not possible that there should exist things in the exotic categories, so that the entire exotic area is best forgotten. The task is not to relate its commitments to the familiar class, but to teach people to do without them, rather as atheists do not seek to understand talk about God in some preferred terms, but want instead to abandon it altogether. In this spirit one might want to eliminate reference to abstract objects such as properties or facts, or to values or even to minds.

Put like this the enterprise of metaphysics sounds eminently reasonable, and one can imagine well-conducted dispute in all three areas: motives for selecting a familiar class, differing views about the relationship it bears to the exotics, and different attitudes to the exotics. But the problem of a method for conducting such enquiry still remains, and we should recognize that philosophy has contained nearly as many thinkers who count themselves as radically opposed to metaphysics as ones who accept the title. In the modern (post-seventeenth century) Western tradition the first philosopher resolutely hostile to metaphysics was David HUME (1711–76) (chapter 31) (Hume 1978). Following him there were always philosophers, especially in Britain, of a more cautious empiricist bent, but few were tough-minded enough to believe with Hume that books of metaphysics should be consigned to the flames, as containing nothing but sophistry and illusion.

Whether or not it has a method, metaphysics is swayed by larger winds that blow in the prevailing culture. It is widely realized that before the Enlightenment the prevailing tone of philosophy was THEOLOGICAL (chapters 15 and 24). It was supposed that the world was the production of an intelligent, rational, caring and perfect being, who possessed a complete understanding of its nature. We imperfect beings could do something to approximate to this understanding, but the insight we obtained in such areas as mathematics and logic afforded us only glimpses of the perfect rational understanding of the whole order of nature that God would possess (Craig 1987). The familiar class of facts with which people were relatively content included God's nature, purposes, values and relationship to creation. The abandonment of this picture of the world by Hume and other Enlightenment figures did not, however, mark the end of metaphysics. On the contrary, the scientific revolution of the seventeenth century replaced one kind of familiar fact with others: notably, those of physical science and those describing the course of perceptual experience. But this 'Galilean worldview', named after Galileo (1564–1642), contained the seeds of its own metaphysical thickets, namely those surrounding the issue of idealism. When mind is sharply distinguished from matter, as it became in this worldview, the uncomfortable and apparently impassable gulf between them is most naturally closed either by making the mind material, or by making the material mental. Idealism is the umbrella title for philosophies that take the latter course. For the idealist, facts about mental life form the familiar class, and ones about the physical world need some kind of certification from them. An idealist, therefore, would be receptive to the kind of instrumental interpretation of physical science mentioned above, in which scientific descriptions are taken as instruments for prediction and control of the course of perceptual experience. Whichever priority is assumed, the problem of providing this certification dominated philosophy from the time of Descartes until the present. Indeed, perhaps the high-water mark of metaphysical speculation was reached with the attempts to marry idealism with a religious worldview in the nineteenth century. According to the accepted story, under the influence of KANT (1724–1804) (chapter 32), but forgetting the tightly critical boundaries that Kant himself put upon metaphysics, it was believed that transcendent results – which go beyond the limits of experience and concern God, freedom, immortality and above all the ultimate spiritual nature of the universe – could be established by a variety of *a priori* arguments. Kant's mistrust of transcendent reasoning was brushed aside by Fichte (1762–1814) and most influentially by HEGEL (1770–1831) (chapter 33), and the metaphysician became the specialist in the nature of THE ABSOLUTE (p. 743), or underlying ground of the cosmic order, which was identified variously with God, pure Freedom, or final Self-consciousness, and which provided some sort of goal to the cumulative historical process. An almost religious belief in progress, coupled with a genuinely religious emphasis on the nature of the SPIRIT (p. 742), and above all its elevated moral tone, gave absolute idealism its hold on the minds of Europe.

The dominant contemporary spirit reverses this direction, privileging facts about the physical and seeking to understand statements about mind and consciousness in its terms. This is known as physicalism, or less often materialism (the word physicalism is preferred because physics itself asserts that not everything that exists is material; the world includes such items as forces and fields). Physicalism and idealism share the goal of relating mind and matter in some intelligible way, but differ over what is familiar and what exotic. The need for additional tasks of the same kind may be less obvious in advance of critical reflection. The point to remember is that whatever a philosopher might put forward by way of doubts about the possibility of metaphysics, the philosophical need for a theory relating central kinds of fact may be driven by wider aspects of the world-picture characteristic of a given time.

Hume was an opponent of metaphysics even though he bequeathed to his successors the paradigm metaphysical problems of modern philosophy. His own attitude was simply that such problems were forever insoluble. The difficulty is that it is hard to believe that metaphysical questions are unanswerable until we try to answer them. Perhaps the problems seem formidable because we are prejudiced in our choice of a familiar class (Hume himself favoured facts about the successions of our own ideas or 'perceptions' as especially basic or familiar, a choice that frequently amazes contemporary thinkers); perhaps we are blind to subtle and insightful ways of relating the exotics to it; perhaps we do not realize that we ought to get rid of exotics that refuse to be accommodated. It is difficult to believe that the entire field can be seen, in advance and from the armchair, to be a no-go area. But there has been one school this century which believed exactly that.

Perhaps the one thing that is best known about the school known as the Vienna Circle, or the logical positivists, was their resolute hostility to metaphysics. It is instructive to see how this hostility flourished, but then eventually crumbled. The positivists were influenced by the empiricism of Hume, and also by the *Tractatus Logico–Philosophicus* of WITTGENSTEIN (1889–1951) (chapter 39) (Wittgenstein 1922), a work which purports to set bounds to the limits of meaningful language. Metaphysics lies outside the bounds, representing language that has gone on holiday. The positivists held that all true thought was empirical; anything straying beyond the use of scientific method also strayed beyond the boundaries of meaning. But metaphysical theses are not properly empirical; they seemed typically to be argued about from the armchair and to bear no visible relationship to scientific thought or experiment. Hence they do not admit of verification or falsification, and are not only unscientific, but also strictly meaningless (they may be allowed some kind of emotional effect, but nothing that permits of assessment as true or false). Instead of metaphysics, all that was left to philosophy was describing the correct methods and structures of empirical science.

Positivism failed in its crusade against metaphysics, largely because of its own instability. For while in one breath it was proclaiming the subject dead, in another it was itself making remarkably confident choices in all three of the areas in which metaphysics characteristically makes choices. Positivism needed a familiar class of empirically sound and basic judgements. It needed views about what counts as a satisfactory accommodation with that class, notably so that the theories of physical science were allowed to be respectable, whereas others were not. And, finally, it had severe views about the areas that were not, by these lights, respectable. Metaphysics soon revenged itself, for all three areas gave trouble, and in all three the movement found itself pulled in different directions, making different choices and indulging in classically metaphysical dispute. Aware of this, later positivist writings grudgingly allowed a place for what looked like metaphysical assertions as recommendations about which LANGUAGE GAMES (p. 9) to play. Thus, the doctrine that there exists mind as well as matter would be construed not as an important description of a fundamental fact about reality, but as a recommendation to speak in terms of minds as well as in terms of matter (to play the mental language game). The recommendation might be useful or not, but could not be regarded as true or false. A similar attitude is characteristic of the later work of Wittgenstein (1953), which is shot through with warning that statements that might seem to be certain kinds of description of reality in fact function in different ways. Wittgenstein's exact intentions are endlessly disputed. But, at least as applied to minds and matter, any pragmatism in the approach is itself acutely uncomfortable. Consider, for instance, the simple proposition that other people besides myself are conscious in the way that I am. This seems to be a metaphysical thesis, although classifying it as one may itself represent a philosophical choice. It is certainly one that we all believe. But it is extremely strange to suppose that the question whether other people are conscious could be construed as the question of whether it was useful for me to enter the language game of reacting to them as having minds (this gloss on the question had in fact been put by William JAMES (1842–1910) (chapter 36) much earlier, especially in *Pragmatism*, and has not received a generally warm welcome). We should also notice that even if we allow the idea that what sound like descriptions of fundamental reality are construed as recommendations about language, there is still argument about what to select as familiar, what is exotic, what should be eliminated and what the relationships are between all these classes. So even the pragmatist gloss may make less difference than might appear at first sight.

Absolute Presuppositions

Their own metaphysical prejudices were invisible to the positivists. The thought that this is an inevitable feature of the philosophical condition is another, different, reason for despair about the possibility of metaphysics. This reason was voiced most notably by R. G. COLLINGWOOD (1889–1943) (pp. 436–9) (especially in *An Essay in Metaphysics*, 1940), and marked a point at which his thought comes surprisingly close to that of both the earlier and later philosophy of Wittgenstein. In this conception, there are commitments that we must have that are not capable of being assessed as true or false, but that nevertheless have the greatest intellectual importance. In Wittgenstein's metaphors, they function as the riverbed within which thought flows, or as the hinges on which ordinary judgement and discourse turn; Collingwood called them the absolute presuppositions of the thought of a time. Because they are presupposed in every activity of thought, they cannot themselves be assessed for truth: in another metaphor, they can be shown but not said. For Collingwood, indeed, they could only be shown historically. That is, at the end of an epoch it would be possible for successors to look back and to find that a particular metaphysics had structured its thought. But at the time the basic structures would themselves be invisible, because they were themselves involved in all seeing (Hegel himself may have thought something similar; the famous remark from the preface to his *Philosophy of Right* (Hegel 1991) that 'when philosophy paints its grey on grey, then has a form of life grown old. The owl of Minerva takes wing only with the coming of the dusk' can be seen as the claim that philosophical reflection can only exist with hindsight). If this is right, the trap that caught the positivists is therefore universal; however much we aspire to care and objectivity in choosing our familiar facts, and a way of relating exotics to them, we will be working within an historically contingent framework whose main structures will be beyond our own vision, and incapable of our own assessment. Collingwood was an historian, and other episodes in the history of philosophy support his view, for it is easier to see absolute presuppositions at work in the thought of particular writers (and their contemporaries) when significant time has passed, and easy to fear that our successors will marvel at similar blindness in our own appreciation of the way we think. An example I have mentioned already is Hume's choice of the sequence of perceptions as the basic familiar fact: a choice that seems extraordinarily wrong-headed to nearly all contemporary philosophers. Once more, however, many philosophers are reluctant to admit there should exist any aspects of our own thought that cannot themselves be identified and even critically assessed. While such episodes in the history of philosophy may nourish our modesty, there seems to be no alternative to continuing to 'work from within', or in other words to do the best we can from within our own best understandings. The thought that one day these may come to look local and parochial is like the similar thought, in moral philosophy, that there might one day be a people to whom our own best judgements seemed inadequate. Perhaps there might, but while we cannot see our way to this improvement, we can, and must, simply soldier on as best we can.

There surfaces here a debate that has preoccupied many recent writers. This is the dispute between realism and its opponents. For the realist it is important that there is no residual reference to us (our language, our sensibilities, our conceptual scheme) when we consider the world. The realist wants real objectivity – a world of facts that are frequently entirely independent of us and that would be as they are whatever our powers of detecting and exploring them. The realist is therefore fundamentally opposed to the view that what we understand and investigate is as much a function of our constitution and our ways of thought as it is of anything independent of us. In a common metaphor, the realist believes that a good conceptual scheme 'carves reality at the joints'; nature is conceived as possessing its own structure and articulation, and good theory only reflects this. This carnivorous metaphor outrages idealists of many varieties, and even philosophers who would scarcely count themselves as idealists. The central problem is that belief that we succeed in carving nature in some especially appropriate way seems to require a way of comparing our own classifications and the kinds of concept we use, with a pre-existent, naturally ordained structure of properties. But no such comparison can be made, nor is it plain what, apart from ordinary scientific utility, could justify us in supposing that some properties are intrinsically natural whereas others are not. This problem received forceful expression in Goodman (1955); for an example of industrial-strength realism, see Lewis (1983); for mistrust of the metaphor see Taylor (1993).

The choice between realism and its opponents has echoes in many areas. For example, the realist is particularly apt to privilege some familiar class, usually that of physical theory, as being especially well-adapted to nature's joints. By comparison other commitments may seem to have less to do with the real way that things are. For instance, the sizes and shapes of things around us may seem to be more objective, more independent of us, than their colours, which seem to be largely a function of the nature of our visual systems. Idealists, impressed by the mind's contribution to any scheme of thought, including that of physics, are typically less partisan. At their most tolerant, they may, as pluralists, become happy to countenance almost all language games or conceptual schemes as alike reflecting the particular perspective of some user; no scheme is privileged by having a unique and special relationship with the way things are, and all are justified in so far as they embody a form of life or way of reacting to the world and coping with it. Pluralism here makes contact with PRAGMATISM (chapter 36), or the view that what ultimately justifies any mode of description of the world is its utility in enabling us to cope with our problems. For the pluralist there may be no urgent task of relating anything familiar to anything exotic, for both alike are conceived of as being no more than one mode of description among others. Pluralism, therefore, serves as yet another avenue from which metaphysics comes to look to be a chimera – and dislike of old-fashioned metaphysics on this ground is one of the characteristics of the postmodernist mistrust of traditional philosophy. But, once more, it is not so obvious that one can be satisfied with pluralism without already having done enough metaphysics to gain the necessarily relaxed attitude to the different categories of being and their relationships.

2 Analysis and Logic

Metaphysics needs a method, but what method can there be? It is generally said that the most influential and respected Anglo-American thought this century marks a complete change of direction from the ambitious and speculative metaphysical system-building characteristic of the previous period. For the first half of this century in Anglo-American philosophy, and for some time afterwards in some places, the problem of method for metaphysics was governed by the ideal of analysis. Faced with a metaphysical problem such as the nature of mind, the philosopher would assemble the central terms with which we talk about mind: thought, sensation, will or whatever; careful attention to what is meant by these terms would reveal the way we conceptualize the nature of mind. The model for such a procedure would be that of the analytical chemist, discovering the nature of a substance by breaking it into components. The negative part of this aim is clear enough. When meanings are obscure and unclear, the inferences that we are permitted to make are uncertain too, and it is this uncertainty that allows for fanciful and monstrous system-building. But if meaning were correctly located, in ways first made possible by the new logical tools developed by FREGE (1848–1925) and RUSSELL (1872–1970) (chapter 37), then those inferences would be systematized and established, and correct methods finally distinguished from impostors. Analytic technique was partly important purely as a defence against wild theorizing. In this sense the method of analysis was not new, but only a new label for procedures that are as old as philosophy. In many of his dialogues, SOCRATES (chapters 22 and 23) challenges his audience to state exactly what they mean by a disputed term; MEDIEVAL PHILOSOPHY (chapter 24), as much as later empiricism, is dominated by the aim of precise clarifications of meaning. But a number of considerations changed the impact of this work of clarification on metaphysics. One was the expansion of logic, suggesting a wholly new range for analytic techniques. Far the most influential example of this expansion in action was the theory of descriptions, revealed by Russell (1905); a 'paradigm of philosophy' whereby judgements that we seem to be making about non-existent 'things' are revealed to have quite a different LOGICAL FORM (p. 790), and to make no such commitments.

Analysis also provided the principal goal for the satisfactory accommodation between the familiar and the exotic. This is the goal of REDUCTION (p. 312), in which the right attention to meaning reveals that what seem to be claims about a puzzling and exotic area are in fact claims of a familiar, homely kind. Specific problems about exotic facts and things do not arise, for they are shown to be ordinary, familiar facts and things. For example, if claims about behaviour are thought to be relatively intelligible, but claims about minds seem by contrast mysterious, then the solution might be to analyse claims about minds as disguised claims about behaviour, or dispositions to behaviour. If logical truth or logical proof are felt to be intelligible, but claims about numbers mysteriously abstract and dangerously non-empirical, the solution would be to analyse claims about numbers as disguised recipes for purely logical inferences. The programmes this approach gave rise to – the two examples given are BEHAVIOURISM (pp. 174–6) and LOGICISM (pp. 790–1), but there were many more – not only dominated much philosophical thinking in the first half of the twentieth century, but go on directing a large proportion of current research effort. If it succeeds, analysis provided an extraordinarily elegant and economical answer to the problem of the relationship of the familiar to the exotic. For if by analysis we lay bare the real 'logical form' or structure of our thought, and it turns out that the facts and things we need to refer to are not what they seem to be at first glance, then the problem is solved by absorption of the exotic into the familiar – the final and simplest kind of solution to the problem of their relationship. We are shown to have no commitments beyond the familiar and the unpuzzling.

It is important to notice that analytical philosophy arose not primarily as a crusade against metaphysics, but only against the undisciplined perversions of metaphysics, which seemed to the major early analysts to surround them. It is in fact notable that the pioneering works of MOORE (1873–1958) (chapter 38) and Russell are themselves preoccupied with questions of what there really is. The familiar class, for Frege, Moore and Russell, included some beliefs that others might regard with suspicion, most notably belief in abstract objects. Moore himself at one time held the distinctly metaphysical-sounding thesis that all that really exists are propositions; Frege remained wedded to but puzzled by the distinctively metaphysical belief in the existence of abstract objects. Russell's empiricism led to flirtations both with doctrines not unlike those of the idealist Berkeley, and with neutral monism (the belief that the same primitive 'stuff', ordered in different ways, makes up on the one hand the mental and on the other hand the physical world). What drove analytical philosophy was not originally hostility to metaphysics, but belief that the correct method for pursuing it had finally been found.

One objection to the method used to be made by more speculative or ambitious philosophers, writing under titles like *Clarity is not Enough*. With concerns echoing those which first arose in ANCIENT GREEK PHILOSOPHY (chapters 22 and 23), they worried that the true nature of mind or other metaphysical topics might not be revealed by analysis, because what is analysed is a compendium of common-sense prejudice or folk-lore which is not particularly likely to enshrine the metaphysical truth. This worry has been revised in a different, scientific, tone of voice more recently. Since common-sense concepts were formed in pre-scientific days, there is no particular reason to respect them as a source of metaphysical or any other kind of truth. Indeed, some philosophers think the right reaction to such concepts is the response we mentioned above, namely eliminativism, which is the doctrine that everyday thought about some topic is sufficiently infected with errors for its categories to be wholly unreliable. Everyday opinions about the nature of mind in principle deserve no more respect than everyday opinions about the nature of mass or the flight of projectiles, and concepts within which everyday thought frames its opinions may be quite worthless, like those of Aristotelian physics. Thought couched in these terms does not need analysis, but elimination (Churchland 1989; Stich 1983).

This is certainly possible. But to turn the possibility into a real likelihood, we must at least correctly identify what the common-sense scheme actually requires. What is common sense committed to, and which parts of it may need eliminating? Here there is a need for work at least significantly like that of the analytical philosopher: we would need to know exactly what the commitments implicit in the common-sense scheme are, and this means correctly locating what is meant by the salient terms.

Let me give a simple example. Suppose someone remarks that one doctrine of every-day common sense is that people often behave as they do because of what they think. Suppose it is then pointed out that science tells us that physics is a closed system: physical events, such as bodies moving, must have physical causes. But, goes the objection, the description of someone as thinking something is not a physical description of them. Hence, it must be an error to believe that people behave as they do because of what they think. This is a simplified version of an argument that has obvious eliminativist leanings, for once people accept that it is wrong to think of people as behaving as they do because of what they think, then the idea of people as thinkers at all is also fairly immediately threatened. For if thought does not cause behaviour, it does not seem to do anything else either. But the argument is scarcely compelling as it stands. It raises a host of questions, and they are analytic in their nature. Is the 'because' in 'people behave as they do because of what they think' actually a causal notion? If it is, does this kind of causal explanation compete with other (neurophysiological) causal explanations, or is it compatible with them? Might it make sense to suggest that mental events are identical with physical events, and are therefore in good standing as physical causes of things? To assess the argument we must first clear up such questions, but clearing up such questions is investigating the very topics that the analytical philosopher took as primary. I return below to discussing some of the moves that have attracted attention in connection with these topics.

The Flight from Analysis

Even if eliminativism cannot entirely do without analysis, in the last forty years, and especially in the last twenty, analysis has officially lost much of its lustre as an ideal. Partly the failure of positivism taught philosophers that theory can take us beyond evidence – that concepts that may not have met strict empiricist or positivist standards for meaning are nevertheless perfectly proper. To theorize properly on the basis of data is to invent new conceptual structures. But then, the kinds of thing said when we make use of those structures will not be equivalent in meaning to the things said without them. New theoretical concepts have their own meanings, and it is futile conservatism to deny this by trying to analyse their content in old terms. The flight from analysis was also propelled from other directions. One was the failure of many of the reductionist programmes, few of which gave convincing reasons for supposing that the exotic was just the familiar in disguise. Another was a gradual disenchantment with the foundational role attributed to meaning in the analytic paradigm. Quine (1951) convinced many that the equations of meaning demanded by analysis could not be self-sufficient 'semantic' facts known merely by knowing the languages concerned, but would themselves equally represent deep theoretical and scientific choices. For example, if statements about physical objects are analysed into statements about courses of experience (phenomenalism) this will not be the result of a neutral semantic equation, but will represent a theoretical (metaphysical) conviction about what there is and the way it is to be understood. In other words, semantics is driven by science or even metaphysics as much as the other way round. It was also realized that metaphysics ought to be able to proceed even where semantics is silent. For example, in the theory of value it is notorious that value terms resist analysis into terms without evaluative implications (it is, after all, their distinct meanings that define them as value terms), but this failure of analysis surely should not halt the enterprise of trying to understand the specific nature of valuing as a human activity, not by purely semantic investigation, but by reflecting on the psychological, socio-logical, or even biological role of valuing (Gibbard 1990). Values would be domesticated, but not by analysis, and perhaps similar progress can be made with other areas.

Two final elements can be discerned in the move from analysis. We have seen that the analytic paradigm was good at presenting a preferred relation between the exotic and the familiar: the one is absorbed in the other. But it is not so good at telling us what to choose as familiar in the first place. And in fact just this point has engendered kinds of conflict to which the analytic paradigm provides no ready solution. Like Hume, twentieth-century PHENOMENALISTS (pp. 53–4) found the stream of perceptions familiar, and the physical world exotic. Others exactly reverse the priority. Frege and Russell found LOGIC (chapter 4) familiar, and MATHEMATICS (chapter 11) exotic; others think that logical relations are even more in need of theory than the properties of mathematical struc-tures. Some think that categorical properties are familiar, and that we ought to analyse DISPOSITIONS AND POWERS (p. 702) in terms of them; others again reverse the priority, believing that categorical properties are dangerously exotic, whereas science deals famil-iarly with powers and dispositions. In the absence of any method of settling such ques-tions of priority, analysis is rudderless, for we do not even know in which direction to work.

Perhaps the most sustained and influential case on behalf of a fundamentally analytic method in the second half of the twentieth century is that made by Michael Dummett (b. 1925). In many writings, but most visibly in *The Logical Basis of Metaphysics* (1991), Dummett has argued that the foundation for metaphysics, and indeed its entire legiti-mate domain, lies in the THEORY OF MEANING (chapter 3). Citing the stagnation and dead-lock that ensues when rival metaphysicians attempt direct descriptions of reality, Dummett believes instead that we must take as our subject not so much reality as the way we think about reality. However, there is no investigation of thought of this kind which is not also an investigation of language and logic. This means we must approach metaphysical problems from the 'bottom-up', recognizing that the problem is that of 'the correct model for meaning for statements of the disputed class' (Dummett 1991: 12). A meaning-theory, as Dummett conceives of it, will give us this model. It must provide a clear view of how our words function, for as things stand we use words with various meanings, but we do not know what it is that we are doing. We have no clear overview of our own practices, and in this sense do not understand ourselves. A meaning-theory will give a representation of what a person learns when learning a language; it will provide a 'workable account of a practice that agrees with that which we in fact observe' (ibid.: 14). Such a transparent understanding of our meanings would certify the correct logic to be used, for it is meaning that confers validity or inva-lidity on an inference; hence it would settle disputes such as that between realists and their opponents, anti-realists in disputed areas.

One surprising thing about such a meaning-theory is that its construction can proceed, according to Dummett, entirely innocently of metaphysics. It is the neutral basis of metaphysics, and nowhere owes anything to metaphysical doctrines or choices. And another surprising aspect is that it is itself sufficiently powerful to settle metaphysical controversy: by adjudicating between rival conceptions of truth offered by realists and their opponents, 'it will resolve these controversies without residue' (ibid.). Dummett is not quite promoting a purely *a priori* method for metaphysics, for the data on which a meaning-theory would be constructed would in one sense be empirical: they would concern the inferential practices of competent users of the language. Nevertheless the data are, in principle, available to any competent language user purely by reflection upon that practice. There is no appeal to general scientific facts or empirical facts lying outside the sphere of language use. Yet the reflection will deliver results that can settle outstanding metaphysical dispute.

The pattern of Dummett's thought is clearly influenced by his own favourite example of metaphysical controversy, that between CLASSICAL MATHEMATICIANS AND INTUITIONISTS (pp. 363–7). In this example it is plausible that the dispute is metaphysical in essence, with the classicists thinking of mathematics as objective, real, independent of us, or 'out there', and the intuitionists thinking of mathematical truth as extending no further than mathematical proof (constructivism). It is also plausible that the heart of the dispute is the correct logic for mathematical proof and inference. The classical mathematician believes in bivalence (the logical law that every proposition is either true or false), whereas for the intuitionist, since there is no guarantee that every proposition is provable or disprovable, bivalence cannot be assumed. And finally, Dummett believes that the issue of the correct logic hinges upon questions that would be tackled by a meaning-theory, in the sense that he conceives of it: the intuitionists believe that classical mathematicians deceive themselves into thinking that they can make sense of notions that are in fact senseless. Deciding whether they are right about that would be the function of just the kind of perspicuous representation of meaning that Dummett advocates.

Nevertheless there are grave difficulties with the programme as it is presented. The most obvious is that it is inconceivable that a meaning-theory with the powers Dummett describes should be constructed in the innocent way that he also requires. Descriptions of what our words mean are historically among the most theory-laden of philosophical claims. They are put forward, naturally, by philosophers who take themselves to inhabit a world of one kind or another, and who believe that our mental powers take one shape or another. We need only remember empiricists and positivists of all kinds, whose conception of what we could mean by a term disallows understanding of anything not given in perceptual experience. But on top of this philosophical choice, the conception of perceptual experience was in turn not purely empirical, or obtained in some neutral scientific spirit. Rather, it was the locus of fierce doctrinal dispute, for instance between perceptual atomists such as Hume and Russell, and more holistic idealists such as Bradley (1846–1924) or Neurath (1882–1945). An even more central and prolonged dispute over the best way to conceive of understanding is represented by the problem of universals, which surfaced above in the dispute between those who do and those who do not think of science as carving nature at the joints. To some realists, meanings reflect natural similarities among things which guide and constrain the application of concepts to new cases; to others of an anti-realist persuasion they do not, but the rules that govern application are a free-standing human construction. But neither side conceives themselves as riding roughshod over empirical facts about the nature of language use.

Dummett is not, of course, denying the obvious fact that persons who think of meta-physics, ontology, perception and epistemology one way will give different descriptions of meaning from those who think of it another way. His claim is that whether or not this is in fact so, it need not be so. The impact of these intruders on a meaning-theory is, somehow, capable of being avoided. But saying that this is possible is far from showing how it is possible, and Dummett's own explorations in this direction have not proved reassuring. In his famous paper, 'The Philosophical Basis of Intuitionistic Logic' (1978), for example, he explained the Wittgensteinian doctrine that meaning is use as implying that we cannot be understood to mean anything we cannot be observed to mean, thereby betraying a fondness for observation that is not at all epistemologically or metaphysically neutral – on the contrary, it is one of the principal planks of posi-tivism (the less contentious doctrine would be that we cannot be understood to mean anything that we cannot be thought of as meaning, leaving the relationship of thought to observation to be fought over another day).

Even more remarkable is the belief that a satisfactory meaning-theory will exhaust the field of metaphysics. We can see the magnitude of this claim by a simple example. Suppose we think of the domain of THEOLOGY (chapter 15) as a part of metaphysics. Then is there really a prospect of an innocent, theologically neutral meaning-theory, not only telling us what is meant by the various terms used by religious thinkers, but *also* telling us the metaphysical truth about such matters? Surely the gap cannot be bridged: anything innocent enough to qualify on the first score must leave the truth of theological claims undecided; anything strong enough to decide them (for instance, the claim that a term like 'God' derives its meaning from God, who must therefore exist for us to think as we do) is not the innocent, neutral starting point that Dummett requires and promises. The same dilemma is visible in other areas, such as ethics. Careful atten-tion to the nature of evaluative language is certainly a necessary part of any worth-while philosophy of ethics, but without a wider view of the nature of human choice, desire and action it will not itself settle disputes between one and another metaphysics of value. And semantic doctrines that bear on such disputes, such as the view that ethical language is essentially prescriptive in function, or the view that ethical predi-cates work in much the same way as colour predicates, are not the neutral, purely empirical outcome of a meaning-theory, but represent instead wider philosophical thought about the way ethical commitments actually function. For a final example, consider the descriptions that are offered of the language in which we talk about neces-sity and possibility. The best-known semantics for these languages are thoroughly 'real-istic', conceiving of us as referring to possible worlds, and describing the inferences we make in classical quantificational terms (if we are talking about possible worlds, neces-sity becomes equivalent to 'all' and possibility to 'some', and the logic is then under-stood classically). The semantic success of this kind of description is undoubted, but its philosophical significance is controversial in the extreme. Those, like Lewis, whose metaphysics is driven entirely by semantics embrace the real existence of different worlds to ours; others reject any such metaphysical implications, and maintain that reference to possible worlds is some kind of useful fiction. The example shows clearly how an overview of the logic of an area can leave its metaphysics almost entirely in the dark. In spite of Dummett's impassioned and weighty advocacy, the prospects, then, for a neutral semantic methodology for metaphysics are not all that bright.

The strength of Dummett's position was its insistence that if metaphysics gives us more than vaguely agreeable pictures, then its content should be reflected in our practice. That is, if a doctrine such as realism means anything, it must make a difference whether or not we adopt it, and this difference must be manifested somewhere in our thought and language. The mathematical example is one in which the classical mathematician allows different inferences from the intuitionist; the difference is therefore one of logic. It is not, however, clear to what extent this case generalizes – certainly, many people who think of themselves as anti-realists about ethics have no objection to classical logic as a systematization of correct inference in that sphere. Kant thought that it was precisely because mathematics was our own construction that we had the right to pursue it in the certainty that every mathematical proposition is true or false. A metaphysics is an overall structure determining which explanations of our practices we find acceptable: it determines what is familiar, what exotic, what counts as an acceptable accommodation and what is intolerable to us. The difference that realism or anti-realism makes is not necessarily one of logic. It comes out primarily in what we accept as explanations of our practice, including explanations of the correctness or otherwise of various patterns of inferences, and it is because of this that classical logical practice can happily coexist with an anti-realist explanation of its appropriateness.

Dummett's conception of the subject is almost unique in the contemporary scene in its insistence on a starting-point that is uncontaminated by scientific and metaphysical doctrines and ideologies. Much more common is the view that such doctrines will themselves be historically conditioned and therefore possibly changeable. It is important to notice that in detail the nature of such changes is often controversial. For example, it has been claimed by Rorty (1979) that the philosophy of mind and its problems are historically quite local, being mainly the upshot of the rise of Cartesian philosophy in the early seventeenth century. To others this is incredible, since it is possible to point to the universal human preoccupation with such possibilities as life after death or the transmigration of souls as a sure sign that the relationship of mind to body has seldom been fully under control. Again, some see the distinction between primary qualities on the one hand – such as extension and mass, which are thought of as real qualities of objective, independent bodies – and secondary qualities on the other hand – such as colour or taste, which are thought of as inherently subjective or mind-dependent – as the local upshot of the science of the same period. But others point to the foundation of the distinction in Greek thought, and its appearance in various forms in Indian or Chinese thought, and argue that the basis is not a particular scientific ideology, but is found in relatively universal or *a priori* considerations.

3   Naturalism and Identity

The authority of logic lay behind the analytic ideal, for logical relationships are those that are laid bare by analysis. When this authority falters, as I have described it doing, the authority of science is the natural substitute, and it is in its shelter that metaphysics is currently mainly conducted. Metaphysics, on this view, is not discontinuous with science. It is theorizing as pursued by the scientist, sometimes on the basis of familiar data and sometimes in the light of new scientific results. This is the *naturalistic* self-image, most forcibly propounded by the American philosopher W. V. O. Quine (b. 1908), and dominant in the minds of many or most contemporary philosophers. In this view, it is perfectly proper to attempt, for example, a metaphysics of MIND AND BODY (chapter 5). It is to be done in the spirit of science, with an up-to-date understanding of neurophysiology, computer science, ecology, evolutionary biology, or any other subject that rings the area. The philosopher marshals the results of the sciences, and propounds a concept of the mind–body relationship that best makes the results fit together, just as the scientist marshals the results of empirical enquiry, and propounds a concept of the nature of things that best makes those results fit together. The metaphysicians' activity differs only in the level of abstraction required, and indeed any difference from the activity of theoretical science is likely to be vague and provisional. Success in philosophizing would most dramatically be shown if the results of philosophical enquiry actually played a role in driving scientific progress.

It is easy to understand why the naturalistic self-image is so popular. First of all, it answers the question of how metaphysics is possible. It is continuous with science, and, since science is possible, so is metaphysics. Secondly, it allows the philosopher some of the prestige and glory of the scientist. It is reassuring to ally philosophical reflection with the most secure and intellectually privileged elements of the contemporary culture. Perhaps philosophy is always something of a free-loader when it comes to continuity with the most prestigious activities. When theology ruled the universities, philosophy and theology were continuous; in the first part of this century, and after the spectacular successes of modern logic, philosophy was deemed continuous with logic; then a little later with linguistics, and now philosophy marches into the future hand-in-hand with science. (The process is of course not as simple as that. Philosophy has had the scientific self-image on-and-off since Aristotle. But other paradigms have also had their day.) Thirdly, the assimilation of metaphysics to science solves the problem of method. In the abstract, it is difficult to know how to conduct metaphysical enquiry. How is one to go about solving the mind–body problem, or discussing the nature of necessity? In distant times, the answer might have been by reflection on what the deity created, by reflection on the logic of mental or modal discourse, or by reflection on the language of mental ascription or modal embeddings. But the current answer is more reassuring: scientifically.

With so much to motivate contentment with this answer, it may be well to wonder whether an element of wish-fulfilment has crept in. Is it possible that the self-image of philosophy as being continuous with science is largely fantasy – that we have been captured by the most superficial resemblances between philosophical and genuinely scientific activity? Might it be that science-envy has led philosophers to see themselves through a comfortable modern haze? Of course, if approaching a subject scientifically simply means attempting to follow it through in a disciplined way, taking account of the known facts, building on our predecessor's labours, using the best ways we have of distinguishing the good from the bad or the true from the false, then philosophy as properly practised, like any other discipline, must be pursued scientifically. But in that sense a novelist or poet may also practise their craft scientifically; the obstacle remains that such activities may bear only the most superficial resemblance to the practice of natural sciences.

The reason for this is clear if we consider what we want from a satisfactory relationship between the exotic and the familiar. Suppose we are happy with scientific facts: in the case of people, let us suppose these are facts about their behaviour and their brains. The naturalist will believe that in an important sense brains and behaviour is all that there is. What then is there to say about mind? The simplest answer is that mental states or events or properties are states, events, or properties of the preferred natural kind. The equation would be presented as like that between water and H_2O, or between lightning and electrical discharge. An enormously important shift took place when these equations emerged as new paradigms of method in metaphysics, largely in the 1970s, and it was due to the work of writers such as Putnam (1975) and Kripke (1980). It came to be believed that we can relate an exotic area to a domestic one in a less hazardous way than by concentrating on equations of meaning. All we may need is an identity claim about the things and properties in question. We do not also need the claim that the very same thing is meant by talking in terms of one and in terms of the other. It is sufficient, for instance, to understand water in scientific terms to know that water *is* H_2O; we do not also need the requirement that the two terms mean the same. Similarly, we would bring mind and consciousness down to natural earth if we could identify mental states, processes and events, with physical states, processes and events. We do not also have to claim that it means the same to talk in either way. Identity of things and properties became the ruling relationship to search for, not identity of meaning.

However, casual acquaintance with the modern literature shows that philosophical discussion of such an equation is not very much like scientific discussion of these equations. There, one would find various kinds of empirical evidence and theory. In the philosophical case we have a general belief that mind must be thought of as fundamentally physical, and then we conduct a great deal of armchair theorizing about the nature of the sustaining equations and identities. This theorizing does not proceed with very convincing examples of actual identities to hand, nor, indeed, is it even known whether convincing 'type–type' identities exist. Thus, it is always true that lightning is an electrical discharge, or water is H_2O, but it may not always be true that a mental event such as a pain coexists with a type of physical event, or whether pain might be 'variably realized' in different brains or different psychologies. It is here that philosophers discuss whether the equation is contingent or necessary, whether it relates types of mental events to types of physical events or whether it is sufficient that each mental event is identical with some – possibly different – kind of physical event, whether it matters that description of a person's mentality often invokes relations with the environment, history and culture, and so on. Without this kind of discussion the equation is of little interest, but it is this theorizing that is insufficiently like anything the scientist does that casts doubt on the Quinean paradigm.

In fact, it may be claimed that the entire discussion of such identities waits upon a piece of analysis that is, unfortunately, not yet completed. We know how to assess questions of identity when the subjects are *things*; we may know how to assess them in cases like that of water or lightning, where what is at question is the way in which a natural kind of event is constituted. But do we know how to assess cross-category identities when the subjects are facts, events, states or properties? What does it mean, for example, to say that my state when I enjoy a glass of wine is identical with the state of some part of my brain, or that the event of my enjoyment is identical with some such event, or that the property of enjoying the wine is identical with some neurophysiological property? Such identity claims do not wear their meanings on their sleeve; nor does a metaphysics centred on asserting them. We do not even know whether each of the abstract categories involved – property, state, event or fact – relates to identity in the same way, or whether very different criteria are needed in each case. To give a simple parallel, some philosophers hold that if a padlock opens by having three notches in line, then it makes sense to say that the state or property of being unlocked is, in this padlock (not others), that of having three notches in line; other philosophers doubt if the equation makes sense, or whether, if it does, it is of any metaphysical use (Lewis 1966; Blackburn 1993).

It does not follow that these questions will be investigated by exactly the techniques modelled on analytical chemistry, and developed by Russell, Moore, Carnap and their followers. But support for this conception of the subject comes from the following thoughts. Suppose we need to locate a way of thinking accurately, in order to gain an understanding of the categories it uses. Then the primary data are the *inferences* that structure the area. These are conveniently thought of as of three kinds. There are things that enable us to make inferences to doctrines in the area (sometimes called the assertibility conditions of such doctrines), there are inferences among such doctrines, and there are things we may infer from them, or their consequences. Staying with the example of mind, the statement that someone is enjoying their glass of wine may be inferred from certain aspects of their behaviour; it enables us to infer that they believe that there is nothing poisonous about the wine (and many other things of the kind), and it enables us to infer (with less confidence) that they are likely to stay put for some while, and unlikely to start doing push-ups or spit on the carpet. The analytic ideal suggests that such inferences, and many like them, give the statement its identity. Not to make them would eventually show that someone does not fully understand what is involved in enjoying a glass of wine; it would reveal incompetence with the notions involved. But identifying these inferences is, in effect, the project of analysis. A term is analysed, in the classical tradition, precisely when we understand what licenses its application, and what consequences may be drawn from it.

The problem that many authors find with this line of thought is that the inferences in question do not seem to come in statement-sized bundles. The mental world is full of surprises and caveats: behaviour that is indicative of enjoying a glass of wine in one person may not be so in another; what else a person wants or believes when they enjoy a glass of wine may be almost indefinitely variable, and for all we know there may be cultures in which doing push-ups or spitting on the carpet is exactly what we would expect by way of showing such enjoyment. The phenomenon, often called the 'holism of the mental', means that straightforward identification of the patterns of inference associated with understanding a mental ascription is not to be expected. Once more, enjoying a glass of wine is something that can be 'variably realized' in different psychologies, evidenced by different behaviour and giving rise to different expression, depending on a whole range of other factors.

Identities nevertheless remain popular instruments for relating the familiar to the exotic. But there are cases that raise more obvious difficulties than that of mind. Consider the project of giving a naturalistic theory of values. Suppose it is pursued on the water–H$_2$O model, by finding a property with which a value such as goodness may plausibly be identified. Let us suppose for simplicity's sake that a property is selected, such as that of creating happiness. This is thought of as a natural, empirically respectable property, it being a fairly ordinary fact about the world (however hard to assess in some cases) that some things cause happiness and others do not. So the metaphysician naturalizes values by making the equation. Admittedly, saying that something is good is not just saying that it creates happiness – Moore (1903) refuted that idea. Nevertheless, the identity-inclined metaphysician insists, the properties are the same. The puzzle with such an idea is that it is quite unclear which of the problems that ethics generates it actually solves. It leaves untouched any investigation of the particular 'take' on the creation of happiness that is had by those who think that it is good, as opposed to those who are indifferent to it, or even who think that it is bad. It does not by itself tell us what kind of mistake is made by these other people. Is it an objective mistake, or a more subjective one; is their error an empirical error, or one of logic? What, indeed, does it mean to see the creation of happiness under the ethical heading? While such questions remain, the identity seems itself a poor contribution to the overall project of giving a naturalistic understanding of our engagement with values.

The Limits of Ontology

Although doing metaphysics by means of the identity of property, state, event or fact is popular, it introduces a particular attitude to its problems: one in which the primary questions are ones of what exist; ones of *ontology*. The central question becomes whether we have two things or one, whether the things are events, properties, states, facts or other more homely items. This is also a contrast with the approach of analysts like Dummett. For the analyst, the unit of significance is the entire sentence; there is no self-standing investigation into the kinds of thing that parts of sentences such as predicates stand for (however, as Taylor (1993) remarks, realists have often felt motivated to expound the existence and nature of such items as universals and properties). But many problems, such as that of value, suggest that not all metaphysical issues are well approached in these terms. Another example where ontology scarcely seems to be the issue is the problem of natural law or necessity. This problem, brought into prominence by Hume (1978), is that of gaining some conception of any necessity underlying the brute empirical order of events. Events, as we apprehend them, happen one after another in contingent patterns that the natural scientist discovers. Descriptions of the way they fall out may be all right; they form the familiar class. What is exotic and hard to think about is a reason why they must fall out as they do, or why the universe must be ordered as it is, or why the order that is discovered must continue to govern its evolutions in the future. The theological worldview could take refuge in the necessity thought to attach to God's existence and to God's goodness in continuing to sustain the same natural order; when such an answer no longer appeals to people's minds there is urgent need for something to fill its place. The problem is essentially metaphysical, for what we are looking for is some conception of the holding of a law of nature: something lying behind or above the actual pattern of events and constraining them to fall out as they do. Now will such a problem be eased by an ontological doctrine? Many suppose it can. They believe that if we can say, sufficiently seriously, that natural laws exist, then everything is fine. It would not be sufficiently serious to say this but only to mean that there are some regularities that are so central to the enterprise of science that they deserve central and privileged places in the ways we systematize our understanding of the patterns of events. The problem is to gain any conception of what it is for these real natural laws to exist, or how things of the nature they need to have are even possible. How can there exist a strait-jacket, whose nature at one time governs how things must fall out at later times or at all other times (Blackburn 1993: chs 3, 5)? More ontology just provides more things, but things and their continued good behaviour are part of the problem, and so do not seem to be any part of the solution.

A final, even clearer example in which ontology cannot be the central issue is the problem of free will. Realizing that we ourselves, physically, are determined complexes, or at best are permitted only such departures from determination as the random events of quantum mechanics allow, philosophers friendly to free-will may struggle to find a further 'part' of us, such as a Cartesian, ghostly, governing agency. But the dilemma is not escaped by these means, for it returns to plague whatever extra is added, for it remains to be explained how it is itself neither wholly determined nor wholly random. The additional ontology is no help with the solution.

Problems with identity have led many naturalists to back down a little, and stake their faith on a different, and at first sight more tractable relation: that of supervenience.

4   Supervenience

Whether or not it makes sense to identify mental and physical events, or ethical and natural properties, at least we ought to think that the mental arises out of the physical, and the ethical out of the natural. This is commonly put by saying that the mental supervenes on the physical, and the ethical on the natural. What does this mean? The fundamental idea is that once the physical aspects of the world are completely fixed, so are the mental. And once the natural facts about a world are completely fixed, so is the question of its ethics – which actions are right and wrong, or who behaved well or badly. Once the familiar is fixed, so is the exotic. If we think in terms of God creating a world, then all he has to do, according to this idea, is to create the physical world. He will thereby have done sufficient to fix the mental facts, or the ethical facts. There is no second creative task to complete.

This idea promises many of the benefits of identity claims, without involving itself in the issues of the previous section. It needs no controversial metaphysics of facts, states of affairs or properties, nor any method of resolving disputed identity claims involving these notions. But it gives the same sense that there is in reality 'nothing but' the underlying, physical or natural world. At least it removes one kind of metaphysical distance between the two categories; the distance that would be were there a second creative task to complete, so that we could imagine the physical being as it is, but without the mental overlay, or the natural being as it is, but without the ethical overlay.

It is notable that to give us this advantage, the supervenience claim must somewhere involve a necessity. There would be a second creative task to complete if, as well as creating physics, God had to shop for one among several possible ways in which physics is able to fix the mental (in this world). If this relationship were contingent, capable of taking different forms in different possible worlds, then clearly there would be a second creative task to complete. It would not be strictly true that physics fixed everything; only physics plus whatever it is as well as physics that links everything else to it.

It is, I believe, worthy of note that the best understood examples of supervenience do not quite give us this sort of necessity. Many examples involve a reference to perception, as when the face in the picture supervenes upon an array of dots. It is certainly true that to create the face no more is necessary than to create the array of dots. But that seems to be because the world contains perceivers such as ourselves; relative to different perceptual powers there would no longer be a face in the picture. So, strictly, God had to do more to create the face in the picture than just arrange the dots; he also had to generate the perceptual sensitivities capable of responding to just that array in just that way. Similarly, to create secondary qualities, such as those of colour, it is not only necessary to create a world in which surfaces reflect light in various ways, but also to create the kinds of perceptual systems that detect the variations in just that way. In these cases, instead of the reassuring, physicalist-sounding thesis that everything supervenes on the underlying physics, we only get that it supervenes on the underlying physics and the relations between physics and perceivers. Granted, a full-blown physicalist will promise that this relation in turn supervenes upon the physics of the surface and the physics of the perceiver, but, so far, this remains simply a promise. We do not have, in cases like this, reassuring examples of the necessity that supervenience claims require.

In the case of ethics it is quite unsatisfactory simply to cite the supervenience of values on natural facts, and then to hope that this makes the intelligible bridge required. The problem is obviously to explain the necessity in question. Granted that any two worlds that are identical in all natural features are identical in all ethical features, why should this have to be so? What, logically or metaphysically, prevents there being a dimension of freedom, the extra thing that God has to do to fix the fact–value links? Explaining supervenience here marks a constraint on satisfactory theory. Some believe that it can be met by citing the parallel with perceptual supervenience claims such as the ones discussed above; others deny this, but think that attention to the purposes for which we value things can only be met by a value system obeying the supervenience constraint. There arises a kind of pragmatic justification for this aspect of the logic of the activity (Blackburn 1993). Once more the issue is one of explanation, and different metaphysical choices are primarily significant because of the different explanatory packages they offer.

5   Conclusion

I have structured this survey round the problem of method in metaphysics, and some of the most influential suggestions about the source of metaphysical method and of metaphysical authority. I have also sketched some of the ways in which authoritative suggestions – analysis, meaning-theory and scientific reduction – have proved at best aids, but never final arbiters of metaphysical success. My own belief is that metaphysics is better regarded as an ocean into which all intellectual rivers flow. When the problems are as abstract and the kinds of explanation required are so difficult to formulate, there is bound to be influence from many different sources: the self-conception of a given period, the scientific paradigms of that period, the most influential examples of intellectual success, even the ethical and political agenda, as well as conceptions of the role of the given time. This is not a cause for regret, but it may perhaps arm us with a cautious scepticism when candidates for metaphysical certainty present themselves.

6 Time

What is time? We may be at a loss to answer this rather bald, abstract question. But suppose we approach it via the more tractable question of how we become aware of the passage of time. To this, the answer is surely through awareness of *change*, either in the external world – the ticking of a clock, the movement of clouds in the sky, the setting of the sun – or in our own thoughts. But if awareness of time and awareness of change are the same thing, then perhaps the best answer to our first question is this: time just *is* change.

ARISTOTLE (chapter 23) attributed this answer to some of his predecessors. And, as with many of his predecessors' opinions, he found fault with it. Time could not be the same thing as change, he said, for first change can go at different rates, speed up or slow down, but not so time, and secondly change is confined to a part of space whereas time is universal. What are we to make of these objections? Surely time does speed up or slow down, or at least it appears to do so. For people in love, a few hours spent together will pass all too swiftly, whereas time will hang heavily during a labour of unremitting tedium. But such phenomena are easily dismissed as illusory. We can be deceived about spatial matters, such as the shape or size of an object, or its distance from us, so why not also about temporal matters? To see whether it makes sense to suppose that *time itself* could pass at different rates, consider how we measure the rate of other kinds of change: the speed of a passing bus, for example. We measure the distance it covers against time. Or consider a kettle on a stove. Its rate of heating is given by measuring the rise in temperature against time. So rate of change is variation in some dimension in so many units of time. How, then, would we measure the rate of passage of time? Why, against time, presumably. But this leads to the conclusion that the rate of the passage of time must never vary. For how long could five minutes take if not five minutes? But Aristotle's objection perhaps misses the point. It is true that time could not be identified with particular changes, such as the crumbling of a sand castle. But to identify time with change is surely to identify time with change *in general*. Now it is not at all clear that change in general – that is, the sum of all changes in the universe – could intelligibly be regarded as proceeding at varying rates. Try to imagine every change in the world suddenly doubling in speed. Does that idea make sense? Aristotle would not have thought so. For one thing, we could not possibly *notice* such a change in rate, for we only notice the change in the rate of some change when comparing it with other changes. We notice the shortening of days with the onset of winter by measuring the time between sunrise and sunset against conventional timepieces or our own biological clocks.

The idea that time is to be identified, not with particular changes, but with change in general seems also to avoid Aristotle's second objection, that change is confined to parts of space, whereas time is universal. Only individual changes are spatially con-fined, but the totality of change covers the whole of space.

These considerations may have removed one ambiguity in the notion of change, but there remains another. What kind of change do we suppose time to be? Do we think that time is the same as the sum of all the ordinary changes of which we can directly be aware, such as the changing colour of a leaf, and also those which underlie per-ceivable changes, though not themselves perceivable, such as the motion of molecules? Or are we instead thinking of the passage of time itself, the inexorable movement of things once present into the ever-distant past? Of course, a philosopher who said that time was to be defined as the passage of time would not get much of a following, since such a definition defines time in terms of itself. We need to have some way of defining the passage of time. This is most vividly described (though some philosophers would object to this way of describing it) as the change in events as they cease to be future, become present, and then increasingly past.

One way of capturing the distinction above is in terms of first- and second-order change. *First-order change* is change in the properties of things in the world, where 'things' are conceived of as items that persist through time, such as trees, atoms and persons. *Second-order change* is change in first-order changes, namely the shifting degree of futurity or pastness of such first-order changes. Second-order change, the changing of changes, is the passage of time. So when we say time is change, is this first-order change or second-order change?

Suppose we mean first-order change. Now, it might seem to us that we could imagine every process in the universe coming to a stop – perhaps after the so-called 'heat-death' of the universe, where all energy is perfectly evenly dispersed – and yet time continu-ing to pass. Endless aeons of time might pass in a completely dead, motionless universe. To put it in terms of the distinction above: second-order change need not imply ongoing first-order change. But where we have second-order change, we have time. So maybe time can exist in the absence of first-order change? Aristotle did not think so, on the grounds that, were all (first-order) change to cease, we would cease to notice the passage of time. But we might be more cautious than Aristotle in making perceivabil-ity a criterion of intelligibility. Perhaps there are some states of affairs which we could never even in principle detect.

What if instead we define time as *second*-order change? This, more subtle, position looks unassailable. How could time exist unless it also passed? To see how things might be otherwise, we need to introduce at this point another distinction, due to the Cambridge philosopher and older contemporary of Russell and Moore, J. E. McTaggart (1866–1925). McTaggart distinguished between what he called the A-series and the B-series, representing different ways of defining positions in time. To define the *A-series* position of an event is to define the time of the event as past (by varying degrees), present or future (by varying degrees). To define the *B-series* position of an event is to define the time of the event in terms of its relations with other events, that is whether it is earlier than, later than or simultaneous with those other events. The most striking difference between these two series is that, whereas the A-series position of an event is constantly changing, its B-series position remains fixed. If an explosion takes place, and is followed by a fire, then these two events remain forever in this relation to each other: one is earlier than the other. To say that time consists of an A-series is another way of stating the view that time is the same as second-order change.

But if time just consists of the A-series, what becomes of the B-series? The natural and plausible answer is that the difference between the two series is one only of language, not of reality. In reality, B-series positions are a direct consequence of A-series positions. Thus, if my getting out of bed this morning is now *past*, my having lunch is *present*, and my taking a stroll in the park is *future* (A-series positions), then getting out of bed is *earlier than* the lunch, and both are *earlier than* the stroll (B-series positions). Once the A-series positions are fixed, so are the B-series positions. Or, as one might put it, it is A-series facts which make B-series statements true or false.

McTaggart, however, invites us to consider an intriguing alternative (although he later rejects it): that time in reality consists solely of a B-series. Now this idea is not immediately intelligible, and it has to be said that McTaggart does not help us very much to make sense of it, no doubt because he himself thought that, ultimately, it does not make sense. But we can try to do so in ways which go beyond McTaggart's own discussion. To raise a similar question to one asked earlier: if time is just a B-series, what becomes of the A-series? Now we cannot reply here that the A-series is fixed by the B-series and leave it at that, because there is a very obvious sense in which the B-series cannot determine the A-series. The fact that the battle of Hastings is earlier than the battle of Trafalgar does not completely fix the A-series positions of these events. The A-series positions are only partially fixed: we can say, for example, that if the battle of Trafalgar is present, then the battle of Hastings must be past, but its position in the B-series does not tell us whether the battle of Trafalgar is present or not. Some philosophers take this as proof that a description of time in purely B-series terms, in terms of what comes before what, leaves out important facts. But perhaps all the above considerations lead to is the conclusion that the relation between the two series is not straightforward. We need to bring in some further component. What could that be?

Consider this more promising account of the two series. During a particularly heavy downpour, I say, with characteristic understatement, 'It's raining'. I am making an A-series statement, in that I am attributing presentness to the rain. But on the account we are now considering what makes my statement true is the purely *B-series* fact that my statement is simultaneous with the raining. After the sky has cleared, I say 'It *was* raining'. Again, what makes this A-series statement, attributing pastness to the rain, true is the purely B-series fact that my statement occurs after the rain. So what B-series facts – facts, that is, about the B-series positions of events – are able to do is to fix the truth or falsity of A-series statements. This theory is sometimes called the *tenseless theory* of time. It is capable, it seems, of reconciling the notion that time in reality simply consists of a B-series, with the intuitive belief that statements such as 'It's now raining', or 'I had my lunch an hour ago', can be true or false.

One consequence of the view that time consists simply of a B-series is that time does not flow: there is in reality no recession of events into the past. What could motivate such a view? A number of arguments have been put forward in its defence, the best known arising from a famous argument of McTaggart's, in which he attempted to prove the unreality, not only of the A-series, but of time itself. There is no space to do justice to that argument here, but three other considerations in favour of the B-series view (that there is in reality no A-series, only a B-series) can be stated briefly: (a) the plausibility of the account given above of how A-series statements can be made true simply in virtue of B-series relations between those statements and the events they describe; (b) the fact that we cannot make sense of the rate of the flow of time varying, which in turn makes us question the idea of a rate of flow, and hence of a flow at all; (c) the apparent unanswerability of the question 'Why is D now?' (where 'D' stands for today's date) except in purely B-series terms: D is correctly describable as 'now' simply because the question is asked on the date it mentions.

The B-series, or tenseless, theory of time faces challenges of its own: how can it account for change, or the direction of time? Such an account may be forthcoming, but there is at least one intuitive belief concerning time with which it comes into conflict, namely the belief that the future is *unreal*: there are no future facts in the way that there are present facts. On the B-series view, in contrast, all times are equally real, and this is perhaps the most striking of its consequences.

Further Reading

This chapter emphasizes twentieth-century metaphysics, but readers might also wish to consult the metaphysical works of historical figures discussed in other chapters, especially Hume, *A Treatise of Human Nature* and Kant, *Critique of Pure Reason*. Craig (1987) explores the great modern change from a divine to a human context of metaphysical thought.

Russell (1905) was long considered a model for analytical treatment of metaphysical questions. Wittgenstein (1922), while having a metaphysical character of his own, inspired the strenuously anti-metaphysical attitude of the Vienna Circle. The pragmatism of Peirce, James (1907), and Dewey influenced many recent American writers, including Quine (1951), Goodman (1955), Putnam (1975) and Rorty (1979, 1989). The criticism of positivism in Quine and Wittgenstein (1953) led to new perspectives on the possibility of metaphysics, especially that of Strawson (1959), whose focus on describing the contours of our ordinary conceptual scheme has been rejected in the eliminativism of Churchland (1989) and Stich (1983). Kripke (1980) and Lewis (1983) have provided different accounts of the importance of modal logic (dealing with necessity and possibility) for metaphysics. Dummett (1978, 1991) has argued that logic and the theory of meaning are the basis for metaphysics, especially for dealing with the fundamental conflict between realism and anti-realism, a question also considered in Blackburn (1993).

Time

HISTORICALLY IMPORTANT TEXTS ON TIME

Any list of these would include Book IV of Aristotle's *Physics*, Augustine's *Confessions*, the Leibniz–Clarke correspondence, and Kant's *Critique of Pure Reason* (see especially the Transcendental Aesthetic and the First Antinomy of Pure Reason).

HISTORY OF THE PHILOSOPHY OF TIME

An excellent overview of theories of time from the Presocratics to the later middle ages is provided by Sorabji (1983). There is a useful, if brief, discussion of Aristotle, Leibniz and Kant in Van Fraassen (1985). Both ancient and modern writers are discussed in Turetsky (1998).

INTRODUCTIONS AND ANTHOLOGIES

Apart from Van Fraassen's book mentioned above, Swinburne (1981) covers a good range of topics in the philosophy of space and time. A lively introduction, in dialogue form, to issues such as the beginning and end of time, the passage of time, the nature of eternity, and the relationship between time and freedom is Smith and Oaklander (1995). Le Poidevin and MacBeath (1993) is a collection of important readings, some of which are accessible to the non-specialist. It includes J. E. McTaggart's attempted proof of the unreality of time. The most comprehensive recent introduction to space and time, which discusses at length the question of whether time flows, is Dainton (2001).

SPECIFIC TOPICS

The relationship between time and change, and issues concerning the topological structure of time (e.g. whether it has a beginning/end, whether it is infinitely divisible, and whether it is like an open line or a closed circle) are very clearly discussed in Newton-Smith (1980). The direction of time is the subject of Price (1996). The A-series/B-series distinction, the tenseless theory of time, and related topics such as the direction of time, the nature of change and the possibility of time-travel, are presented with considerable depth and originality in the second edition of Mellor (1998). Smith (1993) is a detailed and sustained attack on the tenseless theory. A closely related issue, that of the reality of the future, is the topic of Lucas (1989) and of Faye (1989), which also tackles the relationship between time and causality, as does Tooley (1997). The various interconnections between time and ethics are pursued in Cockburn (1997). The significance of the tenseless theory of time, and that of its rivals, for a variety of debates in philosophy is the subject of a collection of readings: Le Poidevin (1998).

PHILOSOPHY OF SPACE-TIME PHYSICS

The Special and General Theories of Relativity have had an enormous impact on philosophical thinking about time. An engaging, though not particularly easy, introduction to the interaction of the physics and philosophy of space and time is Ray (1991). An important and wide-ranging text is Sklar (1974). Nerlich (1994) is an important collection of Nerlich's writings on space, time and relativity.

References

Aristotle 1983: *Aristotle's Physics, Books III and IV* (translated with notes by E. Hussey). Oxford: Clarendon Press.

Augustine, Saint 1961: *Confessions* (translated by R. S. Pine-Coffin). Harmondsworth: Penguin Books.

Blackburn, S. 1984: *Spreading the Word: Groundings in the Philosophy of Language*. Oxford: Oxford University Press.

——1993: *Essays in Quasi-Realism*. New York: Oxford University Press.

Churchland, P. 1989: *A Neurocomputational Perspective: The Nature of Mind and the Structure of Science*. Cambridge, MA: MIT Press.

Cockburn, D. 1997: *Other Times: Philosophical Perspectives on Past, Present and Future*. Cambridge: Cambridge University Press.

Collingwood, R. 1940: *An Essay in Metaphysics*. Oxford: Clarendon Press.

Craig, E. 1987: *The Mind of God and the Works of Man*. Oxford: Oxford University Press.

Dainton, B. 2001: *Time and Space*. London: Acumen Press.

Dummett, M. 1978: The Philosophical Basis of Intuitionistic Logic. In *Truth and Other Enigmas*, London: Duckworth.

——1991: *The Logical Basis of Metaphysics*. Cambridge, MA: Harvard University Press.

Faye, J. 1989: *The Reality of the Future*. Odense: Odense University Press.

Gibbard, A. 1990: *Wise Choices, Apt Feelings*. Cambridge, MA: Harvard University Press.

Goodman, N. 1955: *Fact, Fiction and Forecast*. London: London University Press.

Hegel, G. 1991 [1821]: *The Philosophy of Right* (translated by H. B. Nisbet, edited by A. W. Wood). Cambridge: Cambridge University Press.

Hume, D. 1978 [1739–40]: *A Treatise of Human Nature* (edited by P. H. Nidditch). Oxford: Clarendon Press.

James, W. 1907: *Pragmatism: A New Name for Some Old Ways of Thinking*. New York: Longmans.

Kant, I. 1933: *Immanuel Kant's Critique of Pure Reason*, Second Impression (translated by N. K. Smith). London: Macmillan.

Kripke, S. 1980: *Naming and Necessity*. Cambridge, MA: Harvard University Press.

Le Poidevin, R. (ed.) 1998: *Questions of Time and Tense*. Oxford: Clarendon Press.

Le Poidevin, R. and MacBeath, M. (eds) 1993: *The Philosophy of Time*. Oxford: Oxford University Press.

Leibniz, G. W. and Clarke, S. 1956: *The Leibniz–Clarke Correspondence* (edited by H. G. Alexander). Manchester: Manchester University Press.

Lewis, D. 1966: An Argument for the Identity Theory. In *Philosophical Papers*, vol. 1. New York: Oxford University Press.

——1983: New Work for a Theory of Universals. *Australasian Journal of Philosophy*, 61.

Lewis, H. D. (ed.) 1963: *Clarity is not Enough*. New York: Humanities Press.

Lucas, J. 1989: *The Future*. Oxford: Blackwell.

Mellor, D. H. 1998: *Real Time II*. London: Routledge.

Moore, G. E. 1903: *Principia Ethica*. Cambridge: Cambridge University Press. Revised edition edited by T. R. Baldwin, Cambridge: Cambridge University Press, 1993.

Nerlich, G. 1994: *What Spacetime Explains*. Cambridge: Cambridge University Press.

Newton-Smith, W. H. 1980: *The Structure of Time*. London: Routledge and Kegan Paul.

Price, H. 1996: *Time's Arrow and Archimedes' Point*. New York: Oxford University Press.

Putnam, H. 1975: The Meaning of 'Meaning'. In *Mind, Language and Reality: Philosophical Papers*, vol. 2. Cambridge: Cambridge University Press.

Quine, W. V. O. 1951: Two Dogmas of Empiricism. In *From a Logical Point of View*, New York: Harper.

Ray, C. 1991: *Time, Space and Philosophy*. London: Routledge.

Rorty, R. 1979: *Philosophy and the Mirror of Nature*. Princeton, NJ: Princeton University Press.

——1989: *Contingency, Irony and Solidarity*. Cambridge: Cambridge University Press.

Russell, B. 1905: On Denoting. *Mind*, 14.

Sklar, L. 1974: *Space, Time and Space-Time*. Berkeley: University of California Press.

Smith, Q. 1993: *The Language of Time*. New York: Oxford University Press.

Smith, Q. and Oaklander, L. N. 1995: *Time, Change and Freedom*. London: Routledge.

Sorabji, R. 1983: *Time, Creation and the Continuum*. London: Duckworth.

Stich, S. 1983: *From Folk Psychology to Cognitive Science*. Cambridge, MA: MIT Press.

Strawson, P. 1959: *Individuals: An Essay in Descriptive Metaphysics*. London: Methuen.

Swinburne, R. G. 1981: *Space and Time*, 2nd edn. London: Macmillan.

Taylor, B. 1993: On Natural Properties in Metaphysics. *Mind*, 102.

Tooley, M. 1997: *Time, Tense and Causation*. Oxford: Clarendon Press.

Turetsky, P. 1998: *Time*. London: Routledge.

Van Fraassen, B. 1985: *An Introduction to the Philosophy of Time and Space*, 2nd edn. New York: Columbia University Press.

Wittgenstein, L. 1922: *Tractatus Logico–Philosophicus*. London: Routledge.

—— 1953: *Philosophical Investigations*. Oxford: Blackwell.

Discussion Questions

1   How is metaphysics possible? How do metaphysical questions arise?

2   Does metaphysics discover the broad structure of reality or describe how our conceptual scheme structures our thought about reality?

3   Must all possible conceptual schemes have certain features in common?

4   How might a programme of revisionary metaphysics be justified?

5   Can metaphysics be assessed without considering its ethical and political implications?

6   Is metaphysics the science of Being?

7   Does metaphysics have an acceptable method?

8   Why is metaphysics preoccupied with its own possibility?

9   Is metaphysics a function of what we find familiar and what we find puzzling? Can what we find familiar change?

10   Are there limits beyond which metaphysics should not go? Does the whole of metaphysics attempt to go beyond these limits?

11   If metaphysical questions are unanswerable, should metaphysics be abandoned?

12   Are metaphysical claims meaningless?

13   Are we able to determine whether the absolute presuppositions of our thought are true or false?

14   Can philosophical reflection exist only with hindsight? What does your answer tell us about the nature of metaphysics?

15   Can we eliminate all residual reference to ourselves when we consider the world?

16   Does any conceptual scheme have a unique and special relationship with the way things are?

17   What kind of justification can there be for any way of describing the world?

18   Have philosophers been right to move away from analysis as a method for metaphysics?

19   Should we accept Russell's theory of descriptions as a paradigm of philosophy?

20   In a reductionist programme, how do we determine what requires reduction and what it should be reduced to?

21   Do common-sense concepts need elimination, not analysis?

22   Can semantics be metaphysically neutral?

23   Can logic and a theory of meaning settle metaphysical controversies?

24   Is metaphysics continuous with science?

25   Should metaphysicians search for identity of things and properties rather than for identity of meaning?

26   Why do philosophers and scientists have different questions to ask about identities?

27   Are the basic questions of metaphysics questions of ontology?

28   Should metaphysics deal with supervenience rather than identity?

29   To what extent should explanatory success determine our choice of metaphysical position?

30   Should we identify time with change?

31   Does a description of time purely in terms of whether events are earlier than, later than or simultaneous with other events leave out important facts about time?

32   Does time flow?

33   Are the past, present and future equally real?

3

Philosophy of Language

MARTIN DAVIES

Philosophy of language deals with questions that arise from our ordinary, everyday conception of language. (Philosophy of linguistics, in contrast, follows up questions that arise from the scientific study of language.) But saying this does not yet give a clear idea of the sorts of questions that belong distinctively in philosophy of language. Wittgenstein (1953, §119) said, 'The results of philosophy are the uncovering of one or another piece of plain nonsense and of bumps that the understanding has got by running its head up against the limits of language.' On this conception, philosophy is about the ways in which we understand and misunderstand language, about how we come to mistake plain nonsense for something that is intelligible, and about what cannot be expressed in language. So, on this view, virtually all of philosophy is concerned with questions about language. It is, indeed, true that language has loomed large in the philosophy of the last hundred years or so. But there is still a specific, recognizable area of the discipline that is philosophy of language. It begins from one absolutely basic fact about language, namely, that expressions of a language have meaning, and can be used to talk about objects and events in the world. For philosophy of language, the central phenomenon to be studied is linguistic meaning. This chapter introduces some of the ways in which that study proceeds. Readers might also like to look at the closely related chapters on PHILOSOPHY OF LOGIC (chapter 4), PHILOSOPHY OF MIND (chapter 5), FREGE AND RUSSELL (chapter 37), and WITTGENSTEIN (chapter 39).

1 Introduction: Questions of Meaning

Questions about meaning are central in the philosophy of language. These questions are of two kinds. On the one hand, there are questions about the meanings of particular linguistic expressions (words, phrases and whole sentences); on the other hand, there are questions about the nature of linguistic meaning itself. Questions of the first kind belong to *semantics* (section 4); questions of the second kind belong to *metasemantics* (section 5).

The business of semantics includes questions about the meanings of subject expressions – including PROPER NAMES (chapter 37) (*Theaetetus, Fido*) and DESCRIPTIVE PHRASES (pp. 798–9) ('the man in the gabardine suit', 'the present king of France') – and of PRED-ICATE (chapter 4) expressions like 'is sitting', 'barks', 'is a spy' and 'is bald'. It also includes questions about the meanings of complete subject–predicate sentences ('Theaetetus is sitting', 'The present king of France is bald'). There are important philosophical questions about the meanings of other subject terms, including pronouns ('I', 'you', 'she', 'he', 'it', 'they') and demonstratives ('this', 'that', 'this knife', 'that butter'), and also about the meanings of expressions that go beyond the terms in the basic combination of subject and predicate. Expressions in this latter category include adjectives ('large' as it occurs in 'large flea', 'small' as it occurs in 'small elephant', 'good' as it occurs in 'good person' and in 'good philosopher', 'false' as it occurs in 'false sentence' and in 'false nose'), modal adverbs ('possibly', 'necessarily), manner adverbs ('slowly', 'clumsily'), and many more.

Still within the domain of semantics, and closely related to questions about the meanings of words, phrases and sentences, are questions about the ways in which the meanings of words determine, or at least constrain, the meanings of the phrases and sentences in which they occur. Even if we know what kind of thing the meaning of a sentence is (the meaning of 'Fido barks' or of 'The man in the gabardine suit is a spy'), we also need to understand how component words and phrases make their contributions to the meanings of complete sentences.

On the other side of the semantics versus meta-semantics divide are questions about the nature of linguistic meaning itself. Some of these questions are ontological. Are meanings entities; and, if so, what kinds of entities are they? One putative answer might be that the meanings of complete sentences are *propositions*, and that answer would lead, in turn, to questions about the nature of propositions themselves. An alternative answer might be that, if the meanings of sentences are entities, then they are *states of affairs*. Someone following up this alternative might say that in order for a sentence to be true, the state of affairs that is the sentence's meaning needs to be a state of affairs that *obtains*. *Facts* might then be identified with states of affairs that obtain, and true sentences would be said to be true in virtue of facts. In this case, the answer to the ontological question about meanings would lead to a version of the correspondence theory of truth.

Other meta-semantic questions concern the elucidation or analysis of the concept of meaning. Can we, for example, give any kind of philosophical analysis of the concept of linguistic meaning; and, if we can, what kinds of ideas can legitimately be used in the analysis? How, in general, is the meaning of a linguistic expression related to its *use*? How is the concept of meaning related to the concept of *truth*? In particular, for a complete sentence, what is the relation between the meaning of the sentence and the conditions under which an utterance of the sentence would be true?

The everyday idea of meaning or significance is related to the idea of what is conveyed or communicated in the use of language. In recent philosophy of language, a standard assumption in meta-semantics has been that there is such a thing as the *literal meaning* of linguistic expressions, and that the total communicative significance of a linguistic act is the product jointly of the literal meanings of the expressions used and of contextual factors. According to that meta-semantic view, semantics is the study of the literal meanings of expressions, and of the way that the literal meanings of complex expressions (phrases and sentences) are determined by the literal meanings of their component words. Strictly speaking, questions about the interaction between literal meaning and contextual factors belong, not to semantics, but to *pragmatics* (section 6).

2 Theories of Meaning

Answers to semantic questions and answers to meta-semantic questions can be given by propounding what might be called *theories of meaning*; but that phrase has two very different senses. In the first sense, a theory of meaning answers semantic questions by specifying the meanings of linguistic expressions. In the second sense, a theory of meaning answers meta-semantic questions by providing an elucidatory account of the nature of linguistic meaning.

Consider semantic questions first. These are questions about the meanings of words and phrases, and about the ways in which these contribute to the meanings of whole sentences. For the words, phrases and sentences of a particular language, someone might seek to answer these questions in a very explicit way, by providing a certain kind of formal, axiomatized theory. The idea would be that the axioms of this theory should specify explicitly the meanings of the words of the language under study, and that rules of inference should then permit the derivation, from those axioms, of *theorems* specifying the meanings of phrases, and ultimately of whole sentences in that language. In the case of any given sentence (say, 'Fido barks'), the derivation of a meaning-specifying theorem would make use of the axioms of the theory that specify the meanings of the words occurring in that sentence (in this case, the words 'Fido' and 'barks'). This derivation of a theorem from axioms could reasonably be said to display how, in the language under study, the meanings of the component words contribute to the meaning of the complete sentence. A theory that shows how the meanings of sentences depend on the meanings of their parts is sometimes said to be *compositional*.

The construction of theories of the kind envisaged here is not a trivial matter. We might start off by supposing that a typical theorem would say something like:

> The meaning of the sentence 'Fido barks' is the proposition that the particular dog Fido engages in the activity of barking.

or, avoiding the explicit talk about propositions:

> Th1   The sentence 'Fido barks' means that the particular dog Fido engages in the activity of barking.

We might also suppose that the axioms from which this theorem is to be derived would say things like:

> Ax1   The word 'Fido' means a particular dog, namely, Fido.
> Ax2   The word 'barks' means the activity of barking.

But, even in the context of this extremely simple example, we can see that we would immediately confront at least two important issues. The first issue concerns the difference between subject terms and predicate terms (here, between 'Fido' and 'barks'); the second issue concerns the derivational route from the axioms to the theorem (here, from Ax1 and Ax2 to Th1).

2.1   The difference between subject terms and predicate terms

The issue about the difference between subject terms and predicate terms is this. The two axioms that we proposed have the same form. In each case, the axiom says that an expression stands in the meaning relation to something in the world – in one case, a dog, in the other case, an activity. So, those axioms do not really explain why these two words – 'Fido' and 'barks' – can go together to make up a sentence, whereas other pairs of words – such as two nouns – cannot together yield a sentence, but merely constitute a list.

We can make this point more vivid if we consider, for a moment, nouns that are closely related to predicate terms. Consider, for example, the noun 'barking'. This noun can, of course, occur in sentences: 'The barking of the neighbourhood dogs kept me awake'. Indeed, it can function as the subject term in a sentence: 'Barking is fun'. But the noun 'barking' cannot be juxtaposed with the word 'Fido' to make a sentence. Similarly, consider the noun 'baldness'. If we juxtapose this noun with a subject term, then what we get – say, 'The present king of France baldness' – is not a sentence. (In order to see that it is just a list, we can imagine it as an account of the topics discussed at a meeting.)

The point, in short, is that there seems to be an important difference in meaning between predicate terms, such as 'barks' and 'is bald', and other closely related expressions. The meanings of the predicate terms somehow fit them for combining with subject terms to form sentences, while the meanings of those other expressions ('barking', 'baldness') do not so fit them. Now, suppose that we were asked to offer a meaning-specifying axiom for the noun 'barking' in the style of Ax1 and Ax2. We would be virtually bound to say:

The noun 'barking' means the activity of barking.

But this says just the same about the meaning of the noun 'barking' as Ax2 says about the meaning of the verb 'barks'. Similarly, the model for axioms that we have established thus far would suggest that for the verb phrase 'is bald', and for the noun 'baldness', the axioms should be:

The phrase 'is bald' means the property of baldness.
The noun 'baldness' means the property of baldness.

But, as we just saw, while 'barks' and 'is bald' can function as predicate terms in sentences, 'barking' and 'baldness' cannot. There must be a difference in meaning between 'barks' and 'barking', and between 'is bald' and 'baldness'; but the axioms that we have proposed do not reveal what this difference might be.

2.2   The derivational route from axioms to theorems

The issue about the route from axioms to a theorem is this. The derivation of a theorem from axioms is supposed to have the status of a logical PROOF (pp. 347–9), and it should make use of well-understood, and well-behaved, logical resources. So, suppose that we apply these requirements to the theorem that we have highlighted (Th1) and the two axioms (Ax1 and Ax2).

Certainly the theorem does not follow from the axioms just by way of the logical resources of the propositional calculus or the PREDICATE CALCULUS (p. 367), for example. The inference from Ax1 and Ax2 to Th1 is not a logically valid one. In order to obtain a valid inference, we would need to add an extra premise, in the form of another axiom.

Clearly, if we were to add the hypothetical statement:

> If the word 'Fido' means a particular dog, namely, Fido, and the word 'barks' means the activity of barking, then the sentence 'Fido barks' means that the particular dog Fido engages in the activity of barking.

then we could proceed from this statement plus Ax1 and Ax2 to the conclusion Th1 by way of familiar logical rules of inference. The form of the inference would be:

> A, B, if A and B then C; therefore, C.

which is clearly valid. But there would be good reasons to aspire after something more general than this hypothetical statement about the specific words 'Fido' and 'barks'. We should seek an axiom that speaks in general terms of the effect of putting together two terms – subject and predicate – to make a simple sentence.

Provided that we can find some account of what a subject term is and what a predicate term is, something along the following lines might suggest itself:

> Ax3 If a subject term M means something, say, X, and a predicate term N means something, say, Y, then the sentence made up of M followed by N means that X engages in, or exemplifies, Y.

This is pleasingly general in the way that it talks about M and N and their meanings X and Y, and it is a generalization that we can, it seems, instantiate in order to yield the more specific hypothetical statement about the subject term 'Fido' and the predicate term 'barks'. If that is right, then the conclusion Th1 can be validly derived from Ax1, Ax2 and Ax3. So, by making explicit the generalization in Ax3, we have made some progress with the requirement that the derivation of a meaning-specifying theorem from axioms is supposed to have the status of a logical proof.

Furthermore, we could instantiate the same generalization, Ax3, to give a hypothetical statement about the subject term 'Theaetetus', the predicate term 'is sitting', and the sentence that they go together to make up. Taken in conjunction with specific axioms about the meanings of 'Theaetetus' and 'is sitting', this hypothetical statement would enable us to derive a theorem specifying the meaning of the sentence 'Theaetetus is sitting'.

But, although this looks promising (apart from the issue about subject terms and predicate terms), there are still legitimate causes for concern as to whether statements like Ax1, Ax2 and Ax3 interact with standard logical resources in a well-behaved way. In fact, most work in semantics proceeds on the assumption that, in order to be sure of the logical status of our derivations, we should not make use of axioms and theorems that talk explicitly about meaning. We shall return to this point later (section 4.1).

The Notion of Meaning and Standard Logic

In standard logical systems we have a principle – in essence, Leibniz's Law – saying, among other things, that if Fido = Rover then from any statement about Fido we can infer the corresponding statement about Rover, and vice versa. If we now imagine that one and the same dog has two names, 'Fido' and 'Rover', we can ask whether from the premise:

Fido = Rover

plus:

Ax1   The word 'Fido' means a particular dog, namely, Fido.

it follows that:

Ax1′   The word 'Fido' means a particular dog, namely, Rover.

Either answer – 'yes' or 'no' – is potentially problematic.

If Ax1′ does follow, then we can see – by a few more steps – that everything that can be said about the meaning of the word 'Fido' can be equally truly said about the meaning of the word 'Rover'. Furthermore, the same will go for any pair of words that pick out the same object in the world, such as the pair 'Hesperus' and 'Phosphorus', which both pick out the planet Venus. But we should want to leave it open, at this early stage of our enquiry, whether such pairs of words can be distinguished in point of their meaning. Indeed, ahead of detailed theoretical considerations, we might reasonably expect that such pairs of words would sometimes differ in meaning, despite picking out the same object.

So perhaps we should prefer the alternative that says that Ax1′ does not follow from Ax1 plus the premise that Fido = Rover. But, in that case, we shall have to admit frankly that we are departing from what is familiar, and moving to a kind of theory whose logical behaviour is not so well understood.

We have been considering theories of meaning, in the first of two possible senses of that phrase. These are theories that seek to answer semantic questions. A semantic theory may be a theory in a quite formal sense (with axioms and rules of inference by means of which theorems can be derived) and we have noted that there is an issue about the role of the notion of meaning in formal derivations or proofs. But, apart from the worry about logical good behaviour, a semantic theory might take the concept of meaning as an unanalysed, and unexplained, primitive notion. After all, it is the job of a semantic theory to tell us what linguistic expressions *mean*. A theory of meaning in the second sense – a meta-semantic theory – will, in contrast, set out to explain the concept of meaning in other terms. A meta-semantic theory will provide an analysis, or some other kind of philosophical elucidation, of the notion of linguistic meaning, perhaps by plotting connections between that notion and the notion of use, or the notion of truth.

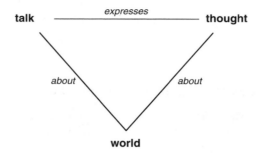

Figure 3.1 The relationship between talk, thought and the world, which is explored in the philosophy of language, the philosophy of mind and metaphysics.

3 Language, Mind and Metaphysics: Questions of Priority

A semantic theory relates pieces of language to pieces of the world. We use language to talk about the world, and to express our thoughts, which are also about the world. (The aboutness of thoughts is often called *intentionality*.) Talk, thought and world form a triangle, and in philosophy of language, PHILOSOPHY OF MIND (chapter 5), and META-PHYSICS (chapter 2) we move around this triangle (figure 3.1).

Thus, for example, we might try to give a philosophical account of some distinctions in reality – say, between OBJECTS AND PROPERTIES (pp. 726–7), or between particulars and universals – in terms of differences among words, or in terms of differences in the realm of thought, provided that we already had some understanding of those linguistic or mental differences. Or, going the other way about, we might assume some account of the metaphysical differences, and use it in our philosophical work in the domains of talk or thought. We shall shortly consider just such a question of relative priority between philosophy of language and metaphysics.

There are also important questions of priority between philosophy of language and philosophy of mind. Indeed, any strategy for elucidating the concept of linguistic meaning will inevitably depend on our general view of the order of priority as between talk and thought. We need to be clear, first, just what notion of priority is at issue here. Then we shall consider three possible views about language and mind.

3.1 Philosophical priorities: language and mind

The kind of priority that concerns us here is priority in the order of philosophical analysis or elucidation. To say that the notion of X is *analytically prior* to the notion of Y is to say that Y can be analysed or elucidated in terms of X, while the analysis or elucidation of X itself does not have to advert to Y. Thus to say that the notion of BELIEF (chapter 1) is analytically prior to the notion of KNOWLEDGE (chapter 1), for example, is to say that knowledge can be analysed in terms of belief, while a good analysis of belief does not need to reintroduce the notion of knowledge. (This is just to say what the claim would amount to, not whether it would be correct.)

Analytical priority should be distinguished from ontological priority and from epistemological priority. To say that X is *ontologically prior* to Y is to say that X can exist without Y, although Y cannot exist without X. For example, it might plausibly be said that individuals are ontologically prior to nations. To say that X is *epistemologically prior* to Y is to say that it is possible to find out about X without having to proceed via knowledge about Y, whereas finding out about Y has to go by way of finding out about X. So it is plausible, for example, that the positions and trajectories of medium-sized material bodies are epistemologically prior to the positions and trajectories of subatomic particles. We can find out about material bodies without investigating subatomic particles but, it might be said, our route to knowledge about subatomic particles has to go via observations of material bodies.

Having distinguished these three kinds of priority, we can make the working assumption that they are logically independent of each other. According to that assumption we can, for example, suppose that the notion of X is analytically prior to the notion of Y, without being obliged to hold that X is either ontologically or epistemologically prior to Y. Our question about the order of analytical priority as between language and mind relates, particularly, to the notion of linguistic meaning and the notion of intentionality (aboutness) for mental states. The three possible views that we need to be aware of are these.

Mind first: This is the view that it is possible to give a philosophical account of the intentionality of *thoughts* without essentially adverting to language, and that the notion of linguistic meaning can then be analysed in terms of the thoughts that language is used to express.

Language first: This is the view that an account of linguistic meaning can be given without bringing in the intentionality of thoughts, and that what a person's thoughts are about can then be analysed in terms of the use of language.

No priority (both together): This is the view that there is no way of elucidating the notion of what a person's thoughts are about without bringing in the notion of linguistic meaning, nor the other way around. The two notions have to be explained together.

(There is in fact a fourth possible view, which involves a different kind of no priority claim, namely that the two notions are quite unrelated. But this view, while possible, is quite implausible.)

All three views have adherents. The no analytical priority view is characteristic of the work of Donald Davidson (b. 1917), who couples it with ontological and epistemological no priority claims. Thus, Davidson (1975) argues that there can be no thought without language nor language without thought, and that there is no finding out in detail what a person believes without interpreting the person's speech (Davidson 1974). The language first view finds expression in Michael Dummett's (b. 1925) writings (see Dummett 1973, 1991, 1993), while the mind first approach is taken by Paul Grice (1913–88) (Grice 1989; see also Schiffer 1972). Given what we have assumed about the logical independence of the three kinds of priority, we can see that one option that is available to us is to agree with Davidson in denying the ontological or epistemological priority of mind over language, and yet to follow Grice in trying to analyse the notion of linguistic meaning in terms of the thoughts that language is used to express.

3.2   Philosophical priorities: language and the world

Our example of a question of relative priority as between philosophy of language and metaphysics comes from the work of Peter Strawson (b. 1919) (Strawson 1959, Part II; 1970a) on subject terms and predicate terms. The distinction in language between subject and predicate terms is intuitively closely related to the metaphysical distinction between objects or particulars, on the one hand (corresponding to subject terms), and properties or universals, on the other (corresponding to predicate terms). Can we use the metaphysical distinction to help us understand the linguistic one? (As we have already seen, we certainly need some account of the subject–predicate distinction.) Or should we, alternatively, seek a more purely logico-linguistic account of the difference between subject terms and predicate terms, and then try to understand the metaphysical distinction in terms of the linguistic one?

One aspect of the subject–predicate distinction to which Strawson gives considerable attention is what he calls the *asymmetry of subjects and predicates regarding negation*. We can explain the basic idea like this. When a subject–predicate sentence ('Theaetetus is sitting') is negated ('It is not the case that Theaetetus is sitting', or 'Theaetetus is not sitting'), the negation can be taken together with the predicate term to yield a new expression ('not sitting') that is of the same kind – a new predicate term. But the negation cannot be taken together with the subject to yield a new expression ('not Theaetetus') that is of the same kind – a new subject term. In short, predicate terms have negations while subject terms do not.

In order to provide (at least the beginnings of) an explanation of this fact about language, Strawson invites us to consider propositions in which, as he puts it, a general character or kind (or property or universal) is assigned to, or predicated of, a particular, or spatio-temporal individual. The important point is that these general characters come in incompatibility groups *vis-à-vis* such empirical particulars, while the particulars do not conversely come in incompatibility groups *vis-à-vis* the general characters. Thus, for example, consider the various colours (general characters) and the sundry items of furniture in the room (spatio-temporal individuals). An item of furniture cannot be more than one colour (all over); whereas more than one item of furniture can be the same colour. Or consider the various postures that people can adopt (general characters) and the philosophers in a courtyard. Perhaps Theaetetus is sitting, and so not standing or lying, while Theodorus is also sitting and Socrates is standing. As both examples illustrate, general characters come in groups that 'compete' for spatio-temporal individuals; whereas the individuals do not come in groups that 'compete' for the general characters. There is at least the prospect, here, of an explanation of the linguistic distinction between subject terms and predicate terms that appeals to the metaphysical distinction between spatio-temporal individuals and the general characters that they may exemplify.

This approach exhibits an order of explanation that is the opposite of the one that is usually associated with the German mathematician and philosopher Gottlob FREGE (1848–1925) (chapter 37). On the Fregean approach, the metaphysical or ontological category of objects is to be read off from an antecedently fixed linguistic category of logical subject terms (roughly, names). So someone adopting this approach would need to be able to give a purely logico-linguistic criterion for an expression to be a name. It is not an easy matter to discharge this obligation without smuggling back in something like the distinction between objects and properties. Strawson himself, after reviewing some of the logico-linguistic marks of the subject–predicate distinction that might be drawn on in the Fregean order of explanation, remarks:

> The general relative natures of the terms combined in the fundamental combination of predication – the differences or alleged differences between subjects and predicates – have so far been discussed in almost exclusively formal terms, in terms belonging to formal logic itself or to grammar. To understand the matter fully, we must be prepared to use a richer vocabulary, a range of notions which fall outside these formal limits. We assume that the subject–predicate duality, and hence the differences so far remarked on, reflect some fundamental features of our thought about the world. (Strawson 1974a: 13–14)

Now, it would not, in fact, be quite accurate to say that Strawson awards absolute priority to metaphysics; but we can, at least, say that he does not award a pre-eminent role to philosophy of language. In this, Strawson's position contrasts with that of Dummett. As we have already noted, when it comes to the question of priority as between language and mind, Dummett adopts the language first option. As we can now add, he also takes a Fregean view on the question about language and metaphysics. So, Dummett does regard the philosophy of language as pre-eminent. Indeed, he once wrote:

> We may characterize analytical philosophy as that which follows Frege in accepting that the philosophy of language is the foundation of the rest of the subject. (Dummett 1978: 441)

This may not be an entirely happy characterization of analytical philosophy as a whole – since it would leave many analytical philosophers on the wrong side of the classification – but it does indicate one influential line of thought within analytical philosophy.

We should not, however, think that the only possible reason for interest in philosophy of language is that it might hold the key to questions in philosophy of mind and metaphysics. Questions about meaning are no less deep, and no less important, for the fact that, in order to investigate them fully, we may well need to draw on resources coming from other areas of philosophy.

4 Semantic Theories: Davidson's Programme

We have already met the idea of a formal, axiomatized theory that permits the systematic derivation of theorems specifying the meanings of complete sentences drawn from some language (section 2). The sentences might be simple or complex, and the language might be a formal language or a natural language. If we were interested in actually constructing theories of this type, then we might do well to proceed by stages.

The first and simplest stage would involve just a finite stock of sentences from a formal language, and would treat each of the sentences as an unstructured unit.

Perhaps there are just three sentences, 'A', 'B' and 'C', where 'A' means that Theaetetus is sitting, 'B' means that Fido barks, and 'C' means that the man in the gabardine suit is a spy. In this case, the idea of an axiomatized semantic theory is simple to the point of triviality. For we can just take three axioms, one stating the meaning of each of the three sentences, and then the project of deriving a meaning-specifying theorem for each sentence of the language quite literally involves taking no steps at all.

The second stage would involve subject–predicate sentences from a formal language. We might have three predicate terms, 'F', 'G' and 'H' and three subject terms, 'a', 'b' and 'c', allowing us to construct nine subject–predicate sentences, among which, let us suppose:

'Fa' means that Theaetetus is sitting
'Gb' means that Fido barks

and

'Hc' means that the man in the gabardine suit is a spy.

If we want to be able to derive a meaning-specifying theorem for each sentence in a systematic way, then we might hope to formulate a theory in which there is an axiom talking about the meaning of each subject term and an axiom talking about the meaning of each predicate term (rather along the lines of Ax1 and Ax2 in section 2 above).

At these first two stages, the total number of sentences under consideration is finite. The third stage would involve an infinite collection of sentences built from some finite stock by applying constructions over and over. We might take the three sentences, 'A', 'B' and 'C', from the first stage, and allow the application of a negation operator '¬'. This would give three more sentences, '¬A', '¬B', '¬C' (meaning that Theaetetus is not sitting, that Fido does not bark, and that the man in the gabardine suit is not a spy, respectively), and then three more, '¬¬A', '¬¬B', '¬¬C', and then three more, indefinitely. Alternatively, we could allow the application of a conjunction operator to two sentences at a time to give 'A&B', 'A&C', 'B&C' and (if we mark the order of the conjuncts) also 'B&A', 'C&A', 'C&B' and (if we allow repetition of conjuncts) 'A&A', 'B&B', 'C&C' (thus, nine new sentences to add to the original three). Then, applying the conjunction operator again, we get '(A&B)&C', '(A&C)&C', '(B&C)&C' and '(A&B)&(A&C)', and many more – in fact, 144 new sentences to add to the twelve.

We could, of course, allow the application of both the negation operator and the conjunction operator, to give us sentences like 'A&¬B'. Suppose that we do that, and then try to provide an axiomatized semantic theory for this simple, but infinite, collection of sentences. Along with axioms stating the meanings of our three building blocks, 'A', 'B' and 'C', we shall need an axiom saying something about the meaning of '¬' and one saying something about the meaning of '&'.

A first thought in this direction might be to suggest these two axioms:

'¬' means negation
'&' means conjunction.

But it is quite unclear how, from this axiom about '¬', say, and the axiom stating the meaning of 'A', we could derive a theorem specifying the meaning of '¬A'. What looks more promising, for the negation operator, is something like:

> If S is any sentence at all, then the sentence made up by putting '¬' together with S means the negation of whatever S means.

This builds into the specification of the meaning of the operator an indication that it is indeed an *operator* that can be applied to any sentence to yield a new sentence. Something similar can be done for the conjunction operator; but we shall not pause any longer over these details. (In fact, this also suggests how we might make some progress with the issue about the difference between subject terms and predicate terms, discussed in section 2.1. We could build into the axiom for a predicate term an indication that it is indeed a predicate – an expression that can go together with a subject term to make a sentence.)

A formal language with subject terms and predicate terms, plus a couple of sentence-building operators, is clearly very far indeed from the rich complexity of natural language. But, apart from the difference of scale, the step from formal languages to natural languages might seem simple in principle. If we know how to provide an axiomatized semantic theory for a formal language with subject terms and predicate terms, for example, then we also know how to provide a theory for a similarly structured fragment of natural language that uses real words and phrases instead of letters ('Theaetetus' instead of 'a', 'is sitting' instead of 'F').

However, in many cases, the relationship between sentences of a formal language and sentences of a natural language is much less clear. There is a tiny indication of this already in the case of negation, where the formal language operator attaches at the front of a complete sentence whereas natural language negation usually occurs within the predicate term ('is *not* sitting', 'does *not* bark'). And, quite generally, the complexity of the relationship between formal and natural languages is shown by the difficulty of the task (familiar to most philosophy students) of regimenting into logical notation arguments that are expressed in natural language. So, one question that has to be faced is just how to regard the relationship between the superficial forms of natural language sentences, on the one hand, and the regimented forms (sometimes called *logical forms*; see Sainsbury 1991) to which an axiomatized semantic theory could be applied, on the other hand.

Even if we ignore these differences between formal languages and natural languages, it is still the case that we have so far only envisaged a semantic theory for a simple subject–predicate language with sentence operators. Subsequent stages of the project of constructing semantic theories would involve bringing further types of expression within the scope of the enterprise.

We should, however, pause here to notice that, while it is clear that axiomatized semantic theories could be of interest to logicians, and – to the extent that they display the meanings of particular kinds of expressions such as pronouns, demonstratives, adjectives and so on – also to linguists, still it may not be evident why they should merit a philosopher's attention. In fact, the project of constructing compositional semantic theories has been a central concern in recent philosophy of language, and Davidson's work in particular reveals several reasons for focusing philosophical attention on semantic theories (Davidson 1967a; and many other papers collected in Davidson 1984). We shall review five of these reasons.

4.1   The format of semantic theories

The first reason for paying attention to axiomatized semantic theories concerns the proper format for the theorems that such a theory is supposed to yield. Since these theorems are supposed to be meaning-specifying, the initially obvious format would be one that relates a sentence to its meaning. If meanings are themselves regarded as entities of some kind, then we might expect a format like:

The meaning of sentence S is *m*.

If meanings are not regarded as entities, then we might expect instead:

Sentence S means *that p*.

Thus, on the first alternative, if meaning-specifying theorems are explicitly to relate sentences to propositions, say, then an example of such a theorem might be:

The meaning of the sentence 'Theaetetus is sitting' is the proposition that Theaetetus is sitting.

On the second alternative, similarly, an example might be:

The sentence 'Theaetetus is sitting' means that Theaetetus is sitting.

If, for some general reason, those formats have to be rejected – if the concept of meaning cannot, after all, figure in the theorems of a compositional semantic theory – then that would be a significant meta-semantic result.

Davidson (1967a) does indeed reject both those formats, and argues that the target theorems of a semantic theory should, instead, exhibit the format:

Sentence S is true if and only if *p*

(where 'if and only if' ('iff') expresses the *material biconditional*). Since theorems like this specify conditions under which a sentence is true, Davidson is said to favour *truth-conditional semantics*. Davidson's argument for this conclusion comes in two steps.

The first step is intended to rule out the idea that, to each word, each phrase and each sentence, there should be assigned some entity as its meaning. In this step, the so-called *Frege argument* (Frege 1892: 62–5; cf. Quine 1960: 148–9) is used to show that, under certain assumptions, all true sentences would be assigned the same entity. Clearly, no such undiscriminating assignment of entities could be an assignment of meanings, since it is certainly not correct that every true sentence has the same meaning. (Essentially the same line of argument allows Davidson (1969a) to conclude that there is no point in saying that true sentences correspond to facts. The Frege argument shows that, under certain assumptions, there is only one fact. For further discussion, see Neale 1995.)

The Frege Argument

The Frege argument shows that if an equivalence relation, E, on sentences meets two conditions then it classifies all true sentences as equivalent, and likewise all false sentences. The two conditions are these.

If two sentences are logically equivalent then they are equivalent according to E.

If two sentences are the same except for the fact that, where one contains a subject term i, the other contains another subject term, j, referring to the same thing, then they are equivalent according to E.

Suppose that we take any two true sentences. Let us choose, say, 'Penguins waddle' and 'The earth moves'. Then, firstly, the sentence

(1)   Penguins waddle

is logically equivalent to

(2)   The number that is 1 if penguins waddle and is 0 if penguins do not waddle is 1.

So, by the first condition, (1) and (2) are equivalent according to E. Similarly,

(3)   The earth moves

and

(4)   The number that is 1 if the earth moves and is 0 if the earth does not move is 1

are equivalent according to E.

But secondly, the subject term in (2), namely 'The number that is 1 if penguins waddle and is 0 if penguins do not waddle', refers to the number 1, since penguins do indeed waddle. And the subject term in (4), namely 'The number that is 1 if the earth moves and is 0 if the earth does not move', also refers to the number 1. So, sentences (2) and (4) are the same except for the fact that, where one contains a (rather lengthy) subject term, the other contains another (equally lengthy) subject term referring to the same thing. By the second condition, then, sentences (2) and (4) are equivalent according to E.

Putting all this together, (1) is equivalent to (2), and (2) to (4), and (4) to (3). So, (1) is equivalent to (3) according to E; and that is what we needed to show.

The second step in Davidson's argument for the truth-conditional format points out that the 'means that p' construction presents logical difficulties, so that the formal derivations of meaning-specifying theorems will be highly problematic (see section 2.2). In contrast, the truth-conditional format is logically well understood. The way in which theorems specifying truth conditions for complete sentences are derived from axioms assigning semantic properties to words and phrases can, to a considerable extent, be carried over from the work of Alfred Tarski (1902–83) on certain formal languages (Tarski 1944, 1956).

This second step in the argument is technical in character, and it is a matter of dispute whether a compositional semantic theory making direct use of the 'S means that p' format is feasible. (See Schiffer 1972: 162; Taylor 1982; Davies 1984.)

As for the status of the first step in the argument, it is now widely agreed that there are reasons for rejecting Davidson's use of the Frege argument. The Frege argument can only establish that all true sentences would be assigned the same entity as their meaning if it is legitimate to suppose that the equivalence relation of having the same meaning would meet the two conditions that figure in the argument. But this is very far from being obvious. So, pending further argument to the contrary, we can admit that it would be possible for a compositional semantic theory to work by assigning an entity to each sentence as its meaning or semantic value. In particular, one possibility would be to assign to each sentence a certain kind of structured entity – a state of affairs with objects and properties as constituents. The situation semantics programme of Barwise and Perry (1983) constitutes one development of this possibility (see also Taylor 1976; Forbes 1989).

4.2   The correctness of semantic theories

The second reason for philosophical interest in semantic theories relates to the conditions of adequacy or correctness on any such theory. Whatever is the right format for a semantic theory, we need some account of the conditions under which a theory in that format is the *correct* theory for the language of a particular speaker or group of speakers. We need to know, for example, what makes it correct to say that, in our language, the particular string of letters 'p'–'e'–'n'–'g'–'u'–'i'–'n'–'s' . . . and so on means that penguins waddle.

In order to be able to consider a possible reformulation of this question, we need to make use of the notion of an abstract or possible language. In the abstract, a language can be considered to be a collection of sentences together with a stipulated assignment of meanings to those sentences. So, for example, there are possible languages in which there is a sentence made up of those same letters – 'Penguins waddle' – but with the meaning that the earth moves. Given the notion of a possible language, the question whether a semantic theory is correct for the language of a given group of speakers can be reformulated as the question whether the possible language for which the semantic theory is stipulated to be correct is the *actual language* of a given group (Lewis 1975; Peacocke 1976; Schiffer 1993). What is sometimes called the *actual language relation* is thus a relation between languages (in the abstract) and groups of language users. Under the reformulation that we are envisaging, conditions of adequacy on semantic theories become constraints on the actual language relation.

Any philosophical elucidation of the key semantic concept used in semantic theories, such as meaning or truth, can be transposed into a condition of adequacy on those theories (or, equivalently, into a constraint on the actual language relation). Thus, suppose for example that an elucidation of the concept of meaning says that any sentence S has meaning m in the language of a group G if and only if some condition $\mathbf{C}(S, m, G)$ holds. This can be transposed into a condition of adequacy as follows:

If a semantic theory for the language of a group G delivers a theorem saying that the meaning of sentence S is *m* then it should be the case that **C**(S, *m*, G).

Similarly, it can be transposed into a constraint on the actual language relation:

A possible language in which S has the meaning *m* is the actual language of a group G only if **C**(S, *m*, G).

This kind of transposition can be carried out in the opposite direction too. Any condition of adequacy on semantic theories (or any constraint on the actual language relation) can help us elucidate the key semantic concept used in those theories. Thus, for example, consider semantic theories that adopt the truth-conditional format:

Sentence S is true if and only if *p*.

Tarski's (1956) Convention T imposes a condition of adequacy on such theories; namely, the condition that the sentence that fills the '*p*' place should *translate* (or else be the very same sentence as) the sentence S.

This condition of adequacy on truth-conditional semantic theories constitutes a partial elucidation of the semantic concept of truth in terms of the concept of translation. Intuitively, the concept of translation is very closely related to the concept of meaning; and what Convention T requires, in effect, is that the sentence that fills the '*p*' place should have the same meaning as the sentence S. If a truth-conditional semantic theory meets that condition, then the truth condition specifications that it yields are guaranteed to be correct. Thus, Convention T's elucidation of the semantic concept of truth involves a connection between that concept and the concept of meaning:

If a sentence S means that *p* then S is true iff *p*.

But Convention T provides no further help with the concept of meaning itself.

One way to shed further light on the concept of meaning – and so, via Convention T, on the concept of truth – would be to spell out other conditions of adequacy on specifications of meanings (or of truth conditions). The concept for which we seek elucidation here is the concept of meaning (or truth conditions) in the language of any group. The concept of meaning is the same whether we consider a group of English speakers or a group of Chinese speakers; so we expect that a condition of adequacy should relate to groups in a very general way. One quite general thing that we can say about specifications of meaning is that they help us to describe members of a group as engaging in linguistic acts. The theorems of a semantic theory for the language of a group, G, can license the redescription of utterances of sentences by a member of G as acts of saying or assertion. For example, if the semantic theory says that a sentence S means that Theaetetus is sitting, then we might reasonably construe an utterer of S as saying or asserting that Theaetetus is sitting. Construing a person's utterances as particular linguistic acts is one aspect of *interpretation*, and what we have just seen is that we can make a link between the theorems of a semantic theory and the project of interpreting the members of a language community.

A semantic theory can play a role in facilitating an overall interpretation of the behaviour of members of a group, by offering a way of understanding their specifically linguistic behaviour. If there are legitimate constraints on ways of interpreting people, then these may yield constraints on the particular aspects of interpretation that are licensed by a semantic theory. In short, the needs of interpretation may lead us to conditions of adequacy on meaning specifications, or truth condition specifications, and so to elucidations of the concepts of meaning and truth.

In Davidson's programme, this idea of a link between semantic theories and interpretation is implemented by describing the constraints on the project of *radical interpretation*. This is the imaginary project of constructing an overall scheme of interpretation for language users about whom we know nothing at the outset. One putative constraint on radical interpretation is that speakers should be so interpreted that what they say about the world – and, presumably, what they believe about the world – turns out to be by and large correct. This is the *Principle of Charity* (see Davidson 1967a, 1973). Thus, for example (Davidson 1984: 169):

> A theory of interpretation cannot be correct that makes a man assent to very many false sentences: it must be generally the case that a sentence is true when a speaker holds it to be.

The Principle of Charity has significance outside philosophy of language, since it appears to offer some prospect for ANTI-SCEPTICAL ARGUMENTS (pp. 51–6), in particular for arguments to the conclusion that most of what we ourselves say and think is correct (Davidson 1983).

But in later work by Davidson and others (Grandy 1973; McDowell 1976; Wiggins 1980) the Principle of Charity has given way to a principle that focuses on intelligibility, rather than on correctness: speakers should be so interpreted that what they say and believe about the world turns out to be by and large reasonable or intelligible. As Davidson (1984: xvii) himself says: 'The aim of interpretation is not agreement but understanding'. Sometimes a speaker's being wrong is quite understandable, while being right would be almost miraculous. An eloquent statement of this principle – sometimes called the *Principle of Humanity* – is provided by Wiggins (1980: 199):

> Let us then constrain the theory . . . that provides sentence by sentence interpretations of the language L by the requirement that [it] should combine with a plausible anthropology . . . in such a way that *in concert* the two theories make the best sense possible . . . of the total life and conduct of L-speakers.

If the semantic theory that provides sentence by sentence interpretations were to make use of the 'S means that *p*' format, then the Principle of Humanity could be conceived as a condition of adequacy on that semantic theory, roughly along the following lines:

> If the semantic theory delivers a theorem saying that S means that *p* then it should be the case that interpreting utterances of S as expressions of the proposition that *p* contributes to making the best sense possible of the total life and conduct of speakers.

This condition of adequacy would help us to elucidate the concept of meaning and thence, via the meaning–truth connection, the notion of truth. But it is also possible to regard the Principle of Humanity as providing direct elucidation of the concept of truth, without explicitly going via the concept of meaning.

One way to do this is to introduce a purely formal predicate 'T' that applies to sentences and then to consider theories that deliver theorems of the form:

Sentence S is T if and only if *p*.

We can impose a condition of interpretational adequacy on such a theory, roughly along the lines of:

> If the semantic theory (canonically) delivers a theorem saying that S is T iff *p* then it should be the case that interpreting utterances of S as expressions of the proposition that *p* contributes to making the best sense possible of the total life and conduct of speakers.

(We need the restriction to *canonical* proofs of T-condition specifying theorems because, for any given sentence S, a theory will deliver many different theorems of the required form: see Davies 1981: ch. 2.) And then we can see that if a theory meets this condition of adequacy its predicate 'T' will apply to precisely the true sentences of the language under study. Wiggins (1980) regards this as showing the way to a 'substantial theory of truth'. Truth simply *is* the property that plays the 'T'-role specified by the condition of adequacy that the Principle of Humanity furnishes (see also McDowell 1976: section 1; Wiggins 1997).

4.3   Semantic theories and mental states

Some aspects of natural languages pose particular problems for a semantic theorist working within the Davidsonian framework. One of these aspects is the use of natural language to report on people's mental states. So a third reason for being interested in semantic theories is that reflection on these theories may yield insight into the meanings of sentences about mental states, and so, also, insight into the nature of those mental states themselves.

To see how the problems arise, consider a belief report sentence like:

(BRep)   Theaetetus believes that Fido barks.

Intuitively, the meaning of this sentence depends on the meaning of the name 'Theaetetus', the meaning of the verb 'believes', and the meaning of the contained sentence 'Fido barks'. So we might have some expectations about the way in which a meaning-specifying theorem for (BRep) would be derived in a compositional semantic theory. We might expect that the derivation would involve, firstly, proving a meaning-specifying theorem for the contained sentence 'Fido barks', and then using that, plus axioms about the meanings of 'Theaetetus' and 'believes', in order to prove the target theorem for the belief report sentence.

In the framework of truth-conditional semantic theories, similarly, we might expect that the proof of a truth-condition-specifying theorem for the belief report sentence would make use of a theorem for 'Fido barks' plus axioms about 'Theaetetus' and 'believes'. But we can see – at least, in an impressionistic kind of way – why this is liable to be problematic.

Statements about people's mental states display some of the same logical properties as statements about meaning (see the box in section 2). With statements about meaning, it is not usually thought to be the case that from:

Fido = Rover

plus:

Sentence S means that Fido barks

it follows that:

Sentence S means that Rover barks.

This logical behaviour is a departure from standard logical systems, and it raises a question about the logical resources that would be needed in a semantic theory using the 'Sentence S means that p' format. It also helps to motivate use of the alternative 'Sentence S is true iff p' format, since that is logically well behaved. Thus, for example, from:

Fido = Rover

plus:

Sentence S is true iff Fido barks

it certainly does follow that:

Sentence S is true iff Rover barks.

But while this well-understood logical behaviour is one of the attractions of truth-conditional semantic theories, it also makes it hard for truth-conditional theories to give an adequate treatment of sentences that report on people's mental states.

With statements about belief, it is not usually thought to be the case that from:

Fido = Rover

plus:

Theaetetus believes that Fido barks

it follows that:

Theaetetus believes that Rover barks.

The first belief report might be true, while the second was false, for example. This is one aspect of what is called the *intensionality* of belief reports.

The problem posed for truth-conditional semantics is that it is hard to see how a truth-condition-specifying theorem for the sentence:

(BRep)   Theaetetus believes that Fido barks

can be derived in the way that we envisaged, without also involving the denial of the aspect of the intensionality of belief reports that we just highlighted. The derivational route that we envisaged goes via a truth-condition-specifying theorem for the contained sentence 'Fido barks', to the effect that the contained sentence is true iff Fido does indeed bark. Given the assumption that:

Fido = Rover

we can move from this theorem:

(FF)   'Fido barks' is true iff Fido barks

to:

(FR)   'Fido barks' is true iff Rover barks.

But now, consider whatever route leads from the original theorem (FF) to a truth-condition-specifying theorem for the belief report sentence (BRep), to the effect that it is true iff Theaetetus does indeed believe that Fido barks. Given the assumption that Fido = Rover, an exactly similar route will also lead via (FR) to the conclusion that the same sentence (BRep) is true iff Theaetetus believes that Rover barks. So, given the assumption that:

Fido = Rover

we are driven to the overall conclusion that:

Theaetetus believes that Fido barks iff Theaetetus believes that Rover barks.

But this goes flatly against the presumed intensionality of belief reports.

The issues here are controversial, and there have certainly been proposals for bringing within the compass of truth-conditional semantics sentences that are usually reckoned to exhibit intensionality (see Davidson 1969b). For now, however, it is enough to notice that attention to compositional semantic theories could bring questions about mental states into sharper focus.

4.4   *Semantic theories and epistemology*

The fourth reason for directing philosophical attention onto the construction of semantic theories is epistemological. We have indicated the way in which a finite set of axioms

109

can permit the derivation of a meaning-specifying theorem for each of infinitely many sentences. So in the case of a given language with infinitely many sentences, someone who knew the facts stated by the finitely many axioms of a compositional semantic theory would thereby be in a position to come to know what each sentence of the language means. The existence of finitely axiomatized semantic theories thus sheds light on an epistemological problem: how is it possible for a finite being to master an infinite language?

So far as the purely formal notion of an axiomatized theory goes, the set of axioms of a theory does not have to be finite. But Davidson (1965) uses the requirement that a language should be learnable (and learnable by a finite being) to motivate a *finite axiomatization constraint* on semantic theories. Since Davidson favours truth-conditional semantic theories, this yields the idea that the aim of a semantic theorist is to construct finitely axiomatized theories of truth conditions for (regimented fragments of) natural languages – building, so far as possible, on the work of Tarski. The sorts of theories envisaged are sometimes spoken of as Tarski–Davidson truth theories, and there is a very considerable body of work – much of it quite technical in character – in pursuit of this aim.

We should note, however, that there is some dispute over the finite axiomatization constraint. At least one prominent philosopher of language (Schiffer 1987: ch. 7) argues that it may be possible for a speaker to master a language, even though no finitely axiomatized truth-conditional semantic theory can be provided for it.

Even if there is a finitely axiomatized semantic theory for a language, there is still a pressing question about the explanatory relevance of the existence of such a theory. Knowledge of the facts stated by the axioms of a compositional semantic theory would suffice, in principle, for knowledge as to what each sentence of the language means. But ordinary speakers of a natural language usually lack conscious knowledge of any compositional semantic theory for their own language. So the question that presses is how the mere existence of a finitely axiomatized semantic theory, unknown to ordinary language users, can solve the epistemological problem that they apparently face.

One approach to answering this question begins by considering a wider range of knowledge that ordinary language users have. Along with knowing what the sentences of their language mean, ordinary speakers of English also know, for example, that in the sentence:

Nigel shaved him

the word 'him' cannot refer back to Nigel, while in the sentence:

Nigel wanted Bruce to shave him

the word 'him' can refer back to Nigel. They know that the sentences:

Less than two books were on the table
More than one book was on the table

sound fine, while:

> Less than two books was on the table
> More than one book were on the table

sound somehow wrong – despite the fact that 'Less than two books' is equivalent to 'At most one book', and 'More than one book' is equivalent to 'At least two books'. And we could multiply examples of speakers' linguistic knowledge indefinitely.

Ordinary language users have conscious access to these pieces of knowledge. But they do not have conscious knowledge of any set of axioms or rules from which these particular pieces of knowledge follow. Theoretical linguists articulate sets of linguistic (especially, syntactic) rules or principles called *grammars*. But the explanatory claims of theoretical linguistics do not end with the mere existence of grammars from which particular pieces of linguistic knowledge could be derived. In a famous passage, Noam Chomsky (b. 1928) says:

> Obviously, every speaker of a language has mastered and internalized a generative grammar that expresses his knowledge of his language. This is not to say that he is aware of the rules of the grammar or even that he can become aware of them . . . Any interesting generative grammar will be dealing, for the most part, with mental processes that are far beyond the level of actual or even potential consciousness. (Chomsky 1965: 8)

According to Chomsky (1965, 1986, 1995), then, ordinary language users possess a body of linguistic knowledge which is, for the most part, inaccessible to consciousness. For this reason, it is often spoken of as *tacit knowledge*. It is because they have this body of tacit knowledge of linguistic rules that they are able to know the vast host of particular things about their language.

While Chomsky is concerned primarily with knowledge of syntax, it seems that the idea that ordinary language users possess a body of tacit knowledge could also be applied in the area of semantics. Thus, one way of answering the question about the explanatory relevance of the existence of compositional semantic theories would be to credit ordinary language users with tacit knowledge of the axioms of such a theory (see below, section 5.3). Some philosophers of language are critical of any appeal to the notion of tacit knowledge, claiming that it embodies conceptual confusions (Baker and Hacker 1984). But accounts of the notion of tacit knowledge, particularly as it applies to semantic theories, have been offered (see Evans 1981a; Davies 1986, 1987, 1989; Peacocke 1986, 1989), and the proposal that ordinary language users have tacit knowledge of the axioms of truth-conditional semantic theories has been developed in some detail (see Higginbotham 1985, 1986, 1988, 1989a, 1989b).

We should note, however, that there are other proposals for answering the epistemological question about compositional semantic theories and ordinary language users' knowledge about the meanings of complete sentences. For example, Dummett (1976, 1991) makes use of a notion of *implicit* knowledge that is importantly different from Chomsky's idea of tacit knowledge, and Wright (1986) sees the construction of compositional semantic theories, not as an articulation of language users' actual knowledge, but as a matter of RATIONAL RECONSTRUCTION (p. 386).

4.5   Semantic theories and metaphysics

The fifth reason for philosophical interest in semantic theories is that the task of bringing specific linguistic constructions within the scope of a compositional semantic
theory sometimes sheds light on issues in other areas of philosophy, and particularly
in metaphysics. We have already discussed the relationships between philosophy of
language, philosophy of mind and metaphysics, so we shall be rather brief here.

Semantic theories for natural languages have to deal with pronouns ('I', 'you', 'she',
'he', 'it', 'they'), demonstratives ('this', 'that', 'this knife', 'that butter') and other indexical expressions ('now', 'then', 'today', 'tomorrow', 'here', 'there'). Questions about the
semantic contributions of these expressions (see Kaplan 1989) inevitably highlight
issues in ontology, as well as in philosophy of mind. For, when we consider the mental
states that are typically expressed using these expressions, we find that they are mental
states that involve thinking about persons, things, times and places in particular ways.
So an adequate account of the thoughts expressed by the use of these expressions seems
to involve a commitment to talking about *ways of thinking* or, in Fregean terminology,
about SENSES (pp. 793–6) (see Frege 1918; Perry 1977, 1979; Evans 1981b, 1982;
Peacocke 1981, 1983, 1986, 1992: ch. 4; Forbes 1987; Davies 1982).

Another example of a link between recent work in philosophy of language and issues
in metaphysics – this time not mediated by philosophy of mind – is provided by work
on the semantics of names ('Theaetetus'), definite descriptions ('the man in the gabardine suit') and modal adverbs ('necessarily'), on the one hand, and metaphysical issues
about necessity and essentialism, on the other (Kripke 1980; Wiggins 1976). A key
claim in this area has been that names are, while definite descriptions typically are not,
rigid designators. A subject term is said to be a rigid designator if it designates the same
object with respect to all different possible situations, so long as we hold the meaning
of the term constant.

To see the importance of the notion of rigid designation to questions about essentialism, consider the sentence:

Necessarily, the tallest animal in the courtyard is human.

To set the scene, suppose that Theaetetus is the tallest of a group of people talking
together in the courtyard, and that there are no non-human animals in the courtyard
other than a dog, Fido, and some fleas. Now, whether the sentence containing the modal
adverb 'Necessarily' is true depends on whether the truth of the subject–predicate
sentence:

The tallest animal in the courtyard is human

is a matter of *necessity* or *contingency*. This subject–predicate sentence is true as evaluated with respect to the described situation; but could it have been false, without any
change in its meaning?

Clearly, the answer is that the sentence could easily have been false. If Theaetetus
and his friends had not been in the courtyard, then Fido would have been the tallest
animal, and Fido is not human. So the question over the modal status of the

subject–predicate sentence (whether it is necessarily or contingently true) does not turn on any interesting metaphysical question about whether human beings are essentially, or merely contingently, human, for example.

Now consider the sentence:

Necessarily, Theaetetus is human.

Whether this sentence is true depends on whether the truth of the subject–predicate sentence:

Theaetetus is human

is a matter of necessity or contingency; and this time the question of modal status does seem to turn on a question about essentialism. Might this particular human being, Theaetetus, have been other than human?

The definite description 'The tallest animal in the courtyard' is a non-rigid designator. With respect to the situation as described, it designates Theaetetus, while with respect to an alternative possible situation, it designates Fido – and without any difference in the meanings of the words ('tallest', 'animal' and so on) that make up the definite description. In contrast, the name 'Theaetetus' is a rigid designator. With respect to the situation described, or with respect to the imagined alternative, that name designates Theaetetus – so long as it retains its meaning. What we have just seen is that, where the subject term is a rigid designator, a question about the truth of a sentence containing a modal adverb leads directly to a question about the essential properties of a particular object.

Davidson's own work provides a third example of a link between semantic theories and issues in metaphysics – particularly of the way in which the construction of a semantic theory may reveal the metaphysical commitments of the conceptual scheme that is expressed in a natural language. Sentences that contain action verbs plus adverbs, such as:

John buttered the toast slowly, in the bathroom

pose a challenge for semantic theories because, after we deal with the subject ('John') and the predicate ('buttered the toast'), it is unclear how we should cope with the adverbs. We shall not pause over the details of the challenge that adverbs pose, but simply note that Davidson (1967b, 1969c, 1985; see also Wiggins 1986) argues that, in order to bring these sentences within the scope of a truth-conditional semantic theory, we need to regiment them as involving quantification over *events*. Roughly, the idea is that an adverbially modified action sentence should be regimented in logical notation as beginning with '$(\exists e)$ –' (in English: 'there is an event which –') so that, for example, the sentence about John and the toast is regimented as equivalent to:

There is an event e which is a buttering of the toast by John, is slow, and is (that is, occurred) in the bathroom.

If this is correct, then our ordinary talk about people doing things, like buttering toast, carries metaphysical commitments, not only to material things like people and toast, but also to an ontology of events.

Adverbs and Events

Davidson's proposal leads to questions about the notion of logical form, about alternative metaphysical theories of events, and about the role of material bodies as the *basic particulars* in our conceptual scheme (Strawson 1959: ch. 1).

Firstly, the proposal can be motivated in either of two ways, corresponding to two rather different ideas of logical form (Evans 1976). On the one hand, there is a pattern of inference to be explained. From 'John buttered the toast slowly, in the bathroom' we can validly infer each of:

John buttered the toast slowly.
John buttered the toast in the bathroom.
John buttered the toast.

If the adverbially modified sentence is regimented as involving a conjunction ('*e* is a buttering of the toast by John & *e* is slow & *e* occurred in the bathroom') then these inferences can be seen as valid in virtue of the logical properties of '&' (Davidson 1967b). On the other hand, the regimentation might be seen as required simply in order to bring the sentences within the scope of a compositional truth-conditional semantic theory (Evans 1976). This motivation might not seem very convincing, since an alternative scheme of regimentation (involving operators that modify the predicate terms corresponding to natural language verbs) appears to be available (Strawson 1974b). But the apparent alternative is not, in the end, formally viable (Taylor 1985; Davies 1991).

Secondly, the proposal leads naturally to the question whether the detailed semantic behaviour of adverbs might provide us with grounds for choosing between two conceptions of events. On the one hand, Davidson (1967b, 1969c) regards events as particulars that can be described in many different ways. One and the same event might be both a *pulling* of a trigger, a *firing* of a rifle and a *killing* of a president, for example. On the other hand, a number of theorists (Goldman 1971; Kim 1976; Taylor 1985) propose that events should be much more finely discriminated – with firings, pullings and killings distinguished from each other. There is a substantial metaphysical difference between these accounts, but it turns out that purely semantic considerations do not provide any compelling reason for favouring one over the other (Davies 1991).

Thirdly, the proposal raises questions about an argument for Strawson's thesis that material bodies are, while events and processes are not, basic particulars in our conceptual scheme. Part of what this thesis comes to is that our ability to pick out individual events in our thought and talk depends on our ability to pick out individual material objects, but not vice versa. At one point, Strawson's argument turns crucially on the claim that our most basic understanding of the conceptually true sentence 'Every animal was born' involves possession of the concept of being born, but not possession of the concept of a birth as an individual particular. Clearly, this argument needs to be assessed in the light of Davidson's proposal for regimenting such sentences as 'This animal was born quickly, in the barn'.

5   Analysing the Concept of Meaning: Grice's Programme

In the last section we considered five ways in which semantic theories might reward philosophical attention. The philosophical significance of meta-semantic theories is much more obvious; for they are attempts at an immediately recognizable philosophical project – a project of conceptual elucidation, or even conceptual analysis. Thus, for example, the programme begun by Grice (1957, 1968, 1969) aims at an analysis of the concept of literal meaning in a public language in terms of psychological concepts such as intention and belief. In this section we shall give an outline description of Grice's programme for analysing the notion of literal meaning. (Grice's papers on the analysis of the concept of meaning are collected in Grice 1989.)

The analytical project can be regarded as having two stages. The first stage aims to characterize a concept of *speaker's meaning* that corresponds, roughly, to the idea of communicating, or attempting to communicate, a proposition (trying to get across a message). The second stage then aims to use that concept of speaker's meaning, along with the notion of a *conventional regularity*, to construct an analysis of the concept of literal linguistic meaning. The basic idea is that a sentence has as its literal meaning the proposition that it is conventionally used to communicate.

Since the project is an analytical one, it is naturally regarded as being subject to a requirement of non-circularity. The accounts of speaker's meaning and of conventional regularity – notions that are drawn on in the analysis of literal linguistic meaning – should not themselves make essential appeal to linguistic notions. Thus, Grice's programme presumes that mind is analytically prior to language. But the success of Grice's programme is not similarly conditional on any ontological or epistemological priority of mind over language (Avramides 1989; cf. Evans and McDowell 1976: xv–xxiii). As we mentioned in section 3.1, it is logically consistent to pursue Grice's analytical programme while accepting Davidson's claims about no ontological priority, and no epistemological priority, of mind over language (though it is true that it would be surprising for someone to combine Grice's analytical views with the no ontological priority claim – no thought without talk).

The claim of no epistemological priority of mind over language says that it is not possible to find out about a person's mental states first, and only then to go on to investigate the meanings of the person's utterances. Rather, the assignment of both meanings and mental states, such as beliefs and intentions, is a single integrated epistemological project governed by the Principle of Charity or the Principle of Humanity (section 4.2). But Davidson goes beyond this epistemological claim. His view is that, by spelling out the constraints on interpretation, we provide all the philosophical elucidation that can be provided of the concept of linguistic meaning. The constraints on interpretation are of two kinds. On the formal side, there is, for example, the finite axiomatization constraint on the semantic theory that is used (in concert with a plausible anthropology) for interpretation. On the empirical side, there are the constraints of agreement (Charity) or intelligibility (Humanity). But the problem with these empirical constraints is that they seem to leave a lacuna.

An interpretation deploys a semantic theory, which generates an assignment of meanings to sentences, in order to provide a description of language users as engaging in certain speech acts (saying and asserting things, for example) and as having certain propositional attitudes (believing and intending things, for example). The Principle of Humanity constrains the specifications of meaning by imposing the requirement that the resulting overall description of the language users in terms of meanings, speech acts and propositional attitudes should make them out to be reasonable or intelligible. But the Principle of Humanity does not itself tell us which combinations of meanings, speech acts and propositional attitudes can be intelligibly attributed.

On the face of it, an account of which combinations are coherent would be provided by articulating the analytical connections between the concept of meaning, the concepts of various speech acts like saying and asserting, and the concepts of propositional attitudes like believing and intending. There might, for example, be conceptual connections that require that anyone who asserts that p does so by using a sentence that literally means that p, and that anyone who asserts that p intends an audience to take him or her (the speaker) to believe that p. Whether there are connections like this, and if so, what exactly they are, is not a trivial question; it is something that requires detailed investigation. The bold proposal of Grice's analytical programme is that there are connections of this kind that actually permit the analysis of the concept of linguistic meaning (and the concepts of the various speech acts; Schiffer 1972: ch. 4) in terms of propositional attitudes.

Grice's analytical project begins from a distinction between *natural* and *non-natural* meaning (Grice 1989: 214). We are talking about natural meaning (or *indicator* meaning) when we say, for example:

Those spots mean (indicate) measles.
Those clouds mean (indicate) rain.

This notion of meaning – which is just a matter of causal co-variation between two kinds of states of affairs – is not the concern of Grice's programme, though it takes on considerable importance in recent work in philosophy of mind, aimed at providing an account of the contents of psychological states themselves (see Dretske 1981, 1986).

Spots indicate measles and clouds indicate rain whether or not anyone takes them in that way, and whether or not anyone intends them to be taken in that way. The various notions of meaning that Grice proposes to analyse are distinguished from natural meaning by the fact that they involve, in one way or another, the intentions of a perpetrator or utterer.

If we are aiming at an analysis of the notion:

Sentence S means that p in the language of group G

then a first suggestion might be this:

Members of G use the sentence S to *say* (to each other) that p.

There are several reasons why this would not be adequate, but the one that concerns us now is that the concept of *saying* seems already to depend on the concept of literal meaning. In order to say something (for example, to say that penguins waddle), a speaker has to use an expression that literally means that thing (here, a sentence that literally means that penguins waddle). So any analysis along these lines would be circular.

It might be replied to this that there is something stipulative about this conception of saying – that is not obligatory to equate saying with *strictly and literally saying*. It might also be replied that perhaps, in the end, we shall have to be satisfied with an analysis that is circular – a circular analysis might be elucidatory provided that the circle of inter-defined terms is large enough. There is some justice in both these replies. But still, a second suggestion for an analysis of the concept of literal meaning might be this:

Members of G use the sentence S to *communicate the message* that *p*.

The advantage of this second suggestion is that the concept of communicating (or getting across) a message does not seem to reintroduce the concept of literal meaning. A person can get across a message even though the sounds used have no literal meaning at all.

However, there is still a problem with this second suggestion. A sound that has no literal meaning can be used by one member of a group to communicate a message to another. The perpetrator of the sound, realizing that the sound has no literal meaning, might rely on some resemblance between the sound produced and some other sound, for example, the sound of an angry dog (see Schiffer 1972: 7, for this example). But then, the same sound might be used by each member of the group when he or she wants to get across the message that he or she is angry. So the conditions in the suggested analysis would be met. But this still might not be a case of literal meaning; and, intuitively, the reason for this is that each person who uses a sound like an angry dog to communicate anger might take himself or herself to be making an innovative use of a resemblance between sounds.

When we have a case of literal meaning, in contrast, it seems that the reason why we use a particular sound is just that it does have the appropriate literal meaning. A little more accurately, we can say that when we make communicative use of an expression with a literal meaning, we rely upon a shared recognition on the part of speaker and hearer that the expression can be used – has been used – in just that way. Communicative use of an expression that has a literal meaning is a rationally self-perpetuating practice; and this fits well with the idea that literal meaning is conventional meaning, since a convention is arguably a rationally self-perpetuating regularity. (The notion of convention is most famously explored by Lewis 1969.)

5.1 Speaker's meaning

We have reached the basic idea that a sentence has as its literal meaning the proposition that it is conventionally used to communicate. Grice's programme aims to develop a detailed philosophical analysis along the lines of this basic idea. The first stage of that programme aims to characterize a concept of *speaker's meaning* roughly corresponding, we said, to the notion of communicating, or attempting to communicate, a proposition. However, we should notice that, given the overall aim of the programme, it is not essential that the concept of speaker's meaning should coincide with any antecedently given notion. It would be consistent with the overall aim that speaker's meaning should come to be regarded as a theory-internal construct.

In Grice's own exposition, the notion of speaker's meaning (utterer's occasion meaning) to be analysed is:

Utterer U meant something by his or her utterance x directed at an audience A.

The putative analysis initially offered by Grice (1957) is as follows (Grice 1989: 92):

U uttered x intending
(1) A to produce a particular response r;
(2) A to think (recognize) that U intends (1);
(3) A to fulfil condition (1) on the basis of his fulfilment of condition (2).

In the case where the speaker is attempting to communicate the message that p to the audience, the primary intended response in clause (1) is that A should believe that p. If we feed this into the analysis, and also unpack clause (3) a little, then we have the proposal that:

Utterer U meant that p by his or her utterance x directed at an audience A

should be analysed as:

U uttered x intending
(1) A to believe that p;
(2) A to think (recognize) that U intends (1);
(3) A's recognition of U's primary intention (1) to be at least part of A's reason for believing that p.

The utterance type that U uses might or might not have a literal linguistic meaning; and if it does then the communicated message might or might not coincide with that literal meaning. But, crucially, this analysis of speaker's meaning does not itself make use of the notion of literal meaning, and so is available for deployment in a non-circular analysis of that notion.

A host of revisions and extensions have been visited on Grice's initial three-clause analysis (Grice 1969; Strawson 1964; Schiffer 1972). Various counter-examples seem to show that Grice's three conditions are neither sufficient nor necessary for speaker's meaning.

There are two main kinds of reason why the three conditions might not be *sufficient* for the intuitive notion of communicating a message or telling somebody something. Firstly, there is nothing in the three conditions to require that there should be some property of the utterance that the utterer should intend or expect to guide the audience towards recognition of the primary communicative intention (Grice 1989: 94). Secondly, the three conditions do not rule out certain kinds of convoluted plans for influencing a person's beliefs in ways that are not, intuitively, straightforwardly communicative (Grice 1969; Strawson 1964; Schiffer 1972: 17–18). We shall not take time over the details here, but the upshot is that – at least so far as sufficiency is concerned – a better analysis of:

Utterer U meant that p by his or her utterance x directed at an audience A

would be:

(1) U intended A to believe that p;
(2) there is some feature F of the utterance x such that U intended A to recognize U's primary intention (the intention in (1)) in part by recognizing x to have F;
(3) U intended A's recognition of U's primary intention to be at least part of A's reason for believing that p;
(4) U did not intend that A should be deceived about U's intentions (such as those in (1), (2) and (3)).

The point of clause (4) is, specifically, to rule out cases where U intends A to be deceived about U's intentions as to how A should arrive at the belief that p (Grice 1989: 99). It is not supposed to rule out the possibility that U might intend A to be deceived about other intentions that U has. For example, clause (4) is certainly supposed to allow that an act of speaker's meaning might also be a case of lying.

The main reason why the three or four conditions might be regarded as not *necessary* for speaker's meaning is that there are so many things that ordinary speakers do with sentences that would not be included under the three- or four-clause analysis. Indeed, there are many quite literal uses of sentences where the speaker does not even intend to produce in the hearer a belief corresponding to the literal meaning of the sentence (so not even clause (1) would be satisfied). Grice (1989: 105–9) reviews several of these cases, including examination answers, confessions, reminding, giving a review of already known facts, spelling out the conclusion of an argument, and talking to a counter-suggestible person. Davidson (1984: 111) also mentions 'stories, rote repetitions, illustrations, suppositions, parodies, charades, chants, and conspicuously unmeant compliments'.

There are various suggested remedies for the problems that these examples are supposed to pose. But, for present purposes, it is enough to note that the massive variety of literal uses of language is not necessarily problematic for the putative analysis of speaker's meaning, if the fundamental model for speaker's meaning is the case of telling someone something with the intention of providing new knowledge. Arguably, that notion of speaker's meaning – with straightforward telling as the central case – can be analysed roughly along the lines of Grice's four-clause definition. But if we retain an analysis of speaker's meaning on which the majority of uses of language turn out not to be cases of speaker's meaning, then we must take that fact into account in the second stage of the analytical programme.

5.2   *Conventional meaning*

Given the basic idea that a sentence has as its literal meaning the proposition that it is conventionally used to communicate, the second stage of the programme should characterize the concept of convention, and most recent work in the Gricean tradition makes use of developments of Lewis's (1969) notion of a convention as a rationally self-perpetuating regularity in behaviour. According to Lewis (1975: 164–6) a convention is a regularity R in action, or in action and belief, that meets the following conditions:

(1)   everyone conforms to R;
(2)   everyone believes that everyone else conforms to R;
(3)   the belief in (2) furnishes each person with a reason to conform to R;
(4)   there is a general preference for general conformity to R, rather than slightly less than general conformity;
(5)   there is at least one alternative regularity which would serve reasonably well; and
(6)   the facts listed in (1)–(5) are matters of *common knowledge*.

The most straightforward way to employ this notion and that of speaker's meaning in tandem in an analysis of literal linguistic meaning is to say:

Sentence S means that *p* in the language of group G iff there is a convention in G to use utterances of S in order to communicate that *p* (that is, in order to mean that *p*, in the sense of speaker's meaning).

In a slogan:

Speaker's meaning + Convention = Literal meaning.

This would need to be refined to allow for the ambiguity and context-dependence characteristic of natural language. But, much more importantly, the suggested analysis imposes a requirement that is far too strict to be a necessary condition for literal meaning.

We have already seen that the four-clause definition of speaker's meaning makes it a relatively rare phenomenon. So there can certainly be literal meaning even where there is no regularity of speaker's meaning (as presently defined). If we want to give an analysis of the concept of literal meaning along the lines of the slogan, then we need to weaken the notion of speaker's meaning, or weaken the notion of convention (or weaken both). (The analyses of literal meaning suggested by recent theorists all depart in one way or another from that most straightforward way of pursuing the second stage of Grice's programme. See Bennett 1976; Blackburn 1984: ch. 4; Davies 1981: ch. 1; Lewis 1975; Peacocke 1976; Schiffer 1972: ch. 5.)

Let us first consider weakening the notion of convention. The trouble with the notion of convention does not seem to lie in the idea of rational self-perpetuation, but rather in the commitment to there being a regularity that members of the group actually conform to. The sentence 'Penguins waddle' literally means, in our language, that penguins waddle. But there is not a regularity of using that sentence to communicate the message that penguins waddle. It is not the case, for example, that whenever anyone wants to get across the message that penguins waddle he or she uses that sentence. There are surely other ways in which that same message might be communicated. But more important for present purposes is that, although people do sometimes use the sentence 'Penguins waddle', it is not regularly used with the intentions specified in the four-clause definition of speaker's meaning.

Grice (1989: 126) himself suggests moving from speaker's meaning to literal meaning via the notion of 'having a certain procedure in one's repertoire'. It would not be adequate to say:

> Sentence S means that *p* in the language of group G iff each member of G has it in his or her repertoire to use utterances of S in order to communicate that *p* (that is, in order to mean that *p*, in the sense of speaker's meaning).

That proposed definition fails to build in the idea of rational self-perpetuation (cf. Schiffer 1972: 132–6). But a more plausible analysis could be built from the concept of speaker's meaning (as presently defined) plus a concept analogous to the concept of convention but with the notion of regularity replaced by the notion of having a certain procedure in one's repertoire. Thus Grice (1989: 127) suggests that more is required than each member of the group G having the communicative procedure in his or her repertoire:

> At least some (many) members of group G have in their repertoires the procedure [to use utterances of S in order to communicate that *p*], the retention of this procedure being for them conditional on the assumption that at least some (other) members of G have, or have had, this procedure in their repertoires.

If we do not weaken the notion of convention, then we have to introduce a concept weaker than speaker's meaning. Some literal uses of language that fall outside the scope of speaker's meaning as presently defined might well fall within the scope of a revised notion in which clause (1) is replaced by:

(1)′   U intended A *actively* to believe that *p*.

Arguably, examples of reminding are covered by this modification. Some other literal uses are covered by a different modification:

(1)″   U intended A to believe that U believed that *p*.

Arguably, this deals with the case of examination answers. But in order to make it plausible that we have covered all, or at least most, literal uses of language, we need to abstract away from these details about just what attitude U intends A to take to the proposition that *p*.

The completely general form would be:

(1)‴   There is *some* propositional attitude Ψ, such that U intends that A should Ψ that *p*.

We could take clause (1)''', together with clauses (2)–(4) of the four-clause definition of speaker's meaning, to define a new notion of *weak speaker's meaning*. This might then be combined with the notion of convention in a putative analysis of literal meaning (Peacocke 1976; Davies 1981).

However the details are worked out, a Gricean analysis of the concept of literal meaning for sentences presents the use of a public language as a psychologically highly complex matter. On a Gricean account, everyday literal use of language for communication involves beliefs about beliefs, intentions about beliefs, beliefs about intentions about beliefs, and much more. It may seem implausible that such complicated propositional attitudes are involved in the ordinary use of language and this may motivate an objection to Grice's programme for analysing the notion of literal linguistic meaning. But, on the other hand, the psychological plausibility of Gricean accounts has been defended (Loar 1981). There are important questions here. But even if they are answered in Grice's favour, there are further difficulties to be faced. For we have not yet taken any account of the internal structure of sentences.

5.3   Expression meaning and the structure of language

The way in which component words and phrases make their contributions to the meanings of complete sentences is the starting-point for Davidson's programme in philosophy of language (see section 3). But the analysis of the concept of literal meaning as it applies to expressions smaller than complete sentences is an extremely difficult problem within Grice's programme (Grice 1968; Schiffer 1972: ch. 6; Loar 1976, 1981: 253–60). Whether or not it is an absolutely insoluble problem is, at best, not clear. The issues here are very complex, and we shall only give a brief indication of the way in which the difficulty arises.

In essence, the problem is that the structure of language presents a dilemma for the general idea that literal meaning is a matter of there being conventions to use expressions with certain intentions. The primary link between meaning and convention has to be made either at the level of words and phrases, and ways of putting them together (such as subject–predicate combination), or else at the level of complete sentences. Either alternative presents problems.

Suppose that we opt for the first alternative. Then, we shall credit language users with having procedures for using words, and phrases, and ways of putting them together, and also with knowledge that they and others have these procedures. We need to credit speakers with this knowledge, in order to maintain the idea of rational self-perpetuation. But it is here that the problem with this first alternative is presented. For the semantic rules that govern the use of sub-sentential components, and ways of combining components, are far from obvious. (That is why the construction of compositional semantic theories is a challenging project.) So, on the first alternative, it is practically inevitable that the analysis of meaning will commit us to attributing to ordinary language users beliefs and knowledge that they do not have: detailed beliefs and knowledge about the components and construction of their sentences (Loar 1981: 256).

Suppose, instead, that we try the second alternative. In that case, literal meaning will be grounded in rationally self-perpetuating regularities of use of complete sentences. But the problem this time is that there are many perfectly meaningful sentences that are never used at all (*meaning without use*); and there are many others that are used, but would never be used to communicate the proposition that is their literal meaning (*meaning despite use*). An example of the latter kind is provided by the sentence: 'No head injury is too trivial to be ignored' (Bennett 1976: 17). This sentence is sometimes used; but it is typically used with the intention that the hearer should believe that no head injury is *sufficiently* trivial to be ignored.

A possible response to this dilemma would be to avoid the first alternative and adopt the second alternative, but only for those sentences for which there is a practice of literal use. According to this response, the Gricean notion of conventional meaning would not apply directly to unused sentences. So there would remain the problem of extending the notion of literal meaning from the core of used sentences to the rest of the sentences in the language. One plausible suggestion for dealing with this problem – perhaps the only plausible suggestion – is that an account of literal meaning applicable to all sentences, whether used or not, should explicitly advert to the psychological mechanisms that underpin the use of sentences in the core set (Loar 1976: 160; see also Schiffer 1987: 249–55; 1993). According to this suggestion, the analysis of literal meaning would be extended from used sentences to unused sentences in two steps.

Firstly, consider a speaker who participates in a conventional practice of using a sentence with a certain literal meaning. We assume that the speaker's assignment of a meaning to the sentence is underpinned by cognitive mechanisms that correspond closely to some of the axioms of a compositional semantic theory for the language. In particular, we assume that the cognitive mechanisms subserving the assignment of a meaning to a sentence include mechanisms corresponding to the semantic theory's axioms for the words (and ways of combining words) in that sentence.

Secondly, consider an unused sentence that is built from words that occur in used sentences (and is built in ways that are also found in used sentences). Then we allow the literal meaning for the unused sentence to be determined by the semantic axioms that correspond to certain cognitive mechanisms; namely, the mechanisms that are implicated in the speaker's assignment of meanings to regularly used sentences built from those same resources. (Strictly speaking, this deals only with the problem of meaning without use. But a similar strategy could be adopted to deal with the problem of meaning despite use.)

A natural way of implementing this suggestion would be to make use of Chomsky's notion of tacit knowledge. Instead of saying, rather vaguely, that there are cognitive mechanisms corresponding in the appropriate way to axioms of a semantic theory, we could say that those axioms are tacitly known (see above, section 4.4). Indeed, Loar (1981: 259) suggests that 'the Chomskyan idea of the internalization of the generative procedures of a grammar has got to be invoked to ... make sense of literal meaning' (see also Davies 2000).

Appealing to the notion of tacit knowledge of a compositional semantic theory may be the best way for a Gricean to solve the problem of meaning without use. But we do not have any detailed prospectus for a marriage between Chomsky's and Grice's rather different projects in the study of language. It is certainly not obvious just how Gricean the resulting union could be (Chomsky 1976: 55–77; 1980: 81–7; 1986: 19–24; see also Laurence 1996, 1998, for a Chomskyan account of literal meaning presented as a competitor to a Gricean or 'convention-based' account).

In summary, then, we can say that there is something of a consensus that Grice's programme faces serious problems. Lycan (1991: 84) lists some of them:

> that most sentences of a language are never tokened at all; that since hearers instantly understand 'novel' sentences, this cannot be in virtue of pre-established conventions or expectations directed on those sentences individually; that sentences are ambiguous and have more than one standard linguistic meaning; that sentences are often (not just abnormally) used with other than their standard meanings; and that indeed some sentences are normally used with other than their standard meanings.

In the last few paragraphs we have sketched a possible strategy for responding to some of these problems. But we should also note that one of the most authoritative exponents of Grice's programme has, after considering just such a strategy, reached the conclusion that the project of analysing literal meaning in terms of intentions and beliefs (IBS: *intention-based semantics*) cannot be carried through (Schiffer 1987: 261): 'I have exhausted my wits . . . I cannot see how to devise an IBS account of expression-meaning that does not require us to have knowledge that we seem not to have'.

5.4   Minimalism about meaning and truth

Schiffer (1987: 10) goes beyond the claim that Grice's analytical programme cannot be completed to the more general conclusion that there is no correct and substantive theory of meaning, in the sense of a philosophical theory about the nature of linguistic meaning, to be given. According to Schiffer, there are no such entities as meanings to be assigned to sentences and, given that Grice's analytical project cannot be completed, there is no prospect of a philosophical analysis of the concept of meaning. There is still room for a theory about how language understanding takes place, about the information processing that goes on in our heads when we hear an utterance. But, as Schiffer says, 'such a theory would not be a *philosophical* theory' (ibid.: 269).

This 'no-theory' theory of meaning is a species of *minimalism* about meaning. According to the minimalist view (Johnston 1988), meaning has no substantial nature and so there is nothing substantive for a theory about meaning to say. Such general elucidation of the notion of linguistic meaning as may be required is provided, not by a substantive theory or conceptual analysis, but by truisms or platitudes, such as:

> If a sentence S means that *p* then utterances of S can be used to say that *p*.

Someone working within Grice's programme might hope to provide an analysis of the notion of a speaker using an utterance of S to say that *p* and, in that way, to provide a substantive, if partial, account of the notion of meaning. But the minimalist says that there is no such analysis to be provided.

The minimalist may go on to say that the platitudes about meaning highlight a connection between meaning and *use*: understanding S, or knowing that S means that *p*, is a matter of being able to use utterances of S to say that *p*. If that is right, then knowledge of meaning may appear to be so closely connected to language use that it cannot play any role in the causal explanation of language use. This claim about the lack of an explanatory role for knowledge of meaning is, indeed, one aspect of minimalism about meaning. But the proposal that there is a close connection between meaning and use seems to go against the strictest construal of the 'no-theory' theory of meaning. For the proposal that meaning is closely connected with use, or even that meaning *is* use (Wittgenstein 1953; Horwich 1998), does seem to be a substantive piece of philosophical theory concerning the notion of meaning.

It may be useful, here, to distinguish two versions of the 'no-theory' theory of meaning. The strict version says that there is nothing substantive at all to be said about meaning – not even that meaning is use. This might be accompanied by the suggestion that there is nothing more to know about meaning than is constituted by acceptance of such trivial-seeming statements about meaning as:

> The sentence 'Fido barks' means that Fido barks.
> The sentence 'The man in the gabardine suit is a spy' means that the man in the gabardine suit is a spy.
> The sentence 'Theaetetus is sitting' means that Theaetetus is sitting.

And so on. The more moderate version of the 'no-theory' theory of meaning allows that there may be something of philosophical interest to be said about linguistic meaning. It would be consistent with the moderate 'no-theory' theory to offer a philosophical theory according to which facts about meaning are determined by facts about use. But the moderate 'no-theory' theory still insists that there is no substantive philosophical theory about meaning that can be packaged as an analysis of the concept of meaning along the lines of:

> Sentence S means that p iff _ S _ p _.

Certainly there is nothing of the kind that Grice was aiming to provide.

The idea that meaning depends on use, or that meaning is constituted by use, is not obviously inconsistent with the aim of providing an analysis of the notion of linguistic meaning. After all, Grice's analytical programme might be regarded as one way of developing the idea that meaning depends on use:

> Sentence S means that p iff S is conventionally used to communicate the message that p.

But it is certainly possible to offer a 'use theory' of meaning while explicitly disavowing any analytical ambitions. The term 'use theory of meaning' is usually applied to meta-semantic theories that appeal to the notion of use and also meet the requirement for being a moderate 'no-theory' theory of meaning.

A use theory of meaning, in this sense, is sometimes coupled with minimalism (or a *deflationary* theory) about truth (Horwich 1990, 1998). The main claim made by a minimalist about the notion of truth is that there is nothing more to grasping the notion of truth than accepting instances of the schema (Horwich 1990: 7):

(E)　　It is true that p if and only if p

such as:

> It is true that Fido barks iff Fido barks.
> It is true that the man in the gabardine suit is a spy iff the man in the gabardine suit is a spy.
> It is true that Theaetetus is sitting iff Theaetetus is sitting.

Because (E) uses the expression 'It is true that – ', it does not speak of the truth of sentences. There is a clear difference between:

> The sentence 'Fido barks' is true iff Fido barks.

which is about a linguistic expression, 'Fido barks', and the instance of (E):

> It is true that Fido barks iff Fido barks.

which might be said to concern the *proposition* that Fido barks. So what we have described so far is minimalism about truth for propositions, or minimalism about 'It is true that'.

But a minimalist about truth for propositions is likely to maintain, in addition, that there is nothing more to grasping the notion of truth as it applies to sentences (or utterances of sentences) than acceptance of statements of the following kind:

> (An utterance of) the sentence 'Fido barks' is true iff Fido barks.
> (An utterance of) the sentence 'The man in the gabardine suit is a spy' is true iff the man in the gabardine suit is a spy.
> (An utterance of) the sentence 'Theaetetus is sitting' is true iff Theaetetus is sitting.

In these statements the same sentence occurs first in quotation marks and then without quotation marks, and statements of this form are said to encapsulate the *disquotational* conception of truth (Field 1994: 250; see also Field 1986).

Even if minimalism about truth for propositions is plausible, minimalism about truth as it applies to sentences may seem to face a challenge. As we saw in section 4.2, Tarski's Convention T can be conceived as a partial elucidation of the concept of truth for sentences in terms of the concept of translation or the concept of meaning. We also observed that conditions of adequacy on semantic theories (or equivalently, constraints on the actual language relation) can help us to elucidate the concept of meaning and thence, via the meaning–truth connection, the concept of truth for sentences. And we described the way in which Wiggins (1980) offered a 'substantial theory of truth' by imposing a condition of adequacy (based on the Principle of Humanity) directly on Tarski–Davidson theories of truth conditions. By offering the prospect of substantial philosophical elucidation of the concept of truth, these considerations seem to threaten minimalism about truth for sentences.

But the minimalist about truth can respond to this threat of unwanted substantiveness. He might, for example, focus on the application of Tarski's Convention T to the case where a theory of truth conditions for a language is given in an extension of that same language. For, in that case, what Convention T requires of:

Sentence S is true if and only if p

is simply that it should meet the 'disquotational' condition that the sentence that fills the 'p' place should be the sentence S itself, as in:

The sentence 'Fido barks' is true iff Fido barks.

And he might combine this with insistence that there is nothing more substantive to be said about the conditions under which a theory of truth conditions is correct and, in particular, nothing substantive to be said about the actual language relation (Field 1994: section 6).

Alternatively, a minimalist about truth who also holds a use theory of meaning (Horwich 1998) may offer his own account of the meaning–truth connection:

If a sentence S means that p then S is true iff p

drawing on no resources that go beyond the use theory of meaning plus disquotational equivalences such as:

(An utterance of) the sentence 'Theaetetus is sitting' is true iff Theaetetus is sitting.

It is plausible, in this case, that the threat of unwanted substantiveness flowing across the meaning–truth connection can be met provided that the use theory of meaning is indeed a moderate 'no-theory' theory. Minimalism about truth avoids a potential problem and, to that extent, gains a measure of support, by being coupled with a moderate 'no-theory' theory of meaning, such as a use theory.

There is also a relation of support in the opposite direction. As Horwich (1998: 113) says:

> By itself, the deflationary [minimalist] view of truth does not motivate the use theory of meaning. But it provides a vital part of the argument by showing that a common reason for rejecting the theory was based on a mistake.

If there were a substantive philosophical theory of truth then, because of the meaning–truth connection, there would be at least a substantive necessary condition on: Sentence S means that p. This would not amount to an analysis of the notion of linguistic meaning, but it would go against the spirit of the 'no-theory' theory of meaning. So a moderate 'no-theory' theory of meaning, such as a use theory, is more plausible when it is accompanied by minimalism about truth.

A use theory of meaning and minimalism about truth for sentences are mutually supporting. Each allows the other to avoid a problem. The combination might be called 'semantic deflationism' (ibid.: 11) – or, perhaps better, 'meta-semantic deflationism'. This deflationary position on meaning and truth is opposed not only to Grice's analytical programme, but also to Davidson's programme with its focus on the construction of compositional, truth-conditional semantic theories. The evaluation of meta-semantic deflationism is a pressing task for the philosophy of language.

6 Pragmatics: Conversational Implicature and Relevance Theory

A sentence that literally means that *p* can be used to communicate a message other than the proposition that *p*. Thus, suppose that someone asks you, 'Would you like more coffee?' and that you answer: 'Coffee keeps me awake'. In a suitable context, this answer can convey the message that you do not want any more coffee (Sperber and Wilson 1995: 34); in a different context (as when you are obliged to stay alert through a boring lecture) it might convey the message that you do want some more coffee. But neither of these possible messages is any part of the literal meaning of the sentence 'Coffee keeps me awake'. In each case, the communicated message is, rather, something implied (in some sense) in the context, by what is literally and explicitly said.

The distinction between semantics and pragmatics is, roughly, the distinction between (1) the significance conventionally or literally attached to words, and thence to whole sentences, and (2) the further significance that can be worked out, by more general principles, using contextual information. Grice's theory of *conversational implicature* is the seminal contribution to recent pragmatic theory. It is a theory – or the beginning of a theory – of how this further significance is generated.

6.1   Conversational implicature

The theory of conversational implicature was first developed in the context of examples such as these.

> *and*: Strawson (1952) discusses differences between the connectives of propositional logic and the corresponding words of English, and he notes that 'a statement of the form "p and q" may carry an implication of temporal order' (ibid.: 81).
>
> *or*: Strawson also notes that 'the alternative statement [statement of the form "p or q"] carries the implication of the speaker's uncertainty as to which of the two it was' (ibid.: 91).
>
> *but*: The statement 'She was poor but she was honest' carries the implication that there is some kind of contrast between being poor and being honest.
>
> *looks*: The statement 'That looks red to me' carries the implication that it is in some way doubtful whether the object really is red.

We can ask whether these implications are all of the same kind. Are they the products of special features of key words in the sentences – 'and', 'or', 'but', 'looks' – or are they generated by some kind of interaction between the literal meanings of the sentences that are uttered and some very general conversational principles?

Grice's (1961) first exposition of the idea of conversational implicature is particularly concerned with the example of 'looks'. He wants to maintain that the statement 'That looks red to me' is literally true, even when the object in question quite obviously *is* red, so that there is no question of any doubt about its colour. In that paper, Grice develops two notions – the *detachability* and the *cancellability* of an implication – that we can use to help us to identify conversational implicatures and to distinguish them from *conventional implicatures*.

In the example with 'looks', the implication is not detachable. This means that there is no form of words that can be used to state just what 'That looks red to me' can be used to state (that has the same truth conditions as 'That looks red to me'), but without carrying the implication. The obvious candidates – 'That appears red to me', 'That seems red to me' – carry the same implication that there is some doubt about the object's colour. On the other hand, the implication is cancellable. It is quite consistent to override the implication of a doubt by saying: 'That looks red to me . . . and it really is red – there's no doubt about it'. In the examples with 'and' and 'or', the implication is likewise cancellable but not detachable; and, indeed, that is the typical profile for conversational implicature.

In the case of 'but', however, the profile is reversed. The implication is detachable, but not cancellable. The implication is detachable (as Grice uses that term) because there is another word, 'and', that makes just the same contribution to truth conditions as 'but', but does not generate the same implication: 'She was poor and she was honest' does not carry the implication of a contrast between poverty and honesty. The implication is not cancellable because it would be extremely odd – indeed, inconsistent, in some sense – to say: 'She was poor but she was honest, though of course I do not mean to imply that there is any contrast between poverty and honesty'.

In the case of the word 'but', then, the implication that is generated appears to be a feature of the literal or conventional meaning of that specific word – even though it is not a feature that helps to determine the truth conditions of sentences containing the word. In the other cases – 'and', 'or', 'looks' – the implication is generated by some more general principles governing conversation. Grice (1961: 94) offers a conversational principle that at least applies to the cases of 'or' and of 'looks'. He suggests that the implications are generated, in those cases, by the assumption that there is in operation a general principle something like:

One should not make a weaker statement rather than a stronger one unless there is a good reason for so doing.

If someone makes a disjunctive statement, then the hearer can suppose – given this conversational principle – that the speaker is not in a position to make a stronger statement by using just one of the disjuncts. Similarly, 'That looks red to me' is intuitively a weaker statement than 'That is red', and a speaker's use of the weaker statement about how it looks to her (or appears to her, or seems to her) generates the implication that she is not in a position to make the stronger statement about how it is in reality. The example with 'and', however, is not dealt with by this conversational principle.

In a later paper, Grice (1975) offers a more fully worked out theory that covers the example of 'and' as well. (Grice's papers on pragmatics are collected in Grice 1989.) The fundamental idea is that participants in a conversation expect each other to observe a *Co-operative Principle*:

Make your conversational contribution such as is required, at the stage at which it occurs, by the accepted purpose or direction of the talk exchange in which you are engaged.

This principle is elaborated by Grice into a series of maxims. He groups these maxims under four headings: Quantity, Quality, Relation and Manner. Examples of the maxims include (one example from each category):

Make your contribution as informative as is required (for the current purposes of the exchange).
Do not say that for which you lack adequate evidence.
Be relevant.
Be orderly.

The first of these sample maxims is one of the maxims of Quantity, and does the work of the earlier conversational principle. The last is one of the maxims of Manner, and is used to explain the implicature generated by 'and'.

The way that conversational implicatures are discerned involves the hearer in inference. Suppose that a participant in a conversation says – quite literally and explicitly – that p, and gives no indication that he is not observing the Co-operative Principle and the maxims. Then, on Grice's theory, a conversational implicature that q is generated if the supposition that the speaker believes that q is required in order to make his literally saying that p consistent with the presumption that he is operating in accordance with the maxims 'or at least the Co-operative Principle' (ibid.: 31).

According to Grice, conversational implicatures can be worked out or calculated using the Co-operative Principle and the maxims together with information about the literal meaning of the sentence used, information about the context, and other background assumptions. There is no way of telling, ahead of time, what background assumptions might be helpful in working out an implicature. So this aspect of communication involves a great deal that is not specifically to do with language. Furthermore, on Grice's view, the Co-operative Principle and the maxims themselves are not specific to language, but are simply the instantiations to the case of conversation of principles and maxims that it would be reasonable to observe in any co-operative activity – such as cooking a meal, or helping a friend to change the wheel on a car.

The mechanism of conversational implicature can be used to communicate more than is literally said – more than the literal meaning that is encoded in the words that are used. If an implicature turns out to be false, then the hearer may well be misled; but the speaker has not, strictly speaking, spoken falsely. This distinction between what is false, and what is only misleading, is of considerable general philosophical importance. If Bruce is standing squarely in front of a standard letter box in the United Kingdom in good daylight, and says, 'That looks red to me', then what he says may be misleading, to the extent that it suggests that there is some doubt about the colour of the letter box. But still, what he says is true: the letter box does look red to Bruce. (Grice (1961) uses this point to defend a version of the sense data theory of perception.)

6.2 Three problems for Grice's pragmatic theory

Although Grice's pragmatic theory is important and has been influential, there are some quite serious problems with it. Here we mention three.

The first problem is that the theory provides no account of how the various maxims are to be weighted against each other. Thus consider the following example:

A: Where does C live?
B: Somewhere in the South of France.

Grice's own gloss on the example is as follows (Grice 1989: 32–3):

> There is no reason to suppose that B is opting out [from the Co-operative Principle and the maxims]; his answer is, as he well knows, less informative than is required to meet A's needs. This infringement of the first maxim of Quantity [Make your contribution as informative as is required (for the current purposes of the exchange)] can be explained only by the supposition that B is aware that to be more informative would be to say something that infringed the maxim of Quality, 'Don't say what you lack adequate evidence for', so B implicates that he does not know in which town C lives.

If we look at this gloss in the light of Grice's account of the generation of implicatures, then we see that it is implicit that measuring up to the maxim of Quality excuses violating the maxim of Quantity, when there is a clash between them. The maxim of Quality is thus implicitly ranked as more important than the maxim of Quantity. But there is nothing explicit in Grice's account about the relative ranking of the maxims.

In Grice's pragmatic theory, the Co-operative Principle is developed in a large number of maxims, but no general account is provided of the relationships between the maxims. It would thus be tempting to look for some one overarching aim in conversation, which would justify a single overarching maxim.

The second problem arises from the fact that what is conversationally implicated is supposed to be part of the message that is communicated: it is supposed to fall within the scope of speaker's meaning. It is unclear how, given this fact, Grice's pragmatic theory can allow for the open-ended character of many implicatures – seen clearly in the open-ended interpretation of metaphor. What Grice actually says about open-endedness is this (Grice 1989: 39–40):

> Since, to calculate a conversational implicature is to calculate what has to be supposed in order to preserve the supposition that the Co-operative Principle is being observed, and since there may be various possible specific explanations, a list of which may be open, the conversational implicatum in such cases will be disjunction of such specific explanations; and if the list of these is open, the implicatum will have just the kind of indeterminacy that many actual implicata do in fact seem to possess.

But what is conversationally implicated is supposed to fall within the scope of speaker's meaning and it is far from clear that it makes sense to say that the proposition that a speaker overtly intended to communicate was an indefinitely extended disjunction. The problem here is that it is unclear exactly what belief the speaker would intend the speaker to end up with (clause (1) of the definition of speaker's meaning in section 5.1), and equally unclear exactly what intention the speaker would intend the hearer to recognize her as having (clause (2)).

We need to allow that, although sometimes a speaker may overtly intend the hearer to recognize a specific conversational implicature as the communicated message, this case lies at one end of a spectrum. Further along the spectrum there are cases where the speaker intends that the hearer will recognize one or more implicatures in a more or less closely demarcated range. Further along again, there are cases where the speaker is doing little more than to invite the hearer to explore a space of possible implicatures.

What this suggests is that we might do best to focus on the ways – some specifically intended, others not – in which a hearer can *exploit* what a speaker literally and explicitly says. Conversational implicatures, meeting the standards of speaker's meaning, would then be regarded as the limiting case of a much more general phenomenon.

The third problem is that the account of the generation of conversational implicatures is under-specified. To see this, consider what Grice says about metaphor and irony (ibid.: 34). In each case (metaphor: 'You are the cream in my coffee'; irony: 'X is a fine friend') what is literally and explicitly said is obviously something that the speaker believes to be false. So, on the face of it, the speaker is flouting one of the maxims of Quality: Do not say what you believe to be false. So the hearer has to find a proposition q such that, by supposing the speaker to believe that q, the hearer can see the speaker as nevertheless observing the Co-operative Principle.

In the case of metaphor, Grice's (ibid.) gloss is:

> The most likely supposition is that the speaker is attributing to his audience some feature or features in respect of which the audience resembles (more or less fancifully) the mentioned substance.

In the case of irony, it is:

> Unless A's utterance is entirely pointless, A must be trying to get across some other proposition than the one he purports to be putting forward. This must be some obviously related proposition; the most obviously related proposition is the contradictory of the one he purports to be putting forward.

But Grice provides no explanation of the way in which the particular relationship between literal meaning and communicated message is to be calculated in each case (but see Grice (1978) for some further discussion).

6.3   Relevance theory

Dan Sperber and Deirdre Wilson (1981, 1986a, 1986b, 1995; Wilson and Sperber 1981) have developed a pragmatic theory that is based on a quite general account of the way in which a hearer makes use of available information. They propose that the key to a theoretical understanding of communication – and, indeed, of cognition in general – is provided by the notion of *relevance*. Thus:

> Our suggestion is that humans tend to pay attention to the most relevant phenomena available; that they tend to construct the most relevant possible representations of these phenomena, and to process them in a context that maximizes their relevance. Relevance, and the maximization of relevance, is the key to human cognition. (Sperber and Wilson 1986b: 586)

In order to explain the notion of relevance, we need to make clear the idea of a *context* that Sperber and Wilson use.

In relevance theory, a context is 'a subset of the hearer's assumptions about the world' (Sperber and Wilson 1995: 15) that provides potential premises to be used in inferences. The idea is that, at any given point in a conversational exchange, the hearer has some assumptions 'in the forefront of his attention'. When a new proposition is introduced – say, as the result of a communicative act on the part of the speaker – the newly introduced proposition and the pre-existing context interact inferentially, so as to produce *cognitive effects*. An implication that depends on the new proposition and also on some of the assumptions in the context is said to be a *contextual implication* of the new proposition; and contextual implication is the simplest example of a cognitive effect.

Relevance is a matter of having cognitive effects (Sperber and Wilson 1986b: 586):

> We claim that information is relevant if it interacts in a certain way with your existing assumptions about the world.

Roughly, the more cognitive effects a proposition has, the more relevant it is. However, the cost of deriving cognitive effects has to be taken into account as well. So we add a second condition; namely, that the less effort that is required in order to derive cognitive effects from a proposition, the more relevant it is. The notion of relevance then provides an account of utterance interpretation via a *Communicative Principle of Relevance* (Sperber and Wilson 1995: 158):

> Every act of ostensive communication communicates the presumption of its own optimal relevance.

This says, roughly, that an utterance carries a guarantee that it can yield an adequate range of cognitive effects without too much processing effort. (For further discussion of the presumption of optimal relevance, see ibid.: 266–71.)

Relevance theory avoids the first of the three problems for Grice's pragmatic theory – that it provides no account of the relative weight attached to the various maxims – by having a single principle take over the work that is done by the Co-operative Principle and the various maxims.

Relevance theory avoids the second problem for Grice's account – that it does not easily allow for the open-endedness of interpretation – because a speaker can communicate to a hearer that worthwhile cognitive effects can be obtained without too much effort, yet not make plain to the hearer just what those cognitive effects will be. Relevance theory thus allows for varying degrees of determinacy of cognitive effects. At one end of the spectrum are the cases that Grice's pragmatic theory handles well. The speaker makes it completely clear what the intended cognitive effects are, overtly

133

intends the hearer to recognize a specific implicature as the communicated message, and can be held as responsible for the truth of the implicature as if she had asserted it outright. At the other end of the spectrum are cases in which the speaker provides a guarantee of relevance, but leaves it totally up to the hearer to explore a range of cognitive effects. Such exploration is likely to involve considerable processing effort, but the speaker communicates that the effort will be repaid (see ibid.: 193–202).

Sperber and Wilson avoid the third problem for Grice's account by giving detailed and substantive accounts of metaphor and irony. The key ideas are that metaphor is a kind of *loose talk* while irony is an *echoic* use of language (see ibid.: ch. 4).

Loose talk – as when someone who lives just outside the city limits of Paris says, 'I live in Paris' – is a pervasive feature of ordinary language use. Relevance theory accounts for loose talk by saying that the utterance of a sentence that is strictly speaking false may be a highly effective way of communicating a whole set of propositions that can be easily derived as logical or contextual implications from the initial piece of (mis-)information. A hearer can use a presumption of relevance to select some implications and ignore others. According to relevance theory, metaphor is a kind of loose talk. The perpetrator of a metaphor intends a hearer to derive a set of contextual implications from a proposition that is literally false (Sperber and Wilson 1986a: 548):

> The most creative metaphors require of the hearer a greater effort in building an appropriate context, and deriving a wide range of implications. In general, the wider the range of potential implicatures and the greater the hearer's responsibility for constructing them, the more creative the metaphor.

The echoic use of language is also widespread. Thus consider the following exchange (Sperber and Wilson 1981: 556):

(a) I've got a toothache.
(b) Oh, you've got a toothache. Open your mouth, and let's have a look.

Here, the second speaker echoes the first speaker's utterance, thereby indicating that it has been heard and understood and also expressing a reaction to it. Often, an echoic utterance is used to convey a speaker's attitude towards the thought of the person whose utterance is echoed, as in the following example (Sperber and Wilson 1995: 239):

> *He*: It's a lovely day for a picnic.
> [They go for a picnic and the sun shines.]
> *She* (happily): It's a lovely day for a picnic, indeed.

It is a very short step from here to a clear example of irony (ibid.):

> *He*: It's a lovely day for a picnic.
> [They go for a picnic and it rains.]
> *She* (sarcastically): It's a lovely day for a picnic, indeed.

According to relevance theory, irony is a kind of echoic use of language: 'The speaker dissociates herself from the opinion echoed and indicates that she does not hold it herself' (ibid.). In general, the interpretation of an utterance as ironical involves the recognition of the utterance as echoic, the identification of the person or kind of person whose utterance (real or imagined) or thought is being echoed, and the recognition that the speaker's attitude towards this thought is one of rejection or dissociation (ibid.: 240).

There is an important similarity between relevance theory's account of irony and the account of metaphor. Both metaphor and irony are said to involve the use of 'very general mechanisms of verbal communication' (ibid.: 242). There is no need for a distinctive theory of *figurative* language; the relevance-theory accounts of metaphor and irony are continuous with accounts of utterances that are neither metaphorical nor ironical.

Implication and Implicature

We can convey some of the basic ideas of relevance theory by looking at an example involving a question, along with four possible answers (based on Wilson and Sperber 1981). We are to assume that the set of background assumptions shared between speaker and hearer already includes the assumption that Bruce is a philosopher, but does not include the assumption that Bruce is boring.

Q: Are you inviting Bruce to your party?
A: (a) No, I am not inviting Bruce.
   (b) Bruce is a philosopher, and I am not inviting any philosophers.
   (c) I am not inviting any philosophers.
   (d) I am not inviting anyone who is boring.

Each of these four replies could serve to communicate the same message – the negative answer to the question. That message is literally and explicitly expressed in (a), but is less directly conveyed in each of (b)–(d). In the case of (b), the message that the speaker is not inviting Bruce can be inferred from what is literally and explicitly said. In the case of (c), that message can be inferred from what is literally and explicitly said together with a shared background assumption. In the case of (d), the message can be inferred from what is explicitly said together with an additional premise, namely, the proposition that Bruce is boring. The idea is that, in order to maintain the presumption that the speaker's utterance is relevant in case (d), the hearer of that answer will supply the additional premise.

To give a description of even this simple example, we need at least four notions:

- the proposition that is literally and *explicitly expressed* in an utterance;
- a proposition that is *logically implied* by what is explicitly expressed;
- a proposition that is contextually or *pragmatically implied* – where the inference relies on both the proposition explicitly expressed and other premises drawn from the set of background assumptions (the context); and
- a proposition that is not already part of the context, but is supplied as an *additional premise*.

135

These four notions can be used to describe cases of a hearer's exploiting information provided by the speaker, as well as cases – such as the example here – where the speaker overtly intends to communicate a message that is not explicitly expressed.

It may not be immediately obvious how Grice's notion of conversational implicature maps onto this relevance theory framework. In the example given, answer (b) would certainly not be a case of conversational implicature on Grice's account, since 'the truth of a conversational implicatum is not required by the truth of what is said' (Grice 1989: 39). Answer (c) does pass that test, but in fact the Gricean notion of conversational implicature corresponds more closely to that of an additional premise, as in answer (d).

6.4 Pragmatic contributions to explicit content

Grice's pragmatic theory offers an account of the way in which an implicature that q can be worked out, given that the speaker literally and explicitly advances the proposition that p. This may suggest that pragmatic principles are not involved in discerning that a speaker has explicitly advanced a certain proposition. But that idea would not be correct. Thus, Sperber and Wilson (1995: 175–6):

> We regard verbal communication, then, as involving two types of communication process: one based on coding and decoding, the other on ostension and inference. The coded communication process is not autonomous: it is subservient to the inferential process. The inferential process is autonomous: it functions in essentially the same way whether or not combined with coded communication (though in the absence of coded communication, performances are generally poorer). The coded communication is of course linguistic: acoustic (or graphic) signals are used to communicate semantic representations. The semantic representations recovered by decoding are useful only as a source of hypotheses and evidence for the second communication process, the inferential one. Inferential communication involves the application, not of special-purpose decoding rules, but of general-purpose inference rules, which apply to any conceptually represented information.

On this view, pragmatic principles are involved in the recognition of the proposition that is explicitly expressed. They are also involved when a hearer discerns what attitude the speaker takes towards the proposition expressed, or what kind of speech act – an assertion, a command, a question – the speaker is performing. Let us consider the recognition of speech acts first and then the recognition of the proposition explicitly expressed.

If we are to appreciate what is involved in discerning what kind of speech act a speaker is performing then it is important to distinguish the idea of a kind of speech act from the grammatical notion of *mood*. The mood of an uttered sentence – indicative, imperative, interrogative – is part of its encoded literal meaning. But uttering a sentence in a particular mood does not guarantee the performance of a particular kind of speech act. Uttering a sentence in the indicative mood, for example, is not the same thing as making an assertion. An indicative sentence can be used to express a conjecture or to make a joke; it can be used ironically or questioningly. Nor is there any further conventional sign, over and above the mood of the uttered sentence, that guarantees that an act of assertion has been performed. Uttering a sentence in a serious tone of voice, for example, does not inevitably make the utterance into an assertion.

It is true that there are some conceptual connections between moods and kinds of speech acts, and an adequate theory of language and its use must spell those connections out. Davidson (1979) makes the proposal that uttering a sentence in a non-indicative mood (for example, the imperative mood or the interrogative mood) is rather like making a pair of utterances. An utterance of 'Put on your hat' is rather like an utterance of 'My next utterance is imperatival in force' (or 'My next utterance constitutes an act of commanding') followed by an utterance of the indicative sentence 'You will put on your hat'. Whether or not Davidson's proposed account is ultimately satisfactory, it certainly establishes a connection 'between the mood indicators and the *idea* of a certain illocutionary act' (Davidson 1984: 275). But the crucial point for present purposes is that even though the presence of a particular mood may constitute a prima facie reason for taking an utterance to be a speech act of a particular kind, still that prima facie reason may be overridden by all manner of other considerations. There are no 'special-purpose decoding rules' for calculating what kind of speech act a speaker is performing.

We turn now to the recognition of the proposition explicitly expressed. It is beyond dispute that the literal meanings of words and the ways in which words are put together to make sentences may leave us far short of determinate truth conditions. A familiar example is provided by the sentence 'I am tired'. This sentence does not, by itself, have determinate truth conditions; the conditions for the truth of a particular utterance of 'I am tired' depend on who is speaking.

But this kind of case of the underdetermination of truth conditions by literal meaning is apt to be misleading. For it is very plausible that there is a rule of language that specifies the way in which the truth conditions of an utterance of 'I am tired' depend on a particular feature of the context in which it is made, namely, the speaker in that context. (Here, we use the ordinary notion of context, rather than the relevance-theory notion of a set of assumptions.) In general, however, the step from the literal meaning of a sentence to the truth conditions of an utterance of that sentence in context is not governed by any such neat rules of context-dependence.

For a pronoun, such as 'he', 'she' or 'it', there is no rule that assigns a reference on the basis of some predetermined feature of the context in which the pronoun is uttered. It is not true, for example, that the reference of 'he' is always the nearest male in the context or the last-mentioned male in the context. It may be said that the reference of 'he' is always the most *salient* male in the context; but there is no limit to the information that might, in principle, be involved in an assessment of salience in a context. What goes for the assignment of reference to pronouns goes also for the removal of lexical ambiguity, the resolution of vagueness or indeterminacy, and the restoration of ellipsis. These are all sensitive to global features of the discourse situation.

Thus, many aspects of the recognition of the proposition explicitly expressed by an utterance involve pragmatic interpretation; they are matters of inference rather than of decoding (Sperber and Wilson 1986b: 585):

> Pragmatic interpretation seems to us to resemble scientific theorizing in essential respects. The speaker's intentions are not decoded but non-demonstratively inferred, by a process of hypothesis formation and confirmation which, like scientific theorizing and unlike grammatical analysis, has free access to contextual information.

6.5   Utterance interpretation and public language meaning

The fact that even explicit content – even an initial proposition from which further inferences might be drawn – depends on pragmatic, as well as semantic, factors is of the greatest importance for a theoretical understanding of the communicative use of language. But we must also note that this fact has been used to cast doubt on the theoretical significance of the very notion of literal meaning in a public language.

A hearer not only uses inference and contextual information in order to bridge the gap between literal meaning and explicit propositional content and then to draw out contextual implications. A hearer may also use those same resources in order to revise his assessment of a speaker's literal meanings themselves. Literal meaning provides an outline that is then filled in under the guidance of a presumption of optimal relevance. But if no way of filling in the outline measures up to this presumption, then the outline itself may be redrawn. This is what usually happens when a speaker makes a slip of the tongue or commits a malapropism.

It may happen, then, that a speaker and a hearer bring to a discourse different assignments of meanings to words. A hearer may begin with one set of expectations and, finding them unfulfilled, may set about devising a new assignment of meanings to words to serve for the discourse in which he is engaged. This process of assigning new meanings is like pragmatic interpretation. It involves non-demonstrative inference rather than decoding, and there is no limit to the information on which it might draw.

Davidson says that, in devising a new assignment of meanings, a hearer will operate in essentially the same way as a radical interpreter: he will try to make the best sense possible of the speaker's total life and conduct (section 4.2). Thus (Davidson 1984: 278):

> agreement on what a speaker means by what he says can surely be achieved even though a speaker and hearer have different advance theories as to how to interpret the speaker. The reason this can be is that the speaker may well provide adequate clues, in what he says, and how and where he says it, to allow a hearer to arrive at a correct interpretation.

The notion of convention looms large in a Gricean analysis of literal meaning. But the moral that Davidson draws from consideration of a hearer's ability to revise his assignment of meanings to a speaker's words is that conventions are, in the end, of merely practical significance (ibid.: 279):

> Knowledge of the conventions of language is thus a practical crutch to interpretation, a crutch we cannot in practice afford to do without – but a crutch which, under optimum conditions for communication, we can in the end throw away, and could in theory have done without from the start.

A convention is a rationally self-perpetuating regularity in the behaviour of members of a group. Literal linguistic meaning is, on a Gricean account, meaning that is assigned as a matter of convention. The assignment of meanings is shared by members of the group and is perpetuated through time. But, Davidson says, it is not essential for successful linguistic communication that there should be an assignment of meanings that is shared between speaker and hearer over an extended period of time.

All that is needed is that the speaker and the hearer should be able to converge on an assignment of meaning at the time of their communicative exchange.

Utterance interpretation always involves the inferential processes of pragmatic interpretation; decoding of shared literal meanings is never sufficient by itself. Where literal meanings are not shared, pragmatic interpretation (or similar processes of non-demonstrative inference) may in principle still allow the hearer to work out what proposition the speaker was trying to communicate. Sperber and Wilson (1995: 176) say that pragmatic interpretation is autonomous while decoding is not autonomous. The conclusion that Davidson draws is that all utterance interpretation is to be seen, for theoretical purposes, on the model of radical interpretation. Since shared literal meanings are not crucial for successful communication, a philosophical theory of linguistic communication will not assign a crucial role to the notion of public language meaning.

It is not clear that the facts about utterance interpretation really license the conclusion about the theoretical dispensability of the notion of literal linguistic meaning. Nor is it obvious that the facts about communication undermine the Gricean analytical programme. After all, Grice himself began with the notion of speaker's meaning, a notion of communication that is supposed to be analytically prior to the notion of literal meaning. But we shall not attempt to adjudicate these issues here.

How much importance attaches to the notions of a shared public language and of literal linguistic meaning? If the notion of literal linguistic meaning is to be retained, can anything more be said about meaning than meta-semantic deflationism suggests? If there is more to be said, then what concepts might be drawn on in a substantive theory about the nature of meaning? Does the notion of convention have a role to play? Should a philosophical account of meaning appeal to the concept of tacit knowledge that figures in theoretical linguistics? These are among the important questions for future philosophy of language.

Further Reading

Philosophy of language is an area where most of the reading that is recommended to students is in the form of articles. The collection edited by Martinich (2001) contains 41 papers. These offer good coverage of some of the main topics in this chapter and also include 13 articles on referring expressions such as names, definite descriptions and demonstratives. Peter Ludlow's excellent anthology, *Readings in the Philosophy of Language* (1997), offers 42 papers, including 17 on referring expressions. Adrian Moore's more compact *Meaning and Reference* (1993) has 14 papers, some of which take up questions that we have noted, but have not discussed, in this chapter. Evans and McDowell (1976) contains high-quality papers at an advanced level. Hale and Wright (1997) offer authoritative and sophisticated surveys of many of the topics touched on in this chapter.

Useful recent textbooks, at a fairly introductory level, include Devitt and Sterelny (1999), Lycan (2000) and Taylor (1998). Among older books, Blackburn (1984) is engaging and challenging, and offers good coverage of both Davidson's and Grice's programmes. Mark Platts's *Ways of Meaning* (1979; 2nd edn, 1997) is useful for an accessible – though far from neutral – account of Davidson's programme.

For Davidson's programme, his book of essays, *Inquiries into Truth and Interpretation* (1984), is essential reading. 'Truth and Meaning' (1967a) is a good place to start and is widely reprinted in anthologies. For an introduction to Chomsky's approach to the study of language, the first chapter of the seminal *Aspects of the Theory of Syntax* (1965) can be combined with a more recent paper, such as 'Language and Problems of Knowledge' (1990). Chomsky (2000) is a collection of recent papers engaging with philosophy of language. Larson and Segal (1995) offer a very thorough grounding in the approach to semantic theory that combines elements from Davidson's and Chomsky's work, as proposed by James Higginbotham.

For Grice's programme, his *Studies in the Way of Words* (1989) is a rich resource. 'Utterer's Meaning and Intentions' (1969) covers many of the essential points in his attempt to analyse the concept of literal meaning. The first thirty pages or so of Schiffer (1972) provide an authoritative introduction to Grice's programme, and the introduction to the second edition (1988) sets the programme against a background of more recent concerns. Strawson (1970b) offers an important comparison of Davidson's and Grice's programmes. Schiffer (1987) has been massively influential in persuading most philosophers of language that Grice's analytical programme cannot be carried through. It is not, however, a book for beginners in this area. Reading on minimalism about meaning and truth should begin with Horwich (1998) and Field (1994).

Grice (1975) should be the starting-point for reading on conversational implicature. Sperber and Wilson (1986b) provides an excellent introduction to their book *Relevance: Communication and Cognition* (1995). For readers who are particularly interested in metaphor, the few comments in Grice (1975) could lead on to Searle (1979) and Davidson (1978), and then to Sperber and Wilson's excellent 'Loose Talk' (1986a). Davis (1991) covers the key topics in pragmatic theory thoroughly (35 papers in all) with classic papers by Grice, several papers by Sperber and Wilson, and a fine section on metaphor and irony.

References

Avramides, A. 1989: *Meaning and Mind: An Examination of a Gricean Account of Language.* Cambridge, MA: MIT Press.

Baker, G. P. and Hacker, P. M. S. 1984: *Language, Sense and Nonsense: A Critical Investigation into Modern Theories of Language.* Oxford: Blackwell.

Barwise, J. and Perry, J. 1983: *Situations and Attitudes.* Cambridge, MA: MIT Press.

Bennett, J. 1976: *Linguistic Behaviour.* Cambridge: Cambridge University Press.

Blackburn, S. 1984: *Spreading the Word.* Oxford: Oxford University Press.

Chomsky, N. 1965: *Aspects of the Theory of Syntax.* Cambridge, MA: MIT Press.

—— 1976: *Reflections on Language.* London: Fontana/Collins.

—— 1980: *Rules and Representations.* Oxford: Blackwell.

—— 1986: *Knowledge of Language: Its Nature, Origin, and Use.* New York: Praeger.

—— 1990: Language and Problems of Knowledge. In A. P. Martinich (ed.) (2001) *The Philosophy of Language*, 4th edn. Oxford: Oxford University Press.

—— 1995: *The Minimalist Program.* Cambridge, MA: MIT Press.

—— 2000: *New Horizons in the Study of Language and Mind.* Cambridge: Cambridge University Press.

Davidson, D. 1965: Theories of Meaning and Learnable Languages. In Y. Bar-Hillel (ed.) *Logic, Methodology and Philosophy of Science*, Vol. 2. Amsterdam: North Holland. Reprinted in D. Davidson (1984) *Inquiries into Truth and Interpretation.* Oxford: Oxford University Press.

—— 1967a: Truth and Meaning. *Synthèse*, 17, 304–23. Reprinted in Davidson (1984), Ludlow (1997), Martinich (2001) and Moore (1993).

—— 1967b: The Logical Form of Action Sentences. In N. Rescher (ed.) *The Logic of Decision and Action.* Pittsburgh: University of Pittsburgh Press. Reprinted in Davidson (1980) and Ludlow (1997).

—— 1969a: True to the Facts. *Journal of Philosophy*, 66, 748–64. Reprinted in D. Davidson (1984) *Inquiries into Truth and Interpretation*. Oxford: Oxford University Press.

—— 1969b: On Saying That. In D. Davidson and J. Hintikka (eds) *Words and Objections: Essays on the Work of W. V. Quine*. Dordrecht: Reidel. Reprinted in Davidson (1984), Ludlow (1997) and Martinich (2001).

—— 1969c: The Individuation of Events. In N. Rescher (ed.) *Essays in Honor of Carl G. Hempel*. Dordrecht: Reidel. Reprinted in D. Davidson (1980) *Essays on Actions and Events*. Oxford: Oxford University Press.

—— 1973: Radical Interpretation. *Dialectica*, 27, 313–28. Reprinted in D. Davidson (1984) *Inquiries into Truth and Interpretation*. Oxford: Oxford University Press.

—— 1974: Belief and the Basis of Meaning. *Synthèse*, 27, 309–23. Reprinted in Davidson (1984) and Martinich (2001).

—— 1975: Thought and Talk. In S. Guttenplan (ed.) *Mind and Language*. Oxford: Oxford University Press. Reprinted in D. Davidson (1984) *Inquiries into Truth and Interpretation*. Oxford: Oxford University Press.

—— 1978: What Metaphors Mean. *Critical Inquiry*, 5, 31–47. Reprinted in Davidson (1984), Davis (1991) and Martinich (2001).

—— 1979: Moods and Performances. In A. Margalit (ed.) *Meaning and Use*. Dordrecht: Reidel. Reprinted in D. Davidson (1984) *Inquiries into Truth and Interpretation*. Oxford: Oxford University Press.

—— 1980: *Essays on Actions and Events*. Oxford: Oxford University Press.

—— 1983: A Coherence Theory of Truth and Knowledge. In E. LePore (ed.) *Truth and Interpretation: Perspectives on the Philosophy of Donald Davidson*. Oxford: Blackwell.

—— 1984: *Inquiries into Truth and Interpretation*. Oxford: Oxford University Press.

—— 1985: Adverbs of Action. In B. Vermazen and M. B. Hintikka (eds) *Essays on Davidson: Actions and Events*. Oxford: Oxford University Press.

Davies, M. 1981: *Meaning, Quantification, Necessity: Themes in Philosophical Logic*. London: Routledge and Kegan Paul.

—— 1982: Individuation and the Semantics of Demonstratives. *Journal of Philosophical Logic*, 11, 287–310. Reprinted in P. Ludlow (ed.) (1997) *Readings in the Philosophy of Language*. Cambridge, MA: MIT Press.

—— 1984: Taylor on Meaning-theories and Theories of Meaning. *Mind*, 93, 85–90.

—— 1986: Tacit Knowledge, and the Structure of Thought and Language. In C. Travis (ed.) *Meaning and Interpretation*. Oxford: Blackwell.

—— 1987: Tacit Knowledge and Semantic Theory: Can a Five per cent Difference Matter? *Mind*, 96, 441–62.

—— 1989: Tacit Knowledge and Subdoxastic States. In A. George (ed.) *Reflections on Chomsky*. Oxford: Blackwell. Reprinted in C. Macdonald and G. Macdonald (eds) (1995) *Philosophy of Psychology: Debates on Psychological Explanation*. Oxford: Blackwell.

—— 1991: Acts and Scenes. In N. Cooper and P. Engel (eds) *New Inquiries into Meaning and Truth*. Hemel Hempstead: Simon and Schuster.

—— 2000: Persons and their Underpinnings. *Philosophical Explorations*, 3, 43–62.

Davis, S. (ed.) 1991: *Pragmatics: A Reader*. Oxford: Oxford University Press.

Devitt, M. and Sterelny, K. 1987: *Language and Reality: An Introduction to the Philosophy of Language*. Oxford: Blackwell (2nd edn, 1999).

Dretske, F. 1981: *Knowledge and the Flow of Information*. Oxford: Blackwell.

—— 1986: Misrepresentation. In R. Bogdan (ed.) *Belief: Form, Content and Function*. Oxford: Oxford University Press. Reprinted in S. P. Stich and T. A. Warfield (eds) *Mental Representation: A Reader*. Oxford: Blackwell.

Dummett, M. 1973: *Frege: Philosophy of Language*. London: Duckworth.

———1976: What is a Theory of Meaning? (II). In G. Evans and J. McDowell (eds) *Truth and Meaning: Essays in Semantics.* Oxford: Oxford University Press. Reprinted in M. Dummett (1993) *The Seas of Language.* Oxford: Oxford University Press.

———1978: *Truth and Other Enigmas.* London: Duckworth.

———1991: *The Logical Basis of Metaphysics.* Cambridge, MA: Harvard University Press.

———1993: *The Seas of Language.* Oxford: Oxford University Press.

Evans, G. 1976: Semantic Structure and Logical Form. In G. Evans and J. McDowell (eds) *Truth and Meaning: Essays in Semantics.* Oxford: Oxford University Press. Reprinted in Evans (1985) and Ludlow (1997).

———1981a: Semantic Theory and Tacit Knowledge. In S. Holtzman and C. Leich (eds), *Wittgenstein: To Follow a Rule.* London: Routledge and Kegan Paul. Reprinted in G. Evans (1985) *Collected Papers.* Oxford: Oxford University Press.

———1981b: Understanding Demonstratives. In H. Parret and J. Bouveresse (eds) *Meaning and Understanding.* Berlin: W. de Gruyter. Reprinted in Evans (1985) and Ludlow (1997).

———1982: *The Varieties of Reference.* Oxford: Oxford University Press.

———1985: *Collected Papers.* Oxford: Oxford University Press.

Evans, G. and McDowell, J. (eds) 1976: *Truth and Meaning: Essays in Semantics.* Oxford: Oxford University Press.

Field, H. 1986: The Deflationary Conception of Truth. In G. Macdonald and C. Wright (eds), *Fact, Science and Morality: Essays on A. J. Ayer's Language, Truth and Logic.* Oxford: Blackwell.

———1994: Deflationist Views of Meaning and Content. *Mind,* 103, 249–85.

Forbes, G. 1987: Indexicals and Intensionality: A Fregean Perspective. *Philosophical Review,* 96, 3–31.

———1989: *Languages of Possibility: An Essay in Philosophical Logic.* Oxford: Blackwell.

Frege, G. 1892: On Sense and Reference. In P. Geach and M. Black (eds) (1970) *Translations from the Philosophical Writings of Gottlob Frege.* Oxford: Blackwell. Reprinted in Ludlow (1997), Martinich (2001) and Moore (1993).

———1918: The Thought: A Logical Inquiry. In P. F. Strawson (ed.) (1967) *Philosophical Logic.* Oxford: Oxford University Press. Reprinted in P. Ludlow (ed.) (1997) *Readings in the Philosophy of Language.* Cambridge, MA: MIT Press.

Goldman, A. I. 1971: The Individuation of Action. *Journal of Philosophy,* 68, 761–74.

Grandy, R. 1973: Reference, Meaning and Belief. *Journal of Philosophy,* 70, 439–52.

Grice, H. P. 1957: Meaning. *Philosophical Review,* 66, 377–88. Reprinted in P. F. Strawson (ed.) *Philosophical Logic.* Oxford: Oxford University Press; Grice (1989) and Martinich (2001).

———1961: The Causal Theory of Perception. *Proceedings of the Aristotelian Society, Supplementary Volume,* 35, 121–52. Reprinted in Grice (1989) and in G. Warnock (ed.) (1967) *The Philosophy of Perception.* Oxford: Oxford University Press.

———1968: Utterer's Meaning, Sentence-meaning, and Word-meaning. *Foundations of Language,* 4, 1–18. Reprinted in Grice (1989) and in J. Searle (ed.) (1971) *Philosophy of Language.* Oxford: Oxford University Press.

———1969: Utterer's Meaning and Intentions. *Philosophical Review,* 78, 147–77. Reprinted in Grice (1989) and Ludlow (1997).

———1975: Logic and Conversation. In P. Cole and J. Morgan (eds) *Syntax and Semantics, Volume 3: Speech Acts.* New York: Academic Press. Reprinted in Grice (1989), Davis (1991) and Martinich (2001).

———1978: Further Notes on Logic and Conversation. In P. Cole (ed.) *Syntax and Semantics 9: Pragmatics.* New York: Academic Press. Reprinted in H. P. Grice (1989) *Studies in the Way of Words.* Cambridge, MA: Harvard University Press.

———1989: *Studies in the Way of Words.* Cambridge, MA: Harvard University Press.

Hale, B. and Wright, C. (eds) 1997: *A Companion to the Philosophy of Language*. Oxford: Blackwell.

Higginbotham, J. 1985: On Semantics. *Linguistic Inquiry*, 16, 547–93.

——1986: Linguistic Theory and Davidson's Program in Semantics. In E. LePore (ed.) *Truth and Interpretation: Perspectives on the Philosophy of Donald Davidson*. Oxford: Blackwell.

——1988: Is Semantics Necessary? *Proceedings of the Aristotelian Society*, 88, 219–41.

——1989a: Elucidations of Meaning. *Linguistics and Philosophy*, 12, 465–518. Abridged version reprinted in P. Ludlow (ed.) (1997) *Readings in the Philosophy of Language*. Cambridge, MA: MIT Press.

——1989b: Knowledge of Reference. In A. George (ed.) *Reflections on Chomsky*. Oxford: Blackwell.

Horwich, P. 1990: *Truth*. Oxford: Blackwell. Second edition (1998) Oxford: Oxford University Press.

——1998: *Meaning*. Oxford: Oxford University Press.

Johnston, M. 1988: The End of the Theory of Meaning. *Mind and Language*, 3, 28–42.

Kaplan, D. 1989: Demonstratives. In J. Almog, J. Perry and H. Wettstein (eds) *Themes from Kaplan*. Oxford: Oxford University Press.

Kim, J. 1976: Events as Property-exemplifications. In M. Brand and D. Walton (eds) *Action Theory*. Dordrecht: Reidel.

Kripke, S. 1980: *Naming and Necessity*. Oxford: Blackwell. Excerpts reprinted in Ludlow (1997) and Martinich (2001).

Larson, R. and Segal, G. 1995: *Knowledge of Meaning: An Introduction to Semantic Theory*. Cambridge, MA: MIT Press. Excerpt reprinted in P. Ludlow (ed.) (1997) *Readings in the Philosophy of Language*. Cambridge, MA: MIT Press.

Laurence, S. 1996: A Chomskian Alternative to Convention-based Semantics. *Mind*, 105, 269–301.

——1998: Convention-based Semantics and the Development of Language. In P. Carruthers and J. Boucher (eds) *Language and Thought: Interdisciplinary Themes*. Cambridge: Cambridge University Press.

Lewis, D. 1969: *Convention*. Cambridge, MA: Harvard University Press.

——1975: Languages and Language. In K. Gunderson (ed.) *Language, Mind and Knowledge*. Minneapolis: University of Minnesota Press. Reprinted in Lewis (1983) and Martinich (2001).

——1983: *Philosophical Papers: Volume 1*. Oxford: Oxford University Press.

Loar, B. 1976: Two Theories of Meaning. In G. Evans and J. McDowell (eds) *Truth and Meaning: Essays in Semantics*. Oxford: Oxford University Press.

——1981: *Mind and Meaning*. Cambridge: Cambridge University Press.

Ludlow, P. (ed.) 1997: *Readings in the Philosophy of Language*. Cambridge, MA: MIT Press.

Lycan, W. G. 1991: Review of Avramides, *Meaning and Mind: An Examination of a Gricean Account of Language*. *Mind and Language*, 6, 83–6.

——2000: *Philosophy of Language: A Contemporary Introduction*. London: Routledge.

McDowell, J. 1976: Truth Conditions, Bivalence, and Verificationism. In G. Evans and J. McDowell (eds) *Truth and Meaning: Essays in Semantics*. Oxford: Oxford University Press.

Martinich, A. P. (ed.) 2001: *The Philosophy of Language*, 4th edn. Oxford: Oxford University Press.

Moore, A. W. (ed.) 1993: *Meaning and Reference*. Oxford: Oxford University Press.

Neale, S. 1995: The Philosophical Significance of Gödel's Slingshot. *Mind*, 104, 761–825.

Peacocke, C. 1976: Truth Definitions and Actual Languages. In G. Evans and J. McDowell (eds) *Truth and Meaning: Essays in Semantics*. Oxford: Oxford University Press.

——1981: Demonstrative Thought and Psychological Explanation. *Synthèse*, 49, 187–217.

——1983: *Sense and Content*. Oxford: Oxford University Press.

——1986: *Thoughts: An Essay on Content*. Oxford: Blackwell.

—— 1989: When is a Grammar Psychologically Real? In A. George (ed.) *Reflections on Chomsky*. Oxford: Blackwell.

—— 1992: *A Study of Concepts*. Cambridge, MA: MIT Press.

Perry, J. 1977: Frege on Demonstratives. *Philosophical Review*, 86, 474–97. Reprinted in Perry (1993) and Ludlow (1997).

—— 1979: The Problem of the Essential Indexical. *Noûs*, 13, 3–21. Reprinted in J. Perry (1993) *The Problem of the Essential Indexical and Other Essays*. Oxford: Oxford University Press.

—— 1993: *The Problem of the Essential Indexical and Other Essays*. Oxford: Oxford University Press.

Platts, M. 1979: *Ways of Meaning: An Introduction to a Philosophy of Language*. London: Routledge and Kegan Paul. Second edition (1997) Cambridge, MA: MIT Press.

Quine, W. V. O. 1960: *Word and Object*. Cambridge, MA: MIT Press.

Sainsbury, R. M. 1991: *Logical Forms: An Introduction to Philosophical Logic*. Oxford: Blackwell. Second edition, 2001.

Schiffer, S. 1972: *Meaning*. Oxford: Oxford University Press. Second edition, 1988.

—— 1987: *The Remnants of Meaning*. Cambridge, MA: MIT Press.

—— 1993: Actual-language Relations. In J. E. Tomberlin (ed.) *Philosophical Perspectives, 7: Language and Logic*. Atascadero, CA: Ridgeview Publishing.

Searle, J. R. 1979: Metaphor. In A. Ortony (ed.) *Metaphor and Thought*. Cambridge: Cambridge University Press. Reprinted in S. Davis (ed.) 1991: *Pragmatics: A Reader*. Oxford: Oxford University Press.

Sperber, D. and Wilson, D. 1981: Irony and the Use–mention Distinction. In P. Cole (ed.) *Radical Pragmatics*. London: Academic Press. Reprinted in S. Davis (ed.) 1991: *Pragmatics: A Reader*. Oxford: Oxford University Press.

—— 1986a: Loose Talk. *Proceedings of the Aristotelian Society*, 86, 153–71. Reprinted in S. Davis (ed.) 1991: *Pragmatics: A Reader*. Oxford: Oxford University Press.

—— 1986b: Pragmatics and Modularity. In A. M. Farley, P. T. Farley and K.-E. McCullough (eds) *The Chicago Linguistic Society Parasession on Pragmatics and Grammatical Theory*. Reprinted in S. Davis (ed.) 1991: *Pragmatics: A Reader*. Oxford: Oxford University Press.

—— 1995: *Relevance: Communication and Cognition*, 2nd edn. Oxford: Blackwell.

Stoljar, D. 2001: The Deflationary Theory of Truth. In E. Zalta (ed.) *The Stanford Encyclopedia of Philosophy*. Stanford, CA: The Metaphysics Research Lab at the Center for the Study of Language and Information, Stanford University, URL = http://plato.stanford/archives/spr2001/entries/truth-deflationary/.

Strawson, P. F. 1952: *Introduction to Logical Theory*. London: Methuen.

—— 1959: *Individuals: An Essay in Descriptive Metaphysics*. London: Methuen.

—— 1964: Intention and Convention in Speech Acts. *Philosophical Review*, 73, 439–60. Reprinted in Strawson (1971) and Davis (1991).

—— 1970a: The Asymmetry of Subjects and Predicates. In H. E. Kiefer and M. K. Munitz (eds) *Language, Belief and Metaphysics*. New York: State University of New York Press. Reprinted in P. F. Strawson (1971) *Logico-Linguistic Papers*. London: Methuen.

—— 1970b: Meaning and Truth. Inaugural Lecture at the University of Oxford. Reprinted in Strawson (1971) and Martinich (2001).

—— 1971: *Logico-Linguistic Papers*. London: Methuen.

—— 1974a: *Subject and Predicate in Logic and Grammar*. London: Methuen.

—— 1974b: On Understanding the Structure of One's Language. In *Freedom and Resentment and Other Essays*. London: Methuen. Reprinted G. Evans and J. McDowell (eds) (1976) *Truth and Meaning: Essays in Semantics*. Oxford: Oxford University Press.

Tarski, A. 1944: The Semantic Conception of Truth and the Foundations of Semantics. *Philosophy and Phenomenological Research*, 4, 341–75. Reprinted in A. P. Martinich (ed.) 2001: *The Philosophy of Language*, 4th edn. Oxford: Oxford University Press.

——1956: The Concept of Truth in Formalized Languages. In A. Tarski, *Logic, Semantics, Meta-mathematics*. Oxford: Oxford University Press.

Taylor, B. 1976: States of Affairs. In G. Evans and J. McDowell (eds) (1976) *Truth and Meaning: Essays in Semantics*. Oxford: Oxford University Press.

——1982: On the Need for a Meaning-theory in a Theory of Meaning. *Mind*, 91, 183–200.

——1985: *Modes of Occurrence: Verbs, Adverbs and Events*. Oxford: Blackwell.

Taylor, K. 1998: *Truth and Meaning: An Introduction to the Philosophy of Language*. Oxford: Blackwell.

Wiggins, D. 1976: The *de re* 'Must': A Note on the Logical Form of Essentialist Claims. In G. Evans and J. McDowell (eds) *Truth and Meaning: Essays in Semantics*. Oxford: Oxford University Press.

——1980: What Would be a Substantial Theory of Truth? In Z. van Straaten (ed.) *Philosophical Subjects*. Oxford: Oxford University Press.

——1986: Verbs and Adverbs, and Some Other Modes of Grammatical Combination. *Proceedings of the Aristotelian Society*, 86, 273–304.

——1997: Meaning and Truth Conditions: From Frege's Grand Design to Davidson's. In B. Hale and C. Wright (eds) 1997: *A Companion to the Philosophy of Language*. Oxford: Blackwell.

Wilson, D. and Sperber, D. 1981: On Grice's Theory of Conversation. In P. Werth (ed.) *Conversation and Discourse*. London: Croom Helm.

Wittgenstein, L. 1953: *Philosophical Investigations*. Oxford: Blackwell.

Wright, C. 1986: Theories of Meaning and Speakers' Knowledge. In C. Wright, *Realism, Meaning and Truth*. Oxford: Blackwell.

Discussion Questions

1   Is the meaning of a sentence a kind of thing?

2   How is the notion of meaning related to the notion of truth?

3   Is there such a thing as the literal meaning of linguistic expressions?

4   What relations exist between semantic and meta-semantic theories of meaning?

5   Are there good reasons to develop an axiomatized theory of meaning?

6   How does the difference between subject terms and predicate terms help us to understand the nature of sentences?

7   If two terms pick out the same object, can everything that is said about the meaning of one term be equally said about the meaning of the other?

8   Is there an order of priority among philosophy of language, philosophy of mind and metaphysics? If so, what sort of priority is involved?

9   Does the metaphysical distinction between objects and properties help us to understand the linguistic distinction between subjects and predicates?

10   Why do predicate expressions have negations, while subject expressions do not?

11   Does understanding sentences of a formal language help us to understand sentences of a natural language?

12   Should the proper format for theorems of axiomatized semantic theories say what sentences mean or give the conditions under which they are true?

13   Is it possible to avoid the conclusion that for a semantic theory specifying meanings, all true sentences are equivalent?

14   Does the notion of a possible language help to determine whether a semantic theory is correct for the actual language of a given group?

15   How does the condition of adequacy imposed by Tarski's Convention T help to elucidate the semantic concept of truth and its connection with the concept of meaning?

145

16   How might the needs of interpretation lead us to specify conditions of adequacy on specifications of meanings or of truth conditions?

17   Does 'radical interpretation' help to establish a link between semantic theories and interpretation?

18   Can truth conditional semantic theories give an adequate treatment of sentences about our mental states?

19   Does the notion of 'tacit knowledge' help to establish the explanatory relevance of systematic semantic theories?

20   How valuable is the notion of a rigid designator for dealing with questions about essentialism?

21   Does ordinary talk about people doing things carry a metaphysical commitment to an ontology of events?

22   Can we satisfactorily analyse the concept of literal meaning in terms of speaker's meaning and conventional regularity?

23   Do propositional attitudes like believing and intending have a role in the analysis of the concept of linguistic meaning?

24   Is the claim that 'meaning is use' a substantive theory concerning the notion of meaning?

25   How might minimalist theories of truth and meaning support one another?

26   How important is the distinction between semantics and pragmatics for an account of meaning?

27   How can we communicate more than we literally say?

28   Does a theory of conversational implicature need one overarching maxim? Can a principle of relevance satisfy this need?

29   Are pragmatic, as well as semantic, factors involved in determining the explicit content of what we say?

30   Is a shared assignment of meanings an essential feature of linguistic communication?

31   Is there any significant difference between ordinary and radical interpretation?

4

Philosophy of Logic

A. W. MOORE

Logic is concerned with reasoning. In particular, it is concerned with the distinction between good and bad reasoning. One of its aims is to formulate completely general criteria for this distinction. This is largely a matter of making precise the conditions under which an argument is valid. It is also a matter of saying what validity is. The latter is the prerogative of the philosophy of logic. The philosophy of logic is the philosophical core of logic, in which the essence of the rest of the discipline comes under scrutiny. Since much of our reasoning, if not all of it, is ineliminably verbal, a large part of the philosophy of logic is concerned with questions about language. This chapter traces a route through such questions, among others, taking as its starting-point a characterization of logic proffered by P. F. Strawson. Because of the nature of Strawson's characterization, two ideas serve to structure the entire discussion: the idea of a proposition, that is, the idea of that which is true or false; and the idea of possibility.

1 Introduction

P. F. Strawson once characterized logic as 'the general theory of the proposition' (Strawson 1967: 1). At this level of abstraction we can do no better. But what is a proposition? And what is such a theory? An initial answer might be:

A proposition is the sort of thing that is true or false. Logic deals primarily with certain relations that hold between propositions, namely those which depend on which combinations of truth and falsity are possible. These relations are called logical relations. Two which are of central concern are consistency and consequence. A proposition is consistent with others when it is possible for them all collectively to be true. (The truth of the others allows for the truth of it.) A proposition is a consequence of others when it is not possible for all of the others to be true yet it to be false. (The truth of the others demands the truth of it: if they are all true, then it must be true too.) Consequence is the relation that holds between the premises and the conclusion of a valid argument.

Each part of this answer requires clarification. In particular, attention settles on the three key terms 'true', 'false' and 'possible'. The interesting thing is that, because logic also has a philosophical component, the very process of providing such clarification is itself part of logic. More precisely, it is part of philosophical logic. Logic subdivides into two: *formal logic* and *philosophical logic*. Formal logic is concerned with the codification of these logical relations. Philosophical logic, or the *philosophy of logic* – unlike other writers, I intend no distinction between these terms – is concerned more generally with what makes these relations the relations that they are. Thus philosophical logic stands to formal logic in something like the relation in which the PHILOSOPHY OF SCIENCE (chapter 9) stands to science. One is engaged in the former when one enquires into the character, scope and preconditions of the latter.

Very well, then; let us set about clarifying the rough account of logic proffered above, beginning with the idea of a proposition.

2 Propositions

'A proposition is the sort of thing that is true or false.' Does this mean that propositions are bits of language? More specifically, does it mean that they are declarative sentences? Suppose we say yes. Still, it behoves us to say considerably more. Quite apart from the many grammatical and philosophical issues that arise from distinguishing declarative sentences from other bits of language, there are (for want of a better word) metaphysical issues that arise concerning what status 'bits of language' are supposed to have in this context. Consider: how many sentences are there in the box below?

> THE CAT IS ON THE MAT
> THERE IS AN APPLE ON THE TABLE
> THE CAT IS ON THE MAT

One could as well answer two as three. There is no special mystery about this, nor one correct answer. It is clear that the question can be taken in two ways, and it is reasonably clear also what the two ways are. Philosophers have introduced some technical terms to mark the distinction. In this case they would say that there are three *sentence-tokens* and two sentence-*types*: two of the tokens are of the same type. Philosophers speak similarly of word-tokens, letter-tokens and so forth, and of their corresponding types. If the province of logic is declarative sentences, then the question arises: declarative sentence-tokens or declarative sentence-types?

The more attractive answer, in many ways, is declarative sentence-types. It seems alien to the very spirit of the discipline to suppose that the subject matter of logic is nothing but certain inscriptions or noises that happen to have been made. Surely, when logicians consider propositions of the form 'No As are Bs', say, what they mean to be considering are the indefinitely many propositions of that form that *could* be produced, even though most of them have never come within the ambit of anyone's consciousness and probably never will. Types are better suited to this role than tokens. For, once the type–token distinction has been drawn, there is no obstacle to admitting types that lack tokens. A sentence-type can be thought of as a particular sequence of word-types. It is true that each of the word-types will have tokens. (This is something of a palliative for those who are concerned that sentence-types are unduly abstract.) But it may well be that no one has ever actually concatenated those words in that order to produce that sentence.

The problem with types, in fact, is more basic. They are not the sort of things that are true or false. Consider the type 'I am hungry'. In itself, this is neither true nor false. At most it is true *relative* to certain people and certain times, or as (potentially) uttered by certain people at certain times. Of course, we could surrender the idea that propositions are, 'in themselves', either true or false, and we could dismiss the contrary suggestion as one of the many infelicities of the rough account of logic with which we started. But that would mean paying a price: there would be a considerable loss of simplicity. An alternative would perhaps be to focus on sentences that did not contain any of the troublesome words or constructions, such as 'I', which occasion this kind of context-dependence. Whether there are any such sentences in natural language is dubious. Perhaps they exist in the language of MATHEMATICS (chapter 11). Perhaps '2 + 2 = 4' is an example. But our hope, if we took this approach, would be that such sentences could at least be artificially constructed. A further hope would be that such sentences could be used to say anything that could be said by means of any other declarative sentences. (We should have to hope this if we did not want logic to be restricted in its application. And it is an important point that it would be a further hope. Someone might well agree that such sentences could be constructed and yet be sceptical about how much could be achieved by their means.) An example of such a sentence might be something of the form '*S* is hungry at *t*', where the 'is' was to be understood tenselessly, and where the terms replacing *S* and *t* picked out a person and a time respectively. It might be protested that there would still be a dimension of relativity, in that a sentence could mean different things in different languages, and so be true in one language and false in another. But we could stipulate that by a 'sentence' we meant something considered as belonging to a particular language. No, the real problem with this approach is that it would represent logic as being concerned with entities whose nature and very existence were a matter of genuine controversy. Some of this controversy will come to the fore later (see section 3.1 below).

The original objection to construing propositions as declarative sentence-types was that declarative sentence-types are not in themselves the sort of things that are true or false. Before we try circumventing our current difficulties by reverting to declarative sentence-tokens, let it be noted that neither are they, in themselves, the sort of things that are true or false. Consider the three tokens in the box on page 148, for example. None of these is either true or false. This is because they appear there for purely illustrative purposes. They are not being used to assert anything. (In fact it would be impossible for tokens of those types to be used to assert anything without a good deal of stage-setting which I, writing this chapter, lack. Which cat? Which mat? What table?) Even when a token is used to assert something we should be wary of classifying it as true or false without qualification. Suppose that Smith, as he sets off to a meeting, pins a note to his door saying 'I am out'. And suppose that the following day, because he does not want to be disturbed, he pins the very same note to his door. Then the sentence-token on his note exhibits a disconcerting inconstancy: first true, then false.

(Or are there two distinct sentence-tokens here? Is something a sentence-token only as used in a certain way?)

These difficulties combine to suggest that we do best to stop thinking of propositions as bits of language at all. The difficulties also suggest a more satisfactory construal. Propositions are what are actually asserted, or, more generally, what could be asserted, *by means of* bits of language. Smith pins his note to his door one day and thereby asserts, or perhaps conveys, a true proposition. He does the same thing the following day and asserts, or conveys, a quite different proposition, this time false. When I say 'I am hungry' I assert a particular proposition. You, using a quite different sentence, say of me a little while later, 'He was hungry', and assert the very same proposition. Propositions are the message carried by the linguistic medium. But they do not depend for their existence on the contingencies and vicissitudes of actual communication. There are countless propositions that are never asserted. Logic is thus able to retain that aura of abstraction which first inclined us against construing propositions as sentence-tokens. On the other hand, propositions are entities with which we can have direct commerce, as they had better be if logic is to impinge on our ordinary thinking and reasoning in the way that it certainly does. Indeed, they enjoy a further advantage here over sentences (whether types or tokens). For our commerce with propositions can take a variety of forms. They can be thought, or entertained, or hoped, even where no sentence is directly involved, and certainly where no sentence is being used to assert anything. There is therefore no puzzle about how logic can have application in such cases, again as it certainly can. (My unexpressed hopes can be inconsistent.) Above all, propositions, on this construal, are true or false. What better then than to think in these terms? Strawson himself certainly seemed to be doing that when, in the context already referred to, he characterized propositions as what we specify by 'that'-clauses when we say things of the form 'I hope that p', 'Suppose that p', 'It follows that p', 'It is possible that p' and suchlike.

But we must be cautious. This account, for all its attractions, and partly, no doubt, because of them, glides over some of the deepest problems in the philosophy of logic. That which language is used to convey – MEANING (chapter 3) – would be regarded by many as the very stuff of logic. To take it for granted, as has just effectively been done, is to take for granted a good deal of what we, as philosophers of logic, ought precisely to be questioning. How exactly, for example, does your utterance of 'He was hungry' relate to my utterance of 'I am hungry'? In what way can two utterances share a meaning when the sentence-types concerned do not? Is it merely captious to point out that your utterance, unlike mine, conveys (affirms? presupposes?) my sex? Are propositions completely extra-linguistic? Can the same proposition be asserted by saying 'There is an apple on the table' as by saying 'Il y a une pomme sur la table'? If so, could that proposition have existed even if there had been no language? Some philosophers, notably W. V. O. Quine, are sceptical about whether there is any way through this morass of questions; and they turn their scepticism on the questions themselves. Quine gives an account of logic which is not in terms of meaning and which eschews propositions, on this construal, altogether (Quine 1970: ch. 1).

One elegant way to cut through the entire debate would be to stop trying to identify propositions with anything extra-logical. That is, we could think of logic as having *its own distinctive subject matter*, a kind of idealization of anything that we might normally think of as true or false. This subject matter could then serve as a model for various aspects of our ordinary thinking and reasoning. Propositions would be rather like the rational agents studied by economists, or the frictionless planes studied by physicists.

One advantage of taking this approach is that it would vindicate bringing to bear a simple true–false dichotomy on the vagueness, indeterminacy, ambiguity, inexactitude, hyperbole, figurativeness and vivid colouring of so much of what we ordinarily say and think; and on the countless uses to which we put declarative sentences where it is unclear whether an assessment in terms of truth and falsity is even appropriate, still less what principles should govern it if it is: we tell jokes, we write fiction, we define words, we praise, blame, approve and disapprove. For there is no doubt, again, that logic can have application when we do these things. A joke can be internally inconsistent. One expression of approval can be a consequence of others. On this approach we could see these facts as being no more puzzling than the fact that a car can move along a road in accordance with principles about frictionless planes. Another advantage of this approach is that it would take any *mystique* out of the fact, which was perhaps beginning to assume a spurious significance, that propositions are the sort of things that are true or false. That, now, could be viewed as nothing more than a defining characteristic (cf. Wittgenstein 1967: §§136; 1961: 6.111). There would still be much that needed to be said about what propositions are like. But there would be some prospect now that it could be said, indirectly, through work in *formal* logic, rather than as part of some philosophical propaedeutic.

Let us turn now to the other key term that occurred in the original rough account of logic: 'possible'.

3 Possibility

It is a fundamental feature of logical appraisal that it relates to possible combinations of truth and falsity, and not, directly, to truth and falsity themselves. In particular, a valid argument can have a false conclusion, and an invalid argument can have a true one. Consider the two following (somewhat regimented) arguments.

> Mothers are always shorter than their fully grown sons
> George is fully grown
> Elizabeth is George's mother
> Therefore Elizabeth is shorter than George

> If he is guilty, then his alibi is flawed
> His alibi is flawed
> Therefore he is guilty

The first of these arguments is valid. It is immaterial if Elizabeth is in fact taller than George. The second argument is invalid. Again, it is immaterial if the person concerned is in fact guilty. In assessing an argument as valid or invalid, we are interested only in whether the conclusion is a consequence of the premises. It does not matter how the conclusion and the premises stand in relation to reality. What matters is how they stand in relation to one another. (It is impossible for mothers always to be shorter than their fully grown sons if this does not include Elizabeth and her fully grown son, George. It is not impossible for a man's alibi, which is flawed if he is guilty, to be flawed anyway.) There is nothing more to this, really, than linguistic stipulation. It is simply a question of how we are going to use the word 'valid'.

Such linguistic stipulation does, however, point to a problem. Since our chief interest with respect to the truth or falsity of propositions is to know which are actually true and which are actually false, the question arises: why is logical appraisal of any interest?

The answer, in a nutshell, is that although logical appraisal does not bear directly on which propositions are true and which are false, it does do so indirectly. If an argument is valid, and its premises are true, then its conclusion is true. If an argument is valid and its conclusion is false, then at least one of its premises is false. If one proposition is inconsistent with others, then it, or one of the others, is false. Logical appraisal thus has a vital normative role to play. Given various things that we already know, it can determine which other things, beyond those, we ought to think or are entitled to think. It can similarly guide us whenever we are exploring different options for what to think, which is itself often an indispensable precursor to choosing the right one. We shall make singularly little progress in our efforts to discriminate between the true and the false without some articulated awareness of what the possibilities are, and in particular, without the kind of awareness that enables us to tell, by dint of reasoning, how the things that we already know and things that we do not yet know are capable of fitting together.

To see further what kind of possibility is involved here, and how it is involved, let us look at some examples of reasoning. As the examples will serve to remind us, reasoning rarely takes the rather stilted form exemplified above: rarely is one involved in assessing an argument whose premises and conclusion are all stated explicitly, in that order. Consider the following three problems.

(1)   Seven cards are laid out in front of you and you see the following array.

You are told that each card also has a single letter on the reverse.
Question: Which cards, if any, do you not need to turn over to test the hypothesis that every card with an 'A' on one side has a 'C' on the other?

(2)   A man needs to transport a lion, a goat and a cabbage across a river. He can only transport one at a time. If the lion is left unattended with the goat, it will eat it. If the goat is left unattended with the cabbage, it will eat it.
Question: What should he do?

(3)   A man walks from *A* to *B*, setting off at 2 p.m. and arriving an hour later at 3 p.m. The following day he takes the same route back from *B* to *A*. Again he sets off at 2 p.m. and again he arrives at 3 p.m. You are not told whether his rate of progress is uniform on either day.

Question: Is there guaranteed to be some point, on the route from *A* to *B*, such that the man reaches that point at precisely the same time on both days?

Here are the three solutions.

(1)   You do not need to turn over the three cards showing a 'C'. In every other case it would be possible for a letter on the reverse to upset the hypothesis – in the case of the two cards showing an 'A', by being anything other than a 'C', and in the case of the cards showing a 'B' or a 'G', by being an 'A'. In the case of the three cards showing a 'C', however, the hypothesis would remain intact whatever was on the reverse.

(2)   The man should first transport the goat over. Then he should return to pick up either the lion or the cabbage and transport it over. Then he should return, with the goat, to pick up whichever of the lion and the cabbage he has not yet transported over and do so, leaving the goat behind. Finally, he should return to pick up the goat and transport it over. Each move is effectively dictated. This is because, for the purposes of this problem, two positions, which differ only in that the lion and the cabbage are interchanged, are equivalent. So the man effectively has, at each stage, only one option which will not lead directly back to a position that he has already been in.

(3)   Yes, there is guaranteed to be such a point. The easiest way to see why is to think, not of one man undertaking these two journeys on successive days, but of two men undertaking equivalent journeys on the same day. One of them takes an hour to walk from *A* to *B*. The other, during that same period, walks from *B* to *A*. The question posed is equivalent to the question of whether the two men are guaranteed to pass each other. And of course, they are.

There is a fundamental three-step process which occurs at different points in all three solutions. The first step of this process is to identify some relevant range of possibilities; the second step is to eliminate some of these possibilities using the parameters of the question; and the third step is to reach a verdict on some specified question concerning the possibilities that remain. Application of the process may well involve some special trick or method: there is no single mechanical procedure that governs all our reasoning. (We can go further. There is no single mechanical procedure for determining whether or not an arbitrary argument is valid. This is something that can actually be proved: it is called Church's theorem (see Boolos and Jeffrey 1989: ch. 15).) Let us identify applications of the process within each of the three solutions.

Problem (1)   Here the process is applied to each individual card. The first step, in this case, is to identify, as the relevant range of possibilities, the different things that can appear on each side of the card. The second step is to eliminate all those possibilities that conflict with the information given and the stated hypothesis. The third step is to determine, of the possibilities that remain, whether they exclude any letter's appearing on the reverse of the card: if so, this is one of the cards that needs to be turned over.

153

Problem (2)   Here the process is applied at each individual crossing. The first step is to identify as the relevant range of possibilities the different combinations of man, lion, goat and cabbage which can undertake that crossing. The second step is to eliminate all the possibilities that violate the constraints of the problem. The third step is to determine, of the possibilities that remain, which constitute progress relative to the desired overall outcome. The key here is to recognize the equivalence, for the purposes of the problem, of some of the positions.

Problem (3)   Here the process is applied globally. The first step is to identify as the possibilities the different ways in which the man can walk from *A* to *B* and back again. The second step is to eliminate all except the possibilities that respect the constraints of the problem. But here the third step is already relevant. The trick is to allow the second step to be informed by the third. Exact times, we can see, are irrelevant to the eventual solution to the problem. So the uneliminated possibilities can be thought of *simply* as those in which each journey lasts an hour. Then further abstraction shows that even the fact that the journeys occur sequentially is irrelevant: one of them can be thought of as being superimposed on the other. (It is an obvious heuristic aid to think of two men undertaking such journeys at the same time.) The third step, having done this work, is now a formality. It is to determine, of the possibilities that remain, whether there is any that does not involve a cross-over point.

All of this may seem a far cry from 'the general theory of the proposition'. In fact, however, these techniques of identifying, eliminating and investigating possibilities, differently highlighted in each of the three cases, are but different means of ascertaining possible combinations of truth and falsity for a given range of propositions. The identification of possibilities is a matter of specifying some relevant feature to which the truth or falsity of the propositions is sensitive. The elimination of possibilities is a matter of supposing some of those propositions to be true or false. And the investigation of the remaining possibilities is a matter of ascertaining what follows concerning the truth or falsity of other propositions. Thus if it is true that every card with an 'A' on one side has a 'C' on the other, and it is true that a specified card has an 'A' on one side, then certain other propositions concerning that card must be false – for example, that the letter on the other side is a 'W'. The three propositions that every card with an 'A' on one side has a 'C' on the other, that a particular card has an 'A' on one side and that the letter on the other side of that same card is a 'W' are *inconsistent*: it is not possible for them all collectively to be true. In fact the initial possibilities are themselves (in the last analysis) propositions. It is their truth or falsity, ultimately, which determines the truth or falsity of all the other propositions under consideration, in accordance with which combinations of truth and falsity are possible.

But what kind of possibility is this? Is there one particular kind of possibility that is the special concern of logic? Is there, for that matter, one particular kind of possibility that is involved in all three of these problems?

The first thing we should be clear about here is that there are indeed different kinds of possibility. These are of varying degrees of stringency. For example, it is *scientifically* possible, though not *technologically* possible, for me to travel round the world in a minute. It is *mathematically* possible, though not scientifically possible, for me to travel round the world in a microsecond. (It is scientifically impossible because it would mean violating the physical law that nothing can travel faster than the speed of light.) On the other hand, it is not even mathematically possible for me to travel round the world infinitely many times in an hour, provided that my speed is constant. It is mathematically possible for me to travel round the world infinitely many times in an hour by doing so the first time in half an hour and then doubling my speed after each circuit. In other ways this is not possible. Exactly which these other ways are is a matter of deep philosophical controversy. However that may be, it is natural to suppose that there does eventually come some one, minimally stringent, kind of possibility which covers all the others and which is the special concern of logic. Thus, for example, it is *absolutely* impossible – we might say, *logically* impossible – for me to travel round the world and not do so at the same time. (Actually, we had better beware of describing this or any other sense as 'minimally stringent'. Imperfections in our own mental faculties mean that there will always be an epistemic kind of possibility which cuts right across all the others. There is always a chance, given an impossibility of some other kind, that it will be an *epistemic* possibility because whatever it is about it which makes it not a possibility is too complex or subtle for us to grasp. But putting to one side that complication, the idea that there is an ultimate, absolute kind of possibility seems right. And so does the idea that logic is concerned with it (see Wittgenstein 1961: 6.3–6.3751).)

It is extraordinarily difficult, however, to give an adequate account of this kind of possibility, or even to agree on whether various problematic cases are instances of it. Is it, for example, absolutely impossible for today to be Thursday if tomorrow is Saturday? Or for 2 + 2 to be equal to 5? Or for a water molecule to be composed of hydrogen and carbon? Or for a surface to be both white and transparent? Or, indeed, for the man involved in problem (3) to avoid reaching some point at the same time on both days? Could he not do so if, say, space and time were each quantized (in some suitably chunky way)?

Attempts to explicate absolute possibility – or logical possibility, as we might as well call it – fall into four broad categories. Some cast it as a METAPHYSICAL (chapter 2) notion; some as an idealized EPISTEMIC (chapter 1) notion; some as a SEMANTIC (chapter 3) notion; and some as a syntactic notion. On the metaphysical approach, logical possibility is a matter of the broad and ultimate structure of reality. On each of the other three approaches, the logically possible is what cannot be ruled out in a certain way; or rather, to put it in its more convenient inverted form, the logically impossible is what can be ruled out in a certain way. On the epistemic approach, something is logically impossible if it can be ruled out *a priori*, that is, roughly, without direct appeal to experience. On the semantic approach, something is logically impossible if it can be ruled out purely by virtue of the meaning of its linguistic expression. And on the syntactic approach, something is logically impossible if it can be ruled out purely by virtue of the (grammatical) structure of its linguistic expression. Each of these approaches faces innumerable difficulties. To assess them one must grapple with problems that lie at the very heart of philosophical logic. I shall confine myself to discussion of the third and fourth approaches.

3.1 The semantic approach

On the semantic approach, it is logically impossible for an aunt to be a man, say, because it is part of the very meaning of the word 'aunt' that aunts are female. Nothing similar precludes an aunt being 150 years old. To understand the sentence 'Some aunts are male' is already to be in a position to see that it is an incorrect thing to say. To understand the sentence 'Some aunts are 150 years old', however, is not yet to be in such a position, even though it too is an incorrect thing to say (since, as it happens, no aunt is as old as that). The former sentence is said to be *analytic*, the latter *synthetic*.

So long as one limits one's attention to simple examples of this kind, one might be forgiven for thinking that nothing more needs to be said to establish a reasonably firm account of logical possibility. But in fact much more needs to be said. We have been given no real guidance when it comes to assessing the problematic cases cited earlier. Can one tell that it is incorrect to say '2 + 2 = 5' just by understanding the sentence? If we were told more about 'understanding' – indeed, if we were told more about what it is to do one thing 'just by' doing another – we might be able to make a stab at that question. As it is, the question is impenetrable.

We should anyway be suspicious about whether the meaning of a sentence like '2 + 2 = 5' can, by itself, impose constraints of this kind. Recall Quine's hostility to the view that propositions are the message carried by the linguistic medium (see section 2 above). That hostility was to the very idea of a clearly delineated and determinate meaning attaching to each of our sentences. Unsurprisingly, it carries over into hostility to the semantic conception of logical possibility. On Quine's view, if, at some point in the future, English-speakers are prepared to describe certain people as 'male aunts', in spite of their earlier insistence that such a thing is impossible, then there will be nothing to rule out their having changed their mind rather than their language or their having come to a different view about what aunts, or some of them at least, are like (Quine 1961c).

Once the distinction between difference in language and difference in view has been blurred in the way it has been here, it may seem a small step to the conclusion that nothing is impossible in any 'absolute' way. For there is nothing we deny which it might not have been correct to say. Suppose, for example, that we had counted differently. Suppose we had counted: '1, 2, 3, 5, 4, . . . '. In that case it would have been correct to say '2 + 2 = 5'. And on the current reckoning, there is no principled way of resisting the move from here to the conclusion that 2 + 2 would have been equal to 5.

But this line of thought is confused. What is blurred, on the current reckoning, is the distinction between a situation in which we come to say different things because of changes in our language and a situation in which we come to say different things because of changes in our thinking. This is enough to cast doubt on the determinacy of meaning, and in particular on whether meaning is sufficiently determinate to sustain the semantic conception of logical possibility. But there may still be some perfectly clear and pertinent distinctions to be drawn between its being correct to say '2 +

$2 = 5$' and $2 + 2$'s being equal to 5. In particular, if some *other* conception of logical possibility can be sustained, then the first of these may count as a logical possibility and the second not.

In general, it is important to distinguish between talk about bits of language and talk, by means of those bits of language, about other things: the former is often signalled by the use of inverted commas. This distinction is nicely illustrated by the fact that, whereas cats have four legs, 'cats' – note the singular verb coming up – has four letters. I myself doubt whether this distinction is always clear in its application. For example, when it is said that Albert, who knows precious little physics, has picked up that $e = mc^2$, I doubt that it is clear whether what has been said concerns the *sentence* '$e = mc^2$' or the physical law itself. But I do not doubt that the distinction is an important one. And I see nothing in Quine's views about meaning to prevent him from acknowledging it.

Where Quine's views may be problematic for him, incidentally, is alongside his insistence that there are certain privileged sentence-types that can be classified as true or false without relativization. This is an apt point at which to pick up on that difficulty.

The existence of such sentence-types was mooted earlier (see section 2 above), during our initial discussion of propositions. Putative examples were '$2 + 2 = 4$' and a specially constructed sentence of the form 'S is hungry at t'. It was suggested that these sentence-types might be suitable candidates for the title of 'proposition'. Part of Quine's interest in them is that this is a suggestion he favours. Certainly it is a suggestion that seems to go well with his general scepticism about meaning, which prevents him from construing propositions as the message carried by the linguistic medium (Quine 1960: 208 – where, it should be noted, he reserves the term 'proposition' for what he takes to be the objectionable construal). In fact, however, there is tension. The tension surfaces when it comes to saying which the privileged sentence-types are. It will not do to say that they are those declarative sentence-types whose tokens are either all true or all false. Some tokens of declarative sentence-types are not used to assert anything, as we saw in section 2 above. Nor will it do to say, coining a suitable phrase, that they are those declarative sentence-types whose assertoric tokens are either all true or all false. Some declarative sentence-types do not have any assertoric tokens: indeed, some (most) do not have any tokens at all. Nor will it do to say that they are those declarative sentence-types whose potential assertoric tokens are either all true or all false. That includes the sentence 'I am a 150-year-old aunt', which ought, intuitively, to be excluded. (Being false relative to *all* people and *all* times is not the same as being false without relativization.) Nor indeed will it do to say that they are those declarative sentence-types whose potential assertoric tokens are guaranteed to be either all true or all false. That includes the sentence 'I do not exist'. What we have to say, intuitively, is that they are those declarative sentence-types whose potential assertoric tokens are guaranteed to be either all true or all false by the fact – and this is where the tension surfaces – that they all carry the same message, or, if you like, that they all have the same content. Quine's only recourse, given this tension, seems to be to draw up a list of words, phrases and other linguistic devices, such as 'I', 'ten years ago' and the use of the present tense, and to identify the privileged declarative sentence-types as those which are free of these devices. However, this would scarcely be illuminating.

3.2   The syntactic approach

Let us turn now to the fourth approach to logical possibility, the syntactic approach. On this approach, it is logically impossible for a green apple not to be an apple, say, because it is part of the very structure of the expression 'green apple' that it applies only to what 'apple' applies to. Not that this is as straightforward as it seems. It is not part of the very structure of the expression 'artificial apple' that it applies only to what 'apple' applies to. Anyone who took this approach would have to insist that 'green apple' and 'artificial apple' had different structures, despite appearances. Structure would sometimes show up only after analysis. Such analysis might involve additional words. For example, the structure of 'green apple' might incorporate the word 'and'. (Something is a green apple if it is green *and* an apple.) This in turn would fit with the most popular version of this approach, according to which there are certain designated words such as 'and', 'not', 'every' and 'is' (or perhaps formalized counterparts of these) whose role in an expression, or in an expression's analysans, determines the structure of that expression. By way of clarification: suppose one starts with an expression, or its analysans. And suppose that one keeps these designated words fixed and replaces every other subsidiary expression by a schematic symbol (traditionally just a letter) which serves to indicate which grammatical category it belongs to. Then what results will represent the structure of the expression. For example, the structure of 'Not every apple is green' is something like 'Not every A is B', where 'A' indicates a sortal noun and 'B' an adjective. 'Not every carrot is pink' presumably has the same structure. So do 'Not every number is prime', 'Not every count is bloodthirsty' and many more. The logically impossible is then what can be ruled out purely by virtue of the structure, in this sense, of its linguistic expression. If we allow ourselves to talk about declarative sentences as being true or false, we can put it like this: the logically impossible is what can be expressed by a declarative sentence that is not only false but such that any other declarative sentence with the same structure is also false. It is logically impossible for a green apple not to be an apple, then, because there are no true sentences with the structure 'There is something which is B and an A and not an A'.

As before, there is a good deal here that calls out for clarification. But the most obvious and the most pressing question is this: what is so special about the designated words? Why does 'and' count, and not 'carrot'? Why does 'not' count, and not 'count'? One intuition is that the designated words are words that are not allied to any specific subject matter: they can be used to talk about anything whatsoever. Interesting attempts have been made to lend some precision to this intuition. Notoriously, however, no generally accepted account of the designated words has emerged, either from this direction or from any other. There is a generally accepted *label*. Such words are standardly referred to as 'logical constants'. And most people who have worked in this area have agreed about which words are clearly logical constants, which words are clearly not and which are problematic cases. But it remains an open question what, if anything, this consensus is a response to. Quine, characteristically, is inclined to play down the distinction between logical constants and other expressions. The clearest possible way of demarcating the former, in his view, would be by compiling a list (Quine 1970: especially ch. 2). But again, that would scarcely be illuminating.

Let us, however, grant the distinction, for the sake of argument. On the syntactic approach to logical possibility, the most straightforward way of defining consistency, inconsistency, consequence and other logical relations is by first transposing talk of the structure of sentences into talk of the structure of propositions. We can then say, for example, that one proposition is inconsistent with others when any set of propositions with the same structure as these contains at least one proposition that is false. Similarly for the other relations. Thus, take the following argument:

No fish are mammals
All whales are mammals
Therefore no whales are fish

We can say that this argument is valid (in other words, that the conclusion is a consequence of the two premises) on the following grounds. No matter what triple of propositions you consider with the following structure

No *A*s are *B*s
All *C*s are *B*s
No *C*s are *A*s

if the first two are true, then so is the third; or, equivalently, there is no triple of propositions with this structure such that the first two are true and the third is false.

But this engenders the following worry. How can we be sure that we are not at the mercy of limited linguistic resources? Perhaps the reason why there is no such triple of propositions is that we do not have the linguistic wherewithal to construct them. It is true that on some views of what propositions are, propositions do not depend for their existence on any particular linguistic resources. But that serves only to redirect our anxiety: how can we be sure that our talk about the structure of sentences is an adequate base for our talk about the structure of propositions?

One natural reply, reined to the example above, is that it is not just that there are no triples of the specified kind, it is that there could not possibly be. That is of little avail, however, when our aim is precisely to elucidate the relevant sense of 'possibly'.

A quite different and more sophisticated reply would involve allaying the worry directly by showing that our linguistic resources are indeed adequate for these purposes. This can be shown, at least on most standard conceptions of the matter: it is enough, in fact, that we can do elementary arithmetic (Quine 1970: ch. 4). However, it can be shown only thanks to the fact that we are able to provide an independent account of what it is that is being shown.

The more one thinks about this problem, the more likely it is that one's attention will be drawn away from language to reality itself. (This shift of attention reflects one important shift in the evolution from a traditional ARISTOTELIAN (chapter 23) conception of logic to its modern descendant.) Reconsider the schematic symbols '*A*', '*B*' and '*C*' in the example above. What ultimately matters is not how these symbols might be replaced by sortal nouns, but how they might be assigned items *of the kind that sortal nouns 'stand for'*, to use a deliberately loose phrase. It is immaterial if, in some cases, no sortal nouns actually fit the bill. (Thus the example concerning fish, mammals and whales would have been pertinent even if there had never been any such words as 'fish', 'mammal' or 'whale', nor any other words equivalent in meaning to these.) For this reason, when logicians circumscribe all the possible 'interpretations' of a symbol, what they usually do is to bypass language and go straight to the items themselves.

Here we arrive at a set of ideas, in particular, the idea of 'standing for', which are fundamental to philosophical logic, whether or not the syntactic approach to logical possibility is correct. They are ideas about the very relationship between language and reality. To elucidate them is a basic task for any philosophy of logic. This is therefore an apt point at which to turn to some of the issues associated with that task.

3.3   Issues of sense and reference

There are various more or less crude intuitions entangled here, and they need to be disentangled. They also need to be refined. The crudest intuition is that each bit of language acts as a label for some bit of reality: the name 'Jupiter', for example, acts as a label for one of the planets in the solar system. (This is clearly much less plausible in the case of a word like 'and'.) A much more sophisticated intuition is that each expression of some grammatically basic kind has a feature, determined by that kind, which is directly relevant to the truth or falsity of any proposition in which the expression occurs (or which it can be used to express – how one puts it will depend on one's view of propositions). This intuition, of course, is directly informed by the ideas being canvassed above.

Now it was part of the genius of arguably the greatest logician of all time, Gottlob FREGE (chapter 37), to extricate from these intuitions a deep and precisely worked out conception of 'standing for'. Frege invented logic in its modern guise. And, in the course of doing so, he first distinguished certain basic grammatical categories, then gave, for each one, an account of what any expression in that category stands for. He called this the *reference* of the expression ('Bedeutung' in the original German: 'Bedeutung' is usually translated as 'meaning', but for Frege it was serving as a technical term).

At the basis of Frege's grammar, alongside declarative sentences themselves, are what he called *names*. (Eventually he reckoned declarative sentences themselves as names (Frege 1964: §2).) These are the singular noun phrases that stand for particular things. (The term 'things' is to be understood in the most generous way possible. Examples of names are 'Jupiter', 'the positive square root of 16', 'the number of symphonies written by Schumann' and 'joy'. The second and third of these have the same reference, namely the number 4.) One of Frege's chief concerns, once he had introduced the idea of a name and its reference, was to show that there is a crucial difference between understanding a name and knowing what its reference is. For instance, someone who has it on good authority that the reference of a name in Urdu is the number 4 does not thereby understand the name. Again, someone who understands perfectly well the two names 'the positive square root of 16' and 'the number of symphonies written by Schumann' cannot tell, without further knowledge, that they have the same reference. Frege accordingly introduced what he called senses. A name's sense, he said, is what we grasp when we understand it. Two names with the same reference can have different senses. But two names with the same sense (synonyms) cannot have different references. The name's sense therefore *determines* its reference.

Indeed, as Frege also said, the name's sense contains the *mode of presentation* of its reference. In grasping the sense, we think of the reference in a certain way. The whole apparatus, including the sense–reference distinction itself, is then extended to expressions in each of the other basic grammatical categories (Frege 1993a, 1993b).

It is a little ironical that the notion of sense should emerge so directly from the syntactic approach to logical possibility. For if the notion could be given suitable philosophical grounding, then it would be perfectly suited to ground, in turn, the semantic approach to logical possibility. Senses are precisely the determinate meanings that Quine rejects.

Grice on Meaning

There have been many and varied attempts to supplement Frege's work in this area in an effort to rescue senses from Quine's sceptical attacks, or at least in an effort to explicate meaning in a way that could, if successful, be pitted against Quine. For example, H. P. Grice famously analysed meaning in a way that made it look, perhaps not completely determinate, but determinate enough (Grice 1967). His analysis was in terms of certain complex psychological states. The first thing Grice did was to delimit what kind of meaning is at stake. He called this *non-natural meaning*, in contrast to the kind of meaning that is involved when an apple's brown skin 'means' that it is rotten. He then distinguished between what an expression means and what someone means by uttering it (on a given occasion). He took the latter to be the more appropriate point of entry for analysis: for an *expression* to mean what it does is for people to mean what they do by uttering it. Finally, he argued that for someone to mean what he does by uttering an expression is for him to intend his utterance to produce some particular effect in an audience by means of the recognition of this very intention.

This analysis has no influence over Quine himself, however. Quine's scepticism about senses simply gets trained on the psychological states themselves. This may look like unreasonable recalcitrance on Quine's part. But consider. How much would Grice's analysis show even if it were correct? There would still be a question about whether the psychological was in any way more basic than the semantic. It would be just as inviting to say that Grice had demonstrated certain intimate interconnections between the psychological and the semantic. After all, it is very implausible that we could divine what a person intends in uttering an expression without first finding out what the expression means. It may even be that the person could not so much as have that intention without the expression first having that meaning. So anyone such as Quine, reflecting on all of this and sceptical about the very idea of meaning involved, is bound to be sceptical about the psychology involved too.

A more immediate worry about Frege's ideas was given celebrated expression by Bertrand RUSSELL (chapter 37). Russell shared Frege's interest in what the latter had called names. He insisted, however, that they form a very heterogeneous class. On Russell's view, it is only by ignoring the crucial distinction between apparent structure and real structure – a distinction which Frege himself, ironically, had done so much to draw to our attention – that we are led to assimilate all these Fregean names in the first place. If we use Frege's own techniques of analysis, we can separate such names into fundamentally different kinds. Many of Frege's conclusions then begin to look unwarranted.

Russell argued as follows (Russell 1956a, 1993). Some Fregean names, the ones that Russell himself was prepared to call names, are simple indefinable words whose meanings do not depend on the meanings of any constituent expressions. (It is hard to give examples because Russell thought that proper nouns, such as 'Plato', could be defined – in this case, presumably as something like: 'the author of *The Republic*'. Russell's own views about what would count as examples underwent various changes. At one point he held that the only two examples were 'I' and 'this' (Russell 1988: 26).) To understand one of these names – a Russellian name – is to know what its reference is. The Fregean names to which this does not apply are definite descriptions – singular noun phrases of the form 'the *A*'. But these function very differently. To see why, consider a definite description that is not in fact satisfied by anything, say 'the planet between Mercury and the Sun'. In Fregean terms, this is a name with a sense but no reference. Now suppose we understand it as *purporting* to have a reference in the same way in which a Russellian name does. What then are we to say about a sentence such as 'The planet between Mercury and the Sun is green'? We are forced to say that, since it is not about anything in the way in which it purports to be, there cannot be any question of truth or falsity: no genuine proposition *is* in play. But surely a genuine proposition is in play. After all, it would be perfectly possible for someone to think, mistakenly, that the planet between Mercury and the Sun is green. We must therefore understand the description differently. We must disregard the sentence's apparent structure, and stop thinking of the description as a proper constituent of it.

This leads to Russell's alternative analysis. On that analysis, 'The planet between Mercury and the Sun is green' is equivalent to the conjunction of the following three propositions.

(1)   There is at least one planet between Mercury and the Sun
(2)   There is at most one planet between Mercury and the Sun
(3)   Any planet between Mercury and the Sun is green

It is clear from this analysis that a genuine proposition is indeed in play. Moreover, given that there are no planets between Mercury and the Sun, we can see from (1) that the proposition is false.

Russell believed that once these ideas had been generalized, and once a suitably deep level of analysis had been reached, there would be no need to invoke senses. Senses are just a Fregean gloss on hidden structural complexity. The only semantic relation between language and reality, ultimately, is that which holds between expressions and their references.

This account is obviously very congenial to Quine. One of its bonuses, which Quine himself has pursued, is a no-nonsense view of what reality must be like in order for any proposition to be true – or false (Quine 1961b). In particular, we are spared the drastic expedient which many have felt it necessary to adopt, of positing references for the offending descriptions (for instance, in the case of 'the planet between Mercury and the Sun', an 'unreal' planet between Mercury and the Sun): this expedient flirts with incoherence in the case of sentences which are used, or seem to be used, precisely to deny that such references exist (for instance, 'There is no such thing as the planet between Mercury and the Sun'). All that reality contains, on Quine's view, is what it is truly and clearly said to contain at the end of Russellian analysis: the things of which it is said that at least one is thus and so, or at most one is such and such, or each which is thus is also so, and so forth.

Strawson, meanwhile, recoiling from what he sees as Russell's over-zealous efforts to burrow beneath the linguistic surface, has tried to rescue part of Frege's original conception of names, though with less concern to respect the demands of formal logic (Strawson 1993). Much of Russell's zeal, Strawson thinks, reflects insufficient sensitivity to how words are actually handled, and to the role that attendant circumstances play in this. Such insensitivity is in turn due to a failure to take into account distinctions blurred when we left behind our initial discussion of propositions in section 2. In particular, talk of whether or not there is a proposition 'in play' – this is my way of putting it, not Russell's or Strawson's – obscures the distinction between sentence-types and sentence-tokens. Meaning, says Strawson, attaches to the types, truth and falsity to the tokens, or at least to assertions made by means of those tokens. The two things are quite separate. It is perfectly possible for a meaningful sentence-type, which can be uttered in suitable circumstances in making an assertion that is true or false, to be uttered in unsuitable circumstances in failing to make an assertion that is true or false. The latter is what happens when someone says 'That is green' without succeeding in indicating anything, or when someone says 'The thing on the table is green' when nothing is on the table. The same thing happens, presumably, when someone says 'The planet between Mercury and the Sun is green' (though in this case there appears to be no such thing as a suitable context). There now seems to be no reason why we should not assimilate definite descriptions to other Fregean names, in the way in which Frege did. The fact that definite descriptions can sometimes be used without reference, in such a way that there is no question of truth or falsity, is quite compatible with their being meaningful, with the sentence-types in which they occur being meaningful, and with whoever uses such a sentence-type in unsuitable circumstances having a genuine but mistaken thought that he or she has said something true.

This dispute between Russell and Strawson means that if someone were to utter the sentence 'The planet between Mercury and the Sun is green', Russell would say that they had asserted something false, whereas Strawson would say that the question of truth or falsity did not arise. Again, Russell would say that it was part of what had been asserted that there is a planet between Mercury and the Sun, whereas Strawson would say that this was something 'implied' by the utterance about the suitability of the circumstances. Russell's account seems the more barbarous of the two. It certainly involves some butchering of our pre-theoretical intuitions. But is this such a bad thing? Such butchering often occurs in logic, for a gain in simplicity. There is a useful analogy here which it is worth digressing to consider. Recall the definition of consequence with which we have been operating: one proposition is a consequence of others when it is not possible for all of the others to be true yet it false. Very few people flinch at this definition when first presented with it. Yet it already involves considerable butchering. Take a set of propositions such that it is not possible for them all to be true, still less for them all to be true and some other proposition false. A simple example would be the pair of propositions that God exists and that God does not exist. The definition above forces us to recognize any arbitrary proposition – the proposition that grass is pink, say – as a consequence of these. Hardly the verdict of pre-theoretical intuition! But this is the price we pay for a simple, workable definition. Similarly, perhaps, with Russell's account.

One thing that must certainly be said in favour of Russell's account is that it is especially helpful when it comes to highlighting the ambiguity in certain sentences, for example 'This time yesterday the thing on the table was green'. There are two ways of subjecting this sentence to Russellian analysis. Either 'this time yesterday' governs all three of the conjuncts, and the sentence is concerned with what was then on the table, or 'this time yesterday' is part of the inner structure of the third conjunct, and the sentence is concerned with how the thing on the table then was.

However this dispute is to be resolved, one thing of fundamental importance that emerges from the work of Frege, Russell, Quine and Strawson – an importance they would all acknowledge – is a certain basic structural feature of propositions which allows us to recognize on the one hand names, used to refer to particular things, and on the other hand their predicative complements, true or false *of* these things and thereby able to combine with the names to produce propositions which are true or false, full stop. The question of what underlies and explains this structure is one of the deepest in philosophical logic. It is well beyond the scope of the current chapter to make a proper attempt at answering it. But here is the sketch of a possible answer. If any expressions are to have meaning, then some of them must sometimes be used as single-expression sentences, like 'Green', which – to make the point yet one more time – are neither true nor false in themselves, but only as (potentially) uttered in certain circumstances, in the expressing of different propositions. Such variation is of the essence of the meaning of these expressions. Precisely their function is to draw attention to recurring yet transitory features of reality. But if their use as single-expression sentences is to be emulated in any other than the relevant circumstances (say, because an episode from the past is under discussion), then language itself had better be able to simulate the relativization. The expressions must count as true or false *of* certain things to which reference is made by means of other expressions.

4   Marginalia

Let us take stock. Logic, I suggested at the outset, is the general theory of the proposition. A proposition is the sort of thing that is true or false; and logic is concerned primarily with which combinations of truth and falsity are possible. Since then I have been concerned with clarifying these ideas. But it is important to see also how they might be challenged and/or supplemented.

4.1   *Beyond truth and falsity*

Some people have thought that logic extends beyond the realm of the true and the false. For instance, there is talk of erotetic logic and of imperatival logic: these are concerned, respectively, with questions and commands. (In some cases the issue is not whether logic extends to the given territory. The issue is whether the given territory is outside the realm of the true and the false. For instance, no one doubts that there can be inconsistency in ethics. But there is fierce debate about whether there can be truth and falsity there.) To say that logic extends beyond the realm of the true and the false is to say that logical relations apply in certain cases in which the concepts of truth and falsity (strictly speaking) do not. To the extent that this is so, I think the best explanation is of the kind I sketched in section 2: though logic is the theory of that which is true or false, that which is true or false can sometimes serve as a model for that which is not.

A more urgent worry concerns the innocuousness of the true–false dichotomy itself. The dichotomy certainly harbours paradoxes. The most familiar of these can be illustrated as follows.

> THE PROPOSITION EXPRESSED
> INSIDE THIS BOX IS FALSE

If the proposition expressed inside the box is true, then it is false. If it is false, then it is true.

Much work has gone into trying to solve such paradoxes (see Sainsbury 1988: ch. 5). I shall not rehearse any of that work now. But what seems clear is that a satisfactory solution will teach us to be more circumspect in our application of the concepts of truth and falsity. Fewer things will seem apt for assessment as true or false.

Philosophers of the anti-realist school think that there is, over and above this, a much more radical circumspection waiting to be learned. Anti-realism is a revisionary philosophy of logic whose investigation has been pioneered by Michael Dummett, though he has never himself gone as far as endorsing it (Dummett 1976, 1978b, 1978c, 1991). The main target of anti-realist circumspection is an inveterate assumption that informs all orthodox work on formal logic, namely that if something is apt for assessment as true or false, then it must be one or the other. This assumption comes so naturally that it seems by turns the merest tautology, then just a rule of the game, then the deepest metaphysical principle about reality, more ultimate than logic itself.

The anti-realist challenge to this assumption concerns propositions whose truth or falsity we cannot determine. An example might be the proposition that Aristotle sneezed at least once on his first birthday. What is the harm in our assuming that such a proposition is either true or false, even if we cannot tell which? The harm, according to anti-realists, is that it blocks a satisfactory account of our grasp of the proposition. Their argument is as follows. Our grasp of a proposition is a matter of knowing what would make it true and, derivatively, what would make it false. On any view of propositions, such a grasp is a kind of linguistic understanding. As such, it must admit of public ratification. For if there were an expression whose understanding did not admit of public ratification, then nobody could ever *show* that they had understood it, which means that it could not be used for purposes of communication, which means that it would not have a meaning, which means that there would be no such *thing* as understanding it. But in order for our grasp of a proposition to admit of public ratification, the proposition had better not be true without our being able to tell that it is, or false without our being able to tell that it is false.

There are two objections to this argument on grounds of self-stultification. The first runs as follows. By insisting that our understanding of expressions must admit of public ratification, anti-realists are in effect locating the meaning of expressions in how we actually use them. So they are endorsing our standard linguistic practices. But one of our standard linguistic practices is to regulate what we say by the assumption that any proposition is either true or false.

Anti-realists will reply that they are endorsing our standard linguistic practices only to the extent that those practices admit of endorsement. It is perfectly proper to reject some of those practices for not harmonizing with others, or for being otherwise internally incoherent.

The second objection is more complex. Consider the following proposition.

(P)   There is at least one proposition whose truth or falsity we cannot determine.

Now as far as the anti-realist argument goes, it is only if (P) is true that there is any harm in our assuming that every proposition is either true or false. But is (P) true? Well, on an anti-realist conception, only if we can tell that it is – in other words, only if there is at least one proposition such that we can tell that we cannot determine its truth or falsity. But if there is such a proposition, then we can tell, in particular, that we cannot determine its truth. The only way of telling that, however, again on an anti-realist conception, is by determining its falsity. So we arrive at a contradiction. It follows that (P) cannot be true. Hence, as far as the anti-realist argument goes, there cannot be any harm in assuming that every proposition is either true or false.

Anti-realists have a number of ways of responding to this objection. Most straightforward, and most heroic, is to *concede* that there cannot be any harm in making the assumption, but still not to make it. This is itself an instance of anti-realist circumspection. It is to concede that the assumption cannot be false, but still not to accept it as true. Whatever the merits of taking this stance, both the original objection and the stance itself are in my view of the utmost philosophical significance.

4.2   Beyond possibility

Let us now reconsider possibility. We can proceed here via the distinction between an argument's being valid and its being good. An argument is good if it provides good reasons for accepting its conclusion. This is not of course a definition. The word 'good' has been relocated rather than eliminated. Moreover, there may be deep reasons of principle why a definition is not available. However that may be, what I have said will suffice for current purposes.

Now there are all sorts of ways in which a valid argument may not be a good one. It may beg the question. Or we may know one of its premises to be false. Or, differently, we may know that not all of its premises can be true. An extreme example of the last of these would be the bizarre case alluded to in section 3.3:

God exists
God does not exist
Therefore grass is pink

Conversely, there are all sorts of ways in which a good argument may not be a valid one. Its premises may all be known to be true, and they may lend the conclusion a degree of support that is very high – but still inconclusive. Take the following example:

This die has been rolled fifty times
It has come up six every time
Therefore it is not fair

Suppose that both the premises are true. Still it is not impossible for the conclusion to be false. The argument is not valid. But it is compelling.

Good invalid arguments of this kind differ from their valid counterparts in resting not on which combinations of truth and falsity are *possible*, but on which are *probable*, or perhaps (in some sense) *reasonable*. There are correspondingly weaker versions of the logical relations. We can call these 'confirmation relations'. We encounter them most frequently, and most interestingly, when we are drawing conclusions about the unobserved from premises about the observed (as, for instance, when someone concludes that the stranger speaking to her on the telephone has only one head), something that we do constantly, unexceptionably, but again, for the most part, invalidly.

I have said more than once that logic is concerned 'primarily' with logical relations, that is with which combinations of truth and falsity are possible. I have not ruled out the possibility that logic extends to these confirmation relations as well. I think it does. They come under the auspices of *inductive* logic, or INDUCTION (chapter 9), as opposed to the *deductive* logic that has been our sole concern so far. (It is not uncontroversial that there is such a thing as inductive logic (Popper 1972).) It is a further question, however, whether *formal* logic extends to these confirmation relations, or rather, whether there is some codification of these confirmation relations which is of a piece with the codification that formal logic supplies of logical relations. I agree with Nelson Goodman that this is the most urgent question facing the inductive logician (Goodman 1979: especially ch. 3). Goodman is famous for having pointed inductive logic in a new direction. In the past it has been concerned with the problem of justifying our reliance on confirmation relations. This is what Goodman calls the old problem of induction. He thinks that that problem can be dissolved. The new problem is to *define* confirmation relations by taking a cue from formal logic and setting up appropriate rules. This is a problem of description rather than of justification.

The problem may well be intractable. But one thing that Goodman has demonstrated quite clearly is that, whatever role structure plays in logical relations – a defining role, if the syntactic approach to logical possibility is correct – it has no prospect of playing an analogous role here. This is because, given any good inductive argument, its structure, under any reasonable construal of structure, will always be shared by some other argument that is crazy. It will always be possible artificially to construct an expression, or a cluster of expressions, which can be used to illustrate precisely this fact. To see how, consider the following argument:

All emeralds observed before now have been green
Therefore, all emeralds are green

This argument is a good one. The fact that all emeralds observed before now have been green is a good reason for thinking that all emeralds are green. But now we can invoke Goodman's celebrated term 'grue', which applies to things observed before a certain future time if they are green and to other things if they are blue. Suppose that 'grue' is put in place of 'green' in the above argument. The resultant argument is clearly a bad one. The fact that all emeralds observed before now have been grue (hence green) is no reason for thinking that all emeralds are grue (hence, in some cases, blue). The confirmation relation that held in the original case has been lost.

In giving his own solution to this problem, Goodman defines confirmation relations in terms of those arguments that we do in fact endorse, or have endorsed in the past. He therefore tries to find a grounding in our actual practices for what is essentially normative – to distinguish between what is crazy and what is not crazy by appeal to the commitments that we are ourselves prepared to make. This brings with it a shift of philosophical interest from the more formal questions about meaning which concern the deductive logician to substantive questions about how we actually classify things together. Self-consciousness about *that* forces us into a notoriously delicate position. For how we actually classify things together can seem on the one hand completely natural and on the other hand completely arbitrary. Several of the deepest problems in philosophy (and not just in the philosophy of logic) are involved in working towards a proper resolution of this dissonance.

Anyone familiar with the work of Ludwig WITTGENSTEIN (chapter 39) will recognize hints of some of his preoccupations in that last paragraph. It is apt for me to finish in Wittgensteinian territory, if only because it gives me a chance to explain, half-apologetically, why I have made no mention of him before now – except in a couple of references.

Wittgenstein's work, as is well known, was divided into two phases. (The *locus classicus* of the earlier phase was Wittgenstein (1961), that of the later phase, Wittgenstein (1967).) In the earlier phase, his aim was to draw the limits of what can be thought and expressed. In his efforts to realize this aim, he assigned the most fundamental of roles to logical relations (relying heavily on the work of Frege and Russell). For he believed that the limits of what can be thought and expressed were set by logic itself. It would not be an exaggeration to describe his early work as an attempt at a 'general theory of the proposition'. Later he repudiated much of this attempt. He shrugged off his earlier aspirations to generality, and began to look more intently at less formal and less abstract issues concerning the different ways in which normativity and meaning reside in our different practices – issues of the very kind that have just come to light. He remained convinced, however, that a proper grasp of logical relations was crucial to a proper understanding of the problems of philosophy. And, in both the earlier phase and the later phase, he made contributions to the philosophy of logic of unrivalled depth and significance. Yet I have so far left him completely out of account. Why?

Part of the explanation lies in Wittgenstein's own ambivalent and idiosyncratic attitude to the philosophy of logic. In his early work, the philosophy of logic subserved and contributed to a unified network of concerns that were so intimately bound up with one another that it is actually somewhat misleading to describe him as practising the philosophy of logic at all, in so far as this suggests one separable activity among others. Later, in aiming for something more piecemeal and more exploratory, he came to deplore the kind of systematic theorizing about logic and its foundations that I have been attempting to survey in this chapter. To have reckoned with all of that in the context of such a survey would have taken us too far afield. The fact remains that there can be no satisfactory progress in the philosophy of logic that does not take Wittgenstein's insights and strictures fully into account. This indicates perhaps just one respect among many in which my survey has had to be selective to the point of travesty.

Further Reading

The great pioneers of contemporary philosophy of logic are Frege, Russell, Wittgenstein and Quine. I have given a small indication of their views in this chapter. For first-hand knowledge, the following are recommended: in the case of Frege, Frege (1952); in the case of Russell, Russell (1940) and Russell (1956a), in which essays 1–4 and 7 are especially relevant; in the case of Wittgenstein, Wittgenstein (1961 and 1967), which are the *locus classicus* of his earlier work and of his later work respectively; and in the case of Quine, Quine (1960, 1961a and 1970).

Other classics include: Carnap (1956), which has had an enduring influence, in particular on Quine; Davidson (1984), a collection of ground-breaking essays which deal, among other things, with fundamental questions about the nature of truth and reference (essays 1–8, 12, 15 and 16 are especially relevant); Dummett (1978a), a collection of extremely influential essays which include some of his most important work on anti-realism (essays 1, 2, 7–9 and 14–17 are especially relevant); Dummett (1981), which not only serves as an invaluable supplement to anyone wishing to understand Frege but has become a classic in the philosophy of logic in its own right; Evans (1985), a collection of brilliant and insightful essays on some of the most demanding issues in the philosophy of logic (essays 1–5, 7, 8 and 12 are especially relevant); Geach (1980), a fascinating, partly historical discussion of reference and quantification; and Kripke (1980), well-known for his highly influential treatment of problems concerning the nature of proper names and necessity.

Excellent introductions to the philosophy of logic, all of them somewhat easier than any of the work cited above, are: Blackburn (1984), which is more concerned with the philosophy of language than with the philosophy of logic, but which does have plenty of relevant material; Putnam (1971), whose focus is somewhat narrow – it is concerned principally with abstract objects – but which provides an engaging and stimulating example of the genre; Strawson (1952), which offers a very provocative 'ordinary language' critique of logic, now slightly dated but still of enormous interest; and finally, Haack (1978) and Sainsbury (1991), both of which are very wide-ranging and very accessible and either of which would be an ideal place to start.

An excellent introduction to formal logic, which pays particular attention to how the formal and philosophical parts of logic relate to one another, is Hodges (1977).

Useful collections are: Moore (1993) (the introduction and essays 1–4, 6–8, 10, 12 and 13 are especially relevant); and Strawson (1967).

References

Blackburn, S. 1984: *Spreading the Word: Groundings in the Philosophy of Language.* Oxford: Oxford University Press.

Boolos, G. S. and Jeffrey, R. C. 1989: *Computability and Logic,* 3rd edn. Cambridge: Cambridge University Press.

Carnap, R. 1956: *Meaning and Necessity: A Study in Semantics and Modal Logic,* 2nd edn. Chicago: University of Chicago Press.

Davidson, D. 1984: *Inquiries into Truth and Interpretation*. Oxford: Oxford University Press.

Dummett, M. 1976: What is a Theory of Meaning? (II). In G. Evans and J. McDowell (eds) *Truth and Meaning: Essays in Semantics*. Oxford: Oxford University Press.

—— 1978a: *Truth and Other Enigmas*. London: Duckworth.

—— 1978b: Truth. In *Truth and Other Enigmas*. London: Duckworth.

—— 1978c: The Philosophical Basis of Intuitionistic Logic. In *Truth and Other Enigmas*. London: Duckworth.

—— 1981: *Frege: Philosophy of Language*, 2nd edn. London: Duckworth.

—— 1991: *The Logical Basis of Metaphysics*. London: Duckworth.

Evans, G. 1985: *Collected Papers*. Oxford: Oxford University Press.

Frege, G. 1952: *Translations from the Philosophical Writings of Gottlob Frege* (translated and edited by P. Geach and M. Black). Oxford: Blackwell.

—— 1964: *The Basic Laws of Arithmetic: Exposition of the System* (translated by M. Furth). Berkeley and Los Angeles: University of California Press.

—— 1993a: On Sense and Reference (translated by M. Black). In A. W. Moore (ed.) *Meaning and Reference*. Oxford: Oxford University Press.

—— 1993b: Letter to Jourdain (translated by H. Kaal). In A. W. Moore (ed.) *Meaning and Reference*. Oxford: Oxford University Press.

Geach, P. T. 1980: *Reference and Generality: An Examination of Some Medieval and Modern Theories*, 2nd edn. Ithaca, NY: Cornell University Press.

Goodman, N. 1979: *Fact, Fiction, and Forecast*, 3rd edn. Brighton: Harvester Press.

Grice, H. P. 1967: Meaning. In P. F. Strawson (ed.) *Philosophical Logic*. Oxford: Oxford University Press.

Haack, S. 1978: *Philosophy of Logics*. Cambridge: Cambridge University Press.

Hodges, W. 1977: *Logic: An Introduction to Elementary Logic*. Harmondsworth: Penguin Books.

Kripke, S. A. 1980: *Naming and Necessity*. Oxford: Blackwell.

Moore, A. W. (ed.) 1993: *Meaning and Reference*. Oxford: Oxford University Press.

Popper, K. 1972: Conjectural Knowledge: My Solution to the Problem of Induction. In *Objective Knowledge: An Evolutionary Approach*. Oxford: Oxford University Press.

Putnam, H. 1971: *Philosophy of Logic*. New York: Harper and Row.

Quine, W. V. O. 1960: *Word and Object*. Cambridge, MA: MIT Press.

—— 1961a: *From a Logical Point of View: Logico-Philosophical Essays*, 2nd edn. New York: Harper and Row.

—— 1961b: On What There Is. In *From a Logical Point of View: Logico-Philosophical Essays*, 2nd edn. New York: Harper and Row.

—— 1961c: Two Dogmas of Empiricism. In *From a Logical Point of View: Logico-Philosophical Essays*, 2nd edn. New York: Harper and Row.

—— 1970: *Philosophy of Logic*. Englewood Cliffs, NJ: Prentice-Hall.

Russell, B. 1940: *An Inquiry into Meaning and Truth*. London: Allen and Unwin.

—— 1956a: *Logic and Knowledge* (edited by R. C. Marsh). London: Allen and Unwin.

—— 1956b: On denoting. In *Logic and Knowledge* (edited by R. C. Marsh). London: Allen and Unwin.

—— 1988: Knowledge by Acquaintance and Knowledge by Description. In N. Salmon and S. Soames (eds), *Propositions and Attitudes*. Oxford: Oxford University Press.

—— 1993: Descriptions. In A. W. Moore (ed.) *Meaning and Reference*. Oxford: Oxford University Press.

Sainsbury, R. M. 1988: *Paradoxes*. Cambridge: Cambridge University Press.

—— 1991: *Logical Forms: An Introduction to Philosophical Logic*. Oxford: Blackwell.

Strawson, P. F. 1952: *Introduction to Logical Theory*. London: Methuen.

—— (ed.) 1967: *Philosophical Logic*. Oxford: Oxford University Press.

—— 1993: On Referring. In A. W. Moore (ed.) *Meaning and Reference*. Oxford: Oxford University Press.

Wittgenstein, L. 1961: *Tractatus Logico-Philosophicus* (translated by D. F. Pears and B. F. McGuinness). London: Routledge and Kegan Paul.

—— 1967: *Philosophical Investigations*, 3rd edn (translated by G. E. M. Anscombe). Oxford: Blackwell.

Discussion Questions

1   What kind of theory is a theory of propositions?

2   What makes logical relations the relations that they are?

3   How useful is the distinction between sentence-tokens and sentence-types for understanding the nature of propositions?

4   How does the requirement that propositions be true or false constrain our account of what propositions are?

5   Are propositions bits of language?

6   How are propositions related to assertions?

7   Is it helpful to say that propositions are what we specify by 'that'-clauses?

8   Can our account of logic do without meaning and propositions?

9   Does logic have its own distinctive subject matter?

10   What kinds of possibility are there? Is there one particular kind of possibility which is of concern to logic?

11   What is the role of consistency in logic?

12   Is there a difference between our knowledge that it is incorrect to say 'Some aunts are male' and our knowledge that it is incorrect to say 'Some aunts are 150 years old'?

13   Can the logical impossibility of a claim be determined just by understanding the meaning of the sentence expressing it?

14   How determinate does meaning have to be in order to sustain the semantic conception of logical possibility?

15   Can we distinguish sentence-types that can be classified as true or false without relativization, from other sentence-types?

16   What kind of analysis and what kind of structure of expressions can help us to understand logical impossibility?

17   Can we do anything more than compile a list of logical constants to shed light on their special role in determining logic?

18   How can we be sure that our talk about the structure of sentences is an adequate base for our talk about the structure of propositions?

19   Could inadequate linguistic resources mislead us about what is logically impossible?

20   Do expressions of different grammatical kinds contribute differently to the truth or falsity of propositions?

21   Can meaning be analysed in terms of psychological states?

22   How can we determine whether there is one kind of name or many logically heterogeneous kinds of names?

23   Is the only semantic relation between language and reality, ultimately, that which holds between expressions and their references?

171

24   In our account of propositions, to what should we assign meaning and to what should we assign truth and falsity?

25   What explains the basic structure of propositions, according to which names and predicates combine to produce propositions which are true or false? Why is this a deep question?

26   Can there be propositions that are neither true nor false?

27   If confirmation relations are defined in terms of our actual practice concerning confirmation, are they defined in terms of something completely arbitrary?

5

Philosophy of Mind

WILLIAM G. LYCAN

The philosophy of mind abounds in arresting questions: issues of consciousness, personal identity, survival of one's physical death, freedom of the will, mental illness, the role of mind in behaviour, the nature of emotion, the comparison between human and animal psychologies, and many more. But each of these issues ultimately depends on a single, fundamental question, called simply 'the mind–body problem': what is a mind, per se, and what is its relation to body, or to the physical in general? Accordingly, this chapter will focus on that question and some proposed answers.

1 Mind–Body Dualism

The first answer to the mind–body problem proposed in the modern period was that of DESCARTES (chapter 26), who held that minds are wholly distinct from bodies and from physical objects of any sort. According to *Cartesian dualism*, minds are purely spiritual and radically non-spatial, having neither size nor location. On this view, a normal living human being or person is a duality, a mind and a body paired (though there can be bodies without minds, and minds can survive the destruction of their corresponding bodies). Mysteriously, despite the drastic distinctness of minds from bodies, they interact causally: bodily happenings cause sensations and experiences and thoughts in one's mind; conversely, mental activity leads to action and speech, causing the physical motion of limbs or lips.

Cartesian dualism has strong intuitive appeal, since from the inside, our minds do not *feel* physical at all; and we can easily imagine their existing disembodied or, indeed, their existing in the absence of any physical world whatever. And until very recently, in fact, the philosophy of mind has been dominated by Descartes's 'first-person' or from-the-inside perspective. With few exceptions, philosophers have accepted the following claims: (1) that one's own mind is better known than one's body, (2) that the mind is metaphysically in the body's driver's seat, and (3) that there is at least a theoretical *problem* of how we human intelligences can know that 'external', everyday physical objects exist at all, even if there are tenable solutions to that problem. We subjects are immured within a movie theatre of the mind, though we may have some defensible ways of inferring what goes on outside the theatre.

Midway through the twentieth century, all this suddenly changed, for two reasons. The first reason was the accumulated impact of logical positivism and the verification theory of meaning. Intersubjective verifiability or testability became the criterion both of scientific probity and of linguistic meaning itself. If the mind, in particular, was to be respected either scientifically, or even as meaningfully describable in the first place, mental ascriptions would have to be pegged to publicly, physically testable verification-conditions. Science takes an intersubjective, 'third-person' perspective on everything; the traditional first-person perspective had to be abandoned for scientific purposes and, it was felt, for serious METAPHYSICAL (chapter 2) purposes also.

The second reason was the emergence of a number of pressing philosophical objections to Cartesian dualism. Here are a few:

(1) Immaterial Cartesian minds and ghostly non-physical events were increasingly seen to fit ill with our otherwise physical and scientific picture of the world, uncomfortably like spooks or ectoplasm themselves. They are not needed for the explanation of any publicly observable fact, for neurophysiology promises to explain the motions of our bodies in particular and to explain them completely. Indeed, ghost-minds could not very well help in such an explanation, since nothing is known of any properties of spookstuff that would bear on public physical occurrences.

(2) Since human beings evolved over aeons, by purely physical processes of mutation and natural selection, from primitive creatures such as one-celled organisms which did not have minds, it is anomalous to suppose that at some point Mother Nature (in the form of population genetics) somehow created immaterial Cartesian minds in addition to cells and physical organs. The same point can be put in terms of the development of a single human zygote into an embryo, then a foetus, a baby and finally a child.

(3) If minds really are immaterial and utterly non-spatial, how can they possibly interact causally with physical objects in space? (Descartes himself was very uncomfortable about this. At one point he suggested *gravity* as a model for the action of something immaterial on a physical body; but gravity is spatial in nature even though it is not tangible in the way that bodies are.)

(4) In any case it does not seem that immaterial entities could cause physical motion consistently with the conservation laws of physics, such as that regarding matter–energy; physical energy would have to vanish and reappear inside human brains.

2 Behaviourism

What is an alternative to dualism? Carnap (1932–3) and Ryle (1949) noted that the obvious verification-conditions or tests for mental ascriptions are behavioural. How can the rest of us tell that you *are in pain*, save by your wincing-and-groaning behaviour in circumstances of presumable disorder, or that you *believe that broccoli will kill you*, save by your verbal avowals and your avoidance of broccoli? If the tests are behavioural, then (it was argued) the very meanings of the ascriptions, or at least the only facts genuinely described, are not ghostly or ineffable but behavioural. Thus *behaviourism* as a theory of mind and a paradigm for psychology.

In academic psychology, behaviourism took primarily a methodological form. Psychological behaviourists claimed (1) that psychology itself is a science for the prediction and control of behaviour, (2) that the only proper data or observational input for psychology are behavioural, specifically patterns of physical responses to physical stimuli, and (3) that *inner* states and events, either neurophysiological or mental, are not proper objects of psychological investigation – neurophysiological states and events are the business of biologists, and mental states and events, so far as they exist at all, are not seriously to be mentioned. Officially, the psychological behaviourists made no metaphysical claims; minds and mental entities might exist for all they knew, but this was not to be presumed in psychological experiment or theorizing. Psychological theorizing was to consist, à la logical positivism, of the subsuming of empirically established stimulus–response generalizations under broader stimulus–response generalizations.

In philosophy, behaviourism did (naturally) take a metaphysical form: chiefly that of *analytical behaviourism*, the claim that mental ascriptions simply *mean* things about behavioural responses to environmental impingements. Thus, 'Edmund is in pain' means, not anything about Edmund's putative ghostly ego, or even about any episode taking place within Edmund, but that either Edmund is actually behaving in a wincing-and-groaning way or he is disposed so to behave (in that he would so behave were something not keeping him from doing so). 'Edmund believes that broccoli will kill him' means just that, if asked, Edmund would assent to that proposition, and, if confronted by broccoli, Edmund would shun it, and so forth.

But it should be noted that a behaviourist metaphysician need make no claim about the meanings of mental expressions. One might be a merely *reductive behaviourist*, and hold that although mental ascriptions do not *simply mean* things about behavioural responses to stimuli, they are ultimately (in reality) made true just by things about actual and hypothetical responses to stimuli. (On the difference between analytic reduction by linguistic meaning and *synthetic* reduction by *a posteriori* identification, see section 3 below.) Or one might be an *eliminative behaviourist*, and hold that there are no mental states or events at all, but only behavioural responses to stimuli, mental ascriptions being uniformly false or meaningless.

Any behaviourist will subscribe to what has come to be called the *Turing Test*. In response to the perennially popular question 'Can machines think?', Alan Turing (1964) replied that a better question is that of whether a sophisticated computer could ever pass a battery of verbal tests, to the extent of fooling a limited observer (say, a human being corresponding with it by mail) into thinking it is human and sentient. If a machine did pass such tests, then the putatively further question of whether the machine really *thought* would be idle at best, whatever metaphysical analysis one might attach to it. Barring Turing's tendentious limitation of the machine's behaviour to verbal as opposed to non-verbal responses, any behaviourist, psychological or philosophical, would agree that psychological differences cannot out-run behavioural tests; organisms (including machines) whose actual and hypothetical behaviour is just the same are psychologically just alike.

175

Besides solving the methodological problem of intersubjective verification, philosophical behaviourism also adroitly avoided a number of the objections to Cartesian dualism, including (1)–(4) above. It dispensed with immaterial Cartesian egos and ghostly non-physical events, writing them off as metaphysical excrescences. It disposed of Descartes's admitted problem of mind–body interaction, since it posited no immaterial, non-spatial causes of behaviour. It raised no scientific mysteries concerning the intervention of Cartesian substances in physics or biology, since it countenanced no such intervention. Thus it is a *materialist* view, as against Descartes's immaterialism.

Yet some theorists were uneasy; they felt that in its total repudiation of the inner, the private and the subjective, behaviourism was leaving out something real and important. When this worry was voiced, the behaviourists often replied with mockery, assimilating the doubters to old-fashioned dualists who believed in ghosts, ectoplasm or the Easter Bunny; behaviourism was the only (even halfway sensible) game in town. Nonetheless, the doubters made several lasting points against it. Firstly, people who are honest and not anaesthetized know perfectly well that they experience, and can introspect, actual inner mental episodes or occurrences, that are neither actually accompanied by characteristic behaviour nor merely static hypothetical facts of how they would behave if subjected to such-and-such a stimulation. Place (1956) spoke of an 'intractable residue' of conscious mental states that bear no clear relations to behaviour of any particular sort; see also Armstrong (1968: ch. 5) and Campbell (1984). Secondly, contrary to the Turing Test, it seems perfectly possible for two people to differ psychologically despite total similarity of their actual and hypothetical behaviour, as in a LOCKEAN (chapter 29) case of 'inverted spectrum': it might be that when you see a red object, you have the sort of colour experience that I have when I see a green object, and vice versa. For that matter, a creature might exhibit all the appropriate stimulus–response relations and lack a mental life entirely; we can imagine building a 'zombie' or stupid robot that behaves in the right ways but does not really feel or think anything at all (Block and Fodor 1972; Kirk 1974; Block 1981; Campbell 1984). Thirdly, the analytical behaviourist's behavioural analyses of mental ascriptions seem adequate only so long as one makes substantive assumptions about the rest of the subject's *mentality* (Chisholm 1957: ch. 11; Geach 1957: 8; Block 1981); for example, if Edmund believes that broccoli will kill him and he is offered some broccoli, he would shun it only if he does not want to die. Therefore, the behaviourist analyses are either circular or radically incomplete, so far as they are supposed to exhaust the mental generally.

So matters stood in stalemate between dualists, behaviourists and doubters, until the mid-1950s, when U. T. Place (1956) and J. J. C. Smart (1959) proposed a middle way, a conciliatory compromise solution.

3 The Identity Theory

According to Place and Smart, contrary to the behaviourists, at least some mental states and events are genuinely inner and genuinely episodic after all. They are not to be identified with outward behaviour or even with hypothetical dispositions to behave. But, contrary to the dualists, the episodic mental items are neither ghostly nor non-physical. Rather, they are neurophysiological. They are identical with states and events occurring in their owners' central nervous systems; more precisely, every mental state or event is numerically identical with some such neurophysiological state or event. To be in pain is, for example, to have one's c-fibres, or more likely a-fibres, firing in the central nervous system; to believe that broccoli will kill you is to have one's B_{bk}-fibres firing, and so on.

By making the mental entirely physical, this *identity theory of the mind* shared the behaviourist advantage of avoiding the objections to dualism. But it also brilliantly accommodated the inner and the episodic as behaviourism did not. For, according to the identity theory, mental states and events actually occur in their owners' central nervous systems. (Hence they are inner in an even more literal sense than could be granted by Descartes.) The identity theory also thoroughly vindicated the idea that organisms can differ mentally despite total outward behavioural similarity, since clearly organisms can differ neurophysiologically in mediating their outward stimulus–response regularities; that would afford the possibility of inverted spectrum. And of course the connection between a belief or a desire and the usually accompanying behaviour is defeasible by other current mental states, since the connection between a B- or D-neural state and its normal behavioural effect is defeasible by other psychologically characterizable interacting neural states. The identity theory was the ideal resolution of the dualist–behaviourist impasse.

Moreover, there was a direct deductive argument for the identity theory, hit upon independently by David Lewis (1966, 1972) and D. M. Armstrong (1968). Lewis and Armstrong maintained that mental terms were *defined* causally, in terms of mental items' typical causes and effects. For instance, the word 'pain' *means* a state that is typically brought about by physical damage and that typically causes withdrawal, favouring, complaint, desire for cessation, and so on. (Armstrong claimed to establish this by straightforward 'conceptual analysis'. More elaborately, Lewis held that mental terms are the theoretical terms of a common-sensical 'folk theory', and with the positivists that all theoretical terms are implicitly defined by the theories in which they occur. That common-sense theory has since come to be called 'folk psychology'; see sections 12 and 13 below.) Now if by definition pain is whatever state occupies a certain causal niche, and if as is overwhelmingly likely, scientific research will reveal that that particular niche is in fact occupied by such-and-such a neurophysiological state, it follows straightway that pain is that neurophysiological state; QED. Pain retains its conceptual connection to behaviour, but also undergoes an empirical identification with an inner state of its owner. (An advanced if convoluted elaboration of this already hybrid view is developed by Lewis 1980; for meticulous discussion, see Block 1978; Shoemaker 1981; Tye 1983; Owens 1986.)

Notice that although Armstrong and Lewis began their arguments with a claim about the meanings of mental terms, their 'common-sense causal' version of the identity theory was itself no such claim, any more than was the original identity theory of Place and Smart. Rather, all four philosophers relied on the idea that things or properties can sometimes be identified with 'other' things or properties even when there is no synonymy of terms; there is such a thing as synthetic and *a posteriori* identity that is nonetheless genuine identity. While the identity of triangles with trilaterals holds simply in virtue of the meanings of the two terms and can be established by reason alone, without empirical investigation, the following identities are standard examples of the synthetic *a posteriori*, and were discovered empirically: clouds with masses of water droplets; water with H_2O; lightning with electrical discharge; the Morning Star with Venus; Mendelian genes with segments of DNA molecules; and temperature with mean molecular kinetic energy. The identity theory was offered similarly, in a spirit of scientific speculation; one could not properly object that mental expressions do not mean anything about brains or neural firings.

So the dualists were wrong in thinking that mental items are non-physical but right in thinking them inner and episodic; the behaviourists were right in their materialism but wrong to repudiate inner mental episodes. But alas, this happy synthesis was too good to be true.

4   Machine Functionalism

Quite soon, Hilary Putnam (1960, 1967a, 1967b) and Jerry Fodor (1968b) pointed out a presumptuous implication of the identity theory understood as a theory of 'types' or *kinds* of mental items: that a mental state such as pain has *always* and *everywhere* the neurophysiological characterization initially assigned to it. For example, if the identity theorist identified pain itself with the firings of c-fibres, it followed that a creature of any species (earthly or science-fiction) could be in pain only if that creature had c-fibres and they were firing. But such a constraint on the biology of any being capable of feeling pain is both gratuitous and indefensible; why should we suppose that any organism must be made of the same chemical materials as we are in order to have what can be accurately recognized as pain? The identity theorist had over-reacted to the behaviourists' difficulties and focused too narrowly on the specifics of biological humans' actual inner states, and in so doing they had fallen into species chauvinism.

Putnam and Fodor advocated the obvious correction: what was important was not its being c-fibres (*per se*) that were firing, but what the c-fibre firings were doing, what they contributed to the operation of the organism as a whole. The *role* of the c-fibres could have been performed by any mechanically suitable component; so long as that role was performed, the psychology of the containing organism would have been unaffected. Thus, to be in pain is not *per se* to have c-fibres that are firing, but merely to be in some state or other, of whatever biochemical description, that plays the same causal role as did the firings of c-fibres in the human beings we have investigated. We may continue to maintain that pain 'tokens' – individual instances of pain occurring in particular subjects at particular times – are strictly identical with particular neurophysiological states of those subjects at those times – in other words, with the states that happen to be playing the appropriate roles; this is the thesis of 'token identity' or 'token' materialism or physicalism. But pain itself, the kind, universal or 'type', can be identified only with something more abstract: the causal or functional role that c-fibre firings share with their potential replacements or surrogates. Mental state-types are identified not with neurophysiological types but with more abstract functional roles, as specified by state-tokens' causal relations to the organism's sensory inputs, behavioural responses, and other intervening psychological states. *Functionalism*, then, is the doctrine that what makes a mental state the type of state it is – a pain, a smell of violets, a belief that koalas are dangerous – is its distinctive set of functional relations, its role in its subject's behavioural economy.

Putnam compared mental states to the functional or 'logical' states of a computer: just as a computer program can be realized or instantiated by any of a number of physically different hardware configurations, so can a psychological 'program' be realized by different organisms of various physiochemical composition, and that is why different physiological states of organisms of different species can realize one and the same mental state-type. Where an identity theorist's type-identification would take the form, 'To be in mental state of type M is to be in the neurophysiological state of type N', Putnam's *machine functionalism* (as I shall call it) has it that to be in M is to be merely in some physiological state or other that plays role R in the relevant computer program (that is, the program that at a suitable level of abstraction mediates the creature's total outputs given total inputs and so serves as the creature's global psychology). The physiological state 'plays role R' in that it stands in a set of relations to physical inputs, outputs and other inner states that matches one-to-one the abstract input–output–logical-state relations codified in the computer program.

Functionalist Levels of Description

The functionalist, then, mobilizes three distinct levels of description but applies them all to the same fundamental reality. A physical state-token in someone's brain at a particular time has a neurophysiological description, but it may also have a functional description relative to a machine program that the brain happens to be realizing, and it may further have a mental description if some mental state is correctly type-identified with the functional category it exemplifies. And so there is after all a sense in which 'the mental' is distinct from 'the physical'. Though presumably there are no non-physical substances or stuffs, and every mental token is itself entirely physical, mental characterization is not physical characterization, and the property of being a pain is not simply the property of being such-and-such a neural firing. Moreover, unlike behaviourism and the identity theory, functionalism does not strictly entail that minds are physical; it might be true of non-physical minds, so long as those minds realized the relevant programs.

5   Cognitive Psychology

In a not accidentally similar vein, behaviourism has almost entirely given way to 'cognitivism' in psychology. Cognitivism is roughly the view that (1) psychologists may and must advert to inner states and episodes in explaining behaviour, so long as the states and episodes are construed throughout as physical; (2) human beings and other psychological organisms are best viewed as in some sense *information-processing* systems; and (3) the vehicle of information processing is internal representation, a repertoire of brain states that represent features of the external world. As cognitive psychology sets the agenda, its questions take the form, 'How does this organism receive information through its sense-organs, represent the information, process it, store the result, and then mobilize its total information in such a way as to result in intelligent behaviour?' The working language of cognitive psychology is highly congenial to the functionalist, for cognitivism thinks of human beings as systems of interconnected functional components, interacting with each other in an efficient and productive way. This was nowhere better exemplified, in the early days of the cognitivist revolution, than in Chomsky's (1959) review of Skinner (1957), which argued for a functionalist information-processing account of language use, against the best behaviourist model.

6 Artificial Intelligence and the Computer Model of the Mind

Meanwhile, researchers in computer science have pursued fruitful research programmes based on the idea of intelligent behaviour as, for given input, the output of skilful information-processing. *Artificial Intelligence* (AI) is, roughly, the project of getting computing machines to perform tasks that would usually be taken to demand human intelligence and judgement. Computers have achieved some modest success in proving theorems, guiding missiles, sorting mail, driving assembly-line robots, diagnosing illnesses, predicting weather and economic events, and the like. A computer just is a machine that receives, interprets, processes, stores, manipulates and uses information, and AI researchers think of it in just that way as they try to program intelligent behaviour. An AI problem takes the form, 'Given that the machine sees this as input, what must it already know and what must it accordingly do with that input in order to be able to . . . [recognize, identify, sort, put together, predict, tell us, and so on]? And how, then, can we start it off knowing that and get it to do those things?' So we may reasonably attribute such success as AI has had to self-conscious reliance on the information-processing paradigm.

This encourages the idea that *human* intelligence and cognition generally are matters of computational information-processing. Indeed, that idea has already filtered well down into the everyday speech of ordinary people, as anyone can verify by talking with children for a while. This tentative and crude coalescing of the notions *cognition, computation, information* and *intelligence* raises two general questions, one in each of two directions: (1) to what extent might computers approximate to minds? (2) to what extent do minds approximate to computers?

The first question breaks down into three more, which differ sharply and importantly from each other. (1a) What intelligent tasks will any computer ever be able to perform? (1b) Given that a computer performs interesting tasks X, Y and Z, does it do so in the same way that human beings do? (1c) Given that a computer performs X, Y and Z and that it does so *in the same* way humans do, does that show that it has psychological and mental properties, such as (real) intelligence, thought, consciousness, feeling, sensation, emotion and the like? Sub-question (1a) is one of engineering, (1b) is one of cognitive psychology and (1c) is philosophical; theorists' answers will depend accordingly on their commitments in these respective areas. But for the record let us distinguish three different senses or grades of 'AI': AI in the weakest sense is cautiously optimistic as regards (1a); it says these engineering efforts are promising and should be funded, for their own sake. AI in a stronger sense says that the engineering efforts can well serve as modelling of human cognition, and that their successes can be taken as pointers toward the truth about human functional and representational organization. AI in the strongest sense favours an affirmative answer to (1c) and some qualified respect for the Turing Test: it says that if a machine performs intelligently *and* does so on the basis of a sufficiently human-like information-processing aetiology, then there is little reason to doubt that the machine has the relevant human qualities of mind and sensation. On this view, any system or organism that (genuinely) realizes such-and-such a program or flow chart would have mental states like ours. Thus, if we could build a machine to certain functional specifications, we could artificially create a thinking, feeling machine. Some theorists welcome this consequence warmly, and look forward to the day. Others find the prospect grotesque and preposterous, a reduction of functionalism to absurdity. (AI in the strongest sense is very strong, but notice carefully that it does not presuppose affirmative answers to either (1a) or (1b).) The opposite issue, that of assimilating minds to computers, is very close to the philosophical matter of functionalism. But here too there are importantly distinct sub-questions, this time two: (2a) Do human minds work in very like the way computers do as computers are currently designed and construed – for instance, using flipflops grouped into banks and registers, with an assembly language collecting individual machine-code operations into subroutines and these subroutines being called by higher-level manipulations of real-world information according to programmed rules? (2b) Regardless of architecture, can human psychological capacities be entirely captured by a third-person, hardware-realizable design of *some* sort that could in principle be built in a laboratory? Subquestion (2a) is currently much discussed (see section 12 below), but is not particularly philosophical. (2b) is tantamount to the fate of functionalism strictly so-called.

The computer model of the mind has opponents of several sorts; of these, perhaps the best known are Dreyfus (1979) and Searle (1980). Dreyfus is thoroughly pessimistic in regard to (1a) and gives an emphatically negative answer to (2a). Drawing on the PHENOMENOLOGICAL tradition of HUSSERL and HEIDEGGER (chapter 41), Dreyfus challenges several of the assumptions underlying classical AI, and diagnoses some of AI's known failures as stemming from those assumptions. In particular, Dreyfus argues that, in real life as opposed to the toy 'micro-worlds' constructed by AI researchers, such standard AI tasks as problem solving and language understanding presuppose unpredictably relevant and nearly endless knowledge of the world (consider just the general problem of understanding ambiguous sentences in context); but no human being's knowledge of the world could ever be made explicit, or even completely formalized in a set of representations and rules. Rather, human knowledge and understanding inhere non-discursively in our biology, our bodily embedding in our environment, our interests and our cultural surround – of which digital computers have at best distant analogues (see also Haugeland 1979).

More recently, however, Dreyfus has granted that *connectionist* AI (see section 12 below) evades his main criticisms of classical AI (see especially Dreyfus and Dreyfus 1986).

Searle offers a hypothetical case in which a human program is executed, not by a mechanical or biological computer in the normal way, but by a simple human being who is given 'inputs', say on index cards, and following some rules written in a manual, writes some 'outputs' on new index cards and drops those in an 'output' bin. Suppose the 'inputs' are sequences of Chinese characters, the program is that which a functionalist would say constitutes a human Chinese speaker's understanding of the

Chinese language, and consequently the 'outputs' are grammatical utterances of Chinese also; but the functionary who does the simple rule-following operation is a monoglot English-speaker and only just bright enough to follow the program's very simple instructions. There is here no actual understanding of Chinese, Searle claims, but only a computational imitation of a real Chinese speaker and understander. Thus, sub-questions (1c) and (2b) are answered firmly in the negative.

A number of differing rejoinders are available to partisans of AI in its strong and strongest senses (they are made by various commentators in the *Behavioral and Brain Sciences* symposium – see Searle 1980). The hypothetical example is not really possible, even if we seem to be able to imagine it; or, though it is possible, its protagonist would (contra Searle) really understand Chinese; or, though Searle is right about the example as described, it can be accommodated by an only slightly modified functionalist theory (in particular, see section 10 below).

And Morality?

It may be wondered whether materialist theories of the mind and/or functionalist theories have any interesting implications for morality and ethics. Three materialists take this up explicitly: Smart (1963: ch. 8) tries to exhibit a materialist basis for morals; Michael Levin (1979: ch. 7) addresses the specific charge that materialists cannot allow freedom of the will or whatever else may be necessary to make room for moral responsibility; Lycan (1985) explores some moral consequences of the computational view of the mind. A main purpose of Dennett's (1978) is also to show why moral responsibility and the mental vernacular that supports it are possible despite Dennett's instrumentalist – sometimes fictionalist – treatment of the mental (see section 11 below).

---

7 Homuncular Functionalism and Other Teleological Theories

As we saw, machine functionalism supposed that human brains may be described at each of three levels, the first two scientific and the third familiar and common-sensical. At the first level, biologists would map out human neurobiology and provide neurophysiological descriptions of brain states. At the second level, psychologists would (eventually) work out the machine program that was being realized by the lower-level neurophysiology and would describe the same brain states in more abstract, computational terms. At the third level, psychologists would also explain behaviour, characterized in everyday terms, by reference to stimuli and to intervening mental states such as beliefs and desires, type-identifying the mental states with functional or computational states as they went. Such explanations would themselves presuppose nothing about neurophysiology, since the relevant psychological–computational generalizations would hold regardless of what particular biochemistry might happen to be realizing the abstract program in question.

Machine functionalism has more recently been challenged on a number of points, that together motivate a specifically teleological notion of 'function' (Sober (1985) speaks aptly of 'putting the function back into functionalism'): we are to think of a thing's function as what the thing is *for*, what its job is, what it is supposed to do. There are five challenges.

Firstly, the machine functionalist still conceived psychological explanation in the logical positivists' terms of subsuming observed data under wider and wider universal laws. But Fodor (1968a), Dennett (1978) and Cummins (1983) have defended a competing picture of psychological explanation, according to which behavioural data are to be seen as manifestations of subjects' psychological capacities, and those capacities are to be explained by understanding the subjects as systems of interconnected components. Each component is a 'homunculus', in that it is thought of as a little agent or bureaucrat operating within its containing subject; it is identified by reference to the function it performs. And the various homuncular components co-operate with each other in such a way as to produce overall behavioural responses to stimuli. The 'homunculi' are themselves broken down into sub-components whose functions and interactions are similarly used to explain the capacities of the subsystems they compose, and so again and again until the sub-sub- . . . components are seen to be neurophysiological structures. Thus biological and mechanical systems alike are hierarchically organized, on the principle of what computer scientists call 'hierarchical control'. (An automobile works – locomotes – by having a fuel reservoir, a fuel line, a carburettor, a combustion chamber, an ignition system, a transmission and wheels that turn. If one wants to know how the carburettor works, one will be told what its parts are and how they work together to infuse oxygen into fuel; and so on.) But nothing in this pattern of explanation corresponds to the subsumption of data under wider and wider universal generalizations.

The second challenge is that the machine functionalist treated functional 'realization', the relation between an individual physical organism and the abstract program it was said to instantiate, as a simple matter of one-to-one correspondence between the organism's repertoire of physical stimuli, structural states and behaviour, on the one hand, and the program's defining input–state–output function on the other. But this criterion of realization was seen to be too liberal; since virtually anything bears a one–one correlation of some sort to virtually anything else, 'realization' in the sense of mere one–one correspondence is far too easily come by (Block 1978; Lycan 1987: ch. 3); Searle's 'Chinese-understanding' set-up would be an example. Some theorists have proposed to remedy this defect by imposing a teleological requirement on realization: a physical state of an organism will count as realizing such-and-such a functional description only if the organism has genuine organic integrity and the state plays its functional role properly for the organism, in the teleological sense of 'for' and in the teleological sense of 'function'. The state must do what it does as a matter of, so to speak, its biological purpose. (Machine functionalism took 'function' in its spare mathematical sense rather than in a genuinely functional sense. One should note that, as used here, the term 'machine functionalism' is tied to the original liberal conception of 'realizing'; so to impose a teleological restriction is to abandon machine functionalism.)

Thirdly, of the machine functionalist's three levels of description, one is commonsensical and two are scientific, so we are offered a starkly two-levelled picture of human psychobiology. But that picture is unbiological in the extreme. Neither living things nor even computers themselves are split into a purely 'structural' level of biological–physiochemical description and any one 'abstract' computational level of machine–psychological description. Rather, they are all hierarchically organized at many levels, each level 'functional' with respect to those beneath it but 'structural' or concrete as it realizes those levels above it. This relativity of the 'functional'–'structural' or 'software'–'hardware' distinction to any specified level of organization has repercussions for functionalist solutions to problems in the philosophy of mind (Lycan 1987: ch. 5), and for current controversies surrounding Connectionism and neural modelling in AI.

Fourthly, the teleologizing of functional realization has helped functionalists to rebut various objections based on the 'qualia' or 'feels' or experienced phenomenal characters of mental states (Lycan 1981; Sober 1985; and see section 8 below).

Finally, Van Gulick (1980), Millikan (1984), Dretske (1988), Fodor (1990a) and others have argued powerfully that teleology must enter into any adequate analysis of the *intentionality* or aboutness or referential character of mental states such as beliefs and desires, by reference to the states' psychobiological functions (see sections 9 and 10 below). Beliefs, desires and other *propositional attitudes* such as suspecting, intending and wishing are directed upon states of affairs which may or may not actually obtain (for instance, that the Republican candidate will win), and are about individuals who may or may not exist (such as King Arthur). Franz Brentano (1838–1917) (1973) drew a distinction between psychological phenomena, which are directed upon objects and states of affairs, even non-existing ones, and physical objects, which are not so directed. If mental items are physical, however, the question arises how any purely physical entity or state could have the property of being 'directed upon' or about a non-existent state of affairs or object; that is not the sort of feature that ordinary, purely physical objects (such as bricks) can have. According to the teleological theorists, a neurophysiological state should count as *a belief that broccoli will kill you*, and in particular as *about broccoli*, only if that state has the representing of broccoli as in some sense one of its psychobiological functions. If teleology is needed to explicate intentionality, and machine functionalism affords no teleology, then machine functionalism is not adequate to explicate intentionality.

All this talk of teleology and biological function seems to presuppose that biological and other 'structural' states of physical systems really do have functions in the teleological sense. The latter claim is, to say the least, controversial. Some philosophers dismiss it as hilariously false, as a superstitious relic of primitive animism, Panglossian theism or at best the vitalism of the nineteenth century; others tolerate it but only as a useful metaphor; still others take teleological characterizations to be literally true but only relative to a convenient classificatory or interpretive scheme (Cummins 1975). Only a few writers (Wimsatt 1972; Wright 1973; Millikan 1984; and a few others) have taken teleological characterizations to be literally and categorically true. This may seem to embarrass teleologized functionalist theories of mind.

Fortunately for the teleological functionalist there is now a vigorous industry whose purpose is to explicate biological teleology in naturalistic terms, typically in terms of aetiology. For example, a trait may be said to have the function of doing F in virtue of its having been selected for because it did F; a heart's function is to pump blood because hearts' pumping blood in the past has given them a selection advantage and so led to the survival of more animals with hearts. Actually, no simple aetiological explication will do (Cummins 1975; Boorse 1976; Bigelow and Pargetter 1987), but philosophers of biology have continued to refine the earlier accounts and seek to make them into adequate naturalistic analyses of genuine function.

Functionalism, and cognitive psychology considered as a complete theory of human thought, inherit some of the same difficulties that earlier beset behaviourism and the identity theory. These remaining obstacles fall into two main categories: qualia problems and intentionality problems.

8 Problems with Qualia and Consciousness

The *quale* of a mental state or event (particularly a *sensation*) is that state or event's *feel*, its introspectible 'phenomenal character', its nature as it presents itself to *consciousness*. Many philosophers have objected that neither functionalist metaphysics nor any of the allied doctrines aforementioned can 'explain consciousness', or illuminate or even tolerate the notion of *what it feels like* to be in a mental state of such-and-such a sort. Yet, say these philosophers, the feels are quintessentially mental – it is the feels that make the mental states the mental states they are. Something, therefore, must be drastically wrong with functionalism.

'The' problem of consciousness or qualia is familiar. Indeed, it is so familiar that we tend to overlook the most important thing about it: that its name is Legion, for it is many. There is no *single* problem of qualia; there are at least nine quite distinct objections that have been brought against functionalism (some of them apply to materialism generally).

(1) Early critics of the identity theory argued that our immediate mental access to qualia militates against their being features of any purely neurophysiological item.

(2) Saul Kripke (1972) made ingenious use of modal distinctions against type or even token identity, arguing that unless mental items are *necessarily* identical with neurophysiological ones, which they are not, they cannot be identical with them at all. Kripke's close reasoning has attracted considerable critical attention.

(3) Block (1978) and others have urged various counter-example cases against functionalism – examples in which some entity seems to realize the right program but which lacks one of mentality's crucial qualitative aspects. (Typically the 'entity' is a group of human beings, such as the entire population of China acting according to an elaborate set of instructions, but Searle's type of set-up would also serve. Neither, it seems, would be *feeling* anything on its own.) Predictably, functionalists have rejoined by arguing, for each example, either that the proposed entity does not in fact succeed in realizing the right program (for example, because the requisite teleology is lacking) or that there is no good reason for denying that the entity does have the relevant qualitative states.

(4) Farrell (1950), Gunderson (1970, 1974) and Nagel (1974) have worried over first-person–third-person asymmetries and the perspectivalness or subjective-

point-of-view-ness of consciousness. Science is designed to *abstract away from* perspective and subjectivity; materialism seems to deny the reality of the first-person experience.

(5) Nagel (1974) and Jackson (1982) have appealed to a disparity in knowledge, as a general anti-materialist argument: I can know what it is like to have such-and-such a sensation only if I have had that sensation myself; no amount of objective, third-person scientific information would suffice. In reply, functionalists have offered analyses of 'perspectivalness', complete with accounts of 'what it is like' to have a sensation, that make those things compatible with functionalism. Nagel and Jackson have argued, further, for the existence of a special, intrinsically perspectival kind of *fact*, the fact of 'what it is like', which intractably and in principle cannot be captured or explained by physical science. Functionalists have responded that the arguments commit a logical fallacy (specifically, that of applying Leibniz's Law in an intentional context; some have added that in any case, to 'know what it is like' is merely to have an ability, and involves no fact of any sort, while, contrariwise, some other theorists have granted that there are facts of 'what it is like' but insisted that such facts can after all be explained and predicted by natural science.

(6) Jackson (1977) and others have defended the claim that in consciousness we are presented with mental individuals that themselves bear phenomenal, qualitative properties. For instance, when a red flash bulb goes off in your face, your visual field exhibits a green blotch, an 'after-image', a *thing* that is really green and has a fairly definite shape and exists for a few seconds before disappearing. If there are such things, they are entirely different from anything physical to be found in the brain of a (healthy) human subject. Belief in such 'phenomenal individuals' as genuinely green after-images has been unpopular among philosophers for some years, but it can be powerfully motivated (see Lycan 1987: 83–93).

(7) A number of philosophers, most notably Sellars (1963), have stressed the ultra-smoothness, homogeneity or grainlessness of phenomenal feels, and contended for this reason that those feels cannot peacefully be dissolved into a metaphysic of little brute particles and their erratic motion through the void.

(8) If human beings are functionally (even teleologically) organized systems of physical components and nothing more, then their 'behaviour' is only the mechanical, physically determined outcome of physical inputs and internal energy transformations. The inputs are themselves only the physical impacts of environmental causes, which causes are themselves the results of events completely external to us. We are merely automata. (It is no accident that Putnam's original inspiration was the Turing Machine.) But we know from the inside that this is false. Our conscious choices and our deliberate actions are entirely up to us; they feel entirely free. If I simply wish to raise my hand, then nothing can stop me from doing so unless quite externally and by making news (such as a madman suddenly pinning me to the floor or a Phantom Jet hurtling through the wall of the building).

(9) Levine (1983, 1993) has complained of an 'explanatory gap': that no functionalist theory can *explain why* such-and-such a sensation feels to its subject

in just the way it does. The question, 'But why do such-and-such functional goings-on constitute or produce a sensation like *this?*' seems always open. Some functionalists contend that a functionalist psychology could indeed explain such facts; others try to show why it need not, consistently with the truth of functionalism.

This is a formidable array of objections, and, on the face of it, each is plausible. Materialists and particularly functionalists must respond in detail. Needless to say, materialists have responded at length; some of the most powerful rejoinders are formulated in Lycan (1987, 1996). Yet recent years have seen some reaction against the prevailing materialism, including a re-emergence of some neo-dualist views, as in Robinson (1988), Hart (1988), Strawson (1994) and Chalmers (1996).

9　Problems with Intentionality

The problem arising from our discussion of Brentano was to explain how any purely physical entity or state could have the property of being about or 'directed upon' a non-existent state of affairs. The standard functionalist reply is that propositional attitudes have Brentano's feature because the internal physical states and events that realize them *represent* actual or possible states of affairs. What they represent (their *content*) is determined at least in part by their functional roles.

There are two main difficulties. One is that of saying exactly how a physical item's representational content is determined; in virtue of what does a neurophysiological state represent precisely *that the Republican candidate will win?* An answer to that general question is what Fodor has called a *psychosemantics*, and several attempts have been made.

The second difficulty is that ordinary propositional attitude contents do not supervene on the states of their subjects' nervous systems, but are underdetermined by even the total state of that subject's head. Putnam's (1975) *Twin Earth* and *index-ical* examples show that, surprising as it may seem, two human beings could be mole-cule-for-molecule alike and still differ in their beliefs and desires, depending on various factors in their spatial and historical environments. Thus we can distinguish between 'narrow' properties, those that are determined by a subject's intrinsic physical composition, and 'wide' properties, those that are not so determined. Representational contents are wide, yet functional roles are, ostensibly, narrow. How, then, can propositional attitudes be type-identified with functional roles, or for that matter with states of the brain under any narrow description?

Functionalists have responded in one of two ways. The former is to understand 'function' widely as well, specifying functional roles historically and/or by reference to features of the subject's actual environment. The latter is simply to abandon functionalism as an account of content in particular, giving some alternative psychosemantics for propositional attitudes, but preserving functionalism in regard to attitude types. (Thus what makes a state a desire that P is its functional role, even if something else makes the state a desire that P). These options will be explored briefly in section 10; and the rest of this chapter will be devoted to problems raised by the propositional attitudes. In section 13 we shall note the impact of the 'narrow'–'wide' distinction on the ontological status of folk psychology itself.

Emotions

In alluding to sensory states and to mental states with intentional content, we have said nothing specifically about the emotions. Since the rejection of behaviourism, theories of mind have tended not to be applied directly to the emotions; rather, the emotions have been generally thought to be conceptually analysable as complexes of more central or 'core' mental states, typically propositional attitudes such as belief and desire (and the intentionality of emotions has accordingly been traced back to that of attitudes). Armstrong (1968: ch. 8, section 3) took essentially this line, as do Solomon (1977) and Gordon (1987). However, there is a literature on functionalism and the emotions; see Rey (1980) and some of the other papers collected in Rorty (1980). Griffiths (1997) takes a generally functionalist view, but argues that 'the emotions' do not constitute a single kind. Some psychological literature on the topic is collected in Clark and Fiske (1982) and Scherer and Ekman (1984).

10   The 'Language of Thought' Hypothesis

Our basic problem about intentionality is to explain how a purely physical system or organism can be in states having such features.

A key point to note is that intentional or representational features are semantical features: beliefs are true, or false; they *entail* or imply other beliefs; they are (it seems) composed of concepts and depend for their truth on a match between their internal structures and the way the world is; in particular their 'aboutness' is very naturally regarded as a matter of mental *referring*. Some philosophers, most notably Sellars (1963), Fodor (1975, 1981, 1987) and Field (1978), have taken the semantic nature of beliefs as a strong clue to the nature of intentionality itself, suggesting that beliefs and thoughts have their intentionality in virtue of properties they share with other semantically characterized items, the sentences of public natural languages such as English and Chinese.

Sellars argued (against the behaviourists) that people's intentional states are indeed inner and are indeed representations. They are physical states of the central nervous system. Nonetheless (*contra* Brentano) they are physical states *that have semantical properties*. They have those properties in virtue of the functional roles they play in their owners' behavioural economies, closely analogous to the inferential roles that corresponding linguistic tokens play in public, entirely physical language games. To put the thesis slightly more formally: for a subject S to think or 'occurrently believe' that P is for there to be a state of S's central nervous system that bears the semantic content that P; the state bears that content in much the same sense and in much the same way that a sentence of English or another natural language means that P. Let us call this the *representational theory of thinking*.

It is tempting to gloss the representational theory by speaking of a *language of thought*, and its leading proponents have given in to that temptation. Fodor argues that representation and the inferential manipulation of representations require a medium of representation, no less in human subjects than in computers. Computers employ machine languages of various kinds; it is reasonable to posit one or more human 'machine languages' in which human thought and cognition take place. On the other hand, there are obvious disanalogies between private thought and public speech, so if we are to take representationalism seriously we must specify, in at least a preliminary way, what similarities are being claimed.

On the representationalist's behalf, let us say that physically realized thoughts and mental representations are 'linguistic' in the following sense: (1) they are composed of parts and are syntactically structured; (2) their simplest parts refer to or denote things and properties in the world; (3) their meanings as wholes are determined by the semantical properties of their basic parts together with the grammatical rules that have generated their overall syntactic structures; (4) they have truth-conditions (that is, putative states of affairs in the world that would make them true), and accordingly they are true or false depending on the way the world happens actually to be; (5) they bear logical relations of entailment or implication to each other. Thus, according to the representational theory: human beings have systems of physical states that serve as the elements of a lexicon or vocabulary, and human beings (somehow) physically realize rules that combine strings of those elements into configurations having the complex representational contents that common sense associates with the propositional attitudes. And that is why thoughts and beliefs are true or false just as English sentences are, though a 'language of thought' (Mentalese, or Brainese) may differ sharply in its grammar from any natural language.

The arguments for the representational theory take a number of impressively different forms (Fodor 1981, 1987; Devitt and Sterelny 1987; Lycan 1988). Though they are formidable, the theory has also come in for a good deal of criticism, and there too the arguments take a number of impressively different forms. Some leading objections are these:

(1) Chisholm (1972) and others have pointed out that the meanings of natural-language sentences are conventional, and so depend on the beliefs and intentions of human speakers. Beliefs and intentions are propositional attitudes. How, then, without circularity or regress, can attitude content be explicated in terms of meaning in the public-linguistic sense?

(2) Dennett (1978) argues on several grounds that the idea of 'sentences in the head', implemented as inscriptions scrawled in brain chalk upon a brain blackboard, is fanciful, not to say grotesque. (Though his target seems to be a stronger and more outlandish version of representationalism than the one sketched above.)

(3) Dennett further argues that tacit propositional attitudes, such as your unconsidered belief that I am less than 12 feet tall, can hardly be internal representations, because there are far too many of them. You also believe that I am less than 12-plus-n feet tall for any real number n.

(4) Churchland and Churchland (1983) (cf. Churchland 1989) contend that the 'language of thought' idea is distinctly *unbiological*. When one recalls that human beings are card-carrying members of the animal kingdom and that we have evolved in the usual way by natural selection, our linguistic abilities, and

189

our cognitive functions on any highly linguisticized account of them, seem to be an evolutionary afterthought at best, and a tiny fragment of the psychology that actually gets us around in the world. P. S. Churchland (1986) and P. M. Churchland (1986, 1989) compellingly depict a brain that works by connectionist networking (see section 12 below) and by physically hardwired coordinate transformation, not by digital-computer-like inferential computation over syntactically structured sentences or logical formulas (see also the complaints raised by Dreyfus (1979) against classical AI).

(5) While public language is (again) conventional in each of several ways, there is obviously nothing social or conventional about the workings of the brain. The 'reference' of the alleged language-of-thought's vocabulary items must be natural. The English word 'dog' is an arbitrary vocable, which is socially attached by the English-speaking community to dogs, but the Mentalese word for 'dog' must somehow be naturally connected to dogs, without human intervention. That is hard to swallow.

(6) The search for an adequate psychosemantics is debilitating at best. If thoughts and beliefs can be about Margaret Thatcher or about Santa Claus because the neurophysiological states that realize them somehow semantically refer to Margaret Thatcher or Santa Claus, and if the neurophysiological states do their referring in virtue of some physical, functional or otherwise naturalistic property they have, what is that property? We may imagine that our thoughts of Thatcher stand in some historical relation to Thatcher herself, but our thoughts of Santa Claus do not stand in any historical relation to Santa Claus himself, for he does not exist. Nor, in trying to say what it is in virtue of which some neurophysiological state 'refers to' anything, may we invoke unexplicated propositional attitudes or representational content, and that proves to be a biting constraint.

Psychosemantics admits of (so far) two basic lines of approach, which are reconcilable though entirely distinct in origin.

The first is the causal–historical approach, in the spirit of Kripke (1972) and Putnam (1975), according to which a mental–brain item M refers to a thing X just in case X figures appropriately in M's causal history or aetiology. Practitioners of this approach cash the important qualifier 'appropriately' in any number of hopeful ways; any successful way will have to account for reference to *non-existent* things, which is no small task in itself and multiply hard given that one may not, on pain of circularity, invoke unexplicated propositional-attitude contents.

The second approach is teleological, as mentioned in section 7. The teleological approach began life as 'indicator semantics', the idea that M represents X just in case M is a reliable indicator of X (see Dretske 1981; Stalnaker 1984); but in order to account for false representations, that idea was soon teleologized. The main hurdle for teleosemantics is to secure full generality: human mental states can be about anything, but so far as the external world is concerned, no individual brain state can have more than a few psychobiological functions at a time; how can neurophysiological states be about anything but food, shelter, predators and sexual partners? Fodor (1990a, although written earlier) was the first teleological theorist to solve that problem –

however quickly and however inadequately. (He has since vigorously repudiated his original solution in a book that, sardonically, has the identical title (Fodor 1987, and in 1990b, 1994); he has moved to a variation on indicator semantics that he calls the 'asymmetric dependence' theory (Fodor 1994).) It is not clear whether Fodor's (1990a) solution can be extended to the vast range of beliefs and thoughts that are about things other than physically present environmental objects: mathematics, literature, philosophy, religion. The teleological view gives no hint as to how such topics are just as ready objects of thought as are nearby cows, cats, desktop computers and buildings.

11   Instrumentalism

The identity theorists and the functionalists (machine or teleological) joined common sense and current cognitive psychology in understanding mental states and events both as *internal to human subjects* and as *causes*. Beliefs and desires in particular are thought to be caused by perceptual or other cognitive events and as in turn conspiring from within to cause behaviour. If Armstrong's or Lewis's theory of mind is correct, this idea is not only common-sensical but a conceptual truth; if functionalism is correct, it is at least a metaphysical fact.

In rallying to the inner-causal story, as we saw in section 3, the identity theorists and functionalists broke with the behaviourists, for behaviourists did not think of mental items as entities, as inner, or as causes in any stronger sense than the bare hypothetical. Behaviourists either dispensed with the mentalistic idiom altogether, or paraphrased mental ascriptions in terms of putative responses to hypothetical stimuli. More recently, other philosophers have followed them in rejecting the idea of beliefs and desires as inner causes and in construing them in a more purely operational or instrumental fashion. D. C. Dennett (1978, 1987) has been particularly concerned to deny that beliefs and desires are causally active inner states of people, and maintains instead that belief-ascriptions and desire-ascriptions are merely calculational devices, that happen to have predictive usefulness for a reason that he goes on to explain. Such ascriptions are often objectively true, he grants, but not in virtue of describing inner mechanisms.

Thus Dennett is an INSTRUMENTALIST (pp. 294–5) about propositional attitudes such as belief and desire. (According to a contemporary interpretation, an 'instrumentalist' about Xs is a theorist who claims that although sentences about 'Xs' are often true, they do not really describe entities of a special kind, but only serve to systematize more familiar phenomena. For instance, we are all instrumentalists about 'the average American homeowner', who is white, male and the father of exactly 1.9 children.) To ascribe a 'belief' or a 'desire' is not to describe some segment of physical reality, Dennett says, but is more like moving a group of beads in an abacus. (It should be noted that Dennett has more recently moderated his line: see Dennett 1991.)

Dennett offers basically five grounds for his rejection of the common-sensical inner-cause thesis. (1) He thinks it quite unlikely that any science will ever turn up any distinctive inner-causal mechanism that would be shared by all the possible subjects that had a particular belief. (2) He offers numerous objections to 'language of thought psychology', which is the most popular inner-cause theory. (3) He compares the belief–desire interpretation of human beings to that of lower animals, chess-playing computers and even lightning-rods, arguing that (3a) in their case we have no reason to think of belief-ascriptions and desire-ascriptions as other than mere calculational–predictive devices and (3b) we have no *more* reason for the case of humans to think of belief-ascriptions and desire-ascriptions as other than that. (4) Dennett argues from the verification conditions of belief-ascriptions and desire-ascriptions – basically a matter of extrapolating rationally from what a subject ought to believe and want in his or her circumstances – and then he boldly just identifies the truth-makers of those ascriptions with their verification-conditions, challenging inner-cause theorists to show why instrumentalism does not accommodate all the actual evidence. (5) He argues that in any case if a purely normative assumption (the 'rationality assumption', which is that people will generally believe what they ought to believe and desire what they should desire) is required for the licensing of an ascription, then the ascription cannot itself be a purely factual description of a plain state of affairs.

Stich (1981) explores and criticizes Dennett's instrumentalism at length (perhaps oddly, Stich (1983) goes on to defend a view nearly as deprecating as Dennett's, though clearly distinct from it). Dennett (1981) responds to Stich, bringing out more clearly the force of the 'rationality assumption' assumption. (Other criticisms are levelled against Dennett by commentators in the *Behavioral and Brain Sciences* symposium that is headed by Dennett (1988).)

A close cousin of Dennett's view, in that it focuses on the rationality assumption, is Donald Davidson's (1970) *anomalous monism*. Unlike Dennett's instrumentalism, it endorses token physicalism and insists that individual mental tokens are causes, but it rejects on similarly epistemological grounds the possibility of any interesting materialistic type-reduction of the propositional attitudes.

12   Eliminativism and Neurophilosophy

Dennett's instrumentalism breaks fairly radically with common sense and with philosophical tradition in denying that propositional attitudes such as belief and desire are real inner causal states of people. But Dennett concedes – indeed, he urgently insists – that belief-ascriptions and desire-ascriptions are true, and objectively true, nonetheless. Other philosophers have taken a less conciliatory, still more radically uncommonsensical view: that mental ascriptions are not true after all, but are simply *false*. Common sense is just mistaken in supposing that people believe and desire things, and perhaps in supposing that people have sensations and feelings, disconcerting as that nihilistic claim may seem.

Following standard usage, let us call the nihilistic claim 'eliminative materialism', or 'eliminativism' for short. It is important to note a customary if unexpected alliance between the eliminativist and the token physicalist: the eliminativist, the identity theorist and the functionalist all agree that mental items are, *if anything*, real inner causal states of people. They disagree only on the empirical question of whether any real neurophysiological states of people do in fact answer to the common-sensical mental categories of 'folk psychology'. Eliminativists praise identity theorists and functionalists for their forthright willingness to step up and take their empirical shot. Both eliminativists and token physicalists scorn the instrumentalist's sleazy evasion. (But eliminativists agree with instrumentalists that functionalism is a pipe-dream, and functionalists agree with instrumentalists that mental ascriptions are often true and obviously so. The three views form an Eternal Triangle of a not uncommon sort.)

Paul Feyerabend (1963a, 1963b) was the first to argue openly that the mental categories of folk psychology simply fail to capture anything in physical reality and that everyday mental ascriptions were therefore false. (Rorty (1965) took a notoriously eliminativist line also, but, following Sellars (1963), tried to soften its nihilism; Lycan and Pappas (1972) argued that the softening served only to collapse Rorty's position into incoherence.) Feyerabend attracted no great following, presumably because of his view's outrageous flouting of common sense. But eliminativism was resurrected by Paul Churchland (1981) and others, and defended in more detail.

Churchland argues mainly from the poverty of 'folk psychology'; he claims that historically, when other primitive theories such as alchemy have done as badly on scientific grounds as folk psychology has, they have been abandoned and rightly so. P. S. Churchland (1986) and Churchland and Sejnowski (1990) emphasize the comparative scientific reality and causal efficacy of neurobiological mechanisms: given the scientific excellence of neurophysiological explanation and the contrasting diffuseness and type-irreducibility of folk psychology, why should we suppose – even for a minute, much less automatically – that the platitudes of folk psychology express truths?

P. S. Churchland's intense interest in neuroscience and her distrust of the categories of folk psychology are matched within a sector of the AI community, in an equally intense upsurge of 'neural modelling'. In particular, what is called 'connectionism' or Parallel Distributed Processing ('PDP' for short; McClelland et al. 1986) has aroused much current interest as an AI research programme that diverges from the standard deployment of 'rules and representations' (as outlined in section 10 above) and from the idea of linear or monotonic theorem-proving from a pre-loaded database. PDP employs (although in practice it only simulates) an array of 'units', each being connected by ligatures to other units and each having an 'activation potential' that is directly affected by the potentials of adjoining units; the obvious, and intended, allusion is to the brain's neural nets. Some units are designated as inputs, others as outputs; the rest are 'hidden', and mysteriously regulate output when they are given input according to various algorithms. A major focus of PDP research is on *learning over time*; connectionist networks are good at learning pattern recognition tasks.

Connectionism is an engineering approach within AI. But the term has caught on among both psychologists and philosophers, and is now often used neologistically, as naming either (1) a psychological theory, roughly that such-and-such behavioural capacities are explained by connectionist architecture actually realized in organisms' brains; or (2) a philosophical contention reminiscent of Ryle (1949), roughly that intelligent human capacities, including thinking and rationality, are somehow holistically emergent from connectionist architecture in the brain rather than being a matter of the manipulation of internal beliefs or other representations according to rules.

Some philosophers take connectionism in one or another of its several senses to refute – or at least embarrass – the idea that human cognition is a matter of hosting internal representational states such as beliefs and desires; see particularly Churchland (1989) and Ramsey, Stich and Garon (1991). But, logically speaking, connectionism seems entirely compatible with representationalism (Smolensky 1988; Bechtel 1987), and arguably it is *an instance of* representationalism (Fodor and Pylyshyn 1988; Lycan 1991). The matter needs considerable further examination; see also Bechtel (1992).

13   The Status of 'Folk Psychology'

In the previous section we were introduced to the somewhat strange idea that mental terms and mental entities themselves are at risk. The idea that mental terms are the theoretical terms of a folk science – the 'theory' theory, as Morton (1980) calls it – was first urged by Sellars, Feyerabend and Quine in the 1960s. After an understandable period of incredulity, the 'theory' theory became widely accepted. But as we have seen, the 'theory' theory leads in a disconcerting direction. If the only reason we have for accepting the existence of mental entities is the utility and presumed truth of folk psychology, and if folk psychology should turn out to be largely *false* or seriously infirm in some other way (as scientific theories and especially folk theories often do), then presumably some version of eliminativism is correct.

We have already looked at some eliminativist arguments. In this section we shall turn to a special issue regarding propositional attitude content – the issue of *methodological solipsism* in Putnam's (1975) phrase – and examine its consequences for the cogency of folk psychology.

Suppose, for the sake of argument, that we attribute representational content to the internal states of computers – as in real life we do, however anthropomorphically. A computer sometimes thinks this or wants that; at the very least, it computes this or computes that, such as the GNP of Monaco, the outcome of a presidential election or the balance of our bank account.

Now, to take a key example of Fodor's (1980), it is quite possible that two computers, programmed by entirely different users for entirely different purposes, should happen to run physically in parallel. They might go through precisely the same sequence of electrical currents and flipflop settings and yet have their outputs interpreted differently by their respective users, especially if what they write to their screens is all in numerical form. One of them would naturally and correctly be described as figuring out the GNP of Monaco, while the other would just as naturally and correctly be described as figuring out the batting averages of the New York Yankees. The point, plain enough when we think about it, is simply that *what* a machine is computing is not fully determined by the physical or even the abstract-functional operations that are going on entirely inside the machine. What the machine is computing depends to some extent on something outside the machine itself – users' intentions, causal-historical chains (see sections 9 and 10 above), teleology, interpretation by observers or just the convenience of the beholder.

The point is not particularly surprising. But Putnam (1975) drew a broader conclusion, that was developed to startling effect by Fodor (1975) and by Stich (1983): as it is with computers, so it is with humans. The representational content of a human subject's propositional attitudes is underdetermined by even the total state inside that subject's head. As we noted in section 9 above, intentional properties are not determined by their subject's intrinsic molecular constitution.

194

The fact that attitude contents are 'wide' rather than 'narrow' raises serious problems about the vaunted role of propositional attitudes in the explaining of behaviour, and attendant methodological questions for psychology (Fodor 1980; Stich 1983). But for our purposes in this section, the main question is this: if the representational content of a propositional attitude depends on factors outside the physical boundary of its owner's skin, what are those factors, and more importantly, can we still suppose that the attitude contents are genuine properties of the owner-subject? The spectre of elimination reappears; perhaps it is not really, objectively true of people that they believe this or desire that.

The question of what the environmental factors are is just the question of psychosemantics again. But what about the ontological status of people's beliefs and desires themselves? There are several different possible positions:

(1) The external semantical interpretation of an organism's internal physical–functional states is entirely up for grabs: any interpretation that suits anyone's convenience is good enough, and if two interpreters' interpretations conflict, neither is correct to the exclusion of the other. (Schiffer (1981) discusses this possibility sympathetically, and construes Quine's (1960) famous doctrine of the 'indeterminacy of translation' as getting at this position.) If we fall in with this view, we can hardly call it a hard fact that a subject believes one thing rather than another.

(2) The semantical interpretation of beliefs is not up for grabs; it is at least loosely determined by various contextual factors, and some interpretations are correct while others are just wrong. But the contextual factors in question are intolerably vague and messy, and social and interest-infested, making them quite unsuitable for incorporation into any genuine science. To ascribe the belief that P to someone is no more scientific, explanatory or useful than is calling something 'nice'. (2) is the position of Stich (1983).

(3) The semantical interpretation of beliefs is loosely determined by various contextual factors, and some interpretations are correct while others are just wrong, and this is what it is for the subject to believe one thing rather than another. Some complex causal-historical and/or teleological feature of the subject's environment makes it objectively true that the subject believes so-and-so rather than such-and-such, whether or not the feature is scientifically interesting or well-behaved. (Lycan (1988) defends this view.)

(4) There is nothing messy, interest-relative or whatever, about the contextual factors in question, even though they extend outside the boundary of the skin. They are a matter of *simple* nomological or teleological fact. This position was endorsed by 'indicator' semanticists, among others.

(1) is essentially an eliminative view, and certainly flouts the folk-psychological thesis that propositional attitudes *qua* propositional attitudes are real causal constituents of the world. (2) allows that attitude ascriptions may be true (however interest-infested), so that people do believe one thing rather than another, but still rejects the folk-psychological view that the attitudes genuinely cause behaviour. (3) and (4) are entirely compatible with folk psychology. (2) and (3) differ from each

other, it seems, only in degree, so the real issue so far is that of whether (2) or (3) is more plausible.

There is a further and deeper issue. Even if we grant that (2) is true or even that (1) is true, why should we care about wide properties at all? What explanatory need do they fulfil? Surely it is only narrow properties that figure in the causal explanation of behaviour. Among others, Horgan and Woodward (1985), Burge (1986) and Fodor (1987) try to answer that deeper question; Devitt (1990) investigates further.

One may of course dispute the 'theory' theory itself as a thesis about mental concepts. Ryle (1949) and Wittgenstein (1953) staunchly opposed it before it had explicitly been formulated. More recent critics include Morton (1980), Malcolm (1984), Baker (1988), McDonough (1991) and Wilkes (1993).

Further Reading

Beakley and Ludlow (1992) offer classical and contemporary readings on the philosophy of mind. Block (1980) contains classic works on the mind–body problem in vol. 1, while vol. 2 takes up special topics, including the imagery debate, the philosophy of linguistics and innate ideas. Campbell (1984) provides a fine introduction to the mind–body problem. Churchland (1984) introduces the mind–body problem from the neurophilosophical point of view. Fodor (1968b) is a founding document of functionalism. Haugeland (1981) contains important papers from the 1970s on Artificial Intelligence. Lycan (1990, 1999) is the successor to Block (1980) and offers some general writings on the mind–body problem and some more specialized readings in the philosophy of cognitive science. Rosenthal (1991) contains classical and contemporary readings on mind and cognitive science.

References

Armstrong, D. M. 1968: *A Materialist Theory of the Mind*. London: Routledge and Kegan Paul.

Baker, L. R. 1988: *Saving Belief*. Princeton, NJ: Princeton University Press.

Beakley, B. and Ludlow, P. (eds) 1992: *The Philosophy of Mind*. Cambridge, MA: Bradford Books/MIT Press.

Bechtel, W. 1987: Connectionism and the Philosophy of Mind: An Overview. *Southern Journal of Philosophy*, 26 (supplement), 17–41. Reprinted in W. Lycan (ed.) 1990: *Mind and Cognition: A Reader*. Oxford: Blackwell.

——1992: The Case for Connectionism. *Philosophical Studies*, 71, 119–54. Reprinted in W. Lycan (ed.) 1999: *Mind and Cognition: An Anthology*. Oxford: Blackwell.

Bigelow, J. and Pargetter, R. 1987: Functions. *Journal of Philosophy*, 84, 181–96.

Block, N. J. 1978: Troubles with Functionalism. In W. Savage (ed.) *Minnesota Studies in the Philosophy of Science, Vol. 10: Perception and Cognition*. Minneapolis: University of Minnesota Press, 261–325. Excerpts reprinted in Lycan (1990, 1999).

——(ed.) 1980: *Readings in Philosophy of Psychology*, 2 vols. Cambridge, MA: Harvard University Press.

——1981: Psychologism and Behaviorism. *Philosophical Review*, 90, 5–43.

Block, N. J. and Fodor, J. A. 1972: What Psychological States are Not. *Philosophical Review*, 81, 159–81. Reprinted in Block (ed.) 1980: *Readings in Philosophy of Psychology*, 2 vols. Cambridge, MA: Harvard University Press.

Boorse, C. 1976: Wright on Functions. *Philosophical Review*, 85, 70–86.

Brentano, F. 1973 [1874]: *Philosophy from an Empirical Standpoint*. London: Routledge and Kegan Paul.

Burge, T. 1986: Individualism and Psychology. *Philosophical Review*, 95, 3–45.

Campbell, K. 1984: *Body and Mind*, 2nd edn. Notre Dame, IN: University of Notre Dame Press.

Carnap, R. 1932–3: Psychology in Physical Language. *Erkenntnis*, 3, 107–42. Excerpt reprinted in W. Lycan (ed.) 1990: *Mind and Cognition: A Reader*. Oxford: Blackwell.

Chalmers, D. 1996: *The Conscious Mind*. Oxford: Oxford University Press.

Chisholm, R. M. 1957: *Perceiving*. Ithaca, NY: Cornell University Press.

—— 1972: Contributions to 'The Chisholm–Sellars Correspondence on Intentionality'. In A. Marras (ed.) *Intentionality, Mind, and Language*. Urbana: University of Illinois Press.

Chomsky, N. 1959: Review of B. F. Skinner. [See Skinner 1957.] *Language*, 35, 26–57.

Churchland, P. M. 1981: Eliminative Materialism and the Propositional Attitudes. *Journal of Philosophy*, 78, 67–90. Reprinted in Churchland (1989) and in Lycan (1990, 1999).

—— 1984: *Matter and Consciousness*. Cambridge, MA: Bradford Books/MIT Press.

—— 1986: Some Reductive Strategies in Cognitive Neurobiology. *Mind*, 95, 279–309.

—— 1989: *A Neurocomputational Perspective*. Cambridge, MA: Bradford Books/MIT Press.

Churchland, P. S. 1986: *Neurophilosophy*. Cambridge, MA: Bradford Books/MIT Press.

Churchland, P. S. and Churchland, P. M. 1983: Stalking the Wild Epistemic Engine. *Noûs*, 17, 5–18.

Churchland, P. S. and Sejnowski, T. 1990: Neural Representation and Neural Computation. In W. Lycan (ed.) 1990: *Mind and Cognition: A Reader*. Oxford: Blackwell. Reprinted in Lycan (1999).

Clark, M. S. and Fiske, S. T. 1982: *Affect and Cognition*. Hillsdale, NJ: Lawrence Erlbaum Associates.

Cummins, R. 1975: Functional Analysis. *Journal of Philosophy*, 72, 741–64. Reprinted in N. J. Block (ed.) 1980: *Readings in Philosophy of Psychology*, 2 vols. Cambridge, MA: Harvard University Press.

—— 1983: The Nature of Psychological Explanation. Cambridge, MA: MIT Press/Bradford Books.

Davidson, D. 1970: Mental Events. In L. Foster and J. W. Swanson (eds) *Experience and Theory*. Amherst: University of Massachusetts Press. Reprinted in N. J. Block (ed.) 1980: *Readings in Philosophy of Psychology*, 2 vols. Cambridge, MA: Harvard University Press.

Dennett, D. C. 1978: *Brainstorms*. Montgomery, VT: Bradford Books.

—— 1981: Making Sense of Ourselves. *Philosophical Topics*, 12, 63–81. Reprinted in W. Lycan (ed.) 1990: *Mind and Cognition: A Reader*. Oxford: Blackwell.

—— 1987: *The Intentional Stance*. Cambridge, MA: Bradford Books/MIT Press.

—— 1988: Précis of *The Intentional Stance*. *Behavioral and Brain Sciences*, 11, 495–505.

—— 1991: Real Patterns. *Journal of Philosophy*, 88, 27–51.

Devitt, M. 1990: A Narrow Representational Theory of the Mind. In W. Lycan (ed.) 1990: *Mind and Cognition: A Reader*. Oxford: Blackwell. Reprinted in W. Lycan (ed.) 1999: *Mind and Cognition: An Anthology*. Oxford: Blackwell.

Devitt, M. and Sterelny, K. 1987: *Language and Reality*. Cambridge, MA: Bradford Books/MIT Press.

Dretske, F. 1981: *Knowledge and the Flow of Information*. Cambridge, MA: Bradford Books/MIT Press.

—— 1988: *Explaining Behavior*. Cambridge, MA: Bradford Books/MIT Press.

Dreyfus, H. L. 1979: *What Computers Can't Do*, 2nd edn. New York: Harper and Row.

Dreyfus, H. L. and Dreyfus, S. 1986: *Mind Over Machine*. New York: Free Press, Macmillan.

Farrell, B. A. 1950: Experience. *Mind*, 50, 170–98.

Feyerabend, P. 1963a: Materialism and the Mind–Body Problem. *Review of Metaphysics*, 17, 49–66.

—— 1963b: Mental Events and the Brain. *Journal of Philosophy*, 60, 295–6.

Field, H. 1978: Mental Representation. *Erkenntnis*, 13, 9–61.

Fodor, J. A. 1968a: The Appeal to Tacit Knowledge in Psychological Explanation. *Journal of Philosophy*, 65, 627–40.

—— 1968b: *Psychological Explanation*. New York: Random House.

—— 1975: *The Language of Thought*. New York: Thomas Y. Crowell.

—— 1980: Methodological Solipsism Considered as a Research Strategy in Cognitive Psychology. *Behavioral and Brain Sciences*, 3, 63–73.

—— 1981: *Representations*. Cambridge, MA: Bradford Books/MIT Press.

—— 1987: *Psychosemantics*. Cambridge, MA: Bradford Books/MIT Press.

—— 1990a: Psychosemantics. In W. Lycan (ed.) 1990: *Mind and Cognition: A Reader*. Oxford: Blackwell.

—— 1990b: *A Theory of Content*. Cambridge, MA: Bradford Books/MIT Press.

—— 1994: *The Elm and the Expert*. Cambridge, MA: Bradford Books/MIT Press.

Fodor, J. A. and Pylyshyn, Z. W. 1988: Connectionism and Cognitive Architecture: A Critical Analysis. *Cognition*, 28, 3–71.

Geach, P. 1957: *Mental Acts*. London: Routledge and Kegan Paul.

Gordon, R. M. 1987: *The Structure of Emotions*. Cambridge: Cambridge University Press.

Griffiths, P. 1997: *What Emotions Really Are*. Chicago: University of Chicago Press.

Gunderson, K. 1970: Asymmetries and Mind–Body Perplexities. In M. Radner and S. Winokur (eds) *Minnesota Studies in the Philosophy of Science, Vol. 4: Analyses of Theories and Methods of Physics and Psychology*. Minneapolis: University of Minnesota Press.

—— 1974: The Texture of Mentality. In R. Bambrough (ed.) *Wisdom: Twelve Essays*. Oxford: Oxford University Press.

Hart, W. D. 1988: *Engines of the Soul*. Cambridge: Cambridge University Press.

Haugeland, J. 1979: Understanding Natural Language. *Journal of Philosophy*, 76, 619–32. Reprinted in W. Lycan (ed.) 1990: *Mind and Cognition: A Reader*. Oxford: Blackwell.

—— (ed.) 1981: *Mind Design*. Cambridge, MA: Bradford Books/MIT Press.

Horgan, T. and Woodward, J. 1985: Folk Psychology is Here to Stay. *Philosophical Review*, 94, 197–226. Reprinted in Lycan (1990, 1999).

Jackson, F. 1977: *Perception*. Cambridge: Cambridge University Press.

—— 1982: Epiphenomenal Qualia. *Philosophical Quarterly*, 32, 127–36. Reprinted in Lycan (1990, 1999).

Kirk, R. 1974: Zombies vs. Materialists. *Aristotelian Society Supplementary Volume*, 48, 135–52.

Kripke, S. 1972: Naming and Necessity. In D. Davidson and G. Harman (eds) *Semantics of Natural Language*. Dordrecht: D. Reidel.

Levin, M. 1979: *Metaphysics and the Mind–Body Problem*. Oxford: Oxford University Press.

Levine, J. 1983: Materialism and Qualia: The Explanatory Gap. *Pacific Philosophical Quarterly*, 64, 354–61.

—— 1993: On Leaving Out What It's Like. In M. Davies and G. Humphreys (eds) *Consciousness*. Oxford: Blackwell.

Lewis, D. 1966: An Argument for the Identity Theory. *Journal of Philosophy*, 63, 17–25.

—— 1972: Psychophysical and Theoretical Identifications. *Australasian Journal of Philosophy*, 50, 249–58. Reprinted in N. J. Block (ed.) 1980: *Readings in Philosophy of Psychology*, 2 vols. Cambridge, MA: Harvard University Press.

—— 1980: Mad Pain and Martian Pain. In N. J. Block (ed.) *Readings in Philosophy of Psychology*, Vol. 1. Cambridge, MA: Harvard University Press.

Lycan, W. 1981: Form, Function, and Feel. *Journal of Philosophy*, 78, 24–50.

——1985: Abortion and the Civil Rights of Machines. In N. Potter and M. Timmons (eds) *Morality and Universality*. Dordrecht: D. Reidel.

——1987: *Consciousness*. Cambridge, MA: MIT Press/Bradford Books.

——1988: *Judgement and Justification*. Cambridge: Cambridge University Press.

——(ed.) 1990: *Mind and Cognition: A Reader*. Oxford: Blackwell.

——1991: Homuncular Functionalism meets PDP. In W. Ramsey, S. P. Stich and D. Rumelhart (eds) 1991: *Philosophy and Connectionist Theory*. Hillsdale, NJ: Lawrence Erlbaum Associates.

——1996: *Consciousness and Experience*. Cambridge, MA: MIT Press/Bradford Books.

——(ed.) 1999: *Mind and Cognition: An Anthology*. Oxford: Blackwell.

Lycan, W. and Pappas, G. 1972: What is Eliminative Materialism? *Australasian Journal of Philosophy*, 50, 149–59.

McClelland, J. L., Rumelhart, D. E. and the PDP Research Group 1986: *Parallel Distributed Processing: Explorations in the Microstructure of Cognition*. Cambridge, MA: Bradford Books/MIT Press.

McDonough, R. 1991: A Culturalist Account of Folk Psychology. In J. Greenwood (ed.) *The Future of Folk Psychology*. Cambridge: Cambridge University Press.

Malcolm, N. 1984: Consciousness and Causality. In D. Armstrong and N. Malcolm, *Consciousness and Causality: A Debate on the Nature of Mind*. Oxford: Blackwell.

Millikan, R. G. 1984: *Language, Thought, and Other Biological Categories*. Cambridge, MA: Bradford Books/MIT Press.

Morton, A. 1980: *Frames of Mind*. Oxford: Oxford University Press.

Nagel, T. 1974: What is it Like to be a Bat? *Philosophical Review*, 83, 435–50. Reprinted in N. J. Block (ed.) 1980: *Readings in Philosophy of Psychology*, 2 vols. Cambridge, MA: Harvard University Press.

Owens, J. 1986: The Failure of Lewis' Functionalism. *Philosophical Quarterly*, 36, 159–73.

Place U. T. 1956: Is Consciousness a Brain Process? *British Journal of Psychology*, 47, 44–50. Reprinted in Lycan (1990, 1999).

Putnam, H. 1960: Minds and Machines. In S. Hook (ed.) *Dimensions of Mind*. New York: Collier Books.

——1967a: The Mental Life of Some Machines. In H.-N. Castañeda (ed.) *Intentionality, Minds, and Perception*. Detroit, MI: Wayne State University Press.

——1967b: Psychological Predicates. In W. H. Capitan and D. Merrill (eds) *Art, Mind, and Religion*. Pittsburgh, PA: University of Pittsburgh Press. Reprinted under the title 'The Nature of Mental States' in N. J. Block (ed.) 1980: *Readings in Philosophy of Psychology*, 2 vols. Cambridge, MA: Harvard University Press.

——1975: The Meaning of 'Meaning'. In K. Gunderson (ed.) *Minnesota Studies in the Philosophy of Science, Vol. 7: Language, Mind and Knowledge*. Minneapolis: University of Minnesota Press.

Quine, W. V. O. 1960: *Word and Object*. Cambridge, MA: MIT Press.

Ramsey, W., Stich, S. P. and Garon, J. 1991: Connectionism, Eliminativism, and the Future of Folk Psychology. In W. Ramsey, S. P. Stich and D. Rumelhart (eds) 1991: *Philosophy and Connectionist Theory*. Hillsdale, NJ: Lawrence Erlbaum Associates.

Ramsey, W., Stich, S. P. and Rumelhart, D. (eds) 1991: *Philosophy and Connectionist Theory*. Hillsdale, NJ: Lawrence Erlbaum Associates.

Rey, G. 1980: Functionalism and the Emotions. In A. O. Rorty (ed.) 1980): *Explaining Emotions*. Berkeley and Los Angeles: University of California Press.

Robinson, W. S. 1988: *Brains and People*. Philadelphia, PA: Temple University Press.

Rorty, A. O. (ed.) 1980: *Explaining Emotions*. Berkeley and Los Angeles: University of California Press.

Rorty, R. 1965: Mind–Body Identity, Privacy, and Categories. *Review of Metaphysics*, 19.

Rosenthal, D. (ed.) 1991: *The Nature of Mind*. Oxford: Oxford University Press.

Ryle, G. 1949: *The Concept of Mind*. New York: Barnes and Noble.

Scherer, K. R. and Ekman, P. 1984: *Approaches to Emotion*. Hillsdale, NJ: Lawrence Erlbaum Associates.

Schiffer, S. 1981: Truth and the Theory of Content. In H. Parret and J. Bouveresse (eds) *Meaning and Understanding*. Berlin: Walter de Gruyter.

Searle, J. 1980: Minds, Brains and Programs. *Behavioral and Brain Sciences*, 3, 417–24.

Sellars, W. 1963: *Science, Perception and Reality*. London: Routledge and Kegan Paul.

Shoemaker, S. 1981: Some Varieties of Functionalism. *Philosophical Topics*, 12, 93–119.

Skinner, B. F. 1957: *Verbal Behavior*. New York: Appleton–Century–Crofts.

Smart, J. J. C. 1959: Sensations and Brain Processes. *Philosophical Review*, 68, 141–56.

——1963: *Philosophy and Scientific Realism*. London: Routledge and Kegan Paul.

Smolensky, P. 1988: On the Proper Treatment of Connectionism. *Behavioral and Brain Sciences*, 11, 1–23.

Sober, E. 1985: Panglossian Functionalism and the Philosophy of Mind. *Synthèse*, 64, 165–93. Revised excerpt reprinted in Lycan (1990, 1999) under the title 'Putting the Function Back Into Functionalism'.

Solomon, R. 1977: *The Passions*. New York: Doubleday.

Stalnaker, R. 1984: *Inquiry*. Cambridge, MA: Bradford Books/MIT Press.

Stich, S. 1978: Autonomous Psychology and the Belief–Desire Thesis. *Monist*, 61, 573–91. Reprinted in W. Lycan (ed.) 1990: *Mind and Cognition: A Reader*. Oxford: Blackwell.

——1981: Dennett on Intentional Systems. *Philosophical Topics*, 12, 39–62. Reprinted in Lycan (1990, 1999).

——1983: *From Folk Psychology to Cognitive Science*. Cambridge, MA: Bradford Books/MIT Press.

Strawson, G. 1994: *Mental Reality*. Cambridge, MA: Bradford Books/MIT Press.

Turing, A. 1964: Computing Machinery and Intelligence. In A. R. Anderson (ed.) *Minds and Machines*. Englewood Cliffs, NJ: Prentice-Hall.

Tye, M. 1983: Functionalism and Type Physicalism. *Philosophical Studies*, 44, 161–74.

Van Gulick, R. 1980: Functionalism, Information, and Content. *Nature and System*, 2, 139–62.

Wilkes, K. 1993: The Relationship Between Scientific and Common Sense Psychology. In S. Christensen and D. Turner (eds) *Folk Psychology and the Philosophy of Mind*. Hillsdale, NJ: Lawrence Erlbaum Associates.

Wimsatt, W. 1972: Teleology and the Logical Structure of Function Statements. *Studies in History and Philosophy of Science*, 3, 1–80.

Wittgenstein, L. 1953: *Philosophical Investigations* (translated by G. E. M. Anscombe). New York: Macmillan.

Wright, L. 1973: Functions. *Philosophical Review*, 82, 139–68.

Discussion Questions

1 If minds are immaterial and non-spatial, how can they interact with bodies?

2 Could the success of neurophysiology eliminate the mind from explanations of what we do?

3 To what extent should the philosophy of mind be constrained by our current view of science?

4 If a machine could pass the Turing Test, what would be the consequences for the philosophy of mind?

5 When you see a red object, could you have the sort of colour experience I have when I see a green object, and vice versa?

6   Are mental states and events identical with states and events in our central nervous systems? What notion of identity is involved in this claim?

7   Are mental terms defined causally?

8   Does an adequate account of the mind require distinct levels of description, all applied to the same fundamental reality?

9   How should cognitive psychology and philosophy of mind be related?

10   Does work in artificial intelligence help to answer philosophical questions about human intelligence?

11   Can human psychological capacities be entirely captured by a third-person, hardware-realizable design that could be built in a laboratory?

12   Could a human being's knowledge ever be completely formalized in a set of representations or rules?

13   Do we need a teleological notion of function for our account of the realization of psychological states and psychological explanation?

14   How can a mental state be about something? How can a mental state be about something which does not exist?

15   Can there be an adequate naturalistic analysis of teleological function?

16   Does functionalist metaphysics leave out the most important feature of the mental: what it feels like to be in a mental state of any certain sort?

17   If mental items are not necessarily identical with neurophysiological ones, can they be identical with them at all?

18   Can we explain consciousness?

19   If you have an after-image, does it show that functionalism is mistaken?

20   Do we know from the inside that we are not merely automata?

21   How is the representational content of a state of the brain determined?

22   If functional roles are 'narrow' and representational contexts are 'wide', can propositional attitudes be identified with functional roles?

23   Are intentional features semantic features?

24   What is a 'language of thought'? Can there be an adequate theory of thinking which denies that there is a language of thought?

25   Does the causal history of a mental item determine what that item refers to?

26   Can the ascription of beliefs and desires be objectively true, but not in virtue of describing causally active inner states of people?

27   To what extent does our ascription of beliefs and desires to people depend upon the assumption that people will generally believe and desire what they ought to believe and desire?

28   Does connectionism offer greater insight into philosophical problems than the standard 'rules and representations' model of artificial intelligence?

29   Are mental terms theoretical terms of a folk science? Should we be prepared to give them up in favour of the terms of a superior theory?

30   If the representational contents of a propositional attitude depend on external factors, are the contents genuine properties of the subject? What are the consequences of your answer for the ontological status of beliefs and desires?

6

Ethics

JOHN SKORUPSKI

In radically different ways, philosophers from Socrates to Wittgenstein have found in ethics a source of deep philosophical perplexity. Virtues, principles and consequences for human well-being have all been proposed as the most important focus of ethical understanding. Intertwined with these are concerns about rationality, impartiality and moral freedom. Philosophers have also asked questions about ethics: for example, if there are special moral facts, how could we know them; without such facts, what else could make ethical judgements true or false? This chapter considers general theories of ethical value as general theories of reasons for action, focusing on the powerful and illuminating utilitarian and Kantian contractarian theories. Readers will want to consult chapters on POLITICAL AND SOCIAL PHILOSOPHY *(chapter 8),* HUME *(chapter 31),* KANT *(chapter 32),* BENTHAM, MILL AND SIDGWICK *(chapter 35) and on* APPLIED ETHICS *(chapter 16),* BIOETHICS, GENETHICS AND MEDICAL ETHICS *(chapter 17),* ENVIRONMENTAL ETHICS *(chapter 18) and* BUSINESS ETHICS *(chapter 19). Chapters about several other historical figures contain discussions of their moral philosophy, and chapters on* EPISTEMOLOGY *(chapter 1),* METAPHYSICS *(chapter 2),* PHILOSOPHY OF MIND *(chapter 5),* AESTHETICS *(chapter 7) and* PHILOSOPHY OF RELIGION *(chapter 15) can help to understand issues raised here.*

1 The Scope of Ethics

Reflection about ethics has been a vital component of all the traditions of philosophizing that we know. China, Greece, India and medieval and modern Europe all asked basic ethical questions. What is the good? What makes a life a good life? What are the virtues of a human being? Is there one good, or one unified scheme of virtues? What duties do we have to each other or to ourselves? So far as we have records of non-literate cultures and their oral traditions, we find the same questions being asked there too.

They are philosophical questions if they examine moral habits and teachings in a reflective way. CLASSICAL GREECE (chapters 22 and 23) also moved to a second level of philosophical reflection: it asked questions about such questions. Can they have objective answers? If so, what kind of knowledge of these answers can we have? Are they matters of reason or feeling? These higher-order issues are often called *meta-ethical*. A striking feature of the Western tradition in philosophy is the urgency with which it has recurrently worried about them, from its Greek beginnings. And in this century meta-ethical questions have been pursued with an urgency and a perseverance never known before. We shall have to say something about meta-ethics as well as about ethical questions themselves.

But first, what is the scope of ethics as such? It does not deal with the whole domain of value. If I enquire into the beautiful or the sublime I am more likely to be doing AESTHETICS (chapter 7) than ethics, though my interest might certainly be ethical as well, in one way or another. Ethics, one may suggest, is concerned with *morality*, rather than with art. True, but it does not stand to morality quite as aesthetics stands to art. It has wider scope, since questions about the relations between morality and art belong to it, as do questions about the relations between morality and prudence or between morality and reason. So if I ask what makes a piece of music beautiful, or what makes a good tennis technique, I am not asking an ethical question, on even the widest sense of 'ethical'; but if I ask what place in my life, or in other people's lives, music or tennis, together with the skills and excellences proper to them, should have, then I am asking an ethical question. I can ask an ethical question about morality itself – what role in life should morality play? Ethical questions have a certain detachment and comprehensiveness which give them a governing role in the philosophy of value. Questions of PROFESSIONAL ETHICS (chapter 16) in business, medicine or journalism have a similar governing role, bearing on the nature of the profession, its place in social life and the consequent application of general ethical principles to it.

Ethical questions have this governing role because ethical enquiry is concerned quite generally with reasons for ACTION (pp. 734–6). Not all reasons are reasons to act. There are reasons to believe and reasons to feel: indeed, we deal in reasons at every turn. To be alive and awake is to be alive to reasons for believing, doing, feeling. You, for example, have reason to believe that I did not change the oil in your car; you have reason to feel irritated; you have reason to take action – to deduct something from my bill. Our evaluations of a person regularly turn on how that person responds or fails to respond to reasons in one or other of the three domains of belief, feeling and action. Personality is the manner of one's sensitivity to reasons in all three of them. An irritable person is more irritated than he or she has reason to be. A credulous person believes when there is insufficient reason to believe. A precipitate person acts when there is no reason to act.

Even at its widest, though, ethics does not deal with this whole normative domain of reasons. It does not deal with whether a conclusion is rightly or wrongly drawn from premises, with whether evidence is good or bad, or with what hypothesis we ought to adopt. Such questions are the province of LOGIC (chapter 4). Ethics in its widest sense stands to questions about what there is reason to do, as logic in its widest sense stands to questions about what there is reason to believe. It is the normative theory of conduct, as logic is the normative theory of belief. Through its concern with action and reasons for action ethics also becomes concerned with character, as it bears on action and reasons for action. (The word 'ethics' derives from the Greek *ethos*, which means 'character', or, in plural, 'manners'.) And, through that concern with character, it becomes concerned with questions about what there is reason to feel, and how reasons to feel connect with reasons to act. But the best way to make this clearer is to turn directly to some of the feelings with which ethics is concerned. Of these, three at least are fundamental: blame, admiration and desire.

2   Blame, Admiration and Desire

Blame is a central category of morality. So much so that one may characterize morality by reference to it. For we have many ways of disapproving of actions – holding an action morally wrong is only one. An action may be idiotic or tasteless, but not morally wrong. To call it morally wrong is a more serious matter. 'It was worse than immoral, it was tasteless', would be a quip, like Boulay de la Meurthe's comment (on the execution of the Duc d'Enghien) – 'It was worse than a crime, it was a mistake'. The quip could make a point, say in the spirit of Oscar Wilde, but it would do so precisely by paradox.

What is it then that marks the special disapproval or hostility conveyed in calling something morally wrong? To call the action morally wrong is to blame the agent. Blame is an act or attitude whose notional core is a feeling, in the way that feeling sorry is the notional core of apology – I mean that, even when the feeling is not actually present, it is nevertheless invoked in every act of apology or blame. Call this emotional core of blame 'the blame-feeling' – it disposes to punish, as feeling sorry disposes to make amends. Moreover, just as apologizing is already making amends to some degree, so public blame (and also self-blame in the form of guilt) already is a degree of punishment. This often makes people reluctant to 'apportion blame'. There is, it should be noted, a wider sense of the word 'blame', in which we may, for example, blame the car's faulty brakes for the accident – in other words, identify them as its relevant cause. But we certainly feel no similar reluctance to blame in that sense.

The relation between this wider and the narrower, moral, sense of blame is a fascinating and deep issue in ethics, but we must pass it by. Characterizing the morally wrong as the blameworthy in the narrow sense, we can say that the morally right is that which it would be morally wrong not to do. Similarly, we can say 'X is morally obligatory' or 'X morally ought to be done' will hold just if the non-performance of X is blameworthy. Of course it is true and important that we admire people for going beyond the morally obligatory – 'beyond the call of duty' – even though we do not blame them for not doing so. We can say that admiration of such actions is moral admiration, because we admire them for the reasons that impelled them, and those reasons are moral reasons. For example, lack of consideration for others' feelings, when it reaches a certain point, becomes blameworthy thoughtlessness. But there are degrees of care for others' feelings that go well beyond what we would expect, on pain of blame, from people in general, but which we still admire when we meet with them. (There are also excesses of solicitousness of course.) The outstandingly and the ordinarily thoughtful person are impelled by the same reasons – consideration for others' feelings. And we can say that those reasons are moral reasons – as against, say, prudential or aesthetic reasons, since their absence from a person's mind beyond a certain point becomes blameworthy.

Now for another important point: 'blameworthy' means 'ought to be blamed'. Is this 'ought' itself a moral 'ought'? No such circularity is involved, for as we have noticed 'ought' in general can be defined in terms of reasons – in this case reasons to adopt a feeling, or feeling-based attitude. To say that an action is blameworthy is to say that there is adequate reason, taking everything into account, to blame the agent for doing it.

This is a special case of a general pattern, in which we assess reasons for feeling an emotion. So with many other terms of appraisal – 'irritating', 'despicable', 'frightening', 'moving', 'tasteless' and so on. Two things seem to be involved in such appraisals: firstly, the appraiser, in typical cases, spontaneously feels the emotion and, secondly, he expects others to feel it. But a certain normativity is built in: he feels the emotion to be *appropriate*, and believes that other good judges will share it. 'I must say I was rather bored – but I was feeling tired and distracted, and I probably didn't understand what the point of it was.' So in this case I do not judge that it really was boring. I am disqualifying myself as a good judge. The internal criteria of appropriateness for such feelings can be debated with great exactness and subtlety, and the 'common pursuit of true judgement' in aesthetic or moral appraisal turns on such debate. Not that commitment to the thought that other judges, who suffer from no disqualifying defect or limitation, would confirm my judgement is special to the moral and the aesthetic: it is a general logical feature of judgement as such.

Judgements about the blameworthy or the admirable, then, are judgements about when it is reasonable to respond with blame or admiration. If the emotional core of *morality* is the blame-feeling, admiration is the feeling fundamental to systems of *ideals*. I have in mind the ideals of character and excellence which play so large a part in shaping the way we live our lives. It is all too easy for ethics to ignore them, for example by making an over-simple contrast between morality and prudence. Admiration for, and debate about, physical courage, style, 'cool', imagination, presence of mind, skill, wit, resourcefulness, sensitivity, fitness, good looks and many other such things drives a great part of life – and of criticism of ways of living. These are not moral valuations, though in some cases they shade into them. Whatever one feels about, for example, obtuseness, cravenness, leaden lack of style or clumsiness – perhaps contempt, derision, embarrassment or pity – it need not be the blame-feeling.

They are not prudential valuations either. Prudential valuations build on the notion of one's well-being, of what one should pursue as an end when one's own best INTERESTS (pp. 760–1) are exclusively in question. In this case the relevant affective core is neither admiration nor the blame-feeling, but desire. The well-being of an individual comprises whatever is found in itself desirable to that individual. And 'desirable' stands to what there is reason to desire as 'admirable' and 'blameworthy' stand to what there is reason to admire and blame.

Questions about what is desirable, for people in general or for a particular person, are questions about the ends of life. They are as much a matter of deliberation and debate as questions about what is admirable and blameworthy. When John Stuart MILL (chapter 35) argued that happiness is desirable because it is what people desire as an end 'in theory and in practice', he was not wasting his time. It is still less trivial that happiness, as he attempted to show, is the only thing desirable. Whether he was right or wrong about this, his method was sound. To reach a conclusion about what ends are intrinsically desirable I must try to reflect, without self-delusion, on what I desire and why – and if I find that I differ from others in my conclusions, I must ask whether my desires might yield to greater experience or knowledge and, indeed, whether my ideas about what those desires really are might not be distorted by personal ideals, conventional proprieties or just sheer wishful thinking.

Here too, then, there is a 'common pursuit of true judgement' – a reflective examination of one's own spontaneous feelings, carried out in dialogue with others who similarly examine theirs. But there is a difference. Though the pursuit may be common, the conclusion need not be, and is not likely to be, that what is desirable for me is just the same as what is desirable for you. Not only will different people differ on what makes them happy; they are also, despite Mill's suggestion to the contrary, quite likely to differ on how desirable happiness is to them, as against, say, knowledge, freedom or achievement. In contrast, suppose I find that many people are moved by a piece of music that I find cacophonous or dull, and that discussion and further listening does not lead me to find anything moving in it. I am unlikely (philosophical preconceptions aside) to conclude that it is 'moving to them' but not 'moving to me'. I may conclude, no doubt silently, that their appreciation is shallow – or with greater humility, that my own is. What is desirable for me may not be desirable for you – but aesthetic valuations do not naturally relativize in this way; moral valuations still less.

This difference certainly deserves further examination. (Distinctions are needed: for example, between particular objects that we desire – this oyster, a weekend in Vienna – and the categorial ends in virtue of which we desire them; or again, between wanting a thing and liking it when you get it.) Overall, however, it remains true that examination of one's own spontaneous responses, together with discussion with others, is the criterion of all valuation – including the aesthetic and the moral, and also the prudential. That is not to say that one can *define* an evaluative predicate – 'tedious', 'tasteless', 'desirable', 'delightful', 'kind' – in terms of the responses of good judges. However informed and sensitive such judges may be it is logically possible that they are wrong – that what strikes them as tasteless is not tasteless but innovative, and so on. Of course if 'good judges' are simply *defined* as 'judges who get it right', then it will be a logical truth that a thing is tedious just if good judges would find it so. But it will then be circular to define the tedious as that which good judges find tedious. Reflective agreement is, it is true, *ultimate*, in the sense that the only way of appealing against it is by forging a new reflective agreement – but it is never guaranteed to be *incorrigible*. Nor, when I judge that something is tasteless, am I judging that others will or would find it tasteless. My eye is on the object, not on what other people might think about the object.

3 Character, the Virtues and Freedom

How do virtues and vices fit into the picture that we have drawn? How, in particular, are they connected with blame, which we have made central to the notion of morality? They are connected in this way: they are traits of character which we could be *blamed* for not attempting to attain or lose. They are also connected in this way: they directly dispose to actions which are morally right or wrong. The various virtues involve spontaneous sensitivity to various types of reasons for acting, and the various vices similarly involve insensitivity to various types of reasons for acting.

This is not to say that we are blamed for our vices as such, as against our avoidable failures to resist them or to try to mend them. It is a basic principle that 'ought implies can' – that what I ought to do I can do. And it is also true that blame makes sense only in respect of that which ought not to have been done. So if I am in fact unable to mend my character then I cannot be blamed for failing to do so – though I can be blamed for not striving hard enough to resist its characteristic impulses on particular occasions.

This distinction, between changing my character and resisting its impulses, is a vital one to ordinary moral thought. I may be cruel, and I may not be able to do much to make myself less cruel; that is, to rid myself of those characteristic impulses to cruel acts. But I can still try to refrain from acting cruelly when I am tempted to. A person who has no control over his cruel actions is not just cruel but pathologically cruel. He does not, on this point at least, have the important kind of moral freedom that we attribute to anyone who we think of as a moral agent, and which we presuppose when we blame. Thus if I blame you for a cruel joke, for example, I assume you could have resisted the impulse to make it. If I become convinced that you are utterly unable to resist such impulses (even, say, when it is greatly to your personal advantage to do so) I am more likely to see you as mad, or at any rate as obsessed, than as bad.

This is the way in which moral freedom is presupposed in attributions of moral responsibility. It is rightly pointed out, for example, that the fact that I was free to do what I wanted to do does not suffice to show that I was morally free, because the want itself may have been so obsessive as to undermine my moral freedom. Drug addicts are not morally free even when they do what their craving compels them to do. They are the slaves of their addiction. Two kinds of thing may be happening here. Firstly, their craving may be so strong as to cloud their judgement – though there are good reasons for them to resist it, the craving itself stops them from seeing them. Secondly, the craving may not cloud their judgement, but it may impair their ability to act on it – they see clearly enough that they have good reason not to do what they crave to do, but they are unable to stop themselves.

In both these cases their moral freedom is attenuated, and their moral responsibility diminished. Thus if we suppose craving to have driven a person to some crime, then both cases, if established on the evidence, could reasonably be recognized by a judge as being, to some degree, extenuating. In general, moral freedom is a function of the total economy of one's character – the degree to which one's feelings are under the control of one's capacity to recognize reasons, instead of outrunning its control or even reducing or controlling the capacity itself. Moral freedom, so conceived, is one of the virtues, which a human being can have in greater or lesser degree. But it also has a special role in the economy of character: it is a precondition of moral agency as such, and it is facilitated by all the other virtues, since these are affective dispositions to act on particular kinds of good reasons. One can envisage, as a logical possibility, the person who sees the right clearly and, by great effort, is able to act on it, despite ever-present vicious impulses. But it is easier for one who has virtuous rather than vicious impulses in the first place to be morally free.

Moral freedom is rationality, understood as the capacity of rational self-government. This doctrine appears in PLATO's (chapter 23) conception of justice in the soul and has been continually reasserted in the Western ethical tradition. But if we are natural objects, whose behaviour is governed by causal laws, can we be in this sense morally free? This is the philosophical problem of 'free will and determinism'.

Free Will and Moral Freedom

Many philosophers have denied that, if our behaviour is governed by causal laws, we can be morally free. But others have seen no inconsistency. The issue is important for ethics, because blame, and thus morality, presuppose moral freedom. In particular, blame presupposes that the responsible agent could have refrained from acting on the motives which in fact he *did* act on – had there been reason to do so. In blaming, then, we judge that a person had the capacity to refrain – and the distinctions we make (is that person just a casual smoker or an addict?) seem not to turn at all on the truth or otherwise of any global thesis about causal determination of human behaviour. Before we blame an agent, we want to know, among other things, whether he could have refrained from doing what he did. In particular, we want to know whether he could have recognized the reasons for refraining, and refrained, given that his desires stood as they did. This is a question about his capacity of rational self-control. We are not asking whether a world is possible in which all the causes of his action stood as they did, and the action did not occur. If determinism is true, there is indeed no such world; but how does this bear on rational self-control, and thus on the issue of moral freedom?

Certainly a closer examination might yet show some connection. It is up to the philosopher who thinks that the truth of determinism would undermine moral freedom – the power of acting or not acting, according to the determinations of reason – to show what the connection is. There have been plenty of attempts to establish a connection. The resilience of the dispute bears witness to its intractability.

4   An Ethical Theory: The Case of Utilitarianism

We have spoken of how judgements about what is desirable, blameworthy and admirable are based on examination of one's feelings and discussion with others, and of how they ground the interacting value-spheres of prudence, morality and excellence in activity and character. But we have said nothing about how such judgements give us reason to act. Since ethics, on our account, is the general study of reasons for action, this important question is ethical.

One could say that ethical 'theory' simply consists of considered, thoughtful answers to it. Then it would hardly be controversial that there is such a thing. But it is controversial – because 'theory' suggests something more than a set of piecemeal and personal answers, however thoughtful. It promises system and objectivity, and many people doubt that answers to ethical questions can achieve those aims. Their doubts are not factious. By now in the history of ethics – in our world of ethical cultures which seem invincibly fragmented and disparate – they must be taken seriously. There is no point, however, in abstract claims and counter-claims about how ambitious ethical theory should be. We will make more progress by taking something which everyone agrees to be an ambitious ethical theory – UTILITARIANISM (chapter 35) – considering its structure and various objections to it, and asking, finally, when and in what way these become objections to 'ethical theory' as such. In this way we will see what difficulties face the idea of *system*; difficulties facing the idea of *objectivity* will be considered in section 11.

Utilitarianism is the thesis that the well-being of each and every individual has intrinsic ethical value, that the greater the well-being the greater its value, and that nothing else has intrinsic ethical value.

The phrase 'intrinsic ethical value' calls for explanation. Let us say that a property has ethical value if there is reason to do whatever is likely to produce or preserve it, increase its degree and so on. It has intrinsic ethical value if that reason consists just in the fact that the property *is* that property, and does not derive from any further facts about its connections with other properties. Why talk about 'properties'? The ethical value of objects and states of affairs, the reasons for acting that they give rise to, whether intrinsic or extrinsic, always seems to reside in something *about* them – they have value in virtue of features or properties that they have. Indeed this seems true for value of any kind: the value of a thing always stems from some feature or property that it has. A currently common way of putting it is to say that the value of a thing always supervenes on some properties that it has. If a certain value supervenes on some properties then anything which has just those properties will have just that value – a difference in value entails a difference in those properties.

For the utilitarian, the only thing that has intrinsic ethical value is a property of individuals, a property they can have to greater or lesser degree: that of being or faring well. The greater the well-being the greater the ethical value; that is, the greater the reason to produce or preserve it. Utilitarians will wish to spell out what well-being consists in. They will then have to consider what ends are desirable, by the method of self-examination and discussion considered in section 2. But our interest now is in the structure of the utilitarian view rather than its doctrine of what well-being, or 'utility', comprises.

The utilitarian holds that the ethical value of well-being is not affected by whose well-being it is – or at least that is true if the only individuals under consideration are human beings. But utilitarians have always freely granted that the well-being of all individuals which can be said to be sentient, or perhaps (if this is different) to have desires, should be taken into account. Now this is still a smaller class than that of individuals which can be said to have well-being at all. Living things in general can fare well or badly, and a green ethicist might hold that all such varieties of well-being have intrinsic ethical value. But utilitarians have not held that view, nor have they held that the well-being of all sentient individuals has equal ethical value. The well-being of non-human animals has an intrinsic ethical value, but it is not as great as that of human beings. Deep issues lurk here, not only for utilitarians, about what these differences of ethical value, as between the well-being of different types of individual, supervene upon.

At any rate, whatever the class of individuals whose well-being is to be taken into account, the utilitarian takes general well-being to be a positive function of the well-being of all of them, and of nothing else – a function in which the utility of every individual is taken impartially into account. Ethical value then consists in general well-being and in nothing else. But note that 'general well-being' is an abstraction constructed out of the well-being of concrete individuals. No 'general being' enjoys 'general well-being'. Only in the well-being of concrete individuals does ethical value, according to the utilitarian, really reside.

Classical utilitarianism is usually taken to hold that general well-being is fixed by the sum of the well-being of all individuals. Henry SIDGWICK (chapter 35), the third of the great trio of British utilitarians, suggested that it might also be taken as the average: that is, that the greatest ethical value is realized when average, rather than aggregate, well-being is at its highest. Either of these views assumes that one can add up the levels of well-being of different individuals – it assumes that that project makes *sense*, not that it can actually be done. The practical question of measurement becomes important if one wants to apply utilitarianism, for example in welfare economics. But even as a pure ethical theory classical utilitarianism does require that comparative questions like these are intelligible: would the increase in X's well-being offset the decrease in Y's? Would X's increase be greater than the loss of Y's and Z's?

They certainly sometimes make sense. I can ask myself whether a book will give greater pleasure to Kate or Julia. I can even ask myself whether Kate would get more pleasure out of this book than Julia and Anna would from two other books at half the price. Some very rough comparing and summing is going on there. The notion of a sum of well-being may be sufficiently well-defined in some areas, for some purposes, to be meaningful, even if it is not in all. We do seem to use it. But do such questions always – even in principle – make sense? And how important to utilitarianism is it that they always should?

John Stuart Mill would have conceded that they do not always make sense, for he thought that one can distinguish between quality and quantity of happiness. Happiness, he thought, was what well-being consists in, but some forms of happiness are 'higher' – or perhaps, deeper, truer or more valuable – in some way other than that in which having two chocolate ices is more valuable than having one. So perhaps there can be discontinuity here, in the sense that, in some contexts at least, a person may reasonably be unwilling to trade off a higher pleasure for any quantity of a lower one. He prefers the former to the latter but it will not make sense to say that he finds it n times as good. For if it did, he ought to be willing to sacrifice a particular higher experience for n or more of the lower ones. This at least gestures towards complications which are genuinely present in our thinking about what makes for a good life. We should certainly bear in mind that it may be intelligible to order possible states (perhaps only partially) by the level of well-being they produce, even if it is not generally possible to say what fraction the well-being in state X is of the well-being in state Y.

The utilitarian's basic idea was that considerations of well-being provide the only intrinsic reasons for action, and that in assessing the strength of such reasons one should consider impartially the well-being of all individuals affected. The only thing that this requires is that we should be able in principle to *order* distributions of well-being by their ethical value. Utilitarianism then holds that ethical value is a function of such distributions and of nothing else. It holds further that the function is positive: if the well-being of one or more individuals goes up, without any other change, then ethical value goes up. And finally it requires that the function be impartial. But what is involved in this notion of impartiality?

5 Impartiality

Maximizing the sum of individuals' well-being, if it makes sense to talk in this way at all, certainly looks impartial. No individual's well-being is given greater weight in the addition than that of any other. No one has his or her well-being multiplied by two or divided by three. This is one way of implementing the principle 'Everybody to count for one, nobody for more than one' – which in *Utilitarianism* Mill attributed to Bentham and which he took to express the principle of impartiality (Mill 1963, X: 257). He was, it should be noted, talking only of the well-being of humans – if non-humans are considered as well, as we noted in the previous section, it ceases to be so plausible that impartiality forbids weighting some individuals' well-being more heavily than others. That is a point about the connection between weighting and impartiality. But another point is that adding up – with or without weighting – is only one way of being impartial. Not only is Sidgwick's idea of maximizing the average of well-being equally impartial, so is a wide variety of other distributive principles.

Consider the DIFFERENCE PRINCIPLE (pp. 260–1) proposed by John Rawls. According to one version of this (Rawls 1972: 83), resources should be so distributed as to make the worst-off group of individuals as well-off as it is possible for them to be; after that, the next worst-off group should be made as well-off as possible, and so on up the scale. Rawls himself does not propose this principle as a comprehensive ethical theory. He presents it as an account of 'justice as fairness' in the POLITICAL (chapter 8) realm, an account with which he hopes people with a variety of comprehensive ethical views will be able to agree. But we could also treat it as a proposal about how impartiality should be understood in a comprehensive ethical theory, a proposal which would share with classical utilitarianism the feature that it takes ethical value to be a positive impartial function of individual well-being and of nothing else. Nor is it the only possible proposal which shares this feature with classical utilitarianism; there are many others.

The difference principle favours the worst off, in that it attaches an ethical priority to improvements in their well-being. But it can also be said to count everybody for one, nobody for more than one in this sense: it is indifferent to which concrete individual is under consideration. It takes account of no property of the individual other than his or her comparative well-being.

A distinctive feature of classical utilitarianism is that it takes an equal amount of well-being to be of equal ethical value, however it is distributed across individuals. This is not true of the difference principle, because a benefit to worse-off people will have greater ethical value than a benefit to the better-off. Note, however, that this contrast assumes that it *makes sense* to think of a given amount of well-being being distributed in various ways across individuals. Where it does not make sense to talk about moving about an equal amount of well-being it will not make sense to talk of summing or averaging either. The difference principle does not require that such talk should make sense, though it does require that we should be able to compare the *levels* of different individuals' well-being. Not that this is an ethical argument in its favour; it simply shows that as we get more sophisticated about what it makes sense to say, we will have to find subtler ways of implementing these competing distributive principles in competing welfare functions. But all of them are impartial.

How then should we understand the term 'utilitarianism' today? Critics have done their worst with it, and a case can certainly be made for burying it. But any other term, such as 'welfarism', is at least as misleading and open to distortion. And 'utilitarianism' has the merit of invoking a historically definite tradition. I suggest that we should interpret it *generically* – as naming a class of ethical theories, all of which hold that overall ethical value is some positive impartial function of individual well-being. On this weak definition, what I have called classical utilitarianism becomes a particular – and particularly simple – species of utilitarian ethical theory. 'Generic utilitarianism' generalizes it by allowing (1) distributive principles other than the aggregative principle of the classical utilitarians; and (2) different interpretations of well-being to the classical view of it as consisting exclusively of happiness. It generalizes in the way that is done when one shifts from the Euclidean paradigm of GEOMETRY (p. 348) to a class of geometries of which Euclid's is only one: by allowing certain axioms of the original theory to be varied. What distributive principle, and what account of human ends, to adopt remains open to debate among generic utilitarians.

6   What Can an Ethical Theory be Expected to Do?

Utilitarianism is a fully general theory of ethical value and so a fully general theory of reasons for acting. But two further elucidations are required.

The first is simply a reminder that there are non-ethical forms of value. Utilitarianism is a general theory of *ethical* value, not a general theory of value, so it does not have anything directly to say about those other forms. For example, what makes a piece of archeological evidence valuable is its bearing on archeological questions about the past, not its effect on general well-being. The value of the evidence lies in the reasons it gives for believing one thing rather than another: a general account of what makes evidence valuable is a task for the epistemologist, not the ethicist. Similarly, when we judge a piano recital to be superb – or dreary – we appeal to the internal standards of that activity, the aesthetics of piano-playing.

However, we can also ask, in one or another larger context, whether it is worth pursuing an admittedly valuable piece of evidence, or putting on a brilliant piano performance. The question might be, for example, whether we should fund the piano recital or the archeological dig. Consider a pianist who plays only for himself, or a desert-islander who pursues evidence about the history of the island that will never be known to others. The aesthetic value of the performance, like the archeological value of the evidence, is quite unrelated to how many people derive well-being from it. But if the utilitarian is right, how many people derive well-being from it is very relevant to its ethical value. If the pianist enjoys his piano-playing, that gives it ethical value. If others do too, that gives it even greater ethical value. Forms of non-ethical value are translated into reasons for action via their ethical value. The utilitarians do not reduce other forms of value to ethical value; they propound a substantive doctrine of what connection there is between the two. To say that great piano-playing should be pursued or funded for its own sake, irrespective of its contribution to well-being, is to adopt another doctrine, incompatible with utilitarianism.

212

The second elucidation can be made by distinguishing between a theory of ethical value and a theory of decision. Utilitarianism is a fully *general* theory of ethical value but that is not the same as saying that it is a fully developed one. It is concerned with intrinsic reasons for action and in that sense offers, as the classical utilitarians said, a 'test', or 'standard' or 'criterion' of conduct. But it is another question whether it can be developed into rules or procedures for deciding what to do. It does not follow directly from the utilitarian theory of ethical value that we should all, at every moment, follow the decision rule: 'do that action which produces greatest ethical value'. We may not know what action has greatest ethical value. It may be that attempts to follow such a decision rule would be highly counter-productive. And so on. A limiting possibility is that ethical value is greatest in a world in which no individual even believes that utilitarianism is true. In this case utilitarianism would be 'self-effacing'. It would itself imply that the best world is one in which it is not believed. These are not objections to utilitarianism. To say that utilitarianism is self-effacing is not to say that it's self-undermining.

Utilitarianism is not committed to the view that the morally right action is the optimal action – that is, the action that produces the greatest well-being, or even that 'optimal action' is in every situation even in principle well-defined. Not only is it consistent with utilitarianism to adopt the account of morality which I gave earlier, it is in fact the account that Mill himself gave. Our everyday moral thinking is by no means wholly impartial in the way the utilitarian theory of ethical value is. We believe that we have special obligations to some people because of the relation in which we stand to them – of kinship, neighbourliness, fellow-citizenship, contract. We believe that we have duties arising from our 'station in life'. We have very specific moral responses to our and others' actions in their context, responses which are certainly not pulled down from an ethical theory, utilitarian or any other.

But ethical theory need not claim that those responses are pulled down. We can recognize that they stem from spontaneous moral feelings, as discussed in section 2. Certainly utilitarianism is committed to this: where it can be shown that general well-being would be improved if a given way of doing things was changed, then it should be. That is what is meant by calling general well-being a test of conduct. Another ethical theory, such as contractualism (see section 9 below), would have the same commitment for the test of conduct which it favoured.

If we could never plausibly show, of any practice, that general well-being would be increased by changing it, then utilitarianism would have no cutting edge – though it could still be true. Similarly, if versions of generic utilitarianism differ in their distributive structure or their view of the ends of life but do not differ in what changes they recommend, then the distinction between them makes no practical difference.

Introducing a utilitarian standard in fact makes subtle but very important differences, as introducing standards of SCIENTIFIC METHOD (chapter 9) made to our beliefs about the world. In neither case, however, does the effect come through a 'linear' derivation, of moral rules from a welfare function, or of specific scientific hypotheses from canons of scientific method. In both cases the new or newly refined standards operate on an *existing* cosmological or moral tradition, changing it but doing so in a holistic and conserving way. 'Where it doesn't itch, don't scratch' is Quine's formula for this method of conservative holism. It applies to ethical method too.

Certainly the classical utilitarians sometimes talked in a 'linear' way, but they also had their conservative–holist moments. Mill particularly emphasized this element of conservative holism because he was responding to criticisms of Bentham and other early utilitarian radicals on precisely this point. Sidgwick then systematized the strategy at length. All this must be remembered if we are to avoid setting up over-simple contrasts between utilitarian and other views of morality.

The attraction of generic utilitarianism is two-fold. In the first place it seems perfectly possible to ask why one should obey a particular set of moral rules, say the Ten Commandments. If such responses as that they are self-evident or that they are laid down by a god seem unsatisfying, one reason at least is that we want to know the point or purpose of the rules. And once the question 'What purpose does this rule serve?' is accepted as proper, the generic utilitarian's answer, referring us to the standard of general well-being, is very compelling. To be told that adultery is wrong because of the hurt it causes, directly and through breakages of trust, is a bit more satisfying, though undoubtedly also a good deal more debatable, than to be told that its wrongness is self-evident or that it is forbidden in the Bible.

7   The Plurality of Value

One may ask about utilitarianism, or any ethical theory, what its credentials are. What sort of thing could show it to be correct? Where does it fit on the intellectual map?

Spontaneous impressions of when an emotion is in place, stabilized by self-examination and discussion, generate internal criteria governing its reasonableness – norms of right feeling. The same goes for epistemic norms, which consist in judgements about what there is reason to believe – norms of right belief.

These appraisals are entwined into our ends. Finding out about ancient cultures, for example – if that is your objective you should pay attention to valuable pieces of evidence. Even more obviously, if you want to play the piano well, you should be interested in what makes a performance musical, perceptive, moving.

But though they are in this way entwined in our ends, they do not tell us what our ends should be. Logic or archeological method tells you what evidence is important for getting at the truth about the ancient past, but neither method tells you that that ought to be your objective or that you ought to pursue the truth. Internal criteria tell you what performance is not merely technically accurate, but beautiful, insightful or profound. But they cannot tell you how much time to spend on it, or what resources to put to it.

Exactly the same, it would seem, must apply to the blameworthy – at least if we think of that as determined solely by the internal criteria of the blame-feeling. Such criteria will tell us what is 'morally right' or 'morally wrong', but not what reason we have to pursue the former and avoid the latter. Just as one could write a book about the The Art of the Pianist, or about Good Method in Archeology, without saying anything about how important these activities are compared to others, so one could write a book about The Art of Moral Goodness, without saying anything about how important it is to pursue moral goodness.

Some philosophers have argued as though these internal criteria proper to various types of activity and experience are the only ones we need. They would say that there is no space for what I have called the ethical question to arise. Is there really a question to be asked about why I should avoid doing what is morally wrong, shun boring or frightening situations, seek to achieve the qualities in myself that I find admirable in others?

Emotion can shape one's action through the links between emotion and desire, and desire and action. Guilt, boredom and fear are emotions that give rise to a desire to eliminate or avoid their object. Others, such as aesthetic delight, give rise to the opposite desire. But what are the connections at the level of reasons? Why should I avoid doing what is boring or blameworthy? Consider this: if a thing is boring (blameworthy) then there is reason not to do it. Is this a truth of logic? It does not seem so. The truth of logic is rather this: if a thing is boring (blameworthy) then boredom (blaming the person who does it) is an appropriate, justified, reasonable response. The logical connection is with norms of feeling rather than norms of action.

Doing things that are boring or blameworthy is likely to make one bored or guilty – states that most of us find unpleasant. And surely one has reason to avoid doing what is unpleasant. This last proposition is obvious enough, and makes the logical link with reasons for action. But it also gets us into the territory of ethical theory. For it is a normative proposition about reasons for action, and we can ask what its source is. But first there is an important point about the status of the moral to be considered.

A Special Status for Morality?

Morality is surely not on all fours with other norms of feeling. One can bring out the asymmetry, for example, in this way. If I honestly find a movie very boring I am quite likely to judge a person who does not find it boring rather unfavourably – perhaps as a pretty uncritical enthusiast. Or I may be led to question my own taste instead. But even if I remain convinced that the movie is boring, I can hardly argue that the *uncritical enthusiast* has reason to avoid it. He after all, uncritical fellow that he is, will enjoy it.

Can we take the same line about immoral, as against uncritical, people? If we did, we could still form an unfavourable assessment of someone who felt no guilt about doing something blameworthy – finding him shameless or blameworthy. But we could not claim that he had a reason to refrain from the immoral act.

There is no symmetry here. I should avoid doing something morally wrong because it is morally wrong, not because it will make me feel guilty, which is unpleasant. Even if it does not make me feel guilty, I still have reason not to do it. Consider a connoisseur of singing who sees that a particular piece of singing is beautiful but no longer gets anything out of it – the uninvolved connoisseur. He has no reason to attend the performance. Compare the uninvolved moral connoisseur – who sees what is right and wrong but no longer feels committed to it. He still has reason to do the right and avoid the wrong. It does not depend on how interested he feels. We want to maintain this ethical principle:

If X is morally wrong then there is reason not to do X.

And we do not think its truth depends on the holding of some further condition which may or may not obtain. For example, whether there is reason for me not to do the morally wrong does not depend on what my objectives are, or whether it will be unpleasant, or even on whether it will degrade my character. One may put this by saying that moral

> reasons are categorical, so the ethical principle may be called *the principle of moral categoricity*.
>
> It is by no means uncontroversial. It has been influentially denied by, among others, Phillipa Foot and Bernard Williams (Foot 1978: chs 7–14; Williams 1981: ch. 8). One could deny it on the grounds that moral reasons are not categorical, or more strongly, on the grounds that no reasons are. But if we endorse it we must conclude that moral norms cannot be grounded solely in spontaneous blame-feelings. They must also be responsive to ethical considerations.

Both sides in the dispute about moral categoricity must give some ethical account of when it is that one has reason to act. Two ideas can be put forward by those who deny moral categoricity:

(1)   You have reason to pursue what is good for you and avoid what is bad for you.
(2)   You have reason to do whatever will promote the objectives you have.

Reasons for acting morally will then depend on what is good for you or on what your objectives are. But where do these ideas come from? They seem to be products of rational reflection alone, just as much as is any other ethical doctrine about reasons for action. So, as well as the whole diverse range of emotion-based values that are *data* for ethical reflection, there seems to be something else, from which it stems: practical reason.

8   Practical Reason

Practical reason concerns reasons to act, as theoretical reason concerns reasons to believe. Since we have repeatedly distinguished between reasons to act, to believe and to *feel*, should we not expect a third division of reason, dealing with reasons to feel? It might be called 'aesthetic reason'.

If 'practical' and 'theoretical' reason were simply labels for the disposition to make judgements about reasons to act and reasons to believe, a tripartite division like that would be right. But no such term as 'aesthetic reason' is in common use. The reason is that 'practical' and 'theoretical reason' do not just label dispositions; they invoke a view about the source of those dispositions, the view that judgements about reasons to act and reasons to believe are exercises of *reason*. So the notion of 'aesthetic reason' limps. For though we constantly make judgements about what there is reason to feel, these judgements are not deliverances of *reason*. To say that they were would be to say that there are rationally evident principles specifically concerned with reasons to feel. Similarly, practical reason exists if there are rationally evident principles yielding reasons for action. And theoretical reason exists if there are rationally evident principles yielding reasons for belief. But, surely, in the case of feeling there are no such principles. We may be reasonable in our feelings, or unreasonable, but it is not rational insight into principles of right feeling that tells us so. In so far as reason comes in, it does so in its theoretical guise, through rational assessment of the beliefs which our feelings presuppose. Pascal said that the heart has its reasons which reason knows nothing of ('Le coeur a ses raisons que la raison ne connaît point': *Pensées*: iv, 277). He was speaking in a different context but his aphorism aptly fits the present point.

But is there such a thing as practical reason? We distinguish between reasonable and unreasonable feelings, even though there are no *a priori* principles of justified feeling. So does the distinction between reasonable and unreasonable action require that there be *a priori* principles of justified action? Come to that, does the distinction between reasonable and unreasonable beliefs require *a priori* principles of justified belief? We shall touch on this again in section 11. For the moment we simply note the contemporary tendency to group reasons to act with reasons to feel, rather than, as was traditional, with reasons to believe. It assumes, rightly or wrongly, that whereas rational belief does presuppose rationally evident principles of reasoning, rational action does not.

Idea (2) in the previous section is closely related to this, or a version of it. It says that a person has reasons for action only in relation to his objectives. The only concept of a reason for acting that we have is one that makes a reason a relation between an objective, an actor and an action, thus: there is reason for a person P whose objective is O to do X. That will hold when P's doing X is a way of bringing about O. How strong the reason is will depend on how effective doing X is – how probable it makes the achievement of O, and how much it impedes the achievement of P's other objectives. This may be called 'instrumentalism' (because it says that reason's only practical function is to select appropriate instruments for achieving objectives). Instrumentalism deflates practical reason into instrumental reason, but it does not deny that there are true reason-statements – only that there are true categorical ones. To hold that there are true categorical reason-statements is to take a more ambitious view of practical reason.

Among those who affirm the more ambitious view the most influential by far has been KANT (chapter 32). He held that some reasons for acting are categorical – in his terminology, categorical and not merely hypothetical imperatives. He also, very influentially, held that the only categorical reasons are moral reasons. But before considering Kant let us note some other ethical theories that must also accept the categorical nature of practical reason.

A reason for an actor to do something is categorical if it holds irrespective of that actor's objectives. This cuts a line between (1) and (2). For according to (1) you have reason to pursue what is good for you, irrespective of whether that is your objective. The person who holds that this is the *only* categorical reason for acting is the *rational egoist*. Because acting selfishly might be bad for you, rational egoists need not recommend selfishness in the usual sense. Their position is also distinct from the instrumentalist's. For what is meant by a person's objectives? The strictly instrumentalist view is that a person's objectives are those that a person in fact has, and which are basic rather than derived from more basic ones that that person in fact has. We are not talking about basic objectives that people would have if they had full rational insight, or wanted what reason tells them to want, and so on. These notions are not available to the instrumentalist. One might argue that instrumentalism itself must endorse at least one categorical principle – on pain of collapsing into pure scepticism about practical reason: 'You ought to do whatever will promote your objectives, irrespective of what they are'. It must indeed endorse that principle, but it is another question whether it has to see it as a substantial deliverance of reason (see section 11).

If it can deny that it is, then it can in that sense be said to reject all categorical principles of practical reason.

Utilitarians, like rational egoists, must accept a categorical principle of practical reason. They cannot be instrumentalists, for they are not just saying that *if* one's objective is to promote general good then one has reason to promote general good. Theirs is a fundamental thesis about ethical value. It says that one has reason to promote general good whether or not one wishes to. The well-being of every individual is a source of categorical reasons for every individual.

The contrast between categorical and instrumental conceptions of practical reason is a major watershed in ethics, and since utilitarianism is so often crudely lumped with instrumentalist notions of reason it is worth stressing that cogent utilitarianism, on the contrary, like Kantianism, falls on the categorical and not the instrumental side. That was clearer to Mill than Bentham, and clearer to Sidgwick than Mill. But let us now turn to Kant's ethical doctrine.

Kant thought the complete set of moral principles could be established by means of a test whose soundness is itself derived from pure reason. This test is the categorical imperative proper:

> Act as if the maxim of your action were to become through your will a universal law of nature.

When it is applied to any maxim of action it is supposed to determine in a clearcut way – and supposedly without appeal to any empirical data – whether that maxim is or is not a categorically binding moral principle. For Kant, the moral simply *is* the rational.

So much in Kant's ethics is momentous and deep that it is easy to forget, or to allow oneself to obscure, the quite incredible ambitiousness of this central doctrine, which is the backbone of the theory. It remains incredible, even when we notice the various ways in which Kant thinks 'anthropological' facts about humans and their circumstances shape the details of morality. One should not gloss over this incredibility, because Kant's greatness as a philosopher, when combined with it, has been ruinous for more defensible doctrines of practical reason, which have suffered collateral damage from the collapse of Kant's over-ambitious project. Because reason cannot have the monopoly in determining right and wrong which Kant, the great defender of reason, sought to give it, it is thought that it can play no part at all. An extreme form of ethical rationalism rebounds into extreme forms of ethical irrationalism. Hence it remains important to draw up an account of what in Kant's ethics must be jettisoned and what can be retained.

9   The Categorical Imperative and Contractualism

Critics on all sides in the nineteenth century (among others, Hegel, Mill, Schopenhauer and Nietzsche) pointed out that though Kant's substantive moral teaching has a very definite and distinctive content, his categorical imperative is too formal to yield any such substantive results. Consider the maxim, 'Break your promise when it is to your advantage to do so'. Kant suggests that it would be self-contradictory to suppose it a universal law, because if everyone complied with it there would be no such thing as 'promising'. As it stands, this is wrong: to get a contradiction one must add contingent, non-formal, assumptions, such as that it is generally known that everyone breaks their promise when it is to their advantage to do so. But this assumption is contingent.

Reason and Autonomy

Kant also requires that we should be able to *will* that the maxim be a universal LAW OF NATURE (pp. 645–8), and this has seemed a more promising line of thought. Can I really will that everyone should break their promise when it is to their advantage to do so? It is easy to be misled here. For Kant, the will in question must be a *purely* rational will: it is simply the moving force of pure reason. It cannot appeal to ends that we happen, contingently, to have. Kant certainly talks as though the will is determined by the mere idea of universal law, and this part of his doctrine does fall to his nineteenth-century critics. But he also, less explicitly, takes it that there are ends that pure reason requires us to have: *persons*, that is rational beings, are the only ends certifiable as intrinsic ends by pure reason alone. This leads him to another, for many people deeply resonant, version of the categorical imperative:

> Act in such a way that you always treat humanity, whether in your own person or in the person of another, never simply as a means, but always at the same time as an end.

Resonant as this is, it is not wholly clear. What is it to treat a person, a rational being, as an end? One view, which seems to be Kant's, is that it is to refrain from actions which impede others or oneself from the exercise of rationality. Now, for Kant, rationality is moral freedom (the notion we discussed in section 3) or, in his word, autonomy. This is one of the most impressive, as well as one of the most central, elements of Kant's moral philosophy. His view is that reason itself requires that we should respect, not infringe upon, the autonomy of beings which can be autonomous.

Kant's link between reason and autonomy is a substantial claim, but attempts to extract it from conjuring tricks on statements like 'reason itself requires that reason be respected' should be resisted. We do have a notion of rational autonomy (as emerged in section 3) and we do, I believe, think that rationally autonomous beings have special moral claims in virtue of their rationality. But we do not think, as Kantian doctrine would require, that only rational beings have moral claims, and we do not think that their only claim on us is respect for their rationality – in other words, abstention from anything that would impede or diminish their moral freedom. In any case, Kant's formalism prevents him from giving definite content to the notion of practical rationality. On his account, rationality consists in seeing what the universal law of reason requires, and this universal law says only that one should respect rationality: nothing in this tells us what respect for rationality, and hence rationality, requires. So in the end the charge of emptiness laid against Kant's categorical imperative stands.

The missing ingredient is the notion of an individual's good. It seems that Kant thought this notion inappropriately 'anthropological' for a purely rational end. However, the notion of an individual's good is not itself anthropological – only when we give an account of what the good *consists in for a human being* do we descend to anthropology. If we equip pure reason with the abstract notion of individual good, we can see various ways of combining it with the doctrine of rational will. For example, if rationality itself tells rational agents to pursue their good, they cannot rationally will that a maxim should be a universal law of nature, where such a law of nature would be to their disadvantage. Or we could take respect for persons to mean concern for their good, reading the categorical imperative as the injunction to treat the good of all persons as something to be promoted impartially. The good of individuals, conceived impartially, becomes the object of rational will, so that a maxim could be willed to be a universal law of nature, and thus adopted as a moral law, only if universal compliance with it would promote the general good.

Either way, we drop the Kantian idea that rationality itself is the only rational end, and substitute the non-Kantian idea that the good of individuals is the only rational end. So either of these developments, towards rational egoism or (if good is identified with well-being) towards utilitarianism, is a decisive break with Kant.

Let us consider a little further the first idea, which places the categorical imperative against a background of rational egoism. Can a rational egoist 'will' that 'Break your promises whenever it is to your advantage' should be a universal law?

Well, a rational egoist thinks it is a universal law of reason. But perhaps he or she cannot will it to be a universal 'law of nature', or something with which everyone always complies. It is not that such universal compliance would be inherently self-contradictory, as Kant thought; rather, it is that it looks likely to be to his disadvantage. And if it is likely to disadvantage him, he cannot will it, or do anything to bring it about. But suppose we modify Kant's test, as follows:

> Accept as a moral principle only that maxim which you can will to be a universal law of nature.

A rational egoist who endorses this test of moral principles will not accept the principle of breaking promises when it is advantageous to do so as a moral principle. On the contrary, since he can will that people should universally comply with their promises – it would be to his advantage if they did – he accepts 'Keep your promises' as a moral principle.

This modification of Kant's test for moral principles puts us on the road to contractualism. A form of contractualism which is quite close to it is the simple view that moral rules are those which rational egoists could 'agree' to – promote as public rules of conduct. Another modification replaces rational egoism by instrumentalism – moral rules are those to which instrumentally rational agents could agree. This moves another step away from Kant, since it appears to drop the idea that there are any categorically rational principles, egoistic or other – but, by the same token, it appears to some as attractively hard-headed.

Though these forms of contractualism have been influential in recent moral and political philosophy, they have a straightforward and pretty unappetizing corollary: one has reason to obey a moral principle only if it is to one's advantage to do so, or if it promotes one's objectives to do so. The egoist or instrumentalist construction of morality can give me reason to seek, in whatever way I can, to influence people into accepting various 'moral' precepts, but it does not give me reason (even in cases like the PRISONER'S DILEMMA (pp. 393–5)) to act in accordance with those moral precepts myself when it is to my advantage, or promotes my objectives, not to do so. If one accepts the principle of moral categoricity considered in section 7, such a conclusion must be rejected, and with it the theory that gives rise to it.

Another recent form of contractualism is closer in spirit to Kant. The Kantian idea of treating persons as ends can be read as requiring that we do not take unfair advantage of them, and a contractualist view of morality based on this reading can treat moral rules as those which could be willed by a reasonable person – one who pursues his or her well-being or objectives while accepting that all must have an equally fair chance to do so. The rules of morality are rules which no reasonable person would reject. Thomas Scanlon (1982) provides an influential defence of this view. I will call it Kantian contractualism, though its affinity to Kant's ethics is a matter for scholarly debate which will not be pursued here.

A Comparison

Since Kantian contractualism is often presented as an alternative to utilitarianism, it is worth considering the similarities and differences between the two ethical theories. And here the proper basis for comparison is with generic utilitarianism, rather than classical aggregative utilitarianism in particular.

Both recognize impartiality, or 'fairness', as a categorical ethical principle located outside morality – so they both diverge from pure instrumentalism and pure egoism. Moral principles, for the Kantian contractualist, are those compliance with which would advantage all in a fair manner, a manner which respects their dignity as persons. In particular, they would be the sub-group of such principles which we could agree to sanction by penalties of blame for non-compliance. Now should these principles simply establish constraints of fairness, rather minimally conceived – a level playing-field for competition among individuals who pursue their own ends? Or does Kantian contractualism lead us to something stronger – a maximizing principle of justice such as Rawls's difference principle?

The upshot of this stronger option would be a test of conduct coextensive with one or another version of generic utilitarianism. Kantian contractualists would say that their way of setting up the test, by reference to a hypothetical agreement, is likely to lead away from the classical utilitarians' views of impartiality, which allow some individuals to be disadvantaged 'unreasonably' for the sake of offsetting advantages to others. They may be right in this. But it remains debatable whether the right objection to classical utilitarianism's aggregative principle is that it is unfair. It may be unreasonable, in the way that applying similar aggregative principles of distribution within one's own life (allowing some period of one's life to fall to limitlessly increasing depths of misery for the sake of compensating advantages in other periods) may seem unreasonable. But in the latter case the unreasonableness is not connected with unfairness.

On the whole Kantian contractualism looks much closer to generic utilitarianism than to the egoistic or instrumentalist forms of contractualism with which we started. The utilitarian principle is strictly agent-neutral, in that it assigns value to the well-being of an individual irrespective of that individual's relation to the agent who is deliberating. Kantian contractualism, likewise, appeals to an agent-neutral principle of fairness. The reason I should do what is morally right is that it would be unfair not to do so. Whether or not the notion of fairness can ultimately carry this weight, it is at least clear that there is no pretence here of founding morality or justice on pure egoism or instrumentalism. Nor is there any attempt to get a substantive theory of the right from purely formal considerations, as Kant sometimes gives the impression of trying to do. Both generic utilitarianism and Kantian contractualism are committed to the view that there are principles of practical reason that are categorical but not merely formal.

10   Reason, Morality and Religion

Some people feel that to distinguish between reason and morality, as utilitarianism and contractualism do, is to draw an invidious line. Moral judgements, they feel, are rationally evident in their own right. Moral life has its own internal rationality. The idea that criteria of practical reason stand outside it alienates us from it.

If the utilitarian or the contractualist view alienate us from morality, that is a lamentable consequence but not an objection to their truth. The philosophical question has to centre on whether moral judgements are indeed, contrary to utilitarians and contractualists, evident in their own right. That they are so is the view of the moral intuitionist. I use this term here simply to name the view that certain moral judgements are rationally evident in their own right, without assuming any particular epistemological account of what it is for something to be rationally evident.

We have already seen that judgements about what is admirable or blameworthy, like other judgements about what it is reasonable to feel, have an internal discipline based on reflection about one's spontaneous feelings and discussion with others. But this internal discipline does not itself connect them with reasons for action; still less could it underwrite the principle of moral categoricity (see sections 2 and 7).

For the moral intuitionist, the truth or otherwise of moral judgements is known directly by purely rational reflection. This in itself still does not show why the fact that something is morally wrong – which, by the intuitionist's hypothesis, I know through pure rational reflection – gives me reason not to do it. But if the intuitionist gives pure rational reflection as big a role as this, he is hardly upping the stakes very much if he adds that I also know that I have reason not to do what is morally wrong by pure rational reflection.

Utilitarians or contractualists who grant the principle of moral categoricity cannot be as direct about it as that. They must, rather, derive the categoricity of moral reasons from the ethical principles that they hold to be primitively categorical – the general good, or fairness. Moral reasons, they can say, are those reasons for action that, given human circumstance, people should observe and should incur blame for failing to observe. If they are conservative holists (section 6) they will not claim to derive them in a linear way from their ethical criteria, but will feel free to ground them in our spontaneous dispositions to blame. In other words, they will accept that the guidance for action and evaluation given by these dispositions is legitimate in the absence of a well-made case against it; but they will insist that it *is* corrigible by a well-made case based on their preferred ethical criterion.

Their criticism of the intuitionist will be that the latter confuses spontaneous judgements about what is admirable and blameworthy with purely rational intuitions. That is a purely philosophical criticism and to my mind a very powerful one. If I examine my responses I find emotions that give rise to judgements about the admirable and the blameworthy, but I find no detailed purely rational intuitions. It is not reason that directly tells me, in concrete circumstances, whether to tell a lie to save a friend. And the utilitarian or contractual theorist can go on to draw a social consequence. When a spontaneous response of admiration and blame get transmuted in this way into a supposed rational intuition, he or she may say – with no appeal allowed to a higher court of ethical judgement, no standard of rational criticism independent of our feelings of admiration and blame – then an important source for regenerating morality is lost. Where those feelings strongly cluster around something, for example feelings of blame around homosexuality, or feelings of admiration around certain kinds of male domineering, we cannot detach from those feelings, stand back, and ask what is wrong with homosexuality or how much we really want that kind of leadership of the pack to be admired. I am not saying that this is a compelling criticism, since intuitionists can reply, firstly, that the question against them has been begged when what they claim to be rational moral intuitions are treated as feelings of admiration and blame; and, secondly, that these intuitions can be criticized from within, when they come into conflict with each other, without any appeal to an 'external' ethical criterion.

Certainly the question whether there are such rational intuitions is philosophically the basic one. The case against is simply that reason does not give us detailed moral responses. Of course the detaching language of the utilitarian or the contractualist has its own dangers, of estrangement from our moral legacy and manipulative social engineering. Ideally we would have a standard of rational criticism which yet somehow lay within morality, and did not treat it as an object. That is one of the most powerful attractions of Kant's ethics. The categorical imperative promised to give a standard of rational criticism which fulfilled this ideal. But it turned out to be empty unless it smuggled in ethical principles of fairness or general well-being, or covertly converted moral feelings into deliverances of pure reason.

Human reason and human moral feelings could be fully integrated if both flowed from some source wiser than the human. Here is a route from morality to religion which has real power for many people. If both reason and moral feeling are implanted in us as responses to the moral law laid down by GOD (chapter 15), then we could safely stay within the circle of morality without being forced into a chilly external standpoint in which reason could come into conflict with sentiments transmitted by tradition.

But two great difficulties stand in the way of this thought. The first is that any argument of this shape – something which is ethically or otherwise desirable can be guaranteed to exist only if God does, so God exists – is invalid. We have no reason to suppose that the world is as it is desirable that it should be. Some independent argument is needed to establish the existence of a wise and benevolent divinity.

The second difficulty has to do with the autonomy of good. In Plato's *Euthyphro* (1961: 10a) Socrates asks 'whether the pious or holy is beloved by the gods because it is holy, or holy because it is beloved of the gods'. One can similarly ask whether the morally good is so because it is commanded by God, or commanded by God because it is morally good. Not a few religious believers cleave to the first answer. So do some atheists: it is implicitly assumed in Nietzsche's assertion that 'God is dead' (Nietzsche 1974: section 125), though Nietzsche played with the fantasy that, after the death of God, new values, beyond moral good and evil, could be created by the imposition of sufficiently forceful human will.

But this voluntarism, theological or Nietzschean, is incompatible with the categoricity of morality. If morality is the command of God, it makes perfectly good sense to ask what reason I have to obey it. Punishment and reward in the after-life, it may be said, give me a self-interested reason. To offer that as the only answer is to propose a pretty shabby philosophy of life; but setting aside its shabbiness consider its logic. I have that reason because my well-being gives me reason to act. But that locates categorical reason outside morality. We must still accept a categorical reason, independent of the command of God, and on this approach we have simply succeeded in locating it in egoism rather than morality. This is the God-assisted transition from rational egoism to morality. And note that we have attached no meaning to 'God is good' other than (perhaps) 'God obeys God's commands'. The same logical points also apply to motives for obeying God's law that are not shabby – love of God, as well as fear of hell.

The other response, in which God's goodness consists in his *recognition* of the good, seems much sounder. It recognizes the autonomy of good and in general the autonomy of reasons. The theist can argue that a benevolent God has implanted our MORAL SENTIMENTS (pp. 716–17) in us as reliable guides to the good, and that gives the theist a way of being reconciled with them. It is consistent with this to hold that the good is something autonomous, independent of God's will, and independently recognizable by us.

This was the view of Kant, one of the great proponents of the autonomy of reason:

Even the Holy One of the gospel must first be compared to our ideal of moral perfection before we can recognize him as such . . . where do we get our concept of God as the highest good? Solely from the Idea of moral perfection which reason traces *a priori*. (Kant 1964: 29)

If the good is categorical it is autonomous, and if it is autonomous then it is transparent to rational beings. God's power and knowledge may allow him to implant reliable rules of conduct in us, but it does not give him greater insight into its *a priori* structure.

Once reason has been isolated in this way, a question remains about its power to inspire. One can love God, but can one love impartial practical reason? Does it make one love virtue? Can one rise above self-interest and limited sympathy without becoming desiccated, if one has no emotional medium in which to do it?

Virtue is naturally loveable, because it is based on what we spontaneously admire. Moral example can make us love the good of others. But is it not likely that only a religious or spiritual perspective can solidly and reliably make us see others' well-being as of no more or less account than our own? Well, even if the thought that there is nothing special about me is given to me by reason, it can still be a moving and liberating experience. If one wishes to call it a spiritual experience, so be it. But it need involve no theistic framework.

224

We must turn finally to the promised meta-ethical discussion: if judgements about reasons are autonomous, what justifies us in making them and what makes them right or wrong?

11   Meta-ethics

The judgements we make about our reasons to act, believe or feel, may be called 'normative' judgements. It is illuminating to keep them all in mind, even though our concern is meta-ethical. For questions which are often asked about the status of ethical judgements in particular can usually be raised in general, about all of them. One can ask about all normative judgements, not just the ethical ones, whether they can be assessed as true or false, correct or incorrect; and if they can be, what makes them so, and how we know them to be so.

Framed in this way, the questions go to the heartland of philosophy. Only the roughest sketch map of its geography can be provided here. Consider to begin with, then, this very common question: are normative judgements, or can they be, 'objective'?

The word is virtually irresistible – and virtually guaranteed to sow confusion. It sounds as though its opposite ought to be 'subjective'; but as soon as we are pressed on the matter we find that we really have no notion of what a 'subjective judgement' might be.

What causes our embarrassment here? A judgement must have a CONTENT (pp. 843–5): one judges that something is so; one can also suppose it to be so, wonder whether it is, hope that it is, and so on. To *judge* that it is so is to judge the proposition that it is so correct. In other words, if there is no proposition – no content of judgement to be judged correct or incorrect – there is no scope for judgement. The very notion of judgement requires a distinction between the act of judging and its content, the proposition which is judged correct or incorrect. But that distinction is available only if we are also able to separate in principle between what seems to the judger to be so, or to be correct, and what is so, or what is correct. It must be *possible* that what seems to the judger to be so is not so. And this possibility supplies objectivity: an objective discourse is one for which it can be maintained. If it cannot be maintained, there is no scope for objectivity – but neither is there scope for judgement. What we should really be asking, when we ask whether normative judgements are objective, is simply whether they are genuine judgements at all. It was just this question that David HUME (chapter 31) answered in the negative, for the moral case, when he said that 'Morality . . . is more properly felt than judg'd of' (Hume 1978: 470).

Hume allowed for propositions, and hence judgements, such as 'All fathers are parents', which in his terminology merely express 'relations of ideas'. We may say that they are true by definition. These cases apart, however, he took propositions to be *factual* – their truth depended on whether or not they corresponded to facts. (The notion of truth by definition certainly requires very careful examination, but we need not delve into it here: if there are no such truths Hume's thesis would simply be that *all* propositions are factual.)

It is not easy to fit normative propositions in general into either of Hume's categories. A normative proposition looks like this:

If *p* then there is reason to believe, do or feel so-and-so.

For example:

(1)   If the available data are deducible from hypothesis H and no other hypothesis available to us is simpler than H then there is some reason for us to believe H.

(2)   If action A promotes someone's well-being then there is reason for me to do A.

It is not plausible that propositions of this kind are true by definition. (What definition? Of what word or words?) So if propositions are either true by definition or factual, they must be factual – or not genuine propositions, despite appearances.

Hume himself thought they could not be regarded as factual and he was clear that this conclusion applied to *all* supposed normative 'propositions', not just ethical ones. There are a number of routes to this conclusion. The simplest is the sheer implausibility of fitting the correspondence theory of truth to such purported propositions as (1) and (2). To what fact, in what domain of reality, would the truth of (1) correspond? Is it some fact of meta- or ultra-physics, beyond the facts of physics? The same question applies to (2). The fact that doing A would promote someone's well-being gives me reason to do A: are we to regard that as a *further* fact? A somewhat expanded version of this line of thought, which we may call (with a sideways glance in Kant's direction) the thesis of the autonomy of norms, stresses that cognition is of facts and reasons, so that the dualism of fact and norm is inherent to it. Facts 'in the world' give reasons; but *this* cannot itself be a fact in the world. No fact can correspond to a normative proposition, about what there is reason to believe, do or feel.

The point can also be developed EPISTEMOLOGICALLY (chapter 1) by appeal to the empiricist thesis that a factual proposition can only be known *a posteriori*, by empirical enquiry. How else could I establish the existence of a fact independent of my judgement, yet corresponding to its content? But normative propositions are not known by empirical enquiry. Indeed, they are – in the particular case of propositions about what gives me reason to believe what – *presupposed* by empirical enquiry.

If we follow Hume we must accept that normative 'propositions' are not genuine propositions, and that normative 'judgements' are not properly speaking judgements but rather expressions of an affective attitude or a decision or volition. Responses of this broadly Humean kind have been popular this century, and have been developed to high levels of sophistication by logical positivists in the 1930s and more recently by others. They remain strikingly influential in contemporary cultures, not least among many who consider themselves opposed to logical positivism. But it is an equally interesting point that in philosophy at least they seem for the moment to be losing ground.

What are the alternatives? One may deny Hume's claim that all propositions are either 'true by definition' or factual. Or one may deny his empiricism, holding that there are, for example, 'moral facts', or 'logical facts', that can be known but that our knowledge of them is not empirical. Or finally one may take the sceptical option: holding that while normative propositions are genuine propositions, purporting to correspond to a special domain of facts, we can have no knowledge of any such domain, or there can *be* no such domain. But this kind of extreme posture tends to be attractive only so long as one refuses to think it through fully.

My own preference is for the first response, that of denying Hume's claim that all propositions are either true by definition or factual. This response is broadly Kantian in respecting the autonomy of the normative, but it does not force us into Kant's rationalism. It can recognize that 'the heart has its reasons which reason knows nothing of'. But unlike Hume, it fully acknowledges the cognitive or propositional status of normative claims. It is a false dichotomy to say that morality is more properly felt than judged of. It is judged of on a basis that includes feeling.

This view distinguishes between normative and factual statements – the former obeying an epistemology of self-examination and discussion and the latter an epistemology of correspondence. Unlike the realist view that there are normative facts, to which true normative propositions correspond, it does not hold that there is something that makes normative propositions true or false, or correct or incorrect – in the realist's correspondence sense. In particular, the correctness of a normative proposition does not *correspond* to the fact that verdicts on it are ideally convergent. That is not its 'truth condition': it has no non-trivial one. So it is not made true by a fact about what people would agree to in an ideal contract, either.

The shift back towards 'objectivity' – towards recognizing normative judgements generally, and moral judgements in particular, as genuine judgements – has been a notable feature of moral philosophy in the last thirty years. It is striking that this shift has been happening even as rejection of normative objectivity has widened and deepened in the general culture of the Western world. Will the general culture respond to this objectivist turn in a generation or two, as it responded to the anti-objective turn of philosophers in the 1920s and 1930s? We can only wait and see.

Further Reading

For each section, a few readings are suggested which discuss its topics, lead on to additional reading and often take a quite different view from that adopted here.

(1) The Scope of Ethics: ch. 5, 'The Object of Morality', in Mackie (1977); ch. 1, 'Introduction', in Sidgwick (1922); Parts I and II of Singer (1991); and ch. 1, 'Socrates' Question', and ch. 2, 'The Archimedean Point', in Williams (1985).

(2) Blame, Admiration and Desire: Part 1 of Griffin (1986); Hurka (1983); Skorupski 'The Definition of Morality' in Phillips Griffiths (1993); ch. 10, 'Morality, the Peculiar Institution', in Williams (1985); and Gibbard (1990).

(3) Character, the Virtues and Freedom: Aristotle (1954); chs 7–14 in Foot (1978); Glover (1970); 'Freedom and Resentment' in Strawson (1974); and Wallace (1994).

(4) An Ethical Theory: The Case of Utilitarianism: Part 2 of Griffin (1986); 'Utilitarianism' in vol. 10 of Mill (1963–); and Smart and Williams (1973).

(5) Impartiality: Rawls (1972); Darwall (1983); and Nagel (1991).

(6) What Can an Ethical Theory be Expected to Do?: Daniels (1979); ch. 6, 'Ethical Principles and Methods' and ch. 13, 'Philosophical Intuitionism', in Sidgwick (1922); and Part 1, 'Self-Defeating Theories', in Parfit (1984).

(7) The Plurality of Value: MacIntyre (1981); ch. 11, 'Morality as a System of Hypothetical Imperatives', in Foot (1978); ch. 8, 'Internal and External Reasons', in Williams (1981); McDowell (1978).

(8) Practical Reason: 'Of the Influencing Motives of the Will' (II, III, i) and 'Of Virtue and Vice in General' (III, II) in Hume (1978); Kant (1964); Book 2, ch. 1, 'The Principle and Method of

Egoism' and concluding chapter, 'The Mutual Relations of the Three Methods', in Sidgwick (1922); 'Autonomy, Obligation, and Virtue: An Overview of Kant's Moral Philosophy' in Schneewind (1992); and Allison (1990), an advanced study of Kant's ethics.

(9) The Categorical Imperative and Contractualism: Gauthier (1986); 'Could Kant Have Been a Utilitarian?' in Hare (1993); Scanlon, 'Contractualism and Utilitarianism' in Sen and Williams (1982); and O'Neill (1989).

(10) Reason, Morality and Religion: Chapter 8, 'Intuitionism', in Sidgwick (1922); 'Values and Secondary Qualities' in McDowell (1985); Dancy (1993); and Berg, 'How Could Ethics Depend on Religion?', ch. 46 in Singer (1991).

(11) Meta-ethics: Smith (1995) and McNaughton (1988).

References

Allison, H. E. 1990: *Kant's Theory of Freedom*. Cambridge: Cambridge University Press.

Aristotle, 1954: *The Nichomachean Ethics*. Oxford: Oxford University Press.

Berg, J. 1991: How Could Ethics Depend on Religion? In P. Singer (ed.) *A Companion to Ethics*. Oxford: Blackwell.

Dancy, J. 1993: *Moral Reasons*. Oxford: Blackwell.

Daniels, N. 1979: Wide Reflective Equilibrium and Theory Acceptance in Ethics. *Journal of Philosophy*, 76.

Darwall, S. 1983: *Impartial Reason*. Ithaca, NY: Cornell University Press.

Foot, P. 1978: *Virtues and Vices and Other Essays in Moral Philosophy*. Oxford: Blackwell.

Gauthier, D. 1986: *Morals by Agreement*. Oxford: Oxford University Press.

Gibbard, A. 1990: *Wise Choices, Apt Feelings*. Oxford: Clarendon Press.

Glover, J. 1970: *Responsibility*. London: Routledge and Kegan Paul.

Griffin, J. 1986: *Well-Being, Its Meaning, Measurement, and Moral Importance*. Oxford: Clarendon Press.

Hare, R. M. 1993: Could Kant Have Been a Utilitarian? *Utilitas*, 5.

Harman, G. 1977: *The Nature of Morality: An Introduction to Ethics*. New York: Oxford University Press.

Hume, D. 1978 [1739–40]: *A Treatise of Human Nature* (edited by L. A. Selby Bigge) (2nd edition with text revised and variant readings by P. H. Nidditch). Oxford: Clarendon Press.

Hurka, T. 1983: *Perfectionism*. Oxford: Oxford University Press.

Kant, I. 1964 [1785]: Groundwork of the Metaphysic of Morals. In *The Moral Law* (translated and analysed by H. J. Paton). New York: Harper and Row.

McDowell, J. 1978: Are Moral Requirements Hypothetical Imperatives? *Proceedings of the Aristotelian Society*, supp. vol. 52.

——1985: Values and Secondary Qualities. In T. Honderich (ed.) *Morality and Objectivity: A Tribute to J. L. Mackie*. London: Routledge and Kegan Paul.

MacIntyre, A. 1981: *After Virtue: A Study in Moral Theory*. London: Duckworth.

Mackie, J. L. 1977: *Ethics: Inventing Right and Wrong*. Harmondsworth: Penguin Books.

McNaughton, D. 1988: *Moral Vision: An Introduction to Ethics*. Oxford: Blackwell.

Mill, J. S. 1963–: *Utilitarianism*, in *The Collected Works of John Stuart Mill*, vol. 10. London and Toronto: Routledge and University of Toronto Press.

Nagel, T. 1991: *Equality and Partiality*. London: Oxford University Press.

Nietzsche, F. 1974: *The Gay Science* (translated with commentary by W. Kaufmann). New York: Vintage Books.

O'Neill, O. 1989: *Constructions of Reason: Explorations of Kant's Practical Philosophy*. Cambridge: Cambridge University Press.

Parfit, D. 1984: *Reasons and Persons*. Oxford: Clarendon Press.

Plato 1961: *Euthyphro* (translated by L. Cooper). In E. Hamilton and H. Cairns (eds) *The Complete Dialogues of Plato*. Princeton, NJ: Princeton University Press.

Rawls, J. 1972: *A Theory of Justice*. Oxford: Oxford University Press.

Scanlon, T. 1982: Contractualism and Utilitarianism. In A. Sen and B. Williams (eds) *Utilitarianism and Beyond*. Cambridge: Cambridge University Press.

Scheffler, S. 1992: *Human Morality*. Oxford: Oxford University Press.

Schneewind, J. B. 1992: Autonomy, Obligation and Virtue: An Overview of Kant's Moral Philosophy. In P. Guyer (ed.) *The Cambridge Companion to Kant*. Cambridge: Cambridge University Press.

Sidgwick, H. 1922: *The Methods of Ethics*. London: Macmillan.

Singer, P. (ed.) 1991: *A Companion to Ethics*. Oxford: Blackwell.

Skorupski, J. 1993: The Definition of Morality. In A. Phillips Griffiths (ed.) *Ethics*. Cambridge: Cambridge University Press.

Smart, J. J. C. and Williams, B. 1973: *Utilitarianism For and Against*. Cambridge: Cambridge University Press.

Smith, M. (ed.) 1995: *Meta-Ethics*. Aldershot: Dartmouth Publishing.

Strawson, P. F. 1962: Freedom and Resentment. In *Freedom and Resentment* (1974). London: Methuen. Reprinted in G. Watson (ed.) (1982) *Free Will*. Oxford: Oxford University Press.

Wallace, R. J. 1994: *Responsibility and the Moral Sentiments*. Cambridge, MA: Harvard University Press.

Williams, B. 1981: *Moral Luck*. Cambridge: Cambridge University Press.

—— 1985: *Ethics and the Limits of Philosophy*. London: Fontana Paperbacks.

Discussion Questions

1   What makes a question an ethical question?

2   Could we accept moral judgements while seeing no reason to act on them? Could other reasons outweigh moral reasons?

3   Is there a special moral sense of blame? Can we understand morality without understanding blame?

4   Is morality dispensable?

5   Is every excellence of character a moral virtue? If not, what makes an excellence a moral virtue?

6   Do the ends of life stand outside morality or are they objects of moral assessment?

7   Can there be experts in morality – or in any other kind of normative judgement?

8   If moral freedom is a matter of degree, how much moral freedom is required for moral responsibility?

9   What notion of rationality is involved in the claim that moral freedom is rationality?

10   Is moral freedom compatible with our being governed by causal laws?

11   In what sense, if any, can there be ethical theory?

12   Are utilitarians right in holding that only the well-being of individuals has intrinsic ethical value? What rival views might there be?

13   If the well-being of some animals has less ethical value than the well-being of humans, does the well-being of some humans have less ethical value than the well-being of others?

14   What grounds might there be for choosing among different impartial principles for distributing well-being among individuals?

15   If standards of value are internal to different human activities, is it a mistake to seek a fully general ethical theory?

16   Is it a truth of logic that if a thing is blameworthy, we have reason not to do it?

17   How can reason be practical?

18   Does the claim that Kant's formalism cannot yield substantive results misunderstand the role of the categorical imperative in his ethical thinking?

19   What does it mean to treat a person as an end?

20   Should I do what is morally right because it is unfair not to?

21   Are moral judgements rationally evident in their own right?

22   Can morality be complete without religion?

23   What, if anything, makes ethical and other normative judgements true or false?

24   Are ethical views expressions of affective attitude, for example, rather than real judgements?

7

Aesthetics

SEBASTIAN GARDNER

Reflection on beauty and art gives rise to a rich and diverse field of philosophical issues. The first part of this chapter outlines the view of aesthetic experience and judgement which forms the background to contemporary discussions in aesthetics. Art is then examined in three parts, concentrating on the key concepts of representation, expression and meaning. Attention is drawn to the relation of topics in aesthetics to those in ethics, metaphysics and philosophy of mind, and to the place of aesthetics in some of the great systems in the history of philosophy.

The experiences that we have when we listen to music, read poetry and look at paintings or scenes in nature, have a distinctive immediate, emotional and contemplative character, and lead us to describe what we experience in a special vocabulary, and to use terms such as 'beautiful', 'exquisite', 'inspiring', 'moving' and so on. Philosophy employs the term 'aesthetic' to circumscribe this kind of experience. The appreciation of art provides the most complex and intense form of aesthetic experience, in which we are set apart from the real world and our powers of imagination are fully engaged, in dramatic contrast with everyday practical life. A less marked form of aesthetic awareness suffuses our perception of the world. Some degree of aesthetic receptivity is shown by the quiet influence that architecture exerts on our feelings, and the choices that we make daily in designing our environment manifest aesthetic preferences. The ability to respond aesthetically, and the opportunity to appreciate art, are important components of well-being. A world without aesthetic qualities would be an inferior, if not uninhabitable, world, and a person without any capacity for aesthetic response, if imaginable, would not qualify as a fully developed human being.

Many questions naturally occur to us in the course of thinking about and discussing works of art. What makes an object qualify as a work of art? What is the relation between form and content in a work of art? Does a work of art put us in touch with the mind of the artist? What are we to think when critics disagree about the meaning of a work? Why do we attach such importance to art? And so on. The philosophy of art aims to reflect on these largely familiar questions in a systematic way.

In addition to topics in the philosophy of art, there are a number of more abstract, less familiar questions concerning the nature of aesthetic experience in general to be considered. What explains the special character of aesthetic experience? Does a judgement that an object is beautiful report a fact about the object? Or does it express a feeling of the subject's? What is beauty? Thinkers in the eighteenth century, above all HUME (chapter 31) and KANT (chapter 32), took up these questions, and their view of aesthetic experience provides the broad framework within which most contemporary, analytical aesthetics operates. The first part of this chapter describes this framework, and the unresolved philosophical questions associated with it.

1 Aesthetic Experience and Judgement

Hume and Kant regard aesthetic judgement as exemplifying taste. Taste, in eighteenth-century aesthetics, refers to the special mental faculty, or special mode of employment of mental faculties, exercised in aesthetic judgement. What more this means can be grasped by attending to two absolutely central features of aesthetic judgement, insisted on by Hume (1965) and Kant (1987).

The first is that aesthetic judgement rests, fundamentally, on a felt response to an object (Kant 1987: §1). Aesthetic judgement on an object cannot be passed second-hand: it requires personal acquaintance. The testimony of others may make me confident that I will find a newly published novel rewarding; but I cannot declare it to be so until I have read it myself. The condition of felt response is reflected in the fact that an aesthetic judgement, like an avowal of emotion, can be made sincerely or insincerely.

The second feature, closely connected to the first, is that rules or principles play no role, or only a highly diminished role, in aesthetic judgement (ibid.: §8). It cannot be inferred that a piece of music is rapturous simply because it is in a particular key and orchestrated for certain instruments; or that a painting is dynamic because its composition has a certain geometric form. No laws connect the aesthetic qualities of an object with its sensory, non-aesthetic properties.

The point is not just that we are ignorant of rules for aesthetic judgement, or unable to agree on them, but that there would be little point in trying to formulate a set of rules: we could not use rules to produce in ourselves felt responses to objects; we could not, in cases of disagreement, reasonably ask another person to relinquish his or her judgement on the grounds that it conflicted with the rules; and whenever our own responses departed from the rules, we would quite rightly repudiate the rules rather than our responses. The fact that rules are otiose in determining the aesthetic qualities and value of objects reflects the fact that aesthetic interest is directed essentially towards particular objects, appreciated for their own sake, and not towards the formulation of general truths. To judge according to rules is to miss the uniqueness of objects, and so to fail to judge aesthetically. The place of rules, in guiding aesthetic judgement, is taken by particular, *exemplary* aesthetic objects; 'established models', as Hume calls them.

Hume and Kant agree, further, in rejecting the view (of earlier, classical and rationalist aesthetics) that aesthetic qualities are objective. Aesthetic objectivism maintains that aesthetic qualities are properties inhering in objects, and that aesthetic experience gives us knowledge of these properties. These properties may be identified with the object's formal properties, such as 'ideal proportion'; or they may be regarded as *sui generis* and irreducible to formal properties (Moore 1984: §§112–21; McDowell, in Schaper 1983). (These varieties of aesthetic objectivism bear comparison with naturalism and intuitionism in ethics, respectively.)

Aesthetic subjectivism denies that aesthetic qualities inhere in objects, and maintains that what it is for an object to be beautiful is for it to yield a certain response in the subject. In aesthetic experience I am *affected* by the object, and my response does not consist in knowledge of its properties. The object's formal and other non-aesthetic properties are merely what occasions the response. Aesthetic subjectivism, we will see, comes in various degrees of sophistication (which again may be compared with different forms of subjectivism in ethics).

Several very powerful considerations militate in favour of aesthetic subjectivism. Firstly, as Hume observes, and as we all recognize, the tastes and verdicts of different individuals and cultures vary enormously. (Lest this be doubted: Johnson said of Shakespeare that he has 'faults sufficient to obscure and overwhelm any other merit'; Voltaire compared Shakespeare's works to a 'dunghill'.) If aesthetic qualities are really out there, inhering in the object, why do we not all pick up on them? The point is not just that divergence is a fact of aesthetic life, but that we lack agreed methods for bringing divergent judgements into line. As was said earlier, rules cannot be appealed to. And aesthetic disagreement is unlike disagreement about colour, where conditions of physiological normality and standard lighting can be checked independently. Aesthetic qualities are deeply elusive: the 'positioning' of the observer needed to discern aesthetic qualities involves a plethora of temperamental and culturally parochial factors, all strongly indicative of subjectivity.

The second point was stressed by Kant (1987: §1). Pleasure is essential to the experience which grounds an aesthetic judgement. Pleasure, like pain, is, however, a mental state that does not represent a property of its object; as Kant says, pleasure 'designates nothing whatsoever in the object'. The necessary connection of aesthetic judgement with pleasure is readily explained by the subjectivist, but it presents aesthetic objectivism with an enormous difficulty: how can there be properties inherent in objects which *necessarily* generate pleasure simply through being apprehended – if not on the theological supposition that the world has been metaphysically tailored to delight us? Such properties would be metaphysically queer in the extreme. (This objection to aesthetic objectivism may be compared with Hume's objection to ethical objectivism, that it fails to capture the necessary connection of moral judgement with the will.)

This objection can be amplified. Objectivism, because it holds that aesthetic qualities inhere in objects, necessarily introduces a distinction between reality and appearance, between how things are and how things seem. Objectivism therefore implies that, even when an aesthetic judgement has withstood all of the toughest tests, we can still be mistaken about it: it is still possible that the object lacks the aesthetic quality attributed to it and is really aesthetically worthless. But this seems mad. It is simply not intelligible that our greatest art could 'really', appearances to the contrary, be worthless. Successful 'appearances' of aesthetic quality are as good as – indeed they are the same as! – the real thing: for aesthetic reality precisely *consists* in appearances.

Put another way, the usual motivation for objectivism in philosophy – namely, showing that our experiences and theories put us in touch with the world as it really is, independently of our means of representing it – has no relevance to the context of aesthetic experience, which has instead a strong similarity to the context of personal relationships, in which rewards other than the gaining of knowledge are sought primarily. The cognitive demand that mind should 'fit the world' does not apply to aesthetic interest, which is in this respect closer to desire than belief – what we want is for the world to fit us.

If, however, aesthetic subjectivism is common-sensical and philosophically plausible, it appears to carry a highly uncommon-sensical and unwelcome implication. If aesthetic qualities do not inhere in objects, what is to prevent the same object being judged beautiful by one person and ugly by another – both being equally justified in their pronouncements? If, as Hume puts it, 'All sentiment is right', there is no such thing as rightness or wrongness in aesthetic matters. In that case, an aesthetic judgement merely reports the speaker's mental state, and aesthetic preferences are on a par with gustatory preferences. It follows that aesthetic judgements cannot be contested or supported with reasons. This position, like emotivism in ethics, to which it corresponds, is inconsistent with common sense (Kant 1987: §56).

Thus the *problem of taste*: of how to maintain the subjective felt basis of aesthetic judgement, without collapsing into unrestricted RELATIVISM (pp. 395–7). Hume and Kant respond to the problem of taste in different ways.

Hume contends that a 'standard of taste' – a basis for accepting some judgements of taste as correct and rejecting others as incorrect – is both philosophically defensible and visibly at work in the way that we actually conduct our aesthetic affairs. The standard of taste lies not in the object but in the sensibility of the subject. Aesthetic sensibility varies in its 'delicacy': 'When the organs are so fine as to allow nothing to escape them, and at the same time so exact as to perceive every ingredient in the composition, this we call delicacy of taste' (Hume 1965: 11). A correct aesthetic judgement is one that issues from a delicate sensibility operating under ideal conditions, which include the cultivation of taste through practice, the ability to make relevant comparisons, and freedom from prejudice. We defer to the judgement of those whose sensibilities we acknowledge to be superior, that of the 'critics'. (The concept of an IDEAL OBSERVER (p. 470) plays an analogous role in Hume's moral theory.)

It follows that for Hume, aesthetic judgements do not identify aesthetic qualities inhering in objects, but nor do they simply report the subject's experiences. An object's possession of an aesthetic quality consists in its being 'fitted' to generate a certain response in us. This distances Hume from the kind of unsophisticated subjectivism which ends up in relativism.

Hume's solution to the problem of taste depends on contingent facts of nature. Firstly, the fact that some 'particular forms or qualities [in objects] are calculated to please, and others to displease'. Secondly, the contingent uniformity of human sensibility, the sameness in 'the original structure of the internal fabric' of our minds – by which is meant, not that we are all equally competent aesthetic judges, but that our sensibilities are *all of a kind*. Where sensibilities differ, the differences are not arbitrary: aesthetic judgements diverge because of differences in delicacy, and other determinable deficiencies of taste; if the sensibilities of two subjects are equally delicate and their conditions of judgement otherwise the same, their judgements will coincide.

Kant and the Normative Aspect of Aesthetics

Kant rejects the kind of account proposed by Hume. Recall that the problem of taste is one of *justification*. The question is, on what grounds can we regard certain aesthetic judgements as being correct? For Kant, there is nothing in Hume's position which accounts for this, the normative aspect of aesthetic judgement. Hume does not validate the claim, implicit in all aesthetic judgement, that one's response is *appropriate* to the object, and that others *ought* to concur. Kant interprets this demand for agreement strongly, as applying to all other people without exception. On Kant's view, Hume offers only a causal, psychological explanation of why we do, as a matter of fact, defer to the judgements of 'critics' – he does not say why we *ought* to do so.

Kant's solution to the normative problem is, in essence, very simple, although his presentation of it is extremely intricate. Suppose that, in making an aesthetic judgement, we abstract from everything that might pertain to our contingent, natural, individually variable constitutions, and base our judgements solely on conditions that are strictly universal, in the sense of being available and common to all human beings. Suppose, that is, we base our aesthetic judgement on the bare form of the object and its interaction with our basic, universal mental powers of perception and understanding. (Kant's reasoning here recapitulates his analysis of moral judgement in terms of the categorical imperative.) Kant argues that this 'universal' standpoint can be achieved through freeing our awareness of the object from desire and practical concern (what he calls 'disinterestedness'), and from our conceptual understanding of it. When these stringent conditions are met, the judgement we make is valid for everyone. We then have what Kant calls a 'pure judgement of taste', which has 'universal validity'. Kant argues that it is indeed possible for the mere form of an object to delight us: certain perceptual forms stimulate our mental faculties optimally, by engendering in us a 'harmonious free play of imagination and understanding', awareness of which is pleasurable. Kant also gives a metaphysical interpretation of aesthetic experience: it makes us conscious of a connection that we have with the world, and with one another, which lies beyond the empirical world. Beauty therefore has a semi-religious and moral significance for Kant (he calls beauty the 'symbol of the good').

Even if we grant that Kant's theory of mental harmony accounts for the experience of beauty, a cost attaches to Kant's solution to the problem of taste. Purifying aesthetic judgement in the way that Kant requires leaves us with an austere, if not impoverished view of aesthetic experience – as consisting of nothing but an estimation of form. This limitation shows up in Kant's inability to do justice to the psychologically rich diversity of experience which art offers.

We are left, then, with a choice: between accepting Hume's account, without (Kant argues) any way of securing the normative aspect of aesthetic judgement; and accepting Kant's account, at the price of excluding from aesthetic experience our cultural identities, and everything in our psychological constitutions that is not strictly universal (which, the Humean will argue, leaves all too little). The task of providing a single account which incorporates and combines the insights of Hume and Kant remains.

A number of other issues remain unresolved within the framework of aesthetic subjectivism, including the formulation of the doctrine itself. Granted that aesthetic qualities are subjective, quite how subjective are they? Are they, for instance, on a par with colours and other secondary qualities of objects? Some theories maintain that they are. Others deny that aesthetic qualities are on a par with colours and compare them with 'looks' or 'aspects' of objects, or describe them as 'powers' to produce experiences. Another, more radical, possibility is that aesthetic judgements are not descriptive at all. WITTGENSTEIN (chapter 39) (1978) suggests that aesthetic judgements are more like gestures and exclamations. On this view, the function of an aesthetic judgement is not to say anything about an object, but to 'put across' an experience. (These options are explored in Sibley 1959, 1965; Sibley and Tanner 1968; Wollheim 1980: essay 6; Hungerland, in Osborne 1972; Meager 1970; and Scruton 1974.)

It is also necessary, as both Hume and Kant saw, to clarify the nature and role of reasons and criticism in aesthetic contexts. That aesthetic judgements can be justified distinguishes them from mere likings, and makes them, in a broad sense, rational. It is the job of the critic to identify the sources of a work's aesthetic qualities and determine what responses are appropriate (a further role for criticism, to be discussed later, is interpretation). But aesthetic reason-giving differs fundamentally from reason-giving in other contexts and has a number of peculiarities, which make it hard to understand (Beardsley 1982: ch. 12; Scruton 1979: ch. 5). It does not consist in inferring one proposition from another; it makes no use of rules, unlike moral reason-giving; and it makes no use of induction or generalizations, unlike reason-giving in science. Even the notion of consistency has little application to aesthetic judgements: liking Wagner does not mean that one ought to dislike Mozart. The problem, in sum, is that aesthetic reasons operate independently from all of the conditions that appear integral to the very concept of a reason.

Two further unresolved issues may be pointed out in conclusion. The first, bequeathed by Kant's notion of disinterestedness, concerns the importance of the concept of an 'aesthetic attitude'. Some theorists have claimed that aesthetic experience *consists in* the adoption of a special attitude in which objects are attended to dispassionately and 'for their own sake'. Indeed, Schopenhauer identifies the point of art with the metaphysical liberation from life that aesthetic contemplation, which does not involve the will, brings in its wake (Schopenhauer 1969, 1: third book). The distinctive phenomenology of aesthetic experience makes this idea alluring, but what can be said about the aesthetic attitude, other than that it differs from and excludes practical and cognitive attitudes? Saying that an object is enjoyed 'for its own sake' really means that it is 'not enjoyed for any ulterior end'. Because descriptions of the aesthetic attitude tend to remain fundamentally negative, it is unclear what value the concept has, stripped of the metaphysical interpretation that makes it significant for Schopenhauer (see, however, Beardsley 1982: ch. 16).

A second issue concerns the concept of beauty, which has undergone a dramatic reversal of fortunes in the history of aesthetics. Classical aesthetics takes it for granted that beauty is the only, or at least the fundamental, aesthetic quality. Some modern writers propose by contrast that 'beautiful' is merely a catch-all term, roughly equivalent to 'aesthetically commendable', and that there is, as ordinary language implies, a limitless plurality of aesthetic qualities, encompassing elegance, grace, poignancy and so on. There is, however, a philosophical issue here which needs to be addressed. The idea that beauty is not just one aesthetic quality among many, but is somehow pre-eminent and accounts for the unity of aesthetic experience, is compelling, and anyone who denies this in favour of the 'pluralist' view is challenged to find an alternative account of the unity of the aesthetic. A recent defence of the concept of beauty is in Mothersill (1984).

2   The Essence of Art

HEGEL (chapter 33) asserts that art 'pervades what is sensuous with mind', and that art accordingly has 'a higher rank than anything produced by nature, which has not sustained this passage through the mind' (Hegel 1993: 15, 34). Whether or not Hegel's view of the superiority of art is justified, the philosophy of art, to which we now turn, shares Hegel's conception of art as a synthesis of mind with something other than itself, in which the mind 'recognizes itself'; and his rejection of the view that a work of art is simply an artefact possessing aesthetic qualities of a kind also found in nature. Theories of art attempt to elucidate the nature of the connection with the mind which makes an object a work of art. Such attempts assume that the concept of art picks out more than a merely nominal, or historically accidental phenomenon – that art has, in short, an essence.

2.1   Definitions of art

Attempts have been made to capture the essence of art in a simple definitional formula. Two representative examples are the definition of art as the imitation of beautiful nature, and the definition of art as the communication of feeling.

If we consider such definitions, it is clear that they are wide open to counter-examples. Not every work of art is an imitation of beautiful nature, or communicates feeling: novels are rarely if ever beautiful, instrumental music is not imitative and much visual art does not communicate feeling. And even if these formulae provided necessary conditions for art, they could hardly provide sufficient conditions: some industrial machinery is beautiful, waxworks are imitative, racist propaganda communicates feelings.

One response to the failure of definitions of this simple kind is scepticism. It has been claimed that the difficulty of defining art is a reflection of there *not being* an essence of art. Proponents of this view (discussed in Tilghman 1984) have often appealed to Wittgenstein's notion that family resemblances between instances of a concept may be all that there is to be found.

A recent, much-discussed attempt to define art – which is built on the Wittgensteinian denial that art has an essence, but maintains that a definition is nevertheless possible – is the *institutional theory*. The institutional theory accepts that works of art cannot be defined in terms of their intrinsic, perceptible properties, and turns instead to their extrinsic, social properties. The theory says that something is a work of art if a member of the artworld has conferred on it the status of being a candidate for appreciation, or if it has been created in order to be presented to the artworld (Dickie 1984). The artworld is a nebulous entity that includes artists, critics and some portion of the general public. 'Work of art' is, on this account, an 'honorific' term: being a work of art is a non-perceptible property which depends upon an object's place in a cultural context (analogous

237

to being 'in public ownership' or 'sacred'). This approach receives an additional stimulus from the way in which some avant-garde art of this century – paradigmatically, Duchamp's ready-made *Fountain*, a mass-produced urinal entered for exhibition unaltered by the artist – appears to have repudiated all traditional criteria for art.

There is, however, something missing at the heart of the institutional theory. It tells us *that* members of the artworld bestow the status of art on some objects rather than others; but not why they do so. It thus leaves out of account the *reasons* for calling something a work of art – the conditions taken to *justify* application of the concept. This is something that ought to figure in a philosophical, as opposed to a sociological, treatment of the concept of art (Wollheim 1980: essay 1).

Proponents of the institutional theory seek to deflect this criticism by saying that they are concerned with the 'classificatory' sense of art, not the 'evaluative' sense in which to call something a work of art is to recommend it for appreciation. But this invites the further objection that it is simply a mistake to separate the classificatory sense of art from the evaluative. Evaluation is just as integral to the concept of art as it is to moral concepts. We do not first classify objects as art, and then discover that they happen to be aesthetically rewarding: conceptually, there is only one move here.

What moral is to be drawn from these attempts to define art? It cannot be ruled out that a complex definition, perhaps combining the concepts of imitation and communication in a complex way and adding further conditions, could be devised to encompass all and only those objects that we consider to be works of art, and at the same time respect the evaluative nature of the concept of art. But what the difficulty of reading off an adequate definition of art from the surface of our ordinary conception of art may be taken to show, more importantly, is that no definition of art can be expected, and in any case cannot hold much interest, in advance of a *theory* of art. A theory of art does not require there to be a simple, manifest property shared by each and every work of art; it allows that what unifies art – its essence – may not be visible at its surface, and probes beneath the surface to locate it.

A theory of art may take one of two forms. It may aim directly at developing a single concept capturing the essence of art. Or it may proceed by building up from an examination of the various specific dimensions of works of art. The first, more traditional approach is explored below; the second, more modest approach favoured in contemporary aesthetics, is explored in the following section.

2.2   Theories of art

Of the numerous and enormously varied theories of art that have appeared in the history of aesthetics, three may be singled out as having greatest importance. These are the mimetic, formalist and expression theories.

Even if the concept of imitation, as ordinarily understood, does not straightforwardly define art, it may be supposed that the concept can be *developed* beyond its ordinary scope. On this claim rests the theory that art consists in *mimesis* – a Greek term rendered approximately by 'imitation', 'copying' or 'representation' (see Plato 1955; Aristotle 1987; and chapter 23 of this volume). The object of mimesis is usually identified with nature, inclusive of human nature. Although, as observed earlier, some art, such as instrumental music, appears to be non-representational, it is open to the mimetic theorist to contend otherwise: in antiquity it was thought that music imitates the order and harmony of the cosmos and the soul. The mimetic theory construes the connection of art with the mind asserted by Hegel in the following way: works of art carry over the mind's fundamental function of *representing* the world.

Granted that the concept of representation is open to being extended, the mimetic theory is open to an objection (Hegel 1993: LXI–LXVII). Even if we accept that it is natural to enjoy imitation and the skill exhibited therein, as Aristotle observes, why should we find imitation valuable in the *special* way that art is found valuable? The values connected conceptually with representation are cognitive, truth-orientated values such as accuracy and comprehensiveness. These have some role in art – verisimilitude of plot and character in literature for instance – and certainly truth is something we value. But truth does not capture the real interest of art. A work of art must come into its own in the field of our experience, and not disappear from our attention in the manner of a transparent window on to the world or vehicle for communicating truths about it. The mimetic theory thus appears to misconstrue the value of art.

The mimeticist's conception of representation accordingly needs to be tightened up. Representation which is *artistic* must be circumscribed in subject and mode: it must be of particular kinds of things, represented in a particular way. It is therefore no accident that mimetic theorists have characteristically gone on to claim that art must *idealize* its subject matter. But once the mimetic theory has undergone this modification, the essence of art has been shifted away from bare representation, in the direction of whatever it is about art that *enables* it to idealize its subjects.

A strong candidate for this role is artistic form. Where the mimetic theory ties art down to the real world, *formalism* allows the work of art to float free, insisting that only form, the complex arrangement of parts unique to each individual work, has artistic significance. Only what is internal to the work is relevant to its status as art; any outward references, to a real or imaginary world, are irrelevant. The concept of form can be made more or less narrow; at its narrowest, only sensory parts and their relations are intended. Formalists differ over the continuity of form in art with form in nature: Kant holds that artistic form must be recognizably of a kind with natural form; Bell (1914: ch. 1), the boldest recent exponent of formalism, holds that artistic form, labelled 'significant form', is in effect exclusive to art. Appreciation of art consists, for the formalist, not in merely recognizing form, but in responding to it: Kant's theory of mental harmony has already been mentioned; Bell posits a unique kind of 'artistic emotion' accompanying the recognition of significant form. According to formalism, what the mind recognizes of itself in works of art is its power of locating *order in perception*, exercised to a specially heightened degree.

The weakness of formalism most frequently indicated by its critics concerns the concept of form, which is argued to be too indefinite to play the role that is asked of it. Asked to specify the kind of form that matters in art, the formalist uses notions such as 'balance' or 'uniformity amidst variety'; but it proves impossible to define these in a way that prevents them from applying to any object whatsoever. The formalist is consequently pushed to declare that artistic form is *indefinable*. Bell embraces this claim, but his theory is then charged with vacuousness: he explains significant form in terms of the 'artistic emotion' that it induces, but then refers us back to 'significant form' for our understanding of artistic emotion.

Whatever the force of this point against Bell, there is another objection to be pressed. Is our interest in form really as uncontaminated with ulterior, worldly concerns as formalists suppose? Formal values may sometimes be of self-sufficient aesthetic interest, but much more commonly they serve non-formal ends: form is the vehicle through which a work articulates its non-formal meaning, apart from which form tends to become artistically uninteresting and merely decorative. In other terms, the attempt to disentangle form from content leaves, on the side of form, an insufficiently significant residue.

This objection to formalism may be pressed on behalf of the mimetic theory; but it also points in the direction of the *expression* theory. The connection of art with feeling, we said earlier, cannot consist in a straightforward equation of art with the communication of feeling. The expression theory of art seeks to offer a more sophisticated and persuasive account of the central place of emotion in art.

The rudiments of the expression theory lie in writings of the Romantics, but it was first formulated philosophically by Croce (1992), who bound it up with the tenets of German idealism. The more accessible version of the theory presented by Collingwood (1937) detaches it from METAPHYSICS (chapter 2), and understands artistic expression as a special form of self-expression. Artistic expression is a process in which the artist begins with an indefinite and inchoate emotional state, for which he or she labours to find a uniquely apt concrete articulation, and in so doing transforms his or her mental state into something definite, tangible and intelligible. What the artist creates does not describe his or her state of mind, so much as *incorporate* it; analogously to the way in which bodily expressions such as smiles and grimaces embody mental life.

Since the product of expression cannot be known before the process is complete, expression cannot consist in exercising a technique: it must take whatever particular shape is commanded by the particular emotion which the artist's mind is impelled to clarify. Because expression is not undertaken with any further end in view, artistic creation contrasts with instrumental activities, in which means and ends are distinct; these Collingwood calls 'craft', and opposes to 'art proper'. Mistaken, 'technical' conceptions of art – which include the conception of art as mimesis or communication of feeling – arise from a failure to grasp this distinction.

On the side of artistic appreciation, the theory claims that the audience retraces in the course of appreciating a work of art the route pursued by the artist: their appreciation re-enacts the artist's creative process and thereby retrieves his or her psychological state (Elliott, in Osborne 1972). The relation of the audience to the work of art thus mirrors the artist's understanding of his or her own mind. The capacity of a work of art to transmit the artist's psychological state is a necessary consequence of successful expression. The expression theory, by giving primacy to the perspective of the artist rather than (as on the mimetic and formalist theories) that of the audience, offers a very strong interpretation of Hegel's claim that the mind 'recognizes itself' in works of art: works of art do not merely exhibit mental features, they, as it were, *contain* mind.

The expression theory's emphasis on the psychology of the artist exposes it to criticism. The mimeticist will object that not only emotions, but also ideas, which refer to the world, are expressed by art, whose legitimate subject is not restricted to the artist's own mind. At the other extreme, the formalist will challenge the expression theory to say how a supremely self-contained and self-sustaining work such as a Ming vase, can be construed as a product of personal expression.

240

The first objection can be met by explaining that what the theory means by emotion is any mental state, however permeated with concepts and thought, that has some emotional charge. The condition that emotion be present is plausible, for most people would agree that mere beliefs without any psychological resonance do not provide sufficient material for art. The scope of the thoughts embedded in the artist's emotion is furthermore left open, which means that the artist's moral and spiritual view of the world and conception of life are proper material for expression, and that what a work of art expresses need not include a personal, biographical reference to the artist.

The formalist's objection cannot be met by expanding the terms of the theory, and obliges the expression theorist to adopt a semi-stipulative measure. The theory must declare that objects possessing only formal virtues do not qualify as full-blooded instances of works of art. This move is obviously acceptable only on the assumption that art's centre of gravity lies in the psychology of the artist; it will be rejected by the formalist as begging the question, and as betraying the theory's fundamentally parochial, pro-Romantic bias.

Of the three theories considered, it is fair to say that – if a monopoly is to be granted – then the expression theory has strengths that give it the edge over the mimetic theory and formalism. These strengths also account for the theory's continued hold on our thinking about art. It may also be pointed out in its favour, that the expression theory allows the understanding of art to draw on the resources of psychological theory (Wollheim 1987); an ultimate verdict on the theory will depend in part on what value is found in such developments.

The Semiotic Theory of Art

A fourth theory, which is not traditional but dominates much contemporary discourse about art, should be mentioned in conclusion. This is the semiotic theory of art, which proposes that works and forms of art be analysed in terms of logico-linguistic categories such as signification, reference, denotation, and syntactic and semantic rules. Goodman (1976), the principal exponent of the semiotic theory, analyses representation and expression in such terms. The semiotic theory of art is also assumed by structuralist and poststructuralist literary theory, which grafts linguistic science and philosophical theories of language onto the study of literature. On the semiotic theory, art is a symbol system much like language, and not just in the metaphorical sense in which an expression theorist might grant that art is a 'language of emotion'.

What the worth of the semiotic theory turns on can be indicated with reasonable assurance. The theory derives its motivation from, firstly, a rejection of the primacy of psychological and experiential concepts (these, it claims, are not autonomous and need to be understood in terms of language and signification); and, secondly, a belief in the radically conventional nature of art (which it grounds on a blanket rejection of philosophical realism). Both strands are explicit in the work of Goodman, and in structuralism and poststructuralism. It follows that the semiotic theory's austere perspective on art must be rejected by anyone who wishes to maintain that art is essentially connected with certain forms of experience; as it may also be, on the supposition that human psychology sets universal, non-conventional parameters to art. This last idea provides the basis for a fifth theory of art, the naturalistic, which will be described in section 4 below.

3   The Dimensions of Art

Recent work in analytical philosophy of art has adopted the second, more piecemeal and empirical, approach described earlier to the construction of a theory of art. Rather than aim directly at a general, overarching characterization of art, it has concentrated on the specific dimensions which constitute works of art, in the belief that an accurate picture of art as a whole will emerge out of a proper understanding of its parts. Representation, expression and meaning have been closely analysed, in terms of the specific forms that they take in each of the arts. This section traces the debates surrounding these concepts in terms of the form of art most strongly associated with each: representation in painting, expression in music, and meaning in literature.

(Issues concerning the ontology of works of art, the nature of fiction, emotional response to fiction, and metaphor, also belong in this context, and would be included in a fuller account of analytic philosophy of art.)

3.1   Representation

When we look at Titian's *The Rape of Europa* we do not see, or do not *just* see, pigment distributed across the two-dimensional surface of a canvas: we see a woman borne across the sea aloft a white bull. Paintings represent or depict things, both real and imaginary.

We are concerned here with what paintings represent in a visual, as opposed to interpretative, sense. A painting of a man clutching a stone may represent St Jerome, and a lute with a broken string in a still-life may represent Discord. In order to make such iconographic identifications, however, a human figure and a musical instrument must first be seen in the picture, and this is a perceptual matter; it is something that art historical scholarship could not do for us. Visual representation is something we take for granted. When we cease to do so, a philosophical question arises: what makes pictorial representation possible? The mimetic theory of art, it should be noted, does not answer this question: it merely assumes that pictorial representation is possible.

The philosophical puzzle surrounding pictorial representation comes into focus when one reflects on the difficulties associated with the common-sensical view of how pictures work. Common sense says that pictorial representation consists in *resemblance*: a painting represents X by looking like X. This may at first seem to be not just self-evident, but the only possible answer. This common-sense view of pictorial representation is reflected in the idea that deception provides the test for successful representation – as illustrated by the story of Zeuxis's painting of vines, which, according to Pliny, deceived the birds into flying down to consume the grapes he had depicted.

It is, however, simply and plainly false that canvases marked with pigments resemble the things that they represent. *The Rape of Europa* does not even begin to share the physical dimensions of the scene that it represents! In fact, each canvas resembles nothing so much as other canvases – but it does not, of course, represent them.

This objection may seem too blunt, for it may seem to have missed the obvious point that for a canvas to represent something, it must be seen, not as a mere physical object, but *as a picture*. But this just restates the problem, which now becomes: what is it for a canvas to be seen as a picture?

It may then be ventured that what the resemblance theory really means, is that a painting of X represents X when it affords us an experience which is like the experience of really perceiving X. Sometimes this is put by saying that the canvas gives us an 'image' which is the same as that which we would receive from the real thing.

Relocating the resemblance at the level of an experience or image, rather than that of the canvas, does not, however, advance our understanding for, once again, what is wanted is an account of *how* the two-dimensional, differentiated surface of Titian's painting can be made to 'have the look' – afford the visual experience or create the image – of a woman carried on the back of a bull.

Very quickly it comes to seem that resemblance does not provide the explanation of pictorial representation. In its place, theorists turn to other, less obvious notions. (However, for a recent defence of pictorial representation in terms of experienced resemblance, see Peacocke 1987.)

The case against resemblance was first set out, at length and with sophistication, by Gombrich (1960). Gombrich attacked in particular the assumption, which accompanies the resemblance view, that there is such a thing as an 'innocent eye' – that an artist can simply 'copy what he sees' by attending to his visual experience, in advance of any interpretation of the world.

Goodman (1976: ch. 1) carries this line further by rejecting altogether the idea that pictorial representation is a matter of perception. On Goodman's account, depiction is a species of denotation: knowing what a picture represents is purely a matter of interpretation, which requires a grasp of a 'symbol system'. Realism in painting is just a function of the familiarity of a symbol system, the ease with which it imparts information.

As was said earlier, the motivation for Goodman's semiotic view is very general. There is, however, much to query in his claim that pictures are interpreted. It seems to us that pictures give us visual experiences, and that this is how they differ from prose descriptions, maps, company logos, road signs and other visual symbols that need to be read. Goodman's theory implies that this impression of difference is an illusion. But if so, what does the illusion of having a visual experience consist in – if not in having a visual experience?

Gombrich himself does not assimilate pictorial representation to interpretation completely. On Gombrich's account, a painting represents X by giving us an *illusion* of X. How illusions are created is explained in terms of the representational practices evolved in the history of art. Art develops through a process of 'making and matching'. Visual 'schema' are originally fabricated semi-arbitrarily in order to represent objects, without resemblance playing any kind of role. They are then modified by artists in the light of their perceptual experience, a historical process which results in increasingly life-like representations (a process which Gombrich models on POPPER'S (pp. 287–90) conception of the development of scientific theories). Resemblance lies, if anywhere, at the end of the history of pictorial art, not at its beginning.

It is true that some visual representations – such as Escher's *trompe l'oeil* drawings – create illusions, but it is not true that most paintings have this effect: in looking at a painting we do not find ourselves having to correct a tendency to *mistake* its content for reality, as the concept of illusion would imply. Furthermore, the illusion theory entails that in seeing what a painting represents, we stop being aware of the material canvas, as the illusion takes hold. This, however, contradicts the fact that appreciating a painting involves simultaneous, complex awareness of its brushwork and what it represents (see Wollheim 1974: ch. 13).

Representation and Seeing In

The weaknesses of the views considered so far suggest that we need to posit a form of visual perception which is, as it were, inherently imaginative. Wollheim's theory does this (Wollheim 1980: essay 5; 1987: 46–77). It proposes that pictorial representation engages a species of perception which Wollheim calls 'seeing in'. Wollheim argues for this claim as follows. An important clue as to the underlying nature of the experience of painting lies in the fact that paintings give us experiences of something absent or non-existent. Now this is something that occurs also in dreams, daydreams and hallucination. It may be ventured that pictorial representation exploits and cultivates a power that the mind possesses innately: the power to generate visual experiences out of itself. When this capacity is exercised in the course of perceiving the external world and fused with perception of external objects – as it is in numerous contexts outside painting: things are seen in Rorschach ink-blots, clouds and damp-stained walls – we then have seeing in. Seeing in is not involved in reading maps or interpreting visual signs; here there is no experience of an absent object. On this theory, what it is for Vermeer's *View of Delft* to represent a townscape is for the canvas to be marked in a way that allows us to see a townscape in it. Seeing in does not presuppose a resemblance between the canvas and what the painting represents; according to Wollheim, no systematic account can be given of how the marking of a canvas determines what is seen in it. Wollheim (1987) proceeds to develop a general account of painting which shows how its value as an art presupposes its rootedness in seeing in and other psychological powers.

3.2 Expression

It is not long before the fugue recedes into its initial calm. Soon, a final crescendo leads us to what appears to be a triumphant conclusion. But no; at the very moment when victory seems to be in our grasp, the music loses all confidence, comes to a halt on a chord that is far from final, and then sinks despondently back into the minor key. Could disillusionment be more graphically expressed? It is the cry of despair; the hoped-for consolation has failed to materialize. (Hopkins 1982: 383)

This passage describes emotions expressed in the final movement of Beethoven's Piano Sonata Op. 110. The expressive qualities of works of art are a sub-class of their aesthetic qualities, distinguished by the employment of terms whose primary use lies in describing people's emotions. Expressive qualities are integral to the beauty and meaning of music. Since the nineteenth century, many have believed that music's incomparable power of expression secures for it a position of supremacy among the arts (Walter Pater claimed that 'all art constantly aspires towards the condition of music').

Describing music in expressive terms exemplifies a broad tendency to talk about works of art as if they were sentient entities: they are described as having 'organic unity', 'vitality' and so on. And yet we do not, of course, really believe or mean to imply that works of art *have* feelings. So, given that a musical work is at one level just a sequence of sounds, just as a painting is nothing but a pigmented canvas, the fundamental problem of expression in art, brought out most sharply by music, is the following: how is it possible for a work of art to express emotion?

The obvious answer would seem to be that musical works have expressive qualities because they serve, as the expression theory of art says, as vehicles for expressing the emotions of the composer. This is, however, no answer. Even if the expression theory of art is accepted, nothing in it explains how it is possible for a composer to use patterns of sound to express emotion. It merely takes that fact for granted.

If it does not help to think of the emotion expressed by music as located in the mind of the composer, it is equally mistaken to attempt to locate it in the mind of the listener: that is, to analyse a musical work's expression of an emotion as its power to arouse that emotion in the listener. Bluntly: we are not *ourselves* made melancholic, or frozen with grief, by music that we would describe in those terms – fortunately. The listener does not *have* the emotion which the music expresses, in the same sense as she has emotions in life. In listening to music, the emotion which is expressed seems to be located 'out there' in the music, not in oneself. The heart of the problem lies in understanding how emotion can be 'objectified' in this fashion – how it can be ascribed neither to the composer nor to the listener, but rather somehow hover, suspended, between them.

Further reflection shows that being moved by music consists, typically, not in simply recognizing or sharing the emotion expressed by music, but in *reacting* to it – in the way that a person may respond to the emotional condition of another, for example, by responding to their distress with pity. The relation is one of sympathy rather than empathy. We are familiar with this structure in the context of representational art, where, in drama, literature and painting, we feel for the protagonist. Its appearance in music reinforces the difficulty of musical expression, since instrumental music precisely lacks the representational content that would make emotional response to music intelligible as a case of participating in a fiction (it has no characters or plot).

At this point, one option is to reconceive the problem of musical expression as merely one of language: of finding an adequate logical characterization of how terms are used in the ascription of expressive qualities. An account of this sort – which appears to cut rather than untie the Gordian knot – is again advanced by Goodman (1976: 85–95).

An alternative way out of the problem is musical formalism, a position defended by Hanslick (1986). Hanslick grants that music has emotional effects on listeners; but he denies that there is any genuine sense in which music expresses emotion. Hanslick has both an argument for denying that music can express emotion, and an account of why we should come to suppose falsely that it can. For music to express emotion, there would have to be an intrinsic relation between them. Hanslick argues that this is impossible, on the grounds that emotions are intentional: they have objects and involve thoughts and concepts; whereas instrumental music lacks objects and does not involve thoughts or concepts. Since music is incapable of presenting any object – what it presents is only itself – it cannot have an intrinsic relation to emotion.

What music can do, Hanslick argues, is express what he calls 'musical ideas', which are its dynamic properties: 'The content of music is tonally moving forms' (ibid.: 29). Tonality provides a sort of auditory space within which the melody, harmony and rhythm of music move (see Scruton 1983: ch. 8; 1997: chs 2–3). Hanslick draws an analogy with the visual movement found in arabesque ornamentation.

Like music, episodes of emotion have dynamic properties, in addition to and independently from their conceptual content, since they involve changes in intensity and bodily feeling. Because music and episodes of emotions share dynamic properties, it is possible for us to fill in, arbitrarily, the musical idea expressed by a piece of music with some particular emotion supplied by our own emotional repertoire: giving us the illusion that the music expresses that particular emotion. For Hanslick, musical appreciation stops properly at the beauty of musical form. Anything else is merely personal emotional association.

Despite its subtlety, Hanslick's repudiation of emotion is not easy to accept: describing musical works in terms of their expressive qualities seems to be, not just natural, but indispensable for justifying our estimates of their artistic value. The thought that music is intrinsically expressive should not be given up unless absolutely necessary. Can anything be salvaged?

Although music does not speak or behave, an analogy between the recognition of emotion in music and in people can be suggested. Perhaps music derives its expressive power from its resemblance to emotionally expressive features of human bodily behaviour, physiognomy and speech (Kivy 1989). That would explain the phenomenological similarity between hearing emotion in music, and perceiving emotion in the body or voice of another person: in both cases, mental life seems to have been made sensuously palpable.

This theory is in a position to deflect Hanslick's objection that music lacks the conceptual components necessary for an intrinsic connection with emotion. Bodily and vocal features can express emotional states without communicating their objects: we can recognize that a person is distressed from the way they look or sound, without knowing what they are distressed about.

The human analogy theory soon encounters difficulties, however. It shares the weakness of the resemblance theory of pictorial representation – namely, the difficulty of locating relevant resemblances. What exactly are the features shared by music and human bodies? Just as canvases are unlike the things represented in pictures, a plain description of music in terms of key, rhythm and so on reveals little that is common to music and human bodies. It is true that both tempo and bodily movement can be slow, but such properties are no more emotionally definite than Hanslick's 'musical ideas': if a sad piece of music is slow, what makes its slowness that of sadness rather than serenity? The objection then arises that significant likenesses between music and human bodies can only be identified after the music has been redescribed in expressive terms, such as '*ponderously* slow'. Only once music has been experienced as expressive does it become possible to model it imaginatively on the human figure. Musical expression remains unexplained.

A second theory that appeals to a resemblance between music and emotion is that of Langer (1942: ch. 8). On Langer's theory, musical works are symbols of a special kind. Unlike the discursive symbolism of language, music shares the 'logical form' of

246

emotion and, by virtue of doing so, articulates and *presents* emotion, as language cannot. Here it is the *inner* aspect of emotion, rather than its outer bodily expression, which music is said to mirror ('Music is our myth of the inner life': ibid.: 245).

A similar problem, however, confronts Langer's theory. In what non-metaphorical sense does emotion have 'logical form'? And in any case, the notion of formal similarity is so plastic and open-ended that it can surely be found between any emotion and any piece of music. Again, the alleged isomorphism of music with emotion seems to be either non-existent, or insufficiently definite to explain musical expression.

If neither the outer nor the inner aspect of emotion has a connection with music which accounts for its expressiveness, it may seem that enquiry grinds to a halt. Budd (1985) concludes, after intensive examination of the above theories, and others, that none succeeds). One remaining avenue, however, is to suppose that the connection of music with emotion is more direct than we have hitherto assumed it must be: that it does not take a detour via resemblance.

A clue to the explanation of expressive qualities may lie in the fact that the mind has, as Hume put it, a natural propensity to spread itself on to the world, and experience objects as emotionally coloured. Projection, as this may be called, is a well-attested psychological phenomenon. If this is joined with a second, equally Humean assumption, to the effect that certain objects in the world are fitted by nature to serve as recipients for the projection of specific emotional states, then we are on the way to a conception of artistic expression as reposing on, and cultivating, a natural tendency of ours to dye objects in the world with our emotions (Wollheim 1980: sections 15–19; 1987: 80–7). If Hanslick's repudiation of emotion is to be avoided, an assumption along these lines seems to be at least necessary.

3.3   Meaning

That works of art have meaning – over and above their representational content, and aesthetic and expressive qualities – is implied by the fact that works of art allow for, and call for, understanding. Questions of meaning in art are best approached through the concept of INTERPRETATION (pp. 384–90). Interpretation aims to identify the meanings of works of art, and is one of the functions of criticism. Questions of interpretation arise of course in all the arts – is Beethoven's *Missa Solemnis* a Christian or a Romantic work? Does Titian's *The Flaying of Marsyus* celebrate the triumph of spirit over body, or that of body over spirit? – but it is literature, and literary criticism, that put the issues surrounding interpretation in sharpest focus.

Of all the arts, literature allows least scope for aesthetic response to operate independently of interpretation: a liking for a literary work not accompanied by so much as a rudimentary grasp of its meaning fails altogether to qualify as an appreciation of it. This is due to the fact that the medium of literature, natural language, is, unlike pigment, sound or stone, inherently meaningful; which, plausibly, allows literary works to bear more conceptually complex meanings than works in other media; for which reason literary works generate greater interpretative controversy.

It is hard to find a great literary work for which different interpretations have not been proposed. Is *Hamlet* correctly understood in terms of Freud's theory of the Oedipus complex? Does *Paradise Lost* represent Satan as a moral being 'far superior to his God', as Shelley claims? Do Shakespeare's sonnets comprise a unified narrative charting the course of Shakespeare's own experience? Are Kafka's writings religious or political parables, or articulations of the personal angst evident in his diaries and letters? Does a proper appreciation of Yeats's poetry presuppose knowledge of his mytho-logical system? To each of these questions critics have returned opposite answers.

Two questions are forced on us by differences in interpretation. Firstly, can biographical information concerning the author serve as legitimate evidence for or against a certain interpretation? Secondly, can we talk of one interpretation as being the correct interpretation of a work?

The starting-point for the first question is the attack made by Wimsatt and Beardsley on what they call the 'intentional fallacy' (in Newton-de Molina 1984). On their view, critics err in supposing that information about the author, or any kind of evidence 'external' to a poetic text (for instance, about its original cultural circumstances), can elucidate its meaning as a literary object; all that is pertinent to the meaning of a poem can be gleaned by careful attention to the words on the page. To suppose otherwise is to commit the fallacy of confusing a psychological fact about the author with a fact about the poem, of failing to distinguish a causal explanation of a work from a literary interpretation of it.

Two opposing views of the relation between the meaning of a literary work (textual meaning) and the intentions of the author (authorial meaning) can be staked out. *Intentionalism* identifies textual meaning with authorial meaning: what the text means is what the author meant (Wollheim 1980: essay 4). *Anti-intentionalism* denies that textual meaning is authorial meaning, and asserts its autonomy: textual meaning resides objectively in the work, 'embodied in the language', and has nothing to do, conceptually, with what the author may have meant (if the two happen to be the same, that is a coincidence without significance, for the anti-intentionalist). These positions have connections with traditional theories of art: the expression theory is straightforwardly committed to intentionalism, formalism to anti-intentionalism (the mimetic theory is uncommitted).

What, then, are the main considerations in the argument over intentionalism? There is much to be said, but some of the most important points are the following.

On the one hand, it seems right that a literary work, considered as a work of art, should be judged in terms of the experience of reading it; if meanings do not show up in an optimally sensitive reading of the text, then, although the author may have wished to convey them, they simply do not form part of what the text means. A poem stands or falls on its own merits. This is Wimsatt and Beardsley's strongest argument for anti-intentionalism.

It can, however, be countered by the intentionalist. While it is true that the author's intentions must be realized in the text and concretely apprehended there in order for the work to be artistically successful, when a work is successful, intentionalism is true: what we grasp is the author's meaning. The intentionalist may add that, although 'external' evidence cannot transform an artistic failure into a success, attention to such evidence may make it easier to see what meaning is contained in the words on the page. The intentionalist can also point out that, since we rarely approach literary works without some awareness of the author's historical circumstances, other writings and so on, there is in fact no firm or deep distinction between internal and external evidence, contrary to what the anti-intentionalist supposes.

The intentionalist's case can be strengthened further by drawing attention to the fact that estimates of sincerity, maturity and perceptiveness are important for our responses to literary works. Literature is flawed if it exhibits mawkishness, self-indulgence or crudity of moral vision; the fine consciousness of life and ethical complexity of George Eliot and Henry James is valued. Literary vices and virtues are qualities of moral personality apparently ascribed in full-blooded intentionalist spirit to the author, in so far as he or she is manifest in his or her work. (Amplifying this approach, see Leavis 1986: part 4.)

The anti-intentionalist will complain that here the intentionalist has once again converted an aesthetic into a non-aesthetic matter, and is treating the text as material for literary biography, as if it were the critic's job to pass moral judgement on the author. We do value qualities such as sincerity in literature, but these are properties of texts: they indicate strengths in the work itself.

We have, then, intuitions favouring each of intentionalism and anti-intentionalism. Neither set of arguments is obviously decisive. Wimsatt and Beardsley did not, therefore, establish that intentionalism involves a fallacy. They did, however, define anti-intentionalism as a theoretical option, and indicate the methodological repercussions of the issue. If intentionalism is true, then the study of literature may cast its net wide and draw, in addition to literary biography, on other disciplines – history, psychology or anthropology – concerned with factors contributing, consciously or unconsciously, to the author's meaning. If anti-intentionalism is true, then external information ought to be bracketed out.

The second question raised by differences of interpretation, which concerns the notion of correctness, can again be formulated in terms of a sharp opposition. On the monistic view, there is for each work a uniquely correct interpretation. Whether it can be identified conclusively, and gain universal acceptance, is another matter. Monists say that where interpretations differ, and yet seem equally well-supported, their conflict can be overcome by a 'super-interpretation', which incorporates what is true in each of the interpretations which it supersedes.

Pluralism denies that there is, even in principle, a uniquely correct interpretation for each work; it maintains that a number of different interpretations can meet the condition of, not correctness, if correctness is taken to imply uniqueness, but 'legitimacy'. Pluralists differ over the criteria for legitimacy of interpretation and how restrictive these should be. The arguments between monism and pluralism engage closely with the issue of intentionalism versus anti-intentionalism.

The pluralist focuses in the first instance on the notion of textual meaning. Correctness of interpretation presupposes that textual meaning is determinate. Wimsatt and Beardsley help themselves to the assumption that literary works have objective, determinate meanings, but the pluralist challenges the monist to say where this determinacy comes from: for even if the meaning of each individual word composing a text is determinate – a claim which is itself vulnerable in view of the ubiquity of metaphor in literature – the meaning of the work as a whole is far from being a straightforward function of the dictionary meanings of the words composing it. As we would ordinarily put it, there is 'room for interpretation', and this, according to the pluralist, means that there is room for a *number* of interpretations. Easiest, then, is for the monist to embrace intentionalism: since, if intentionalism is true, a source of determinacy is readily supplied by the author's intention.

The pluralist's second argument draws on a tenet of aesthetic subjectivism: namely, that felt response is at the core of the aesthetic. Literary interpretation should serve the kind of interest appropriate to literary works, and literary interest, as a case of aesthetic interest, centres on response. The proper goal of interpretation is therefore to enhance our experience of the work, to offer a reading which makes it mean as much as possible to us. Since the perspectives of readers will always differ, the interpretation that is optimal for one reader will not be optimal for another. Multiple interpretations of a work are therefore to be expected, and should be welcomed. To meet this argument on its own terms, the monist would have to defend the – evidently controversial – claim that there is for each text one interpretation which is universally optimal.

Arguments between monism and pluralism tend to converge on the following scenario. The monist says that if pluralism is true, then 'anything goes' in interpretation, an implication which the monist claims reduces pluralism to absurdity – *The Ancient Mariner* cannot be interpreted as a poem about issues of power and gender in late twentieth-century culture. The pluralist objects that the notion of a uniquely correct interpretation fosters dogmatism, and disregards both the richness of texts and the diversity of human interests which may legitimately be expressed in literary interpretation.

These (unresolved) philosophical issues gain a special urgency from their relevance to the present, turbulent and logomachic climate of literary studies, where theoretical and ideological commitments are explicitly adopted and appealed to in interpreting texts. The dominant deconstructionist conception of literary meaning at work here is fundamentally a form of pluralism, adopted on wholly general philosophical grounds: the very concept of determinacy of meaning is rejected, in all, not just literary contexts. To this is added a radically idealist view of literary meaning which reverses the ordinary conception of the relation of meaning and interpretation: the meaning of a literary work is conceived as created, rather than grasped by interpretation. The point of literature, on this picture, is not aesthetic: literature exists for the sake of interpretation.

4 The Point of Art

We come finally to the question of the point of art. What value does art have? What is art *for*? This is not a demand for a 'justification' of art in the same sense as a justification of morality is thought to be required – that would be an inappropriate demand, since the creation and appreciation of art do not share the necessity of moral obligation. The question is rather whether we can articulate and vindicate our sense of the importance of art. The fact, observed earlier, that art is an evaluative concept, means that an account of the point of art is not a mere coda to aesthetic enquiry: it should fall out conceptually from a theory of art.

That art does have some point is not beyond all doubt (Passmore 1991). It has already been seen how the mimetic theory encounters difficulties on this score. Positive reasons for scepticism about the value of art are not hard to unearth: they derive from art's essential connections with pleasure, play and imagination, its freedom from reason and practical purposes. The sceptic will insist that art has the same sort of value as any other form of entertainment. Plato's notorious critique of art, in book ten of the *Republic*, goes further, by suggesting that art's preoccupation with appearance entrenches our ignorance of reality, and that its effects may be psychologically and morally harmful (see Janaway 1995).

The distinction of ends and means figures prominently in many discussions of the point of art, and is usually employed critically: some accounts are said to reduce art to a 'mere' means, others to recognize correctly that art is an end.

This contrast is, however, not altogether felicitous, for two reasons. Firstly, art, so long as it has some value, can always be redescribed as a means to whatever value it realizes. Secondly, it is not clear what can be meant by describing art, or its appreciation, as an end. Certainly individual works of art have to be approached in their own terms and contemplated 'for their own sake'; but it would be a mistake to move from this fact about aesthetic attention, that it terminates in its object and does not 'think ahead', to the claim that art is its own point and cannot have extrinsic value. Formalists such as Bell and Hanslick, who describe works of art as ends in themselves, seem to make this mistake.

What the denial that art is 'merely a means' – and the aestheticist slogan 'art for art's sake' – may be trying to say, is that the value of art realized by art cannot be realized by anything else, or cannot be realized in the same way. Thus interpreted, the doctrine meets with our agreement: we recoil from hedonistic, moral, didactic or other instrumental attitudes to art, to the extent that these suggest that other things could be substituted for art *without loss*, or that the complexity of art is redundant. Tolstoy's (1930) theory of art as the transmission of moral feeling, for example, makes little effort to distinguish art from other, potentially more efficient, ways of achieving that end. It follows that so long as art is viewed as having a *necessary* role in relation to the kind of value in question, and the complexity of art is taken account of, there is nothing necessarily wrong with assigning a hedonistic, moral, didactic or other goal to art. Schiller (1989), for instance, argues that the goal of art, as a component of 'aesthetic education', is to overcome the metaphysical contradictions in human nature in order that we may attain full 'humanity'; this goal is 'extra-aesthetic', but Schiller regards aesthetic education as the only way in which it can be achieved.

What forms may accounts of the value of art then take?

They may, first, be divided according to how closely they relate the value of art to the values of life. In a perspective such as that of Leavis, art is properly and inextricably bound up with the values of life: the '*raison d'être* of the work' is to 'have its due effect and play its part in life'; the 'essential business of criticism' is to locate 'the creative centre where we have the growth towards the future of the finest life' (Leavis 1986: 283). At the other extreme, Bell holds that art is autonomous and has value only to the extent that it distances us from life: 'to appreciate a work of art we need bring with us nothing from life, no knowledge of its ideas and affairs, no familiarity with its emotions . . . In this world the emotions of life find no place. It is a world with emotions of its own' (Bell 1914: 25–7).

The deeper distinction to be made among accounts of the value of art, however, is between those that are naturalistic, and those that are metaphysical; a distinction that was foreshadowed by the contrast of Hume and Kant.

Naturalistic accounts ground art in human nature. The contingent fittedness by nature of certain objects to our minds proposed by Hume provides the starting point. To exhibit the point of art, it needs to be shown how works of art engage fundamental and important mental activities (Dewey 1934). Psychoanalysis provides one example of this approach (Wollheim 1987). The question of the point of art is therefore answered by saying that art is *natural*: art exists because it is natural for us to create and appreciate it. As such, art is a 'form of life' (Wollheim 1980), as necessary a component of human existence as language, culture and politics. The naturalistic view affirms that art responds to the psychological needs of human beings, but it denies that the functions which art performs could be specified, or fulfilled, through other means. When art is pictured as a necessary part of the human order, and the appreciation of art as a natural component of human well-being, the point of art merges with that of human life itself.

The naturalistic view of art therefore qualifies as a fifth theory of art, in addition to those considered earlier (it may, but need not, be formulated so as to incorporate the expression theory). By showing how the various dimensions of art map on to psychological processes, it accounts for the unity of art in terms of the unity of the mind, and locates the essence of art with reference to human psychology.

Metaphysical accounts of the point of art are, of necessity, more speculative and less pinned down to the empirical features of art than naturalistic accounts. They will also, of course, depend explicitly on a general philosophical outlook, which naturalistic accounts do not need to do. This does not, or should not, mean that they simply squeeze art into a preformed metaphysical system: they may, on the contrary, allow art a role in forming the system itself. This is what we find, in different ways, in Kant, Hegel, Schopenhauer, Schiller and Nietzsche (German idealism has been notably more accommodating to art than any other philosophical tradition).

The basic demand to which metaphysical accounts of art answer – and which naturalistic accounts cannot properly satisfy – derives from what might be called the 'transfigurative' aspect of our experience of art: the sense that the transformation of reality which art effects, and which locates in it a kind of value that we find consoling, is more than a fanciful embellishment. Tragedy exhibits the transfigurative power of art most clearly. The aspiration to achieve, through art, a justification of the world 'as an aesthetic phenomenon', as Nietzsche (1993: 32) put it, is a further part of the legacy of Romanticism, and has not disappeared from the demands that we put on art.

Further Reading

As an introduction to aesthetics, Richard Wollheim's short *Art and its Objects* (1980), which offers both an overview and a distinctive approach to the subject, and Malcolm Budd's *Values of Art* (1995) are both excellent. Other, plainer introductions are Charlton (1970) and Sheppard (1987). Hanfling (1992) contains a series of essays specifically written as a unified introduction to aesthetics, but of sufficient length to present many arguments in detail.

It is important to have a grasp at first-hand of the classic writings in aesthetics, few of which make difficult reading. Hofstadter and Kuhns (1964) is a first-rate, currently available anthology. Carritt (1931) is more comprehensive but the extracts are shorter. Two other excellent anthologies that also serve this end, and intersperse selections from the classics with modern writings, are Dickie and Sclafani (1977) and Rader (1979). Both are organized thematically and contain helpful bibliographies (as does Wollheim 1980). The historical development of aesthetics is traced by Beardsley (1966), which is also useful as a reference book. Cooper (1992) contains helpful entries on most figures and topics.

A number of books may be singled out as offering more complex discussions with the stress on a particular topic or perspective. Danto (1981) is stimulating and addresses many problems, but with the accent firmly on contemporary art. Budd (1985) gives detailed and lucid analytical treatment of some central aesthetic theories. Wollheim (1974) brings issues in aesthetics in relation to philosophy of mind and psychoanalysis. Scruton (1974) also emphasizes the contribution of philosophy of mind, together with that of philosophy of language; Scruton (1983) relates aesthetics to cultural issues. Goodman (1976) has been highly influential. Savile (1982) focuses on questions of value, in the idealist tradition. Walton (1990) attempts to provide a general theory of artistic representation.

Important articles are collected in Dickie and Sclafani (1977), Barrett (1965), Margolis (1978) and Osborne (1972).

With respect to particular topics in aesthetics, as broken down in this chapter: Hume needs no commentary, but Kant's *Critique of Judgement* is extremely difficult, and it is best to read either Kemal (1992) or McCloskey (1987) alongside. Three comprehensive treatments of aesthetic experience and judgement are Beardsley (1982), Scruton (1974), and Mothersill (1984). Definitions of art are explored in Davies (1991). Theories of art, and accounts of its point, are best approached through the classic writings. For detailed treatment of the debates surrounding each of the dimensions of art, Schier (1986) deals with pictorial representation, Budd (1985) with expression, and Newton-de Molina (1984) with literary meaning and interpretation.

References

Aristotle 1987: *Poetics* (translated by S. Halliwell). London: Duckworth.

Barrett, C. (ed.) 1965: *Collected Papers on Aesthetics*. Oxford: Blackwell.

Beardsley, M. C. 1966: *Aesthetics From Classical Greece to the Present*. Tuscaloosa: University of Alabama Press.

——1982: *The Aesthetic Point of View*. Ithaca, NY: Cornell University Press.

Bell, C. 1914: *Art*. London: Chatto and Windus.

Budd, M. 1985: *Music and the Emotions*. London: Routledge and Kegan Paul.

——1995: *Values of Art: Pictures, Poetry and Music*. Harmondsworth: Penguin Books.

Carritt, E. F. 1931: *Philosophies of Beauty*. Oxford: Clarendon Press.

Charlton, W. 1970: *Aesthetics*. London: Hutchinson.

Collingwood, R. G. 1937: *The Principles of Art*. Oxford: Oxford University Press.

Cooper, D. (ed.) 1992: *The Blackwell Companion to Aesthetics*. Oxford: Blackwell.

Croce, B. 1992 [1902]: *The Aesthetic as the Science of Expression and of the Linguistic in General* (translated by C. Lyas). Cambridge: Cambridge University Press.

Danto, A. 1981: *The Transfiguration of the Commonplace*. Cambridge, MA: Harvard University Press.

Davies, S. 1991: *Definitions of Art*. Ithaca, NY: Cornell University Press.

Dewey, J. 1934: *Art as Experience*. New York: Putnam.

Dickie, G. 1984: *The Art Circle*. New York: Haven.

Dickie, G. and Sclafani, R. J. (eds) 1977: *Aesthetics: A Critical Anthology*. New York: St Martin's Press.

Gombrich, E. H. 1960: *Art and Illusion*, 2nd edn. New York: Pantheon.

Goodman, N. 1976: *Languages of Art*. Indianapolis: Hackett.

Hanfling, O. (ed.) 1992: *Philosophical Aesthetics*. Oxford: Blackwell in association with the Open University.

Hanslick, E. 1986 [1854]: *On the Musically Beautiful* (translated by G. Payzant). Indianapolis, IN: Hackett.

Hegel, G. W. F. 1993 [1820–9]: *Introductory Lectures on Aesthetics* (translated by B. Bosanquet). Harmondsworth: Penguin Books.

Hofstadter, A. and Kuhns, R. (eds) 1964: *Philosophies of Art and Beauty*. New York: Harper and Row.

Hopkins, A. 1982: *Talking About Music*. London: Pan.

Hume, D. 1965 [1757]: Of the standard of taste. In *'Of the Standard of Taste' and Other Essays*. New York: Bobbs-Merrill.

Janaway, C. 1995: *Images of Excellence: Plato's Critique of the Arts*. Oxford: Oxford University Press.

Kant, I. 1987 [1790]: *'Critique of aesthetic judgement'*, Part I of *Critique of Judgement* (translated by W. S. Pluhar). Indianapolis: Hackett.

Kemel, S. 1992: *Kant's Aesthetic Theory: An Introduction*. London: Macmillan.

Kivy, P. 1989: *Sound Sentiment*. Philadelphia, PA: Temple University Press.

Langer, S. 1942: *Philosophy in a New Key*. Cambridge, MA: Harvard University Press.

Leavis, F. R. 1986: *Valuation in Criticism and Other Essays*. Cambridge: Cambridge University Press.

McCloskey, M. 1987: *Kant's Aesthetics*. London: Macmillan.

Margolis, J. (ed.) 1978: *Philosophy Looks At the Arts*. Philadelphia, PA: Temple University Press.

Meager, R. 1970: Aesthetic Concepts. *British Journal of Aesthetics*, 10, 303–22.

Moore, G. E. 1984 [1903]: *Principia Ethica*. Cambridge: Cambridge University Press.

Mothersill, M. 1984: *Beauty Restored*. Oxford: Clarendon Press.

Newton-de Molina, D. (ed.) 1984: *On Literary Intention*. Edinburgh: Edinburgh University Press.

Nietzsche, F. 1993 [1871]: *The Birth of Tragedy* (translated by S. Whiteside). Harmondsworth: Penguin Books.

Osborne, H. (ed.) 1972: *Aesthetics*. Oxford: Oxford University Press.

Passmore, J. 1991: *Serious Art*. London: Duckworth.

Peacocke, C. 1987: Depiction. *Philosophical Review*, 96, 383–409.

Plato 1955: *Republic* (translated by H. D. P. Lee). Harmondsworth: Penguin Books.

Rader, M. (ed.) 1979: *A Modern Book of Esthetics*, 5th edn. New York: Holt, Rinehart and Winston.

Savile, A. 1982: *The Test of Time*. Oxford: Clarendon Press.

Schaper, E. (ed.) 1983: *Pleasure, Preference and Value*. Cambridge: Cambridge University Press.

Schier, F. 1986: *Deeper Into Pictures*. Cambridge: Cambridge University Press.

Schiller, F. 1989 [1793–5]: *On the Aesthetic Education of Man* (translated by E. Wilkinson and L. A. Willoughby). Oxford: Clarendon Press.

Schopenhauer, A. 1969 [1819]: *The World as Will and Representation*, 2 vols (translated by E. F. J. Payne). New York: Dover.

Scruton, R. 1974: *Art and Imagination*. London: Methuen.

——1979: *The Aesthetics of Architecture*. London: Methuen.

——1983: *The Aesthetic Understanding*. London: Methuen.

——1997: *The Aesthetics of Music*. Oxford: Clarendon Press.

Sheppard, A. 1987: *Aesthetics*. Oxford: Oxford University Press.

Sibley, F. 1959: Aesthetic Concepts. *Philosophical Review*, 68, 421–50.

——1965: Aesthetic and Non-aesthetic. *Philosophical Review*, 74, 135–59.

Sibley, F. and Tanner, M. 1968: Symposium on 'Aesthetics and Objectivity'. *Proceedings of the Aristotelian Society*, supplementary volume 42, 31–72.

Tilghman, B. R. 1984: *But is it Art?* Oxford: Blackwell.

Tolstoy, L. 1930 [1898]: *What is Art?* (translated by A. Maude). Oxford: Oxford University Press.

Walton, K. 1990: *Mimesis as Make-Believe*. Cambridge, MA: Harvard University Press.

Wittgenstein, L. 1978: *Lectures and Conversations on Aesthetics, Psychology and Religious Belief*. Oxford: Blackwell.

Wollheim, R. 1974: *On Art and the Mind*. Cambridge, MA: Harvard University Press.
—— 1980: *Art and its Objects*, 2nd edn. Cambridge: Cambridge University Press.
—— 1987: *Painting as an Art*. London: Thames and Hudson.

Discussion Questions

1 What makes a judgement aesthetic?

2 Are the aesthetic qualities of an object any less objective than its colour?

3 Can arguments about aesthetic value be resolved, and what does it signify if they cannot?

4 Can it be shown, or must it merely be assumed, that aesthetic judgements differ from gustatory preferences?

5 In what ways, if any, can reasons be given for aesthetic judgements?

6 Are there any limits on what can be an object of aesthetic attention?

7 In what respects are aesthetic judgements like moral judgements, and in what respects are they unlike?

8 What can criticism of art hope to contribute to our appreciation of art?

9 In what respects can one's relation to works of art be compared with one's relations to other people?

10 Does aesthetic experience presuppose an aesthetic attitude?

11 Is it plausible to claim that beauty is the fundamental concept in aesthetics?

12 Does it matter if art cannot be defined?

13 What is the relation between form and content in art, and does either have greater importance than the other?

14 To what extent is it appropriate and profitable to compare art with language?

15 Does the concept of resemblance have any role to play in elucidating pictorial representation?

16 Can it be explained how music expresses emotion?

17 What assumptions are needed to uphold the claim that literary works have objective meanings, and are those assumptions acceptable?

18 Must each literary work have one correct interpretation?

19 Does the meaning of a literary work reside in the mind of its author, in the text itself, or in neither of these?

20 Is the correct interpretation of a literary work the one that makes it mean most to us?

21 Does the study of literature need to be guided by literary theory?

22 Does psychology have importance for aesthetics?

23 Do we need art?

24 Is it ever legitimate to view art as serving moral or political ends?

25 Is a paradox involved in the enjoyment of tragedy and, if so, how should it be resolved?

26 In what sense might it be true that art is a social rather than individual phenomenon?

27 Does emotional response to fiction require what Coleridge calls a 'willing suspension of disbelief'?

28 Is it more than just a contingent truth that art has a history?

29 How can one be moved by the plight of Anna Karenina, when one knows her to be merely fictional?

30 What distinguishes metaphor from nonsense?

31 Does survival of the test of time provide a criterion for artistic achievement?

32 Is photography a form of art?

33 Can it be maintained that any one form of art is superior to the others?

34 Is architecture 'frozen music'?

35 Can anything be made of the thought that music has 'metaphysical meaning'?

36 What makes a painting artistically significant?

8

Political and Social Philosophy

DAVID ARCHARD

Social and political philosophy has experienced a dramatic revival in recent decades. This chapter considers the background of work in the years after 1945, before examining the writings on justice of the main architects of this revival, John Rawls and Robert Nozick. Subsequently discussed are the ideal of equality, the problem of pluralism and the principle of neutrality, the communitarian, feminist and Marxist critiques of liberalism, and the significance of community. The final section considers the nature of political philosophy and its relation to politics.

1 Introduction

In a now celebrated phrase, Peter Laslett announced that 'for the moment, anyway, political philosophy is dead'. He did so in his 1950 introduction to the first collection of essays entitled *Philosophy, Politics and Society*. The sixth series was published in 1992, and the intervening years show clearly enough that the reports of death were greatly exaggerated, or at least that the moment was merely a passing one. The last fifty years, and the last thirty in particular, have witnessed a quite astonishing regeneration of social and political philosophy, understood in Laslett's own terms as the concern of philosophers with 'political and social relationships at the widest possible level of generality' (Laslett 1950: vii). The work has displayed a range of views, fertility of imagination, rigour of argumentation, care in critical analysis, and concern to address contemporary problems which are ample testimony to the considerable strengths of philosophy in the English-speaking world.

In the 1950s these strengths were far more selectively deployed. The study of politics was, to simplify greatly, divided between the empirical social sciences and philosophy. Exponents of the former were optimistic that political science could offer value-free but well-founded explanatory theories of its object. For its part philosophy disdained substantive political evaluation and restricted itself to the logical and linguistic analysis of political discourse.

The title of Daniel Bell's 1960 book, *The End of Ideology*, concisely defined an historical moment, and its subtitle, 'On the Exhaustion of Political Ideas in the Fifties', spelled out what was intended. Bell's text was a series of sociological essays about

America, but its grander claims carried further afield. The 1930s and 1940s testified to the sheer awfulness of the practical realization of ideologies like fascism and Stalinism which made simplifying and absolute claims to truth about humanity, history and reason. These years also reconciled intellectuals to the virtues of a more moderate and modest political programme. Capitalism could be tamed by a welfarist state the economy mixed, and fundamental freedoms adequately protected by democratic constitutionalism. There was no further need for ideologies in the sense of millenarian visions of utopia yet to be realized. The exhaustion of ideologies in this narrow sense seemed also to betoken a disenchantment with politics in general, a retreat from the traditional concern of political philosophy to prescribe the good society.

This was mirrored in the work of philosophers. The 1950s was the high tide of CONCEPTUAL ANALYSIS (pp. 2–3), and in an emblematic text, *The Vocabulary of Politics*, T. D. Weldon (1953) characterized the enduring questions of political philosophy as misplaced, resting on false assumptions and the misuse of unanalysed fundamental terms. Correctly understood, these questions are merely 'confused formulations of purely empirical difficulties' (ibid.: 192). It is proper for philosophers to analyse the language and foundational claims of ideologies, but the evaluation of political states of affairs and institutions is more appropriately reserved for politicians and political scientists.

However, it would be a mistake to over-simplify. From 1945 into the 1960s there was serious and important work in political philosophy. Karl Popper (1945) sought to rebut totalizing political theories such as those of PLATO (chapter 23) and MARX (chapter 34). But he did so by defending an ideal of the 'open society', and the politics of piecemeal reform rather than wholesale social engineering. F. A. von Hayek was entering upon his lifelong defence of a position which is echoed in important current views (Gray 1984). Hayek affirmed the ideal of justice as individual freedom under the LAW (chapter 13), and defended the idea that the economic and social world displays a spontaneous, impersonal pattern. It is simply inappropriate, and ultimately destructive of freedom, for governments to impose upon this world according to a redundant ideal of 'social' justice.

The work of Isaiah Berlin is especially noteworthy, for he anticipates some major themes in the philosophical liberalism that is now dominant. For Berlin, a plausible politics must start from a recognition of a plurality in valid yet conflicting ends of life. There is no single ideal of the good life, and the proper goal of politics is to make possible the pursuit by individuals of their several ends (Kocis 1980). Berlin (1958) famously distinguished two senses of liberty, one characterized as the absence of obstructions, and the other characterized in terms of self-mastery. He argued for the former, 'negative' liberty, as the 'truer and more humane ideal' than the latter, 'positive' liberty. At the same time Berlin urged a clear separation of the notions of liberty and equality. He conceded that the degree of social inequality may determine the conditions that make liberty worth having, but insisted that these conditions do not enter into the definition of liberty.

2   John Rawls and Robert Nozick on Justice

These various writings are important, but it is those of John Rawls that are now taken to signify the beginning of a distinctly new era. The publication of Rawls's *A Theory of*

Justice (1972) has proved a landmark, radically changing the character of English-speaking political philosophy and supplying the ineliminable background against which all subsequent discussion has been conducted. 'Political philosophers now must either work within Rawls's theory or explain why not' is fitting tribute from one whose own views are at a great distance from Rawls's (Nozick 1974: 183).

A Theory of Justice is much lauded but it is also now an extensively criticized text. Rawls's presuppositions, methodology and conclusions have all been subjected to such extensive criticism that it is important to be clear how and why his text set the scene. First, *A Theory of Justice* is a work of substantive political philosophy. Although Rawls engages in the analysis of concepts, this serves rather than substitutes for the evaluation of political institutions. *A Theory of Justice* is more. It defends a single, unified vision of the good society – one that is recognizably liberal. Rawls gives philosophical voice to a doctrine of democratic constitutional liberalism which can with merit be urged as the only feasible theory for contemporary Western society.

Second, Rawls seeks to combine a recommendation of the ideal polity with a plausible account of HUMAN NATURE (pp. 672–3). This involves not just a theory of human MOTIVATION (p. 392) taken from the SOCIAL SCIENCES (chapter 12). It also – and less noticed – comprises a view of the manner in which citizens can be brought to recognize and accept as both fair and realistic the formal terms of their coexistence.

Third, Rawls has provided political philosophy with an agenda. He does not just offer a theory of justice. He supplies an account of the priority of individual liberty, the defensible limits of egalitarianism, and the rule of law.

Fourth, Rawls's work puts contemporary political philosophy back into contact with its own history. The work and concerns of past writers, such as HOBBES (chapter 28), LOCKE (chapter 29), Rousseau, HUME (chapter 31), MILL (chapter 35) and KANT (chapter 32), are given renewed pertinence.

Fifth, *A Theory of Justice* is nevertheless a response to the particular circumstances of modernity. It is not just a principled affirmation of the virtues of liberalism against the postwar background of disillusionment with more extreme ideologies. It can be seen as an attempt to affirm these virtues in the context of a more local crisis, that is the challenge posed to the ideal of American democratic constitutionalism by the civil rights movement and the war in Vietnam. More generally again, Rawls, as did Berlin, insists that value pluralism is an unavoidable feature of modern existence to which politics must adequately respond.

The ideas of *A Theory of Justice* can best be laid out by answering a number of broad questions. First, why is a theory of justice needed? Because publicly agreed terms of social cooperation are both necessary and possible. Individuals benefit from living and working together so long as they can be assured that social existence is well-ordered and stable. Yet there is a predisposition to conflict inasmuch as individuals want different and not necessarily compatible things out of their life together. Agreed PRINCIPLES (pp. 733–6) are needed to regulate interaction, and determine the proper division of benefits and costs among the members of society. Such principles are possible to the extent that individuals can see them to be necessary, and their particular terms can be agreed under appropriate conditions.

The Primacy of Justice

Justice has primacy in three senses. It is the first virtue of social institutions. This does not mean that society cannot display other virtues, only that without at least the assurance of justice these would have little or no value. Second, truth is a demand made of a system of thought in so far as it relates to reality. Justice is demanded of a polity in so far as it must relate to the real world. The circumstances of justice are those first noted by David Hume, namely limited benevolence and moderate scarcity. Humans are not well-enough disposed to make sacrifices for others, and material resources are not available in sufficient quantity to make formal agreement on terms of cooperation unnecessary.

Rawls adds to this understanding of circumstances the facts of modern value pluralism. Individuals have different but not necessarily compatible aims. My pursuit of my life's ends will conflict with your pursuit of yours. Agreement on how to reconcile such a conflict is necessary but possible only if no one set of individual values is affirmed over the others.

Third, any theory of justice specifies and guarantees an equality of citizenship which supplies an assurance that no individual may be sacrificed for society's greater good. Justice has primacy in that this assurance is not to be compromised.

What is a theory of justice? It is a theory of the publicly agreed, final principles which define the fundamental terms of social co-operation. It is a theory of those principles which regulate the institutions, the 'basic structure' of society. It does not prescribe particular outcomes; nor does it provide a criterion for evaluating actions or the character and dispositions of individuals. It is a theory of *social* justice, which must also coincide with our considered and reflective MORAL JUDGEMENTS (pp. 225–7). Rawls's notion of 'reflective equilibrium' allows for, indeed encourages the possibility of, mutual adjustment in both theory and judgements. Yet any theory of justice must capture what is essential to and shared by different accounts of justice, namely that 'institutions are just when no arbitrary distinctions are made between persons in the assigning of basic rights and duties and when the rules determine a proper balance between competing claims to the advantages of social life' (Rawls 1972: 5).

What then is *A Theory of Justice?* Rawls's theory assures citizens equal LIBERTY (pp. 762–3), and a distribution of all other goods that maximizes the expectations of the least well off. More formally and completely:

First Principle
Each person is to have an equal right to the most extensive total system of equal basic liberties compatible with a similar system of liberty for all.

Second Principle
Social and economic inequalities are to be arranged so that they are both:
(a) to the greatest benefit of the least advantaged, consistent with the just savings principle, and
(b) attached to offices and positions open to all under conditions of fair equality of opportunity. (Rawls 1972: 302)

The first part of the second principle is familiarly known as the 'difference principle', and the two principles are in lexical order. That is to say that inequalities regulated by the second principle are only permitted when equality of liberty under the first principle has been guaranteed.

Provided that these principles apply or very nearly apply to the basic institutions of society then that society is just. And individuals have a duty to abide by the rules of a just society. Although Rawls offers a CONTRACTUALIST (pp. 672–7) argument for the rules themselves, the duty to abide by them is not itself contractually based. In part three of *A Theory of Justice* Rawls offers an account of the acquisition of a sense of justice. This grows out of the basic attachments and relationships which constitute any society: family, friendship and broader associations. There is in the well-ordered society a concordance of fair rules and a sense of justice. Citizens can recognize that the rules are just and acknowledge their duty to abide by them. Fairness and feasibility coincide.

Lastly, *A Theory of Justice* is a theory of THE RIGHT AND THE GOOD (pp. 598–601). The just society is not one which realizes the good life of its community. It is one which permits its members to pursue their own conception of the good under certain conditions. First, the pursuit of the good is constrained by the right, that is the publicly agreed principles of justice. Second, these principles determine the distribution of primary social goods – rights, liberties, powers and opportunities, income and wealth – which are the desired prerequisites of any particular pursuit of the good. Third, people pursue different ideals of the good life. 'Human good is heterogeneous because the aims of the self are heterogeneous' (Rawls 1972: 554). It would be a disastrous mistake for a polity to try to impose upon its members any one particular ideal of life. Rawls has continued to believe that, in any modern society, there will be a plurality of conscientiously sought ends, and that any state, presuming or prescribing to the contrary, would have to employ extensive coercion to secure its single vision.

The final question to be answered is, Why *A Theory of Justice*? This asks what justification Rawls offers for his own principles. Rawls famously employs a contractualist methodology: the principles of justice are those that rational, self-interested, but mutually disinterested individuals would choose in an original situation specified chiefly in terms of the parties' selective knowledge. The contractualist method has been the subject of a great deal of criticism: why should a hypothetical contract bind? Why would individuals choose as Rawls claimed they would? Would not individuals choose differently in a different original position? Moreover Rawls himself has subsequently denied that the contractarian argument has independent justificatory force and views it only as a heuristic device which serves to illustrate the force of a claim whose real justification lies elsewhere.

However, the question then presses of what *does* justify the principles of justice, and it presses the more since Rawls has become concerned with the issue of how a just society can be well-ordered, that is be viewed as legitimate by its citizens. Before considering this question it is necessary to examine a fundamental, and influential, critique of Rawls's understanding of justice.

This is to be found in Robert Nozick's *Anarchy, State and Utopia* (1974), which is rightly paired with Rawls's *A Theory of Justice* when the contemporary resurgence of political philosophy is discussed. The foundations of Nozick's arguments are RIGHTS (pp. 690–1) and OWNERSHIP (pp. 690–1). The rights possessed by individuals are fundamental, and define a moral space surrounding each person whose invasion constitutes a wrong. Following Locke, Nozick holds the basic rights to be those to life, liberty, and 'estate' or property. For Nozick, these rights are 'side-constraints' upon action, and have infinite moral weight. That is, no amount of good consequences, including even an overall diminution of rights violations, can justify a single violation of one of these rights. Nozick does not offer a systematic defence of his understanding of rights. At most he claims the underlying justification to be the Kantian view of INDIVIDUALS AS ENDS (p. 736), leading separate, different, consciously and deliberatively shaped lives, which should not be sacrificed or used as means to others' ends.

Nozick is egalitarian to the extent of holding that all humans equally possess these fundamental rights. He also endorses an initial equal distribution of ownership in respect of our selves. Each owns his or her own body, and its powers, capacities and abilities. Nozick believes that through an exercise of this initial self-ownership further entitlements to bits of the world are generated. He considers only one form of argument to show how this generation of entitlements might occur. This is John Locke's famous claim that one acquires rights to that with which one has mixed one's labour. Unfortunately Nozick devotes four incisive pages to expose seemingly unanswerable difficulties in the Lockean account (Nozick 1974: 174–8). This seems to leave Nozick with his own problem of unfounded entitlements, and so some critics have charged. But Nozick is appealing to the plausible background assumption that unowned objects are there to be owned, and that some sort of fruitful exercise of one's own powers grounds an entitlement to ownership of these objects. That is, provided certain conditions upon legitimate acquisition are met.

Entitlements

What occupies Nozick is less the process of acquisition than the limits which may be set upon its scope. Nozick borrows again from Locke and urges the acceptance of one fundamental proviso: 'A process normally giving rise to a permanent bequeathable property right in a previously unowned thing will not do so if the position of others no longer at liberty to use the thing is thereby worsened' (ibid.: 178). Nozick's concern is to show that this proviso can be met by an established distribution of property entitlements, when one considers that there may no longer be any unowned objects for individuals to acquire. His answer is that individuals unable to appropriate are nevertheless better off living under a system permitting private property than they would be if no original appropriations had been permitted.

The account of entitlements is completed by acknowledging that those who hold bits of the world are entitled freely to transfer them if and to whomsoever they choose. It follows that those who receive such freely transferred holdings are themselves now entitled to hold them. Thus everything which is not unowned is legitimately owned if acquired justly (by some process which does not violate the Lockean proviso) or freely transferred from one who justly acquired it. A just set of holdings is just that set of holdings which came about in the right way.

In part one of *Anarchy, State and Utopia* Nozick justifies a minimal state. He does so by constructing a plausible tale of how a state of nature might have given way to a state, that is an organization legitimately claiming a monopoly on the use of force within a given territory, without at any stage violating rights. The tale turns on the evolving competition between private agencies formed to protect their clients, with one eventually assuming a monopolistic role and adequately compensating the others for its usurpation of their functions.

Part two of *Anarchy, State and Utopia* is devoted to a defence of the view that such a state, restricted to preventing force, theft and fraud, and enforcing contracts, is morally sufficient. Any greater role for the state is illegitimate. Of course an obvious reason for a greater role would be that people's holdings need to be redistributed in accord with a theory of justice. Nozick's own theory of justice does not require any such action by government. His task is then to show that redistributive theories of justice are mistaken, and what they require of the state illicit.

The distinction Nozick draws is between his own entitlement theory of justice, and patterned or end-state theories. His is a historical theory since the justice of a set of holdings is given by the propriety of the history which led up to it. End-state theories are unhistorical, specifying that a distribution must conform to a prescribed structure. More particularly, patterned theories prescribe a distribution of holdings according to some natural attribute or ordered set of such attributes, such as intelligence or effort. Nozick's critique of non-historical theories is both general and specific. At a general level he insists that no patterned distribution can be maintained without persistent and serious violations of the right to liberty. His reasoning is simple. Voluntary transfers of those holdings initially assured under any patterned distribution will subvert the pattern and transgress the principle underlying the pattern. Such transfers are easy to imagine, and appear eminently unobjectionable inasmuch as they can be simple, consensual, bilateral exchanges. Nozick's own famous example is of fans willingly paying extra to see an especially talented basketball player, Wilt Chamberlain. Such transfers can only be prevented by denying individuals the right to do with their holdings as they choose. Surely no consistent theory of justice can both distribute holdings and deny the individuals to whom they come any effective control over them?

Nozick's specific criticisms are of Rawlsian and egalitarian theories of justice. The fundamental weakness of Rawls's theory is that it proceeds as if individuals did not already have claims to ownership of themselves and bits of the world. A cake spontaneously given to a group might be divided among its members in a way close to Rawls's principles; a cake which I have baked or whose ingredients you have provided will be divided in quite another way. Rawls is simply wrong to discount the various entitlements individuals bring to any determination of who gets what. People, not least, are entitled to their natural assets, and, consequently, to any rewards that may flow from these. Rawls is mistaken to think that these assets are a collective resource, or that the difference principle which reflects this assumption would be acceptable to the well-off who are required to make a comparatively greater sacrifice so that the worst-off benefit.

Nozick finds no justification either for any egalitarian principle. A demand for equality of material condition reduces to an unsubstantiated claim that the function of society is to meet the needs of its members, and simply discounts the fact that things are already attached to particular individuals. Equality is not required for self-esteem, which in fact thrives on comparable differences. At base the demand for equality is driven by envy.

Nozick's theory of justice permits the government no interventionist role beyond the rectification of injustices by the terms of the entitlement principle. It is ironic then that,

263

given the logistic difficulties in tracking back and forward between past wrongs and present holdings, Nozick should suggest the difference principle as a rough rule of thumb for rectifying injustices (ibid.: 231). Otherwise holdings must be left as they have come legitimately to stand. That this may result in great disparities of wealth and life prospects is regrettable but no injustice. The rich may choose to be philanthropists but they do no wrong in not being. And it would violate their rights to require that they assist the less fortunate. This seems harsh but it is not obviously wrong-headed. Liberal critics chide Nozick for offering a 'libertarianism without foundations', but this may not be quite true.

Nozick's foundations are attractive ones. Individuals do appear to have rights in the sense that it would be fundamentally wrong to do certain things to them in the name of a greater social good. Individuals do also have a claim to ownership of their selves. That this is so can be shown by considering one's reaction to the idea that bodily parts should be redistributed equitably or to benefit the least fortunate in this respect. Do the blind have a claim upon at least one of the eyes of the sighted?

Criticism of Nozick is more appropriately directed at his rendering of these foundations and how he builds upon them. There is little warrant for construing rights in an absolute and exclusively negative manner, not least when appeal is made to Kantian underpinnings. Within a moral community, individuals in need may, on Kant's own principles, have the right to contributions from those who can help them. It is an impossibly stringent requirement of rights merely that they rule out invasions of our moral space and do nothing to sustain us in our satisfaction of basic needs.

Nozick may be right to think that we, severally, own ourselves and may, in consequence and by some form of activity, come to make legitimate claims upon what is unowned. But, arguably, the conditions he sets for legitimate acquisition are too lax and too easily met in ways that favour free-market capitalism. It may very well be possible to concede an initial equality in self-ownership, and the legitimacy of some process of acquisition of unowned objects, but then to specify sufficiently tough conditions of legitimacy to ensure that a final equality of holdings is ensured. Again, the 'Lockean proviso' need not be as easily satisfied by his favoured set of economic arrangements as Nozick assumes, especially once ambiguities in both the sense of 'better off' and the baseline against which comparisons are made are clarified.

Nozick seems to presume throughout that ownership is full and exclusive ownership by individuals, and that anything less amounts to a violation of liberty rights. Yet Nozick forgets that, for Locke, individuals made claim through their labouring not upon what was unowned, but what was communally owned. In his Wilt Chamberlain example Nozick assumes that individuals within the patterned distribution have holdings with which they are free to do as they choose. All forms of redistribution, including taxation, are implausibly stigmatized as coercive interferences with freedom. Yet it is possible that individuals might choose to limit in advance departures from a favoured pattern of distribution, and do so in the name of a liberty-preserving equality of condition.

In sum, Nozick's theory is not so much libertarianism without foundations, as libertarianism with unwarranted conclusions. His case against anarchy may be accepted. His claim that state minimalism is utopian in a positive sense remains unproven.

3   Equality

Both Rawls and Nozick are egalitarians to the extent that they are, in their different ways, committed to the view that human beings are entitled to an equality of regard or treatment in some fundamental respect. Rawls's theory assures citizens equal liberty and Nozick holds that all humans equally possess fundamental rights. All contemporary social and political philosophy affirms that humans are entitled to equality of something, which suggests that the crucial question is not 'Why equality?' but 'Equality of what?' (Sen 1992). Of course a demand for equality in respect of some good is consistent with, indeed may demand, inequality in respect of some other good. This is true of Nozick's libertarianism which claims that an equal distribution of individual liberty must lead to an unequal distribution of income and property. A demand for equality in some good may take priority over other values, as is the case with Rawls's insistence upon the lexical priority of equal liberties.

But although Rawls's first principle of justice formally guarantees equal citizenship, the difference principle tolerates social and economic inequality. Rawls sees no inconsistency here, though he concedes – as did Berlin – that differential access to resources will qualify the worth of equal liberty. The more you have the more you can make of a freedom shared equally with others in society. Socialist critics of liberalism have always insisted that this is unsatisfactory, arguing that real equality of freedom demands an equalization of resources. Some feminists have also argued that the public or legal equality of the genders is undermined by, and yet serves to disguise, a fundamental inequality of social power. This characterizes all male–female relationships within patriarchal society, and its elimination will require more far-reaching reform of society than simply instituting a principle of equal citizenship.

Walzer's (1983) argument is important in this context. He suggests that there are different spheres of justice, each being specified by a set of goods to be distributed and a consequent principle of their fair distribution. The unequal distribution of some good need not in itself be unjust, but if this distribution determines the distribution of some other good then that is unfair. It is not necessarily wrong that some people have more money than others; it is if their greater wealth buys them political power, office or greater personal health.

Walzer's approach highlights the fact that our favoured account of equality depends on what it is that we wish to see equally distributed. Contemporary egalitarianism defends three broad fields of application of equality. For a welfare egalitarian the ideal is a 'condition of equal well-being for all persons at the highest possible level of well-being' (Landesman 1983). The central problem for welfare egalitarianism is that it seems committed to taking account of those pleasures some humans may take from seeing others do less well, and is also committed to the satisfaction of some acquired expensive tastes.

Resource egalitarianism assigns to each individual a bundle of goods which is envied by no other individual. The central problem for this version of egalitarianism is that natural assets (skills, talents and abilities) are unequally distributed and in consequence people benefit differentially from their use of equally distributed resources. Yet to include personal talents among resources which are equalized means that the talented are, in effect, the slaves of the untalented.

Contemporary egalitarians are now inclined to agree that individuals should not be compensated for the effects of free choices (such as, obviously, choosing to develop an expensive taste), but should be compensated for those factors affecting them which are due to 'brute luck' (such as, obviously, a handicap). On Dworkin's (1981) influential argument, a principle of liberal equality should be 'endowment-insensitive' but 'ambition-sensitive'. That is, it should permit individuals' lives to flourish or founder as a result of the choices they make, but not in consequence of their natural or social endowments. Such a principle may not be easy to render determinate and relies upon a specification of the scope of free choice. Moreover it should be noted that individuals may not choose the circumstances which cause freely chosen preferences to be more or less expensive.

Capability or opportunity egalitarians demand the equalization of the capacity to lead the life that the individual values or chooses to live. They thereby avoid the problem faced by resource egalitarians of how the same set of resources may, according to the circumstances, be differentially convertible into achievable standards of living. They also avoid the problems of welfare egalitarianism which neglects those aspects of good life which do not reduce to well-being and which cannot acknowledge the fact that some people, subject to enduring conditions of significant inequality, may adapt their preferences (and states of well-being) to these conditions and not, in consequence, experience a significantly lesser degree of welfare. Capability egalitarians, however, must provide a ranking of capacities which cannot be purely quantitative – a life does not necessarily go better the more things one can do. But if such a ranking does not reduce to one of opportunities for greater or lesser welfare, it is in danger of being an objective list resting upon a contentious account of the human good.

Finally, any egalitarianism must answer criticisms of both practice and principle. Egalitarianism may simply be inconsistent with certain immutable features of human motivation. It may not be possible to combine, within the individual, the attitude of universal impartiality and personal partiality (Nagel 1991). Again, a society in which equality is guaranteed may lack the incentives necessary for maximizing the total social product and thereby improving the well-being of all. Egalitarianism must also meet Nozick's challenge that the case for equality is unproven, and anyway trumped by more fundamental ideals, such as freedom or self-ownership: a prior commitment to liberty undermines any guarantee of equality, and, correlatively, equality can only be maintained by the denial of individual freedom. The disputed relationship between equality and liberty may prove to be the most enduring and pressing issue of political philosophy. The fact that we have thereby come full circle to the work of Berlin and Hayek certainly suggests an underlying continuity of concern in the subject.

4   Pluralism and Neutrality

Rawls responded to criticisms of *A Theory of Justice* in a series of articles which culminated in his second major book, *Political Liberalism* (Rawls 1993). Its concern is with the good order of a modern liberal democratic society. It does not defend a particular theory of distributive justice, although Rawls continues to think that his own two principles are suitable to regulate the basic structure of a well-ordered society. Whereas *A Theory of Justice* started from Humean circumstances of justice, *Political Liberalism* starts from the modern condition of value pluralism, namely that people entertain, for good reasons, different and probably incompatible comprehensive philosophical doctrines. *Political Liberalism* also repudiates the main arguments for the two principles of *A Theory of Justice*. The contractarian argument was only a 'device of representation'; no metaphysical understanding of the self was or needs to be presupposed; and it is a mistake to think agreement to the principles of justice could rely on deep-lying acceptance of a broader moral doctrine of fairness.

Nevertheless, *Political Liberalism* argues that a political conception of justice could command the support of an 'overlapping consensus' of various comprehensive doctrines in the society whose basic structure it regulates. A just society of free and equal citizens could thus endure over time even though deeply divided in its basic religious, moral and philosophical outlooks.

Some critics fear that Rawls's theory only represents a pragmatic accommodation to the possibilities of consensus within particular societies. Yet *Political Liberalism* does not simply defend the politics of compromise and *modus vivendi*. It is an attempt to specify the terms of co-operation that can withstand the test of public and rational negotiation, commanding the freely given assent of equals. The worry should rather be that Rawls can no longer show why the well-ordered society must be one regulated by certain principles of justice, and vice versa. Rawls's idea of an 'overlapping consensus' may be so indeterminate as to yield very many different outcomes. Or it may deliver a specific outcome by prescriptively stipulating what shall and shall not count as reasonable doctrines. Moreover, it may miss the real nature of negotiating political difference in its representation of views and disagreement as 'reasonable'.

The last part of *A Theory of Justice* sketched an account of the development in the citizens of the just society of the requisite sense of justice. It offered a theory of moral education through the relationships of association within that society. In *Political Liberalism* Rawls forswears this kind of account. But to that extent any theory of political justice is 'thinner' and less plausible. Indeed there is a general problem of the basic liberal approach. Rawls's conviction remains that, short of an unacceptable coerced unanimity, a domain of public agreement can be secured and clearly separated from the sphere of the heterogeneous private good. In this he remains faithful to the liberal vision of a society in which all equally and freely pursue their different lives constrained by public terms of fair coexistence. Yet such a vision may be impaled on the horns of a dilemma. Either the terms of public agreement are so insubstantial as to yield only an empty form of political community. Or they are made substantial only by violating the requirement that disputed understandings of the good be restricted to the private sphere. A liberal political order may demand a culture of and education in liberal values. The good of society may not be so readily separable from the good of its citizens' private lives.

Finally it may be held unreasonable to ask people to exclude their deeply held comprehensive views from the terms of their political activity. Citizens are required to frame and articulate their demands in the language of a public reason which is political and independent of any particular comprehensive view. In a frequently invoked metaphor individuals must come 'naked to the public square' by setting aside views that are deeply important to and perhaps even constitutive of their selves. Moreover a liberal political culture is cut off from the substantive comprehensive views that may historically have nourished it, leaving it deracinated and its citizens alienated.

Rawls's starting point in *Political Liberalism*, as it is now for many other political philosophers, is value pluralism. This should not be confused with relativism or scepticism about the good. Such pluralism is rather taken to be an inevitable result of the conscientious exercise by distinct individuals of a similar capacity for reasoning. An expectation of reasonable disagreement is an acknowledgement of an evident fact about modern life and a rejoinder to a long Enlightenment tradition which holds reason to generate convergence on the truth.

Pluralism must not merely be expected but also tolerated because value monism can only be secured through coercive state interference with individual liberty of conscience, and because pluralism need not spell disaster if it can still provide the basis of harmonious social and political co-operation. The problem may be that the toleration of value pluralism presupposes some foundational value – such as the autonomy whose exercise by different individuals generates it. Yet if pluralism goes, as it were, all the way down there is no reason to think that any value can be privileged and not be the subject of reasonable disagreement between individuals.

Value pluralism is honoured, arguably, if and only if the state, in its laws and policies, remains neutral between its citizens' different conceptions of the good. This doctrine of official neutrality on the question of the good is viewed by many as definitive or constitutive of contemporary philosophical liberalism (Dworkin 1978; Ackerman 1980: 10–12). A distinction is normally drawn between neutrality with respect to the justification or aim offered by government for its activity and with respect to its consequences or outcome, most preferring to understand neutrality in the first sense. Thus, going back to a much earlier liberal thinker, John Locke defended political intolerance of Catholics (non-neutral in its consequences) not because Catholics were doctrinally in error (non-neutral in its justification) but because Catholics, in owing allegiance to the foreign jurisdiction of Rome, represented a danger to the good order of the state (neutral in its justification) (Locke 1689).

The manner in which political neutrality can be achieved is represented either negatively, as the bracketing out of whatever is the subject of disagreement, or positively, as the operation of a shared public political reason. Neutrality will be defended by appeal to the value of equality or that of individual autonomy. On the first a state does not treat its citizens as equals if it favours one citizen's views of the good over others. On the second it is more important that individuals lead the lives they see as good rather than be led to live the life that the state thinks of as good. In addition a doctrine of neutrality will be seen as a necessary protection against the excessive, and dangerous, exercise of state power over individuals.

Value pluralism, and the associated principle of neutrality, stand opposed to perfectionism, the doctrine that there are specifiable human excellences such that some forms of human life are superior in themselves to others. Rawls rejects perfectionism, but some liberals have insisted that, nevertheless, his own account of human good is too thin, and that we can make judgements about the relative worth of different forms of existence. This need not be inconsistent with a commitment to egalitarianism and tolerance (Haskar 1979; Galston 1980). Moreover, there is a suspicion that Rawlsian liberalism is, at base, inconsistent. If it is strictly neutral then it cannot subscribe to any normative understanding of individuals, that they should, for instance, strive to be purposive, autonomous creatures. But such a view seems presupposed by Rawls. If, on the other hand, liberalism does include some foundational moral judgements about human beings, then it cannot reasonably claim objectivity for these judgements and refuse it for judgements about the good life.

It also seems clear that a liberal democratic culture will flourish to the extent that its citizens acquire and practise certain virtues, those for instance of tolerance, civility, respect for others and a willingness to make sacrifices for the common good. Now whether such virtues are learnt in childhood, or got through good habits, a liberal society must surely take the decision to encourage those social forms which facilitate the acquisition of such virtues.

Autonomy and Liberalism

In this context Joseph Raz (1986) is a revisionist liberal. He doubts whether liberty should be the central value, and defends instead the primacy of autonomy. His understanding of autonomy is that only a life chosen from among several moral options is autonomous. Further, Raz believes that, while not all forms of life are valuable, there may be several incompatible ones that are. Autonomy requires a plurality of moral life choices, and this in turn requires the creation and maintenance of social forms conducive to autonomy. The government has a duty to preserve these forms but, crucially, may do so in non-coercive ways. Subsidies and taxation can effectively render certain choices attractive or unattractive relative to others. Thus, Raz bites the bullet, holding that a liberal political culture should sustain its own core values, and not aspire to an implausible ideal of neutrality. Liberalism can be tolerant of diversity, interventionist and anti-perfectionist.

In similar terms William Galston's liberalism embraces and supports a set of distinctive liberal purposes that guide liberal public policy and shape liberal justice. These require the practise of and a civic education in liberal virtues, and the maintenance of a liberal public culture. Liberalism has a thick enough theory of the good life to be able to rule out certain practices and encourage others: 'it is not the absence of an account of the good that distinguishes liberalism from other forms of political theory and practice. It is rather a special set of reasons for restricting the movement from the good to public coercion' (Galston 1980: 180). Liberalism is not neutral; rather its governance is not morally costly in its use of coercive state power.

5   Critics of Liberalism: Communitarianism, Feminism, and Analytical Marxism

There are three broad movements deserving consideration for their critiques of liberalism: communitarianism, feminism and Marxism.

5.1   Communitarianism

The writers gathered under this title – Roberto Unger (1975), Michael Sandel (1982), Michael Walzer (1983), Charles Taylor (1985), Alasdair MacIntyre (1981, 1988) and Richard Rorty (1989, 1991) – are disparate and do not consciously subscribe to a common manifesto. It is more accurate to speak of family resemblances than a single, shared programme. In the respects in which they are all communitarian they offer not so much an alternative political view to liberalism as a criticism of its presuppositions. Communitarians invoke community in criticisms which are both normative and descriptive, although the distinct kinds of criticism are not always carefully distinguished (Caney 1992; Taylor 1989).

The central descriptive criticism concerns the nature of the self or individual, and charges liberalism with subscribing to an inadequately 'thin' understanding of the 'self'. The facts specifying the social and historical situation of each person constrain the kinds of self-understanding she can reach, and the choices she will make. The Rawlsian individual is not 'embedded' in any place or time; she is so emptied of substantial, individuating features as to make it difficult to describe her as choosing a life. How can a self-less person be said to have any conception of the good or make choices of ends?

This criticism may rest on a misunderstanding. Rawls's concern is not to define idealized choosers of the good so much as to specify the relevant considerations entering into a jointly agreed determination of the public rules of fair co-operation. As he insists in his later work, his theory of justice is not metaphysical but political and assumes no particular understanding of the self. At the same time the criticism may be overstated. To claim that individuals are wholly defined, and their identity completely constituted by their membership of some community at some historical moment, is effectively to deny them any kind of meaningful choice over their lives. It also seriously undermines any claim they might make to be MORAL AGENTS (chapter 6). And to the extent that the communitarian claim is qualified by phrases such as 'to a large extent' it is hard to see what distinguishes the communitarian from the liberal.

The normative criticisms of communitarianism are threefold. First, the priority which Rawls accords the virtue of justice is alleged to derive from an impoverished understanding of political association. Rawls claims that justice is the first virtue of social institutions, that it is required to deal with limited benevolence, moderate scarcity and modern value pluralism, and that it is needed to protect individuals from being sacrificed for the society's greater good. According to communitarian critics, however, justice is only the ideal of societies which do not display community. Communities proper do not need to be just, and would not be communities if they felt such a need. Michael Sandel (1982) characterizes justice as a remedial virtue, binding up in the best way possible a second-best form of social co-operation.

The sense in which justice has primacy for Rawls has already been indicated, and Sandel's criticism appears misplaced. Resolution in the face of death is not less of a human virtue for being redundant in immortal creatures. Sandel does not claim, as have some Marxists for instance, that the circumstances of justice will disappear in the future. He says only that some communities do not display them. But these – most notably the family – cannot be the models for society as a whole. The family has those characteristics which make its members benevolently disposed to one another –

270

closeness, and affectivity rooted in natural relationships – because it is not simply a smaller kind of society but something quite different altogether. Societies cannot be familial communities.

The second normative claim of communitarianism is that membership of a political community is a good which liberalism neglects, ignores, or whose sense it cannot successfully capture by its own terms. Political association is viewed by liberals and libertarians as an INSTRUMENTAL GOOD (pp. 216–18). It realizes the compromises necessary for individuals to derive mutual advantage from co-operating. There is no other sense of being together as citizens than is required to bring about this end. Rawls and Nozick both talk of community, or even communities, growing up within this framework. But these seem inessential and somehow added onto the basic terms of political association.

This would not be so serious a criticism were it not for the further claim that a liberal theory of justice needs more. Sandel charges that Rawls defends a difference principle without foundations. Acceptance of this principle requires a willingness to see one's natural assets as communally owned, and yet Rawls's theory allows for no community which could lay such a claim to ownership. On Rawls's account I see my talents as for others to derive benefits from, yet there is no reason why I should see myself as joined to these others. Here we meet again the problem for liberalism of showing how a just society can also be well-ordered and whether political legitimacy must rest upon a sense of community which liberalism is incapable of supplying.

The third normative communitarian claim is that what is good and just for individuals is defined by the community to which they belong. Alasdair MacIntyre (1981, 1988) is associated with the view that an individual's good is inseparable from the ROLE (p. 388), office or social position he fills. Michael Walzer (1983) makes the further claim that, since the goods to be distributed have particular SOCIAL MEANINGS (pp. 384–90), the justice of their distribution is relative to these meanings. As these meanings have particular social and historical location, so do the associated principles of justice.

However, the besetting danger of any appeal to the existence of distinct understandings of the good and the just is RELATIVISM (pp. 395–7). This society is just by its own lights; that society is just by its own lights. And never shall the two be compared. Further, shared understandings determine not only what is just but what is unjust. Yet these particular judgements may violate what, plausibly, ought to be UNIVERSAL MORAL STANDARDS (pp. 733–6). Imagine a society by whose understanding of the master–slave relationship 20 lashes a day are fair and sufficient. If a master administers 25 he is unjust and if only 15 he behaves generously. But surely any beating is wrong, and any 'rules' of slavery are unjust, whatever the members of the society believe.

With regard to the communitarians' normative claims the liberal will respond that liberalism does not dispute the value of community nor need it neglect its significance. The liberal will press the communitarian to clarify precisely what sort of political proposals are distinctive of communitarians, worrying that, where they are spelled out, such proposals suggest an illiberal concession to whatever happens to be the shared understandings and practices of a particular time and place (Gutman 1985). At best communitarianism prompts liberalism to demonstrate how its constitutive values are

271

consistent with the maintenance and reproduction of a good order which, arguably, needs a shared sense of community.

5.2   Feminism

FEMINISM (chapter 20) offers two quite distinct kinds of criticism of philosophical liberalism. The first concentrates on the silence of liberal political theory and, being consciously *ad hominem*, of its male theorists about women's place in a just society. More particularly this silence is compounded by assumptions about what this place actually is and should remain. A formal commitment to the equality of all is gainsaid by an endorsement of patriarchalism, which is not always only implicit. Patriarchalism here means the doctrine of the subordination of women to male power.

The Public and the Private

The crucial assumption underpinning liberal patriarchalism is that to the distinction between public and private spheres of activity corresponds a difference of nature between men and women, and the roles for which these natures best suit them. The woman is confined to the family where her biology equips her to bear, rear and care. The woman is thus doubly oppressed: excluded from the public, political sphere where the liberal principle of equality operates, and the inferior of her male provider within the private household.

In terms of oppression related to the distinction between public and private spheres, Susan Moller Okin (1989) accuses Rawls of perpetuating liberal patriarchalism. He never broaches the issue of sexual justice, yet assumes both the continued existence of the institution of the family, and, more pertinently, the traditional sexual division of labour within this institution. Okin can reasonably claim that a family whose structure is deeply unjust cannot, as Rawls expects, be the appropriate institution for acquiring a sense of justice. Okin's critique of the family is nevertheless not a radical one. She merely insists that Rawlsian principles of justice be universal in scope and extend to all institutions, including the family.

The second line of feminist criticism concerns the alleged maleness of a preoccupation with justice and rights. Appeal is made to a distinctive female ethics which emphasizes attachment, responsibility, context and particularity as opposed to independence, rights, abstraction and universality. The idea that women speak in another moral 'voice' to that of men is due principally to the work of Carol Gilligan (1982) in the psychology of moral development. But the contrast between an ethics of care and one of justice now enjoys wide currency in moral and political philosophy. Gilligan herself does not see these moral outlooks as mutually exclusive; nor does she see each of them as necessarily associated with one particular gender. Indeed she seems to favour an account of moral development which emphasizes the socializing role of parents, whatever their gender.

From the standpoint of social and political philosophy this particular line of criticism bites only if the prevailing liberal accounts of the good society may be judged defective for omitting mention of care. It begs too many questions to suggest that justice applies in the public sphere, and care in the private. It would also grossly over-simplify to suggest that social co-operation could be governed either by rules of justice or by an ethos of care. Indeed there are reasons to agree with the Rawlsian view that justice has primacy. Care alone cannot determine who should be in receipt of what goods. And where care fails or falls short of what is desired, justice specifies what can be legitimately expected of others. Nevertheless, the opposition between care and justice highlights – as does the communitarian critique – the extent to which a society governed solely by respect for rights and a 'sense of justice' may not generate any real sense of relatedness and interdependence among its members.

5.3 Analytical Marxism

As the title implies analytical Marxists have displayed the virtues of anglophone philosophy in general, that is argumentative rigour, scrupulous attention to the text, and careful conceptual analysis. Whether such work is Marxist is debatable. It certainly eschews wholesale subscription to every aspect of Marx's work, and prefers instead separately to appraise the distinct claims that may be said to constitute this theory. It has rejected a certain understanding of history, TELEOLOGICAL (pp. 319–20) and HEGELIAN (chapter 33) in origin, and, in the case of Jon Elster (1985) at least, embraced a robust METHODOLOGICAL INDIVIDUALISM (pp. 397–9) that is very unfamiliar among Marxists. It has been willing to jettison what many would see as central Marxist claims, for instance the LABOUR THEORY OF VALUE (chapter 34), and has increasingly conceded the attractiveness of non-Marxian theories in political philosophy.

However, analytical Marxism has insisted upon the specific character of capitalism, and sought to explicate the manner both in which such a society is fundamentally flawed, and in which socialism represents a feasible and desirable alternative. Yet there are deep problems with such an approach. In the first instance it needs to be shown that Marx had a theory of justice by which CAPITALISM (pp. 755–6) can be judged unjust. This task confronts a familiar paradox. Marx employs a language with apparent moral import, yet explicitly disdains moral criticism and theory (Lukes 1985). The paradox is not easy to resolve, and any resolution may simply have to accommodate the fact that Marx was not consistent in his outlook (Geras 1985).

Second, if capitalism is unjust then for Marxists that injustice must inhere in some significant feature of the relationship between capitalist and proletarian. Two candidates suggest themselves. The first is that the capitalist exploits the proletarian. Yet on any plausible account of exploitation that can be offered it is arguable that some form of exploitation may characterize every society, including socialism. Moreover, the difference in ownership of resources which defines the capitalist relation need not be unfair. It may have arisen in a perfectly legitimate fashion, for instance through the superior efforts, talents, assiduity and prodigality of the capitalist. The idea of a 'cleanly generated capitalism' conforms to Robert Nozick's prescription of a just distribution that has arisen by just steps from an originally just situation.

The second candidate for explaining the injustice of the capitalist relation is coercion. Workers may be unfairly forced to work for their employers. The difficulty is that for any one worker the alternatives to employment are not so stark and restrictive as would be required to establish coercion. This is especially true in a modern welfare society where it must also be acknowledged that avenues of escape from one's class do exist for the talented and hard working.

Difficulties in appreciating the specific inequity of capitalism are compounded by imprecision in the recommendations of socialist justice. Notoriously Marx said little about the lineaments of the future society, and what he did say suggests utopianism in the pejorative sense of this word. Talk of a society 'beyond justice' might imply the view that the circumstances of justice will be transcended. This is unrealistic. Or it might imply the irrelevance of any evaluative criteria to such a society. This is dangerously naive. Marxists can engage with other contemporary political philosophers on the grounds of equality, emphasizing the deep, structured inequalities of present capitalist society and the manner in which these inequalities corrupt any formal equality of civic rights. But if they are to be radical egalitarians they may differ little from some liberals, or be beset by difficulties which derive from their commitment to principles, such as that of self-ownership, which liberals do not share (Cohen 1990).

There is a final important point. Any theory which indicts the present society of fundamental injustice and recommends a future perfect society needs an account of the means of transforming the first into the second. Traditionally Marxism relied on some combination of the historical guarantee of revolutionary change and the uniquely important role of the proletariat. Analytical Marxism is not teleologically optimistic and has tended to reticence about proletarian activism. This is partly due to its individualist presuppositions, which make it hard to appreciate the factors disposing to and inhibiting COLLECTIVE AGENCY (pp. 397–9). It is also due to the need for an account of why what is in the interests of the majority of society's members coincides with the morally desired emancipation of all. This is increasingly difficult, for there is no longer a group of individuals who satisfy the various requirements of that orthodoxy – being the exploited bulk of capitalist society with nothing to lose and everything to gain by overthrowing that society and its injustices.

Analytical Marxism has performed a signal service by bringing Marxism within the fold of contemporary political philosophy. But it may have done so at the price of exposing serious if not fatal shortcomings in Marxism. And to the extent that analytical Marxists have become political philosophers they have arguably ceased to be Marxists.

6   Individuals and Communities

A standard charge against liberalism is that it is individualistic. Methodological individualism is discussed elsewhere, and the various senses in which liberalism might be said to neglect community were considered in the section on communitarianism. What needs to be examined here is the significance political philosophy should accord to groups or communities, and the relationship of individuals to these collective entities. For while each of us is an individual we are also social creatures, belonging to particular tribes, cultures, religions, races and nations. To deny these facts would be productive of an implausible theory and an impoverished political practice.

There are at least two ways in which group identity is significant. In the first instance there is the question of how the state should treat the existence within its jurisdiction of stable, enduring, well-defined groups with their own history, culture and way of life.

This is the problem of cultural pluralism. In the second instance there is the question of where the boundaries of any state or jurisdiction should be drawn and what role should be played in this context by nationhood. This is the problem of nationality and nationalism.

6.1   Cultural pluralism

Although political philosophy has, from its inception with the Greeks, tended to assume the cultural or ethnic homogeneity of the 'people' whose obligation a legitimate state commands and to whom a set of principles of justice may apply, the fact is that all modern societies comprise distinct stable groups whose members identify themselves – and are identified by others – by reference to some combination of shared race, religion, nationality, language, culture or history. How should the state respond?

It could insist on denying the fact of difference either by enforcing a 'republican' ideal wherein citizens have no allegiances or identities other than those which constitute them as members of the polity, or by supporting assimilationist practices whereby members of cultural minorities must acquire the identity of the dominant community. Such measures of compulsory homogenization are widely perceived as unfair in denying to individuals something of great value, namely the expression of their own particular communal identity.

A culturally pluralist state, by contrast, honours the existence of plural identities by measures which may range from underwriting the right of persons belonging to minorities to enjoy their own culture, to 'communalist' measures which positively protect and preserve the distinct groups recognized within society.

Liberals are unwilling to see the warrant for such measures in the existence of group rights which do not straightforwardly reduce to the rights of the individual members of the group in question. Rather they have argued that the protection of groups can be defended in so far as doing so protects and advances the interests of individuals as members of groups (Raz 1986: 207–9). The value of a culture is said to be that of cultural membership, its value to the individuals who are members (Buchanan 1991). In an original and arresting argument, Kymlicka (1989) rejects the idea of group rights but commends a policy of actively seeking to preserve cultures. He does so by arguing that our cultural membership is a good in so far as it provides the necessary context from within which we are able to make and evaluate meaningful, rational, autonomous choices of life. Charles Taylor (1992) has tried to defend a liberalism which might permit the state to nourish and protect a particular culture, so long as it was also able to secure the rights of those who do not share the dominant culture.

The major problem is that liberalism may be left with no other criterion for appraising different cultures than the extent to which they nurture the kind of individuals favoured by liberals. Should a liberal society tolerate a minority culture which does not respect autonomy, even if it supplies its members with an otherwise worthwhile life? Is cultural pluralism a good thing only if the various cultures are all consistent with liberal ideals of individuality? Moreover any account of cultural pluralism must acknowledge the possible disadvantages of diversity. These may include the increased possibility of social conflict, and the undermining of the shared sense of community which is necessary for good political order.

6.2   *Nationalism and nationality*

Political philosophy has, until recently, remained largely silent on the questions of nationalism or nationality; or it has dismissed such questions as somehow unworthy of philosophical consideration (Pettit and Goodin 1993: 7). Yet there is no more salient fact about the contemporary world, nor any more potent source of conflict and violence, than the existence, actual and disputed, of nations. It is also noteworthy that political philosophy has assumed the existence of distinct nation-states and concerned itself with the application to such entities of principles of justice, equality and rights (Canovan 1996).

Although they are closely related terms, often used as synonyms, and frequently hyphenated, 'state' and 'nation' have distinct meanings. A nation is a community of people bound together over time by some significant, shared characteristic such as language, race or culture. A state is an independent, sovereign political association of people inhabiting a bounded territory. Nationalism, as a doctrine, makes the factual claim that humanity is and always has been naturally divided into nations. The normative claims of nationalism are that nations should be states and that states should be nations.

Contemporary philosophical defenders of nationalism (Miller 1995; Tamir 1993) have sought to answer the criticisms of claims of nationalism, and to show that a defence of nationalism is consistent with, indeed demanded by, a proper defence of liberalism. To the charge that nations are fictive products of modernity, defenders of nationalism will insist that modern nations do have premodern ethnic origins, and that even false beliefs can have instrumental value if they sustain a valuable sense of community.

States should be nations because a principle of nationality may supply the 'fellow feeling' J. S. Mill thought necessary for good government (Mill 1975: ch. 16) or for the acceptance of redistributive principles of justice (Miller 1995). Nations should be states because democratic self-government is coextensive with national self-determination, and because membership of a nation being a constitutive element of individual identity and well-being, statehood is an essential means of protecting nationality.

To those who insist that the defence of nationality represents an unwarranted partiality inconsistent with the cosmopolitanism which properly realizes the global scope of any acceptable political philosophy, the friends of nationalism will insist that it is necessary to make an accommodation with the realities of the modern world. Further partiality is not morally unjustified so long as its demonstration remains constrained by a recognition of the minimum owed to those who are not one's own co-nationals.

However, critics of nationalism will reply that since there is no well-bounded territory containing an ethnically homogeneous population the demands of nationalism are productive of grossly unacceptable political results: at best discrimination against national minorities within the state, at worst the forcible expulsion and slaughter of these minorities. Moreover the number of potential, aspirant nation-states greatly exceeds the number of possible viable states, and internal secession would continue to the point of non-viability.

Sympathetic political philosophical treatments of nationality may thus stop short of conceding the full demands of nationalism, arguing, for instance, that those ends thought to require the coincidence of nation and state may be served by something less, such as federalism (Buchanan 1991). Unsympathetic treatments of nationality may insist that it is possible to construct a non-national principle of political community, around for instance loyalty to the constitutive principles of a particular polity (Habermas 1992). Both camps may seek to defuse the sting of nationalism by encouraging a political disassociation of 'nation' and 'state'. This may be managed through the development of trans- and international institutions, the protection of subnational ethnic plurality, and the provision for decentralized political representation.

Political philosophy cannot now ignore the brute facts of nationality. A proper acknowledgement of these facts should consist in a recognition of what can be changed and what cannot, and, in consequence, of the fact that whatever value national identity has may be secured only at the expense of inseparable disadvantages.

7 Political Philosophy and Politics

This last section considers what is political philosophy and what is politics. First, then, what is it thought that a political theory should do? I do not mean by this the question of whether a theory should be about justice, the state, the class struggle, or whatever. I mean what is a theory taken to be doing when it answers a self-chosen question such as 'What is justice?' There are four broad sorts of answer.

The first is that a theory should be built upon FOUNDATIONS (pp. 40–1) that are universally recognized and evident truths; its procedure of argumentation and reasoning should similarly be unexceptionable and acceptable to any rational person. It is likely that these foundations will comprise some understanding of the individual human being.

Both Rawls's *A Theory of Justice* and Nozick's *Anarchy, State, and Utopia* may be represented as political theory in this foundational sense. The problem with this approach is that it risks being empty or contentious. Either the foundational understanding of the human being commands universal agreement in virtue of being emptied of real substantive content, or is a recognizably interesting view but thereby partial and controversial. A familiar criticism of Rawls is that his contracting individuals are not those of any time and place, but historically and culturally located agents – Western, liberal men.

A response to these problems is self-consciously to adopt a stance that is rooted in one's own culture and history. Borrowing Plato's famous metaphor, Michael Walzer contrasts a philosophical attitude that walks out of the cave and seeks the high ground of universal objectivity with one that takes its stand in the cave and with its inhabitants. This 'way of doing philosophy is to interpret to one's fellow citizens the world of meanings that we share' (Walzer 1983: xiv). The problems with this approach are threefold. First, as has already been noted, it courts relativism: the good society is each and every society that judges itself to be good by its own lights. Second, a society's practices, however unjust they may seem to the reasonable outsider, are not open to criticism if, on the inside, that society lacks the shared meanings which could inform such a critique. Third, the approach tends to conservatism. It implies that a society's meanings are defined by its existing practices. But there is no space from which to judge these practices. Or, put another way, the meanings by which the practices could be judged appear to float outside the society (Cohen 1986).

Rawls appears to have moved from his original foundationalism towards this second understanding of political theory. In *Political Liberalism* (Rawls 1993) he views the liberal conception of justice as expressing ideas implicit within the institutions and public culture of constitutional democratic regimes. Yet this is not a simple shift from universal to particular, from transcendental rules of justice to the particular virtues of American constitutionalism. 'Kantianism in one country' is a fine and witty definition of Rawls's political philosophy. It is possible, and plausible, to believe that modern democracy is an historical achievement which institutes general moral principles – equality of respect for individual choices of life, and the public justifiability of agreed rules of social co-operation. Actually existent institutions may do no more than approximate to these ideals, but they nevertheless aspire to them.

At the same time Rawls would now insist that political philosophy is turned to when a society's shared understandings break down and come into conflict. Philosophy resolves these conflicts by ascending to abstractions which are nevertheless also somehow uncovered through fundamental ideas deep and implicit within the society's culture (ibid.: 44–6). This is somewhat mysterious. It may also betray a false optimism that the plurality of fundamental beliefs which characterizes modern society is, at some level, eliminable. On the other hand, if the implication is that we can reach outside the terms of our present, public culture for values which validate it, then too many crucial questions have been begged. This at least is the charge of Richard RORTY (pp. 783–4) (1989, 1991). Whether or not democratic liberalism stands at the end of ideological history is a question which anglophone philosophy is on the whole ill-equipped to acknowledge or answer, not least because it lacks the means to theorize ideas of modernity and historical progress. Philosophy in the English-speaking world is notoriously incapable of 'reflexive social understanding'; that is, being in a position to interrogate itself about its relation to the society and history in which it is situated (Williams 1980).

One way to open a space between presently shared meanings and preferred alternatives is given by the third approach to political philosophy which may be termed CRITIQUE (chapter 32). Marx famously remarked that science would be unnecessary if reality and appearance coincided. His scientific concern was to disclose the real workings of capitalism which could not be apparent to those who lived and worked under it.

Analogously the task of political philosophy may be to reveal what our shared meanings do not and cannot say about our political world. The function of critique is to display these gaps and thus the distance between actuality and the moral pretensions generated by that actuality. To the extent that analytical Marxism shares many of the premises and concepts of contemporary philosophical liberalism, it may be said to have eschewed critique in favour of criticism. However, feminist political theory does aspire to critique when it seeks to show how unspoken assumptions – about women's nature, the public–private divide, the family – explain why liberalism is both silent about, and yet eloquent in its implicit endorsement of, women's continued subordination.

The fourth and final approach to political philosophy is hostile to any misjudged rationalist ambitions theory might have. It repudiates the idea that political association must self-consciously realize any desired end or purposes. Instead it sees the tasks of political theory as more modest and restricted. It is the articulation of the commonly acknowledged rules of conduct which inform our actual practices. It salutes the historical achievements of modern liberalism, not least the emergence of 'individuality' and 'civility'; that is, law and civic order. Yet it refuses to see these eminently practical achievements as conforming to universal, objective principles that may be laid bare. Political theorizing should be faithful to the knowledge already presupposed in our practice; it should 'pursue the intimations' of established traditions.

The author of this approach is Michael Oakeshott (1962, 1975). His sceptical and nuanced conservatism does not figure large in most surveys of contemporary political philosophy, perhaps because he speaks at a tangent to its main concerns. Yet his work has been influential in a British conservatism, ably represented by Roger Scruton (1984), which keeps its distance from both American philosophical liberalism and the free market, anti-statism that often passes for contemporary right-wing thinking. At the same time there is in such work a Hegelian sensitivity to history and practice which importantly distinguishes it from the simple appeal to shared meanings which characterizes the second approach.

Our second important question is, 'What is politics?' That is, what is the scope of political activity, what distinguishes it from other forms of human activity, and what is its importance? Here it is best to consider a number of oppositions. First, there is that between what we could call instrumental and expressivist understandings of politics. According to the instrumental understanding, politics is a means used by essentially independent individuals to secure the agreements which are necessary if they are to obtain the benefits of co-operation and avoid the costs of non-agreement. It is the politics of bargaining, compromise, accommodation, and achieving a *modus vivendi*. The political sphere is like a market-place in which individuals come to make their separate deals and then return to live their lives. Politics has no further function than is necessary to facilitate and protect the agreements made.

On the EXPRESSIVIST (pp. 384–90) understanding, political activity is itself valuable. It is an important way in which human beings express themselves as social, co-operative creatures enjoying an interdependent existence. This is the politics of participation, community and republican citizenship. The political sphere is a forum in which people come together as citizens, and a vital constituent of the full life led by all. Politics is impoverished to the extent that it falls short of exhibiting this character.

On the whole liberals, and certainly libertarians, have favoured the former understanding. Their preference derives from according a primary importance to liberty and believing that individual purposes will be various. Political activism, of the sort envisaged by expressivists, is unlikely to be spontaneously universal, and will be unacceptable if coerced. Perhaps in part for this reason liberals, despite a clear preference for it as a regime, have had little to say about how democracy should actually work and what particular form it should take. Democracy tends to be seen as merely the formalized process by which SOCIAL CHOICES (pp. 391–5) are generated from the rational preferences of individuals. Famous paradoxes and difficulties characterize the translation of many individual choices into a single public choice.

By contrast there is an important and influential deliberative model of democratic politics. A key figure is Jürgen Habermas (1992), who has sought to demonstrate the principled presuppositions of everyday communication, such as the speaker's implicit claims to be truthful, right and sincere. From these foundations he defends a view of moral norms as those which would, and could, be agreed upon by the members of a communicative community who recognize only the force of the better argument. The relevance of such ideas to an ideal of deliberative or discourse politics whereby individuals reach reasoned agreement on the collective good is evident. The problems are also clear. If the model is intended to be a description of the actual political world it is at best unrealistic, and arguably undervalues disagreement and contestation as constitutive features of political activity. Politics may be ineliminably agonistic. If the model is an ideal then it needs to be shown that it does not import and employ values, such as equality, which cannot be found solely in the nature and presuppositions of conversational speech.

The concern of socialists and feminists with democratic theory and practice is attributable in part to the expressivist ideal of political participation as a good (Pateman 1970). It is also due to a worry about reconciling the formal equality of political citizenship with the various inequalities, of race, class, and gender, which characterize civil society.

Related to but distinct from the instrumental–expressivist distinction is that between public and private, already introduced in section 5. As this distinction is now understood, the public comprises the political, legal and economic, the world in which individuals work, vote and are accountable to the rest of society for their actions. The private is the personal and familial, the sphere of the household in which individuals love, play and generally retreat from the public world.

To this distinction corresponds differences of motivation, relatedness and loyalty. The public world is cold, impersonal, governed by abstract rules, in which independent and mutually disinterested individuals meet. The private is the emotionally warm haven in which individuals are bound by particular relationships of affection, loyalty and mutual interdependence.

Liberals have, on the whole, refused to see the private as political. Indeed the private sphere is that with which the state has no business and into which it should not intrude. This is plausible in so far as liberals have characterized private activity as self-regarding in J. S. Mill's sense; that is, whose harmful effects, if any, are confined to the agent. Consensual sexual behaviour and procreative decisions, according to liberals, are paradigmatically private in this regard.

It is to feminism that we owe a critique of the public–private divide. This insists first that the scope and character of the private is determined publicly by law and policy. It is not that the private domain pre-exists and limits that of the public. Rather the terms of privacy are set within the public sphere. Indeed the very inauguration of the private, and civil society, may be due to an unnoticed but deeply illegitimate 'sexual contract' in which the male first subordinated the female to serve his sexual purposes (Pateman 1988).

Second, the private is political if 'political' extends to describe any structure or relationship in which some individuals exercise significant power over others. The family is the object of interest here. The traditional institution is marked by a familiar sexual division of labour with the husband dominant over the wife. Any characterization of familial relations as private amounts to a public endorsement of their continuing inequity.

Even on their own principles liberals should be interested in the family. For it can support or undermine broader social justice. This is not only in so far as the family is, as noted earlier, a site of moral education, a place where a sense of justice is learned. It is also that the family is the major means by which assets – property as well as natural endowments – are transferred across generations. Differences between familial situations remain a crucial obstacle to securing equality of opportunity (Fishkin 1983).

The final opposition sets the political against the economic. Although the economic is included within the public sphere, there is a tendency among liberals to be relatively indifferent towards various economic arrangements. These, to simplify their view, are to be preferred on grounds of efficiency not morality. In *A Theory of Justice* Rawls leaves open the choice between a private property economy and socialism (Rawls 1972: 258). In *Political Liberalism* he maintains that the question is 'not settled at the level of first principles of justice', but depends on the contingencies of a country's particular institutions and historical circumstances (Rawls 1993: 338). But the economic is political in three important regards.

First, liberal principles of justice apply to the distributive sphere, that is they determine who gets what goods once they are produced. But principles restricted to distribution leave out of account the productive sphere, concerning what is produced by whom. Decisions may be taken as to what goods are produced and in what quantities. It can sometimes seem as if the goods to be distributed in liberal theories of justice have just dropped from heaven, quite explicitly in Bruce Ackerman's (1980) account, where he speaks of manna.

Second, there is a stronger claim associated with Marx that production determines distribution; that is, that a distribution of goods to be consumed is a consequence of how production itself is organized. If this determinist thesis is true then principles of distributive justice are in an important sense beside the point.

Third, the economic sphere is one to which political considerations directly apply. Work constitutes a significant part of an individual's life. In itself it can be rewarding or frustrating, self-realizing or alienating. It can be self-directed or performed under conditions of subordination to another. Work is also instrumentally valuable in so far as payment for employment determines one's level of subsistence and the character of one's work affects one's social status and self-esteem.

It is important then to recognize that employment – an individual's right to it, and the determination of its conditions – are proper subjects for political inquiry. Socialists have attended to these issues. They have defended an extension of democracy to the work place, and have been more generally concerned about the proper balance between market and state control, private and public ownership.

8   Conclusion

Political philosophy is alive and well. It was not quite moribund in 1950 but the post-1970 revival now makes it appear so. The current dominance of philosophical liberalism may irk those who feel that its approach pre-emptively biases consideration of important matters and ignores crucial facts. But those who feel that way must recognize that it is to liberals that we owe the revival of political philosophy and our present ability to speak to the problems of our social and political existence. We may not wish to speak in the language of liberalism. But then philosophers can no longer, as Weldon once argued, be silent, and the onus is on those who dissent to perfect and practise the alternative languages of political criticism.

Further Reading

Of the general surveys of social and political philosophical work, Kymlicka (1990) is the best. It is comprehensive, incisive and judicious. Plant (1991) is well-informed and successfully brings out many of the main concerns of contemporary political theory (though he unaccountably ignores feminism). Pettit (1980) and Brown (1986) are also useful if more narrowly concerned with the main theories of distributive justice. *Philosophy and Public Affairs* remains the flagship journal of political philosophy in the present era. Goodin and Pettit (1993) is a volume in the present series. It contains extended essays on various disciplinary contributions to the subject, shorter entries on major ideologies, and short notes on special topics. The contributors are distinguished practitioners of the subject, the writing is almost uniformly excellent, and the whole text supplies an illuminating picture of post-Rawlsian political philosophy.

The Oxford Political Theory series, edited by David Miller and Alan Ryan, contains excellent books by distinguished and particularly well qualified contributors on particular topics within contemporary political philosophy.

On Rawls the literature is voluminous. Daniels (1975) collects the best of the earlier critical essays, and other standard commentaries are Barry (1973) and Wolff (1977). Kukathas and Pettit (1990) compares 'early' and 'late' Rawls, but before publication of *Political Liberalism*.

Paul (1981) does for Nozick what Daniels does for Rawls, and Wolff (1991) offers an unprejudiced but critical account of Nozick's theory.

Mulhall and Swift (1996) provides a fine, clearly written review of the debate between liberals and their communitarian critics, even if it struggles somewhat to find the common themes in communitarianism. In addition to Gutman (1985), the following also supply useful evaluations of communitarianism: Kymlicka (1988) and Buchanan (1989).

G. A. Cohen has worried at and about the legacy of Marx and its relationship to current political philosophy with more acuity and assiduity than anyone. Cohen (1988) collects together some of his best pieces.

Kittay and Meyers (1987) gives a good sense of Gilligan's impact upon moral and political thinking. Jaggar (1983) is a standard introduction to feminist political theory, while Grimshaw (1986) is also clearly written and relevant.

An introduction to British conservatism is provided by Covell (1986), and Franco (1990) offers a comprehensive, if cautious account of his subject.

Kymlicka (1995) is a comprehensive collection of important articles on cultural and national pluralism, while Beiner (1999) offers a fine collection of pieces by leading theorists on the topic of nationalism.

Chambers (1996) is a very good evaluation of the ideal of Habermasian deliberative democracy within the context of Rawlsian political philosophy.

References

Ackerman, B. 1980: *Social Justice in the Liberal State*. New Haven, CT: Yale University Press.
Barry, B. 1973: *The Liberal Theory of Justice*. Oxford: Clarendon Press.

Beiner, R. (ed.) 1999: *Theorizing Nationalism*. Albany: State University of New York Press.

Berlin, I. 1958: Two Concepts of Liberty. In *Four Essays on Liberty*. Oxford: Clarendon Press.

Brown, A. 1986: *Modern Political Philosophy*. Harmondsworth: Penguin Books.

Buchanan, A. 1989: Assessing the Communitarian Critique of Liberalism. *Ethics*, 99 (July), 852–82.

——1991: *Secession: The Morality of Political Divorce from Fort Sumter to Lithuania and Quebec*. Boulder, CO: Westview Press.

Caney, S. 1992: Liberalism and Communitarianism: A Misconceived Debate. *Political Studies*, 40, 273–89.

Canovan, M. 1996: *Nationhood and Political Theory*. Cheltenham: Edward Elgar.

Chambers, S. 1996: *Reasonable Democracy: Jürgen Habermas and the Politics of Democracy*. Ithaca, NY: Cornell University Press.

Cohen, G. A. 1978: *Karl Marx's Theory of History: A Defence*. Oxford: Oxford University Press.

——1988: *History, Labour, and Freedom: Themes from Marx*. Oxford: Clarendon Press.

—— 1990: Marxism and Contemporary Political Philosophy, or: Why Nozick Exercises some Marxists more than he does any Egalitarian Liberals. *Canadian Journal of Philosophy*, supplementary volume 16, 363–87.

Cohen, J. 1986: Review of Walzer, *Spheres of Justice*. *Journal of Philosophy*, 83: 8, 457–68.

Covell, C. 1986: *The Redefinition of Conservatism*. Basingstoke: Macmillan.

Daniels, N. (ed.) 1975: *Reading Rawls*. Oxford: Blackwell.

Dworkin, R. 1978: Liberalism. In S. Hampshire (ed.) *Public and Private Morality*. Cambridge: Cambridge University Press.

——1981: What is Equality? Part 1: Equality of Welfare and Part 2: Equality of Resources. *Philosophy and Public Affairs*, 10: 3, 185–246, and 10: 4, 283–345.

Elster, J. 1985: *Making Sense of Marx*. Cambridge: Cambridge University Press.

Fishkin, J. S. 1983: *Justice, Equal Opportunity, and the Family*. New Haven, CT: Yale University Press.

Franco, P. 1990: *The Political Philosophy of Michael Oakeshott*. New Haven, CT: Yale University Press.

Galston, W. A. 1980: *Justice and the Human Good*. Chicago: University of Chicago Press.

Geras, N. 1985: The Controversy about Marx and Justice. *New Left Review*, 150, 47–85.

Gilligan, C. 1982: *In a Different Voice*. Cambridge, MA: Harvard University Press.

Goodin, R. E. and Pettit, P. (eds) 1993: *A Companion to Contemporary Political Philosophy*. Oxford: Blackwell.

Gray, J. 1984: *Hayek on Liberty*. Oxford: Blackwell.

Grimshaw, J. 1986: *Feminist Philosophers*. Brighton: Wheatsheaf.

Gutman, A. 1985: Communitarian Critics of Liberalism. *Philosophy and Public Affairs*, 14: 3, 308–22.

Habermas, J. 1992: Citizenship and National Identity: Some Reflections on the Future of Europe. *Praxis International*, 12, 1–33.

——1996: *Moral Consciousness and Communicative Action* (translated by Christian Lenhardt and Shierry Weber Nicholsen). Cambridge, MA: MIT Press.

Haksar, V. 1979: *Equality, Liberty and Perfectionism*. Oxford: Oxford University Press.

Jaggar, A. M. 1983: *Feminist Politics and Human Nature*. Totowa, NJ: Rowman and Allanheld.

Kittay, E. F. and Meyers, D. T. (eds) 1987: *Women and Moral Theory*. Savage, MD: Rowman and Littlefield.

Kocis, R. A. 1980: Reason, Development, and the Conflict of Human Ends: Sir Isaiah Berlin's Vision of Politics. *American Political Science Review*, 74: 1, 38–52.

Kukathas, C. and Pettit, P. 1990: *Rawls: A Theory of Justice and its Critics*. Cambridge: Polity Press.

Kymlicka, W. 1988: Liberalism and Communitarianism. *Canadian Journal of Philosophy*, 18, 2 (June), 181–204.

—— 1989: *Liberalism, Community, and Culture*. Oxford: Clarendon Press.

—— 1990: *Contemporary Political Philosophy*. Oxford: Clarendon Press.

—— (ed.) 1995: *The Rights of Minority Cultures*. Oxford: Oxford University Press.

Landesman, B. 1983: Egalitarianism. *Canadian Journal of Philosophy*, 13, 27–56.

Laslett, P. 1950: Introduction. In P. Laslett (ed.) *Philosophy, Politics and Society*. Oxford: Blackwell.

Locke, J. 1689: *Epistola de Tolerantia*. English translation, *A Letter on Toleration* (introduction and notes by J. W. Gough). Oxford: Clarendon Press.

Lukes, S. 1985: *Marxism and Morality*. Oxford: Clarendon Press.

MacIntyre, A. 1981: *After Virtue*. London: Duckworth.

—— 1988: *Whose Justice? Whose Rationality?* London: Duckworth.

Mill, J. S. 1975 [1861]: Considerations on Representative Government. In *Three Essays*. Oxford: Oxford University Press.

Miller, D. 1995: *On Nationality*. Oxford: Clarendon Press.

Mulhall, S. and Swift, A. 1996: *Liberals and Communitarians*, 2nd edn. Oxford: Blackwell.

Nagel, T. 1991: *Equality and Partiality*. Oxford: Oxford University Press.

Nozick, R. 1974: *Anarchy, State and Utopia*. Oxford: Blackwell.

Oakeshott, M. 1962: *Rationalism in Politics*. London: Methuen.

—— 1975: *On Human Conduct*. Oxford: Clarendon Press.

Okin, S. M. 1989: *Justice, Gender, and the Family*. New York: Basic Books.

Pateman, C. 1970: *Participation and Democratic Theory*. Cambridge: Cambridge University Press.

—— 1988: *The Sexual Contract*. Cambridge: Polity Press.

Paul, J. (ed.) 1982: *Reading Nozick*. Oxford: Blackwell.

Pettit, P. 1980: *Judging Justice*. London: Routledge and Kegan Paul.

Pettit, P. and Goodin, R. (eds) 1993: *A Companion to Contemporary Political Philosophy*. Oxford: Blackwell.

Plant, R. 1991: *Modern Political Thought*. Oxford: Blackwell.

Popper, K. 1945: *The Open Society and its Enemies*, 2 vols. Vol. 1: Plato. Vol. 2: Hegel and Marx. London: Routledge and Kegan Paul.

Rawls, J. 1972: *A Theory of Justice*. Oxford: Oxford University Press.

—— 1993: *Political Liberalism*. New York: Columbia University Press.

Raz, J. 1986: *The Morality of Freedom*. Oxford: Clarendon Press.

Rorty, R. 1989: *Contingency, Irony and Solidarity*. Cambridge: Cambridge University Press.

—— 1991: *Objectivity, Relativism and Truth*. Cambridge: Cambridge University Press.

Sandel, M. 1982: *Liberalism and the Limits of Justice*. Cambridge: Cambridge University Press.

Scruton, R. 1984: *The Meaning of Conservatism*, 2nd edn. Basingstoke: Macmillan.

Sen, A. 1992: *Inequality Re-examined*. Oxford: Clarendon Press.

Tamir, Y. 1993: *Liberal Nationalism*. Princeton, NJ: Princeton University Press.

Taylor, C. 1985: *Philosophy and the Human Sciences: Philosophical Papers*, Vol. 2. Cambridge: Cambridge University Press.

—— 1989: Cross-Purposes: The Liberal Communitarian Debate. In N. Rosenblum (ed.) *Liberalism and the Moral Life*. Cambridge, MA: Harvard University Press.

—— 1992: *Multiculturalism and The Politics of Recognition* (commentary by A. Gutman, edited by S. C. Rockefeller, M. Walzer and S. Wolf). Princeton, NJ: Princeton University Press.

Unger, R. M. 1975: *Knowledge and Politics*. New York: Free Press.

Walzer, M. 1983: *Spheres of Justice*. New York: Basic Books.

Weldon, T. D. 1953: *The Vocabulary of Politics*. Harmondsworth: Penguin Books.

Williams, B. 1980: Political Philosophy and the Analytical Tradition. In M. Richter (ed.) *Political Theory and Political Education*. Princeton, NJ: Princeton University Press.

Wolff, J. 1991: *Robert Nozick*. Cambridge: Polity Press.

Wolff, R. P. 1977: *Understanding Rawls*. Princeton, NJ: Princeton University Press.

Discussion Questions

1　Are equality and liberty incompatible ideals?

2　Is value pluralism an ineliminable feature of modern society?

3　Are there any feasible ways in which the circumstances of justice could be transcended?

4　How egalitarian is the 'difference principle'?

5　What roles does the contractarian argument play in Rawls's theory of justice?

6　Should a theory of justice be 'metaphysical' or 'political'?

7　Is the distribution of natural assets morally arbitrary?

8　Are rights 'side constraints' on actions?

9　Can we be said to own ourselves?

10　Is justice a matter of legitimate acquisition of goods, whatever the pattern of their distribution?

11　What should there be equality of?

12　Should autonomy rather than liberty be the central value of liberalism?

13　Is the idea of a 'liberal community' a contradiction in terms?

14　Does liberalism depend on an unacceptable conception of the individual?

15　Is a caring society morally preferable to a just one?

16　Can the family ever be a force for justice?

17　What for Marxists is wrong with capitalism?

18　Is 'analytical Marxism' Marxism at all?

19　Can political philosophy go beyond what we happen here and now to believe and value?

20　Is the human being a *political* animal?

21　Is anything really private in the sense of being beyond the public gaze and public concern?

22　Is the ideal of official neutrality on the question of the good life either feasible or desirable?

23　Why should minority cultures be protected or preserved?

24　Does justice lie beyond, between or within nations?

25　What inequalities in our material circumstances are permissible?

26　Is liberal nationalism an oxymoron?

27　Are we all liberals now?

9

Philosophy of Science

DAVID PAPINEAU

The philosophy of science can usefully be divided into two broad areas. On the one hand is the epistemology of science, which deals with issues relating to the justification of claims to scientific knowledge. Philosophers working in this area investigate such questions as whether science ever uncovers permanent truths, whether objective decisions between competing theories are possible and whether the results of experiment are clouded by prior theoretical expectations. On the other hand are topics in the metaphysics of science, topics relating to philosophically puzzling features of the natural world described by science. Here philosophers ask such questions as whether all events are determined by prior causes, whether everything can be reduced to physics and whether there are purposes in nature. You can think of the difference between the epistemologists and the metaphysicians of science in this way. The epistemologists wonder whether we should believe what the scientists tell us. The metaphysicians worry about what the world is like, if the scientists are right. Readers will wish to consult chapters on EPISTEMOLOGY *(chapter 1),* METAPHYSICS *(chapter 2),* PHILOSOPHY OF MATHEMATICS *(chapter 11),* PHILOSOPHY OF SOCIAL SCIENCE *(chapter 12) and* PRAGMATISM *(chapter 36).*

1 The Epistemology of Science

1.1 The problem of induction

Much recent work in the epistemology of science is a response to the problem of induction. Induction is the process whereby scientists decide, on the basis of various observations or experiments, that some theory is true. At its simplest, chemists may note, say, that on a number of occasions samples of sodium heated on a Bunsen burner have glowed bright orange, and on this basis conclude that in general *all* heated sodium will glow bright orange. In more complicated cases, scientists may move from the results of a series of complex experiments to the conclusion that some fundamental physical principle is true. What all such inductive inferences have in common, however, is that they start with particular premises about a *finite* number of past observations, yet end up with a general conclusion about how nature will *always* behave. And this is where the problem lies. For it is unclear how any finite amount of information about what has happened in the past can guarantee that a natural pattern will *continue* for all time.

After all, what rules out the possibility that the course of nature may change, and that the patterns we have observed so far turn out to be a poor guide to the future? Even if all heated sodium has glowed orange up till now, who is to say it will not start glowing blue sometime in the next century?

In this respect induction contrasts with deduction. In deductive inferences the premises guarantee the conclusion. For example, if you know that *Either this substance is sodium or it is potassium*, and then learn further that *It is not sodium*, you can conclude with certainty that *It is potassium*. The truth of the premises leaves no room for the conclusion to be anything but true. But in an inductive inference this does not hold. To take the simplest case, if you are told, for properties *A* and *B*, that *Each of the As observed so far has been B*, this does not guarantee that *All As, including future ones, are Bs*. It is perfectly possible that the former claim may be true, but the latter false.

The problem of induction seems to pose a threat to all scientific knowledge. All scientific discoveries worth their name are in the form of general principles. Galileo's law of free fall says that '*All* bodies fall with constant acceleration'; Newton's law of gravitation says that '*All* bodies attract each other in proportion to their masses and in inverse proportion to the square of the distance between them'; Avogadro's law says that '*All* gases at the same temperature and pressure contain the same number of molecules per unit volume'; and so on. The problem of induction calls the authority of all these laws into question. For if our evidence is simply that these laws have worked so far, then how can we be sure that they will not be disproved by future occurrences?

1.2   *Popper's falsificationism*

One influential response to the problem of induction is due to Sir Karl Popper (1902–94). In Popper's (1959a, 1963, 1972) view, science does not rest on induction in the first place. Popper denies that scientists start with observations, and then infer a general theory. Rather, they first put forward a theory, as an initially uncorroborated conjecture, and then compare its predictions with observations to see whether it stands up to test. If such tests prove negative, then the theory is experimentally falsified, and the scientists will seek some new alternative. If, on the other hand, the tests fit the theory, then scientists will continue to uphold it – not as proven truth, admittedly, but nevertheless as an undefeated conjecture.

If we look at science in this way, argues Popper, then we see that it does not need induction. According to Popper, the inferences which matter to science are refutations, which take some failed prediction as the premise, and conclude that the theory behind that prediction is false. These inferences are not inductive, but deductive. We see that some *A* is not-*B*, and conclude that it is not the case that *All As are Bs*. There is no room here for the premise to be true and the conclusion false. If we discover that some body falls with *increasing* acceleration (say because it falls from a great height, and so is subject to a greater gravitational force as it nears the earth), then we know for sure that all bodies do not fall with constant acceleration. The point here is that it is much easier to disprove theories than to prove them. A single contrary example suffices for a conclusive disproof, but no number of supporting examples will constitute a conclusive proof.

So, according to Popper, science is a sequence of conjectures and refutations. Scientific theories are put forward as hypotheses, and they are replaced by new hypotheses when they are falsified. However, if scientific theories are always conjectural in this way, then what makes science better than astrology, or spirit worship, or any other form of unwarranted superstition? A non-Popperian would answer this question by saying that real science proves its claims on the basis of observational evidence, whereas superstition is nothing but guesswork. But on Popper's account, even scientific theories are guesswork – for they cannot be proved by the observations, but are themselves merely undefeated conjectures.

Popper calls this the 'problem of demarcation': what is the difference between science and other forms of belief? His answer is that science, unlike superstition, is at least *falsifiable*, even if it is not provable (Popper 1959a: ch. 2). Scientific theories are framed in precise terms, and so issue in definite predictions. For example, Newton's laws tell us exactly where certain planets will appear at certain times. And this means that if such predictions fail, we can be sure that the theory behind them is false. By contrast, belief systems like astrology are irredeemably vague, in a way which prevents their ever being shown definitely wrong. Astrology may predict that Scorpios will prosper in their personal relationships on Thursdays, but when faced with a Scorpio whose spouse walks out on a Thursday, defenders of astrology are likely to respond that the end of the marriage was probably for the best, all things considered. Because of this, nothing will ever force astrologists to admit their theory is wrong. The theory is phrased in such imprecise terms that no actual observations can possibly falsify it.

Popper himself uses the criterion of *falsifiability* to distinguish genuine science, not just from traditional belief systems like astrology and spirit worship, but also from Marxism, psychoanalysis and various other modern disciplines that he denigrates as 'pseudo-sciences'. According to Popper, the central claims of these theories are as unfalsifiable as those of astrology. Marxists predict that proletarian revolutions will be successful whenever capitalist regimes have been sufficiently weakened by their internal contradictions. But when faced with unsuccessful proletarian revolutions, they simply respond that the contradictions in those particular capitalist regimes have not yet weakened them sufficiently. Similarly, psychoanalytic theorists will claim that all adult neuroses are due to childhood traumas, but when faced by troubled adults with apparently undisturbed childhoods, they will say that those adults must nevertheless have undergone private psychological traumas when young. For Popper, such ploys are the antithesis of scientific seriousness. Genuine scientists will say beforehand what observational discoveries would make them change their minds, and will abandon their theories if these discoveries are made. But Marxists and psychoanalytic theorists frame their theories in such a way, argues Popper, that no possible observations need ever make them adjust their thinking.

1.3   The failings of falsificationism

At first sight Popper seems to offer an extremely attractive account of science. He explains its superiority over other forms of belief, while at the same time apparently freeing it from any problematic dependence on induction. Certainly his writings have struck a chord within the scientific community. Popper is one of the few philosophers ever to have become a Fellow of the Royal Society, an honour usually reserved for eminent scientists.

In the philosophical world, however, Popper's views are more controversial. This is because many philosophers feel that his account of science signally fails to solve the problem with which he begins, namely, the problem of induction (for example, see Ayer 1956: 71–5; Worrall 1989). The central objection to his position is that it only accounts for negative scientific knowledge, as opposed to positive knowledge. Popper points out that a single counter-example can show us that a scientific theory is wrong. But he says nothing about what can show us that a scientific theory is right. Yet it is positive knowledge of this latter kind that makes science important. We can cure diseases and send people to the moon because we know that certain causes *do* always have certain results, not because we know that they *do not*. Useful scientific knowledge comes in the form 'All As are Bs', not 'It's false that all As are Bs'. Since Popper only accounts for the latter kind of knowledge, he seems to leave out what is most interesting and important about science.

Popper's usual answer to this objection is that he is concerned with the logic of pure scientific research, not with practical questions about technological applications. Scientific research requires only that we formulate falsifiable conjectures, and reject them if we discover counter-examples. The further question of whether technologists should *believe* those conjectures, and rely on their predictions when, say, they administer some drug or build a dam, Popper regards as an essentially practical issue, and as such not part of the analysis of rational scientific practice.

But this will not do. After all, Popper claims to have solved the problem of induction. But the problem of induction is essentially the problem of how we can base judgements about the future on evidence about the past. In insisting that scientific theories are just conjectures, and that therefore we have no rational basis for *believing* their predictions, Popper is simply denying that we can make rational judgements about the future.

Consider these two predictions: (1) when I jump from this tenth-floor window I shall crash painfully into the ground; (2) when I jump from the window I will float like a feather to a gentle landing. Intuitively, it is more rational to believe (1), which assumes that the future will be like the past, than (2), which does not. But Popper, since he rejects induction, is committed to the view that past evidence does not make any beliefs about the future more rational than any others, and therefore that believing (2) is no less rational than believing (1).

Something has gone wrong. *Of course* believing (1) is more rational than believing (2). In saying this, I do not want to deny that there is a *problem* of induction. Indeed it is precisely *because* believing (1) is more rational than believing (2) that induction is problematic. Everybody, Popper aside, can see that believing (1) is more rational than believing (2). The problem is then to explain *why* believing (1) is more rational than believing (2), in the face of the apparent invalidity of induction. So Popper's denial of the rational superiority of (1) over (2) is not so much a *solution* to the problem of induction, but simply a refusal to recognize the problem in the first place.

Even if it fails to deal with induction, Popper's philosophy of science does have some strengths as a description of pure scientific research. For it is certainly true that many scientific theories start life as conjectures, in just the way Popper describes. When Einstein's general theory of relativity was first proposed, for example, very few scientists actually *believed* it. Instead they regarded it as an interesting hypothesis, and were *curious* to see whether it was true. At this initial stage of a theory's life, Popper's recommendations make eminent sense. Obviously, if you are curious to see whether a theory is true, the next step is to put it to the observational test. And for this purpose it is important that the theory is framed in precise enough terms for scientists to work out what it implies about the observable world – that is, in precise enough terms for it to be falsifiable. And of course if the new theory does get falsified, then scientists will reject it and seek some alternative, whereas if its predictions are borne out, then scientists will continue to investigate it.

Where Popper's philosophy of science goes wrong, however, is in holding that scientific theories never progress beyond the level of conjecture. As I have just suggested, theories are often mere conjectures when they are first put forward, and they may remain conjectures as the initial evidence first comes in. But in many cases the accumulation of evidence in favour of a theory will move it beyond the status of conjecture to that of established truth. The general theory of relativity started life as a conjecture, and many scientists still regarded it as hypothetical even after Sir Arthur Eddington's famous initial observations in 1919 of light apparently bending near the sun. But by now this initial evidence has been supplemented with evidence in the form of gravitational red-shifts, time-dilation and black holes, and it would be an eccentric scientist who nowadays regarded the general theory as less than firmly established.

Such examples can be multiplied. The heliocentric theory of the solar system, the theory of evolution by natural selection and the theory of continental drift all started life as intriguing conjectures, with little evidence to favour them over their competitors. But in the period since they were first proposed these theories have all accumulated a great wealth of supporting evidence. It is only those philosophers who have been bemused by the problem of induction who view these theories as being no better than initial hypotheses. Everybody else who is acquainted with the evidence has no doubt that these theories are proven truths.

1.4   Bayesianism

If we insist, against Popper, that we are fully entitled to believe at least some scientific theories on the basis of past evidence, then we are committed to finding some solution to the problem of induction. One currently popular account of the legitimacy of induction is found within Bayesianism, named after Thomas Bayes (*c*.1701–61) (Horwich 1982; Howson and Urbach 1989).

Bayesians are philosophers who hold that our beliefs, including our beliefs in scientific theories, come in degrees. Thus, for example, I can believe to degree 0.5 that it will rain today, in the sense that I think there is a 50 per cent likelihood of rain today. Similarly, I might attach a 0.1 degree of belief to the theory that the strong nuclear and electro-weak forces are the same force – I think it unlikely, but allow that there is a one-in-ten possibility it may turn out true.

As these examples indicate, Bayesians think of degrees of belief as the extent to which you subjectively take something to be PROBABLE (pp. 167–8). Accordingly, they argue that your degrees of belief ought to satisfy the axioms of the probability calculus. (See the box below for the Dutch Book Argument for this thesis.) It is important to realize, however, that while Bayesians think of degrees of belief as probabilities in this mathematical sense, they still think of them as *subjective* probabilities. In particular, they allow that it can be perfectly rational for different people to attach *different* subjective probabilities to the same proposition – you can believe that it will rain today to degree 0.2, while I believe this to degree 0.5. What rationality does require, according to the Bayesians, is only that if you have a subjective probability of 0.2 for rain, then you must have one of 0.8 for its not raining, while if I have 0.5 for rain, then I must have 0.5 for its not raining. That is, both of us must accord, in our different ways, with the theorem of the probability calculus that Prob(p) = 1 − Prob(not-p).

At first sight, this element of subjectivity might seem to disqualify Bayesianism as a possible basis for scientific rationality. If we are all free to attach whatever degrees of belief we like to scientific theories, provided only that we are faithful to the structure of the probability calculus, then what is to stop each of us from supporting different theories, depending only on individual fads or prejudices? But Bayesians have an answer; namely, that it does not matter what prejudices you start with, as long as you revise your degrees of belief in a rational way.

Bayesians derive their account of how to revise degrees of belief, as well as their name, from Bayes's theorem, originally proved by Thomas Bayes in a paper published in 1763. Bayes's theorem states:

$$\text{Prob}(H/E) = \text{Prob}(H) \times \text{Prob}(E/H)/\text{Prob}(E).$$

The simple proof of this theorem is given in the box. But the philosophical significance of the theorem is that it suggests a certain procedure for revising your degrees of belief in response to new evidence. Suppose that H is some hypothesis, and E is some newly discovered evidence. Then Bayesians argue that, when you discover E, you should adjust your degree of belief in H in line with the right-hand side of the above equation: that is, you should increase it to the extent that you think E is likely given H, but unlikely otherwise. In other words, if E is in itself very surprising (like light bending in the vicinity of the sun) but at the same time just what you would expect given your theory H (the general theory of relativity), then E should make you increase your degree of belief in H a great deal. On the other hand, if E is no more likely given H than it would be on any other theory, then observing E provides no extra support for H. The movement of the tides, for example, is no great argument for general relativity, even though it is predicted by it, since it is also predicted by the alternative Newtonian theory of gravitation.

Note in particular that this strategy for updating degrees of belief in response to evidence can be applied to inductive inferences. Consider the special case where H is some universal generalization – all bodies fall with constant acceleration, say – and the evidence E is that some particular falling body has been observed to accelerate constantly.

If this observation was something you did not expect at all, then Bayesianism tells you that you should increase your degree of belief in Galileo's law significantly, for it is just what Galileo's law predicts. Of course, once you have seen a number of such observations, and become reasonably convinced of Galileo's law, then you will cease to find new instances surprising, and to that extent will cease to increase your degree of belief in the law. But that is as it should be. Once you are reasonably convinced of a law, then there is indeed little point in gathering further supporting instances, and so it is to the credit of Bayesianism that it explains this.

The Bayesian account of how to revise degrees of belief seems to make good sense. In addition, it promises a solution to the problem of induction, since it implies that positive instances give us reason to believe scientific generalizations.

There are, however, problems facing this account. For a start, a number of philosophers have queried whether Bayes's theorem, which after all is little more than an arithmetical truth, can constrain what degrees of belief we adopt in the future (see the box below). And even if we put this relatively technical issue to one side, it is unclear how far the Bayesian account really answers the worry raised above, that the subjectivity of degrees of belief will allow different scientists to commit themselves arbitrarily to different theories. The Bayesian answer to this worry was that Bayes's theorem will at least constrain these different scientists to revise their degrees of belief in response to the evidence in similar ways. But, even so, it still seems possible that the scientists will remain on different tracks, if they start at different places. If two scientists are free to attach different prior degrees of belief in Galileo's law, and both update those degrees of belief according to Bayes's theorem when they learn the evidence, will they not still end up with different posterior degrees of beliefs?

The standard answer to the objection is to appeal to *convergence* of opinion. The idea is that, given enough evidence, everybody will *eventually* end up in the same place, even if they have different starting-points. There are a number of theorems of probability theory showing that, within limits, differences in initial probabilities will be 'washed out', in the sense that sufficient evidence and Bayesian updating will lead to effectively identical final degrees of belief. So in the end, argue Bayesians, it does not matter if you start with a high or low degree of belief in Galileo's law – for after 1,000 observations of constantly falling bodies you will end up believing it to a degree close to 1 anyway.

However, interesting as these results are, they do not satisfactorily answer the fundamental philosophical questions about inductive reasoning. For they do not work for all possible initial degrees of belief. Rather, they assume that the scientists at issue, while differing among themselves, all draw their initial degrees of belief from a certain range. While this range includes all the initial degrees of belief that seem at all intuitively plausible, there are nevertheless other possible initial degrees of belief that are consistent with the axioms of probability, but which will not lead to eventual convergence. So, for example, the Bayesians do not in fact explain what is wrong with people who never end up believing Galileo's law because they are always convinced that the course of nature is going to change tomorrow. Of course, Bayesians are right to regard such people as irrational. But they do not explain why they are irrational. So they fail to show why all thinkers must end up with the same attitude to scientific theories. And in particular they fail to solve the problem of induction, since they do not show why all rational thinkers must expect the future to be like the past.

Bayesianism

The Dutch Book Argument

The axioms of probability require that

(1) $0 \leq \text{Prob}(P) \leq 1$, for any proposition P
(2) $\text{Prob}(P) = 1$, if P is a necessary truth
(3) $\text{Prob}(P) = 0$, if P is impossible
(4) $\text{Prob}(P \text{ or } Q) = \text{Prob}(P) + \text{Prob}(Q)$, if P and Q are mutually exclusive.

Bayesians appeal to the Dutch Book Argument to show why subjective degrees of belief should conform to these axioms. Imagine that your degrees of belief did not so conform. You believe proposition P to degree y, say, and yet do *not* believe not-P to degree $1 - y$. (You thus violate the conjunction of axioms (2) and (4), because P or not-P is a necessary truth.) Then it will be possible for somebody to induce you to make bets on P and not-P in such a way that you will lose whatever happens. A set of bets that guarantee that you will lose whatever happens is called a 'Dutch book'. The undesirability of such a set of bets thus provides an argument that any rational person's subjective degrees of belief should satisfy the axioms of the probability calculus.

Bayes's Theorem

The conditional probability of P given Q – $\text{Prob}(P/Q)$ – is defined as $\text{Prob}(P \text{ and } Q)/\text{Prob}(Q)$. Intuitively, $\text{Prob}(P/Q)$ signifies the probability of P on the assumption that Q is true. It immediately follows from this definition that

$$\text{Prob}(H/E) = \text{Prob}(H) \times \text{Prob}(E/H)/\text{Prob}(E)$$

This is Bayes's theorem. As you can see, it says that the conditional probability $\text{Prob}(H/E)$ of some hypothesis H given evidence E is greater than $\text{Prob}(H)$ to the extent that E is improbable in itself, but probable given H.

Bayesian Updating

Bayesians recommend that if you observe some evidence E, then you should *revise* your degree of belief in H, and set your new $\text{Prob}_{t'}(H)$ equal to your *previous* conditional degree of belief in H given E, $\text{Prob}_t(H/E)$, where t is the time before you learn E, and t' after. Bayes's theorem, applied to your subjective probabilities at t, then indicates that this will *increase* your degree of belief in H to the extent that you previously thought E to be subjectively improbable in itself, but subjectively probable given H.

   This Bayesian *recommendation*, that you revise your degree of belief in H by setting it equal to your old conditional degree of belief in H given E, should be distinguished from Bayes's *theorem*. Bayes's theorem is a trivial consequence of the definition of conditional probability, and constrains your degrees of belief at *a given time*. The Bayesian recommendation, by contrast, specifies how your degrees of belief should change *over time*. Bayes's theorem is uncontentious, but it is a matter of active controversy whether there is any satisfactory way of defending the Bayesian recommendation (Hacking 1967; Teller 1973).

1.5   *Instrumentalism versus realism*

At this stage let us leave the problem of induction for a while and turn to a different difficulty facing scientific knowledge. Much of science consists of claims about *unobservable* entities like viruses, radio waves, electrons and quarks. But if these entities are unobservable, how are scientists supposed to have found out about them? If they cannot see or touch them, does it not follow that their claims about them are at best speculative guesses, rather than firm knowledge?

It is worth distinguishing this problem of unobservability from the problem of induction. Both problems can be viewed as difficulties facing *theoretical* knowledge in science. But whereas the problem of induction arises because scientific theories make *general* claims, the problem of unobservability is due to our *lack of sensory access* to the subject matter of many scientific theories. (So the problem of induction arises for general claims even if they are not about unobservables, such as 'All sodium burns bright orange'. Conversely, the problem of unobservability arises for claims about unobservables even if they are not general, such as 'One free electron is attached to this oil drop'. In this section and the next, however, it will be convenient to use the term 'theory' specifically for claims about unobservables, rather than for general claims of any kind.)

There are two general lines of response to the problem of unobservability. On the one hand are *realists*, who think that the problem can be solved. Realists argue that the observable facts provide good indirect evidence for the existence of unobservable entities, and so conclude that scientific theories can be regarded as accurate descriptions of the unobservable world. On the other hand are *instrumentalists*, who hold that we are in no position to make firm judgements about imperceptible mechanisms. Instrumentalists allow that theories about such mechanisms may be useful 'instruments' for simplifying our calculations and generating predictions. But they argue that these theories are no more true descriptions of the world than the 'theory' that all the matter in a stone is concentrated at its centre of mass (which is also an extremely useful assumption for doing certain calculations, but clearly false).

Earlier this century instrumentalists used to argue that we should not even *interpret* theoretical claims literally, on the grounds that we cannot so much as meaningfully talk about entities we have never directly experienced. But nowadays this kind of semantic instrumentalism is out of favour. Contemporary instrumentalists allow that scientists can meaningfully *postulate*, say, that matter is made of tiny atoms containing nuclei orbited by electrons. But they then take a SCEPTICAL (pp. 45–56) attitude to such postulates, saying that we have no entitlement to *believe* them (as opposed to using them as an instrument for calculations).

An initial line of argument open to realism is to identify some feature of scientific practice and then argue that instrumentalism is unable to account for it. One aspect of scientific practice invoked in this connection has been the unification of different kinds of theories in pursuit of a single 'theory of everything' (Friedman 1984); other features of science appealed to by realists have included the use of theories to *explain* observable phenomena (Boyd 1980), and the reliance on theories to make novel *predictions* (Smart 1963). For, so the realist argues, these aspects of scientific practice only make sense on the assumption that scientific theories are *true* descriptions of reality. After all, says the realist, if theories are simply convenient calculating devices, then why expect different theories to be unifiable into one consistent story? Unification is clearly desirable if our theories all aim to contribute to the overall truth, but there seems no parallel reason why a bunch of instruments should be unifiable into one big 'instrument of everything'. And similarly, the realist will argue, there seems no reason to expect a mere calculating instrument, as opposed to a true description of an underlying reality, to yield a genuine explanation of some past occurrence, or a reliable prediction of a future one.

However, this form of argument tends to be inconclusive. There are two possible lines of response open to instrumentalists. They can offer an instrumentalist account of the relevant feature of scientific practice. Alternatively, they can deny that this feature really is part of scientific practice in the first place. As an example of the first response, they could argue that the unification of science is motivated, not by the pursuit of one underlying truth, but simply by the desirability of having a single all-purpose calculating instrument rather than a rag-bag of different instruments for different problems. The second kind of response would be to deny that unification is essential to science to start with. Thus Nancy Cartwright argues that science really *is* a rag-bag of different instruments. She maintains that scientists faced with a given kind of problem will standardly deploy simplifying techniques and rules of thumb which owe nothing to general theory, but which have shown themselves to deliver the right answer to the kind of problem at hand (Cartwright 1983).

Similar responses can be made by instrumentalists to the arguments from explanation and prediction. Instrumentalists can either retort that there is no reason why the status of theories as calculating instruments should preclude them from giving rise to predictions and explanations; or they can query whether scientific theories really do add to our ability to predict and explain to start with. Not all these lines of response are equally convincing. But between them they give instrumentalism plenty of room to counter the initial realist challenge.

1.6   Theory, observation and incommensurability

A different line of argument against instrumentalism focuses on the distinction between what is observable and what is not. This distinction is crucial to instrumentalism, in that instrumentalists argue that claims about observable phenomena are unproblematic, but claims about unobservables are not. However, a number of writers have queried this distinction, arguing that observation reports are not essentially different from claims about unobservables, since they too depend on theoretical assumptions about the underlying structure of reality. Norwood Hanson (1958) has argued, for example, that scientists before and after Copernicus *saw* different things when they looked at the Sun: whereas pre-Copernicans regarded the Earth as stationary and so saw the Sun revolving round it, post-Copernican scientists saw the Sun as stationary and the Earth as rotating. Similarly, Hanson (1963) argues that the photographic plate which looks like a squiggly mess to a lay observer is seen as displaying a well-defined electron–positron pair by an experienced particle physicist. Examples like these undermine the distinction between what is observable and what is not, since they show that even judgements made in immediate response to sensory stimulation are influenced by fallible theories about reality.

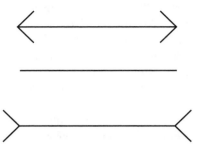

Figure 9.1 The Müller–Lyer. Although all three lines are the same length, the top line, with inward-pointing arrowheads, appears to be shorter, and the bottom line, with outward-pointing arrowheads, appears to be longer, than the 'neutral' middle line.

Nor is the point restricted to recherché observations of astronomical bodies or subatomic particles. Even immediate perceptual judgements about the colour, shape and size of medium-sized physical objects can be shown to depend on theoretical assumptions implicit in our visual systems. Perhaps the best-known illustration is the Müller–Lyer illusion (see figure 9.1), which shows how our visual system uses complex assumptions about the normal causes of certain kinds of retinal patterns to draw conclusions about the geometry of physical figures. And analogous illusions can be used to demonstrate the presence of other theoretical presuppositions in our visual and other sensory systems.

As I said, in the first instance the unclarity of the observable–unobservable distinction counts against instrumentalism rather than realism. After all, it is instrumentalism, not realism, which *needs* the distinction, since instrumentalism says that we should be sceptical about unobservable claims, but not observable ones, whereas realism is happy to regard both kinds of claims as belief-worthy, so does not mind if they cannot be sharply distinguished.

However, there is another way of responding to doubts about the theory–observation distinction. For note that the arguments against the observable–unobservable distinction do not in fact vindicate the realist belief-worthiness of claims about *unobservables*; rather, they attack realism from the bottom up, and undermine the belief-worthiness of claims about *observables*, by showing that even observational claims depend on fallible theoretical assumptions. Obviously, if there is no observable–unobservable distinction, then all scientific claims are in the same boat. But on reflection it seems that the boat they all end up in is the instrumentalist boat of sceptical disbelief, not the realist one of general faith in science.

A number of influential recent philosophers of science, most prominently T. S. Kuhn (1962) and Paul Feyerabend (1976), have embraced this conclusion wholeheartedly, and maintained that no judgements made within science, not even observational judgements, can claim the authority of established truth. Rather, they argue, once scientists have embraced a theory about the essential nature of their subject matter, such as geocentrism, or Newtonian dynamics, or the wave theory of light, they will interpret all observational judgements in the light of that theory, and so will never be forced to recognize the kind of negative observational evidence that might show them that their theory is mistaken. Kuhn and Feyerabend independently lit on the term *incommensurable* to express the view that there is no common yardstick, in the form of theory-independent observation judgements, which can be used to decide objectively on the worth of scientific theories. Instead, they argue, decisions on scientific theories are never due to objective observational evidence, but are always relative to the presuppositions, interests and social milieux of the scientists involved.

Kuhn's and Feyerabend's blanket relativism has provoked much discussion among philosophers of science, but won few whole-hearted converts. Much of the discussion has focused on the status of observations. Most philosophers of science are prepared to accept that all observational judgements in some sense presuppose some element of theory. But many balk at the conclusion that observations therefore never have any independent authority to decide scientific questions. After all, they point out, most simple observations, such as that a pointer is adjacent to a mark on a dial, presuppose at most a minimal amount of theory, about rigid bodies, say, and about basic local geometry. Since such minimal theories are themselves rarely at issue in serious scientific debates, this minimal amount of theory-dependence provides no reason why observations of pointer readings should not be used to settle scientific disputes. If a scientific theory about the behaviour of gases, say, predicts that a pointer will be at a certain place on a dial, and it is observed not to be, then this decides against the theory about gases. It is not to the point to respond that, in taking the pointer reading at face value, we are making assumptions about rigid bodies and local geometry. For nothing in the debate about gases provides any reason to doubt these assumptions. And this of course is why scientists take such pains to work out what their theories imply about things like pointer readings – since observations of pointer readings do not depend on anything contentious, they will weigh with all sides in the scientific debate.

So, despite the arguments of Kuhn and Feyerabend, nearly all philosophers are realists about pointer readings and similar observable phenomena. But this still leaves us with the original disagreement between realism and instrumentalism about less directly observable entities. For, even if claims about pointer readings are uncontroversially belief-worthy, instrumentalists can still argue that theories about viruses, atoms and gravitational waves are nothing more than useful fictions for making calculations.

The realist response, as I said, is that the observable facts provide good indirect evidence for these theoretical entities, even if we cannot observe them directly. However, there are two strong lines of argument that instrumentalists can use to cast doubt on this suggestion. In the next two sections I shall discuss 'the underdetermination of theory by evidence' and 'the pessimistic meta-induction from past falsity'.

1.7   The underdetermination of theory by evidence

The argument from underdetermination asserts that, given any theory about unobservables that fits the observable facts, there will be other incompatible theories that fit the same facts. And so, the argument concludes, we are never in a position to know that any one of these theories is the truth.

Why should we accept that there is always more than one theory that fits any set of observable facts? One popular argument for this conclusion stems from the

'Duhem–Quine thesis'. According to this thesis, any particular scientific theory can always be defended in the face of contrary observations by adjusting auxiliary hypotheses. For example, when the Newtonian theory of gravitation was threatened by observations of anomalous movements by the planet Mercury, it could always be defended by postulating a hitherto unobserved planet, say, or an inhomogeneous mass distribution in the Sun. This general strategy for defending theories against contrary evidence seems to imply that the adherents of competing theories will always be able to maintain their respective positions in the face of any actual observational data.

Another argument for underdetermination starts, not with competing theories, but with some given theory. Suppose that all the predictions of some particular theory are accurate. We can construct a 'de-Ockhamized' version of this theory (reversing William of Ockham's 'razor' which prescribes that 'entities are not to be multiplied beyond necessity'), by postulating some unnecessarily complicated unobservable mechanism which nevertheless yields a new theory with precisely the same observational consequences as the original one.

Both of these lines of reasoning can be used to argue that more than one theory about unobservables will always fit any given set of observational data. Does this make realism about unobservables untenable? Many philosophers conclude that it does. But this is too quick. For we should recognize that there is nothing in the arguments for alternative underdetermined theories to show that these alternative theories will always be *equally well-supported by the data*. What the arguments show is that different theories will always be *consistent* with the data. But they do not rule out the possibility that, among these alternative theories, one is vastly more plausible than the others, and for that reason should be believed to be true. After all, 'flat earthers' can make their view consistent with the evidence from geography, astronomy and satellite photographs, by constructing far-fetched stories about conspiracies to hide the truth, the effects of empty space on cameras, and so on. But this does not show that we need take their flat-earthism seriously. Similarly, even though Newtonian gravitational theory can in principle be made consistent with all the contrary evidence, this is no reason not to believe general relativity. Nor is our ability to 'cook up' a de-Ockhamized version of general relativity a reason to stop believing the standard version unencumbered with unnecessary entities.

Nevertheless, as I said, many contemporary philosophers of science do move directly from the premise that different theories are consistent with the observational evidence to the conclusion that none of them can be regarded as the truth. This is because many of them address this issue from an essentially Popperian perspective. For if you follow Popper in rejecting induction, then you will not believe that evidence ever provides positive support for any theory, except in the back-handed sense that the evidence can fail to falsify it. Accordingly you will think that all theories that have not been falsified are on a par, and in particular that any two theories that are both consistent with the evidence are equally well-supported by it.

So the arguments for underdetermination do present a problem to Popperians, since Popperians have no obvious basis for discriminating among different theories consistent with the data. But, as I pointed out above, these need not worry those of us who diverge from Popper in thinking unfalsified theories can be better or worse supported by evidence, for we can simply respond to the underdetermination arguments by observing that some underdetermined theories are better supported by the evidence than others.

Now that we have returned to Popper, it is worth noting that the Duhem–Quine argument also raises a more specific problem for Popperians. Recall that Popper's overall philosophy raised the 'problem of demarcation', the problem of how to distinguish science from other kinds of conjecture. Popper's answer was that science, unlike astrology, or Marxism and psychoanalytic theory, is falsifiable. But the Duhem–Quine argument shows that even such eminently scientific theories as Newtonian physics are not falsifiable in any straightforward sense, since they can always save themselves in the face of failed predictions by adjusting auxiliary hypotheses.

Not only does this cast doubt on Popper's dismissal of Marxism and psychoanalysis as unscientific, but it seems to undermine his whole solution to the demarcation problem. If such paradigmatic scientific theories as Newtonian physics are not falsifiable, then it can scarcely be falsifiability that distinguishes science from non-science. Still, this is Popper's problem, not ours (see Harding 1975). If we do not reject induction, then we do not have a problem of demarcation. For we can simply say that what distinguishes successful scientific theories from non-science is that the observational evidence gives us inductive reason to regard scientific theories as true.

The arguments in the latter part of this section have presupposed that a certain kind of inductive argument is legitimate. The kind of inductive argument relevant to underdetermination is not simple 'enumerative' induction, from observed As being Bs to 'All As are Bs', but rather inferences from any collection of observational data to the most plausible theory about unobservables that is consistent with that data. But these are species of the same genus; indeed, enumerative inductions can themselves be interpreted as treating 'All As are Bs' as the most plausible extrapolation consistent with the observed As being Bs. My attitude to this more general category of inductive inferences remains the same as my attitude to enumerative induction, which I outlined earlier. We do not yet have an explanation of why inductive inferences are legitimate, and to that extent we still face a problem of induction. But it is silly to try to solve that problem by denying that inductive inferences are ever legitimate. And that is why the underdetermination of theory by data does not constitute a good argument for instrumentalism. For to assume that we are never entitled to believe a theory, if there are others consistent with the same data, is simply to assume the illegitimacy of induction.

The Underdetermination of Theory by Observational Data (UTD)

There are two arguments for the UTD. The first is based on the Duhem–Quine thesis, originally formulated by the French philosopher and historian Pierre Duhem (1861–1916) and later revived by the American logician W. V. O. Quine (b. 1908). Duhem (1951) and Quine (1951) point out that a scientific theory T does not normally imply predictions P on its own, but only in conjunction with auxiliary hypotheses H.

$$T \,\&\, H \Rightarrow P$$

So when P is falsified by observation, this does not refute T, but only the conjunction of T & H.

not-P $\Rightarrow$ not-(T & H)

So T can be retained, and indeed still explain P, provided we replace H by some alternative, H', such that

T & H' $\Rightarrow$ not-P.

This yields the Duhem–Quine thesis: any theoretical claim T can consistently be retained in the face of contrary evidence, by making adjustments elsewhere in our system of beliefs. The UTD follows quickly. Imagine two competing theories T_1 and T_2. Whatever evidence accumulates, versions of T_1 and T_2, conjoined with greatly revised auxiliary hypotheses if necessary, will both survive, consistent with that evidence, but incompatible with each other.

The other argument, first put forward by physicists like Henri Poincaré (1854–1912) and Ernst Mach (1838–1916) at the turn of the twentieth century, has a different starting-point. Imagine that T_1 is the complete truth about physical reality, and that it implies observational facts O. Then we can always construct some 'de-Ockhamized' T_2 which postulates more complicated unobservable mechanisms but makes just the same observational predictions O. (Glymour 1980: ch. 5.)

For example, suppose we start with standard assumptions about the location of bodies in space-time and about the forces acting on them. A de-Ockhamized theory might then postulate that all bodies, including all measuring instruments, are accelerating by 1ft/sec.^{2} in a given direction, and then add just the extra forces required to explain this. This theory would clearly have exactly the same observational consequences as the original one, even though it contradicted it at the unobservable level.

To bring out the difference between the two arguments for UTD, note that the Duhem–Quine argument does not specify exactly which overall theories we will end up with, since it leaves open how T_1's and T_2's auxiliary hypotheses may need to be revised; the de-Ockhamization argument, by contrast, actually specifies T_1 and T_2 in full detail, including auxiliary hypotheses. In compensation, the Duhem–Quine argument promises us alternative theories whatever observational evidence may turn up in the future; whereas the de-Ockhamization argument assumes that all future observations are as T_1 predicts.

1.8   The pessimistic meta-induction

I turn now to the other argument against realism. This argument takes as its premise the fact that past scientific theories have generally turned out to be false, and then moves inductively to the pessimistic conclusion that our current theories are no doubt false too. (This is called a 'meta-induction' because its subject matter is not the natural world, but scientific theories about the natural world.)

There are plenty of familiar examples to support this argument. Newton's theory of space and time, the phlogiston theory of combustion, and the theory that atoms are indivisible were all at one time widely accepted scientific theories, but have since been recognized to be false. So does it not seem likely, the pessimistic induction concludes, that all our current theories are false, and that we should therefore take an instrumentalist rather than a realist attitude to them? (See Laudan 1981.)

This is an important and powerful argument, but it would be too quick to conclude that it discredits realism completely. It is important that the tendency to falsity is much more common in some areas of science than others. Thus it is relatively normal for theories to be overturned in cosmology, say, or fundamental particle physics, or the study of primate evolution. By contrast, theories of the molecular composition of different chemical compounds (such as that water is made of hydrogen and oxygen), or the causes of infectious diseases (chickenpox is due to a herpes virus), or the nature of everyday physical phenomena (heat is molecular motion), are characteristically retained once they are accepted.

Nor need we regard this differential success rate of different kinds of theories as some kind of accident. Rather, it is the result of the necessary evidence being more easily available in some areas of science than others. Paleoanthropologists want to know how many hominid species were present on earth 3 million years ago. But their evidence consists of a few pieces of teeth and bone. So it is scarcely surprising that discoveries of new fossil sites will often lead them to change their views. The same point applies on a larger scale in cosmology and particle physics. Scientists in these areas want to answer very general questions about the very small and the very distant. But their evidence derives from the limited range of technological instruments they have devised to probe these realms. So, once more, it is scarcely surprising that their theories should remain at the level of tentative hypotheses. By contrast, in those areas where adequate evidence is available, such as chemistry and medicine, there is no corresponding barrier to science moving beyond tentative hypotheses to firm conclusions.

The moral is that realism is more defensible for some areas of science than others. In some scientific subjects firm evidence is available, and entitles us to view certain theories, like the theory that water is composed of H_2O molecules, as the literal truth about reality. In other areas the evidence is fragmentary and inconclusive, and then we do better to regard the best-supported theories, such as the theory that quarks and leptons are the ultimate building blocks of matter, as useful instruments which accommodate the existing data, make interesting predictions, and suggest further lines for research.

At first sight this might look like a victory for instrumentalism over realism. For did not instrumentalists always accept that we should be realists about *observable* things, and only urge instrumentalism for uncertain theories about unobservable phenomena? But our current position draws the line in a different place. Instrumentalism, as originally defined, takes it for granted that everything *unobservable* is inaccessible, and that all theories about unobservables are therefore uncertain. By contrast, the position we have arrived at places no special weight on the distinction between what is observable and what is not. In particular, it argues that the pessimistic meta-induction fails to show that falsity is the natural fate of all theories about unobservables, but only that there is a line *within* the category of theories about unobservables, between those theories that can be expected to turn out false and those whose claims to truth are secure. So our current position is not a dogmatic instrumentalism about all unobservables, but merely the uncontentious view that we should be instrumentalists about that sub-class of theories which are not supported by adequate evidence.

1.9   Naturalized epistemology of science

In the last decade or so a number of philosophers of science have turned to a *naturalized* approach to scientific knowledge (Kitcher 1992). In place of traditional attempts to establish criteria for scientific theory-choice by *a priori* philosophical investigation, the naturalized approach regards science itself as a subject for *a posteriori* empirical investigation. Accordingly, naturalized epistemologists look to the history, sociology and psychology of science, rather than to first principles, to identify criteria for the acceptability of scientific theories.

One apparent difficulty facing this kind of naturalized epistemology of science is that it is unclear how empirical investigation can ever yield anything more than *descriptive* information about how scientists actually operate. Yet any epistemology of science worth its name ought also to have a *normative* content – it ought to *prescribe* how scientists should reason, as well as describe how they do reason. David HUME (chapter 31) first pointed out that there is a logical gap between 'is' and 'ought'. A naturalized epistemology based on the empirical study of science seems fated to remain on the wrong side of this gap.

However, there is room for naturalized epistemologists to reply to this charge. They can agree that the empirical study of science cannot by itself yield prescriptions about how science ought to be done. But empirical study can still be *relevant* to such prescriptions. Suppose it is agreed that *technological fertility*, in the sense of generating technological advances, is a virtue in a scientific theory. Then the history, sociology and psychology of science might be able to show us that certain kinds of research strategies are effective at developing technologically fertile theories. More generally, given any agreed theoretical end Y, empirical study can show that research strategy X is an effective *means* to that end. The empirical study of science can thus yield the *hypothetical prescription* that, if you want Y, then you *ought* to adopt means X. It is this kind of hypothetical prescription that naturalized philosophers of science seek to establish: they look to the history, sociology and psychology of science to show us that scientists who *choose* theories on grounds X will in general *achieve* theories with characteristic Y.

Can the naturalized study of science tell us which research strategies are an effective means to theoretical *truth*? Different naturalized philosophers of science give different answers to this question. Many are suspicious of the idea of theoretical truth, and instead prefer to stick to the study of how to achieve more practical ends like technological fertility, simplicity and predictive accuracy. However, there seems no good reason for this restriction. There is nothing obviously incoherent in the idea of looking to the empirical study of science to tell us which research strategies have proved a good way of developing true theories. Indeed, the discussion of the 'pessimistic meta-induction' in the previous section amounted to the sketch of just such an investigation, in that it appealed to the history of science to decide whether or not the standard procedures of scientific theory-choice succeed in identifying true theories. It is not difficult to imagine more detailed and specific studies of this kind of issue.

Let me now return briefly to the issue with which I began, namely, the problem of induction. It is possible that the naturalized study of how to get at the scientific truth will enable us to make headway with this problem. For an empirical investigation into science might be able to show us that a certain kind of *inductive* inference is in general a reliable guide to scientific truth. And this would then provide a kind of vindication of that inductive method (see Papineau 1993: ch. 5).

It is true that this kind of defence of induction will inevitably involve an element of circularity. For when we infer that certain kinds of induction are *in general* a reliable guide to truth, on the basis of evidence from the history of science, this will itself be an inductive inference. It is a matter of some delicacy, however, whether this circularity is vicious.

Defenders of this naturalized defence of induction will point out that, from their point of view, a legitimate criterion of theory-choice need not be an *a priori* guide to truth, but only an empirically certifiable one. Given this, the original argument against induction, that it is not logically valid, will not worry naturalized philosophers of science. Induction may not provide any *a priori* guarantee for its conclusions; but from the naturalized point of view, this does not show that induction is in any way illegitimate, since it leaves it open that induction may be an empirically reliable guide to the truth. And if there is nothing to show that induction is illegitimate, naturalized philosophers of science can then argue, why should we not use it to investigate the worth of inductive inferences? Maybe this is less satisfying a defence of induction than we might originally have hoped for. But perhaps it is defence enough.

2 The Metaphysics of Science

2.1 *Causation*

Many issues in the metaphysics of science hinge on the notion of *causation*. This notion is as important in science as it is in everyday thinking, and much scientific theorizing is concerned specifically to identify the *causes* of various phenomena. However, there is little philosophical agreement on what it means to say that one event is the cause of another.

Modern discussion of causation starts with David Hume, who argued that causation is simply a matter of CONSTANT CONJUNCTION (p. 720). According to Hume (1978), one event causes another if and only if events of the type to which the first event belongs regularly occur in conjunction with events of the type to which the second event belongs. This formulation, however, leaves a number of questions open. Firstly, there is the problem of distinguishing genuine *causal laws* from *accidental regularities*. Not all regularities are sufficiently lawlike to underpin causal relationships. Being a screw in my desk could well be constantly conjoined with being made of copper, without its being true that these screws are made of copper because they are in my desk. Secondly, the idea of constant conjunction does not give a *direction* to causation. Causes need to be distinguished from effects. But knowing that A-type events are constantly conjoined with B-type events does not tell us which of A and B is the cause and which the effect, since constant conjunction is itself a symmetric relation. Thirdly, there is a problem about *probabilistic causation*. When we say that causes and effects are constantly conjoined, do we mean that the effects are always found with the causes, or is it enough that the causes make the effects probable?

Many philosophers of science during the past century have preferred to talk about *explanation* rather than causation. According to the covering-law model of explanation, something is explained if it can be deduced from premises which include one or more laws. As applied to the explanation of particular events, this implies that one particular event can be explained if it is linked by a law to some other particular event. However, while they are often treated as separate theories, the covering-law account of explanation is at bottom little more than a variant of Hume's constant conjunction account of causation. This affinity shows up in the fact that the covering-law account faces essentially the same difficulties as Hume: (1) in appealing to deductions from 'laws', it needs to explain the difference between genuine laws and accidentally true regularities; (2) it omits the requisite directionality, in that it does not tell us why we should not 'explain' causes by effects, as well as effects by causes; after all, it is as easy to deduce the height of a flagpole from the length of its shadow and the laws of optics, as to deduce the length of the shadow from the height of the pole and the same laws; (3) are the laws invoked in explanation required to be exceptionless and deterministic, or is it acceptable, say, to appeal to the merely probabilistic fact that smoking makes cancer more likely, in explaining why some particular person developed cancer?

In what follows I shall discuss these three problems in order (treating them as problems that arise equally both for the analysis of causation and the analysis of explanation). After that I shall consider some further issues in the metaphysics of science.

The Covering-Law Model of Explanation

According to this model (originally proposed by Hempel and Oppenheim (1948) and further elaborated in Hempel (1965)) one statement (the *explanandum*) is explained by other statements (the *explanans*) if and only if the explanans contains one or more *laws*, and the explanandum can be *deduced* from the explanans. In the simplest case, where the explanandum is some particular statement to the effect that some individual *a* has property E, we might therefore have:

a has C
For all x, if x has C, then x has E
a has E

For example, we might deduce that a piece of litmus paper turned red, from the law that all litmus paper placed in acid turns red, together with the prior condition that this piece of litmus paper was in fact placed in acid. The model can accommodate more complicated explanations of particular events, and can also allow explanations of laws themselves, as when we deduce Kepler's law that all planets move in ellipses, say, from Newton's law of universal gravitation and his laws of motion.

As applied to the explanation of particular events, the covering-law model implies a symmetry between *explanation* and *prediction*. For the information that, according to the model, suffices for the explanation of some known event should also enable us to predict that event if we did not yet know of it. Many critics have fastened on this implication of the model, however, and pointed out that we can often predict when we do not have enough information to explain (as when we predict the height of the flagpole from its shadow) and can often explain when we could not have predicted (as when we explain X's cancer on the basis of X's smoking).

These examples suggest that genuine explanations of particular events need to cite genuine causes, and that the reason the covering-law model runs into counter-examples is that it adds nothing to the inadequate constant conjunction analysis of causation, except that it substitutes the term 'law' for 'constant conjunction'. To get a satisfactory account of explanation we need, firstly, to recognize that explanations of particular events must mention causes, and, secondly, to improve on the constant conjunction analysis of causation.

There is a variant of the covering-law model which allows non-deterministic explanation as well as deterministic ones. This is termed the 'inductive–statistical (I–S)' model, by contrast with the original 'deductive–nomological (D–N)' model. An example would be:

a drinks 10 units of alcohol per diem
For *p* per cent of *xs*, if *x* drinks 10 units of alcohol per diem, *x* has a damaged liver
a has a damaged liver

Here the explanandum cannot be *deduced* from the explanans, but only follows with an *inductive* probability of *p*; and the inference appeals to a *statistical* regularity, rather than an exceptionless *nomological* generalization. In Hempel's original version of this model, it was required that the probability of the explanandum be *high*. A better requirement, however, as explained in the section on probabilistic causation below, is that the particular facts in the explanans need only make the probability of the explanandum *higher* than it would otherwise have been.

2.2   Laws and accidents

There are two general strategies for distinguishing laws from accidentally true generalizations. The first stands by Hume's idea that causal connections are mere constant conjunctions, and then seeks to explain why some constant conjunctions are better than others. That is, this first strategy accepts the principle that causation involves nothing more than certain events always happening together with certain others, and then seeks to explain why some such patterns – the 'laws' – matter more than others – the 'accidents'. The second strategy, by contrast, rejects the Humean presupposition that causation involves nothing more than happenstantial co-occurrence, and instead postulates a relationship of 'necessitation', a kind of 'cement', which links events that are connected by law, but not those events (like being a screw in my desk and being made of copper) that are only accidentally conjoined.

There are a number of versions of the first Humean strategy. The most successful, originally proposed by F. R. Ramsey (1903–30), and later revived by David Lewis (1973), holds that laws are those true generalizations that can be fitted into an ideal system of knowledge. The thought here is that the laws are those patterns that are somehow explicable in terms of basic science, either as fundamental principles themselves, or as consequences of those principles, while accidents, although true, have no such explanation. Thus, 'All water at standard pressure boils at 100°C' is a consequence of the laws governing molecular bonding; but the fact that 'All the screws in my desk are copper' is not part of the deductive structure of any satisfactory science. Ramsey neatly encapsulated this idea by saying that laws are 'consequences of those propositions which we should take as axioms if we knew everything and organized it as simply as possible in a deductive system' (Ramsey 1978: 130).

Advocates of the alternative non-Humean strategy object that the difference between laws and accidents is not a *linguistic* matter of deductive systematization, but rather a *metaphysical* contrast between the kind of links they report. They argue that there is a link in nature between *being at 100°C* and *boiling*, but not between *being in my desk* and *being made of copper*, and that this is nothing to do with how the description of this link may fit into theories. According to D. M. Armstrong (1983), the most prominent defender of this view, the real difference between laws and accidents is simply that laws report relationships of natural *necessitation*, while accidents only report that two types of events *happen* to occur together.

Armstrong's view may seem intuitively plausible, but it is arguable that the notion of necessitation simply restates the problem, rather than solving it. Armstrong says that necessitation involves something more than constant conjunction: if two events are related by necessitation, then it follows that they are constantly conjoined; but two events can be constantly conjoined without being related by necessitation, as when the constant conjunction is just a matter of accident. So necessitation is a stronger relationship than constant conjunction. However, Armstrong and other defenders of this view say very little about what this extra strength amounts to, except that it distinguishes laws from accidents. Armstrong's critics argue that a satisfactory account of laws ought to cast more light than this on the nature of laws.

2.3   The direction of causation

Hume said that the earlier of two causally related events is always the cause, and the *later* the effect. However, there are a number of objections to using the earlier–later 'arrow of time' to analyse the directional 'arrow of causation'. For a start, it seems in principle possible that some causes and effects could be simultaneous. More seriously, the idea that time is directed from 'earlier' to 'later' itself stands in need of philosophical explanation – and one of the most popular explanations is that the idea of 'movement' from earlier to later depends on the fact that cause–effect pairs always have a given orientation in time. However, if we adopt such a 'causal theory of the arrow of time', and explain 'earlier' as the direction in which causes lie, and 'later' as the direction of effects, then we will clearly need to find some account of the direction of causation which does not itself assume the direction of time.

A number of such accounts have been proposed. David Lewis (1979) has argued that the asymmetry of causation derives from an 'asymmetry of overdetermination'. The overdetermination of present events by past events – consider a person who dies after simultaneously being shot and struck by lightning – is a very rare occurrence. By contrast, the multiple 'overdetermination' of present events by future events is absolutely normal. This is because the future, unlike the past, will always contain multiple traces of any present event. To use Lewis's example, when the president presses the red button in the White House, the future effects do not only include the dispatch of nuclear missiles, but also his fingerprint on the button, his trembling, the further depletion of his gin bottle, the recording of the button's click on tape, the emission of light waves bearing the image of his action through the window, the warming of the wire from the passage of the signal current, and so on, and on, and on.

Lewis relates this asymmetry of overdetermination to the asymmetry of causation as follows. If we suppose the cause of a given effect to have been absent, then this implies the effect would have been absent too, since (apart from freaks like the lightning–shooting case) there will not be any other causes left to 'fix' the effect. By contrast, if we suppose a given effect of some cause to have been absent, this does not imply the cause would have been absent, for there are still all the other traces left to 'fix' the cause. Lewis argues that these counterfactual considerations suffice to show why causes are different from effects.

Other philosophers appeal to a probabilistic variant of Lewis's asymmetry. Following Reichenbach (1956), they note that the different causes of any given type of effect are normally probabilistically independent of each other; by contrast, the different effects of any given type of cause are normally probabilistically correlated. For example, both obesity and high excitement can cause heart attacks, but this does not imply that fat people are more likely to get excited than thin ones; on the other hand, the fact that both lung cancer and nicotine-stained fingers can result from smoking does imply that lung cancer is more likely among people with nicotine-stained fingers. So this account distinguishes effects from causes by the fact that the former, but not the latter, are probabilistically dependent on each other.

2.4   Probabilistic causation

The just-mentioned probabilistic account of the *direction* of causation is normally formulated as part of a more general *theory of probabilistic causation*. Until relatively recently philosophers assumed that the world fundamentally conforms to deterministic laws, and that probabilistic dependencies between types of events, such as that between smoking and lung cancer, merely reflected our ignorance of the full causes. The rise of quantum mechanics, however, has persuaded most philosophers that determinism is false, and that some events, like the decay of a radium atom, happen purely as a matter of chance. A particular radium atom may decay, but on another occasion an identical atom in identical circumstances might well not decay.

Accordingly, a number of philosophers of science have put forward models of causation which require only that causes probabilify, rather than determine, their effects. The earliest such model was the 'inductive–statistical' version of the covering-law model of explanation (Hempel 1965). Unlike deterministic 'deductive–nomological' explanations, such inductive–statistical explanations required only that prior conditions and laws imply a *high* probability for the event to be explained, not that this event will certainly happen. However, even this seems too strong a requirement for probabilistic causation. After all, smoking unequivocally causes lung cancer, but even heavy smokers do not have a *high* probability of lung cancer, in the sense of a probability close to 1. Rather, their smoking increases their probability of lung cancer, not to a high figure, but merely from a low to a less low figure, but still well below 50 per cent. So more recent models of probabilistic causation simply require that causes should *increase* the probability of their effects, not that they should give them a high probability (Salmon 1971).

This kind of model needs to guard against the possibility that the probabilistic association between putative cause and putative effect may be *spurious*, like the probabilistic association between barometers falling and subsequent rain. Such associations are not due to a causal connection between barometer movements and rain, but rather to both of these being joint effects of a *common cause*, namely, in our example, falls in atmospheric pressure. The obvious response to this difficulty is to say that we have a cause–effect relationship between A and B if and only if A increases the probability of B, and this association is not due to some common cause C. However, this is obviously incomplete as an analysis of causation, since it uses the notion of (common) *cause* in explaining causation.

It would solve this problem if we could analyse the notion of common cause in probabilistic terms. It seems to be a mark of common causes that they probabilistically '*screen off*' the associations between their joint effects, in the sense that, if we consider cases where the common cause is present and where it is absent separately, then the probabilistic association between the joint effects will disappear. For example, if it is given that the atmospheric pressure has fallen, then a falling barometer does not make it any more likely that it will rain; and similarly, if the atmospheric pressure *has not* fallen, a faulty falling reading on a barometer is no probable indicator of impending rain. (Numerically, if C is a common cause, and A and B its joint effects, we will find that A and B are associated – $\text{Prob}(B/A) < \text{Prob}(B)$ – but that C and its absence render A irrelevant to B – $\text{Prob}(B/A \& C) = \text{Prob}(B/C)$ and $\text{Prob}(B/A \& \text{not-C}) = \text{Prob}(B/\text{not-}C)$.) It remains a matter of some debate, however, whether this characteristic probabilistic structure of common causes is enough to allow a complete explanation of causation in probabilistic terms, or whether further non-probabilistic considerations need to be introduced.

2.5   Probability

Philosophical interest in probabilistic causation has led to a resurgence of interest in the philosophy of probability itself. Probability raises philosophical puzzles in its own right, quite apart from its connection with causation. What exactly is the 'probability' of a given event? The only part of the answer that is uncontroversial is that probabilities are quantities that satisfy the axioms of the probability calculus I specified earlier when discussing Bayesianism. But this leaves plenty of room for alternative philosophical views, for there are a number of different ways of interpreting these axioms.

One interpretation is the *subjective* theory of probability, which equates probabilities with subjective degrees of belief. This is the interpretation assumed by Bayesian confirmation theory. Most philosophers are happy to agree that subjective degrees of belief exist, and that the Dutch Book Argument (see the above box on Bayesianism) shows why they ought to conform to the axioms of probability. But many, if not all, philosophers argue that we need a theory of objective probability in addition to this subjective account.

One possible objective interpretation is the *frequency* theory, originally put forward by Richard von Mises (1957). According to this theory, the probability of a given kind of result is the number of times this result occurs, divided by the total number of occasions on which it might have occurred. So, for example, the probability of heads on a coin toss is the proportion of heads in some wider class of coin tosses.

This theory, however, faces a number of difficulties. For a start, it has problems in dealing with 'single-case probabilities'. Consider a particular coin toss. We can consider it as a member of the class of all coin tosses, or of all tosses of coins with that particular shape, or of all tosses made in just that way, or so on. However, these different 'reference classes' may well display different frequencies of heads. Yet intuitively it seems that there ought to be a unique value for the probability of heads on a particular toss of a particular coin. Perhaps this difficulty can be dealt with by specifying that the single-case probability should equal the relative frequency in the reference class of all tosses that are *similar in all relevant respects* to the particular toss in question. But there remain difficulties about which respects should count as 'relevant' in this sense.

In addition, there is the problem that many of these more specific reference classes will only be finite in extent. Coins with a certain distinctive shape may only be tossed in some given way ten times in the whole history of the universe. Yet the probability of heads on these tosses is unlikely to be equal to the relative frequency in the ten tosses, for luck may well yield a disproportionately high, or low, number of heads in ten tosses. Because of this, frequency theorists standardly appeal, not to actual reference classes, but to hypothetical infinite sequences, and equate the probability with the *limit* that the relative frequency *would* tend to *if* the relevant kind of trial were repeated an infinite number of times. Critics of the frequency theory object that this reliance on hypothetical infinite reference sequences makes probabilities inadmissibly abstract.

Because of these difficulties, many contemporary philosophers of probability have adopted the '*propensity*' theory of probability in place of the frequency theory. The earliest version of this theory, proposed by Popper (1959b), simply modified the frequency theory by specifying that only those relative frequencies generated by repeated trials on a given 'experimental set-up' should count as genuine probabilities. This arguably deals with the problem of single-case probabilities, but it still leaves us with hypothetical reference classes. To avoid this, later versions of the propensity theory do not define probabilities in terms of frequencies at all, but simply take probabilities to be primitive propensities of particular situations to produce given results.

This kind of propensity theory does not seek to define objective probabilities in terms of frequencies, but in effect simply takes single-case probabilities as primitive (see Mellor 1971). But it can still recognize a connection between probabilities and frequencies. For, as long as propensities are assumed to obey the axioms of the probability calculus (though this assumption itself merits some debate), it will follow that, in a sufficiently long sequence of independent trials in each of which the propensity to produce B is p, the overall *propensity* for the observed frequency of B to differ by more than a given amount from p can be made arbitrarily small, in accord with the Law of Large Numbers. (Note how the italicized second use of 'propensity' in this claim prevents it serving as a definition of propensities in terms of frequencies.)

Both the frequency theory and the propensity theory have their strengths. The frequency theory has the virtue of offering an explicit definition of probability, where the propensity theory takes probabilities as primitive. On the other hand, the propensity theory has no need to assume hypothetical reference sequences, whereas these are essential to the frequency theory.

It may seem that the frequency theory, because it offers an explicit definition, is better able than the propensity theory to explain how we find out about probabilities. But this is an illusion. The trouble is that the frequency theory's explicit definition is in terms of frequencies in INFINITE SEQUENCES (p. 355). But our evidence is always in the form of frequencies in *finite* samples. So the problem of explaining how we can move from frequencies in finite samples to knowledge of probabilities is as much a problem for the frequency theory as for the propensity theory. (There are various suggestions about how to solve this 'problem of statistical inference', none of them universally agreed. My present point is merely that this problem of statistical inference arises in just the same way for both frequency and propensity theorists.)

In the face of continued debate about the interpretation of objective probability, some philosophers have turned to physics, and in particular to the notion of probability used in quantum mechanics, to resolve the issue. Unfortunately, quantum mechanics is no less philosophically controversial than the notion of probability. There are different philosophical interpretations of the formal theory of quantum mechanics, each of which involves different understandings of probability. Because of this it seems likely that philosophical disputes about probability will continue until there is an agreed interpretation of quantum mechanics.

The Interpretation of Quantum Mechanics

Modern quantum mechanics says that the state of any given system of microscopic particles is fully characterized by its 'wave function'. However, instead of specifying the exact positions and velocities of the particles, as is done in classical mechanics, this 'wave function' only specifies *probabilities* of the particles displaying certain values of position, and velocity, *if* appropriate measurements are made. *Schrödinger's equation* then specifies how this wave function evolves smoothly and deterministically over time, analogously to the way that Newton's laws of motion specify how the positions and velocities of macroscopic objects evolve over time – except that Schrödinger's equation again only describes changes in probabilities, not exact values.

On the orthodox interpretation of quantum mechanics, quantum probabilities change into actualities only when 'measurements' are made. If you measure the position of a particle, say, then its position assumes a definite value, even though nothing before the measurement determined exactly what this value would be.

There is something puzzling about this, however, since any overall system of measured particle and measuring instrument is itself just another system of microscopic particles, which might therefore be expected to evolve smoothly according to Schrödinger's equation, rather than to jump suddenly to some definite value for position. To account for this, the orthodox interpretation says that in addition to the normal Schrödinger evolution, there is a special kind of change which occurs in 'measurements', when the wave function suddenly 'collapses' to yield a definite value for the measured quantity.

The 'measurement problem' is the problem of explaining exactly when, and why, these collapses occur. The story of 'Schrödinger's cat' makes the difficulty graphic. Suppose that some unfortunate cat is sitting next to a poison dispenser which is wired up to emit cyanide gas if an electron emitted from some source turns up on the right half of some position-registering plate, but not if the electron turns up on the left half. The basic quantum mechanical description of this situation says that it is both possible that the electron will turn up on the right half of the plate and that it will turn up on the left half, and therefore both possible that the poison is emitted and that it is not, and therefore both possible that the cat is alive and that it is dead. One of these possibilities only becomes actual when the wave function of the whole system collapses. But when does that happen? When the electron is emitted? When it reaches the plate? When the cat dies or not? Or only when a human being looks at the cat to see how it is faring?

There seems no principled way to decide between these answers. Because of this, many philosophers reject the orthodox view that physical systems are completely characterized by their wave functions, and conjecture that, in addition to the variables quantum mechanics recognizes, there are various 'hidden variables' which always specify exact positions and velocities for all physical particles. It is difficult, however, for such *hidden variable theories* to reproduce the surprising phenomena predicted by quantum mechanics, without postulating mysterious mechanisms that seem inconsistent with other parts of physics.

A more radical response to the measurement problem is to deny that the wave function ever does collapse, and somehow to make sense of the idea that reality contains both a live cat and a dead cat. This 'many-worlds' interpretation of quantum mechanics flies in the face of common sense, but its theoretical attractions are leading an increasing number of philosophers to take it seriously.

2.6 Teleology

We normally explain some particular fact by citing its *cause*: for example, we explain why some water freezes by noting that its temperature fell below 0°C. There are cases, however, where we seem to explain items by citing their *effects* instead. In particular, this kind of explanation is common in biology. We often explain some biological trait by showing how it is useful to the organism in question: for instance, the explanation of the polar bear's white fur is that it camouflages it; the explanation of human sweating is that it lowers body temperature, and so on. Similar explanations are also sometimes offered in anthropology and sociology.

Until fairly recently most philosophers of science took such functional or teleological explanations at face value, as an alternative to causal explanation, in which items are explained, not by their causal antecedents, but by showing how they contribute to the well-being of some larger system. Carl Hempel's covering-law model of explanation embodied an influential version of this attitude. According to Hempel, causal explanations and functional explanations are simply two different ways of exemplifying the covering-law model: the only difference is that in causal explanations the *explaining fact* (lower temperature) temporally precedes the *explained* fact (freezing), whereas in functional explanations it is explained fact (white fur) that comes temporally before the consequence (camouflage) which explains it.

Most contemporary philosophers of science, however, take a different view, and argue that all explanations of particular facts are really causal, and that functional explanations, despite appearances, are really a *subspecies* of causal explanations. On

311

this view, the reference to future facts in functional explanations is merely apparent, and such explanations really refer to past causes. In the biological case, these past causes will be the evolutionary histories that led to the natural selection of the biological trait in question. Thus the functional explanation of the polar bear's colour should be understood as referring us to the fact that their *past* camouflaging led to the natural selection of their whiteness, and not to the fact that they may be camouflaged in the *future*. Similarly, any acceptable functional explanations in anthropology or sociology should be understood as referring us *back* in time to the conscious intentions or unconscious selection processes which caused the facts to be explained (see Wright 1973; Neander 1991). (There remains the terminological matter of whether functional explanations understood in this way ought still to be called 'teleological'. Traditional usage reserves the term 'teleology' for distinctively non-causal explanations in terms of future results. But most contemporary philosophers are happy to describe disguised causal explanations that make implicit reference to selection mechanisms as 'teleological'.)

2.7   Theoretical reduction

Another philosophical question about subject matters like biology is whether they can be reduced to lower-level (in the sense of ontologically more basic) sciences like chemistry and physics. Obviously, this is an issue that arises not just for biology, but also for such other 'special' natural sciences as geology and meteorology, and also for such human sciences as psychology, sociology and anthropology.

One science is said to 'reduce' to another if its categories can be defined in terms of the categories of the latter, and its laws explained by the laws of the latter. *Reductionists* argue that all sciences form a hierarchy in which the higher can always be reduced to the lower. Thus, for example, biology might be reduced to physiology, physiology to chemistry, and eventually chemistry to physics.

Reductionism can be viewed either historically or metaphysically. The historical question is whether science characteristically progresses by later theories reducing earlier ones. The metaphysical question is whether the different areas of science describe different realities, or just the one physical reality described at different levels of detail. Though often run together, these are different questions.

Taken as a general thesis, historical reductionism is false. Recall the earlier discussion of the 'pessimistic meta-induction from past falsity'. This involved the claim that new theories characteristically show their predecessors to be false. To the extent that this claim is true, historical reductionism is false: for a new theory can scarcely explain why an earlier theory was true, if it shows it is false.

In the earlier discussion I argued that there are some areas of science, like molecular biology and medical science, to which the pessimistic meta-induction does not apply. If this is right, then we can expect that in these areas new theories will indeed normally reduce old ones. But I did not dispute that there are other areas of science, like cosmology and fundamental particle physics, in which the normal fate of old theories is to be thrown out. It follows that we must reject historical reductionism, understood as the thesis that all science proceeds by new theories reducing old ones.

This does not mean, however, that metaphysical reductionism is false. Even if science proceeds towards the overall truth by fits and starts, there may be general reasons for expecting that this overall truth, when eventually reached, will reduce to physical truth.

One possible such argument stems from the *causal interaction* between the phenomena discussed in the special sciences and physical phenomena. Biological, geological and meteorological events all unquestionably have physical effects. It is difficult to see how they could do this unless they are made of physical components.

It is doubtful, however, whether this suffices to establish full-scale reductionism, as opposed to the weaker thesis (sometimes called 'token-identity') according to which each *particular* higher-level event is identical with some *particular* physical event. Thus, for example, it might be true that one animal's aggressive behaviour can be equated with a given sequence of physical movements, and another animal's aggressive behaviour can be equated with another sequence of physical movements, without there being any uniform way of defining 'aggressive behaviour', for all animals, in terms of physical movements. The case-by-case token-identity will explain how each instance of aggressive behaviour can have physical effects, like causing intruding animals to move away. But without any uniform definition of 'aggressive behaviour' in terms of physical movements there is no question of reducing ethology (the science of behaviour) to physics, and so no question of explaining ethological laws by physical laws. Instead, the laws of ethology and other special sciences will be *sui generis*, identifying patterns whose instances vary in their physical make-up, and which therefore cannot possibly be explained in terms of physical laws alone (see Fodor 1974).

Acknowledgements

I would like to thank Stathis Psillos for helping me with this chapter.

Further Reading

For an introduction to the problem of induction, and Popper's solution, see Popper (1959a), especially chapter 1. The problem and Popper's solution are further discussed in O'Hear (1989). There are two excellent introductions to Bayesian philosophy of science: Horwich (1982) and Howson and Urbach (1989).

The best modern defence of instrumentalism is Van Fraassen (1980). Churchland and Hooker (1985) offers a good collection of essays on the realism–instrumentalism debate. Kitcher (1993) contains a strong defence of realism.

The classic works on the theory-dependence of observation and the incommensurability of theories are Hanson (1958), Kuhn (1962) and Feyerabend (1976). A good collection of essays on these issues is Hacking (1981). The best sources for the underdetermination of theories by evidence and the pessimistic meta-induction are respectively Quine (1951) and Laudan (1981). For a survey of recent work on naturalized epistemology, see Kitcher (1992).

Most modern discussions of explanation begin with the title essay in Hempel (1965). Explanation and its relation to causation are further explored by the essays in Ruben (1993). Armstrong (1983) provides an excellent account of the general problem of distinguishing laws from accidents, as well as his own solution. Chapter 7 of O'Hear (1989) contains a good introduction to both probability and probabilistic causation. The best contemporary non-specialist discussion of the problems of quantum mechanics is to be found in chapters 11–13 of Lockwood (1989).

313

The view that events discussed in the special sciences are token-identical but not reducible to physical events is defended in Fodor (1974).

References

Armstrong, D. 1983: What is a Law of Nature? Cambridge: Cambridge University Press.

Ayer, A. J. 1956: The Problem of Knowledge. London: Macmillan.

Boyd, R. 1980: Scientific Realism and Naturalistic Epistemology. In P. Asquith and R. Giere (eds) PSA 1980 vol. 2, 613–62. East Lansing, MI: Philosophy of Science Association.

Cartwright, N. 1983: *How the Laws of Physics Lie*. Oxford: Oxford University Press.

Churchland, P. and Hooker, C. (eds) 1985: *Images of Science*. Chicago: University of Chicago Press.

Duhem, P. 1951 [1906]: *The Aim and Structure of Physical Theory* (translated by P. Wiener). Princeton, NJ: Princeton University Press.

Feyerabend, P. 1976: *Against Method*. London: New Left Books.

Fodor, J. 1974: Special Sciences. *Synthèse*, 28, 97–115.

Friedman, M. 1984: *Foundations of Spacetime Theories*. Princeton, NJ: Princeton University Press.

Glymour, C. 1980: Theory and Evidence. Princeton, NJ: Princeton University Press.

Hacking, I. 1967: Slightly More Realistic Personal Probability. *Philosophy of Science*, 34, 311–25.

——(ed.) 1981: *Scientific Revolutions*. Oxford: Oxford University Press.

Hanson, N. R. 1958: *Patterns of Discovery*. Cambridge: Cambridge University Press.

——1963: *The Concept of the Positron*. Cambridge: Cambridge University Press.

Harding, S. (ed.) 1975: *Can Theories be Refuted?* Dordrecht: Reidel.

Hempel, C. 1965: *Aspects of Scientific Explanation*. New York: Free Press.

Hempel, C. and Oppenheim, P. 1948: Studies in the Logic of Explanation. *Philosophy of Science*, 15, 135–75.

Horwich, P. 1982: *Probability and Evidence*. Cambridge: Cambridge University Press.

Howson, C. and Urbach, P. 1989: *Scientific Reasoning*. La Salle, IN: Open Court.

Hume, D. 1978 [1739]: *A Treatise of Human Nature* (edited by P. H. Nidditch). Oxford: Clarendon Press.

Kitcher, P. 1992: The Naturalists Return. *Philosophical Review*, 101, 53–114.

——1993: *The Advancement of Science*. New York: Oxford University Press.

Kuhn, T. S. 1962: *The Structure of Scientific Revolutions*. Chicago: Chicago University Press.

Laudan, L. 1981: A Confutation of Convergent Realism. *Philosophy of Science*, 48.

Lewis, D. 1973: *Counterfactuals*. Oxford: Blackwell.

——1979: Counterfactual Dependence and Time's Arrow. *Noûs*, 13, 455–76.

Lockwood, M. 1989: *Mind, Brain and the Quantum*. Oxford: Blackwell.

Mellor, D. 1971: *The Matter of Chance*. Cambridge: Cambridge University Press.

Mises, R. von 1957: *Probability, Statistics and Truth*. London: Allen and Unwin.

Neander, K. 1991: The Teleological Notion of Function. *Australasian Journal of Philosophy*, 69, 454–68.

O'Hear, A. 1989: *An Introduction to the Philosophy of Science*. Oxford: Clarendon Press.

Papineau, D. 1993: *Philosophical Naturalism*. Oxford: Blackwell.

Popper, K. 1959a: *The Logic of Scientific Discovery*. London: Hutchinson.

——1959b: The Propensity Interpretation of Probability. *British Journal for the Philosophy of Science*, 10, 25–42.

——1963: *Conjectures and Refutations*. London: Routledge and Kegan Paul.

——1972: *Objective Knowledge*. Oxford: Clarendon Press.

Quine, W. V. O. 1951: Two Dogmas of Empiricism. In *From a Logical Point of View*. New York: Harper.

Ramsey, F. 1978 [1929]: General Propositions and Causality. In D. H. Mellor (ed.) *Foundations*. London: Routledge and Kegan Paul.

Reichenbach, H. 1956: *The Direction of Time*. Berkeley: University of California Press.

Ruben, D.-H. (ed.) 1993: *Explanation*. Oxford: Oxford University Press.

Salmon, W. 1971: *Statistical Explanation and Statistical Relevance*. Pittsburgh, PA: University of Pittsburgh Press.

Smart, J. 1963: *Philosophy and Scientific Realism*. London: Routledge and Kegan Paul.

Teller, P. 1973: Conditionalization and Observation. *Synthèse*, 28, 218–58.

Van Fraassen, B. 1980: *The Scientific Image*. Oxford: Clarendon Press.

Worrall, J. 1989: Why Both Popper and Watkins Fail to Solve the Problem of Induction. In F. D'Agostino and I. Jarvie (eds) *Freedom and Rationality*. Dordrecht: Kluwer.

Wright, L. 1973: Functions. *Philosophical Review*, 82, 139–68.

Discussion Questions

1   Is it any less rational to accept induction than it is to accept deduction?

2   Is it always a mistake to save a theory when it has been falsified?

3   How can we show that it is more rational to believe some hypotheses than to believe others?

4   How do scientific theories move beyond the stage of conjecture?

5   Is belief a matter of degree?

6   Does Bayes's theorem help us to deal rationally with evidence?

7   Do scientific claims about unobservable entities differ in status from scientific claims about observable entities?

8   Is instrumentalism mistaken if it cannot account for some features of scientific practice? How can we determine what features are really a part of scientific practice?

9   Are general theories or piecemeal procedures more important to our basic characterization of science?

10   Does all observation depend on theoretical assumptions? What are the implications of your answer for an account of unobservables?

11   'Given any theory about unobservables which fits the observed facts, there will always be other incompatible theories which fit the same facts.' Does this make realism about unobservables untenable?

12   Can we be realists in some areas of science and instrumentalists in others?

13   Should we look to the history, sociology, and psychology of science, rather than to first principles, to identify criteria for the acceptability of scientific theories?

14   Can a naturalized study of science tell us which research strategies are an effective means to theoretical truth?

15   Is there any good reason for a philosopher to prefer to talk about explanation rather than causation?

16   How can we distinguish laws from accidentally true generalizations?

17   Must we posit an ideal system of knowledge in order to understand the notion of 'law'? What if there cannot be such a system?

18   Do scientific laws involve necessity? In what sense?

19   How can we explain the direction of causation?

20   Can we accept a model of causation according to which causes probabilify, rather than determine, their effects?

21 What problem poses greater difficulties for frequency theories of probability: 'single-case probabilities' or a reliance on hypothetical infinite reference sequences?

22 If 'propensities' are primitive, can a propensity theory give us any insight into the nature of probability?

23 How are interpretations of quantum mechanics relevant to philosophical disputes about probability?

24 Can we give up common sense in favour of a 'many-worlds' reality containing both Schrödinger's cat alive and Schrödinger's cat dead?

25 Are teleological explanations an alternative to causal explanations or a kind of causal explanation?

26 How can we determine whether all sciences form a hierarchy in which the higher can always be reduced to the lower?

27 Do different areas of science describe different realities, or just one physical reality at different levels of detail?

10

Philosophy of Biology

ELLIOTT SOBER

Philosophy of biology is a branch of the PHILOSOPHY OF SCIENCE (chapter 9). Some of its characteristic questions concern the relationship of biology to the rest of science; others are internal to the methods and results of biology itself. Philosophy of biology also bears a diverse set of relationships to other areas of philosophy. Questions about vitalism and reductionism closely parallel discussions of the mind–body problem in PHILOSOPHY OF MIND (chapter 5). Evolutionary theory's relationship to the argument from design brings it into contact with the PHILOSOPHY OF RELIGION (chapter 15). And the idea that human evolution has implications about morality and human nature connects it with ETHICS (chapter 6).

1   The Subject Matter of Biology

1.1   The definition of life

Biology is conventionally defined as the science of life. Philosophers, and scientists when they wax philosophical, wonder what being alive amounts to. Should life be defined in terms of the molecule DNA? Well, we know that organisms pass traits to their offspring by transmitting genes to them, and genes are made of DNA. These offspring begin life as one-celled organisms; the genes they contain and the environments they occupy then lead them to grow into multi-cellular organisms containing many different types of cell. Thus, DNA is fundamental to the processes that comprise heredity and development.

DNA and RNA are central to organic processes as they occur on earth. But must life be based on DNA and RNA? Could other molecules play the same role in heredity and development? What we earthlings call 'organic chemistry' is the chemistry of carbon compounds, but could life forms, if they exist in other galaxies, be built out of silicon? Perhaps it is parochial to think of life in terms of the physical structures that happen to mediate life processes on earth. Is it possible to provide more general and more abstract criteria for what it takes to be alive?

As already mentioned, organisms reproduce, pass traits to their offspring, and develop in the course of their lifetimes. In addition, they extract energy from their environment and use this energy to repair tissue damage and to engage in homoeostatic processes that keep some of their characteristics constant despite the flux that occurs in their environments. Not all living things do all of these, but most do most. Perhaps 'alive' is a cluster concept of the sort described by WITTGENSTEIN (chapter 39); being alive means that the system engages in one or more of these characteristic life processes. We best conceive of these life processes in a way that leaves open how many types of physical structure can instantiate them.

Although biology is the science of life, *being alive* is not a theoretical concept in biology. Biology has developed as a discipline without having anything terribly precise to say about exactly what its domain of inquiry is. ARISTOTLE (chapter 23) once observed that it is a mistake to demand more precision of a concept than is needed. Perhaps 'alive' is not a crisply delimited category in nature (for parallel remarks about the notion of 'mind', see Sober 1990).

1.2   Vitalism, supervenience and reductionism

How are the biological properties and processes just listed related to physical properties and processes? This question precisely parallels the mind–body problem in the philosophy of mind. Just as Cartesian dualism maintains that individuals have mental properties in virtue of possessing minds that are made of a non-physical substance, so there is a position in philosophy of biology that holds that living things have biological properties in virtue of containing a non-physical substance (a Bergsonian *elan vital*) that animates them with life. This is *vitalism*, in one of the many senses that that term has acquired.

If vitalism were true, the SUPERVENIENCE THESIS (pp. 80–1) much discussed in the philosophy of mind would be false. This thesis maintains that if two individuals were physically identical and lived in physically identical environments, then they would be identical in all respects. They would have the same psychological properties, and they would have the same biological characteristics as well. The slogan that sums up supervenience is 'no difference without a physical difference'. Supervenience is a synchronic claim, different from the diachronic claim that constitutes the thesis of causal determinism.

Most biologists and philosophers of biology believe that the supervenience thesis is correct. For example, if two organisms are physically identical and live in physically identical environments, then they must have the same fitness value (Rosenberg 1978, 1985; Mills and Beatty 1979; Brandon 1978; Sober 1984). An organism's fitness is its ability to survive and reproduce. In part, the supervenience thesis has been accepted because the alternative seems never to have led to anything substantial in science. Science has made great strides in understanding the physical bases of respiration, digestion, reproduction and other biological processes. But the hypothesis that living things possess an immaterial something has led to nothing. Still, the question may be asked of how strongly the track records of physicalism on the one hand and vitalism on the other establish that the supervenience thesis is true (Sober 1999a).

Although physicalism in the form of the supervenience thesis is widely accepted, most philosophers of biology reject the claim that biology reduces to physics. Their reasons recapitulate the discussion of FUNCTIONALISM (pp. 178–9) and multiple realizability in philosophy of mind. Although an organism's fitness supervenes on its physical properties and the physical properties of its environment, fitness is not itself a physical property. What do a fit orchid and a fit otter have in common? There is no physical property, or set of physical properties, that defines what fitness is. Fitness is multiply realizable. The theory of natural selection states generalizations in terms of the concept of fitness; since fitness is not a physical property, the theory of natural selection cannot be reduced to physics. This is anti-reductionism without vitalism. There are no immaterial substances in the subject matter of biology, but biological properties describe similarities that exist in spite of physical differences. Every fit organism is a physical thing, but fitness is not a physical property. Similar reasoning has led some philosophers to argue that Mendelian genetics cannot be reduced to theories in molecular biology (Kitcher 1984); however, there is room to explore what these theories amount to, and also to question how reductionism should be understood (Waters 1990; Sober 1999b).

The multiple realizability argument against reductionism presupposes a very specific conception of what reductionism requires. However, there are a number of contending philosophical analyses of reduction that need to be evaluated to decide how that concept should be understood. Nagel (1961) set the agenda for subsequent discussion by arguing that one theory reduces to another if the first can be deduced from the second, once appropriate 'bridge laws' are provided that connect the vocabularies of the different theories to each other. Schaffner (1976) observed that false theories are sometimes reduced to true ones by showing that the reduced theory is a good approximation of the reducing theory (for example, Newtonian mechanics is sometimes said to reduce to the theory of special relativity on the grounds that relativistic particles approach Newtonian trajectories as they slow down); however, this poses a problem for Nagel's account, since a false theory cannot be deduced from a true one if the bridge laws are true. Schaffner suggested that the reducing theory must correct the reduced theory, and that the two theories must exhibit an appropriate analogy. Other proposals have been made and it has been recognized that 'reduction' and 'reductionism' each have multiple meanings (Wimsatt 1979; Dupré 1993; Rosenberg 1994).

1.3 Teleology

Philosophers of biology have for a long time debated how the concept of teleology (goal-directedness) is treated in modern biology. If it forms a part of that science, does this count against reductionism? After all, it seems clear that teleology has had no place in physics since the seventeenth century. The answer is that philosophers have endorsed various reductionist accounts of what function claims mean, but that the reduction involved is not to physics, but to the general concept of causality. Since causal concepts are widely used in the rest of science, we may draw the conclusion that there is nothing irreducible about teleological discourse in biology.

Most philosophical discussion of this issue derives from the work of Wright (1973, 1976) and Cummins (1975). Wright defended an *etiological* account of function. To describe the function of the heart is to say why organisms have hearts. Hearts evolved in the lineages leading to modern organisms because hearts helped organisms to circulate their blood. The organ was not retained because it made noise. The function of the heart, therefore, is to pump blood, not to make noise. This is not to deny that organisms sometimes benefit from the fact that hearts make noise; for example, babies

319

are comforted by hearing their mothers' heartbeat, and patients are diagnosed when physicians listen to their heartbeats. But, according to Wright, these benefits are not part of the heart's function if they did not help cause the heart to evolve. Wright's account crisply distinguishes function from fortuitous benefit.

The etiological account faces some interesting objections. Scientists were making function claims long before evolutionary theory was developed. What could Harvey have meant by his claim that the function of the heart is to pump blood? In addition, the Wrightian pattern is sometimes present in traits that do not have a function. If a man fails to exercise because he is obese, and he remains obese because he fails to exercise, are we prepared to say that the function of obesity is to prevent exercise? For these and other reasons, non-etiological accounts of function are of interest (Boorse 1976).

Cummins's proposal was to understand function claims as summarizing a kind of analytic decomposition. If the organism has certain capacities, then the function of its organs may be understood in terms of how they contribute to those capacities. To say that the function of the heart is to pump blood is to describe what hearts now do, not why they evolved. Function claims are like descriptions of the workings of an assembly line; the whole factory is able to produce a product because the various stations along the assembly line make their separate contributions to that end result. Cummins's proposal has been criticized for its liberality. According to Cummins, the heart has as many functions as it has effects on the containing system. The heart pumps blood, but it also makes noise, and it weighs a couple of pounds. Each of these constitutes a function that the heart has, because each contributes to some property of the organism as a whole. Cummins pointed out that we may not be equally interested in all of these effects, which is why we may be disinclined to talk about the function of the heart's noisiness or weight. However, for Cummins, there is no objective, interest-independent distinction between function and fortuitous benefit.

Wright's etiological account and Cummins's alternative have been refined, and the debate continues (see Allen, Bekoff and Lauder 1998; Buller 1999). However, it is worth considering the possibility that both concepts are needed in biology (Sober 1993; Godfrey-Smith 1993, 1994). It is important to distinguish the reason a trait evolved from the beneficial effects the trait has once it is present. But it also is important to analyse the workings of the current organism. Which account captures the real meaning of the word 'function' may be less important than the fact that both are, broadly speaking, causal accounts. Wright focuses on phylogeny, whereas Cummins focuses on ontogeny. Again, we must realize that 'function' is not a theoretical term used in biology, but is an informal concept that is used to talk about biological issues. Clarity is important if we are to avoid miscommunication, but clarity does not always require univocity.

2   The Structure of Evolutionary Theory

Although philosophers generally agree with Dobzhansky (1973) and other biologists that evolution is the central unifying idea in biology, a good deal of work goes on in biology that is not evolutionary in its content. Evolution is standardly defined as changes in the genetic composition of populations. But ecologists, physiologists, anatomists and molecular biologists often look at properties and processes found in populations, organisms and organic molecules that do not involve genetic change. Some philosophical work has been done on these non-evolutionary subjects, but the fact remains that evolutionary theory has been the central focus of philosophy of biology.

2.1 Darwin's two-part hypothesis

For a long time, philosophy of biology languished in the shadow of philosophy of physics. In part this was because philosophy of science for many years was developed by philosophers who knew about physics, but often knew little about other sciences; in addition, these philosophers often viewed physical theories like Newtonian mechanics, relativity theory and quantum mechanics as paradigms. Questions about the philosophy of science were posed and answered with these physical theories in mind; the net result was that other sciences had to measure up to these physical standards, or be viewed as second rate. This 'physics worship' was not just a consequence of the personal inclinations of the philosophers involved; it also was grounded in the philosophical theses that these philosophers often defended. Reductionism and claims about the unity of science (Oppenheim and Putnam 1958) conferred upon physics a privileged status.

If relativity theory and quantum mechanics are one's paradigms, then it makes sense to define science as the search for laws of nature. Laws are usually taken to be universal generalizations that do not mention any place, time or individual, and which are empirical and nomologically necessary. Newton's universal law of gravitation, for example, does not mention any individual place, time or thing; it describes the gravitational attraction that must exist between any two objects that have mass. If science is the search for laws, the question immediately arises of how Darwin's theory of evolution can count as scientific. It is difficult to find a law of evolution in Darwin's writings. His major insight was to formulate, test and apply the following two hypotheses: (1) all the organisms now on earth share common ancestors – there is a single *tree of life*; (2) natural selection was an important cause of the characteristics that living things on earth are observed to have. Neither of these claims is a law; both are historical hypotheses about the earth's past.

Nomothetic Sciences and Historical Sciences

Rather than consign the claims for the single tree of life and natural selection to the background of Darwin's achievement and promote some universal claim to the centre of our attention, it is better to recognize that not all sciences have the search for laws as their primary goal. *Nomothetic* sciences are like this, but *historical* sciences are not. The contrast in physics between mechanics and astronomy illustrates this difference. In mechanics the main goal is to discover the laws of motion. One may want to discover the truth values of singular statements about particular objects in order to test proposed laws, but this information about particulars is merely a means to an end. In astronomy the main goal is to discover facts about the composition and history of objects in the cosmos. One may use laws of nature to test singular historical hypotheses, but this information about laws is merely a means to an end. Darwin's theory of evolution is first and foremost a historical hypothesis; it is an attempt to reconstruct the history of the living things we find around us. Darwin's theory of evolution and Newton's theory of gravitation are different, not just in their subject matters, but in their logical structure.

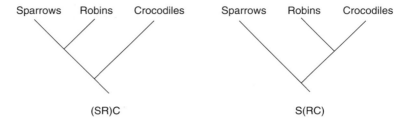

Figure 10.1

2.2 Phylogenetic inference

Darwin argued that the best explanation of many of the similarities we observe among different species is the hypothesis that they share common ancestors. However, not all similarities have this evidential significance; for example, the fact that sharks and dolphins both are shaped like torpedoes can easily be explained by the hypothesis that this shape was useful for each group of organism to move efficiently through water. We would expect to find the torpedo shape even if the two groups had arisen independently. In contrast, those similarities that cannot be explained by the functional requirements of similar environments provide better evidence of common descent. This is why vestigial organs are such telling indications of shared ancestry. Why do human foetuses have gill slits, if they are not related to organisms in which gill slits are useful? The logic of these inferences conforms to the Likelihood Principle: a set of observations is said to favour one hypothesis over another precisely when the first hypothesis confers on the observations a higher probability than the second one does (Sober 1988, 1993, 1999c; Royall 1997). A similarity S exhibited by two species is evidence that they have a common ancestor precisely when Pr (S/common ancestry) > Pr (S/separate ancestry).

If all species on earth share common ancestors, the question remains as to which species are closely related and which are related only more distantly. The methodology of this problem has been intensively studied in evolutionary biology. One principle that is often used is termed *phylogenetic parsimony*. It was independently proposed by Hennig (1966) and by Edwards and Cavalli-Sforza (1964). Consider the two phylogenetic trees depicted in figure 10.1. The tips of the trees represent present-day species or superspecific taxa; interior nodes represent ancestors. The (SR)C tree represents the hypothesis that sparrows and robins have a common ancestor that is not an ancestor of crocodiles; the S(RC) tree represents the claim that robins and crocs are more closely related to each other than either is to sparrows.

We know by observation that sparrows and robins have wings, but crocodiles do not. Can this observation be used to discriminate between the two genealogical hypotheses? If we assume that the species at the root of the tree lacked wings, then we are saying that sparrows and robins share a derived character (an apomorphy) that crocodiles do not possess. The (SR)C tree is more parsimonious than the S(RC) tree in this case, because (SR)C is able to explain the observations at the tips of the tree by

322

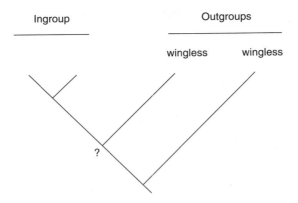

Figure 10.2

postulating a single change in character state (from wingless to winged) in the tree's interior, whereas S(RC) requires two such changes to explain the observations. On the other hand, if the species at the root of the trees had wings, then sparrows and robins would share an ancestral character (a plesiomorphy), and the two hypotheses would be equally parsimonious, since each could explain the observations by postulating a single change in character state. Thus, the principle of phylogenetic parsimony asserts that derived similarities are evidence of relatedness, while ancestral similarities are not.

How is one to determine whether wings or lack of wings is the ancestral condition in the problem just described? The principle of parsimony addresses this question as well. Even if we don't know how robins, sparrows and crocodiles are related, we still may know that these three groups are more closely related to each other than any of them is to various other groups (for example, daffodils). If the outgroup species depicted in figure 10.2 all lack wings, then phylogenetic parsimony dictates that we should conclude that winglessness is the ancestral condition for the ingroup as well.

To infer phylogenetic relationships, why should parsimony be used, rather than a criterion of overall similarity, which accords evidential significance to derived and ancestral similarities alike? Some have argued that Popperian considerations concerning FALSIFIABILITY (pp. 287–90) suffice to justify phylogenetic parsimony (see, for example, Eldredge and Cracraft 1980; Wiley 1981); others have suggested a likelihood analysis instead (Sober 1988).

Phylogenetic inference provides an interesting context for considering philosophical questions about the role of a parsimony principle in scientific reasoning. Although philosophers often complain that it is unclear what it means for one theory to be simpler or more parsimonious than another, it is clear enough what it means for one genealogical hypothesis to provide a more parsimonious explanation of the observations than another. And in answer to the question of why we should use parsimony to infer genealogical relatedness, it seems unsatisfactory to reply that a preference for parsimonious hypotheses is part of what it means to think scientifically. Why is it 'unscientific' to use overall similarity as one's guide? Parsimony is not an end in itself; if a preference for parsimonious explanations is justified, it is justified because it provides a means of achieving some more ultimate epistemic end.

2.3   Adaptationism

Natural selection is one among several processes that can influence the evolution of a trait. Since a lineage starts evolving with some pre-existing set of ancestral traits, the characteristics exhibited by descendants may show the influence of that ancestral condition. For example, suppose an ancestral bear species has a fur thickness of 5 cm. The climate then gets colder, so that the optimal fur thickness for one of its descendants would be 12 cm. If the descendant achieves a fur thickness of, say, 10 cm, one may want to attribute this outcome both to natural selection and to *phylogenetic inertia*, sometimes called *ancestral influence* (Orzack and Sober 2001). Another factor that can prevent natural selection from moving species to optimal trait values is the underlying genetics. For example, if the fittest phenotype is coded by a heterozygote, it will be impossible for all individuals to exhibit that optimal phenotype. In similar fashion, random genetic drift, correlation of characters, and other factors can prevent natural selection from causing the fittest available phenotype to evolve (Sober 1993).

The debate about 'adaptationism' that has been going on for the last twenty-some years in evolutionary biology does not concern Darwin's tree of life hypothesis; nor does it concern the modest claim that natural selection has influenced most of the phenotypic traits that species exhibit. Rather, the question concerns the power of natural selection. Is selection merely *one* among several important influences on trait evolution, or is it the *only* important influence (Orzack and Sober 1994; Sober 1993)? Can phylogenetic inertia and genetic constraints be ignored in predicting the descendant bear's fur thickness? Adaptationism embodies a relatively *monistic* conception of trait evolution; its alternative is *evolutionary pluralism* (Gould and Lewontin 1979).

Adaptationism, Pluralism and Methodology

Separate from the substantive debate about the processes that have governed evolution, the debate about adaptationism has had an important methodological dimension. Gould and Lewontin (1979) accused adaptationists of endorsing 'just-so stories' – of accepting explanations uncritically. Adaptive hypotheses need to be tested rigorously, which means that they should be tested against non-adaptive alternative explanations. Gould and Lewontin also suggested that adaptationism violates Popper's injunction that scientific hypotheses should be falsifiable. Notice that neither of these criticisms, even if they were correct, would show that pluralism is true and monism is false as claims about nature. The fact that a proposition has been accepted uncritically does not entail that the proposition is false.

The charge that adaptationism is untestable should not be taken at face value. It is true that if one adaptationist hypothesis is rejected, then another can be invented. This is because adaptationism is an *ism* – it specifies the *kind* of explanation that all or most traits have without saying anything in detail about what *specific* adaptationist hypotheses are true. Consider, for example, the fact some species reproduce sexually while others reproduce asexually. Adaptationists will insist that this variation exists because sexual reproduction is better in some circumstances and asexual reproduction is better in others. However, this general claim does not tell us why selection favours sexual reproduction in some cases and asexual reproduction in others. Adaptationism is a research programme in something like the sense that Lakatos (1978) described (Mitchell and Valone 1990); the failure of one or several adaptationist models does not mean that the research programme is bankrupt. The same point applies to evolutionary pluralism: if one pluralistic model fails, another can be invented, but this does not show that pluralism should be rejected. It is important that scientists rigorously test specific hypotheses, whether they are adaptationist or pluralistic in form; however, the *isms* that govern research programmes are not so easily tested. Only the accumulation of successes and failures over the long run will tell us whether adaptationism is true as a claim about nature (Orzack and Sober 1994).

2.4   The units of selection controversy

Whether or not the concept of *function* is understood historically (section 1.3), it is pretty clear that evolutionists use the concept of *adaptation* in this way. To say that wings are an adaptation for flying does not mean that wings now are useful because they help organisms to fly; it means that wings evolved because they helped organisms to fly. The relevant consideration is in the past tense, not the present. Wings could be an adaptation for flying even if it now is *dis*advantageous for the organisms in question to leave the ground. Historical origin and present advantage are not automatically linked. Notice also that wings can be adaptations for flying even if adaptationism is wrong in what it says about wings; to say that natural selection helped cause the trait to evolve does not mean that selection was the only important influence on the trait's evolution.

When Darwin argued that this or that trait is an adaptation, he usually had in mind that the trait evolved because it helped individual organisms to survive and reproduce. For example, predators have sharp teeth because individuals with sharp teeth do better in the struggle for existence than individuals that have dull teeth. The explanation is not that the trait evolved because it helped the whole species, or the whole ecosystem. The adaptations that Darwin discussed are mainly *individual* adaptations. These individual adaptations evolved by the process of *individual selection*, wherein individuals compete with other individuals in the same species.

There were a few occasions, however, in which Darwin saw things differently. Why are there sterile workers in some species of social insect? This is not because sterile individuals do better in surviving and reproducing than fertile individuals. Rather, Darwin argued that nests that contain sterile workers do better than nests that do not. Darwin introduced the idea that some traits are *group* adaptations – they evolved because they helped groups, not because they helped individual organisms. These adaptations evolved by the process of *group selection*, wherein groups compete with other groups in the same species.

Darwin thought that group selection is required to understand important features of human morality. Here is how he analysed the problem in *The Descent of Man*:

It must not be forgotten that although a high standard of morality gives but a slight or no advantage to each individual man and his children over the other men of the same tribe, yet that an increase in the number of well-endowed men and advancement in the standard of morality will certainly give an immense advantage to one tribe over another. There can be no doubt that a tribe including many members who, from possessing in a high degree the spirit of patriotism, fidelity, obedience, courage, and sympathy, were always ready to aid one another, and to sacrifice themselves for the common good, would be victorious over most other tribes; and this would be natural selection. At all times throughout the world tribes have supplanted other tribes; and as morality is one important element in their success, the standard of morality and the number of well-endowed men will thus everywhere tend to rise and increase. (Darwin 1981: 166)

The character traits that Darwin describes are disadvantageous to individuals, but advantageous to groups. A courageous man who risks his life in warfare is less fit than a coward in the same group who plays it safe; yet groups that include courageous individuals are fitter than groups that include only cowards.

Biologists came to use the term 'altruistic' for traits that are deleterious to individuals but advantageous to groups. This terminology is potentially confusing, since altruism, so defined, describes the fitness costs and benefits of the trait, not how or even whether the individual thinks and feels. Sterile workers in a nest of social insects and the warriors whom Darwin described are both altruistic in the evolutionary sense, even though the warriors have views about their own behaviour while the insects presumably do not. And just as a mindless organism can be an evolutionary altruist, it also is possible for a behaviour that enhances the actor's own fitness to be motivated by desires that are psychologically altruistic (Sober and Wilson 1998).

The idea that evolution involves both individual selection and group selection was standard fare in the heyday of the Modern Synthesis in evolutionary biology, roughly from 1930–60. Biologists invoked individual selection to explain some traits and group selection to explain others. Mathematical population geneticists, such as R. A. Fisher, J. B. S. Haldane and Sewall Wright, briefly expressed reservations about the ability of group selection to cause altruistic traits to evolve, but these theoretical points were not given much credence by biologists in the trenches; these biologists thought they observed altruism in nature and they sought to explain altruism in the only way they knew how – by invoking the hypothesis of group selection.

This complacent pluralism about the units of selection was shattered in the 1960s, when group selection was attacked by a number of biologists. The most thorough and devastating critique was G. C. Williams's (1966) book *Adaptation and Natural Selection*. Williams touched a nerve and his vigorous rejection of adaptations that exist for the good of the group spread quickly through the evolution community. The arguments that Williams advanced were popularized ten years later by Richard Dawkins (1976) in his widely read book *The Selfish Gene*. The idea that *some* traits evolve because they benefit the group was replaced by *genic selectionism* – the idea that *all* traits evolve because they are good for the gene. However, not all biologists subscribed to this new viewpoint; they argued that group selection had been rejected prematurely (for example, Lewontin 1970; Wilson 1980; Wade 1978). Since then, *multi-level selection theory* – the view that selection occurs at all levels of the biological hierarchy – has been making a comeback (Sober and Wilson 1998).

Assessing Group Selection: An Empirical or Conceptual Controversy

This scientific controversy is philosophically interesting because group selection was rejected in the 1960s for a number of reasons, and these reasons differ so much in character that it is unclear what in the controversy is empirical and what is conceptual. The schizophrenic character of the arguments that biologists produced may be illustrated by their discussion of the evolution of sex ratio – the mix of males and females that a population exhibits. Williams (1966) treats this as an empirical test case for group selection. He notes, following Fisher (1957), that individual selection would favour an even sex ratio, whereas group selection would sometimes favour a female-biased sex ratio (the latter because groups maximize their productivity by having the smallest number of males consistent with all the females being fertilized). Williams claims that the sex ratios observed in nature are uniformly even, and concludes that the empirical hypothesis of group selection is mistaken, at least as it pertains to the evolution of sex ratio.

A year later, W. D. Hamilton published a paper called 'Extraordinary Sex Ratios'. Hamilton (1967) reported that female-biased sex ratios are very common in the social insects. One might expect that this empirical finding, interpreted through the lens of Williams's argument, would have led biologists to conclude that group selection is implicated in the evolution of sex ratio. However, this is precisely how the model was *not* interpreted. The reason is that Hamilton's paper provides a mathematical theory for understanding how uneven sex ratios evolve. Solving Hamilton's equations allows one to identify the fittest (the 'unbeatable') sex ratio strategy that an individual female should follow in determining her mix of sons and daughters; this formalism was widely interpreted as showing how individual selection could promote the evolution of a female-biased sex ratio. One of the few biologists who did not interpret Hamilton's model in this way was Hamilton himself; Hamilton says, though only in a footnote, that his model represents the action of group selection. Although Hamilton embraced the idea of group selection in 1967 and later publications, his followers were more Hamiltonian than Hamilton himself.

Williams (1992) concurs with Hamilton's interpretation. Yet many biologists continue to view group selection as beyond the pale, and they cite Hamilton and Williams as having shown why.

Sterelny and Kitcher (1988) argue in favour of genic selectionism on the grounds that all adaptations can be interpreted as evolving because they benefit the genes that code for them. Biased sex ratios, extreme altruism and so on, can all be brought under the rubric of the selfish gene. The reason group selection is the wrong way to think about nature is not that it is empirically disconfirmed; rather, the problem is that it is insufficiently general. Although all adaptations can be treated as genic adaptations, it is false that all adaptations can be interpreted as group adaptations. According to Sterelny and Kitcher, the solution to the units of selection problem involves adopting a convention, not answering a factual question about the history of life. For them, the fact that a trait can be interpreted as a genic adaptation, no matter what the trait is like, is a point in favour of the genic convention. However, those who think that the units of selection problem is an empirical issue view this as a defect, not a strength, of the framework that Sterelny and Kitcher recommend (Wimsatt 1980; Sober and Lewontin 1982; Lloyd 1988; Sober and Wilson 1994, 1998).

2.5   Are there laws of evolution?

Although Darwin's fundamental contribution was the formulation, test, and application of two historical hypotheses (see also Kitcher 1993: ch. 2), the broad subject of modern evolutionary theory includes much more than historical hypotheses. The subject is peppered with what biologists call 'models'. These are mathematical statements that describe what the evolutionary consequences would be of specified initial conditions. For example, Fisher's analysis of sex ratio is an if/then statement. Fisher (1957) described a sufficient condition that ensures that a population with an uneven sex ratio will evolve towards an even sex ratio, and remain there. Fisher's theory has all the earmarks of a law of nature, save one. It is general, it does not refer to any place, time or individual, and it has counterfactual force. However, Fisher's model is an *a priori* mathematical truth. This does not mean that the claim that Fisher's model applies to a real world population is *a priori*; whether the population exhibits random mating and satisfies the other assumptions of the model is an empirical matter, and whether the population exhibits an even sex ratio is an empirical matter as well. The antecedent is empirical and the consequent is too, but the conditional is *a priori* (Sober 1984, 1993).

Empirical generalizations exist in evolutionary biology, but they often fail to have the modal force that laws are supposed to have. Cope's Rule, for example, says that species evolve in the direction of increased size. This is, at best, a rule of thumb that summarizes a pattern found in the fossil record (Hull 1974). The problem is not just that there are exceptions (a law, after all, can be probabilistic), but that there is nothing in our understanding of the evolutionary process that tells us that evolution must have this sort of directionality. A fundamental property of natural selection is that it is 'opportunistic'. If growing larger is advantageous, selection will push the population along that trajectory; but if growing smaller is advantageous, selection will favour that outcome, instead. It is an accident of circumstance whether the environment favours one transition rather than the other. If the history of life on earth happens to contain more environments of the first kind than of the second, Cope's Rule will be true as a statistical generalization, but it will not be a law.

The same point holds about increasing complexity. To be sure, complexity has often increased; however, there also are many cases in which complexity has declined. For example, the evolution of parasites from their free-living ancestors often involves the loss of organs; selection often leads organisms to lose features that they no longer need. Still, if life started simple, an increase in complexity was bound to occur. Biologists generally regard this as an artefact of the initial conditions that obtained, not as reflecting some resolute directionality in the evolutionary process itself. As an analogy, consider a game played on a one-row checker board that has a thousand squares. The game is played in a sequence of steps; at each step, a coin is tossed to decide how the checker will be moved. Heads means the checker moves one square to the right and tails means that it moves one square to the left. Of course, if the coin lands tails when the checker is on the left-most square, the checker can't move to the left; in this case, one must toss the coin again. The same applies if the checker is on the right-most square when the coin lands heads. Since the coin is fair, there is no directionality in the laws that govern the checker's trajectory. The laws entail no net tendency for the checker to move to the right or to the left. However, an asymmetry can be introduced by the checker's initial location. Suppose we begin the game with the checker in the left-most square. After fifty tosses, the checker will almost certainly occupy a square that is to the right of where it began (Maynard-Smith 1988; Gould 1989; Sober 1994a).

I so far have suggested that there are two types of generalization in evolutionary biology that fail to be scientific laws in the usual sense. The conditional statements that comprise mathematical models are *a priori*, and empirical generalizations about evolutionary trends often are accidentally true, if true at all. This does not show that there are no laws. Are there any? Beatty (1995) has argued that there are none, not just none in evolutionary biology, but none in biology as a whole. His reason for this claim is that every biological generalization is true in virtue of a contingent evolutionary process's making it so. For example, if the organisms in a population obey Mendel's law of independent assortment, this is because evolution led this regularity to evolve. If selection had favoured some other pattern of heredity, that pattern might have evolved instead. This is Beatty's *evolutionary contingency thesis*.

One question that needs to be considered about Beatty's argument is depicted in the following diagram:

$$\frac{E \Rightarrow (\text{If P then Q})}{t_0 \qquad t_1 \qquad\qquad t_2}$$

If the evolutionary regularity 'If P then Q' holds true between times t_1 and t_2 only because contingent evolutionary events E happened to take place at time t_0, then it makes sense to say that the regularity is contingent. However, this leaves it open that the more complex conditional 'if E occurs, then (if P then Q) will be true later' holds true *non*-contingently (Sober 1997a). This point does not establish that biological laws exist, but it does show that one cannot establish that there are no laws just by pointing out that regularities depend on earlier contingencies. Furthermore, if causality entails the existence of laws (a metaphysical claim that should not be accepted uncritically; Anscombe (1975), for example, denies it), then the causal dependency of 'If P then Q' on E *entails* the existence of a law.

Sensitivity to Initial Conditions

Gould (1989) has emphasized the idea that evolutionary outcomes often exhibit a great deal of *sensitivity to initial conditions*. Even a small change in the conditions that obtained millions of years ago would have made a huge difference in the distribution of life forms that we find on earth now. If a certain meteor strike had not occurred, the dinosaurs would not have gone extinct; if the dinosaurs had not gone extinct, mammals would not have proliferated; and if the mammalian explosion had not occurred, no mammal resembling *Homo sapiens* would have made its appearance. According to Gould, 'replaying the tape' would reveal that many of the interesting features of the life forms we find around us are accidents of history.

The claim that there is sensitivity to initial conditions has the following form: although X_1 leads to Y_1, it also is true that X_2 leads to Y_2, where X_1 and X_2 are very similar, while Y_1 and Y_2 are very different. The usual gloss on this claim is that there are two *laws*:

X_1 leads to Y_1 and X_2 leads to Y_2. Thus, the sensitivity thesis does *not* entail that there are no biological laws. Notice also that Gould is not claiming that *all* features of living things exhibit sensitivity to initial conditions; he is merely calling attention to the importance of this phenomenon. It is perfectly possible that some features of life are *robust* (that is, *in*sensitive to perturbations in initial conditions) while others are not. The frequency of evolutionary *convergence* shows that similar outcomes often arise from rather different starting points. What is sorely needed in this area are biologically well motivated theories concerning which features should be robust and which should exhibit sensitivity. Evolutionary biology very much needs to move this problem beyond the reporting of piecemeal intuitions about examples.

3 The Philosophical Significance of Evolutionary Theory

3.1 The argument from design

The two parts of Darwin's theory of evolution by natural selection both conflict with at least one traditional reading of Genesis. First, the theory postulates a single tree of life, and thus contradicts the claim that different groups of organisms were separately created. Second, the theory postulates the mindless process of natural selection as the cause of life's adaptive features, and thus contradicts the claim that adaptive features arose by the intelligent design of a creator. There are additional, though less central, points of conflict as well; for example, Darwin held that the earth is ancient while one literal reading of the Bible says that the earth is young.

Not only does the theory of evolution conflict with one set of religious *doctrines*; it also conflicts with an influential *argument* for the existence of God – the ARGUMENT FROM DESIGN (pp. 478–80). The fifth of THOMAS AQUINAS's (chapter 24) five ways of proving the existence of God contends that things that 'act for an end' must either have minds or be produced by an intelligent designer. In the century in Britain preceding Darwin's publication of the *Origin*, this argument was repeatedly elaborated. It was not simply *one* argument for the existence of God; it became the *fundamental* argument.

Perhaps the most famous formulation of the design argument is that given by William Paley, in his book *Natural Theology* (1805). Paley proposed an analogy. If you were walking across a heath and found a stone, you would not dream of concluding that the stone was produced by an intelligent designer. However, if you found a watch, you would conclude without hesitation that the watch was produced by a watchmaker. The difference between the watch and the stone is that the watch exhibits *adaptive complexity*. The watch as a whole measures out equal intervals of time, and the parts of the watch conspire to allow the watch to perform that function; were any of those parts even modestly different from the way they are, the watch would not keep time. Paley then argues that what is true of the watch also holds for many features of organisms. The vertebrate eye, for example, also exhibits adaptive complexity. Paley concludes that organisms are the result of intelligent design no less than the watch is the handiwork of a watchmaker.

Philosophers have not always agreed on what the form of the design argument is. For example, HUME (chapter 31), in his *Dialogues Concerning Natural Religion* (1779), published some thirty years before Paley's *Natural Theology* appeared, suggests that the design argument is an analogical argument that has the following form:

Watches are produced by intelligent design.
Organisms are like watches.

Organisms were produced by intelligent design.

The double line separating premises from conclusion indicates that the argument is not intended to be deductively valid. Hume suggests that the strength of the analogical argument depends on the degree to which watches and organisms resemble each other – the more similar they are, the more strongly the premises support the conclusion. He then points out that there are many dissimilarities – watches are made of metal and glass, organisms breathe, and so on. Hume concludes that the design argument is a very weak analogical argument.

A more charitable reading of the argument from design construes it as an *inference to the best explanation* (pp. 42–3) (what C. S. PEIRCE (chapter 36) called an *abductive* argument), one that does not depend on there being any strong degree of overall similarity between organisms and artefacts. According to this reading of the argument, Paley is using the Likelihood Principle to discriminate between two hypotheses:

O_d Organisms were created by an intelligent designer.
O_r Organisms were produced by random mindless processes.

Paley claims that the observed adaptive complexity of organisms is rendered much more probable by the former hypothesis than by the latter. Paley discusses the watch on the heath to make vivid the power of this type of inference in an uncontroversial example. The adaptive complexity of the watch favours the first of the following hypotheses over the second:

W_d The watch was created by an intelligent designer.
W_r The watch was produced by random mindless processes.

The point of the analogy is just to explain how the Likelihood Principle works. It does not matter how similar or dissimilar watches and organisms are overall, so long as they share the single feature of adaptive complexity (Sober 1993).

While he studied at Cambridge, Darwin read Paley and greatly admired Paley's discussion of adaptive contrivances. Darwin eventually came to reject the argument from design, and to move towards agnosticism, because he thought he saw so many features of organisms that conflict with the hypothesis that organisms were created by a benevolent, omniscient and omnipotent designer. For example, Darwin was revolted by the parasitic wasps that lay their eggs on paralysed caterpillars; when the eggs hatch, they eat their hosts alive, leaving the brain until last (Desmond and Moore 1991). If an intelligent designer built so much suffering into the living world, this designer does not deserve our reverence. Darwin saw the living world as saturated with pain and death; this is what one should expect according to the hypothesis of evolution by natural selection, but not what one should expect according to the hypothesis of intelligent design as Darwin understood that hypothesis. This is a version of the ARGUMENT FROM EVIL (pp. 480–3). The argument is not best put by saying that the quantity of evil found in the world *deductively entails* that there is no God; rather, the observations are claimed to play the non-deductive role of favouring atheism over theism.

This Darwinian argument is a likelihood argument, just like Paley's, but Darwin considers a hypothesis that Paley does not, and he considers an observation that differs from the one on which Paley focused. The hypothesis of evolution by natural selection does not claim that living things change their features at random. A process is random when its possible outcomes are equiprobable, or nearly so. Tossing a coin, spinning a roulette wheel, drawing cards from a deck – these are examples of random processes. However, natural selection is a process in which some traits have much higher probabilities of spreading than others. The rule that governs selection processes is that fitter traits tend to increase in frequency and less fit traits tend to decline. In addition to elaborating a hypothesis that Paley did not consider, Darwin also emphasized the ubiquity of adaptive imperfections. Vestigial organs, for example, are not what one should expect to find if living things were created from scratch by a benevolent, intelligent and powerful engineer. However, since natural selection works on the array of variation that ancestral populations happen to contain, it is no surprise that these processes leave traces of ancestral forms that have no adaptive rationale.

Paley anticipated one aspect of this Darwinian argument. He says that we should infer a watchmaker when we see the watch, even if the watch turns out to be imperfect. Paley emphatically denies that imperfect adaptation undercuts the design argument. To be sure, Paley delighted in what he took to be the many perfections found in nature. However, it is clear that he did not think of this as part of his argument for the existence of a designer. Rather, the ostensible perfection of nature comes in later, as evidence that bears on the designer's characteristics. Adaptive complexity, even when imperfect, proves there is a designer. Further details then show that this designer is benevolent.

What, then, is the logical status of the design argument, and how is Darwin's theory related to it? Darwin and his successors have claimed that imperfect adaptations favour evolutionary theory over intelligent design (see, for example, Gould 1980). Should they concede that perfect adaptation would favour intelligent design over purely random mindless processes? I suggest that this interpretation concedes too much to Paley. Even a perfect watch is no evidence of intelligent design unless we have independently attested auxiliary information about the intentions and abilities that the putative designer would have if he existed. What probability does the design hypothesis confer on the features of the watch that we observe? We observe, for example, that the watch is made of metal and glass. How probable is it that an intelligent designer would use these materials? If intelligent designers *never* use these materials, the design hypothesis will be *less* likely than the hypothesis of random mindless processes. However, if we assume that intelligent designers *often* use metal and glass, we reach the opposite verdict. And if we simply *do not know* what the putative intelligent designer would be inclined to do, we will be *unable to compare* the likelihoods of the two hypotheses.

Paley is right that we do not and should not hesitate to infer a watchmaker from the observed features of the watch; this is because we know a great deal about the inclinations and abilities that human designers have. However, when we shift from watch to organism, the situation changes. What do we know about the desires and abilities of this putative designer of organisms? I suggest that we do not know enough to compare the likelihoods of the two hypotheses. Paley's analogy between watch and organism in fact conceals a deep disanalogy. As a result, the design argument fails on its own terms; there is no need to bring in Darwinian theory to see this. It is not true that the observed features of organisms put the design hypothesis to the test and that what we observe disconfirms the hypothesis; rather, the present suggestion is that the design hypothesis is untestable (Sober 1993, 1999d). Defenders of the design argument are not entitled to assume without argument propositions that describe the features that organisms would have if they were produced by an intelligent designer. Critics of the argument are not entitled to do this, either.

3.2   Species, essentialism and human nature

Species have long been a favourite example that philosophers cite when they discuss *natural kinds*. For example, MILL (chapter 35) in his *System of Logic* (1874) claims that *human being* is a natural kind, but the class of *snub-nosed individuals* is not, on the grounds that 'Socrates is a human being' allows one to predict many other characteristics that Socrates has, but 'Socrates is snub-nosed' does not. Aristotelian essentialism burdens the concept of natural kind with a more substantial characterization. Natural kinds not only have predictive richness; in addition, they have ESSENCES (pp. 112–13). The essence of a natural kind is the necessary and sufficient condition that members of the kind must satisfy in order to be members. An individual's possessing this essence is what makes it belong to the kind in question. In addition, it is a necessary truth that all and only the members of the kind have this essential property. The essence also does a good deal of explanatory work; the fact that an individual has this species-typical essence explains many other features that the individual possesses.

Besides citing biological species as examples, philosophers often point to the chemical elements as paradigm natural kinds. Gold is a kind of substance; its essence is said to be the atomic number 79. This atomic number is what makes a lump of matter an instance of gold. And atomic number explains many other properties that gold things have. Kripke (1972) and Putnam (1975) have suggested that science is in the business of empirically discovering the essences of natural kinds. Formulated in this way, essentialism is not established by the existence of trivial necessary truths. It is a necessary truth that all human beings are human beings, but this does not entail that there is an essence that human beings have. It is also important to separate the claim that kinds have essences from the claim that individuals in the kind have essential properties (Enç 1986). The fact that gold has one atomic number and lead another does not entail that an individual cannot persist through time as it changes from being made of lead to being made of gold.

The example of the chemical elements illustrates a further feature that kind essences are supposed to have. Gold's essence is *purely qualitative*; 'atomic number 79' does not refer to any place, time or individual. In principle, gold could exist at any place or at any time. What makes two things members of the same natural kind is that they are similar in the requisite respect. There is no requirement that they be causally or spatio-temporally related to each other in any way.

Although philosophers who accept this essentialist picture of the chemical elements usually think that chemistry has already discovered the essences that various chemical kinds possess, they must admit that biology has to date not delivered the goods with respect to biological species. If biological species have essences and these essences are not beyond the ken of science, then the essentialist must claim that biology will eventually reveal what these species essences are. However, there are strong reasons to think that Darwin's theory of evolution undermines this essentialist picture of biological species (Hull 1965; Mayr 1975; Sober 1980). It is not just that biology has not discovered these species essences *yet*; rather, the way species are conceptualized in evolutionary theory suggests that species simply do not have essences. They are not natural kinds, at least not on the usual essentialist construal of what a natural kind is.

The reasons for this conclusion need to be stated carefully. The fact that species evolve is, *per se*, not a conclusive argument against essentialism. Just as the essentialist can agree that lead might be transmuted into gold, so the essentialist can agree that a lineage might be transformed from one species into another. And the fact that there are vague boundaries between species is not, in itself, a refutation of essentialism, either. If a piece of matter is transformed from lead to gold, perhaps there will be intermediate stages of the process in which it is indeterminate whether the matter belongs to one natural kind or the other (Sober 1980).

Unfortunately, there still is disagreement in evolutionary biology about how the species category should be understood. Perhaps the most popular definition is Mayr's (1963, 1970) *biological species concept* (for others, see Ereshefsky 1992). Its anti-essentialist consequences are to a large degree also the consequences that other species concepts have, so we may examine it as an illustrative example. Mayr's basic idea is that a biological species is an ensemble of local populations that are knit together by gene flow. The individuals within local populations reproduce with each other. And migration between local populations means that there is reproduction between individuals in different populations as well. This system of populations is reproductively isolated from other such systems. Reproductive isolation can be a simple consequence of geographical barriers, or it can mean that the organisms have behavioural or physiological features that prevent them from producing viable fertile offspring even when they are brought together. A consequence of reproductive isolation is that two species can evolve different characteristics in response to the different selection pressures imposed by their different environments. However, the different phenotypes that evolve are not what make the two species two; it is reproductive isolation, not physical dissimilarity, that is definitive.

Mayr (1963) initially allowed two populations to belong to the same species if there was actual or potential interbreeding between them, but he later changed the definition so that actual interbreeding was required (Mayr 1970). This raises the question of what the time scale is on which interbreeding must take place. How often must individuals in different local populations reproduce with each other for the two populations to belong to the same species? Indeed, the same question can be posed about individuals living in the same local population. Another detail that needs to be added to the sketch just provided concerns individuals that exist at different times. Human beings who are alive now are not having babies with human beings who lived thousands of years ago. Reproduction is something that occurs between contemporaneous individuals. So what makes human beings now and human beings thousands of years ago members of the same species? A necessary condition is that human beings now are descended from human beings a thousand years ago. But this is clearly not sufficient; otherwise, a present-day species could not be descended from a different, ancestral, species. Finally, I should note that Mayr's definition excludes the possibility of asexual species, and this is another of its features that has made it controversial.

The thing to notice about Mayr's definition is that qualitative similarity is neither necessary nor sufficient for conspecificity. Members of the same species may have very different characteristics. And if creatures just like tigers evolved independently in other galaxies, they would not belong to the species to which earthly tigers belong. What makes for conspecificity are the causal and historical connections that arise from reproductive interactions. Biological species and chemical elements are very different in this regard.

Evolutionary biologists talk about species in the same way they discuss individual organisms. Just as individual organisms bear genealogical relationships to each other, so species are genealogically related. Just as individual organisms are born, develop and die, so individual species come into existence, evolve and go extinct. These considerations led Hull (1978, 1988) to develop Ghiselin's (1974) suggestion that *species are individuals, not natural kinds*. There is room to doubt, however, that species are as functionally integrated as individual organisms often are. The parts of a tiger depend on each other for survival; excise an arbitrary 30 per cent of a tiger, and the whole tiger dies. However, the extinction of 30 per cent of a species rarely causes the rest of the species to go extinct. This suggests that individuality (in the sense of functional interdependence of parts) comes in degrees, and that species are often less individualistic than organisms often are. Still, Hull and Ghiselin's main thesis remains; perhaps it should be stated by saying that species are *historical entities* (Wiley 1981).

Similar points apply to higher taxonomic categories. Although ordinary language may suggest that carnivores all eat meat and that mammals all nurse their young, this is not how biologists understand *Carnivora* and *Mammalia* as taxa. These taxa are understood genealogically; they are *monophyletic groups*, meaning that they include an ancestral species and all of its descendants (Sober 1992). Pandas belong to *Carnivora* because they are descended from other species that belong to *Carnivora*; the fact that pandas are vegetarians does not matter. Superspecific taxa, like species themselves, are conceptualized as big physical objects; they are chunks of the genealogical nexus. And just as species are often not very individualistic, superspecific taxa are even less so (Ereshefsky 1991).

The chemical kinds do not comprise an *ad hoc* list. Rather, there is a theory, codified in the periodic table of elements, that tells us how to enumerate these chemical kinds and how they are systematically related to each other. To say what the chemical kinds are, we can just consult this theory; we do not, in addition, have to go out and do field work. No such theory exists in biology for species and higher taxa; field work is basically the only method that science has for assembling a list of species. The terms 'botanizing' and 'beetle collecting' both allude to this feature of systematic biology. Species and higher taxa are things that happen to come into existence owing to the vagaries of what transpires in the branching tree of life.

It does not follow that there are no natural kinds in evolutionary biology. Perhaps sexual reproduction is a kind; perhaps being a predator is another. What makes it true that two organisms each reproduce sexually, or that both are predators, is that they are similar in some respect; it is not required that they be historically connected to each other. The sexual species do not form a monophyletic group, and neither do the predators. These kind terms appear in models of different evolutionary processes; there are models that explain why sex might evolve, and models that describe the dynamics of predator–prey interactions. Although Darwin's theory of evolution undermines essentialist interpretations of species and higher taxa, it is another matter whether essentialism is the right way to understand these other, non-taxonomic, theoretical concepts.

If biological species lack essences, then *Homo sapiens* lacks an essence. If the essentialist is right about chemical kinds, then it makes sense to ask what the nature of gold is. But what could it mean to talk about 'human nature'? Taken literally, the idea of human nature is the idea that there is an essence that all human beings, and only they, possess. This thought is at the root of ARISTOTLE's (chapter 23) ethical theory. It also is at the root of many normative claims to the effect that this or that human behaviour is 'unnatural'. This peculiar expression can be given a sensible biological reading, if 'natural' is simply equated with the idea of *being found in nature*. Understood in this way, everything that human beings do, both the good and the bad, is natural. However, when 'natural' and 'unnatural' are *not* used in this way, it is important to demand that an explanation be given of what the terms are supposed to mean. Normative ethical claims should not be permitted to masquerade as biology.

3.3   Evolutionary epistemology

Evolutionary epistemology is a field divided into two research programmes (Bradie 1994). First, there are attempts to use ideas from evolutionary biology to explain various features of human cognition. Second, there is the attempt to develop theories of cultural and scientific change that are analogous to theories of biological evolution. These lines of inquiry are independent of each other, so that the success or failure of the one does not automatically entail the success or failure of the other. Nor is either research programme particularly unified; this means, for example, that one evolutionary model of scientific change might fail miserably, while another succeeds admirably.

Sociobiology (Wilson 1975) and evolutionary psychology (see the papers collected in Barkow, Cosmides and Tooby 1992) provide examples of the first type of evolutionary epistemology. Sociobiologists usually focus on different features of human behaviour and seek to explain them as adaptive responses to ancestral environments. The debate about adaptationism, discussed earlier, grew out of the vociferous controversy that engulfed sociobiology. Critics of sociobiology believed that sociobiology's methodological defects were just the tip of the iceberg; the real problem, they thought, was the pervasive influence of naive adaptationism in evolutionary biology as a whole (Gould and Lewontin 1979). Evolutionary psychology differs from sociobiology, not by being less adaptationist, but by shifting its focus from behaviour to cognitive mechanisms as the items requiring evolutionary explanation. Evolutionary psychologists tend to think of the mind as a highly modularized set of devices, each having evolved as a solution to a different adaptive problem; they also tend to think that cognitive adaptations vary very little among human beings. Both the modularity hypothesis and the universality hypothesis have been questioned (Sterelny and Griffiths 1999; Wilson 1994).

This first type of evolutionary epistemology has also been pursued by philosophers. For example, there has been considerable debate about whether, or in what circumstances, natural selection can be expected to favour belief acquisition devices that are *reliable* – that is, that produce mostly true beliefs (Stephens 2001). There also has been investigation of when natural selection will favour innate and inflexible characteristics, and when it will favour traits that are learned and plastic (Godfrey-Smith 1991, 1996; Sober 1994b). Godfrey-Smith (1996) also explores the hypothesis that mentality evolved as a response to environmental complexity (Sober 1997b).

Examples of the second kind of evolutionary epistemology may be found in proposals developed by Popper (1973), Campbell (1974) and Hull (1988), which view scientific change as the result of a competition among theories, with the fittest theory surviving. This does not mean that theories survive because they enable those who believe them to have more babies; nor do evolutionary epistemologists propose that scientific theories are passed from individual to individual by genetic transmission. Whereas models of biological evolution standardly measure fitness in terms of reproductive output and treat genes as the mechanism of inheritance, evolutionary models of scientific change replace genetic transmission with teaching and learning, and think of fitness as an idea's propensity to spread. Fit ideas are *attractive*, regardless of whether they affect biological survival and reproduction (Sober 1993).

There are some obvious disanalogies between biological models of evolution by natural selection and selectionist models of scientific change. For one thing, novel biological variation arises by random mutation; this means that what causes a mutation to occur has nothing to do with whether the mutation will be useful. In contrast, it seems clear that novel scientific ideas are often invented with the goal of being useful; scientists don't make up hypotheses at random. However, this and other disanalogies do not undermine the claim that the ideas in a scientific community compete with each other; and that there is a selection process in which some ideas spread while others disappear from the scene. Thus, it seems clear that scientific change can be described as a selection process. The substantive task is to say how the concept of fitness should be understood in this context. What makes one idea more attractive than another in a scientific community? Surely there are many factors that can influence an idea's attractiveness, and the mix of features that make an idea attractive in one scientific context may differ from the mix that matters in another. Perhaps some episodes of scientific change are driven largely by observational evidence, while others occur because of religious, metaphysical or political commitments. Evolutionary epistemologists who want to model scientific change as a selection process must address the questions that historians of science debate when they consider 'internal' versus 'external' factors. Merely saying that scientific change occurs by a selection process is not enough.

Another variety of evolutionary epistemology may be found in models of *cultural group selection* (Boyd and Richerson 1985). As Darwin observed in his discussion of human morality, groups compete with each other, and groups with more adaptive ideologies will out-compete groups whose ideas are less fit. Again, there is no requirement that these ideational elements are transmitted genetically; groups may vary simply because the individuals in one generation faithfully teach their mores to the next. Group

337

competition may mean that people in one group kill the members of others, or it may simply mean that the conquerors impose their mores on the conquered. Indeed, the spread of ideas may not involve 'conquest' at all, if people in one group freely adopt ideas from another.

3.4 Evolutionary ethics

HUME's (chapter 31) distinction between *is* and *ought* – between claims that are purely descriptive and claims that are normative – must be borne in mind when we ask what relevance evolutionary theory has for questions about morality. Darwin suggested that evolutionary theory helps us understand why human morality has some of the features that it has. It remains to be seen how much of the content of human morality can be explained in this way, and how much should be thought of as arising by non-adaptive cultural processes. For example, some cultures impose restrictive norms on the clothing that men and women may wear, while others encourage personal innovation. Even if evolutionary theory has nothing to say about why *this* pattern of variation exists, it is possible that the theory has an important bearing on *other* patterns (Sober and Wilson 1998).

What can evolutionary theory tell us about which normative ethical claims, if any, are true? Although many social Darwinists thought that evolutionary outcomes are always good (because they thought that evolution is inherently 'progressive'), there has also been a strong tradition that maintains that evolutionary outcomes are often morally deplorable. Just as Darwin did not rejoice in the behaviour of parasitic wasps, so Huxley (1997) thought that the point of morality was to combat the instincts we inherit; more recently, and in the same vein, G. C. Williams (1989) has suggested that nature is a 'wicked old witch'.

Another line of thinking in evolutionary ethics holds that evolutionary considerations show that there can be no objective normative truths. The claim is not just that the moral principles we now happen to hold are mistaken; the claim is stronger – that no moral convictions can be true (Ruse and Wilson 1986). Evolution has created in us the illusion that there are objective moral standards; there is an adaptive advantage in believing this fiction. In reply, it should be noted that the mere fact that our moral beliefs are produced by evolution does not show that there are no moral truths. After all, our simple mathematical beliefs may be the result of evolution, but that does not show that there are no mathematical truths (Kitcher 1994). However, more needs to be said here, since the subjectivist does not have to maintain that the non-existence of moral truths deductively follows from the claim that the morality we accept is the product of evolution.

A better formulation of subjectivism maintains that it is exceedingly improbable that the morality we accept is true, given that it is produced by evolution. After all, natural selection causes traits to evolve because they provide reproductive benefits. Why should a process bent on maximizing reproduction lead us to moral beliefs that are true? The thing to notice about this line of thought is that it does not entail that there are no moral truths; rather, it advances the more modest hypothesis that the moral beliefs we presently have are not true. In addition, this argument fails to attend to the fact that evolution has given human beings the capacity to reason; if this capacity can lead us to discover theoretical truths in science that provide no practical benefit in terms of survival and reproduction, why should reason not also be able to lead us to discoveries about the good and the right? Perhaps there are reasons to doubt this, but the mere fact that natural selection aims to maximize reproduction should not lead us to embrace ethical subjectivism.

A slightly different argument for ethical subjectivism maintains that we can provide a fully satisfactory explanation of why we behave the way we do, and also explain why we accept the moral principles we do, without postulating a realm of ethical truths (Harman 1977; Ruse and Wilson 1986). Objectivism about ethics is *unparsimonious*; a simpler explanation of human thought and behaviour traces these phenotypic features back to the social context of human culture and the biological context of human evolution. The right reply to this argument for subjectivism is that normative ethical principles are not in the business of explaining why people think and act as they do. The point of morality is to regulate behaviour, not to explain it. One might just as well argue that objective epistemological norms do not exist because they are not needed to explain why people think as they do. Psychology is in the business of explaining how people in fact think; epistemology, however, is in a normative line of work (Sober 1993).

Acknowledgements

I am grateful to David Hull and Christopher Stephens for their help in the preparation of this chapter.

References

Allen, C., Bekoff, M. and Lauder, G. (eds) 1998: *Nature's Purposes: Analyses of Function and Design in Biology*. Cambridge, MA: MIT Press.

Anscombe, E. 1975: Causality and Determination. In E. Sosa (ed.) *Causation and Conditionals*. Oxford: Oxford University Press.

Barkow, J., Cosmides, L. and Tooby, J. (eds) 1992: *The Adapted Mind: Evolutionary Psychology and the Generation of Culture*. Oxford: Oxford University Press.

Beatty, L. 1995: The Evolutionary Contingency Thesis. In G. Wolters and J. Lennox (eds) *Concepts, Theories, and Rationality in the Biological Sciences: The Second Pittsburgh–Konstanz Colloquium in the Philosophy of Science*. Pittsburgh: University of Pittsburgh Press.

Boorse, C. 1976: Wright on Functions. *Philosophical Review*, 85, 70–86.

Boyd, R. and Richerson, P. 1985: *Culture and the Evolutionary Process*. Chicago: University of Chicago Press.

Bradie, M. 1994: Epistemology from an Evolutionary Point of View. In E. Sober (ed.) *Conceptual Issues in Evolutionary Biology*, 2nd edn. Cambridge, MA: MIT Press.

Brandon, R. 1978: Adaptation and Evolutionary Theory. *Studies in the History and Philosophy of Science*, 9, 181–206.

—— 1990: *Adaptation and Environment*. Princeton, NJ: Princeton University Press.

—— 1996: *Concepts and Methods in Evolutionary Biology*. Cambridge: Cambridge University Press.

Buller, D. (ed.) 1999: *Function, Selection and Design*. Series in Philosophy and Biology. New York: State University of New York Press.

Campbell, D. 1974: Evolutionary Epistemology. In P. Schilpp (ed.) *The Philosophy of Karl Popper*. La Salle, IN: Open Court.

ELLIOTT SOBER

Cummins, R. 1975: Functional Analysis. *Journal of Philosophy*, 72, 741–64. Reprinted in E. Sober (ed.) (1994) *Conceptual Issues in Evolutionary Biology*, 2nd edn. Cambridge, MA: MIT Press.

Darwin, C. 1981 [1871]: *The Descent of Man, and Selection in Relation to Sex*. Princeton, NJ: Princeton University Press.

Dawkins, R. 1976: *The Selfish Gene*, 2nd edn. Oxford: Oxford University Press.

Desmond, A. and Moore, J. 1991: *Darwin – the Life of a Tormented Evolutionist*. New York: Times Warner.

Dobzhansky, T. 1973: Nothing in Biology Makes Sense Except in the Light of Evolution. *American Biology Teacher*, 35, 125–9.

Dupré, J. 1993. *The Disorder of Things*. Cambridge, MA: Harvard University Press.

Edwards, A. and Cavalli-Sforza, L. 1964: Reconstruction of Evolutionary Trees. In V. Heywood and J. McNeill (eds) *Phenetic and Phylogenetic Classification*. New York: Systematics Association Publication, 6, 67–76.

Eldredge, N. and Cracraft, J. 1980: *Phylogenetic Patterns and the Evolutionary Process*. New York: Columbia University Press.

Enç, B. 1986: Essentialism Without Individual Essences: Causation, Kinds, Supervenience and Restricted Identities. *Midwest Studies in Philosophy*, 11, 403–26.

Ereshefsky, M. 1991: Species, Higher Taxa, and the Units of Evolution. *Philosophy of Science*, 58, 84–101.

——(ed.) 1992: *The Units of Evolution: Essays on the Nature of Species*. Cambridge, MA: MIT Press.

Fisher, R. 1957 [1930]: *The Genetical Theory of Natural Selection*, 2nd edn. New York: Dover Books.

Fox Keller, E. and Lloyd, E. (eds) 1992: *Keywords in Evolutionary Biology*. Cambridge, MA: Harvard University Press.

Ghiselin, M. 1974: A Radical Solution to the Species Problem. *Systematic Zoology*, 23, 536–44.

Godfrey-Smith, P. 1991: Signal, Decision, Action. *Journal of Philosophy*, 88 (12), 709–22.

——1993: Functions: Consensus Without Unity. *Pacific Philosophical Quarterly*, 74, 196–208.

——1994: A Modern History Theory of Function. *Nous*, 28 (3), 344–62.

——1996: *Complexity and the Function of Mind in Nature*. Cambridge: Cambridge University Press.

Gould, S. 1980: *The Panda's Thumb*. Harmondsworth: Penguin Books.

——1989: *Wonderful Life*. New York: W. W. Norton.

Gould, S. and Lewontin, R. 1979: The Spandrels of San Marco and the Panglossian Paradigm: A Critique of the Adaptationist Programme. *Proceedings of the Royal Society of London B*, 205, 581–98. Reprinted in E. Sober (ed.) (1994) *Conceptual Issues in Evolutionary Biology*, 2nd edn. Cambridge, MA: MIT Press.

Hamilton, W. 1967: Extraordinary Sex Ratios. *Science*, 156, 477–88.

Harman, G. 1977: *The Nature of Morality: An Introduction to Ethics*. Oxford: Oxford University Press.

Hennig, W. 1966: *Phylogenetic Systematics*. Urbana: University of Illinois Press. (Revision and translation of Hennig's 1950 *Grundzuge einer Theorie der phylogenetishen Systematik*.)

Hull, D. 1965: The Effect of Essentialism on Taxonomy: 2000 Years of Stasis. *British Journal for the Philosophy of Science*, 15, 314–26; 16, 1–18.

——1974: *Philosophy of Biological Sciences*. Englewood Cliffs, NJ: Prentice-Hall.

——1978: A Matter of Individuality. *Philosophy of Science*, 45, 335–60. Reprinted in E. Sober (ed.) (1994) *Conceptual Issues in Evolutionary Biology*, 2nd edn. Cambridge, MA: MIT Press.

——1988: *Science as a Process*. Chicago: University of Chicago Press.

Hull, D. and Ruse, M. (eds) 1998: *Philosophy of Biology*. Oxford: Oxford University Press.

Hume, D. 1947 [1779]: *Dialogues Concerning Natural Religion*. New York: Thomas Nelson and Sons.

Huxley, T. 1997 [1893]: Evolution and Ethics. In A. Barr (ed.) *The Major Prose of Thomas Henry Huxley*. Athens, GA: University of Georgia Press.

Kitcher, P. 1984: 1953 and All That: A Tale of Two Sciences. *Philosophical Review*, 93, 335–73. Reprinted in E. Sober (ed.) (1994) *Conceptual Issues in Evolutionary Biology*, 2nd edn. Cambridge, MA: MIT Press.

——1993: *The Advancement of Science*. New York: Oxford University Press.

——1994: Four Ways of Biologicizing Ethics. In E. Sober (ed.) *Conceptual Issues in Evolutionary Biology*, 2nd edn. Cambridge, MA: MIT Press.

Kripke, S. 1972: Naming and Necessity. In G. Harman and D. Davidson (eds) *The Semantics of Natural Language*. Dordrecht: Reidel.

Lakatos, I. 1978: Falsification and the Methodology of Scientific Research Programmes. In *The Methodology of Scientific Research Programmes: Philosophical Papers*, vol. 1. Cambridge: Cambridge University Press.

Lewontin, R. 1970: The Units of Selection. *Annual Review of Ecology and Systematics*, 1, 1–14.

Lloyd, E. 1988: *The Structure and Confirmation of Evolutionary Theory*. Westport, CT: Greenwood Press.

Maynard-Smith, J. 1988: Evolutionary Progress. In M. Nitecki (ed.) *Evolutionary Progress*. Chicago: University of Chicago Press.

Mayr, E. 1963: *Animal Species and Evolution*. Cambridge, MA: Harvard University Press.

——1970: *Populations, Species, and Evolution*. Cambridge, MA: Harvard University Press.

——1975: Typological versus Populational Thinking. In *Evolution and the Diversity of Life*. Cambridge, MA: Harvard University Press. Reprinted in E. Sober (ed.) (1994) *Conceptual Issues in Evolutionary Biology*, 2nd edn. Cambridge, MA: MIT Press.

Mill, J. S. 1874: *A System of Logic*, 8th edn. Harper and Brothers.

Mills, S. and Beatty, J. 1979: The Propensity Interpretation of Fitness. *Philosophy of Science*, 46, 263–88. Reprinted in E. Sober (ed.) (1994) *Conceptual Issues in Evolutionary Biology*, 2nd edn. Cambridge, MA: MIT Press.

Mitchell, W. and Valone, T. 1990: The Optimization Research Program: Studying Adaptations by their Function. *Quarterly Review of Biology*, 65, 43–52.

Nagel, E. 1961: *The Structure of Science*. London: Routledge and Kegan Paul.

Oppenheim, P. and Putnam, H. 1958: Unity of Science as a Working Hypothesis. In H. Feigl, G. Maxwell and M. Scriven (eds) *Minnesota Studies in the Philosophy of Science*, vol. 2. Minneapolis: University of Minnesota Press.

Orzack, S. and Sober, E. 1994: Optimality Models and the Long-run Test of Adaptationism. *American Naturalist*, 143, 361–80.

——2001: Adaptationism, Phylogenetic Inertia, and the Method of Controlled Comparisons. In *Adaptationism and Optimality*. Cambridge: Cambridge University Press.

Paley, W. 1805: *Natural Theology*. Rivington.

Popper, K. 1973: *Objective Knowledge*. Oxford: Clarendon Press.

Putnam, H. 1975: The Meaning of Meaning. In K. Gunderson (ed.) *Language, Mind and Knowledge: Minnesota Studies in the Philosophy of Science*, vol. 7. Minneapolis: University of Minnesota Press.

Rosenberg, A. 1978: The Supervenience of Biological Concepts. *Philosophy of Science*, 45, 368–86.

——1985: *The Structure of Biological Science*. Cambridge: Cambridge University Press.

——1994: *Instrumental Biology, or the Disunity of Science*. Chicago: University of Chicago Press.

Royall, R. 1997: *Statistical Evidence – A Likelihood Paradigm*. London: Chapman & Hall.

Ruse, M. 1973: *The Philosophy of Biology*. London: Hutchinson University Library.

Ruse, M. and Wilson, E. 1986: Moral Philosophy as Applied Science. *Philosophy*, 61, 173–92.

Reprinted in E. Sober (ed.) (1994) *Conceptual Issues in Evolutionary Biology*, 2nd edn. Cambridge, MA: MIT Press.

Schaffner, 1976: Reductionism in Biology: Prospects and Problems. In R. S. Cohen et al. (eds) *PSA 1974*. Dordrecht: Reidel.

Sober, E 1980: Evolution, Population Thinking, and Essentialism. *Philosophy of Science*, 47, 350–83. Reprinted in E. Sober (ed.) (1994) *Conceptual Issues in Evolutionary Biology*, 2nd edn. Cambridge, MA: MIT Press.

——1984: *The Nature of Selection*. Cambridge, MA: MIT Press. (Second edition (1994) Chicago: University of Chicago Press.)

——1988: *Reconstructing the Past: Parsimony, Evolution, and Inference*. Cambridge, MA: MIT Press.

——1990: Putting the Function Back Into Functionalism. In W. Lycan (ed.) *Mind and Cognition: A Reader.* Oxford: Blackwell.

——1992: Monophyly. In E. Fox Keller and E. Lloyd (eds) *Keywords in Evolutionary Biology*. Cambridge, MA: Harvard University Press.

——1993: *Philosophy of Biology*. Boulder, CO: Westview Press. (Second edition 1999.)

——1994a: Progress and Direction in Evolution. In J. Campbell and W. Schopf (eds) *Creative Evolution?!* Boston: Jones and Bartlett.

——1994b: The Adaptive Advantage of Learning and *a priori* Prejudice. In *From a Biological Point of View*. Cambridge, MA: Cambridge University Press.

——1997a: Two Outbreaks of Lawlessness in Recent Philosophy of Biology. In L. Darden (ed.) *PSA 1996*, 458–67.

——1997b: Is the Mind an Adaptation for Coping with Environmental Complexity? *Biology and Philosophy*, 12, 539–50.

——1999a: Physicalism from a Probabilistic Point of View. *Philosophical Studies*, 95 (1–2), 135–74.

——1999b: The Multiple Realizability Argument Against Reductionism. *Philosophy of Science*, 66 (4).

——1999c: Modus Darwin. *Biology and Philosophy*, 14 (2), 253–78.

——1999d: Testability. *Proceedings and Addresses of the American Philosophical Association*, 73 (2), 47–76.

Sober, E. and Lewontin, R. 1982: Artifact, Cause, and Genic Selection. *Philosophy of Science*, 47, 157–80.

Sober, E. and Wilson, D. 1994: A Critical Review of Philosophical Work on the Units of Selection Problem. *Philosophy of Science*, 61, 534–55. Reprinted in D. Hull and M. Ruse (eds) *Philosophy of Biology*. Oxford: Oxford University Press.

——1998: *Unto Others – the Evolution and Psychology of Unselfish Behaviour*. Cambridge, MA: Harvard University Press.

Stephens, C. 2001: When is it Selectively Advantageous to Have True Beliefs? Sandwiching the Better Safe than Sorry Argument. *Philosophical Studies*, 105, 161–89.

Sterelny, K. and Griffiths, P. 1999: *Sex and Death: An Introduction to the Philosophy of Biology*. Chicago: University of Chicago Press.

Sterelny, K. and Kitcher, P. 1988: The Return of the Gene. *Journal of Philosophy*, 85, 339–61.

Wade, M. 1978: A Critical Review of Models of Group Selection. *Quarterly Review of Biology*, 53, 101–14.

Waters, C. K. 1990: Why the Anti-reductionist Consensus Won't Survive the Case of Classical Mendelian Genetics. *PSA 1990*, vol. 1, 125–39. Reprinted in E. Sober (ed.) (1994) *Conceptual Issues in Evolutionary Biology*, 2nd edn. Cambridge, MA: MIT Press.

Wiley, E. 1981: *Phylogenetics: The Theory and Practice of Phylogenetic Systematics*. London: John Wiley.

342

Williams, G. 1966: *Adaptation and Natural Selection*. Princeton, NJ: Princeton University Press.

——1989: A Sociobiological Expansion of Evolution and Ethics. In J. Paradis and G. C. Williams (eds) *T. H. Huxley Evolution and Ethics: With New Essays on its Victorian and Sociobiological Context*. Princeton, NJ: Princeton University Press.

——1992: *Natural Selection: Domains, Levels and Challenges*. Oxford: Oxford University Press.

Wilson, D. 1980: *The Natural Selection of Populations and Communities*. Menlo Park, CA: Benjamin Cummings.

——1994: Adaptive Genetic Variation and Human Evolutionary Psychology. *Ethology and Sociobiology*, 15, 219–35.

Wilson, E. 1975: *Sociobiology: The New Synthesis*. Cambridge, MA: Harvard University Press.

Wimsatt, W. 1979: Reduction and Reductionism. In P. Asquith and H. Kyburg (eds) *Current Research in Philosophy of Science*. Philosophy of Science Association, 352–77.

——1980: Reductionistic Research Strategies and their Biases in the Units of Selection Controversy. In T. Nickles (ed.) *Scientific Discovery*, vol. 2. Dordrecht: Reidel.

Wright, L. 1973: Functions. *Philosophical Review*, 82, 139–68. Reprinted in E. Sober (ed.) (1994) *Conceptual Issues in Evolutionary Biology*, 2nd edn. Cambridge, MA: MIT Press.

——1976: *Teleological Explanations: An Etiological Analysis of Goals and Functions*. Berkeley: University of California Press.

Discussion Questions

1   What constitutes being alive?

2   How should we understand fitness?

3   If biological properties supervene upon physical properties, can biology be reduced to physics?

4   Is reductionism compatible with the multiple physical realizability of biological properties?

5   What is required for one theory to be reducible to another?

6   How should we understand the role of function in biology?

7   Must we take account of our explanatory interests to distinguish between the function and the fortuitous benefit of an organ?

8   Are both Newton's theory of gravitation and Darwin's theory of evolution scientific?

9   How can we determine which species are closely related and which are related only more distantly?

10   What is the role of parsimony in scientific reasoning?

11   Can we explain why natural selection does not always result in species having optimal traits?

12   Is natural selection merely *one* among several important influences on trait evolution, or is it the *only* important influence?

13   What is the difference between testing hypotheses and testing research programmes?

14   Why in biology is it important to recognize that historical origin and present advantage are not automatically linked?

15   Do more than one unit of selection have a role in the evolutionary process?

16   Is the choice between individuals and groups as the units of selection a matter of adopting a convention rather than a matter of answering a factual question about the history of life?

17 Are there any laws of evolution?

18 How can *a priori* models have a part to play in empirical science?

19 Does the adaptive complexity of organisms justify the argument from design?

20 Could species, as understood in evolutionary theory, have essences?

21 What makes human beings now and human beings thousands of years ago members of the same species?

22 Are species individuals or natural kinds? What could count as natural kinds in evolutionary biology?

23 What follows from the claim that species are historical entities?

24 Is evolutionary psychology more securely based than sociobiology?

25 Is biological evolution a good model for explaining social and cultural change?

26 What are the consequences for philosophy of accepting a modularity account of the mind?

27 Can natural selection help to explain the existence and character of human mentality?

28 Does an evolutionary theory of the character of human morality help us to assess moral claims?

29 Do evolutionary considerations undermine the claim that there are objective moral truths?

11

Philosophy of Mathematics

MARY TILES

Since the time of ancient Greece, mathematics has been intimately tied to philosophy, both as a model of knowledge and as an object of philosophical reflection. Are numbers real? What is a proof? Is mathematics more certain than other knowledge? Can finite minds have knowledge of infinity? How can mathematics apply to the world? In this chapter, changing philosophical conceptions of mathematics, changes in the historical context of mathematical thought and changes in mathematics itself are explored in relation to a basic question: how can theoretical reasoning about non-concrete mathematical objects be both secure and so useful? Platonic, Aristotelian and Kantian approaches to mathematics are examined in their own right and to place in context the problems and proposed solutions of the major modern schools of logicism, formalism and intuitionism. Recent developments which do not seek foundations for mathematics are also considered. Many of the discussions of great historical figures in this volume, especially FREGE AND RUSSELL (chapter 37), are relevant to the present chapter. Readers will also wish to consult chapters on EPISTEMOLOGY (chapter 1), METAPHYSICS (chapter 2), PHILOSOPHY OF LANGUAGE (chapter 3), PHILOSOPHY OF LOGIC (chapter 4) and PHILOSOPHY OF SCIENCE (chapter 9).

Introductions to the philosophy of mathematics often begin where Körner's (1960) influential introduction began, outlining three positions: logicism, formalism and intuitionism. These were the three contending schools to emerge from nineteenth-century mathematical moves to provide rigorous foundations for mathematical analysis (including infinitesimal calculus). The problem for the philosophy of mathematics has been that (1) these seemed to represent all the reasonable positions available, and (2) in the light of Gödel's incompleteness theorems and other results proved by Turing, Church, Skolem and Tarski in the 1930s, neither logicism nor formalism seemed a philosophically viable position. Intuitionism, whilst having its philosophical credentials intact, was unacceptable to most mathematicians because it involved discarding parts of classically accepted mathematics. This apparent impasse partly explains the decline of interest in the philosophy of mathematics since the first part of this century, when for a while, with the work of Russell and Whitehead, and the Vienna Circle logical positivists, it seemed to occupy centre stage.

Hao Wang, in his perceptive retrospective analysis of the philosophy of mathematics of this period (Wang 1968), explains this trajectory in terms of the wider movements of analytic philosophy, which were initially strongly empiricist and which consequently inherited a hostility toward abstract objects. Mathematics presents a significant challenge to empiricism, as was made painfully evident by the prominence of mathematics in Einstein's relativity theories and in the development of quantum mechanics. How is empiricism to give an adequate explanation of the certainty, clarity, universality and applicability of mathematics? Wang's answer is that the above mentioned developments in logic and the foundations of mathematics show that analytic empiricism cannot meet this challenge. It is therefore only as philosophy in general begins to move beyond analytic empiricism that more fruitful approaches to philosophy of mathematics can begin to be explored.

But how exactly is such a move to be made? Because the three foundational schools originated in the work of philosophically minded mathematicians who were seeking to resolve sophisticated conceptual problems that had arisen in the context of ongoing mathematical research, much of the work in foundations is itself technical and mathematical in character. There is no sharp line where mathematics ends and philosophy begins. Indeed, one of the striking features of the development of mathematics in the twentieth century was the way in which attempts to solve philosophical and conceptual problems generated new mathematics. Thus from the standpoint of the early twenty-first century, work in the foundations of mathematics can by no means be ignored, but it may need to be re-evaluated. What is its status? What exactly does it tell us about contemporary mathematics? These questions must now be added to the philosophical agenda. So one of the ways of moving beyond the presuppositions built into philosophy of mathematics by analytic empiricists is to recontextualize their work on logic and foundations in the hope of understanding its motivations, achievements and shortcomings. A first step is to sketch, using broad strokes, major features in the landscape of Western philosophical reflection on mathematics, many of which were already put in place by the ancient Greeks.

1 Basic Tasks for a Philosophy of Mathematics

The basic puzzle, of which the challenge to empiricism is but a specialized variant, is to explain how theoretical reasoning about highly abstract objects can be so useful. The features of mathematics which seemed to mark it off from other disciplines are that its objects are not encountered in the world of sense experience, and yet, perhaps as a consequence, mathematical claims can be provided with proofs which seem to establish them with an exactness and certainty unparalleled in other branches of knowledge. But how is it that people shut away from the outside world, thinking, calculating and proving theorems about things which we can never hope to see or touch (numbers such as 2, 1 million, π, or structures such as circles, rings and vector spaces), produce results which other, very practical people find so useful in their dealings both with the everyday world and with the esoteric worlds of high-tech science? What right have we to be so confident of the correctness of these results?

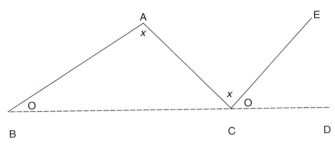

Figure 11.1 Proof that the internal angles of a triangle add up to the sum of two right angles.

The straightforward answer to this last question is that mathematicians are able to offer proofs of their results. For example, as geometers before the time of Aristotle realized, measurements of the internal angles of plane triangles do not yield one exact result, but results that cluster round two right angles, and, because measuring gives no insight into why this clustering should occur, it affords no assurance that a 'rogue' triangle might not some day be found whose internal angles had a markedly different sum. A proof, on the other hand, that shows why, given what it is to be a triangle, its internal angles must add up to two right angles, assures us that no rogue triangle exists. One such proof is shown in figure 11.1.

Such a proof is possible only if it can be assumed that all the lines involved are perfectly straight and have no thickness (something which is not true of the lines in the diagram). Lines which have thickness do not meet in points and if they have wriggles in them there is no sense to be given to an exact measurement of the angle between them. So even to have internal angles whose sum is exactly equal to two right angles is possible only for a perfect plane triangle, which we could not encounter in experience. The theorem proved below will hold more or less exactly for those triangles we encounter to the extent that they are more or less perfectly triangular.

There is an important assumption made here about the applicability of results proved about idealizations: a result proved about an idealization will hold for situations which approximate to that ideal in direct proportion to the closeness with which they approximate to the ideal. This assumption has traditionally underwritten applications of mathematics, but, with recent work in chaos theory, it has been shown not to be valid for systems exhibiting sensitive dependence on initial conditions (Stewart 1989: chs 7, 14). This work opens up new questions about the connection between proofs and the use of results proved.

But how can we tell that a purported proof really is a proof? All proofs have to start from some assumptions (we assumed above some properties of parallel lines and of addition of angles). How can we be certain that these are correct? Furthermore, how can we be sure that all inferences are made correctly? To ask for a proof for every assumption will lead to an infinite regress. So if there are to be any proofs there must be some self-evident starting-points, which can be known to be necessarily true and which are neither capable of, nor stand in need of, further justification.

This means that if mathematics is a discipline in which proofs are required then it must be one which exhibits a systematic hierarchical order. Some propositions concerning mathematical entities will appear as first principles, accepted without proof: these are the foundations upon which subsequent knowledge must be built. Basic theorems are proved from first principles: these theorems are in turn used to prove further results, and so on. This is the sense in which, so long as mathematicians demand and provide proofs, their discipline must necessarily be organized along lines approximating the pattern already to be found in the *Elements of Geometry* of Euclid (which dates from around 300 BC) – a work which for centuries served as an exemplar.

The question of what principles of inference are generally valid (rationally compelling, or truth-preserving) is traditionally assigned to LOGIC (chapter 4). But one may wonder whether there are not some specifically mathematical principles of inference. Take, for example, Euclid's principle that if $A = B$ and $C = D$, then $A + C = B + D$. Is this a logical principle (a specific application of the SUBSTITUTIVITY OF IDENTICALS (p. 800))? Is it a basic principle of the theory of part and whole? If so, does this belong to logic or to mathematics? Or is it a specifically mathematical principle governing extensive magnitudes?

At this point it is already possible to see how concern for principles of valid deductive inference and for the nature and status of first principles becomes a natural part of any philosophy of mathematics that takes proof to be that on the basis of which mathematical propositions gain their aura of privileged certainty, or necessary truth. However, to equate the philosophy of mathematics with studies in logic and foundations would seem to ignore one half of the combination of features that make mathematics so philosophically puzzling and intriguing. It leaves out questions concerning the utility of mathematics.

So far we have the following schema of questions structuring the problematic of philosophical reflections on mathematics:

Basic Problem
How can theoretical reasoning about non-concrete mathematical objects be both so secure and so useful?

If the question of security is presumed to be answered by the fact that theoretical reasoning produces proofs of mathematical propositions, then we have to distinguish between first principles and results proved from them, to get something like the following subsidiary problems:

1   What is the nature and status of the first principles of mathematics?
   1.1   Can its first principles be identified?
   1.2   How can these first principles be known with certainty?
2   How is mathematical knowledge acquired?
   2.1   *Discovery*: How are discoveries made? How are results established or proofs found?
   2.2   *Justification*: What constitutes a proof? What principles of inference are available? What is their nature and what grounds have we for thinking them reliable?

3 Given the answers under (1) and (2), how is the applicability of proved mathematical results to be explained? Do the answers under (1) and (2) assure us that we have
   a right to expect mathematical results to have applications and that in their
   application established results will be reliable?

2 Basic Responses

Mathematics since the sixteenth century has been a highly dynamic discipline. Over
this period, methods of problem-solving and of proof have undergone many changes.
Philosophers have tended to take the ability to provide proofs to be the distinguishing
characteristic of mathematics. But if proof methods change and are likely to continue
to change, philosophic analyses of proof methods, and opinions about the foundations
of mathematical claims derived from these analyses, will be historically conditioned.
Similarly, the kinds of applications made of mathematics are continually changing.
Any account of the applicability of mathematics will thus also have different problems
to address depending on the period in which it is being offered. This means that a
response to the basic problem which may be adequate at one period of history may
be inadequate at a later period and so require considerable modification. This can be
illustrated by seeing how the configuration of the basic problem, and hence of viable
solutions to it, changed in the seventeenth century and then again in the nineteenth
century. In this way we can indicate, albeit very sketchily, the historical context of
analytic empiricist responses.

   For the purposes of a schematic overview of the philosophical terrain, it is possible
to view philosophies up to the late seventeenth century as proposing variations on what
we may call Platonic realist or Aristotelian conceptualist responses to the basic question. (These labels indicate the classical ancestry of these responses but should not be
read literally as Plato's realism or Aristotle's conceptualism.)

2.1 Platonic realism

For the Platonic realist the problem dissolves once it is realized that the cosmos has an
eternal and unchanging underlying order, or harmony, and that the principles of this
order are essentially mathematical. This kind of view can be traced back to the
Pythagoreans who based a vision of a harmoniously ordered universe on their discovery of the association between musical harmonies and numerical ratios. It found
one of its most explicit expressions in the work of Kepler (1571–1630), the famous
astronomer. In his *Harmonice Mundi* (1940) he supposes the universe to be the work
of a God who is not only a geometer but also a musician. The planets therefore make
heavenly music as they orbit the Sun.

   The same conception surfaces in many other authors of various periods. For Newton
(1642–1727) in his *Opticks* (1931), the division of the spectrum into seven colours is
numerically correlated with the harmonic division of a single string which yields the
notes of the octave. Einstein's (1879–1955) often-quoted rejection of the claims of
quantum mechanics to be a fundamental physical theory – 'God does not play dice' –

reveals a similar attitude. It also found expression in the drive to mathematical elegance and unity which resulted in his theory of general relativity and in his unsuccessful quest for a grand unified field theory, a quest continued by those working on the theory of superstrings (Davies and Brown 1988).

If the universe is mathematically ordered, this would explain the utility of mathematics but not how we can come to mathematical knowledge or the specially secure status of that knowledge. For the realist who was either Christian, or a NEO-PLATONIST (p. 595) (or someone who was both), this was readily explicable. The Christian God created not only the universe, but also human beings; we were created with an intellect that is a finite image of God's infinite intellect. This faculty was given to us precisely so that we might come to a secure knowledge of the existence of the God who created us and to a limited knowledge of God's nature. Thus God created human beings with an intellect that is innately equipped to grasp mathematical principles and to recognize them as true beyond all doubt. This requires that the intellect be exercised in the right way, namely, by turning away from sensual distractions to focus on things intellectual and the realm of pure abstractions (see, for example, Descartes 1985–91b; Augustine 1990: Bk VI, 1955, Bk II). For the neo-Platonist, the human soul (microcosm) was an integral part of the universe (macrocosm) and capable of resonating in sympathy with the world soul. The microcosm and macrocosm thus mirror each other in such a way that the harmonies of one will be recognized by and affect the other. On either account mathematical knowledge is a matter of insight, of intellectual intuition, or a seeing in the light of reason which is analogous to a religious revelation. When the mind is properly focused the first principles of mathematics will be revealed with irresistible clarity and distinctness, for they are integral to the intellect's own nature.

But because the human intellect is limited and finite it does not comprehend all things immediately in its intellectual vision; it only comprehends those things that are simple and basic. (In the mind of God all things are immediately intuited; God never needs to engage in reasoning or to make inferences. Neither does the world soul; its structures are integral to itself and immediately known to it.) Human minds have to approach progressively more complex and complete knowledge in stages. Reasoning and deductive proof do not in themselves confer the intellectual intuition that is true knowledge, but reason and intuition are, for finite minds, the necessary route to it (see Spinoza 1992; Descartes 1985–91a). It is hardly surprising then to find that such philosophers give priority to methods of discovery and routes to insight, over methods of justification. Proofs are less justifications than records of the real interconnections of things, the interconnections which explain, for example, why triangles must have internal angles equalling the sum of two right angles. These interconnections can be grasped in a single act of intellectual vision, by one who truly understands, but can only be recorded sequentially.

Thus for the Platonic realist the cosmos is an ordered whole. Mathematics expresses the principles of this order and gives insight into it. The route to mathematical knowledge is supernaturally linked to its utility, through the idea that the senses reveal to us only the changing phenomenal world of sense experience. To acquire knowledge of the eternal principles underlying the order of that world it is necessary to turn away from the senses and to (re-)unite the human intellect (or soul) with the intellect which orders the world (or with the world soul).

2.2   Aristotelian conceptualism

By contrast the Aristotelian conceptualist's cosmos, although structured, is in the first instance a collection of individual things that undergo change, and whose order is partly contingent and partly a product of the natures of the things making up the universe. To comprehend the universe is thus to know the natures of individual (kinds of) things. Logic gives us some insight into the principles of the ordering of individual things into species and genera based on their specific qualities (differentia). But, in addition, it is necessary, by observation and reflection, to discover the causal principles, the forces, the powers and potentialities of the things that govern their behaviour.

Mathematics deals with things that do not change. Moreover, it can only ever yield principles that concern relations between things, because numbers are assigned only after selection of a unit of measure and geometry deals only with shapes, which in turn are characterized by the relations between their parts, and with spatial relations between shapes. This means that mathematics can never yield insight into the natures, or the principles of change, of individual things or, hence, into the causal principles that govern the universe. Arithmetic is the science of discrete magnitudes and geometry is the science of continuous magnitudes. Magnitudes themselves are a product of measurement and hence of human measuring activities. It is in experience that we encounter the various kinds of magnitudes and invent measurement systems that are appropriate to them and to our purposes.

When we invent measures, discriminate between shapes and become, for practical purposes, interested in spatial relations, for example, or the relative motions of the planets, mathematics can help us describe in systematic ways the various kinds of orders that we are interested in and to co-ordinate our various measuring units. Thus astronomy uses geometry and arithmetic to help connect the various temporal units – such as day, lunar month and solar year – in ways that make construction of a calendar possible. Geometry applied to measurements made on the ground makes building plans and maps possible. Mathematics is useful because measurement is useful and this utility arises out of the practical contexts in which measures were devised. We can have more complete knowledge here than of the natural world because it is a human invention and just as we do not have to examine the natural world to find out how to use the words of a language or to determine whether an action is or is not legal according to the legal system of a specific city or country, so we would not expect to look to the world to resolve questions about magnitudes and their relations.

But in this case would there not be as many different mathematical systems as there are legal systems? Yet one of the experiences which gives support to claims about the universal necessity of mathematics is that although different cultures have developed different numeral systems, units of measurement, methods of calculation and mathematical problem-solving, there is remarkable agreement at the level of results. Merchants speaking different languages can nevertheless bargain their way to agreed prices, adapting to different currency and measurement systems. Two plus two does not make five or three in the arithmetic of any culture.

Aristotelian conceptualists accommodate this in a way not wholly dissimilar from Platonic realists. This is not surprising since both believed in a universal human nature and emphasized intellect as an important distinguishing mark of humanity; a human

351

is a rational animal. Thus for ARISTOTLE (chapter 23), LOCKE (chapter 29), BERKELEY (chapter 30) and even HUME (chapter 31), the human mind comes into the world disposed to impose certain kinds of structures on it. Humans are born able to start making certain basic discriminations on the basis of qualitative similarity and difference and to learn to make many more. In fact, if it is assumed that all experience is of particulars, then all relating one thing to another, whether with respect to colour, taste and smell, or with respect to size, shape, place and time, must be a function of the human mind. To be able to do this the human mind must have, in addition to innate capacities for sense perception, innate relation-imposing capacities. Reflection on these yields the basic concepts for more abstract disciplines, including mathematics; concepts such as unity, number, size, shape and indefinitely continued repetition. These abstract concepts, presupposed in ordering experience, can be said to be first in the order of understanding, or simple with respect to the intellect, because, although they may be explicitly acquired, if at all, only after intellectual reflection, they are nonetheless presupposed in all experiential knowledge.

Where the realist sees in these simple, innate intellectual concepts indications of a supernatural order, the conceptualist sees only structures of the human mind in terms of which it orders the natural world of particulars. Mathematical first principles thus involve concepts derived from reflection on innate human intellectual capacities to distinguish between, and to relate, particulars. In this sense they are simple innate ideas, ideas which are first in the order of understanding although not in the order of human experience, because they can only come to be known by turning away from the world and reflecting on the way in which the intellect functions. They are potentially self-evident to all human beings because they are explicit expressions of principles that are implicit in the innate, natural operation of the human intellect.

More complex concepts, however, must be built up from these simples by explicit processes of definition. Not all cultures will necessarily develop the same complex concepts, although all start from the same simples and all are measuring aspects of things in the same physical world; the definition of any complex concept should therefore be explicable to anyone, irrespective of cultural location. Results concerning more complex concepts must be proved by appeal to their definitions and to first principles, and they must proceed by deductive syllogistic reasoning. Proofs, in other words, are demonstrations in the sense outlined by Aristotle in his *Posterior Analytics* (1941a: 93a16–96a19). Since complex mathematical concepts are the work of humans, there is no ground of proof beyond the definition of complex concepts in terms of simple concepts. It can sometimes appear that more is involved because it does take work to arrive at good definitions. This is because many measurement-related concepts arise first in practical contexts where computation or diagrammatic reasoning is involved. It is only when the question of the reliability of such reasoning arises that it becomes necessary to think about explicitly defining concepts, such as a circle, a straight line, subtraction, multiplication or division. A good definition will be required to justify core components of successful computational and measurement practices, but may not preserve (or justify) every component. From this way of looking at things, justification in the form of proof receives more emphasis than discovery, for there does not appear to be much to discovery beyond giving useful definitions and deducing their consequences.

3   New Procedures, New Problems: Analytic Geometry and the Infinite

So we have two approaches to resolving the basic problem. Do we then sort out our metaphysics and on that basis take our pick? If we see the world as consisting of changeable particulars should we accept a version of Aristotelian conceptualism, whereas if we see the world as an interrelated whole governed by unchanging mathematical principles of harmony should we accept some form of Platonic realism? That would surely be too simple, yet up to the seventeenth century the choice could have looked very much like this. This was in part because mathematics itself did not constitute a large or complex domain. It came in the form of arithmetic and geometry, which dealt with discrete and continuous magnitudes respectively. However, with the Renaissance revival of neo-Platonism and of mathematics came new ambitions, which began with the extension of the domain of arithmetic by algebra and continued via the use of algebraic techniques in geometry to the development of infinitesimal calculus and its use in Newtonian mechanics.

By the late seventeenth century, the mathematical, scientific and political background had shifted in such a way that neither of the old options could seem unproblematic. In the context of the increasing religious intolerance generated by the Thirty Years War in Europe, neo-Platonism became simply too dangerous a position to hold openly because of its obvious heretical implications. To survive, the new mathematical natural philosophy needed to distance itself from that position. Descartes's attempt to underwrite the security of his rational powers (and hence the mathematics to which reasoning led him) with a proof of the existence of a benevolent God who created him, was ingenious, but it failed to convince many people and also trespassed dangerously over the border from philosophy to theology, or from the domain of reason to that of FAITH (pp. 622–4). The strategy of philosophically securing an elevated status for mathematics by supernatural means looked increasingly unattractive, as demarcations were drawn between philosophy and theology, or between what is within the legitimate scope of human reason and what must, if believed, be a matter or faith or revelation.

Aristotelian conceptualism was thus initially the more attractive route, and it certainly attracted empiricist philosophers such as Locke and Hume. But there were factors in both the new developments in mathematics and those in natural philosophy that seemed strongly to favour some form of realism – the view that mathematics deals with a subject matter which exists independently of the human mind.

The development of analytic geometry brought algebraic methods into geometry and saw the gradual emergence of the mathematical concept of a function. This took place in the context of developing a mathematics that was capable of representing change and of expressing principles of change. The equation of a parabola ($y = ax - bx^2$), for example, could be read both as a mathematical definition of that particular conic section and as the principle according to which a projectile moves under the influence of gravity in the absence of air resistance ($s = v_0t - gt^2$).

Geometrical attention shifted to curves that were defined not in words but by algebraic equations, many of which were curves previously excluded from geometry

353

because they are generated mechanically but cannot be defined in terms of ruler and compass constructions. These developments were problematic because they make the tacit supposition that any point on a plane can be assigned a pair of numbers as co-ordinates, once co-ordinate axes have been fixed.

The ancient Greeks already had proof that the hypotenuse of a right-angled isosceles triangle with unit sides must have a length $\sqrt{2}$, but that this length could not be expressed as any ratio. The discovery of the existence of such incommensurable magnitudes was one of the reasons why arithmetic and geometry had been regarded as distinct mathematical disciplines. One studied discrete magnitudes, the other continuous magnitudes and it was not thought possible to reduce the study of continuous magnitudes to that of discrete magnitudes. This attitude was reinforced by paradoxes, such as Zeno's paradox of Achilles and the tortoise, which were taken to show that a continuous magnitude cannot be made up of discrete parts. The history of much of the work in pure mathematics in the eighteenth and nineteenth centuries is the history of how, in spite of such paradoxes, ways were found to effect a reduction of the study of the continuous to a study of the discrete. This reduction is not without cost. The price is having to develop a mathematics of the infinite and admitting the infinite as a foundational concept. The difficulties encountered in this process make it hard to believe that continuous magnitudes are human inventions and thus transparent to the human intellect.

The invention of infinitesimal calculus and its use in mechanics gave added urgency to philosophical questions about whether, and how, it is possible to reason reliably about what is infinitely large or infinitely small. An additional feature of Newtonian mechanics is that its associated view of the physical world is of a world of small material particles moving around in, but not densely populating, space. The forces acting on particles and causing their motions are intimately connected to space and time in two ways. Firstly, they are connected by Newton's second law of motion, which states: force = mass × acceleration. This seemed to Newton to require that space and time form an absolute frame of reference, relative to which absolute motion is distinguished from relative motion (changes in absolute motion being those that result from forces acting on the moving object). For relative motions the second law can be false. A person standing on a railway platform accelerates away from a person in a train, from whose point of view the train is stationary. But there is no force acting on the person or the platform causing them to accelerate away from the train. Secondly, Newton's gravitational theory proposes that there is a gravitational attraction between any two material particles and that this force is directly proportional to the product of the masses of the two particles and inversely proportional to the square of the distance between them. In other words, spatial separation is itself a causal factor as it determines the magnitude of a fundamental force. The mathematics of space as the paradigm continuous magnitude must, it seems, be regarded as dealing with an aspect of the same physical world that is studied by the natural philosophers. If one subscribed to the vision of the world proposed by Newtonian mechanics, it would be hard not to be some form of realist about mathematics. Only by being instrumentalist about Newtonian physics – by regarding it as a mere calculatory device for better predicting and controlling events in the world of everyday human experience – would one be more likely to be attracted to some kind of conceptualism about mathematics.

But note how the ground has shifted in such a way that neither form of position is entirely stable. The new form of realism requires mathematics to relate to an independently existing, natural world of material particles in motion, not to an eternal and unchanging supernatural or spiritual world. It therefore faces serious problems about its ability to say how it can be possible for us to get certain knowledge of this world by mathematical (as distinct from experimental) methods, for this material world is explicitly described as having no affinity with the human intellect. Appeal to the benevolent Christian God certainly remained a possibility for believers, but it would be in a climate where this must be regarded as an act of faith, and thus not as something for which any rational, philosophic justification can be given. The philosophical form of the basic problem would thus have to be dismissed as insoluble and an inappropriate topic of investigation.

The new form of conceptualism also faced serious problems. The first problem area is the notion of the infinite. If the human intellect is finite how can it – either innately, or when prompted by its necessarily limited experience – be the source of a concept of the infinite? Only such a concept would be adequate to a detailed mathematical comprehension of the infinite complexity hidden within continuous magnitudes. Secondly, the problems posed by the new algebraic mathematics, and the methods of inference being used to provide solutions, made it quite clear that these forms of inference could in no way be construed as conforming to the pattern of inference from explicit definitions of concepts via deductive logical moves (or syllogisms) to conclusions. Because definitions, even in geometry, frequently came to take the form of algebraic equations, inferences from these involved computation and the handling of equations and inequalities in a central way. All of this is explicitly relational reasoning – it is not assimilable within the framework of Aristotelian syllogistic, which is basically a logic of predication.

Two new variant strategies emerged in response to the changed configuration of mathematics and its uses. One, accompanying an INSTRUMENTALIST ATTITUDE TO SCIENCE (pp. 294–5), was conventionalist or formalist. Since instrumentalism about science was not prominent in the eighteenth and nineteenth centuries, this was not a widely pursued option. The other, proposed by KANT (chapter 32), is a form of constructivism which represents a creative synthesis of elements from both Platonic realism and Aristotelian conventionalism.

The problem of the infinite, for conceptualists, lay in their assumption that to attach any significance to a word, that word must stand for an idea. That idea had in some way to represent, or to present to the mind, something infinite and should have its origin either in human experience or in the nature of the finite, human intellect. How can there be a finite representation of something infinite which adequately expresses the infinity of what is represented? Berkeley (1995: §§19–20) short-circuited this problem by arguing that a sign (or word) can acquire meaning from use; it does not have to stand for an idea. If a word does not stand for an idea it does not represent any reality; however, a sign can be of use even if it has no representative function, or if it forms part of a system that we have developed for classifying, ordering and anticipating experience. This suggests that mathematicians are free to create signs so long as they do not claim to be able to express any superior or arcane knowledge by these means. The problem for such a position, as Berkeley's (1947–57) astute criticisms of Newton's mathematical methods illustrate, is how to ensure that when we try to make use of our new signs we will neither get absurd nor unreliable results.

Difficulties over space and time and the use made of mathematics in Newtonian mechanics formed one of the focuses of Kant's *Critique of Pure Reason*. His formulation of the basic question about mathematics is 'How is *synthetic a priori* knowledge possible?' His answer is to assume that it is possible (since Newtonian mechanics is accepted and is seen to work) and to ask what are the necessary conditions of its possibility. His answer rejects traditional relational accounts of space and time as well as Newton's absolute space and time. He argues effectively that space cannot be reduced to spatial relations but must be thought to be a unity which has its own characteristic properties. One argument he uses (repeated and strengthened by Nerlich 1976) is to point out that the difference between a right hand and a left hand cannot be captured by characterizing the relations between the parts of the hand; rather, it has to do with the way the hand is 'inserted' into space. Nerlich uses the very simple shapes (which he calls 'knees') to illustrate the same point. It is not possible by sliding a right knee around on a flat surface to move it in such a way that it becomes a left knee. This can only be achieved if we lift the right knee up, turn it over and re-insert it in the plane, when it will now be a left knee. Thus the difference between right and left is not intrinsic to the object, but to the way it is 'oriented' in space. Not all surfaces, however, have this characteristic. The surface of a Möbius strip is such that by moving a right knee once around the strip it becomes a left knee. Thus 'orientability', the capacity to produce right–left distinctions, is a feature of space itself, not of things in it.

Kant on Space, Time and Mathematics

Kant's position on space and time is thus non-reductionist, but it is not realist. He does not assert that space and time have any reality independent of human perception. Rather, space and time are forms of human intuition and hence structure all human experience. We do not, and could not, gain these notions from experience because they are preconditions of and are presupposed in all experience. All human experience occurs in time and all experience of things outside our own mental life is experienced as occurring in space as well as time. The foundation of arithmetic is to be found in the temporal structure of our experience, and that of geometry in its spatial structure. These structures are of the world of experience, but they have that status only because the forms of human intuition are what constitute and give form to that world.

That mathematics is grounded back to *a priori* forms of intuition, rather than to innate ideas or structures of the intellect, is significant and indicates Kant's divergence from Aristotelian conceptualism. He distinguishes sharply between logical deduction, reasoning from concepts, and mathematical reasoning, which involves reasoning from the construction of concepts. It is our ability imaginatively to construct mathematical objects in pure intuition that grounds our insight into their properties. We imagine a mathematical point tracing out the curve whose co-ordinates at all times satisfy the equation for a circle, and thereby connect the algebraic definition with what it constructively defines. The algebraic definition of a curve in analytic geometry is thus viewed as a definition in the sense of a recipe for constructing an object, rather than as an Aristotelian definition of a term proceeding by a specification of genus and differentia. It is our ability, in our imagination, to carry out the operations that correspond to functional expressions, which forms the ground that makes mathematical knowledge possible. It is the fact that space and time, as forms of intuition, are such that all items of experience appear as magnitudes that assures us of the universal applicability of mathematics. The very notion of empirical reality and an objective order of experience is argued to require the supposition that the causal order of events is such as to impose determinate mathematical structures on space and time. Thus Kant, using a modified conceptualist strategy, sought to preserve the essentials of the Newtonian framework whilst avoiding the problems that were encountered by postulating absolute space and time.

However, the fact that human intellectual construction forms the ground for mathematical knowledge means that if the infinite is to have any place in mathematics, it can only be as the potential infinity of the unending, never-completed series of which the natural number series is the primary example. No actually infinite construction can be supposed to have been carried out. Kant argues both that human reason is so structured that it will tend, illegitimately, to form the idea of a completed infinite process, and that this is always a source of illusions. If we want to treat infinite series as objects we will not be able to regard them as things that are ever completed. Reasoning concerning them thus cannot obey all the same principles as reasoning about fully determinate objects. In particular, reasoning by reductio ad absurdum cannot be relied upon in such cases.

It was within a broadly Kantian framework that much of the work in mathematics and its foundations was pursued into the nineteenth century, particularly in Germany. Work by Weierstrass (1815–97) and Cauchy (1789–1857) seemed further to justify Kant's position on the infinite. They succeeded in providing definitions of limits and convergence for infinite series that use only the notion of a potential infinite and make no appeal to the actual completion of an infinite sequence of approximations. This work seemed to secure the foundations of analysis without invoking the actual infinite.

4 Foundations

4.1 Logic, set theory and analytic empiricism

Toward the end of the nineteenth century, developments within mathematics and physics, together with wider socio-cultural changes, meant that the Kantian position could no longer be regarded as adequate. In mathematics the discovery of pathological functions – functions such as Weierstrass's everywhere-continuous-but-nowhere-differentiable function

$$f(x) = \sum_{n=0}^{\infty} b^n \cos(a^n x)$$

clearly indicated that geometrical intuition was not an adequate foundation for producing reliable mathematics. It was felt that the theory of real numbers needed to be put on a wholly numerical, arithmetical footing, one which did not at any point appeal to spatial intuition.

357

As a part of attempts to do this and to characterize the order structure required of the real numbers, Cantor (1845–1918) introduced transfinite ordinal numbers, and then, having proved that there can be no one–one correspondence between the natural numbers and the real numbers, introduced distinct infinite cardinal numbers. That is, he not only supposed that there could be a mathematics of the actually infinite, but, having argued that it is necessary to distinguish different sizes of infinite totality, went on to develop an arithmetic of infinite numbers. Disputes over the legitimacy of the proposed introduction of these transfinite numbers, coming on top of those concerning the introduction of Gauss's (1777–1855) imaginary numbers and Hamilton's (1805–65) quaternions, made clarification of the concept of number and of the grounds on which one could legitimately claim to have introduced a new kind of number a pressing issue.

Einstein and the Nature of Mathematical Knowledge

Perhaps most damaging to the Kantian position was the discovery of non-Euclidean geometries and the application of these in Einstein's theories of relativity. In one sense Einstein's procedure was thoroughly Kantian. He argued from the causal structures indicated by the form of laws used in electro-magnetism to the form required for those of mechanics (assuming that fundamental physical theories should conform to the same space-time forms) and read out the implications of this for the geometry of space-time. But this meant that it could no longer be plausibly argued that geometry gives *a priori* knowledge of the space-time structure of the material world.

The net effect of Einstein's use of non-Euclidean geometry in a physical theory was to disestablish the view that mathematics is a source of *a priori* knowledge about the empirical world. Euclidean geometry does not contain, and never had contained, truths about physical space that were guaranteed to be correct in application by their proofs. This appeared to vindicate empiricist claims that synthetic *a priori* knowledge is impossible. When mathematics forms part of empirical, scientific theories, then the correctness or otherwise of its results must be as much an empirical question as that of the correctness or otherwise of a scientific theory. But if proofs do not serve to justify applications, what do they prove? In other words, what exactly is the character and content of mathematical knowledge? If proofs do not establish claims about the world of experience, we seem to be left with the options either of a return to a form of Platonic realism or working toward a view that locates the importance of mathematics in its function and does not see it as making knowledge claims.

The overthrow of the Newtonian framework of classical mechanics was the combined effect of acceptance of relativity theory and of quantum mechanics. Again, one of its philosophical impacts was to give a boost to empiricism, particularly because quantum mechanics was accepted on the basis of its empirical success, despite conceptual problems over the interpretation of its mathematical formalism and conceptual resistance to its indeterminism. Now from an empiricist point of view, a return to a form of Platonic realism about mathematics would seem to be a non-starter. Yet, ironically, the logicist route to an empiricist account of mathematics (pursued by Russell (1919) and Whitehead and Russell (1913)) involves a displaced form of the Platonic realist strategy. Two moves are crucial here: (1) invoking an IDEAL LOGICAL LANGUAGE (p. 797) (for science); and (2) the use of classes, or sets, to define numbers in terms of their potential applications.

Both of these moves had already been made by FREGE (chapter 37) (1884, 1893), who had no commitment to an empiricist epistemology. Frege was concerned to provide a philosophical defence of the claims of mathematics to be a body of objective knowledge. He was reacting on the one hand against what he saw as the naturalistic psychologism of Kantian and other positions that treat knowledge as a matter of relating ideas, and on the other hand, he was reacting against conventionalist claims that mathematicians are free to create new numbers systems, since these are no more than formal symbol systems.

Frege's Realism

Frege appealed to the metaphor of geographic exploration when defending his claim that mathematics is a body of objective knowledge, and he resisted fiercely the suggestion that mathematicians have the right to create new mathematical objects or concepts. His conception of objective knowledge is thus strongly realist. Such knowledge is of an independently existing reality. It is expressed in language, which serves to represent that domain, using sentences which say either truly or falsely how things are. Whether such sentences are true or false depends on the state of the domain referred to and the result is independent of the state of human knowledge and of human cognitive capacities. What is said cannot, therefore, be a function of ideas in the minds of individual language speakers. The meanings of words must be publicly grounded in their linguistic function, which refers to the contribution that they make to fixing the truth conditions of sentences in which they occur. From the point of view of knowledge-expression, the sentence is the primary unit of meaning. These views on language and meaning turn the focus of philosophic attention away from ideas and thought processes, to language and its function in the communication and expression of knowledge; they constitute what has been labelled the 'linguistic turn', which is characteristic of analytic philosophy. This turn made available a broadly Platonic realist strategy, for language is here conceived not as any actually existing natural language, but as an ideal vehicle for the expression of objective knowledge to which all natural languages must approximate to the extent that they succeed in making knowledge-expression possible. The ideal logical language becomes the non-natural intermediary linking human beings to the structures of reality. It takes over some of the roles of the mind of God. We can come to know the structural principles governing faithful representation in this language because we are language speakers, and can reflect on the conditions of the possibility of language functioning in this way – a thought that found its classical expression in Wittgenstein's *Tractatus Logico-Philosophicus* (1922). Logic is an explicit codification of the principles of language in its representative, knowledge-expressing function. Its laws are not inherent in the structure of the human intellect; they are laws of truth, not laws of thought. The structures of such an ideal language, one able accurately to represent reality, must therefore also be reflections of the structure of reality.

Why should it be thought that mathematics, the study of magnitudes, can be reduced to logic, the study of the structure and relations of sentences in their knowledge-expressing function? The link here is the notion of a 'class' or 'set'. The theory of classes, the extensions of concepts, was traditionally a part of logic because Aristotelian syllogistic can, on one interpretation, be treated as a logic of classes and their relations. ('Whales are mammals' is treated as saying that the class of whales is included in that of mammals.) The natural numbers can be treated as measures of the sizes of sets, or classes, so that, for instance, the number 2 can be the measure of all 2-membered sets. It can be shown that negative numbers and rational numbers can be defined as sets (or ordered pairs) of natural numbers. Dedekind (1831–1916) proposed a definition of real numbers as infinite sets (or cuts) of rational numbers (Dedekind 1963). This suggested that 'set', or 'class', may be the single primitive concept from which all other mathematical concepts could be defined, if geometry and analysis could themselves be reduced either to arithmetic or to the study of sets of points.

Cantor (1895) and others were basing their definitions of number on a conception that can already be found in Plato. The number 2, for example, consists of two abstract units; it is the ideal type (the one over many) to which all pairs conform. Cantor suggested that numbers are arrived at by a psychological process of abstraction from collections such as two pencils on a desk. We must imaginatively subtract all the distinguishing qualities of the pencils and their location. If we abstract from everything but their order (the order in which we count) we get an ordinal number (an order type) and if we abstract even this we get a cardinal number (a cardinality type). In other words, the Platonic universal becomes an idea in an individual mind. But Frege ruled out such psychologistic accounts. Instead, he adopted a definition that makes 2, the one over all pairs, simply the class of all pairs. What saves this from circularity is that he defines what it is to be a two-membered class without using any reference to the number 2. A class is by definition a two-membered class if and only if there is a one–one correspondence between it and the class whose only members are 0 and 1. So, to say that there are two pencils on my desk is to say that the class of pencils on my desk is such that there is a one–one correspondence between it and $\{0,1\}$. Thus if I can find one pencil on my desk and pair it with 0 and another and pair it with 1 and there are none left over, I will know that the claim is true; otherwise, it is false. Of course 0 and 1 have themselves to be defined. 0 is defined as the class of classes C such that there is a one–one correspondence between C and the extension of the concept $x \neq x$. 1 is then the class of those classes C such that there is a one–one correspondence between C and the class whose only member is 0.

In this way the number 2 is linked by definition to its potential applications. But to justify the claim that all arithmetic truths can be proved by appeal only to definitions and formally expressed logical laws, the definitions given above must be expressed in the language of formal logic, and must use only concepts belonging to logic. Further, it must be shown that all the normally accepted arithmetic principles can be logically derived from these definitions.

Two things were crucial to this project: firstly, treating '=' as a primitive logical relation and, secondly, assuming, as a principle of logic, that every concept defined over individual objects has a class as its extension. It was also necessary to express in logical terms what it is for a relation to be a one–one correspondence between two classes. This idea can be defined as follows – 'R is a one–one correspondence between A and B if and only if for every x in A there is just one y in B such that x is R-related to y and for every y in B there is just one x in A such that x is R-related to y'. To express this as a logical condition requires a logic of relations capable of handling multiple quantification in a single sentence, and in which it is possible to express the numerical concept 'there is just one'. None of these was available in traditional logic. However, focus on the sentence as the unit of meaning enabled Frege to treat concept expressions and relational expressions (predicates) by analogy with mathematical functions of one, two or more variables, as sentence-forming operators. It was within this expanded logical framework that Frege claimed that arithmetic reduces to logic. What had previously been a major stumbling block to such a claim – the relational character of arithmetical reasoning – was overcome by the integration of a logic of relations with the logic of concepts.

This brilliant strategy, however, came to grief as a result of Russell's paradox, which demonstrated that Frege's system of 'logic' is inconsistent. The paradox arose because it is possible, in this system, to express the concept 'is a class which does not belong to itself'. Since classes are, for Frege, individual objects, and every concept defined over individual objects is assumed to have a class as its extension, this concept too must define a class – say R. Does R belong to itself? If it does then it must be a class which does not belong to itself; clearly a contradiction. But if it does not, then it is a class which does not belong to itself and hence belongs to R (itself).

However, RUSSELL (chapter 37) was attracted to Frege's strategy. If it were possible to show that all mathematics reduced to logic, then this would substantially strengthen the case for the empiricist denial of any autonomy to conceptual knowledge. Russell was an empirical realist: in other words, he assumed that there is a world that exists independently of our experience; it is a world of atomic events (or 'sense data'). The order of occurrence of such events is thus wholly contingent. Objective knowledge of this world, as attempted by natural science, takes the form of a description of global, structural features of the totality of events that constitutes the universe. It takes the form of knowledge of relations between sense data; sensed qualities, since they can only be known subjectively, must drop out of the scientific picture. Thus simple, atomic, sentences will all state that a certain relation holds between two or more sense data.

Because the order of events is contingent, we can never in fact be in a position to know the truth of any global description. Its truth conditions are such that only a non-finite being apprehending the whole space-time universe in a single intuition could directly verify its truth. The form that a direct description of such a world would take would be a list of all the true atomic sentences of the ideal logical language of science. If the use of mathematics in science is to lead to objectively true descriptive statements about this world, every description given using mathematical terms should be an abbreviation that is reducible without residue to some (possibly infinite) complex sentence built out of atomic sentences in such a way that the truth value of the complex is determined by those of its atomic components. In other words, the complex is constructed using (possibly infinite) truth-functions. Thus the definitions of all complex mathematical terms should indicate how, in principle, such an elimination could be effected. Such abbreviations are resorted to only because of the limited capacity of finite human minds. Mathematical truths are those that can be derived, logically, from an unpacking of the definitions of mathematical concepts. They do not say anything about the world, but they do help us make logically correct moves around the shorthand language that we have developed for describing it.

How did Russell propose to avoid the problem Frege ran into? His end solution is the so-called no-class theory which incorporates his 'ramified theory of types'. There are two key ideas here: (1) classes are logical fictions, they are not real individual objects; (2) for this reason, the language which incorporates these fictions must have a hierarchical structure. At the base level we have the empirical world of individuals. Concepts are defined over these and for convenience we introduce names of classes as a shorthand way of talking about all the things to which a given concept applies. These 'classes' clearly cannot be treated as belonging to the original level, but once they have been introduced it is possible to define new concepts using them, and to introduce more classes on a yet higher level. This has the effect of ruling out the possibility that a class should belong to itself and also the possibility of defining the concept 'is a class'; it is only possible to define 'is a class of level n'. However, as Russell admitted, there was no hope of developing mathematics within this framework without two substantial assumptions: the Axiom of Infinity and the Axiom of Reducibility.

The Axiom of Infinity says that there are infinitely many individuals in the universe. This is necessary because Russell could not use Frege's definitions of the natural numbers in quite their original form. The basic idea is still the same – 2 is to be the class of all two-membered classes of individuals – but a different definition of what it is to be a two-membered class is required, namely, one which does not refer to 0 and 1. The solution was to define a two-membered class as the extension of any concept F for which the following is true: 'there are distinct objects x and y which satisfy F and every object which satisfies F is identical either with x or with y'. However, this means that in a universe containing only one object, 2 would be the empty class, and so would 3 and every larger number. Thus to ensure that there are infinitely many natural numbers, there must be assumed to be an infinite universe. This illustrates the impossibility of simultaneously restricting objects to those that actually exist in the empirical world, insisting that mathematical terms be defined in such a way as to build in all their legitimate applications in advance, and claiming that mathematics does not embody any knowledge of or make any substantive claims about that actual world.

The Axiom of Reducibility is required to be able to define real numbers as infinite classes of rational numbers. Basically, it claims that all possible ways of grouping individuals (into 'classes') are already available using concepts definable at the first level of the hierarchy; that is, the introduction of more complex concepts whose definitions make reference to already defined concepts and classes does not in fact make any new discriminations possible; it does not genuinely enlarge our vocabulary for describing the structure of the world. This assumption is, however, equivalent to the claim that the reduction of mathematics to logic was supposed to help establish – the denial that concepts contribute to the content of what we say about the empirical world.

Bostock (1974, 1979), Field (1980), Chihara (1990) and Wright (1983) have made interesting attempts to follow logicist courses somewhat different from Russell's. But in each case, as in Russell's, the question arises of what exactly falls within the scope of logic. A convincing claim to have reduced mathematics to logic would require a clear way of distinguishing between what is and what is not logic, and well-grounded philosophical motivations for making the distinction exactly where one does. One way of making that distinction can be found in Quine's work. From the point of view of empiricism, logic should not introduce any ontology of abstract objects. Thus Quine (1970) limits logic to first order predicate calculus – the only objects talked about are individual objects. Modal logic and higher order logic are discounted, but if mathematics is reducible to logic at all, at least some form of one or both of these kinds of logic seems to be required. The alternative, the one taken by mathematicians and by Quine (1963), is to say that mathematics does not reduce to logic, but can be reduced to axiomatic set theory. Philosophical questions about the status of mathematics then become questions about the status of set theory, since this is the foundation on which everything else can be built. Analytic empiricists tended to accept, increasingly unquestioningly, this focus on foundations where everything comes to rest on logic and set theory. Here again the options of Platonic realism or some form of conceptualism are available. There are those who defend Platonic realism (see Brown 1991; Maddy 1990) by adopting the view that the best explanation for the successful application of mathematics is that it does express knowledge of principles underlying the structure of reality. This neatly turns the basic problem around but leaves one asking about the validity of this style of inference. What other explanations of success in application are there? How are we to adjudicate between competing explanations?

There is a competing explanatory strategy offered by Quine's (1969) NATURALIZED EPISTEMOLOGY (pp. 302–3). Although the Darwinian account of the descent of man has rendered implausible the idea that God created humans with intellects innately equipped to discern the mathematical principles according to which he created the universe, it can be used to underwrite the utility of our innate capacities. Our innate capacities are a product of evolution, that is, partly a matter of chance (random genetic variation) and partly a matter of natural selection, which favours those variations that have up to now proved to have adaptive value. Thus we find certain things self-evident because these things have, in the past, proved useful (they have conferred superior survival value). Adaptive value is, however, relative to the environing experience. We can have no guarantee that experience will not in the future require changes in mathematical theories, just as it may require changes in physical theories. Mathematical theories are no different in kind from other scientific theories; they are just more general and thus more resistant to change, because changing them means wholesale revisions in so many other areas. Acknowledging this, Quine adopts an instrumentalist attitude toward mathematics, by which it does postulate the existence of abstract objects and it does postulate them as real existents, but this is seen as part of the mythology that we have developed for dealing with the physical world. We are realist about such things, but it is (to use a term coined by Putnam) an 'internal realism' in which we can receive no justification that guarantees either ultimate truth or permanent utility.

4.2 Intuitionism, formalism and open questions

What logicist and set theoretic foundationalist approaches to mathematics significantly ignore is the question of how human beings actually acquire and use mathematical knowledge. They focus on questions of justification, relegating the study of methods of discovery to psychology. Wittgenstein and more recently Dummett, together with formalists and intuitionist critics of logicism, pointed out that the proposed logicist reduction, even if successful, begs central questions about the epistemological foundations of mathematics. This is because, to check that a full logical analysis of, for example, 'there are two things which are F' is correct, one must count occurrences of variables. In other words, a grasp of arithmetical concepts is presupposed in being able to read a formal logical language and understand its definitions of numbers. The analysis cannot indicate how we acquire a grasp of numerical concepts and hence cannot explain how we might manage to extend our grasp of finite, natural numbers to an understanding of terms purporting to refer to infinite sets, infinite series or transfinite numbers. These critics take it that one of the tasks of a philosophy of mathematics is to explain with what right human beings with finite capacities can introduce and claim to understand symbols purporting to represent the infinite – symbols whose use was intended to facilitate a knowledge of infinite structures.

Thus in various forms their concern is with the way in which, or the extent to which, a grasp of the infinite can be grounded in apprehension of the finite. Brouwer's (1881–1966) intuitionism was self-consciously Kantian in inspiration (Brouwer 1975). It grounds the arithmetic of natural numbers in the pure form of temporal intuition: the bare two-oneness which is a precondition of being able to apprehend anything as a manifold (a unity having internal complexity), and hence of any knowledge whatsoever. This is used to provide a foundation for analysis, via a theory of the creative subject. Brouwer followed Kant in eschewing use of the actually infinite. He thus rejected set theoretic approaches to the definition of the real numbers. Potentially infinite sequences, the paradigm of which is the natural number sequence, can be objects of knowledge but cannot be treated as if they were fully determinate. Such a sequence can only be known through the principle which generates it, the principle which assures us that it is unending. This may (for a lawless sequence) be simply the ever-available free choice of the creative subject to extend it. As Kant had already argued, reasoning concerning incomplete, potentially infinite totalities cannot validly employ reductio ad absurdum proofs. This is because we have no warrant for asserting that one of P or not-P must be true (the Principle of the Excluded Middle) in advance of generating the sequence to a point where it can be directly determined either that P or that not-P is the case. For some claims we have no guarantee that such a position can ever be reached (for example, regarding the conjecture that there are only finitely many times in the decimal expansion of π that a digit in an odd-numbered place is equal to the digit in the following even-numbered place). Because intuitionists reject the Principle of the Excluded Middle, and proofs based on it, there are many proofs which classical mathematicians accept but which are rejected by intuitionists.

Having rejected the Frege–Russell framework for logic, intuitionists developed a logic that does not take the principle of the excluded middle to be universally valid. Heyting (1956), Dummett (1973) and others taking the linguistic turn, have used this alternative logic as a means of providing a framework for intuitionism which does not appeal to Kantian intuition. An account of the meaning of a mathematical claim is not to be given by stating its truth conditions, but by a specification of the conditions under which one would be entitled to assert it (the proof conditions). This links the understanding of mathematical questions to knowledge of what a proof constituting an answer would look like. In arithmetic, the basic, canonical proofs are computations. Effective computational procedures thus figure prominently in intuitionist and constructivist mathematics. For this reason much of what has been developed has been found to be useful, even by those who do not espouse intuitionist or constructivist views and who do not reject the mathematics that requires use of the actual infinite.

Hilbert (1882–1943) (1926) adopted a position very similar to that of intuitionism with respect to the arithmetic of natural numbers. In his case, however, the founding intuitions were not those of pure imagination, but are derived from the use of tally systems and the progression to written numerals. He thus focuses on mathematics as a tool, or an instrument for solving problems, rather than as an elaboration of innate human intellectual structures. This means that when it comes to the use of infinite numbers and symbols purporting to represent infinitistic operations, Hilbert's response is conventionalist and instrumentalist, rather than conceptualist. While insisting that such signs can have for us no direct representational content, he allows that they may form a legitimate part of mathematics. Symbols have meaning which is derived from their use in formal mathematical systems, and their introduction is justified if it makes possible the solution of pre-existing problems and if the total system, consisting of the new symbols together with the old system which they extend, can be shown to be consistent.

But how can consistency be proved? One way to show that a theory is consistent is to show that it has a model. Thus non-Euclidean geometries were proved consistent relative to Euclidean geometry by showing that they had models in Euclidean geometry. Riemannian plane geometry can be interpreted as geometry on the surface of a Euclidean sphere, for example. But this still leaves open the question of what assures us of the consistency of Euclidean geometry. Hilbert (1899) had provided an axiomatization of Euclidean geometry where the axioms take the form of conditions on relations between points which must be satisfied if a totality of points is to be considered a Euclidean space. He further showed that the real numbers could be used to provide a model for these axioms. This reduces the consistency question to how to ensure the consistency of the theory of real numbers. For both Hilbert and intuitionists the consistency of the arithmetic of natural numbers and of effective computational procedures (finitary arithmetic) is guaranteed by the fact that models can actually be constructed (whether in intuition or on paper). The theory of real numbers, quantification over the totality of natural numbers – when treated as obeying the law of excluded middle – and the use of symbols for infinite sets and transfinite numbers all face the problem that, *ex hypothesi*, it is not possible to find effective methods for constructing models of the infinite totalities that they presuppose. The consistency question thus reduces to how to ground the use of symbols for infinitary objects, or infinitary operations, in the finite. What came to be called Hilbert's Programme was the suggestion that one should try to treat consistency as a formal property of symbol systems. Symbol systems are themselves finite, even if they contain symbols intended to refer to infinite objects or to infinitary operations. They are governed by rules whose correct application can be checked by appeal merely to a capacity to recognize the symbolic forms of formulae, which is something that does not require a grasp of their content. Proofs in such systems are finite symbol structures constructed according to formal rules. For inconsistency to arise it would have to be possible to prove some sentence and its negation; for example, to prove a sentence with a formal structure analogous to 'P and not-P'. If it were possible to show, by reference to the formal, finitary properties of the symbol system that no such formula could be the last line of a proof, then one would have a demonstration of consistency, one which uses only finitary, constructive methods.

Gödel and Consistency

Gödel (1906–78) (1931) proved (in his First Incompleteness Theorem) that it is impossible to complete Hilbert's Programme. He proved, using finitary methods, that if a formal system S capable of expressing arithmetic is consistent, then there is a sentence G expressible in the formal language of S which is such that neither it nor its negation can be proved in S. (G is so constructed that it can be interpreted as saying of itself that it is not provable.) He further showed (in his Second Incompleteness Theorem) that, as a result, an inconsistency arises if it is supposed that S can be proved consistent by finitary methods, for this would make it possible to prove in S that G is not provable in S. Since G is a formal expression of the claim that G is not provable in S, this would also be a proof of G. Hence (by the First Incompleteness Theorem) S would be inconsistent. The key idea behind this proof was to code all symbols of the formal language by numbers. Formulae and proofs, being finite symbol structures, can then also be coded by numbers, in such a way that their symbolic properties correspond to arithmetical properties of their numerical counterparts. Since the formal language was intended to be one that talks about numbers, this device allows the symbol system to have a double interpretation – in talking about numbers, it also talks about its own formulae.

This idea revealed the enormous potential of numbers as devices for coding symbolic and other structures. It is this power that was subsequently exploited to develop digital electronic computers. In this way, mathematics concerned with formal systems and effective computational procedures, which was developed in response to Hilbert's Programme and to the emphasis placed on effective procedures by intuitionism, not only found immense practical application but also led to the development of whole new areas of mathematics, including proof theory, model theory and recursive function theory.

But where does this leave the issue of justifying the use of infinitary mathematics? The exact interpretation of the philosophical import of Gödel's theorem has been much discussed (Detlefsen 1986) and there is no general consensus. What does seem to be agreed is that there is no hope of a complete justificational bootstrapping, using only finitary methods, to provide an unchallengeable legitimation of infinitary methods. Formal systems are themselves potentially infinite. So to prove results about a whole system S, such as C, which states, 'There is no proof in S of any formula of the form "P and not-P"', requires a proof about a potentially infinite totality. But without the assumption that it is legitimate to regard infinite totalities as completed objects (which is the assumption that a finitary consistency proof is trying to justify), there is no justification for asserting that either C or not-C must be true.

Similarly, set theory's ability to deliver definitive answers on foundational questions has been shown to be limited. What have come to be regarded as the core axioms of set theory – namely, the Zermelo–Fraenkel axiom and the Axiom of Choice which, together, we shall call ZFC – do not make possible a resolution of the question that Cantor sought to answer by introducing transfinite numbers, namely, the question of the structure of the continuum. Cantor proved that there can be no one–one correspondence between the real numbers and the natural numbers. He interpreted this result as proof that the cardinal number of the set of real numbers ($2^{\aleph_0}$) is greater than that of the set of natural numbers ($\aleph_0$). He also proved that the cardinal number ($\aleph_1$) of the set of all well-orderings of the natural numbers must be greater than that of the natural numbers, and that there could be no infinite set whose cardinality was greater than $\aleph_0$ but less than $\aleph_1$. That is, $\aleph_1$ is the next infinite cardinal number after $\aleph_0$. Cantor thought it was the case that $2^{\aleph_0}$ must be the same number as $\aleph_1$ (Cantor's Continuum Hypothesis, or CH), but he was unable to prove it. Gödel (1940) produced a model of ZFC (the constructible sets) in which this is the case, but Cohen (1966) produced one in which it is not. Together the results show that ZFC leaves the question undecided. The question remains, if we accept ZFC and use infinite sets, on what ground should we accept or reject CH? What difference, if any, does it make in other areas of mathematics?

These foundational questions require detailed technical work from mathematicians. The larger philosophical questions, however, concern evaluation of the whole foundational trend, a trend which has not, as had been hoped, provided once and for all solutions to questions about the status of mathematics and our justification for relying on it. It has produced lots of new and interesting mathematics and this in itself must surely tell us something about contemporary mathematics. The question is, what exactly does it tell us?

5   Beyond Foundationalism and Analytic Philosophy

Foundationalism is reductionist; it seeks to determine a hierarchical ordering of a given area of knowledge by pushing back to the starting-points from which all the rest deductively follows and hence can be rationally justified. Questions of the status of that whole area of knowledge thus come to focus on the status of these first principles. This presumes that there is some absolute, timeless, universal sense of rational order, or of what constitutes a rational justification. Yet as the historical outline presented here already shows, ideas about standards of rigour in mathematical proofs and about what constitutes logic have changed. The fact that mathematical reasoning was relational was enough at one time to suggest that it did not proceed solely according to principles of deductive logic. Now that relational reasoning has been incorporated into logic in the form of first order predicate calculus, that particular ground for thinking that mathematical reasoning does not reduce to logical deduction has been removed. But what are the grounds for thinking that first order predicate calculus is the ultimate, canonical form of logic? There are many potential challengers. Mathematicians have studied any number of formal 'logics', including modal logics, and many-valued logics and relevant logics. Information technology in its pursuit of the development of expert systems has in the past few years spurred a growth of interest in non-monotonic logics. Should we be monist or pluralist about logic? So long as foundationalism was the prevailing philosophic attitude toward accounts of knowledge in mathematics or any other area, it had to be presumed that there is just one system of logic, that which reveals the absolute, timeless, universal, rational order of knowledge and which provides an account of what constitutes a rational justification for belief. But foundationalism in other areas of epistemology has in the last half of this century increasingly been challenged. These assumptions about rationality no longer appear self-evident. Yet, as Bloor (1973) was aware when launching the strong programme in the sociology of knowledge, mathematics would be a test case for that programme, as it was for the analytic empiricists. It might be a bastion of a fixed, eternal rational order around which defenders of claims to universal rationality can rally. But the standards of rationality could prove less than fixed and the order presupposed by foundationalists could prove unnecessary to explain the development of actual mathematics or its applications. If this were true, then the claims of foundationalism and of access to universal standards of rationality would look shaky indeed. Bloor takes many of his cues from the anti-foundationalist later philosophy of WITTGENSTEIN (chapter 39) (1963, 1967) which emphasizes the way in which forms of life – social practices of which mathematics and language are integral parts – inform our sense of what is or is not rational. Wittgenstein's view of mathematics is non-reductionist. Moreover, he repeatedly emphasizes what he calls the 'motley of mathematics' – the variety to be found in its various branches and in their applications. He raises the question that other philosophers did not at that time dream of raising – questions of how it is determined what a proof proves and of how the logical 'must' acquires its force. He regarded mathematics as an integral part of the framework of linguistic conventions, which we develop in the context of trying to live with others in a material world. These conventions are learnt by training, that is, in repetitive, corrected practice in certain kinds of contexts. The meaning (or content) of a linguistic sign thus derives wholly from its customary uses. These uses themselves derive from forms of life in which they are embedded; for example, calculating as part of exchanging money for goods of various kinds. In normal circumstances the question of justification will not arise and can receive no answer beyond 'That is the way we do it'. This is because use is the bedrock of understanding. But as we know from the occurrences of ethical and practical dilemmas, elements of human practices can come into conflict with one another. It is in such circumstances that reflective conceptual analysis is required to make explicit what has been implicitly presumed in the practices that conflict (for instance, between reliance on both geometric intuition and on algebraic definitions in analytic geometry) and to resolve the conflict where possible by reference to values drawn from the wider framework of the form of life in which the practices are embodied.

Wittgenstein himself seems to have had a very narrow conception of the source of conceptual problems (an idea parallel to Kant's view that the human mind is prone to delude itself with illusions based on mistaking ideas of reason for real things). He thought that our everyday language tends to mislead us into belief in abstract objects. We tend to believe that wherever we have an expression that functions grammatically as a name, there must be something that it names. Analysis proceeds by revealing the logical grammar of problematic nouns – the grammar implicit in the practices of use which determine their content – and shows that the apparent names do not function as names. In this way Wittgenstein argues that neither numbers nor expressions for private sensations serve to stand for objects. But sociologists of knowledge, even when taking cues from Wittgenstein, do not necessarily limit themselves, in advance, concerning the possible sources of conceptual problems. Wittgenstein thought that the role of the philosopher in mathematics should be that of conceptual analyst, not reviser of practice. However, his own analyses led him to be highly critical of set theory and of the use of infinitistic methods. Indeed, it is hard to see how analyses intended to reveal how language misleads us could fail to be critical in their intent, by aiming to revise aspects of practice. Only if philosophers could work from a vantage point wholly outside the practices they analyse could their activity avoid being potentially revisionary. But, since participation in practice is, for Wittgenstein, the ground of understanding linguistic expressions employed in them, philosophers cannot begin their work from a stance of distanced non-engagement. Wittgenstein likened the role of philosopher to that of anthropologist; and, indeed, the philosopher faces the same problems of reflexivity as the anthropologist – the philosopher, and his or her studies, become part of the object he or she is studying and so modify it.

This reflexivity is strikingly illustrated by the work of the mathematician–philosophers, such as Frege, Russell, Hilbert and Brouwer, whose foundational studies profoundly changed the way mathematics is done. In an effort to resolve conceptual problems encountered within existing mathematical practices, they sought to clarify and codify the assumptions built into those practices. But to do so they had to forge new mathematical instruments and invent new terminology to provide explicit expression for principles and structures that had previously had only practical embodiments. Even as they examined the bases of existing mathematics they were in the process of changing it, and they left a subsequent generation to examine these bases of the mathematics so produced; that pattern of development is discussed by Bachelard (1928).

If we stand back from the foundational enterprise and its tendency to focus on limited segments of pure mathematics, it is evident that there are also forces for change in mathematics that derive from its applications. Once mathematics is examined in the context of the world in which it is employed, questions about its authoritative status may be treated as questions of social or political authority. Such authority will be linked to its utility and the power that it confers, and the fact that it reflects values of twenty-first-century culture, but not those of Plato's Athens (Latour 1987: ch. 6). Some research conducted from this point of view suggests that it may indeed be fruitful to explore the relations between changing standards of proof, the demands placed on a proof, and changing patterns of application; such changes may alter the kinds of reliability about which assurance is sought. For example, the increased use of computers in science (for computer modelling) and in technology (particularly the military technology of smart weapons) has already renewed the question of what constitutes a proof and has led to the quasi-empirical exploration of fractal geometry via computer graphics. In what circumstances, if any, might hundreds of pages of computer printout constitute a proof? MacKenzie (1993) reports on the case, which nearly came to court, of the VIPER computer chip. Its manufacturers claimed to have a proof of its reliability. A prospective purchaser challenged this claim, saying that what was touted as a proof was not. Computer chips are physical embodiments of complex mathematical structures. Assuming that the physical transcription is correct, there still remains the question of whether a chip made to that design will actually perform the function for which it was designed. It would be desirable to have a proof answering this question in advance of the chip's deployment in, for example, a weapons system. Moreover, since claims made in this context are part of commercial transactions, they also come under legal jurisdiction. This means that the question of what does or does not constitute a proof needs to be agreed in such a way that a legal ruling is possible. Here are two social demands on the notion of proof. They are demands that are not guaranteed to be compatible or realizable, and they are demands that arise because of the kind of application given to a particular sub-branch of mathematics. That branch itself owes much of its development to its intended military applications. Whether, how, or the extent to which these demands can be met, is a matter of reflective mathematical and conceptual analysis, combined with technical research.

Such demands push pure mathematical work in directions that it might not otherwise have taken, and they force changes in the concept of proof. What are the constraints within which such change can occur? Are there any objective constraints? If so, what is their origin? These are the kind of questions that come to the fore if foundationalism is discarded. They go back to the basic problem of the philosophy of mathematics and lead us to look afresh at the nexus of proof, discovery and application. This nexus has by now become very diverse and very complex because of the prominence of mathematics in our science and technology. This in turn means that to have any understanding of that science and technology, we must also understand the sources of the power of contemporary mathematics.

Further Reading

In many ways Frege's *Grundlagen* remains one of the best introductions to the philosophy of mathematics of the early part of this century. This could be coupled with the commentary by Dummett (1991). The selection of readings in Benacerraf and Putnam (1983) is excellent and provides a broad-based introduction to foundational approaches to the subject. Crucial papers from the period 1879–1931 are to be found in Van Heijenoort (1967). Shanker (1988) is a useful collection of papers assessing the significance of Gödel's theorem. Hofstadter (1979) provides an excellent introduction to the concept of a formal system and a sense of both its power and its wider conceptual connections. Tiles (1989) provides an historical introduction to philosophical aspects of set theory in relation to the continuum hypothesis.

An historical overview of developments in mathematics and their impact on views about its status is provided by Kline (1980). Another way into the subject is through explanations of the conceptual challenges posed by and faced in mathematics that are written for non-mathematicians. Of these, Dantzig (1930) remains a useful introduction to the intriguing aspects of numbers. The more recent Reid (1992) covers some of the same ground. Davis and Hersch (1983) gives a broader sampling of the kinds of issues raised by mathematics and of their history, as does Stewart (1987). Stewart (1989) is an excellent, eminently readable historical treatment of the relation between chaos and order, and it keeps mathematics in the context of its relation to physical theory. It begins with a discussion of the Newtonian vision of a clockwork universe and is mainly concerned with the origins of chaos theory. Somewhat different in character, but an interesting challenge to foundationalist approaches, is Lakatos (1976).

Readers might be interested in the early history of philosophical reflections on mathematics. Most of Aristotle's remarks are to be found in *Metaphysics* (1941b: I, M, N). Much of Plato's position we get from Aristotle's reports, the originals having been lost. But there are some remarks in *Republic* (1961a: Books 6 and 7). The *Timeaus* (1961b) was, however, the work which inspired many of the neo-Platonists, via Plotinus. Yates (1964) and French (1972) give some idea of the character of Renaissance neo-Platonism. Caspar's (1959) biography of Kepler gives insight into the way in which his vision of the place of mathematics in the world was integrated with his astronomical work.

References

Aristotle, 1941a: *Posterior Analytics*. In R. McKeon (ed.) *The Basic Works of Aristotle*. New York: Random House.

——1941b: *Metaphysics*. In R. McKeon (ed.) *The Basic Works of Aristotle*. New York: Random House.

Augustine, St, Bishop of Hippo 1955: *The Problem of Free Choice* (translated by M. Pontifex). Westminster, MD: Newman Press.

——1990: *De Musica* (commentary by Pizzani and Melanese). Palermo: Edizioni Augustinus. Translation in L. Schopp et al. (1947–) *The Fathers of the Church*, vol. 4. Washington, DC: Catholic University of America.

Bachelard, G. 1928: *Essai sur la connaissance approchée*. Paris: J. Vrin.

Benacerraf, P. and Putnam, H. (eds) 1964: *Philosophy of Mathematics: Selected Readings*. Englewood Cliffs, NJ: Prentice-Hall. Revised edition, Cambridge: Cambridge University Press (1983).

Berkeley, G. 1947–57 [1734]: *The Analyst or A Discourse Addressed to an Infidel Mathematician*. In *The Works of George Berkeley, Bishop of Cloyne* (edited by A. A. Luce and T. E. Jessop). London: Thomas Nelson and Sons.

——1995 [1710, 1713]: *Principles of Human Knowledge and Three Dialogues* (edited and introduced by Howard Robinson). Oxford: Oxford University Press.

Bloor, D. 1973: Wittgenstein and Mannheim on the Sociology of Mathematics. *Studies in the History and Philosophy of Science*, 4, 2, 173–91.

Bostock, D. 1974: *Logic and Arithmetic, Vol. 1: Natural Numbers*. Oxford: Clarendon Press.

——1979: *Logic and Arithmetic, Vol. 2: Rational and Irrational Numbers*. Oxford: Clarendon Press.

Brouwer, L. E. J. 1975: Consciousness Philosophy and Mathematics. Proceedings of 10th International Congress of Philosophy, Amsterdam 1940. Reprinted in *L. E. J. Brouwer, Collected Works, Part 1* (edited by A. Heyting). Amsterdam: North-Holland.

Brown, J. R. 1991: *The Laboratory of the Mind: Thought Experiments in the Natural Sciences*. London: Routledge.

Cantor, G. 1895: Beiträge zur Begrundung der transfiniten Mengenlehre, Part I. *Mathematische Annalen*, 46, 481–512. Translated by P. E. B. Jourdain (1915) *Contributions to the Founding of the Theory of Transfinite Numbers*. Chicago: Open Court, and New York: Dover (1955).

Caspar, M. 1959: *Kepler*. London: Abelard-Schuman.

Chihara, C. 1990: *Constructibility and Mathematical Existence*. Oxford: Clarendon Press.

Cohen, P. J. 1966: *Set Theory and the Continuum Hypothesis*. New York: W. A. Benjamin.

Dantzig, T. 1930: *Number: The Language of Science*. London: Allen and Unwin.

Davies, P. C. W. and Brown, J. (eds) 1988: *Superstrings: A Theory of Everything*. Cambridge: Cambridge University Press.

Davis, P. J. and Hersh, R. 1983: *The Mathematical Experience*. Harmondsworth: Penguin Books.

Dedekind, R. 1963 [1888] Was sind und was sollen Zahlen? Braunschweig: Vieweg. Translated by W. W. Beman (1901) *Essays on the Theory of Numbers*. Chicago: Open Court, and New York: Dover (1963).

Descartes, R. 1985–91a [1629]: *Rules for the Direction of our Native Intelligence*. In J. Cottingham, R. Stoothoff and D. Murdoch (eds) *The Philosophical Writings of Descartes*. Cambridge: Cambridge University Press.

——1985–91b [1641]: *Meditations on First Philosophy*. In J. Cottingham, R. Stoothoff and D. Murdoch (eds) *The Philosophical Writings of Descartes*. Cambridge: Cambridge University Press.

Detlefsen, M. 1986: *Hilbert's Program*. Dordrecht: Reidel.

Dummett, M. 1973: The Philosophical Basis of Intuitionistic Logic. In *Proceedings of the Logic*

Colloquium, Bristol, July 1973, ed. H. E. Rose and J. C. Shepherdson. Amsterdam: North-Holland (1975). Reprinted in P. Benacerraf and H. Putnam (eds) 1983: *Philosophy of Mathematics: Selected Readings*. Cambridge: Cambridge University Press.

——1991: *Frege: Philosophy of Mathematics*. London: Duckworth.

Euclid 1956: *The Thirteen Books of Euclid's Elements* (translated by T. L. Heath). Cambridge: Cambridge University Press. Second edition, New York: Dover.

Field, H. 1980: *Science Without Numbers*. Oxford: Blackwell.

Frege, G. 1884: *Die Grundlagen der Arithmetik*. Breslau: Koebner. Translated by J. L. Austin, 1959: *The Foundations of Arithmetic*. Oxford: Blackwell.

——1893: *Grundgesetze der Arithmetik, Band. 1*. Jena: Verlag Hermann Pohle. Translated by M. Furth, 1964: *The Basic Laws of Arithmetic*. Berkeley and Los Angeles: University of California Press.

French, P. J. 1972: *John Dee: The World of an Elizabethan Magus*. London: Routledge.

Gödel, K. 1931: Uber formal unentscheidare Sätze der Principia Mathematica und verwandter Systeme. *Monatshefte für Mathematik und Physik*, 38. Translated as 'On formally undecidable propositions of *Principia Mathematica* and related systems', in J. van Heijenoort (ed.) 1967: *From Frege to Gödel: A Source Book in Mathematical Logic, 1879–1931*. Cambridge, MA: Harvard University Press.

——1940: The Consistency of the Continuum Hypothesis. *Annals of Mathematics Studies*, 3.

Heyting, A. 1956: *Intuitionism: An Introduction*. Amsterdam: North-Holland. Selections reprinted in Benacerraf and Putnam (1964) and (1983).

Hilbert, D. 1899: *Grundlagen der Geometrie*. Stuttgart: Teubner. Seventh edition translated as *Foundations of Geometry*. Lasalle, IL: Open Court (1971).

——1926: On the Infinite. Delivered before a congress of the Westphalian Mathematical Society. Originally published in *Mathematische Annalen*, 95, 161–90. English translation in Benacerraf and Putnam (1964) and (1983).

Hofstadter, D. R. 1979: *Gödel, Escher, Bach: An Eternal Golden Braid*. New York: Basic Books; Hassocks, Sussex: Harvester Press.

Kepler, J. 1940 [1619]: *Harmonice Mundi, Gesammelte Werke*, Vol. 6. Munich: H. Beck. Translated as *The Harmonies of the World*. Chicago: Encyclopaedia Britannica (1990).

Kline, M. 1980: *Mathematics: The Loss of Certainty*. Oxford: Oxford University Press.

Körner, S. 1960: *The Philosophy of Mathematics: An Introductory Essay*. London: Hutchinson.

Koyré, A. 1973: *The Astronomical Revolution*. Paris: Hermann; London: Methuen.

Lakatos, I. 1976: *Proofs and Refutations*. Cambridge: Cambridge University Press.

Latour, B. 1987: *Science In Action*. Cambridge, MA: Harvard University Press.

MacKenzie, D. 1993: Negotiating Arithmetic, Constructing Proofs. *Social Studies of Science*, 23, 1, 37–65.

Maddy, P. 1990: Realism in Mathematics. Oxford: Clarendon Press.

Nerlich, G. 1976: *The Shape of Space*. Cambridge: Cambridge University Press.

Newton, I. 1931 [1730]: *Opticks or A Treatise of the Reflections, Refractions, Inflections and Colours of Light*. London: Bell and Sons; New York: Dover (1952).

Plato 1961a: *Republic*. In E. Hamilton and H. Cairns (eds) *The Collected Dialogues of Plato*. Princeton, NJ: Princeton University Press.

——1961b: *Timaeus*. In E. Hamilton and H. Cairns (eds) *The Collected Dialogues of Plato*. Princeton, NJ: Princeton University Press.

Quine, W. V. O. 1963: *Set Theory and its Logic*. Englewood Cliffs, NJ: Prentice-Hall.

——1969: Epistemology Naturalized. In *Ontological Relativity and Other Essays*, New York and London: Columbia University Press.

——1970: *Philosophy of Logic*. Englewood Cliffs, NJ: Prentice-Hall.

Reid, C. 1992: *From Zero to Infinity*. Washington, DC: The Mathematical Association of America.

Russell, B. 1919: *Introduction to Mathematical Philosophy*. London: Allen and Unwin.

Shanker, S. G. (ed.) 1988: *Gödel's Theorem in Focus*. Beckenham: Croom Helm; New York: Methuen.

Spinoza, B. 1992: *Ethics with the Treatise on the Emendation of the Intellect and Selected Letters*. Indianapolis, IN: Hackett.

Stewart, I. 1987: *The Problems of Mathematics*. Oxford: Oxford University Press.

—— 1989: *Does God Play Dice? The Mathematics of Chaos*. Oxford: Blackwell.

Tiles, M. 1989: *The Philosophy of Set Theory: An Historical Introduction to Cantor's Paradise*. Oxford: Blackwell.

Van Heijenoort, J. (ed.) 1967: *From Frege to Gödel: A Source Book in Mathematical Logic, 1879–1931*. Cambridge, MA: Harvard University Press.

Wang, H. 1968: *Beyond Analytic Philosophy: Doing Justice to What We Know*. Cambridge, MA: MIT Press.

Whitehead, A. N. and Russell, B. 1913: *Principia Mathematica*. Cambridge: Cambridge University Press.

Wittgenstein, L. 1922: *Tractatus Logico-Philosophicus* (translated by C. K. Ogden). London: Routledge.

—— 1963: *Philosophical Investigations*. Oxford: Blackwell.

—— 1967: *Remarks on the Foundations of Mathematics*. Oxford: Blackwell.

Wright, C. 1983: *Frege's Conception of Numbers as Objects*. Aberdeen: Aberdeen University Press.

Yates, F. A. 1964: *Giordano Bruno and the Hermetic Tradition*. London: Routledge.

Discussion Questions

1　In what sense, if any, is mathematics objectively true?

2　Does mathematics need foundations?

3　How can theoretical reasoning about mathematical objects be both so secure and so useful?

4　Is mathematical knowledge different from knowledge in other disciplines?

5　Do we have a right to expect mathematical results to have applications and to be reliable in their applications?

6　Does any account of mathematics depend upon a prior choice of metaphysical perspective? Can there be mathematics without metaphysics?

7　Is grounding mathematics in *a priori* forms of intuition an improvement over grounding it in innate ideas or innate structures of the intellect?

8　Is the infinite in mathematics potentially infinite rather than actually infinite? What difference would this make?

9　Does Einstein's use of non-Euclidean geometries show that geometry does not give *a priori* knowledge of the structure of the physical world?

10　Is the correctness of mathematics as part of a scientific theory any less an empirical question than the correctness of a scientific theory?

11　What is the importance of sets or classes in our account of mathematics?

12　How can we tell whether a realist account of mathematics is the best explanation of the success of applications of mathematics to the world? Even if it is, does this provide a good reason to accept a realist ontology?

13 How can a grasp of the infinite be grounded in apprehension of the finite?

14 Is it always the case that P is true or that not-P is true?

15 What is the place of effective computational procedures in mathematics?

16 Can extending our success at problem solving justify the introduction of new mathematical symbols, even if they do not have any direct representational content?

17 If we discard foundationalism, what are the consequences for our account of proof, discovery and application?

18 Are there any specifically mathematical principles of inference?

19 Can there be an adequate finite representation of something infinite?

20 If space and time are part of nature, is mathematics a natural science? If so, can we understand mathematical certainty?

12

Philosophy of Social Science

MARTIN HOLLIS

Philosophical problems arise from our attempts to gain insight into ourselves and our social institutions, to comprehend other societies, and to make sense of social change. The following chapter brings together a complex array of questions in the philosophy of social science by critically exploring two crucial distinctions: scientific explanation versus interpretative understanding and individualism versus holism. Relations are traced with other major fields of philosophy: EPISTEMOLOGY (chapter 1), METAPHYSICS (chapter 2), PHILOSOPHY OF MIND (chapter 5), ETHICS (chapter 6), POLITICAL AND SOCIAL PHILOSOPHY (chapter 8) and PHILOSOPHY OF SCIENCE (chapter 9). Discussions of recent work on rationality and social relativism lead to a final agenda of unresolved problems.

If the climate of Africa became suddenly cooler and wetter, the social effects would be enormous. Agriculture would change character as some crops became easier to grow and others harder. As the demand for both sorts shifted, some people and groups would become richer and others poorer. As some rose in social esteem and others fell, social roles and relations would change. With shifts in status and the distribution of power, political effects would start to emerge. We need not speculate further to see that whole societies could be transformed.

Such changes would not simply be dictated by the change in climate, however large. What happened would depend on how people and groups responded. Some millet farmers would fare better than other millet farmers, and some kinds of farmer better than other kinds. In different places, traders, middlemen, bureaucrats or holders of public office would play different parts. Again, without speculating further, we can see that any uniformities in the response would have to lie deep below the surface of events and that, even so, local conditions and individual initiatives would matter.

Observers trying to make sense of events would have, very broadly, two directions of approach. One would be to connect the variety of reaction with differences in social structure and organization, thereby presuming that there are social systems, whose responses to pressure are transmitted to their components in ways which vary with the system. This approach could be termed 'top down'. The other would be to treat macroscopic changes as fusions of microscopic changes by a process whose final elements were at least local and perhaps individual. This approach could be termed

	Explanation	Understanding
Holism	Systems	Cultures
Individualism	Rational choices	Subjective meanings

Figure 12.1   The four keys to analysing social action.

'bottom up'. It is not immediately plain whether these approaches are conflicting or complementary.

Meanwhile the idea of 'making sense of events' is not a clear one and we can usefully gloss it, again very broadly, in two ways. One relies on notions of *explanation* that are familiar from the natural sciences and their philosophy, where the aim is to identify the causes which produce, generate or perhaps are merely correlated with what happens next. The other appeals to ideas of *understanding* that are familiar to students of history or everyday life, who seek to identify the meaning of action (in some sense of that elusive phrase). Here too it is not obvious in advance whether explanation and understanding can finally be combined, however sharply we may want to contrast them at the start.

The last two paragraphs might suggest that 'top down' goes with explanation and 'bottom up' with understanding. That is not the intended message, however. This chapter sets off from a presumption that analysis can proceed in either direction by either method. Abstractly speaking, we start with the two-by-two matrix shown in figure 12.1, which provides the framework for the chapter. Ignoring what is written in the four boxes for the moment, let us take note of the columns and rows.

Our leading question will concern the columns – the claims of Explanation and Understanding to hold the key to social scientific knowledge. Are the phenomena of the social world to be explained after the manner of the natural sciences or understood in some manner special to the study of social life? That is a complex question with three aspects. One aspect is *methodological*, inviting philosophical discussion of scientific method and of whether there is a single, universal method for natural and social sciences alike. One aspect is *epistemological*, posing the Problem of Knowledge in general and the Problem of Other Minds in particular. The third aspect is *ontological*, to do with what there is (or 'the study of being', to translate the ancient Greek terms involved literally). We shall be asking what general kinds or categories of phenomena there are in the social world, what sort of method is best able to reveal how it works and what warrants claims to knowledge of these matters.

The rows pose questions of analytical priority. They bid us think whether the social world is to be analysed finally into particulars, especially agents and actions ('individualism'), or into structures ('holism'), or whether both have an irreducible claim to feature in the final account. In deciding whether analysis can best proceed 'top down' or 'bottom up' we shall again be engaged in methodology, EPISTEMOLOGY (chapter 1) and ONTOLOGY (chapter 2).

But, as I have just said, the chapter is chiefly organized round the distinction between Explanation and Understanding. Section 1 will explore the case for naturalistic explanation in the social sciences, the theme being that, since human beings belong to the natural order, the social world presents no final obstacle to the methods that serve the natural sciences so well. Section 2 will mount a rival case for interpretative understanding, the theme here being that, since social actors view social life from the inside, the social sciences must make sense of it by doing likewise. Section 3 will examine the scope for collaboration between explaining and understanding, thereby identifying some fertile philosophical questions that remain unsettled, as the short concluding section will point out by way of summary.

1 Explanation

The sole foundation for belief in the natural sciences is this idea, that the general laws dictating the phenomena of the universe are necessary and constant. Why should this principle be any the less true for the development of the intellectual and moral faculties of man than for the other operations of nature?

This beguiling question comes from a book written in 1794 amid the European ferment of ideas known as the Enlightenment. The author is the Marquis de Condorcet (1743–94), mathematician, philosopher and social scientist, and the book offers what its title calls a *Sketch for a Historical Picture of the Progress of the Human Mind* (1955). Condorcet traces the historical development of human society and rejoices in the amazingly rapid progress made in the two centuries since the scientific revolution. He looks forward to an enlightened future where 'the sun will one day shine only on free men who own no other light than their reason'. His theme, and the key to this progress, is recognition that 'Truth, happiness and virtue are bound together by an indissoluble chain'.

Such optimism may ring hollow two centuries later; and Condorcet himself died in prison shortly after finishing the book, a victim of the French Revolution in which he fervently believed. But his linking of truth, happiness and virtue stems from a vision of humanity and social order which still influences the social sciences and their philosophy. If nature includes HUMAN NATURE (pp. 672–3), the progress of knowledge will find no radical obstacle in 'the intellectual and moral faculties of man'. A new science of human beings will bring us knowledge of human nature and hence the power to school and satisfy our desires. Virtue comes into the story in so far as we use this power for the benefit of humanity, thus creating a free and enlightened social order.

The quotation serves to introduce naturalism, to give it its current name, under the three aspects mentioned above. The ontology is naturalistic. Nature, as pictured by Condorcet, is an ordered realm of objects governed by natural laws. It includes 'man' and 'the intellectual and moral faculties of man', whose development has been among 'the other operations of nature'. Although this stops short of saying that human beings are solely physical creatures, it does imply that the human mind is not the sort of non-physical thinking substance (*res cogitans*) claimed by DESCARTES (1596–1650) (chapter 26) and Cartesian dualists. As a contemporary put it, 'Man is not fashioned out of a more precious clay; Nature has used only one and the same dough, in which she has merely varied the leaven.' This exactly captures the moving spirit of naturalism in the human sciences.

The claim that the laws of nature are general, dictate the phenomena of the universe and are 'necessary and constant' ushers in a naturalistic idea of scientific knowledge and how to acquire it. The method which Condorcet took to be the foundation of the scientific revolution was one of identifying the hidden laws of nature and using them to explain phenomena. By reason we can discern the laws and thus detect the underlying causal order of the universe.

If this broad sketch were enough to work with, we could proceed at once to questions about the intellectual and moral faculties of human beings. But, as the chapters on EPISTEMOLOGY (chapter 1) and the PHILOSOPHY OF SCIENCE (chapter 9) make clear, the sketch can be filled in several ways. So objections to one naturalistic account of the social realm may not be objections to all. Although readers will need to refer to those other chapters to make full sense of this one, we can usefully pick out some key issues which are especially relevant to the philosophy of social science.

Condorcet's remark that the laws of nature are 'necessary and constant' gestures to an old dispute, which has affected the social sciences from the start. On the one hand there is the RATIONALIST (chapters 26 and 27) contention that nature is constant because its laws hold of necessity; on the other, there is the empiricist retort, still novel at the end of the eighteenth century, that there is nothing necessary about nature itself and that any 'necessity' is therefore only a matter of how our minds work. We attribute necessity to what, if we reflect carefully, we know only to be constant in its workings. Although today's philosophers usually deem this contrast too stark and simple, as we shall note in a moment, it remains a useful pointer to some radical differences of approach to social theory.

The rationalist contention goes with a strongly determinist vision of nature as a system driven by hidden forces. This vision had inspired Descartes and Newton (1642–1727), the leading seventeenth-century philosophers of the scientific revolution. In a popular image of the time, the world is like a perfect watch, with 'Wheels and Springs so out of sight that we have been long a-guessing at the movement of the Universe' (Fontenelle 1929). In the mechanical universe, whatever happens *must* happen, given the previous state and the laws of nature, and science advances by demonstrating these necessities. Scientific knowledge, therefore, cannot depend on SENSE EXPERIENCE (chapter 26), since, in the words of an old adage, 'the senses reveal no necessities'. It depends instead on our intellectual faculty of 'intuition', aided by mathematical models which allow demonstrative reasoning. Newtonian mechanics and Cartesian geometrical physics are classic examples.

Applied to the social world, this ambitious scheme has striking implications. Its firm distinction between 'phenomena' and 'laws' suggests some kind of social or psychological physics, of whose explanatory elements we, as actors, may be unaware. Moreover, if we too are like watches driven by hidden wheels and springs, our cherished free will may turn out to be an illusion. Many social scientists have accepted these implications, starting with Thomas HOBBES (1588–1679) (chapter 28), whose influence on social and political philosophy has been pervasive. In *Leviathan* Hobbes (1990) presents human beings as mechanical individuals for whom the will is merely 'the last appetite in deliberating' (ibid.: ch. 5). We are driven by an urge for self-preservation and 'a perpetual and restless desire for power after power, that ceaseth only in death' (ibid.: ch. 11). We know this, he maintains, by discerning 'laws of reason' which account for human behaviour. Yet, by harnessing this knowledge, we can learn to make and maintain the social order without which human beings will destroy one another. 'Reason is the pace, increase of science the way, and the benefit of mankind the end' (ibid.: ch. 5).

Leviathan remains a leading example of an individualist account, in which social arrangements emerge from the interplay of individuals rationally seeking self-preservation. For a notable example of a structural account, I recommend the *Preface to A Contribution to the Critique of Political Economy* (1971) by Karl MARX (1818–83) (chapter 34). There we are told that the economic structure of society is 'the real foundation, on which rises a legal and political superstructure and to which correspond definite forms of social consciousness . . . It is not the consciousness of men which determines their being but, on the contrary, their social being which determines their consciousness.' Here too the appeal to hidden forces goes with a denial of familiar notions of free will. Yet Marx too, at least in other works and other moods, holds that men make their own history, even though not under conditions chosen by themselves, and that science can strengthen this power by revealing what is feasible. Questions of freedom and determinism are thus far from straightforward and we shall return to them.

Meanwhile, Hobbes and Marx both belong in the left-hand column of figure 12.1 and serve nicely to illustrate the bottom and top boxes respectively. But this is not to say that it is yet clear what sense attaches to 'necessity' in these and in similar accounts. Perhaps there is indeed good reason to think that laws of nature are not merely 'constant', and that, for instance, what goes up must, in some sense, come down because of the laws of gravity. But it is far from plain than any 'must' involved in the power of forces or the relation of causes to effects is the kind of 'must' involved in truths of mathematics. Even in the seventeenth-century image of the world as a watch the compulsion envisaged is as much to do with mechanisms as with formulae. Two distinct ideas are involved, one of logical necessity and one, more mysteriously, of natural necessity. Although this is not the moment to explore the latter, the ambiguity helps to clear the way for the rise of empiricism and the denial that necessity of any kind is a feature of the working of nature.

Here the classic source is David HUME (1711–76) (chapter 31), especially *A Treatise of Human Nature* (Hume 1978a), which was intended to lay the foundations for 'a complete system of the sciences'. It is evident, Hume said in the introduction, that all sciences relate to human nature. 'Even *Mathematics, Natural Philosophy, and Natural Religion* are in some measure dependent on the science of MAN; since they lie under the cognizance of men, and are judged by their powers and faculties.' Hence a science of human beings, grounded in an empirical study of 'Logic, Morals, Criticism and Politics', would comprehend everything which can tend to the improvement of the human mind. The method was to be 'experience and observation', applied to 'men's behaviour in company, in affairs and in their pleasures'. The aim was 'explaining all effects from the simplest and fewest causes'.

To undermine the grand pretensions of Reason, Hume drew a sharp distinction between 'matters of fact and existence' and 'relations of ideas'. Matters of fact are always contingent and known to us by experience. Any 'necessity' to them can only be due to our mental habit of expecting established correlations to continue, since genuine necessities, like those of mathematics, lie solely in relations of ideas. Thus we have no warrant in experience for holding that causes necessitate their effects, produce them or make them happen. As far as our knowledge of objects and events goes, a cause is merely immediately prior to, contiguous with and regularly conjoined with what we label its effect. 'Real' connections only reflect our expectation that regular sequences will be repeated in like conditions.

By this account social science is concerned with 'men's behaviour in company, in affairs and in their pleasures', without any presumption that scientific determinism denies human freedom. A similarly empiricist and individualist line is taken by John Stuart MILL (1806–73) (chapter 35) in *A System of Logic* (1961), whose Book 6 'On the Logic of the Moral Sciences' remains the best worked out manifesto for empiricism in social science. Chapter 7 of Book 6 opens with this challenging declaration:

> The laws of the phenomena of society are, and can be, nothing but the laws of the actions and passions of human beings united together in the social state. Men, however, in a state of society, are still men; their actions and passions are obedient to the laws of individual human nature. Men are not, when brought together, converted into another kind of substance, with different properties; as hydrogen and oxygen are different from water, or as hydrogen, oxygen, carbon, and azote, are different from nerves, muscles, and tendons. Human beings in society have no properties but those which are derived from, and may be resolved into, the laws of nature of individual man.

If that still sounds determinist, it is meant to. Mill, like Hume, takes the compatibilist line that free action is caused action whose causes lie in the desires and character of the agent, guided by beliefs about its likely success in satisfying these desires. Free action thus presupposes a regular and predictable world and is given all the more scope as science learns to chart the precise regularities. If this neat reconciliation of freedom and determinism is tenable, many awkward problems for a scientific approach to human behaviour vanish. Here readers may wish to pause and consider whether it is indeed tenable. Hobbes (1990: ch. 21), Hume (1978a: I, 8) and Mill (1961: VI, 2) offer a useful starting-point.

Hobbes, Hume and Mill together give us a strong case for believing that the intellectual and moral faculties of man are no obstacle to the extension of science to the social world. They agree that, in Hobbes's words, 'Reason is the pace', even if Hobbes is a rationalist and Hume and Mill empiricists. They agree that science advances by discovering causal laws and that determinism is no threat to human freedom, properly conceived. All three are squarely in the main line of modern philosophy, in short, and that is a good, clear way to begin. But matters cannot be kept so straightforward, I fear, and we must next think more deeply about scientific method. As we saw, Hume's corrective to a confusion about necessity was to dispense with it altogether as a real-world component of causal laws or causal explanation. That is splendidly bold. But is it satisfactory?

Does science need some stronger distinction between laws and regularities than Hume's empiricism offers? We can best focus the question with the help of a recent example. It comes from a 1970 social science textbook on scientific method, where the authors use it to illustrate the style of explanation which they recommend (Przeworski and Teune 1970). They introduce a typical French worker, Monsieur Rouget, and enquire, 'Why does M. Rouget, age twenty four, blond hair, brown eyes, a worker in a large factory, vote Communist?' They then remark that 'to explain the vote of M. Rouget, one must rely on probabilistic statements that are relevant for voting behaviour and have been sufficiently confirmed against various sets of evidence'. When this process of evidence gathering is complete, they suggest, an explanation will emerge in the following form:

1   M. Rouget is a young male worker employed in a large factory in a social system where the church plays an important role.
2   Young workers in large factories vote Left with a probability of .60 to .70, and in those systems in which the role of the church is strong, men vote Left more often than women; *therefore it is highly likely* (probability of .80) that
3   M. Rouget votes for a party of the Left.

The guiding idea here is that to explain behaviour is to arrive at reliable generalizations from which it could have been predicted with high PROBABILITY (pp. 308–10). Whether such generalizations count as causal depends solely on how well the predictions derived from them fare. In Humean spirit, there is nothing more to it by way of causal connections or hidden mechanisms. A so-called law of nature is simply a well-enough confirmed hypothesis and the only test of a hypothesis is its predictive success.

This account of explanation is usually known as the covering law model and its rule of application as the hypothetico-deductive method. Figure 12.2 presents it in diagramatic form, taken (slightly simplified) from another textbook, Richard Lipsey's *Introduction to Positive Economics* (1972).

The diagram shows a process of formulating hypotheses or theories, deducing their implications and testing them against experience. When observation confirms the theory, 'no consequent action is required'; when it does not, the theory is to be amended or replaced. Again, there is no suggestion that causal laws have more to them than what is involved in this filtering process, which, in both textbooks, has to do solely with degrees of probability.

How satisfactory is this idea of explanation? On the credit side, it is as simple and elegant as one could wish, especially if one is impressed by the empiricist case for holding that only experience can justify claims to knowledge of the world. But there are several large objections.

If we focus these doubts on Monsieur Rouget, we soon wonder whether the proposed form of explanation even begins to tell us why he votes Communist. That he belongs to a group of which some 80 per cent votes Communist may be relevant, but is hardly revealing. Why do age, sex and the size of the factory and the strength of the church matter, whereas colour of hair and eyes do not? Here are three kinds of answer, each opening further lines of enquiry.

(1)   Post-empiricist
The explanation offered is inadequate not because it fails to unearth hidden causes but because it is too sketchy. We need more of a web of correlations, compactly stated

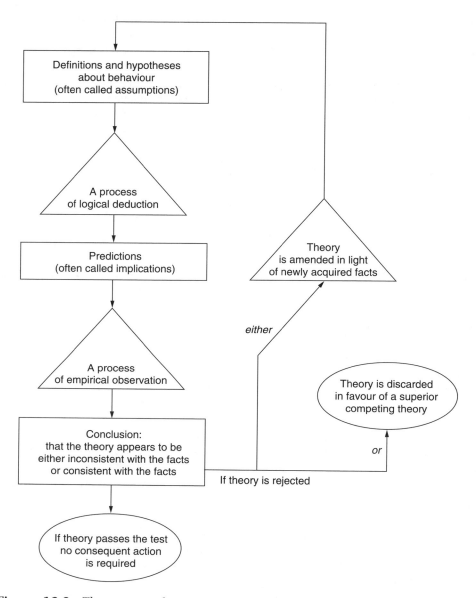

Figure 12.2 The covering law model of explanation, which use the hypothetico-deductive method to form hypotheses, deduce implications and test them against evidence.

and elegantly ordered so that they have greater predictive power for a larger set of cases. Empiricism is right to maintain that explanations stand or fall solely by the test of experience and thus rely wholly on what experience can tell us. But experience is never brute and its verdicts never unambiguous. It always involves the application of concepts, in the spirit of Kant's remark that percepts without concepts are blind. The mind is not a blank tablet on which experience writes, but an active interpreter bringing theories to bear. Hence there are no facts that are neutral between all interpretations and, in explaining anything, we are *choosing* which theory to prefer.

This first answer has two principal sources. One is Karl Popper's idea of science as 'Conjectures and Refutations', to cite the title of the famous paper in Popper (1969). Popper argues that observation is never theory-free and can never establish or even confirm the truth of a hypothesis or conjecture. But it can in principle *refute* the genuinely empirical ones (as opposed to the 'pseudo-scientific', which, like Marxism or psychoanalysis, in his view, are so organized that they can be squared with all possible experience). But progress is possible because refutation is a moment of objective truth, even if confirmation is not. This is not radical enough for the other main source, PRAGMATISM (chapter 36), especially Quine (1953), where there are no moments of unvarnished truth independent of all webs of interpretation. Refutations are decisive only if we choose to regard them as such. Explanation becomes holistic, with consequences that I cannot trace in this chapter. Meanwhile the reasons for picking out M. Rouget's age and sex but not his hair and eyes are pragmatic. They instance reliable regularities which mesh well with wider patterns in our interpretation of social life.

(2) Realist

No explanation has yet been offered either for M. Rouget's vote or for the leftist tendency of the groups to which he belongs. To ask, 'Why?' bids us identify *causes* – psychological or social processes, or both. Indeed it may be that processes depend in turn on causal mechanisms – powerful particulars whose powers do not somehow derive from 'laws of nature' but, in sum, are the reality of those laws. In any case, the old idea of structures and forces external to the enquiring mind remains a necessary presupposition of science. If it is asked how we can know that there are any, and hence how we are entitled to such an ontology, the answer is that science can and should proceed by inference to the best explanation.

Whether the best explanation is psychological or social (or both) raises the 'vertical' question of individualism and holism. The individualist case has traditionally depended, as in Hobbes, Hume and Mill, on conscious or unconscious motives inherent in human nature and on an account of how these motives can generate social organizations through the interplay of individuals. In so far as the motives are conscious, there is scope for rational reconstructions of action and so for the kind of interpretative approach that is discussed below. But any such internal story is finally subordinate to a naturalistic canon of causal explanation. The leading realist analysis of causation, which is described in chapter 9 on the Philosophy of Science, will serve nicely.

The holist case often involves a further claim on behalf of functional explanation. Like the planetary system, which is mechanical, or a termite colony, which is organic, social systems have various equilibrium conditions. When these conditions are breached, the system tends to correct the disturbance or shift towards a fresh equilibrium. The behaviour of parts of the system can thus be explained by functional demands arising from the properties of the system as a whole. The treatment of the class struggle in a crude version of 'vulgar' Marxism, where the consciousness of humans is wholly determined by their social being, is a classic example. Here M. Rouget's membership of the industrial proletariat is crucial (although the ideology purveyed by the church might mute the conflict between the economic forces and relations of production). Classic too are some of the instances of social explanation given by Emile Durkheim (1858–1917) in the course of insisting that social facts be treated as things. Like Marx, he does not belong squarely in the top-left quadrant of figure 12.1, if his works are read as a whole. But the brief argument in *The Rules of Sociological Method* (1964) that there will always be crime because all societies need crimes to stigmatize for the sake of increasing social integration is a gem.

Although functional thinking is no longer as common and explicit as it was until the 1960s, it has by no means vanished. It occurs latently, for instance, even in that most individualist of social sciences, neo-classical economics. Here the picture of individual firms pursuing their self-interest by rational calculation is tempered by a conviction that, if they falter, they will be driven out of business by the operation of market forces. These forces apparently constitute an economic system that demands efficiency and, unless subjected to political interference, achieves it, to the general benefit of the economy. Without plunging into a discussion of how seriously neo-classicists really take the idea of market forces within an economic system, we can plausibly suggest this as an example of explanatory realism with both psychological and social components and functionalist aspects. M. Rouget's interests need not be identical with those of the firm for which he works.

(3) Interpretative

It is strange to suppose, as Przeworski and Teune seem to, that we can try to explain M. Rouget's vote without enquiring how he sees his situation. No doubt we can make sense of what termites do without interviewing any termites. But M. Rouget is not a termite and his social world is not an external structure in which he is enclosed. Or, if it is largely external to him, that does not make it external to all its inhabitants collectively. In that case explanations need to start, and perhaps even to finish, by understanding the situation from within. That promises a potentially different account of why age and sex matter but hair and eyes do not, and one which is not directly consonant with naturalism. This brings us to the idea of understanding.

2 Understanding

Meaning, according to Wilhelm Dilthey (1833–1911), is 'the category which is peculiar to life and to the historical world'. Dilthey was one of a group of German idealists interested in the study of history. Prompted in part by the work of HEGEL (chapter 33), Dilthey came to the view that human life can be understood only by applying categories, like 'purpose' and 'value', which have no place in our knowledge of the physical world. These categories address the connectedness of life and make us realize that the meaning of its episodes must be understood by seeing it as a whole. But nothing external to humanity is involved. 'Life does not mean anything other than itself. There is nothing in it which points to a meaning beyond it' (Dilthey 1926: VII, 24).

This strikes a bold note on which to open our discussion of INTERPRETATIVE (pp. 247–50) understanding. It not only sets the historical world apart from the natural but also bids us to think holistically. Leaving the merits of holism until later, let us start with the idea of meaning.

Varieties of Meaning

When M. Rouget casts his vote in an election, his action has meaning in several senses, three of which are especially relevant. Firstly, we can ask what he means by it. What is his intention, purpose, reason or motive? How does he expect other people to interpret his action? These are questions about what we might term 'subjective meaning' – what is going on in M. Rouget's conscious mind. Secondly, we can ask what the action itself means – exactly what action is being performed, considered from a public point of view. Actions are usually taken from stock, as is clearest if we think about utterances. The words 'pandas are black and white' have a public meaning which can be found, for instance, by use of a dictionary or phrase book. They do not change their public meaning if the speaker utters them by mistake or believing that they mean something else or supposing that a panda is a kind of bird. Similarly what move one makes in a game depends on the rules of the game and commonly has no meaning outside those rules. These are matters of what we might term 'intersubjective meaning'.

Thirdly, we can ask the significance of actions, seeking perhaps to set them in a wider context or to treat them as a sign of an underlying process. There are many variants, ranging from background articles on current affairs in newspapers to ambitious attempts to probe what is hidden, as when Freudians treat slips of the tongue as clues to the unconscious or when historians seek to trace the underlying movement of history. The common element is a readiness to find meanings which the actors grasp only dimly or are not aware of at all. We might term these 'objective meanings', while noting that we shall need to enquire whether accounts of underlying significance couched in terms very remote from the actors' own belong under the heading of causal explanations.

Philosophically, the neatest way to make meaning central is to pose the problem of other minds. How does one person or group of persons know what is in the mind of another? This too is a problem of knowledge but it differs from those raised earlier in that it involves a 'double hermeneutic' ('hermeneutic' comes from the ancient Greek *hermeneus*, an interpreter). Section 1 gave us good reason to accept that facts do not simply obtrude but involve interpretation. Hence, we might say, there is a single hermeneutic in all our knowledge of the world, including our observation of human behaviour. But when we interpret behaviour as action, we are interpreting twice: once in identifying the behaviour and again in ascribing its meaning as action. To know what is in other minds, we must be able to manage this double hermeneutic.

The problem, as traditionally posed, is that each of us has a kind of self-knowledge, which is denied us in our knowledge of others. We understand their thoughts, emotions and desires, the meaning (in the first sense above) of their words and actions, by inferences whose starting-point is their behaviour. These inferences cross a divide which it is natural to describe as one between physical and mental or between the outward and inward aspects of a person. Yet, unlike standard inductive inferences, there is no independent way of checking conclusions in some cases, so as to have a reliable warrant for others. How, then, do we manage, epistemologically, to progress from a single to a double hermeneutic?

Let us focus the problem on the interpretation of behaviour as action. Consider, for example, blinking and winking. There is no obvious or immediate physical difference. Yet blinks belong wholly to a physiological story of response to stimulus, whereas winks are a vehicle for information – hints, reservations, conspiracy, warnings; they are, in short, speech-acts. How do we know a blink from a wink and how do we identify exactly what a wink conveys?

This is a good moment to turn to Max Weber (1864–1920) and the methodological essay at the start of *Economy and Society* (1922). Weber says there that 'the science of society attempts the interpretative understanding of social action'. In 'action' he includes 'all human action when and in so far as the acting individual attaches subjective meaning to it'. By 'social action' he means action 'which takes account of the behaviour of others and is thereby oriented in its course'. Thus cyclists entering traffic engage in social action, whereas someone putting up an umbrella does not. The former take account of other actors, the latter takes account only of the weather. There is subjective meaning in both cases, since that merely requires an intention of some kind, whereas in social action the intention relates to the intentions of others.

Weber suggests that identifying intentions is a two-step process. The first is 'direct understanding' or 'empathy', by which one knows, for instance, that a man swinging an axe is chopping wood or that a marksman is aiming a rifle. In other words, there is a process akin to perception, which lets us identify intentions, and hence actions, directly. The second step is 'explanatory understanding' by which we might come to know that the woodcutter is earning a living or the marksman taking part in a vendetta. This is done by assigning the action to 'a complex of meanings'. It can be done 'historically', where we trace the exact history and motive of a particular action, or 'sociologically', where we fill in a social context like that of revenge-killing, or 'ideal-typically', where we conduct a RATIONAL RECONSTRUCTION (p. 436) of what is going on. I shall pursue this last suggestion in a moment.

Notice that the appeal to 'empathy' effectively by-passes the other-minds problem by refusing to treat the identification of some actions as the conclusion of an inference from behaviour. To revert to our first example, we do not infer that someone winked from premises about the movements of one eyelid; we perceive the wink, even though an ignorant alien observer might perceive nothing of the sort. This may be a shrewd move, since the problem, as traditionally posed, threatens to be insoluble. If one can get away with it, there is much to be said for simply introducing a datum level of actions as a distinctive feature of Understanding. But it clearly risks begging the question and calls for further thought about the relation between behaviour and action.

Meanwhile, the move may be vulnerable from a different direction. Weber is assuming that we can, sometimes at least, identify intentions like 'aiming a rifle' without presupposing social practices. This is an individualist assumption and, if it is wrong, holism comes swiftly into play. It need not be holism on any grand Hegelian scale. The counter-suggestion is only that to by-pass the traditional other-minds problem is to go directly to the *public* meaning of action. Whereas Weber starts from what an agent means by an action (our first sense of Meaning above), a holistic account starts from our second sense – what the action means. This may seem a minor shift but it goes with a wide-spread recent rejection of the Cartesian *cogito* as the foundation of our knowledge of the world and of other minds. The broader theme is that subjective meanings are possible only because we share an everyday world with other people.

The key philosophical text here is perhaps *Philosophical Investigations* (1953) by Ludwig WITTGENSTEIN (1889–1951) (chapter 39). In so far as actions are typically moves in some 'game' of social life, they cannot be identified independently of the game to which they belong. This is plainest for actions that are literally moves in a game, for instance the playing of a tile in mah-jong, where the subjective meaning cannot be analytically prior to the intersubjective meaning. Wittgenstein bids us regard social action in general in this sort of way. Social life is made up of institutions or practices, best understood by analogy with games. Crucially, games have two sorts of rules. One sort is regulative and governs the best choice of moves at each turn. For instance, success in mah-jong depends on knowing some useful rules of thumb and in knowing whether the other players know them too. The other sort is constitutive and governs the very possibility of making moves at all. The constitutive rules of mah-jong define the procedures, pieces and purpose of the game and *must* be followed by the players, on pain of failing to take any part in the game.

Important to this fertile analogy is the fact that there is nothing (except the presence of constitutive rules) which all games have in common:

> Don't say: There *must* be something common, or they would not be called 'games' – but *look and see* whether there is something common to all. For if you look at them you will not see something that is common to *all*, but similarities, relationships, and a whole series of them at that. (Wittgenstein 1953: §66)

There is only a complex network of similarities, overlapping and criss-crossing, or 'family resemblances'. There is no further common core to 'board games, . . . Olympic games and so on'. So we should not expect social practices to display any universal common core either. They vary within and between societies and there is nothing more global to it. 'What has to be accepted, the given, is – one could say – *forms of life*' (ibid.: 226).

The primary understanding of action, then, is not as an expression of subjective meaning but as the following of a rule by an agent who, in a famous Wittgensteinian phrase, 'knows how to go on'. This may sound deterministic. It can seem a small step from presenting social actors as rule followers to presenting them as creatures of the rules which they follow. But that can be avoided, if the rules of the games of social life are not taken to be so complete, detailed and pervasive that they cover every possible situation in advance. On one interpretation of Wittgenstein, rules are always open-ended and are constructed to cover new cases in the course of play. (For a plausible example of this process, think how legal rules evolve through the interplay of judicial interpretations in courts of law.) In that case we have a fertile holistic approach which does not turn the actors into cultural dopes. Instead, the actors retain a positive interpretative role.

Even so, it does not leave as much room for individual initiative as an individualist might wish. It suggests not only that the 'games' of social life are analytically prior to the 'moves' made within them and that all social actions are 'moves', but also that social actors are *essentially* players. If so, it conflicts with the common belief that we are individuals who choose whether to play and what to play. Furthermore, this belief extends to the conviction that what we cannot do separately we can often do collectively. For example, many theories of political freedom and democracy presume that the institutions, rules and practices of a society can be changed by collective decision. An analysis that worked *wholly* 'top down' in the Understanding column of figure 12.1 would thus be politically contentious, even if it left some room for players to manoeuvre within the game.

On the other hand, an analysis which worked *wholly* 'bottom up' in the Understanding column would seem wilfully blind to the point that reasons for social action are commonly bound up with the roles that people play. So let us next try embedding social actors in their social roles without thereby denying that they are individuals. If social norms are indeed as much constructed in the course of interaction as laid down in advance of it, there should be room for an individualist story about this process of construction. To tell it, we need to stress that roles enable as well as constrain action.

Roles

A 'role' is standardly defined as a set of normative expectations attached to a social position. Thus a professorship is a social position and professors are expected to do research, teach students and so on. These expectations are *normative* in that those dealing with professors are *entitled to* presume that the role will be played as required and to complain if it is not. But the requirements of the role are not expressible in a complete list of explicit rules to cover every situation. No such complete list could be specified and role players have to be left to interpret the role in some general spirit. Professors are required to be scrupulous about giving credit for ideas borrowed from others and to be conscientious and fair-minded when judging students' work; but what counts as scrupulous, conscientious and fair-minded cannot be specified in detail. That depends too much on the exact circumstances of each new case in ways that call for judgement by the actors. Roles thus take on shape as they are played and, singly and collectively, we choose much of that shape. It is a constrained choice but still a choice and, although the choices sum to define the role more closely, the shifting character of the social scene contrives to undefine it at the same time. The requirements of roles both constrain and enable the role players.

I do not wish to assert dogmatically that this is the right way to conceive of roles. But, if it is a plausible way, then it offers scope for a social individualism that is philosophically challenging on several grounds. Although there is space only for what may seem a very bald list, think of what follows as a pointer to a compromise in the Understanding column of figure 12.1 between the pure individualism of the bottom box and the thoroughgoing holism of the top one.

Firstly, we need to think further about the notion of a reason for action. There are two ideas of practical reason in common use in the social sciences. One is instrumental or what Weber, in the essay cited earlier, terms *Zweckrationalität* – the rational choice of the most effective means to the agent's ends. This, elaborated in decision theory, is basic for economics and 'economic' theories of human behaviour, as will emerge in the next section. It confines practical reason to deliberation about the likely consequences of alternative actions. The other is expressive or what Weber terms *Wertrationalität*, where the agent attaches such value to the goal or to the performance of the action that consequences do not matter. This sounds like the kind of rationality – or lack of it – that turns social actors into what I have called cultural dopes. But that need not be its implication, if we treat it as rule-following, as in the paragraphs above, and so set for a more human *homo sociologicus* the task of deliberating about what is required of him or her. Yet neither of these accounts seems to yield an analysis of practical reason that does justice to the concept of a person as someone capable of moral conduct. Nor can they be readily combined, as we shall see presently.

Secondly, mention of MORAL CONDUCT (chapter 6) invites the thought that expressive action often expresses the character of the agent, rather than the demands of a social position. Is the self not more than the sum of the roles that it plays? That leads to tangled questions of personal identity and deep into the PHILOSOPHY OF MIND (chapter 5). Can persons be kept distinct from both personalities and *personae*? If 'personality' refers to psychological character and 'persona' (as in *dramatis persona*, a character in a play) refers to people as manifested in social relations, is there anything further and non-physical that is special to a person? Neither 'personality' nor 'persona' captures the elements of self-awareness and self-direction which many thinkers hold to be crucial for what it is to be a person. A promising starting-point is to invoke the distinction made by William JAMES (chapter 36) between the 'I' and the 'me': 'the self as knower' and 'the self as known' (James 1958, 1962). But there is no avoiding deeper matters than we can pursue here and, it must be said, they make the other-minds problem all the harder.

Thirdly, questions about the nature of human freedom remain urgent. Those concerning moral, political and social freedom are touched on below, although chiefly dealt with elsewhere (see chapters 6 and 8). Meanwhile, we noted earlier that the problem of free will that faces anyone applying a deterministic philosophy of natural science to the social world is not indisputably settled by adopting compatibilism. One attraction of a method of Understanding that allows for self-direction on the part of social actors is that it seems less deterministic. The idea that we help to create the social order to which we belong is intriguing but does not abolish the problem either. The initial holistic suggestion that social actors are the transmitters rather than the creators of the meaning of their actions still needs very careful amendment if it is not to suck us into a residual social determinism. Nor should we forget that we have not addressed the difficulties of relating an active, autonomous self to the physical world that it inhabits.

Anyone seeking a compromise between individualism and holism to conclude this section therefore has a great deal of unfinished business. So it seems wiser to end the section with some summary remarks about Understanding. It starts by making sense of action 'from within' by disclosing both the meaning of the action and what the actor meant by it. That can demand two sorts of account, one identifying the relevant practices and forms of life, the other seeking the actors' aims and reasons. For both it is helpful to suggest that we proceed on the assumption that the action is rational. But this form of words conceals a deep division. In calling action rational we often mean that the agent has particular reasons for it, which are good reasons or at least seem to him or her to be so. That is to stress the actor's meaning. But we may also mean that the action is rational in the sense of being appropriate and in accord with the relevant rules, especially if we are seeking to understand actions that stem from the demands of roles. That is to stress the rule-governed character of social actions. It is not obvious how these two sorts of account finally relate to one another. Yet it is certainly fertile to ask.

There may also be deeper questions about the meaning of HISTORY (chapter 14) that show themselves when historians and social theorists try to identify epochs and movements. Such attempts continue to inspire many philosophers, especially those influenced by Hegel. On the other hand, they infuriate others, and Popper's fulminations in *The Poverty of Historicism* (1957) are not to be missed. There is nothing brief to say about whether the historical world is open to a dialectical interpretation that calls for a vaultingly ambitious concept of understanding. But it is worth noting that, even if Popper were right to deny it, nothing would follow about the success of naturalism. The Weberian and Wittgensteinian reflections deployed in this section stand without presupposing any hidden dialectics and we have yet to discuss the relation between understanding and explanation.

3   Explaining and Understanding

Without adequacy on the level of meaning, our generalizations remain mere statements of *statistical* probability, either not intelligible at all or only imperfectly intelligible . . . On the other hand, from the point of view of sociological knowledge, even the most certain adequacy on the level of meaning signifies an acceptable *causal* proposition only to the extent that there is a probability . . . that the action in question *really* takes the course held to be meaningfully adequate.

This is Weber's (1922) view of how sections 1 and 2 relate. (It too comes from the opening essay in *Economy and Society,* with his italics.) It sounds entirely reasonable. On the one hand, we have statistics about people like M. Rouget; but it makes scarcely more sense to learn that 65 per cent of young workers in large factories vote Left than that 65 per cent of men with brown eyes ride bicycles. So we also need a meaningful story, which presents M. Rouget's world from the inside by means of a rational reconstruction. On the other hand, there is no inherent guarantee that a rational reconstruction yields a true story. To ensure that, we need a high empirical probability that the story is causally adequate too.

On reflection, however, this resolution is not so neat. Weber has adopted the Humean thesis that causal propositions are to be construed as statements of statistical probability. But, as we saw in section 1, there are grounds for rejecting this analysis in favour of one involving real connections or causal powers or both. In that case, statistical generalizations do not relate adequacy on the level of meaning directly to whatever 'really' moves M. Rouget at a causal level. This in turn reveals an ambiguity in Weber's resolution. Is he saying that the social world does indeed work as a meaningfully adequate, rationally reconstructed account claims, provided only that people like M. Rouget are statistically common enough? Or is he saying that such accounts provide an essential clue to a causal level, where the elements that do the 'real' explanatory work may be of a very different sort? It is thus open to us to conclude either that the actors are usually self-propelled and know what they are doing, at least when their accounts tally, or that their social being commonly determines their consciousness; either that their social being is distinct from the fabric of meanings and causes it or that causal explanations must finally be couched in cultural terms. In other words, the tale could still end with any of the possibilities in figure 12.1.

In what follows, I shall focus on two separate centres of current debate. One concerns the right sort of way to read the 'economic' theories of behaviour mentioned earlier, thus continuing our discussion of rationality as an individualist key to social analysis. The other is the vexed question of rationality and relativism, where the dispute between Explanation and Understanding is broadly holistic on both sides. The conclusions of this chapter, given the present state of philosophy and social theory, will consist largely of an agenda.

3.1   Rationality and the theory of games

'The first principle of economics is that every agent is actuated solely by self-interest.' This much-quoted remark comes from F. Y. Edgeworth's engagingly titled book *Mathematical Psychics* (1886) and captures what is widely taken to be the key to the most forceful individualist analysis of social action, institutions and practices. As noted earlier, one of Weber's routes to explanatory understanding is by 'ideal-typical rational reconstruction' of action. This means interpreting actions as the choices made by rational agents in order to achieve their ends or to satisfy their preferences. 'Ideal-typical' refers to what is nowadays often called a 'rational choice' or 'economic' approach, which works by way of an idealized model of a world where all agents are perfectly rational. We can best begin with a brief outline of such a model.

Start by defining a perfectly rational agent as an agent with complete and consistent preferences, perfect information and perfect powers of calculation. His or her preferences range over the consequences of each action open to him or her. Information includes knowing what these consequences would be and how likely they are to occur. Calculation then identifies the rational choice in the circumstances. For example, Jack is a farmer choosing whether to breed goats or pigs. He would rather have pigs but they cost more and are more prone to disease. So he must calculate whether the greater 'utility' of pigs is more than offset by the greater costs and risks. In theory at least, he can compare the expected utility of goats and pigs by ranking their utility, net of costs, after discounting it for the risk that it would not materialize. A rational agent never chooses a course of action whose expected utility is less than that of another available to him.

The concept of UTILITY (chapter 35) here owes most to Jeremy BENTHAM (1748–1832) (chapter 35) and the utilitarians. Bentham held that all actions are subject to a 'principle of utility', defined as 'that property in any object, whereby it tends to produce benefit, advantage, pleasure, good or happiness . . . to the party whose interest is considered'. The principle guides each rational agent to do what, as modern economists put it, maximizes his or her expected utility. Whether an action is rational is finally a matter of the mental satisfaction which its consequences bring to the agent (Bentham 1970: ch. 1).

It may sound as if Bentham assumed human beings to be selfish, self-seeking creatures. The same impression is conveyed by Edgeworth's remark that 'the first principle of economics is that every agent is actuated solely by self-interest'. But, even if people are in fact all too often self-seeking, the principle of utility does not say so. It implies nothing about the specific character of preferences and tells us only that people are motivated to seek what will best satisfy whatever they happen to desire. Similarly Hume, while insisting that action is always motivated by passion, made it clear that not all passions are selfish:

> Ambition, avarice, self-love, vanity, friendship, generosity, public spirit: these passions, mixed in various degrees, and distributed through society, have been, from the beginning of the world, and still are, the source of all the actions and enterprises, which have ever been observed among mankind . . . Mankind are so much the same, in all times and places, that history informs us of nothing new or strange in this particular. (Hume 1978b: VIII, I, 65)

Thus saints can be as rational as sinners. Whether action is rational depends solely on whether it is instrumental in furthering the agent's passions or preferences.

This becomes still more explicit in recent utility theory, where a conscious effort is made to remove all trace of psychology and to treat rationality as consistency between preferences, actions and (expected) outcomes (see especially Savage 1954). Whereas Hume thought in terms of motivating passions, modern exponents of the pure theory of rational choice dispense with passions and require only that a rational agent has a consistent preference-order over possible outcomes. What makes rational choice theory (or decision theory) complex is not the complexity of human psychology but the problems of dealing with risk and uncertainty. We might wish to doubt Hume's claim that mankind are 'so much the same, in all times and places that history informs us of nothing new or strange in this particular'. It is at least harder to doubt the blander claim that all rational actions have a single, universal logic.

We next apply this model of individually rational action to more than one agent. Whether Jack does well to choose pigs over goats may depend on whether Jill chooses to breed goats or pigs on the neighbouring farm. If the pay-off to his action depends on her strategy and vice versa, then they are playing a 'game', in a sense defined by the theory of games and far removed from Wittgenstein's. Perhaps they intend to sell their animals in a small village market which will absorb some goats and some pigs but not a glut of either. Then they may be playing a co-ordination game, as shown in figure 12.3. Here each has a choice between the two strategies, Goats and Pigs, and the game has four (2 × 2) possible outcomes. Each outcome (or cell of the matrix) yields a pay-off to each player, shown as utility numbers (Jack's first and then Jill's). What exactly these numbers represent is a philosophically interesting question; but, for present purposes, let us take them to register how each player ranks the outcomes, with a higher number signifying a greater preference. Thus figure 12.3 shows both players equally well satisfied by either way of co-ordinating, where one opts for pigs and the other for goats.

Jill

	Pigs	Goats
Pigs	1, 1	2, 2
Goats	2, 2	1, 1

Jack

Figure 12.3   The co-ordination game: strategies faced by Jack and Jill for breeding pigs or goats.

This particular game has two pure 'solutions': if Jack chooses pigs, Jill's best strategy is goats, in which case Jack's best choice is indeed pigs; if Jack chooses goats, Jill's best strategy is pigs, in which case Jack's best choice is indeed goats. So there is no single best strategy for either, or none better than tossing a coin. If the game is to be played several times, however, Jack and Jill would both welcome the help of a convention to steer them towards one of the pure solutions. If it were the practice, for instance, that pigs are men's work or goats are women's work, and if each knew that the other knew this, then each would presumably opt accordingly for what game theorists term the 'salient' strategy. At any rate, as soon as a relevant convention is established, both players are well served and neither has any reason to depart from it.

The idea is simple but can be used to prompt a powerful individualist analysis of institutions. We are being invited to regard the basic rules or norms of any society as conventions that are of mutual benefit to rational individuals with separate interests. It seems very plausible to suggest that rules or norms which solve co-ordination problems exist and persist because they do so. More generally still, it also seems plausible to suggest that society and its basic institutions can be analysed as an association of individuals, regulated to mutual advantage.

Is it not simpler still to suppose that Jack and Jill, instead of looking round for a convention or waiting for one to emerge, will make a direct agreement? Yes it is; but that presupposes the existence of language and a practice of making agreements. In the most ambitious versions of the theory of the social contract nothing is presupposed and even language is treated as a set of conventions and practices which let individuals gain the mutual benefits of communication. Game theory therefore starts with games where initial choices are to be made without prior communication and where any emergent conventions exist without being enforced by any kind of sanctions.

Even if co-ordination is a basic game, it does not hold the key to all norms or institutions. No less crucial is the game known as the prisoner's dilemma, shown in figure 12.4. Here, let us suppose, Jack and Jill have a mutual interest in giving back any animals that stray across the boundary between their farms. (Jack has specialized in pigs and Jill in goats; so strays can be eaten but not used for the more profitable business of breeding.) But, since there is no way of proving what happens to a missing animal, each does better still to keep the other's strays and does worst of all by being the only one to return them. If each is a rational agent with the preference order given in figure 12.4, they will fail to achieve their mutual interest. Jack will reason that he

Jill

	Keep	Return
Keep	2, 2	4, 1
Return	1, 4	3, 3

Jack

Figure 12.4 The prisoner's dilemma: strategies faced by Jack and Jill for dealing with animals that stray on to their farms.

does better to keep Jill's strays, if she does not return his, and better to keep her strays, even if she does return his; so he does better to keep hers, *whatever she does*. Jill reasons similarly. The outcome is therefore worse for *both* than it would be if both acted co-operatively.

It might seem that they can improve on this inferior outcome by making an agreement and promising to keep it. But that will not help them, if they have the same instrumental view of agreements and promises as they so far have of other matters. Suppose that each now prefers that both keep the agreement than that neither does, but most prefers to break it (secretly, no doubt) while the other keeps it, and least prefers to keep it while the other breaks it. Then the situation is still that in figure 12.4, and each will break the agreement, thus again producing a mutually inferior outcome.

The last paragraph is contentious. It takes a line most famously put forward by Hobbes, who was cited above for his view of human beings as mechanical individuals with 'a perpetual and restless desire for power after power, that ceaseth only in death'. Hobbes goes on in *Leviathan*, chapter 13, to argue that men can live at peace only if they can create 'a common power to keep all in awe', which can then enforce any agreements made; and in chapter 17 he says: 'Covenants, without the Sword, are but Words, and of no strength to secure a man at all'. This argument lies at the core of his version of the social contract, which is thus strikingly different from versions grounded in the rationality of co-operating for simple mutual advantage. Here lie the origins of an enduring dispute between 'conflict' and 'consensus' models of society.

The difference might seem to turn on opposing views of human nature and whether we have enough genial passions, like Hume's 'friendship, generosity, public spirit', to make co-operation natural. But, although this may be relevant if we ask how widespread examples of the prisoner's dilemma game are, it does not affect the logic of the game. Rational choice theory implies that players with the preferences shown in figure 12.4 will choose not to co-operate, regardless of how they acquired the preferences. Reasons for action always look forward to the consequences of action and never back to how the situation came about. If the fact that a promise has been made is to serve as a reason for keeping it, the theory needs recasting.

Meanwhile enough has been said to show why 'Rational choices' belong in the bottom-left quadrant of figure 12.1. In its standard form, rational choice theory slots the agent into a causal sequence between whatever gives rise to his or her preferences and the actions which his or her internal computer directs. That threatens its status as an individualist theory. But if it is not defence enough to point out that actions result from individual preferences, there is still the case for holding that institutions are the outcome of previous interactions among individuals. On the other hand, it is at least interesting to try recasting the theory so that agents can distance themselves from their preferences and can act on other than consequentialist reasons. That would make it a candidate for the bottom-right quadrant, a form of individualism which is adequate at the level of meaning along the lines indicated when we were discussing role-playing in the previous section.

3.2 Rationality and relativism

Although nothing has yet been said to prove it, it is hard to resist the idea that social action cannot be identified and described without seeing the actors' situation from within. So let us now assume for the sake of argument that the first step in the analysis of any social phenomenon belongs to Understanding. Even so, the last step may still belong to Explanation. We may need understanding to identify what is going on and yet also need an explanation of how and why it occurs. The implications of this thought lead us to a current dispute about rationality and RELATIVISM (pp. 295–7).

It used to be common to meet behaviourists who regarded social actors as very inferior guides to their own behaviour. Scientists, they maintained, have an access to the brain, the body, the human environment and the mechanics of interaction, which mere agents cannot aspire to. Therefore quantitative, and hence objective, evidence always trumps qualitative, and hence merely subjective, reports from the inside. Moreover, it is no objection that behavioural explanations often use concepts alien to those in which the actors think. After all, biology does not need to take a worm's eye view or worry about any subjective meaning attaching to what worms do; there is nothing inherently special about human life among the other operations of nature.

This attitude has receded and most social scientists or philosophers are now willing to start by describing social phenomena in terms which the actors would understand and assent to. This is effectively to grant that social events are significantly more historically and culturally located than those studied by physics. But naturalists do not regard this as a damaging concession, provided that an interpretative account of what happens is finally subordinate to a naturalistic account of how and why it happens. Then action can be identified from within and explained from without: a compromise favouring naturalism.

A major complication, however, is the recent growth in the sociology of science, encouraged by Thomas Kuhn's work on the structure of scientific revolutions (Kuhn 1970). The Enlightenment view of science has always been that it is a search after truth under the guidance of reason. Kuhn put up a strong case for believing that reason cannot do everything asked of it, because all systems of thought rely on 'paradigms' which govern what counts as reasonable. A PARADIGM (pp. 10–11) has two key features. One is cognitive – a set of very general presuppositions about the nature of things, for example the Ptolemaic world view or the Copernican one which replaced it. The other is social – a set of institutional practices that entrench the presuppositions in the life of a society, for example those that maintain the professional conduct, status and influence of neo-classical economists. Since both features regulate a canon of rational belief and action, paradigms are not subject to rational criticism from the sort of external, absolute standpoint to which the Enlightenment aspired. There can be no such standpoint.

If reason does not determine our most general beliefs, what does? One influential answer has been to extend the sociology of knowledge to include the study of whatever passes for 'knowledge' – science and epistemology no less than, say, religion and theology. In some versions, the theme is that cognitive systems are generated by the working of social systems, with these causal relations being a subject for an objective social science (Barnes and Bloor 1982). But this seems to leave an allegedly objective social science as an exception to the claim that all cognitive systems have social determinants. Other versions are careful to include the sociology of knowledge in the sociology of knowledge. This, however, prompts a still more radical thought.

If science, natural and social, is ultimately a practice among practices, then explanation cannot finally be contrasted with understanding by opposing an external standpoint to an internal one. Explanation is a vital part of the game of science, or even the purpose of that game, but it cannot be a device for doing the impossible, namely stepping out of the game altogether in order to reveal the nature of reality. So, although it remains important to understand the claims to objectivity made in the practice of science, this can only be an exercise in seeing from within. Hence a line which set out to give understanding the first turn and explanation the second presumably ends by giving a final turn to understanding.

Meanwhile, there is something odd about this sharp contrast between cognitive systems and social systems. The former do not float in thin air and the latter do not consist of unthinking bodies. Although it is useful to draw distinctions among the many activities that comprise a social world, it is not as if we were unpicking a fabric whose threads were either social or cognitive but none of them both. Weber's distinction between the level of meaning and the causal level cannot be taken as one between separate orders of being. In relating explanation to understanding, we are trying to make sense of a single world.

The preceding paragraphs raise an urgent question about relativism, which we should next make explicit. The Enlightenment story of science relies on notions of rationality which connect reason directly with truth. The broadest idea is that there is a rational order in nature and that reason can discern the truth about it. If there is less of a rational order in the human world, that is because humans are imperfectly rational, at least when it comes to constructing social arrangements. But that simply gives reason the further task of discerning how to improve them. It will be clear by now that this story has come under heavy fire of late. In effect, critics have been trying to relativize reason by suggesting that rationality is always a matter of conforming to the rules of a particular practice. If practices, in turn, are relative to particular groups and societies, then truth too becomes unattainable or, if you prefer, a matter of conformity to local custom.

It is ironic to find Enlightenment thinkers, who set out to destroy dogma with the aid of reason, being attacked for making reason a dogma. But, if it is indeed one, then it is liberating to have it exposed as such. This, accordingly, has become a theme in recent political philosophy, especially where the target is the state as the embodiment of a domineering rational–legal order. Some LIBERTARIANS, FEMINISTS and COMMUNITARIANS (chapters 8 and 20) in particular have sought to base ideas of autonomy and respect for persons on a rejection of claims to justify centralized power by appeal to rational authority. Their case often involves a defence of relativism, apparently strengthened by insisting that, to recall the quotation from Dilthey, 'life does not mean anything other than itself. There is nothing in it which points to a meaning beyond it.'

But other libertarians, feminists and communitarians find this a dangerous line. If there is nothing beyond forms of life by which to judge forms of life, there can be no external standpoint for criticizing the state. Indeed, if life has no meaning outside existing forms of life, then we presumably need to love, honour and obey the ones we have. In that case relativism, allied with hermeneutics, is not liberating at all. Since this is not a chapter on political philosophy, I shall not try to umpire the dispute. But its existence should make us wary of relativism in epistemology too, if that were to clear the way to maintaining that a closed society is as entitled to its way of life as an open one.

Yet we should not assume that to endorse the claims of Understanding is thereby to internalize reason and truth to practices. That would be to run into deep trouble with the notorious 'hermeneutic circle'. Here lies a problem too ramified for this chapter, but there is just room for a pointer to it. Suppose that each culture or 'form of life' were self-contained in a sense which includes the possession of rules defining what is real. Thus suppose, for instance, that whether witches exist is, at heart, a question about whether there are cultures with rules for identifying and dealing with witches, so that the reference as well as the meaning of 'witch' is determined internally. Suppose, roughly speaking, that witches exist wherever belief in witches is cognitively and socially entrenched. Then generalize the idea, so that nature at large ceases to be independent of rules determining what it is rational to believe about the world. That would make it plausible to suggest that each culture determines what is real and what is rational for itself. This sounds an attractive suggestion, even if it takes a bold imagination to fancy that what holds for witches also holds for rabbits. But it poses the other-minds problem in an acute form. In order to penetrate another culture, we would have to establish what it held to be rational before we could know what it held to be real; and we would have to establish what it held to be real before we could know what it held to be rational. That is the 'hermeneutic circle'.

To escape it, I think, one must either avoid internalizing reason and truth to practices or insist that some practices are universal. That is no doubt easier said than done. In mentioning it, I mean only to suggest that defenders of objective reason in hermeneutics need not give up without a struggle.

4   Conclusions

What can we conclude about the four keys to analysing social action offered in the quadrants of figure 12.5? It would make for a tidy ending if one of them were a master key. But that is unlikely. Start with the least promising claimant, 'systems' (top left), and try thinking of actions wholly as responses to changes in the actors' environment. For each actor singly, the environment includes other actors; for all collectively, it is an external structure – 'society' or perhaps 'nature'. For this to be at all plausible as an explanatory master key, it needs the backing of an ambitious functional or

	Explanation	Understanding
Holism	Systems	Cultures
Individualism	Rational choices	Subjective meanings

Figure 12.5 Conclusions: the four keys to analysing social action revisited.

EVOLUTIONARY THEORY (pp. 320–30). Such theories do certainly have champions in some realms of science. For instance, bees adapt and evolve as their environment changes. Their normal behaviour, singly and collectively, can be presented as being what is required if the hive is to function in its environment. But, even so, this can hardly be the whole story. Bees are too fascinatingly particular, and humans much more so. Curiosity swiftly beckons us into the bottom-left quadrant.

Individual bees are wonderfully intricate creatures, whose interactions are amazingly complex. For instance, a scout will return to the hive and perform an elaborate dance whose movements, it seems, communicate the distance, direction, quantity and quality of the nectar which it has located. But, even though we might therefore deem bees to have a language, their behaviour is always an effect of environmental events on a complex mechanism. Is this also how we want to construe the explanatory individualism of the bottom-left quadrant, as applied to human beings? That is unclear. On the one hand, rational choice theory, extended to include game theory, certainly sets out to analyse collective phenomena into their individual components. Social conventions and hence enduring social institutions can be presented as the sums and deposits of individual choices. On the other hand, the 'individuals' involved are automatic translators of given preferences into expected utilities, no more particular than different data sets fed into the same computer program. Whatever establishes the preferences could plausibly be said to dictate the choices.

Here compatibilism is philosophically crucial. If the conditions for freedom and individuality are satisfied, provided that actions are rationally consistent with particular preferences, then rational choice theory is an individualist theory of the sort wanted. While preferences remain given, and so exogenously determined, it cannot claim to provide a sole master key; but it can claim to supply an essential link between social structure and social action. Yet the individuality of human beings still seems different in kind from the particularity of individual bees. If so, we are drawn into the bottom-right quadrant in search of what is special about persons.

As we cross into the Understanding column, the nature of action changes. It ceases to be independently describable behaviour caused by a mental state and becomes what the agent means by it. 'Subjective meanings' are the stuff of action, which is no doubt why Weber's method of understanding begins with empathy. Actors interpret their situation creatively and express themselves in bringing their intentions to bear on it. Intersubjective rules and meanings are proposed, negotiated and left open to renegotiation. Yet, whatever its merits as an account of social experience at first hand, this is too anarchic for even a hermeneutically inclined social science, and makes for a hopelessly one-sided analysis of roles and role-play. We cannot resist asking what the 'Cultures' of the top-right quadrant have to offer.

The key idea here is that rules enable as well as constrain. Constitutive rules engender the 'games' in which social actions are 'moves'; regulative rules give rise to reliable expectations about which moves will be played. The idea conveyed by calling the rules 'cultural' is that a culture is a web of shared meanings external to each of its members, yet internal to all collectively. That is suggestive for the difference between natural facts and social facts, for instance between African weather and African politics. It recalls Wittgenstein's remark that 'What has to be accepted, the given, is – one could say – *forms of life*', apparently offering 'forms of life' as a master key. But it is hard to believe that they are so self-propelled, although I regret that there has not been room to discuss recent attempts to trace the progress of the human mind (to recall the title of Condorcet's book) in unified theories about the dynamics of cultural history. Meanwhile, my comment about African weather and African politics is double-edged. The external world of nature still constrains and enables the life of societies, providing common problems and scarce resources. We are back with the top-left quadrant.

Presumably then, there is no unique master key. Human beings make some of their own history in circumstances partly of their own choosing, with greater scope if they know 'how to go on'. This knowledge mixes explanation and understanding in ways that elude social scientists and philosophers, or at least defy summary. So the chapter can best end with an agenda of questions about the borders between the quadrants. Are the reasons that prompt role-players causes of action after the manner of natural causes? Can players of the games of social life be seen consistently both as followers of rules and as makers of choices? In making sense of social facts, do we need concepts both prior to those of individual psychology and alien to those of natural science? What form of determinism, if any, shall a social science bring to bear on a world whose inhabitants claim to be its creators? How peculiar, in short, are the intellectual and moral faculties of human beings?

Nor should we forget the original Enlightenment hope that the social sciences would bring moral and political progress. A final question, then, is whether truth, happiness and virtue are indeed bound together by an indissoluble chain.

Further Reading

For a general background in the philosophy of science see the Further Reading for chapter 9. But I will just recommend Chalmers (1982) as a masterly start. Among many general introductions to the philosophy of social science, Ryan (1970) has proved durable. It is rich in instructive examples, although more positivist in approach than one might wish for now. Keat and Urry (1975) is harder, but casts its net wider. Three interesting, recent introductions, which give scope to Understanding, are those by Doyle and Harris (1986), Rosenberg (1988) and Braybrooke (1991). Anyone wanting to see the theme of this chapter deployed in full might try Hollis (1994).

Positivism remains important and so, therefore, does Mill (1961) Book VI, lately edited by A. J. Ayer. Milton Friedman's (1953) paper speaks volumes. But the tide has turned. Winch (1958) has become classic. It makes a fertile Wittgensteinian case for the distinctness of the social sciences. A contrary view is taken by Bhaskar (1979). Like his *Scientific Realism and Human Emancipation* (1986), it is deep but difficult reading. That goes generally for much anti-Positivist work; but Geuss (1981) is a clear initial guide. Several of the issues raised in these references lead to heated argument about relativism, as in the essays rounded up in Wilson (1970) and Hollis and Lukes (1982).

There is clearer water for disputes between individualism and holism, at any rate on the individualist side. That owes much to Jon Elster's series of lucid and imaginative books insisting that 'the elementary unit of social life is the individual human action'. I suggest starting with *Explaining Technical Change* (1983) chs 1–3, *Logic and Society* (1978) chs 4 and 5, and *Ulysses and the Sirens* (1984), rather than the more recent (Elster 1989). There is an accessible literature on rational choice and game theory; for instance, Hargreaves Heap et al. (1992). Holism is harder going, but Ruben (1985) puts an exact analytical case.

References

Barnes, B. and Bloor, D. 1982: Relativism, Rationalism and the Sociology of Knowledge. In M. Hollis and S. Lukes (eds) *Rationality and Relativism*. Oxford: Blackwell.

Bentham, J. 1970 [1789]: *An Introduction to the Principles of Morals and Legislation*. London: Athlone Press.

Bhaskar, R. 1979: *The Possibility of Naturalism*. Hassocks: Harvester Press.

——1986: *Scientific Realism and Human Emancipation*. Hassocks: Harvester Press.

Braybrooke, D. 1991: *Philosophy of Social Science*. Englewood Cliffs, NJ: Prentice-Hall.

Chalmers, A. F. 1982: *What is This Thing Called Science?* 2nd edn. Milton Keynes: Open University Press.

Condorcet, M. de 1955 [1795]: *Sketch for a Historical Picture of the Progress of the Human Mind* (translated by J. Barraclough). London: Weidenfeld and Nicolson.

Dilthey, W. 1926: *Gesammelte Werke* (edited by B. Groethuysen). Stuttgart: Teubner.

Doyle, L. and Harris, R. 1986: *Empiricism, Explanation and Rationality*. London: Routledge and Kegan Paul.

Durkheim, E. 1964 [1895]: *The Rules of Sociological Method* (translated by S. Solovay and J. Mueller). New York: Free Press.

Edgeworth, F. Y. 1886: *Mathematical Psychics*. London: Routledge and Kegan Paul.

Elster, J. 1978: *Logic and Society*. New York: Wiley.

——1983: *Explaining Technical Change*. Cambridge: Cambridge University Press.

——1984: *Ulysses and the Sirens*. Cambridge: Cambridge University Press.

——1989: *Nuts and Bolts*. Cambridge: Cambridge University Press.

Fontenelle, B. de 1929 [1688]: *The Plurality of Worlds* (translated by J. Glanvill). London: Nonesuch Press.

Friedman, M. 1953: Methodology of Positive Economics. In *Essays in Positive Economics*, Chicago: University of Chicago Press.

Geuss, R. 1981: *The Idea of a Critical Theory: Habermas and the Frankfurt School*. Cambridge: Cambridge University Press.

Hargreaves Heap, S., Hollis, M., Lyons, B., Sugden, R. and Weale, A. 1992: *Choice: A Critical Guide*. Oxford: Blackwell.

Hobbes, T. 1990 [1651]: *Leviathan* (edited by R. Tuck). Cambridge: Cambridge University Press.

Hollis, M. 1994: *The Philosophy of the Social Sciences*. Cambridge: Cambridge University Press.

Hollis, M. and Lukes, S. (eds) 1982: *Rationality and Relativism*. Oxford: Blackwell.

Hume, D. 1978a [1739]: *A Treatise of Human Nature*. Oxford: Oxford University Press.

———1978b [1748]: *An Enquiry Concerning Human Understanding*. Oxford: Oxford University Press.

James, W. 1958: *The Principles of Psychology*. New York: Dover Books.

———1962: *Psychology: Briefer Course*. London: Collier Books.

Keat, R. and Urry, J. 1975: *Social Theory as Science*. London: Routledge and Kegan Paul.

Kuhn. T. S. 1970: *The Structure of Scientific Revolutions*, 2nd edn. Chicago: Chicago University Press.

Lipsey, R. 1972: *Introduction to Positive Economics*. New York: Harper and Row.

Marx, K. 1971 [1859]: *Preface to A Contribution to the Critique of Political Economy*. London: Lawrence and Wishart.

Mill, J. S. 1961 [1843]: *A System of Logic*. London: Longworth. Book VI, edited by A. J. Ayer, London: Duckworth (1988).

Popper, K. 1957: *The Poverty of Historicism*. London: Routledge.

———1969: *Conjectures and Refutations*. London: Routledge.

Przeworski, A. and Teune, H. 1970: *The Logic of Comparative Social Enquiry*. New York: J. Wiley and Sons.

Quine, W. V. O. 1953: Two Dogmas of Empiricism. In *From a Logical Point of View*, Harvard, MA: Harvard University Press.

Rosenberg, A. 1988: *Philosophy of Social Science*. Oxford: Clarendon Press.

Ruben, D.-H. 1985: *The Metaphysics of the Social World*. London: Routledge and Kegan Paul.

Ryan, A. 1970: *The Philosophy of the Social Sciences*. London: Macmillan.

Savage, L. J. 1954: *The Foundations of Statistics*. New York: J. Wiley.

Weber, M. 1922: *Economy and Society*, ed. G. Roth and C. Wittich. Berkeley: University of California Press.

Wilson, B. (ed.) 1970: *Rationality*. Oxford: Blackwell.

Winch, P. 1958: *The Idea of a Social Science*. London: Routledge and Kegan Paul.

Wittgenstein, L. 1953: *Philosophical Investigations*. Oxford: Blackwell.

Discussion Questions

1   Does the study of society require both causal explanation and interpretative understanding?

2   Do persons and the roles they fill both have importance for social explanation?

3   Can a social science cope with human autonomy?

4   How are social facts related to facts about individuals?

5   Does any account of natural science provide a model on which social science might reasonably be based?

6   How important is the notion of a 'form of life' to the understanding of society?

7   If we are concerned about human freedom, should we be more worried by a social science which binds individuals by social laws or a social science which reduces individuals to mere carriers of culture?

8   Is it a mistake to seek a universal social science to cover all societies?

9   Do we need more than rational choice theory and game theory to analyse social institutions?

10   If social explanation is in terms of base and superstructure, how can we determine what is the base and what is the superstructure?

11   What are the implications of the claim that social understanding is essentially historical?

12   How do different conceptions of rationality affect our account of social science?

13   Is individualism or holism a better approach to understanding social institutions and practices?

14   Do moral notions like justice have a legitimate role in social explanation?

15   Can ideal types help to explain social action?

16   How is it possible to understand other societies?

17   In what sense should social science seek objectivity?

18   Are there good reasons to confine accounts of behaviour and institutions in a society to concepts available to members of that society?

19   Can an account of society based on hermeneutics explain social change?

20   Does an analysis of social action in terms of rule-following imply that social actors follow rules automatically?

21   What concept of the person is most suitable for social science?

13

Philosophy of Law

N. E. SIMMONDS

The philosophy of law lies at the intersection of a number of problems. These concern the relationship between law and morality; the logical status (as descriptive or prescriptive) of propositions of law; the possibility of separating adjudication from politics; and the distinction between law and organized force. Legal positivists have insisted on a morally neutral concept of law, wherein a legal system consists of posited rules ascertainable by reference to factual criteria. The natural law tradition, by contrast, draws attention to law's rootedness in notions of justice and the common good. Modern debates have often centred on the process of adjudication, in particular upon the question of the extent to which judges may properly rely upon their personal moral judgement, and how far they are limited to the application of technical legal rules.

For most of us, most of the time, law seems to be nothing more than a set of governmental arrangements whereby transactions are regulated and undesirable forms of conduct discouraged. Why should this give rise to philosophical problems? Or rather, why should it give rise to philosophical problems other than the problems of APPLIED ETHICS (chapters 16–19), which may arise in relation to any set of human arrangements?

A convincing answer to this question will require us to outline a number of puzzling features of the phenomenon of law. The philosophy of law lies at the intersection of these puzzles, and seeks to construct a coherent understanding of the nature of law in such a way as to resolve the puzzles. Some problems are of a kind that might occur to any thinking person, while others spring from the technical understanding and experience of lawyers. Some problems are generated by the special role that law enjoys within modern political life, while others arise only against the background of specific philosophical commitments imported from areas of enquiry such as EPISTEMOLOGY (chapter 1) or ETHICS (chapter 6). Philosophers of law hope to offer solutions that are both enlightening and integrated, in the sense that a single theory of law should provide a basis for the resolution of all the central problems.

Unsurprisingly, a diversity of theories has been offered. The debate is significantly complicated, however, by the fact that different legal philosophers and jurists conceive of the debate in quite different ways: they disagree about the nature and status of legal theory just as much as they disagree about the nature and status of law. Some theories purport to be purely 'analytical' or 'clarificatory', while others argue that an adequate solution to the philosophical problems of law requires a theory that has a prescriptive aspect and that is rooted in POLITICAL PHILOSOPHY (chapter 8); some theories defend claims about the 'necessary' constituents of the 'concept' of law, while others seek a reflective understanding of specific social practices. These disagreements will inevitably complicate our survey.

1   Problems of Jurisprudence

1.1   Law and force

Law may at times strike us as being nothing more than a set of governmental arrangements worth studying for practical purposes, but devoid of philosophical interest. We do not always, however, think of law in this mundane guise. We treat the idea of law as a moral *aspiration* that is systematically connected to a range of other values. We contrast the rule of law with political regimes that are based solely on force; we think of law as having deep connections with individual LIBERTY (pp. 258–64) and with JUSTICE (chapter 8); we speak of law as imposing obligations upon us, and as conferring rights. The law seems to be both mundane and aspirational: a mundane set of arrangements, and at the same time an embodiment of aspirations that have a central place within our political morality.

This ambivalence of law manifests itself at every turn. We might think, for example, of the relationship between law and force. We contrast forms of government based on 'the rule of law' with government based merely on organized force. Indeed the object of law might be thought to be the elimination of force from human relations, and its replacement by peaceful compliance with shared rules. The 'rule of law' seems to represent a situation where citizens and officials regulate their conduct by publicly recognized rules that are accepted as binding on all concerned. Yet are not legal systems simply very well organized and systematic structures of violence? Is the binding force of law any more than its backing by coercive sanctions? Unlike a gang of robbers, the state authorities can deploy overwhelming force against those who defy them, and they will generally use that force in regular and predictable ways. But does that make them the embodiment of a value to be radically contrasted with rule by force?

The attempted answers to such questions are often divided into two different groups. On the one hand are theories (generally called 'natural law theories') claiming that law is in its essential nature connected with the values of justice, right and the common good. A governing regime can truthfully claim to govern by law only if its actions and decrees are devised to serve the common good or to do justice. If a government simply exploits a subject population without even the pretence of seeking to do justice, it governs by force, not by law, however many of the trappings of legitimacy it may assume.

On the other hand, so-called 'legal positivist' theories insist on a morally neutral concept of law. Such theories are inclined to analyse law in terms of purely formal features, such as the presence of organized sanctions, or the publication of black-letter rules (namely, rules which are established in a definite verbal formulation, such as the provisions of a statute or an explicitly formulated rule laid down by a judge) which are quite independent of the good or bad content of the law, and the good or bad intentions of the law-makers. Like natural law theories, positivist theories vary widely in their reasons for advocating such a neutral concept of law, as well as in their conceptions of the nature of the philosophical enquiry. The contrast between 'natural law' and 'legal positivism' is therefore a slippery one which needs to be handled with care, but it can serve as a preliminary organizing device.

1.2   Positivism and reductionism

Law tells us what we 'ought' to do; it confers rights; it imposes obligations. Do not these terms import a dimension of moral authority? How can we speak of law as imposing obligations and conferring rights unless we regard the law as morally binding? If law is simply an apparatus of rules established by those who happen to have extensive coercive force at their disposal, how could it ever alter our rights and obligations?

The mere possibility of asking such questions demonstrates that, even if the positivist could convince us that all laws are posited rules emanating from authoritative sources, this would not suffice to establish the separation of law and morals. KANT (chapter 32), for example, argued in *The Metaphysics of Morals* that, even in a system of wholly posited laws, one would still require a basic natural law that established the moral authority of the lawgiver. In the absence of some such acknowledged moral claim upon our conduct, how could we view the law as a source of obligation?

The positivist reply to this line of argument consists in the claim that a legal obligation is not a species of moral obligation, nor is a legal right a species of moral right. Law may or may not impose moral obligations on us, the positivist claims: moral obligatoriness is not a logically necessary feature of law. Law does impose legal obligations on us, but these are not moral obligations and they involve no commitment to the law's moral authority or moral bindingness.

Having claimed that legal rights and obligations are not a species of moral right or obligation, the positivist is faced with the task of explaining what they are. Earlier versions of positivism tended to respond to this challenge by adopting a REDUCTIONIST (pp. 312–13) stance. They claimed that the apparently prescriptive language of law could be analysed reductively as a disguised form of descriptive or predictive language. When I state that you have a legal obligation to pay me £100, I seem to be making a prescriptive claim about how you *ought* to behave. But in fact (it was argued) all that my assertion actually means is that if you do *not* pay me £100 you are likely to suffer a sanction. In this way, propositions of law concerning legal rights and obligations could be treated as factual statements about the issuing of certain commands, predictions of the likely reactions of courts or the likelihood of suffering sanctions.

This type of reductionist analysis appealed to positivists because it seemed to translate legal concepts into terms that were free of all moral connotations. The analysis encountered some rather obvious difficulties, however. For example, I may *not* be likely to suffer a sanction if I fail to pay you £100 (I may be out of the jurisdiction and have no intention of returning, or it may be clear that you would not dream of suing for such a small sum), but it may nevertheless be the case that I have a legal obligation to pay. Similarly, courts generally invoke the existence of certain legal obligations incumbent on the litigants as a *reason* for deciding the case one way rather than another, and as a *justification* for imposing a sanction. This would make no sense if, correctly analysed, statements about legal obligations were *predictions* of the reactions of courts or the imposition of sanctions.

More modern positivists have therefore sought to analyse propositions of law in a way that preserves their prescriptive character without equating them with moral judgements. This has proved to be a very delicate balancing act.

The legal positivist Hans Kelsen (1881–1973) sought to avoid reductionism by treating legal discourse as based on a fundamental presupposition to the effect that the regime which is in effective control within a certain territory ought to be obeyed. He called this presupposition 'the basic norm'. To invoke such a basic norm looks at first like an abandonment of positivism, since the need for some such basic assumption seems to be precisely the point that is being made by Kant in his above mentioned remark from *The Metaphysics of Morals*. Yet Kelsen argued that this basic presupposition of legal science can be deployed simply for the purpose of grounding a cognition of positive law, and without collapsing questions of legal doctrine back into moral questions about justice. He described the basic norm as the minimum element of natural law without which a (non-reductionist) cognition of law is impossible.

Other approaches have been explored by those legal theorists who have found the notion of a basic normative presupposition unattractive. H. L. A. Hart (1907–93), for example, argues in his book *The Concept of Law* (1961) that reductionist theories of law proceed from the external viewpoint of someone observing the workings of a legal system, rather than the viewpoint of a participant in that system. To avoid the errors of reductionism, legal theory needs to reproduce the viewpoint of a participant within the system. Such a participant regards the legal rules as standards that ought to be complied with. Statements about legal rights and obligations do not predict sanctions, but draw conclusions about the applicability of legal rules to particular circumstances. The 'internal' point of view from which such language is deployed need not, Hart argues, be an attitude of moral approval of the law; nor need it be expressive of a judgement as to law's moral bindingness. The internal point of view rests on a judgement that the law ought to be obeyed, but this 'ought' need not be a moral 'ought'. A great many diverse considerations might underpin the conclusion that one 'ought' to obey the law. Legal theory can be neutral, it is argued, on what those considerations might be.

The problem with this way of avoiding reductionism in legal theory is that very little middle ground seems to be left between the viewpoint of the external observer and the judgement that law is morally binding. Someone who obeys the law purely from fear of sanctions would seem to take an *external* view, since his only concern will be with identifying those forms of conduct that are in fact likely to incur sanctions. If the participant's internal point of view is not one of simple sanction-avoidance, what can it be other than a belief in law's moral bindingness? The legal theorist could simply exclude such questions as irrelevant, thereby treating the 'ought' as foundational for legal discourse, while bracketing out all questions about what reasons underpin the 'ought' judgement. This approach, however, seems to depend upon a fundamental normative presupposition in very much the same way that Kelsen's theory does. It is therefore doubtful whether Hart succeeded in offering a genuine alternative to Kelsen's approach.

1.3 Law and politics

The debate between legal positivism and natural law is commonly thought of as a debate with an ancient and continuous history. Philosophers from SOCRATES (chapter 22) to the present day have reflected on the relationship between might and right, and have asked whether law is simply a body of decrees issued by those enjoying a monopoly of coercive power, or whether it is an expression of moral right which serves to concretize the abstract requirements of justice. Yet in more recent times these fundamental issues have acquired from the circumstances of modernity a peculiar salience and a distinctive character. New questions have arisen, and old ones have acquired new resonances, as a result of the central role that conceptions of law play in modern political life.

The ancient understanding of politics placed questions about the nature of the good life at the centre of political enquiry. Political institutions were thought to exist in order to inculcate and make possible a way of life that would be worthy and excellent. Such a fully valuable life was to be attained within public life by participation in the political affairs of one's collectivity. The private realm, which consists of labour, the family and the household economy, was considered to be a realm of necessity that was of value only in so far as it made a public political life possible. In the modern world, however, these priorities have been largely reversed. Political philosophers since HOBBES (chapter 28) have tended to search for a form of politics that would leave each individual free, so far as possible, to pursue his or her own conception of a good and excellent life. On this approach, the private realm is seen as a critically important area of autonomy within which the individual can choose and pursue wholly personal goals and projects. The existence of such private areas of autonomy necessitates the clear demarcation and enforcement of individual entitlements. Law and the state exist primarily to sustain the clear areas of entitlement that comprise the private realm.

To the extent that it emphasizes the role of individual entitlements, together with the need for PLURALISM (pp. 266–9) and autonomy, the modern conception of politics takes on a profoundly jurisprudential character. For it is law that defines and enforces entitlements, and the possibility of coherent and determinate principles of law is a necessary foundation for the modern view. Yet, if modern LIBERAL (chapter 8) political thought tends to promote individual autonomy above collective participation, the latter value nevertheless has a vital part to play, and a part that adds a further dimension to the problems of legal philosophy. For the modern world no longer regards the structures of civil society, the economy and the family as immutable structures forming a natural horizon within the parameters of which political life must be conducted. We are deeply aware of the mutability of such structures and of their openness to transformation through politics. In valuing democracy, we value our ability to decide collectively upon the general profile that our social structures should exhibit. In this sense, we value our ability to pursue collective projects of social reform.

Liberal politics, therefore, values both collective project pursuit and (in the form of the liberal's concern for liberty or autonomy) individual project pursuit. But these two values compete. A society which allowed its overall character to be determined solely by the uncoordinated actions and transactions of individuals pursuing their own projects would forfeit any power of collective control over its general profile and structure. On the other hand, a society which sought to regulate collectively every facet of its existence would inevitably erase any scope for autonomous individual project pursuit.

It is the possibility of a stable legal system that renders the liberal scheme of values coherent. If the rule of law is possible, collective project pursuit can find its sphere of expression within political decisions concerning the general rules which are to be enacted in law, and the general entitlements which are to be conferred. Action within the scope of such rules and entitlements will then be protected whether or not it serves to advance the goals of the collectivity as a whole.

This conception of the rule of law assumes, however, that one can identify and apply the rules and principles of existing law without reopening the political questions of collective project pursuit that may have led to the enactment of those rules and principles. It assumes that a judge can determine whether or not a citizen has acted within the scope of his or her legal rights without asking whether that citizen's actions serve to advance desirable collective goals. If these assumptions are false, then one's entitlements will extend only so far as one's actions serve collective goals. In other words, the value of individual autonomy will be wholly subordinated to the demands of collective project pursuit.

A major area of investigation in the philosophy of law concerns the attempt to sustain a viable distinction between law and politics. This debate has largely been conducted in the context of general theories of law and adjudication, but it has also involved detailed studies of particular areas of legal doctrine with a view to assessing the extent to which they can resolve disputes without collapsing all questions back into basic issues of collective goals and distributive policies.

1.4   Legal positivism and the criteria of validity

Legal positivism offers a morally neutral conception of law. It claims that valid laws may be identified by reference to criteria of a purely factual nature. H. L. A. Hart, for example, argues that every legal system contains a basic 'rule of recognition', accepted by officials, which identifies certain sources (such as decisions of courts or enactments of the legislature) as sources of law. A rule that emanates from an appropriate source is a valid rule regardless of its justice or injustice. Correspondingly, a rule that does not emanate from an appropriate source is not a valid rule, no matter how just or reasonable it may be.

Hart's legal positivism has much to recommend it. It offers pleasingly clear-cut answers to a number of questions, and seems to provide a simple way in which a distinction between legal doctrine and political dispute may be maintained. If, however, the theory is construed as an attempt to elucidate the criteria of validity actually employed by lawyers, the theory seems less convincing. Expert lawyers frequently disagree about what the existing legal rules are. For example, many lawyers believe that the English law of contract contains a doctrine of 'common mistake', holding that a contract is void if it was entered into on the basis of a fundamental mistake shared by both parties. Other lawyers deny the existence of any such doctrine. But if lawyers employ criteria of a factual kind in order to establish the content of the law, how is this type of disagreement possible?

Rather than providing a simple refutation of Hart's legal positivism, however, such examples raise the question of whether his theory aims simply to record the criteria of validity implicit in lawyers' practices, or whether it might not be seen as proposing a revised conception of law, constructed in the light of more general theoretical considerations. Hart was Professor of Jurisprudence at Oxford University during the 1950s and 1960s, and he worked in close collaboration with members of the Oxford ordinary language school of philosophy. This leads many to assume that his object in legal theory was the unearthing and articulating of deep criteria that lawyers and citizens unconsciously employ in making judgements about legal validity. Yet we shall see later that there are good grounds for rejecting this interpretation of Hart's work.

1.5   Law and adjudication

When courts come to apply legal rules, they are frequently confronted by difficult questions of interpretation. Factual situations do not come neatly packaged and labelled in legal vocabulary, and there can be ample scope for doubt about whether a particular legal rule should or should not be applied in the individual case. Can such questions be resolved by reference to formal semantic rules? Generally, the meaning of an utterance will be a function of formal linguistic rules in conjunction with the implications of the pragmatic context of the utterance. But legal rules frequently lack any obvious pragmatic context: they may have been enacted long ago with intentions that are now obscure, but they nevertheless purport to regulate the present. It may be tempting to interpret legal rules in the light of desirable policy objectives, but this threatens to collapse fundamentally the distinction between law and politics.

Different theorists have drawn different conclusions. Hart sought to sketch out a middle course between two extreme positions which he called 'formalism' and 'rule-scepticism'. By 'formalism' he meant the view that all conceivable cases can be decided by applying pre-existing rules of law, without any need to ask questions about non-legal considerations such as justice or social policy. 'Rule-scepticism', on the other hand, is the view that judges are never really bound by rules, so that the decisive factors in each case are always extra-legal considerations of social policy. Hart argued that formalism ignores the fact that language exhibits an 'open texture': while words have a 'core of settled meaning' they also possess a 'penumbra of uncertainty' where it will be unclear if the word is properly applicable or not. In so far as legal rules are linguistic entities they too will exhibit this 'open texture'. Cases of penumbral uncertainty will inevitably arise in any conceivable system of laws, and such cases can only be resolved by the court exercising its discretion. On the other hand, rule-sceptics (Hart argued) overestimate the extent of penumbral uncertainty and ignore the fact that the great majority of cases fall within the 'core of settled meaning' of the rule.

Hart's response to the rule-sceptics is not entirely satisfactory. In the first place his argument places great reliance on the assumption that legal rules have a definite verbal formulation. This is, of course, true of statutory rules, but within the common law developed by the courts it is not true. The binding part of a precedent is called the *ratio decidendi*, a phrase which refers to that part of the court's reasoning (as published in its judgement) which was necessary to justify the conclusion reached. All other observations made in the judgements are said to be *obiter dicta*. The distinction between *ratio* and *obiter* is extremely pliable, since a later court may take a different view from the original court about what exactly was necessary to the decision. Even where a court does offer a definite verbal formulation of the rule that it is applying, such a rule never becomes law *simply* by virtue of having been so pronounced, for it is always possible that a later court may treat the rule as *obiter*. In this way, courts constantly modify the rules in the course of applying them.

Suppose that we, as judges, have to decide a case that is somewhat similar to an earlier precedent. The court in the earlier case laid down a principle, the wording of which appears to apply exactly to the case in front of us. It will nevertheless be possible for us to avoid applying the principle as formulated in the earlier case if we can identify facts in the present case that were absent from the earlier case, and those facts appear to justify deciding the two cases differently. We will say that the principle as formulated in the earlier case was 'too wide', was not necessary for the decision in the earlier case (since a narrower principle, containing an exception for cases with facts like those of the present case, would have served equally well), and was therefore *obiter*. We will then decide our case by reference to a revised version of the earlier principle, now including an exception for cases exhibiting facts of the kind found in the present case.

The apparent pliability of the distinction between *ratio* and *obiter*, combined with the resulting tendency of courts to modify rules in the course of applying them, raises a problem of rule-scepticism that is not addressed by Hart. For if courts can alter the rules whenever they think it best (on grounds of justice, for example) then they are not really bound by rules: to be bound by a rule involves having to apply it even when you think that its application is *not* for the best.

Is it possible to argue that courts may *alter* the law while still being *bound* by the law? Hart's successor at Oxford University, Ronald Dworkin (b. 1931), has developed a theory which seems to explain how that might be possible, but only by radically breaking with the assumptions of legal positivism. Dworkin argues that law does not consist solely of rules deliberately established in precedents and statutes. In his view, law also includes general principles which are implicit within the established black-letter provisions. Judges have the task of constructing a coherent moral theory that provides an appropriate abstract justification for the established rules and institutions. They may interpret and modify established rules in a way that brings them more closely into line with the overarching abstract justification. Thus, even when judges *modify* established legal rules they are doing so in the application of deeper legal principles.

On the one hand, Dworkin's theory resembles rule-scepticism in its denial that black-letter rules, viewed in abstraction from considerations of justice, provide reliable guides to judicial decision in most cases. On the other hand, the theory resembles formalism, since it claims that the judge need never step outside the law to decide the case on extra-legal grounds of social policy. Every case, in Dworkin's view, can be decided by reference to the law: but law comprises much more than the black-letter rules allowed for by the positivist.

2   The Enterprise of Legal Theory

Even after we have become familiar with the range of problems outlined so far, we may remain uncertain about the type of solution that they require or invite. We need a general theoretical account of the nature of law that will, for example, explain the relationship between law and force, elucidate the criteria of legal validity and clarify the nature of adjudication. Yet what type of theory is being sought here? Would such a theory be *descriptive*, as talk of investigating the 'nature' of law seems to suggest? Descriptive of what? What facts about law are accessible only to philosophical enquiry and unknown to conventional legal or social scientific scholarship?

Or would such a theory be *prescriptive*? Would it be offering moral ideals and critical standards for the evaluation of legal systems? And, if so, is it not misleading to express the search for such a theory in the language of an investigation into law's 'nature'?

The philosophy of law is often said to be divided into two fields, known as 'analytical jurisprudence' and 'normative jurisprudence'. Analytical jurisprudence claims, not to offer prescriptions (which is the job of its normative partner), but to 'analyse' concepts, including the concept of law. Different theorists have inevitably had somewhat different conceptions of what such analysis might amount to.

The form of analysis developed by the legal positivist John Austin (1790–1859) sought to dispel problems by breaking down the concept of 'law' into simpler elements that would be more transparent. Thus Austin claimed that laws were the commands of a sovereign person or body in an independent political society. Each of these terms ('sovereign', 'command' and so on) was then defined in more basic and, Austin hoped, more transparent terms. The 'sovereign' in a society was to be identified not by any legal criterion (this would render the theory circular), nor by a moral standard (which would convert the theory into a natural law theory), but by direct reference to observable facts about patterns of behaviour. Thus the 'sovereign' was said to be that person or body that is habitually obeyed by the bulk of the population, and is not itself in the habit of obeying any other determinate person or body.

Despite the considerable influence that Austin's theory came to exert in late nineteenth-century England, it exhibited a number of serious defects. In many legal systems it is not possible to identify any person or body satisfying Austin's definition of sovereignty: power and obedience are divided according to shared constitutional rules. Moreover, Austin's theory is thoroughly reductionist in character, claiming that propositions about legal duties are statements about the likelihood of suffering sanctions in certain circumstances.

Hart endeavoured to develop a version of legal positivism that would overcome the limitations of Austin's approach while remaining faithful to the basic objectives of legal positivism. Thus Hart sought to demonstrate that valid laws could be identified by criteria of a factual, non-moral kind, without running into the difficulties encountered by Austin's account of the sovereign; and that propositions of law (about legal obligations and rights) could be distinguished from moral judgements without adopting a reductionist analysis that denied their prescriptive character.

Hart took the view that Austin's account of the sovereign was misconceived in so far as it attempted to identify a fundamental source of law by direct reference to

411

observable behavioural patterns. What was required, in Hart's view, was not the notion of a basic 'habit of obedience' but the notion of the acceptance of a rule. An accepted rule differs from a mere habit of obedience in that, in addition to a regular pattern of conforming conduct (which Hart called the 'external aspect'), a rule involves the existence of a critical reflective attitude on the part of participants (the 'internal aspect'): the pattern of conforming conduct is thought of as a standard that ought to be complied with; those who deviate are criticized; and the criticism is thought of as justified.

Hart on Primary and Secondary Rules

Austin's theory also lacked another distinction developed by Hart: the distinction between primary and secondary rules. Primary rules are rules directly regulating conduct, such as rules prohibiting theft or violence. Secondary rules are rules that regulate the identification, modification and application of other rules. Hart claimed that the invention of secondary rules was as important as the invention of the wheel, and described it as representing the step from the pre-legal to the legal world. A social order containing only primary rules would exhibit various defects such as inflexibility and inefficiency. Most importantly, if such a society were of any complexity it would be likely to exhibit great uncertainty about the scope and content of its primary rules. Uncertainty of this kind could be overcome by adopting a basic 'rule of recognition' which stipulated some criterion by which the society's primary rules might be identified. A very simple rule of recognition might provide that all the rules carved on a certain stone tablet were to be obeyed. Developed legal systems will have highly complex rules of recognition, identifying sources of law such as enactments of the legislature and decisions of the courts, and regulating the relations between those various sources.

As we noted earlier, Hart sought to avoid the reductionism of Austin's theory and to preserve the prescriptive character of propositions of law by reproducing the 'internal point of view' of the participants. Hart's object was to elucidate the meaning of propositions of law by exhibiting their role within a specific social context. Propositions of law (reporting the content of legal rights, duties, powers and so forth) derive their significance from a social context characterized by the existence of a basic rule of recognition. But they are not *descriptions* of that social context. They express conclusions about the applicability of the rule of recognition and the rules derived from it. They are, as it were, prescriptive judgements made from the viewpoint of a specific system of rules. One might compare them, by analogy, with judgements about what is required by the rules of a game. Such judgements are, within the parameters of the game, prescriptive; but they bracket out all questions about whether there is good reason for playing the game in the first place.

Hart's theory does not purport to offer moral prescriptions: it represents an enterprise of conceptual clarification, which Hart conceives as being prior to substantive moral or empirical inquiries into law. But what exactly does Hart take 'conceptual clarification' in this context to be?

The central objective of Hart's positivism is a defence of what he calls the 'separation of law and morals'. This 'separation' has two main facets. One aspect involves the claim that legal validity is a matter of a rule's derivability from a basic rule of recognition in a legal system: a rule that emanates from an appropriate source is valid irrespective of its justice or injustice (and, similarly, the justice of a rule does not make it law if it does not emanate from an appropriate source). A regime exhibiting certain formal features (acceptance by officials of a basic rule of recognition, combined with general compliance with the laws flowing from that basic rule) is a legal system irrespective of whether it pursues justice or exploitation.

The other aspect of the separation of law and morals is the claim that knowledge of the content of the law does not, in itself, have any bearing on what one should do from a moral point of view. There may or may not be a moral obligation to obey the law. If there is, then knowledge of the law will give precise content to that obligation, but such an obligation is not entailed by the concept of legal validity. It is not part of the concept of law that it is morally binding.

Why did Hart believe that we should accept these claims about the concept of law? His long association with the Oxford ordinary language school of philosophy has led some to assume that Hart saw himself as simply unearthing and laying before us the criteria that are implicit in our ordinary usage of the word 'law'. It should be obvious, however, that ordinary usage is unlikely to provide an enlightening guide on these issues. To a large extent ordinary usage simply expresses and evinces the ambivalences articulated within theoretical debate.

Dworkin has drawn a distinction between 'borderline' disputes and 'pivotal' disputes. In a borderline dispute, we have a shared criterion but disagree about the extent of its applicability: for example, we agree on some general concept of 'art' but disagree about whether that concept is applicable to photography. In a pivotal dispute, we have no shared criterion: here our disagreement about photography is merely symptomatic of a deeper disagreement about the essential nature of art. Dworkin appears to suggest that Hart viewed legal theory as being concerned with borderline disputes, whereas (in Dworkin's view) legal theory is concerned with a pivotal dispute.

This clearly misrepresents Hart's conception of legal theory. Hart himself pointed out, in the introduction to his *Essays in Jurisprudence and Philosophy* (1983), that his analysis of the concept of 'law' was not intended as a piece of ordinary language philosophy. In Hart's view, the uncertainties surrounding the concept of law require a choice to be made between rival theoretical standpoints: they cannot be resolved simply by close attention to ordinary usage. Nor do they require a simple decision on the applicability of the concept's 'penumbra'. The 'core of settled meaning' of the concept of 'law' may reflect, not a shared criterion, so much as agreement on a range of instances where diverse theoretical positions and criteria happen to overlap. Thus we may all agree that the enactments of legislatures in France, the United Kingdom and Canada are central instances of 'law', yet we may have quite different reasons for so regarding them. In your view the critical fact may be the moral authority of those legislatures, or the justice of their enactments, while in my view it may be the effective control that they exert over their territory.

Hart's reason for adopting a positivist theory of law appears to be his belief that positivism reflects the most important features of law as a social phenomenon. Such a judgement obviously requires criteria of 'importance' and, if the theory is to play a clarificatory role as a preliminary to substantive enquiry, the criteria should be drawn from values that are as weak and widely shared as possible. Reconstruction of Hart's

413

arguments in *The Concept of Law* suggests that his point is as follows. Given the very minimal and widely shared goal of survival, and given certain very general facts about human nature and circumstances (Hart speaks here of a 'minimum content of natural law') it can be demonstrated that societies require rules of conduct. In a society of any complexity, shared rules will be sustainable only if they are publicly identifiable by means of a rule of recognition. The provision of such a set of publicly identifiable rules is a function of law.

Hart's theory develops an account of law's nature that emphasizes its central role in providing publicly ascertainable rules. Only rules identifiable by reference to the basic rule of recognition are acknowledged by Hart to be instances of 'law'. More open-ended criteria of justice or fairness, even though admitted in forensic debates and regarded by lawyers as legal doctrinal arguments, are treated by Hart as extra-legal considerations that may be looked to when the legal rules fail to yield a determinate answer. The justification for semantic regimentation of this kind is not that it reflects ordinary usage, nor that it adjudicates on penumbral uncertainties, but that it reflects the most important and distinctive features of law, judged from the viewpoint of human survival.

Once the minimal element of evaluation involved in Hart's view of law is exposed, however, it can be difficult to prevent it spreading so far as to endanger the positivism of the theory. For example, Hart claims that positivism clarifies the issue that is faced by a citizen who has to decide whether to obey an unjust law. In Hart's view it is better and more honest to say, 'This is law, but because it is unjust I should perhaps disobey it', rather than, 'Because this rule is unjust, it is not law'. Yet why, we might ask, should one way of expressing the point be thought clearer than the other?

The most plausible answer is one that involves a *rejection* of Hart's strict separation of law and morals. If publicly ascertainable rules are necessary for survival, that seems to give us a moral reason for complying with them even when they are unjust. After all, if people were prepared to comply only when they considered the rules to be perfectly just, there would be no point in having a system of publicly ascertainable rules in the first place. These moral reasons for compliance continue to apply even when they are outweighed by conflicting considerations (the rule is, let us say, *grossly* unjust). The best reason for insisting on continuing to apply the label 'law' even to unjust rules is that this usage acknowledges the continued force and applicability of the moral considerations stemming from the need for a system of publicly ascertainable rules. To refuse to acknowledge the legal validity of an unjust rule would be to treat it as a mere non-entity lacking all moral significance, and so would be to deny the continued relevance of the need for publicly ascertainable rules.

Hart is concerned to defend two theses, which we might call 'the exclusivity of sources' and 'the moral neutrality of propositions of law'. 'The exclusivity of sources' is the idea that legal validity is a matter of derivability from the rule of recognition, and not a matter of the rule's just or unjust content. 'The moral neutrality of propositions of law' is the idea that knowledge of one's legal duties does not in itself entail any judgements about how, from a moral point of view, one should behave. Yet the most powerful reasons for advocating the exclusivity of sources require the rejection of the 'moral neutrality' thesis. This would be totally unacceptable if it forced on us the view that law is morally *conclusive* of how one should behave. No such move is required, however. The 'moral neutrality' thesis should be abandoned in favour of a much weaker claim, that can be labelled 'the moral non-conclusivity of law'. This thesis claims that propositions of law are indeed a species of moral judgement: they are judgements about the applicability of those moral reasons flowing from the need for a body of publicly ascertainable rules. Yet such judgements can never be morally *conclusive*, since they embody only one range of moral considerations which will need to be balanced against many other factors.

3 From Positivism to Natural Law

Legal positivism originated in opposition to theories of natural law. Some positivists rejected the claims to objective knowledge of morality that formed the bedrock of the natural law tradition. Kelsen, for example, adopted an ETHICAL NON-COGNITIVIST (p. 440) stance which denied the possibility of knowledge of moral norms or values. The central core of his work was the attempt to demonstrate that scientific knowledge of positive *legal* norms was in fact possible. It is in the context of this project that we should interpret his remark (mentioned earlier) about the basic norm as the minimum element of natural law without which a cognition of law is impossible.

Hart's positivism was closer to a tradition of thought initiated by Jeremy BENTHAM (1748–1832) (chapter 35). Bentham did not wish to deny that we can have knowledge of moral right and wrong. In fact, his legal positivism was in many respects the consequence of his view that the PRINCIPLE OF UTILITY (chapter 35) (requiring that we should act so as to maximize the greatest happiness of the greatest number) is the supreme principle of morality. This utilitarian stance led him to regard theories of natural law as being founded on confusion and posing a threat to ordered liberty under law.

The opening salvo of Bentham's positivist assault on natural law was directed against the work of the English judge and jurist Sir William Blackstone (1723–80). Blackstone was the author of the first systematic exposition of English law, published as the *Commentaries on the Laws of England* in 1765. Prior to Blackstone, one acquired a knowledge of English law by immersion in its chaos of details. Law books were mostly huge compendia of legal knowledge arranged on no very rational principle. Adopting models drawn from continental legal scholarship, Blackstone arranged the institutions of English law around a basic scheme of natural rights. In accordance with the view of natural law writers such as John LOCKE (chapter 29) (1632–1704), Blackstone treated English law as the concretization and enforcement of people's natural rights. The law was not simply a massive list of disorderly rules, but a systematic body of principles. It was capable of systematic study and exposition precisely because and in so far as it was based on principles of natural law. Consequently, Blackstone's account of English law was inclined to pass smoothly from exposition of the law to justification, since the very scheme of exposition was structured by natural law precepts.

In Bentham's opinion, this type of natural law theory confused questions about what the law *is* with questions about what it *ought to be*. The exposition of existing legal rules is one thing, he argued, while their critical evaluation is another. It does not follow from the *existence* of a legal rule that it is morally *right*. Nor does it follow from the immorality of a rule that it is not law. Bentham believed that confusion of these different questions was likely to induce either supine conformity without any preparedness to criticize the law (since it would be assumed that the law, being law, must be right) or, alternatively, irresponsible anarchism (since it could be claimed that any particular rule which is considered to be unjust is therefore not law at all).

It is doubtful if Blackstone was really guilty of the crude confusions that Bentham claimed to discover in his work. Much of Bentham's fire was directed not so much at Blackstone's view of the relationship between law and morals as at Blackstone's emphasis on natural *rights* as the basis of morality. Bentham considered all talk of natural rights to be 'nonsense' and he believed that such talk merely served to divert our attention away from the only relevant considerations: considerations of utility.

Indeed Bentham's whole theory of law was fundamentally shaped by what he took to be the requirements of utility. He developed an elaborate analytical framework for the intellectual reconstruction of positive law, by means of which he sought to explain the entire apparatus of legal concepts (including rights, duties, powers and property) in terms of a general theory that viewed law as a set of commands backed by sanctions. For Bentham, such reconstruction served an essentially practical point, by making law and legal thinking more closely fitted to its role as an instrument of utility, and by eliminating the confusions that so often (in Bentham's view) obscured the true requirements of utility and insulated the law from the demands of reform. His aim was not to *explicate* legal thinking so much as to revise it.

The move away from Bentham's clear UTILITARIAN (chapter 35) objectives, and towards a more purely 'analytical' jurisprudence, commenced with the work of Bentham's own disciple, John Austin, whom we mentioned earlier. Austin's theory of law is in many respects a simplified version of Bentham's. But, whereas Bentham might have presented the theory as a deliberate proposal to *revise* ordinary assumptions about law, Austin seems to intend his theory as an *explication* of those assumptions. Indeed, far from mounting an assault on the vested interests of lawyers in the way that Bentham might have wished, Austin's version of legal positivism provided a powerful underpinning for the lawyer's claim to be an expert in a technical and self-contained area of knowledge distinct both from morality and from politics.

Austin and his disciples thus introduced into legal theory a basic uncertainty concerning the status of investigations into the nature of law. This uncertainty continues to dog the subject.

Superficial examination of the writings of legal positivists might lead one to believe that their theories treat law in entirely formal terms, involving no judgement about law's purpose or value. Yet if the legal positivist is to offer an integrated solution to the various problems outlined at the start of this chapter, some features must be selected from the immensely complex social phenomena of law and given a central role within the theory, so that they may serve as a point of focus around which other features can be arranged. Thus Hart chooses to emphasize the lawyer's reliance upon rules emanating from a limited number of authoritative sources (especially legislative enactments and judicial decisions). Other features of law are either reinterpreted or marginalized. This selection of focus expresses Hart's judgement about the fundamental purpose or function of law: the provision of a body of publicly ascertainable rules as a basis for the ordering of conduct in a world characterized by disagreement. Yet the ghostly influence of Austin seems to induce in Hart a desire to leave this basic foundation of his theory understated and relatively unexplored. As the contemporary natural lawyer John

Finnis (b. 1940) aptly puts it, 'Hart's method points out a land which is left to his readers and hearers to hazard to enter.'

Finnis on Natural Law

In Finnis's view, the tradition of natural law thought has been misunderstood and misrepresented by legal positivists. Positivists have tended to assume that the central thesis of natural law theory is the claim that legal validity is a matter of moral bindingness (or, perhaps, of justice) so that a rule that is not morally binding (or not just) cannot be said to be legally valid. As it is traditionally, if somewhat misleadingly, put: *lex injusta non est lex* ('an unjust law is not a law'). Positivists regard this claim as simply being confusing, and prefer to apply the label 'law' to all the rules emanating from particular formal sources within a legal system, irrespective of their moral status. Yet, as we have seen, the claim that this way of thinking is clearer, and reflects the most distinctive and important features of the social phenomena of law, itself requires some evaluative stance from which we can make the required judgement of 'importance'.

Finnis claims that natural lawyers have never really wished to deny validity in the lawyer's sense to unjust or immoral rules. Rather, their object has been to explore the land to which Hart's method points. In other words, they believe that a coherent theory of law can only be the consequence and expression of a deeper moral and political theory. In fact, Finnis claims, we understand the nature of law by grasping the way in which law is the solution to a problem of practical reason.

With this end in view, Finnis develops an account of the objective 'goods' or 'forms of human flourishing' which we will pursue if we are fully rational. These goods can be pursued only within a community, and the maintenance of a community that sustains the ability of each individual to pursue the objective goods amounts to 'the common good'. The common good is therefore not an aggregative conception, involving the 'maximization' of individual goods, but a framework of institutions and conditions making individual pursuit of a good life possible. The existence of an appropriate community requires the co-ordination of conduct around shared rules, and the provision of such a set of rules is the central task of law.

In one sense, therefore, Finnis's conception of law is not dissimilar to Hart's. They both view law as a set of publicly ascertainable rules. Finnis, however, believes that this conclusion is to be arrived at only by means of an understanding of law's relationship with the requirements of practical reason. In its 'focal' sense, law serves the common good, and this relationship to the common good inevitably shapes our thinking about law, and the vocabulary (using terms such as 'rights' and 'duties') we use to describe law. Legal institutions may at times be used for purposes of oppression or exploitation, but these are degenerate instances of law which we can only understand by grasping the ways in which they resemble, and yet diverge from, law in its 'focal' instances. The traditional maxim *lex injusta non est lex*, Finnis concludes, was intended to highlight the degenerate nature of such uses of law.

Finnis has performed a great service in overturning hitherto prevailing caricatures of natural law theory. Yet he seems to underestimate the significance of Hart's apparent desire to construct his theory of law from a standpoint (of the aim of 'survival') which is both weak and widely shared. Hart's reliance upon such a minimal evaluative starting-point reflects an understanding of his enterprise as a clarificatory one which is prior to substantive moral enquiry or empirical investigation. Hart hopes to construct a coherent concept of law that may be employed as a tool in moral and empirical debate, thereby overcoming the problems which arise when different participants in debate employ different conceptions of law; or, still worse, when controversial moral or empirical theories about law are introduced in the guise of definitions of 'law'. Finnis appears to view Hart's minimalism as a failure to explore fully the underpinnings of his own theory; but it is probably better to regard it as a refusal to build the clarificatory enterprise on a richly controversial foundation when a weak and minimal foundation will serve equally well.

4 Theory as Interpretation

Philosophy is often thought to be characterized by a concern for the necessary and universal. Particular, contingent facts are thought of as matters for empirical enquiry, not philosophical reflection. Thus the philosophy of law traditionally concerns itself with features of law that are logically necessary, as defining features of a supposedly universal concept of law. The peculiar characteristics of this or that particular legal system are matters for social science rather than philosophy. Writers such as Hart and Finnis offer concepts of law that purport to be universal. They do not simply describe characteristic features of the legal systems of the United Kingdom or Australia: rather, they offer us criteria for saying of *any* form of social ordering whether or not it should be regarded as an instance of law.

Familiar though this conception of philosophy may be, it is not beyond challenge. We may reflect upon the meaning and significance of practices within our own society and culture, without any pretension to universality, and such reflections may bear many of the hallmarks of philosophical thought. Indeed, we may discover that it was the desire reflectively to understand our own practices that drove us into the search for universal and necessary features in the first place.

The theory of law developed by Dworkin adopts a focus that is culturally specific rather than universal, and that seeks a reflective understanding of our own practices. According to Dworkin, the philosophical debate concerning the nature of law is not, when properly understood, a search for a semantic definition of 'law', or a search for a universal concept. Rather it arises out of the adoption of an 'interpretive attitude' in relation to our own practices. The interpretive attitude raises a question about the general point or rationale of a practice, not as a theoretical but as a practical issue: the ultimate question is how best to continue the practice.

Questions such as those concerning the nature of law reflect disputes about the meaning or point of our legal practices. Such disputes cannot be resolved by reference to the intentions or understandings of the participants in the practice, because the participants will themselves be embroiled in the dispute. Thus a society might have practices of courtesy, involving raising one's hat to people in certain circumstances, or opening doors for them. Yet the participants in these practices might disagree about the underlying point of courtesy. Is the object to express a judgement of respect about the recipient of courtesy? Or, quite to the contrary, is the object to provide a neutral, non-judgemental, way of dealing with people regardless of what you think of them? The choice between rival interpretations of this kind might make a difference to what we would see as an appropriate way of continuing the practice. Should we, for example, make a special effort to raise our hats to soldiers returning from a war?

If we cannot have recourse to the intentions and understandings of the participants, how are we to choose between rival interpretations of a practice? Dworkin offers a general theory of interpretation which he calls 'constructive interpretation'. On this view, the best interpretation will satisfy two criteria, of 'fit', and of 'appeal'. Criteria of fit concern the ability of the interpretation to accommodate the uncontroversially observable features of the practice. An interpretation need not be a perfect fit, but it must come up to a certain threshold of adequacy. Within the constraints of fit, we must choose the interpretation that makes the practice into the most appealing practice it can be from a moral point of view.

We noted above that there is room for some uncertainty about whether philosophical enquiry into the nature of law is intended to be descriptive or prescriptive. Dworkin's theory of interpretation presents legal theory as having both a descriptive and a prescriptive aspect. Interpretive theories of law will be descriptive to the extent that they must satisfy the constraints of fit; they will be prescriptive in so far as one must choose the morally most appealing interpretation amongst those that satisfy the constraints of fit.

A theory of law (or any other interpretation of a practice) will, Dworkin holds, involve three stages. At the 'pre-interpretive' stage we must achieve a rough preliminary identification of the practices we are discussing. Dworkin concedes that even the pre-interpretive stage involves interpretation (every description of human conduct involves interpretation), but the interpretations involved at this stage may be wholly uncontroversial. Next comes the 'interpretive' stage, where we must arrive at a general interpretation of the meaning, point or rationale of the practice, choosing (within the constraints of fit) the interpretation that makes the practice into the best practice it can be from a moral point of view. Finally comes the 'post-interpretive' stage, where we revise our original understanding of what the practice requires in the light of the interpretation now adopted (for instance, we decide that, since courtesy is an expression of one's judgements of respect, it requires us to raise our hats to soldiers returning from a war, but not to the local squire).

This account of the nature of legal theory, and the view of interpretation on which it depends, raise a large number of questions. Some positivists feel, for example, that important questions are begged when a prescriptive, justificatory aspect is built into one's conception of the legal theoretical enterprise. Is it not the whole object of positivism, they ask, to present law as being morally neutral? On the other hand, one can argue that Dworkin actually overestimates the contrast between his conception of legal theory and that held by Hart and others. For, as we have seen, Hart's theory also adopts an interpretation of the point of law (the provision of a set of publicly ascertainable rules) and then revises our ordinary understanding in the light of that interpretation.

Dworkin also seems oblivious to the way in which an interpretive and culturally specific view of the tasks of legal theory fundamentally erodes the distinction between philosophy and sociology (formerly policed by the distinction between the universal or the necessary and the particular or the contingent). In resisting attempts to collapse the philosophy of law into sociology, Dworkin maintains that the interpretation of a practice is necessarily prior to a study of its social or historical context. We may well wish to challenge this claim, however. When viewed in isolation, a practice may have an apparent meaning that is subverted once it is relocated in its social context. Practices of male courtesy towards women, for example, may take on a different meaning when located in the context of a male-dominated society within which women are generally subordinated. Equally, an understanding of the historical context may well be necessary if we are to grasp the genesis and character of the interpretive disputes that arise: such disputes are, after all, not free-floating, but arise out of historically produced fractures and tensions within formerly unproblematic practices. An historical and sociological enquiry may therefore be necessary if philosophy is to attain a fully transparent and self-conscious understanding of the interpretive disputes in which it hopes to engage.

Dworkin's neglect of law's social context is particularly ironic since, as we shall see, he views law as a deep expression of equality and interprets in this light the lawyer's concern for consistency and principle. Radical critics of law, such as MARXISTS (chapter 34) and FEMINISTS (chapter 20), might well agree that law involves a 'discourse' of equality; but they would point out that the apparent meaning of this discourse is subverted once we locate law in the context of a deeply hierarchical society founded on oppression and domination. The law then appears not as the expression of a deep concern for equality, but as an attempt to mystify and misrepresent social relations by presenting them as being founded on equality.

5   Law as Integrity

Having outlined Dworkin's views on the nature of legal theory, what of his substantive conclusions about the nature of law? What interpretation of our legal practices does he adopt?

Dworkin considers three rival interpretations or theories of law, which he calls 'conventionalism', 'pragmatism' and (his own preferred theory) 'law as integrity'. Each theory is evaluated against the descriptive criteria of 'fit' and the prescriptive criteria of moral 'appeal'.

Conventionalism resembles legal positivism in its emphasis on the public ascertainability of legal rules, but it proffers this view in the context of a wider interpretation of the point of law. According to the conventionalist, the point of law is to give citizens fair warning of the circumstances in which the state's coercive powers will be used, and to protect the expectations formed in reliance on this warning. In Dworkin's view, this theory fails to fit the facts of law, since it cannot explain the ability of courts to innovate by granting new remedies in cases that are not clearly covered by any existing rules. What if the conventionalist responds by saying that the value of protecting expectations must be traded off against the demands of flexibility, so that some judicial innovation in cases not covered by existing rules is permissible? In that case, Dworkin argues, conventionalism will fail *prescriptively* since it proposes an irrational way of trading off flexibility against the protection of expectations. If such a trade-off is the point of law, it is best effected case-by-case, so that the expectations engendered in each case can be identified and weighed.

Pragmatism is a theory that proposes precisely such a case-by-case approach. The pragmatist is really a species of rule-sceptic, since he or she holds that judges should not view themselves as being *bound* by pre-existing legal rules. Rather, the judge's task should be to give the decision that will have the best consequences, all things considered. The expectations that have been created by the publication of legal rules must be taken account of by the pragmatist judge when he or she tries to determine which decision will be for the best. It may frequently be the case, therefore, that the pragmatist judge has very powerful reasons for applying pre-existing legal rules. Yet such reasons are never conclusive in advance of the particular facts of the case: they must always be weighed against other conflicting considerations.

Pragmatism in its turn is rejected by Dworkin, and he turns to the development of his own theory. This hinges on the value of 'integrity' in law. Dworkin claims that we expect the law to express and embody some more or less coherent moral vision. While the law may contain competing moral values we would not expect it to strike wholly arbitrary compromises between rival moral positions, even if such compromises gave expression to the prevailing balance of power (in terms of numbers of votes) between the advocates of rival positions. We value the moral coherence or integrity of the law quite independently of the value we put on the law's justice, for we expect the law to exhibit a certain deep moral coherence even when we personally subscribe to some rival moral vision.

When the state employs its coercive apparatus in accordance with a coherent moral position, it treats its citizens as equals. The point of law, Dworkin claims, is to ensure that governments treat their citizens as equals in that sense. The lawyer's concern with principles and consistency is a concern not with the public ascertainability of rules but with the moral coherence that is a deep expression of equality.

Dworkin on Adjudication

How then should a judge set about the task of adjudication? At this point Dworkin brings his theory of interpretation into play once again. A judge is to decide cases by reference to the morally best interpretation of the materials of law. Rather than thinking of the judge as confronted by a finite number of black-letter rules which, once exhausted, throw us back on to extra-legal considerations of social policy, the judge confronts an enormous array of statutes and cases which must be subjected to a process of interpretation. The judge must find interpretations of these materials that discover within them some coherent moral vision. Such interpretations must satisfy the constraints of fit, and within those constraints must make the law as good as it can be from a moral point of view. In fact, Dworkin claims, this process of interpretation is of a piece with the investigations of legal theory so that jurisprudence (or the philosophy of law) is but the first and most abstract stage of adjudication.

This theory offers an elegant solution to a number of intractable problems. For example, we noted earlier the way in which it enables us to explain how judges can modify the established rules of law while still being bound by law, a feature of adjudication which poses severe difficulties for most other theories. Some serious problems remain, however. On Dworkin's theory, judges must decide cases not by reference to what they consider to be just in the abstract, but by reference to the conception of justice that they find embodied in the existing law. Yet, in deciding what that conception is, they must rely upon their personal moral viewpoint. Since it is quite likely that the 'constraints of fit' will prove not so constraining after all, is there not ample scope here for different judges to reach dramatically diverse conclusions about what the existing law is? Indeed, Dworkin insists that it is up to each citizen to decide for himself or herself what is required by law, and it is in principle possible for a citizen to be correct when all the judges are wrong. Of course, convergence in legal judgements may be secured by pre-existing convergence in moral judgement. But is it not plausible to suggest that a major object of having law is to make it possible for us to have shared rules even in a world characterized by serious and far-reaching moral disagreements?

The perceived need for authoritative rules in a context of moral diversity makes conventionalism seem attractive. Dworkin's criticisms of conventionalism are in fact somewhat misconceived, for they assume that the conventionalist is concerned with the protection of expectations that have been formed in reliance on published rules, and this type of concern could be adequately accommodated by a pragmatist approach. But a better account of conventionalism would see it as being concerned to *encourage the formation* of stable mutual expectations about conduct, and a pragmatist approach to adjudication would be inferior to conventionalism when judged by this objective.

Some problems with Dworkin's analysis stem from the character of a modern legal order. When Blackstone systematized his exposition of English law around a handful of basic natural rights, the law was mainly concerned to enforce rights of property and to deal with obvious wrongs such as theft or assault. Also, the law had been mainly developed by judges, who were concerned to preserve the coherence of their decisions with the existing fabric of law. Once the law is largely a product of statute, and the statutes are enacted in pursuit of a host of very loosely related or even conflicting social policies, is there any good reason to expect it to exhibit a high degree of moral coherence?

The growing muddle and complexity of most modern legal orders might, in fact, provide a powerful explanation of Dworkin's own theory. Lawyers regularly construct theories as a basis for the decision of cases, in the sense that they need to generalize from certain specific instances, or to find a perspective from which to interpret specific statutory words. Yet the lawyer's theories operate at a very low level of abstraction. What is so striking about Dworkin's vision of law is the abstract philosophical plane on to which he drives legal doctrinal argument. Such abstraction, however, may itself be a response to the growing complexity and incoherence of the law. If one is determined to seek coherence, one must seek it at ever more abstract levels. Legal positivism might be seen as the opposite response to the same problem: faced by growing incoherence at the level of general principles, one focuses more and more narrowly and exclusively upon black-letter rules.

Dworkin's theory can be compared and contrasted with the work of Lon Fuller (1902–78). Fuller's work seems to have influenced Dworkin in several fundamental respects, although the influence is not acknowledged. Like Dworkin, Fuller sees the judge as being confronted by a task that cannot be reduced to the application of a basic rule of recognition. Adjudication is, in Fuller's view, a purposive enterprise guided by the complex moral aspiration of 'fidelity to law'. Whereas Dworkin connects the value of law to a left-liberal concern for equality, Fuller interprets the central value of law in terms of a more conservative concern for liberty and order under the governance of general, prospective and published rules. In many cases, fidelity to law will require adherence to posited rules; but, Fuller claimed, to imagine that this represents the ultimate guiding principle of adjudication is to confuse fidelity to law with 'subservience to authority'. Thus, a power to modify the rules in some cases may be consistent with the judge's fundamental duty. On appropriate occasions, fidelity to law may require a refusal to apply the rules established by authority (as where, for example, those rules are so vague as to defeat the idea of governing conduct by prospective rules: an idea that Fuller takes to be an integral part of the concept of 'law'). In some situations, the judge's duty may give rise to intractable moral dilemmas: enforcing a hopelessly vague statute may undermine the ideals of clarity that are inherent in the rule of law, but assuming a power to strike down such statutes may itself give rise to great uncertainty. A complex process of moral and philosophical reflection is therefore *internal* to the application of law.

6 Unger and the Critical Legal Studies Movement

We saw earlier that liberalism requires a firm distinction between law and politics. Political debate and decision results in the enactment of certain rules and the conferment of certain entitlements. Action within the scope of such rules and entitlements should be protected even when it does not serve the general welfare, or advance the political objectives of the collectivity. Yet can we apply the rules and decide upon the exact scope of the entitlements without reopening the political questions of social policy or distributive justice that resulted in their enactment?

The suggestion that we cannot successfully separate legal doctrine from politics lies at the heart of the arguments put forward by the Critical Legal Studies movement (CLS), a loose association of leftist lawyers centred in the United States. Much of the work of CLS takes the form of detailed studies of particular areas of legal doctrine, with a view to demonstrating the doctrine's open-endedness, incoherence, or its tendency to collapse back into basic political issues. When CLS adherents seek to offer more general theoretical statements, they frequently exhibit a high degree of confusion and a lack of clarity which poses severe obstacles to interpretation. This provides us with a justification for focusing on the work of one leading figure who has exerted a powerful influence on CLS even if his views are not altogether typical of the movement generally. The work of Roberto Unger exhibits a much higher degree of sophistication than most other CLS writings, and merits consideration even in a very brief survey of legal philosophy.

In Unger's first book, *Knowledge and Politics* (1976), he identified two problems that are internal to liberal political theory, which he called 'the problem of legislation' and 'the problem of adjudication'. The problem of legislation concerns the question of how liberal political theory can find a basis for generating just rules for the conduct of social life given its commitment to neutrality between conceptions of the good life. This problem is a central topic within political philosophy, and we shall leave it on one side in order to focus on a problem that is specific to the philosophy of law, namely, 'the problem of adjudication'. Here Unger argued that, even given the enactment of authoritative legal rules, those rules could not be applied in specific cases without collapsing the issue back into political value judgements. He saw this claim as following from liberalism's rejection of 'essentialism', which is understood as the thesis that words have stable meanings by virtue of representing fundamental 'essences'. Liberalism's moral neutrality (as Unger characterized it) required a rejection of essentialism, and yet liberalism's faith in law could not be sustained *without* essentialism.

In effect, Unger was arguing that, once legal theory abandoned *formalism* (which is the claim that all cases can be resolved simply by applying legal rules without reference to any other considerations), it would have no way to avoid collapsing adjudication into politics. In his later work, *The Critical Legal Studies Movement* (1986), Unger employed the term 'formalism' in a wider sense to refer to all theories that assert the existence of a distinction between legal doctrine and open-ended ideological controversy: he claimed that 'formalism' in its more narrow and conventional sense is simply the extreme end point of the same general thesis. Unger argued that when we come to apply legal rules, we are forced back into deeper questions about the principles underpinning the rules: we are forced to assume that the rules represent a morally coherent and defensible scheme of human association (an assumption that Unger terms 'objectivism', and which we may find best exemplified by Dworkin's theory of law). Yet this assumption, he claims, is unsustainable. Law already represents within itself the conflict between rival social visions. For every principle that we discover in the legal doctrine, therefore, we will also find a counter-principle that tends to subvert it. There may be a way in which the principle and counter-principle are conventionally balanced against each other, but this balance will not itself be grounded in any deeper principle. Rather, it is an expression of the erroneous assumption that social arrangements have to take more or less the form that they presently do. Once we grasp the essentially plastic and revisable nature of our forms of association, Unger argues, we will see that there is no reason why the counter-principles should not be extended at the expense of the principles. This 'deviationist' form of doctrinal argument reveals the hollowness of legal doctrine's claim to be separable from politics, while simultaneously revealing the doctrine's potential as an instrument of revolutionary social transformation.

It is doubtful whether Unger's argument is successful. As John Finnis has pointed out, on the assumption that the law is pursuing a plurality of different 'goods' or moral values, there is no reason why the particular balance struck between those goods should itself be required by a deeper principle; there may be different, equally reasonable, ways of striking the balance. Alternatively, a more conservative view might point out that, if a part of law's object is to stabilize mutual expectations about conduct, one would expect the law to reflect those forms of human association that currently exist; the mere fact that they could be otherwise would, from this perspective, be irrelevant.

7 Philosophical Reconstruction of Legal Doctrine

The juxtaposition of Dworkin's emphasis on the internal coherence of law with Unger's assertion of its conflict-ridden incoherence has spawned an upsurge of philosophically informed studies of particular areas of legal doctrine. The aim has been to identify the general moral theories or values that appear to underpin major legal institutions such as contract, tort, liability and criminal law.

The most well-established field for this type of philosophical research has long been criminal law and the penal system. Bentham offered a sweeping justification of punishment in utilitarian terms, backed up by corresponding justifications for such features of criminal law as the mental defences (criminal responsibility generally requires either intention or foresight on the defendant's part), the defence of duress, and the exclusion of liability for the insane. Such utilitarian accounts have been relentlessly opposed by rival theories, often drawing their inspiration from Kant.

More recently, theorists have turned their attention to private law, particularly contract and tort. Here the major split has been between those theorists who see private law doctrines as being inextricably connected to wider conceptions of distributive justice or aggregate welfare, and rival theorists who seek to confine such distributive or aggregative concerns to the tax and welfare sectors of the law, and who seek to explain private law in terms of the value of 'corrective justice'. Amongst the former group, scholars of 'the economic analysis of law' have been prominent, generally seeking to explain and justify legal doctrines as instruments of efficient resource allocation or wealth maximization. Inevitably, these debates are connected both with general questions about the nature of law and with wider issues of political philosophy.

Further Reading

Cotterrell (1989), Lyons (1984) and Simmonds (1986) provide elementary introductions to the subject. After that, it is probably best to tackle Hart (1961), Fuller (1969), Finnis (1980) and Dworkin (1986). Dworkin's earlier books also repay detailed study. Hart (1983) contains a number of very important and immensely lucid essays.

Kelsen's work provides a very different form of legal positivism from that of Hart, and the best place to begin is with Kelsen (1992). The 1992 English translation contains a very valuable introduction by Stanley Paulson.

Joseph Raz is one of the most important contemporary writers on the philosophy of law, and he has developed a sophisticated defence of positivism that is strongly influenced by both Hart and Kelsen, in The Authority of Law (1979), and in numerous other publications. His work is also notable for the connections that it develops between philosophy of law and theories of practical reason. For various views on the relationship between law and practical reason, see Raz (1975), MacCormick (1978), Beyleveld and Brownsword (1986) and Finnis (1980).

Recent debates on the moral underpinnings of legal doctrines may be explored by reading Fried (1981), Coleman (1992) and Hart (1968).

Unger (1976) is a rather wayward book that is inclined to resort to crude caricatures. Nevertheless, it contains some arguments that are interesting, and which have exerted a powerful influence on the critical legal studies movement. Unger (1986) contains a powerful critique of Dworkin (referred to as 'the rights and principles school') in its early pages. This might be compared with the essay by Finnis, in Eekelaar and Bell (1987). Kelman (1987) and Altman (1990) provide useful guides to the confused debate surrounding critical legal studies.

425

References

Altman, A. 1990: *Critical Legal Studies: A Liberal Critique*. Princeton, NJ: Princeton University Press.

Austin, J. 1955 [1832]: *The Province of Jurisprudence Determined*. London: Weidenfeld and Nicolson.

Beyleveld, D. and Brownsword, R. 1986: *Law as a Moral Judgment*. London: Sweet and Maxwell.

Coleman, J. 1992: *Risks and Wrongs*. Cambridge: Cambridge University Press.

Cotterrell, R. 1989: *The Politics of Jurisprudence*. London: Butterworths.

Dworkin, R. 1978: *Taking Rights Seriously*, revd edn. London: Duckworth.

——1985: *A Matter of Principle*. Cambridge, MA: Harvard University Press.

——1986: *Law's Empire*. London: Fontana.

Eekelaar, J. and Bell, J. (eds) 1987: *Oxford Essays in Jurisprudence*, 3rd series. Oxford: Clarendon Press.

Finnis, J. 1980: *Natural Law and Natural Rights*. Oxford: Clarendon Press.

Fried, C. 1981: *Contract as Promise*. Cambridge, MA: Harvard University Press.

Fuller, L. 1969: *The Morality of Law*, 2nd edn. New Haven, CT: Yale University Press.

Hart, H. L. A. 1961: *The Concept of Law*. Oxford: Clarendon Press.

——1968: *Punishment and Responsibility*. Oxford: Oxford University Press.

——1983: *Essays in Jurisprudence and Philosophy*. Oxford: Oxford University Press.

Kelman, M. 1987: *A Guide to Critical Legal Studies*. Cambridge, MA: Harvard University Press.

Kelsen, H. 1992 [1934]: *Introduction to the Problems of Legal Theory* (translated by B. L. Paulson and S. L. Paulson). Oxford: Clarendon Press.

Lyons, D. 1984: *Ethics and the Rule of Law*. Cambridge: Cambridge University Press.

——1993: *Moral Aspects of Legal Theory*. Cambridge: Cambridge University Press.

MacCormick, N. 1978: *Legal Reasoning and Legal Theory*. Oxford: Clarendon Press.

Raz, J. 1975: *Practical Reason and Norms*. London: Hutchinson.

——1979: *The Authority of Law*. Oxford: Clarendon Press.

——1980: *The Concept of a Legal System*, 2nd edn. Oxford: Clarendon Press.

Simmonds, N. E. 1986: *Central Issues in Jurisprudence*. London: Sweet and Maxwell.

Unger, R. M. 1976: *Knowledge and Politics*. New York: Free Press.

——1986: *The Critical Legal Studies Movement*. Cambridge, MA: Harvard University Press.

Discussion Questions

1 Can a single theory of law deal satisfactorily with all the major puzzling features of legal thought and practice?

2 Is it more important for philosophers to analyse the concept of law or the social practices of which law is a part?

3 What, if anything, distinguishes the rule of law from a regime based solely on force?

4 Are legal rights and obligations species of moral rights and obligations?

5 Can a reductionist programme deal with the apparently prescriptive language of law?

6 Does Kelsen's basic norm allow law to be prescriptive without being absorbed into moral questions about justice?

7 How minimal is the 'minimum element of natural law' required for a positivist account of law?

8   Should we accept Hart's claim that an adequate positivist account of legal obligation can be provided by taking account of the 'internal' viewpoint of a participant of a legal system?

9   What importance does the modern notion of autonomy have for the theory of law?

10   Discuss the claim that rules are laws if they emanate from an appropriate source, whether or not they are just.

11   Must we choose between the 'formalist' position that all conceivable cases can be decided by pre-existing rules of law and the 'rule-sceptical' position that all legal cases are decided by extra-legal factors?

12   Do judges have the task of constructing a coherent moral theory? Can different judges construct different theories?

13   What is the importance of a rule of recognition in the theory of law?

14   Does legal positivism provide a middle way between supine acceptance of the law and irresponsible anarchism?

15   Should philosophy of law be a matter of reflectively understanding law in a particular society rather than the determination of a universal theory?

16   Is it a fault of Dworkin's interpretive and culturally specific theory that it erodes the distinction between philosophy and sociology?

17   Should we value moral coherence or integrity in law even if we subscribe to a different moral view?

18   How does Fuller's 'fidelity to law' differ from subservience to authority?

19   What are the consequences if we cannot separate legal doctrine from open-ended ideological controversy?

20   Does the possibility of striking different balances among the plurality of moral values pursued by the law undermine the authority of the actual balance struck by the law?

14
Philosophy of History
LEON POMPA

Historians are concerned with the human past, with what happened, and how and why it happened. But the past is a difficult object of study. It is beyond the reach of perception and requires special methods of enquiry which may lead to results that fail to satisfy the criteria of knowledge that perception satisfies. Its contents are almost limitless and can be studied in greater and lesser degrees of detail, requiring decisions of selection which may affect historians' claims to truth. It contains the deeds and practices of past individuals and communities which may be sufficiently different from our own that we cannot be sure that we can reach any true explanation or understanding of them. Finally, historians must express their results in forms that may also affect the epistemological status of their claims. Modern philosophy of history has engaged with all of these difficulties. An underlying concern has been to establish how far the capacity of historians to reach objective truth is affected by the difficulties which arise in each of these areas of enquiry. This will be the central question in this chapter, starting with what historians themselves consider the least philosophically puzzling aspects of their activity and proceeding to those that they consider more problematic.

1   Knowledge of Historical Fact

Historians normally adopt a realist view of knowledge, involving three claims: that individual events, actions and occurrences really took place in the past; that true historical statements or historical facts are statements about some of these occurrences; and that these statements are known because sufficient evidence for them is available in the present. Thus, when we know that Napoleon lost the Battle of Waterloo, we know that a certain event, Napoleon's losing the battle, took place in the past. We know this because we know that the statement that it did take place is true, and we know that the statement is true because there is sufficient evidence in the present to justify our claim to know it. But this threefold conception is deceptively simple and has been challenged at every stage. I shall consider each of these in turn.

It is clear that this whole view would be at risk if we had reason to doubt that there was a real past at all. Such a reason was first offered by Bertrand RUSSELL (chapter 37), who pointed out that it is logically possible for the world to have come into existence five minutes ago, with a population having a complete range of 'memories' of apparently prior times (Russell 1921: 159–60). But if the world came into existence five minutes ago, not only would most of our memories be false but so would almost all of our historical knowledge. It might be thought that we can avoid this conclusion by appealing, as historians normally do, to the evidence presently available to us. But this will not help for, according to the hypothesis, everything would now be as it is, including all that historians think of as evidence for the past. Hence, were there no past before five minutes ago, nothing that we take as evidence for that past could really be evidence for it.

Russell took his hypothesis seriously enough to suggest that our supposed 'knowledge' of the past should be translated into statements about the present contents of mind because he believed that, through perception, we are directly acquainted with the reality that makes statements about the present true in a way in which we cannot be with regard to the past. The hypothesis has been subject to a number of objections (Danto 1965: 83–4), but I shall concentrate on one which depends upon important features of the nature of historical evidence. According to this objection, it does not follow from the logical possibility of the hypothesis either that the world began five minutes ago or that we cannot know whether or not it did, because 'present evidence would not be what it is if no past had existed' (Gorman 1982: 72). To understand the force of this objection it is necessary to note two points. Firstly, it is an important feature of historical language that it contains what are called 'past-entailing' or 'past-referring' terms. These are terms 'whose correct application to some present object or event *logically* involves a reference to some earlier object or event'. Thus to describe somebody as having a scar entails that at some earlier time he or she suffered a wound (Danto 1965: 71–2). Secondly, the use of some artefact as a piece of historical evidence requires use of such past-entailing terms. Thus when an historian describes some document as a letter written by Gladstone, he or she is making a past-entailing assertion. For he or she is applying to a document which exists in the present a description which entails that some event happened in the past, namely that Gladstone wrote this letter (Gorman 1982: 56–8). Thus, given the past-entailing nature of the descriptions under which documents count as historical evidence, the refutation takes the form of asserting that we cannot maintain our present past-entailing conception of historical evidence and admit that the hypothesis could be true.

It might seem, however, that this fails to refute Russell's hypothesis, since it is part of the latter that, even if the world came into existence five minutes ago, everything in it would remain the same *for us*, including therefore our present conception of historical evidence. So we would continue to describe present artefacts in past-entailing terms, even though the events 'entailed' never took place. In fact, however, the refutation is substantially correct. For Russell must allow for the reality of *some* period of time – let us say his 'five minutes' – before which the past may not have existed, in order to allow us to understand the doubt expressed in the hypothesis. This means that he must allow that some past-entailing descriptions, namely those that relate something now present to something in the past five minutes, are true. But if this is so, he must show how it is possible that some past-entailing terms really have the implications for the past that we take them to have while others, which are of precisely the same kind and satisfy

429

precisely the same criteria, do not. But this cannot be shown. For the consistent use of criteria is necessary not only for historical thought but for any coherent thought whatsoever. Hence the sceptical challenge could be maintained not as a challenge about the reality of some *part* of the past but only as a challenge about the reality of the *whole* of the past. But this would be self-defeating since the contrast between a real past (the 'five minutes') and an unreal past, which is needed to make the hypothesis coherent, would then be lost.

So far, therefore, there is no reason to doubt that there was a real past. But realism involves the view that the past to which historians are committed is also an *independent* past; in other words, it is a past filled with events that occurred *irrespective of whether or not we shall ever come to know of them*. Historians conceive of their task as discovering the contents of this past but not of *creating* it. This view has, however, been challenged from an idealist point of view, via a theory now generally known as 'constructionism' (Nowell-Smith 1977). The constructionist thesis accepts that historians come to know truths about the past. But the past to which these relate is not the real past, as we normally understand it – that is, as an independent past of real events which await discovery. It is seen as a peculiarly 'historical' past that exists as something that we construct from present evidence. Accordingly, were we to come into possession of new evidence and construct it differently, not only would our knowledge alter but so also would the historical past itself. But if this is so, the standard historical belief in realism, and the conception of knowledge which presupposes it, would be false.

The principal reason given for this claim is that since the real past no longer exists, it can have no part to play in the verification of the historian's account. Accordingly, it is claimed, the past that the historian brings into view is not the past as it might have been in itself but one that exists relative only to its capacity to explain our beliefs about the evidence. The idea that historians discover a past that existed independently of our knowledge of it is therefore rejected in favour of the idea of a past that exists only as a construction to explain present evidence (Goldstein 1976, 1977). It should be noted, although it cannot be pursued here, that this view has affinities with some forms of scientific ANTI-REALISM (pp. 294–5).

Constructionism involves the same assumption as Russell made: that because historical statements are about a past which we can no longer perceive, there is something problematic about its ontological status. But this is a very doubtful assumption. Most kinds of knowledge, both everyday and scientific, are about what is currently unobservable. Our memories, for example, are about what we cannot now perceive. So, too, are our beliefs about the speed of light or the existence of neutrons. Were it the case, therefore, that a statement about something that is unobservable cannot be about an independent reality, the range of statements about what we take to be real entities would need to be replaced by a range of statements about constructed entities. To take a simple case, one person's reason for claiming to know the colour of Queen Elizabeth II's coronation dress may be that he remembers having seen it on Coronation Day, while another's may be that she has consulted the order books of the royal dress makers – she has, that is, undertaken some simple historical research. If the constructionist account is correct, the two claims cannot be about the same dress, for each will be about a dress that exists only in relation to the mode in which our knowledge of it is constructed. Thus there will be two dresses, one existing as part of an 'historical' past and the other as part of a 'memorial' past, rather than, as we would normally think, one dress which we can know about in either of two different ways. This conclusion, moreover, will apply to the constituents of all of our different kinds of knowledge that go beyond simple reports of what is present to perception. Thus the book in the past that I remember will differ not only from that whose history I reconstruct but from that whose past physical or chemical properties can be analysed in terms of theories proper to chemistry or physics. But in this case we shall be unable to use our knowledge, say, of the chemical properties of some past object to help us in our historical thinking about that object, perhaps by helping us to date it, since the object whose past chemical properties we construct will be a different object from that whose historical existence we construct. Thus there would be a number of different objects 'existing' in a number of different realities, each relative to a particular mode of research, rather than, as the realist believes, objects existing in one and the same reality, whose different properties can be known by different kinds of research.

This thesis certainly conflicts with our everyday view of the real world. But this is perhaps not too important since, while philosophy should not ignore everyday belief, it cannot be wholly constrained by it. More importantly, it conflicts with the requirement that we must think of all knowledge as being about one single reality because, unless we do so, we shall be unable to relate the products of our different disciplines to one another. Constructionism, and the strong verificationism upon which it depends, must be rejected because it leads to results that conflict with this requirement.

These points do not, however, rule out historical knowledge being reached by the use of argument in the way in which the constructionists suggest. They show only that there is no reason to believe that the arguments result in statements about some peculiarly 'historical' past rather than about a real past which we can know in a variety of different ways. How they do this has been shown in an account that emphasizes the need for historical evidence to be described in past-entailing terms in the way indicated above (Gorman 1982: 56–68). When the historian has carried out his research correctly and checked for authenticity, he will be in possession of an evidential statement such as 'Here, before us . . . is a letter written by Gladstone', the truth of which both entails and requires that Gladstone wrote the letter. Thus there is a relationship of mutual entailment between past-referring *evidential* statements and historical statements, in virtue of which we can truly assert the latter on the strength of the former.

But while this shows how evidential statements, *if true*, entail true historical statements about a real past, it leaves room for a third and final sceptical doubt. For in order to arrive at an evidential statement such as that about Gladstone's letter, we need both to employ a theory of interpretation and to be satisfied that it is the correct one. Because the example given is in English, this is a point that is often overlooked by English speakers, where we just assume that we are using the correct language. But the fact that a theory of interpretation is employed becomes evident if we consider the case where the evidential statement is in some language which we do not understand. Then we need to turn to dictionaries and grammar books to enable us to translate the language of the document. This, of course, is rarely difficult, although it can become so in practice when historians are dealing with documents in old and relatively unknown languages. But it illustrates the fact that a theory of interpretation is always in use, even if not explicitly.

431

The sceptical doubt that now arises, however, concerns the justification of the theory of interpretation that is employed. For recent work in the PHILOSOPHY OF LANGUAGE (chapter 3) has shown that there is always the possibility of more theories of interpretation than any which we employ. It follows that we cannot, especially when dealing with the past, simply rest content with the belief that we are employing the correct theory of interpretation, the one enabling us to justify the claim that we are in possession of *true* past-entailing statements. We require some reason to support this belief. Thus, to revert to the example of Gladstone's letter, it is a fact that we have a theory of interpretation under which the word 'Gladstone' is taken to be the name of a particular historical individual. Moreover, our use of 'Gladstone' is linked to the use of many other similarly functioning names, such as 'Disraeli' and 'Queen Victoria'. If we are wrong in our interpretation of the word 'Gladstone', we shall be wrong also about all these connected names. The doubt is not therefore simply about our right to interpret a single name in a certain way but about our right to rely upon the whole theory governing the interpretation of that and many other names.

This doubt about justifying any theory of interpretation we employ provides a threat not only to our knowledge of the past but to a considerable amount of our knowledge of the present, since our use of past-entailing terms means that much of what we take to be knowledge of the present involves truths about the past. We think of ourselves, for example, as having personal and communal histories that interlink in innumerable ways. Indeed, such beliefs comprise an important component in our conception of personal identity. Thus if it were not true, say, that there was a 1914–18 war, all that part of people's personal histories which involve reference to the war would be false. In so far, therefore, as much knowledge of the present involves claims about the past, the sceptical threat to historical knowledge also threatens much of our knowledge of the present.

One possible response to this doubt is to point to the fact that our present procedure leads to coherence in our claims about the past. Claims about Gladstone are linked to claims about Disraeli, the Irish problem and so on. But an appeal to coherence alone is inadequate to justify a theory of interpretation. For there are many other possible theories of interpretation which could lead to equally coherent sets of claims which are incompatible with those that we now accept.

A Framework of Basic Historical Facts

Another way of countering the doubt concerning justification for our theory of interpretation would be by supporting the theory by linking it to some knowledge of the past reached by a different route. If it could be shown, for example, that, prior to his examination of the evidence, the historian already knows that Gladstone existed, we could use that knowledge to justify his or her use of a theory of interpretation in which the word 'Gladstone' is the name of that historical individual. The problem then would be not how to defend the theory of interpretation that allows the historian to conclude that an individual called Gladstone existed and wrote the letter in front of him or her, but the much simpler problem of deciding whether the historian can show that the letter was written by the Gladstone of whose existence he or she already knows or whether it was written, perhaps forged, by some other person.

But how is it possible to support this refutation which, at the moment, amounts to little more than asserting what the sceptic is questioning: that we know *some* things at least about what happened in the past? What we need here is an account of how, *independently of argument from evidence under a theory of interpretation*, we can have some such knowledge. Since others have not written on this subject, I must here fall back upon my own suggestion that some of our knowledge of the past has actually come from the past – in other words, that it is transmitted within societies with appropriate institutional mechanisms, from the past to the present, and that, in virtue of existing in such a society, the historian is in possession of knowledge of a framework of basic facts with which to support his or her theory of interpretation (Pompa 1993). Thus, instead of arguing from evidence under a theory of interpretation to, say, Gladstone's existence, the historian takes his or her inherited knowledge of Gladstone's existence as justification for a theory of interpretation in which that existence is presupposed. On this view, any attempt to interpret the evidence in such a way as to throw doubt upon Gladstone's existence would be disallowed and any theory of interpretation that seems to allow such doubt would be rejected as unjustified. The suggestion, therefore, is that our theory of interpretation is justified because it presupposes some historically acquired knowledge of the past. The historian is then entitled to use it to discover new facts about the past that are not part of our inherited knowledge.

It should be noted, however, that this suggestion conflicts with the widely held FALLIBILIST (pp. 39–40) theory of knowledge, according to which no belief is in principle immune from the possibility of revision, including therefore the most central of our present historical beliefs, such as that there was a Crimean War. But the reply to the fallibilist must be that although it is a LOGICAL POSSIBILITY (pp. 151–6) that the Crimean War never occurred, it is not an *epistemological possibility*. For we can allow that it is an epistemological possibility only if we can envisage some way in which some future historian could try to justify the claim that the war never occurred without accepting the sort of theory just outlined. But if he is unable to do this, he will be open to sceptical doubt about his or her theory of interpretation and therefore about his or her claims to knowledge about the past.

2 Explanation and Understanding

The discussion so far lends support to the belief that historians can produce knowledge of what actually happened in the past. But a large part of their work is concerned with explaining what happened. The analysis of the proper way in which to do this has been the source of a major controversy involving two opposing viewpoints: that they should offer 'scientific' explanations or that they should focus upon a humanistic form of understanding.

The view that explanations in history either are or should be of the same form as those in the natural sciences was advanced in a particularly strong way by Carl Hempel (b. 1905) who, building upon the work of Karl Popper (1902–94) in the PHILOSOPHY OF SCIENCE (chapter 9), advanced a general thesis (Hempel 1959) about what it is for something to be an explanation. The thesis, subsequently known as the COVERING LAW MODEL (pp. 304–5) or the deductive–nomological theory, involves two points: that to explain an event is to show it to be predictable; and that to be shown to be predictable, the event must be shown to be subsumable under some set of causal laws. Thus, although historians normally explain the occurrence of particular events, such as the 1914–18 war, in terms of a combination of particular causes – such as the development of national rivalries for political supremacy in Europe in the nineteenth century or the common need for new sources of raw materials and new markets to maintain the industrialization of Western Europe – this can be an explanation only if the particular causes cited are instances of a causal law or laws to the effect that whenever there is a build up of national rivalries for political supremacy and a common need for new sources of raw materials and new markets, a war breaks out. Hempel realized that the sorts of generalizations mentioned in this example were not laws in the sense that they held without exception and, indeed, that properly supported causal laws were rarely, if ever, used by historians. For this reason he referred to the explanations that historians actually give as 'explanation sketches', claiming that they offered more or less vague indications of the relevant laws and pointed the way for the further empirical research necessary to establish them as required in a fully supported explanation. On this account, therefore, historical explanations are incomplete explanations of the same form as those to be found in the physical sciences.

A strength of the covering law model is that it satisfies one feature that one would expect of any explanation, namely, that it should explain why one event occurred rather than some other (Donagan 1966). It does this because, by subsuming an event under causal laws, it shows that the event had to occur. This means, however, that the kind of explanation it offers is deterministic and this, as we shall see, has been the main underlying reason for the strongest objections to it.

Objections to the theory divide into two kinds. First there are those that emphasize that historical explanations do not, as a matter of fact, conform to it. There have been many objections of this sort (White 1965: 14–104, offers a reformulation of the theory; see also Donagan 1966: 142–6), but these cannot be conclusive. If the theory claims that this is the form that any fully supported explanation *must* take, objections that historical explanations do not take this form can be met by the reply that historians are failing to offer fully supported explanations. For this reason, I shall concentrate on objections of the second kind, which claim that the subject matter of history is such that the theory is wrong in principle.

The first of these objections, which has weighed particularly strongly with historians, is that the theory fails to recognize the uniqueness of the events and individuals featuring in history (Oakeshott 1933: 154). There was, and can be, only one 1914–18 war. Hence, if historians succeed in explaining what caused this unique event, it cannot be by conforming to the requirements of the covering law model since the laws in question hold between different *kinds* of events rather than unique events. But the claim to uniqueness must be treated with care, for much depends upon the sort of uniqueness in question. The covering law model does not deny, for example, that the events that it offers to explain, such as the occurrence of the 1914–18 war, are unique. It must insist, of course, that these events, although unique, are describable in general terms, in order to be subsumable under laws about kinds of things. But it can hardly be denied that although events are unique in being the particular events that they are, they must also be describable in general terms, for this is necessary in order for us to be able to say anything at all about them. The 1914–18 war was a unique event, but to talk about it we must bring it under the general term 'war', a term that can be applied to many other unique events. Hence the mere appeal to the uniqueness of historical events is an insufficient objection to the covering law model.

What historians sometimes mean, however, when they appeal to uniqueness, is the way in which the occurrence of events depends upon the activities of unique individuals *about whose behaviour there can be no laws*. If there can be no laws about the behaviour of individuals, the explanation of any events that their behaviour affects cannot involve subsumption under general laws. Nevertheless, while some covering law theorists have accepted that different individuals are unique, they have rejected the claim that this precludes the application of the model, on the grounds that there can be laws about unique individuals. We can explain what a particular individual does, for example, by asserting that he or she always acts like that, which involves referring to his or her dispositions (White 1965: 47–53). There is, however, an important difference between causal laws and the dispositions of individuals to act in certain ways. For causal laws necessitate events and hence will support deductive predictions about them. The dispositions of individuals, on the other hand, are simply patterns of behaviour that are characteristic of them; explanations and predictions based on knowledge of them lack the rigorous character that the covering law model requires. One can explain somebody's acting in a certain way by reference to his or her general tendency to do so, but that does not mean that he or she may not upon occasion act in an entirely different way in the same sort of situation: a fact that we acknowledge when we say that what he or she did was out of character. We cannot both admit this possibility and maintain that explanation in terms of dispositions carries the same implications of law-governed predictability as is required by the covering law model.

The issue of individuality is given increased importance by the fact that historians are not usually concerned with the individual as such but with the individual in particular historical roles, such as that of the King or Queen of England. We can be interested in Elizabeth Tudor as the individual she was, but this is largely to understand her behaviour as Queen Elizabeth I of England, which involves her acting in a certain role or set of roles, and how, as the unique individual she was, she affected the character of the roles that she occupied. This raises the issue of ROLE THEORY (p. 388). Very roughly, we may note that the occupancy of a role involves the possession of powers and responsibilities that range from those that are fairly specific, even legally defined, to others that are relatively indeterminate – and even in areas of legal definition there is considerable flexibility in the ways in which the individual may properly behave in the role. As a result, the behaviour of the individuals who occupy the roles can have as much effect on the nature of the roles as the requirements of their role upon their behaviour. Tracing this interplay is among the most important ways in which historians seek to explain the historical development of roles. Thus, there has been ongoing discussion as to how far changes in the respective powers of Parliament and Monarchy in sixteenth-century England were due to Elizabeth's conduct in her role. This does not mean that these changes may not have been affected also by religious, social and economic changes but, since these further changes also involve reference to individuals in their roles, the relationship between individual and role still remains at the centre of the discussion. Given its flexibility, it seems that there could be no laws able to explain either this relationship or the historical development of roles to which it has contributed (Berlin 1966: 23–4). Thus the covering law model is in principle inapplicable here.

These difficulties suggest that the failure of the covering law model is due to an incorrect assimilation of explanation in history to explanation in the natural sciences. An alternative viewpoint, which stresses the primacy of understanding over explanation, has built upon the work of R. G. Collingwood (1889–1943), who distinguished between the subject matter of science, which is the physical world, and that of history, which is the world of human activity. Accordingly, he argued, historical explanations differ from scientific explanation because human activity is always an expression of thought, which it is the historian's task to understand. 'When an historian asks "Why did Brutus stab Caesar?" he means "What did Brutus think, which made him decide to stab Caesar?"' (Collingwood 1993: 213–15). Thus we explain the agent's action by establishing his or her reason for deciding to do what he or she did. The mistake of thinking that historical explanations are the same in kind as those in the natural sciences stems from a failure to recognize this distinction in subject matter.

Rational Reconstruction

Collingwood's claims have been very influential in the development of an alternative model of historical explanation, involving what is often called a RATIONAL RECONSTRUCTION (p. 386). The central idea here is that the historian's principal task is to understand human ACTION (pp. 384–8) in a specifically human way, which he or she does by showing some event to be an INTENTIONAL ACT (p. 386) undertaken in accordance with beliefs that rendered it sensible to the agent in question (Dray 1957, 1980, 1993; Martin 1977). The action is explained when we understand why the agent decided to act in that way. This, however, is only a part of the explanation since, as Collingwood insisted, historians are interested not only in why people acted in certain ways but also in the success or failure of their actions. Hence, once the agent's reasons and beliefs are established, they must undergo further critical examination, since the success or failure of actions often depends upon the merits or defects of the beliefs and reasons behind them. Thus, it may be that although the agent's actions made good sense from his or her point of view, some of the relevant beliefs were false, as were the beliefs the Romans held about Hannibal's position at the Battle of Trasimeno. Once, however, the historian has established what the Romans believed and that those beliefs were false, he or she can use this knowledge to explain their defeat.

If historians attempt to understand actions in terms of rational reconstruction, the explanation will be true only if they can establish what the agent's reason for acting really was. It has been argued, however, that to do this they must establish the additional facts that the agent was rational and that, in the agent's kind of situation, rational agents invariably do the kind of thing which he or she did. The need for a covering law is thus re-introduced, this time relating the beliefs of rational agents in certain kinds of situations to certain kinds of actions (Hempel 1974: 98–105). This is a useful objection to consider, for it highlights the difference between the deterministic assumptions of the covering law model and the voluntarist assumptions of the rational reconstruction model. The objection assumes that an appeal to an agent's rationality will suffice only if his or her behaviour was an instance of some sort of *causal law* governing the behaviour of rational agents. But this is what the rational reconstruction model denies. According to the latter, when we say that an agent was rational we are saying that his or her action was caused by a decision based upon an appraisal of his or her situation undertaken in the light of, *but not caused by*, his or her knowledge of certain standards of appropriateness. When we act we must have some idea of what it is appropriate to do to achieve our ends. But standards are not laws. They are simply beliefs about the sorts of things one ought to do, either for their own sake, as in the case of moral standards, or in order to achieve certain ends, and there can be many different beliefs of both kinds. The fact that we make use of standards when considering what to do does not *necessitate* that some particular action be done on a particular occasion – hence the fact that an agent's action is a consequence of a decision taken in the light of standards does not mean that it was caused or necessitated by them.

The crucial weakness in the covering law model to which this points is thus not the assumption that the historian can explain the occurrence of something only by showing why that action occurred rather than some other action; rather, the weakness is the further assumption that he or she can do this only by showing that that action *had* to occur. But this is a requirement that neither can nor needs to be met. To show why one action occurred rather than another, it is sufficient to show why that action rather than the other *in fact* occurred and to do this the historian need only show why, from among the historically available options (the options available to a given individual in a specific historical society), one course of action seemed preferable to the others.

The importance of standards in this conception, however, gives rise to a problem which does not beset the covering law theorist. For standards vary in different historical societies. The Greeks, for example, consulted the oracles for advice in certain situations. Because we do not ourselves normally consult oracles (although some people do), we may wonder whether the Greek standard of rationality was the same as ours and, if it was not, whether we can understand rational reconstructions of Greek actions in the way in which we can understand those of our contemporaries. This difficulty has been exacerbated, moreover, by the claim that standards are peculiar to, and part of, the lived experience of specific societies. We understand the standards of our own society because they are rules which we are *taught* how to follow by living in our society. But since we cannot share the lived experience of past societies and be taught their rules of conduct, we can have no way of understanding them. Even if we manage to make statements about them, they will not come out as standards the rationality of which we can grasp. This position, sometimes called historicism, relativizes the notion of rationality to particular historical societies and in doing so challenges our right to claim to understand why people in those societies acted as they did.

One might try to counter this difficulty by pointing out that, despite it, historians do succeed in making the activities of past societies intelligible to us. But this might seem to beg the question, which concerns how far we *really* understand the kind of rationality in dispute. A more effective response is to question whether *historical* societies have the self-contained character suggested. For to talk of an historical society is often just a way of talking about earlier phases of the career of some present society. It is sometimes thought that historicism is provided some support by the difficulties that anthropologists encounter when trying to grasp the rules which can make sense of the practices of primitive societies. But this is an unhelpful parallel for, while anthropologists often start with no knowledge whatsoever of the language of the societies they study, this is not so in the historical case. As argued in the previous section, the historian is not completely alien to the past which he or she seeks to understand, for the society in which an historian finds himself or herself is a product of that past. It carries within it many social and linguistic practices, some of which are developments, and others remnants, of earlier practices. If present standards have arisen from earlier ones, there seems no reason in principle preventing the historian from working backwards to their earlier stages. If this is so, we can refute this version of an historicist argument by appealing to the fact that we do not find understanding all standards in earlier parts of history as impossible as the objection suggests. Certainly there seems to be no more difficulty in understanding the Greeks' recourse to the Delphic Oracle than a contemporary non-believer might find in understanding a believer's recourse to prayer. It could be argued, of course, that non-believers have *no understanding at all* of religious practice. But this would limit the concept of understanding to what we believe and that is far too severe a standard. We can, surely, understand early cosmological theories even if we do not believe them. Moreover, the attempt to limit what we can understand to what we believe would have sceptical implications for much shared everyday understanding that we take to be quite unproblematic. But investigation of this possibility is beyond the scope of this chapter.

The scope of rational reconstruction extends beyond action in the strict sense to include what has been made – including the different political and economic institutions, technologies and artistic creations of the past – by enabling us to understand the point of these creations and, through this, to understand why they have changed. In histories of art, for example, past influences play a very important part, as in the case of the effect which the rediscovery of classical architecture and sculpture had upon Renaissance art and architecture. But rational reconstructions are required here precisely because the influence of the rediscovery of the classical world lay in the way the Renaissance artists and architects assimilated classical thought into their own and through that saw the expanded range of possibilities which they could incorporate into their aims.

Nevertheless, rational reconstructions are not the only kind of explanations to be found in history. Collingwood claimed that all historical explanation should be in terms of the agent's thought, but this was certainly an overstatement. The political supremacy of Athens depended upon a fleet of very expensive triremes, a fleet which Athens could not have built without the discovery of new sources of silver. Even if an explanation of Athenian success involves establishing the reasons why the city took the unusual decision to invest this wealth in building the triremes, the explanation cannot omit this discovery, without which Athens could not even have considered the decision. Humans live in a natural environment and many of their practices derive from trying to cope with this environment. Reference to it can therefore never be wholly omitted. But to recognize this is not to readmit the covering law model. It is simply to accept that while historians are primarily concerned with understanding historical actions, they often need to refer to the natural world to achieve this.

438

It must be mentioned, however, that many philosophers do not accept that a person's reason for doing something can be a cause of doing it. They argue that an action is an event, albeit of a special kind, and events can be brought about only by other events. This is an issue much debated in the PHILOSOPHY OF MIND (chapter 5). Here, however, we need note only that, even if this were correct, it would give no support to the covering law theory as we have been considering it. For if reasons can be causes only if they are in some sense *physical* events, they will need to be stripped of the descriptions under which they are cited as reasons, including, for example, 'ambitious for literary fame' or 'felt maltreated', whereas the covering law theory requires that there be laws about the behaviour of agents under these descriptions, including laws about would-be literati or maltreated subjects.

3   Objectivity and Value

The previous sections support the claim that historians are primarily concerned with what is of interest in the past from a human point of view. In this case, however, they must also be concerned with human values. This raises no problem for the rational reconstruction model itself, provided that the historicist difficulty can be overcome, since many actions are undertaken in the light of an agent's values. It has been argued, however, that the historian's own value judgements must affect his or her account in a number of ways and it is possible that this may affect the claim that historians can give true accounts of what really happened.

Past and Present Viewpoints

We may see one way in which the issue concerning value judgements arises by asking whose point of view the historian is interested in recapturing. If the historian were *confined* to seeing things in terms of rational reconstructions it would seem that it must be the point of view of historical agents, since it is their view of their situation that the reconstruction is concerned to elucidate. But historians do not confine their accounts in this way and often they explain things in their historical context by reference to factors unknown and even unknowable within that society.

Whether they should do this has been a source of controversy, reflecting different views about the value of studying history. One view (Lovejoy 1959) is that its most important value lies in its capacity to enable us to grasp the possibilities of other ways of living and, hence, of other sets of values than our own. This suggests that the historian should be primarily concerned with the past in its own terms and as a contrast to the present. Others, however, have claimed that its value lies in its capacity to enable us to understand certain aspects of the present. But this means that our concern will be with those parts that link up with current interests. It has sometimes been held that these two viewpoints are incompatible although historians usually interweave them both. They frequently make claims about the truth that conflict with what was believed at the time, often because their knowledge of what subsequently occurred enables them to show that the agent's views were mistaken. More importantly, however, they often describe and give significance to things in ways which, because they require hindsight, were unavailable to past agents.

The role of hindsight can most easily be shown by attending to a particular kind of sentence which historians use, now known as a 'narrative sentence' (Danto 1965: 143ff.). A narrative sentence is one in which an event or person is described in the light of a connection with something that occurred later. Its truth can therefore be known only by someone who knows the truth about the later event and not by anyone at the time of the earlier event. The earlier event is thus seen as part of a temporal whole. To use one of Danto's own examples, an historian may assert that when Petrarch climbed Mount Ventoux he opened the Renaissance, to emphasize Petrarch's significance in the set of events that constitute the Renaissance. The truth of such an assertion could not have been known by anybody who witnessed Petrarch's ascent since he or she could not know the future. Nevertheless, the description is not incompatible with something which the eye-witness could have known, namely, Petrarch's ascent of Mount Ventoux. All that is happening, therefore, is that the same event is being described from two different temporal perspectives and in the light of its connection with different events. Since the statements are compatible, however, it is not the case that if statements which reflect one reason for studying the past are true, those reflecting the other must be false. Thus these different views of the value of studying the past give rise to no problems about the objectivity of the accounts offered.

There are, however, two other ways in which it has been claimed that value judgements have a determining influence upon how the historian construes the past, and these may have consequences for the objectivity of the accounts offered. To see why this is so, it is necessary to allude briefly to the current debate about the cognitive or non-cognitive status of VALUE JUDGEMENTS (pp. 4–6). Cognitivists hold that value judgements are either true or false. If this is so, and if historical accounts presuppose such judgements, then the truth or falsity of historical accounts will depend upon that of the particular judgements made. Non-cognitivists, however, claim that value judgements are expressions of attitude or emotion and, as such, that they have no truth values. If this is so and if historical accounts presuppose them, they will turn out to be accounts expressive of certain attitudes towards the past but not accounts which can be said to be true or false. Thus, although the individual statements and explanations they contain can still be true, the account as a whole cannot be true. There remains the further possibility, however, that historical accounts do not presuppose value judgements, in which case their objectivity will not be affected by them.

The first argument to be considered concerns the question whether, since historians cannot include everything in their accounts, they must use value judgements in their selection of what to include. Many reasons have been offered to show that they must, but here I can consider only one: that the historian must decide which events were more important than others and, since there are no objective criteria of importance, this requires historians to make their own value judgements about them (Dray 1993: 42–6). Whether their accounts are true will then depend, at least in part, upon whether their judgements of importance are true.

Attempts to meet this claim by arguing that there are objective criteria of importance have not been generally accepted. The most plausible suggestion is that historians should choose those events that have the widest range of causal consequences. But since not all the causal consequences of an event can be taken into account – indeed, it is not clear how they can even be calculated – it seems that only the most important should be taken into account. In this case, however, further judgements of importance will be required. It has been noted also that this criterion has little relevance to histories which describe and interpret the main characteristics of an age, such as G. M. Young's *Victorian England: Portrait of an Age*. 'What', it has been asked, 'would we think of a volume-length "portrait" of Victorian England that ignored the working-class movement?' Such an omission would need justification and the only one available seems to be that what was included was more important than what was excluded (Dray 1993: 42).

It is not clear, however, that this argument must lead to the conclusion that the historian cannot avoid making *his or her own* value judgement. To see this, it is worth considering two possible objectivist responses, relating to the two different reasons for studying history mentioned above. If the portrait is meant to be a portrait of a people as they saw themselves to be – and this is what Young claims in his Introduction – the historian will not get very far in his or her research without making the *empirical* discovery that the state and activities and condition of the working class were widely perceived as a matter of importance by very large parts of the population, including workers, factory owners, politicians, philanthropists and many others. It is true that the historian needs to know which sources he or she should consult to learn this, but this is precisely what a well-trained historian is taught to know. An historian starting research with the hypothesis that the working class was not a cause of concern to the Victorians would surely need to abandon this if the sources indicated that it was wrong. This implies that the sources have, in a certain sense, a capacity to speak to the historian. They were not, of course, produced to speak to historians but they were produced to speak to somebody, and it hardly requires a value judgement to hear what they were saying, what worries they were expressing or, if many are about the same thing, to conclude that that was a matter of widespread concern. The historian may, therefore, need to abandon an initial hypothesis in view of what the sources reveal and, if this is so, there is no reason to believe that doing so involves making a value judgement. It is true, of course, that there may be areas of life where there was no such consensus of importance, but if this is so, it is surely an historian's duty to report this fact.

But, as noted above, historians often write from the point of view of the bearing of the past upon present interests and for an historian of this sort the fact that the Victorians thought the development of the working class was important would not provide a criterion for including it in an account of Victorian England. But although this is true, an alternative objective criterion for the inclusion of the development of the working class in this sort of account can be found in the importance that the historian can show that development had for certain later changes. Would it, one might ask, have been so misleading for an historian of this sort to have omitted an account of the development of the working class in favour of something else had that development not come to transform almost the whole subsequent structure of British social, economic, political and constitutional life? What must be remembered here is that historical reality is a process of ongoing but continuous change and that, as the worlds in which historians find themselves differ, different aspects of the past become relevant to an understanding of the present. On this view, what determines an historian's selection of material is not what he or she personally holds important, but what that historian can find to explain the things involved in a society's perception of itself. The reason why a

441

contemporary historian of this kind would give more prominence to an account of the working class than, say, an historian in the late nineteenth century, must surely be that the working class now affects so many more aspects of the structure of our present world, and is so much a part of what we take that world to be, that a portrait of the period in which it first arose that omitted that development would no longer be acceptable.

This is a consequentialist but not a narrowly causal criterion. It could be argued, however, that, since it appeals to what we think important about the present, all that it does is make judgements of importance about the past consequent upon others about the present. But this seems implausible. For it is surely an objective fact that the working class now occupies a certain place in the economy, that it has institutions which claim to speak for it and to protect its interests, and that this is part of our shared understanding of our present world. Accordingly, historians must include in their accounts whatever they can find to explain this fact if their intention is to explain the present in terms of the past. Moreover, in removing the basis of selection from the individual historian's own judgement of importance to the self-perception of the society for which the historian writes, this criterion provides a shared basis on the strength of which individual historians can reasonably ask one another to justify their selection of some things in preference to others.

The second objection that raises questions about the relation between value and objectivity is the argument from characterization. The claim here is that before deciding that a certain item is sufficiently important to be included in an account, in the case of certain kinds of history at least, the historian must first decide whether the item should be characterized in such a way as to make it the right kind of candidate for inclusion and that such a decision again requires a value judgement by the historian. The sorts of histories which most obviously seem to raise this difficulty are histories of art and religion, where it must be decided whether a certain work is genuinely a work of art or a certain action genuinely religious before deciding whether to include it in the relevant history. But the case can, it has been argued, be extended also to political history, where it can be asked whether the actions of the IRA or the PLO are acts of terrorism or acts of war. The judgements made will decide the kinds of history for which they are candidates for inclusion (Dray 1980: 45; 1993: 49–51).

In considering this view it is not necessary to deny that events find their way into their relevant histories only as characterized or under certain descriptions. The question at issue is solely the basis of the characterization. The first point to be noted is that we would lose our capacity to talk about anything, past or present, were there not a widespread basis of shared characterizations. The IRA, for example, may describe its actions as executions rather than murders, but this claim cannot be taken as literally true in the absence of the institutional legal and judicial procedures that must operate before something can be an execution. In describing its acts as executions rather than murders the IRA may be expressing its rejection of the legitimacy of British rule in Ulster, but that is not sufficient to turn murders into executions unless the acts issue from alternative legal and judicial processes, the legitimacy of which is established. This example, of course, raises the question of political legitimacy, which is too large to be discussed here. Nevertheless, it remains the case that we must have a shared basis of characterization, and hence shared criteria of characterization, before we can discuss anything. This does not eliminate the existence of borderline cases, but it does mean that the majority of cases must be unarguable and, indeed, that it is by reference to them that we can identify and discuss borderline cases.

It must be noted, however, that criteria are normally implicit and often cannot be made explicit without reference to objects that exemplify them. This is evident when we turn to histories, even of those areas which seem most appropriate for the characterization argument. For here it is noticeable that the historical process itself has produced the characterization as works of art or as religions of the things that constitute the subject matter of most histories of art or religion. But these cannot simply be disregarded in favour of new characterizations which an historian might wish to propose. It would surely be very odd if an historian who was also a devout Christian, were to exclude the rituals at Delphi as a candidate for inclusion in a history of religion simply because they involved no beliefs which accorded with those of orthodox Christianity or none which he or she personally was prepared to evaluate as 'genuinely' religious. The claim that they should be excluded on these grounds cannot be correct since, by parity of argument, an historian belonging to any other faith would be entitled to write a history of religion for which Christianity is not a candidate. Indeed, on this line of reasoning, there would be nothing to block the claim that one religion was the only appropriate candidate for a history of all religion. It would be equally unacceptable, for the same reasons, if an historian of Italian art were to exclude the works of Michelangelo as candidates for his or her account. Surely such cases raise questions about the claim that a history of art or religion has been produced rather than questions about the entitlement of the works and institutions to be characterized as appropriate candidates for inclusion in these histories. Thus, there is what might be called a 'verdict of history' but this is not a verdict that historians have reached; instead it is one that has arisen through the internal historical development of their subject matter. This is not to deny that criteria may change, but, if they do, this can only be as a consequence of major new developments in their subject matter and not of historians' value judgements.

As with the argument from selection, it might be replied that this does not show that value judgements have no part to play in the characterization of historical phenomena, since it merely replaces the part played by the historian's value judgement by shared characterizations which have arisen through past value judgements. But if the argument is correct, there is a significant difference between the two positions, for it means that the historian must respect the state that the historical development of the subject matter has reached, with all the characterization of material that that involves, and cannot be thought of as being in a position to reconstruct it *ab initio*, as it were, according to his or her own values.

As noted above, borderline cases will inevitably remain, but there is no harm in this provided that they are so recognized. An historian is unlikely to command much support, however, in attempts to make these central and to rearrange all other items of characterization accordingly. It is difficult to imagine what sort of history might be produced by an historian who accepted an IRA killing as a central case of an execution and tried to write a history of politics, with attendant revisions of the notion of political authority, on such an assumption. It is even more difficult to believe that such a history, if written, would be accepted as a true account of the past.

4   Narrative and Realism

Historians have traditionally presented the results of their research in the form of a narrative. That this is as it ought to be has been challenged by the development of new schools of historians. These include, for example, econometric historians who use quantitative economic techniques to establish 'objective' accounts of the causes of social and political change or the French *annaliste* school, which gives preference also to quantitative techniques and treats individuals and events as relatively superficial consequences of deeper underlying structures and processes, the existence of which can be discerned only over different lengths of time. Nevertheless, despite calls for further developments of these kinds of history, narratives have remained the most characteristic way of presenting historical knowledge and there has been a strong debate about their epistemological status and their ontological implications.

The basic issue arises from claims about the nature of narrative itself. Narratives must have some form in virtue of which we can follow what they say and various analyses of their typical form have been proposed (Gallie 1964; White 1965; Danto 1965; White 1973). In all of these analyses it is agreed that, although a narrative presupposes a chronological sequence of events, it goes beyond this in various ways; for instance, by connecting different events and actions through their necessary conditions (Gallie 1964) or by explaining later aspects of the object of enquiry in terms of earlier causes (White 1965). But, drawing upon modern literary theory, two challenging claims have been made about narratives in general: firstly, that narratives are literary artefacts and, as such, constructions of the literary imagination; secondly, that there are many different forms that a narrative might take and nothing to determine that an author, whether historian or novelist, should adopt one rather than another. Thus, there is indeterminacy at the level of narrative construction. Applying these considerations to historical narratives, it has been claimed that we cannot think of the past as a determinate reality of which a narrative *as a whole* is true for there is no one right way of composing an historical narrative about the past and, hence, of claiming that through it we have captured the meaning of the past. Rather, there are a number of different, irreconcilable ways of creating narratives about the past and, through them, of *imposing* upon it a variety of meanings that it does not possess of itself. Since meaning is not an objective feature of the past, it cannot be claimed that the historical narratives, which project meaning upon it, are expressions of objective truth (White 1973: 1–42; Mink 1978). To mention one point in illustration of this view, it is a necessary feature of a story that it should have a beginning, middle and end. But reality has no beginnings, middles and ends. Hence, when we think about the past in terms of beginnings, middles and ends, as narratives invite us to do, we are imposing upon it a structure which it does not itself possess. One must note, however, that the claim allows that some things in the narrative can be true, such as the facts that it cites or the explanations that it offers. For were this not possible, the distinction between fact and fiction would be destroyed. But the anti-realist's intention is not to challenge this distinction. It is, rather, to preserve the historian's right to present us with a variety of different but incompatible ways of thinking about the past. It is only the way in which the narrative organizes these into a coherent whole, it is claimed, which cannot express a further truth about real connections in the past. Thus, to think, as the realist does, that the narrative as a whole asserts something that is true of the past, in the way in which some of its constituent parts do, is a mistake. It is the mistake, as it has been put, of thinking of the past as 'an untold story waiting to be told' (Mink 1978).

The controversy is therefore about whether, in constructing a narrative about the past, the historian must inevitably falsify it. Although this claim has been applied only to narrative histories, it has implications for other forms of history, many of which have narrative elements in them. An interpretative history such as Young's *Victorian England* contains many passages of narrative. Indeed, it is difficult to see how any form of history which involves tracing and explaining at least some developments can fail to contain narrative elements. Moreover, although the claim has not been extended to other forms of history such as econometric history, it would seem that, in so far as all kinds of historical accounts require some form of literary expression, objections of the same kind must apply to them.

Before discussing this position, one other reason that has been advanced for it should be mentioned, namely that a narrative contains much that involves hindsight. This, as we saw earlier, is true. Thus, an historian can talk, retrospectively, of 'hopes unfulfilled, plans miscarried, battles decisive and ideas seminal'. But, it is claimed, these are aspects of stories and not of life, for in life there are only 'hopes, plans, battles and ideas' (Mink 1970). Hence, by using hindsight, the historian falsifies the past. But this argument cannot be correct for, although it is true that we can only *know* certain things at certain times, there is no reason why we should take what we know only at certain times, for instance, while the event is occurring, as the sole way of characterizing reality. For, as we saw when discussing narrative sentences, the descriptions that historians offer retrospectively are not incompatible with those that can be given at the time of the event. There can only be a 'hope unfulfilled' if there was a 'hope' in the first place. But the fact that the former presupposes the latter is not a reason for believing that only the latter can be true. Nor can the role of retrospective descriptions be denied by confining the concept of reality to life as we experience it, for it is part of life as we experience it that we see our situation, at any particular moment, in terms of fulfilled or unfulfilled hopes, successful or unsuccessful plans and so on, and abandon or revise our further hopes and plans in the light of this knowledge. Thus, it is false that, as this objection asserts, retrospectivity is a feature of narratives but not of life.

Given the strongly anti-realist implications of these claims about narratives, it is hardly surprising that there has been a strong realist reaction against them. One of these builds upon the point just made: that, contrary to what the anti-realists assert, we both live out narratives in our own lives and understand our lives in terms of those narratives. Hence, it is appropriate to understand the lives of others in the same way (MacIntyre 1981: 197ff.). But while this is an adequate response to anti-realist objections to retrospectivity, it cannot be an adequate response to the more fundamental claims about the relation of narratives to reality. For a narrative history is not merely an account of the way in which individuals have lived out their lives. The focus may, as we saw earlier, be upon the human past, but the latter requires social, economic and natural contexts, many of which will impinge upon individuals in ways unknown to them. The historian will, of course, draw upon these in giving a narrative account, but in doing so he or she is going well beyond the sort of understanding which we have when we try to understand ourselves in narrative terms. Historical reality does not consist solely of human agents and there is therefore no reason why we should conclude that because lived experience has a narrative structure, the same must be true of historical reality.

A stronger and much simpler realist defence is to challenge the anti-realist's way of setting up the problem. We can do this by accepting the claim that stories need structures and authors. If, therefore, the realist is committed to the notion of past reality as 'an untold story waiting to be told', he or she is indeed committed to an incoherent conception, since past reality would then both need but not have an author. However, this can be shown to be an unacceptable way of presenting the problem by the fact that, if this is so, *all* claims about the past, including those that the anti-realist wishes to accept, would be incoherent. To see this, let us consider the case of some statement made by an historian about the past which was never made by anyone in the past. Statements are less complex than narratives but they also require a literary structure, usually a sentence, and an author. Hence, if, as the anti-realist claims, the narrative realist is committed to the conception of the past as an 'untold story waiting to be told', a statement realist would be committed to the conception that part of the past, that which the anti-realist needs to accept to preserve the distinction between fiction and history, involves the equally incoherent notion of 'unstated sentences waiting to be stated'. On this view, then, the idea of any independent historical reality whatsoever must be abandoned as incoherent. But this would produce a scepticism that applies not merely to narrative histories, but to any claims of any sort about the past. Since, however, as we saw in the first section, a scepticism of this sort would itself be incoherent, the anti-realist argument which entails it cannot be correct.

The use of narratives thus cannot have the implications that the anti-realist claims. Nevertheless, to reject the anti-realist view is not the same as to understand how narratives relate to the past. From considerations presented earlier, it might seem that they do so by telling us what happened and by showing us how to understand why it happened. But this seems to do scant justice to the role of the narrative itself which, as the anti-realists have rightly insisted, involves relating individuals, events and contexts of many different kinds and from different points of view, including those of the agents and the historian. Furthermore, neither would it explain the fact, troubling for realists, that historians disagree so much in their overall accounts, nor would it identify the source of their disagreements.

One promising suggestion involves the notion of an historical narrative as providing a special form of 'configurational understanding' which is characteristic of history (Mink 1987; Dray 1993). There are two aspects to this idea, which may be taken separately. The first is that the narrative integrates different parts of the past as parts of a temporal whole. This can be quite easily understood if we return to the idea of a narrative sentence. Here some event or institution is described in the context of a larger-scale event or process which did not end until after the termination of the original event or institution. It is clear, however, that historians could not maintain claims to the truth of such sentences if they were to connect earlier and later events in an arbitrary way. We can describe Petrarch's ascent of Mount Ventoux as the opening of the Renaissance, but hardly as the opening of the Industrial Revolution. Nor is this just a matter of time-scale, for events very distant from one another can be related in narrative sentences.

What is required is what has been called a 'colligatory concept' *of an appropriate type* (Walsh 1967). A colligatory concept is one that refers to some large-scale underlying movement or some developing idea, within which the events or individuals in whom the historian is interested will be seen in various sets of relationships and thus acquire different kinds of significance. But what determines whether such a concept is of the appropriate type? Why, for example, is the Renaissance but not the Industrial Revolution appropriate for Petrarch? There are two parts to the response to this question. The first is that the historian must be able to show that the new relationships which he or she can trace by adopting this viewpoint are empirically true. There is no reason in principle why any colligatory concept may not be used in the attempt to understand the significance of the activities of any individual. But a minimum condition of appropriateness must be that the historian can provide empirical support for the possibilities opened up. The second is that a colligatory concept must not be one which merely allows events to be reclassified in general terms – a murder as an execution, for example. It must be one that refers to specific historical items, such as the Renaissance or the French Revolution. Thus, colligating under appropriate concepts is a specifically historical form of understanding because it involves understanding specific historical phenomena in the light of their relationships to other specific phenomena, the character of which can be ascertained only with historical hindsight.

If this is one of the main characteristics of historical narratives, it might seem that it can explain what is a problem for realists, the existence of apparently irresolvable large-scale disagreement between historians. For the same events and people can be brought under different appropriate colligatory concepts. To see this, one merely needs to think of the significance of Luther's Ninety-Five Theses against the abuse of indulgence in relation, for example, to the histories of the Roman and Protestant churches, to theology, to changes of relationships between churches and states and to the development of the modern Protestant conscience. In fact, however, while the use of different colligatory concepts can explain how historians come to give different narrative accounts of the same events, it could show that these differences are irresolvable only if the colligatory concepts were contradictory. But since they are concepts of specific large-scale historical phenomena, which are known to have existed, they cannot be contradictory. When such disagreement occurs, therefore, it can be put down only to disagreement about the relative importance of the themes referred to by the colligatory concepts in question. But there is no reason why historians should think that these accounts are incompatible, unless they believe that there is one and only one way in which historical reality can truly be described. But, as we saw earlier, a realist can accept that there is only one reality, to parts of which all true statements and accounts refer, without needing to deny that there are many different ways of referring to and describing that one reality.

It is necessary to turn to the second aspect of this conception of historical narrative: the notion that it is a *configuration*. This concept has been much used in trying to characterize how narratives express their truth. It arises from a reluctance to accept either of two alternatives. The first is that narratives state the truth, for in this case it might seem that their truth was little more than a function of the statements and explanations that they contain. The alternative is that a narrative is simply a literary way of dressing up the results of the historian's research and, in this case, one cannot ascribe to the narrative as such any truth value at all. The main claim made in connection with the concept of configuration, however, is that historical narratives go beyond the explanatory value of their contents to a form of understanding, in which the parts are related to a whole, as described above, but in such a manner that the historian's conclusions cannot be grasped other than by the way in which they are expressed in the narrative. Thus, rather than state the truth, the narrative displays it. One analogy used here is with music, where it is often claimed that there is no way of understanding what a piece of music is about other than by listening to it. In the same way, it is suggested, it is not possible to understand the historical narrative other than by grasping the relationships between parts and whole in just the way in which, by the end, it has displayed them.

The analogy with music, however, is both helpful and unhelpful. It is helpful in the sense that one can contrast listening to a piece of music sequentially, as it were, noting how one theme is related to or develops out of another, and grasping, by the end, the piece *as a whole*. In the latter case, one can gain a much more complex understanding of the same parts of the piece by seeing, for example, how some foreshadow what comes later. Similarly, since narratives presuppose chronological sequences, they have a sequential structure – yet the historian enables us to understand the parts of a chronological sequence in many different ways, by relating them to different sets of relations and contexts through the use of colligatory concepts and through a capacity to see reality retrospectively. The analogy with music is unhelpful, however, in that it is not clear that music is about something in the same sense that an historical narrative is about something. The interrelationships that one can come to grasp in the musical example do not refer to anything that stands outside the piece of music. But those which one should come to grasp in a narrative history, even if one can do so only by the way in which they are presented in the narrative account, must be features of that which the narrative is about, that is, historical reality. Moreover, this attempt to give the narrative a unique cognitive value by presenting it as a way of displaying the character of a whole rather than stating it, runs into the difficulty that historians can and do detach their conclusions from their narratives and argue their merits in a way that is incompatible with the suggestion that conclusions are undetachable from the narrative. For we can, and do, ask whether two different narrative accounts of the same historical event are substantially in agreement or not, and, having allowed for differences that might arise because they are addressed to different readers, we can fairly easily decide. These difficulties do not refute the account we are considering of what narratives, in virtue of being narratives, relate, but they cast doubt upon the claim that narratives exhibit this in virtue of their own internal configuration. There seems no reason therefore to deny that narratives are implicit statements of truths about the past which are different in kind from those stated by any of their parts, but which can nevertheless be made explicit should that be required.

It remains to be asked, however, whether some historical disagreements are in principle irresolvable. The suggestion that they are has been powerfully defended upon the grounds that ultimately they may depend upon different METAPHYSICAL (chapter 2) or evaluative presuppositions (Walsh 1967, 1986). This can be illustrated by reference to the different ways in which Marxist and Whig historians have written narrative accounts of the nineteenth century. For the Marxist, the unifying theme is the collapse of capitalism, while for the Whig it is the growth of freedom. But behind these obvious differences, there lie different metaphysical conceptions of the nature of human beings. For the Marxist, human beings are pre-eminently producers of their own means of subsistence, and all that follows is to be explained in the light of the needs of the related technological, economic and ideological systems that develop necessarily to enable this to be done (see chapter 34). For the Whig, on the other hand, humans are essentially free, and the underlying theme of human history is the creation of the set of institutions that could best satisfy their inalienable right to liberty. Hence, where the Marxist historian sees the development of so-called 'liberal' institutions in the nineteenth century as concealed expressions of the needs of capitalism in a particular phase, the liberal sees them as the collective constructions of people becoming ever more aware of their inalienable rights (Mandelbaum 1971). These are, of course, incompatible metaphysical views and there is no way of resolving them other than by metaphysical discussion of the sort in which historians do not normally engage. It could be argued that if this is so, they ought to engage in it. But this is too optimistic, for disagreement could be removed once and for all only if the possibility exists of establishing the truth of some metaphysical system once and for all. But this seems an impossible dream. In the end, therefore, claims to the objectivity of large-scale historical accounts must be relativized to the metaphysical perspective upon which they rest. But although this imposes an ultimate limit upon the kind of objectivity to which history can aspire, it does not show that historical knowledge is any less reputable than any other kind of knowledge. For there is no branch of knowledge whose conclusions are not subject to the same qualification. The fact that there appears to be less disagreement in, say, the natural sciences than in history, is simply a consequence of the fact that the theories of natural science involve agreed assumptions about the nature of reality, but not that they involve none at all, whereas historians often do not agree about at least some of their assumptions.

5 Conclusion

Historians live within, share the interests of, and write for, specific historical societies. They seek objective truth but, if the main elements in the previous discussion are correct, the degree of objectivity that can be claimed for their final accounts must be relativized in various ways: to the self-perception of their societies, to their own implicit metaphysical assumptions and also, perhaps, to their evaluative standards. But such relativization does not mean that they are not warranted ways of thinking of the past. It could only mean this if the historian could escape the temporal and conceptual constraints of his or her situation to achieve some God's-eye viewpoint from which to see the whole. But it is not clear that the idea of such a whole and such a viewpoint is intelligible. The fact that historical knowledge must be from a perspective cannot therefore vitiate it. It does, however, put an end to the old hope of a once-and-for-all universal history, for historical knowledge is not simply aggregative in the way that such a hope requires. The present is not simply an addition to the past but a development of it; and, as new presents come into being, so must new temporal standpoints from which we can discern, if they exist, new relationships between different parts of the past or between present and past, requiring new colligatory concepts. But this alone would not mean that what can now be discerned must be false for, as we have seen, colligatory concepts cannot be contradictory. The ultimate reason, therefore, why any account as a whole must be thought revisable lies in the fact that the perspective from which it operates involves revisable metaphysical assumptions.

Further Reading

There are three excellent general introductions. Gorman (1992) is explicitly written as an introduction to analytic philosophy through philosophy of history, but includes an account of econometric history which I have had to omit here. Walsh (1967) remains a clear and helpful discussion of some of the above issues. Dray (1993) is more comprehensive and more detailed, containing an excellent assessment of the varieties of causal judgement in history, which I have again had to omit, while also putting the case for the ineliminability of value judgements at its strongest. For an excellent, extended defence of Collingwood's approach to historical understanding, see Dray (1995). McCullagh (1984), while too difficult to be an introduction, has excellent chapters on historical generalizations, historical causes and causal significance, together with a wealth of examples.

Constructionism retains its appeal and readers should consult Goldstein (1976) and the essays in *History and Theory*, 1977, 4, for the start of the debate and, for later developments, Michael Krausz's 'History and its objects' in *The Monist*, 74. The problem of interpretation has received greater attention by European writers. For a comprehensive but difficult discussion, leading to results different from those outlined here, Gadamer (1975) is indispensable.

The scientific conception of causal explanation has remained important. For a devastating attack on the covering law model itself and an impressive argument for its replacement by a more comparative conception of causal explanation, which nevertheless remains naturalistic, see Miller (1987). For a completely anti-positivist view, see Hart and Honoré (1985). To the writings on Understanding discussed in the chapter should be added Von Wright (1971) and Winch (1958).

The ontological and epistemological implications of narrative continue to be a source of much dispute. For both sides of the debate, see the articles in *History and Theory*, 1986, 4, and 1987, 4. For a strong defence of its epistemological adequacy, and an equally strong denial of it, see Carr (1986) and Ankersmit (1983), respectively.

References

Ankersmit, F. R. 1983: *Narrative Logic*. The Hague: Martinus Nijhoff.
Berlin, I. 1966: The Concept of Scientific History. In W. H. Dray (ed.) *Philosophical Analysis and History*. New York: Harper and Row.
Carr, D. 1986: *Time, Narrative and History*. Bloomington: University of Indiana Press.
Collingwood, R. G. 1993: *The Idea of History*, revd edn. Oxford: Oxford University Press.
Danto, A. C. 1965: *Analytic Philosophy of History*. Cambridge: Cambridge University Press.
Donagan, A. 1966: The Popper–Hempel Theory Reconsidered. In W. H. Dray (ed.) *Philosophical Analysis and History*. New York: Harper and Row.
Dray, W. H. 1957: *Laws and Explanation in History*. Oxford: Oxford University Press.
——1980: *Perspectives on History*. London: Routledge and Kegan Paul.
——1993: *Philosophy of History*, 2nd edn. Englewood Cliffs, NJ: Prentice-Hall.
——1995: *History as Re-enactment: R.G. Collingwood's Idea of History*. Oxford: Oxford University Press.
Gadamer, H.-G. 1975: *Truth and Method*. London: Sheed and Ward.
Gallie, W. B. 1964: *Philosophy and the Historical Understanding*. London: Chatto and Windus.

Goldstein, L. J. 1976: *Historical Knowing*. Austin: University of Texas Press.

—— 1977: History and the Primacy of Knowing. *History and Theory*, 16, 4.

Gorman J. L. 1982: *The Expression of Historical Knowledge*. Edinburgh: Edinburgh University Press.

—— 1992: *Understanding History: An Introduction to Analytical Philosophy of History*. Ottawa: University of Ottawa Press.

Hart, H. L. A. and Honoré, T. 1985: *Causation and the Law*, 2nd edn. Oxford: Clarendon Press.

Hempel, C. G. 1959 [1942]: The Function of General Laws in History. In P. Gardiner (ed.) *Theories of History*. New York: Free Press.

—— 1974: Reasons and Covering Laws. In P. Gardiner (ed.) *The Philosophy of History*. Oxford: Oxford University Press.

Krausz, M. 1974: History and its Objects. *The Monist*, 74, 2.

Lovejoy, A. O. 1959: Present Standpoints and Past History. In H. Meyerhoff (ed.) *The Philosophy of History in Our Time*. New York: Doubleday.

McCullagh, C. B. 1984: *Justifying Historical Descriptions*. Cambridge: Cambridge University Press.

MacIntyre, A. 1981: *After Virtue*. Notre Dame, IN: University of Notre Dame Press.

Mandelbaum, M. 1971: *History, Man and Reason: A Study in Nineteenth-Century Thought*. Baltimore, MD: Johns Hopkins University Press.

Martin, R. 1977: *Historical Explanation: Re-enactment and Practical Inference*. Ithaca, NY: Cornell University Press.

Miller, R. W. 1987: *Fact and Method*. Princeton, NJ: Princeton University Press.

Mink, L. O. 1970: History and Fiction as Modes of Comprehension. *New Literary History*, I.

—— 1978: Narrative Form as a Cognitive Instrument. In R. H. Canary and H. Kozicki (eds) *The Writing of History: Literary Form and Historical Understanding*. Madison: University of Wisconsin Press.

—— 1987: *Historical Understanding* (edited by B. Fay, E. O. Golob and R. T. Vann). Ithaca, NY: Cornell University Press.

Nowell-Smith, P. 1977: The Constructionist Theory of History. *History and Theory*, 16, 4.

Oakeshott, M. 1933: *Experience and Its Modes*. Cambridge: Cambridge University Press.

Pompa, L. 1993: The Possibility of Historical Knowledge. *Supplementary Proceedings of the Aristotelian Society*.

Russell, B. 1921: *The Analysis of Mind*. London: George Allen and Unwin.

Von Wright, G. H. 1971: *Explanation and Understanding*. London: Routledge and Kegan Paul.

Walsh, W. H. 1967: *An Introduction to Philosophy of History*, 2nd edn. London: Hutchison.

—— 1986: Fact and Value in History. In M. C. Doeser and J. N. Kraay (eds) *Facts and Values*. Dordrecht: Martinus Nijhoff.

White, H. 1973: *Metahistory: The Historical Imagination in Nineteenth-Century Europe*. Baltimore, MD: Johns Hopkins University Press.

—— 1978: The Historical Text as Literary Artefact. In R. H. Canary and H. Kozicki (eds) *The Writing of History: Literary Form and Historical Understanding*. Madison: University of Wisconsin Press.

White, M. 1965: *Foundations of Historical Knowledge*. New York: Harper and Row.

Winch, P. 1958: *The Idea of a Social Science*. London: Routledge and Kegan Paul.

Young, G. M. 1936: *Victorian England: Portrait of an Age*. Oxford: Oxford University Press.

Discussion Questions

1   Is it logically possible that the world came into existence five minutes ago? If it is, what implications would it have for our knowledge that there was a real past more than five minutes ago?

2   Is the past in which historians believe a past that could exist in its own right, or can it exist only as a construction from present historical evidence?

3   What is a past-entailing expression? What is its function in enabling us to infer from historical evidence to historical statements?

4   Can we justify our belief that we are in possession of a theory of interpretation which gives us access to historical truths?

5   Is the covering-law theory adequate as an account of the logical form of historical explanations?

6   Can there be laws about the behaviour of individuals? If there can, how would this affect the character of historical explanations?

7   Can there be laws about the development of historical roles?

8   Is historical understanding different in kind from historical explanation? If it is, what does it enable us to grasp which historical explanations do not?

9   Are historical explanations deterministic?

10   How can the transmission of influence in history be made intelligible?

11   What is historicism? Does it render the understanding of the past in its own terms impossible?

12   Is there an incompatibility between understanding the past as a contrast to the present and understanding it in relation to the present?

13   What are the logical features of narrative sentences? What is their function in historical accounts?

14   If historical accounts depend upon value judgements, how does this affect their truth?

15   Must historians make judgements of importance when deciding what to include in their accounts? If they must, on what would these judgements depend?

16   Events can be candidates for specific kinds of history only if they are characterized in certain ways. On what does their characterization depend?

17   How would a history of politics be affected by the judgement that a killing by the IRA was a central case of an execution rather than a murder?

18   Must historians appeal to their own religious beliefs when deciding what might be appropriate for inclusion in a history of religion? What would be the consequences for histories of religion if they must?

19   Must narrative histories impose on the past meanings that it cannot possess?

20   What is a colligatory concept? Does it introduce a specifically historical form of understanding into history?

21   How do historical narratives relate to what they are about?

22   Are there some disagreements in history that cannot be resolved? If so, what is the source of their irresolvability?

23   Can historical accounts reach a degree of truth such that all future histories merely add later truths to them? If not, how does the future of reality affect them?

15

Philosophy of Religion

CHARLES TALIAFERRO

Philosophy of religion explores philosophical issues that arise from reflection on the nature and truth of religious belief and the meaning of religious practices. If the field is defined broadly enough, then the historical record of the beginning of philosophy marks the beginning of philosophy of religion. The field includes philosophical arguments for and against belief in a Creator of the cosmos, comparative treatments of the Divine, accounts of the meaning of religious language and faith, the ethical implications of religious commitments, the relation between faith, reason, experience and tradition, concepts of the miraculous, the afterlife, the sacred revelation, mysticism, prayer, salvation and other religious concerns.

This chapter reviews the current practice of the philosophy of religion, highlighting arguments on the nature of religious belief, the intelligibility of competing conceptions of God and the debate over the role of evidence in shaping religious convictions, and it examines some recent work on arguments for and against belief that there is a God. Philosophy of religion is integrally related to metaphysics, epistemology, ethics, the philosophy of mind and to other areas, not the least of which is the history of philosophy itself, as virtually all the seminal historical figures of philosophy held views that bear on religious matters.

1 Overview of the Current State of the Field

Philosophy of religion has grown substantially since the 1970s to become one of the largest fields within philosophy. Fruitful new works in philosophy of religion have launched a host of new journals, societies, institutes and websites dedicated to it. (For a sampling of these resources see the Further Reading at the end of this chapter.) The popularity of the field may be due in part to increased awareness of the diversity of religious traditions and communities. It is less likely than before for someone in the West to grow up with only one religious alternative to secular life. It is therefore quite natural for many to employ the tools of philosophy in their investigation and assessment of different religious and secular values. Philosophy of religion is the second most requested philosophy course by students in the United States. Another reason for growth in the field is the retreat of a restrictive, empirical theory of meaning and evidence called logical positivism (sometimes referred to as 'verificationism').

Logical positivism has deep roots in empiricism (see HUME, chapter 31), but its epicentre in the twentieth century was a group of philosophers who met in the 1920s and 1930s at the University of Vienna called the Vienna Circle. Logical positivists insisted that much of traditional metaphysics, including the belief that there is a God, is incapable of evidential testing and therefore meaningless.

There were many versions of the empiricism promoted by logical positivism, but the following empiricist principle is representative: for a propositional claim to be meaningful it must either be about the bare formal relations between ideas such as those enshrined in mathematics and analytic definitions ('A is A', 'triangles are three-sided'), or there must in principle be perceptual experience providing evidence of whether the claim is true or false. Ostensibly factual claims that have no implications for our experience are empty of content. Metaphysical claims like 'The Absolute is outside of time' and 'There are Platonic properties' were thereby swept away as nonsense. In line with this form of logical positivism, A. J. Ayer (1910–89) and others claimed that religious beliefs were meaningless. How might one empirically confirm that God is omnipresent or loving, or that Krishna is an avatar of Vishnu? In an important debate in the 1950s, philosophical arguments about God were likened to debates about the existence and habits of an unobservable gardener. The idea of a gardener who is not just invisible but who also cannot be detected by any sensory faculty seemed nonsense. Using this garden analogy and others crafted with the same design, Antony Flew (see his essay in Mitchell 1971) made the case that religious claims do not pass the empirical test of meaning. The field of philosophy of religion in the 1950s and 1960s was largely an intellectual battlefield where the debates centred on whether religious beliefs were meaningful or conceptually absurd.

Empirical verificationism is by no means dead. Some critics of the belief in an incorporeal God continue to advance the same critique as that of Flew and Ayer, albeit with further refinements. Michael Martin (1990) and Kai Nielsen (1982) are representatives of this approach. Despite these efforts, empiricist challenges to the meaningfulness of religious belief are now deemed less impressive than they once were.

The charge that positivism is itself meaningless has been advanced on the grounds that the empiricist criterion of meaning itself does not seem to involve the formal relation between ideas as with tautologies, nor does it appear to be empirically verifiable. How might one empirically verify whether the principle is correct? At best, the principle of verification seems to be a recommendation as to how to describe those statements that logical positivists are prepared to accept as meaningful. But then, how might a dispute about which other statements are meaningful be settled in a non-arbitrary fashion? To religious believers for whom talk of 'Brahman' and 'God' is at the centre stage of meaningful discourse, the use of the principle of empirical verification will seem arbitrary and question-begging. If the principle is tightened up too far, it seems to threaten various propositions that at least appear to be highly respectable, such as scientific claims about physical processes and events that are not publicly perceptible. For example, what are we to think of states of the universe prior to all observation, or physical strata of the cosmos that cannot be observed directly or indirectly but only inferred as part of an overriding SCIENTIFIC THEORY (chapter 9)? Or what about the mental states of other persons, which may ordinarily be reliably judged, but which, some argue, are underdetermined by external, public observation? A person's subjective states – how one feels – can be profoundly elusive to external observers and even to the person concerned. Also worrisome was the wholesale rejection of ethics. Are we willing to give up a normative account of ethics and all value judgements? The latter question had some force against an empiricist like A. J. Ayer, who regarded ethical claims as lacking any truth value and yet at the same time construed empirical knowledge in terms of having the right to certain beliefs. Can an ethics of belief be preserved if one dispenses with ethics altogether?

The strict empiricist account of meaning was also charged as meaningless on the grounds that there is no coherent, clear, basic level of experience with which to test propositional claims. The experiential 'given' is simply too malleable, often reflecting prior conceptual judgements and, once one appreciates the open-textured character of experience, it may be proposed that virtually any experience can verify or provide some evidence for anything. A mystic might well claim to experience the unity of a timeless spirit everywhere present. A. J. Ayer allowed that in principle mystical experience might give meaning to religious terms. Those who concede this appeared to be on a slippery slope leading from empirical verificationism to mystical verificationism. A growing number of philosophers were led to conclude that the empiricist challenge was not decisive. Critical assessments of positivism can be found in work by, among others, Alvin Plantinga (1967, 1974, 1993), Richard Swinburne (1977, 1979), and John Foster (1985). Ronald Hepburn summarizes a widely held conviction: 'There can be no shortcut in the philosophy of religion past the painstaking examination and re-examination of problems in the entire field . . . No single, decisive verification-test, no solemn Declaration of Meaninglessness, can relieve us of the labour' (Hepburn 1963: 50).

Once verificationism was called into question, the floodgates opened and the philosophy of religion came to include highly speculative accounts of God's nature, power, knowledge and goodness. In addition, debate got under way in the cross-cultural philosophy of religion (comparing religious conceptions of the self, the afterlife, the experience of the Divine and Nirvana) in ways that would have seemed entirely unworthy of attention earlier. The abandoning of strict empiricism cleared the way for the return of many of the projects that were at the heart of MEDIEVAL (chapter 24) or ANCIENT (chapters 22 and 23) philosophy of religion.

Another factor shaping contemporary philosophy of religion and also contributing to its growth has been the belief that philosophy need not be practised in a strictly uniform fashion, with common starting assumptions and methodology. A single model of philosophy made sense in a tight empiricist framework or in a widely upheld rationalism, but it is frequently argued that neither of these positions (nor any substitute) demands universal assent by all intellectually responsible enquirers, which means that the path is clear for a variety of philosophical projects. The term 'evidence' is derived from the Latin *ex videre* meaning 'from seeing' and, according to some philosophers today, it is less than obvious that a secular way of seeing reality should receive any prior evidential privilege over a religious way of seeing reality. This more free-wheeling, contextualized treatment of evidence has led some philosophers to do their work from within different religious traditions (see Beaty (1990) as an example of this approach to the philosophy of religion). There is, for example, a huge contemporary philosophical literature on different views specific to the Christian faith (topics like the Trinity, the

Incarnation and atonement) and interfaith dialogue (philosophical comparisons between the concepts of God across religions) that has currency among 'the believers', but does not have built into it the need to justify all its projects to a secular, external sceptic. This outlook receives some support from philosophers who repudiate any over-arching treatment of truth which is independent of historical conceptual schemes.

With philosophy of religion revivified, a number of philosophers whose primary work is in other areas have been drawn to it in order to articulate their views. So different arguments and concepts about space and time, free will and determinism, which are at home in METAPHYSICS (chapter 2), the PHILOSOPHY OF MIND (chapter 5) and the PHILOSOPHY OF MATHEMATICS (chapter 11), have been explored in reference to the idea of God – for instance, it is not unusual to see contemporary discussions on the nature of truth to be put in terms of a debate about whether there can be a God's-eye point of view of reality.

2 Religious Beliefs and Religious Forms of Life

A natural way to begin the philosophical exploration of religion is to outline the various metaphysical claims about the cosmos and God, to check the claims with reference to standard moves in metaphysics (the way one would argue about the nature of the material world or about numbers), and then to examine the claims in terms of epistemology (why do we think the metaphysical claims are true?), and ethics (is the theory of values elaborated in the religion credible?). This kind of philosophical inquiry customarily employs the following terms and categories. *Theism*, common to traditional Judaism, Christianity and Islam, is the view that the cosmos is created and kept in existence by an omnipresent, omniscient, omnipotent, supremely good being. It preserves some distinction between God and the creation, according to which the two are not identical however interwoven they might be. Typically, the term 'theism' is used to designate *monotheism*, though contexts may arise when it will be quite important to note explicitly the differences between monotheism (there is one God), *polytheism* (there are many gods) and tritheism (there are three Gods or gods – this usage comes into play in philosophical work on the Trinity in Christianity). *Henotheism* is the recognition of one God for purposes of devotion and worship without denying the existence of other Divine beings. The term 'theism' can be used today with some flexibility, so that it would still be possible to call oneself a theist if one were a monotheist who believed God was omnipresent and all the rest except for being omnipotent. Some self-described 'theists' claim God is 'almighty' (very powerful) without being omnipotent. *Pantheism* is the view that all is God, while Panentheism occupies a position midway between theism and pantheism. For panentheists, while it is not strictly true that everything is God, everything is lodged or embedded within God, making the two interdependent.

This metaphysical approach to religion allows for the relatively neat division between various forms of belief in the Divine as distinct from atheism (from the Greek *atheos*, 'without god', a term commonly used to deny theism as well as all other notions of the Divine) and agnosticism (from the Greek *agnosis*, meaning 'without knowledge' and designating the thesis that the Divine is unknown or, in an extreme form, that the Divine cannot be known).

Three obstacles to this way of proceeding should be noted, the first two only briefly. Firstly, the term 'religion' is not at all easy to define and so the boundaries of the philosophy of religion are likewise difficult to lay out with precision. A necessary condition for being a 'religion' cannot be the belief that there is a God (Theravada Buddhism is a religion which, in the main, is atheistic). Definitions that require the promotion of reverence or awe for what is believed to be sacred are difficult to use with much confidence because of the vagueness of the terms 'reverence' and 'awe', and there is also the problem that some religions may not enshrine these 'religious emotions'. Consider, for example, religious practices that appear to treat the Divine only as a vehicle for ensuring healthy crops, much like Euthyphro's economic approach to God in PLATO's (chapter 23) dialogue *Euthyphro*, and note the prevalence of many today who repudiate all religion and yet seek to live with reverence for life. Debates over such matters (Is capitalism a religion? Is Marxism?) can very quickly appear philosophically sterile. What follows of philosophical interest if capitalism is defined as a religion? The way philosophers usually handle the problem of defining religion is by noting the major traditions recognized today as 'religions' and casting the field of philosophy of religion as enquiry into those specific religions and *the traditions and practices resembling them*. On this view, religions include Judaism, Christianity, Islam, Hinduism, Buddhism, Taoism, Sikhism, and those traditions that resemble one or more of them. If it is plausibly argued that a secular, atheist humanism has many religious characteristics and should be considered as one religion among the others, this may have important political and social consequences (perhaps in terms of government protection or persecution), but settling the matter does not seem to involve very high stakes philosophically. All it means for philosophers of religion is that the primary topic of what is considered their field has widened somewhat.

A second worry is that the systematic categorizing of religions by registering their metaphysical commitments will invariably depreciate the enormous diversity within any given religious tradition. For example, there are important figures within the great traditions of Judaism, Christianity and Islam who sometimes adhere to views that seem either atheistic, agnostic, pantheist or panentheist. There is also considerable cross-referencing today in which religious practitioners will describe themselves as Buddhist Christians and the like. All one can do here is simply exercise caution, being ready heavily to qualify one's description of the different religious traditions as one works at close range on religious figures and movements.

A third obstacle to consider is more potent philosophically and emerges largely from the work of Ludwig WITTGENSTEIN (1889–1951) (chapter 39). In his early philosophical development, Wittgenstein deeply influenced the empiricism of the Vienna Circle, while his mature work took a very different turn with its open-ended approach to the many different ways in which language may be used. Following Wittgenstein's later views on truth, belief and forms of life, some philosophers of religion have gone so far as to contend that all religions are principally matters of practice and that metaphysical concerns are latent and marginal.

Wittgenstein launched an attack on what has been called the picture theory of meaning, according to which statements may be judged true or false depending upon whether reality matches the picture represented by the belief. This understanding of truth and beliefs – essentially the correspondence theory of truth in which the statement 'God exists' is true if and only if God exists – seemed to Wittgenstein to be misguided. It gives rise to insoluble philosophical problems and it misses the whole point of having beliefs, which is that their meaning is to be found in the life in which they are used. By shifting attention from the referential meaning of words to their use, Wittgenstein promoted the idea that we should attend to what he called 'forms of life'. As this move was applied to religious matters, a number of philosophers have either denied or at least played down the extent to which religious forms of life involve metaphysical claims. Norman Malcolm (1975), B. R. Tilghman (1993) and D. Z. Phillips (1970) have all promoted this approach to religion. It may be considered *non-realist* in the sense that it does not treat religious beliefs as straightforward metaphysical claims that can be adjudicated in a realist manner as either true or false. By their lights, the traditional metaphysics of theism got what it deserved when it came under attack in the mid-twentieth century by radical empiricists and under the earlier philosophical attacks in the eighteenth century by David HUME (1711–76) (chapter 31), because the traditional, cognitive outlook profoundly misconstrued what it meant to be religious.

This challenge, then, appears to place in check much of the way philosophers in the West have approached religion. When, for example, LOCKE (1632–1704) (chapter 29), BERKELEY (1685–1753) (chapter 30), Hume, Butler (1692–1752) and Reid (1710–96) argued for and against the justification of belief in God, metaphysics was at the forefront. And the same is largely true of ancient or medieval philosophical reflection about the Divine. When St Thomas AQUINAS (1224–74) (chapter 24) articulated his proofs for God's existence he was engaged in fully fledged metaphysics. In terms of the history of the field, the Wittgensteinian stance is closest to Kantianism, radically recasting and yet continuing the Kantian move of locating the role of religious belief in terms of ethical practices. KANT (1724–1804) (chapter 32) opposed metaphysical arguments supporting religious traditions, claiming that none was successful, but he then went on to argue that there were practical, moral grounds for acting on the basis of a religious view of life and history.

Several points can be made on behalf of twentieth-century non-realism. Firstly, it has some credibility based on the sociology of religion. In the practice of religion itself it appears that we have something more (one might well say something deeper) than 'mere' metaphysical theorizing. Religion seems pre-eminently to be focused upon how we live. Phillips has looked at different religious practices such as prayer and the belief in an afterlife, concluding that both are intelligible and that the motives behind each can be held intact without any of the metaphysical baggage traditionally linked with them. Prayer to God by parents for the recovery of a child's health may be understood as an expression of their anguish and an effort to centre their hope on the child's getting better and not as an attempt to influence God's will. A second reason that might be offered (considered in greater detail in section 4) is that the classical and contemporary arguments for specific views of God have seemed unsuccessful to many philosophers (though not to all). Tilghman takes this line and argues that if the traditional arguments for God's existence are reinterpreted as part of religious life and not treated as if they were scientific truth-claims, then they have an intelligibility and force that they otherwise lack. So, if one expects to argue convincingly to the existence of a Divine designer on the basis of the appearance of design in the cosmos, one is in philosophical trouble. One is in far better shape casting religious references to God's design of the cosmos in terms of religious practices like living with respect for humanity. It might appear that this non-realism would lead religious adherents into some highly paradoxical positions. Does it make sense for there to be Christian atheists, for example? But this worry might be met, at least in part. After all, if the Wittgensteinian critique holds, is not the atheist as much committed to the unacceptable picture theory as the theist? If so, then the non-realist can understand religious life as neither atheist nor theist. Finally, on behalf of non-realism, it may be noted how such a stance receives support from more than the Wittgensteinian movement, but also by the current revival of PRAGMATISM (chapter 36), especially in North America, and the appropriation of some of the work of HEIDEGGER (1889–1976) (chapter 41). There is currently a renewed interest in John DEWEY's (1859–1952) (chapter 36) emphasis on practice over theorizing, and with Heidegger's stress on coping and activity as opposed to conscious, detached reflection. Practice, then, rather than metaphysical theories seems predominant in these philosophical outlooks.

Non-realist views have their critics from the vantage point both of atheists, such as Michael Martin (1990) and theists, such as Roger Trigg (1989). By way of a preliminary response it may be pointed out that even if a non-realist approach is adopted this would not mean altogether jettisoning the more traditional approach to religious beliefs. If one of the reasons advanced on behalf of non-realism is that the traditional project fails, then the traditional project will still need investigating and, assuming that if it has failed the failure is not overwhelmingly obvious, constant rethinking. This is similar to a move in reply to a Kantian philosophy of religion. As Kant built his case against traditional metaphysics, in part, on the basis that theoretical, metaphysical reason leads to contradictory positions (for example, that the world has an origin and that the world does not have an origin), the ongoing assessment of the tenability of a Kantian stance requires rethinking of the metaphysical approach and checking to see if the contradictions are in fact unavoidable.

A more substantial reply to Wittgensteinian non-realism has been the charge that it undermines the very intelligibility of religious practice. Let us concede that practice is antecedent to theory, which is a concession not shared by all. If one has a religious practice, such as prayer to God or Buddhist meditation to see through the illusion of having a substantial ego, the development of some sort of theory of the cosmos to make sense of this practice seems inevitable. Once such a theory is in place, it is intelligible to raise the question of its truth. While Malcolm has proposed that it makes sense to believe *in* God without believing *that* God exists, others have submitted that lack of belief that God exists makes belief in God meaningless. Belief *that* X is prior to belief *in* X. One may hope that something will occur (a child recovers from illness) without the accompanying belief it will occur, but it is more puzzling to suppose one can trust in a child recovering or a Divine being, without believing there was some reality there to rely upon. While non-realism might seem to lay the groundwork for greater tolerance between religions (and between religions and the secular world) because it subverts the battle over which religion has a true picture of the cosmos, critics have lamented the loss of a normative way of choosing between religions, ways that seem to be used in commonplace reflection on the merits of religion. So today it is still not at all unusual for people to claim they have changed religions (or stayed with their own or abandoned all religion), for reasons like the appeal to religious experience, answered or unanswered prayer, miracles or the lack of them, moral and cultural relativism, an overwhelming sense of the reality of good and evil, and so on.

While realists and non-realists are at odds in debate, each side can learn from the other. Non-realists can consider the realist approach to divine attributes and a philosophy of God as reflections of a religious form of life. A philosophical treatment of God's goodness may reveal important insights about practical religious forms of life. On the other hand, the non-realist approach to religion may caution realists against approaching religion as a mere theoretical, abstract enterprise.

3 Divine Attributes

Most philosophy of religion in the West has focused on different versions of theism. Ancient philosophy of religion wrestled with the credibility of monotheism and polytheism in opposition to scepticism and very primitive naturalistic schemes. For example, should Plato's view that God is singularly good be preferred to the portrait of the gods that was articulated in Greek poetic tradition, according to which there are many gods and they are often imperfect and subject to vice and ignorance? The emergence and development of Judaism, Christianity and Islam on a global scale secured the centrality of theism for philosophical enquiry, but the relevance of a philosophical exploration of theism is not limited to those interested in these religions and the cultures in which they flourish. While theism has generally flourished in religious traditions amid religious practices, one may be a theist without adopting any religion whatever, and one may find theistic elements (however piecemeal) in Confucianism, Hinduism, some versions of Mahayana Buddhism, as well as in the religions of some smaller-scale societies. The debate over theism also has currency for secular humanism and religious forms of atheism as in Therevada Buddhist philosophy. In addition, theism may be deemed philosophically interesting in so far as it provides an arena for studying the nature and limits of certain concepts used to describe human life, such as human knowledge, power, creativity and goodness. All these are utilized in theism when God is described as all-knowing, powerful, creative and good. This generates much philosophical work, analysing how these terms function on a transcendent level, noting in particular how our use of them may be informed or undermined by different theories of human life. As God is also described in some theistic traditions as necessarily existing, immutable (unchanging), eternal and incorporeal, this invites philosophical study of the meaning of such notions and the justification of the ensuing idea of a being with either all or most of these supreme attributes.

It will be useful first to get a clearer idea about the general ways in which the language about God has been treated and then to consider some specific cases of philosophical reflection on the attributes of God.

Terms applied both to God and to any aspect of the world have been classified as either *univocal* (sharing the same sense), *equivocal* (used in different senses) or *analogical*. There is a range of accounts of analogous predication, but the most common – and the one assumed here – is that terms are used analogously when their use in different cases (John limps and the argument limps) is based on what is believed to be a resemblance (John's leg is impaired and the argument is weak in some respect). It seems clear that many terms used to describe God in theistic traditions are used analogously, as when God is referred to as a fountain. More difficult to classify are descriptions of God as good, personal, knowing and creative. Heated philosophical and theological disputes centre on unpacking the meaning of such descriptions, disputes that are often carried out with the use of thought experiments.

In thought experiments, hypothetical cases are described – cases that may or may not represent the way things are. In these descriptions, terms normally used in one context are employed in expanded settings. Thus, in thinking of God as omniscient, one might begin with a non-controversial case of a person knowing that a proposition is true, taking note of what it means for someone to possess that knowledge and of the ways in which the knowledge is secured. A theistic thought experiment would seek to extend our understanding of knowledge as we think of it in our own case, working toward the conception of a maximum or supreme intellectual excellence befitting the religious believers' understanding of God. Various degrees of refinement would then be in order, as one speculates not only about the extent of a maximum set of propositions known but also about how these might be known. That is, in attributing omniscience to God, would one thereby claim God knows all in a way that is analogous to the way we come to know truths about the world? Too close an analogy would produce a peculiar picture of God relying upon, for example, induction, sensory evidence or the testimony of others. One move in the philosophy of God has been to assert that the claim 'God knows something' employs the word 'knows' univocally when read as picking out the thesis that God knows something, while it uses the term in only a remotely analogical sense if read as identifying *how* God knows (Swinburne 1977).

Here a medieval distinction comes into play between the *res significata* (what is asserted – for instance, that God knows X) and *modus significandi* (the mode or manner in which what is signified is realized or brought about – for instance, how God knows X). We might have a good grasp of what is meant by the claim that a being is omniscient while being sceptical about grasping how a being might be so. Thought experiments aimed at giving some sense to the Divine attribute of omniscience have been advanced by drawing attention to the way we know some things immediately (bodily positions, feelings and intentions), and then by extending this, coaxing us into conceiving a being that knows all things about itself and the cosmos immediately (see Beaty (1990) for a constructive view, and Blumenfeld in Morris (1987b) for criticism).

Utilizing thought experiments and language in this way, philosophical theology has a stake in the soundness and richness of the imagination, picturing the way things might be 'in one's mind's eye', whether or not this relies on any actual imagery. Philosophers are now more cautious about drawing such inferences as we are increasingly aware of how some features of an imagined state of affairs might be misconceived or overlooked. Even so, it has been powerfully argued that if a state of affairs appears to one to be possible after careful reflection, checking it against one's background knowledge in other areas, then there is at least some warrant in judging the state of affairs to be a *bona fide* possibility (Sorensen 1992). Understanding the current debate over the limits of our thinking about God and the Divine attributes can be sharpened by distinguishing between three important cases: a case of claiming to conceive of *a possible state of affairs*, a case in which one conceives of *the impossibility of a state of affairs*, and a case in which one simply *fails to conceive of a state of affairs*, perhaps

461

accompanied by an argument to the effect that the state of affairs cannot be conceived regardless of whether it is possible or impossible. A strong atheist strategy is to argue that even the best candidates for conceiving of God represent something impossible; the idea of God is as incoherent as the idea that one equals three. Not all atheists take this tack, however; some allow that while it is possible that God exists, God does not exist. Some theists have been fairly agnostic when it comes to conceiving of God's very being, assuming that virtually all language about God is highly analogical at best and that univocal language is appropriate chiefly when making claims about what God is not (for instance, that God is not a material object, not wicked or contingent). The idea of God can be approached through the use of imagination (the *via imaginativa*) and varies to the extent that it employs positive attributions (the *via positiva*) or negative (the *via negativa*). While Brian Davies (1993) adopts a more qualified, *via negativa* philosophy of God, Swinburne (1977) adopts a theism that is more informed by the *via positiva*.

As these strategies become more explicit it becomes easier to note the ways in which philosophy of religion intersects with other areas of philosophy. Consider this with respect to the philosophy of mind. According to certain forms of eliminative materialism, the very notion of possessing such things as beliefs, desires or love rests on confusions; only physical objects, states and entities exist. Adopting this radical eliminativism will probably lead to scepticism about the intelligibility of there being an all-knowing, loving, non-physical being in line with classical treatments of God. If, on the other hand, one adopts a dualist understanding of the human person according to which we are non-physical minds, souls or persons who are materially embodied, this scepticism will be tempered. Supposing that there is a non-physical supreme mind will not seem intellectually confused from the very start. A range of philosophers attribute their reservations about theism to their scepticism about dualism (Kenny 1979; Barnes 1972) and for this reason a substantial number of theists have linked their defence of theism to a defence of the intelligibility of dualism (for instance, Swinburne 1977; Taliaferro 1994). Some theistic philosophers do not think one need go quite so far to defend the intelligibility of dualism; all that is required is to defend the possibility that God is non-physical and possesses the divine attributes regardless of how we happen to be constituted. On this view, God might be non-physical and person-like even if all created persons are exclusively physical. Thus, William Alston (1991a) defends the coherence of theism on the basis of a neutral, functionalist reading of human persons. Alston thinks that so long as we are not eliminativists and we recognize mental terms as intelligible as they function in human life, theism can be defended without having recourse to dualism. Such three-way debate is quite common between those claiming to have good reason to believe that a given idea of God is incoherent, those claiming equally good reason to conclude it is conceptually coherent, and those claiming that the question of God's existence is left unresolved despite all such pro and contra argument.

God and Ineffability

Before concentrating on specific attributes, consider the prospects for a religiously motivated robust agnosticism according to which God or ultimate reality is completely beyond description or conception. St Anselm (1033–1109) held that God is greater than that which can be conceived. What if all concepts must by their very nature fail in making any reference to the Divine, even in highly nuanced, analogous ways, not because there is no God, but because there is one? This proposal is sometimes put as the claim that God is ineffable (from the Latin, *ineffabilis*, for 'not being capable of being expressed'). The insistence on God's ineffability has played a role in the mysticism and thought of important figures in the great monotheistic traditions, and in Buddhist and Hindu traditions as well.

Qualifications about the adequacy of our concepts to represent the Divine are common in religiously sympathetic philosophical systems. Achieving philosophical proficiency in mapping out a robust understanding of the Divine may require an order of experience far beyond what we now have or could ever have. Perhaps, as Joseph Albo (*c.*1380–*c.*1444) put it in the fifteenth century, 'To Know God's nature one would have to be God Himself'. It does not seem obviously wrong to suppose that certain conceptual schemes allow us to obtain only a very thin understanding of ultimate reality, but problems arise when it is claimed that ultimate reality or God are altogether beyond *all* conceptual descriptions no matter how tenuous and circuitous. Philosophers like Plantinga (1980) have objected that this kind of strict ineffability is incoherent, because, firstly, to be described as ineffable is itself a description; secondly, descriptions like 'if it is, it is' are irresistible; and, thirdly, we have good reason for thinking there can be no such ineffable X 'out there'. Even if these charges fail, it is very difficult to see what use positing an ultimately ineffable X would have, religiously, practically, philosophically or scientifically. Denying the existence of X might make as much (or as little) sense as affirming it. Fortunately or unfortunately, very few religions rule out in principle all conceptualizing of God, even if they are quite wary of such theorizing, and so philosophers of religion can still engage in conceptual analysis without having to admit from the outset that they are already cut off from the religions they are attempting to explore philosophically.

In proceeding to treat divine attributes some selectivity is in order. I shall cover those that have occasioned the most intense philosophical scrutiny in recent years.

3.1 Omnipotence

Some of the most vigorous philosophical debate has centred on whether it makes sense to think of God as a supreme, maximally powerful being responsible for the origin and continued conservation of the cosmos. Begin with a claim like 'God can do anything whatever' or 'All things are possible for God' and one is bound to run into obstacles that may be classified as external or internal. External difficulties would hinder any being whatever from being omnipotent, while internal problems would prevent us from recognizing as omnipotent God as conceived in the three main monotheistic traditions. Consider external problems first.

The external barrier here might be purely logical or it may take on broader metaphysical dimensions. There are problems with supposing that anything or anyone can do what is logically impossible. Can God make $2 + 2 = 6$? It would appear to be nonsense to suppose that this could be done by any being. The problem has an additional metaphysical edge if one assumes that there are certain truths, such as 'time is onedirectional', which are necessary but not due to bare logical relationships (its denial does not involve a contradiction). Grant that there are necessary metaphysical truths and it seems that nothing can be omnipotent, because nothing can alter such meta-physically necessary truths. These problems are often treated at one stroke by insisting that what is or *should be* meant by the claim that there is an omnipotent being is that if a being is omnipotent, it can do anything that is logically or metaphysically possible. This approach has the implication that the mathematical and time-bending tasks mentioned above are idle pseudo-tasks or absolute nonsense. This is no worse than 'con-ceding' that an omnipotent being cannot make the concept of justice jump around the number 7 or eat happiness.

This strategy of defining the possibility of Divine omnipotence is fairly common and has antecedents going back to medieval philosophy of religion. It is sometimes refined to take into account different levels and sequences of action. Consider the question of whether God could make something that God could not control. It would appear so, given a certain conception of freedom of the will. Arguably, a being is free only if it is not completely under the control of another being. If God creates a free creature, has God ceased to be omnipotent because now there is a being God cannot control? Presumably, these sorts of 'limits' on Divine freedom can be cast in terms of God's being limited by the limits God introduces. To expect an omnipotent being to be able to make a creature both free and not free at the same time would be akin to expecting that an omnipotent being could make something that is square while lacking four right angles.

Can we envisage a maximal power that is deeper than, or behind, the laws of logic? Perhaps there is some room to move if one adopts an anti-realist treatment of abstract objects and of LOGIC (chapter 4), according to which logical laws are merely the codifi-cation of human designs and language. Alternatively, one might follow DESCARTES (1596–1650) (chapter 26) who thought that God was responsible for the creation of necessary truths. This has not been widely accepted by theists on the grounds that the-istic voluntarism would undermine the necessity of logical and metaphysical truths. If God could make A = A, then God would have the power to make ¬A = A and thus the law of identity would be contingent and not necessary. A group of contemporary philosophers has sought to bolster Descartes's stance, however.

Plantinga (1974), Menzel and Morris (1986) and others propose preserving the necessity of logical and metaphysical truths and yet insist that they are true in virtue of God's creative will, a creative will which could not be otherwise. The necessity of A = A and other such truths is thereby affirmed and accounted for by a deeper Divine necessity. This revival of Descartes's position may be articulated using the convention of talking of possible worlds. A possible world may be said to be a way things could be. The actual world is one possible world; in a different possible world you wrote this chapter and I did not. Using this terminology, one could say that, in all possible worlds, God wills that A = A, and so on for all necessary truths. This revised version of Descartes's stance has been commended on the grounds that it preserves the desired necessities, that it offers some account of the truths at issue rather than leaving the necessities suspended in Platonic strata, and that the explanation it offers has greater simplicity than rival accounts.

Is there an ultimate limit to what, in principle, we could credit to a maximally pow-erful being? Could there be a being that could take credit even for its own existence and constitution? Could God have created God? The idea that any being could create itself (*causa sui* means 'cause of itself') has been dismissed on the grounds that to create itself a being would have to exist already, which is an absurdity; but it has recently been suggested that if creating itself did not require a first moment of existing, the prospect for *causa sui* might improve. One proposal by Menzel and Morris is that in an important respect God could be like a machine. Imagine a machine – the Menzel–Morris machine – that creates matter from nothing. It has always existed and has continuously replaced all its parts systematically, not all at once (in which case it would have to cease to be and then create itself) but incrementally (for instance, on Mondays it would replace its right side, on Tuesdays its left). With every cycle of replacement, would it not have created itself? The standard move in the philosophy of God is to resist these possibilities (perhaps it is absurd to think of God as a machine or having parts or being in time), and to think instead that, if there is a God, God's being God is not something God could have brought about or altered. Perhaps God did not make God omnipotent, but that does not mean God is harnessed by something external to God or is somehow defective.

Consider now some internal obstacles to imagining omnipotence, especially as these are borne out in the monotheistic traditions. God is believed to be non-physical. If so, can God remain God and yet swim? God is thought of as existing necessarily. If so, can God cease to be? God is thought of as necessarily good. Does this mean that God could not bring about an evil state of affairs, without there being some overriding ethical reason to do so? Would this mean that there could be something more powerful than the God of these religious traditions, namely a being that could swim, cease to be, commit evil acts and so on?

Some ways of handling these puzzles include proposing that God can do such things as swim (God can assume a body), bring about evil and so on. Alternatively, one can concede that God cannot do these things, but deny that omnipotence requires doing any act possible for some conceivable creature; rather an omnipotent being has maximal power, such that there can be no being more powerful. Perhaps God cannot commit suicide, but an omnipotent God would nonetheless possess a scope of power that cannot be surpassed by beings capable of self-annihilation. Another response to these paradoxes has been to re-examine the relation between Divine attributes and the motivation for ascribing them to God. Schlesinger (1988) and Morris (1987a), among others, have contended that the rationale behind ascribing great-making qualities to God is to make explicit the idea that God is perfect. What one is after, then, is locating those properties that, together, form the greatest compossible set of properties. On this schema, two properties are compossible if they can both be instantiated simultaneously of the same being. If God's being perfectly good in any way limits God's being all-powerful, it does so only in a fashion that, overall, contributes to the excellence of God. God would be less great, less worthy of worship if God could commit evil. This shifting of attention from bare power to thinking of power in terms of values has been heralded by some feminist and social critics of religion as a healthy departure from a more male-based celebration of a power that only too quickly turns into oppressive, suffocating pictures of the Divine. The Morris–Schlesinger strategy is in the same spirit of earlier tactics, such as that of Boethius (*c*.480–524) in the sixth century, who concluded that the ability to commit evil was far from being a positive power or sign of greatness. In his dialogue *The Consolation of Philosophy* (Boethius 1969) there is the following exchange:

'There is nothing that an omnipotent God could not do.' 'No.' 'Then, can God do evil?' 'No.'
'So that evil is nothing, since that is what He cannot do who can do anything.'

3.2   Omniscience

The belief that God is all-knowing has had a vital role in a host of religious convictions about God's role as the creator of the cosmos and reliance upon God's wisdom, love and providence. Philosophically, omniscience is typically defined in terms of knowing all propositions, or (with some elaboration) knowing with respect to all true propositions that they are true and with respect to all false propositions that they are false. Some of the debate on omniscience stems from philosophical debate over the nature of propositions. Some propositions contain indexical terms (terms having their reference determined according to which person is using them). If you think that some true propositions containing first-person indexical terms, like 'I am in pain now', can only be known by the individual 'I' who is entertaining them, then you would not be able to cast omniscience in terms of knowing all true propositions. On this view, indefinitely many propositions could be true but known only by particular individuals. My knowing that Smith is in pain would involve my knowing a different proposition to be true than that known by Smith. He knows 'I am in pain' and I know 'Smith is in pain'. This puzzle is sometimes dealt with by denying the existence of such hyper-private propositions (Kvanvic 1986). More sustained debate, with less promise of resolution, has occurred over the scope of omniscience.

Omniscience and Freedom

Are omniscience and freedom compatible? Imagine there is a God who knows the future free action of human beings. If God does know you will freely do some act A, then it is true that you will indeed do A. But if you are free, would you not be free to avoid doing A? Given that it is foreknown you will do A, it appears you would not be free to refrain from the act. Initially this paradox seems easy to dispel. If God knows about your free action, then God knows that you will freely do something and that you could have refrained from it. God's foreknowing the act does not make it necessary. Does not the paradox only arise because we confuse two propositions: 'Necessarily, if God knows X, then X' with 'If God knows X, then necessarily X'? AUGUSTINE (354–430) (chapter 24), Boethius, Anselm, Aquinas and others sought to preserve the reality of freedom along with God's foreknowledge, and this is a stance widely represented today. The problem is retained, however, when the point is pressed concerning the grounds for foreknowledge. If God does know you will freely do X, then it appears that there must now be a fact of the matter about what you will and will not do, and thus some residual sense in which your freely doing X is not something that can be altered. If the problem is put in first-person terms and one imagines God foreknows you will freely turn the next page, then an easy resolution of the paradox seems elusive. Imagine God tells you what you will freely do. Under such conditions, is it still intelligible to believe you have the ability to do otherwise if it is known by God as well as yourself what you will indeed elect to do?

Various replies have been given, of which I note three. Some adopt what is called compatibilism, affirming the compatibility of free will and determinism, and conclude that foreknowledge is no more threatening to freedom than determinism. A second position involves adhering to the radically libertarian outlook of insisting that freedom involves a radical, indeterminist exercise of power, and concludes that God cannot know future free action. What prevents such philosophers from denying that God is omniscient is that they contend there are no truths about future free actions. Prior to someone's doing a free action, there is no fact of the matter that he or she will do a given act. This is in keeping with ARISTOTLE's (chapter 23) philosophy of time and truth. Aristotle thought it was neither true nor false prior to a given sea battle whether a given side would win it. Some theists, such as Swinburne (1977), adopt this line today, holding that the future cannot be known. If it cannot be known for metaphysical reasons, then omniscience can be read as knowing all that it is possible to know. That God cannot know future free action is no more of a mark against God's being omniscient than God's inability to make square circles is a mark against God's being omnipotent. Other parties, including Linville (1993), deny the original paradox. They insist that God's foreknowledge is compatible with libertarian freedom and seek to resolve the quandary either by claiming that God is not bound in time (God does not so much *fore*know as eternally know) or by arguing that the unique vantage point of an omniscient God prevents any impingement on freedom. God can simply know the future without this having to be grounded on the future somehow being already fixed. Some advocates of this position hold that God knows not just what will occur, but what would occur given all possible future events. God knows whether you will freely turn the page and also knows whether you would freely do so if any number of other events were to occur prior to the act (for instance, God knows what you would do if you saw an elephant just now, even though you are not seeing one). This kind of knowledge of possible free choices is referred to as *middle knowledge*, as it designates knowledge mid-way, as it were, between *what will occur* and *what could occur*. Middle knowledge involves knowing *what would happen under all possible conditions*.

3.3   Eternal or everlasting?

Could there be a being that is outside time? In the great monotheistic traditions, God is thought of as without any kind of beginning or end. God will never, indeed, can never, cease to be. Some philosophical theists hold that God's TEMPORALITY (see chapter 2) is very much like ours in the sense that there is a before, during and an after for God – or a past, present and future for God. This view is sometimes referred to as the thesis that God is *everlasting* (Wolterstorff 1982). Those adopting a more radical stance claim that God is independent of temporality, arguing either that God is not in time at all, or that God is 'simultaneously' at or in all times. This is sometimes called the view that God is *eternal* as opposed to everlasting (Leftow 1991). Why adopt the more radical stance? One reason, already noted, is that if God is not temporally bound, there may be a resolution to the problem of reconciling freedom and foreknowledge. As Augustine put it in *The City of God*: 'For He does not pass from this to that by transition of thought, but beholds all things with absolute unchangeableness; so that of those things which emerge in time, the future, indeed, are not yet, and the present are now, and the past no longer are; but all of these are by Him comprehended in His stable and eternal presence' (Augustine 1972: XI, 21). If God is outside time, there may also be a secure foundation explaining God's immutability (changelessness), incorruptibility and immortality. Furthermore, there may be an opportunity to use God's standing outside of time to launch an argument that God is the creator of time.

Those affirming God to be unbounded by temporal sequences face several puzzles which I note without trying to settle. If God is somehow at or in all times, is God simultaneously at or in each? If so, there is the following problem. If God is simultaneous with Rome burning in 410, and also simultaneous with your reading this book, then it seems that Rome must be burning at the same time you are reading this book. A different problem arises with respect to omniscience. If God is outside of time, can God know what time it is now? Arguably, there is a fact of the matter that it is now, say, midnight on 1 July 1996. A God outside of time might know that at midnight on 1 July 1996 certain things occur, but could God know when it is *now* that time? The problem is that the more emphasis we place on the claim that God's supreme existence is independent of time, the more we seem to jeopardize taking seriously time as we know it. Finally, while the great monotheistic traditions provide a portrait of the Divine as supremely different from the creation, there is also an insistence on God's proximity. For some theists, describing God as a person or person-like (God loves, acts, knows) is not to equivocate. But it is not clear that an eternal God could be personal.

3.4   The goodness of God

All known world religions address the nature of good and evil and commend ways of achieving human well-being, whether this be thought of in terms of salvation, liberation, deliverance, enlightenment, tranquillity or an egoless state of Nirvana. Notwithstanding important differences, there is a substantial overlap between many of these conceptions of the good as witnessed by the commending of the Golden Rule ('Do unto others as you would have them do unto you') in many religions. Some religions construe the Divine as in some respect beyond our human notions of good and evil. In Hinduism, for example, Brahman has been extolled as possessing a sort of moral transcendence, and some Christian theologians have likewise insisted that God is only a moral agent in a highly qualified sense. To call God good is for them very different from calling a human being good (Davies 1993). Belief in the supreme goodness of God has, however, been a mainstay of the great monotheistic traditions, and belief in the goodness of God has also had considerable force independent of these traditions. Disputes over the goodness of God lay at the heart of the initial quarrel between philosophy and poetry. Plato was so repelled by the moral incoherence of the polytheism displayed in the poetry of Hesiod and Homer, with the complicity of the gods in infanticide, patricide, murder, rape and adultery, that he proposed banning poets from his ideal republic.

Here I note some of the ways in which philosophers have articulated what it means to call God good. In treating the matter, there has been a tendency either to explain God's goodness in terms of standards that are not God's creation and thus, in some measure, independent of God's will, or in terms of God's will and the standards God has created. The latter view is termed *theistic voluntarism*. A common version of theistic voluntarism is the claim that for something to be good or right simply means that it is willed by God and for something to be evil or wrong means that it is forbidden by God.

Theistic voluntarists face several difficulties: moral language seems intelligible without having to be explained in terms of the Divine will. Indeed, many people make what they take to be objective moral judgements without making any reference to God. If they are using moral language intelligibly, how could it be that the very meaning of such moral language should be analysed in terms of Divine volitions? New work in the PHILOSOPHY OF LANGUAGE (chapter 3) may be of use to theistic voluntarists. According to a causal theory of reference, 'water' necessarily designates H_2O (it is not a contingent fact that water is H_2O), notwithstanding the fact that many people can use the term 'water' without knowing its composition. Similarly, could it not be the case that 'good' may refer to that which is willed by God even though many people are not aware of or even deny the existence of God? Another difficulty for voluntarism lies in accounting for the apparent meaningful content of claims like 'God is good'. It appears that in calling God good the religious believer is saying more than 'God wills what God wills'. If so, must not the very notion of goodness have some meaning independent of God's will? Also at issue is the worry that if voluntarism is accepted, the theist has threatened the normative objectivity of moral judgements. Could God make it the case that moral judgements were turned upside down? Could God make cruelty good? Arguably, the moral universe is not so malleable. In reply, some voluntarists have sought to understand the stability of the moral laws in light of God's immutably fixed, necessary nature. Recall the similar move in the Cartesian strategy of anchoring the necessity of logic and metaphysics in God's very being. For sympathetic treatments of voluntarism, see Adams (1987) and Owen (1965).

By understanding God's goodness in terms of God's being (as opposed to God's will alone), we come close to the non-voluntarist stand. Aquinas and others have held that God is essentially good in virtue of God's very being. All such positions are non-voluntarist in so far as they do not claim that what it means for something to be good is that God wills it to be so. The goodness of God may be explained in various ways, either by arguing that God's perfection requires God being good as an agent or by arguing that God's goodness can be articulated in terms of other Divine attributes such as those outlined above. For example, because knowledge is in itself good, omniscience is a supreme good. God has also been considered good in so far as God has created and conserves in existence a good cosmos. Debates over the problem of evil (if God is indeed omnipotent and perfectly good, why is there evil?) have poignancy precisely because they challenge this chief judgement over God's goodness. This debate is considered in the last section.

The choice between voluntarism and a more internalist picture is rarely strict. Some theists who oppose a full-scale voluntarism allow for partial voluntarist elements. According to one such moderate stance, while God cannot make cruelty good, God can make some actions morally required or morally forbidden which otherwise would be morally neutral. Arguments for this have been based on the thesis that the cosmos and all its contents are God's creation. According to some theories of property, an agent making something good gains entitlements over the property. The crucial moves in arguments that the cosmos and its contents belong to their Creator have been to guard against the idea that human parents would then 'own' their children (they do not, because parents are not radical creators like God), and the idea that Divine ownership would permit *anything*, thus construing our duties owed to God as the duties of a slave to a master (a view to which not all theists have objected). Theories spelling out why and how the cosmos belongs to God have been prominent in all three monotheistic traditions. Plato defended the notion, as did Aquinas and Locke. (See Brody (1992) for a current defence of Locke's version of Divine ownership.)

One other effort worth noting to link judgements of good and evil with judgements about God relies upon the ideal observer theory of ethics. According to this theory, moral judgements can be analysed in terms of how an ideal observer would judge matters. To say an act is right entails a commitment to holding that if there were an ideal observer, it would approve of the act; to claim an act is wrong entails the thesis that if there were an ideal observer, it would disapprove of it. The theory can be found in work by Hume, Adam Smith (1723–90), SIDGWICK (1838–1900) (chapter 35), Hare (1996) and Firth (1970). The ideal observer is variously described, but typically is thought of as impartial, omniscient regarding non-moral facts (facts that can be grasped without already knowing the moral status or implications of the fact – for instance, 'He did something bad' is a moral fact; 'He hit Smith' is not), and as omnipercipient (Firth's term for adopting a position of universal affective appreciation of the points of view of all involved parties). The theory receives some support from the fact that most moral disputes can be analysed in terms of different parties challenging each other to be impartial, to get their empirical facts straight, and to be more sensitive – for example, by realizing what it feels like to be disadvantaged. The theory has formidable critics and defenders. If true, it does not follow that there is an ideal observer, but if it is true and moral judgements are coherent, then the idea of an ideal observer is coherent. Given certain conceptions of God in the three great monotheistic traditions, God fits the ideal observer description (and more besides, of course). Should an ideal observer theory work, a theist would have some reason for claiming that atheists committed to normative, ethical judgements are also committed to *the idea of a God* or a *God-like being*.

3.5   Other aspects of the philosophy of God

I note very briefly some additional, recent work in the philosophy of God. With respect to transcendence, there is considerable debate over whether God is best thought of as an individual being or as Being itself. Some resist thinking of God as an individual because they think of individuals in terms of one thing among others. That is, if there is an individual, it must be thought of as part of a genus. But, by hypothesis, God is *sui generis* (one of a kind or a genus unto itself) and hence not an individual. Also high on the list of transcendent properties, some philosophers have rekindled the notion that God is ultimately simple, without parts and not possessing distinguishable attributes. It makes sense to distinguish the Divine attributes, as we have done above, but this should be seen as an artificial device, not reflecting any real distinction within the Godhead. The appeal of this philosophical theism will depend upon one's theory of properties, just as the earlier debate on being and individual will depends upon one's overall ontology. For a defence of God as BEING (p. 62) see Davies (1993), and for Divine simplicity see Kretzmann and Stump, in Morris (1987b).

On Divine immanence, much of the debate has turned on claims about whether God is impassable (not subject to passions). If one adopts a high, non-temporalist view of God's eternity, one will be more likely to affirm the impassability of God as, arguably, undergoing passion requires change. One might still allow for *certain* change for God, sometimes called 'Cambridge change' (because it satisfies the criterion of change suggested by Russell and others in Cambridge without involving real change in the subject), but this will not be a substantial change on God's side. An example of Cambridge change would be the change in Jones when he becomes shorter than Smith as a result of Smith's getting taller while Jones remains the same size. A Cambridge change regarding God might be for God to be thought about by Jones on one day but not on another. The only 'real' alteration is on Jones's side, not God's. Would recognizing that God can undergo Cambridge change be enough to make philosophical sense of the idea that God suffers and feels pleasure over the different ills and goods of the cosmos? Perhaps God can suffer and feel pleasure in creation, but does so in some non-temporal fashion or possibly at each time God is in different affective states. Those who believe God *does* feel passion tend to believe God is everlasting and thus in time. How one decides such issues will have an impact on how one construes higher-order Divine properties like God's omnipresence. Thus, if one accepts that God is subject to passions, God's being everywhere present might involve a full host of Divine properties – for example, God would know what is occurring everywhere, God could exercise maximal power without limit (except, perhaps, by the limits of logic and necessary metaphysical truths), no place would exist without God's conserving, creative power, and there would be the additional Divine attribute of affective responsiveness to values. Thus, for God to be present in the cosmos would mean, in part, that God feels sorrow and pleasure in response to its ills and goods.

4 Evidence, Religious Experience and Secular Explanations

There is currently some philosophical unease about whether metaphysics or epistemology should have priority. Modern Western philosophy may be seen to have followed Descartes in championing epistemology over metaphysics. On Cartesian grounds, each individual must start from himself or herself and then work outward, eventually achieving a knowledge of God, other people and the external world. It is a hallmark of some philosophy now that it takes deliberate issue with this approach. Thus, it has been held that any starting-point of an epistemological kind will already house within it certain assumptions about what exists. Are we all able to agree on a common starting-point? A common criticism of Descartes is that if you begin with his *Meditations*, you will never escape an exasperating scepticism. We simply lack the self-evident axioms and the clear and evident ideas required to have any sort of constructive philosophy of the world. As the effort to build up one's understanding of the world from a Cartesian foundation is losing its appeal, there have been widespread repercussions in the philosophy of religion.

One way of carrying out philosophy of religion along non-foundationalist lines has been to build a case for the comparative rationality of a religious view of the world. It has been argued that the intellectual integrity of a religious world view can be secured if it can be shown to be no less rational than the available alternatives. It need only achieve intellectual parity. John Hick (1990) and others emphasize the integrity of religious ways of seeing the world that are holistic, internally coherent, and open to criticism along various external lines. On the latter front, if a religious way of conceiving the world is at complete odds with contemporary science, that would count as good grounds for revising the religious outlook. The case for religion need not, however, be scientific or even analogous to science. If Hick is right, religious ways of seeing the world are not incompatible with science, but complementary. Independent of Hick but in the same spirit, Plantinga (1993) has proposed that belief in God's existence may be taken as properly basic and fully warranted without having to be justified in relation to standard arguments for God from design, miracles and so on. Plantinga argues that the tendency to believe in God follows natural tendencies of the human mind. This stance comprises what is commonly referred to as *Reformed Epistemology* because of its leaning on work by the Reformed theologian John Calvin (1509–64), who maintained that we have a sense of God (*sensus divinitatus*) leading us to see God in the world around us. Plantinga has thereby couched the question of justification within the larger arena of metaphysics. By advancing an intricate, comprehensive picture of how beliefs can be warranted when they function as God designed them, he has provided what some believe to be a combined metaphysical and epistemic case for the rationality of religious convictions.

Who has the burden of proof in a debate between a theist and an atheist? Antony Flew (1984) thinks it is the theist. By his lights, the theist and atheist can agree on a whole base line of truths (such as the findings of the physical sciences). The question then becomes, why go any further? Flew wields a version of Ockham's razor, arguing that if one has no reason to go further, one has reason not to go further. His challenge has been met on various fronts, with some critics claiming that Flew's burden of proof argument is wedded to an outmoded foundationalism, that any burden of proof is shared *equally* by atheists and theists, or that the theist has an array of arguments to help shoulder a greater burden of proof. The position of *fideism* is a further option. Fideism is the view that religious belief does not require evidence and that religious faith is self-vindicating. Karl Barth (1886–1968) advocated a fideistic philosophy. Hick and Plantinga need not be considered fideists because of the major role each gives to experience, coherence and reflection. (For a superb study of fideism, see Penelhum 1983.)

Perhaps the justification most widely offered for religious belief concerns the occurrence of religious experience or the cumulative weight of testimony of those claiming to have had religious experiences. Putting the latter case in theistic terms, the argument appeals to the fact that many people have testified that they have felt God's presence. Does such testimony provide evidence that God exists? That it is evidence has been argued by Gellman (1997), Yandell (1993), Alston (1991a, b), Davis (1989), Gutting (1982), Swinburne (1979) and others. That it is not (or that its evidential force is trivial) is argued by Martin (1990), Mackie (1985), Nielsen (1982) and others. In an effort to stimulate further investigation, I shall briefly sketch some of the moves and counter-moves in the debate.

472

The Importance of Religious Experience: Objections and Replies

Objection: Religious experience cannot be experience of God for experience is only sensory and if God is non-physical, God cannot be sensed.

Reply: The thesis that experience is only sensory can be challenged. Yandell (1993) marks out some experiences (as when one has 'a feeling' someone is present but without having any accompanying sensations) that might provide grounds for questioning a narrow sensory notion of experience.

Objection: Testimony to have experienced God is only testimony that one *thinks* one has experienced God; it is only testimony of a conviction, not evidence.

Reply: The literature on religious experience testifies to the existence of experience of some Divine being on the basis of which the subject comes to think the experience is of God. If read charitably, the testimony is not testimony to a conviction, but to experiences that form the grounds for the conviction.

Objection: Because religious experience is unique, how could one ever determine whether it is reliable? We simply lack the ability to examine the object of religious experience in order to test whether the reported experiences are indeed reliable.

Reply: As we learned from Descartes, all our experiences of external objects face a problem of uniqueness. It is possible in principle that all our senses are mistaken and we do not have the public, embodied life we think we lead. We cannot step out of our own subjectivity to vindicate our ordinary perceptual beliefs any more than in the religious case.

Objection: Reports of religious experience differ radically and the testimony of one religious party neutralizes the testimony of others. The testimony of Hindus cancels out the testimony of Christians. The testimony of atheists to experience God's absence cancels out the testimony of 'believers'.

Reply: Several replies might be offered here. Testimony *to experience the absence of God* might be better understood as testimony *not to experience God.* Failing to experience God might be justification for believing that there is no God only to the extent that we have reason to believe that if God exists God would be experienced by all. Theists might even appeal to the claim by many atheists that it can be virtuous to live ethically with atheist beliefs. Perhaps if there is a God, God does not think this is altogether bad, and actually desires religious belief to be fashioned under conditions of trust and faith rather than knowledge. The diversity of religious experiences has caused some defenders of the argument from religious experience to mute their conclusion. Thus, Gutting (1982) contends that the argument is not strong enough fully to vindicate a specific religious tradition, but that it is strong enough to overturn an anti-religious naturalism. Other defenders use their specific tradition to deal with ostensibly competing claims based on different sorts of religious experiences. Theists have proposed that more impersonal experiences of the Divine represent only one aspect of God. God is a person or is person-like, but God can also be experienced, for example, as sheer luminous unity. Hindus have claimed the experience of God as personal is only one stage in the overall journey of the soul to truth, the highest truth being that Brahman transcends personhood.

How one settles the argument will depend on one's overall convictions in many areas of philosophy. Currently it is popular to see the individual arguments favouring and opposing God's existence as part of cumulative, mutually supportive lines of reasoning. This view stresses the holistic character of concepts, such as the view that concepts cannot be isolated but must be seen as part of conceptual frameworks. The holistic, interwoven nature of both theistic and atheistic arguments can be readily illustrated. If you diminish the implications of religious experience and have a high standard regarding the burden of proof for any sort of religious outlook, then it is highly likely that the classical arguments for God's existence will not be persuasive. Moreover, if one thinks that theism can be shown to be intellectually confused from the start, then theistic arguments from religious experience will carry little weight. Testimony to have experienced God will have no more weight than testimony to have experienced a round square, and non-religious accounts of religious experience – like those of Freud (a result of wish-fulfilment), Marx (a reflection of the economic base) or Durkheim (a product of social forces) – will increase their appeal. If, on the other hand, you think the theistic picture is coherent and that the testimony of religious experience provides some evidence for theism, then your assessment of the classical theistic arguments might be more favourable, for they would serve to corroborate and further support what you already have some reason to believe. From such a vantage point, appeal to wish-fulfilment, economics and social forces might have a role, but the role is to explain why some parties do not have experiences of God and to counter the charge that failure to have such experiences provides evidence that there is no religious reality. Some interconnections among theistic arguments and among anti-theistic arguments will be noted below.

5   Four Arguments about the Existence of God

We have already covered considerable ground that is traversed in arguments supporting and opposing theism. I will map some of the strategies that are employed in four additional areas where recent philosophical activity has been focused. I will recount what appear to be strong and lively versions of the various arguments and leave readers to explore matters further, rather than offer the dozen or so versions of each argument that are now under debate.

5.1   Ontological arguments

There is a host of arguments under this title; all of them are based principally on conceptual, *a priori* grounds which do not involve *a posteriori* empirical investigation. If a version of the argument works, then it can be deployed using only the concept of God and some modal principles of inference, that is, principles concerning possibility and necessity. The argument need not resist all empirical support, however, as I shall indicate.

The focus of the argument is the thesis that, if there is a God, then God's existence is necessary. God's existence is not contingent – God is not the sort of being that just happens to exist. That this is an accurate picture of what is meant by God may be shown by appealing to the way God is conceived in Jewish, Christian and Islamic traditions. This would involve some *a posteriori*, empirical research into the way God is thought of in these traditions. Alternatively, a defender of the ontological argument might hope to convince others that the concept of God is the concept of a being that exists necessarily by beginning with the idea of a maximally excellent being. If there were a maximally excellent being what would it be like? It has been argued that among its array of great-making qualities (omniscience and omnipotence) would be necessary existence. Once fully articulated, it can be argued that a maximally excellent being, which existed necessarily, could be called 'God'.

The ontological argument goes back to St Anselm, but I shall explore a current version relying heavily on the principle that if something is possibly necessarily the case, then it is necessarily the case (or, to put it redundantly, it is necessarily necessary). The principle can be illustrated in the case of propositions: $1 + 1 = 2$ does not seem to be the sort of thing that might just happen to be true. Rather, either it is necessarily true or necessarily false. If the latter, it is not possible, if the former, it is possible. If one has good reason to believe it is possible that $1 + 1 = 2$, then one has good reason to believe that $1 + 1$ does indeed, necessarily equal 2. Do we have reason to think it is possible God exists necessarily? In support of this, one can also appeal to *a posteriori* matters, noting the extant religious traditions that uphold such a notion. There does not appear to be anything amiss in their thinking of God as existing; if the belief that God exists is incoherent this is not obvious. Indeed, a number of atheists think God might exist, but conclude God does not. If we are successful in establishing the possibility that God necessarily exists, the conclusion follows that it is necessarily the case that God exists.

There have been hundreds of objections and replies to this argument. Perhaps the most ambitious objection is that the argument can be used with one minor alteration to argue that God cannot exist. Assume all the argument above but also that it is possible God does not exist. Atheists can point out that many theists who believe there is a God at least allow for the bare possibility that they could be wrong and there is no God. If it is possible that there is no God, then it would necessarily follow that there is no God. Replies to this objection emphasize the difficulty of conceiving of the nonexistence of God. The battle over whether God is necessary or impossible is often fought over the coherence of the various divine attributes discussed in section 3. If you think these attributes are compossible, involve no contradictions and violate no known metaphysical truths, then you may well have good grounds for concluding that God is possible and therefore necessary. However, if you see a contradiction, say, in describing a being who is at once omniscient and omnipotent, you may well have good grounds for concluding that God's existence is impossible.

Another objection is that it makes no sense to think of a being existing necessarily; propositions may be necessarily true or false, but objects cannot be necessary or contingent. Some philosophers reply that it makes no less sense to think of an individual (God) existing necessarily than it does to think of propositions being necessarily true.

A further objection is that the ontological argument cannot get off the ground because of the question-begging nature of its premise that if there is a God, then God exists necessarily. Does admitting this premise concede that there is some individual thing such that *if it exists, it exists necessarily*? Replies have claimed that the argument only requires one to consider an ostensible state of affairs, without having to concede initially whether the state of affairs is possible or impossible. To consider what is involved in positing the existence of God is no more hazardous than considering what is involved in positing the existence of unicorns. One can entertain the existence of unicorns and their necessary features (that necessarily if there were unicorns, there would exist single-horned beasts) without believing that there are unicorns.

Finally, consider the objection that, if successful in providing reasons to believe that God exists, the ontological argument could be used to establish the existence of a whole array of other items, like perfect islands. Replies to this sort of objection have typically questioned whether it makes sense to think of an island (a physical thing) as existing necessarily or as having maximal excellence on a par with God. Does the imagined island have excellences like omniscience, omnipotence (a power which would include the power to make indefinitely many islands) and so on?

Classical, alternative versions of the ontological argument are propounded by Anselm, Spinoza and Descartes, with current versions by Plantinga (1974), Hartshorne and Malcolm (both in Hick and McGill 1967), and Dore (1984); classical critics include Gaunilo and Kant, and current critics are many, including Rowe (1993), Barnes (1972) and Mackie (1985).

5.2   Cosmological arguments

Arguments in this vein are more firmly planted in empirical, *a posteriori* reflection, but some versions employ *a priori* reasons as well. There are various versions. Some argue that the cosmos had an initial cause outside it, a First Cause in time. Others argue that the cosmos has a necessary, sustaining cause from instant to instant. The two versions are not mutually exclusive, for it is possible both that the cosmos had a First Cause and that it currently has a sustaining cause.

The cosmological argument relies on the intelligibility of the notion of something which is not itself caused to exist by anything else. This could be either the all-out necessity of supreme pre-eminence across all possible worlds used in versions of the ontological argument, or a more local, limited notion of a being that is uncaused in the actual world. If successful, the argument would provide reason for thinking there is at least one such being of extraordinary power responsible for the existence of the cosmos. At best, it may not justify a full picture of the God of religion (a First Cause would be powerful, but not necessarily omnipotent), but it would nonetheless challenge naturalistic alternatives and bring one closer to theism.

Both versions of the argument ask us to consider the cosmos in its present state. Is the world as we know it something that necessarily exists? At least with respect to ourselves, the planet, the solar system and the galaxy, it appears not. With respect to these items in the cosmos, it makes sense to ask why they exist rather than not. In relation to scientific accounts of the natural world, such enquiries into causes make abundant sense and are perhaps even essential presuppositions of the natural sciences. Some proponents of the argument contend that we know *a priori* that if something exists there is a reason for its existence. So why does the cosmos exist? If we explain the contingent existence of the cosmos (or states of the cosmos) only in terms of other contingent things (earlier states of the cosmos, say), then a full cosmic explanation will never be attained. At this point the two versions of the argument divide. Arguments to a First Cause in time contend that a continuous temporal regress from one contingent existence to another would never account for the existence of the cosmos, and they conclude that it is more reasonable to accept there was a First Cause than to accept either a regress or the claim that the cosmos just came into being from nothing. Arguments to a sustaining cause of the cosmos claim that explanations of why something exists now cannot be adequate without assuming a present, contemporaneous sustaining cause. The arguments have been based on the denial of all actual infinities (Craig 1980) or on the acceptance of some infinities (for instance, the coherence of supposing there to be infinitely many stars) combined with the rejection of an infinite regress of explanations solely involving contingent states of affairs (Taylor 1963). The latter has been described as a vicious regress as opposed to one that is benign. There are plausible examples of vicious infinite regresses that do not generate explanations: for instance, imagine that I explain my possession of a book by reporting that I got it from A who got it from B, and so on to infinity. This would not explain how I got the book. Alternatively, imagine a mirror with light reflected in it. Would the presence of light be successfully explained if one claimed that the light was a reflection of light from another mirror, and the light in that mirror came from yet another mirror, and so on to infinity? Consider a final case. You come across a word you do not understand; let it be 'onggggt'. You ask its meaning and are given another word which is unintelligible to you, and so on, forming an infinite regress. Would you ever know the meaning of the first term? The force of these cases is to show how similar they are to the regress of contingent explanations. Versions of the argument that reject all actual infinities face the embarrassment of explaining what is to be made of the First Cause, especially since it might have some features that are actually infinite. In reply, Craig and others have contended that they have no objection to potential infinities (although the First Cause will never cease to be, it will never become an actual infinity). They further accept that prior to the creation, the First Cause was not in time, a position relying on the theory that time is relational rather than absolute. The current scientific popularity of the relational view may offer support to defenders of the argument.

It has been objected that both versions of the cosmological argument set out an inflated picture of what explanations are reasonable. Why should the cosmos as a whole need an explanation? If everything in the cosmos can be explained, albeit through infinite, regressive accounts, what is left to explain? One may reply, either by denying that infinite regresses actually do satisfactorily explain or by charging that the failure to seek an explanation for the whole is arbitrary. The question 'Why is there a cosmos?' seems a perfectly intelligible one. If there are accounts for things in the cosmos, why not for the whole? The argument is not built on the fallacy of treating every whole as having all the properties of its parts. But if everything in the cosmos is contingent, it seems just as reasonable to believe that the whole cosmos is contingent as it is to believe that if everything in the cosmos is invisible, the cosmos as a whole would be invisible.

Another objection is that rather than explaining the contingent cosmos, the cosmological argument introduces a mysterious entity of which we can make very little philosophical or scientific sense. How can positing at least one First Cause provide a better account of the cosmos than simply concluding that the cosmos lacks an ultimate account? In the end, the theist seems bound to admit that why the First Cause created at all was a contingent matter. If, on the contrary, the theist has to claim that the First Cause had to do what it did, would not the cosmos be necessary rather than contingent?

Some theists come close to concluding that it was indeed an essential feature of God that creation had to occur. If God is supremely good, there had to be some overflowing of goodness in the form of a cosmos (see Kretzmann and Stump in Morris (1987b) on the ideas of Dionysius the Areopagite). But theists typically reserve some role for the freedom of God and thus seek to retain the idea that the cosmos is contingent. Defenders of the cosmological argument still contend that its account of the cosmos has a comprehensive simplicity lacking in alternative views. God's choices may be contingent, but not God's existence and the Divine choice of creating the cosmos can be understood to be profoundly simple in its supreme, overriding endeavour, namely to create something good. Swinburne (1977) has argued that accounting for natural laws in terms of God's will provides for a simple, overarching framework in terms of which to comprehend the order and purposive character of the cosmos. At this point we move from the cosmological to the teleological arguments.

Defenders of the cosmological argument include Swinburne (1979), Taylor (1963), Meynell (1982), Reichenbach (1972) and Rowe (1993); prominent opponents include Flew (1984), Martin (1990) and Mackie (1985).

5.3   Teleological arguments

These arguments focus on characteristics of the cosmos that seem to reflect the design or intentionality of God or, more modestly, of one or more powerful, intelligent God-like agents. Part of the argument may be formulated as providing evidence that the cosmos is the sort of reality that would be produced by an intelligent being, and then arguing that positing this source is more reasonable than agnosticism or denying it. As in the case of the cosmological argument, the defender of the teleological argument may want to claim only to be giving us *some* reason for thinking there is a God. Note the way the various arguments might then be brought to bear on each other. If successful, the teleological argument may provide some reason for thinking that the First Cause of the cosmological argument is purposive, while the ontological argument provides some reason for thinking that it makes sense to posit a being that has Divine attributes and necessarily exists. Behind all of them an argument from religious experience may provide some initial reasons to seek further support for a religious conception of the cosmos and to question the adequacy of naturalism.

One version of the teleological argument will depend on the intelligibility of purposive explanation. In our own human case it appears that intentional, purposive explanations are legitimate and can truly account for the nature and occurrence of events. In thinking about an explanation for the ultimate character of the cosmos, is it more likely for the cosmos to be accounted for in terms of a powerful, intelligent agent or in terms of a naturalistic scheme of final laws with no intelligence behind them? Theists employing the teleological argument will draw attention to the order and stability of the cosmos, the emergence of vegetative and animal life, the existence of consciousness, morality, rational agents and the like, in an effort to identify what might plausibly be seen as purposively explicable features of the cosmos. Naturalistic explanations, whether in biology or physics, are then cast as being comparatively local in application when held up against the broader schema of a theistic metaphysics. Darwinian accounts of biological evolution will not necessarily assist us in thinking through why there are either any such laws or any organisms to begin with. Arguments supporting and opposing the teleological argument will then resemble arguments about the cosmological argument, with the negative side contending that there is no need to move beyond a naturalistic account, and the positive side aiming to establish that failing to go beyond naturalism is unreasonable.

In assessing the teleological argument, we can begin with the objection from uniqueness. We cannot compare our cosmos with others, determining which have been designed and which have not. If we could, then we might be able to find support for the argument. If we could compare our cosmos with those we knew to be designed and if the comparison were closer than with those we knew to be undesigned, then the argument might be plausible. Without such comparisons, however, the argument fails. Replies to this line of attack have contended that were we to insist that inferences in unique cases were out of order, then we would have to rule out otherwise perfectly respectable scientific accounts of the origin of the cosmos. Besides, while it is not possible to compare the layout of different cosmic histories, it is in principle possible to envisage worlds that seem chaotic, random or based on the laws that cripple the emergence of life. Now we can envisage an intelligent being creating such worlds, but, through considering their features, we can articulate some marks of purposive design to help us judge whether the cosmos was designed rather than created at random. Some critics appeal to the possibility that the cosmos has an infinite history to bolster and reintroduce the uniqueness objection. Given infinite time and chance, it seems likely that something like our world will come into existence, with all its appearance of design. If so, why should we take it to be so shocking that our world has its apparent design and why should explaining the world require positing one or more intelligent designers? Replies repeat the earlier move of insisting that if the objection were to be decisive, then many seemingly respectable accounts would also have to fall by the wayside. It is often conceded that the teleological argument does not demonstrate that one or more designers are *required*; it seeks rather to establish that positing such purposive intelligence is reasonable and preferable to naturalism. Defenders of the argument this century include Schlesinger (1977) and Swinburne (1979). It is rejected by Mackie (1985), Martin (1990) and others.

One feature of the teleological argument currently receiving increased attention focuses on epistemology. It has been contended that if we do rely on our cognitive faculties, it is reasonable to believe that these are not brought about by naturalistic forces, forces that are entirely driven by chance or are the outcome of processes not formed by an overriding intelligence. An illustration may help to understand the argument. Imagine coming across what appears to be a sign reporting some information about your current altitude (some rocks in a configuration giving you your current location and precise height above sea-level in metres). If you had reason to believe that this 'sign' was totally the result of chance configurations, would it still be reasonable to trust it? Some theists argue that it would not be reasonable, and that trusting our cognitive faculties requires us to accept that they were formed by an overarching, good, creative agent. This rekindles Descartes's point about relying on the goodness of God to ensure that our cognitive faculties are in good working order. Objections to this argument centre on naturalistic explanations, especially those friendly to evolution. In evolutionary epistemology, one tries to account for the reliability of cognitive faculties in terms of trial and error leading to survival. A rejoinder by theists is that survival alone is not necessarily linked to true beliefs. It could, in principle, be false beliefs that enhance survival. In fact, some atheists do think that believing in God has been crucial to people's survival, though the belief is radically false. Martin (1990) and Mackie (1985), among others, object to the epistemic teleological argument; Plantinga (1993), Creel (1995) and Taylor (1963) defend it.

A more sustained objection against virtually all versions of the teleological argument takes issue with the assumption that the cosmos is good or that it is the sort of thing that would be brought about by an intelligent, completely benevolent being.

5.4   Problems of evil

If there is a God who is omnipotent, omniscient and completely good, why is there evil? The problem of evil is the most widely considered objection to theism in both Western and Eastern philosophy. There are two general versions of the problem: the *deductive* or *logical* version, which asserts that the existence of any evil at all (regardless of its role in producing good) is incompatible with God's existence; and the *probabilistic* version, which asserts that given the quantity and severity of evil that actually exists, it is unlikely that God exists. The deductive problem is currently less commonly debated because it is widely acknowledged that a thoroughly good being might allow or inflict some harm under certain morally compelling conditions (such as causing a child pain when removing a splinter). More intense debate concerns the likelihood (or even possibility) that there is a completely good God given the vast amount of evil in the cosmos. Consider human and animal suffering caused by death, predation, birth defects, ravaging diseases, virtually unchecked human wickedness, torture, rape, oppression and 'natural disasters'. Consider how often those who suffer are innocent. Why should there be so much gratuitous, apparently pointless evil?

In the face of the problem of evil, some philosophers and theologians deny that God is all-powerful and all-knowing. MILL (1806–73) (chapter 35) took this line, and panentheist theologians today also question the traditional treatments of Divine power. By their lights, God is immanent in the world, suffering with the oppressed and working to bring good out of evil, although in spite of God's efforts, evil will invariably mar the created order. Another response is to think of God as being very different from a moral agent. Davies (1993) and others have contended that what it means for God to be good is different from what it means for an agent to be good. Those who think of God as *Being* as opposed to *a being* have some reason to adopt this position. A more desperate strategy is to deny the existence of evil, but it is difficult to reconcile traditional monotheism with moral scepticism. Also, in so far as we believe there to be a God worthy of worship and a fitting object of human love, the appeal to moral scepticism will carry little weight. The idea that evil is a privation of the good, a twisting of something good, may have *some* currency in thinking through the problem of evil, but it is difficult to see how it alone could go very far to vindicate belief in God's goodness. Searing pain and endless suffering seem altogether real even if they are analysed as being philosophically parasitic on something valuable. The three great monotheistic traditions, with their ample insistence on the reality of evil, offer little reason to try to defuse the problem of evil by this route. Indeed, classical Judaism, Christianity and Islam are so committed to the existence of evil that a reason to reject evil would be a reason to reject these religious traditions. What would be the point of Judaic teaching about the Exodus (God liberating the people of Israel from slavery) or Christian teaching about the Incarnation (Christ revealing God as love and releasing a Divine power that will, in the end, conquer death), or the Islamic teaching of Mohammed (the holy prophet of Allah who is all-just and all-merciful) if slavery, hate, death and injustice do not exist?

In part, the magnitude of the problem of evil for theism will depend upon one's commitments in other areas of philosophy, especially ethics, epistemology and metaphysics. If in ethics you hold that there should be no preventable suffering for any reason, no matter what the cause or consequence, then the problem of evil will conflict with accepting traditional theism. Moreover, if you hold that any solution to the problem of evil should be evident to all persons, then again traditional theism is in jeopardy, for clearly the 'solution' is not evident to all. Debate has largely centred over the legitimacy of adopting some position in the middle: a theory of values that would preserve a clear assessment of the profound evil in the cosmos as well as some understanding of how this might be compatible with the existence of an all-powerful, completely good Creator. Could there be reasons why God would permit cosmic ills? If we do not know what those reasons might be, are we in a position to conclude that there are none or that there could not be any? Exploring different possibilities will be shaped by one's metaphysics. For example, if you do not believe there is free will, then you will not be moved by any appeal to the positive value of free will and its role in bringing about good as offsetting its role in bringing about evil.

Theistic responses to the problem of evil distinguish between a *defence* and a *theodicy*. A defence seeks to establish that rational belief that God exists is still possible (when the defence is employed against the logical version of the problem of evil) and that the existence of evil does not make it improbable that God exists (when used against the probabilistic version). According to the defence response, no creature should expect to be able to solve the problem of evil; it is beyond our epistemic capacities to stand in judgement here. Some have adopted the defence strategy while arguing that we are in a position to have rational beliefs in the existence of evil and in a completely good God who hates this evil, even though we are unable to see how these two beliefs are compatible. A theodicy is more ambitious, and is typically part of a broader project, arguing that it is reasonable to believe that God exists in light of the good as well as the evident evil of the cosmos. In a theodicy, the project is not to account for each and every evil, but to provide an overarching framework within which to understand at least roughly how the evil that occurs is part of some overall good – for instance, the overcoming of evil is itself a great good. In practice, a defence and a theodicy often appeal to similar factors, the first and foremost being what many called the Greater Good Defence.

Evil and the Greater Good

In the Greater Good Defence it is contended that evil can be understood as either a necessary accompaniment to bringing about greater goods or an integral part of these goods. Thus, in a version often called the *Free Will Defence*, it is proposed that free creatures who are able to care for each other and whose welfare depends on each other's freely chosen action constitute a good. For this good to be realized, it is argued, there must be the *bona fide* possibility of persons harming each other. The free will defence is sometimes used narrowly only to cover evil that occurs as a result, direct or indirect, of human action. But it has been speculatively extended by those proposing a defence rather than a theodicy to cover other evils which might be brought about by supernatural agents other than God. According to the Greater Good case, evil provides an opportunity to realize great values, such as the virtues of courage and the pursuit of justice. Reichenbach (1982), Tennant (1930) and Swinburne (1979) have also underscored the good of a stable world of natural laws in which animals and humans learn about the cosmos and develop autonomously, independent of the certainty that God exists. Some atheists accord value to the good of living in a world without God, and these views have been used by theists to back up the claim that God might have reason to create a cosmos in which Divine existence is not overwhelmingly obvious to us. If God's existence *were* overwhelmingly obvious, then motivations to virtue might be clouded by self-interest and by the bare fear of offending an omnipotent being. Further, there may even be some good to acting virtuously even if circumstances guarantee a tragic outcome. John Hick (1978) so argued and has developed what he construes to be an Irenaean approach to the problem of evil (named after St Irenaeus of the second century). On this approach, it is deemed good that humanity develops the life of virtue gradually, evolving to a life of grace, maturity and love. This contrasts with a theodicy associated with St Augustine, according to which God created us perfect and then allowed us to fall into perdition, only to be redeemed later by Christ. Hick thinks the Augustinian model fails whereas the Irenaean one is credible.

Some have based an argument from the problem of evil on the charge that this is not the best possible world. If there were a supreme, maximally excellent God, surely God would bring about the best possible creation. Because this is not the best possible creation, there is no supreme, maximally excellent God. Following Adams (1987), many now reply that the whole notion of a best possible world, like the highest possible number, is incoherent. For any world that can be imagined with such and such happiness, goodness, virtue and so on, a higher one can be imagined. If the notion of a best possible world is incoherent, would this count against belief that there could be a supreme, maximally excellent being? It has been argued on the contrary that Divine excellences admit of upper limits or maxima that are not quantifiable in a serial fashion (for example, Divine omnipotence involves being able to do anything logically or metaphysically possible, but does not require actually doing the greatest number of acts or a series of acts of which there can be no more).

Those concerned with the problem of evil clash over the question of how one assesses the likelihood of Divine existence. Someone who reports seeing no point to the existence of evil or no justification for God to allow it seems to imply that if there were a point they would see it. Note the difference between *seeing no point* and *not seeing a point*. In the cosmic case, is it clear that if there were a reason justifying the existence of evil, we would see it? Rowe (1993) thinks some plausible understanding of God's justificatory reason for allowing the evil should be detectable, but that there are cases of evil that are altogether gratuitous. Defenders like Hasker (1989) and Wykstra (1984) reply that these cases are not decisive counter-examples to the claim that there is a good God. These philosophers hold that we can recognize evil and grasp our duty to do all in our power to prevent or alleviate it. But we should not take our failure to see what reason God might have for allowing evil to count as grounds for thinking that there is no reason.

Some portraits of an afterlife seem to have little bearing on our response to the magnitude of evil here and now. Does it help to understand why God allows evil if all victims will receive happiness later? But it is difficult to treat the possibility of an afterlife as entirely irrelevant. Is death the annihilation of persons or an event involving a transfiguration to a higher state? If you do not think that it matters whether persons continue to exist after death, then such speculation is of little consequence. But suppose that the afterlife is understood as being morally intertwined with this life, with opportunity for moral and spiritual reformation, transfiguration of the wicked, rejuvenation and occasions for new life, perhaps even reconciliation and communion between oppressors seeking forgiveness and their victims. Then these considerations might help to defend against arguments based on the existence of evil. In so far as one cannot rule out the possibility of an afterlife morally tied to our life, one cannot rule out the possibility that God brings some good out of cosmic ills.

5.5 Other arguments

I have not been able to cover the many other arguments for and against the existence of God, but I shall now mention a few of these. The argument from miracles starts from specific extraordinary events, arguing that they provide reasons for believing there to be a supernatural agent or, more modestly, reasons for scepticism about the sufficiency of a naturalistic world view. The argument has attracted much philosophical attention, especially since David Hume's rejection of miracles. The debate has turned mainly on how one defines a miracle, understands the laws of nature, and specifies the principles of evidence that govern the explanation of highly unusual historical occurrences.

There are various arguments that are advanced to motivate religious belief. One of the most interesting and popular is a wager argument often associated with Pascal (1623–62). It is designed to offer practical reasons to cultivate a belief in God. Imagine that you are unsure whether there is or is not a God. You have it within your power to live on either assumption and perhaps, through various practices, to get yourself to believe one or the other. There would be good consequences of believing in God even if your belief were false, and if the belief were true you would receive even greater good. There would also be good consequences of believing that there is no God, but in this case the consequences would not alter if there were no God. If, however, you believe that there is no God and you are wrong, then you would risk losing the many goods which follow from belief that God exists and actual Divine existence. On this basis, it may seem reasonable to believe there is a God.

In different forms the argument may be given a rough edge (for example, imagine that if you do not believe in God and there is a God, hell is waiting). It may be put as an appeal to individual self-interest (you will be better off) or more generally (believers whose lives are bound together can realize some of the goods comprising a mature religious life). Objectors worry about whether one ever is able to bring choices down to just such a narrow selection – for example, to choose either theism or naturalism. Some think the argument is too thoroughly egotistic and thus offensive to religion. For a recent defence of the argument see Rescher (1985).

6 New Directions in the Field

Growth in the philosophy of religion shows no sign of abating. There are currently efforts to explore cross-cultural philosophy of religion, to articulate feminist challenges to traditional religions, to address postmodern versions of religion, and to consider a host of practical, moral and social problems from the standpoint of a philosophically articulate religious ethic, focusing on environmental, medical and political concerns. Specific issues internal to religious traditions are also receiving increased attention with philosophical speculation on the afterlife, heaven, hell, the sacraments, the meaning of revelation and the nature of religious communities.

Acknowledgements

The author gratefully acknowledges comments on earlier versions of this chapter, especially from M. Okerlund, C. Gossett, G. Gentry, M. Lazenby, C. Granneman and the Columbia University Philosophers of Religion.

Further Reading

Readers new to the philosophy of religion may begin with any of the introductory texts mentioned in the first section of the references, supplemented by one or more of these useful anthologies containing important papers or excerpts from books: Quinn and Taliaferro (1996) includes 78 original essays spanning the history of the field in Eastern and Western philosophy. Mitchell (1971) contains papers on the early debates about the meaning of religious language, and includes early papers by Flew and Mitchell. Morris (1987) is an extremely useful collection on the concept of God, with papers by Kretzmann, Stump, Blumenfeld and Rowe.

Other valuable collections are edited by Pojman (1987), Rowe and Wainwright (1989), Brody (1992), Hick (1970), Geivett and Sweetman (1992), Hudson (1991), Beaty (1990) and MacDonald (1991).

Readers interested in exploring particular topics discussed in the chapter can turn to the books and articles in the second section of references.

Journals that are particularly strong in addressing the philosophy of religion are: *The International Journal for Philosophy of Religion, Religious Studies, Faith and Philosophy, Sophia, The Journal of Religion, The Journal of Religious Ethics, The Heythrop Journal for Philosophy and Theology, The Annual of the Society of Christian Ethics, American Catholic Philosophical Quarterly* and the *Thomist*. Papers in philosophy of religion are published in virtually all the main philosophy journals in the English-speaking world. There are regular sessions about philosophy of religion on the programmes of the annual meetings of the three divisions of the American Philosophical Association, as well as on the programme of the annual meeting of the American Academy of Religion. Societies interested in the philosophy of religion include: the Society for Philosophy of Religion (in the UK), the Society of Christian Philosophers, the Philosophy of Religion Society, the Society for Philosophy of Religion (in the USA), the American Catholic Philosophical Association, the American Humanist Association, the American Maritain Association, the

Fellowship of Religious Humanists, the Jesuit Philosophical Association, the Society for Medieval and Renaissance Philosophy, and the Society for Philosophy and Theology. Addresses and websites for many of these organizations are found in the *Directory of American Philosophers*, a publication of the Philosophy Documentation Center, Bowling Green State University.

References

Introductory texts
Abraham, W. 1985: *An Introduction to the Philosophy of Religion*. Englewood Cliffs, NJ: Prentice-Hall.

Anderson, P. S. 1997: *A Feminist Philosophy of Religion*. Oxford: Blackwell.

Clark, B. and Clark, B. R. 1998: *The Philosophy of Religion*. Oxford: Blackwell.

Davies, B. 1993: *An Introduction to the Philosophy of Religion*. Oxford: Oxford University Press.

Evans, S. C. 1985: *Philosophy of Religion*. Downers Grove, IL: Intervarsity Press.

Hick, J. 1990: *Philosophy of Religion*, 4th edn. Englewood Cliffs, NJ: Prentice-Hall.

Morris, T. V. 1991: *Our Idea of God*. Downers Grove, IL: Intervarsity Press.

Peterson, M. et al. 1991: *Introduction to the Philosophy of Religion*. Oxford: Oxford University Press.

Rowe, W. 1993: *Philosophy of Religion*. Belmont, CA: Wadsworth.

Taliaferro, C. 1998: *An Introduction to Contemporary Philosophy of Religion*. Oxford: Blackwell.

Tilghman, B. R. 1993: *An Introduction to Philosophy of Religion*. Oxford: Blackwell.

Wainwright, W. 1988: *Philosophy of Religion*. Belmont, CA: Wadsworth.

Other books and articles
Adams, R. M. 1987: *The Virtue of Faith*. Oxford: Oxford University Press.

Alston, W. 1991a: *Perceiving God*. Ithaca, NY: Cornell University Press.

——1991b: The Inductive Argument from Evil. *Philosophical Perspectives*, 5, 29–68.

Augustine 1972 [426]: *The City of God* (translated by H. Bettenson). Harmondsworth: Penguin Books.

Barnes, J. 1972: *The Ontological Argument*. London: Macmillan.

Beaty, M. (ed.) 1990: *Christian Theism and the Problems of Philosophy*. Notre Dame, IN: University of Notre Dame Press.

Beaty, M. and Taliaferro, C. 1990: God and Concept Empiricism. *Southwest Philosophy Review*, 6: 2.

Boethius 1969 [524]: *The Consolation of Philosophy* (translated by V. E. Watts). Harmondsworth: Penguin Books.

Brody, B. (ed.) 1992: *Readings in the Philosophy of Religion*. Englewood Cliffs, NJ: Prentice-Hall.

Brown, D. 1987: *Continental Philosophy and Modern Theology*. Oxford: Blackwell.

Clayton, J. 1987: Religions, Reasons and Gods. *Religious Studies*, 23.

Craig, W. 1979: *The Kalam Cosmological Argument*. New York: Barnes and Noble.

——1980: *The Cosmological Argument from Plato to Leibniz*. New York: Barnes and Noble.

Craig, W. L. and Smith, Q. 1993: *Theism, Atheism, and Big Bang Cosmology*. Oxford: Clarendon Press.

Creel, R. 1995: *Divine Impassibility*. Cambridge: Cambridge University Press.

Davis, C. 1989: *The Evidential Force of Religious Experience*. Oxford: Oxford University Press.

Dore, R. 1984: *Theism*. Dordrecht: D. Reidel.

Evans, S. 1996: *The Historical Christ and the Jesus of Faith: The Incarnational Narrative as History*. Oxford: Clarendon Press.

Firth, R. 1970: Ethical Absolutism and the Ideal Observer. In W. Sellars and J. Hospers (eds) *Readings in Ethical Theory*. Englewood Cliffs, NJ: Prentice-Hall.

Flew, A. 1984: *God, Freedom and Immortality*. Buffalo, NY: Prometheus Books.

Forrest, P. 1996: *God Without the Supernatural: A Defense of Scientific Theism*. Ithaca, NY: Cornell University Press.

Foster, J. 1985: *Ayer*. London: Routledge and Kegan Paul.

Geivett, R. and Sweetman, B. (eds) 1992: *Contemporary Perspectives on Religious Epistemology*. Oxford: Oxford University Press.

Gellman, J. 1997: *Experience of God and the Rationality of Theistic Belief*. Ithaca, NY: Cornell University Press.

Griffiths, P. 1994: *On Being Buddha*. Albany: State University of New York Press.

Gutting, G. 1982: *Religious Belief and Religious Skepticism*. Notre Dame, IN: University of Notre Dame Press.

Hare, J. E. 1996: *The Moral Gap*. Oxford: Oxford University Press.

Hasker, W. 1989: *God, Time, and Knowledge*. Ithaca, NY: Cornell University Press.

——1999: *The Emergent Self*. Ithaca, NY: Cornell University Press.

Helm, P. 1988: *Eternal God*. Oxford: Oxford University Press.

Hepburn, R. W. 1963: From World to God. *Mind*, 72.

Hick, J. 1966: *Rational Theistic Belief Without Proof*. London: Macmillan.

——(ed.) 1970: *Classical and Contemporary Readings in the Philosophy of Religion*. Englewood Cliffs, NJ: Prentice-Hall.

——1978: *Evil and the God of Love*. New York: Harper and Row.

Hick, J. and McGill, A. (eds) 1967: *The Many Faced Argument*. New York: Macmillan.

Howard-Snyder, D. (ed.) 1996: *The Evidential Argument from Evil*. Bloomington: Indiana University Press.

Hudson, Y. (ed.) 1991: *The Philosophy of Religion*. London: Mayfield Publishing.

Hughes, G. 1995: *The Nature of God*. London: Routledge.

Hume, D. 1947 [1779]: *Dialogues Concerning Natural Religion* (edited by N. Kemp Smith). London: Nelson.

Kant, I. 1960: *Religion Within the Limits of Reason Alone* (translated by T. M. Greene and H. H. Hudson). New York: Harper and Brothers.

Kenny, A. 1979: *The God of the Philosophers*. Oxford: Clarendon Press.

Kerr, F. 1988: *Theology After Wittgenstein*. Oxford: Blackwell.

Kvanvic, J. 1986: *The Possibility of an All-Knowing God*. London: Macmillan.

Leftow, B. 1991: *Time and Eternity*. Ithaca, NY: Cornell University Press.

Levinas, E. 1961: *Totality and Infinity* (translated by A. Lingis). Pittsburgh: Duquesne University Press.

Linville, M. 1993: Divine Foreknowledge and the Libertarian Conception of Human Freedom. *Journal of the Philosophy of Religion*, 33.

MacDonald, S. 1991: *Being and Goodness*. Ithaca, NY: Cornell University Press.

Mackie, J. 1985: *The Miracle of Theism*. Oxford: Clarendon Press.

Malcolm, N. 1975: The Groundlessness of Religious Beliefs. In S. Brown (ed.) *Reason and Religion*. Ithaca, NY: Cornell University Press.

Martin, M. 1990: *Atheism*. Philadelphia, PA: Temple University Press.

Menzel, C. and Morris, T. V. 1986: Absolute Creation. *American Philosophical Quarterly*, 23, 353–62.

Meynell, H. 1982: *The Intelligible Universe*. Totowa, NJ: Barnes and Noble.

Mitchell, B. (ed.) 1971: *The Philosophy of Religion*. Oxford: Oxford University Press.

——1973: *The Justification of Religious Belief*. London: Macmillan.

——1994: *Faith and Criticism*. Oxford: Oxford University Press.

Morris, T. V. 1986: *The Logic of God Incarnate*. Ithaca, NY: Cornell University Press.

—— 1987a: *Anselmian Explorations*. Notre Dame, IN: University of Notre Dame Press.

—— (ed.) 1987b: *The Concept of God*. Oxford: Oxford University Press.

Neville, R. C. 1995: Religions, Philosophies, and Philosophy of Religion. *International Journal for Philosophy of Religion*, 38.

Nielsen, K. 1982: *An Introduction to the Philosophy of Religion*. New York: St Martin's Press.

—— 1996: *Naturalism Without Foundations*. Buffalo, NY: Prometheus Press.

Oppy, G. 1995: *Ontological Arguments and Belief in God*. Cambridge: Cambridge University Press.

Owen, H. P. 1965: *The Moral Argument for Christian Theism*. London: George Allen and Unwin.

Padgett, A. 1992: *God, Eternity and the Nature of Time*. New York: St Martin's Press.

Penelhum, T. 1983: *God and Skepticism*. Dordrecht: D. Reidel.

Phillips, D. Z. 1970: *Concept of Prayer*. London: Routledge and Kegan Paul.

Plantinga, A. 1967: *God and Other Minds*. Ithaca, NY: Cornell University Press.

—— 1974: *The Nature of Necessity*. Oxford: Oxford University Press.

—— 1980: *Does God Have a Nature?* Milwaukee, MN: Marquette University Press.

—— 1993: *Warrant*, 2 vols. Oxford: Oxford University Press.

Pojman, L. (ed.) 1987: *Philosophy of Religion: An Anthology*. Belmont, CA: Wadsworth.

Proudfoot, W. 1976: *God and Self*. Lewisburgh: Bucknell University Press.

—— 1985: *Religious Experience*. Berkeley: University of California Press.

Quinn, P. and Taliaferro, C. (eds) 1996: *A Companion to Philosophy of Religion*. Oxford: Blackwell.

Reichenbach, B. 1972: *The Cosmological Argument*. Springfield, IL: Thomas Press.

—— 1982: *Evil and a Good God*. New York: Fordham University Press.

Rescher, N. 1985: *Pascal's Wager*. Notre Dame, IN: University of Notre Dame Press.

Rhees, R. 1969: *Without Answers*. New York: Schocken Books.

Rowe, W. and Wainwright, W. J. (eds) 1989: *Philosophy of Religion: Selected Readings*. New York: Harcourt Brace Jovanovich.

Schlesinger, G. 1977: *Religion and Scientific Method*. Dordrecht: D. Reidel.

—— 1988: *New Perspectives on Old-Time Religion*. New York: Oxford University Press.

Sessions, L. 1994: *The Concept of Faith: A Philosophical Investigation*. Ithaca, NY: Cornell University Press.

Sharma, A. 1990: *A Hindu Perspective on the Philosophy of Religion*. New York: St Martin's Press.

Smart, J. J. C. and Haldane, J. J. 1996: *Atheism and Theism*. Oxford: Blackwell.

Sorensen, R. A. 1992: *Thought Experiments*. Oxford: Oxford University Press.

Soskice, J. M. 1984: *Metaphor and Religious Language*. Oxford: Oxford University Press.

Stiver, D. 1996: *The Philosophy of Religious Language*. Oxford: Blackwell.

Swinburne, R. 1977: *The Coherence of Theism*. Oxford: Clarendon Press.

—— 1979: *The Existence of God*. Oxford: Clarendon Press.

—— 1996: *Is There a God?* Oxford: Oxford University Press.

—— 1998: *Providence and the Problem of Evil*. Oxford: Oxford University Press.

Taliaferro, C. 1994: *Consciousness and the Mind of God*. Cambridge: Cambridge University Press.

Taylor, R. 1963: *Metaphysics*. Englewood Cliffs, NJ: Prentice-Hall.

Tennant 1930: *Philosophical Theology*. Cambridge: Cambridge University Press.

Tracy, T. F. (ed.) 1994: *The God Who Acts*. University Park: Pennsylvania State University Press.

Trigg, R. 1989: *Reality at Risk*. London: Harvester.

—— 1993: *Rationality and Science: Can Science Explain Everything?* Oxford: Blackwell.

Wainwright, W. 1981: *Mysticism: A Study of Its Nature, Cognitive Value, and Moral Implications*. Madison: University of Wisconsin Press.

—— (ed.) 1996: *God, Philosophy, and Academic Culture*. Atlanta, GA: Scholars Press.

Westphal, M. 1984: *God, Guilt, and Death*. Bloomington: Indiana University Press.

Whitehead, A. N. 1978: *Process and Reality*. New York: Free Press.

Wierenga, E. 1989: *The Nature of God*. Ithaca, NY: Cornell University Press.

Wolterstorff, N. 1976: *Reason Within the Bounds of Religion*. Grand Rapids, MI: Eerdmans.

——1982: God Everlasting. In S. M. Cahn and D. Shatz (eds) *Contemporary Philosophy of Religion*. Oxford: Oxford University Press.

Wykstra, S. 1984: The Humean Obstacle to Evidential Arguments from Suffering. *International Journal for Philosophy of Religion*, 16, 73–93.

Yandell, K. 1993: *The Epistemology of Religious Experience*. Cambridge: Cambridge University Press.

Zagzebski, L. T. 1991: *The Dilemma of Freedom and Foreknowledge*. New York: Oxford University Press.

Discussion Questions

1   On the merits and problems of verificationism: How might an empiricist go about assessing the meaningfulness of the claim that God is non-physical, all-good and creative? If God is non-physical, does it follow that God cannot be perceived? If it is allowed that we can perceive (or somehow experience) God, can God's being omnipotent or being everywhere present be something perceivable? What about the other Divine attributes? Assuming an empiricist theory of meaning and the existence of God, how would God know about the cosmos? To be omniscient, would God have to have a massive number of (or perhaps infinitely many) sensory experiences?

2   Assess non-realist approaches to religious belief. Most versions of non-realism assume a substantially 'all or nothing' position. Could a modified version of non-realism be defended in which, say, the practice of prayer is treated cognitively, while belief in the afterlife is treated along non-realist lines? Is it intelligible to have faith in God without believing that God exists? Does it make any more (or less) sense to have hope that God will do something without belief that there is a God?

3   Given your understanding of the following terms, as used to describe human beings, would using them as predicates to describe a supremely excellent, non-physical reality, require using them analogically or could they be used univocally?: knowledgeable, powerful, creative, good, intelligent, loving and wise. Alternatively, do you think any of them would have to be used equivocally?

4   How might one's theory of persons affect one's theory about God? Could it be that all created persons are physical while God is a person that is non-physical? How many of the traditional, theistic Divine attributes could be preserved on the assumption that God is physical? In what respects can or should one's view of God be influenced by one's understanding of gender and race?

5   Illustrate some of the ways in which one's philosophy of religion is influenced by other areas of philosophy, including metaphysics, epistemology, ethics, the philosophy of language and the philosophy of history. Alternatively, consider a case where one's views in the philosophy of religion will have an influence on one's view of these other areas.

6   Critically analyse the following argument. If God is all-powerful, God can make a stone too heavy for anyone to lift. If God is all-powerful, God can lift any stone. God is not all-powerful, because God cannot create a stone too heavy for anyone to lift

(because God can lift any stone) or God cannot lift any stone (if God succeeded in creating a stone too heavy for God to lift).

7   Is the existence of freedom compatible with foreknowledge? If not, can even God be free?

8   Analyses of omniscience typically focus on the scope of God's knowledge. Should the way in which God knows be considered as part of the meaning of what it is to be omniscient? If a being knew all true propositions but only had this knowledge by virtue of the testimony of others or through reliable but circuitous means (having to rely on highly technical equipment) would you consider this being to have the divine attribute of omniscience?

9   If a being is omnipotent, must it also be omniscient? To what extent, if any, can a being create itself? What is your view of the Menzel–Morris machine?

10   Do you find coherent the thesis that God is eternal? If God were eternal, could God know what time it is now? Could God have created time?

11   What is your assessment of the ideal observer theory and how this might articulate a God's-eye ethical point of view? Can theistic voluntarism be defended?

12   Can the failure to experience God be employed in a plausible argument providing evidence that there is no God? What is the difference between experiencing the absence of God and not experiencing God?

13   Assess the arguments for and against God's existence in this chapter, including: arguments from religious experience, ontological arguments (consider both the traditional theistic version and the version cited above in which one argues against God's existence), cosmological arguments, teleological arguments, the problem of evil, arguments from miracles and wager arguments. How might these arguments be interconnected, so that the force of one argument depends on the others?

14   Does one need a successful theistic argument, such as the teleological, cosmological or ontological argument, in order for the belief that there is a God to be justified? Is there a burden of proof that is borne more by the religious believer than the naturalist?

15   In what way, if any, may traditional or other conceptions of an afterlife be employed in addressing the problem of evil?

16   What are the ethical implications of there being a good God who is affectively responsive to the cosmos – grieved by the ills and taking pleasure in goods such as justice and friendship?

16

Applied Ethics

JOHN HALDANE

Recent philosophy has returned to a traditional concern with providing critical assessment of conduct and institutions. Under the term 'applied ethics' areas as diverse as health care, warfare, business and the environment have been subject to close scrutiny in terms of rival ethical theories or within the scope of a specific ethical theory. The chapter examines the rise of applied ethics against the background of twentieth-century developments in ethics and political philosophy and suggests that there are dangers in its current popularity. It considers a precedent for applied ethics and examines its possible future development. Readers may wish to read this chapter together with the chapters on BIOETHICS, GENETHICS AND MEDICAL ETHICS *(chapter 17),* ENVIRONMENTAL ETHICS *(chapter 18) and* BUSINESS ETHICS *(chapter 19).*

1 What is Applied Ethics?

In trying to understand what applied ethics is, and how it has developed within English-speaking philosophy over the last twenty to thirty years, it is useful to begin by making a threefold or three-level distinction, between MORALITY (chapter 6), MORAL THEORY (pp. 212–14) and META-ETHICS (pp. 225–7). The first of these consists of individual claims about what is of moral value, such as honesty and loyalty, and about what ought to be done or avoided in general and on particular occasions: for instance, always help those in great need, or never inflict unnecessary pain. Sometimes claims of these sorts come in groups and constitute a moral outlook or system. When this is so it becomes possible to speak of a *morality* or an *ethic* – such as a Christian morality or an ecological ethic. A morality in this sense is a body of moral claims usually expressing a certain kind of concern or commitment.

It is likely, but not logically required, that a morality will be accompanied by one or more PRINCIPLES (pp. 733–6) by reference to which particular claims are justified. This brings us to the second of the three levels, for the articulation of such principles within a systematic structure is what constitutes a *moral theory*. Here it is important to note two points: first, that one can make moral claims, and more generally possess a morality, without having a moral theory; and, second, that the same moral claims, and even the same moralities or ethics, are compatible with different moral theories. Thus, for example, one may hold that lying is wrong without having a systematic account of what makes it wrong, and moreover this moral claim might be justified by quite distinct theories such as those of consequentialism, deontology or DIVINE LAW (pp. 223–4). The immorality of lying might, for example, be taken to derive from its tendency to cause unhappiness, its intrinsic wrongness or its being at variance with a divine commandment.

The third level is different from the other two inasmuch as it is not concerned with what is right or wrong, good or bad, and with why things are so, but rather concerns the logical status of moral claims and moral theories. *Meta-ethics* is the most philosophical and abstract form of thinking about morality. It addresses such METAPHYSICAL (chapter 2) and EPISTEMOLOGICAL (chapter 1) questions as whether values are objective, and what that might mean and whether thoughts about them can constitute genuine knowledge.

While a number of things now go by the description of 'applied ethics' the central aspect of this consists in the more or less systematic application of moral theory to particular moral problems (in terms of the threefold division, the application of second-level to first-level thinking). In its earlier stages these were principally life and death issues, such as those of abortion, euthanasia, suicide or warfare. More recently, however, there has been a considerable increase of interest among college and university students, professional philosophers and those outside higher education in the examination of moral issues, and this interest has led to an extension of medical ethics from questions of abortion and euthanasia and to the development of new fields of applied ethics such as *business ethics, computer ethics, environmental ethics, gender ethics, journalism ethics, reproductive ethics* and so on. Indeed, the point has now been reached at which there are very few if any areas of human activity that are not the subject of some named branch of applied ethics. Whether this is a good thing is itself an interesting and important question.

2   The Rise of Applied Ethics

The rise and expansion of this area of philosophy is due to a number of causes, some more creditable to its practitioners than others. To begin with there is the fact that for the first half of the twentieth century English-speaking moral philosophy consisted almost exclusively of meta-ethics. The main concerns of this were, and remain, whether values and requirements are features of the world or merely products of human preference and commitment, and whether the language of morality is descriptive, expressive or prescriptive. Discussions of these questions became ever more distant from actual moral thinking, in part because by their nature they were abstracted from particular moral outlooks, but also because the language in which they were presented was a technical philosophical one owing nothing to familiar ethical vocabularies. Although during this period the study of meta-ethics produced some very good analytical philosophy, moral problems were left entirely unaddressed and the intermediary level of moral theory was also neglected.

This can now seem very odd because throughout the same period there had been two world wars, the rise of ideological totalitarianism, widespread attempts at genocide, and the development and use of weapons of mass destruction. But however it was that philosophers judged it none of their professional business to discuss these matters, the pressure increased for systematic moral thinking about fundamental values and the basis of conduct. By the mid-1960s a change in attitudes and practice was becoming apparent. The experience of students and academics in the United States was perhaps the most important social factor in the rise of applied ethics. Questions of civil rights, of sexual ethics, of the morality of warfare and of bioethics became prominent themes of public debate and the society began to divide between conservatives and radicals, absolutists and relativists. Setting aside the question of particular viewpoints, what became clear and was felt to be something of a scandal was that professional moral philosophy appeared to have nothing to say about these important moral issues.

In earlier times, a professional response might have been that a philosopher has no more business saying how one should act than a chemist has saying whether there should be more or fewer synthesized compounds in the world – in each case the professional duty is to understand the nature of reality, not to change it. But this sort of reply came to seem unacceptable. First, from its earliest days, philosophy has been concerned with both theoretical and practical reasoning. As well as asking what one should believe about the world – that is, what is true? – it has addressed the question about how one should act in it – that is, what is it good to do? Second, developments in meta-ethics themselves steadily weakened the case for non-involvement. One widely held reason for thinking that moral philosophy could not provide a guide to action was the belief that to the extent that systematic reflection showed anything about morality it revealed it to be a matter of subjective attitudes or commitments about which there could be no rational argument. One might perhaps show that someone was acting irrationally given the moral values and outlook he or she possessed (for instance, by being inconsistent), but one could not demonstrate that it was contrary to reason to have those values and outlook, for they were simply matters of subjective preference. By the late 1960s, however, meta-ethical subjectivism had begun to lose ground to more objectivist views. In the United Kingdom there was a revival of ethical naturalism in the form of the thesis, advanced by writers such as Elizabeth Anscombe, Philippa Foot and Peter Geach, that moral claims relate to human well-being and are assessable as true or false, reasonable and unreasonable, by reference to this objective norm. In the United States, meanwhile, other earlier traditions were being revived, in particular certain forms of ethical rationalism which argue that questions of conduct can be answered by reference to standards of what are universally reasonable rules of action.

Some of the most interesting developments in North America which influenced the course of applied ethics there and elsewhere emerged out of POLITICAL PHILOSOPHY (chapter 8) and in turn are traceable to certain strands in modern epistemology. Clear and historically important examples of this are to be found in John Rawls's book *A Theory of Justice* (1971). There he is concerned to articulate principles of JUSTICE (pp. 258–64) that might underlie the political institutions and practices of a liberal state. In order to arrive at these, he employs a version of social contract theory inviting us to consider what principles we would rationally choose to have regulate our lives if we were not to know in advance what our social circumstances would be. This procedure thereby gives a form of rational justification for such principles. However, in thinking at a theoretical level about what principles do or would guide our conduct, it soon becomes apparent that such rationales may not entirely square with our moral inclinations and pre-reflective judgements. Here we face a problem of whether to revise the principles or abandon the moral intuitions. Rawls's discussion of this issue involves the idea of reflective equilibrium. The general principles implicit in our attitudes to real or imagined situations may need to be amended in the face of contrary judgements of further, often borderline, specific cases. By the same token, where a principle itself is shown to be well-attested in other circumstances we may then need to revise our intuitive judgement of the troublesome case. The point here is that we should seek to maximize coherence in our moral and social outlook, and such 'equilibrium' is plausibly a rational requirement of reflection on questions of value and conduct.

Whatever the rights and wrongs of this sort of moral epistemology, it, and the revival of other broadly objectivist ethical theories, provided both an example and an impetus to applied ethics. In general one finds two methods being employed: firstly, that just described – that is, the derivation of principles from pre-theoretical moral judgements and their extension to other cases, constrained by demands of consistency and coherence; and, secondly, the direct application of well-established moral theories, such as UTILITARIANISM (chapter 35), to determine general policies and to resolve particular problems. Since the 1970s the employment of these methods, by writers such as Richard Hare, Anthony Kenny, Thomas Nagel, Peter Singer, Mary Warnock and Bernard Williams, has produced some interesting work on ethical and social questions which will survive just as well as contemporary research in more theoretical areas of philosophy.

Earlier, however, I suggested that not all features of the growth in applied ethics are to be welcomed. What I had in mind was the unseemly rush of some philosophers and those on the fringes of the subject to become part of what has proven to be a rapidly expanding and institutionally successful area of academic practice. It is not just that opportunism is undignified. The point is rather that through poor-quality products the very activity risks falling into disrepute, and thereby an opportunity for practical philosophy to re-establish itself as a major aspect of serious study may be lost as other philosophers turn against what they perceive to be intellectually shallow work, and the public patrons of applied ethics come to feel dissatisfied with it.

The Moral Danger of Applied Ethics

This latter prospect also raises a *moral* concern akin to that which partly motivated Socrates in his attack on the Sophists, the purveyors of moral and political wisdom in the Greek city-states of the fifth century BC. Although it is often supposed otherwise, even by those who should know better, moral philosophy is no easier to practise than any other area of the subject. Unlike philosophy of language, say, its initial starting-points are usually commonplaces of reflective experience: for example, the question of truth-telling often involves dilemmas, but the attempt to structure satisfactory arguments about such matters involves deep and difficult problems, with the consequence that error and confusion are all too common. The suggestion of the Sophists and of some contemporary applied ethicists – that there are skills the more or less mechanical employment of which will yield answers to moral questions – is both a disservice to philosophy and a corrupting influence on the consciences of those whom it claims to be assisting. Moreover, as SOCRATES (chapter 22) saw, there is a danger that when sophistry is exposed, people's reaction is not to seek better counsel but to conclude that there can be no sound reasoning about questions of value and conduct, supposing instead that these are just matters of personal preferences. It would be a terrible irony if the recent rise of applied ethics led in due course to the spread of moral irrationalism.

3   A Neglected Precedent

Although the *term* is a recent one, there is in fact nothing new in the general *idea* of applied ethics. While it is true that there have been periods, such as the earlier half of the twentieth century, when philosophers were almost exclusively concerned with speculative questions, I noted earlier that from antiquity the importance of practical as well as theoretical philosophy has been recognized. It is worth observing, therefore, that there was (and to some extent remains) a very long and well-developed tradition of thinking about practical problems in the light of general principles, namely that of *moral casuistry*.

It should be said immediately that the term 'casuistry' is now most often used perjoratively to condemn some piece of thinking as attempting a specious justification or as involving equivocation or hypocrisy. Interestingly, this critical usage arose from perceived or imagined abuses of practical reasoning similar to those attributed to the Sophists. In this connection see, for example, the ridiculing of Jesuit casuistry by PASCAL (1623–62) (pp. 483–4) in his *Provincial Letters* (1967). However, the authentic tradition derives from the sincere effort to apply rigorous standards of critical argument to the resolution of questions of conduct. Historically, it developed through moral theology as Christians tried to work out the detailed implications of scriptural texts and the teachings of the early Church Fathers. In the middle ages, writers such as Thomas AQUINAS (1225–74) (p. 619) advanced quite complex theories of moral reasoning in which various elements of ethical judgement (*synderesis* and *conscientia*) were connected with an account of right reasoning (*recta ratio*). This tradition survived the Reformation and was further developed by both Catholic and Protestant authors, such as Francisco Suarez (1548–1617) and Hugo Grotius (1583–1645), and later still, in increasingly secular versions, by Immanuel KANT (1724–1804) (chapter 32) and Jeremy BENTHAM (1748–1832) (chapter 35).

As well as being concerned with the *forms* of moral reasoning, the SCHOLASTIC (pp. 621–2) casuists were interested in resolving major dilemmas in particular fields of human activity, such as in sexual matters, economic affairs and the conduct of warfare. Their writings on the form and substance of morality contain many insights that are still worth recovering. One aspect of these writings relevant to the assessment of applied ethics as it is now practised is the way in which the casuists related moral problems and moral theory. The present-day expressions 'applied ethics' and 'applied philosophy' suggest a two-stage process. Firstly, one works out some general philosophical principles, then one applies them to a given issue. On this account there need be nothing philosophical about the second stage; rather it should be an algorithmic or mechanical process. For the medieval and modern casuists, by contrast, the treatment of particular cases is itself an exercise of moral reasoning no less than is the working out of general principles. Indeed, there need not be two distinct tasks involved. Rather, the determination of the general and the particular may be aspects of a single complex procedure similar in some respects to the establishment in Rawlsian methodology of a state of 'reflective equilibrium'.

A further mark of the difference between casuistry or practical moral philosophy and applied ethics is revealed in the fact that whereas contemporary writers usually suppose that there are no topic-specific moral values but only topic-indifferent general principles, the medievals and moderns tended to develop accounts of virtues and values specific to the different departments of life. Thus, for example, chastity was thought of as a distinctly sexual virtue and not an instance of, for example, prudence. Similarly, the medieval prohibition on usury derived from reflections on the values implicit in distinctive forms of social relationships. Perhaps the most important area of casuistical thought, however, was in relation to large-scale violence, concerning which it developed the doctrine of just war with its various topic-specific moral values, such as that of non-combatant immunity.

4 The Future of the Subject

Contemporary moral philosophers concerned with practice might therefore do better to adopt something of the approach of casuistry and practical philosophy rather than to think, as at present, in the somewhat limiting terms suggested by the phrase 'applied ethics'. There is certainly need and considerable scope for the philosophical study of the practice of thinking about practice – that is to say, there is a requirement for a 'meta-philosophical' account of moral reasoning.

If such an enquiry were to lead to a reconception of the subject of normative ethics along the lines suggested in connection with earlier styles of thought, that would certainly have implications for its future development. As it is, there can be little doubt but that the growth of publications, college and university courses, in-service professional training sessions, and other forms of activity concerned with the philosophical treatment of moral and social questions will continue at more or less its present rate until at least the end of the twentieth century.

It is impossible to be confident about developments beyond that point, but it seems likely that applied ethicists will look for new fields of operation. For the most part, that will involve seeking out existing areas of life that have not yet been made the subject of academic moral enquiry; but it will also lead to greater novelty as technology extends the limits of the possible and thereby changes patterns of behaviour, and as other factors bear upon the structure of personal and social relationships. We have seen how the development of electronic data-gathering and data-recording has given rise to increased concerns about privacy, and how reproductive technology has prompted worries about the proper limits of control over the creation of life. Doubtless at this very moment someone is writing a book on the ethics of 'virtual reality' technology, and there will soon be other writings on the moral dimensions of technologies not as yet generally known of, nor even, perhaps, yet invented.

As these interests develop so will the publishing and other services that cater for them. Thirty years ago there were no academic philosophy journals concerned primarily or even largely with normative, first-order moral and social questions. Today, such journals abound and more are created every year. The present range includes the following: *Agriculture and Human Values, Bioethics, Business Ethics, Business and Professional Ethics Journal, Criminal Justice Ethics, Environmental Ethics, Environmental Values, Ethics and Animals, Ethics and Medicine, International Journal of Applied Philosophy, International Journal of Moral and Social Studies, International Review of Economics and Ethics, Journal of Agricultural Ethics, Journal of Applied Philosophy, Journal of Business Ethics, Journal of Environmental Ethics, Journal of Medical Ethics, Journal of Medicine and Philosophy, Journal of Religious Ethics, Journal of Social Philosophy, Philosophy and Public Affairs, Philosophy and Technology, Public Affairs Quarterly, Social Philosophy and Policy* and *Social Theory and Practice*. However the subject develops, there will be no shortage of journals – such, for good and ill, is academic professionalism.

Further Reading

Hare (1981) offers an advanced but clearly presented account of the author's 'prescriptivist' theory of morality developed in relation to different levels of thinking about moral problems. Kenny (1985) provides a series of clearly argued and well-balanced essays, the core of which concern the ethics of war and nuclear deterrence. Nagel (1979) has written a collection of subtly argued essays many of which develop deontological ways of thinking in connection with various moral problems. Singer (1979) is a clear and direct account of utilitarian theory and of its application to a range of life and death issues. It is very useful for seeing the attractions and the problems of consequentialism. Warnock (1992) presents a selection of writings by a philosopher who is prominent in public life in the United Kingdom, which explore the possibilities and limitations of philosophy in relation to practical problems. Williams (1981) offers a collection of influential essays by another prominent public philosopher developing the idea of the importance of personal character in relation to morality.

References

Most of the following books are collections of essays by one or more authors. However, Rachels (1979), Singer (1986) and Velasquez and Rostankowski (1985) are anthologies containing, in whole or in part, some of the most influential papers in various fields of applied ethics published in the last twenty to thirty years.

General works in applied ethics
DeMarco, J. P. and Fox, R. M. (eds) 1986: *New Directions in Ethics: The Challenge of Applied Ethics.* London: Routledge and Kegan Paul.
Evans, J. D. G. (ed.) 1987: *Moral Philosophy and Contemporary Problems.* Cambridge: Cambridge University Press.
Griffiths, A. P. (ed.) 1985: *Philosophy and Practice.* Cambridge: Cambridge University Press.
Hare, R. M. 1981: *Moral Thinking.* Oxford: Clarendon Press.
——1989: *Essays in Ethical Theory.* Oxford: Clarendon Press.
Kenny, A. 1985: *The Ivory Tower: Essays in Philosophy and Public Policy.* Oxford: Blackwell.
Louden, R. B. 1992: *Morality and Moral Theory.* Oxford: Oxford University Press.

Nagel, T. 1979: *Mortal Questions*. Cambridge: Cambridge University Press.
Nuttall, J. 1993: *Moral Questions*. Cambridge: Polity Press.
Pascal, B. 1967 [1656]: *Provincial Letters* (translated by A. J. Krailsheimer). Harmondsworth: Penguin Books.
Phillips, D. Z. 1992: *Interventions in Ethics*. London: Macmillan.
Rachels, J. (ed.) 1979: *Moral Problems*. New York: Harper and Row.
Singer, P. 1979: *Practical Ethics*. Cambridge: Cambridge University Press.
——(ed.) 1986: *Applied Ethics*. Oxford: Oxford University Press.
——(ed.) 1991: *A Companion to Ethics*. Oxford: Blackwell.
Spaemann, R. 1989 [1982]: *Basic Moral Concepts* (translated by T. J. Armstrong). London: Routledge.
Velasquez, M. and Rostankowski, C. (eds) 1985: *Ethics: Theory and Practice*. Englewood Cliffs, NJ: Prentice-Hall.
Warnock, M. 1992: *The Uses of Philosophy*. Oxford: Blackwell.
Williams, B. 1981: *Moral Luck*. Cambridge: Cambridge University Press.
Winkler, E. and Coombs, J. (eds) 1993: *Applied Ethics: A Reader*. Oxford: Blackwell.

Animal rights
Frey, R. 1983: *Rights, Killing and Suffering*. Oxford: Blackwell.
Regan, T. 1983: *The Case for Animal Rights*. Berkeley: University of California Press.

Business ethics
Beauchamp, T. and Bowie, N. 1979: *Ethical Theory and Business*. Englewood Cliffs, NJ: Prentice-Hall.
Velasquez, M. 1982: *Business Ethics*. Englewood Cliffs, NJ: Prentice-Hall.

Environmental ethics
Attfield, R. 1991: *The Ethics of Environmental Concern*, 2nd edn. Athens, GA: University of Georgia Press.
Rolston, III, H. 1988: *Environmental Ethics: Duties to and Values in the Natural World*. Philadelphia, PA: Temple University Press.

Gender issues
Gilligan, C. 1982: *In a Different Voice: Psychological Theory and Women's Development*. Cambridge, MA: Harvard University Press.
Jaggar, A. 1983: *Feminist Politics and Human Nature*. Totowa, NJ: Rowman and Littlefield.

Medical ethics
Harris, J. 1985: *The Value of Life: An Introduction to Medical Ethics*. London: Routledge and Kegan Paul.
Sommerville, A. et al. 1993: *Medical Ethics Today*. London: British Medical Association.

Punishment
Honderich, T. 1984: *Punishment: The Supposed Justifications*. Harmondsworth: Penguin Books.
Primoratz, I. 1989: *Justifying Legal Punishment*. Atlantic Highlands, NJ: Humanities Press.

Sex
Scruton, R. 1986: *Sexual Desire*. London: Methuen.
Soble, A. (ed.) 1980: *Philosophy of Sex*. Totowa, NJ: Rowman and Littlefield.

War

Glover, J. 1987: *Causing Death and Saving Lives*. Harmondsworth: Penguin Books.

Teichman, J. 1986: *Pacifism and the Just War*. Oxford: Blackwell.

Walzer, M. 1977: *Just and Unjust Wars*. Harmondsworth: Penguin Books.

Discussion Questions

Questions about applied ethics

1   Should all areas of human activity be subject to a branch of applied ethics?

2   How close should the main philosophical problems of ethics be to actual moral thinking and familiar ethical vocabularies?

3   How can we judge whether it is the professional business of moral philosophers to discuss matters such as totalitarianism, genocide, warfare, civil rights and sexual ethics?

4   Does either a conception of human well-being or a notion of universally reasonable rules of action provide a satisfactory basis for the objective assessment of conduct and institutions?

5   How can we determine whether there are right methods in applied ethics?

6   Are debates in applied ethics more likely to entrench or to challenge well-established moral theories, like utilitarianism or Kantian ethics?

7   Does applied ethics corrupt our consciences? How can this danger be avoided?

8   How should practical philosophy relate thought about general principles and thought about particular cases? What are the consequences of your answer for the possibility of applied ethics?

9   Are there different values and different virtues specific to different departments of life? How should we understand applied ethics in the light of your answer?

10   How might a meta-philosophical account of moral reasoning help us to choose between 'applied ethics' and 'casuistry' as the main form of moral philosophy about practice?

11   In what new fields might applied ethics find a field of operation?

Questions within applied ethics

12   What distinguishes just wars from unjust wars?

13   Is destroying a culture a wrong in addition to killing the people who are the bearers of that culture?

14   Is there any moral difference between abortion and infanticide?

15   Can we respect the autonomy of mental patients?

16   Do animals have rights?

17   Does the fact that humans live in an environment give rise to moral constraints on how we should treat that environment?

18   Does the market answer all questions of business ethics?

19   Should pornography be banned?

17

Bioethics, Genethics and Medical Ethics

REBECCA BENNETT, CHARLES A. ERIN, JOHN HARRIS AND SØREN HOLM

Bioethics investigates ethical issues arising in the life sciences (medicine, health care, genetics, biology, research and so on) by applying the principles of MORAL PHILOSOPHY (chapter 6) to these problems. Medical ethics and genethics (ethical issues arising from the discipline of genetics) are subsets of bioethics.

1 Bioethics

1.1 Methodology

There is often much confusion about what the methodology of bioethics is. Bioethics is characterized as a multidisciplinary mode of enquiry. Health care professionals, life scientists, philosophers, theologians, lawyers, economists, psychologists, sociologists, anthropologists and historians are among those who are typically involved in bioethical enquiry. However, while a wide range of disciplines are actively involved in bioethics, the central method of bioethics is moral philosophical enquiry. Bioethics, rather than being a multidisciplinary mode of enquiry, is a branch of APPLIED ETHICS (chapter 16), which is characteristically informed by multidisciplinary expertise and findings. As Ronald Green puts it: 'while ethics and moral philosophy may sometimes represent a relatively small part of the actual work of bioethics, they form in a sense the confluence to which all the larger and smaller tributaries lead, and, more than any other single approach, the methods of ethics and philosophy remain indispensable to this domain of inquiry' (Green 1990: 182).

Applied ethics involves the application of the principles and methods of moral philosophy to practical problems. Bioethics, a branch of applied ethics, applies these principles and methods of moral philosophy to issues arising in the life sciences.

1.2 Theoretical approaches

Within bioethics a number of theoretical approaches have been used as the basis for ethical analysis of concrete bioethical problems. All the major approaches in moral philosophy have also been applied within bioethics, although often in forms that are somewhat simplified in comparison to the most advanced contemporary developments of these approaches. KANTIAN ETHICS (chapter 32) is for instance often appropriated in bioethics as if it consisted only of the two formulations of the CATEGORICAL IMPERATIVE (pp. 735–6), and bioethical consequentialism often neglects the problems of precisely specifying the maximand in a preference CONSEQUENTIALIST (pp. 30–1) theory. The popularity of the different approaches has waxed and waned over time, and at least one approach specific to bioethics has been developed, the so-called principlist or Four Principles approach.

Because deontology, consequentialism and virtue ethics are central theoretical approaches in modern moral philosophy they will not be presented here, but in the list of references the main works of the most important proponents of each of these frameworks within bioethics are presented. It is also important to note that phenomenological, existentialist, discourse-ethics, and postmodern approaches are prevalent in that part of the bioethics literature which is not written in English, and which is therefore often neglected in the Anglo-American literature.

Three approaches that are not especially common, or entirely absent, within moral philosophy in general have gained some currency within bioethics: (1) intuitionism; (2) the Four Principles; (3) Pluralist views. As will become apparent, all three approaches can be seen as three different types of reaction to two perceived deficiencies in moral philosophy:

1   The lack of agreement at the basic level of moral philosophy. This is exemplified in the interminable debate between consequentialists and deontologists.
2   The perception that theoretical elegance has been prioritized to the detriment of realistic applicability to real-life ethical problems.

Intuitionism in bioethics is often derived from the writings of the later WITTGENSTEIN (chapter 39), especially his considerations about rules and rule-following in *Philosophical Investigations*. It entails the most radical rejection of the main traditions in moral philosophy, and claims that the reasons behind ethical decision-making cannot be formulated in statable rules, and even if such rules could be stated they would underdetermine the decision to be made in every realistic situation calling for ethical judgement. Bioethical intuitionists therefore criticize mainline bioethics for being much too simplistic, and for neglecting the importance of the agents' pre-reflective ethical judgements. Intuitionists will maintain that if agents immediately feel revulsion at the thought of infanticide, then this is a moral fact which cannot easily be set aside. A 'primitive' intuitionism will place all emphasis on immediate 'gut feelings' as the bedrock of moral judgement, and will thus stand in danger of removing the possibility of moral debate, but more sophisticated intuitionists will try to avoid this danger.

The Four Principles approach (4PA) is the only commonly used approach that is truly indigenous to bioethics. The approach was invented by Thomas Beauchamp and James Childress in the first edition of their very influential *The Principles of Biomedical Ethics* in 1979. It was popularized in Europe by Ranaan Gillon in a series of articles in the *British Medical Journal*, later collected in the book *Philosophical Medical Ethics* (Gillon 1986). The 4PA posits four principles that are thought to occupy a middle level and to mediate between an upper level of conflicting moral theories and a lower level of common morality. It is claimed that the four principles are supported by both deontological and consequentialist moral theories, and that they also emerge from a rational reconstruction of common morality (i.e. the immediate moral intuitions/judgements) of ordinary people. The four principles are:

Respect for autonomy
Non-maleficence
Beneficence
Justice

The four principles are not rank-ordered in the 4PA. In the consideration of a moral problem an agent is first to consider which of these four principles are applicable in the situation by looking at the content and scope of each principle. If two or more principles are applicable, and if they do not support the same decision, the agent must specify the content of each principle and balance the principles against each other in order to reach a final solution. The 4PA has attained great popularity in medical ethics, although its impact on academic bioethics seems to be waning. The attractions of the 4PA are undoubtedly (1) its simple structure, (2) its apparent ability to make a deeper understanding of, and engagement with, moral theory unnecessary, and (3) its apparent congruence with common features of moral thinking. The diminution of the impact of the 4PA on academic bioethics can be traced to six kinds of critiques pointing out that (1) the derivation of the four principles from moral theory is problematic; (2) the degree to which common morality can be said to support the four principles is questionable; (3) the four principles must either be seen as contentless labels or their content must be seen as culturally determined within a specific culture; (4) although Beauchamp and Childress deny a rank-ordering of the principles, their examples of application give respect for autonomy much greater emphasis than for instance justice; (5) the four principles do not cover the whole moral domain; and (6) the guidelines for specification and balancing are so vague that the 4PA in many circumstances radically underdetermine the solution to a given problem.

The label 'Pluralist views' is used here to denote a class of approaches to bioethics that attempt to combine the 'best' insights from deontology, consequentialism and virtue ethics in some form of coherent framework. The impetus for developing a pluralist view is often that all of the 'pure' theoretical approaches lead to strikingly contra-intuitive results when applied to certain bioethical problems. The pluralist views try to solve this problem by, for instance, advocating consequentialism but with certain deontological side-constraints that can remove the 'unwanted side-effects' of pure, unbridled consequentialism. Certain pluralist views stand in the tradition of American PRAGMATISM (chapter 36) (following figures such as Peirce and Dewey), but other modern kinds of pragmatism seem to be very close to pure consequentialism. The main problem for proponents of pluralist views is that the deeper theoretical foundations of the pluralist project are often very difficult to defend because the proponents of 'pure' theories can often exploit the cracks in the foundation where the different theories in the plurality are jointed together.

Ethics and Law

Many areas of 'bioethics', such as artificial reproduction, are heavily regulated by LAW (chapter 13), and this raises the question of the relationship between law and ethics in this field (see Simmonds 1986: chs 5–7). It would be all too simple to suppose that what ethics provides in the way of principles and moral calculus forms the foundation of legislation and judicial reasoning and decision-making, but there is, of course, some overlap between moral philosophy and jurisprudence. This kind of approach is embodied in the work of so-called 'natural lawyers' whose basic tenet holds that the job of the law is to enforce natural rights. Through this explicit commitment to a theory of NATURAL RIGHTS (p. 769), the expository is conflated with the justificatory, and it is the view that this conflation is mistaken and dangerous that led to the development of 'legal positivism', originating in the work of Jeremy BENTHAM (chapter 35). For Bentham, it is the principle of utility, and not traditional faith in natural rights, which should constitute the touchstone by which the law is to be judged. Whilst legal positivists such as H. L. A. Hart would disclaim neither the importance of morality nor the fact that morality can influence law-making, they advocate the divorce of expository jurisprudence from censorial jurisprudence. That is, discovering what the law is should be seen as a distinct enterprise from moral evaluation of the law. In principle, we have well established 'RULES OF RECOGNITION' (p. 412) for deciding what legal rules exist and what rights and duties they confer, and every legal system must possess a fundamental rule of recognition. Positivists would claim that any relationship between legal rights and duties and moral rights and duties is at most coincidental. 'What is the law?' is to be viewed as a very different question to 'Should the law be obeyed?' and, indeed, following Bentham, Hart would charge that it is through this separation that we are put in a position to answer the latter. Now, as Simmonds has argued, legal positivism itself relies on a particular moral approach: 'Positivists wish to portray the law as a body of rules that can be ascertained in some more or less uncontroversial way, quite independently of our differing moral judgements. But . . . this approach itself rests on an understanding of the distinctive significance of law. It is precisely the public nature of law that gives it its moral claim on our conduct' (Simmonds 1986: 95).

The foremost critique of legal positivism in modern times is to be found in the work of Ronald Dworkin (1977). Dworkin argues that law encompasses not only rules, but principles. Whilst valid rules are applied in an 'all-or-nothing' fashion and cannot conflict, principles may conflict and, when they do, resolution is achieved by balancing one against another. (To find one principle decisive in a particular case, however, does not imply that that principle will 'trump' in all cases.) It is through this understanding of the function of principles that we can explain how, for example, legal precedent can be amended or overturned. Now where Dworkin's theory is exclusive of the claims of positivism is in how Dworkin claims legal principles are to be recognized. This is not by reference to a rule of recognition, but through moral and/or political analysis. For Dworkin, whilst a policy is a standard which expresses some goal of the community, a principle is 'a standard that is to be observed . . . because it is a requirement of justice or fairness or some other dimension of morality' (ibid.: 22). And a principle counts as a legal principle if it is a constituent of the 'soundest theory of law that could be offered as a justification for the established legal rules and institutions' (Simmonds 1986: 95).

Thus, whilst legal positivists want to say that law is separate from morality because law has a rule of recognition that provides for a straightforward delineation of what standards apply, Dworkin's counter-argument rests on the fact that developing the 'soundest theory of law' is certainly not straightforward and must include moral and political theoretical considerations. If Dworkin is right, then the legal regulation of medicine and the biosciences will ultimately involve the appeal to moral and political principles.

1.3   The history of bioethics

Modern bioethics can be traced back to two distinct roots. The first root is traditional medical etiquette and ethics and the second is academic moral philosophy. Considerations about the ethical implications of medical practice have always played a role in the self-understanding of the Western medical profession and in the education of medical apprentices and later medical students. This was first given expression in the famous Hippocratic Oath, which probably originated in a minority Pythagorean school in early Greek medicine, but which became important because it resonated with later Christian values. It is, however, important to note that the Hippocratic tradition has never been the only tradition in medical ethics. There have always been several competing traditions. During certain historical periods when there has been no reflection on the content of the rules of medical ethics they have degenerated to pure rules of professional etiquette to be learned by rote, but in other periods the rules have been questioned and the philosophy of the day has been employed in the criticism and reconstruction of medical ethics. It is possible, in the English-speaking world, to locate the beginning of modern professional ethics to the 1827 publication of *Medical Ethics* by the Manchester physician Thomas Percival. Percival's ideas formed the basis of the early ethics codes of the American and British medical associations, and also influenced the codes of the World Medical Association as late as the 1940s and 1950s. The cornerstone of this conception of ethics was the dual responsibility of the professional towards the patient and towards the profession. In the early 1960s this understanding of ethics came under pressure in the increasingly complex health-care systems in the Western world.

The other root of bioethics is academic moral philosophy. In the Anglo-American tradition moral philosophy encountered a barren period in the middle of the twentieth century when the most prominent philosophers turned away from an engagement with real moral problems to discussions of META-ETHICS (pp. 225–7). Moral philosophy thus lost its importance as a corrective to the morally problematic aspects of social policy. During the early 1960s many young philosophers began again to turn to the moral problems of modern society, utilizing the philosophical tools of modern Anglo-American analytic philosophy. This move can be seen as part of the general social unrest resulting in the anti-war, nuclear disarmament and hippie movements. Some of this philosophical attention was turned towards the field we now call bioethics, and formed the second major root of modern bioethics.

1.4   The scope of bioethics

While medical ethics makes up a large and central subsection of bioethics, bioethics extends beyond the realms of medicine and health care to encompass those of the biological sciences more generally, and areas including environmental ethics, ethical issues of sexuality and reproduction. Consider, for example, genethics, the ethics of genetic choice and manipulation.

2   Genethics

Genetics, perhaps more than any other science, created both acute ethical dilemmas and acute existential anxieties. It is genetics that makes us recall not simply our responsibilities to the world and to one another, but our responsibilities for how people will be in the future. It is genetics that is enabling us more and more to determine not simply who will live and who will die, but what all those who will live in the future will actually be like. Genes are special because they have encoded within them all the information required to make not only the parts but also the whole organism and they have one other very special characteristic: they are essentially immortal, or rather the information that they contain is essentially immortal, passed from generation to generation indefinitely and shared between different species. The Human Genome Project aimed at identifying and mapping all of the one hundred thousand or so genes that make up the human genome and is now essentially complete. Locating and understanding the function of all the genes will help us in developing techniques or modifying them in various ways. So far the impetus for this research has been largely therapeutic. The more we know about disease the more we understand the influence of genes. In single gene disorders, such as sickle cell disease, the presence or absence of a particular gene is what determines whether or not the individual will contract the disease. In other cases, for example, the genes for breast cancer (BRCA1 and 2 genes), it is not the presence or absence of a single gene or group of genes that is decisive but rather their presence or absence will act as an important predisposing factor. It is obvious that the ability to influence these genes and their operation is of immense potential benefit. However, genes determine or influence many other features of human beings as well, which range from factors with therapeutic importance like the ability to fight disease, to what one might think of as morally neutral traits, like height, weight, build, hair colour, eye colour and so on.

The therapeutic manipulation of genes (gene therapy) can, in principle though perhaps not always in practice, be carried out either on the somatic line or on the germ line. Somatic changes to genes are one-off changes that affect only the individual whose genes have been manipulated; such changes are not passed on through normal reproduction and die with the individual. Manipulations to the germ line, on the other hand, affect those genes which are passed on through reproduction and consequently if they are changed those changes can be passed on indefinitely from generation to generation. At first sight it seems obvious that if we can make beneficial changes which will remove an inherited disease or mitigate its disastrous effects, then both humanity and economy would seem to indicate a preference for the germ line, since the beneficial changes will be passed on without further interventions being required from generation to generation. However, there is a downside to this: any mistakes or unforeseen consequences will also be built permanently into the genetic make-up of an individual, which will in turn be passed from generation to generation. That is why many have been anxious to confine gene therapy to somatic changes at least until we understand it far better than we do currently. One problem that occurs here is that there may be some beneficial changes that, if they are to be made at all, can only be made in the germ line and this raises the question of whether or not it could be ethical to deny present generations possible effective therapies for fear that the genetic changes may express themselves in disastrous ways perhaps many generations hence.

2.1 Genetic testing and screening

Since genes are associated so strongly with many diseases or adverse conditions, it is possible by using genetic tests either to predict whether individuals or their progeny are likely to be affected by these diseases or indeed to screen whole populations or partial populations. These tests raise many important ethical issues. Where the tests will be performed on embryos, either at the pre-implantation stage (pre-implantation genetic diagnosis: PIGD) or *in utero* (pre-natal diagnosis), many problems arise. One concerns the ethics of attempting to use test results to filter out the presence of particular conditions in future generations. To many this seems unproblematically advantageous, since damaging or disabling conditions may be eradicated and human life made better. To others this seems to constitute discrimination against those with disability and an insult to people currently living with disability. These techniques also raise issues about the moral status of the embryo and whether we are entitled, for example, to terminate pregnancies on the basis of particular features that we know to be present in the embryo. While many think that terminating pregnancy for significant disability is justifiable, genetic tests will also reveal the presence of non-disabling characteristics, for example, gender or skin colour, on the basis of which some might also wish to terminate pregnancies.

Separate questions concern the ethics of making genetic information available through testing and screening so that people may know what to expect in their children and so that societies may know what to expect in future generations and the ethics of acting on that information.

2.2 Cloning

Finally, cloning technology of the sort that was used to create the now world famous 'Dolly the sheep' may be used not only to copy the genotype of the whole organism and produce a genetically identical copy of existing adults, but also can be used at the level of cells to create cells and cell lines that are genetically compatible with the genome of particular individuals so that these may be inserted without fear of rejection and also to create, in principle, limitless numbers of copies of particular genes that might be useful and difficult to produce or to find. While cloning whole organisms has great dramatic appeal, it has limited therapeutic or altruistic utility. On the other hand, cloning cells and cell lines is one of the most promising avenues of scientific research which may lead to the power to help tissue repair itself and regenerate itself in living human organisms and eventually may lead to the, perhaps indefinite, postponement of death. While the ethics of therapy seem unproblematic, the ethics of increasing life expectancy are complicated and raise issues not only of individual but also of global justice.

3   Medical Ethics

Medical ethics is a subset of bioethics and investigates ethical issues arising in medicine and health-care provision by applying the principles of moral philosophy to these problems. While the terms 'bioethics' and 'medical ethics' are often used interchangeably, they do not represent identical disciplines. Although applied ethics relating to medicine and health care may be categorized as either bioethics or medical ethics, the term 'bioethics' represents the application of the principles of moral philosophy to all the life sciences, not just to medicine and health-care provision.

Some of the major issues in medical ethics are discussed below.

3.1   When does life begin?

Many people have thought that the problem of when life becomes morally important, in the ultimate sense, is answered by knowing when life begins. Many of the most popular accounts of personhood, for example, concentrate on attempting to answer the question of when life begins, treating life unproblematically in this context as human life. The event most popularly taken to mark the starting-point of human life is conception. But conception is unhelpful as a threshold of moral importance for a number of reasons. First, conception can result in a hydatidiform mole, a cancerous multiplication of cells that will never become anything but a palpable threat to the life of the mother. Second, even if human life does begin at conception, it is not necessarily the life of an individual; twins may form at any point up to approximately fourteen days following conception.

Cloning also has raised problems for our understanding of when life begins. If one has a pre-implantation embryo in the early stages of development when all of the cells are totipotent, that is, where any of the cells could become any part of the resulting individual, and one splits this early cell mass (anything up to the 100-cell stage) into, say, four clumps of cells, each of the four clumps would constitute a new, viable embryo that could be implanted with every hope of successful development into adulthood. Each clump is the clone or identical twin of each of the others and comes into being not through conception, but because of the division of the early cell mass. Moreover, the four clumps can be recombined into one embryo. This creates a situation where, without the destruction of a single human cell, one human life, if that is what it is, can be split into four and can be recombined again into one. Those who think that ensoulment takes place at conception have an interesting problem to account for the splitting of one soul into four, and for the destruction of three souls when the four embryos are recombined into one, and to account for the destruction of three individuals without a single human cell being removed or killed. These possibilities might give us pause in attributing a beginning of morally important life to a point like conception.

However, if we want to know when life begins to matter morally then it can never be enough to know when life begins; we have to know why life of a particular sort, whenever it begins, is important, and moreover why it is more important than other sorts of lives to which care, respect and resources might also be devoted.

3.2   Speciesism and natural kinds

Some people have attempted to overcome, or rather side-step, this problem by simply stipulating that it is human beings that matter. Although this move certainly avoids the problem, it does so at some cost. It is difficult to imagine how one would defend a moral theory that was founded on the stipulation of an arbitrary preference for one kind of creature over another, particularly when this preference is asserted by self-interested individuals on behalf of their own kind. We are all too familiar with the history of similar claims in which the moral priority and superiority of 'our own kind' has been asserted on behalf of one racial, religious or gender group at the expense of another. Simply stipulating arbitrarily the superiority of our own kind, whether defined by species membership, race, gender, nationality, religion, or any other non-moral characteristic, without further argument is insufficient to establish any moral claim. Membership of a natural kind, or of an ethnic, religious or other grouping, is not of itself a moral property.

3.3   Potentiality

The problem is to distinguish in some morally significant respect, human embryos from the embryos and indeed the adult members of any other species. The one thing human embryos have that members of other species do not is their potential not simply to be born and to be human, but to become the sort of complex, intelligent, self-conscious, multifaceted creatures typical of the human species. There are, however, two difficulties for the potentiality argument.

The first, logical difficulty is straightforward but telling. We are asked to accept that human embryos or foetuses are persons, morally important beings whose interests trump those of other sorts of beings, in virtue of their potential to become another sort of being. But it does not follow logically without further premises, even if we accept that we are required to treat x in certain ways, and even if a will inevitably become x, that we must treat a as if it had become x, at a time or at a stage prior to its having become x.

The second difficulty with the potentiality argument involves the scope of the potential for personhood. If the human zygote has the potential to become an adult human being and is supposedly morally important in virtue of that potential, then what of the potential to become a zygote? Something has the potential to become a zygote, and whatever has the potential to become the zygote has whatever potential the zygote has. Cloning by nuclear transfer, which involves deleting the nucleus of an unfertilized egg, inserting the nucleus taken from any adult cell, and electrically stimulating the resulting newly created egg to develop, can, in theory, produce a new human. This means that any cell from a normal human body has, if appropriately treated, the potential to become a new 'twin' of that individual.

Personhood

The quest for those features that make individuals morally important is often considered to be the same question as the question 'What is a person?' Toward the end of the seventeenth century in his *Essay Concerning Human Understanding*, the philosopher John LOCKE (chapter 29) attempted to answer this question in a way that scarcely has been surpassed. He wrote:

> We must consider what person stands for; which I think is a thinking intelligent being, that has reason and reflection, and can consider itself the same thinking thing, in different times and places; which it does only by that consciousness which is inseparable from thinking and seems to me essential to it; it being impossible for anyone to perceive without perceiving that he does perceive. (Locke 1924: ch. 27, book II)

Locke's definition forms the basis of most accounts of personhood given today. One question that immediately arises is: 'Can someone be more or less of a person?' All of the elements in Locke's definition – intelligence, the ability to think and reason, the capacity for reflection, self-consciousness, memory and foresight – are capacities that admit of degrees. Does this lead us into a hierarchy of persons and hence of moral importance or value? The answer to this question turns on whether or not the degree to which these capacities are required for personhood forms a 'threshold' or a continuum. If a threshold, then once across the threshold the individual is a person. If not, the above problems for personhood accounts of the moral status of individuals remain.

3.4   Abortion and moral status

In contemporary debate the issue of the ethics of abortion has been approached in three major ways. The first treats the ethics of abortion as turning on the moral status of the embryo or foetus. Broadly, if the human individual *in utero* qualifies as a person then it has a moral status which protects its life. A difficulty here is absence of agreement on the defining characteristics of personhood.

The second approach takes a 'women's rights' view of the ethical issue and suggests that it is a woman's right to choose what happens in and to her body and that the ethics of abortion must be seen as a dimension of the moral entitlements of women. A difficulty with such a view is that if the individual *en ventre sa mere* is a person then it is unclear why there does not result an irresolvable conflict or rights or interests.

The third approach attempts to side-step the irreconcilability of these two approaches by suggesting that even if the foetus is a person or has moral importance comparable to that of the mother, it may be seen as making an unjustifiable claim on the mother that she is under no obligation to meet (see Thompson 1971).

3.5   End of life decisions

End of life decisions occur when a decision is made, the effect of which is to end the life of a human individual which could, in principle, have continued. There are many different instances of this: suicide, where a competent individual ends her own life by her own hand; assisted suicide, where such an individual is helped to die; physician-assisted suicide, where the helping hand is that of a physician; and voluntary euthanasia, where the helping hand is that of a non-medically qualified third party. The ethics of all these cases turn principally on the questions of whether or not a competent individual is entitled to control her own destiny, including the timing and manner of her death, and if she is not wholly entitled to exercise this control whether or not there are some circumstances in which this may be legitimate. Some people regard as morally significant whether the steps required to bring about death are active or passive, distinguishing between active euthanasia (sometimes referred to as direct killing) and passive euthanasia (sometimes referred to as indirect killing).

Involuntary and non-voluntary euthanasia

Involuntary euthanasia is the killing of another against their will. This is of course tantamount to murder and will be condemned wherever murder is condemned. Non-voluntary euthanasia is the ending of the life of an individual in any of the manners above described where that individual has not expressed a preference and is at the time of the decision no longer capable of expressing preferences one way or the other. This case usually concerns those individuals who have insufficient competence, for whatever reason, to make an autonomous decision about the ending of their life and who are in such severe pain or distress which is irremediable by normal palliative means, but the question of ending their existence arises. The second class of cases are those who have permanently lost consciousness and who require life-sustaining measures, whether they are in the form of medical treatment or in the form of assisted feeding and hydration. Classic cases of this type are afforded by the condition known as Persistent Vegetative State (PVS). This is the condition which was at issue in two crucial cases of highest juris-diction in the United States and in the United Kingdom, those of Nancy Cruzan and Tony Bland. For brevity we will concentrate on the details of the Bland case. Both Nancy Cruzan and Tony Bland had been left in a persistent vegetative state following accidents. PVS is an unconscious state which, after a year's duration, is generally accepted as per-manent and irreversible. People in PVS do not require life support as this is usually under-stood. They are not on ventilators, for example, although they do require tube feeding and hydration. They are not, nor without assistance will they become, 'dead' according to any of the current criteria or accepted definitions of death. They are not brain-stem dead for example, and because they have spontaneous heartbeat and respiration are not dead by any normal conceptions of death either.

Tony Bland's parents asked the courts to rule that his death could be brought about by withdrawal of feeding and withholding of other life-sustaining measures, including antibiotics, because after withdrawal of feeding he was expected to succumb to infections from which he would die without antibiotics. In advance of the various hearings, it had been expected that the issue in court would turn on whether it was lawful to withdraw feeding and starve someone to death. There were legal precedents for decisions to with-draw life-sustaining medical treatment, but no one considered feeding to be a 'treatment' and hence something that doctors could withdraw on the basis of their judgements as to whether the measure at issue was in the patient's best interests or could be afforded by the health-care system. To their credit the courts did not attempt to stretch the meaning of 'medical treatment' to cover feeding, thus giving the doctors clinical discretion in the matter, but squarely faced the issue of whether or not Tony Bland should continue alive.

Despite disclaimers, the House of Lords decision in the Bland case is regarded by many as in effect one permitting non-voluntary euthanasia. Since Tony Bland was not dead, and would not die unless the Law Lords permitted a definite course of action which would result in his death, their decision to the effect that it was permissible to end his life when it otherwise would have continued indefinitely, effectively brought his life to an end. And indeed, such a decision was sought by Tony Bland's parents for precisely that reason.

If we ask what justified the decision to take steps that would inevitably result in his premature death, the answer raises interesting issues about the legitimacy of ending lives. For if it is believed that the sanctity – the sacredness – of life attaches to the lives of humans, then as a live human Tony Bland does not relevantly differ from others whose lives it is wrong to end. If, however, it is lives of a particular character, lives that are in some sense worth leading, we might arrive at a different answer. Tony Bland, at the time of the courts' deliberations, had a life that he could not lead in any meaningful sense at all. In the words of Lord Keith of Kinkel in his judgement in that case, 'It is, however, perhaps permissible to say that to an individual with no cognitive capacity whatever, and no prospect of ever recovering any such capacity in this world, it must be a matter of complete indifference whether he lives or dies'.

It is widely thought that death is the only event that can bring to an end a valuable life and release others from most, though not all, of the obligations they owe to other people. If this is right, then of course a definition of death is very important and it is now widely accepted that the death of the brain stem (so called 'brain-stem death') is the best criterion of or evidence for death in the ordinary-language or traditional sense. However, in cases such as that of Tony Bland, it may be argued that it is not brain-stem death that indicates the end of human life but the loss of the capacity for consciousness and thought. It is the higher brain, the cerebral cortex, that is generally associated with consciousness and thought, and in PVS it is this section of the brain that has ceased to function. This has led some to suggest that not only can we consider higher brain death as synonymous with the death of that human life in the biographical sense, but further that death should be equated with the loss of higher brain function. However, it is one thing to claim that we may not have the same obligations not to kill and to help sustain the life of those whose higher brain is dead; it is quite another to redefine death to include a permanently unconscious but nevertheless spontaneously breathing individual.

3.6   Health care and justice

The main problem of DISTRIBUTIVE JUSTICE (pp. 258–64) discussed in bioethics is the problem of the distribution of scarce health-care resources. This question may occur in connection with indivisible resources like organs for transplant, but also more commonly in connection with divisible resources like money. The general problem is to distribute a resource in situations where a number of persons either (1) have claims on the resource that cannot be fulfilled simultaneously, or (2) can benefit from the resource but where there is not sufficient for everybody. If the possibility of benefiting from a resource is sufficient to have a claim on that resource, problems (1) and (2) are identical, otherwise they are potentially different problems. For ease of exposition we will assume that possible benefit can be the basis for a valid claim on health-care resources.

If two or more people have a claim on the same resource how should we then decide who should have the resource? Within a consequentialist framework the general answer must be that we should maximize good consequences by our allocation of health-care resources, but this raises the further question of the appropriate specification of the maximand. A popular answer is that we should try to maximize the production of QALYs (Quality Adjusted Life Years), or one of the similar measures like HLYEs (Healthy Life Year Equivalents) or DALYs (Disability Adjusted Life Years) (although for technical reasons DALYs should be minimized, since they measure the burden of disability). The basic idea behind all these measures is that health care should maximize health outcomes and that health outcomes are best measured as the extra life time gained as a result of the use of resources adjusted by some factor designed to reflect that a period without disability, distress, etc. is worth more than a period with these factors. Several problems have been raised concerning QALY maximization, including the following: (1) it discriminates against the elderly and the already disabled; (2) it fails to take account of an important distinction between life-saving and non-life saving interventions; and (3) it fails to take account of the fact that health care may have more than one goal.

Whether or not certain kinds of merit or desert can ground a special claim on resources is a difficult question. For instance, could it be the case that a fireman injured in the line of duty has a special claim to health care, even if it will not bring him or her back to active duty (and thereby open room for a non-desert explanation of the claim)? Such a claim seems to have intuitive merit, but it turns out to be very difficult to explicate exactly what kinds of desert can justify health-care claims.

3.7   Public health versus individual rights

The last two decades have witnessed the gradual evolution of a doctrine of patient autonomy fully endorsed in the writings of most ethicists and at least partially recognized and enforced by the law and observed in medical practice. Patient autonomy is increasingly and rightly perceived as a manifestation of the individual's rights of self-determination and privacy, universally regarded as a pillar of civil liberty. It is acknowledged that the state should refrain from intervention in private lives save where the individual's health-state or lifestyle endangers others. Health, more and more, is a matter of private choice, as is the decision as to whether or not to undergo medical treatment.

While it is held important that individuals are able to exercise their own choices with regard to their health and lifestyle, it is also assumed that nation-states are responsible for the protection of citizens against threats to their lives, including threats from illness or disease. Thus, when considering social policy in the area of public health, we are faced with a 'balancing act' between respecting individual autonomy and the state's responsibility to protect others.

The development of social policy relating to HIV/AIDS illustrates this tension between individual autonomy and public health responsibilities. The threat posed to the community by HIV/AIDS has forced a reconsideration of any concept of absolute autonomy. HIV/AIDS is often seen as a disease centrally related to lifestyle for its association with drug use and sexual conduct. At the same time as age-old problems such as infection surface once more, new difficulties arise to complicate the relationship between public health and private lives.

The emphasis on autonomy in recent years has tended to pre-empt analysis of the responsibilities of the state and of the individual for personal and public health. A number of important questions emerge. Where does the interface between the state's responsibility to protect and promote public health and the individual's civil rights (privacy, freedom, etc.) lie? Where should a line be drawn between public health and private lives? To what extent can the state rely on individual responsibility in health promotion?

Such questions pervade every level of human life. For example, if, by the choice she has made, an individual is responsible, at least in part, for her own ill-health, is her moral claim to care, or to priority in care, so much the less? How are rights and responsibilities for safety and health to be fairly distributed in the work place? How should lifestyle considerations and disease state be accounted for in insurance (life and health)?

3.8 Professional ethics

A cornerstone of modern professional ethics within the health professions is the concept of informed consent. It is generally accepted, and in many jurisdictions also legally enforced, that no medical intervention can be performed on a competent person unless that person has given their free and informed consent. In order for a consent to count as valid informed consent, two information conditions and two consent conditions have to be fulfilled:

Information conditions
1   Information about the nature, purpose, expected effect, and expected side-effects of the intervention has been given.
2   The information mentioned in (1) has been understood to a sufficient degree.

Consent conditions
3   The person is competent to consent.
4   The consent is given freely and without coercion.

The ethical justification of the requirement for informed consent has three partly independent strands, and depending on theoretical orientation one may place the emphasis exclusively on one of these or accept more than one.

The first justification comes from considerations about bodily integrity and the ethically problematic nature of unwanted bodily invasion. The second justification comes from considerations about the right to have autonomous decisions respected. And the third justification comes from considerations about the plurality of values and preferences, and the problems thereby created by making decisions not based on the person's own values.

The other major area in professional ethics is concerned with the classical topics of confidentiality, privacy and the modern topic of data protection. The idea that confidentiality is an important component of the relationship between the doctor and the patient has been upheld in medical ethics ever since the Hippocratic Oath in ancient Greece. It is, however, important to note that the ethical justification for confidentiality has changed over time. The traditional justification was based on the idea that the reputation of the medical profession would suffer if doctors publicly spread the secrets they knew about their patients. This was the main justification for confidentiality until the late 1940s, when a more modern two-pronged justification began to emerge. The current argument for confidentiality has two strands, one generally concerned with the passing of information between health-care professionals or from health-care professionals to outsiders, and one specifically concerned with the passing of information to law enforcement agencies and similar bodies. The first strand of argument proceeds from one of the following premises: (1) there is a right to privacy, (2) there is a right to control personal information (as an extension of a more general right to self-determination), or (3) personal information is a kind of personal property. From all of these premises the conclusion can be derived that the patient has decision control over what health information should be generated and to whom it can be transmitted. This control is not absolute and non-defeasible, but it is strong and can only be defeated by substantial harm to others in cases of non-disclosure of confidential information.

The second strand of argument proceeds in much the same way as the classical justification of professional confidentiality. It posits two premises: (1) it is important that injured and ill persons seek medical attention; (2) if it is generally known that health-care professionals routinely divulge information to law enforcement agencies, it will deter some persons from seeking medical attention when they need it. The conclusion which this strand of the argument seeks to establish is thus that health-care professionals should never or only in very rare circumstances be forced to disclose information to law enforcement agencies.

With the increasing use of information technology in health care, issues concerning data protection have become more and more important. What is at issue here is not the deliberate dissemination of confidential information, but the risks of non-deliberate disclosure and possible misuse of information when it is stored in easily retrievable and linkable form. There are great possible benefits associated with the use of information technology, and the problem is thus to balance these benefits against the inherent risks. Some have tried to analyse these problems in terms of a distinction between sensitive and non-sensitive information, but this is unhelpful in most bioethics contexts because all kinds of health information are or can become sensitive in a range of quite normal circumstances.

3.9   Research ethics

The ethics of research generally and research on human subjects in particular is of increasing importance. Following the Nazi doctors' trial at Nuremberg at the end of the Second World War, there was widespread understanding of the terrible abuse of science that had occurred under the Nazis. This understanding, coupled with a determination to attempt to prevent such abuses in the future, culminated in the formulation of many international protocols governing research, particularly research on human subjects, most prominent of which is perhaps the World Medical Association Declaration of Helsinki and its various amendments. However, in the light of recent massive challenges, not to human rights but to human health, the stringency of the safeguards that have been proposed has increasingly been called into question. For example, the World Medical Association Declaration of Helsinki states (Article 1 Para. 5): 'Concern for the interest of the subject must always prevail over the interest of science and society'. If science and society are construed narrowly as the personal or professional interest of scientists and the interests of society are defined in terms of a particular ideology this protocol seems sound enough. However, the AIDS pandemic has drawn attention to the fact that both the interests of individuals and the interests of society may also require the pursuit of science and that to some extent if individuals are to protect themselves they must be willing to co-operate in this endeavour. This tension is likely to remain with us and is as yet unresolved.

A second principle of the Helsinki Declaration, and one maintained in many other research ethics protocols, requires that such subjects should not be coerced or induced to participate by offers of reward, particularly financial reward. However, in an increasingly consumerist world, individuals more often than not expect to be rewarded or at least compensated for their contribution. Here again there is a tension between what is required to safeguard the rights of the individual and what may be fair or reasonable both in order to avoid exploitation and to enable science to continue. Many have tried to resolve this tension by distinguishing sharply between the reimbursement of reasonable expenses and payment of fees. However, this dividing line is often difficult to draw because if reasonable expenses include lost opportunity costs of using one's time in another way it is difficult to see how the distinction may be maintained.

A further issue, which is of increasing importance in the contemporary world, is the ethics of using animal rather than human subjects in medical research. Many who take a stand on the importance of sentience (the capacity to feel pain or sensation) note that humans and animals, in sharing this capacity, share vulnerability and are entitled to equal protection. Others, bearing in mind, perhaps, considerations of the sort advanced by Lord Keith of Kinkel (above), draw a distinction between most human individuals and most animals which would permit research on the latter but not the former. Finally, some perceive a morally significant hierarchy in animals and would distinguish, for example, primates from other animals in terms of their appropriateness as research subjects. The resolution of these issues depends crucially on the account one feels compelled to give of the acquisition and maintenance of moral status or on the moral significance of sentience.

References

Beauchamp, T. L. and Childress, J. F. 1994: *Principles of Biomedical Ethics*, 4th edn. New York: Oxford University Press.

Bennett, R. and Erin, C. A. (eds) 1999: *HIV and AIDS: Testing, Screening and Confidentiality*. Oxford: Oxford University Press.

Dworkin, R. 1977: *Taking Rights Seriously*. London: Duckworth.

Dyson, A. O. and Harris, J. 1991: *Experiments On Embryos*. London: Routledge.

Englehardt, Jr, H. T. 1996: *The Foundations of Bioethics*, 2nd edn. New York: Oxford University Press.

Gillon, R. 1986: *Philosophical Medical Ethics*. London: John Wiley and Sons on behalf of the *British Medical Journal*.

Glover, J. 1977: *Causing Death and Saving Lives*. Harmondsworth: Penguin Books.

Green, R. M. 1990: Method in Bioethics. *The Journal of Medicine and Philosophy*, 15, 2, April.

Harris, J. 1991: *The Value of Life: An Introduction to Medical Ethics*. London: Routledge and Kegan Paul.

—— 1998: *Clones, Genes and Immortality*. Oxford: Oxford University Press.

Harris, J. and Holm, S. (eds) 1998: *The Future of Human Reproduction: Ethics, Choice and Regulation*. Oxford: Clarendon Press.

Hursthouse, R. 1987: *Beginning Lives*. Oxford: Blackwell.

Locke, J. 1924: *An Essay Concerning Human Understanding* (edited by E. S. Pringle Patterson). Oxford: Clarendon Press.

Oderberg, D. S. 2000: *Applied Ethics: A Non-Consequentialist Approach*. Oxford: Blackwell.

Rachels, J. (ed.) 1986: *Ethical Theory*. Oxford: Oxford University Press.

Simmonds, N. E. 1986: *Central Issues in Jurisprudence: Justice, Law and Rights*. London: Sweet and Maxwell.

Singer, P. (ed.) 1986: *Applied Ethics*. Oxford: Oxford University Press.

Steinbock, B. 1980: *Killing and Letting Die*. Englewood Cliffs, NJ: Prentice-Hall.

Thompson, J. J. 1971: A Defense of Abortion. *Philosophy and Public Affairs*, 1, 1. Reprinted in J. Feinberg (ed.) 1984: *The Problem of Abortion*, 2nd edn. Belmont, CA: Wadsworth Publishing.

Discussion Questions

1   Should we attempt to eradicate disability?

2   Is the selection of the sex or appearance of one's offspring morally unacceptable?

3   Does pre-implantation genetic diagnosis imply that the lives of individuals with disabling conditions, such as deafness, are not worth living?

4   Could cloning become a morally acceptable practice if certain restrictions were made on its use?

5   What is it that gives human life value?

6   Is it possible, in the case of abortion, to balance the rights of the carrying mother against the rights of the unborn child?

7   Is it consistent to argue that there may be both cases where abortion is completely unjustifiable and also cases where abortion is completely justifiable?

8   What moral obligations does a pregnant woman have towards the foetus she is carrying? What implications do these moral obligations have for legislation in this area?

9   Is killing people always wrong and if so, why?

10   Does the withdrawing of treatment, such as in the case of Tony Bland, constitute euthanasia?

11   Is there a defensible moral distinction to be drawn between killing someone and letting them die?

12   Advance Directives aim to represent our interests when we lose the capacity for consent. Should Advance Directives always be followed?

13   Examine the justice of prioritizing health care according to desert. In particular what effect should a patient's responsibility for his own disease have on determining access to treatment? Is it fair that someone who has contributed to their own ill-health should be treated with the same urgency as an 'innocent victim'?

14   Do individuals who believe themselves to be HIV-positive have a moral obligation to forewarn others of their positive status?

15   Do people have a right to remain in ignorance of their health state? Is this 'right' affected if the person has a communicable disease?

16   Why is consent to treatment important? Under what circumstances would it be appropriate to treat a person without their consent?

17   Should patients always be told the truth about their condition?

18   Should medical confidentiality be absolute or are there circumstances in which health-care professions should breach patient confidentiality?

19   Is it acceptable to conduct research on human subjects without their informed consent if it is very unlikely that they will be harmed by the research?

18

Environmental Ethics

HOLMES ROLSTON, III

Environmental ethics is theory and practice about appropriate concern for, values in, and duties regarding the natural world. By classical accounts, ethics is people relating to people in justice and love. Environmental ethics starts with human concerns for a quality environment, and some think this shapes the ethic from start to finish. Others hold that, beyond inter-human concerns, values are at stake when humans relate to animals, plants, species and ecosystems. According to their vision, humans ought to find nature sometimes morally considerable in itself, and this turns ethics in new directions.

1   The Environmental Turn

Humans are the only self-reflective, deliberative moral agents. Ethics is for people. But are humans the only valuable, valuing agents in an otherwise value-free world? Humans co-inhabit Earth with five to ten million species. Nature has equipped *Homo sapiens*, the wise species, with a conscience. Perhaps conscience is less wisely used than it ought to be when, as in classical Enlightenment ethics, it excludes the global community of life from consideration, with the resulting paradox that the self-consciously moral species acts only in its collective self-interest toward all the rest. Environmental ethics claims that we humans are not so 'enlightened' as once supposed, not until we reach a more considerate ethic.

If someone had been attempting to foresee the future of philosophy at the middle of the twentieth century, one of the most surprising developments would have been the rise of environmental philosophy. Environmental ethics remained unknown until the mid-1970s. That was to change rapidly. Philosophers have published dozens of anthologies and systematic works in the field, and courses are taught in several hundred universities and colleges on many continents. There are four professional journals. The International Society for Environmental Ethics (ISEE) has 400 members in 20 countries. The World Congress of Philosophy (1998) devoted four sections to environmental philosophy, with dozens of other related papers.

The website bibliography of the ISEE contains 8,000 articles and books not only by philosophers, ethicists and theologians, but also by policy-makers, lawyers, environmental professionals, foresters, conservation and wildlife biologists, ecologists, economists, sociologists, historians, developers and business persons – all with an ethical concern about human uses of the natural environment. Although the first edition of this book contained no chapter on environmental ethics, this second edition includes this ethical revising.

Philosophers have thought about nature for millennia. Although there is an ethic implicit in many of these world views, this was never much developed in the West. Following the Enlightenment and the scientific revolution, in secular philosophies nature came to be regarded as a valueless realm, governed by mechanistic causal forces. Values arose only with the interests and preferences of humans. In the prevailing Judeo-Christian theologies, God created a good Earth with myriads of creatures, and subjected these to human dominion. For four centuries, Western philosophy and THEOLOGY (chapter 15) were both dominantly humanistic, or, in current vocabulary, anthropocentric.

Environmental ethics applies ethics to the environment, analogously to ethics applied to BUSINESS (chapter 19), MEDICINE (chapter 17), engineering, LAW (chapter 13) and technology. Such humanist applications may be challenging: limiting population growth or development, questioning consumerism and the distribution of wealth, advocating the inclusion of women or aboriginal peoples, or fearing global warming.

Environmental quality is necessary for quality of human life. Humans dramatically rebuild their environments; still, their lives, filled with artefacts, are lived in a natural ecology where resources – soil, air, water, photosynthesis, climate – are matters of life and death. Culture and nature have entwined destinies, similar to (and related to) the way minds are inseparable from bodies. So ethics needs to be applied to the environment.

At depth, however, environmental ethics is more radical in 'applying ethics' (so many advocates claim) outside the sector of human interests. Contemporary ethics has been concerned to be inclusive: the poor as well as the rich, women as well as men, future generations as well as the present. Environmental ethics is even more inclusive. Whales slaughtered, wolves extirpated, whooping cranes and their habitats disrupted, ancient forests cut, Earth threatened by global warming – these are ethical questions intrinsically, owing to values destroyed in nature, as well as also instrumentally, owing to human resources jeopardized. Humans need to include nature in their ethics; humans need to include themselves in nature.

Somewhat ironically, just when humans, with their increasing industry and technology, seemed further and further from nature, having more knowledge about natural processes and more power to manage them, the natural world has emerged as a focus of ethical concern. Human power to affect nature has dramatically escalated, as with species loss or global warming. Exploding populations raise concerns that humans are not in a sustainable relationship with their environment. Nor have they distributed the benefits derived from natural resources equitably. Nor have they been sensitive enough to the welfare of the myriads of other species.

The plan here is to outline six levels of concern: humans, animals, organisms, species, ecosystems, Earth. These will be criss-crossed with over a dozen differing approaches to environmental ethics: humanistic ethics, animal welfare ethics, biocentrism, deep ecology, land ethics, theological environmental ethics, ethics of ecojustice, communitarian ethics with circles of concern, environmental virtue ethics, axiological environmental ethics, political ecology, sustainable development ethics, bioregionalism, ecofeminism, postmodern environmental ethics, and an ethics of place.

2   Humans: People and their World

Humans are helped or hurt by the condition of their environment, and that there ought to be some ethic concerning the environment can be doubted only by those who believe in no ethics at all. Ethics will have a concern for what humans have at stake there – benefits, costs, and their just distribution, risks, pollution levels, rights and torts, environmental sustainability and quality, the interests of future generations. An anthropocentric ethics claims that people are both the subject and the object of ethics. Humans can have no duties to rocks, rivers, nor to wildflowers or ecosystems, and almost none to birds or bears. Humans have serious duties only to each other. Anthropocentrists may wish to save these things for the benefits they bring. But the environment is the wrong kind of primary target for an ethic. Nature is a means, not an end in itself. Man is the measure of things, said Protagoras, an ancient Greek philosopher, setting the tone of philosophy since.

Humans deliberately and extensively rebuild the spontaneous natural environment and make the rural and urban environments in which they reside. We care about the quality of life in these hybrids of nature and culture. Ethics arises to protect various goods within our cultures; this, historically, has been its principal arena. As philosophers frequently model this, ethics is a feature of the human SOCIAL CONTRACT (pp. 622–7). People arrange a society where they and the others with whom they live do not (or ought not) lie, steal, kill. This is right, and one reason it is right is that people must co-operate to survive; and the more they reliably co-operate the more they flourish. One way of envisioning this is the so-called ORIGINAL POSITION (p. 261), where one enters into contract, figuring out what is best for a person on average, oblivious to the specific circumstances of one's time and place. This is where a sense of universality, or at least pan-culturalism, in morality has a plausible rational basis.

A great deal of the work of environmental ethics can be done from within the social contract. Most of environmental policy is of this kind. Humans need to be healthy. Health, however, is not simply a matter of biology from the skin-in. Environmental health, from the skin-out, is equally as important. It is hard to have a healthy culture on a sick environment. More than that, humans desire a quality environment, enjoying the amenities of nature – wildlife and wildflowers, scenic views, places of solitude – as well as the commodities – timber, water, soil, natural resources. Supporting environmental health and a quality environment can certainly be counted as duties within a social contract.

Environmental ethics, by this account, is founded on what we can call a human right to nature. The World Commission on Environment and Development claims: 'All human beings have the fundamental right to an environment adequate for their health and well-being' (1987b: 9). This includes the basic natural givens: air, soil, water, functioning ecosystems, hydrologic cycles and so on. These could previously be taken for granted. But now the right must be made explicit and defended. Note that is not any claim against or for nature itself; rather it is a claim made against other humans who might deprive us of such nature.

The four most critical issues that humans currently face are peace, population, development and environment. All are interrelated. Human desires for maximum development drive population increases, escalate exploitation of the environment and fuel the forces of war. Those who exploit persons will typically exploit nature as readily – animals, plants, species, ecosystems and the Earth itself. Ecofeminists have found this to be especially true where both women and nature are together exploited. The interests of environmental ethics done from perspectives of political ecology, sustainable development, bioregionalism, ecojustice, from an ethics of stewardship, or human virtues in caring, or a sense of place – all these tend to be humanistic and to recognize that nature and culture have entwined destinies. Bryan G. Norton (1991) claims that fully enlightened anthropocentrists and more naturalistic environmentalists will almost entirely agree on environmental policy, what he calls a 'convergence hypothesis'.

3   Animals: Beasts in Flesh and Blood

Ethics is for people, but is ethics only about people? Wild animals do not make man the measure of things at all. There is no better evidence of non-human values and valuers than spontaneous wild life, born free and on its own. Animals hunt and howl, find shelter, seek out their habitats and mates, care for their young, and flee from threats. They suffer injury and lick their wounds. Animals maintain a valued self-identity as they cope through the world. They defend their own lives because they have a good of their own. There is somebody there behind the fur or feathers.

An animal values its own life for what it is in itself, without further contributory reference, although of course it inhabits an ecosystem on which its life-support depends. Animals are value-able, able to value things in their world, their own lives intrinsically and their resources instrumentally. So there can and ought to be an animal welfare ethic; or, some prefer to say, an animal rights ethic.

Such ethicists may still say that value exists only where a subject has an object of interest, only now recognizing that the pleasures and pains of non-human subjects must be considered. At least some of what counts in ethics is generic to our kinship with animals, not just specific to our species. Common sense first and science later teaches that we human animals have many similarities with non-human animals. No one doubts that animals grow hungry, thirsty, hot, tired, excited, sleepy. The protein coding sequences of DNA for structural genes in chimpanzees and humans are more than 99 per cent identical.

Confronted with such facts, we have to philosophize over them. The conclusion seems to follow that, whatever our unique differences as *Homo sapiens*, there is also a kinship with others. By parity of reasoning, it seems that what humans value in themselves, if they find this elsewhere, they ought also to value in non-human others. We value what does not stand directly in our lineage but is enough like ourselves that we are drawn by spillover to shared phenomena manifest in others. The principle of universalizability demands that an ethicist recognize corresponding values in fellow persons. Growth in ethical sensitivity, or virtue, has often required enlarging the circle of neighbours to include other races and cultures. But these widening circles do not end with reciprocating moral agents. A communitarian ethics finds enlarging concentric circles around the moral self: family, local community, nation, humankind, and – in a surrounding though more remote circle – animals.

A moose does not suffer the winter cold, as we might (humans having evolved in the tropics). Perhaps the warbler is not glad when it sings. But one must not commit the humanistic fallacy of supposing no natural analogues to what humans plainly value. We have every logical, biological and psychological reason to value positive degrees of kinship. There will arise conflicts of interest. There might even be bad kinds (rattlesnakes?), but prima facie, at least, these kindred lives count. They are good adapted fits in their places, co-evolved with others. Presumptively, animal life is an EVOLUTIONARY SUCCESS (pp. 320–30) and a good thing.

Some may think it logically or psychologically impossible to value kinds of experience that we cannot share (those of the snakes). True, animal lives do not coincide with our own, and there are realms of experience that we cannot reach and which are difficult to evaluate. But neither should we underestimate the human genius for thoughtful appreciation and considerable respect for alien forms. Meanwhile, the claims of kindred animals ought to count in environmental ethics.

4   Organisms: Respect for Life

A biocentric ethics asks about appropriate respect toward all living things, not only the wildlife and farm animals, but now the butterflies and the sequoia trees. Otherwise, most of the biological world has yet to be taken into account: lower animals, insects, microbes, plants. Over 96 per cent of species are invertebrates or plants; only a tiny fraction of individual organisms are sentient animals. Considering plants makes the differences between biocentrism and an animal rights ethic clear.

A plant is a spontaneous life system, self-maintaining with a controlling genetic programme (though with no controlling centre, no brain). A plant is not a subject, but neither is it an inanimate object, like a stone. Plants, quite alive, are unified entities of the botanical although not of the zoological kind; that is, they are not unitary organisms highly integrated with centred neural control, but they are modular organisms, with a meristem that can repeatedly and indefinitely produce new vegetative modules, additional stem nodes and leaves when there is available space and resources, as well as new reproductive modules, fruits and seeds.

Plants do not have ends-in-view, and in that familiar sense they do not have goals. Yet the plant grows, reproduces, repairs its wounds and resists death, maintaining a botanical identity. All this, from one perspective, is just biochemistry – the whir and buzz of organic molecules, enzymes, proteins – as humans are too, from one perspective. But from an equally valid – and objective – perspective, the morphology and metabolism that the organism projects is a valued state. *Vital* is a more ample word now than *biological*. We could even argue that the genetic set is a *normative set*; it distinguishes between what *is* and what *ought to be* – not of course in any moral or conscious sense – but in the sense that the organism is an axiological system. The genome is a set of conservation molecules. A life is spontaneously defended for what it is itself.

An objector can say, 'The plants don't care, so why should I?' But plants do care – using botanical standards, the only form of caring available to them. The plant life *per se* is defended – an intrinsic value. Though things do not matter *to* trees, a great deal matters *for* them. We ask, 'What's the matter *with* that tree?' If it is lacking sunshine and soil nutrients, we arrange for these, and the tree goes to work and recovers its health. Such organisms do 'take account' of themselves; and we should take account of them.

For classical ethicists, all this seems odd. Plants are not valuers with preferences that can be satisfied or frustrated. It seems curious to say that wildflowers have rights, or moral standing, or need our sympathy, or that we should consider their point of view. But biocentrists claim that environmental ethics is not merely an affair of psychology, but of biology. The concentric circles keep expanding. Every organism has a *good-of-its-kind*; it defends its own kind as a *good kind*. Perhaps man is the only deliberative measurer of things, but man does not have to make himself the only measure he uses. Life is a better measure.

Adaptive Fits and Inclusive Ethics

Ethics and biology have had uncertain relations over recent centuries. An often-heard argument forbids moving from what *is* the case (a description of biological facts) to what *ought to be* (a prescription of duty); any who do so commit the NATURALISTIC FALLACY (pp. 805–6). On the other hand, if spontaneous natural lives are of value in themselves, and if humans encounter and jeopardize such value, it would seem that humans ought not to destroy values in nature, not at least without overriding justification producing greater value. Perhaps some of these plant kinds are bad kinds (poison oak?), but again, as with the animals, in their place they are adapted, they are presumptively well suited for life in their niches. The counter-risk is a fallacy of mislocated value, a humanistic mistake taking value to lie exclusively in the satisfaction of our human preferences. The problem is that, despite the excellence of our increasingly scientific accounts in biology, nature has been mapped philosophically as a moral blank space, as value-free in and of itself. Theologically, we forgot God's good creation.

Ethics is significantly a matter of respecting others for what they are in themselves, apart from my self-interests. That is altruism. But a humanistic ethic is not really yet 'altruistic' toward any non-human others; even an animal rights ethic finds value only in our animal cousins. Environmental ethics, the most altruistic of ethics, takes accounts of all other living organisms. This nowhere denies trade-offs and degrees of significance and value. Given our own biological needs, humans too have to make a way through the world, and this requires defending ourselves (against poison oak) and capturing values present in plants and animals, for food and shelter. Humans do so not only as biological agents but as moral agents. We have, if you like, a right to eat; we also have a responsibility to respect the vitalities of the fauna and flora around us. A full ethics is inclusive of every living organism.

5   Species and Biodiversity: Lifelines in Jeopardy

At the species level, responsibilities increase. So does the intellectual challenge of defending duties to species. What are species? The question is scientific, one to be answered by biologists. Have humans duties to them? The question is ethical, to be answered by philosophers. On a biological level, species are historical lineages. *Ursus arctos* (the grizzly bear) is a dynamic ongoing bear-bear-bear sequence, a specific form of life historically maintained over generations for thousands of years. The sow devotes her life to her cubs. The individual represents (re-presents) a species in each new generation. It is a token of a type, and the type is more important than the token.

Moral Concern for Species Lines

As with plants, classical ethicists will find species often (though not always) to be useful natural resources. But they find species obscure objects of direct moral concern. Species, though they can be endangered, cannot 'care' – so returns the objection we heard before. They just come and go. Around 98 per cent of the species that have inhabited Earth are extinct. Most ethicists say that one ought not needlessly to destroy endangered species; virtuous persons are not vandals. But many will give humanistic reasons, and think this enough.

More radical environmental ethicists claim that one ought to respect these life lines. Biological identity need not attach solely to the individual centred or modular organism, an animal or a plant. Biological identity can be reasserted genetically over generations, persisting as a discrete, vital pattern over time. The life that the individual has is something passing through the individual as much as something it intrinsically possesses, and a comprehensive respect for life finds it appropriate to attach duty dynamically to the specific forms of life. The value resides in the dynamic form; the individual inherits this, exemplifies it and passes it on.

The appropriate survival unit is the appropriate location of persistent valuing, where the defence of life goes on in regeneration, as individual members of a species are given over to survival of their kind. Plants and animals not only defend their own lives; they defend their kinds. Such kinds are the dynamism of life. A shutdown of the life stream on Earth is the most destructive event possible. In threatening Earth's biodiversity, the wrong that humans are doing is stopping the historical vitality of life. Every extinction is an incremental decay in this stopping life. 'Ought species *x* to exist?' is a distributive increment in the collective question, 'Ought life on Earth to exist?' Since life on Earth is an aggregate of many species, when humans jeopardize species, the burden of proof lies with those who wish deliberately to extinguish a species and simultaneously to care for life on Earth.

Few past philosophers have even raised the question of duties to species, much less answered it. Now such duty is becoming clearer. If it makes any sense to claim that one ought not to kill individuals without justification, it makes more sense to claim that one ought not to extinguish species lines, without extraordinary justification. This is a kind of super-killing.

6 Ecosystems: The Land Ethic

Aldo Leopold, a forester–ecologist and prophet of environmental ethics, claimed, famously: 'A thing is right when it tends to preserve the integrity, stability, and beauty of the biotic community. It is wrong when it tends otherwise.' 'That land is a community is the basic concept of ecology, but that land is to be loved and respected is an extension of ethics' (Leopold 1969: 224–5, viii–ix). In a holistic ethic, this ecosystemic level in which all organisms are embedded also counts morally – in some respects more than any of the component organisms, because the systemic processes have generated, continue to support, and integrate tens of thousands of member organisms. The appropriate unit for moral concern is the fundamental unit of development and survival. That, we were just saying, is species lines. But a species is what it is where it is, encircled by an ecology.

In an axiological ethics, here is systemic value, as well as instrumental and intrinsic value. Value lies in processes as well as in products. To value individuals among the fauna and flora and not the evolutionary and ecological processes is like valuing the eggs that the golden goose produces more than the goose able to produce them. It would be a mistake to value the goose only instrumentally. A goose that lays golden eggs is systemically valuable. How much more so is an ecosystem that generates myriads of species, or even, as we soon see, an Earth that produces billions of species, ourselves included.

A land ethic might seem a naturalistic ethic, but people are living on this land, and so nature and culture soon mix. Trying to map the human environments, we are valuing three main territories: the urban, the rural and the wild – all three of which are necessary if we are to be three-dimensional persons. Nature is much present in the hybrid habitats of rural landscapes; we need an ethic for agro-ecosystems. Wildlife can extensively remain on landscapes put to multiple use; and so we need an ethic of wildlife management. We need an ethic for forests and farmlands, for the countryside. Nature is present in, and a support of, our cities as well.

People on Landscape: Environmental Policy and Managing Nature

Environmental ethics has to be directed to human dominated, managed, disturbed (and often degraded) landscapes. Such a land ethic must be informed about ecosystem health, but more focused on human ecology, on political ecology. Government and business are large influences in our lives; both have vast amounts of power to affect the environment for good or ill. Social systems make humans behave as they do toward their environment, and any effective reformation will have to be worked out in reformed, more environmentally sensitive social institutions. Environmental ethics cannot be an ecosystem ethic pure and simple; there is only an ethic about humans relating to their ecosystems, in the economies in which they live.

Environmental ethics must be corporate; action must be taken in concert: green politics, green business. The natural environment is crucially a 'commons', a public good. Policies will need to relate such a commons to capitalism, ownership of the means of production, market forces, the concerns of labour, real estate development policies, property rights of individuals, population control, equitable distribution of the products made from natural resources. There is no 'invisible hand' that guarantees an optimal harmony between a people and their landscape, or that the right things are done in encounter with fauna, flora, species, ecosystems, or regarding future generations.

Humans are mostly moved to act in their self-interest; and they will do so to the degradation of the environment – unless environmental policy gives them incentive otherwise. Short-term self-interest will get out of hand, especially when coupled with social power. Thus, to respect ecosystems and keep them healthy, to ensure environmental quality even in a humanistic ethics, there is a need for laws to regulate private and business use; these regulations are imposed in the longer-range public interest by the forces of democracy.

What about spontaneous wild nature? Wilderness areas and nature reserves are part of our global environment, and yet not our human habitat. The wild is an environment that humans need and ought to respect; they may like to visit there. But the wild is not an environment in which we can reside and still be human. 'Man is by nature a political animal', said Aristotle – the animal who builds and inhabits a *polis*, a town. That is why, some say, ethics arises to govern conduct in the *polis*, with its social contract, orienting behaviour to protect the goods of human nature and culture. Hence, they say, ethics does not belong in the wild. It is for people, in urban or rural environments.

But, again, a more radical environmental ethics, resolving to be quite inclusive and comprehensive, holds that humans can and ought to set aside wild areas for what they are in themselves, areas which we try to manage as little as possible, or to manage human uses of them so as to let nature takes its course, as far as we can. Virtuous persons ought to respect the integrity, the freedom of life in all its wildness. True, humans are the dominant species on the landscape, which they must manage. But humans are also a moral species, who can and ought to respect evolutionary ecosystems – at least on representative parts of the landscape.

An 'ethics of place' has a tendency to see values largely as those that human inhabitants 'place' on nature. The English love their countryside. But ought this ethic not also be sensitive to values that are already 'in place' before we humans arrive to dwell there (warblers defending the good of their kind)? Part of the needed ethic does demand a constructed sense of place; a person needs an embodied sense of residence. Another part respects nature as it is found to be in itself, oblivious to the specific circumstances of a person's particular time and place. The personal view must be complemented by a regional view, indeed a global view.

Bioregionalism emphasizes living on regional landscapes. The most workable ethic is where persons identify with their geography. People are likely to be most motivated by what they have at stake on their at-home landscapes. True, one ought to have concern for endangered species, vanishing wildlife, intrinsic natural values or wilderness conservation; but that is not what orients day-to-day behaviour. What is politically possible is concern about the countryside of everyday experience. After all, ecology is about living at home (Greek: *oikos*, 'house'). That is where the land ethic really operates. That is where people can act, where they vote and pay taxes. They need to be 'natives', as much as 'citizens'. Michel Serres (1995: 20) argues that 'the old social contract ought to be joined by a natural contract'.

A bioregion, says Kirkpatrick Sale (1985: 43), is 'a place defined by its life forms, its topography, and its biota, rather than by human dictates; a region governed by nature, not legislature'. A focus on bioregions permits 'ecosystem management', a much lauded goal. Bioregionalism appeals to geographers, landscape architects, developers, state legislators, county commissioners – all those charged with decisions about a quality environment. Humans need to learn to 'reinhabit' their landscapes. This is environmental ethics on a human scale.

Aldo Leopold concludes with a land ethic that he recommends universally. It is no accident, however; rather, it is essential that the earlier pages of his *Sand County (Wisconsin) Almanac* remember a January thaw, the spring flowering of *Draba*, the April mating dance of the woodcock. Leopold's biographical residence is the personal backing to his ethic. An environmental ethic needs roots in locality.

Taking a model from ecology, the deep ecology movement emphasizes the ways in which humans, although individual selves, can and ought to extend such selves through a webwork of connections. The human 'self' is not something found from the skin-in, an atomistic individual set over against other individuals and the rest of nature. Ecology dissolves any firm boundary between humans and the natural world. Ecology does not know encapsulated egos over against their environment. Ecological thinking is a kind of vision across boundaries. Humans have such entwined destinies with the natural world that their richest quality of life involves a larger identification with these communities. Such transformation of the personal self will result in an appropriate care for the environment.

Ecofeminists may add that women are better suited for such caring than men – at least men too much dominated by the 'dominion' view, too much inclined to be managers.

7 Earth: Ethics on the Home Planet

Views of Earth from space are the most impressive photographs ever taken. They are the most widely distributed ever, having been seen by well over half the persons on Earth. Few are not moved to a moment of truth, at least in their pensive moods. The whole Earth is aesthetically stimulating, philosophically challenging and ethically disturbing. 'I remember so vividly', said Michael Collins, 'what I saw when I looked back at my fragile home – a glistening, inviting beacon, delicate blue and white, a tiny outpost suspended in the black infinity. Earth is to be treasured and nurtured, something precious that *must* endure' (Collins 1980: 6). There is a vision of an Earth ethic in what he sees.

But, reply the anthropocentrists, that this is 'our home planet' reveals the real focus of ethical concern: humans and their sustainable future. Humans can and ought to be held responsible for what they are doing to their Earth, which is their life-support system. But – so this argument goes – these are duties owed by people to other people; caring for the planet is a means to this end.

Environmental ethics on global and regional scales is inextricably coupled with development ethics. The Rio Declaration begins: 'Human beings are at the centre of concerns for sustainable development. They are entitled to a healthy and productive life in harmony with nature'. The United Nations World Commission on Environment and Development declares: 'Sustainable development is development that meets the needs of the present without compromising the ability of future generations to meet their own needs'. That applies to agriculture, forestry, water use, pollution levels, industry, resource extraction, urbanization, national policies and strategies. 'Sustainable' coupled with 'development' expects continued growth, but not such as degrades opportunities and environments for the future.

Ethics – this argument claims – ought not to confuse people and their Earth. Earth is a big rockpile like the moon, only one on which the rocks are watered and illuminated in such a way that they support life. Earth is no doubt precious as a means of life support, but it is not precious in itself. There is nobody there in a planet. There is not even the objective vitality of an organism, or the genetic transmission of a species line. Earth is not even an ecosystem, strictly speaking; it is a loose collection of myriads of ecosystems. So any ethicist must be talking loosely, perhaps poetically or romantically, of valuing Earth. Earth is a mere thing, a big thing, a special thing for those who happen to live on it, but still a thing, and not appropriate as an object of intrinsic or systemic valuation. We do not have duties to rocks, air, ocean, dirt or Earth; we have duties to people, or sentient things. We must not confuse duties to the home with duties to the inhabitants. Nature, not ultimately important, is (in the literal sense) provisionally important. Any condition of nature that supplies and sustains such opportunities will be acceptable.

The radical environmental ethic finds, however, that this humanistic account fails to recognize the globally relevant survival unit: Earth and its biosphere. The bottom line, trans-cultural and non-negotiable, is a sustainable biosphere. That is the ultimate expanding circle: the full Earth. The us-and-our-sustainable-resources view is not a systemic analysis of what is taking place. The planet is a self-organizing biosphere, which has produced and continues to support all the Earthbound values. Earth is the source of value, and therefore value-able, able to produce value itself. This generativity is the most fundamental meaning of the term 'nature', 'to give birth'. Do not humans sometimes value Earth's life-supporting systems because they are valuable, and not always the other way round?

True, humans are the only evaluators who can reflect about what is going on in animals, plants, species lines, over evolutionary history, or at global scales, or who can deliberate about what they ought to do conserving it. When humans do this, they must set up the scales; and humans are the measurers of things. Animals, organisms, species, ecosystems, Earth, cannot teach us how to do this evaluating. But they can display what it is that is to be valued. The axiological scales we construct do not constitute the value, any more than the scientific scales we erect create what we thereby measure. Humans are not so much lighting up value in a merely potentially valuable world, as they are psychologically joining ongoing planetary natural history in which there is value wherever there is positive creativity. An axiological ethics ought to optimize the value levels and diversity on Earth, both natural and cultural. To put this theologically, humans are trustees, as well as stewards with dominion.

At depth, such an Earth ethics asks whether the European Enlightenment is compatible with the emerging ecological movement, both theoretically and practically. Science, technology, industry, democracy, human rights, freedom, preference satisfaction, maximizing benefits over costs, consumerism – all these 'management ethics' are outcomes of the Enlightenment world view. And they are all seriously implicated as causes of the environmental crisis. Much of the enthusiastic humanism that the Enlightenment stood for has been a good thing in modern times; but today, with an environmental turn, it needs to be ecologically chastened. Ethics needs to become postmodern.

Development in the West has been based on the Enlightenment myth of endless growth. But in the United States and Europe, whether one considers agricultural development, forests cut, rivers dammed and diverted for water, lands fenced, minerals extracted, or highways and subdivisions built, the next hundred years cannot be like the last hundred years. None of the developed nations have yet settled into a sustainable culture on their landscapes.

On these scales 'sustainable' also means 'fair' or 'just', an ethics of eco-justice. On Earth, the developed nations hold about one-fifth of the world's 5 billion persons, and they produce and consume about four-fifths of all goods and services. The underdeveloped nations, with four-fifths of the world's people, produce and consume one-fifth. Of the 90 million new people on Earth each year, 85 million appear in the Third World, the countries least able to support them, and the result is poverty and environmental degradation in a feedback loop. Meanwhile, the 5 million new people in the industrial countries will put as much strain on the environment as the 85 million new poor.

The over-consumption problem in the developed nations is linked with the under-consumption problem in the developing nations, and this results in increasing environmental degradation in both sets of nations. Sustainable development must close the gap between the rich and the poor, between and also within nations. Even if there were an equitable distribution of wealth, the human population cannot go on escalating without people becoming more and more poor, because the pie has to be constantly divided into smaller pieces. Even if there were no future population growth, consumption patterns cannot go on escalating on a finite Earth. There are three problems: over-population, over-consumption, and under-distribution.

Once the mark of an educated and ethical person could be summed up as *civitas*, the privileges, rights and responsibilities of citizenship. People ought to be upright and moral, productive in their communities, leaders in business, the professions, government, church, education. That was the responsibility that went with one's rights. The mark of a virtuous person today, increasingly, is something more – so environmental ethicists claim. It is not enough to be a good 'citizen', for that is only half the truth; we are 'residents' dwelling on landscapes. A century ago, a call for community was typically phrased as the brotherhood of man and the fatherhood of God. For most of the twentieth century the call was phrased as justice and human rights. In this century such a call must be more ecological and less paternalistic, less humanistic and more global. We are expanding ethics: it is not just what a society does to its slaves, women, blacks, minorities, handicapped, children or future generations, but what it does to its fauna, flora, species, ecosystems and landscapes that reveals the character of that society. We humans are Earthlings and care for the Earth is a developing and an ultimate human virtue.

References

Complete lists of anthologies and systematic works may be found on the International Society for Environmental Ethics website bibliography, under 'Anthologies' and 'Systematic Works'. There is also a list of 'Introductory Articles' and syllabuses of courses at colleges and universities: http://www.cep.unt.edu/ISEE.html

Journals: *Environmental Ethics, Environmental Values, Ethics and the Environment, Journal of Agricultural and Environmental Ethics.*

Botzler, R. G. and Armstrong, S. J. (eds) 1998: *Environmental Ethics: Divergence and Convergence*, 2nd edn. New York: McGraw Hill.

Collins, M. 1980: Foreword. In R. A. Gallant, *Our Universe*. Washington, DC: National Geographic Society.

Des Jardins, J. R. 1997: *Environmental Ethics: An Introduction to Environmental Philosophy*, 2nd edn. Belmont, CA: Wadsworth.

Johnson, L. E. 1991: *A Morally Deep World: An Essay on Moral Significance and Environmental Ethics*. Cambridge: Cambridge University Press.

Leopold, A. 1969 [1949]: *A Sand County Almanac*. New York: Oxford University Press.

Norton, B. G. 1991: *Toward Unity Among Environmentalists*. New York: Oxford University Press.

Pojman, L. P. (ed.) 2001: *Environmental Ethics: Readings in Theory and Application*, 3rd edn. Belmont, CA: Wadsworth.

Sale, K. 1985: *Dwellers in the Land: The Bioregional Vision*. San Francisco: Sierra Club.

Serres, M. 1995: *The Natural Contract*. Ann Arbor: University of Michigan Press.

United Nations Conference on Environment and Development 1992: *The Rio Declaration*. UNCED Document A/CONF.151/5/Rev. 1, June 13.

United Nations World Commission on Environment and Development 1987a: *Our Common Future*. Oxford: Oxford University Press.

United Nations World Commission on Environment and Development 1987b: *Environmental Protection and Sustainable Development: Legal Principles and Recommendations*. London/Dordrecht: Graham and Trotman/Martinus Nijhoff.

Discussion Questions

1   Are humans the only valuable, valuing agents in an otherwise value-free world?

2   Do philosophers have a special role in the development of environmental ethics?

3   Do values arise only with the interests and preferences of humans?

4   Is humanistic philosophy necessarily anthropocentric?

5   How similar is the inseparability of culture and nature to the inseparability of minds and bodies?

6   Do humans need to include nature in their ethics and need to include themselves in nature?

7   Do humans have serious duties only to each other?

8   Are there ethical concerns that go beyond the scope of a social contract?

9   Is the health of the environment of ethical importance as well as the health of human beings within the environment?

10   What weight should environmental ethics give to the values of animals? Who should represent these concerns?

11   What distinguishes an animal rights ethic from an animal welfare ethic?

12   Does kinship to humans give animals moral standing?

13   How can we determine whether the widening circles of ethical concern end with reciprocating moral agents?

14   Does evolutionary success make animal life a good thing?

15   Can we value kinds of experience that we cannot share?

16   What justifies giving moral value to non-sentient living things?

17   Is the biological identity of individuals or species enough to justify moral concern?

18   Plants can thrive or fall ill, and they function to preserve their life or their species. Does this give them moral standing?

19 Are spontaneous natural lives of value in themselves?
20 Do we have duties to species?
21 If the type is more important than the token for animal and plant species, is the same true for the human species? What would be the social and political consequences of this view?
22 Is the fundamental unit of development and survival the appropriate unit for moral concern?
23 How would greater moral sensitivity to the environment affect human social, political and economic systems?
24 Who would be parties to a 'natural contract' that might supplement a social contract?
25 Is an ecological ethic a matter of argument or vision?
26 If Enlightenment values are incompatible with the ecological movement, which should be supported?
27 How might justice and sustainable development be related?

19

Business Ethics

GEORGES ENDERLE

Business and economics have become major driving forces in contemporary societies, in both the national and the international context. Combined with modern technologies, they shape thought and behaviour and have increasing impact on many domains of life: research and development, telecommunications, biotechnology, politics, education, culture, religion and the family. The greater the influence of business and economics, the greater the urgency to ensure that they develop in the right direction. Guidance for business and economics must come from both 'outside' and 'inside': from outside in terms of political pressure, legal regulations, socio-cultural customs and learning; from inside in terms of proactive behaviour of business organizations and business people, self-regulation of industries and business alliances. The outside approach alone cannot achieve this guidance because it lacks the inner commitment of business, but the inside approach is also insufficient because business is only a single part of society and needs additional outside control and guidance. However, the inside approach is becoming more important as economic actors enjoy more freedom and thus bear more responsibility.

1 Introduction

That business and economics should develop 'in the right direction' is a way to express the ethical dimension inherent in this domain. At stake is not only moral practice but also ethical reflection and theory, or 'business and economic ethics' as academic inquiry. The further that globalization advances, the greater and more complex the practical and theoretical challenges become. Until now, the achievements of business ethics have fallen considerably short of what is required. Global transformations are highly complex processes that are incomplete and are poorly understood in their depth and consequences for both global and local societies. From the ethical perspective as well, the challenges are awesome. The questions concern not only intersocietal relations (see Rawls 1999), but also person-to-person relations in multiple institutions across national borders (see Sen 1999b). Business ethics must come to grips with cultural and religious pluralism worldwide within countries and cultures and strive for a common ethical ground in facing common challenges (see *A Global Ethic* 1993; Küng 1998).

Given our current situation, it is advisable to approach business and economic ethics in a global context. However valuable the approaches in particular countries and cultures may be, they have not matched the needs of a globalizing world. For example, Frederick's impressive *A Companion to Business Ethics* (1999) overwhelmingly reflects a US approach, and *Handbuch der Wirtschaftsethik* (Korff et al. 1999) is strongly shaped by German thinking. These contributions are important, but their use is seriously limited outside their home environment.

In contrast, a worldwide survey for the First World Congress of Business, Economics, and Ethics 1996 in Tokyo sought the material from which to develop a comparative conceptual framework to determine the challenges, initiatives and achievements in the emerging field of business ethics (*Journal of Business Ethics*, October 1997). The need for such a framework has been especially felt by those conducting research and teaching business ethics simultaneously in different countries and cultures. This chapter will introduce a conceptual framework for business ethics and then chart the current contours of the field. Finally, it will discuss different theoretical approaches to business ethics before a few concluding remarks.

2   A Conceptual Framework for Business Ethics

The development of a conceptual framework that accommodates different approaches to business ethics can overcome widespread confusion in the field and promote useful dialogue. By concentrating on the interface between empirical and theoretical studies, it can avoid many theoretical controversies, offer strategies for empirical investigations and provide grounding for operationalization and measurement.

A conceptual framework is neither a full-fledged body of knowledge nor a blueprint. Nevertheless, it provides a consistent organization of the key elements, relations and terms of the field under investigation. It can be used by different theoretical approaches and can be specified in a wide variety of ways. It has theoretical implications concerning, for example, the relationship between theory and practice, the philosophical foundations of ECONOMICS (pp. 388–9), the moral status of economic organizations and anthropological assumptions about the MIND–BODY RELATIONSHIP (chapter 5).

Business ethics is a kind of APPLIED ETHICS (chapter 16) and shares common features with other kinds of applied ethics, such as BIOETHICS AND MEDICAL ETHICS (chapter 17), legal ethics, engineering ethics, media ethics and computer ethics. At the same time, approaches to applied ethics and business ethics vary considerably according to different conceptions of ethics, the fields of application and the ways of conceiving the relationship between the ethics and the field.

The conceptual framework developed here relates business ethics to decision-making and action and distinguishes among descriptive ethics, normative ethics and meta-ethics, with a special focus on NORMATIVE ETHICS (pp. 201–4). As a conceptual framework, it does not advance a particular ethical theory, but places much emphasis on the structuring of the field of business ethics and uses a two-legged approach to characterize the relationship between ethics and business.

'Business ethics' is not clearly defined because 'business' itself has various meanings. This can lead to serious misunderstandings, especially when translated into other

Table 19.1   Questionnaire for country- and region-related reports on business ethics

---

1   Semantics of business ethics
What are *key terms* in your country/region to express ethical issues in business? What is the prevailing understanding, definition and field of business ethics?

2   What are major challenges of business ethics in your country/region?
Broad issues? Specific issues? Relevance of *cultural* and *religious* traditions? Impact of *international* business? What are *major reasons* to address these challenges?

3   Business ethics activities in the business world
- What *endeavours* of business people, companies and business associations have been undertaken? Setting up and dissemination of codes of conduct? Ethics training programmes? Positions of ethics officers or the like? Public statements and publications of business leaders? Legislation?
- Are, and if so how are, domestic and foreign companies *evaluated* from an ethical point of view? By consumers, workers, investors and other groups and organizations?
- What expectations, criticisms and requirements are raised by a *broader public*, e.g. governments, political and educational organizations, non-governmental organizations, churches, etc.?
- What are *major reasons* for conducting these business ethics activities? What major factors hinder such activities?

4   Business ethics activities in academia
- What *institutional forms* of business ethics have been established? Chairs, institutes, centres, networks, associations, etc.? Surveys, publications about this institutional aspect?
- What *teaching* activities have been undertaken? Elective and mandatory courses, interdisciplinary seminars, integration in the students' curricula? Surveys, publications about teaching business ethics?
- What *research* activities have been conducted? Surveys, publications about research in business ethics?
- What *consulting* activities have been carried out? Surveys, publications on consulting activities?
- What *paradigm* (conception) of business ethics is involved in these activities?

5   What are common tasks of business and academia in the field of business ethics?
Do they face common challenges? What common challenges? What kind of competences can and does each side bring in?

6   Relationship to business ethics in other countries and regions
What experiences in, and insights from, business practice and academia can your country/region *offer to* people working in business ethics in other countries and regions? What lessons can your country/region *learn from* other countries and regions?

Source: *Journal of Business Ethics*, October 1997, 1477.

languages and cultures. For instance, the famous saying 'The business of business is business' is puzzling for people who are not conversant with English. Because 'business' stands for 'the task or job', 'the economic organization' and 'to make profit', the slogan can read 'the task of the company is to make profit'. However, in terms such as 'business cycle', 'business' is almost equivalent to 'the economy', so that 'business ethics' can be understood as a very broad notion that is comparable to 'economic ethics', the German *Wirtschaftsethik* and the Spanish *ética Económica*. The increasingly used expression 'corporate ethics' concerns the ethics of business organizations as well as ethics in business organization (Berenbeim 1987).

In this chapter, we shall understand 'business ethics' in a broad sense, covering the whole economic domain of life. Understood in this way, business ethics deals with the individual decision-making of economic actors (such as managers and employees), the shaping and conduct of economic organizations, business-related public policies, economic systems, and global economic and financial institutions. We shall assume that this domain can be identified and distinguished reasonably well from other domains of life (such as the political–legal and the socio-cultural domain) and that each domain has a certain autonomy and type of RATIONALITY (pp. 395–7). Given this understanding, we can see that business ethics aims to improve the ethical quality of decision-making and acting at all levels of business.

From a cross-cultural perspective, it is important to distinguish three modes of understanding business ethics: *semantics, practice and theory*. Attitudes toward *speaking* about business ethics and the terms used differ significantly from one cultural setting to another. Moreover, talking about business ethics is usually not identical with ethical *conduct*. To think systematically, or *theorize*, about business ethics is important not only for theoretical reasons, such as the need for consistency, critical scrutiny and independent evaluation, but also for practical reasons, such as the need to clarify conceptual issues in practice, to offer impartial assessment of business conduct and to provide serious consultation to companies. Therefore, although these three modes are interrelated, they are distinct and cannot replace each other. However, the definitive test of the value of business ethics is practice.

2.1 Structuring the field of business ethics: a multiple-level action-oriented approach

Fundamental questions of ethics are 'What should I do?' and 'What should we do?' We are under pressure to act and cannot avoid making decisions. Decision-making and acting are an essential part of human existence. As Alan Gewirth states, 'the independent variable of all morality is human action' (Gewirth 1984: 12). In our pluralistic societies, we face a host of different ethical beliefs and theories. Whether we hold strong convictions on HUMAN RIGHTS (pp. 31–4), believe in the overriding power of SELF-INTEREST (pp. 761–3), adopt a position of ETHICAL RELATIVISM (pp. 395–7) or are sceptical about ethics as a whole, we must make decisions and take actions. We propose an action-oriented approach to business ethics, which takes account of both the *actors* and the *structures* in which they are embedded.

Action involves FREEDOM OF CHOICE (pp. 206–8). We can choose from among different courses of action while being subject to constraints. Actions are never limitless, without boundaries, and the limitations are often the results of previous choices. For example, market conditions and laws and regulations constrain the actions of economic actors who face them and cannot change them immediately. But these human-made constraints are largely the outcome of preceding decision-making processes. Freedom relates both to choice *within* constraints and to choice of constraints (how

534

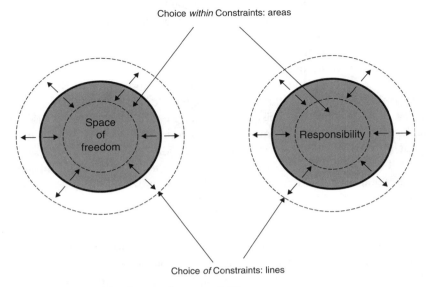

Choice *within* Constraints: areas

Choice *of* Constraints: lines

Figure 19.1 Space of freedom and responsibility.

actors shape the conditions and limitations of their future actions). Both sets of circumstances are essential to a conceptual framework for business ethics (see figure 19.1).

Decisions and actions always are concrete, meaning that they are exposed to the complexities of life. Decision-makers face complex choices with far-reaching consequences that are difficult to foresee and evaluate. They cannot content themselves with analysing different options and determining the conditions of good decisions because they must (as the Chinese say for doing business) 'jump into the sea': make decisions and take actions. Yet concrete human actions characteristically need theory in reaching 'real' decisions and actions. 'Good practice' needs 'good theory' in business ethics as well as in other domains.

Choices *within* constraints and choices *of* constraints necessarily involve an ethical dimension that can be articulated in terms of ethical beliefs and ethical theories. For the purpose of our conceptual framework, we shall introduce the key term, 'responsibility'. Although responsibility does not cover the full range of ethical values and norms, it is a key notion of contemporary morality and has complex practical and theoretical aspects (see Fischer 1986, 1999; French 1984; Glover 1970; Jonas 1984; *Social Philosophy and Policy* 1999). We shall assume that the extent of responsibility is a function of the extent of freedom: the bigger one's space of freedom, the bigger one's responsibility (see figure 19.1). Reflecting the traditional ethical principle 'ought implies can', the determination of the space of freedom of economic actors is crucial for allocating their responsibilities. This concrete notion of 'space of freedom' comes close to Sen's (1999a) concept of a set of real freedoms or 'capabilities' and to the definition of 'human development' as 'enlarg[ing] people's choices' (UNDP 1990: 10).

535

In order to identify the subjects of responsibility as concretely as possible, three different levels of acting are proposed, each of which includes actors with their respective objectives, interests and motivations: the micro-level, meso-level and macro-level. At the *micro-level* the focus is on the *individual*, that is, what actors, as employee or employer, colleague or manager, consumer, supplier or investor, do, can do and ought to do in order to perceive and assume their ethical responsibility. At this level we also consider groups, composed of small numbers of individuals and without organizational structures, making collective decisions and taking collective actions. At the *meso-level* we consider the decision-making and action of economic *organizations*, chiefly business firms, but also trade unions, consumer organizations and professional associations. Finally, at the *macro-level* we consider the *economic system* as such and the shaping of the overall economic conditions of business: the economic order with its multiple institutions and economic, financial and social policies.

At each level the actors are assumed to have spaces of freedom for decision-making with corresponding ethical responsibilities and to be limited by constraints that they cannot change, at least for the time being. No level can substitute for another. Even if all problems at one level were satisfactorily solved, problems at the other levels could remain. This three-level conception, adopted by various business ethics scholars (for example, Goodpaster 1992; Solomon 1993), contrasts with the common distinction between the micro-level and macro-level in economics and sociology (see, for example, Coleman 1990). According to the three-level conception, the individual person is explicitly addressed as moral actor, differing from the decision-maker in micro-economics and micro-sociology. The business organization is considered to be a moral actor, too, although of a special nature. The emphasis of the meso-level expresses the enormous importance of organizations in modern societies and is supported by the New Economics of Organization, which draws a basic distinction between markets and organizations (see Williamson 1985, 1990). Note also the distinction between institutions and organizations. For instance, the institution of the American corporation at the macro-level includes the essential features of all American corporations (Bellah et al. 1992: 3–18), while an individual American corporation, with its particular identity, culture and conduct, is an organization at the meso-level. The central point of this three-level conception is to perceive the links between decision-making, acting and responsibility as concretely as possible and to provide conceptual room for addressing the differences and conflicts of objectives, interests and motivations which are located at the interfaces between different levels. We can ask at each level what can be done and what ought to be done. Under pressure to act, single actors cannot push their responsibility onto other actors, nor can responsibility be delegated from one level to another. When corporate ethics are at stake, the problem must not be personalized or pushed to the system level. If we take concrete decision-making and acting seriously, we do not ask in the first place how other individuals, companies or economic systems ought to behave. Rather the question must be: how I, how my company and how my economic system can perceive and assume ethical responsibility.

Nevertheless, acting responsibly at all levels can require ethical displacement, a technique of resolving a dilemma, or sometimes solving an ethical problem, by seeking a solution on a level other than the one on which the dilemma or problem appears (De George 1993: 97). For example, in order to prevent sexual harassment, an explicit corporate policy and a sustained corporate culture (at the meso-level) might be necessary if a change of attitude and behaviour by individual actors (at the micro-level) is not sufficient. If such organizations and institutions at higher levels do not exist (as is the case in dealing with many international problems), it might be necessary to create them.

Until now the three-level conception has been applied to the national economy or economic domain of life. Given the increasing importance of international issues, we can change this conception, for example by adding an international level or by superimposing a global level under which all issues are subsumed. We propose, however, an extended three-level model to provide sufficient conceptual room for several types of international relations at different levels of acting in the emerging world economy and to identify the actors and their responsibilities in the international context.

In developing our extended conception we must understand the borders between national and international matters at all three levels. At the micro-level special attention is paid to personal (inner-group) relations and responsibilities across national borders; for example, cross-national groups of managers and employees or cross-national families. At the meso-level the focus is on inner-organizational relations and responsibilities across national borders; for example, multinational corporations, international trade unions or consumer organizations. The macro-level includes inner-systemic relations and responsibilities across national borders, incorporated, for instance, in bilateral agreements, regional treaties or global institutions like the World Trade Organization.

Borders can be permeable in various degrees. At one extreme is hermetic seclusion, which characterized the former communist Albania *vis-à-vis* its neighbours; at the other extreme is the complete abolition of all borders and total openness, as proposed by some proponents of globalization. Intermediate states give a differentiated picture of international relations and encompass all cross-national variants, including both imminent conflicts and opportunities for co-operation between various actors. These variants can be classified in four types of international relations: the foreign country type; empire type; interconnection type; and globalization type. Although these types can be found at all three levels, the explanations below refer mainly to the macro-level.

The *foreign country* type is exemplified by the relationship between a small economy or small company and a foreign country, for example Switzerland or Schläpfer Embroideries with Nigeria. The international relations differ significantly from domestic relations and have no relevant repercussions on them. The international relations are added to the national framework and can be relatively easily detached from it. Each country is different. Foreigners have to adapt themselves to the host country, and national borders are relatively impermeable.

Examples of the *empire* type are the relationship between Great Britain and India during British colonialism, and the United Fruit Company in Central America. This type characterizes international relations as a pure cross-national expansion of domestic relations without modification. From the host country's perspective, the asymmetric power relationship often involves misunderstanding, exploitation and repression. Repercussions on the home country are negligible, since national borders are much more permeable from the home to the host country than in the opposite direction.

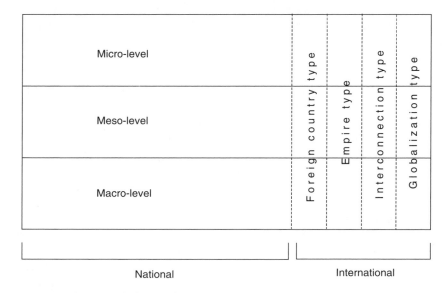

Figure 19.2 National / International

Figure 19.2 The extended three-level conception of business ethics.

The *interconnection* type can be illustrated by the relationship between Italy and the European Union. International relations differ significantly from domestic relations, but are intrinsically interconnected with them. What is beyond national borders has impact on domestic relations and domestic relations have impact on the international relations. Interdependence blurs the notion of a national interest that disregards the interests of other nations and supranational entities. Although they are still important, national borders are pervious to some extent in both directions.

In the *globalization* type, exemplified by global warming, international relations are so important that national borders become irrelevant. Citizens become cosmopolitan; multinational firms become global; and nation-states fade away. This type can in principle comprehend the whole Earth, although until now it is mainly confined to parts of the northern hemisphere.

The proposed typology of international relations (see Enderle and Kamm 2000) can be visualized in figure 19.2. It is easy to figure out the multiple possible combinations of types and levels with their spatio-temporal overlaps and conflicts. The extended three-level conception of business ethics provides a framework to locate the plural affiliations (Sen 1999b) of the economic actors in the current global context.

2.2 The relationship between ethics and business

Business ethics as applied ethics has to reflect on the relationship between ethics and the field of application. From the perspective of the action-oriented approach, equal importance should be given to understanding business and economics and understanding the reasoned ethical orientation. The cognitive and the normative dimensions of the subject matter should be distinguished, but if they are split into two separate realities, business ethics from 'inside' would be impossible. Either the relationship would remain external, or the distinguishing boundary between the cognitive and normative would be blurred, rendering both factual and normative statements meaningless.

In business practice the two dimensions are generally accepted. When a manager faces the problem of soil pollution, for instance, he has to know the nature, causes and possible remedies of this ENVIRONMENTAL HARM (chapter 18), along with the costs involved and legal requirements. In addition, he applies normative standards: whether to follow the principle of sustainable business, whether to respect environmental regulations, and so on. Similarly, when a company struggles with a corrupt business environment, it needs sound ethical guidelines, but also needs to understand the kinds and mechanisms of corruption in order to choose an effective strategy for dealing with this corrupt environment.

In academia, however, the situation seems to be different. While the descriptive–analytical perspective is extensively scrutinized, normative–ethical questions have attracted less attention. These questions relate to the VALUES AND NORMS (pp. 202–4) which ought to guide business decisions and actions and the ways to provide rational justification for these values and norms. Normative ethics is a philosophical undertaking (see Kagan 1998) that faces urgent issues in the context of complex pluralistic societies. In countering widespread acceptance of ETHICAL RELATIVISM (pp. 395–7), it goes beyond the instrumental notions of the normative commonly used in academic business disciplines, such as developing the most efficient strategy to achieve the norm of profit maximization or maximizing the social welfare function within a given utilitarian framework.

The Two-Legged Approach

The two-legged approach gives equal importance to the cognitive and normative dimensions and strives to integrate them in a balanced way. By doing so, it affects the understanding of both business and ethics. Structuring the field of business ethics in this way poses numerous complex questions to ethics, such as the moral status of organizations and systems, the relationship between personal, organizational and systemic ethics, the legitimacy of particular ethical theories in the global context, and the foundation of a global ethic. Business ethics challenges the paradigms of the business disciplines. If management theory, marketing, accountancy, economics and finance are value-free, an integration of cognitive and normative dimensions within the disciplines is excluded, and ethics, at best, has an external role to play. If these paradigms incorporate a normative dimension that is open to ethical reasoning, the integration can be effected from within. Of course, business disciplines are not thereby transformed into ethical disciplines, but they provide bridgeheads into ethics.

Amartya Sen's (1987) distinction between the engineering approach and the ethics-related approach can help us to understand the value of the two-legged approach. The engineering approach primarily focuses on logistical issues: what means should one choose in order to achieve as efficiently as possible, under very simple behavioural assumptions, goals that are given from elsewhere? The ethics-related approach involves a broader understanding of economics and other business disciplines. It also comprehends problems of human motivation and the judgement of social achievements that cannot be disconnected from the ethical questions of the good and the just: how should one live and what is a just society? If business disciplines embrace these questions, the integration of the cognitive and normative dimensions becomes possible within them.

The work of Amartya Sen, the 1998 Nobel Laureate in Economics, shows that such an approach can be consistently developed (see, particularly, Sen 1999b). His scholarship in both ethics and economics is outstanding, but he also explores with great sophistication the interfaces between them and the building of bridges that help the different perspectives interact. Another prominent scholar, Arthur Rich, has pioneered business and economic ethics in German-speaking countries. The guiding principle of his *Wirtschaftsethik* is: 'That which is not economically rational cannot really be humanly just, and that which conflicts with human justice cannot really be economically rational' (Rich 1984: 81).

3 Charting the Emerging Field of Business Ethics

To present the state of business ethics today is a difficult undertaking. Compared to the situation in 1990, hosts of publications in many languages, from scholarly works to corporate statements, have appeared and cannot be fully surveyed. Nevertheless, many recent surveys and encyclopedias are available, and our extended three-level conception may help to organize our presentation.

The most extensive overview in geographic terms can be found in the special issue of the *Journal of Business Ethics*, October 1997, which includes 13 region- and country-related reports on business ethics with extended lists of literature. The reports show that business ethics is an emerging and dynamic field, depending on economic factors, political changes and an awareness of value-conflicts and ethical and environmental demands. Because it is an emerging field, it is much more difficult than in an established field to capture the lasting features of business ethics and to foresee their likely development. Each country and each region has its own business ethics history. Some, like the US and Canada, are old-timers (if 25 years can be called old), and some, like China and South Africa, are 'newcomers'. Of course, such an observation implies a certain understanding of business ethics and does not mean that ethical issues in business and the economy had not arisen before.

From the rich findings of the reports, only a few striking features can be highlighted here. A first characteristic is the relevance of semantics. Because ethical issues in business are not merely rational puzzles, but are deeply rooted in emotions and cultures, the ways of speaking about ethics and the use and meaning of ethical terms are strongly affected by emotional and cultural factors. For instance, the Japanese terms for economy (*keizai*) and business (*keiei*) are not value-free, but already contain a normative ethical component, namely governing the world in harmony (*kei*) and making ceaseless efforts to achieve [these purposes] (*ei*). As a consequence, Japanese business ethics can have a very broad scope and includes different moral agents at various levels of economic activity. In a narrower sense, preferred by many business ethicists in Japan, the term relates to corporate ethics.

A second feature concerns the enormous variety of business environments that are shaped by the historical and societal conditions of countries and regions and, in many cases, by recent dramatic changes. The transition from communist regimes to democracies and market economies in Central and Eastern Europe and Russia, the nearly twenty years of economic reform in China, the abolition of apartheid rule and the building of democracy without discrimination in South Africa, are developments which have far-reaching implications for the specific role of business ethics in these environments. If we ignore these systemic differences at the macro-level, the challenge of business ethics for corporations at the meso-level cannot be understood.

Among the large number of specific business ethics issues mentioned in the reports, corruption, leadership and corporate responsibility attract particular attention. The globalization of the economy has been accompanied by a globalization of *corruption*. Its elimination is considered the most significant challenge for many countries because corruption profoundly affects business relations (meso-level), individual decision-makers (micro-level) and whole economies (macro-level). Numerous reports emphasize the need for a new generation of business leaders. They are considered to be a crucial instrument for implementing organizational integrity through management-driven self-governance programmes in which company values and aspirations play a critical role. Leaders have to incorporate this vision. In spite of broad systemic challenges, the reporters from the countries of Mahatma Gandhi and Nelson Mandela stressed the importance of individual ethics, personal character and integrity.

Not surprisingly, the reports discuss a wide range of issues regarding corporate ethics in the national as well as international context. They raise issues of corporate responsibility concerning the conduct, culture and structure of business organizations (at the meso-level), and these clearly differ from issues at the systemic and individual levels. One of the most common themes in the business ethics literature of North America concerns stakeholder obligations and stakeholder theory and has gained wide international interest. Another export of ideas, from the Cadbury Report in the United Kingdom, concerns corporate governance and has influenced Australia and South Africa in different ways. Finally, deregulation and a growing civil society has intensified the call for effective ways to hold companies accountable, nationally and internationally.

Topic areas of international business ethics were identified and discussed at the First and Second ISBEE World Congress of Business, Economics, and Ethics, 1996 in Tokyo, and 2000 in São Paulo (see Enderle 1999 and ISBEE website at www.isbee.org). Also, many overviews have appeared. *Business Ethics: A European Review* has published a number of European country reports. The *Journal of Business Ethics* has dedicated a whole issue to Spain (1999). *Business Ethics Quarterly* has celebrated its 10th anniversary with a collection of over thirty, mostly US contributions (January 2000). Werhane and Singer (1999) present contributions from Asia and New Zealand. Enderle (1996) compares business ethics in North America and continental Europe and surveys business and corporate ethics in the USA (Enderle 1999). Barkhuysen and Rossouw (2000) report on business ethics as an academic field in Africa. And 'Trends of business ethics in Latin America' were presented at the ISBEE Congress in São Paulo (Arruda 2000).

While surveys and overviews can only introduce one to the field, encyclopedic works can dig deeper and reflect more comprehensive and elaborate conceptions of the field. The 1990s have brought several major works: in the USA, the *Encyclopedic Dictionary of Business Ethics* (Werhane and Freeman 1997), *A Companion to Business Ethics* (Frederick 1999) and the *Encyclopedia of Ethics* (Becker and Becker 1992), with many entries on business and economic ethics; in German-speaking countries, the *Lexikon der Wirtschaftsethik* (Encyclopedia of Business Ethics) (Enderle et al. 1993) and the four-volume *Handbuch der Wirtschaftsethik* (Handbook of Business Ethics) (Korff et al. 1999). Although we cannot provide a thorough comparison between the US and German approaches incorporated in these works, a few remarks might be of interest (see also Enderle 1996).

Four differences between the US (and Canadian) approach and the German (and continental European) approach stand out. First, business ethics in the USA chiefly deals with issues at the individual micro-level, whereas the main emphasis in German-speaking countries (and continental Europe) is on the systemic macro-level. North Americans address an increasing number of issues at the organizational meso-level, but rarely discuss issues at the macro-level. In contrast, Germans are only beginning to be interested in the meso-level of the organization.

Secondly, the US approach emphasizes the freedom and responsibilities of decision-making and acting, with the tendency to overlook their limitations. The German approach underlines the importance of shaping business conditions in an ethically responsible way and tends not to make full use of existing spaces of freedom.

Thirdly, the US approach to business ethics is much more practical than the German one, at least with regard to the micro-level and the meso-level, whereas continental Europeans tend to focus on theoretical issues before addressing, if ever, practical challenges.

Fourthly, there is a multitude of views on an appropriate paradigm of business ethics, and neither North America nor continental Europe has a well-established discipline of business ethics. While academics in German-speaking and Scandinavian countries are likely to be more concerned about the cognitive dimension of business ethics that incorporates the contributions of business disciplines, North American academics deal much more directly and openly with normative issues.

4   Theoretical Approaches to Business Ethics

The discussion of various theoretical approaches to business ethics can be organized according to the extended three-level conception and the cognitive and normative dimensions of the two-legged approach.

4.1   *Foundational issues: productive interdisciplinary communication*

Contrary to a widespread European perception, foundational issues of business and economic ethics have been extensively discussed in English-speaking countries too, though in different forms and beyond narrowly defined business ethics circles. Testimony to this discussion are contributions to the review *Economics and Philosophy*, large parts of Sen's work, the survey 'Taking Ethics Seriously: Economics and Contemporary Moral Philosophy' in the *Journal of Economic Literature* (Hausman and McPherson 1993) and substantive introductions like *Economic Analysis and Moral Philosophy*

Table 19.2 Dissimilarities of business ethics in North America and continental Europe

		North America	*Continental Europe*
1	Semantics	One language (basically) Easy talk about BE	Multiple languages Reluctant talk about BE
2	Level (actor)-focus	MICRO, meso	MACRO, micro
3	Outreach-dimension	Less international	More international
4	Choice parameters	Free choice of actors (choice within constraints)	Constraints of actors (choice of constraints)
5	Arguments for BE	Arguments of scandals and 'good business'	Argument of economization
6	Practice-focus	Strong	Weak
7	Paradigm of BE	Clear normative orientation	Connection with social sciences
8	Teaching BE	Wide acceptance in business schools; beginning integration into curriculum	Beginning efforts; no general acceptance and no integration into curriculum
9	Corporate initiatives	Widespread dissemination of codes of conduct; increasing positions of ethics officers and ethics training programmes	Fair, increasing dissemination of codes of conduct; few ethics training programmes; no ethics officers
10	Role of business ethicists	Teaching mainly future managers; more practice- oriented research; increasing consulting activities	Teaching students in various disciplines; less practice- oriented research; consulting has just begun

Source: Enderle (1996).

(Hausman and McPherson 1996). Following Sen's notion of an ethics-related approach, three broad topic areas can be distinguished. The first topic area, dealing with human motivation, concerns rationality and morality: rationality and utility theory; rationality in positive and normative economics; and rationality, norms and morality. The second topic area, dealing with judgements about social arrangements, concerns evaluating economic and social institutions, policies and outcomes: the informational basis of evaluation; welfare, efficiency, utilitarianism and consequentialism; and liberty, rights, equality and justice. A third topic area, using an engineering approach, deals with moral mathematics, particularly social choice theory and game theory.

In German-speaking countries, the discussion of foundational issues has a long history going back to the 'Historische Schule' in the 'Verein für Socialpolitik' [Historical School of Thought in the German Economic Association] and theoretical struggles in the early twentieth century. In the mid-1980s this professional association established its own Economics and Ethics Division, which has published a series of books with contributions on foundational problems. Moreover, the *Handbuch der Wirtschaftsethik* (Korff et al. 1999) dedicates its entire first volume to determining the relationship between business/economics and ethics. It covers topics from the essential components of modern business ethics (such as work, property and technology) to political–structural implications of modern economies. It also presents various approaches of contemporary business ethicists in German-speaking countries.

Despite the variety of approaches in both scholarly groups, the overall situation can be summarized as follows: 'In the last twenty years, economists and moral philosophers have renewed a conversation that was interrupted during the heyday of positivist methodology in both disciplines. Although there remain considerable gaps between both modes of expression and habits of thought of moral philosophers and economists . . . we hope our presentation has also shown that there is considerable room for productive interdisciplinary communication' (Hausman and McPherson 1993: 723).

4.2   Features of the economic system

At the macro-level we can present a few key features from the focus on the economic system. These features apply not only to closed economies without international relations, but also to economies with different types of inner-systemic relations across national borders. According to the prevailing view in modern theory of economic systems (Kromphardt 1990), we cannot properly characterize an economic system by one single criterion, such as capital as the property regime or the market as the allocation regime. Rather, three sets of criteria are necessary:

1   Ownership and decision-making: who participates in the process of economic decision-making? Who plans and controls production, distribution and consumption, for example, through a high concentration of economic power or a broad participatory economy?
2   Information and co-ordination: with the help of what information system are the individual decisions co-ordinated, for example, by decentralized markets or centralized planning?
3   Motivation: what objectives motivate the various decision-makers; for example, self-interest, the common good or loyalty? Which ways are chosen to implement economic decisions and what type of behaviour is expected?

Only if all three criteria are treated in a balanced manner, can the economic system be adequately understood and ethically evaluated.

The study of economic history can further clarify the notion of the economic system. As North states, two dimensions make up the economy from the historical perspective: '(1) the overall growth of the economy over time and the determinants of that growth (or stagnation or decline) and (2) the distribution of income within that economy in the course of its growth or decline' (North 1972: 468). Both dimensions, the productive and the distributive, are equally important and closely related to each other. This holds true at the macro-level and, with appropriate modifications, also at the meso-level and micro-level. Countries which achieved the 'East Asian Miracle' (World Bank 1993) paid much attention to the interplay between productive and distributive aspects, and many difficulties of economic development in Latin America and the Caribbean can be explained by the neglect of the distributive dimension, that is, by ignoring poverty and inequality as impediments to growth (ECLAC 1999). That the economy is not only a productive system but also includes distribution as an integral part has raised fundamental issues in regional and global economic affairs; for example, the hotly debated distributional problems in the context of the North American Free Trade Area, the European Union, the World Trade Organization and globalization in general.

In addition, the clear articulation of the economic system can prevent the short-sighted equation of the economy with markets and private goods. The theory of public economics (Auerbach and Feldstein 1987) goes far beyond markets and private goods by dealing with public goods, taxation, income maintenance, social insurance and other issues. In the international context too, public goods are becoming a crucial issue (Kaul, Grunberg and Stern 1999; Enderle and Kamm 2000). Therefore, business ethics, if restricted to market morality, is doomed to miss an essential part of the economy.

A final remark concerns the role of the economic system (macro-level) and its relationship with the economic actors at the organizational (meso-level) and individual levels (micro-level). If one assumes that the economic system fully determines all actors and actions in the economic domain (as in the mechanistic paradigm and in Luhmann 1988), there is no need to pay attention to the meso-level and micro-level. However, if we assume that there are extended spaces of freedom at all levels, the actors have relative autonomy and responsibility. This does not minimize the importance of the macro-level, because at this level the main institutions and ground rules of the economy are defined and anchored. With the internationalization of business, systemic issues of the empire, interconnection and globalization types become more important and must be aligned with similar international developments at the meso-level and micro-level.

4.3   Different approaches to corporate ethics

Business organizations have become powerful engines of economic and social change and have extended their structures and activities internationally in multiple forms. The importance of ethics in business enterprises has increased accordingly.

One important approach to corporate ethics is the stakeholder approach. Since Edward Freeman's seminal work in 1984, this approach has gathered much momentum in North America and beyond (Donaldson and Preston 1995; Näsi 1995; Clarkson 1998). Although it is a world view rather than a coherent and elaborated theory, it has found a large consensus over the rejection of a narrow conception of corporate responsibility geared only to the shareholders of the enterprise (Friedman 1970) by including other stakeholders as well. Thus the stakeholders, defined as any group and individual who can affect or are affected by the achievement of a corporation's purpose, include customers, employees, suppliers, competitors, local communities, governments and others. Because businesses are involved in relations with multiple internal and external stakeholders, they bear ethical as well as economic responsibility for shaping these relations. According to supporters of this view, this implies that the stakeholders' voices should be recognized as having some intrinsic value beyond their instrumental value for the corporation. Still, many questions remain open: what specific responsibilities have corporations towards various stakeholders? How can these responsibilities be justified and how should they be balanced? (Enderle and Tavis 1998).

Moreover, the increasing importance of business enterprises has given rise to the development and application of various theories of corporate ethics. They include a KANTIAN (chapter 32) perspective (Bowie 1999), UTILITARIANISM (chapter 35) (Snoeyenbos and Humber 1999), VIRTUE ETHICS (pp. 206–8) (Solomon 1992), a SOCIAL CONTRACT (pp. 672–7) approach (Donaldson et al. 1999), discourse ethics (Ulrich 1993, 1997), dialogue ethics (Steinmann and Löhr 1992) and others. Overviews of many of these approaches are provided by Frederick (1999). The development of corporate ethics is a relatively recent undertaking in the history of ethics and will require further effort to achieve a well-established and balanced view. Some theories (like virtue ethics) concern more the individuals in the corporation than the corporation itself, or draw no clear distinction between the micro-level and meso-level. Other theories (like the Kantian perspective and social contract theory) are fairly well developed at the meso-level, but have little foundation in the systemic level. Other theories (like discourse ethics), with strong foundations, pay too little attention to organizational issues. In addition, only a few theories explicitly address the international dimension (De George 1993; Donaldson et al. 1999; Bowie 1999).

5   Concluding Remarks

This introduction to the ongoing development of business ethics in various parts of the world shows that business ethics faces enormous practical and theoretical challenges. The further that globalization advances, the greater and more complex these challenges become, but struggling and coming to grips with them is exciting as well as urgent and demanding.

Developments in recent decades in many places justify reasonable hope for the future of the field rather than scepticism or cynicism. However, different approaches to business ethics often stand alone and barely learn from each other. Corporate ethics and an appropriate ethics-related concept of the enterprise in the global context need much more elaboration. Systemic issues should be addressed and integrated into the business ethics approaches. The importance of individual decision-making and action should be taken seriously. And the understanding of the multiple forms of international involvement of economic actors should become more sophisticated. Business ethics, too, needs global networking and globalization. The effort will yield a richer understanding that is closer to the complexity of modern business and better able to provide ethical guidance for business practice.

Further Reading

In this chapter several encyclopedic works are mentioned which provide easy access to a large variety of topics in business and economic ethics, along with rich bibliographical information (Enderle et al. 1993; Werhane and Freeman 1997; Frederick 1999; Korff et al. 1999). One can find valuable monographs and topic-related collections of articles in a number of series: the

Ruffin Series in Business Ethics by Oxford University Press (since 1989), Issues in Business Ethics by Kluwer Academic Publishers (since 1990), Studies in Economics, Ethics and Philosophy by Springer (since 1992); and in German, series in Schriften des Vereins für Socialpolitik by Duncker and Humblot (since 1985) and St. Galler Beiträge zur Wirtschaftsethik by Haupt (since 1986). Leading journals of business ethics are: *Business and Professional Ethics Journal* (since 1981), *Journal of Business Ethics* (since 1982, with a content analysis of 1,523 issues in the issue dated 1 July 2000), *Business Ethics Quarterly* (since 1991) and *Business Ethics: A European Review* (since 1992). In addition, journals of management and social sciences have begun publishing articles on business and economic ethics. A bibliography on diskette includes all business ethics articles published from 1992 to July 2001 in six major journals (Enderle and Kamm 2001).

The textbook literature, with a primary focus on corporate ethics, has developed considerably, particularly in the USA. See Boatright (1997), Buchholz and Rosenthal (1998), De George (1999), Donaldson et al. (1999), Hoffman and Frederick (1995), Shaw (1996), Weiss (1994) and Velasquez (1998). Textbooks in other countries are Sorell and Hendry (1994) (UK); Rossouw (1994) (South Africa); Van Luijk (1986) (Netherlands); Kreikebaum (1996) and Steinmann and Löhr (1992) (Germany); Staffelbach (1994) (Switzerland).

Different cultural and intercultural perspectives are addressed by Kumar and Steinmann (1998), Moorthy et al. (1998), Gasparsky and Ryan (1996), Cavanagh (1998), Frederick (1995), Pesqueux (2000), Becker (1996), Yu Xuanmeng et al. (1997) and Chakraborty (2001).

Codes of conduct are discussed from a behavioural research perspective by Messick et al. (1996) and from a global perspective by Williams (2000).

A great deal of literature, especially from North America and varying greatly in quality, deals with the ethics of and for managers and leaders. Outstanding books are Jackall (1988), Levi (1986) and Ciulla (1998).

References

A Global Ethic: The Declaration of the Parliament of World's Religions 1993: London.

Arruda, M. C. (ed.) 2000: *The Ethical Challenges of Globalization: Proceedings Latin America*. São Paulo: EAESP/FGV (see www.isbee.org).

Auerbach, A. J. and Feldstein, M. (eds) 1987: *Handbook of Public Economics*, vol. 2. Amsterdam: North-Holland.

Barkhuysen, B. and Rossouw, G. J. 2000: Business Ethics as Academic Field in Africa: A Survey of Its Current Status. Paper presented at the Second World Congress of Business, Economics, and Ethics. Website: www.nd.edu/~isbee.

Becker, G. K. 1996: *Ethics in Business and Society: Chinese and Western Perspectives*. Berlin: Springer.

Becker, L. C. (ed.) and Becker, C. B. (associate ed.) 1992: *Encyclopedia of Ethics*. New York: Garland Publishing.

Bellah, R. N., Madsen, R., Sullivan, W. M., Swidler, A. and Tipton, S. M. 1992: *The Good Society*. New York: Random House.

Berenbeim, R. E. 1987: *Corporate Ethics*. New York: The Conference Board.

Boatright, J. R. 1997: *Ethics and the Conduct of Business*. Upper Saddle River, NJ: Prentice-Hall.

Bowie, N. E. 1999: *Business Ethics: A Kantian Perspective*. Oxford: Blackwell.

Buchholz, R. A. and Rosenthal, S. B. 1998: *Business Ethics: The Pragmatic Path Beyond Principles to Process*. Upper Saddle River, NJ: Prentice-Hall.

Business Ethics Quarterly. 2000: January issue.

Cavanagh, G. F. 1998: *American Business Values with International Perspectives*, 4th edn. Upper Saddle River, NJ: Prentice-Hall.

Chakraborty, S. K. 2001: *The Management and Ethics Omnibus. Management by Values. Ethics in Management. Values and Ethics for Organizations*. New Delhi: Oxford University Press.

Ciulla, J. B. (ed.) 1998: *Ethics: The Heart of Leadership*. Westport, CT: Quorum Books.

Clarkson, B. E. (ed.) 1998: *The Corporation and Its Stakeholders: Classic and Contemporary Readings*. Toronto: University of Toronto Press.

Coleman, J. S. 1990: *Foundations of Social Theory*. Cambridge, MA: Belknap Press.

De George, R. T. 1993: *Competing with Integrity in International Business*. New York: Oxford University Press.

——1999: *Business Ethics*, 5th edn. Englewood Cliffs, NJ: Prentice-Hall.

Donaldson, T. and Dunfee, T. W. 1999: *Ties That Bind: A Social Contracts Approach to Business Ethics*. Boston: Harvard Business School Press.

Donaldson, T. and Preston, L. E. 1995: The Stakeholder Theory of the Corporation: Concepts, Evidence, and Implications. *Academy of Management Review*, 20, 1, 65–91.

Donaldson, T. and Werhane, P. H. (eds) 1999: *Ethical Issues in Business: A Philosophical Approach*, 6th edn. Upper Saddle River, NJ: Prentice-Hall.

Enderle, G. 1996: A Comparison of Business Ethics in North America and Continental Europe. *Business Ethics: A European Review*, 33–46.

——(ed.) 1999: *International Business Ethics: Challenges and Approaches*. Notre Dame, IN: University of Notre Dame Press.

Enderle, G. and Kamm, D. 1998: Business and Corporate Ethics in the USA: Philosophy and Practice. In B. Kumar and H. Steinmann (eds) *Ethics in International Management*. Berlin: Walter de Gruyter.

——2000: Whose Ethos for Public Goods in a Global Economy? An Exploration in International Business Ethics. *Business Ethics Quarterly*, 131–44. First published in German as 'Welches Ethos für öffentliche Güter in der Weltwirtschaft?' In H. Küng and K.-J. Kuschel (Hg.) 1998: *Weltethos und Wissenschaften*. Munich: Piper.

——2001: Bibliography of Business Ethics Articles (on diskette). Articles published from 1992 to July 2001 in *Business Ethics: A European Review*; *Business Ethics Quarterly*; *Business and Society*; *Business and Society Review*; *Journal of Business Ethics*; *Teaching Business Ethics*. Notre Dame, IN: ISBEE Secretariat (see www.isbee.org).

Enderle, G. and Tavis, L. A. 1998: A Balanced Concept of the Firm and the Measurement of its Long-term Planning and Performance. *Journal of Business Ethics*, 17, 1121–44.

Enderle, G., Homann, K., Honecker, M., Kerber, W. and Steinmann, H. (eds) 1993: *Lexikon der Wirtschaftsethik*. Freiburg: Herder.

Fischer, J. M. (ed.) 1986: *Moral Responsibility*. Ithaca, NY: Cornell University Press.

——(ed.) 1999: Recent Work on Moral Responsibility. *Ethics*, 110, 1, 93–139.

Frederick, R. E. (ed.) 1999: *A Companion to Business Ethics*. Oxford: Blackwell.

Frederick, W. C. 1995: *Values, Nature, and Culture in the American Corporation*. New York: Oxford University Press.

Freeman, R. E. 1984: *Strategic Management: A Stakeholder Approach*. Boston: Pitman.

French, P. A. 1984: *Collective and Corporate Responsibility*. New York: Columbia University Press.

Friedman, M. 1970: The Social Responsibility of Business Is to Increase Its Profits. *New York Times Magazine*, 13 September.

Gasparski, W. W. and Ryan, L. V. (eds) 1996: *Human Action in Business: Praxiological and Ethical Dimensions*. New Brunswick, NJ: Transaction Publishers.

Gewirth, A. 1984: The Epistemology of Human Rights. *Social Philosophy and Policy*, 1, 2, 1–33.

Glover, J. 1970: *Responsibility*. London: Routledge and Kegan Paul.

Goodpaster, K. E. 1992: Business Ethics. In L. C. Becker (ed.) and C. B. Becker (associate ed.) *Encyclopedia of Ethics*. New York: Garland Publishing.

Hausman, D. M. and McPherson, M. S. 1993: Taking Ethics Seriously: Economics and Contemporary Moral Philosophy. *Journal of Economic Literature*, 31, 671–731.

—— 1996: *Economic Analysis and Moral Philosophy*. Cambridge: Cambridge University Press.

Held, D., McGrew, A., Goldblatt, D. and Perraton, J. 1999: *Global Transformations: Politics, Economics and Culture*. Stanford, CA: Stanford University Press.

Hoffman, W. M. and Frederick, R. E. 1995: *Business Ethics: Readings and Cases in Corporate Morality*. New York: McGraw-Hill.

Homann, K. and Blome-Drees, F. 1992: *Wirtschafts- und Unternehmensethik*. Göttingen: UTB.

Jackall, R. 1988: *Moral Mazes: The World of Corporate Managers*. New York: Oxford University Press.

Jonas, H. 1984: *The Imperative of Responsibility: Foundations of an Ethics for the Technological Age*. (Original in German: *Prinzip Verantwortung*.) Chicago: University of Chicago Press.

Journal of Business Ethics 1997: Country- and Region-Related Reports. October.

Journal of Business Ethics 1999: Business Ethics in Spain. 11 November.

Kagan, S. 1998: *Normative Ethics*. Boulder, CO: Westview Press.

Kaul, I., Grunberg, I. and Stern, M. A. (eds) 1999: *Global Public Goods: International Cooperation in the 21st Century*. Published for the United Nations Development Programme (UNDP). New York: Oxford University Press.

Korff, W., Baumgartner, A., Franz, H., Genosko, J., Homann, K., Kirchner, C., Kluxen, W., Küpper, H.-U., Picot, A., Rendtorff, T., Richter, R., Sautter, H. and Schlecht, O. (Hg.) 1999: *Handbuch der Wirtschaftsethik*, 4 vols. Gütersloh: Gütersloher Verlagshaus.

Kreikebaum, H. 1996: *Grundlagen der Unternehmensethik*. Stuttgart: Schäfer-Poeschel.

Kromphardt, J. 1990: *Konzeptionen und Analysen des Kapitalismus, vol. 3: Auflage*. Göttingen: Vandenhoeck and Ruprecht.

Kumar, B. N. and Steinmann, H. (eds) 1998: *Ethics in International Management*. Berlin: Springer.

Küng, H. 1998: *A Global Ethic for Global Politics and Economics*. New York: Oxford University Press.

Levi, I. 1986: *Hard Choices: Decision Making under Unresolved Conflict*. Cambridge: Cambridge University Press.

Luhmann, N. 1988: *Die Wirtschaft der Gesellschaft*. Frankfurt am Main: Suhrkamp.

Messick, D. M. and Tenbrunsel, A. E. (eds) 1996: *Codes of Conduct: Behavioral Research Into Business Ethics*. New York: Russell Sage Foundation.

Moorthy, R. S., De George, R. T., Donaldson, T., Ellos, W. J., Solomon, R. C. and Textor, R. B. 1998: *Uncompromising Integrity: Motorola's Challenge*. Shaumberg, IL: Motorola University Press.

Näsi, J. (ed.) 1995: *Understanding Stakeholder Thinking*. Helsinki: LSR-Publications.

North, D. C. 1972: Economic History. In D. L. Sills (ed.) *International Encyclopedia of Social Sciences*. New York: Macmillan and Free Press.

Pesqueux, Y. 2000: *Le Gouvernement de l'entreprise comme idéologie*. Paris: Ellipses Édition.

Rawls, J. 1999: *The Law of Peoples with 'The Idea of Public Reason Revisited'*. Cambridge, MA: Harvard University Press.

Rich, A. 1984/1990: *Wirtschaftsethik*, vols 1–2. Gütersloh: Mohn. Translated as *The Ethics of Economic Systems*, forthcoming.

Rossouw, D. 1994: *Business Ethics: A Southern African Perspective*. Pretoria: Southern Book Publishers.

Sen, A. 1987: *On Ethics and Economics*. Oxford: Blackwell.

—— 1999a: *Development as Freedom*. New York: Alfred A. Knopf.

—— 1999b: Global Justice: Beyond International Equity. In I. Kaul, I. Grunberg and M. A. Stern (eds) *Global Public Goods: International Cooperation in the 21st Century*. Published for the United Nations Development Programme (UNDP). New York: Oxford University Press.

Shaw, W. H. 1996: *Business Ethics*. Belmont, CA: Wadsworth.

Snoeyenbos, M. and Humber, J. 1999: Utilitarianism and Business Ethics. In R. E. Frederick (ed.) *A Companion to Business Ethics*. Oxford: Blackwell.

549

Social Philosophy and Policy 1999: Responsibility. Summer issue.

Solomon, R. C. 1992: *Ethics and Excellence: Cooperation and Integrity in Business*. New York: Oxford University Press.

Solomon, R. T. 1993: Business Ethics. In P. Singer (ed.) *A Companion to Ethics*. Oxford: Blackwell.

Sorell, T. and Hendry, J. 1994: *Business Ethics*. Oxford: Butterworth-Heinemann.

Staffelbach, B. 1994: *Management-Ethik. Ansätze und Konzepte aus betriebswirtschaftlicher Sicht.* Bern: Haupt.

Steinmann, H. and Löhr, A. 1992: *Grundlagen der Unternehmensethik*. Stuttgart: Poeschel.

Ulrich, P. 1993: *Transformation der ökonomischen Vernunft. Fortschrittsperspektiven der modernen Industriegesellschaft. 3: Auflage.* Bern: Haupt.

—— 1997: *Integrative Wirtschaftsethik. Grundlagen einer lebensdienlichen ökonomie.* Bern: Haupt.

Uncompromising Integrity: Motorola's Global Challenge. Schaumburg, IL: Motorola University Press.

United Nations Development Programme (UNDP) 1990: *Human Development Report 1990.* New York: Oxford University Press.

United Nations, Economic Commission for Latin America and the Caribbean (ECLAC) 1999: Latin America and the Carribean in the World Economy. Santiago, Chile: United Nations.

Van Luijk, H. 1986: *In het belang van de onderneming; aantekeningen voor een bedrijfsethik*, 2nd edn. Delft: Eburon.

Velasquez, M. G. 1998: *Business Ethics: Concepts and Cases*, 4th edn. Upper Saddle River, NJ: Prentice-Hall.

Walton, C. C. 1988: *The Moral Manager*. New York: Harper Business.

Weiss, J. W. 1994: *Business Ethics: A Managerial, Stakeholder Approach*. Belmont, CA: Wadsworth.

Werhane, P. H. and Freeman, R. E. (eds) 1997: *Encyclopedic Dictionary of Business Ethics*. Oxford: Blackwell.

Werhane, P. H. and Singer, A. E. (eds) 1999: *Business Ethics in Theory and Practice: Contributions from Asia and New Zealand*. Dordrecht: Kluwer Academic Publishers.

Williams, O. F. (ed.) 2000: *Global Codes of Conduct: An Idea Whose Time Has Come*. Notre Dame, IN: University of Notre Dame Press.

Williamson, O. E. 1985: *The Economic Institutions of Capitalism*. New York: Free Press.

—— (ed.) 1990: *Organization Theory: From Chester Barnard to the Present and Beyond*. New York: Oxford University Press.

World Bank 1993: *The East Asian Miracle: Economic Growth and Public Policy*. New York: Oxford University Press.

Yu Xuanmeng, Lu Xiaohe, Liu Fangtong, Zhang Rulun and Enderle, G. 1997: Economic Ethics and Chinese Culture. *Chinese Philosophical Studies*, 14. Washington, DC: Council for Research in Values and Philosophy.

Discussion Questions

1   How has globalization shaped the problems addressed by business ethics?

2   Are there advantages to having a comparative conceptual framework with which to discuss business ethics?

3   What is the relationship between theoretical and empirical studies in business and economic ethics?

4   How do different conceptions of business affect our notion of business ethics?

5   How are the semantic, theoretical and practical aspects of business ethics related?

6   Should business ethics be 'action-oriented'? How can we relate freedom, choice, constraint and responsibility in business ethics?

7   What are the consequences for business ethics of the 'concreteness' of action and decision-making in business?

8   How should we understand the relations among problems of ethics that arise at different levels of business and economic life, from the individual actor to the whole economic system? Should one level have priority over the others?

9   How should a theory of business ethics respond to the internationalization of economic relations across national and cultural borders?

10   Can the cognitive and normative aspects of business ethics be separated? What are the consequences of your answer for business and economic disciplines?

11   What is the moral status of organizations?

12   How should business ethics respond to the diversity of historical and social contexts, business practices and problems that arise in different countries?

13   What should be the character of corporate ethics? How can we decide whether corporations should be responsible to stakeholders other than shareholders?

14   To what extent should we seek to reconcile the different approaches to business ethics in North America and continental Europe?

15   What notions of rationality should be used in business ethics and other business disciplines?

16   Can business ethics help us to evaluate social and economic institutions?

17   What is the role of 'moral mathematics' in business ethics?

18   What criteria should be used to characterize an economic system?

19   What is likely to be the character of business ethics as it becomes a mature discipline?

20

Philosophy and Feminism

JEAN GRIMSHAW AND MIRANDA FRICKER

Recent decades have seen intense debates among feminists, especially in France, the United Kingdom and the United States, about the exclusion of women from philosophy, the representation of women in philosophical works, varying reasons the subject itself might be considered 'masculine', and different proposals for a feminist philosophy. Discussions have ranged from areas such as ethics and political philosophy, to areas in which questions of gender arise less spontaneously, like epistemology, metaphysics and philosophy of science. This chapter examines some main features of contemporary feminist philosophy and considers proposals for the future. Jean Grimshaw considers feminism and philosophy (sections 1–4), and Miranda Fricker discusses feminism in philosophy (sections 5–6).

1 Feminism and Philosophy: Introduction

For women who have been in any way sensitized to the issues concerning gender and the situation of women, which have been central to contemporary feminism, to be a woman studying philosophy is to be faced with a set of problems about one's own location within the discipline. Above all other academic disciplines, perhaps, philosophy, in its historical aspect, appears as a history of 'Great Men of Ideas', and in the roll call of 'great' philosophers from the past, women seem to be singularly absent. Women philosophers whose names are known to us have tended, as Michèle Le Doeuff (1991) points out, to be restricted to the role of disciple of, or correspondent with, the 'master'; as in the case of DESCARTES (chapter 26) and Princess Elizabeth of Bohemia (1618–80).

The formal barriers to the independent study of philosophy that existed in the past for women have now largely gone. Quite a lot of women study philosophy; many come to think of it as their 'intellectual home'. Yet relatively few of them 'make it' into academic posts, and those for whom philosophy continues to be central to their lives may also feel that there are ways in which philosophy can be alien and inhospitable to women. Being a woman and a philosopher, as Le Doeuff notes, is *always* something that is problematic, that has to be negotiated.

In the majority of mainstream courses in philosophy, issues concerning philosophy and gender continue to be largely invisible. This was often the case for those women philosophers who are now trying to theorize the relationship between feminism and philosophy. For them, the initial recognition that male philosophers *had* written a great deal about women, and that much of what they had written was riddled with sexism and misogyny, came as a shock. How was it possible that one could have studied philosophy for a long time, yet failed to notice this? How, for example, could one be required to study Rousseau (1712–78) without one's attention being drawn at any point to what he wrote about Sophie and the subordination of women? How could one possibly have studied NIETZSCHE (1844–1900) (chapter 40) without noting the crucial, if problematic, role that the concept of 'woman' plays in his thought? Along with the shock there frequently came a sense of dislocation. This arose from the recognition that whereas the study of philosophy had seemed to be something to which one's gender was irrelevant, much of philosophy in fact assumed and was addressed to a *male* subject.

The first (and essential) stage in thinking about philosophy and gender consisted in highlighting the endemic misogyny of many male philosophers; in noting the ways in which philosophy commonly assumed the exclusion of women (as citizens, as rational subjects, or as MORAL AGENTS (chapter 6), for example), and in charting the ways in which women were devalued or seen as inferior. This history of sexism and misogyny has largely been invisible to the academic philosophical mainstream. If noted, it has been dismissed as unimportant, a kind of local 'accident' whose recognition need not otherwise affect philosophical discussion and theorizing. And indeed, the mere exposure of sexism, however important, is 'negative' in the sense that, by itself, it does not theorize the ways in which such sexism might affect the substance of philosophical theories, what relationship feminism and philosophy might continue to have, or how women might relocate themselves within philosophy.

One strategy adopted by those who were concerned about this exclusion of women has been to attempt to include women in philosophical theories. A paradigm of such attempts at inclusion can be found in the writings of the eighteenth-century feminist, Mary Wollstonecraft (1759–97). In *A Vindication of the Rights of Woman* (1975) Wollstonecraft insisted that the possibility of realizing ideals of rationality and virtue, of which it was commonly thought that only men were capable, should be extended to include women. She noted that Rousseau regarded women as incapable of reason. Not so, she argued; to the extent that women were unable to reason adequately, it was because they had been prevented from so doing by a pernicious system of female education. Rousseau argued that the 'virtue' of a man was entirely different from the 'virtue' of a woman. Wollstonecraft replied that virtue should be the same regardless of sex.

But however important it has been to insist that women are not 'inferior' to men, and are no less capable of reason or virtue, the strategy of simply including women in philosophical theories soon breaks down. Firstly, it is frequently the case that one cannot simply 'include' women whilst leaving the rest of a theory intact. Rousseau is a case in point. His theory of the state and the education of the citizen was wholly premised on a private, patriarchal and rural family life, in which women were to be completely subordinated to men. Secondly, the attempted inclusion of women fails to ask questions about that from which they are excluded; is there a sense, for example, in which some ideals of reason and virtue might themselves be seen as 'masculine'? Much feminist philosophical work has been devoted to asking whether there are deeper senses in which the content of philosophical theories might be seen as 'masculine'. Can philosophy sometimes at least be seen as 'gendered' even in cases where such things as the nature of women and men is not apparently under discussion? Does the enterprise of philosophy itself have some kind of 'deep structure' that might also be seen in this way? The analysis of this kind of 'masculinity' reaches far deeper than merely detecting or analysing overt instances of misogyny or sexism, and it has been approached in more than one sort of way.

2 Philosophy and Masculinity

The first essential premise, on which the analysis of masculinity in philosophy is predicated, is as follows. Perhaps above all other disciplines, philosophy has historically liked to think of itself as based on reason; but a reason which is assumed to be universal and objective. The philosophical subject has often been assumed to be capable of a 'God's-eye view', a 'view from nowhere'; a 'rational mind' that has no class, gender, race, social and historical location, perhaps even, in some philosophical theories, no body. Discussion of the social location of those who practise philosophy has been seen in contemporary terms (often dismissively) as a form of sociology of knowledge which has no relevance to questions about the truth or adequacy of philosophical theories themselves. But from a feminist perspective, questions about the social location of knowers, or those who claim to know, are not extrinsic to philosophy. Rather, they should be at its very heart, since the gendering of philosophy, and its frequent exclusion of women, are based on the denial of this location, on the assumption of a 'universality' which is in fact a concealed partiality. The 'human' subject in philosophy has often turned out to be a male subject.

The process of attempting to theorize the kinds of social location that are of relevance to the study of philosophy has, however, produced some differing views of the ways in which philosophy might be seen as 'masculine'. In her book *Speculum of the Other Woman* (1985), the French feminist philosopher Luce Irigaray, who is also a practising psychoanalyst, offered a reading of the myth of the cavern in Plato's *Republic*. She argued that the myth rested on a profound denial and repression of the mother, the womb, and the fact of male dependence on women, and she interpreted this denial by offering a reinterpretation of the Freudian theory of the death drives. A psychoanalytic approach has been used by other philosophers as well. In an important article published in 1983, Jane Flax argued that philosophical theories arose out of typically *male* social experience, interests, fears and concerns. Drawing on the work of the feminist psychoanalytic writer Nancy Chodorow (1978), who used an approach derived not from orthodox Freudianism but from object-relations theory, she argued that there are typical differences in 'gender personality' between women and men, arising from the fact that it is women who perform the main work of child-rearing. Men, Flax suggested, typically feel a need to distance themselves from the 'world of women', to devalue it, to associate with the world of masculinity 'outside' the home, and to stress a defensive autonomy and separateness against the fear of being engulfed by women. Flax noted features in the philosophy of Plato (chapter 23), Hobbes (chapter 28), Descartes and Rousseau which, she argued, could be interpreted in the light of these typical masculine psychic structures. Such features included individualism, fear of the body and senses, a denial of human interdependence and interconnectedness, and a stress on the radical isolation of the human knower and the human self.

There are, however, considerable problems in this kind of analysis of 'masculinity' in the writings of philosophers. Male philosophers have said very different things; they have certainly not all espoused the kinds of atomistic or individualistic theories that Flax sees as paradigmatically masculine. In addition, there are great problems in trying to give such a general or ahistorical account of male social experience or of the male psyche. These kinds of problems might seem to suggest that trying to look for any very general features of philosophy that might be seen as 'masculine' is something of a hopeless quest, given the importance of historical variability and difference. Even though many male figures in the canon have expressed derogatory views about women in one way or another, these ways have varied greatly. It is commonly the case that whatever is valued in a philosophical theory can be found to be associated with an ideal of masculinity; nevertheless, these ideals vary historically a great deal.

However, despite this difference, one is faced with the fact that misogyny and the exclusion of women seem to be endemic in philosophy, even if they may at times take very different forms. Is it possible to give any sort of general account of the features of philosophy that seem to underpin this constant and dreary history of the devaluation of women, which does not run quite this risk of historical over-generalization? Other approaches that women working in philosophy have adopted in attempting to answer this question depend not so much on looking at the more particular or specific features of individual theories, or on psychoanalytic speculation about the male psyche, but on trying to trace some of the structures of representation and ideology through which phallocentrism and the exclusion and devaluation of women get written into philosophy.

3 Dichotomies: Derrida and Feminism

Feminist writers have noted the constant tendency in philosophical theories towards forms of binarism, to thinking in terms of dichotomies. These are legion in the history of philosophy; they include man–woman, culture–nature, reason–emotion, mind–body, public–private and production–reproduction. They do not always take the same forms, and none of them is universal, but there are nevertheless important historical continuities. Within each dichotomy or binarism there is a hierarchy, a privileged term, and this privileged term is associated with men rather than with women.

The recognition of the importance of such binarisms has not been unique to the work of feminist philosophers. It has characterized much 'postmodern' philosophy as well. Jacques DERRIDA (chapter 42), for example, argues that most of Western metaphysics has been constructed on a system of differences or binarisms in which one term is privileged at the expense of the other. It has been 'phallogocentric', based not only on the assumed logocentric authority and primacy of speech and 'presence' over writing, but also on the assumed phallocentric primacy of the transcendental male subject. Derrida's project of deconstruction aims to destabilize; to privilege the subordinate term in such metaphysical binarisms, and to show how the privileged term is in fact dependent on the subordinate term. Derrida aims, by complex strategies of textual analysis and argument, to prevent the original binarism from reasserting itself.

Derrida is one of the relatively few contemporary philosophers in whose work the concept of 'woman' plays a central role. 'Woman', in Derrida's work, becomes a figure for that which is undecidable, that which can evade the illusory fixity of traditional metaphysical structures of meaning. But feminist reactions to Derrida's work highlight some of the most interesting tensions and difficulties in the project of feminist philosophy. Derrida has been notoriously critical of feminism (and rarely in his own work refers to feminist writings). The reason seems to be as follows. The project of 'deconstruction' aims to subvert and undermine dualisms and dichotomies and to create a space for multiplicity and difference, including sexual difference. But, according to most interpretations of Derrida, he argues that if the feminist project includes any kind of assertion of female specificity – of women's right to the subjectivity that men have been able to assume as theirs – then it simply repeats the old dichotomies. Women, in fact, come to 'speak like men'. Derrida's own desire to 'speak like a woman', then, seems to amount to a desire to perform a vertiginous and elusive textual dance at the margins or in the interstices of traditional philosophical texts. It seems very different from the feminist project of finding a 'voice' for women in philosophy, of allowing women to speak in their own right. Some critics of Derrida have argued that his valorization of 'speaking like a woman' effects yet another erasure of women. To 'speak like a woman' is not the same as 'speaking as a woman'.

Irigaray and Women's Voice in Philosophy

Of course there are dangers, evident in some feminist writing, of simply recapitulating old and oppressive dichotomies. Simply to propose that 'the feminine' should be valued, if it involves no critique of the ways in which 'the feminine' is constructed as the shadow or inversion of the masculine, may reinstate that from which much feminist theory has tried to escape. The problem is to see how women can speak within philosophy, assume the status of philosophical SUBJECTS (pp. 846–7), without this reification of older categories. Luce Irigaray writes that it is the object of her work to 'jam the theoretical machinery'; a great deal of recent feminist philosophical writing has explored ways in which old philosophical dichotomies might be deconstructed so that they are no longer seen as polarized, as exclusive of each other; rather, they are redefined as mutually interdependent. Nevertheless, Irigaray is also concerned that women should find a voice within philosophy. In her work, it is not a question of finding an 'essence' of woman, or of theorizing about women's 'nature'. She does not assume that we could know in advance what women might say, were they to speak 'in their own voice'.

4   Feminism and Philosophy

But how might we suppose that philosophy would change if the insights of feminist philosophical writing were taken seriously? At the present time, whilst there is a great deal of feminist philosophical writing being published, it has seemingly made little impact in many places on the traditional academic teaching of philosophy, or on 'mainstream' publication. 'Feminism' or 'feminism and philosophy' are often at best an 'option' on the margins, a 'special interest', in which it is usually implicitly assumed that only women will take a real interest. This is reflected in such things as the ways in which books are classified in libraries and in bookshops. Philosophical books by women are frequently not included in the shelves labelled 'philosophy'; they are placed under 'gender' or 'women's studies'. The long-term question about the relationship between feminism and philosophy concerns what might be called 'the nature of the hyphen', the 'and' which appears in the title of this chapter itself.

As I suggested earlier, the crucial premise of feminist philosophical writing is that questions about the social and historical location of philosophers are intrinsic to understanding the discipline, and they cannot be dismissed as extraneous or irrelevant. There is a need to recognize that philosophical theories arise from and speak to the concerns of particular social groups at particular periods in history. This view should not be equated with crude kinds of reductionism – the kind, for example, which assumes that discussion of philosophical theories can be reduced to discussion of the psyches of the philosophers who hold them. But it does imply that understanding philosophical theories will necessitate understanding something about the social interests and concerns which gave rise to them – and the power relations by which they may have been shaped.

Feminist philosophers have argued that this is as true of the less apparently 'gendered' areas of philosophy, such as EPISTEMOLOGY (chapter 1), METAPHYSICS (chapter 2) and the PHILOSOPHY OF SCIENCE (chapter 9), as it is of those where issues of gender have a more obvious place, such as ETHICS (chapter 6) or POLITICAL PHILOSOPHY (chapter 8, especially pp. 272–3). Philosophical enquiry should reject the 'false universalism' of supposing that philosophers can speak from nowhere, or construct theories that are universally applicable. The recognition of this has the consequence that the parameters of philosophical enquiry will inevitably change. Boundaries between what is and is not 'philosophy' will shift; one consequence of developing a feminist perspective on philosophy is that one becomes far less worried by the challenge: 'But is this *philosophy?*' – a challenge that has often been used to try to dismiss feminist questioning at the outset. But the critique of 'false universalism' also implies that feminist enquiry itself should recognize its own locatedness, and take into account the fact that the differences of social location, experience and perspective among women themselves may be as important as those between women and men.

But if the most important claim of a feminist approach to philosophy is that philosophical theories are socially located, and have tended to answer to the interests, concerns and experiences of men rather than of women, this still leaves open the important question of what the future of philosophy might be like were feminist perspectives on themselves to become part of the mainstream, rather than a 'special interest' on the sidelines. Women philosophers such as Irigaray have been concerned that women should be able, in philosophy, to assume the position of subjects and speak in their own voice. But the question remains whether the insistence on this voice should be seen as a strategic necessity born of circumstances in which women have often been excluded and silenced, or whether the concerns of women and men are likely to remain irreducibly different in ways that will imply a continuing need for philosophy written for, and mainly by, women themselves.

Approaches to this question vary. Those who believe that women's experiences and concerns will always diverge in some respects from those of men are more likely to continue to insist on the need for 'women's philosophy'. On the other hand, there are those such as Michèle Le Doeuff who believe that the project of feminist philosophy, in the long term, should be a new kind of universalism, different from the older kind of universalism which assumed the possibility of a 'God's-eye view'. Le Doeuff argues that whereas it is commonly assumed that philosophy itself is 'universal' and feminist enquiry merely partial – a form of 'special interest' – it would be more appropriate to say that philosophy has been 'partial' in the sense that it has commonly excluded women both from the possibility of the production of philosophical theories and from being capable of exemplifying the ideals to which philosophical theories have been committed. Le Doeuff sees it as essential to the enterprise of philosophy that it posits 'objects' of thought which are assumed to be of interest to an audience not differentiated by extra-intellectual criteria such as gender. In other words 'feminist philosophy' should not be seen, in the end, as a 'special interest'. It is something that aims to change and inform the mainstream of philosophy, such that questions that now tend to be marginal or invisible will become normal, visible and part of the repertoire of all of those who study philosophy.

But if the production of philosophy arises from social interests and concerns, so also does its reception, and Le Doeuff's conception of an audience undifferentiated by any extra-intellectual criterion may seem to be a form of idealism which is too close to older philosophical ideals of 'universality'. Nevertheless, it highlights what is perhaps the most interesting question about the future of feminist philosophical enquiry. There is an ongoing need to bring the many differing perspectives of women into philosophy, and to continue to address questions about the invisibility and marginalization of these. But feminist enquiry also addresses issues of general human interest and relevance; it is not an orthodoxy committed to a narrow or blinkered set of preconceptions about what should be seen as 'women's issues'. The tension between the project of creating frameworks within which women can speak and think as women, and the project of changing the face of philosophy so that women's perspectives are no longer 'marked' as marginal to the mainstream, is both an essential one in current circumstances, and one whose resolution is perhaps the major task facing feminist philosophy at the moment.

5   Feminism in Philosophy: Two Conceptions

On one conception of feminism's relation to philosophy it is appropriate to think in terms of a conjunction – feminism *and* philosophy – in which feminist consciousness is brought to bear from the outside upon the philosophical tradition. On this conception, a central question arising is the question how far philosophy has been distinctively masculine (hence 'masculist') in its approach, and whether there might be such a thing as a distinctively feminine philosophical voice as yet barely heard in the history of the subject (hence the possibility of a certain 'feminist' approach). The key commitment arising from explorations of this question tends to take the form of an insistence on historicism in our understanding of philosophers and their work. This is borne out in Jean

Grimshaw's account in sections 1–4 of feminism and philosophy, in which she outlines feminist ideas about both the literally and the symbolically masculine character of philosophy. In connection with the first, feminists have concerned themselves with the expression of prejudicial or downright misogynist attitudes towards women by male figures in the canon; and in connection with the second, they have tried to reveal some of the subtler ways in which philosophy might be considered historically to have expressed a masculine point of view. The subtler ways in which a masculine point of view is argued to be implicit in a given philosophical text might be revealed through a psychoanalytic analysis of the psychology expressed there, or through a more sociological analysis designed to reveal that the social experience which informs the writing is a masculine one. Grimshaw's account closes with the aspiration that feminist work should impact on the mainstream rather than remaining 'marked' as marginal. In the spirit of that aspiration, I would like to take up my account where hers leaves off, by outlining a non-conjunctive conception of feminism's relation to philosophy so as to suggest a model for how and why feminism might come to have its deserved impact within the mainstream: feminism *in* philosophy (also see the introduction to Fricker and Hornsby 2000).

This so-to-speak *internal* conception is perfectly compatible with the conjunctive conception – it substantially overlaps with it, and indeed is historically dependent upon it. To differentiate too sharply between the two, by pretending for instance that all feminist philosophy falls neatly into one or other category, would be grossly artificial. With this warning bell sounded, however, the internal view seems worth treating as distinctive when one is aiming to map feminist work in terms of its ambition *vis-à-vis* the mainstream. The ambition might consist, broadly speaking, in one or other of two very different aims: the aim to achieve integration into mainstream debates, or, by contrast, the aim to maintain independence from the mainstream either by way of a sustained marginality or a more extreme intellectual separatism. In this respect, a book such as *Hipparchia's Choice* (Le Doeuff 1991) might represent a revisionist spirit, while *Speculum of the Other Woman* (Irigaray 1985) might be regarded as offering a 'separatist' project that posits the idea of an as yet unheard feminine philosophical voice. Whereas the conjunctive conception fosters either ambition with equal encouragement – this is its strength – the internal conception will tend more exclusively to nurture the sort of work which facilitates dialogue not only with other feminists but also with colleagues to whom the idea of feminist philosophy may still be alien or even suspect – this, in turn, is *its* strength. Here a desirable by-product of doing internal-style feminist work might be to convince such colleagues that at least some of the socializing concerns of feminism might properly be the concerns of *any* philosopher (hence the appropriateness of the integrationist ambition).

Consequently, those who start from the internal conception are far less likely to produce work which engages in wholesale CRITIQUE (p. 278) of philosophy *per se*, and more likely to produce work which goes in for piecemeal localized critical participation in the philosophical discourses of the day. By certain radicalist lights, of course, such a piecemeal approach threatens the integrity of the critical impulse in feminism. The fear is that engagement with the mainstream will erode the radical potential of the feminist stance in philosophy. But the integrationist ambition can be entertained without fear of any such thing, so long as one is entitled to trust a historicist view of what constitutes the discipline: if philosophy is an evolving historical entity, then feminist consciousness can help (re)constitute it by including itself among the critical energies which influence the discipline's ongoing history. Philosophy purports to aspire to an unconstrained self-criticism, and work of the feminism in philosophy kind aspires to prove the point. Integration is thus an active critical ambition, not a desire for mere acceptance. Thus in so far as critical engagement brings transition to both parties, it can be freely admitted that genuine dialogue between a given set of feminist ideas and a given patch of mainstream philosophy will transform the thinking on both sides; but it would be unduly pessimistic to think that this must be a bad thing for the feminist ideas at stake. In any event, if there was ever a case for the separatist approach to feminist philosophy, then the encouragement of integrationist feminist work does not change that. There is room for all kinds of feminist philosophy. The point here is only to characterize an approach which is well-designed to fulfil the undeniably valid aspiration that at least some feminist work should come to lose its mark of marginality by way of the mainstream's gaining the marks of feminist insight.

Like its conjunctive sister-conception, the internal conception incorporates a commitment to historicism (understood inclusively to cover social specificity of all kinds). But while the conjunctive conception tends in particular to problematize the masculinity of the canonical philosopher with a view to diagnosing the extent of the masculinity of philosophy *per se*, the internal conception tends more exclusively to problematize the seemingly compulsory *asociality* of philosophy's idea of the beings it treats. Thus in work of the feminism in philosophy kind there is likely to be a more exclusive use of the sort of HISTORICISM (pp. 437–9) which highlights not so much the social identity of the philosopher, but rather the social specificity of the human subject whose practices – conceptual, linguistic, epistemic, ethical, political – philosophy purports to account for. This is strictly a difference only in emphasis between the two conceptions, for to historicize the HUMAN SUBJECT (pp. 864–8) in this way is really just to insist upon what feminists of almost all stripes have for years called 'difference'. As I have said, the two conceptions of how feminism relates to philosophy are substantially overlapping, and the concern with DIFFERENCE (pp. 868–71) is naturally a major area of overlap. Indeed, here again the genetic dependence of the internal upon the conjunctive conception is apparent: feminism's route to problematizing the asociality of philosophy's human subjects comes to us by way of those debates which problematized the supposedly asocial persona adopted by the philosopher himself (*sic*).

6   Philosophical Commitments

Sometimes it is supposed that a commitment to feminism entails a commitment to oppose certain fundamental commitments of philosophy, its methods and aspirations. The possibility of doing work which flows from the internal conception, however, shows that this is not so. The internal conception remains sternly neutral about certain traditional styles of philosophical argument in a way that has not been typical of a considerable proportion of the work produced by the conjunctive conception, as that conception – being the more inclusive – gives some significant nourishment to the appetite for a wholesale critique of philosophy. Perhaps one of the definitively typical aspirations of philosophy is the aspiration to universal truth, and it is often assumed that there is something in feminism which implies a commitment to the rejection of that universalist aspiration. Certainly there is a great deal of feminist work which does reject it and which characterizes it as a piece of masculism *par excellence*. We can, for example, read Rosi Braidotti's (1991) feminist reworking of the Deleuzian idea of 'nomadism' as a feminist anti-universalism.

But in fact there is nothing in feminism which forces either this characterization or the rejection. On the contrary – and happily for feminism's credentials as a non-dogmatic intellectual attitude under whose influence philosophical debate may flourish – there is room between feminist philosophers, indeed between philosophers of all stripes, for argument about the merits and demerits of the aspiration. While some feminist thinkers may be persuaded by arguments against the very idea of universal truths about human practices, and perhaps against the methods designed to issue in them too (transcendental or other sorts of *a priori* argumentation, for instance), nonetheless the internal conception's emphasis on the sociality of the human subject need not discredit such sources of universalism. On the contrary, its very articulation calls upon at least one instance of universalism, namely the universal claim that all human beings are socially identified individuals. And the possibility that there are some basic universal, even necessary, truths about, say, the nature of sensory experience is perfectly compatible with the irreducible sociality of the human beings that have these experiences. The key corrective impact of feminism in philosophy over this point is that relations of power and identity impinge in many more of the basic human practices which philosophy aims to theorize than has traditionally – complacently – been assumed. Here we ought to recognize one source of justification for a more wholesale suspicion of philosophy that might typically be countenanced on this conception: if history had witnessed an express project of creating a philosophical discourse designed to make questions of power apparently unaskable, because apparently unphilosophical, then it could hardly have hoped to have come up with anything better than the Anglo-American paradigm. There is room, then, for the expression of wholesale suspicion within the internal conception. But such suspicions will not inspire separatism there, only a greater will to participate in the transformation of the tradition.

A second fundamental commitment of philosophy besides the aspiration to universal truth is the commitment to conducting debates at a very high level of abstraction. It is in the nature of philosophy to trade in abstractions, and that is as it should be for a non-empirical discipline. Sometimes it is supposed that there is something in feminism that implies the rejection of abstraction, as if abstraction must be replaced by something else – something which might be gestured at in the idea of social and cultural specificity. (This is the form that the commitment to 'difference' sometimes takes, as if theorizing about people as socially specific subjects were necessarily an enterprise in abandoning abstraction.) Again, there is in fact nothing in feminism which requires the rejection of abstraction *per se*. If there were, then there would be no prospect for feminist philosophy remotely to resemble philosophy as we know it, and so there would be no future for feminist work of the internal sort – but then there would be little prospect for much feminist *theorizing* of any kind. Feminist philosophy would have to be transformed into an utterly empirical enterprise, shedding its *a priori* methodological origins altogether. There are admittedly postmodern forms of feminist philosophy which might embrace such an outcome, or some version of it. Perhaps the value of intellectual pluralism means this is as it should be; the present point is simply that nothing in feminism requires it. Instead the feminist attitude may bring a very different problematization of philosophy's favourite level of abstraction – the level at which human beings are conceived as, simply, rational beings. It may question the obligation to conduct debates at this level, bringing a release from this seeming obligation, not by rejecting abstraction as such, but rather by insisting on the appropriateness, for some areas of philosophy at least, of an abstraction which is so to speak one level lower, so that human beings are conceived not as rational beings simply but as rational–social beings. This would be a conception that relates not to any social location in particular (that would indeed invite empirical questions), but rather one which pictures human beings as always located somewhere or other in relations of SOCIAL IDENTITY AND POWER (pp. 864–8). Such a socialized conception of the human subject liberates the philosophical sensibility in so far as it ushers in a new range of questions which, though one might have been curious about them, had seemed unaskable in the philosophical idiom: questions, for instance, about how a subject's location in the social world – their place, whatever it may be, in relations of identity and power – might impinge upon their participation in various fundamental practices. Thus it also allows in questions about how far the practices themselves may depend upon these social dimensions for their very structure – questions, then, about how far the involvement of identity and power is a *necessary* feature of the practices under scrutiny.

Here we revisit the question of the appropriateness of a universalist aspiration in philosophy, and we arrive at the heart of that aspiration: the idea that philosophy is specially placed to reveal the necessary aspects of human practices. If a philosopher discovers that a given practice – an epistemic or an ethical practice, for instance – exhibits a necessary dependence on operations of power, then an eminently respectable sort of philosophical truth will have been revealed: a necessary truth about that sort of practice (Fricker 1998). Thus the socialized conception of the human subject as a rational–social being (always an abstraction) which is encouraged by the internal conception of feminism's relation to philosophy, is able to produce universalist conclusions of a kind to which the discipline has quintessentially aspired.

Here – as ever in this enterprise of distinguishing different approaches in feminist philosophy – I risk oversimplification. The oversimplification that now looms, however, concerns not so much one or other feminist approach, but rather the character of 'the' philosophical tradition – the question how far 'it' may be described as espousing a strictly *a priori* quest for universal truths. In the continental tradition there is an obviously influential, even definitive, heritage of thought which specifically rejects universalism, or which otherwise launches its own wholesale critique of philosophy (see Derrida 1976). Similarly influential and disruptive currents are to be found too in the Anglo-American tradition, though they might not plausibly be cast as definitive of it. The Wittgensteinian idea of philosophy as a therapeutic enterprise is an obvious case in point; a more recent example is Richard Rorty's *Philosophy and the Mirror of Nature* (1980).

In connection too with the asocial conception of the human subject, it should be acknowledged that there are sub-traditions within analytic philosophy that are in some degree socialized: NATURALIZED EPISTEMOLOGY (pp. 302–3), for instance; or PRAGMATISM (chapter 36); or social-historicist currents of thought in philosophy of science, and in ethics. In these sorts of work, the sociality of human beings – the fact that they always operate as members of some culture or other, or think and deliberate from the context of some tradition or other – is very much in the picture. However, what they lack which feminism introduces is a *fully socialized* conception of this sociality: the difference that the relations of identity and power make to human subjects' participation in the relevant practices of understanding, enquiry or evaluation. This is not to say that there are no practices – that of sensory perception, for instance – accounts of which are quite properly conducted at the level of rational beings, simply. To repeat, part of the impact of feminism in philosophy should be to encourage non-complacency about which, if any, these practices are, so that the different levels of abstraction which philosophy makes available come to be employed more discriminatingly, more imaginatively and more appropriately. Given the asocializing nature of the tradition, this may justify a heuristic of general suspicion regarding claims to sociality's irrelevance; but it does not require any blanket pronouncement to the effect that it is always mistaken or otherwise inappropriate to conduct debates at the highest level of abstraction.

At its most positive, feminism in philosophy is a forward-looking, relentlessly interrogative energy directed at opening up new, more socialized, more politicized questions. Aside from a certain qualified discouragement to wholesale critique, nothing philosophically substantive is dictated in advance, and the internalist stance signals a baseline neutrality regarding philosophy's traditional commitments and aspirations. This is what makes the internal conception a useful one for those with the positive, critical integrationist ambition for feminist work which is pointed to in Jean Grimshaw's account of *feminism and philosophy*, and for which I have attempted to suggest a possible model in this companion account of *feminism in philosophy*.

Further Reading

Anthony and Witt (1993) is an important collection of accessible essays in the analytic style. Braidotti (1991) is not an easy book to read, but it is very useful in particular for its discussion of French philosophy as well as Anglo-American feminist writing, and for its perspectives on the relationship between feminism and postmodernism. Coole (1993) provides a general survey of issues concerning gender in political philosophy. Fricker and Hornsby (2000) is a compendious recent collection put together specifically with the 'internal' conception of feminist philosophy in mind. Gatens (1991) is a recent and wide-ranging discussion of philosophical texts from a feminist point of view, and of feminist perspectives in philosophy. Griffiths and Whitford (1988) offers a collection of essays on feminism and philosophy covering a wide range of topics. Grimshaw (1986) is an accessible introduction to questions concerning women and philosophy, with a particular focus on ethics. Grosz (1990) surveys feminist approaches to philosophy, and offers a very useful account of what it might mean to say that philosophy is 'masculine'. Harding and Hintikka (1983) present a ground-breaking collection of essays which laid the foundations for a great deal of subsequent feminist enquiry into philosophy. Haslanger (1995) is a valuable collection of essays on topics in philosophy of language, epistemology and metaphysics. Irigaray (1985) established the terms of debate for much current French feminist thought and has also been influential in the United Kingdom and the USA. Kourany (1998) is a helpful collection of essays on a range of subjects. The further reading collected in Larrabee (1993) provides excellent background to the issue of whether women speak with a 'different voice' in ethics and the problems surrounding the idea of an 'ethic' of care. Le Doeuff (1991) is written in the form of a series of 'notebooks', and it includes an excellent discussion of Jean-Paul Sartre and Simone de Beauvoir, as well as raising broad issues about the location of women in philosophy and the objectives of feminist philosophy. Lennon and Whitford (1994) offer a useful collection from a feminist perspective, addressing both traditional epistemology and postmodern views. Lloyd (1993) is a 'classic' discussion of ways in which conceptions of 'reason' in Western philosophy have been aligned with notions of 'masculinity'. Nicholson (1990) is an invaluable collection of feminist essays, aiming to show why feminism has both an affinity with and yet also a deep ambivalence about many of the central themes of postmodernism. Nye (1988) surveys misogyny in a wide range of philosophical theories and offers an analysis of possible feminist responses. Pateman and Grosz (1986) contains a lively and interesting collection of essays both on general issues concerning the place of women in philosophy, and on more specific social and political questions. Scheman (1993) offers a wide-ranging, accessible and engaging collection of essays on feminism and philosophy, providing an excellent introduction to some central issues. Spelman (1988) discusses how some feminist thinking has excluded many women in ways that are not unlike the exclusion of women in much of the philosophy that is written by men. Tronto (1993) defends an 'ethic of care', but argues that it should not be contrasted sharply with an ethic based on notions of 'rights' or 'justice'. For feminist works that are continuous with socialized sub-traditions in analytic philosophy, see Nelson (1990) (naturalized epistemology); Seigfried (1996) (pragmatism); Harding (1991) (historicism in the philosophy of science); and Gilligan (1982) (historicism in ethics).

References

Alcoff, L. and Potter, E. 1993: *Feminist Epistemologies*. London: Routledge.

Antony, L. and Witt, C. (eds) 1993: *A Mind of One's Own*. Boulder, CO: Westview Press.

Benhabib, S., Butler, J., Cornell, D. and Fraser, N. 1995: *Feminist Contentions: A Philosophical Exchange*. London: Routledge.

Braidotti, R. 1991: *Patterns of Dissonance*. London: Routledge.

Chodorow, N. 1978: *The Reproduction of Mothering*. Berkeley: University of California Press.

Code, L. 1995: *Rhetorical Spaces: Essays on Gendered Locations*. London: Routledge.

Coole, D. 1993: *Women in Political Theory*, 2nd edn. Brighton: Wheatsheaf.

Derrida, J. 1976: *Of Grammatology*. Baltimore, MD: Johns Hopkins University Press.

Dwyer, S. (ed.) 1995: *The Problem of Pornography*. Belmont, CA: Wadsworth Publishing.

Flax, J. 1983: *Political Philosophy and the Patriarchal Unconscious*. In S. Harding and M. Hintikka (eds) *Discovering Reality: Feminist Perspectives on Epistemology, Metaphysics, and the Philosophy of Science*. London: D. Reidel.

Fricker, M. 1998: Rational Authority and Social Power: Towards a Truly Social Epistemology. *Proceedings of the Aristotelian Society*, vol. 98, part 2.

Fricker, M. and Hornsby, J. (eds) 2000: *The Cambridge Companion to Feminism in Philosophy*. Cambridge: Cambridge University Press.

Garry, A. and Pearsall, M. 1989: *Women, Knowledge and Reality: Explorations in Feminist Philosophy*. London: Unwin Hyman.

Gatens, M. 1991: *Feminism and Philosophy*. Cambridge: Polity Press.

Gilligan, C. 1982: *In a Different Voice: Psychological Theory and Women's Development*. Cambridge, MA: Harvard University Press.

Griffiths, M. and Whitford, M. (eds) 1988: *Feminist Perspectives in Philosophy*. London: Macmillan.

Grimshaw, J. 1986: *Feminist Philosophers*. Brighton: Wheatsheaf.

Grosz, E. 1990: Philosophy. In S. Gunew (ed.) *Feminist Knowledge, Critique and Construct*. London: Routledge.

Harding, S. 1991: *Whose Science, Whose Knowledge?* Buckingham: Open University Press.

Harding, S. and Hintikka, M. (eds) 1983: *Discovering Reality: Feminist Perspectives on Epistemology, Metaphysics, and the Philosophy of Science*. London: D. Reidel.

Haslanger, S. (ed.) 1995: *Philosophical Topics: Feminist Perspectives on Language, Knowledge, and Reality*, vol. 23, no. 2, fall.

Held, V. (ed.) 1995: *Justice and Care: Essential Readings in Feminist Ethics*. Boulder, CO: Westview Press.

Irigaray, L. 1985: *Speculum of the Other Woman*. Ithaca, NY: Cornell University Press.

Jaggar, A. and Young, I. M. (eds) 1998: *A Companion to Feminist Philosophy*. Oxford: Blackwell.

Kourany, J. (ed.) 1998: *Philosophy in a Feminist Voice: Critiques and Reconstructions*. Princeton, NJ: Princeton University Press.

Larrabee, M. J. (ed.) 1993: *An Ethic of Care*. London: Routledge.

Le Doeuff, M. 1991: *Hipparchia's Choice: An Essay Concerning Women, Philosophy, etc*. Oxford: Blackwell.

Lennon, K. and Whitford, M. (eds) 1994: *Knowing the Difference: Feminist Perspectives in Epistemology*. London: Routledge.

Lloyd, G. 1993: *The Man of Reason: Male and Female in Western Philosophy*, 2nd edn. London: Methuen.

Nelson, L. H. 1990: *Who Knows: From Quine to a Feminist Empiricism*. Philadelphia, PA: Temple University Press.

Nicholson, L. (ed.) 1990: *Feminism/Postmodernism*. London: Routledge.

Nye, A. 1988: *Feminist Theory and the Philosophies of Man*. London: Croom Helm.

Pateman, C. and Grosz, E. (eds) 1986: *Feminist Challenges: Social and Political Theory*. London: Allen and Unwin.

Rorty, R. 1980: *Philosophy and the Mirror of Nature*. Oxford: Blackwell.

Scheman, N. 1993: *Engenderings*. London: Routledge.

Seigfried, C. H. 1996: *Pragmatism and Feminism: Reweaving the Social Fabric*. Chicago: University of Chicago Press.

Spelman, E. 1988: *Inessential Woman: Problems of Exclusion in Feminist Thought*. Boston: Beacon Press.

Tronto, J. 1993: *Moral Boundaries*. London: Routledge.

Wollstonecraft, M. 1975 [1792]: *A Vindication of the Rights of Woman*. Harmondsworth: Penguin Books.

Discussion Questions

1   Why, if at all, should being a woman and a philosopher always be 'something that is problematic, that has to be negotiated'?

2   Should women seek to be accepted as citizens, rational subjects and moral agents just like men or should they seek to alter our conceptions of citizenship, rationality and agency?

3   Are class, gender and ethnic origin of equal importance as social and historical locations in shaping our forms of rationality?

4   Does historical variability undermine the possibility of there being any general 'masculine' features in philosophy?

5   Does the feminist project, in asserting female specificity, repeat rather than undermine existing dichotomies?

6   What is the importance of distinguishing 'speaking like a woman' and 'speaking as a woman'?

7   Can women speak within philosophy without reifying the categories they seek to escape?

8   Why might feminists seek to 'jam the theoretical machinery'?

9   How might philosophy change if the weight of feminist philosophical writings were taken seriously?

10   Must feminist philosophers accept the claim that knowing the social and historical location of philosophers is crucial to understanding the discipline?

11   Compare the role of feminist philosophy in an area such as epistemology, metaphysics or philosophy of science, with its role in an area where questions of gender have a more obvious place, such as ethics or political philosophy.

12   Is universalism in philosophy necessarily 'false universalism'? What are the implications of your answer for the role of feminism in philosophy?

13   Are differences among women as important as differences between women and men for feminist enquiry?

14   Are there advantages in distinguishing between 'feminism and philosophy' and 'feminism in philosophy'?

15   Does local piecemeal participation within mainstream philosophy threaten the integrity of feminism's critical impulse?

16   Should feminism challenge philosophy's asocial account of what it studies? If so, how can this best be achieved?

17   To what extent, if at all, should feminism seek to alter the methods and aspirations of philosophy?

18   Does feminist critique add anything valuable to other radical critiques of philosophy?

19   Does theorizing about people as socially specific subjects require abandoning abstraction?

20   How might feminism help us to ask previously unaskable questions in philosophy?

21

Ethnicity, Culture and Philosophy

ROBERT BERNASCONI

The question of the place of ethnicity within philosophy can be understood as the question of reconciling the conception of philosophy as a universal quest for universal truths with the fact that its various historical instantiations are always marked by their spatio-temporal localization. In other words, it is the question of whether philosophical pluralism at the cultural level should be considered a value, rather than a defect, as it was for HEGEL (chapter 33). If it is granted that the different perspectives that different cultures bring to bear enrich philosophy, this not only reopens the debate about the nature of philosophy, but also opens Western philosophy to kinds of critical reflection that have so far been foreign to it.

The question of what is and what is not philosophy is not simply a question of classification. The label 'philosophy' has historically been a name for one of the noblest activities of the human mind, so that to acknowledge a form of thought as a philosophy is to accord it a status; it is a way of acknowledging the seriousness of that thought. Today, even though philosophy in the universities arguably takes itself less seriously than hitherto, it remains the case that to exclude a form of thought from philosophy, or to marginalize it within philosophy, is usually meant to disparage it. Nevertheless, to acknowledge a form of thought as philosophy while keeping in place the criteria which hitherto were used to exclude it can be even more diminishing, because it is no longer treated on its own terms. The idea of ethnic philosophy does not imply that philosophy must renounce the universalism of having something to say to everyone. The problem arises only when a philosophy wants to speak for everyone and in the process silences or ignores alternative voices.

Although it is no longer as customary as it once was to refer differences in philosophical style and content to the cultures from which any given philosophy arises, the question of the relation of philosophy and culture has resurfaced within philosophy as a belated response to multiculturalism. Multiculturalism is an academic movement within the humanities that, by celebrating cultural diversity, challenges the cultural hegemony claimed by certain ethnic groups. It is also a fact of life, particularly in major cities across the world. Multiculturalism in philosophy challenges the established canon of philosophy by insisting on the need for a greater awareness of traditions of philosophy beyond so-called Western philosophy with its origin in Greece. Although many philosophers tend to associate the reference of philosophy to culture with the spectre of relativism, it is apparent that there are distinct cultures, that these are often reflected in philosophy, and that cross-cultural dialogue does take place. One of the tasks of the philosophy of culture is to examine the conditions underlying such a dialogue and the obstacles to it, given that a great deal of misunderstanding and incomprehension still persists between various philosophical traditions.

In the first section of this chapter I recall the fact that philosophy in the West only recently came to locate its origins in Greece and to that extent identify itself as GREEK (chapters 22 and 23). Many Western philosophers do not understand why discussions about multiculturalism within philosophy often quickly come to focus on the alleged Greek origins of philosophy, but one reason is because the Greek tradition of philosophy is still often used as the standard in terms of which disputes about what is and what is not philosophy are judged. In the second section I pass to a consideration of African philosophy. It is impossible in a brief essay to survey the different kinds of philosophy that have a claim to being included in the canon. I focus on African philosophy because it has been preoccupied for almost fifty years with the question of its status as philosophy. That there is an Indian philosophy or a Chinese philosophy tends to be taken for granted in academic discussions across the world, although at the same time they are usually marginalized. By examining the obstacles to a recognition of African philosophy, it is possible to highlight how the dominant conception of philosophy resists challenges to it. In the third section, I broaden the perspective to take account of a variety of different models of cross-cultural or intercultural dialogue. Finally, in the fourth section, I consider one of the most vibrant fruits of intercultural dialogue in contemporary philosophy: the critical re-examination of the Western philosophical canon from viewpoints it has largely excluded. Instead of seeing the question of so-called non-Western philosophy as a question of finding approximations to Western philosophy, where it remains the unquestioned standard, Western philosophers might see it as a way of renewing Western philosophy.

It would be absurd to try to provide in this space a survey of the different kinds of philosophy throughout the world, showing their relation to the specific culture from which they arise. Instead, I have provided an introduction to some of the debates about the relation of philosophy and culture that are taking place both within and outside the academy. Inevitably those debates, in so far as they address the question of whether the balance of what is taught in universities across the world as philosophy should be changed to take account of a broader range of cultures, takes its starting-point in the status quo. That should not be taken to mean that the university has become the privileged or sole site of philosophy. Nevertheless, the institutional realities need to be acknowledged, even as one recognizes so-called Western philosophy as one form of ethnic philosophy among others.

1   History of the Problem in the Context of the Western Philosophical Tradition

In the seventeenth century, European historians of philosophy tended to treat the subject along ethnic lines. Johannes Gerardus Vossius (1577–1649) began his posthumously published *De philosophorum sectis* (1657) with a brief survey of the Barbarian philosophies of Asia (the Chaldeans, the Jews, the Persians, the Indians, the Phoenicians and the Phrygians), and of Africa (the Egyptians, the Ethiopians and the Libyans), before passing to the philosophies of Europe (the Thracians, the Druids and, finally, the Greeks). A century later, Jacob Brucker continued the same practice, although his list was somewhat longer, and included the ancient Arabs, the Etruscans, the ancient Romans and, in an appendix on so-called 'exotic' philosophies, the Buddhists, the Chinese, the Japanese and the Canadians (Native Americans). However, Brucker (1742: 458) identified Thales as the first philosopher, in so far as Thales and his student, Anaximander, introduced the SCIENTIFIC METHOD (chapter 9). The Egyptians, according to Brucker, arrived at their knowledge by custom and chance. Brucker acknowledged that the Greeks themselves placed a high value on Egyptian learning, but, on his account, this was due to the influence of Orpheus, and so far as Brucker was concerned Orpheus brought the Greeks only Egyptian mythology, not philosophy. This was in sharp contrast to Marsilio Ficino, who over two hundred years earlier, temporarily put aside the task of translating Plotinus to translate the *Hermetica* instead (Yates 1964: 12–17). During the Italian Renaissance the return to Egypt took precedence over the return to Greece. Subsequently, the richer sources available for the study of Greek thought, the fact that Egyptian hieroglyphics had not been deciphered, and the doubt placed on the authenticity of the Hermetica, led to Egypt being given an increasingly limited role in accounts of the history of philosophy.

Nevertheless, it was not until the end of the eighteenth century that full-length histories that purportedly covered all of philosophy were written reflecting unambiguously this belief in philosophy's Greek origins. Dietrich Tiedemann in *Geist der spekulativen Philosophie* (published 1791) seems to have been the first to write a full-length history of philosophy that begins with Thales without any acknowledgement of his precursors elsewhere. At the same time European philosophers, particularly but by no means exclusively the Germans, regarded themselves as the legitimate heirs of the Greeks, thereby establishing the idea of a unified tradition.

Various explanations can be given for this restriction of philosophy to the West at this point in its history. One can point, firstly, to the emergence of a narrower conception of philosophy. Brucker, who perhaps did as much as anyone to establish the new canon, was the proponent of an eclecticism that he identified as one of the dominant characteristics of modern philosophy, but this eclecticism was not open to all philosophies. KANT (chapter 32) played a major role in restricting the idea of philosophy further, thereby highlighting the philosophical sectarianism of Western philosophy at the expense of non-Western philosophy.

There was also, secondly, in the eighteenth century a secularization of philosophy that led to a renegotiation of the distinction between myth and reason, so that what had previously been regarded as philosophy was displaced into RELIGION (chapter 15). This is nowhere more evident than in the case of Chinese philosophy, which had been criticized as atheist in response to Christian Wolff's attempt to promote it, but which was subsequently excluded from philosophy as religion. Thirdly, the history of philosophy came to be written in conformity with the new philosophy of history with its belief in progress. To show progress in history, history was written as a narrative. What did not fit into the continuous narrative was regarded as relatively insignificant or an aberration. Fourthly, partly for political motives, the conviction grew that DEMOCRACY (pp. 277–81) was a condition for the possibility of a flourishing philosophical debate. This argument can be found, for example, in both Adam Smith and Voltaire. Fifthly, and perhaps most importantly, there was the development in Europe of a virulent chauvinism, which by the end of the eighteenth century was reinforced by the new conception of race. The existence of highly developed older civilizations, such as those of Egypt or India, contradicted the chronology of creation that Europeans had calculated on the basis of the Bible. Similarly, the existence of highly developed philosophical systems in China and India threatened Europe's self-conception, particularly among those who believed that REVELATION (pp. 622–4), not reason, was the ultimate source of wisdom.

All of these forces were at work in Hegel, who did as much as anyone to establish the philosophical importance of the history of philosophy. Hegel explicitly raised the question of the relation of ethnicity to philosophy when he asked why philosophy, which supposedly was the teaching of absolute truth, appeared restricted to a small number of individuals and to particular peoples at particular times (Hegel 1985: 12). The formulation clearly echoes, however unconsciously, the anxiety of Christians trying to make sense of the fact that the revelation of God's law had apparently been confined to a few. Unlike some other cultures, which maintain that each culture has the religion appropriate to it and so is not committed to missionary activity, the West has tended to see religion in terms of a stark alternative: either one is in the truth or outside it. It is not necessary to explore here Hegel's account of the relation of philosophy to religion in all its complexity, but Hegel took the position that only a few peoples had succeeded in raising themselves to the level of philosophy. The rest had deposited their views of the world in religion (ibid.: 28). Hegel raised the concern that the plurality of philosophies made philosophy appear pointless (ibid.: 16). Pluralism was a condition to be overcome through the systematic presentation of a selective history of philosophy. Only if one made a careful selection of what should be included and restrained the urge to completeness would the progressive unfolding of truth become visible.

Hegel was also involved in an important but largely forgotten debate on the canon. At the beginning of the nineteenth century some Europeans became aware of the richness of Indian philosophy. Most notably, Friedrich Schlegel in *On the Wisdom and Language of the Indians* (1809) attempted to give Hindu philosophy a place within the philosophical canon. It is telling that he attempted to do so by locating Indian philosophy at the origin of the Western tradition. That is to say, he presented Indian philosophy as the forgotten source of a continuous narrative. He proposed a kind of renaissance, somewhat on the model of the Italian Renaissance. Schlegel's efforts did not succeed, in part because he himself converted to Catholicism and so directed his interests elsewhere. Hegel, who was a staunch opponent of Schlegel's conception of philosophy, nevertheless took Indian philosophy sufficiently seriously to discuss it on occasion in his lectures on the history of philosophy, although he rejected its claim to being 'philosophy proper' (Hegel 1994: 346–7).

Today the idea that philosophy began in Greece is under attack. Firstly, there is a question as to why the upholders of philosophy as a universal human possibility should be so keen to insist that philosophy had a single, identifiable, beginning. This seems to be an unwarranted dogmatism, particularly in the face of the fact that even the strict criteria used to privilege the place of Greek philosophy can be met elsewhere, for example, in the discussion of logic attained in India. Secondly, there is a longstanding dispute about why more attention is not paid in the standard histories to the non-Greek sources on which the Greeks clearly drew and which provide evidence of philosophies that preceded them. The point is most often made with reference to the claims of Egypt and has come to be particularly associated with certain African philosophers, such as Cheikh Anta Diop and Theophile Obenga, and African-American philosophers like George James (1954). However, some established classical scholars, such as Burkert (1992) and West (1971), have also insisted on the role of Zoroastrianism, thereby renewing another connection that was readily acknowledged in the seventeenth century but that has tended to be neglected over the last two hundred years.

It would be a mistake to attend only to those moments when some of the central figures of the Western philosophical canon dismissed the representatives of non-Western philosophies without also acknowledging those moments when Western philosophers proved more open to philosophies from elsewhere. Throughout the history of Western philosophy there have been striking examples of thinkers being drawn to what was foreign to them. Indeed, one should probably count the enthusiasm of Thomas AQUINAS (chapter 24) for Greek philosophy and its Arab commentators among them, as it is only the subsequent construction of Western philosophy as a unity that conceals the radical nature of the encounter. Recognition of the existence, if not the significance, of such dialogues is acknowledged even within fairly standard accounts of the history of Western philosophy. Leaving aside the controversy over Greek philosophy's debt to the Egyptians and the Persians, as well as the disputed case of Plotinus's alleged debt to Indian philosophy, one might look at Marsilio Ficino's translation of the Hermetica, LEIBNIZ's (chapter 27) response to the I Ching, Hegel's comments on the Bhagavad-Gita, Heidegger's enthusiasm for Lao Tsu, and so on. Indeed, although HEIDEGGER (chapter 41) dogmatically maintained a conception of philosophy as essentially Western (Heidegger 1958: 31), he nevertheless introduced a conception of poetic thinking that opened the way to a fruitful dialogue with certain aspects of Indian and Chinese philosophy.

Western philosophers who are new to debates about the merits of so-called non-Western philosophies sometimes express surprise about how quickly the focus of the argument shifts from the question of the merits of those philosophies to the question of the construction of the history of philosophy as exclusively Western. Their tendency is to see this thesis about the beginning of philosophy as a contingent HISTORICAL TRUTH (pp. 000–00) which is irrelevant to the question of whether, for example, Confucianism is philosophy. However, proponents of the broader, more inclusive, view of philosophy have made the question of the history of philosophy one of the main sites of contestation because they suspect that this account of history is being employed to legitimate an unduly narrow definition of philosophy and so cannot be left unexamined.

2   The Example of African Philosophy

The most sustained discussion of the question of ethnic philosophy in recent times has taken place in the context of African philosophy, although similar debates can be found with reference to, for example, Latin American philosophy. The debate over the nature, and even the possibility, of African philosophy may be different in character from that occasioned by, for example, Indian or Chinese philosophy, but it indicates very clearly what is at stake when a philosophy's ethnicity is marked. Indeed, it is in part the vehemence with which philosophers in the West like HUME (chapter 31), Kant and Hegel dismissed the intellectual potential of Africans on racial grounds that has led to the tendency for the discussion of African philosophy to be preoccupied with the question of its possibility.

It has become customary to follow Odera Oruka's distinction between four schools of thought or kinds of African philosophy (Oruka 1990). The first, the ethnographical school, describes the world view of a particular African people or collection of peoples. Its best-known exemplar is *Bantu Philosophy*, a work by a Belgian priest, Placide Tempels (1959). He considered it the task of Western philosophers to write the philosophy of the Bantu for them, on the grounds that they were incapable of doing it for themselves. This attitude has contributed to the disrepute into which this approach has fallen. A second approach, that of sage philosophy, focuses on individual indigenous thinkers. It is often thought to be exemplified by Ogotemelli, who became widely known through the work of Marcel Griaule (1965), but Oruka preferred to focus on sages who illustrated a greater capacity for critical thinking (Oruka 1990: 83–162). A third approach, sometimes called nationalist–ideological, was originally associated with the African politicians who led their countries to independence. Julius Nyerere, Leopold Sedar Senghor and Kwame Nkrumah are prime examples. It has now become more broadly identified to include other thinkers who contributed to the critique of colonialism and the development of postcolonial philosophy, such as Sékou Touré and Walter Rodney. Fourthly, some African philosophers have argued that African philosophy is simply Africans doing philosophy according to the same universalist view of philosophy that is widespread among academically trained philosophers. Oruka referred to this as the 'professional (critical) trend'. His list of examples ran from AUGUSTINE OF HIPPO (chapter 24) and Anton Wilhelm Arno, the first African to study philosophy at a German university, to contemporary figures like Paulin Hountondji and Kwasi Wiredu.

To the extent that African philosophers have allowed Western philosophers to provide the definition determining what is and what is not philosophy, they seem to be placed in a double bind: when African philosophy takes Western philosophy as its model, then it seems to make no distinctive contribution and so effectively disappears, but when its specificity is emphasized then its credentials to be considered genuine philosophy are put in question and it is dismissed either as religion or as wisdom literature. African philosophy's preoccupation with establishing its credentials as philosophy, usually according to Western standards, has clearly impeded its development. But it is a task whose importance is obvious in the context of contemporary academic institutions. Kwasi Wiredu and Valentine Mudimbo have each in their own way negotiated the impasse. Wiredu (1996), employing the tools of ANALYTIC PHILOSOPHY (pp. 2–6), has fashioned a synthesis of traditional and modern ideas to articulate the conceptuality of the Akan. Mudimbe (1988), by contrast, used FOUCAULT (chapter 42) to question the discourses through which the academy has theorized African identities.

The problem identified in the context of African philosophy can be stated more generally: does Western philosophy establish the terms according to which any other philosophy is judged or can the latter be recognized as philosophy on its own terms? To accept the former alternative would maintain in force the structural mechanism by which the achievements of these cultures have historically been diminished within the West. The question of ethnic philosophy thus necessarily presents a challenge to the dominant philosophy that has largely defined itself in terms of UNIVERSAL REASON (pp. 395–7). The decisive question is thus the question 'what is philosophy?' It is worth noting, however, that the definition of philosophy is widely employed as an instrument of exclusion between the various sectarian philosophies in the West and not only to confine philosophy to the West. It has, for example, been used in analytic philosophy's polemic against CONTINENTAL PHILOSOPHY (chapters 40, 41, 42). And yet, although philosophers like to proclaim their right to police or otherwise interrogate other academic disciplines, on the grounds that those disciplines are incapable of investigating their own central concepts – for example, the concept of life that sustains BIOLOGY (chapter 10) – philosophers are rarely as 'unphilosophical' as when they are laying down the law about what is and what is not philosophy.

3 Interculturalism in Philosophy

There is a question about the identities used to describe various philosophies, but they are not as problematic as is sometimes claimed. One does not have to be committed to some form of linguistic or cultural RELATIVISM (pp. 395–7) to believe that labels like 'Arabic philosophy', 'the Scottish Moralists' or 'contemporary French philosophy' are informative. Even after Hegel's restriction of 'philosophy proper' to the Greeks and their heirs, the question of the cultural identity of philosophy was not regarded as closed. Hegel had both a broad and a narrow understanding of the Germanic, but in whichever sense he meant it, philosophy was firmly located along a Greek–German axis. It was the practice throughout the nineteenth and twentieth centuries to divide European philosophy along national lines and write, for example, specifically of French or Scottish philosophies. Cultural factors were more often appealed to as a way of explaining why another nation or group did not recognize the truth that was presented to them on a platter, but instead preferred to adhere to false opinions in line with their national characteristics. Of course, terms like 'African philosophy' are less likely to be informative than labels like 'Bantu philosophy' because of their level of generality, but they nevertheless retain a certain usefulness. It is disingenuous to question 'African' as an identity, even given its questionable genealogy, and yet leave the idea of Western philosophy intact. The construction of Africa represents a problem, but no less of a problem than the construction of 'the West' as employed in the phrase 'Western philosophy', particularly if the Greeks are thought of as Western, which is, of course, not how they understood themselves.

There is also a question as to the resources available for theorizing the relation of a specific ethnicity to the philosophies that are said to express or represent it. Reflection about philosophy and ethnicity has the task of establishing the conditions of a genuinely open dialogue. Agreement about the nature of philosophy is not one of those conditions in the way that care about translation is. One of the ways in which philosophy happens is through the translation of the defining experiences of one culture into

573

a language that makes those experiences accessible to people who have not undergone them. Instead of Westerners telling the Bantu what their philosophy was, as Tempels proposed, one of the tasks of Bantu philosophers is, on this model, to articulate the most central ideas of their culture in a way that renders it intelligible to members of very different cultural groups. Philosophy, in this conception, is not merely the expression of world views. It is a vehicle not just for learning about, but also for learning from, other cultures. The critical function of philosophy thereby comes to be understood DIALECTICALLY (pp. 746–7) as that moment within an encounter that can be transforming. There are those who leave such an encounter untouched; but others, if not converted, are at the very least, in T. S. Eliot's phrase, 'no longer at ease, here in the old dispensation' (Eliot 1963: 110). One danger of any attempt to draw ethnic divisions among philosophies is that it lends itself to biological essentialism. Another danger is that a culture can come to be identified with what belongs to its past. In both cases culture can come to be thought of as confined to a static set of beliefs already in place, giving rise to the imposition of the strait-jacket of authenticity. However, an adequate understanding of the operation of how cross-cultural dialogue takes place in practice exposes these dangers more as traps that theories fall into than real possibilities.

Some conceptions of philosophy are better able to accommodate philosophical pluralism than others. From this perspective the debate between Kant and Herder in the 1780s represents a decisive moment in Western philosophy's understanding of its relation to 'rival' traditions, although the issue between them at the time was the PHILOSOPHY OF HISTORY (chapter 14) rather than the history of philosophy. Kant's idea of a cosmopolitanism that took its cue from Europe clearly had more impact on the way the history of philosophy came to be written in the nineteenth century, but one can find in Herder the resources for a certain multiculturalism. Indeed, Herder was unusual in the way he not only gave a place to every culture in the formation of the idea of humanity, but he also allowed for one culture to challenge another. Perhaps because a certain vicious form of cosmopolitanism was gaining ground among the European powers, the Herderian approach was largely neglected. The decisive moment was perhaps when, following Hegel, the model adopted for understanding was that of 'pure self-recognition in absolute otherness' (Hegel 1977: 14). This model remains alive in Gadamerian HERMENEUTICS (p. 397), where the idea of tradition still has a controlling force. The possibility of a different approach is sketched by students of the study of religion. The very conception of religion in the West has been enriched and transformed by an understanding of 'non-Western' religions. It is no longer a question of seeing what in other cultures resembles or prepares for Christianity, as was once the case.

Cross-Cultural Dialogue

The question of philosophy and ethnicity is, therefore, by no means restricted to questions about the philosophical canon, but embraces a concern for establishing the conditions for a cross-cultural genuine dialogue. It is at least arguable that treating the existence of philosophy as a cultural universal, present in some degree in all cultures at least as an impulse, without challenging the status of Western philosophy for philosophy in general, has done more to diminish Indian and Chinese thought than their total exclusion did. It means that they are no longer approached on their terms, but are judged on the basis of alien standards. The role of multiculturalism within philosophy goes beyond recognizing some aspects of, for example, Indian thought as legitimate philosophy according to an already established definition of philosophy. For this reason the phrase 'cross-cultural conversation' can be used to characterize the process by which cultures, which are in any case not discrete units, can engage with each other in a way that is mutually empowering (Balslev 1996: 17). In German discussions the term 'interculturalism' (Kimmerle 1994) has served a similar purpose and it is perhaps preferable to the term 'multiculturalism', which suggests a more static conception.

The existence of Western philosophers who incorporate their knowledge of, usually, Indian or Chinese philosophy into their work shows cross-cultural conversation at work, but to focus on them would be to retain a certain one-sidedness. Sarvepalli Radhkrishnan in India and Kitarô Nishida in Japan are among the best-known examples of cross-cultural conversation outside of Europe and North America. Nishida's philosophical effort was arguably devoted to 'the development and articulation of the logic of oriental experience' (Inagaki 1993: 293), with a strong emphasis on the Buddhist tradition, but his extensive discussions of Western philosophy, particularly of Kant and Hegel, were integral to his performance of this task and in no way a distraction from it. However, for the question of the relation between philosophy and ethnicity, the work of Leopold Senghor, the former president of Senegal, is particularly instructive. Senghor was one of the founders of the Negritude movement, which had arisen in Paris in the 1930s among students from the French colonies who had discovered their racial identity in large measure as a result of the way they experienced themselves as seen in racial terms. But far from trying to be exclusively African, which is how some of its critics represent the Negritude movement, Senghor aspired to a kind of cultural miscegenation to which all cultures could contribute. In direct contrast to the civilization of the Universal that it was offered by the West, and which seemed only another name for explicitly Western ideas, Senghor proposed a universal civilization. The goal was 'to assimilate, not to be assimilated' (Senghor 1964: 39). Among his extensive references to African philosophy, one finds frequent appeals to, for example, Henri Bergson, Pierre Teilhard de Chardin and Martin Heidegger.

Attention to the process of translation helps clarify how understanding across traditions takes place. Many key philosophical terms, like *logos*, *yoga*, *tao*, *zen* or, for that matter *Geist* or *Dasein*, are usually left untranslated. These words have now passed into the English language but without losing any of their foreignness. This shows how the often-heard demand that every philosophy express itself clearly in English is too severe. The lexicon of any language expands to accommodate what is new, especially in the encounter between cultures. One sees this very clearly in the case of Japanese, which initially lacked a word for 'being' and developed one in the course of translating some of the classics of Western philosophy. However, the fact that the Greek word 'philosophy' has itself proved difficult to translate into many of the world's languages does not mean that it makes no sense to talk of philosophy in relation to the cultures that speak those languages.

Philosophy is not static. The Western tradition of philosophy is familiar with the way great philosophers or great movements in philosophy redefine the field. A particularly fruitful conception of the relation of philosophy to culture is now evident in post-Holocaust Jewish philosophy. For example, Emmanuel Levinas not only translated a Hebraic wisdom that he drew from the Talmud into the language of Greek philosophy, but he also enriched that language further by introducing into it a range of experiences that had previously been absent from that tradition. In particular, Levinas claimed that the experience of being persecuted gave access to depths of subjectivity to which previous philosophy had not had access. Although Levinas himself had reservations about labelling his work 'Jewish philosophy', there was a clear continuity between his commentaries on the Talmud, which he explicitly described as translations from Hebrew into the language of the universities, and his directly philosophical works, which needed a further moment of translation in so far as philosophy called, in his view, for different kinds of evidence. Levinas himself had a somewhat conservative conception of the philosophical canon, and he was prone in interviews to dismiss non-Western cultures in outrageous terms (Mortley 1991: 18). Nevertheless, his use of the experience of being persecuted as evidence can serve as a model for other oppressed groups committed to the philosophical articulation and commemoration of the suffering that has helped forge their identity and culture, and who, like Levinas, are committed to resisting the tendency of the traditional aspects of a culture's existence from sinking to the level of folklore (Levinas 1994: 197). A similar relation between philosophy and experience can be found in African-American philosophy, which has been aptly described by Leonard Harris (1983) as a 'philosophy born of struggle'.

4   Re-examining the Eurocentrism of the Canon and Renewing Philosophy

In addition to broadening the philosophical canon and seeking ways to advance the dialogue between the various philosophies included in such an expanded canon, interculturalism in philosophy engages in a re-examination of the major figures of the Western philosophical tradition. Much of the energy animating interculturalism within contemporary philosophy has come from the widespread tendency of contemporary Western philosophers to dismiss as lacking in philosophical significance the fact that many of the most prominent philosophers of the tradition were less critical of the West's exploitation of other societies than many of their contemporaries. In other words, the ethnocentric character of Western philosophy is illustrated not only by the construction of the canon, but also by the fact that, for example, the racism of many of the central figures from the canon is, like their sexism, often ignored. FEMINIST PHILOSOPHERS (chapter 20) have for some time insisted on confronting the philosophical canon with its blindness and its complicity in oppression, but similar criticisms have also long been widespread among other oppressed or neglected groups, and it is merely a matter of time before they too become more widely disseminated through the academy.

That Western philosophy often tries to take credit for the noble ideas it has articulated, while refusing responsibility for the evil that it has underwritten, sometimes in the name of those same ideals, is one of the focal points of postcolonial philosophy. This has led some of the major philosophers of the canon to be scrutinized afresh. For example, LOCKE's (chapter 29) discussion of rights is now seen in the context of his involvement in the African slave trade, in the same way that his account of the origin of private property is now seen in the context of his support for the colonization of North America. Similarly, Kant's cosmopolitanism is contrasted with his advocacy of the concept of race and his opposition to race mixing. And NIETZSCHE's (chapter 40) writings are mined for his remarks on women and Blacks. Although it has often been African-American philosophers who have insisted in the first instance on asking about John Locke's involvement in African slavery, Jewish philosophers who have insisted on recalling Kant's anti-semitism, and women philosophers who have initially raised questions about Nietzsche's sexism, these concerns should not be and have not been confined to members of the offended group. However, many standard commentaries still dismiss these approaches as irrelevant to an understanding of the specific philosophy under consideration.

What significance should be given to the fact that Locke and Kant failed to question the chattel slavery in Africans of which they were well aware, even though they had at their disposal the intellectual resources to challenge it? This failure is regarded by many Western philosophers as merely a contingent fact that tells us nothing significant about their philosophies, still less the tradition to which they belong. Whereas Locke's and Kant's defenders explain that they are merely making the logical point that there is nothing at the core of their philosophies that entails race-based slavery, critics complain that that defines their philosophies too narrowly. This example shows how at the heart of the debate is the question of the definition of philosophy. The recognition that such controversies provide another access to the question of the nature of philosophy gives additional importance to them. The widespread tendency to confine the philosophical study of major figures in the history of philosophy to consideration of their ontological or epistemological arguments, even though these philosophers had widespread interests they considered no less philosophical, is defended as a way of focusing on what is most important in their thought, but at the same time it distorts the relation of philosophy to its historical context. For one thing, it makes it seem that philosophy is unmotivated or unconcerned about the prevailing context.

Extending the Role of Philosophy

What seems, particularly from the outside, as defensiveness on the part of Western philosophy about its own history is also a reflection of its acceptance of a reduced role for philosophy. Western philosophy as practised in universities across the world has become reconciled to its role as a somewhat marginal activity, at least compared with its former centrality. Nevertheless, understanding a text involves an appreciation of what is being attempted in that text. This is not always easy, as attempts to establish the legitimacy of a text as philosophy often involve minimizing some of its central elements. For example, within Indian philosophy one finds *Karman, karmamârga* in the Gita, as the working out of one's own salvation, not only as an idea but also as something to realize. Pannikar has argued that by appealing to this notion one can upset a certain prevalent conception of philosophy and thereby deepen the notion of philosophy. Pannikar concedes that this works by reminding the West of the fact that there is an entire tradition which proclaims the philosophical life without a rupture between theory and praxis (Pannikar 1993: 25). He thereby grants that the insight still would be conducted without reference to India at all! Nevertheless, the argument helps to establish how limited the conception of academic philosophy has become. Similarly, one of the arguments often made as to what Western philosophy can learn from Chinese philosophy is that the former can rediscover through the latter a recognition of the importance of the question: how should one live (Van Norden 1996)? Although there has been a marked increase in work contrasting the discussions of the virtues within the Confucian tradition with those found in classical Greek philosophy, for the moment this still seems a distant possibility.

5 Concluding Remarks

Even if one restricts oneself to the dominant conception of philosophy that is current within Anglo-American philosophy and takes that as one's standard, one will nevertheless be able to find that standard met elsewhere, for example, in select moments in Chinese or Indian philosophy. One would also have to accept that much that, by consensus, passes for philosophy would also not meet that criterion. The point is that there is no single definition of philosophy that covers even everything that is regularly recognized as philosophy within the academy. The flexibility of the conception of philosophy is what allows each major philosopher to redefine the discipline, often in a way that belittles or even excludes from philosophy much that had previously been included. Nevertheless, our familiarity with that procedure does not give Kantians the right to deny that, for example, pre-Kantian metaphysics be called philosophy. Nor should we confuse the legitimacy of a specific tradition of philosophy with all of philosophy. It is true that philosophical debate in the twentieth century has often been conducted by refusing to share the title 'philosophy' with one's intellectual opponents, but the relative flexibility of the conception of philosophy does not have to be used only as a way of narrowing what counts as philosophy. It can equally well serve to expand its boundaries. Just as the study of religion in the West largely ceased during the course of the twentieth century to be a way of promoting Christianity at the expense of non-Western religions, so the study of philosophy in the universities can be redesigned to offer greater opportunity for studying different traditions. Until this happens there will always be a suspicion that, in spite of the pretensions of Western philosophy toward universalism, for the most part Western philosophers will tend to be more provincial in their interests than, for example, many African, Chinese, Indian or Japanese philosophers, who often have mastery of more than one tradition.

Further Reading

The challenge to the Greek origins of philosophy is often associated with the first volume of Martin Bernal's *Black Athena* (1987), but although that book usefully directs attention to the history of the history of philosophy in the eighteenth century, his account is not always reliable. For the historiographical question one would do better to consult the essays by Blackwell and Schneider in Kelly (1997). The case against the Greek origins of philosophy has been made with reference to African and particularly Egyptian philosophy, by Cheikh Anta Diop (1991) and Theophile Obenga (1992). The case for finding the origins of philosophy in the Near East has been made by Burkert (1992) and West (1971).

For an excellent survey of many of the different kinds of philosophy that are at issue in discussions of philosophy's relation to ethnicity, see the collection edited by Deutsch and

Bontekoe (1997). There is a good review of recent debates on the philosophical status of African philosophy in Masolo (1994). Oruka (1990) not only includes some of his most important essays, but also classic essays by Bodunrin and Outlaw. Halbfass (1988) has provided a survey of the relations between Indian and European philosophy that furthers our understanding of intercultural dialogue. The best introduction to Herder as an early exponent of a form of multiculturalism is Berlin (1976), although Berlin does not use that term specifically. For an introduction to cross-cultural conversation, see Balslev (1996). Finally, for an excellent example of a philosopher educated both in the East and the West, steering a course between universalism and relativism, see chapters 20 and 26 of Mohanty (1993).

References

Balslev, A. 1991: *Cultural Otherness: Correspondence with Richard Rorty.* Shimla: Indian Institute of Advanced Study.

——1996: *Cross-Cultural Conversation. (Initiation.)* Atlanta, GA: Scholars Press.

Berlin, I. 1976: Herder and the Enlightenment. In *Vico and Herder.* London: Hogarth Press.

Bernal, M. 1987: *Black Athena, Volume 1: The Fabrication of Ancient Greece, 1785–1985.* New Brunswick, NJ: Rutgers University Press.

Bernasconi, R. 1997: African Philosophy's Challenge to Continental Philosophy. In E. C. Eze (ed.) *Postcolonial African Philosophy.* Oxford: Blackwell.

——2000: Krimkrams: Hegel and the Current Controversy about the Beginning of Philosophy. In C. E. Scott and J. Sallis (eds) *Interrogating the Tradition.* Albany: State University of New York Press.

Brucker, J. 1742: *Historia Critica Philosophiae.* Leipzig: Weidemann.

Burkert, W. 1992: *The Orientalizing Revolution* (translated by M. E. Pinder and W. Burkert). Cambridge, MA: Harvard University Press.

Deutsch, E. and Bontekoe, R. 1997: *A Companion to World Philosophies.* Oxford: Blackwell.

Diop, C. A. 1991: *Civilization or Barbarism* (translated by Yaa-Lengi Meema Ngemi). New York: Lawrence Hill Books.

Eliot, T. S. 1963: Journey of the Magi. In *Collected Poems 1909–1962.* London: Faber.

Gadamer, H.-G. 1989: *Truth and Method* (translated by J. Weinsheimer and D. G. Marshall). New York: Continuum.

Gracia, J. J. 1992: *Philosophy and Its History.* Albany: State University of New York Press.

Griaule, M. 1965: *Conversations with Ogotomméli* (translated by R. Butler). Oxford: Oxford University Press.

Halbfass, W. 1988: *India and Europe.* Albany: State University of New York Press.

Harris, L. (ed.) 1983: *Philosophy Born of Struggle: Anthology of Afro-American Philosophy from 1917.* Dubuque: Iowa State University Press.

Hegel, G. W. F. 1977: *Phenomenology of Spirit* (translated by A. V. Miller). Oxford: Oxford University Press.

——1985: *Introduction to the Lectures on the History of Philosophy* (translated by T. M. Knox and A. V. Miller). Oxford: Oxford University Press.

——1994: *Vorlesungen über die Geschichte der Philosophie. Teil 1* (edited by P. Garniron and W. Jaeschke). Hamburg: Felix Meiner.

Heidegger, M. 1958: *What is Philosophy?* German–English (translated by W. Kluback and J. T. Wilde). London: Vision Press.

Herder, J. G. 1800: *Outlines of a Philosophy of the History of Man* (translated by T. Churchill). New York: Bergmann Reprint.

Hountondji, P. J. 1996: *African Philosophy: Myth and Reality* (translated by Henri Evans). Bloomington: Indiana University Press.

Inagaki, B. R. 1993: The Concept of Creation in the Philosophy of Kitaro Nishida. In G. Fløistad (ed.) *Contemporary Philosophy: A New Survey*, vol. 7. Dordrecht: Kluwer.

James, G. G. M. 1954: *Stolen Legacy*. New York: Philosophical Library.

Kelly, D. R. 1997: *History and the Disciplines*. Rochester, NY: University of Rochester Press.

Kimmerle, H. 1994: *Die Dimension des Interkulturellen*. Amsterdam: Rodopi.

Leibniz, G. W. 1977: *Discourse on the Natural Theology of the Chinese*. Honolulu: University Press of Hawaii.

Levinas, E. 1994: *Beyond the Verse* (translated by Gary D. Mole). London: Athlone Press.

Masolo, D. A. 1994: *African Philosophy in Search of Identity*. Bloomington: Indiana University Press.

Mohanty, J. N. 1993: *Essays on Indian Philosophy*. Delhi: Oxford University Press.

Mortley, R. 1991: *French Philosophers in Conversation*. London: Routledge.

Mudimbe, V. Y. 1988: *The Invention of Africa*. Bloomington: Indiana University Press.

Nishida, K. 1966: *Intelligibility and the Philosophy of Nothingness* (translated by R. Schinzinger). Honolulu: East–West Center Press.

Obenga, T. 1992: *Ancient Egypt and Black Africa* (translated by S. Martinon and A. Shelk). London: Karnak.

Oruka, H. O. (ed.) 1990: *Sage Philosophy: Indigenous Thinkers and Modern Debate on African Philosophy*. Leiden: E. J. Brill.

Panikkar, R. 1993: Satapathaprajñâ. Should We Speak of Philosophy in Classical India? A Case of Homeomorphic Equivalents. In G. Fløistad (ed.) *Contemporary Philosophy: A New Survey*, vol. 7. Dordrecht: Kluwer.

Santinello, G. et al. 1993: *Models of the History of Philosophy, Volume 1: From its Origins in the Renaissance to the 'Historia Philosophica'*. Dordrecht: Kluwer.

Schlegel, F. 1849: On the Indian Language, Literature, and Philosophy. In *The Aesthetic and Miscellaneous Works of Frederik von Schlegel* (translated by E. J. Millington). London: Bohn.

Schneider, U. 1990: *Die Vergangenheit des Geistes*. Frankfurt: Suhrkamp.

Senghor, L. 1964: *Liberté*. Paris: Éditions du Seuil.

Tempels, P. 1959: *Bantu Philosophy* (translated by Colin King). Paris: Presence Africaine.

Van Norden, B. W. 1996: What Should Western Philosophy Learn from Chinese Philosophy? In P. J. Ivanhoe (ed.) *Chinese Language*. Chicago: Open Court.

Vossius, J. G. 1657: *De Philosophorum Sectis*. The Hague.

West, M. L. 1971: *Early Greek Philosophy and the Orient*. Oxford: Oxford University Press.

Wiredu, K. 1996: *Cultural Universals and Particulars: An African Perspective*. Bloomington: Indiana University Press.

Wolff, C. 1985: *Rede über die praktische Philosophie der Chinesen*. Latin–German (translated by M. Albrecht). Hamburg: Felix Meiner.

Yates, F. 1964: *Giordano Bruno and the Hermetic Tradition*. Chicago: University of Chicago Press.

Discussion Questions

1   In what sense is philosophy transcultural?

2   If philosophy is not transcultural, is it condemned to cultural relativism?

3   Why has philosophy as a discipline largely resisted the pronounced tendency toward multiculturalism in neighbouring disciplines?

4   Does it make sense to talk about the beginning of philosophy? If so, what difference does it make where philosophy began?

5   Is there progress in philosophy? How would this be shown?

6   How is the standard established by which what is and what is not philosophy comes to be determined?

7   Is Western philosophy one form of ethnic philosophy among others?

8   What considerations led to the identification of Western philosophy as philosophy proper?

9   What difference, if any, does it make for the question of determining what cultures have philosophy that the word 'philosophy' is derived from Greek?

10   What problems are to be guarded against when construing philosophical divisions along ethnic lines?

11   What is the relation between philosophy and experience? Can culture-specific experiences legitimately provide the basis for a philosophy?

12   What significance should be given to the instances of racism within the history of Western philosophy? Under what conditions should, for example, Locke's or Kant's racism come to alter our views of their philosophy?

13   Does the fact that a mode of thinking is attached to a culture or a way of living count as evidence that it is not philosophical?

PART II
HISTORY OF PHILOSOPHY

22

Ancient Greek Philosophy

ROBERT WARDY

Western philosophy has its origins in ancient Greece, with speculation, problems and arguments stretching from the Presocratics to the major Hellenistic schools. Instead of concentrating on the rich variety of philosophical doctrines explored and defended in this brilliant formative period, the following chapter focuses on the deeply original conceptions of method developed by Socrates, Plato, Aristotle and the Hellenistic Stoics and Epicureans. This study of method provides a framework for understanding conceptions of philosophy, the goals of philosophers and the point of particular philosophical questions not only in ancient Greece, but also in subsequent philosophical periods, including our own.

Why read ancient Greek philosophy? The most obvious answer is that if the history of philosophy is a worthy object of study, then any serious philosopher must know something of the Greek contribution to the subject. This priority is not simply a matter of ancestral piety. It is not merely that Western philosophy began in ancient Greece. Because many of the defining techniques, characteristic preoccupations and perennial difficulties of philosophy arose during its brilliant first phase, anyone working in ignorance of those achievements and failures labours under a significant handicap. This large claim can be given both 'historical' and 'philosophical' specifications. Much MEDIEVAL (chapter 24) and later philosophy is unintelligible to those unacquainted with the Greek material that in large measure set the agenda for subsequent thinkers; while views of the distinctive goals and methods of philosophical investigation will be seriously impoverished if the initial Greek conceptions are left out of account.

Greek philosophy is as good as any philosophy ever done. During the twentieth century it attracted many of the very best philosophical historians, and the explosion in scholarship within recent decades makes even a brief overview of work on a number of central issues impossible. New interpretations of Presocratic philosophy continue to appear, accompanied by renewed reflection on what factors distinguish the momentous new movement of rationalistic investigation from older, mythological patterns of thought (Lloyd 1979: 10–58). Much insight has been gained about the Greek invention of axiomatics, and about how philosophers and mathematicians might have interacted (Barnes 1975; Lloyd 1979: 59–125). Revitalized interest in the theory of the virtues, practical reason and the naturalistic turn in ETHICS (chapter 6) has sharpened the appreciation that Aristotle (384–322 BC) is perhaps the West's most important ethical thinker (MacIntyre 1981; Williams 1985). Advances in the history of EPISTE-MOLOGY (chapter 1) have established that Hellenistic sceptical controversy played a vital part in the evolution of theories of knowledge (Burnyeat 1980; Annas and Barnes 1985). Although Aristotle's LOGIC (chapter 4) continues to benefit from innovative new interpretations (Lear 1980), there is also a steady increase in the illuminating study of hitherto neglected ancient logical systems (Frede 1974; Brunschwig 1980; Barnes 1980; Denyer 1991). A massive project of translation and exegesis is currently making generally available the vast resources of the late commentators on Aristotle, whose philosophical creativity had hitherto been neglected on the erroneous presumption that the exegetical format prohibits originality and because of the sheer difficulty of the largely untranslated, unexplored sources (Sorabji 1987–).

1   Socrates and Dialectical Method

This list is only a very incomplete catalogue of ongoing research. Apart from a few passing illustrations, I shall concentrate exclusively on only one especially vigorous field, the study of dialectical method in ancient Greece. My discussion will still be heavily curtailed, but it will summarize some of ancient thought's most fruitful achievements and indicate current problems which should exercise all philosophers.

Philosophy has been provocatively described as 'footnotes to Plato'. In the contemporary scene it would be more accurate, if no less provocative, to characterize philosophy as answers to Socrates (c.470–399 BC). Why is he of such overwhelming importance? Although the argumentative exploration of reality and illusion which is philosophy was undertaken for the first time in the Greek colonies of Asia Minor roughly a century before his time, the indomitably rationalistic Socrates of the Platonic dialogues has completely dominated the Western portrait of the archetypical philosopher, as can be seen during the Renaissance in Rabelais (c.1494–1553) and Montaigne (1533–92), and during the nineteenth-century intellectual upheaval in Kierkegaard (1813–55) and NIETZSCHE (1844–1900) (chapter 40).

Whether as hero or as villain, Socrates epitomizes the promise and the threat of philosophy. That these evocations of Socrates appear as often on the margins of philosophy as in its main text increases rather than diminishes his stature: the Socratic image connects philosophy with the great movements in literature, politics and religion which collectively give philosophy its place in culture. The Socrates of Plato's *Symposium* is a figure of almost grotesque physical ugliness concealing unequalled intellectual gifts, who devotes unceasing, single-minded effort to the discovery of vital ethical truths through disciplined argument. His effect on almost everyone is unsettling: he shakes their most cherished convictions, and arouses shame at failure to think rationally and live consistently by the light of reason. He inspires a passion beside which ordinary erotic feelings dwindle into insignificance.

Philosophy during the twentieth century in the English-speaking world emerged from infatuation with an exceedingly narrow self-conception as the handmaid of the natural sciences; but it remains a self-contained, highly technical academic discipline largely inaccessible even to highly educated non-specialists. In consequence,

Anglo-American philosophy has sadly almost completely lost the strength it gave to and received from the culture at large, and too easily lapses into esoteric scholasticism. Some responsibility for this isolation must rest with a longstanding feature of philosophy, its claim to transcend merely personal persuasion by conforming solely to the dictates of objective canons of argument; people outside philosophy are not readily inclined to listen to unattractively impersonal, difficult messages. The central enigma of Socrates is that whereas the standards of argument to which he adhered are a model of rigour, he worked not in an academy, but in the market-place and streets of Athens. In the Platonic image of Socrates, irresistible personality and dialectical force, subjective and objective appeal, inextricably combine. Contemporary philosophers worried about the marginalization and inaccessibility of their subject do well to ponder Socrates's universal impact; philosophers complacent about their specialism do even better if forced to awaken from their dogmatic slumbers by the Socratic gadfly (Plato, *Apology*, 30E).

In what sense was Socrates a street-philosopher? As portrayed in the earlier Platonic dialogues, he can do philosophy not by himself, but rather with and against an inter-locutor. He examines anyone whomsoever with a reputation for wisdom (ibid.: 23B), including but not limiting himself to professional thinkers, and deliberately seeks out the politicians, poets and artisans of Athens (ibid.: 21B–22E). (Since the women of ancient Greece did not engage in public affairs, Socrates does not argue with them, but that is not on account of lack of interest; when he describes his attitude towards exis-tence after death, if such there be, he indicates his enthusiasm at the prospect of con-tinuing his characteristic debates with famous men and women in the afterlife (ibid.: 41C).) Why did Socrates carry on in this fashion? As he famously declares, 'the unex-amined life is not worth living for a human' (ibid.: 38A). Although he abstained as much as possible from involvement in political affairs as conventionally understood, his conviction was that the only way to achieve virtue was to understand it; Socratic philosophy, so far from being an academic avoidance of the active life, was the essen-tial means of conducting life properly, and challenged everyone without exception.

The Socratic method of doing philosophy, adversarial co-operation, sounds para-doxical; how did it work? Its Greek name, *elenchos*, occurs outside philosophical con-texts and means 'testing' or 'examination'. Nowhere does Socrates formally delineate, let alone justify, his procedure, but it is possible to derive a description of his standard practice from a consideration of the Platonic dialogues where it is put to work. Socrates gets his interlocutor to offer an answer to the question 'What is X?', where the value of 'X' is usually, if not always, a virtue such as courage, justice or piety. In these dialogues, that there is such a thing as, say, courage is taken for granted; and *what sort of thing* it might be – an item in the world, as people and colours are in their different ways, or a mental item, or a feature of the Greek language – is also never made an object of enquiry. Thus Socratic *elenchos* is a matter of definition, yet vital questions concerning the nature and import of definition are not raised.

Once his partner has offered a candidate definition, Socrates typically proceeds by eliciting his support for further propositions. Sometimes the connection between these propositions and the original definition is immediately obvious, sometimes not; but the eventual result is always an argument using the definition whose conclusion either directly contradicts it, or at least conflicts with assumptions the interlocutor is not willing to surrender. The outcome is consistently negative: Socratic 'examination' is refutation, establishing that a proposed definition of some virtue is unacceptable because it entails contradiction directly or indirectly. Socrates concludes that his partner has no better grasp of the nature of that which is being defined, the *definiendum*, than he himself, and urges that they persevere in the definitional quest, since nothing could be more important than knowledge of what they demonstrably do not know.

The logic of the Socratic *elenchos* has continuously fascinated workers on Greek philosophy, and provoked a series of extremely important studies from the late Gregory Vlastos (1907–91), the leading Socratic scholar of the twentieth century. Vlastos is exercised by two closely interrelated questions. The *elenchos* as described can evidently at best hope to establish the consistency, not the truth, of the interlocutor's beliefs, but it is overwhelmingly obvious that Socrates aspires to objective validity; how can he suppose that his philosophical method might get beyond merely human agreement? Then, in the so-called 'middle' dialogues, the Platonic Socrates is made to propound a collection of TRANSCENDENTAL (chapter 32), METAPHYSICAL (chapter 2) and EPISTEMO-LOGICAL (chapter 1) doctrines strikingly different from anything encountered before in the corpus. It is now common ground to almost all scholars that these pronouncements represent Plato's own later philosophy, supplementing but also largely supplanting the *elenchos*, which is itself perhaps to be identified with the method of the historical Socrates. So Vlastos tries to understand how the real Socrates could justifiably have used the *elenchos* as an instrument reaching beyond consistency to truth, and why Plato ultimately rejected his hero's position.

In 'The Socratic Elenchus' Vlastos (1983) makes a proposal which has excited the greatest interest. He emphasizes that the procedure of eliciting contradiction sketched above is a significantly incomplete description of Socrates's procedure. In addition, it is essential that we recognize that Socrates demands that his interlocutor's responses be *sincere*: the *elenchos* is examination, not of neutral propositions which might be held, but rather of *asserted propositions*, these being the sincere beliefs of Socrates's dialectical partner. This feature of the method is of vital importance to Vlastos because he argues that if the *elenchos* works on commitments rather than bare, unasserted propositions, it can yield substantive results on one, admittedly remarkable, assumption: namely, that the belief-sets of all human beings always contain true propositions on the basis of which it is always possible to refute their false beliefs. Socrates can transcend mere inconsistency because inconsistency with the truth is not just inconsistency – it is falsehood. Finally, we are to understand Plato's eventual renunciation of the *elenchos* – and with it the populism characteristic of authentic Socratic street-philosophy – as the outcome of his dissatisfaction with Socrates's startling epistemological faith, a dissatisfaction issuing eventually in the philosophy transcending ordinary beliefs and experience intimately associated with his name.

Vlastos's proposal has produced intense debate rather than easy consent. His thesis is intrinsically unstable. The leading theme of his later book is that the procedures and convictions of the 'real' Socrates and the later, Platonic 'Socrates' 'contrast as sharply with one another as with any third philosophy you care to mention' (Vlastos 1991: 46). One aspect of this near schizophrenia is the total epistemological naivety, or at least total silence on epistemological topics, of the 'real' Socrates: Vlastos's analysis of the logic of the *elenchos* is inferred from, rather than seen in, the actual text of the dialogues. Thus he must attribute to Socrates highly contentious and undefended, if not indefensible, philosophical tenets, while maintaining that they remain wholly implicit in the practice of their original proponent and only break out in order to be rejected in Plato's subsequent reflections. This scenario strains credibility, and has not won general support; the nature and implications of Socratic questioning continue to trouble readers of Greek philosophy.

It is now easy to see why I labelled the *elenchos* 'adversarial': propositions are asserted by Socrates's partner in the course of the search for a definition, and are refuted on the basis of his further admissions. But how is this method also 'co-operative'? Anticipating or reacting to his interlocutors' irritation at being worsted, Socrates declares time and again that examination of his type is not a personal matter: for example, when in the *Gorgias* he is about to elicit further damaging admissions, he insists that he does this 'not for your sake, but for the argument, so that it will advance in the fashion best able to render what is under discussion clear to us' (Plato, *Gorgias*, 453C). Dialectical argument does not fall within the scope of a personal pronoun; it is neither 'yours' nor 'mine'; rather, it progresses through the phases of critical examination to the intellectual and moral benefit of questioner and answerer alike. Dialectic is ultimately for the sake of knowledge. If it appears to attack or spare the interlocutor, that is a mere appearance. The argument itself is not only our chief but our sole concern: we interact with our partner only because and in so far as he contributes to the investigation. By the same token we do not care about our own dialectical fate as such, that is, whether whatever fragment or figment of truth emerging from the discussion is 'ours'. Truth, on this Socratic conception, is not a commodity accessible at some positions within a hierarchy at the expense of the occupants of other positions; all participants in the discussion share success – arriving at the truth – communally.

Perhaps the most salient characteristic of ancient Greek society is that it was *agonistic*, or competitive: whether in politics, art or athletics, Greeks *competed*. Intellectual life was no exception to this generalization. The prototypes of what we now distinguish as Western philosophy, science, medicine and even mathematics were invented by the Greeks not by dispassionate, disinterested investigation in a calm institutional setting, but rather in an arena of strident, often highly personal, debate. Of the many metaphorical descriptions of philosophy itself that appear in Plato's writings, those likening it to combat predominate: philosophy is a struggle in which one opponent is worsted by another with argumentative weapons. This gladiatorial conception survives to this day – witness the ease with which contemporary philosophers speak admiringly of a 'knock-down argument' – and is largely responsible for the suspicion, hardening into active dislike, in which philosophy is now often held. The view is prevalent that philosophical reason is, together with science, a mere intellectual manifestation of distinctively masculine aggression concealing its violence beneath the ideology of objectivity. This largely FEMINIST (chapter 20), occasionally non-Western, critique of the arrogance of reason deserves to be treated with the utmost seriousness, and we cannot do better than to turn to Socrates, not for a definitive answer, but for highly suggestive indications of where an answer might lie. The *elenchos* does not abjure aggressive argument; it does, however, insist that rational enquiry resides in a special form of disciplined competition aiming at mutual benefit rather than at victimization for its own sake. There is good reason to query the tenability, perhaps even the coherence, of

Socrates's *elenchos*, but philosophers eager to confront the modern attack on their ratio-nalistic pretensions still have everything to learn from his ideal.

I have mentioned Vlastos's insistence that under discussion in Socratic dialectic are sincere beliefs; given the importance of the *definienda*, the virtues, what are examined are a person's deepest commitments, that person's *life*, not academic opinions defended only in school. This assertion raises a final problem for us. Vlastos is emphatically inter-ested in the historical truth; he is anything but insensitive to the fact that information about Socrates is filtered to us through the medium of Plato's writings, among others, but he still avowedly conceives of his task as the *historical* exercise of extracting factual information from documentary sources.

Thinking About Method

Vlastos champions Plato as the historical, not just the philosophical, authority on Socrates. Leaving aside the persistent controversy over the merits of this judgement, what we should recognize is that the 'sincere beliefs' underpinning interlocutors' 'lives' in Plato's writings are words given to characters in dialogues. Socrates and Plato together should encourage the student to think hard about philosophical method, not now in the sense of the *elenchos* as opposed to some other particular mode of enquiry, but in the sense of oral as opposed to written, aporetic as opposed to demonstrative, and 'scientific' as opposed to 'literary'. The real Socrates wrote nothing down; the Platonic Socrates is constantly engaged in argumentative discussion, but is not represented as going off to record his negative results in any sort of treatise. Doubtless in large measure as a conse-quence of the uniform failure of candidate definitions, Socratic philosophy is not a written product, but an oral process; it is something that happens between partners in dialectic, not a body of formulizable doctrine to be learnt by the passive reader. It is almost impossible to exaggerate the significance of this feature of Socratic practice, which sur-vives with modifications throughout ancient philosophy. The core of Greek philosophy remains a live encounter between dialecticians debating a thesis according to more or less well-articulated rules of argumentation, and this undoubtedly led to an especially sophisticated sensitivity to and exploitation of the logic of self-refutation, most ably expounded by Burnyeat (1976a, 1976b, 1990). The first, most difficult and most impor-tant lesson for any aspiring student is that philosophy is properly understood not as a body of ideas, no matter how interesting, but as a living activity of argument undertaken by practitioners who, ideally at least, share standards of rational debate rather than an official set of opinions. Reading Plato's descriptions of Socrates at work is no guarantee that this lesson will be learned, but it can provide matchless insight into how philosophy, as opposed to 'the history of ideas', is actually done.

2   Plato

Platonic dialogue is written philosophy, but it, no less than the Socratic model, challenges unthinking assumptions about how a philosopher should communicate. It is a commonplace of scholarship and culture at large that Plato ranks as a uniquely gifted literary artist as well as a philosopher of genius; yet, all the best intentions notwithstanding, a disastrous tendency persists to conceive of his dialogues as hard philosophical content tricked out in attractive but disposable literary ornament. At least so far as his own writings are concerned, we have no idea of what Plato himself thought about anything. The character 'Socrates' is no more Plato than Hamlet is Shakespeare. The dialogues confront us with arguments whose construction we can observe in fictional debates between fictional characters and which should therefore force us to react to them as products of a fabricated *mise-en-scène*. Some 'literary' factors are potentially as influential as conventionally 'philosophical' ones, and conclusions are always *ad hominem*, rather than of universal import.

The Platonic dialogue is an invitation to argue, not a record of endorsed propositions. It offers an alternative – devastating in its seductive and irritating charm – to the model of the expository treatise, one which constitutes an outstanding prima facie counter-example to our own time's prevalent dogma: that philosophy achieves a probative force beyond fiction by austerely sacrificing the meretricious attractions of literary artifice. To a considerable extent, the potency of Plato's challenge to philosophers' comfortable but limiting presumptions about what they should be doing and how they should be doing it, derives from the methodological self-reflection with which the dialogues abound. Consider this striking exchange from Plato's *Protagoras* (334C–E):

Socrates: 'Being, as it happens, a rather forgetful sort of person, Protagoras, I tend to forget, faced with a lengthy statement, the original point of the argument. Now, suppose I happen to be hard of hearing: if you meant to hold a conversation with me, you would think it necessary to speak more loudly than normal; so now that you are faced by a man with a poor memory, please cut your answers down and make them short enough for me to follow.'

Protagoras: 'What do you mean "make my answers short"? Am I to make them shorter than is necessary?'

Socrates: 'Certainly not.'

Protagoras: 'As short as is necessary, then?'

Socrates: 'Yes.'

Protagoras: 'Am I then to make my answers as short as I think necessary, or as short as you think necessary?'

Socrates's representation of his dissatisfaction with the way his interlocutor has been going on at (what he feels to be) evasive length as merely the upshot of a feeble memory is, of course, a particularly abrasive instance of his celebrated irony. Plato is indirectly inviting us to ponder the relative merits of extended, narrative exposition and sharp, argumentative dialectical interchange. But we must not jump to the conclusion that this is no more than a cryptic invitation to endorse uncritically the procedure of the Socratic 'hero', and reject that of the 'sophistical' villain, Protagoras. Protagoras – who is also a Platonic character – is given an excellent riposte by the philosophical dramatist when he is made to ask *whose* authority arbitrates, who decides just how much is enough. The last thing we attentive, perhaps even argumentative, readers of Platonic dialogues are here encouraged to do is to take anything for granted. The classic dilemma confronting enemies of complacency is how they might attack the tyranny of unthinking convention without themselves, if successful, becoming yet further figures of baleful authority. Plato has certainly become such a figure; but a careful reading of the dialogues should, on the contrary, persuade us that he expended the wealth of his philosophical and literary genius on the most ingenious efforts to frustrate our most likely expectations – that is, to make us think philosophically. Contemporary scholars more readily admit the profound consequences of the dialogue form than in the past, but continue to struggle to come to terms with its daunting implications. Hubbard and Karnofsky (1982) is a highly exceptional effort to help the student catch the repercussions of Plato's format; their 'Socratic commentary' strives to overcome the self-defeating dogmatism of traditional Platonic interpretation by restricting itself exclusively to questions.

3 Aristotle

As with Socrates and Plato, so too in Aristotelian studies it is the case that especially important recent work focuses on methodology. A major concern throughout the history of philosophy has been the discovery, analysis and evaluation of convictions deeply entrenched within a given society or, in the case of especially ambitious philosophical projects, held by humanity at large. We have already seen how Socrates's definitional project skirts the question of *what sort of thing* is being defined. Plato's development of Socratic practice was an answer with a vengeance: postulation of the existence of unqualified, perfect exemplars beyond space and time, the so-called Platonic Forms. Aristotle, however, pursues dialectical investigation by working from what he calls the *endoxa* and the *phainomena*, which it was once standard practice to translate as 'common beliefs' and 'phenomena', respectively. But, largely under the influence of G. E. L. Owen (1922–82) (see Owen 1986; and supplemented by Nussbaum 1986), it is now generally agreed that these renderings are unacceptable for reasons central to the proper understanding of Aristotle's method. *Endoxa* are not merely common beliefs, although they might be widespread; they are *reputable* beliefs, espoused either by 'the many' or 'the wise'. Similarly, *phainomena* are not limited to, although they include, observable 'phenomena'; they are 'appearances' which embrace what people are inclined to accept without prompting, but across a spectrum much broader than the latter-day empiricist connotations of the word 'phenomena' might suggest.

Aristotle's characteristic method when addressing questions in the philosophy of nature as well as in ethics and politics is first of all to gather together these appearances and reputable opinions. Often when collected they seem to conflict, either superficially or in some more serious fashion. This (ostensible) conflict is what he calls an *aporia*, a puzzle. For him the role of the philosopher is to take on not any random problem, but puzzles generated in this way by disharmony in suggestions which deserve a high degree of initial credence. The philosopher's job is essentially conciliatory, to explain that the conflict is a matter of mere appearance wherever this is the case, and, where the difficulty runs deeper, to adjudicate between the opposing views, effecting the minimal adjustments necessary to resolve the conflict.

In Aristotelian dialectic, Greek philosophy attained a degree of analytical subtlety and breadth of scope which has been equalled but never surpassed. Yet the method has troubling implications. The *endoxa* also include what we, at least, are inclined to view as linguistic phenomena: Aristotle draws sweeping conclusions from 'what we say' – that is, what ordinary people say in Greek. The sceptical modern reaction is to ask how his claims about Greek morphology, syntax and usage support substantial propositions valid beyond the confines of his linguistic community, even if they are correct. Furthermore, the fear that a method otherwise admirably inclined to treat untutored opinion with considerable respect might yet spill over into ideological justification for pernicious beliefs and practices finds ample justification in Aristotle's notorious theories that certain people – slaves – are 'living instrumental property' (Aristotle, *Politics*, I.2) and that the female sex is a 'natural deformation' of the male standard, defined by incapacity (Aristotle, *De Generatione Animalium*, A.20 – a devastating critique is to be found in Lear 1988). There is no comparison between Aristotle's methodological self-consciousness and Socrates's silence about how the *elenchos* works, but precisely the same problem which impelled Vlastos to attribute to Socrates an undefended conviction that everyone's belief-set contains some true beliefs about virtue re-emerges when we reflect on Aristotle's philosophical practice: how can he be confident that his dialectic ever achieves objective truth, rather than just coherent (and perhaps coherently false) belief?

Irwin on Aristotle's Dialectic

Irwin (1988) proposes an evolutionary answer to the problem. He argues that Aristotelian dialectic passes through two stages. An initial 'weak' form does indeed aspire to no more than coherence, but it is superseded by 'strong' dialectic, which tries to establish results that are 'true' by the standards of metaphysical realism and valid by reference to the world, not our attitudes. For Irwin, this evolution is possible because 'strong' dialectic proceeds from a privileged subset of beliefs, those which cannot be rejected on pain of forfeiting rationality, such as the principle of non-contradiction. This principle rejects the possibility of a proposition and its negation both being true. Irwin's argument has excited much interest, but is vulnerable on two major fronts. Firstly, even if so-called 'strong' dialectic can be isolated, it is hard to see how anything beyond a very few fundamental principles could meet its forbidding standards and thus yield 'strong' results; since Aristotle's philosophy covers so much more than the foundations of metaphysics and epistemology, most of his dialectical work would remain 'weak'. Secondly, Irwin's reading of Aristotle is unashamedly KANTIAN (chapter 32): his solution attributes to him a type of transcendental argument which gained currency in the history of philosophy long after the Greek period. Furthermore, transcendental arguments themselves might face the same problem of moving beyond coherence to truth.

An alternative approach searches for an answer constructed exclusively from Aristotelian materials (Wardy 1991). The Aristotelian natural world is teleological: that is, many, perhaps all, characteristics of the structure and behaviour of natural kinds are to be explained in terms of what is good for them. Although the import of Aristotle's arguments for teleology is a matter for debate (Sedley 1991; Wardy 1993), it is perfectly clear that Aristotelian teleological explanations are irreducible. They can often be supplemented by causal accounts which cite, say, material processes, but they cannot be reduced to non-teleological explanation. A teleological explanation constitutes a perfectly legitimate reason, complete in itself, for some state of affairs to be as it is. The alternative interpretation of Aristotle's dialectic is simply an application of this global teleology to the human species. For Aristotle, we are *essentially* knowers; a human being is a rational animal endowed with innate speculative curiosity. Since Aristotle's teleological philosophy dictates that no animal kind can be radically frustrated in fulfilling its nature, it follows that the world must be accessible to human enquiry. Just as the lower animals are obliged to struggle to survive, so too we cannot uncritically accept the *phainomena* and *endoxa* without modification – but the real truth is there to be found. Aristotle's confidence in the utility of his dialectical method as an instrument for discovering absolute truth relies on his philosophical biology. Since his biology in turn is derived from an exercise in that very dialectic, the purported 'justification' seems to beg the question. But it might be that dissatisfaction with this circularity is the product of imposing post-Kantian epistemological concerns on Aristotle, with the inevitable result that his thought is either severely distorted or found seriously wanting.

The argument between these candidate solutions to the riddle of Aristotle's method remains unresolved. Quite apart from the obvious intrinsic interest of comprehending his procedure, the debate is a particularly apt illustration within Greek philosophy of an inescapable dilemma in all philosophical historiography. One might feel that the Kantian reading is anachronistic, while the teleological explanation lands Aristotle with a strange position that is totally inaccessible to contemporary philosophers. All historical study entails commitments taking the investigator far beyond mundane factual reportage. In the history of philosophy this commitment is to doing philosophy when doing the history of philosophy. If philosophers are to learn from their past, then they must abandon hope of an easy formula dictating interpretations which succeed in engaging with old arguments while avoiding anachronistic deformation. One of the most valuable gifts the history of philosophy has to offer us can be a glimpse of how *different* philosophy was at other times. By 'different' I mean not just that earlier thinkers propounded a rich variety of doctrines now unfamiliar, although there is no doubt that historical expertise makes available a range of potential ideas easily overlooked by too narrow a concentration on contemporary views. The more challenging sense of 'difference' accessible through history is the realization that the very terms in which the apparently constant problems of philosophy are opposed, the logical and heuristic considerations to which thinkers are sensitive, the standards to which they submit their arguments, might themselves be susceptible to historical change (not necessarily progress). The debate over Aristotelian method exemplifies this most fruitful dilemma, and the expansion of philosophical perspective it encourages.

4 Hellenistic Methodology

If one had to select the single most important development in work on ancient Greek philosophy in recent times, it would doubtless be the renaissance in Hellenistic studies. Until a few years ago the prevailing attitude towards the Hellenistic period even among ancient Greek specialists was dismissive. The usual view left Plato and Aristotle in splendid isolation, the first figures in a parade of great philosophers all too often followed immediately by a contingent from the seventeenth century. Although later Greek philosophers had their able advocates, the relative inaccessibility of the scattered source materials, all too often in the form of biased indirect testimony, exacerbated the neglect into which Hellenistic philosophy had lapsed since the time of the Enlightenment. The publication of a major new study (Long and Sedley 1987) utterly transformed the situation. Their invaluable collection of the sources both in the original languages and in translation with extensive commentary permits all philosophers to penetrate the relatively unknown territory of the Hellenistic period with assurance.

An immediate advantage from some familiarity with Hellenistic philosophy is proof that one hallowed notion, that of the 'timeless' problems of philosophy, crumbles on inspection. To name but the most obvious examples, Hellenistic philosophers invented two issues, determinism and scepticism, which so came to dominate later preoccupations that the unwary are tempted into supposing that these topics are eternally present in philosophy. This mistake at once instils false expectations of what can be reasonably expected when evaluating earlier periods – for example, bewildered surprise at the incapacity of Aristotle's theory of voluntariness to cope with determinism, or grave misconstruals of Plato's epistemological concepts – and prohibits recognition of the sheer creativity of the Hellenistic contribution.

But, as on so many other points we have canvassed, there is a healthy lack of consensus on one particularly important question. In at least some respects, the Greek chapter in philosophical history is surprisingly unified. The period stretching from the Presocratics to the later Neoplatonists is more than a millennium, but even the very latest work falling within it demonstrates an acute appreciation of inherited insights and a largely shared problematic. The remarkable force of this coherence becomes apparent when we reflect that Aquinas (1224–74) is closer to us in time than figures at the two ends of the Greek millennium were to one another. This intellectual cohesion lends Greek philosophy much of its appeal, but readily shades into a highly questionable methodological principle: namely, that ancient philosophers react to the work of their more or less immediate predecessors in obedience to our sense of chronology and importance. Application of this principle has produced the assumption that since Aristotle is a towering figure for us, he must similarly have dominated the formation of Hellenistic philosophy – which is indeed a guiding assumption of much recent scholarship. Central Hellenistic doctrines have been regularly interpreted as products of reflection on Aristotelian insights or as efforts to circumvent some of his criticisms. But an alternative school maintains that Aristotelian philosophy went into rapid eclipse shortly after his death and did not regain prominence until long after the formative phase of Hellenistic philosophy (Sandbach 1985). Long and Sedley themselves differ over this issue, only the former routinely explaining features of Hellenistic positions by adducing an Aristotelian forerunner.

What did the Hellenistic philosophers have to say about our major theme regarding method, the recognition, assessment and exploitation of non-philosophical belief? I stressed that translation of the cardinal term *endoxon* in Aristotle as 'common belief' is a grave error; *reputable* opinion is his dialectical material. Hellenistic method worked with a very different set of assumptions: its dialectic did indeed operate on *general* opinions, designated 'common preconceptions'. The leading schools active in this period shared the concept 'common preconception', but differed sharply over its signification and, of course, what the preconceptions actually were. The Stoics, on one side, argued that Nature, identified as a divine, providential reason informing the entire cosmos, leads us to form certain notions on which we might ultimately build a comprehensive philosophy to guide us through every aspect of life. Their arch-opponents, the Epicureans, denied the existence of any such divine rationality, while arguing that human beings naturally construct reliable preconceptions on the basis of sense perception. Although the schools disagreed about the mechanism responsible for our natural intellectual endowment, they largely agreed on the reality, reliability and philosophical significance of our preconceptions. Both camps also propounded NATURALISTIC (pp. 805–6) ethical theories: life has a goal which is determined by nature itself, and success in living depends entirely on perceiving and conforming to the conditions which might permit us to achieve the good according to nature. For the Epicureans, this goal was pleasure and the absence of pain; for the Stoics, it was 'living according to reason'.

How do 'common preconceptions' have a bearing on the argument between Epicureans and Stoics concerning the real goal of life? Neither school asserted, implausibly, that people apprehended their favoured doctrine in all its detail as a matter of naturally acquired knowledge: that extreme position could not even accommodate the existence of wrong-headed Stoics (or Epicureans) without embarrassment. Instead, *pre*conceptions were made to provide a fundamentally sound initial indication of the truth which is, however, vulnerable to subsequent corruption, and requires elaboration and defence from, of course, the correct philosophy. The result was a brace of fascinating developments in dialectical technique. The Hellenistic thinkers were the first philosophers to adduce the evidence of infantile behaviour in support of their doctrines: Epicureans claimed that babies *naturally* seek pleasure and shun pain, Stoics that they strive for self-preservation and avoid extinction (these arguments received magisterial attention from Brunschwig 1986). Secondly, the common allegiance to a form of innatist epistemology led proponents of rival philosophies to criticize hostile citation of ostensible 'preconceptions' for a variety of intriguing reasons.

It is easy to adopt a jaundiced attitude towards such Hellenistic debate. For any issue, it might seem to us that if it appeared to favour Epicureanism, then its champions would say that it is a trustworthy expression of our natural intellectual equipment, incorrigible within the limits of its only partial articulation of the truth; while the Stoics would protest that, although there certainly are reliable conceptions realizable by grace of providential reason and harmonizing with Stoicism, in this instance social contamination has in some way bastardized the opinion. If, on the other hand, the Stoics claimed the support of a common preconception, the Epicureans could readily reply that in this case spontaneous, true instinct has been adulterated by the admixture of unhealthy social conditioning. The ever-present availability of the charge of corruption-by-society ensured that the testimony of common preconceptions could never control the excesses of inter-school dialectic, which threatens to degenerate into mere polemic. It is clear from Brunschwig's study that although Hellenistic philosophers believed that human nature is manifest at a pre-cultural age, they evinced little inclination to engage in the scrupulous observation of infants evidently called for by this belief; and the search for such data was anything but systematic. Nevertheless, we should avoid too harsh a judgement. The doctrine of preconception encouraged the Stoics in particular to turn to non-philosophical witnesses, especially literary ones, which made their philosophy receptive to an enriching diversity of influences.

If Hellenistic philosophy is vulnerable to heavy criticism of the opportunities it often missed by manipulating, rather than reacting circumspectly to, formulations of common belief, we must remember that this philosophical problem does have a good claim to figure on a cautious list of 'perennial' challenges to philosophers. All but the most obstinately scientistic and increasingly old-fashioned modern thinkers would concede that philosophy cannot avoid deriving substantial impetus from sources clearly related to both Aristotelian *endoxa* and Hellenistic common preconceptions. We, of course, subscribe neither to the proto-Kantianism dubiously attributed to Aristotle, nor to the epistemic teleology to which he undoubtedly subscribed, nor again to the Hellenistic philosophers' ambitious epistemic naturalism. But whether or not we go so far as to characterize our activity as conceptual or linguistic analysis, the fact remains that we are often in the uneasy position of armchair theoreticians obliged to pronounce on what people 'really' believe. If contemporary philosophers do rather better than their pioneering Hellenistic ancestors in assimilating the discoveries of a multiplicity of empirical disciplines, they still face the uncomfortable task of distinguishing in a well-motivated, convincing fashion between innocent belief and the construction put on it by philosophy.

I warned at the outset that my treatment of ancient dialectic would be obliged to omit even the mention, let alone the sustained discussion, of crucial episodes in the history of Greek philosophical methodology. But it would be very wrong to leave the topic without encouraging the reader to connect positive Hellenistic epistemic naturalism with the period's negative epistemological invention, scepticism. The primary challenge confronting ancient sceptics was whether it was possible consistently to maintain that all the schools of dogmatic philosophy had failed to reach the truth, or at least had failed to prove that they had reached it, while nevertheless avoiding an ironically self-refuting dogmatic commitment to the truth of scepticism itself. Further, the vigorous dialectic of the Hellenistic era helped to create and feed another important development in the philosophical deployment of common beliefs, a development which has also only just begun to achieve the scholarly respect it deserves. Philosophers of the so-called sceptical schools, Academics and neo-Pyrrhonists, were not only adept in pitting ordinary beliefs against the philosophical doctrines of their 'dogmatist' rivals – the Stoic, Epicurean, Peripatetic or Platonist – and in alleging intolerable inconsistencies between what opposing schools claimed as 'natural' beliefs, tendencies or practices. They also *displayed* the ordinary beliefs and practices of different places, times and cultures as different, but as equally valid – or equally invalid. All such manipulations of common conceptions were intended to contribute to the desired sceptical end: the suspension of belief in the face of as yet unresolved, and perhaps irresolvable, universal conflicts between ideas, beliefs, perceptions and arguments. One of the most interesting current debates about ancient scepticism precisely concerns the questions whether such suspension extends to all beliefs, and whether, if so, any human life, let alone a desirable one, is possible in such a state (Burnyeat 1980; Frede 1984).

The aim of this limited exercise has been to demonstrate how even a narrowly focused survey of some aspects of the philosophical methods of Socrates, Plato, Aristotle and the Hellenistic schools immediately reveals a provocative mixture of argument and assumption about how philosophy could and should be conducted; the exercise could easily be repeated again and again for many other essential topics. No philosopher can afford to ignore the history of Greek philosophy; but, then again, no philosopher would want to.

Further Reading

Barnes (1980) and Brunschwig (1980) make fascinating companion-pieces, while Brunschwig (1986) is a model of philosophically illuminating historical reconstruction. The works of Burnyeat (1976a, 1976b, 1980, 1990) have all been deservedly hailed as masterpieces (the last is quite possibly the finest modern commentary on a Platonic dialogue). Frede (1974) remains the classic study of Stoic logic. Lear (1988) is the best of the many single-volume introductions to Aristotle for philosophers. No student should be unacquainted with the uniformly brilliant, unfailingly provocative essays collected in Owen (1986).

References

Plato and Aristotle

There are many valuable translations of Plato and Aristotle, but readers might find it helpful to use two standard collections:

Aristotle 1984: *The Complete Works of Aristotle*, 2 vols (edited by J. Barnes). Princeton, NJ: Princeton University Press.

Plato 1961: *The Collected Dialogues of Plato* (edited by E. Hamilton and H. Cairns). Princeton, NJ: Princeton University Press.

In addition, Oxford University Press has published two series of translations with philosophical commentary:

Aristotle, *Clarendon Aristotle* 1975– : Oxford: Oxford University Press.

Plato, *Clarendon Plato* 1973– : Oxford: Oxford University Press.

Other writers

Annas, J. and Barnes, J. 1985: *The Modes of Scepticism: Ancient Texts and Modern Interpretations*. Cambridge: Cambridge University Press.

Barnes, J. 1975: *Aristotle's Posterior Analytics*, translated with notes. Oxford: Clarendon Press.

——1980: Proof Destroyed. In M. Schofield, M. F. Burnyeat and J. Barnes (eds) *Doubt and Dogmatism: Studies in Hellenistic Epistemology*. Oxford: Clarendon Press.

Brunschwig, J. 1980: Proof Defined. In M. Schofield, M. F. Burnyeat and J. Barnes (eds) *Doubt and Dogmatism: Studies in Hellenistic Epistemology*. Oxford: Clarendon Press.

——1986: The Cradle Argument in Epicureanism and Stoicism. In M. Schofield and G. Striker (eds) *The Norms of Nature: Studies in Hellenistic Ethics*. Cambridge: Cambridge University Press.

Burnyeat, M. F. 1976a: Protagoras and Self-refutation in Plato's *Theaetetus*. *Philosophical Review*, 85, 172–95.

——1976b: Protagoras and Self-refutation in Later Greek Philosophy. *Philosophical Review*, 85, 44–69.

——1980: Can the Sceptic Live His Scepticism? In M. Schofield, M. F. Burnyeat and J. Barnes (eds) *Doubt and Dogmatism: Studies in Hellenistic Epistemology*. Oxford: Clarendon Press.

——1990: *The Theaetetus of Plato* (with a revised translation by M. J. Levett). Cambridge: Hackett Publishing.

Denyer, N. C. 1991: *Language, Thought and Falsehood in Ancient Greek Philosophy*. London: Routledge.

Frede, M. 1974: *Die Stoische Logik*. Göttingen: Vandenhoeck and Ruprecht.

——1984: The Sceptic's Two Kinds of Assent and the Question of the Possibility of Knowledge. In R. Rorty, J. B. Schneewind and Q. Skinner (eds) *Philosophy in History: Essays on the Historiography of Philosophy*. Cambridge: Cambridge University Press.

Hubbard, B. A. F. and Karnofsky, E. S. 1982: *Plato's Protagoras: A Socratic Commentary*. London: Duckworth.

Irwin, T. H. 1988: *Aristotle's First Principles*. Oxford: Clarendon Press.

Lear, J. 1980: *Aristotle and Logical Theory*. Cambridge: Cambridge University Press.

——1988: *Aristotle: The Desire to Understand*. Cambridge: Cambridge University Press.

Lloyd, G. E. R. 1979: *Magic, Reason and Experience: Studies in the Origins and Development of Greek Science*. Cambridge: Cambridge University Press.

Long, A. A. and Sedley, D. N. 1987: *The Hellenistic Philosophers: Translations of the Principal Sources, with Philosophical Commentary* (vol. 1) and *Greek and Latin Texts with Notes and Bibliography* (vol. 2). Cambridge: Cambridge University Press.

MacIntyre, A. 1981: *After Virtue*. London: Duckworth.

Nussbaum, M. C. 1986: Saving Aristotle's Appearances. In *The Fragility of Goodness: Luck and Ethics in Greek Tragedy and Philosophy*. Cambridge: Cambridge University Press.

Owen, G. E. L. 1986: Tithenai ta phainomena. In *Logic, Science and Dialectic: Collected Papers in Greek Philosophy* (edited by M. C. Nussbaum). London: Duckworth.

Sandbach, F. H. 1985: *Aristotle and the Stoics*. Cambridge: Cambridge Philological Society.

Sedley, D. N. 1991: Is Aristotle's Teleology Anthropocentric? *Phronesis*, 36, 179–96.

Sorabji, R. (ed.) 1987– : *The Ancient Commentators on Aristotle*. London: Duckworth.

Vlastos, G. 1983: The Socratic Elenchus. *Oxford Studies in Ancient Philosophy*, 1, 27–58.

——1991: *Socrates, Ironist and Moral Philosopher*. Cambridge: Cambridge University Press.

Wardy, R. 1991: Transcendental Dialectic. *Phronesis*, 36, 88–106.

——1993: Aristotelian Rainfall or the Lore of Averages. *Phronesis*, 38.

Williams, B. 1985: *Ethics and the Limits of Philosophy*. London: Fontana.

Discussion Questions

1   Do philosophers today have any reason to study ancient Greek philosophy?
2   How did Greek philosophy help to form the distinctive goals and methods of philosophy?
3   What is the Socratic method in philosophy and why is it important?
4   Can disciplined argument reach ethical truths?
5   How should philosophy be related to the culture at large?
6   In what sense could a philosopher be a 'gadfly'?
7   How can we decide whether philosophy is best conducted in dialogue?
8   In order to achieve virtue in our life, must we understand what virtue is?
9   Can the Socratic method reach beyond consistency to truth?
10   If Plato rejected the Socratic *elenchus*, why did he do so?
11   What is the difference between philosophy as a disciplined competition aiming at mutual benefit and philosophy as individual pursuit?
12   Should either oral philosophy or written philosophy have priority over the other?
13   In what sense should a reader of philosophy be active?
14   What distinguishes philosophy (and the history of philosophy) from the history of ideas?
15   Is there any reason for philosophy to start from reputable beliefs and from what people are inclined to accept?
16   Can Aristotle's dialectic ever achieve objective truth, rather than mere coherence?

17   Can we agree that we have knowledge because we are essentially knowers?

18   Are 'reputable opinions' or 'common preconceptions' a better starting-point for philosophical argument?

19   Did the Stoics or the Epicureans provide a better basis for determining what are our common preconceptions?

20   Did the Hellenistic use of common preconceptions require an epistemic naturalism?

21   Can infantile behaviour tell us anything important about philosophical doctrines?

22   How can we know when dialectic degenerates into mere polemic?

23   How can discoveries in other disciplines have consequences for philosophy?

24   If scepticism is true, is it self-refuting?

25   Are the ordinary beliefs and practices of different places, times and cultures equally valid or equally invalid?

26   What is the scope of the suspension of belief licensed by scepticism?

23

Plato and Aristotle

LESLEY BROWN

Chapter 22 highlights issues of philosophical method in the triumvirate of Greek philosophers: Socrates (who wrote nothing but who set the philosophical agenda), Plato (c.429–347 BC) and Aristotle (384–322 BC). Robert Wardy reminds readers that Plato's works are written as dialogues, fictional debates, and rightly cautions against a too-ready assumption that we can discern Plato's views in the dicta of the fictional Socrates who is the leading speaker in almost all the dialogues.

Yet philosophers through the ages have – rightly or wrongly – thought it proper to try to discern in these dramatic fictions Plato's own favoured arguments and conclusions. In support they can claim the precedent set by Aristotle, who came to Athens from Stagira in northern Greece and studied for twenty years under Plato in the Academy before founding his own school of philosophy. Aristotle's works – best thought of as lectures, some more polished than others – betray no qualms in interpreting Plato's writings as containing theses accepted and argued for by Plato, ones Aristotle often criticizes and sometimes praises. In similarly rash vein, this chapter extracts some themes which are common to Plato and Aristotle's philosophy, often ones on which Aristotle offers a more or less direct response to what he took Plato to be arguing, and which have set a major part of the philosophical agenda in subsequent Western philosophy. But important areas of their writings are omitted, including the contribution by both, but especially by Aristotle, to logic and philosophy of language. Since chapter 22 discusses method, this chapter says little about the richness of dialectical argument that each philosopher, in his different way, presents, and that is such an important, and attractive, feature of their philosophizing.

1 Plato

1.1 Knowledge and reality

Knowledge is recollection: so Socrates argues in several dialogues. The thesis is launched in a remarkable scene in Plato's dialogue, *Meno*, a work in which Socrates and the self-assured Meno discuss what virtue is and whether it is teachable. To show

Meno that, despite many false starts, it is possible to inquire into what virtue is, Socrates summons a young uneducated slave and questions him about a problem in geometry, a problem the boy has evidently never encountered. Thanks to Socrates's questioning and indeed prompting, the slave comes to see the solution, whereupon Socrates convinces Meno that, since the boy had not been taught geometry, he was recollecting the correct answers. Indeed, the slave's soul – argues Socrates – knows these truths for all time, hence must be immortal.

Though the conclusions Plato draws from this episode – that our souls can recollect innate knowledge, and are immortal – are daring and not ultimately convincing, we find here Plato expounding a matter of crucial importance: one's ability to 'draw out truths from within oneself'. Socrates insists that the knowledge he and Meno seek, what the nature of virtue is, no less than mathematical truths as in the experiment, is to be gained by this 'inward inquiry', labelled recollection. The emphasis on what came to be called *a priori* knowledge, together with the idea that such knowledge, in the incarnate state, is recollected from a previous discarnate existence, becomes even more prominent in the *Phaedo* (and, without the explicit claim of recollection, in the *Republic*). But in these dialogues, this picture according to which recollected knowledge is to be had by pure thought, aided by dialectical questioning, is accompanied by a further thesis: Plato's famous theory of Forms.

LEIBNIZ (chapter 27) discerned in the *Meno*'s theory a precursor of his own belief in latent innate knowledge present in all human beings and actualized in everyday cognitive activity. Recollection, on this 'optimistic' view, is open to all, especially with the probing help of a Socrates. But is this Plato's view or is it, as Scott (1995) has argued, a more 'pessimistic' account according to which recollecting is the preserve of philosophers alone through hard intellectual labour? The *Meno*'s choice of a slave-boy as the subject of recollection suggests Leibniz's optimistic view, but Scott's view has more plausibility for the *Phaedo*, where the objects 'recollected' are the Forms.

The Theory of Forms

What are Plato's Forms? We approach this by looking first at how the inquiry proceeds in some dialogues from which the full-blown theory of Forms is absent. In these, Socrates seeks knowledge of what qualities such as piety, self-control and courage are. This is the famous 'What is X?' question (see chapter 22). Attempts to answer the question fail in various instructive ways, and the reader learns, from the way Socrates treats the failed attempts, what is required of a correct answer. It must encompass all and only cases of X (for instance, of courage), and it must show X to be a single quality, and one which explains why all the cases of X (the 'many X's') are X. Finally, it should help the inquirer to settle, in disputed cases, whether something is or is not X. In a new phase of the search into knowledge and its objects, Plato's *Phaedo* and *Republic* go further, and develop the idea that to know what, for example, beauty is, one must get to know the Form beauty, labelled 'the beautiful itself' or 'that which is really beautiful'. This 'X itself', the one X, is contrasted with the many Xs which are changeable, are liable to be the opposite of X as well as X (ugly as well as beautiful, for instance) and, unlike the Form, are known with the help of the senses. The Forms, as Socrates argues for them, are real but immaterial objects, known by the soul's reasoning, not by sight, hearing or any of the bodily senses.

They exist independently of the material world and of the persons who aspire to know them. And the Form of the beautiful is itself beautiful in a manner evidently different from that of the 'many beautifuls' which are beautiful through their relation to the Form, specifically, through what is called 'participation in the beautiful itself'.

Before we look more closely at the theory, a warning. The title 'Plato's theory of Ideas' (often used as an alternative to 'theory of Forms') is best avoided. Though they are immaterial, Plato's Forms are not ideas in the sense made famous by seventeenth-century and eighteenth-century philosophy, nor is the theory idealist in BERKELEY's (chapter 30) sense. Unlike Berkeleyan ideas, Forms do not depend for their existence on minds, not even on the divine mind, although some later thinkers (so-called 'neo-Platonists') developed the theory in that direction. But, as we shall see, though Forms are decidedly not mind-dependent entities, Forms and minds are peculiarly fitted to one another.

The Forms, then, are to serve as objects of knowledge and understanding. But they have several other roles: ontological, semantic and ethical, as well as epistemological. To complement and underpin their EPISTEMOLOGICAL (chapter 1) role, the ONTOLOGICAL (chapter 2) status of Forms is crucial. Forms play a fundamental role in an account of how things are – even, somehow, in an account of how things in the empirical world are, since the X's in the empirical world are X by participation in the Form X. Knowledge, as Socrates often insists, is of being, of what truly and fully is, and that means: of Forms. But how should we understand the claim that only Forms 'truly and fully' are, or have being? Does this mean being as existence, or being as being something or other? Some have accused Plato of confusion here, while others (such as Vlastos) insist that the superior being of the Forms should not be read as a superior kind of existence, but rather a superior (because 'cognitively reliable') way of being X – for example, of being beautiful. Perhaps to pose the question thus is to foist onto ancient thought an anachronistic distinction.

In elaborating the different roles of Forms, it is useful to employ Armstrong's distinction between two conceptions of universals, realist and semantic. On the realist conception, universals are posited as explanatory entities (usually as properties), such that a full account of the world will make reference to them. The discussion in the previous paragraph makes it clear that a Platonic Form is some kind of universal on the realist conception: universal because the Form F is that by virtue of which all the many F's are F, and realist because it is part of the structure of true reality. The 'semantic' conception of universals, by contrast, sees them as the meanings of general terms, of expressions such as 'beautiful' or 'circular' or 'man' or 'horse', and the theory seems to accord Forms this role also. This is shown by a famous passage in *Republic* 10 (596), where Socrates remarks that 'we customarily hypothesize a single Form in connection with each of the many things to which we apply the same name'. But this semantic role must be subordinate to the ontological one, in particular because, on occasion, natural language fails to 'divide nature at the joints' (*Phaedrus*). An example is the term 'barbarian', to which no Form corresponds, since the division of mankind into Greeks and barbarians (unlike that into male and female, for instance) fails to reflect a real, natural, division. In such (rare) cases, the term will not have a corresponding Form, but, in general, investigation of LANGUAGE (chapter 3) is another tool for the philosopher aspiring to discern the role of Forms in structuring reality. This is especially so, as the late dialogue *Sophist* shows, for the investigation of Forms which figure prominently in LOGIC (chapter 4) and DIALECTIC (chapter 22), including, for instance, same and different, or like and unlike.

Finally, in their ethical role, Forms such as justice, virtue and, especially, the Form of the good, which is prominent in the *Republic*, serve as guarantors of objectivity in ETHICAL (chapter 6) and AESTHETIC (chapter 7) questions. Confidence in the existence of ethical and aesthetic Forms is a bulwark against those who would assert that justice and other values are nothing more than the beliefs or conventions of a given person or group. For more on this, see section 4.

Are the various roles compatible? Could there be entities such as Platonic Forms, or is the theory impossibly ambitious, and in the end logically incoherent? A crucial assumption seems to be that a Form – say the Form, beautiful – is itself beautiful in some specially privileged way, a way which is both superior to that in which the many instances of beautiful things are beautiful and which explains or grounds their being beautiful. (Perhaps this idea is an early version of the causal adequacy principle favoured by DESCARTES (chapter 26), that if A causes something to be F, then A must itself be F.) Wardy calls this the notion that Forms are 'IDEAL PERFECT EXEMPLARS' (p. 592). Rather than the innocuous idea that the Form or universal 'beautiful' is simply what all beautiful things have in common, this seems to suggest – incoherently – that the Form can have itself as a property; hence it is labelled the self-predication assumption. An argument sketched in Plato's own dialogue *Parmenides*, and labelled by Aristotle 'the Third Man argument', claims to find a regress here. If (1) we postulate a Form F to be what the group of the many F's have in common, and if (2) the Form F is itself F, then (3) we have a new group of F's, the many F's plus the Form F, for which we must postulate a new Form, F^1, to explain what the new group have in common. And so on in an infinite regress. To rebut this challenge, the theory can try to appeal to a special way in which it is true that the Form F is F, a way which avoids the need to class it, as another F thing, together with the many F's at the third step of the argument. Thus, 'The Form beautiful is beautiful' may be read as 'The Form beautiful is what it is to be beautiful', or alternatively, as 'The Form beautiful explains why ordinary things are beautiful'. But it is hard to accept that either of these gives us an acceptable way of reading the predication 'is beautiful'. Indeed, it is easy to sympathize with those imagined opponents (*Republic* Book 5) who denied that there is a single thing that explains why all beautiful things are beautiful, let alone that the putative single explanans must itself be beautiful.

1.2   The soul

Plato's theory of the soul is developed in tandem with his theory of Forms. Forms, though immaterial, are not mind-dependent, but it is the task of the mind, or the soul, or reason, to come to knowledge of the Forms. We now turn to Plato's psychology, his discussions of the human soul (Greek: *psyche*).

In the *Phaedo*, where the theory of Forms is apparently launched, a view of the soul later called CARTESIAN DUALISM (pp. 650–1) finds vivid expression, and it is linked with the existence of the Forms. 'As surely as those objects [the Forms] exist, so surely do our souls before we are born' (*Phaedo* 76e). Socrates goes on (79–80) to develop a whole string of affinities between souls and Forms, on the one hand, and bodies and 'the many' on the other. The body, like the many sensible objects, is visible to the senses, ever-changing, many-faceted and perishable, while the soul is 'very like' Forms, which are invisible, perceived by intellect, not the senses, unchanging, simple and imperishable. Note especially that a soul, like a Form, is said to be simple, that is uncompounded, lacking parts.

Unsurprisingly, it is in the *Phaedo* that we find the claim that it is the task of the philosopher to try to approximate, in life, to the state of death, that is, to that state in which the soul is separated from the chains of the body. The best state for you, as a human soul, is to be discarnate, independent of the body, the state you were in before and will return to after this existence of yours as a human being. Such is Socrates's claim, and the *Phaedo* contains three daring arguments to try to show that the soul is immortal.

But the *Republic* introduces a more nuanced and more psychologically convincing picture, the famous account of the tripartite (or three-part) soul. 'Do we learn with one part of us, feel angry with another and desire the pleasures of eating and sex with another? Or do we do so with the soul as a whole?' asks Socrates (*Republic* 436a). They reach agreement that the first is correct: that each of us has a three-part soul, with a reasoning element, a spirited element (*thumos*) and a third which is the seat of the bodily desires. Evidence for this comes from inner psychological conflict, and Plato quotes Homer's description of Odysseus rebuking his *thumos* to illustrate how a person's *thumos* is seen as distinct from the part which reflects on what is best for the agent, the reasoning part. Whenever we find ourselves with opposite impulses – as Odysseus did, or as when, though thirsty, we restrain ourselves from drinking through concern for health – in all such cases we can discern opposing *elements* in the soul responsible for these opposing *motivations*. Like Freud two thousand years later, Plato suggests there are no fewer but no more than three distinct psychic parts – hence the label 'the tripartite soul'.

Weakness of Will

In place of the simple dualism of body and soul from the *Phaedo*, the *Republic* presents a highly suggestive picture of a complex human soul with conflicting motivations, a picture which allows and accounts for irrational behaviour, such as choosing what you know is bad for you. This picture differs markedly not just from that in the *Phaedo* but from views Socrates defends in Plato's dialogue *Protagoras* against the common-sense belief in such weakness of will or *akrasia*. There Socrates had argued that only those who miscalculate or make some other mistake can choose and do what is bad for them. On the *Protagoras* account, a person's motivation always mirrors their evaluation of the options; if I fail to do what I claimed to know was better, this simply shows that, at the vital moment of choosing, I in fact valued the worse option more highly, a kind of self-deception. Aristotle regarded this as a denial of *akrasia*, but it might better be thought of as explaining *akrasia* in a special way, one which denies so-called 'clear-eyed *akrasia*', but postulates a kind of self-deception to explain succumbing to temptation. But now in *Republic* it is recognized that desires can and do sometimes get the upper hand in a quite straightforward manner: they exert more motivational force than they should, and the rational part can be powerless against them. (The power of desires is revealed in our dreams, says Socrates – another anticipation of Freudian theory.) Hence education – a prominent theme in *Republic* – must first seek to tame and cultivate the two non-rational parts of the soul.

Despite its greater psychological realism, including allowing 'clear-eyed *akrasia*', the tripartite soul theory invites many questions. Why only three parts of the soul? Considering the huge number of potential inner conflicts might force us to postulate innumerable parts. Again, why speak of parts at all rather than a single person's many and conflicting sources of motivation? How, in particular, should we envisage the rational part? HUME (chapter 31) objected to Plato's idea that reason's role involves both recognizing the good and pursuing it, for Hume thought of reason as capable only of finding means to ends, not of recognizing the value of the ends themselves. Central to Plato's (and Aristotle's) conception of reason is the idea Hume rejected, that reason has its own ends and desires.

1.3 Ethics and politics

In Plato's works we find a highly influential and important discussion of many major questions still hotly disputed in ethics today. Here are some of them. The question of moral realism or objectivism: are there moral truths whose truth is independent of any individual's or society's beliefs and/or customs? The question of moral motivation: why should I be moral? The question of the relation between what God wills or commands or approves of and what is morally right (see chapter 15).

Moral realism. Plato is unswerving in his opposition to those who hold that justice and other moral values are no more than the beliefs of given individuals or societies. Indeed this realism is so deeply entrenched that it is not explicitly argued for. Rather than try to *prove* that moral truths or facts are there to be known – a hopeless endeavour – Plato's dialogues show, or try to show, the reader how to seek moral knowledge. But the different answers are in their own different ways unconvincing. For the idea that the Socratic *elenchos* can yield moral knowledge, see chapter 22. The 'new' claim, that moral knowledge is the apprehension (perhaps through recollection) of transcendent Forms, is less likely to convince readers.

Moral motivation. Here the sceptical challenge: 'why should I be moral?' is skilfully constructed and equally boldly rebutted. Speaking for the sceptics in *Republic*, Socrates's partner in conversation, Glaucon, puts the challenge: what reason do I have to be just (that is, to be moral) if I can get the benefits of the moral behaviour of others and of a reputation for morality myself? Actually being moral benefits others, not myself, says the sceptic. Glaucon reports a SOCIAL CONTRACT (pp. 393–4) theory of morality, one that stresses the costs and benefits to all of living in a society where moral restraints encourage the society's members to 'live and let live'. This theory sees my being moral as a cost to me, but a benefit to others, a cost compensated for (in normal circumstances) by the benefits I derive from the restraint shown by others – they keep their hands off me and my property in return for me leaving them and theirs alone.

But just suppose I could get the benefits at no cost, without having actually to be moral or consistently act morally myself – if, for instance, I had the ring of Gyges, which makes the wearer invisible at will. Would not any sensible person choose to act immorally, in such a scenario? Yes, say the sceptics. No, insists Socrates. Why so?

Socrates's answer is to argue that to be just (that is, moral) is to have a harmoniously ordered soul, that is, one in which reason rules; *thumos* backs up the rule of reason and the lowest, appetitive, part is kept firmly in check. With such a well-ordered soul the just person is far happier than the unjust, whatever material benefits the unjust person enjoys, and whatever hardships or poor reputation the just person suffers. In this way Socrates tries to show that being moral is of supreme value to the moral agent, who thus has every reason to be moral.

Does this give a satisfying answer to the problem of moral motivation? Here are some responses. A: 'This says I should be moral because it is good for me, but that just reduces morality to self-interest, which cannot be right.' B: 'No, it makes morality an intrinsic good, not something which brings other benefits to the agent.' C: 'Even so, in saying morality is valuable in that it is an intrinsic good to the agent, the theory divorces morality from its everyday connection with interpersonal actions and with other-regarding motivations and sentiments.'

1.4 Political theory

We find not one but two different Utopias – sketches of an ideal political community – in Plato; first in the *Republic*, and another in his last work, called *Laws*. Both emphasize the importance of only properly qualified experts having authority. The ideal *polis* in *Republic* is sketched as an analogy to the perfectly just human being: each has three parts, and each is perfect when that part which is naturally fitted to do so controls the whole. In the *polis* this part fitted to rule is a small class of highly educated 'guardians', with the right nature, education and living conditions (no private property or family ties) to fit them for absolute power wielded for the good of the whole *polis*.

Karl Popper's (1966) famous critique of Plato's political philosophy, where he charged it with totalitarianism, has been hotly disputed. Where Popper saw an authoritarian elevation of the good of the state over the happiness of the citizens, more recent writers have seen the proposals as merely paternalistic. That is, the political aim is simply *the happiness of all the citizens*, though this requires benevolent compulsion by the wise guardians of the majority who are ruled by their passions, not reason. Which interpretation is correct? Popper's critics are right that Socrates, in *Republic*, never suggests that the happiness of the whole *polis* could come about without that of all the classes. But can Socrates really allow that members of the lowest class can enjoy a happiness other than that of making their lowly contribution to the happiness of the *polis*?

If not, then Popper's charge that Socrates regards these citizens as little more than cogs in a machine has some truth in it.

Two key themes pervade Plato's writing on politics: the idea that freedom is not a good when exercised by those who lack reason and self-control, and the idea that power should only be entrusted to those with the knowledge of how to use it for good ends. Those espousing liberalism must have an answer to both.

2 Aristotle

It is a commonplace to contrast Aristotle's philosophy with that of Plato, for whom to investigate reality is not to make an empirical inquiry into the natural world of everyday objects but to seek out Platonic Forms, known to the intellect, not to sense-perception. At first blush Aristotle's thought can seem profoundly anti-Platonic.

2.1 Metaphysics and epistemology

2.1.1 Aristotle's empiricism

Our word 'metaphysics' derives from the title of a major work of Aristotle's, though it simply meant 'what comes after the *Physics*'; that is, after his investigations concerning the natural world. The *Metaphysics* opens with the remark that the senses, and sight in particular, are a vital source of knowledge. Learning and knowledge require sense-perception, memory and experience – progressive steps to the formation of the universal grasp of similar things required for knowledge. As well as this emphasis on the need for sense-perception, memory and experience, another apparently direct confrontation with Plato is Aristotle's down-to-earth insistence, in his early work the *Categories*, that 'primary substances' are everyday things like a particular man or a particular ox – a direct rebuttal of Plato's relegation of these to an inferior status to the Forms, and of Plato's claim that particular things get their reality by 'sharing in' the Forms.

Indeed, Aristotle makes frequent attacks on the claims of 'the Platonists' about Forms. He argues that in 'separating' Forms from the everyday things which are supposed to 'share in' them, Plato and his followers make the mistake of treating Forms both as particulars (that is, for Aristotle, as things which cannot be predicated of many things) and as universals. (See especially *Metaphysics* 7, ch. 13.) But on Plato's behalf we could reply that what Aristotle criticizes as Plato's objectionable thesis of the 'separation' of the Forms is merely the plausible claim that universals are prior to particulars in the sense that they could exist uninstantiated. To argue this is not to make a universal at the same time a particular, it could be urged. But while Aristotle firmly believes in universals – as we saw, he believed knowledge must be of what is universal – he rejected the idea that they could exist uninstantiated and thus independently of their particular instances.

2.1.2 Aristotle's rationalism

Despite his rejection of aspects of Plato's metaphysics, Aristotle shares many tenets with Plato. Knowledge, for both, is of what is universal, and, more importantly, requires

608

knowledge of the 'why?' – of the cause or explanation of whatever is being investigated, whether natural objects like a kind of animal or its parts, or phenomena such as eclipses or lightning. In investigating causes it is vital to distinguish what is essential from what is merely accidental or coincidental. A thing's essential properties are those it has in its own right, on which its other properties depend. And in his insistence on the link between knowledge, explanation and essence, Aristotle gives a major role to form, in contrast to matter, and often, like Plato, equates form with essence.

2.1.3 Matter and form in Aristotle

It is easy to grasp the distinction between matter and form in the case of something like a bronze sphere, where the matter or material – bronze – acquires the form – a spherical shape – when poured into a mould by the craftsman. Both matter and form can count as causes, in that each explains some properties of objects: its matter explains why the bronze sphere rings out when struck, its shape explains its rolling down an incline. But generally, Aristotle holds, form is more important in a causal explanation than matter, and he frequently criticizes his predecessors (not including Plato) for focusing on material causes – the basis elements of things – and ignoring form. This is especially so for living things, for whom their form is more than their shape and is closely related to FUNCTION (pp. 319–20). A wooden 'hand' is not a hand, and that of a dead person is only by courtesy called a hand. For Aristotle the form of a living thing is its organization, the basis of the activities (such as flying, hunting, eating mice) characteristic of a thing of that kind. Now in living things their matter is replaced over time and it is the form, thus understood, which persists, and which explains the organism's behaviour; hence form is more properly cause and essence than matter. But Aristotle recognizes that a clear demarcation between form and matter seems to break down; at times he allows that the form of living things must include the 'proximate matter' – the sort of flesh and bones needed for creatures of a given kind to function as they do.

And there is a further, grave, problem in understanding Aristotle's metaphysics: that of whether he regards forms as universal or as particular. While in his early work *Categories* he made concrete individuals such as a particular man or ox the primary substances, he revisits the question 'What is substance?' in the *Metaphysics* and there gives as his considered answer, not the concrete individual, composed of form and matter, but form. Now, if form is the universal, the species form 'man' (that is, what Socrates and Callias share), then it can certainly be the object of knowledge and definition, since these must be of something universal, Aristotle insists. But nothing universal can be a substance – this was in effect Aristotle's objection to Plato. So if, on the new view, form is to be substance, then it must be particular forms, one for Socrates and one for Callias, which Aristotle here intends.

So Aristotle's metaphysics and epistemology have much in common with Plato's. Despite his more down-to-earth approach to the natural world, and his criticisms of the excesses, as he saw it, of Plato's theory of Forms, Aristotle shares Plato's focus on causes, essences and form, and his insistence that reality must be intrinsically intelligible and well-ordered. Indeed, it might be thought that in some of his theses – notably in the famous argument that seeks to show that if there are to be changing substances such as horses, trees and houses, there must be an unmoved mover, God, who is pure form without matter – Aristotle equals or surpasses Plato's metaphysical flights.

2.2   The soul

Here the contrast between Aristotle's view and Plato's is more marked, and, from a contemporary perspective, Aristotle's psychology (theory of the soul) contains far more promising insights. In opposing Plato's view (a precursor of Cartesian dualism, as we saw) that the human soul is something immaterial, independent of the body and capable of surviving its death, Aristotle places his investigation firmly in the context of natural science. Soul, for Aristotle, is simply that in virtue of which living things are alive, and he castigates those who focus their inquiries into soul on human soul and neglect non-human animals, who share many 'psychic functions' with human beings. For Aristotle, this includes functions of living things not now thought of as psychic, such as breathing, growth and nutrition, in addition to thought, perception and memory.

This extension of 'psychological' inquiries to all living things and to the capacities they have as living things grounds many of the distinctive features of Aristotle's account of soul. As in his overall account of reality, he steers a path between the legacy of Plato – here, the account of the soul as an independent entity, the subject of psychological properties such as thinking and memory, and capable of surviving the death of the organism – and that of materialist predecessors who had sought to explain all psychic functions in terms of the material constituents of living things. Famously, Aristotle defined the soul as the form of a natural body, that is, of a body of a living thing with organs. He insists that psychic phenomena such as perception, emotions (for example, anger), memory and thinking cannot occur except in an embodied organism (though he occasionally qualifies this with reference to one kind of faculty – labelled active intellect – which is capable of independent, that is non-embodied, existence).

The insistence that psychic functions require a body goes beyond a claim that the soul can only operate with the help of a body. It is not the soul, but the organism itself, which is the subject of mental phenomena. 'To say that the soul is angry is like saying that the soul is weaving or is building a house. It's better to say, not that the soul is feeling pity, or thinking, or learning, but that the human being is doing so in virtue of the soul' (*De Anima* 1.4). These remarks, together with the insistence that psychic phenomena are necessarily enmattered, may seem to suggest that Aristotle sides with the materialists who seek to account for psychic phenomena purely in terms of the material constituents of the living organism. But to call soul the form of the natural body is very different from thinking of it as the arrangement of the material parts. As we saw above, the form in the case of a living thing is the principle of the organization of that thing, its disposition to behave in all the ways characteristic of that kind of thing. Certainly, since perceiving, being angry, pitying and so on are functions of a necessarily material thing, the soul as the form of a natural body will include descriptions of them in apparently material terms. Aristotle distinguishes two current definitions of anger. One, given by one kind of student of nature, focuses on the material aspect and defines anger as 'the boiling of blood around the heart', while another, the dialectician's, gives the form, defining anger as 'the desire to take revenge'. But a true student of nature, he tells us, should include both aspects. The reason for this is presumably not just that each contributes an essential part of the account of anger, but also that each already incorporates aspects of the partner term. The allegedly material definition – the boiling of blood around the heart – is already an account which presupposes that a living organism is being described – hence one whose form is evidently vital to its being – while the desire to take revenge is itself necessarily enmattered, that is has a physiological basis.

Aristotle's middle path between dualism and materialism, his discussion of psychological phenomena with reference to non-human as well as to human animals, and his foregrounding of the whole living organism as the subject of psychological properties give his psychology considerable appeal. And many will approve his refusal, nonetheless, to accept a REDUCTIONIST (pp. 174–8) account of mental properties. Huge questions remain as to how Aristotle thinks we should understand the relation between accounts which focus on, say, the chemical properties of an organism and accounts which mention such things as the desire for revenge. Such questions remain at the forefront of modern philosophy of mind, though Aristotle is innocent of the modern emphasis on the difficulty of capturing in physiological terms the first-person perspective, and the phenomena of CONSCIOUSNESS (pp. 650–2).

2.3 Ethics

Ethics is the inquiry into the human good, the good for human beings. Everyone agrees that the human good is *eudaimonia* (happiness or flourishing), but beyond that there is much controversy. Setting out reputable opinions on the subject yields the suggestions that *eudaimonia* is pleasure, or virtue or contemplation. Such opinions also reveal that its formal properties include the following: *eudaimonia* is actuality, not potentiality (and this is one reason to exclude the identification of virtue – a potentiality – with *eudaimonia*, though virtue is intrinsically connected with it); it is sought for its own sake and it cannot be made better by the addition of other goods (for this reason it cannot be equated with pleasure). To flesh out the account Aristotle turns to the idea of the function of a human being, and locates this in activities in accordance with reason (broadly understood), concluding that *eudaimonia*, being supremely *good*, consists in activities which manifest the *best* states, that is the *virtues*, of the rational aspect of human beings.

So an account of these virtues is needed; they fall into two categories: virtues of intellect and virtues of character (often called moral virtues). This corresponds to an important division of the rational part of the soul into two: the part which is fully rational, the intellect, and the part which can 'obey reason', which Aristotle labels the desiderative part. This part is the source of desires of many kinds, both physical appetites and desires for fame, honour and revenge, together with the emotions and feelings associated with these desires. The virtues of character, excellent states of this part of the human being, are defined as involving a mean between excess and deficiency; they include courage, temperance, justice and a host of other virtues such as gentleness and generosity. The virtues of intellect are divided into those connected with practical thinking, and those connected with purely intellectual thought. For the

611

majority of the work it seems that *eudaimonia* is to be identified with a life manifesting virtues of all three types, but a rather different picture emerges at the end of the work where contemplation, the activity of the theoretical intellect, is argued to be the best candidate for *eudaimonia*. An attractive way to resolve this tension is to recognize that contemplation would be the best life for those with a divine nature, but cannot be so for human beings, who, unlike the gods, have needs, desires and feelings, and are essentially 'political animals', that is who flourish in communities where social attributes are crucial.

Ethics as the Search for the Highest Human Good

In putting *eudaimonia* at the heart of ethical inquiry, Aristotle's theory may seem to resemble UTILITARIANISM (chapter 35), but there are two major differences. As we have seen, his account of *eudaimonia* in terms of activities manifesting the virtues makes it a far cry from the utilitarian account of happiness as pleasure. Secondly, utilitarianism makes happiness the sole ultimate good and proceeds to explain moral goodness, especially right action, as that which promotes the good. Thus moral goodness has a derivative worth, derived from its contribution to happiness, which is conceived in non-moral terms. By contrast, in characterizing *eudaimonia* as activities manifesting the virtues, Aristotle is operating with a *unified* conception of human good, one in which ethical or moral goodness is an integral part of the good life. And in this respect Aristotle's starting-point differs also from, and is arguably superior to, that of KANT (chapter 32) and neo-Kantians who like to distinguish the good or value of a human being from what is good for a human being, insisting that ethics should concern itself with the first and not the second. It is a strength of Aristotle's approach that his inquiry into 'the human good' does not allow this bifurcation and, *a fortiori*, privileges neither the non-moral good (as utilitarianism does) nor, with the Kantians, the moral good. In searching for the human good, Aristotle distances himself from Plato's inquiry into the Form of the Good, an alleged transcendent good. Aristotle rejects this on the grounds, first, that there could be no such thing, and second, that even if there were it would be of no help in an ethical inquiry into the good for human beings.

2.3.1 Eudaimonia, virtue, function and the good of others

The idea that human beings have a shared function is objectionable if it implies that humans were created for a purpose. But Aristotle's appeal to the human function is simply an appeal to the premise that there are capacities and activities characteristic to human beings, without which a life is less than fully human, and to the claim that this essentially involves the exercise of reason. That the best human life at least involves (though it need not be exhausted by) activities manifesting the best states of a rational nature is relatively uncontroversial. Far more problematic are Aristotle's assumptions (a) that this seemingly vague characterization picks out a sufficiently determinate end and (b) that these 'best states of a rational nature' include the moral virtues, as traditionally understood: courage, temperance, generosity, justice. For what the theory takes to be good about these states is that they are what makes the individual's life go well, but it is a large assumption that justice, in particular, is in the required way good *for the individual*. Whereas Plato had tackled head on the sceptical challenge: why should I be moral? Aristotle quietly avoids it, by simply including justice among his list of moral virtues, an inclusion that a sceptic would challenge, on the grounds that justice is not evidently one of those dispositions that it is best *for the agent to possess*. On Aristotle's behalf we could reply, first, that his work was addressed to well-brought-up young men, who will already be disposed to view justice as a desirable quality for an individual to possess; second, that good grounds for this assumption can be found in the nature of human beings, who flourish in communities and when engaged in co-operative activities with friends and associates.

2.3.2   *Moral virtues, the mean, and 'practical wisdom': Aristotle's version of moral realism*

The famous doctrine of the mean – the thesis that the moral virtues are mean states where the mean is 'relative to us' – involves the following claims. To have and to manifest a moral virtue such as temperance involves feeling an appropriate degree of its associated emotion (desire for bodily pleasures, in the case of temperance) and making the appropriate choice of such pleasures, avoiding excess and deficiency in feeling and action. The mean is what is appropriate, neither too much nor too little, and it is 'relative to us' as human beings, not as different individuals – there are not different virtues according to our different susceptibilities to such pleasures. But what determines what is appropriate? For this one needs, as a complement to a given moral virtue, the intellectual virtue of *phronesis*, practical wisdom. Aristotle's account of this important virtue is fraught with difficulties, but it is clear that he views it as a kind of moral knowledge, a grasp of a moral reality (that the appropriate way to respond in these circumstances is to feel like this and to act in this way). It is evident that his view privileges knowledge of what is morally appropriate in a particular set of circumstances over universal moral truths. Some go further and claim that his view is particularist in refusing to acknowledge any important role for universal moral principles in moral knowledge. Aristotle never makes clear the respective roles of deliberation and insight in *phronesis*, but it is clear that he sees a crucial interdependence between the fully fledged moral virtue and its intellectual counterpart, practical wisdom, such that one cannot first acquire the one and then the other: learning to feel and act in the appropriate way goes hand in hand with acquiring a grasp of what that appropriate way is. And no 'external' criterion of what is appropriate should be demanded; what is appropriate is evident to a person of moral virtue and practical wisdom, but this must not be taken to mean that it is their say-so that makes it appropriate. This theory of moral knowledge and reality avoids the twin extremes of reducing the goodness of a good action to a matter of convention, and of finding it in the strict application of universal principles. And if someone complains that the account is not very informative, that it does not tell us, case by case, where the mean lies, then Aristotle would reply that the complaint misses the point: his theory is meant to show why no such account is possible, and why such knowledge is available only to a good person (whose responses have been properly trained and who has developed practical wisdom in tandem with this) placed in the relevant circumstances.

613

2.4 Political theory

What are we to make of Aristotle's famous dictum that 'man is a political animal'? Certainly this means that human beings are by nature suited to living in a political community, but does Aristotle think that human beings exist for the *polis*, or that the *polis* exists for human beings? If the former, his view would resemble that taken in Plato's *Republic* (a target for Aristotle's sharp criticism), at least on Popper's interpretation of it. Aristotle's claim (*Politics* 1253a: 19–29) that the *polis* is prior to the family and the citizen as a whole organism is to a part such as the hand certainly suggests this disturbing view. But this is misleading.

Aristotle holds, indeed, that a human being's function or characteristic excellence can be perfected only in a *polis*, but he does not think the *polis* defines that function, or that man's function is to serve the *polis*. Rather, the point of a *polis* is to create conditions in which its citizens can live the best life possible. This will include social and political interaction as well as various intellectual pursuits, all pursued for their own sake. Aristotle's political philosophy does not, then, subordinate the citizen to the *polis*. But it has a very different defect, that of holding that citizenship should not be extended to those human beings incapable of living the best human life, and this, for Aristotle, means women, manual workers and those he notoriously labels 'natural slaves'. It is an abiding challenge to political theory to see if it is possible to marry a more inclusive and democratic conception of citizenship to Aristotle's central, and attractive, tenet that the goal of the *polis* – that is, the aim of political arrangements – should be not merely to enable its citizens to live, but to 'live well', that is to provide the conditions under which citizens acquire and exercise the moral and intellectual human virtues.

Further Reading

The best introduction to Plato is to read some of his dialogues, which are literary as well as philosophical masterpieces. They are collected in English translation in a single volume in Hamilton and Cairns (1961) and also in Cooper (1997). Many of the translations in the latter are also published separately by Hackett. An excellent 'taster' collection is *The Last Days of Socrates*, containing three short works (*Euthyphro*, on 'What is piety?', *Apology*, Plato's representation of Socrates's defence at his trial, and *Crito*, on political obligation) and the much longer, more profound and demanding *Phaedo*. See also Grube (1981), which has these four and *Meno*. Ethical issues are discussed in the sparkling *Protagoras* and in *Gorgias*, one of whose characters, Callicles, was the inspiration for Nietzsche's revaluation of values. *Republic*, Plato's most famous work, covers ethics, politics, philosophy of mind, metaphysics and theory of knowledge, as well as philosophy of art. Despite its hyperbolic criticism, Popper's (1966) attack on *Republic* is a classic. Annas (1981) is an excellent introduction to the whole work. *Theaetetus*, whose topic is knowledge and its relation to perception and to opinion, rivals or surpasses *Republic* and *Phaedo* in its brilliance and toughness of argument, but unlike them discusses knowledge and reality without an appeal to the Forms. Three fine works on it (by McDowell, Bostock and Burnyeat) are listed below.

Still on Plato, Kraut (1992) contains a full bibliography and recent articles, including discussions of the order and dating of Plato's writings, and of the debate over whether we should seek, in the dialogues, an account of Plato's own philosophy, and if so, whether 'unitary' or 'developmental'. Kahn (1996) favours the former, but most recent writers assume development both in Plato's ethical views, for example Irwin (1995), and in his metaphysics. Valuable collections of articles on a range of Platonic issues by various writers are Allen (1965), Kraut (1992) and Fine (1999); single-authored collections are Owen (1986) and Vlastos (1981, 1991). Rutherford (1995) is valuable for literary and historical aspects of Plato.

Aristotle's collected works are available in a two-volume translation (Barnes 1984). Substantial selections are available in Ackrill (1987) and in the very useful Irwin and Fine (1995), with notes, glossary and bibliography. It contains parts or all of the following works: on logic: *Categories**, *De Interpretatione**, *Prior and Posterior Analytics**, *Topics*; on natural philosophy: *Physics** and *de Generatione et Corruptione*; on psychology, *de Anima** (*on the Soul*) and *de Motu Animalium*; *Metaphysics**, *Nicomachean Ethics**; *Politics**, *Rhetoric* and *Poetics*. Clarendon Aristotle translations plus commentary are available for all or parts of those asterisked.

Excellent short introductions to Aristotle are Ackrill (1981) and Barnes (1982). Help with the difficult *Metaphysics* can be gained from several volumes of the Clarendon Aristotle series (translation and commentary) and from Witt (1989) or Loux (1991). For *Nicomachean Ethics* (the most important of the ethical works) see translations by Crisp (2000) or Irwin (1999, with useful notes and glossary), and studies by Urmson (1988, a good introduction) and Broadie (1991). Rorty (1980) is a valuable collection of essays on Aristotle's ethics. Barnes (1994) has articles on many aspects of Aristotle's thought, and a good bibliography. Ross (1964) is still a very useful general work.

References

Plato: translations
Cooper, J. M. (ed.) 1997: *Plato: Complete Works*. Indianapolis, IN: Hackett.
Grube, G. M. A. 1981: *Plato: Five Dialogues*. Indianapolis, IN: Hackett.
Hamilton, E. and Cairns, H. (eds) 1961: *The Collected Dialogues of Plato* (including the Letters). Princeton, NJ: Princeton University Press.
Tredennick, H. (trans.) 1993: *The Last Days of Socrates*, revd edn (revised by H. Tarrant). Harmondsworth: Penguin Books (contains *Euthyphro, Apology, Crito, Phaedo*).
The translations with philosophical commentary in the Clarendon Plato series include those on *Phaedo* (D. Gallop), *Protagoras* (C. C. W. Taylor), *Gorgias* (T. H. Irwin) and *Theaetetus* (J. H. McDowell). The *Theaetetus* of Plato, translated by Levett (1990: Hackett), has a long introduction by Burnyeat. Many translations of *Republic* are available; for *Laws*, there is T. J. Saunders (1970: Penguin Books), with introduction and summaries as well as bibliography.

Works on Plato
Allen, R. E. 1965: *Studies in Plato's Metaphysics*. London: Routledge.
Bostock, D. 1988: *Plato's Theaetetus*. Oxford: Clarendon Press.
Fine, G. 1999: *Plato 1 Metaphysics and Epistemology, Plato 2 Ethics Politics Religion and the Soul* (Oxford Readings in Philosophy, also available in a single volume). Oxford: Oxford University Press.
Kahn, C. H. 1996: *Plato and the Socratic Dialogue*. Cambridge: Cambridge University Press.
Kraut, R. 1992: *The Cambridge Companion to Plato*. Cambridge: Cambridge University Press.
Owen, G. E. L. 1986: *Logic, Science and Dialectic* (collected papers). Ithaca, NY: Cornell University Press.
Popper, K. R. 1966 [1945]: *The Open Society and its Enemies, vol. 1: The Spell of Plato*. London: Routledge.

Rutherford, R. 1995: *The Art of Plato*. London: Duckworth.

Scott, D. 1995: *Recollection and Experience: Plato's Theory of Learning and its Successors*. Cambridge: Cambridge University Press.

Vlastos, G. 1981: *Platonic Studies*. Princeton, NJ: Princeton University Press.

——1991: *Socrates, Ironist and Moral Philosopher*. Cambridge: Cambridge University Press.

Aristotle: translations

Ackrill, J. L. (ed.) 1984: *A New Aristotle Reader*. Oxford: Oxford University Press.

Barnes, J. (ed.) 1984: *The Complete Works of Aristotle*, 2 vols. Princeton, NJ: Princeton University Press.

Irwin, T. and Fine, G. 1995: *Aristotle: Selections*. Indianapolis, IN: Hackett.

Works on Aristotle

Ackrill, J. L. 1981: *Aristotle the Philosopher*. Oxford: Oxford University Press.

Barnes, J. 1982: *Aristotle*. Oxford: Oxford University Press.

——(ed.) 1994: *The Cambridge Companion to Aristotle*. Cambridge: Cambridge University Press.

Ross, W. D. 1964 [1923]: *Aristotle*. London: Methuen.

ON METAPHYSICS

Loux, M. J. 1991: *Primary Ousia*. Ithaca, NY: Cornell University Press.

Witt, C. 1989: *Substance and Essence in Aristotle*. Ithaca, NY: Cornell University Press.

ON PSYCHOLOGY

Nussbaum, M. C. and Rorty, A. O. (eds) 1992: *Essays on Aristotle's De Anima*. Oxford: Oxford University Press.

ON ETHICS

Crisp, R. 2000: *Aristotle, Nicomachean Ethics* (introduction and translation). Cambridge: Cambridge University Press.

Irwin, T. H. 1999: *Aristotle, Nicomachean Ethics* (translation, notes and glossary). Indianapolis, IN: Hackett.

Rorty, A. O. (ed.) 1980: *Essays on Aristotle's Ethics*. Berkeley: University of California Press.

Urmson, J. O. 1988: *Aristotle's Ethics*. Oxford: Blackwell.

Discussion Questions

1 If knowledge is recollection, must the soul be immortal?

2 What is virtue? Is virtue teachable?

3 Can ordinary things participate in a Form?

4 Are there good reasons to think that Forms and minds are peculiarly fitted to one another?

5 Can anything satisfy all the roles that Plato assigns to Forms?

6 Does the Form of X have a superior kind of existence or a superior way of being X?

7 Which should have priority: the semantic role of Forms or their ontological role?

8   How does an investigation of language help to discern the role of Forms in structuring reality?

9   Can the theory of Forms guarantee the objectivity of ethics and aesthetics?

10   Does the theory of Forms involve us in an endless regress?

11   Can a single thing explain why all beautiful things are beautiful?

12   Do souls have parts? If so, what are they and how can they be identified?

13   How is weakness of will or *akrasia* possible?

14   What should be our conception of reason? Can reason determine ends as well as means to achieve ends?

15   Why should I be moral if I could get the benefits of morality without having actually to be moral?

16   Is the just person happier than the unjust, even if the balance of material benefits and hardships favours the unjust?

17   Who should have authority? Is the answer the same in a *polis* and in a modern society?

18   Is freedom a good when exercised by those who lack reason and self-control?

19   Is Aristotle's thought anti-Platonic?

20   Is a particular man a substance?

21   How should we draw the distinction between particulars and universals? Are forms particulars or universals?

22   Can universals exist if they are uninstantiated?

23   Does knowledge require an account of the cause or explanation of what is being investigated?

24   Can we distinguish between essential properties of a thing and its accidental properties?

25   Is the essence of a thing its form?

26   Is form more important than matter in causal explanation?

27   What is substance? Should contemporary philosophy be concerned with this question?

28   Must reality be intrinsically intelligible?

29   Can all mental functions be explained in terms of the material constituents of living things?

30   How should we assess the claim that the soul is the form of a natural body?

31   Do psychic functions require a body?

32   Is the soul or the organism itself the subject of mental phenomena?

33   Are considerations of both physiology and desires necessary for an account of anger?

34   Can we avoid reductionism in our account of mental phenomena?

35   What constitutes human happiness or flourishing? Do philosophers have a special role in answering this question?

36   Can we distinguish between virtues of intellect and virtues of character?

37   Do virtues involve a mean between excess and deficiency?

38   Is a life of contemplation the best candidate for *eudaimonia*?

39   Must a good life be ethically good?

40   Would knowing the Form of the Good help us to understand the good for human beings?

41   Does knowledge of universal moral principles have any important role in moral knowledge?

42   Could we have moral virtue without moral wisdom or moral wisdom without moral virtue?

43   What is the role of citizenship in the *polis*? Should citizenship have the same role in modern democratic societies?

24

Medieval Philosophy

JORGE J. E. GRACIA

The concern to integrate revealed doctrine and secular learning distinguishes medieval philosophy from ancient, Renaissance and modern philosophy and determines to a great extent the philosophical problems the medievals addressed and the solutions they proposed for those problems. This chapter examines the way the medievals approached this main theme and illustrates how it affected their choice of philosophical problems and how they dealt with them. In particular, it pays attention to seven problems well discussed throughout the age: the relation of faith and reason, the existence of God, the significance of names used to speak about God, the object of theology and metaphysics, the way we know, universals, and individuation. C. F. J. Martin has contributed 'Understanding Medieval Philosophy: Arguments from Authority'.

The use of the expression 'medieval philosophy' to refer to philosophy in the middle ages is paradoxical because it is hard to find anyone during the period who considered himself a philosopher, whose concerns were purely philosophical, or who composed purely philosophical works. Medieval authors from the Latin West thought of themselves rather as theologians, were primarily interested in theological issues, and very seldom composed purely philosophical works. For them, the philosophers were the ancients, PLATO AND ARISTOTLE (chapter 23), and some of the Islamic authors, like Avicenna of Baghdad (Ibn Sina, 980–1037) and Averroes of Cordoba (Ibn Rushd, 1126–98). There are very few works produced in the period that can be classified strictly speaking as philosophical. Most of the philosophy that we find is contained in books of theology and used to elucidate theological doctrine. Whence the well-known phrase, coined by Thomas Aquinas (c.1225–1274) in reference to philosophy, *ancilla theologiae*, 'servant of theology'. The expression 'medieval philosophy', moreover, has a disparaging connotation derived from the term 'middle ages', used first by Renaissance humanists to refer to what they thought was a barbaric and dark period of Western history found between the two civilized and enlightened ages of classical antiquity and the Renaissance. In spite of the lack of philosophers, the absence of purely philosophical works, and the prejudices of Renaissance humanists, the middle ages is not only the longest period of philosophical development in the West, but also one of the richest. Indeed, in intensity, sophistication and achievement, the philosophical flowering in the thirteenth century could be rightly said to rival the golden age of ancient philosophy in the fourth century BC in Greece and the extraordinary developments in the twentieth century in Europe and America.

The temporal and territorial boundaries of the middle ages are a subject of controversy among scholars. No matter which dates are picked, however, it is clear that both Augustine (354–430) and John of St Thomas (1589–1644) were engaged in the same intellectual programme and therefore belong together. Before Augustine, the intellectual life of the West was dominated by pagan philosophy, and DESCARTES (1596–1650) (chapter 26), generally regarded as the first modern philosopher, was contemporaneous with John. Territorially, we need to include not only Europe, but also the Middle East, where important Greek Orthodox, Jewish and Islamic authors flourished.

A period that extends for more than a millennium is by no means uniform or easily breaks down into smaller units. The first of these might be called Patristic, and began in earnest with Augustine, although its roots went back to the second century BC. It extended to the seventh century, and closed with the death of Isidore of Seville (c.560–636), author of the *Etymologies*, the first of many medieval encyclopedias. Between this time and the Carolingian Renaissance nothing of philosophical importance took place. Thanks to the efforts of Charlemagne (742–814) to establish schools, regularize writing, and gather in his court all the great minds of the times in order to encourage learning and to replicate the greatness of Rome, there was some important intellectual activity at the end of the eighth and the beginning of the ninth centuries, which culminated in the work of John Eriugena (c.810–75).

This period was followed by a dark age which ended with another, more lasting revival of learning in the eleventh and twelfth centuries. The twelfth-century renaissance, as it is often called, produced some of the greatest of all medieval thinkers: Anselm (1033–1109), Gilbert of Poitiers (c.1076–1154), Peter Abelard (c.1079–1142) and the School of Chartres. The period that went from 1150 to about 1225 is of paramount importance. At this time many of the works of the ancients became available to the medievals for the first time, thanks to the conquest of territory by Christians in Spain, and Western scholars engaged in a feverish attempt to assimilate them. Some of these works had been translated from Greek into Syriac in the Middle East, and later were translated into Arabic. From Arabic, they were translated into Latin with the help of Spanish Jews. A few other works were rendered into Latin directly from Greek originals by scholars working in Sicily and Southern Italy. Prior to 1150, the medievals had a rather meagre group of technical philosophical works from Aristotle and his commentators, known as the *logica vetus*. But in a few years not only the whole *Organon*, but most other works of Aristotle, with commentaries by Islamic authors, and many scientific works from antiquity, became available.

The renaissance of the twelfth century and the ferment created by the newly available texts gave rise to what is usually known as scholasticism. This is a method of teaching and learning used in various disciplines, particularly philosophy and theology. The origin of the term is to be found in medieval schools, where a lecturer, particularly one who taught the liberal arts (*trivium* and *quadrivium*) was called *scholasticus*. The aim of the method was to yield knowledge concordant with both human reason and the Christian faith, a *concordia discordantium* of opinions which the medievals regarded as authoritative. The method was practised in the medieval university and used as a tool of Aristotelian logic. As a result, the literary genres used by scholastics reflect university activities and settings. The commentary is, generally speaking, the product of classroom lectures on texts; the *quaestio* is the product of university disputations; and the *summae* were the textbooks of the age.

Among the first scholastics of note were Roger Bacon (*c.*1214–92) and Albert the Great (*c.*1200–1280), but they were followed by a host of towering figures: Bonaventure (*c.*1217–1274), Thomas Aquinas, John Duns Scotus (*c.*1265–1308) and William of Ockham (*c.*1285–1347). In the middle of the fourteenth century, however, scholasticism suffered a nearly irreversible setback through the Black Death (*c.*1347–51), which decimated the universities of Europe. It took more than a hundred years to recover and generate a second period of greatness under the leadership of Spanish scholastics of the sixteenth century, such as Francisco Suárez (1548–1617) and Francisco de Vitoria (*c.*1483–1546).

The distinguishing mark of medieval philosophy is to be found in its double aim: the understanding of Christian faith and its defence against those who attacked it. The effort at understanding produced theological works; the effort at defence produced apologetic works. This does not mean, however, that the medievals were not interested in purely philosophical problems. They were, but most often the reason for their interest was that the solutions to these problems had important implications for Christian doctrine; indeed, the solutions adopted were often governed by the doctrinal principles they wished to defend. In this sense, philosophy was generally subordinated to theology and apologetics.

This attitude separates the philosophy of the middle ages from both ancient and Renaissance philosophy. The approach of medieval philosophy separates it from ancient philosophy because both in classical Greece and Rome, philosophy enjoyed a largely independent status and a predominant position. Philosophy was a pursuit unsubordinated to any other intellectual activity, whose main goal was the understanding of the world and man's place in it. On the other hand, the medieval attitude is quite distinct from that of the Renaissance, because the humanists looked upon the classical past as a model of their activity and, therefore, restored man to the centre of attention and channelled their efforts to the recovery and emulation of classical learning, particularly in the philosophy of Plato. In contrast, philosophy in the middle ages was subordinated to theology, and the centre of intellectual attention was GOD (chapter 15) and his revelation rather than human beings; human beings were studied only as creatures of God made in his image and likeness. The model emulated by the medievals was not to be found in the lives and theories of ancient philosophers, but instead in the lives of saints and their prayers.

The character of medieval philosophy is evident in the philosophical problems medievals chose to address, the way they interpreted philosophical problems they found in ancient texts, and the solutions they gave to most of these problems. Three of the most important problems the medievals inherited from the ancients were the problem of how we know, the problem of God's existence, and the problem of universals. Three problems they raised as a result of their theological concerns and commitments were the problem of the relation between faith and reason, the problem of individuation, and the problem concerned with the language used to talk about God.

1 Faith and Reason

No other issue concerned the medievals more than the relation of faith to reason, for the success of the programme adopted in the age depended to a large extent in turn on the success in working out this relationship. For ancient philosophers, this had not been a concern, for most of them were not religious, so there was no need to reconcile reason to faith, or truths derived from the study of the world independently of faith to a body of revealed truths known by faith. Under this rubric, several and different, if interrelated, issues are contained. The problem is first explicitly formulated in the second century of the Christian era, when some early Fathers of the church questioned the merit of using secular learning by those to whom the truth has been revealed by God. Two sides are easily identifiable. Some rejected the value of secular learning altogether; this position is often called fideism because of its exclusive preference for faith. Others found a place for secular learning in the understanding of faith. Tertullian (c.160–220) argued that there is no place for the learning of infidels in Christianity, and he coined a phrase that has made history: 'I believe because it is absurd' (*Credo quia ineptum*). Among those who saw some merit in the use of secular learning and tried to bring it together with revealed truth was Justin Martyr (d. c.165).

Augustine followed in the footsteps of Justin Martyr and provided the parameters for future discussions of this issue. For him, all truth is one, regardless of the source, so the Christian can and should make use of secular learning. However, it is only in the Christian faith that one can truly understand the world and the place of human beings in it. Christian doctrine completes, illuminates and transforms secular learning, providing answers to questions which are most important and for which non-Christians have no answers. Moreover, it supplies us with an infallible criterion of truth. Anything found in secular learning that contradicts Christian doctrine is false and must be rejected; anything concordant with it may be used as long as it is done in the context of faith.

The controversy between the approach of those denying the value of secular learning and those advocating its use surfaced again in the eleventh and twelfth centuries. This time the focus was upon the use of logic, known then as dialectic, in the understanding of scriptures. Among the anti-dialecticians was Peter Damian (1007–72), who went so far as to reject not just logic, but even grammar because, as he put it, the Devil became the first grammarian when he declined the word *Deus* in the plural. His irrationalism was so strong, and his faith in God's power so great, that he argued that God could bring it about that the past never happened. The most outspoken dialectician was Abelard, known as the Peripatetic from Pallet because of his use of and predilection for Aristotelian logic. In a controversial book, entitled *Sic et non* (Yes and No), Abelard showed that Christian authorities contradict each other, and therefore an understanding of Christian faith requires the use of logic. A more moderate position was adopted by Anselm. Inspired by Augustine, he argued for a measured use of logic, in which understanding begins with faith but is achieved when the doctrines revealed in scriptures are articulated in logical form. His view is encapsulated in two famous formulas: *Credo ut intelligam* (I believe in order that I may understand) and *Fides quaerens intellectum* (Faith seeking understanding).

The relation between faith and reason was also of concern to Islamic and Jewish thinkers during this period. One of the most controversial views on the topic was proposed by Averroes. Adopting a strict Aristotelian model of knowledge as demonstration, he argued that the understanding of scriptures can never reach the level of knowledge, for knowledge is based on demonstrative reasoning, and reasoning founded on premises that are not self-evident can never be considered demonstrative. Theology does not yield knowledge properly speaking, and therefore must be subordinated to philosophy, which does. Averroes's position, as well as the position of those who preferred reason over faith, is usually referred to as rationalism.

In the thirteenth century, both Bonaventure and Aquinas responded to Averroes. Bonaventure rejected the universality of the Aristotelian model of knowledge, though he admitted its competence within its own sphere. Since all things in the created order are, for Bonaventure, signs of the Uncreated Wisdom, each sphere of reality must be seen in its connection to that Wisdom. As a result, although in any one science knowledge can be acquired without revelation, each science and its subject needs to be traced back (*reducere*) to the Uncreated Wisdom for proper appreciation of its role within human life and thought. Hence, Bonaventure privileges Augustinian wisdom over and against Aristotelian science, rejecting the latter as the highest canon of judgement regarding human knowledge.

In contrast to Bonaventure, Aquinas did not reject the Aristotelian model used by Averroes, but rather argued that not all knowledge is of the same sort. Some knowledge has premises which are self-evident principles – as is the case with metaphysics – but some have premises which have been demonstrated in other branches of knowledge – as with optics, which takes its principles from geometry. Theology is based on faith, but it can be considered knowledge because it rests on God's own knowledge, which is the highest one there can be. Aquinas, moreover, made room for both theology and philosophy in the body of all knowledge by arguing that some truths can be known only through faith (for example, Christ is God), some can be known only through reason (for example, all material substances are composed of matter and form), and some can be known through either faith or reason (for example, God exists).

In spite of the efforts of Bonaventure, Aquinas and others, the influence of Averroes continued to be felt well into the sixteenth century and prompted repeated condemnations from various quarters. The most famous of these occurred in 1277, and included even some views which Aquinas himself had held. The popularity of Averroes was most strongly felt in the faculty of arts rather than theology. Among those in the thirteenth century accused of following Averroes too closely was Siger of Brabant (*c.*1235–84). He was charged with holding a doctrine of double truth, according to which there is a truth of faith and a truth of reason, and these truths can and often do contradict each other. Clearly, this was unacceptable to most medievals, for it undermined the overall programme of the age, that is, the integration of revelation and secular learning into a consistent body of doctrine.

Understanding Medieval Philosophy: Arguments from Authority

Let us take a case in point: that of the medieval attitude to arguments from authority. A typical medieval text will contain frequent appeals to authoritative statements, drawn from scripture, from Augustine, say, or from Aristotle or Cicero. This is not a feature of contemporary philosophy: we quote philosophers chiefly to disagree with them, or because a previous author has made our point better and more concisely than we can. We do not – or, at least, we claim we do not – bring in dicta of, for example, Wittgenstein to support our views, with the implication that if Wittgenstein said so it must be so. But the medievals seem to act in just such a way.

One reaction to this is to say that therefore the medievals were not doing what we would call philosophy, and that the study of their philosophy must be principally of historical interest – 'merely' historical interest, some would say, with the implication that medieval philosophy is a suitable study for the historian of ideas, but not for the philosopher. Someone who takes this line will be able to learn from medieval philosophy, at best, what the historian of science might learn from the works of, for example, the phlogiston theorists.

An alternative reaction would be to ignore the appeals to authority as irrelevant – to skip them – and to concentrate on what a contemporary philosopher would regard as the 'real' arguments. Such a philosopher would learn something of philosophical value from the medievals, but not much: he or she would learn from a medieval author solely what could have been learned from a contemporary philosopher who happened to use arguments roughly formally parallel. If such readers learn anything new from the medievals, it will only be because of the mere chance that no contemporary author happens to have hit on roughly parallel arguments.

Neither kind of reader will learn what a reading of the medievals truly can teach in this case: to rethink our current preconceptions and prejudices about the use of authority. Medieval use of authority was conscious and articulate, not blind and all-trusting. As it happens, we profess, in our day, a blind and all-doubting rejection of authority which, by contrast with the nuanced views of the medievals, can be seen as very crude. The medievals accepted the fact, which most contemporary philosophers would implicitly or explicitly deny, that most of the interesting and important things that we know, we know from authority. Since the medievals recognized this fact, they were able to examine it, what weight to give to authority, and when to give it. Since we refuse to recognize the fact, we are all at sea; we blindly accept authority, often enough, without even knowing that we are doing so; and, at moments where a conscious acceptance of authority might be of genuine use to us, we conspire to reject it. By reading the medievals intelligently, avoiding the extremes mentioned above, being aware of how different was their thought from ours, but not for that reason abandoning it as of 'merely historical interest', we can genuinely learn from them to correct the mistakes that our age is too prone to make.

2   God's Existence

Proving that God exists was important for the medievals because GOD'S EXISTENCE (chapter 15) is the angular stone on which the Christian faith rests. It was important in order both to lay down the foundation of all Christian theology and to establish a base for apologetic efforts directed toward Muslims and Jews.

The ancients had already provided some arguments for the existence of God, but it was the medievals who formulated these in elegant and parsimonious ways. These arguments break down into two types: arguments based on the analysis of concepts and arguments based on experience. Of the first, the most famous are the arguments of Anselm in the *Proslogion* and John Duns Scotus in *On the First Principle*. Both have come to be known as versions of the so-called ontological argument, a term first used by Kant to designate them. Of the second type, the most famous are the Five Ways presented in Aquinas's *Summa theologiae*, which comprise both cosmological and teleological arguments.

Anselm's argument derives God's existence from the conception of God as that than which a greater cannot be thought. God exists, for if he did not, that than which a greater cannot be thought would not be that than which a greater cannot be thought. Anselm assumes, in line with his Augustinian–Platonic framework, that something that exists is greater than something that does not, that the notion of that than which a greater cannot be thought is intelligible, and that logical necessity has a bearing on existence. He has been criticized for all three assumptions. But to this day there are strong supporters of the soundness of the argument.

Each of Aquinas's Five Ways begins by taking note of a fact given in experience, such as that some things change. From this they go on to point out, through various steps, that these experiences cannot be explained without recourse to a being who is ultimately responsible for them, and this being is God. The first way argues from the fact that there is change in the world to a first cause of the change. The second argues from the efficient causality we experience in the world to a first efficient cause. The third distinguishes between necessary and contingent beings, and from this concludes that there must be one necessary being whose necessary existence is not derived from any other being. The fourth argues from the gradation found in things to a being who is both the maximum and the cause of those things. And the fifth argues that all things, intelligent or not, act for an end, and there must be an intelligent being who directs them toward their end.

3 The Names of God

Showing that we can know God was as important to the medievals as proving that he exists. Indeed, because the latter implies knowing something about God, one might say that the task of showing that we can know God logically precedes the task of proving he exists.

Several philosophers from antiquity had talked about God. Texts abound in Plato, Aristotle and the Stoics that speak about a single divinity. In all these cases, however, God seems to have been conceived as part of the world. Knowing God, then, was not essentially different from knowing anything else, even if perhaps more difficult, for the terms we use to talk about the world are in principle applicable to God as well. The Christian conception of God, however, changed this. If God is wholly other than creation and transcends it, then it is questionable that the terms we use to speak about the world can also be applied to him.

625

Understanding the Names of God

The background of the controversy over understanding terms used for God is found in both Augustine's writings and an anonymous treatise probably written by a fifth-century Syrian monk who posed as Dionysus the Areopagite, entitled *On the Divine Names*. Controversies over the ways to understand divine names heat up in the twelfth and thirteenth centuries with Moses Maimonides (Moshe ben Maimon, *c.*1135–1204), Aquinas and Scotus. The issue concerns the application and understanding of terms which express perfections, such as 'good' and 'just'; no one held that terms expressing imperfections, such as 'bad' and 'unjust', are applicable to God. If terms of the first sort do not signify anything about God, then it appears that when we use them we do not understand anything in particular about God; and if they do, then it appears that we understand something about God but that he is not fundamentally different from the world. The first makes God unknowable and the scriptures unintelligible; the second makes God part of the world and therefore not divine. Both are unacceptable to an orthodox Muslim, Jew or Christian.

Almost everyone in the middle ages tried to find a solution to this dilemma. Maimonides argued that there are two kinds of terms applicable to God. First, terms that stand for attributes do not signify anything about God himself, but rather are to be understood negatively, as denying something of God. To say that God is good is to say that he is not evil, and to say that he is just is to say that he is not unjust. Second, terms that stand for actions do convey information, but the information they convey is not about God himself but about what God has done for others.

At the other extreme, Scotus argued that, in order for the language we predicate of God to be effective in producing understanding, there must be at least one term that is used univocally (that is, with the same meaning) of God and creatures, and proposed 'being' as such a term. The univocity of this term grounds our knowledge of God and makes it possible to speak intelligibly about him. Aquinas adopted a middle position, between Maimonides and Scotus, with the doctrine of analogy. The terms we predicate of God are not used equivocally (i.e. with different meanings) or univocally, but analogically. 'God is good' does not mean that he is good like we are, or that he is not bad in the sense we are; it means that he is good in proportion to his nature and thus better than we are, in a superlative degree, as the Pseudo-Dionysus had already stated.

4   Theology and Metaphysics

Because God is at the centre of our understanding, there must be a discipline devoted to his study. But which is this discipline? On the one hand, it is clear that the scriptures are the source where we can find revealed knowledge of God. But, on the other hand, the world also contains information about God because, as creator, he has left his imprint on it. Indeed, thirteenth-century theologians found texts of Aristotle in the *Metaphysics* that spoke of a science concerned with God. This gave rise to a heated controversy concerning whether God is studied in theology or in metaphysics.

In the Islamic world already we find differing views with respect to this issue. Avicenna rejected the view that God is studied in metaphysics because no science proves the existence of what it studies and metaphysics proves the existence of God. On the contrary, Averroes argued that God is studied in metaphysics, because his existence is not proven in this science but in physics. On the Latin side, Aquinas distinguished between Sacred Doctrine, that is theology based on scriptures, and what we now call Natural Theology, that is theology based on the study of the world. Moreover, he contrasted both of these disciplines with metaphysics. On the one hand, both Sacred Doctrine and Natural Theology study God: the first studies God as revealed in the scriptures and the second studies God as revealed in creation. On the other hand, metaphysics does not study God primarily, but rather studies being *qua* being, that is, being in so far as it is neither this kind (e.g. human, divine) nor this individual being (e.g. Socrates, God). Metaphysics studies God only secondarily, as the First Cause of being. Scotus agrees with Aquinas to the extent that he too believes that the proper object of study of theology is God, whereas that of metaphysics is being *qua* being.

This apparent agreement between two towering figures did not help to settle the matter, however, for the very understanding of being *qua* being was at issue. Aquinas and his followers argued that being *qua* being is to be understood as the last act (*esse*) and perfection of an essence in an individual entity, and distinct in reality from the essence. But both Scotus and Ockham rejected this conception of being. Indeed, Ockham even rejected the notion that any science has a single object of study. According to him, sciences are merely collections of mental propositions and because these propositions have different subjects, one cannot say that any science has only one subject.

5   How We Know

The problem of how we know beings other than God was introduced into the middle ages by Augustine's dialogue *On the Teacher*. The ostensive problem raised in this work is the purpose of the use of words, but the real underlying concern is the old Platonic issue of whether we can be taught. Plato's answer to this question had been negative: we cannot be taught because the objects of knowledge are immaterial Ideas, and the only way to know these is through a direct encounter with them in a previous life, when we were not fettered to the body. Our only hope for acquiring knowledge in this life is to be reminded through language of the Ideas we once knew. Augustine followed closely on Plato's footsteps but because, as a Christian, he could not accept the pre-existence of the soul, he modified the Platonic scheme. Christ becomes the teacher who places Ideas in our memory and it is there that we encounter them by being reminded of them through words. Augustine's view became known as the Doctrine of Illumination, because he used the Platonic metaphor of light to describe how Christ makes us see ideas: Christ is like the Sun which illumines our minds with knowledge of intelligible realities.

This doctrine turned into one of the most important battlegrounds between Augustinians and Aristotelians in the later middle ages. Almost everyone accepted Augustine's metaphor, but that is where the agreement ended. Bonaventure and Henry of Ghent (*c*.1217–1293), among others, tried to answer some of the questions raised by the doctrine and to resolve some of its ambiguities, but Aquinas and Scotus opposed these interpretations. The first argued that the light about which Augustine was speaking is none other than the natural light of reason, so that illumination is a natural rather than a supernatural process. Scotus, although a Franciscan, opposed his brothers in this. He argued that Henry of Ghent's interpretation of Augustine leads to scepticism, and knowledge is possible without illumination understood in a supernatural way.

6   Universals

Both Aristotle and Plato had made clear that knowledge properly speaking is of the universal, and the authority of Augustine had added further support for this view. Knowledge, in a strict sense, is not about this or that cat, but about cat, not about this man or that man, but about man in general. The medievals generally accepted this, but at the same time most of them held that not just substances in the Aristotelian sense (for example, this cat, this man), but also the features of substances (for example, a cat's black fur colour, a man's humanity) were individual. This posed a host of epistemological and metaphysical problems, one of which is known as the problem of universals.

The Problem of Universals

In the early part of the medieval period, the problem of universals was framed in terms of three questions Porphyry the Phoenician (c.232–304) had asked in the *Isagoge* concerning genera and species, and which the medievals found in Boethius's translation of that work: (1) Are things like animal and man something in the mind only or also something outside the mind? (2) If they are something outside the mind, are they material or immaterial? And (3) are they something separate and different from individual, sensible things, or something in them and like them? Boethius himself gave rather ambiguous answers to these questions, which left much for others to do. Roughly, he held that animal and man are both something in the mind and something outside the mind. They are understood in one way in the mind and exist in another way in things outside the mind; in the mind they are understood as universal, whereas outside the mind they are individual and sensible. Moreover, explicitly adopting an Aristotelian stance, which he justified because he was commenting on a work dealing with Aristotle, he rejected the view that genera and species exist separately from individual things outside the mind.

Challenged by Boethius's answers to his questions about genera and species, subsequent authors developed many positions in the early middle ages. They ranged from the extreme realism of Eriugena, according to whom genera and species are Platonic Ideas, to the extreme nominalism of Roscelin (c.1050–1120), who held they are mere individual utterances. The most sophisticated view was offered by Abelard, who argued that universals are words which are created to be predicated of several things. Although these words do not cause an understanding of any individual thing in particular, but rather of a conception common to many of them which the mind contrives, the cause of their imposition is to be found in the status of individual things. The status itself is not a thing, or any kind of reality, but merely what things are. The status of Socrates and Plato is man, but man is no entity other than Socrates and Plato. In spite of the sophistication of Abelard's theory, there were many questions that it left unanswered and which were taken up by subsequent authors.

In the thirteenth century the terms of the controversy changed somewhat because of the introduction of new terminology found in the recent translations of Aristotle and the commentaries on them by Averroes and Avicenna. Instead of speaking about genera, species or universals, the talk changed to natures. Moreover, the question was framed in terms of their unity and being: what kind of being and unity do natures have? The classic moderate position was taken by Aquinas, who argued that natures can be considered absolutely or in relation to the mind or individual things. Absolutely, only what is included in their definitions belongs to natures. Therefore, they cannot be said to have being or unity, but neither can they be said to lack them. Because the definition of the nature 'man' is 'rational animal', only animality and rationality can be said to belong to man considered absolutely. And because being and unity, just like whiteness, are not present in the definition, these cannot be said to belong to man considered as man, but neither are they supposed not to belong to it. The nature 'man' is as neutral with respect to being and unity, as it is with respect to whiteness. Being and unity belong to natures only when they are considered in relation to the mind or to individual things outside the mind. In relation to the mind, natures are concepts properly speaking and, therefore, are universal and have mental being. In relation to individual things, natures are individual and have individual being. Man, when understood, has both being and unity, the being proper to the mind, where it is found as a concept, and the unity proper to universals, because it can be used to think about not any man in particular but about each and every man. Man, considered in relation to individual men, has both individual being and unity, the being and unity of each man where it is found as their nature.

Both Scotus and Ockham developed views that disagreed with that of Aquinas, but in opposite directions. Scotus moved closer to realism and Ockham closer to nominalism. For Scotus, natures considered absolutely have a being and unity proper to themselves. Thus, in individuals, natures have a double unity and a double being, their own and that of individuals. Man has a being and unity proper to natures, so that in this man there is a double being and unity: the being and unity of the nature and the being and unity of the individual.

Ockham was quite dissatisfied with this view and applied to it his famous Razor, according to which explanations should not multiply entities beyond necessity. For him, there is no such a thing as a nature considered absolutely; there are only universal concepts in the mind and individual things outside the mind. The notion of a nature considered absolutely, whether that nature is conceived neutrally as Aquinas did, or as having some being and unity as Scotus did, is superfluous. The existence of universal concepts in the mind can be explained in terms of the natural capacity of the mind to form a general concept based on the particular experience of individuals.

629

7 Individuation

Those authors who attributed some status to natures in things outside the mind naturally asked themselves the question of what it is in things that makes them individual. If all the terms we predicate of individual things indicate something universal or common in them, what is individual in things? This was a particularly important question for medieval authors, and one which had been generally neglected by the ancients. Both Plato and Aristotle had talked about individuals, but their primary concern was with universals and their status. For the medievals, the order of importance was reversed, because for them God was not universal and had even become an individual person in the world. Moreover, God's creation was conceived as individual and endowed, as Augustine had pointed out, with a value higher than the ideas through which we know it.

The first author to raise questions concerning individuation was Boethius in *On the Trinity*, a treatise devoted to the explanation of how God can be both one substance and three persons. For him, individuality is the result of the bundle of accidents (that is, of features which are not necessary to the thing) substances have, and ultimately, if they have all other accidents in common, of the place they occupy. Although this view is controversial, it enjoyed enormous popularity throughout the early middle ages. After Abelard's challenge in the twelfth century, however, it was generally rejected. He argued that accidents cannot individuate a substance because a substance is prior to its accidents in so far as particular accidents are not necessary for the substance.

Ockham and other conceptualists and nominalists did not think they needed to find a principle of individuation because they held that only individual things exist and universals, or natures, are nothing but concepts produced by mental processes. Realists, however, who held universals or natures are something real outside the mind, had to identify a principle of individuation. A popular view was to hold that substances are individual owing to their matter. In an Aristotelian framework, where substances are composed of matter and form, and form is common, this view makes sense prima facie. Upon further analysis, however, it appears that matter also is common and this makes it difficult for it to individuate. Aquinas's response was to propose that it is not matter by itself that individuates, but rather matter taken together with quantity, which he understood as dimensions. This was unsatisfactory to Scotus, who pointed out that quantity is as common as matter and therefore the combination of the two cannot explain individuality. Instead, he proposed a *sui generis* principle of individuation, a formality he called *thisness*. This is an unanalysable and indefinable principle whose only function is to individuate. Each individual, then, has a common nature with a unity and being proper to itself, and also a principle of individuation which makes it a this. This principle and the common nature are distinguished more than concepts are, but less than real things are; they are distinguished formally.

8 Conclusion

The problems discussed above provide only a small sample of the many that the medievals addressed. Indeed, except for problems only subsequently raised because of advances in science and technology (for example, artificial intelligence), the medievals seem to have touched upon most of the philosophical problems of perennial interest. Although medieval philosophy is significantly different from contemporary philosophy in so far as it is primarily concerned with the integration of revelation and secular learning, nonetheless it has much in common with it. For example, it shares with analytic philosophy an emphasis on linguistic precision, the use of technical language, an argumentative spirit, and the view that philosophical problems can be solved by drawing distinctions. And it shares with continental philosophy a concern with being and the existential issues that affect humans. Much can be found in medieval philosophy, therefore, that should be of interest to contemporary philosophers not just as a matter of antiquarian curiosity, but also as a source of philosophical understanding.

Further Reading

Good general introductions to medieval philosophy are Copleston (1946–75, 1972), Knowles (1988) and Marenbon (1983, 1987). For general information about particular authors, periods and topics, see Gracia and Noone (2002). Important and fairly accessible texts are the *Confessions* (1991) and *On Free Choice of the Will* (1964) of Augustine, *The Consolation of Philosophy* and *The Theological Tractates* of Boethius (1968), and the *Monologion* and *Proslogion* of Anselm (1973). For an introduction to Aquinas, read Copleston (1976) or Kenny (1980). Spade (1999) is a good introduction to Ockham.

References

Medieval philosophers

Abelard, P. 1954: *The Story of Abelard's Adversities* (translated by J. T. Muckle). Toronto: Pontifical Institute of Mediaeval Studies.

Anselm, St 1973: *The Prayers and Meditations of St Anselm* (translated by B. Ward). Harmondsworth: Penguin Books.

Aquinas, St Thomas 1963–75: *Summa theologiae* (edited by T. Gilby). London: Eyre and Spottiswoode.

——1988: *The Philosophy of Thomas Aquinas: Introductory Readings* (edited by C. E. J. Martin). London: Routledge.

Augustine, St 1964: *On Free Choice of the Will* (translated by Anna S. Benjamin and L. H. Hackstaff. Indianapolis, IN: Bobbs-Merrill.

——1991: *Confessions* (translated by H. Chadwick). Oxford: Oxford University Press.

Averroes 1961: *On the Harmony of Religion and Philosophy* (translated by George F. Hourani. London: Luzac.

Boethius 1968: *The Theological Tractates* and *The Consolation of Philosophy* (translated by H. F. Stewart and E. K. Rand). Cambridge, MA: Harvard University Press.

Duns Scotus, J. 1962: *Philosophical Writings: A Selection* (edited and translated by A. Wolter). London: Nelson.

Maimonides 1956: *The Guide for the Perplexed,* 2nd revd edn (translated by M. Friedlander). New York: Dover Publications.

Ockham, William of 1957: *Philosophical Writings: A Selection* (edited and translated by P. Boehner). London: Nelson.

Pseudo-Dionysus 1966: *On the Divine Names and the Mystical Theology* (edited and translated by C. E. Rolt). New York: Macmillan.

Other writers

Broadie, A. 1993: *Introduction to Medieval Logic*, 2nd edn. Oxford: Oxford University Press.

Chadwick, H. 1986: *Augustine*. Oxford: Oxford University Press.

Copleston, F. A. 1946–75: *History of Philosophy*, vol. 2. Westminster, MD: Newman Bookshop.

——1972: *History of Medieval Philosophy*. London: Methuen.

——1976: *Aquinas*. London: Search Press.

Gibson, M. M. T. 1981: *Boethius: His Life, Thought and Influence*. Oxford: Blackwell.

Gilson, E. 1961: *The Christian Philosophy of St Augustine* (translated by L. E. M. Lynch). London: Gollancz.

Gracia, J. J. E. and Noone, T. (eds) 2002: *The Blackwell Companion to Philosophy in the Middle Ages*. Oxford: Blackwell.

Kenny, A. J. P. 1980: *Aquinas*. Oxford: Oxford University Press.

Kirwan, C. 1989: *Augustine*. London: Routledge.

Knowles, D. 1988: *The Evolution of Medieval Thought*, 2nd edn. London: Longman.

Kretzmann, N. and Stump, E. (eds) 1993: *The Cambridge Companion to Aquinas*. Cambridge: Cambridge University Press.

Kretzmann, N., Kenny, A. J. P. and Pinborg, J. (eds) 1982: *The Cambridge History of Later Medieval Philosophy*. Cambridge: Cambridge University Press.

Marenbon, J. 1983: *Early Medieval Philosophy (480–1150): An Introduction*. London: Routledge.

——1987: *Later Medieval Philosophy (1150–1350): An Introduction*. London: Routledge.

Spade, P. V. (ed.) 1999: *The Cambridge Companion to Ockham*. Cambridge: Cambridge University Press.

Discussion Questions

1 'I believe because it is absurd.' Does this leave any role for philosophy?

2 'I believe in order that I may understand.' Can belief enable us to understand?

3 Can we gain knowledge through revelation? How would knowledge gained through revelation be related to other human knowledge?

4 If theology had a legitimate role to play in medieval philosophical thought, how can we decide whether it has a similar role today?

5 Among logic, metaphysics and theology, does one discipline have priority over the others?

6 Is there a single system for understanding and assessing all claims to knowledge?

7 Can some truths be known only through faith, some be known only through reason and some be known through either faith or reason?

8 What explanations are possible if reason and faith appear to contradict one another?

9 What is necessary existence? Does a being than whom no greater can be conceived necessarily exist?

10 Can we use facts given in experience to prove that God exists?

11 Can the terms we use to speak about the world also be applied to a wholly transcendent God?

12 Must God be either unknowable or part of the world and therefore not divine?

13 Can we determine whether a term is used equivocally, univocally or analogically?

14 Can we study 'being *qua* being'?

15 Must any science have a single object of study?

16 Does the metaphor of illumination explain how we acquire knowledge?

17   Is knowledge of man about man in general rather than about this man and that man?

18   Could man be both something in the mind and something outside the mind?

19   Could universals be words that are created to be predicated of several things rather than being a special kind of entity?

20   Is it useful to distinguish between absolute and relative understanding of natures?

21   Must natures either have being and unity or lack being and unity?

22   How should we understand the claim that something has mental being?

23   Which explanations multiply entities beyond necessity?

24   Do natures in individuals have a double unity and a double being, their own and that of individuals?

25   Does our natural capacity to form general concepts based on the particular experience of individuals explain the existence of universal concepts in the mind?

26   What makes something individual?

27   Can *thisness* explain individuation?

28   What can contemporary philosophy learn from medieval philosophy?

25

Bacon

STEPHEN GAUKROGER

Francis Bacon (1561–1626) was instrumental in effecting a major shift in mentality from a contemplative to an empirical approach to the nature of the physical world. His achievement was twofold. First, he transformed the discipline of philosophy from something contemplative which focused above all on moral questions into something practical which focused centrally on questions in natural philosophy (what is now called science). Secondly, he set out an account of procedures for scientific enquiry which has resulted in his being considered one of the founders of modern SCIENTIFIC METHOD *(chapter 9). Applying ideas for reform initially developed in the area of law to natural philosophy, his method takes the form of induction (a procedure that moves inferentially from observable effects to deeper underlying causes) which proceeds by means of elimination of various possible explanations by testing their consequences against experiment or observation.*

1 Introduction

Bacon was brought up in a Renaissance humanist context, and was employed throughout his life in senior legal positions in government, ending up as Lord Chancellor, until his impeachment in 1621. Humanist education centred upon rhetoric, and it was rhetoric and the law that guided his thought. What was unusual about his application of precepts learned from rhetoric and law to natural philosophy was that he used them to propose a fundamental reform of philosophy.

Philosophy as a discipline was at a low ebb in sixteenth- and early seventeenth-century England. A contrast was often drawn in classical terms between the life of contemplation (*otium*) and the life of practical, productive activity (*negotium*), and there was a decisive shift in favour of the latter in sixteenth-century England. There was a stress on practical questions, and the practical uses of learning, and philosophy was widely regarded as a useless discipline which fostered argument for its own sake, never getting anywhere and never producing anything of value. Moreover, morality was widely seen as the key philosophical topic (following the Ciceronian model current in Renaissance Europe generally), and a number of Elizabethan thinkers, most notably the poet Sir Philip Sidney, were arguing that poetry was superior to philosophy, in that philosophy could only discourse on the nature of goodness, whereas poetry could actually move people to goodness, which was the point of the exercise.

Bacon did two things: he shifted philosophy from *otium* to *negotium*, and he made natural philosophy replace MORAL PHILOSOPHY (chapter 6) as the centre of the philosophical enterprise. The combination of these two (and they are intimately connected) is a radical move that marks a decisive break with earlier conceptions of philosophy and, rather importantly, with earlier understandings of just what the job of the philosopher was.

2   The Reform of Philosophy and its Practitioners

Natural philosophy existed in a number of forms in the sixteenth and seventeenth centuries, and there were two extreme forms. The first was exemplified in alchemy, which was an esoteric but practical discipline which had little connection with traditional philosophical practice and which suffered, in Bacon's view, from a lack of structure, so that what few results were achieved were achieved by chance. At the other extreme was scholastic natural philosophy, an intensely theoretical discipline which, in Bacon's view, produced nothing at all, despite its great sophistication, which turned out to be almost exclusively verbal. Bacon wanted something that could deliver the advantages of each of these without any of the disadvantages. He wanted something that would provide a detailed theoretical overview of the natural realm such that natural processes could not only be understood but, more importantly, transformed on the basis of this understanding: this is the context of his famous dictum that 'knowledge is power'. The ultimate aim was to transform natural processes for the common good (where the common good was very much something to be decided by the sovereign, on Bacon's view), and it was this, rather than some contemplative understanding of nature, that provided the rationale for natural philosophy, and by extension philosophy *per se*.

Bacon's first attempts at reform were in the area of LAW (chapter 13) rather than natural philosophy, where he was concerned to systematize the law, provide regular records and reviews of legal decisions, and then try to discover some firm foundations for legal practice. The law worked with elaborate procedures for gathering, assessing and testing evidence. Moreover, it was an area of theoretical sophistication wholly devoted to practical ends. This was exactly the kind of thing that Bacon had in mind for natural philosophy, although natural philosophy was in a far worse state than the law.

3   A Method of Discovery: From Rhetoric to Science

The law did not act as a model in its own right, however: its importance arose from the fact that (especially in a reformed state) it exemplified a rhetorically motivated account of discovery. This holds the key to Bacon's enterprise. His education, like that of any other schoolboy in the West in the early modern era, was in the liberal arts, the study of which underlay a broad range of areas, including law and POLITICS (chapter 8), on the one hand, and the issues of scientific demonstration and discovery on the other, and the most crucial part of the liberal arts in this respect was rhetoric.

At its most general level, the task of rhetoric was the formulation, organization and expression of one's ideas in a coherent and compelling way. It was designed to help one find one's way around the comprehensive body of learning built up from antiquity, to recognize where appropriate evidence and arguments might be found, to provide models which were designed to give one a sense of what was needed if a particular question was to be investigated, or a particular position defended, models that would be shared with those to whom one was expounding or defending one's case. It was designed to help one focus one's mental powers in various ways, to organize one's thoughts in the most economical fashion, as well as providing models to show one how particular kinds of case were best defended, depending on such facts as the availability and complexity of the evidence, and the state of the knowledge, opinions and prejudices of the audience towards which one was directing one's arguments. At a general level, rhetoric was indifferent as to subject matter, in that very comprehensive procedures were recommended that would aid one's investigations or one's case irrespective of whether one were conducting a scientific investigation or a legal one, although at a specific level there would be similarities or analogies (as regards the standing of various kinds of evidence, for example) and dissimilarities (as regards the means by which one collected evidence, for example) between legal cases and those in natural philosophy. The law, taken in a broad sense, was very much a paradigm case for rhetorical writers: rhetorical treatises were often seen explicitly as being directed towards lawyers and legislators, and examples were geared around the kinds of problem case that arose in law. In the light of this, it is only to be expected that using a rhetorical model for knowledge – that is, a model that gives direction on how to collect and assess evidence for a view, how to make a judgement on the basis of that evidence, and how to establish the correctness of one's judgement, using precepts derived from the study of rhetoric – is in many respects using a legal model. These connections are particularly strong in the case of Bacon's attempts to reform natural philosophy.

4   The Doctrine of Idols

If rhetoric is the first ingredient in Bacon's account of method, the second is a distinctive understanding of why the need for method arises. Here Bacon's stress on a psychological dimension to knowledge is important: questions of presentation of knowledge are not only recognized to be important, but have to be understood, where such an understanding is not supplementary to EPISTEMOLOGY (chapter 1) but actually part of it. There is nothing new in this at one level, for it is simply part of a long tradition which begins in earnest with the Roman rhetoricians; but although it borrows from Greek writers, it is rather different from the approach to epistemological questions that we find in the classical GREEK PHILOSOPHERS (chapters 22–3) and HELLENISTIC PHILOSOPHERS (chapter 22). When one thinks of Bacon's general project in this context, it becomes clear that there is something novel here. For natural philosophy had generally been the preserve of Greek philosophy, and had been pursued in a similar way by SCHOLASTIC PHILOSOPHERS (chapter 24). The Roman tradition, with the exception of

Lucretius, had generally speaking not concerned itself with speculative natural-philosophical questions, dealing instead with practical moral, political and legal questions. In thinking of persuasion in terms of a psychological theory, in thinking of psychological theory as part of epistemology, and in thinking of epistemology as being directed primarily towards natural philosophy, Bacon can provide himself with some of the resources to start thinking through natural philosophy, not as a speculative but as a practical discipline.

Idols of the Mind

The psychological dimension to epistemology is brought out fully in Bacon's doctrine of the 'Idols of the Mind'. The second part of the 'Great Instauration', which aims at the renewal of learning, is devoted to the 'Invention of knowledge', and has two components, one of which aims to rid the mind of preconceptions, while the other aims to guide the mind in a productive direction. These components are interconnected, for until we understand the nature of the mind's preconceptions, we do not know in what direction we need to lead its thinking.

In other words, various natural inclinations of the mind must be purged before the new procedure can be set in place. Bacon's approach here is genuinely different from that of his predecessors, as he realizes. Logic or method in themselves cannot simply be introduced to replace bad habits of thought, which Bacon identifies as 'Idols', because it is not simply a question of replacement. The simple application of logic to one's mental processes is insufficient.

In his doctrine of Idols, Bacon provides an account of the systematic forms of error to which the mind is subject, and this is a crucial part of his epistemology. It is in his treatment of internal impediments, the Idols of the mind, that the question is raised of what psychological or cognitive state we must be in to be able to pursue natural philosophy in the first place. Bacon believes an understanding of nature of a kind that had never been achieved since the Fall is possible in his own time because the distinctive obstacles that have held up all previous attempts have been identified, in what is in many respects a novel theory of what might traditionally have been treated under a theory of the passions, one now directed specifically at natural-philosophical practice.

The Idols of the Tribe derive from human nature itself, and affect everyone equally. They are manifested in eagerness to suppose that there is more order and regularity in nature than there actually is; in the tendency to neglect or ignore counter-examples to one's theories; in the tendency to extrapolate from striking cases with which one is familiar to all other cases; in the restlessness of the human mind, which means it is not satisfied with perfectly good fundamental explanations, mistakenly and constantly seeking some more fundamental cause *ad infinitum*; and in the tendency to believe true what one would like to be true. The Idols of the Cave, we are told, 'take their rise in the peculiar constitution, mental or bodily, of each individual; and also in education, habit, and accident'. They include fascination with a particular subject, which leads to over-hasty generalization; the readiness of some minds to focus on differences, and some to focus on similarities and resemblances, while a balance is difficult to attain naturally; the fact that some minds are overly attracted to antiquity and some to novelty; finally, there are those who are concerned wholly with material constitution at the expense of structure (the ancient atomists), and those who are concerned wholly with structure at the expense of material constitution.

These examples bring to light a very significant difference between the Idols of the Tribe and Idols of the Cave. There seems to be a set of routine procedures one can go through to remedy the situation in the latter case, procedures which are provided by the positive part of Bacon's doctrine of 'eliminative induction', whereas the case of Idols of the Tribe is, in most cases, much more difficult to remedy.

The Idols of the Market-place derive, in essence, from the fact that we have to express and communicate our thoughts by means of language, which contains systematic deficiencies: it provides names which refer to things that do not exist, such as 'Fortune' and 'Prime Mover'. The solution here is simply to get rid of the theories that give rise to these fictitious entities. A second kind of case is not so straightforward. It arises because words have multiple meanings, and/or ill-defined meanings, or both, and this is especially so in the case of terms such as 'humid', which have been abstracted from observation. Finally, the fourth kinds of impediment, the 'Idols of the Theatre', are neither innate in the mind nor in language, but are acquired from a corrupt philosophical culture and its perverse rules of demonstration. Here a general remedy is available, namely following Bacon's positive methodological prescriptions.

One of the great values of Bacon's account of the Idols is that it allows him to make the case for method in a particularly compelling way. Indeed, never has the need for method been set out more forcefully, for Bacon's advocacy of method is not simply as an aid to discovery. We pursue natural philosophy with seriously deficient natural faculties, we operate with a severely inadequate means of communication, and we rely on a hopelessly corrupt philosophical culture. In many respects, these are beyond remedy. The practitioners of natural philosophy certainly need to reform their behaviour, overcome their natural inclinations and passions and so on, but not so that, in doing this, they might aspire to a natural, prelapsarian state in which they might know things as they are with an unmediated knowledge. This they will never achieve. Rather, the reform of behaviour is a discipline to which they must subject themselves if they are to be able to follow a procedure which is in many respects quite contrary to their natural inclinations, which is at odds with traditional conceptions of the natural philosopher, and which is indeed subversive of their individuality.

5   Eliminative Induction

What Bacon is seeking from a method of discovery is something that modern philosophers would deem impossibly strong: the discovery of causes which are both necessary and sufficient for their effects. Why place such strong constraints on CAUSATION (pp. 303–12), so that we only call something a cause when the effect always occurs in the presence of this thing and never in its absence? In the final analysis, what Bacon – like ARISTOTLE (chapter 23) before him – is after are the ultimate explanations of things, and it is natural to assume that ultimate explanations are unique. What Bacon's method is designed to do is provide a route to such explanations, and this route takes us through a number of proposed causal accounts, which are refined at each stage. The procedure he elaborates, eliminative induction, is one in which various possibly contributory factors are isolated and examined in turn, to see whether they do in fact make a contribution to the effect. Those that do not are rejected and the result is a convergence on those factors that are truly relevant. The kind of 'relevance' that Bacon is after is, in effect, necessary conditions: the procedure is supposed to enable us to weed out those factors that are not necessary for the production of the effect, so that we are left only with those that are necessary.

The Case of Colour

Bacon provides an example of how the method works in the case of colour. We take as our starting-point some combination of substances that produces whiteness, that is we start with what are in effect sufficient conditions for the production of whiteness, and then we remove from these anything not necessary for the colour. First, we note that if air and water are mixed together in small portions, the result is white, as in snow or waves. Here we have the sufficient conditions for whiteness, but not the necessary conditions, so (second) we increase the scope, substituting any transparent uncoloured substance for water, whence we find that glass or crystal, on being ground, become white, and albumen, which is initially a watery transparent substance, on having air beaten into it, becomes white. Third, we further increase the scope, and ask what happens in the case of coloured substances. Amber and sapphire become white on being ground, and wine and beer become white when brought to a froth. The substances considered up to this stage have all been 'more grossly transparent than air'. Bacon next considers flame, which is less grossly transparent than air, and argues that the mixture of the fire and air makes the flame whiter. The upshot of this is that water is sufficient for whiteness, but not necessary for it. He continues in the same vein, asking next whether air is necessary for whiteness. He notes that a mixture of water and oil is white, even when the air has been evaporated from it, so air is not necessary for whiteness, but is a transparent substance necessary? Bacon does not continue with the chain of questions after this point, but sets out some conclusions, namely that bodies whose parts are unequal but in simple proportion are white, those whose parts are in equal proportions are transparent, proportionately unequal colours, and absolutely unequal black. In other words, this is the conclusion that one might expect the method of sifting out what is necessary for the phenomenon and what is not to take, although Bacon himself does not provide the route to this conclusion here.

One can ask what Bacon's confidence in his conclusion derives from if he has not been able to complete the 'induction' himself. The answer is that it derives from the consequences he can draw from his account. There are two ways in which the justification for the conclusions can be assessed: by the procedure of eliminative induction that he has just set out, and by how well the consequences of the conclusions so generated match other observations. In other words, there is a two-way process, from empirical phenomena to first principles (induction), and then from first principles to empirical phenomena.

639

6   Truth

Closely tied up with Bacon's account of method is his treatment of the question of TRUTH (chapter 36). Bacon goes through a number of what he considers to be inadequate criteria that have been used to establish truth. He rejects criteria depending on antiquity or authority, those deriving from commonly held views, and those relying upon the internal consistency or the capacity for internal reduction of theories, presumably on the grounds, among others, that such criteria do not bear on the question of whether there is any correspondence between the theory and reality. He also rejects 'inductions without instances contradictory', that is, inductions which restrict themselves to confirming a theory, as well as 'the report of the senses'. None of these, he tells us, are 'absolute and infallible evidence of truth, and bring no security sufficient for effects and operations'. That he ties in evidence for the truth of a theory and its usefulness here is no accident, for these are intimately connected, telling us in *Valerius Terminus* that 'the discovery of new works and active directions not known before, is the only trial to be accepted of'. Is Bacon providing a gloss on truth here, maintaining that it has been misconstrued, that to say something is true is exactly the same as saying that it is useful? Or is he saying that something is true, in the ordinary accepted sense, only if it is useful? Whichever, it is a very strong claim on Bacon's part. Are there no useless truths, and are there no falsehoods which have practical application? It is not simply that false premises may lead to true conclusions, but there are cases where approximations which, while false, may have more practical value than the truths of which they are the approximation.

The solution becomes clear when we consider that since antiquity debates on methods of generating truths had hinged on the question of generating informative truths: the aim is to discover something we did not already know. In particular, there was a concern among Aristotle and his Renaissance followers to show that formal modes of reasoning such as the SYLLOGISM (pp. 151–3) were not trivial or circular, because, at the start of the inferential process, we have knowledge *that* something is the case, whereas at the end of it we have knowledge *why* it is the case. In particular what they sought to show was that the kind of knowledge of an observed phenomenon we have through sensation is qualitatively different from, and inferior to, the kind of knowledge we have of that phenomenon when we grasp it in terms of its causes.

This is also what Bacon was seeking. If we think in terms of 'informative truths', Bacon's position makes a little more sense. He is saying that the only way in which we can judge whether something is informatively true is to determine whether it is productive, whether it yields something tangible and useful. And if something does consistently yield something tangible and useful, then it is informatively true. (The 'consistently' here is important if we are to be able to rule out cases where false premises just happen on particular occasions to yield true conclusions, for we can assume that, unlike truths, they will not continue to do this indefinitely.) And the case of approximations can perhaps be dealt with by saying that these derive their usefulness not from their falsity but from their proximity to the truth, although the cases where the approximation is more useful than the true account cannot be handled so easily.

The question of the practicality of truth turns on its informativeness, but there is another dimension to this question which, although it is not explicitly mentioned by Bacon, is of importance in understanding his general orientation. In the humanist thought which is the source from which Bacon derives much of his inspiration, moral philosophy figures very predominantly. Now in this philosophy, being virtuous and acting virtuously are the same thing: there is no separate practical dimension to morality. This is all the more interesting because moral philosophy is a cognitive enterprise, one in which the practical outcome is constitutive of the discipline, something Bacon stresses in the *Advancement of Learning*. If we see natural philosophy as being in some respects modelled on moral philosophy, something which is natural enough in a humanist context, and which is reinforced in the shift from *otium* to *negotium*, then we may be able to make a little more sense of the idea that truth is not truth unless it is informative and productive. Moreover, we may also begin to approach the question of why the natural philosopher is not simply someone with a particular expertise, for Bacon, but someone with a particular kind of standing, a quasi-moral standing, which results from the replacement of the idea (prevalent throughout ancient thought) of the Sage as a moral philosopher with the idea of the Sage as a natural philosopher.

Further Reading

For a general overview of Bacon's thought see Zagorin (1998) and Peltonen (1996). On his natural philosophy and method see Rossi (1968) and Gaukroger (2000). Anderson (1971) provides a detailed summary and assessment of his natural philosophy. Rees has dealt with specific aspects of Bacon's natural philosophy in a number of articles, and his introduction to volume 6 of the new Oxford edition of Bacon provides a good summary of his pioneering work on such topics as Bacon's matter theory and cosmology. Urbach (1987) provides the most comprehensive discussion of Bacon's account of method. Jardine (1974) and Pez-Ramos (1988) concentrate on the role of rhetoric in Bacon's work. Martin (1992) provides a good account of Bacon's thought on legal questions. Webster (1975) looks at the influence of Bacon between the time of his death and the founding of the Royal Society.

References

Bacon
The standard edition is:
Bacon, F. 1857–74: *The Works of Francis Bacon*, 14 vols (edited by J. Spedding, R. L. Ellis and D. Denon Heath). London: Longmans, Green, Reader, and Dyer.
This will eventually be replaced by the following, as the volumes appear:
Bacon, F. 1996–: *The Oxford Francis Bacon*, 12 vols (general editors G. Rees and L. Jardine). Oxford: Clarendon Press.

Other writers
Anderson, F. H. 1971: *The Philosophy of Francis Bacon*. New York: Octogan Books.
Briggs, J. C. 1989: *Francis Bacon and the Rhetoric of Nature*. Cambridge, MA: Harvard University Press.
Eamon, W. 1994: *Science and the Secrets of Nature: Books of Secrets in Medieval and Early Modern Culture*. Princeton, NJ: Princeton University Press.

Farrington, B. 1964: *The Philosophy of Francis Bacon: An Essay on its Development from 1603 to 1609 with New Translations of Fundamental Texts*. Chicago: University of Chicago Press.

Fattori, M. 1997: *Introduzione a Francis Bacon*. Rome: Edizione Laterza.

Findlen, P. 1997: Francis Bacon and the Reform of Natural History in the Seventeenth Century. In D. R. Kelley (ed.) *History and the Disciplines: The Reclassification of Knowledge in Early Modern Europe*. Rochester, NY: University of Rochester Press.

Gaukroger, S. 2000: *Francis Bacon and the Transformation of Early Modern Philosophy*. Cambridge: Cambridge University Press.

Jardine, L. 1974: *Francis Bacon: Discovery and the Art of Discourse*. Cambridge: Cambridge University Press.

Jones, R. F. 1982: *Ancients and Moderns: A Study of the Rise of the Scientific Movement in Seventeenth-century England*. New York: Dover.

Kuhn, T. S. 1977: Mathematical versus Experimental Traditions in the Development of Physical Science. In *The Essential Tension*, 2nd edn. Chicago: University of Chicago Press.

Laudan, L. 1981: *Science and Hypothesis: Historical Essays on Scientific Methodology*. Dordrecht: D. Reidel.

Leary, J. E., Jnr 1994: *Francis Bacon and the Politics of Science*. Ames: Iowa State University Press.

Malherbe, M. 1985: Bacon, *l'Encyclopédie* et la Revolution. *Études Philosophiques*, 3, 387–404.

Martin, J. 1992: *Francis Bacon, the State, and the Reform of Natural Philosophy*. Cambridge: Cambridge University Press.

Milner, B. 1997: Francis Bacon: The Theological Foundations of *Valerius Terminus*. *Journal for the History of Ideas*, 58, 245–64.

Peltonen, M. (ed.) 1996: *The Cambridge Companion to Bacon*. Cambridge: Cambridge University Press.

Pez-Ramos, A. (1988) *Francis Bacon's Idea of Science and the Maker's Knowledge Tradition*. Oxford: Clarendon Press.

Rees, G. 1975a: Francis Bacon's Semi-Paracelsian Cosmology. *Ambix*, 22, 81–101.

——1975b: Francis Bacon's Semi-Paracelsian Cosmology and the *Great Instauration*. *Ambix*, 22, 161–73.

——1977: Matter Theory: A Unifying Factor in Bacon's Natural Philosophy?' *Ambix*, 24, 110–25.

——1979: Francis Bacon on Verticity and the Bowels of the Earth. *Ambix*, 26, 202–11.

——1980: Atomism and 'Subtlety' in Francis Bacon's Philosophy. *Annals of Science*, 37, 549–71.

——1981: An Unpublished Manuscript by Francis Bacon: *Sylva sylvarum* Drafts and Other Working Notes. *Annals of Science*, 38, 377–412.

——1984a: Bacon's Philosophy: Some New Sources With Special Reference to the *Abecedarium novum naturae*. In M. Fattori (ed.) *Francis Bacon: terminologia e fortuna nel XVII secolo*. Rome: Edizione dell'Ateneo.

——1984b: Francis Bacon and spiritus vitalis. In M. Fattori and M. Bianchi (eds) *Spiritus: IVº Colloquio Internazionale del Lessico Intellettuale Europeo*. Rome: Edizione dell'Ateneo.

Rossi, P. 1968: *Francis Bacon: From Magic to Science*. Chicago: University of Chicago Press.

Urbach, P. 1987: *Francis Bacon's Philosophy of Science: An Account and Reappraisal*. La Salle, IL: Open Court.

Vickers, B. (ed.) 1968: *Essential Articles for the Study of Francis Bacon*. Hamden, CT: Archon Books.

Webster, C. 1975: *The Great Instauration: Science, Medicine and Reform, 1626–1660*. London: Duckworth.

Wormald, B. H. G. 1993: *Francis Bacon: History, Politics and Science, 1561–1626*. Cambridge: Cambridge University Press.

Zagorin, P. 1998: *Francis Bacon*. Princeton, NJ: Princeton University Press.

Discussion Questions

1   Is a philosophy that does not have practical consequences deficient? Is there a place for a purely contemplative form of philosophy?

2   Was Bacon being realistic in thinking that one could transform a contemplative and speculative discipline into an empirical one?

3   Can the understanding of nature be separated from the transformation of nature?

4   What does Bacon mean when he maintains that knowledge is power?

5   Could there be a general method of discovery which was indifferent as to area (politics, law, natural science)?

6   Could there be a method of discovery at all, even in a restricted area?

7   Are there psychological obstacles to learning which need at least to be recognized, and at best purged, before we can attain to knowledge?

8   To what extent can the Idols of the Tribe be overcome by Bacon's method of eliminative induction?

9   Is there anything that can be done about the Idols of the Cave? Is Bacon being unduly pessimistic in his account of them?

10   Is the way in which Bacon characterizes language in his account of the Idols of the Market-place satisfactory?

11   Is language really the obstacle to thought that Bacon believes it to be?

12   To what extent can the Idols of the Theatre be purged by following Bacon's methodology?

13   Could simply following Bacon's method of eliminative induction ever enable anyone to discover anything?

14   Is there any way of avoiding circularity in abstracting general principles from a set of facts, and then demonstrating those facts from the abstracted principles?

15   Is there some way of making sure that the methods or procedures one uses yield informative truths?

16   How does the fact (if it is a fact) that approximations, which are strictly speaking false, are sometimes more useful than the truths of which they are the approximations, bear on the claim that usefulness is a sign of truth?

26

Descartes and Malebranche

RICHARD FRANCKS AND
GEORGE MACDONALD ROSS

The seventeenth century was a period of profound transformation in philosophy, science and theology, and in the conception of human life. The scholastic philosophy of the universities was challenged, and many themes still at the centre of philosophical debate were initiated. This and the next chapter are devoted to four major figures, Descartes (1596–1650), Malebranche (1638–1715), Spinoza (1632–1677) and Leibniz (1646–1716). All were powerful metaphysical thinkers, who used reason to criticize both the philosophy of their medieval predecessors and common-sense views of the world. The rival accounts of substance offered by these authors are explored in the context of attempts to establish modern explanatory science. These accounts include Descartes's divinely created extended substance and thinking substances; Malebranche's 'occasional' causes; Spinoza's single substance, God or Nature; and Leibniz's soul-like monads, each existing in isolation but reflecting the whole system of reality according to a divinely created pre-established harmony. With the exception of Malebranche, whose philosophy raises special issues, the focus is on the implications for nature, God and human beings. Readers will wish to consult several of the historical chapters in this volume, but especially those dealing with other seventeenth-century philosophers, HOBBES (chapter 28) and LOCKE (chapter 29). They will also wish to read chapters on EPISTEMOLOGY (chapter 1), METAPHYSICS (chapter 2), PHILOSOPHY OF MIND (chapter 5), PHILOSOPHY OF SCIENCE (chapter 9) and PHILOSOPHY OF RELIGION (chapter 15).

1 Descartes

René Descartes has been referred to since the eighteenth century as the 'father of modern philosophy', but as conceptions of philosophy have altered during that time, so too has the meaning of the title. In the nineteenth century and for most of the twentieth century, English-speaking philosophers have seen Descartes primarily as an EPISTEMOLOGIST (chapter 1), whose work set the agenda for the central philosophical task of showing why we are justified in believing what we believe. At the same time in CONTINENTAL PHILOSOPHY (chapters 41 and 42) Descartes's concentration on the individual thinking self and its relation to its surroundings has led to his being regarded primarily as the originator of the phenomenological and existentialist traditions. No one would deny Descartes's importance in those two areas, but more recent work has given us a rather different Descartes: by looking more closely at the historical context within which Descartes was working, recent philosophers have offered a different perspective on his work, and in so doing have allowed him to keep his title, while changing its meaning back to something nearer to what those who originally gave it to him might have had in mind.

'Philosophy' in the seventeenth century was not the name of a specific academic discipline, but meant more generally something like 'learning' or 'knowledge', construed as any attempt to understand the world by purely natural, rational means. In that context, to say that Descartes was the father of modern philosophy is to say that he was the great champion of the self-proclaimed 'modern' movement of the seventeenth century. That movement was very diverse, very diffuse and very widespread, and was united by little more than the conviction that the traditional learning had failed, but that a secure and practically useful understanding of the world could be achieved if only we would renounce the mistaken methods and assumptions of the past and refound knowledge on a new basis. The movement was variously referred to as the 'New Philosophy', the 'Mechanical Philosophy' and the 'Experimental Philosophy', and the perceived success of its adherents in taking over or replacing the intellectual establishment of the day is a central part of the complex process which later historians came to refer to as the 'Scientific Revolution'.

Descartes did not start the modernist movement, nor was his work the cause of its success. His reputation as the father of the modern view derives from the fact that for many years both before and after his death he was considered its leading theorist and publicist. His carefully worked out and brilliantly presented philosophical vision of the world and humanity's place in it played a large part in establishing the possibility of a viable alternative to the traditional account, and in legitimizing belief in it. The life of Descartes was a classic story of a man with a message in which he passionately believes but which he knows will be unpopular with much of the intellectual, religious and political establishment of his time. He was constantly working to avoid persecution, to win influential people over to his side, and to disguise or suppress his true opinions wherever he thought it necessary, while at the same time inventing a series of superb literary and conceptual devices to propagate his message whenever it was safe to do so.

To present modernism as a viable alternative to traditional learning, Descartes essentially had to do three things: to describe in very general terms the nature of the world according to his version of modernism, to show how that world related to a Christian GOD (chapter 15), and how it related to humanity. We will set out this sketch of his work under those three headings.

1.1 Nature

Descartes saw the whole non-human natural world as a single, deterministic, mechanical system. He held that just as Kepler (1571–1630) had reduced the apparently wandering paths of the planets to simple mathematical laws, or as Galileo (1564–1642) had found similarly simple mathematical laws underlying all the diverse phenomena of falling objects on earth, so in fact all natural phenomena, from the shining of the

Sun to the biting of a flea, could, if properly understood, be seen to be governed by unchanging LAWS OF NATURE (pp. 305–6) such that, if only we knew enough about them, we would see them not as random and isolated events but as the only possible outcomes of the timeless facts of nature. And those unchanging facts, he held, were ultimately the laws of mechanics. The laws of meteorology, for example, and of zoology might appear very different; but underlying both of them are more fundamental laws governing the mechanical interaction of particles of inert matter. The laws of optics, for example, he held to be a consequence of the laws of mechanics, because he saw light as a stream of highly energetic particles which either penetrate or bounce off surfaces in the same way as arrows will either penetrate or bounce off a surface of custard or of steel. Kepler's laws of planetary motion he held to be derivable from mechanics because the planets were pushed along in their orbits by a swirl or 'vortex' of tiny material particles swinging around the sun, in just the same way that a leaf is swirled around by a current of air, or a cork by an eddy in a stream. In biology, too, mechanism ruled: the heart of a living creature beats because of a constant repetition of heating and cooling – themselves mechanical phenomena to be explained by the accelerating and decelerating of particles – which the blood undergoes in moving through the body; a seed grows because of the gradual accretion of some of the particles which are constantly pushed through it by its (mechanical) digestive processes – and so on. Thus the whole of nature comes to be seen as a giant clockwork – the seventeenth century's favourite analogy – wound up by God at creation, and ticking along until the end of the world, powered by an unending series of pushes and pulls, bumps and twists, shakings and swirlings.

At this point the modern reader may be inclined to take a rather patronizing view of Descartes's work: this purely mechanical view seems childishly naive, an obviously inadequate resource for explaining all the phenomena of nature. And indeed, Descartes's biology was a research programme that was never successfully carried out; his anatomy was rejected in favour of that of Harvey (1578–1657); within a generation his cosmology and his optics were being replaced by Newton's (1642–1727); and even his mechanics itself was increasingly abandoned. Two points, though, should be made in his defence. Firstly, Descartes was a pioneer, and however unsuccessful his physical theory may have been in detail, the philosophical vision that inspired it was enthusiastically adopted even by those who abandoned his own cherished discoveries, and in fact still forms the basis of the modern view of the world.

The second point in defence of Descartes's mechanism is more complex, and gives a better view of Descartes's relation both to his predecessors and to his successors. Descartes's world is characterized above all by its intelligibility. As with all those of the modernist party, his constant complaint against supporters of the debased Aristotelianism of the universities was that they left the world mysterious, by postulating incomprehensible faculties, powers, virtues and goals in nature. Instead of explaining such well-known and politically and economically important phenomena as that of the compass, for example, they merely redescribed its behaviour in technical terms which had no content beyond the very phenomena they were invented to explain. Descartes's mechanism, by contrast, succeeded in reducing the unknown to the known, by showing how initially puzzling phenomena can be explained as the operation of an unperceived but perfectly well understood cause, namely the impact of invisible particles. Significantly, this emphasis on explicability was what distinguished the Cartesian world picture from those of many of his contemporaries and successors who proclaimed themselves his fellow modernists. The disagreement with Harvey, for example, over the operation of the heart derives from a rejection by Descartes of Harvey's acceptance of the living power of the heart as something not itself explained; whereas for Harvey the heart is imbued with life, as befits the central organ of the body around which the blood circulates like courtiers around a king, for Descartes it is merely a lump of matter, alternately dilated and contracted by the mechanical pressure of the blood it contains. In the same way, later Cartesians sought unsuccessfully to defend his system of vortices and ether against the Newtonian theory for precisely the same reason: Newton's view contained as a given the fact that all bodies have the power to draw other bodies towards them with no intervening medium through which such force is transmitted. As compared to Descartes's theory, this is a clear betrayal of the modernist ideal, and a re-introduction of the occult powers of the SCHOLASTICS (chapter 24), in that it claims to explain the fact that heavy objects fall to earth not by means of a flow of invisible particles which push them downward, but by imbuing the physical world with the pseudo-property of 'gravitas'.

Vital powers and gravitational attraction were not the only categories of things that Descartes's bare ONTOLOGY (chapter 2) of matter in motion ruled out. And here we return to an aspect of his work which subsequent generations have for the most part accepted. The bare material particles of his mechanical world are equipped only with the mechanical properties of shape, size and motion, and all their other properties must be a function of those few. Thus whereas an ordinary person might say that a sword, for example, was shiny, sharp and dangerous, Descartes would say that in itself the sword is none of those things: in itself, as it really is, the sword is an extended object of a certain size and shape; all its other PROPERTIES (p. 686) are REDUCIBLE (pp. 312–13) either to those bare mechanical properties, or to the interaction of those mechanical properties with the human sensory system. Colour is a classic example, which Descartes and his contemporaries insisted again and again must be removed from the list of an object's real properties. The colour of an object is not a property it possesses, as its shape or its size is, but rather a function of the way in which the shape, size and motion of its constituent parts interact with those of particles that make up rays of light to operate on our sensory system. 'Silver-coloured' and 'shiny', therefore, are words that refer not to properties in the object, but only to experiences that humans typically have when confronted by it.

Descartes's World

The world of Descartes is a bare, mechanical place operating in accordance with time-less laws of motion, and, in itself, it is devoid of most of the properties that could make us feel at home in it. In fact, even the mechanical properties that it does possess turn out to be importantly different from the shape, size and motion with which we are familiar. Their importance for Descartes, and their suitability to explain everything that happens in the natural world, lies not in their familiarity, but in the fact that they are measurable, and so can be expressed and manipulated *mathematically*. Galileo had already written that the book of nature is written in the language of mathematics, and the idea is central to Descartes's more fully worked out metaphysical and epistemological position. For Descartes, what we see when two billiard-balls collide is only an appearance; the reality of the event is appreciated not by the eye of the body, but by the eye of the mind. Thus, the only really accurate account of the event – the one which most fully corresponds to what is really there in the world, purged of any reference to its effects on our sensory apparatus – is a mathematical description, in which size, shape, weight, speed and direction are all expressed (with the help of what we still refer to as Cartesian co-ordinates) as numbers. The outcome of that collision is then expressible as a new set of such numerical values, and the transformation from one set to the other is governed by laws of motion, central among which is that of the conservation of the total amount of motion in the system as a whole.

It is a testimony to the success of Descartes and his fellow modernists in propagating their views of nature that much of that story seems so familiar, indeed obvious, to us today. Our contemporary view is a direct descendant of the philosophical innovations of the seventeenth century, to such an extent that it is hard for us to see how anyone could ever have seen things otherwise. In particular, we take for granted Descartes's funda-mental metaphysical claim that the world of experience, the world of the ordinary person, is not the world as it really is, but only the way that real world *appears* to us. The world as we experience it is a rich and varied succession of qualities and values; the world as it really is, is a stately transformation of number sequences in accordance with immutable laws. The view of the expert is not a fuller and more detailed version of the view of the common person, but a radically different view, which is expressible not in the language of common sense but in the language of mathematics; the real world is simply unavailable to the sensory apparatus of the ordinary person, and is discoverable only by the arcane investigations of the 'philosopher'.

This contrast between the common-sense view and the view of the expert is one of the most striking features of Descartes's writing. Time and again he has to try to per-suade his audience that they cannot trust the way the world appears to be to their senses; they must work out rationally what it is really like. It may appear to the casual observer as if the blood in the arteries and that in the veins is of a different kind, but the philoso-pher can show that in reality they are the same; it may look to the senses as if the earth stands still while the heavenly bodies move around it, but the philosopher can show that in reality the earth moves around the sun.

1.2   God

Descartes was acutely aware, especially after the public condemnation of Galileo in 1633, that many would regard his physical and metaphysical theories as tantamount to heresy, but he himself saw them as perfectly compatible with, and indeed insepa-rable from, his version of Christianity. To see the relation, we need to look more closely at his account of material substance.

Descartes, for all his modernity, was not an atomist. Although he maintained that the properties of objects were a function of the way their minute parts were put together, he did not think that all matter was made up in the end of impenetrable and irreducible atoms. For Descartes, remember, the reality of the world is what can be described numerically, so it follows that just as there is no smallest possible number, so there can be no smallest possible particle or atom. Matter, therefore, must be infinitely divisible. For the same reason, Descartes denied the possibility of a vacuum. If the true description of the world is its mathematical description, and matter just *is* its dimensions ('extension'), then a space between objects, since it possesses shape, size, duration and motion, is every bit as real a physical thing as are the objects on either side of it. There is therefore no such thing as genuinely empty space: just as a room which the common person would say was empty is known by the philosopher to be full of air, so the space between the planets and that above the column of mercury in Torricelli's famous experiment is held by Descartes to be in reality filled with a fine, fluid, 'subtle' matter, through which light and gravity are mechanically transmitted. The relation between objects and the spaces around them must therefore be seen as analogous to that between a whirlpool and the water that surrounds it. A whirlpool can be seen, and can be touched; if it is fast enough, it can feel quite hard, even impenetrable. And yet it is made up of the very same stuff as the water around it: there is nothing in the whirlpool that is not in the water, and there is no more of it in the whirlpool than there is in the rest of the sea. The only difference between the two is relative motion: all the water that we consider as part of the whirlpool is moving in unison, and moving at a high speed relative to the otherwise indistinguishable water around it. That is Descartes's model for the individuation of physical objects in the seamless continuum of extended matter: what we call an object is what we might now describe as a high-pressure area in the material continuum. For Descartes, the ordinary person's pluralist view of a world made up of an indefinite number of separate physical objects is a childish error, from which the man of science must escape. Those separate physical 'objects' are in reality, he says, only adjectival in nature. Just as the shape of an apple or the fall of a leaf are not separate things over and above the apple and the leaf to which they belong, but only 'modes' or 'modifications' of their respective substances, so, according to Descartes, the apple and the leaf themselves, like every other physical object in existence, are not in reality separate things or substances, but only modes of the one single extended substance: they are areas of a continuum differentiated by us 'modally' on the basis of relative motion, but are not 'really' or 'substantially' distinct.

The relation of God to that physical continuum is a double one. On the one hand, God created the material world *ex nihilo* and set its parts in motion, and that original motion has been conserved through all the mechanical interactions which have taken place from that day to this. With the exception of occasional MIRACLES (p. 483), therefore, the whole history of the natural world can be explained purely naturalistically, purely scientifically, through the laws of mechanics.

But that is only part of the story. In addition to creating the universe and setting it in motion, God also sustains it in being from moment to moment. Therefore the reason why, for example, some particular beam of light is reflected from a surface at an angle of 30 degrees is not only because it hit the surface at an angle of 30 degrees, but also because God was at that time maintaining the law of reflection whereby the angle of incidence equals the angle of reflection. In the same way, the reason why a stone lying in a field will continue to lie in that field is not only because no one comes along to move it, but also because God keeps in operation during this period the laws which determine its nature and its structure. In this way God's 'concourse' or 'concurrence' is involved at every moment of history; without the continual involvement of God, the clockwork mechanism of the universe would not tick along regardless, but would fall apart into chaos and nothingness.

In this sense, therefore, the modal relation which we have seen to exist between the properties of an object and the object itself, and also between any given object and extended substance in general, is mirrored in the relation between God and that extended substance itself. Just as to talk about the shape of an object is not to talk about a separate thing, but to talk about one aspect of the object itself, and to talk of an individual object is in reality to talk about one particular aspect of material substance, so to talk about matter at all is, when correctly understood, only a way of talking about one aspect of God. Strictly speaking, God is the only true substance, the only real thing; the material world is only an expression, or a consequence, of God's nature.

These two strands in Descartes's account of God and the world – the divine clockmaker and the one true substance – obviously tend to pull in different directions, and they were developed in different directions by his successors. Their combination in his work means that Descartes had a very strong defence against those who tended to see the new SCIENCE (chapter 9) of nature as tantamount to atheism: Descartes could claim that the investigation of nature, far from being incompatible with Christian duty, was actually co-extensive with the discovery of God's true nature and intentions.

1.3   Humanity

Descartes's mechanist view of nature covers the entire physical world, including the creation of the Earth itself as a consequence of the break-up of a larger vortex of matter. It extends also to the entire plant world, and the entire non-human animal kingdom. The life of an animal is not a mysterious faculty or a vital principle infused into matter, but simply a series of mechanical interactions, exactly like the working life of a machine: an animal has mechanically produced drives and appetites, and it makes its way around the world seeking by mechanical means to achieve those ends with the help of its mechanical sensory system – it is a 'beast machine', a very complex and sophisticated natural robot. The human body is another mechanism of exactly the same kind, with just the same kind of mechanical life which is responsible for all of its natural processes, and most of its desires and aversions, its actions and reactions. But there we reach the limits of mechanical explanation: there is more to a human being than those mechanical properties alone can explain. Unlike any other creature on earth, we can consider the past, the future and the distant present, far beyond the scope of our physical senses; we can sometimes stand back from our desires and choose which ones to satisfy and which to deny; and we can have knowledge of things which are no part of the physical world revealed by the physical senses, notably things such as the truths of mathematics, the minds of other people, and God. Descartes's explanation for these remarkable human capacities is that there is more to a human being than the area of the physical continuum which is his or her body; in addition, human beings also possess a soul, an immaterial substance which can understand and choose, and which is a finite imitation of the infinite immaterial substance which is God.

This, then, is the famous 'Cartesian Dualism', the suggestion that a human being is an area of the physical continuum *together with* an individual thinking mind or soul. The status of each such individual thinking substance is the same as that of the one material substance: it is dependent on God both for its initial creation and for its continued being.

Descartes holds that this theory is obvious from the facts of nature that we have surveyed, but in addition he brought forward a dramatic proof of its truth. In perhaps the most famous single moment in the whole of Western philosophy, he claimed that the existence of the individual thinking substance is indubitable for any thinker. It makes perfect sense, he claimed, for me to pretend that I have no physical body, and indeed that the entire physical world that my senses reveal to me is nothing but a dream, or an illusion created by some evil power. But no matter what mistakes I may make, and no matter how deceived I may be, I must still exist in order to be mistaken. The mere fact that I am able to make judgements at all, even mistaken ones, proves that I exist: *cogito ergo sum*. And the fact that I can think away the entire physical world but cannot think away my own existence surely proves that I myself, the thing that is doing this thinking, cannot be merely a part of that physical world.

The relations between that MIND AND BODY (chapter 5) have always been perceived as problematic. Descartes proposed a system whereby the hydraulic fluids which operate the muscles of the body are all routed through the pineal gland in the centre of the brain, so that by making tiny adjustments in the position of that gland, the soul is able to control the flow of those fluids and in that way to redirect the actions of the body in accordance with its decisions. However quaint the mechanics of that story might seem, the view of human nature which it embodies is one that is very natural and very powerful. The soul, because it is immaterial, is not subject to the effects of physical decay, and so is immortal. It is God-like in its immateriality, and thus is not part of the crude, base material world, although it is tied to it by its incarnation. The actions of the soul are human versions of the divine activities of understanding and willing, the former a perfect but finite copy of God's divine intelligence, the latter prone to misuse and corrupted by the Fall. In making judgements, the understanding presents an idea to the mind, which the will then affirms or denies.

In this way Descartes is able to show that intellectual mistakes and moral and religious deviance are alike, in that both result from the misuse of the free will. Descartes is thus able to represent his project for a refounding of human knowledge as not only a scientific investigation with important practical benefits, but also as a religious and moral reformation of human society and of the human spirit: by coming to see the world as it really is, through the eye of reason, we are liberating our true, active immaterial thinking selves from their subjection to the deceitful physical senses, and we are allowing the pure, immaterial, divine soul to take precedence over the corrupt physical body and achieve a view of the world which is closer to that of God.

This, then, is the metaphysical, psychological and theological underpinning of Descartes's celebrated work in epistemology. His task here was to show that despite the failure of the established authorities as embodied in the universities, and despite the fashionable pessimism of philosophers who were sceptical as to the possibility of any genuine human knowledge, it is indeed possible for us to escape from the world of appearances and establish a stable and useful body of knowledge as to how the world really is, if only we can abandon traditional learning and adopt the new methods of the modernist party.

Again, the device of the *cogito* takes centre stage: because it begins from Descartes's 'hyperbolical' doubt about the ultimate deception, and shows that even in those extreme circumstances genuine knowledge would be attainable, it means that no matter how extreme the sceptical doubts may be, the possibility of certainty cannot coherently be denied, provided only that we escape from the illusory appearances of common sense to the clear understanding of the rational soul. Our common-sense views are part of our animal nature, useful for finding our way around in the world, but deeply misleading as to its true nature; the *cogito* proves that by reason and reflection we can overcome that deception and work out rationally what is really going on. What we must do is to look behind the apparent contingency of events in the world to find the underlying structures which determine them, and our aim is to work towards a unified science of nature which could be laid out like Euclid's Elements as a single axiomatic system of nature, in which all natural phenomena are represented as the inevitable outcome of unchanging universal laws.

2   Malebranche

Cartesianism became the dominant philosophy in Europe during the second half of the seventeenth century, and well into the eighteenth. Not all Cartesians followed Descartes slavishly, and there were a number of independent-minded thinkers who modified his philosophy in various ways, in order to overcome its tensions and ambiguities. By far the most influential of these was Father Nicholas Malebranche. Indeed, he was so influential that all the major figures of the late seventeenth and early eighteenth centuries (Locke, Leibniz, Berkeley, Hume and Reid) found it necessary to attack him in detail, despite, or perhaps because of, the extent to which they had come under his influence. It is a remarkable fact about the history of philosophy, that, outside France, due recognition has been given to his importance only recently.

There are three main areas in which Malebranche diverged significantly from Descartes; namely perception, causation, and our knowledge of the self and of God. We shall examine these in turn.

2.1   *Perception*

We have seen how Descartes made a sharp distinction between the world as represented to us by our senses, and the very different, real world, which is known only to philosophers by the use of reason. In order to understand Malebranche's criticisms, we shall need to look more closely at Descartes's theory of perception and its background.

The dominant theory in Descartes's day was the scholastic theory that material objects are a compound of matter and form. The matter contains all the particular qualities of an object which make it the individual thing it is; and the form contains all the general attributes which make it an individual of a certain kind. For example, if a carpenter constructs a set of chairs, each chair will differ from every other chair in the grain and colour of the wood, minor differences in shape and size, and so on; but all the chairs share one and the same form of a chair, by virtue of which they are all equally chairs, and not tables or any other kind of thing. When we perceive one of these chairs, what happens is that it emits ethereal surfaces, called 'species', which are captured by one or more sense organs (its colour by sight, its hardness by touch, etc.). These are transmitted to the 'common sense', where all the sensory information is brought together to make up the single composite image of the chair of which we are directly aware. So far there is no difference in kind between what happens in the brain of an animal, and what happens in the brain of a human. In both cases, there are images which closely resemble the surfaces of physical objects as they are in themselves. The big difference is that, in addition to having a sensory image of the particular object, humans can, through the use of their reason, abstract its universal form. So although my cat's sensory image of the chair and my image of it may be much the same (allowing for differences in our sense organs), only I can recognize it as having the universal form of a chair.

Both Descartes and Malebranche rejected the scholastic theory of species, and maintained instead that sensations become present to the mind as the result of *motions* emanating from bodies (light waves and sound waves, for example), which give rise to motions in the sense organs and thence in the brain. The sensory characteristics of which we are conscious, such as colours and sounds, are wholly unlike the properties of the objects which cause them. In themselves, objects are nothing other than parcels of extension, moving in various ways. Although the geometrical properties of objects given in sensation are similar in kind to the properties of objects themselves, even these can be very different. To use Descartes's example, the Sun appears to our senses as a flat disc about a foot across, and just beyond the horizon; whereas our scientific idea is of a body far larger then the earth, and millions of miles away. Again, the sensory image of a coin is usually elliptical, even though our true idea of the coin is of something circular.

Where Malebranche parts company with Descartes is over the question of how we have intellectual knowledge of the true natures of things. Descartes made a complete separation between sensory images and intellectual ideas, so that the sensory image of the Sun is a totally different entity from the intellectual idea of it, and only the latter gives us true knowledge. But what grounds do we have for supposing that our intellectual ideas correspond to reality any more than our sensory images? Descartes's answer was to say that God equipped our souls, at conception, with a range of innate ideas, which are faithful copies of the ideas he used when creating the universe. Since God is not a deceiver, these ideas must be correct, and any universal principle which we 'clearly and distinctly' perceive to be true must actually be true of the world.

Malebranche criticized Descartes's theory on a number of grounds. In particular: (1) it is liable to lead to a complete relativism, since God's not being a deceiver is insufficient guarantee that what each individual 'clearly and distinctly perceives' corresponds to a single, objective reality; (2) there are infinitely many intellectual ideas which we might need at some time or other, and it is impossible for a finite mind to contain them all; and (3) some of these ideas are themselves infinite (e.g. the idea of infinite extension), and again they cannot be contained within a finite mind.

His solution was to say that these ideas are not in *our* minds, but in *God*'s mind – in other words, we are granted the privilege of perceiving a subset of God's ideas, without their being transferred into our own minds. This may seem a strange notion; but Malebranche was operating in a Christian context, according to which 'we live, and move, and have our being' in God (Acts 17.28); or, as he put it, 'God is the locus of spirits', or the metaphorical place where they exist. So the validity of our clear and distinct perceptions of intellectual ideas is guaranteed by the fact that we are in direct contact with the mind of God.

As for our perceptions of external objects, Malebranche reverted to the scholastic view that our perceptions contain a mixture of sensory imagery and intellectual form, with the Cartesian proviso that images do not tell us how things are in themselves, but only how our bodies are affected by them. Our knowledge of how things are in themselves depends on the ideas which we see in God – hence his slogan that 'we see all things in God'. Nevertheless, the created universe is separate from God, and it is only its general features which we see in God. The particular differences between one physical object and another are given to us only in sensation, which is provided by our physical bodies.

2.2   Causation

As we saw earlier, Descartes had little to say about the nature of causation, since he took it for granted that God is the only cause. As far as the material world is concerned, he held that God constantly re-creates it from one moment to the next in an infinitesimally different form, so that there is an illusion of continuous development; but in fact its state at one instant is no more the cause of its state at the next instant than one frame of a movie is the cause of the next. His account of causation in the realm of thought is more problematic, since he ascribed to humans complete freedom of will, despite their total subjection to God. Similarly, he had great difficulty accounting for how matter could influence mind, or vice versa, since both were of utterly disparate natures, and it was impossible to conceive of any relationship between the two. His ultimate answer to both questions was that we seem to be faced with a contradiction, since in this life we are bound by the laws of logic; but God is not so bound, and all will be revealed in the afterlife.

Malebranche analysed the concept of causation more deeply. Matter is essentially passive, since it merely transfers forces which are impressed on it. If it were to be a genuine cause, it would need to have its own immaterial, active power, of which we are not directly aware in perception. Causal power is totally beyond our comprehension, and it can only be attributed to God. To treat physical objects as having causal powers is to consider them as deities, which is absurd and heretical. As before, Malebranche discusses the issue in theological terms; yet there remains the essential philosophical point that our sensory experience gives us only a regular succession of events, and the idea of a necessary connection between cause and effect has to be supplied from some alternative source. Subsequent philosophers, such as Hume and Kant, did not agree that the alternative source was God; but they were heavily influenced by Malebranche's insight that necessary causal connections are not given in experience.

Given that God is the only cause, the reason why one event follows another lies in God's mind, which is beyond our comprehension. All we can say is that God wills the second event *on the occasion of* the first event, not that the first event *causes* the second. This is Malebranche's famous doctrine of 'occasional causes'.

The relation between the mind and the body poses a special problem (of which Descartes was acutely aware), since, unlike matter, the mind is essentially active. Here Malebranche uses a different argument to prove that there can be no causal interaction between the two. This is that, since they belong to completely different categories of being, we cannot comprehend any relationship between them, let alone a causal one. For example, if I will to move my arm, the movement of my arm immediately follows the will to move it. But I haven't the slightest idea how. Even if I had a complete knowledge of physiology, I still wouldn't know what to do, as a pure thinking substance, in order to set in motion the chain of events which would result in the raising of my arm. Consequently, the raising of my arm must be caused directly by God on the occasion of my willing it. This is not to say that God is in any way influenced by my act of volition, but rather that only God can understand the reason why the raising of my arm should follow my act of willing.

2.3   The self and God

For Descartes, the only thing we cannot possibly doubt is the existence of the self as a thinking thing. He believed that by bracketing everything which could conceivably be doubted, we arrive at a direct intuition of the essential nature of the thinking self. It is only after this has been established that we can reinstate a belief in God, by deducing his existence from the idea of God we find in our minds.

Malebranche held that Descartes had got things the wrong way round. When we introspect, all we are directly aware of are our inner sensations and thoughts. We do not have any immediate intuition of our essential nature. The idea of our selves as thinking things is an abstract idea, and therefore one which we perceive in God. So the existence of God is a prerequisite of our thinking our own existence, not a consequence to be deduced from it.

Conversely, Descartes held that we have an idea of God, which, although it reveals God to us, nevertheless comes between us and God. For Malebranche, there is no idea of God, and there is no need of one, since God is the locus of all spirits. We have an immediate and direct vision of his infinite essence and existence, even if, as finite beings we cannot fully comprehend it. Consequently, we know God better and with greater certainty than we know ourselves.

In conclusion, for all its Cartesianism, Malebranche's philosophy can be seen as a reversal of the seventeenth-century move towards a greater separation between philosophy and theology, and a return to the almost mystical world view of the Christian Platonist, St Augustine. Nevertheless, the means by which he argued for his position were philosophically rigorous, and he had a profound influence on the subsequent development of seventeenth- and eighteenth-century philosophy, whether or not his overall philosophy was accepted.

Further Reading

For Descartes we first suggest a major source of their writings translated into English: Descartes (1985), and then a more convenient selection of his: Descartes (1988). Readers often concentrate on the *Discourse on Method* (published 1637) and *Meditations on First Philosophy* (published 1641), but we would suggest also reading parts of *Principles of Philosophy* (published 1644), *Replies to Objections to the Meditations* (published 1641–2) and some of Descartes's correspondence. We do not discuss *Passions of the Soul* (published 1649), but that is worth reading as well. Garber (1992) shows the relationship between Descartes's philosophical and scientific aims. The articles in Cottingham (1992) provide a comprehensive and up-to-date exploration of current philosophical responses to Descartes. Hooker (1978) and Moyal (1991) offer extremely useful collections of articles about Descartes.

Malebranche's most important work is *The Search after Truth*, which was first published in 1674–5, and went through a number of revised editions during his lifetime. The standard English translation is Malebranche (1997). Recent commentaries in English include Rome (1963) and Nadler (1992). There are two books which discuss Malebranche's influence as well as his philosophy itself: McCracken (1983) and Brown (1991). Other books contain chapters on Malebranche as well as other seventeenth-century philosophers, for example Yolton (1983) and Jolley (1990).

References

Descartes

Descartes, R. 1985: *The Philosophical Writings of Descartes*, 2 vols (edited and translated by J. Cottingham, J. R. Stoothoff and D. Murdoch). Cambridge: Cambridge University Press.

——1988: *Descartes: Selected Philosophical Writings* (edited and translated by J. Cottingham, R. Stoothoff and D. Murdoch). Cambridge: Cambridge University Press.

Writers on Descartes

Cottingham, J. (ed.) 1992: *The Cambridge Companion to Descartes*. Cambridge: Cambridge University Press.

Garber, D. 1992: *Descartes's Metaphysical Physics*. Chicago: University of Chicago Press.

Hooker, M. (ed.) 1978: *Descartes: Critical and Interpretive Essays*. Baltimore, MD: Johns Hopkins University Press.

Moyal, G. J. D. (ed.) 1991: *René Descartes: Critical Assessments*. London: Routledge.

Malebranche

Malebranche, N. 1997: *The Search after Truth; Elucidations of the Search after Truth* (translated and edited by T. Lennon and P. Olscamp). Cambridge: Cambridge University Press.

Writers on Malebranche

Brown, S. (ed.) 1991: *Nicolas Malebranche: His Philosophical Critics and Successors*. Assen: Van Gorcum.

Jolley, N. 1990: *The Light of the Soul: Theories of Ideas in Leibniz, Malebranche, and Descartes*. Oxford: Clarendon Press.

McCracken, C. 1983: *Malebranche and British Philosophy*. Oxford: Clarendon Press.

Nadler, S. 1992: *Malebranche and Ideas*. Oxford: Oxford University Press.

Rome, B. 1963: *The Philosophy of Malebranche*. Chicago: Henry Regnery.
Yolton, J. 1983: *Perceptual Acquaintance from Descartes to Reid*. Oxford: Blackwell.

Discussion Questions

1   What is the importance of method in philosophy?

2   Is the non-human world a single, deterministic, mechanical system?

3   What would make some laws of nature more fundamental than others?

4   Was Descartes right to demand that scientific theories be intelligible?

5   How can we determine when an account explains and when it merely redescribes a phenomenon?

6   Must properties be measurable if we are to use them in scientific explanation?

7   Is the book of nature written in the language of mathematics? What are the implications of your answer?

8   If what we see is only an appearance, how can we gain knowledge of what really happens in the world?

9   Should Descartes have been an atomist?

10   Can there be genuinely empty space? How are objects related to the spaces around them?

11   If God's concurrence is needed at every moment to sustain the universe, how can the laws of nature be laws?

12   If animals are explicable in purely mechanical terms, can humans be explained entirely in this way as well?

13   Does the fact that I can make judgements, even mistaken ones, prove that I exist?

14   If I can think away the entire physical world, but cannot think away my own existence, does it follow that I am a thinking thing, and not merely part of the physical world?

15   Should we follow Descartes's method of doubt?

16   Why did Malebranche think that our intellectual ideas are a subset of God's ideas?

17   Why does Malebranche use the slogan 'we see all things in God'?

18   Explain why Malebranche denied that physical objects have causal powers.

19   What is Malebranche's doctrine of 'occasional causes'? What problem is it meant to solve?

20   Explain Malebranche's criticism of Descartes's views of the existence of God.

21   In what ways does Malebranche's philosophy show a greater integration of philosophy and theology than Descartes and other seventeenth-century thinkers?

27

Spinoza and Leibniz

RICHARD FRANCKS AND
GEORGE MACDONALD ROSS

This chapter continues the discussion begun in chapter 26 of the seventeenth-century transformation in philosophy, science and theology, and in the conception of human life. It explores the reasoning that led to the great metaphysical systems of Spinoza and Leibniz, focusing on the implications of Spinoza's single substance and Leibniz's monads for philosophy, science and theology.

1 Spinoza

If DESCARTES (chapter 26) was the leading light of the modernist movement, Baruch Spinoza (Benedict de Spinoza) was its most perfect expression. By developing Descartes's vision of a new, scientific understanding of things to its ultimate conclusion, he produced an account of God, the universe and humanity's place in it which was of unparalleled breadth, consistency and beauty. As a result he was excommunicated from his Jewish community, his books were publicly burned, and his name became a byword for wickedness and atheism until a hundred years after his death, when he was rediscovered – and misinterpreted – by the Romantics.

In contrast to Descartes, who was constantly trying out new ways of re-presenting and re-expressing different aspects of his message, Spinoza worked for years to polish and perfect a single, comprehensive and definitive account of how things are. His work is therefore very brief, very dense and deeply obscure. Our survey of Spinoza's thought will use the same three headings of Nature, God and Humanity; but in talking of Spinoza, we must begin with God.

1.1 God

The simplest summary of Spinoza's metaphysics is that he takes Descartes's outline of a mechanistic science of non-human nature and develops it into a unified theory of the whole of being, which he calls 'God or Nature'.

For Descartes, as we saw, God was the one true substance, which underlies and supports all created substances. But Descartes's God was also, and simultaneously, a pre-existing, independent immaterial being who freely chose to bring matter and minds into existence for God's own purposes. Spinoza sees those two elements as inconsistent, and with characteristic ruthlessness he simply eliminates the second: God or Nature is the one substance which exists, the single unchanging reality which underlies all phenomena of any kind, and which a perfect science would reveal.

This pantheistic doctrine was, and remains, startling to many people, and puzzling to even more. God, for Spinoza, is the cause of the world and all it contains – but not in the way that the term is usually understood. God is not a separate entity, whose causation of the world is a creative act which gives it its beginning, in a way analogous to that in which a potter creates a pot. Rather, God is the world itself, as it really is; God stands as the indwelling or immanent 'cause' – or explanation – of the world, in the sense in which we might say that the fundamental laws of physics 'cause' – they underlie, give rise to, or explain – all physical objects and events. God is therefore identified with Nature, not in the sense that God is simply the aggregate of everything that exists, but in so far as God is the fundamental facts of nature which explain all the rest, the unchanging reality behind all appearances whatsoever. God or Nature is therefore the atemporal reality which science seeks to discover, and of which the world as we know it is a temporal expression.

The idea strikes us as an odd mixture of religious vision and scientific research programme, and different readers will produce different Spinozas as they emphasize one or other of those seemingly irreconcilable aspects. Spinoza himself, though, is insistent that the two are united, and that it is only the weak-mindedness and anthropomorphism of Descartes and the Cartesians (and therefore of us as their descendants) which prevents them (and us) from seeing it. Just as he tries to reinterpret the idea of God's causality by removing the misleading analogy with human creativity, and in so doing claims that his God, and only his God, is truly the cause of the world, so he insists that almost all the traditional attributes of God can in truth belong to his God, and to his God alone. God or Nature is infinite (limitless) and eternal (atemporal); it is self-caused (self-explanatory), and necessarily exists (cannot without contradiction be said not to exist). It is omnipotent (the explanation of everything that is possible) and omnipresent; it is all truth and all knowledge, and as we shall see later, in the knowledge of God or Nature lies true blessedness and our only hope of immortality, and to love God or Nature is the only route to perfect freedom. It was God or Nature who chose the Jews and inspired the prophets, because the prophets were men of great understanding, who understood the truths that Spinoza is now revealing, but who expressed that understanding for an ignorant public in picturesque and anthropomorphic language. In fact, the only characteristic of traditional gods which Spinoza's God lacks is personality: God or Nature is not a person, and is not anything like one. It does not have desires or feelings or intentions, and it cannot love or be angry, or be interested in the fate of human beings. To those who maintain that any conception of God must have these features, Spinoza's reply is uncompromising and clear: we naturally tend to see the world in our own human terms, and no doubt in just the same way if triangles could speak, they would insist that God must be eminently triangular.

1.2 Nature

God, then, is the fundamental facts of the world, from which all the phenomena of nature necessarily flow. In the material world, that becomes a straightforwardly

Cartesian story in which all physical phenomena are strictly determined by unchanging universal laws, and all physical laws depend ultimately on laws of motion. Like Descartes, Spinoza denied the possibility of a vacuum, and of atoms, and like Descartes he held that what common sense takes to be individual physical objects are in reality only conventionally individuated modes of an extended continuum, which Spinoza called the Attribute of Extension.

All of that is, and was, familiar. In his account of mental phenomena, though, Spinoza was much more radical. Whereas for Descartes the mental world consists of an indefinite number of individual immaterial thinking substances, some of which are temporarily linked by God to specific areas of the material continuum, Spinoza posits a second, non-material, mental continuum – the Attribute of Thought – of which all mental phenomena are modes, just as all physical phenomena are modes of the Attribute of Extension. The two attributes are co-extensive, and exactly parallel: everything that exists in one has an exact counterpart in the other. In fact, Spinoza claims, those counterparts, and the attributes on which they depend, are in reality the same thing: there is only a single substance, which is expressed in those two different ways (and in countless others unknown to us).

What are we to make of such a story? It has been read in a variety of ways, as equivalent to certain varieties of Buddhist thought, as a return to some kind of primitive animism, and as a mystical poetic vision of a World Soul underlying all the phenomena of nature. It may be all or any of those things; but what it is also is an attempt to extend Descartes's modernism into the mental realm, and by so doing to create a universal explanatory framework for a complete science of nature.

Descartes's view of the mind had been a surprisingly conservative one, in that the appearance/reality distinction which so dominated his account of matter was almost completely absent from it. Whereas he held that the common-sense view of the material world is completely transformed when we come to see it with the eye of reason, the common-sense view of the mind turns out on his view to be surprisingly accurate. The uneducated layman's belief that the mind is some extra, immaterial thing which is united with the body and which leaves it at death is shared by the philosopher. The expert may have a more complete and a more systematic knowledge of the mind's operations than does the person in the street, but that knowledge is still expressed in terms of the categories of the ordinary person's experience, such as willing, understanding, feeling and perceiving. The mind is known, as it were, entirely from within: what it is to think just is to have certain kinds of experience, and there is no deeper level of understanding which explains that experience in the way in which a knowledge of Cartesian physics explains the observable phenomena of the natural world.

Thought

Spinoza's Attribute of Thought is an attempt to provide that deeper level of understanding, and by so doing to give an objective, scientific explanation of the phenomenon of thought precisely parallel to that which Descartes had given of the material world. Just as Descartes extends the concept of materiality from actual solid objects to a universal extension, and in so doing explains away those solid objects as merely local concentrations of a universal stuff, so Spinoza tries to extend the concept of thought from individual thinking agents to a universal mentality, and by so doing seeks to explain away our individual minds as merely local concentrations of a universal characteristic of all things. Everything is extended, even so-called empty space, and when extension is arranged appropriately, the result is what we experience as a solid object. Similarly, everything is mental, even so-called inert objects, and when mentality is arranged appropriately, the result is what we experience as a thinking thing.

The idea is a strange one, but perhaps no more so than the parallel move in the material world, which today we find quite easy to accept. If it can be made to work, it offers a genuinely non-materialist alternative to Cartesian dualism – a basis for a science of nature which sees human beings as natural objects which are to be treated in the same way as any other natural object, but which at the same time preserves human (and potentially animal) subjectivity as an ineliminable feature of the world.

The price he pays for those advantages, though, is one which many people are unwilling to pay. He rules out any possibility of free will, and insists that like all other natural phenomena human beings are entirely determined effects of the underlying facts of nature. The structure of his theory also denies the possibility of any cross-attribute causation: mental acts can never be given physical explanations, or vice versa, but each must be understood through the laws of its own nature. More fundamentally still, he denies the ultimate individuality, and even identity, of the human mind. A mind, for Spinoza, is merely a local concentration of thought, conventionally individuated from other concentrations around it. It is not a separate, individual thing with its own identity and independence, but merely a convenient way of talking about a constantly changing body of interrelated thought, which comes together, develops and changes over time, and eventually dissipates, like a whirlpool in the bath water.

Whether or not we find the picture acceptable, its motivation is clear: when seen through the eye of reason, all the phenomena of nature are seen as precisely that – mere phenomena, generated by the unchanging features of nature which a true science would reveal. The task of understanding is therefore, as Descartes said, to rise above the level of experience, at which we perceive the world as a multiplicity of objects in time and space, and to see things from the point of view of eternity (*sub specie aeternitatis*), as temporary local manifestations of the unchanging facts of nature. But whereas Descartes and his followers saw that task as applying only to material objects, Spinoza seeks to extend it to everything that exists.

1.3 Humanity

The account of humanity which emerges from this metaphysic is a mixture of austerity and passion. As we have seen, Spinoza's overriding conviction that human beings are parts of nature, natural phenomena like any other, and therefore to be understood in the same dispassionate, naturalistic way, leads him to an outright denial of the Cartesian free will: human actions are natural events, like the actions of clouds or rainstorms, and to understand them is to see how they follow necessarily from the unchanging facts of God or Nature. The conventional objection to any such determinism, of course, is that it makes moral judgements impossible, because it makes no sense to praise or to blame what could not have been otherwise, and with typical remorseless logic Spinoza therefore accepts that morality, at least as conventionally understood, is impossible. Terms like 'right' and 'good', he claims, are merely words which we apply to things that we want, and we deceive ourselves if we think they are anything else. Similarly, politics and the legal system are purely pragmatic devices for organizing and directing human action, and to seek any higher purpose or claim any higher justification for our decisions is absurd.

The story depends on his understanding of human beings as purely natural, appetitive creatures in a world of fellow strugglers, both human and non-human. Like any other part of nature, whether it is one we normally think of as conscious or not, we strive to maintain our existence, to develop our natures and to realize our potentials. In so doing we perceive helps and hindrances: some things we find to be beneficial to our development and enable us to survive and to progress; others thwart and obstruct our growth and prevent us from realizing our aims. Those basic facts produce the three fundamental emotional states of Desire, Pleasure and Pain, and he then develops a rigorous and systematic analysis of all other emotions as being built up out of combinations of those three, in a way which is precisely parallel to that in which all change in the material world can be seen to be built up out of the basic facts of motion and resistance.

Yet out of this austere, rational, mechanical account of human existence there arises an understanding of human life and behaviour which is surprisingly rich, and which provides a notion of the good life for human beings which makes clear why his one great work is called the *Ethics*. We are all capable, to some extent, of understanding the world and ourselves, of seeing things as they really are. And that understanding can be enhanced and extended. To the extent that we do understand ourselves and the world around us, to that extent we act rationally, and we know why we act – our actions are grounded in what is internal to us. In that sense, when we think clearly we are in control of our own action, whereas when we act irrationally we are at the mercy of external forces operating on us.

Those forces may be internal or external: when we gaze at the Sun like a fool, and jump to the conclusion that it moves around the Earth, we are passive, enslaved: our belief foisted on us by circumstances. By contrast, when we understand why things appear that way, we are active, free, rational agents – our beliefs are the result of our own thinking processes. In exactly the same way, when we react angrily to an insult we are at the mercy of our own passive emotions, driven hither and thither by alien forces within ourselves. But when we understand why the insult was offered, and understand why we feel as we do in response, we do not magically lose our appetitive nature and rise above the emotional life to a life of pure rationality, but we are nevertheless able to *choose* how to react, and in that sense, even though our action remains as rigorously determined as any other, we are free, *self*-determining agents.

The picture is now almost complete. This notion of freedom, of self-determination, is the only true good for human beings, because the active, rational life is the one which as a matter of fact in the long term is best calculated to produce the stable, prosperous and happy life, and it is that fact of nature which moralists have tried in their misleading way to teach by their systems of good and evil. Because it is an emotional life, and because it is based on a true understanding of oneself and one's surroundings, Spinoza can also claim that it is the Intellectual Love of God, and therefore that it is also the lesson which the great religious teachers of the world, of all faiths, have been trying to put across, once we purge their message of its anthropomorphic and figurative language. And because self-determining, rational, free agents will necessarily tend to agree with others of the same kind, the requirements of civil life and political obligation will also, when properly understood, turn out to be founded on the same conception of human beings in their eternal and unbreakable dependence on God or Nature.

In this way what Spinoza offers is indeed an account of the good life which is firmly grounded in an objective, scientific account of human beings, and which is in turn located within an all-embracing metaphysical structure of all reality. If it were successful it would bring together science and religion, reason and emotion, objectivity and morality in a way which is unique in the modern world. But the price is perhaps too high for most of us to pay. According to Spinoza, all that is wrong with cruelty, all that is wrong with selfishness, is that a life of that kind is not in the long term beneficial either to the agent or to her neighbours. Similarly, all that is wrong with despotism and with totalitarianism is that systems of that kind tend in the long run not to last, and not to be conducive to the best interests of their members. Many people still feel the need for some stronger weapon against their enemies.

2 Leibniz

Philosophers have always been notorious for the strength of their disagreements, and for their inability to resolve them by rational debate. Leibniz was a diplomat by profession, and he applied the techniques of diplomacy to bring about peace and harmony in the world of philosophy. Although his philosophical system had many original features, he presented it not as one new system among many, but as incorporating the common ground on which the warring factions could agree.

His approach can be summed up in his dictum that philosophers are generally right in what they assert, and wrong in what they deny. He liked to illustrate this with an analogy: different views of a town give prominence to some features and hide others, so that observers at various viewpoints will give different descriptions of it. But these descriptions are mutually compatible, as long as individual observers do not deny the existence of features they cannot themselves see. Leibniz's ambition was to achieve a God-like perspective which encompasses everything, and reveals all other perspectives as partial, but true as far as they go.

Unlike the other modern philosophers, who saw themselves as making a more or less complete break with the past, Leibniz accepted *all* philosophers as making positive contributions to philosophical truth – not merely canonical figures such as PLATO (c.429–347 BC) (chapter 23) and ARISTOTLE (384–322 BC) (chapter 23), but more exotic thinkers like Pythagoras (b. c.570 BC) and the Neoplatonists, the much-derided scholastic philosophers, and mystics and alchemists. Again, he was less Eurocentric than most of his contemporaries, and he learned as much as he could about Chinese philosophy, to show how it complemented the Western tradition.

But despite his reconciliatory programme, he was as sharp in his criticisms of his predecessors as anyone. In outlining the main themes of Leibniz's positive philosophy under the same headings of Nature, God, and Humanity, we shall take note of his arguments against Descartes, Malebranche, and Spinoza in particular.

2.1 Nature

Descartes, Malebranche and Spinoza all held that the realm of nature was a unitary whole, whether distinct from, or merely an aspect of God. Two alternative views of the world which they consciously rejected were the atomist view that it derives all its reality from the discrete atoms of which it is composed, and the vitalist view that all physical objects are either living beings, or collections of living beings. Leibniz held that all three views contained part of the truth, and that they could be reconciled by reviving the Aristotelian–scholastic concept of a substantial form.

Firstly, Descartes, Malebranche and Spinoza were right to insist on the systematic wholeness of nature – it is more than just a chaotic jumble of atoms. But Spinoza in particular was wrong to say that only the universe as a whole is a real substance, since it is a compound of its parts, and the parts must be at least as real as the whole. The question is, what are the ultimate parts of which the universe is a compound? Everyone agreed that everyday physical objects like sticks or stones do not qualify, since they are only temporary collections of smaller parts. The atomists held that there are very small parts of matter of various shapes and sizes, which cannot be divided into further parts, and which are the ultimate substances. For Leibniz, size was irrelevant, since whether something is big or small is relative to the observer – a grain of sand too small to be noticed by an elephant would be a mountain to a microbe. From a mathematical point of view, there is no less possibility of subdividing a spherical atom than a cannonball; and it is simply arbitrary to assert that atoms, unlike cannonballs, can never be broken down into their component parts. In short, there is no such thing as the smallest conceivable material atom.

The conclusion Leibniz drew was not (like Descartes, Malebranche and Spinoza) that there are no fundamental units of nature, but that these units are not material particles. In their enthusiasm for the mechanistic view of the world, the modern philosophers had overlooked the crucial distinction between things which are mere collections of parts, and things which are organic wholes. For Descartes, a clock, a cat and the live body of a human being would all be transitory manifestations of matter of the same kind. The main difference between a cat and a clock is that the mechanism is more complicated; the difference between a cat and a human body is that the human body has a temporary special relationship with an immaterial soul. For Leibniz, the clock is a mere collection of parts, whereas both the cat and the live human body are *organisms*. An organism is a being of a completely different kind. At the common-sense level, it has the capacity to initiate motion, to act purposefully, to react to stimuli and to reproduce. But of special significance to Leibniz was his belief that an organism is a unitary whole, in that its parts are peculiar to itself – every organ and every cell (indeed, every part of every cell) bears unique characteristics that link it to the body to which it belongs. So even if the parts of the body become physically separated, they are still parts of the same organism (rather as a family is a single family, even if its members do not live under the same roof). For Leibniz, then, the only fundamental units of nature are organisms, since they alone possess true unity.

In this, Leibniz sided with the vitalists, whose understanding of nature was modelled on the purposeful, vital forces of living beings, and who saw life everywhere. Even though the majority of macroscopic physical objects we see around us are not themselves living organisms, they are in fact composed of tiny organisms. Leibniz appealed to the evidence of the recently invented microscope, which revealed apparently homogeneous substances, such as chalk, blood or semen, as containing masses of tiny creatures. Indeed, since matter is infinitely divisible, he maintained that every organism is a colony of smaller organisms, and so on *ad infinitum*.

However, although Leibniz accepted the metaphysics of the vitalists, he could not go along with their rejection of the new mechanistic science. In order to achieve a reconciliation of the two world views, he drew on the traditional Aristotelian distinction between matter and form. For Aristotle, every being has two aspects: its form (the active principle which each individual shares with other members of the same species) and its matter (the passive principle, which bears the characteristics by which one individual is distinguished from another). In the case of animate beings, the form was identified with the soul. Perhaps influenced by Spinoza's theory that extension and thought are two attributes of the same substance, Leibniz maintained that nature had two aspects: the material aspect, consisting of the bodies of all the organisms of which it is composed; and the vital aspect, consisting of all the forms or souls. The material aspect could be understood only in terms of the mathematical laws governing the interactions of pieces of matter characterized by different shapes, sizes and masses. The vital aspect could be understood only in terms of the life principle of striving for perfection. As with Spinoza, there was a perfect one-to-one correlation between what is true of matter, and what is true of forms, or 'monads' (unities), as he later called them. So, for example, a bullet fired from a gun can be seen equally as blindly obeying the laws of mechanics, and as striving for the best possible state with the greatest economy of effort.

2.2 God

If the universe consists in an infinity of individual substances, how does it form a systematic whole? Leibniz's answer was that God is needed to ensure that the components of the universe interact as harmoniously as possible – indeed, he often referred to his philosophical system as the 'system of universal harmony'. This does not mean that the universe is perfect in all its parts, otherwise it would be an absolutely perfect being, and therefore identical with God. Like Descartes and Malebranche, but unlike Spinoza, Leibniz insisted that God must be distinct from the universe he created. But as a perfect being, God must have created the best universe which it is logically possible to create, so that if it were made better in some respect, it would be worse overall. The evil, pain and ugliness that we see around us are real enough; but the solution to the problem of evil is to recognize that they contribute to a greater good.

Monads and the Harmony of the Universe

So what is it for the universe to be a harmonious system? Monads, being soul-like, have characteristics analogous to those of human souls. In particular, they have something akin to a perceptual state in human souls, only lacking consciousness. In effect, they represent everything that has any influence on them, with greater or less clarity, depending on the strength of the influence. For example, the motion of a particle is affected, however remotely, by all other particles in the universe; and in order to 'know' which direction to move in, it must register all these influences. This led Leibniz to describe monads as 'living mirrors of the universe', each representing all other monads from a distinct and individual point of view. God perceives everything with equal clarity, and without any point of view; whereas created monads are limited by their perspectival point. The harmony of the total system consists in the fact that the perceptions of each individual monad interlock to form a single, consistent view of the universe as perceived by God, like a jig-saw puzzle of infinitely many dimensions. Moreover, since the perceptual state of each monad is constantly changing, the harmony of the universe has to be re-established from one instant to the next.

But how does God bring it about that the whole universe is kept in perfect harmony? Leibniz held that there were three possible theories, which he illustrated with the then-popular metaphor of God as the perfect clock-maker. To keep the account as simple as possible, suppose that God has made just two clocks, which keep in perfect time with each other to eternity. One theory would be that he has devised an invisible mechanism which physically compels the clocks to keep in time (e.g. rods connecting their hands). This would be analogous to saying that the universe is harmonious because there are necessary causal connections between its components. But, as Malebranche had shown, we cannot perceive any such connections, and we cannot conceive how one piece of matter can transfer its energy to another. Moreover, given that the ultimate realities are spiritual monads, it is even more difficult to conceive how anything could pass from one monad to another. As Leibniz himself put it, monads have no windows through which anything can pass in or out.

The second theory is that, as soon as the clocks begin to diverge, the clock-maker adjusts one of them so that they keep telling the same time. Leibniz attributed this theory to Malebranche, since he took him as saying that, when I will to raise my arm, nothing would happen unless God intervened. In the normal course of bodily events, my arm would have remained stationary, or moved in some other way for purely physiological reasons. So, according to Leibniz, Malebranche's theory of occasional causes implies that God perpetually adjusts the mechanism of nature in order to keep it in harmony with human volitions; and any divine intervention of this sort is a miracle. Leibniz rejected occasionalism on the grounds that God would not be perfect if he had to make innumerable miraculous interventions into the working of his creation. As will be evident from our account of occasionalism in the previous chapter, this is probably a misinterpretation of Malebranche, whose position was closer to Leibniz's than the latter realized.

The only alternative is the third theory, which is simply that the clocks were made so perfectly, that they keep in time forever without any invisible connections or miraculous adjustments. In other words, each monad has been pre-programmed with such accuracy, that it spontaneously evolves in perfect harmony with every other monad. For Leibniz, the essence of each individual monad is a unique law or programme, which controls its development, and specifies what state it will be in at any given time. God's perfection consists in his creating an infinite number of monads which will evolve in perfect harmony with each other. In using the analogy of the clocks, Leibniz was restricted by the technology of his day. In modern terms, a better analogy might be two spaceships which are pre-programmed to dock together at a certain point in space, without receiving any information about each other's positions, and without any adjustments from base. It is conceivable that this could be done; but it would require almost divine powers of pre-programming.

So far we have considered God's creative act as analogous to a craftsperson making a machine. But at a deeper and more metaphysical level, Leibniz explained it as one of endowing a concept with reality. Since God is omniscient, his mind contains all possible concepts, in all their possible permutations and combinations. Every logically consistent set of possibilities constitutes a possible world. These possible worlds can be graded as to their perfection – their fullness of being, coherence, variety, orderliness, harmony or beauty, for instance. In the competition for existence, the best of the possible worlds is the one which is actualized.

One of Leibniz's projects was to devise an ideal language for every possible concept, which would make their logical relationships patent (his 'universal characteristic'). If concepts were given numbers rather than names, and the main logical operators reduced to arithmetical operators, it would then be possible to replace fallible human reasoning by purely mechanical computation – and he designed and built a prototype machine for doing just this. In his more mystical moments, he speculated that all concepts were generated out of the binary numbers 1 and 0, with 1 representing pure being, or God, and 0 representing absence of being, or the void. Individual substances are dependent on God like the light radiating from the Sun; and they are distinct from God and from each other because of their varying proportions of darkness or non-being. In effect, the universe is the most perfect number, other than 1 itself.

2.3 Humanity

Leibniz's account of humankind falls somewhere between those of Descartes and Malebranche on the one hand, and of Spinoza on the other. He agreed with Descartes that each human is a distinct substance in its own right; but he also agreed with Spinoza that humans are part of nature, and that there are no special soul-substances which exempt them from the laws of nature.

Leibniz made many detailed criticisms of Descartes's absolute distinction between mind and body, of which one example will suffice here. In a number of his writings, Descartes proposed a theory to account for how the immaterial soul could influence what happens in the body. In essence, his theory was that bodily movements are controlled by tiny particles in the brain ('animal spirits'), which emerge from the nerves attached to the sense organs, and are deflected by the pineal gland into nerves leading to the muscles. The precise positioning of the pineal gland is determined by emotional factors, such as whether the body is in a state of anger or fear; and this in turn determines whether the perception of something dangerous results in fight or flight, for example. However, the soul (which has its seat in the pineal gland) can make infinitesimal adjustments to its position, so that the body fights instead of fleeing, or vice versa.

Leibniz criticized this theory on two grounds. First, the laws of motion which Descartes had formulated were wrong, because he maintained that the total quantity of *motion* in the material universe was constant, without taking into account the *direction* of motion. He thought that the soul could alter the direction of motion of animal spirits in the brain without contravening the laws of material nature. But in fact it is *force* or *energy* which is conserved, and it takes energy to alter the direction of motion of a material particle. So any intervention by the soul would have to add energy to the material world, and contravene the law of the conservation of energy.

Secondly, Descartes leaves it entirely unexplained *how* the soul can influence the direction of motion of particles in the brain. It is not enough to say that the amount of deflection is so infinitesimally small that it can be brought about even by an immaterial substance, since the soul is of a completely different nature from matter, and cannot have any relationship with it. It is not even proper to say that it has its seat in the pineal gland, since an immaterial substance cannot have any location in space. Leibniz suggested that Descartes was thinking of the soul as like the rider of a horse. The horse supplies all the energy for its motion, without any contribution from the rider; but the rider controls the direction in which the horse moves. However, the means by which the rider controls the horse are physical – pulling at the reins, or digging in the spurs. But the soul, as an immaterial substance, has none of these physical means at its disposal, and it is wholly unintelligible how it can exert a physical influence on the functioning of the brain.

Underlying penetrating criticisms such as these, there is a deeper difference between Leibniz and Descartes. Descartes had rejected the prevailing scholastic–Aristotelian theory that the soul is no more than the form of the body, and had reverted to the Platonic and Augustinian theory that they are entirely separate substances in their own right (and with some doubts as to whether body exists at all). Leibniz was more Aristotelian, and he held that souls are inextricably bound up with matter, as its form. Indeed, just as there can be no form without matter, there can be no matter without form – which is why all genuine substances are living beings, with a soul analogous to that of humans.

However, although Leibniz maintained that there is no ontological difference between human beings and other substances, he recognized that they differ sufficiently in degree to give human beings a special status in the scheme of things.

Although most of our perceptions are, like those of other monads, below the threshold of consciousness, some of the time, some of our perceptions are sufficiently clear and distinct to give rise to consciousness – a state in which we do not merely perceive, but are aware of ourselves as perceiving. It is this which distinguishes human beings from other substances. Similarly, our desires and ambitions are not mere unconscious goal-directed behaviour, but set in a context of self-improvement, rationality and moral choice. Drawing on St Augustine's (354–430) (chapter 24) great work, *The City of God*, Leibniz held that humans shared with angels and other superior conscious and rational beings the privilege of being members of the City of God, or the 'realm of grace'.

Just as form and matter are different aspects of the same reality, so are the realms of grace and of nature. As part of nature, all human actions are explicable in purely deterministic, mechanical terms, as motions of particles of matter. But since we are also citizens of the realm of grace, our actions are also describable as the outcome of completely free, rational choices. As scientists, we investigate the causal determinants of human behaviour, but as subjects of God's kingdom we are each contributing to the fulfilment of God's plan for the moral perfection of the universe. Thanks to the gift of reason, we can and should make it our goal in life to raise ourselves above a limited and parochial view of the world, to one which is as close as possible to the divine perspective.

Further Reading

For the two philosophers featured in this chapter we first suggest a major source of their writings translated into English: Spinoza (1985) and Leibniz (1969) and then a more convenient selection of their works: Spinoza (1992) and Leibniz (1995). Readers might seek some understanding of Spinoza's demanding masterpiece, the *Ethics* (published 1677), before turning to his other writings. The fullest accounts of many of Leibniz's ideas appear in his letters, but an overview may be gained from such works as *Discourse on Metaphysics* (written in 1686, published 1846) and the mature accounts in *New Essays on Human Understanding* (written 1704, published 1765), *Theodicy* (published 1710) and the *Monadology* (written 1714). His *Correspondence with Arnauld* (published posthumously in 1846) and *The Leibniz–Clarke Correspondence* (published posthumously in 1717) are classic exchanges which help to explain the grounds for his system.

Readers might begin their additional reading with books comparing all three authors: Cottingham (1988) and Woolhouse (1993).

Freeman and Mandelbaum (1975), Grene (1979), and Grene and Nails (1986) are collections offering wide-ranging critical responses to Spinoza. Donagan (1988) explores Spinoza's doctrines with balance and sophistication, while Bennett (1984) examines the details of Spinoza's system with engaging vigour.

Leibniz's life of brilliant achievement in many fields is explored in Aiton (1985). MacDonald Ross (1984) provides a helpful introductory account. Woolhouse (1993) and Jolley (1995) are collections offering guidance for more advanced work.

References

Spinoza

Spinoza, B. 1985: *The Collected Works of Spinoza*, vol. 1 (edited and translated by E. Curley). Princeton, NJ: Princeton University Press.

—— 1992: *Ethics with the Treatise on the Emendation of the Intellect and Selected Letters* (edited by S. Feldman, translated by S. Shirley). Indianapolis, IN: Hackett.

—— 1994: *A Spinoza Reader* (edited and translated by E. Curley). Princeton, NJ: Princeton University Press.

Writers on Spinoza

Bennett, J. 1984: *A Study of Spinoza's Ethics*. Cambridge: Cambridge University Press.

Donagan, A. 1988: *Spinoza*. London: Harvester Wheatsheaf.

Freeman, E. and Mandelbaum, M. (eds) 1975: *Spinoza: Essays in Interpretation*. La Salle, IL: Open Court.

Garrett, D. 1996: *The Cambridge Companion to Spinoza*. Cambridge: Cambridge University Press.

Grene, M. (ed.) 1979: *Spinoza: A Collection of Critical Essays*. Notre Dame, IN: University of Notre Dame Press.

Grene, M. and Nails, D. (eds) 1986: *Spinoza and the Sciences*. Dordrecht: D. Reidel.

Lloyd, G. 1996: *Spinoza and the Ethics*. London: Routledge.

Leibniz

Leibniz, G. W. 1969: *G. W. Leibniz: Philosophical Papers and Letters* (edited and translated by L. E. Loemker). Dordrecht: D. Reidel.

—— 1995: *G. W. Leibniz: Philosophical Writings* (edited by G. H. R. Parkinson and translated by M. Morris and G. H. R. Parkinson). London: Everyman.

Writers on Leibniz

Aiton, E. J. 1985: *Leibniz: A Biography*. Bristol: Adam Hilger.

Jolley, N. (ed.) 1995: *The Cambridge Companion to Leibniz*. Cambridge: Cambridge University Press.

MacDonald Ross, G. 1984: *Leibniz*. Oxford: Oxford University Press.

Woolhouse, R. S. (ed.) 1993: *G. W. Leibniz: Critical Assessments*. London: Routledge.

Writers on Descartes, Spinoza and Leibniz

Cottingham, J. 1988: *The Rationalists*. Oxford: Oxford University Press.

Woolhouse, R. S. 1993: *Descartes, Spinoza, Leibniz: The Concept of Substance in Seventeenth-Century Metaphysics*. London: Routledge.

Discussion Questions

1 Does Spinoza offer a better universal explanatory framework for a science of nature than Descartes?

2 Should the appearance–reality distinction apply to the mind?

3 Can we explain away individual minds while retaining mentality?

4 What would things be like if seen from the point of view of eternity? Could there be such a viewpoint?

5 How can we decide whether Spinoza is correct in claiming that there is only one substance: God or Nature?

6 Should we accept Spinoza's account of the link between rationality and free action?

7 How valuable is Spinoza's account of the emotions?

8 Should a philosophical system seek to incorporate rather than to reject past philosophical thought?

9 What is at stake in deciding whether nature is a systematic whole?

10 Could the fundamental units of nature be organisms rather than material particles?

11 What are monads? In what sense is each monad meant to reflect all the others?

12 Would pre-established harmony or causal interaction among monads be a better explanation of the harmony of the universe?

13 What is the role of Leibniz's concept of possible worlds? How can we determine whether this is the best of all possible worlds?

14 Could Leibniz's project of devising an ideal language be realized?

15 Does the notion of substance help or hinder philosophical understanding?

16 Does Descartes, Spinoza or Leibniz have the best understanding of human freedom?

17 Does Descartes, Spinoza or Leibniz give the best insight into how the mind and the body are related?

28

Hobbes

TOM SORELL

Modern political theory originates with Thomas Hobbes (1588–1679). In Leviathan and other works, Hobbes presented a bleak picture of violence and disorder as the inevitable condition of humans in the state of nature. Peace, the main concern of politics, could be realized only by a strong sovereign established through a social contract. Subjects would have no rational grounds to challenge the rule of the sovereign so long as peace was maintained. Hobbes, who wrote during the turmoil of the English Civil War, has had wide influence among subsequent political and social theorists. His materialist method is worth examining in his discussion of many other topics.

1 Introduction

Thomas Hobbes is best known as a philosopher of HUMAN NATURE (p. 259) and HUMAN SOCIETY (pp. 690–1). He is famous for maintaining that the natural condition of people is one of war, in which life is 'solitary, poor, nasty, brutish and short', and he was an early social contract theorist: he believed that the STATE (pp. 261–2) could be understood as the outcome of an agreement between free human beings to submit to government. *Leviathan* (1651), published in London, is widely regarded as his masterpiece, and it is the most commonly quoted source of his views about humanity and about the state. It is not, however, Hobbes's only full-length work of political philosophy – there were two others – and it is not the work in which he thought that he had given the best or most rigorous statement of his theory of the state.

Nor was politics Hobbes's only preoccupation as a philosopher. He was a very forthright and thoroughgoing materialist, and, perhaps above all, a contributor to, and systematizer of, some of the new NATURAL SCIENCE (chapters 25–7) of the seventeenth century. In his own opinion he deserved to go down in the history of philosophy as the originator of a true science of natural JUSTICE (chapter 8) or politics, and as an innovator in optics. He also claimed some distinction as the first to boil the whole of philosophy or science down to its 'elements' – the concepts necessary to understand body or matter, man and citizen. His *Elements of Philosophy*, comprising *De Cive* (1642), *De Corpore* (1656a), *De Homine* (1658), published in three volumes between 1655 and 1658, was the largest intellectual project he undertook, occupying as it did nearly two decades of thought and writing. In so far as Hobbes had a complete system of philosophy, it is expounded in this trilogy.

2 Hobbes's Politics

There are two rather different ways in which Hobbes's political writings can be understood. On the one hand, they can be interpreted as partisan interventions in a debate between English parliamentarians and royalists between 1628 and 1650, that is, the period that climaxed in the English Civil War of the early 1640s. In this debate Hobbes's own position was determined by the royalist allegiances of his aristocratic employers. He sided with Charles I, and approved of many of his actions – to do with taxation, the forced billeting of troops in private houses and the curtailment of parliamentary powers – that were highly unpopular in England in the prewar period. Was it these actions that Hobbes's theoretical works of politics were intended to legitimatize? The suggestion fits the early *Elements of Law* (1640) better than *Leviathan*, for the *Elements* were actually written as a sourcebook or brief for aristocrats who spoke in defence of the king in parliamentary debates in 1640, while *Leviathan* seems to justify the actions of any *de facto* sovereign power, including, explicitly, the regime that replaced the monarchy in England after the death of Charles I.

The second reading of Hobbes's politics is as a contribution, albeit a revolutionary contribution, to a lofty debate concerning questions of politics in the abstract, questions discussed in a long line of treatises going back to the Greeks and the Hebrews. This reading fits neither the *Elements of Law* nor *Leviathan* as well as it does the third of Hobbes's three political treatises, *De Cive* (1642). *De Cive* has a certain pre-eminence among Hobbes's three political treatises: it was on the strength of writing this work that Hobbes claimed to have done something original in POLITICAL PHILOSOPHY (chapter 8). *De Cive* was the first book, according to Hobbes, to deal scientifically with the recognized central questions of political philosophy. Other works, he conceded, had taken up those questions, but not by a method that had any chance of putting conclusions beyond dispute. *De Cive*, on the other hand, purported to do for its subject matter – commonwealths or bodies politic and their maintenance – what had only ever been done before for lines and figures. In short, *De Cive* was supposed to expound a science of politics comparable to geometry, with conclusions as compelling to an open mind as those of Euclid (fl. 300 BC).

3 Human Nature and the State of War

De Cive was published in 1642, two years after the *Elements of Law*, and nearly nine years before the appearance of *Leviathan*. It opens (ch. 1, ii) with a strong denial of one of the cardinal principles of ARISTOTLE's (chapter 23) politics, that humans are by nature cut out for life in the *polis*. According to Hobbes, human beings are not naturally made for the political life. They think too much of themselves, put too much value on present gratification, and they are bad at predicting the consequences of their actions. One effect of these tendencies is for people to come into conflict with one another, especially when they feel that they are undervalued in other people's eyes. The conflict can consist of the denigration of one person in the conversation of another person, or it can take the form of outright quarrelling and even violence. And if these are familiar patterns of behaviour when there is LAW (chapter 13) and custom and good manners to restrain people, how much more extreme must the hostility be when these things are absent and naked human nature is allowed to express itself without interference?

What would Life be Like without Law?

Hobbes's answer (Hobbes 1640: Pt I, ch. 14; 1642: ch. 1; 1651: ch. 13) is that, left to do what comes naturally, human beings would quickly find themselves in a state of war. They would have to see to their own survival and happiness guided not by a government's sense of what was conducive to survival and happiness, but only by their conflicting, fluctuating and irremediably diverse private judgements about what was best. Not being required to defer to anyone else's judgements, but not being able, either, to rely on others to seek the good co-operatively or benevolently, people would have rationally to expect the worst from one another and, if they thought that their safety demanded it, take pre-emptive action. Thus, even those who were not naturally greedy or violent might begin to see their own survival and well-being in taking as much of what they wanted as they could, or in killing anyone who might be a potential enemy – which could mean anyone. As for those who were naturally violent and greedy, and who were normally able to get away with it, they would fight and appropriate goods until stopped by people stronger than themselves. Whoever was a potential victim would have a reason to take action against them first. In this way life with no holds barred would quickly degenerate into fearful insecurity and a permanent struggle for survival. Or, as Hobbes puts it, life in the state of nature is war – the anti-social condition *par excellence*.

In relation to the seeds of war in human nature, the argument of *De Cive* is not very different from that of the *Elements of Law* or *Leviathan*. Hobbes maintains in all three treatises that life would be extremely unpleasant if law and coercive government were to disappear; he also holds that any government that does exist is constantly in danger of being subverted, that is, forced by rebels into a state of collapse that re-introduces the war of all against all. The seeds of this war are not only the dangerous passions of individual people, who can be aroused by their circumstances or their corporeal constitutions. The seeds also include the lack of science and capacity for reasoning, for it is only in the absence of these things that the PASSIONS (pp. 716–17) succeed in determining individuals' behaviour. Again, Hobbes believed that people were easily swayed by clever politicians and put in fear of hell by a manipulating clergy. They were thus prone to resent the restrictions of life under government, or to imagine that obedience would cost them salvation. It was a short step from these resentments and fears to civil war.

4   The Laws of Nature and the Rationale for the State

Hobbes's rules for avoiding civil war if a commonwealth exists, and for ending war in the pre-political state of nature, are called laws of nature. Though statements of other 'laws of nature' existed long before the *Elements of Law*, *De Cive* and *Leviathan*, Hobbes's own list (Hobbes 1640: Pt I, chs 16–17; 1642: chs 2–3; 1651: chs 14–15) was unusual, and he claimed he was the first to find an uncontroversial basis for laws of nature. What is more, the basis would make it irrational for anyone to ignore them. It is partly because he was able to identify a single, uncontroversial good that the laws of nature all promoted that Hobbes believed his statement of the laws of nature amounted to a moral science.

The basic good that he identified was the good of peace or the absence of war; or, as he sometimes put it, the good of safety. Because war threatened the possession of all good things, not least life itself, any action that helped to avoid war or to put an end to it, and that did not itself threaten too many goods, was a rationally compulsory thing to do. There were two laws of nature that Hobbes put before the rest: firstly, to seek peace by all means if to do so was not too unsafe; and, secondly, to adopt one particular means of seeking peace if other people agreed to do the same: namely, to lay down rights that get in the way of peace.

In the state of nature, the right that people have to give up in order to secure peace is the 'right of nature' – the right to be one's own judge of what will make one safe and happy. So long as each is his or her own judge of these things, there is no insurance against war. The right must therefore be given up. Hobbes was not thinking of a simple renunciation of this right: he had in mind a transfer of it (Hobbes 1640: Pt 1, ch. 15, iii; 1642: ch. 2, iv; 1651: ch. 14) by most in the state of nature to a few or to one in the state of nature, who would then decide for the many what would make each as safe and happy as possible. The one or the few would become a SOVEREIGN POWER (pp. 261–4), and the many would become subjects of that power, and be obliged to live in keeping with the sovereign's judgements about safety and well-being, as expressed in the sovereign's laws.

The transfer of the right of nature to a sovereign power is what creates a state or commonwealth. Once transferred, the right of nature cannot be taken back, except for the sake of a personal safety which a weak or incompetent sovereign is no longer able to secure. In other words, one gets back one's right of nature if obedience to the sovereign is not after all a means of avoiding war (Hobbes 1640: Pt 2, ch. 1, v; 1642: ch. 6, iii; 1651: ch. 17). On the other hand, if a commonwealth is keeping one safe, one is obliged to obey the sovereign's laws, either by the act that transferred one's right of nature, and by the duty to abide by one's agreements; or by some act of submission if one did not enter the commonwealth from the state of nature.

Drawing back from the details, one can see that Hobbes has both a secular conception of the state, and one that tries to show that the existence of the state is reasonable, not arbitrary. There is no divine right of the sovereign to rule that obliges one to obey, nor yet is it a matter of the sovereign's simply being more powerful than one is oneself. The obedience springs from a transfer of right for the sake of peace. The state is thus seen as a security or peace-keeping device whose existence is in the interest of the many, rather than as a facsimile on earth of a divine ordering of things by nobility or rank or station.

Leaving the State of Nature as a Prisoner's Dilemma

How can it be rational for anyone in the state of nature to lay down his right to protect himself, if by doing so he lays himself open to the attack of someone who decides not to do so, or who pretends to do so? Doesn't it make more sense to stay in the state of nature when others decide to leave it? Hobbes considers the question in the form of scepticism about the need to keep one's agreements. He answers that in the long run it pays to keep one's agreements. If one doesn't, one will be mistrusted by others, who won't enter any further agreements with you, or who may decide to get their revenge for your taking advantage. Any short-term advantage is cancelled out by the subsequent insecurity. Following Gauthier (1969), one may represent the practical choices facing two would-be parties to the social contract as a prisoner's dilemma (see chapter 12):

		B Keeps the contract	B Breaks the contract
A	Keeps the contract	2, 2	4, 1
A	Breaks the contract	1, 4	3, 3

This matrix depicts the rankings placed by A and B on different outcomes in the short term. A and B each like most (give the ranking 1 to) the case in which they themselves break the contract but their opposite number keeps it. Then comes mutual adherence, followed by mutual violation of the contract. Over the long term things change:

		B Keeps the contract	B Breaks the contract
A	Keeps the contract	1, 1	4, 2
A	Breaks the contract	2, 4	3, 3

5   The Obligations of Subjects and the Rights of Sovereigns

The sovereign's subjects are obliged by a sort of agreement among themselves to obey the sovereign's laws; but the sovereign, though he is a beneficiary of the agreement, is not party to it. The many make a gift to a person or body of people of their submission; but the submission does not oblige the sovereign to please the many in return. The sovereign would perhaps be *imprudent* if he did not do his best to arrange for the peace and well-being of his subjects; for if he allows the state to descend into lawlessness, his subjects take back their right of nature, act once more as laws unto themselves and regard no one as their sovereign. In such a case a former sovereign, being only solitary or a small group, is no more secure than anyone else. So it is in the sovereign's interest not to disappoint his subjects. But he is not obliged to do so, and if his laws only bring about a peace in which everyone is safe but living austerely, that does not amount to an injustice against his subjects, even if they are hugely dissatisfied with their lot. On the contrary, the sovereign is left free by his subjects to act as he sees fit to secure peace and well-being; it is the subjects who act unjustly if they try to reinterpret the agreement as one in which they decide how the peace and well-being are to be got, and of what they will consist.

The sovereign, then, has very extensive freedoms or rights (Hobbes 1640: Pt 2, ch. 1; 1642: ch. 6; 1651: ch. 18). He decides what is legal and illegal, who owns what, who is to hold the offices of state, who is to be allowed to preach and make political speeches, how people are to be allowed to trade and associate. He has powers to legislate and to tax and of making war. Nothing less than these rights would enable the sovereign to make and keep the peace. But it is one thing for a sovereign to have these extensive rights; it is another for him to exercise them; and Hobbes lists as one of the principal causes of civil war the fact that sovereigns fail to exercise them. This failure, just as much as the failure of subjects to acknowledge the rights of sovereignty, can disturb the peace.

It is not hard to work out the consequences of Hobbes's theory in relation to the question of whether Charles I was within his rights to force a loan from his rich subjects, to billet soldiers and to circumvent parliament in the period before the Civil War. He was within his rights in all of these areas; and that civil war ensued was as much traceable to a mistaken understanding of the rights of subjects, as to ineptitude in the exercise of sovereign rights.

We have come far enough to see that both readings of Hobbes's politics fit after all. There can be no doubt that, in his three major works on the commonwealth, Hobbes frames his account of the rights of sovereigns (and of the causes of civil war) with the events of England in the 1630s and 1640s in his mind. But it is also true that the theory takes up abstract questions that transcend his historical period and which go back to Plato and Aristotle. Hobbes has an answer to the question of what the state is for, of what human happiness can consist in and what goods are promoted by morality; he is not only operating through his writings as a policy adviser to a certain English king or kings and their entourage.

6 Strengths and Weaknesses of Hobbes's Politics

How successful is Hobbes's theory of subjection and sovereignty as a piece of political philosophy? One of its most distinctive ideas is that peace rather than happiness is what the institution of the state is for. Hobbes thought that the concept of peace was clearer than the concept of happiness, and also that, while people had different, and sometimes irreconcilable, conceptions of happiness, people could reach agreement about what constituted peace. He also believed that people could not rationally repudiate the demands of peace. Against this background, a theory of the state and of morality geared to peace was supposed to make a great advance on preceding theories. Unfortunately, all of the supposed advantages of the concept of peace can be questioned. Firstly, the concept of peace is *not* very clear in Hobbes's writings. It is defined as any time when there is not war. But because Hobbes thinks that war is not only open fight-ing but also includes the vague phenomenon we now call 'cold war', the concept of the absence of war is bound to have the vagueness that the concept of war itself has.

Secondly, Hobbes sometimes seems to identify the chief aim of the state with that of securing peace and sometimes with that of achieving public safety (Hobbes 1651: ch. 30). The public safety, however, he defines in broad and in narrow senses. The narrow sense of safety is protection from physical attack; the broad sense is safety in the narrow sense plus as much well-being as is compatible with safety in the narrow sense. Plainly, if the advisability of obedience to the state is to be judged by the state's success in making people safe in the broad sense, then, since safety in the broad sense is open to many interpretations, there is perhaps too much scope for the conclusion that the state is not fulfilling its functions and that obedience is not due. The expectation of safety from the state starts to become as destabilizing as the expectation of happiness, which is not surprising, since safety in the broad sense overlaps with the concept of happiness.

Hobbes's problems do not disappear if the concept of safety is narrowed down to the concept of safety from physical attack, for individuals in the state never lose their right to judge when they are under threat of physical attack, and they never lose their right to do what they like to protect themselves if they really do think they are under such threat. Stuck in the middle of a riot, for example, they may take up arms and kill if they think that is how to survive. But even in what is outwardly a peaceful state someone may sincerely believe that an underground paramilitary movement is secretly working its way towards a successful takeover of the state and a future policy of genocide; it is unclear that this belief, even if paranoid, would not free an individual from the ties of the social contract. Because Hobbes insists on the inalienability of the right to be one's own interpreter of present dangers, he may leave too much room for pretexts for taking the law into one's own hands: precisely what he prides himself on having excluded.

7   The Rest of Hobbes's Philosophy

Hobbes's politics is not unrelated to the rest of his philosophy – to his materialistic metaphysics, for instance, or his theories of optics. On the contrary, Hobbes thought that his metaphysics, his politics, his optics, as well as other philosophers' findings in other branches of learning, could be arranged into one orderly body of science in general.

Science in general was supposed to begin with 'first philosophy'. This was not a Cartesian first philosophy, nor an Aristotelian one. Hobbes was a critic of DESCARTES (chapter 26), on whose *Meditations* he was one of the first to comment. He denied that there were irreducibly immaterial substances, either finite or infinite; there were no immaterial souls in particular, and nothing in the world like a Cartesian *res cogitans*. In his replies to Bishop Bramhall (1594–1663) in a controversy over free will, Hobbes said that even GOD (chapter 15) was a corporeal spirit; and he insisted that MENTAL ACTIVITY (chapter 5) was motion in the head and in the nervous and circulatory systems. Another kind of Cartesian immaterialism that Hobbes denied was the belief in abstract objects, such as the nature of a triangle. Descartes had insisted on the reality of such things in his fifth *Meditation*; Hobbes, for his part, thought that everything important about triangles could be understood as flowing from linguistic conventions governing the word 'triangle', rather than from triangularity.

Hobbes's positive first philosophy was a set of definitions enabling different kinds of motion in matter to be distinguished. The different branches of the sciences were distinguished by the different kinds of motion they studied. Geometry studied motion in the abstract with many specific properties of moving bodies left out of account; physics included the motions of parts of bodies and the interaction between inanimate bodies and the senses. In optics, Hobbes advocated the theory that we see things as a result of the displacement of a medium and the agitation of the sense organs by the motion of a luminous object, like the Sun. When it came to politics and ethics, Hobbes's claim that all the sciences are sciences of motion is hard to understand. The laws of nature and the arguments for certain kinds of distributions of rights, which are central to the theory of the commonwealth, are not mechanistic, though they are connected to a mechanistic psychology. Hobbes's mechanistic geometry also prompted criticism in its day from mathematicians much more able than Hobbes himself.

The thread running through all of his own contributions to the sciences is a strong antagonism to the old learning of the scholastics, and especially the hero of the scholastics, Aristotle. Hobbes developed his theory of vision in opposition to the Aristotelian theory that we see things by a process of transfer of forms or species from the seen object to the intervening medium to the eye. He developed his politics, as we have seen earlier, partly in opposition to the Aristotelian theory that human beings are animals that are suited to the polity. And he arrived at his materialism partly in opposition to Aristotle's theory that the main branches of science all have discrete and distinctive subject matters which exist in their own ways. For Hobbes, to exist was to be material, and the explanation of everything in nature was to be referred to different types of motion in matter. On the surface, Hobbes followed Aristotle in dividing up sciences according as their subject matter was natural or artificial; but even here he broke the mould, for neither of the sciences he reckoned to be concerned with artefacts, namely geometry and politics, was counted as artificial by Aristotle, and to be artificial for Hobbes was still to be material and the result of motion. To be sure, the motion that gives rise to artefacts is motion initiated by the human will, but the will itself is mechanically explicable; so there was no fundamental distinction for Hobbes between the subject matters of the natural sciences and the sciences of artefacts: both were sciences of motion or mechanistic sciences.

In the case of politics, the subject matter was something made by and out of human beings, namely a commonwealth. The purpose of the science was not, however, primarily explanatory, but productive: Hobbes claimed he would teach how to construct a lasting commonwealth, much as Euclid had taught how to construct circles. Precepts dominate Hobbes's politics; statements about the possible causes of observed effects dominate his contributions to the natural sciences. So a rough way for Hobbes to distinguish between the political or moral sciences and the natural sciences is by way of the difference between ought and is; or, more precisely, between statements of what one ought to do, backed by reasons, and conjectures of causes of observed effects, backed by reasons.

Further Reading

Those working on Hobbes should begin by reading *Leviathan* (1651). Peters (1956) offers a clearly written study of the whole of Hobbes's philosophy, while Sorell (1986) provides a study of Hobbes's metaphysics and politics against the background of his philosophy of science. Gauthier (1978), Oakeshott (1975), Macpherson (1962) and Warrender (1957) are classic appraisals of Hobbes's political thought. Mintz (1970) deals with the context and early reception of *Leviathan*, and Sommerville (1992) is a very clear and comprehensive guide to the historical context of Hobbes's political writings. Johnston (1986) explores the tensions between the scientific pretensions of some of Hobbes's political writings and their persuasive purpose. A short study by Tuck (1989) argues for the importance of philosophical scepticism in Hobbes's thought. Most of the papers in Rogers and Ryan (1988) are accessible, and there is coverage of Hobbes's metaphysics, philosophy of science and politics. Sorell (1996) contains an authoritative biographical account and articles on all aspects of Hobbes's thought, including his mathematics and optics and his theories of law and religion, as well as his metaphysics, politics and philosophy of science.

References

Hobbes

The standard edition of Hobbes's works is divided between his English and Latin writings:

Hobbes, T. 1966a: *The English Works of Thomas Hobbes*, 11 vols, 2nd reprint (edited by Sir W. Molesworth). Aalen: Scientia Verlag.

——1966b: *Opera Latina*, 5 vols, 2nd reprint (edited by Sir W. Molesworth). Aalen: Scientia Verlag.

Individual works, unless cited otherwise, are to be found in the collected works. *Leviathan* is available in several recent editions.

Hobbes, T. 1641: *Third Set of Objections to Descartes's Meditations*. In E. Haldane and G. Ross (eds) 1978: *The Philosophical Works of Descartes*. Cambridge: Cambridge University Press.

——1642: *De Cive*, short title for *Elementorum Philosophiae, Section Tertia, De Cive* (translated by Hobbes into English (1651) as *Philosophical Rudiments Concerning Government and Society*).

——1646: *A Minute or First Draught on Optics*.

——1651: *Leviathan, or the Matter, Form and Power of Commonwealth, Ecclesiastical and Civil*.

——1654: *Of Liberty and Necessity*.

——1656a: *De Corpore*, short title for *Elementorum Philosophiae, Secto Prima de Corpore*, (1655), translated into English as *Elements of Philosophy*, the first section concerning Body, 1656.

——1656b: *The Questions Concerning Liberty, Necessity and Chance, Clearly Stated and Debated between Dr. Bramhall, Bishop of Derry, and Thomas Hobbes of Malmsbury*.

——1656c: *Six Lessons to the Professors of Mathematics ... in the University of Oxford*.

——1658: *De Homine, sive Elementorum Philosophiae Sectio Secunda* (edited by B. Gert, translated by C. T. Wood, T. Scott-Craig and B. Gert, 1962, as *On Man in Man and Citizen*. New York: Humanities Press).

——1662a: *Seven Philosophical Problems*.

——1622b: *Considerations of the Reputation, Loyalty, Manners, and Religion, of Thomas Hobbes of Malmsbury*.

——*c.*1666: *Dialogue Between a Philosopher and a Student of the Common Laws of England*.

——*c.*1668: *Behemoth, or the Long Parliament. Dialogue of the Civil Wars of England*.

——1678: *Decameron Physiologicum or Ten Dialogues of Natural Philosophy*.

——1889 [1640]: *The Elements of Law Natural and Politic* (edited by F. Tonnies). London: Simkin and Marshall.

——1976 [1641 or 1642]: *Thomas White's 'De Mundo' Examined* (translated by H. W. Jones). Bradford: Bradford University Press.

Other writers

Boonin-Vail, D. 1994: *Thomas Hobbes and the Science of Moral Virtue*. Cambridge: Cambridge University Press.

Brandt, F. 1928: *Hobbes's Mechanical Conception of Nature*. London: Hachette.

Brown, S. M. 1959: Hobbes: The Taylor Thesis. *Philosophical Review*, 68.

Dewey, J. 1974: The Motivation of Hobbes's Political Philosophy. In R. Ross, H. Schneider and T. Waldman (eds) *Thomas Hobbes in His Times*. Minneapolis: University of Minnesota Press.

Gauthier, D. 1969: *The Logic of Leviathan: The Moral and Political Theory of Thomas Hobbes*. Oxford: Blackwell.

——1978: *The Logic of Leviathan*. Oxford: Clarendon Press.

Goldsmith, M. 1966: *Hobbes's Science of Politics*. New York: Columbia University Press.

Johnston, D. 1986: *The Rhetoric of Leviathan*. Princeton, NJ: Princeton University Press.

Levin, M. 1982: A Hobbesian Minimal State. *Philosophy and Public Affairs*, 11.

Lloyd, S. A. 1994: *Ideals as Interests in Hobbes's Leviathan*. Cambridge: Cambridge University Press.

McNeilly, F. S. 1968: *The Anatomy of Leviathan*. London: Macmillan.

Macpherson, C. B. 1962: *The Political Theory of Possessive Individualism*. Oxford: Clarendon Press.

Mintz, S. 1970: *The Hunting of Leviathan*. Cambridge: Cambridge University Press.

Nagel, T. 1959: Hobbes's Concept of Obligation. *Philosophical Review*, 68.

Oakeshott, M. 1975: *Hobbes on Civil Association*. Oxford: Blackwell.

Peters, R. 1956: *Hobbes*. Harmondsworth: Penguin Books.

Raphael, D. D. 1977: *Hobbes: Morals and Politics*. London: George Allen and Unwin.

Robertson, G. C. 1886: *Hobbes*. Edinburgh: W. Blackwood.

Rogers, G. A. J. and Ryan, A. (eds) 1988: *Perspectives on Thomas Hobbes*. Oxford: Clarendon Press.

Sacksteder, W. 1982: *Hobbes Studies (1879–1979)*. Bowling Green: Philosophy Documentation Center.

Shapin, S. and Schaffer, S. 1985: *Leviathan and the Air Pump*. Princeton, NJ: Princeton University Press.

Skinner, Q. 1966: The Ideological Context of Hobbes's Political Thought. *The Historical Journal*, 9.

——1996: *Reason and Rhetoric in the Philosophy of Hobbes*. Cambridge: Cambridge University Press.

Sommerville, J. 1992: *Thomas Hobbes: Political Ideas in Historical Context*. London: Macmillan.

Sorell, T. 1986: *Hobbes*. London: Routledge.

——(ed.) 1996: *The Cambridge Companion to Hobbes*. Cambridge: Cambridge University Press.

Taylor, A. E. 1938: The Ethical Doctrine of Hobbes. *Philosophy*, 13.

Thomas, K. 1965: The Social Origins of Hobbes's Political Thought. In K. C. Brown (ed.) *Hobbes Studies*. Oxford: Blackwell.

Tuck, R. 1989: *Hobbes*. Oxford: Oxford University Press.

Warrender, H. 1957: *The Political Philosophy of Hobbes*. Oxford: Clarendon Press.

Zarka, Y. 1987: *La Decision metaphysique de Hobbes – Conditions de la politique*. Paris: Vrin.

Discussion Questions

1   Can we understand Hobbes's contributions to abstract political theory without grasping his role in the political controversies of his time?

2   Why did Hobbes wish to deal scientifically with the questions of political philosophy? Did he succeed?

3   What follows from Hobbes's denial that human beings are made for political life?

4   How can we decide whether people are peaceable or by nature prone to conflict and violence?

5   Is life in the state of nature war?

6   Assess Hobbes's moral psychology in a state of nature and under a coercive government.

7   How does the prisoner's dilemma support Hobbes's claim that it is rational for us to leave the state of nature?

8   Did Hobbes have good reasons for asserting that even strong governments are vulnerable to rebellion and collapse?

9   Do science and a capacity for reasoning prevent the passions from determining an individual's behaviour?

10   Did Hobbes find in peace a single, uncontroversial good on which to base laws of nature?

11   In relinquishing rights in order to secure peace, do Hobbesean actors give up too much?

12   Can we accept Hobbes's account of how one or a few might become a sovereign power? How else might a sovereign power be established?

13   What is a state or commonwealth? Would a transfer of rights from individuals be sufficient to establish a state?

14   Are there circumstances other than renewed hazards of war which would justify rejecting the sovereign's laws?

15   Can we accept that the sovereign has no obligation to maintain the peace, but does so only as a matter of prudence?

16   Would subjects have a reasonable complaint against a sovereign whose laws left them safe, but hugely dissatisfied with their lot?

17   Do subjects act unjustly if they try to decide what constitutes peace and well-being and how they are to be obtained?

18   Was Hobbes right to see danger in a sovereign's failure to exercise rights?

19   Does it make better sense to say that the institution of the state is for peace or for happiness?

20   Can Hobbes's theory be altered to give a greater role to well-being?

21   Is the expectation of safety from the state as destabilizing as the expectation of happiness?

22   Does Hobbes, contrary to his intention, leave too much room for taking the law into one's own hands?

23   Can we avoid any commitment to immaterial things?

24   Can everything important about triangles be understood as coming from linguistic conventions about the word 'triangle'?

25   Does Hobbes succeed in establishing a materialist theory of the mind? Consider especially his account of the will.

29

Locke

R. S. WOOLHOUSE

John Locke is one of the most important European philosophers of the 'early modern' or immediate post-Cartesian period. Born in Somerset, England, in 1632 and educated in Oxford, he died in Essex in 1704. Besides being involved in Protestant politics and public affairs through his employer, Lord Ashley, later Earl of Shaftesbury, he found time to write on a wide variety of broadly philosophical topics: religion, education, economics, political philosophy. He is known primarily for his epistemological masterpiece, An Essay Concerning Human Understanding (published 1690), but also for his Two Treatises of Government (published 1690) and The Reasonableness of Christianity (published 1695). Readers will find it helpful to look at chapters on EPISTEMOLOGY (chapter 1), METAPHYSICS (chapter 2), POLITICAL AND SOCIAL PHILOSOPHY (chapter 8), PHILOSOPHY OF RELIGION (chapter 15), DESCARTES AND MALEBRANCHE (chapter 26), SPINOZA AND LEIBNIZ (chapter 27), HOBBES (chapter 28), BERKELEY (chapter 30) and HUME (chapter 31).

1   The *Essay Concerning Human Understanding*

Locke's *Essay* was begun some twenty years before it was published, and it went through various drafts. It embodies and draws together many of the thought-currents that were commonplace in the latter half of the seventeenth century: negative ones, such as anti-Aristotelianism, and positive ones, such as that of the mechanical philosophy and the new experimental philosophy. A hint of these themes is given in the 'Epistle to the Reader' of the *Essay*, where Locke contrasts the impediments to knowledge thrown up by SCHOLASTIC PHILOSOPHY (chapter 24), with the lasting monuments produced by contributors such as Robert Boyle (1627–91) and Isaac Newton (1642–1727), to 'the commonwealth of learning'. The chemist Robert Boyle was a founder member of the Royal Society of London for the Advancement of Experimental Knowledge, and the mathematician and theoretical physicist Isaac Newton was one of its first presidents. Locke was elected a Fellow to the Society in 1668, not long before he began work on the *Essay*.

Besides thus being a product of its century, the *Essay* had a great influence on the Enlightenment of the next century, whose RATIONALISM (chapters 26 and 27) wears the colours of the individualism which pervades both Locke's expression and his explicit doctrine. Running through the *Essay* is an insistence that opinions are carefully to be weighed, impartially considered and judged on their own merits, by individuals for themselves independently of what others say, particularly those in the majority or in authority.

Though there are METAPHYSICAL AND ONTOLOGICAL (chapter 2) elements in the *Essay*, its main concern is the EPISTEMOLOGICAL (chapter 1) one of the extent to which the human mind has the capacity to acquire knowledge. 'My purpose', Locke says, is 'to enquire into the original, certainty, and extent of human knowledge; together with the grounds and degrees of belief, opinion and assent' (Locke 1975: I, I, ii). It is plain, moreover, that one of Locke's concerns in setting out 'to take a survey of our own understanding, [to] examine our powers, and to see to what things they were adapted' (ibid.: I, I, vii) was to make a response to scepticism about the very possibility of knowledge. He speaks of the sceptical despair, and the tendency to disclaim all knowledge, which can arise when people realize that 'some things are not to be understood' (ibid.: I, I, vi): 'Men, extending their enquiries beyond their capacities . . . 'tis no wonder that they raise questions . . . which never coming to any clear resolution, are proper only to . . . confirm them at last in perfect scepticism' (ibid.: I, I, vii).

His interest in this matter was not purely theoretical. He had a practical interest in the human predicament in general, in the question of what kind of creature GOD (chapter 15) has seen fit to make us and in the question of how, as a consequence, we should arrange and manage our lives and thoughts. He wished, therefore, 'to find out those measures, whereby a rational creature put in that state, which man is in, in this world, may, and ought to govern his opinions, actions depending thereon' (ibid.: I, I, vi).

Locke's general position, as outlined at the very outset of his detailed investigation, is that there is some truth in scepticism: our knowledge does indeed have its limits. There are things of which we are completely ignorant, and there are things about which we can merely opine and believe. But this is no cause for despair for, so Locke believed, our capacities for knowledge are suited to our needs. 'How short soever . . . [people's] knowledge may come of an universal or perfect comprehension of whatsoever is, it yet secures their great concernments' (ibid.: I, I, v).

Yet what *are* our needs and concernments? In Locke's view we are put here by God in this world, with some hope of a life hereafter in another. Our needs are met, therefore, if we know enough for the everyday practicalities of life in this world and, in terms of our duties and obligations to each other and to God, for our salvation in the next. And, in Locke's view, these needs *are* met, or, with some reasonable effort on our part, *can* be met. People should be 'well satisfied with what God hath thought fit for them, since he hath . . . put within the reach of their discovery the comfortable provision for this life and the way that leads to a better' (ibid.: I, I, v).

This is not to say that God has actually given us what knowledge is necessary and useful; the whole of Book I of the *Essay* is devoted to rejecting roundly any suggestion that any of our knowledge or ideas is innate, and possessed from birth. It is rather that God, by equipping us with an understanding, has enabled us to acquire what is necessary; and, without striving against or complaining about its limits, we should make use of that ability. I do not, he says, 'disesteem, or dissuade the study of nature', but only 'that we should not be too forwardly possessed with the opinion, or expectation of knowledge where it is not to be had' (ibid.: IV, XII, xii). This ability, moreover, has been given to each one of us, and each one of us must autonomously make his own individual use of it. Locke is passionately dismissive of those who 'taking things upon trust, misimploy their power of assent, by lazily enslaving their minds to the dictates and dominion of others, in doctrines which it is their duty carefully to examine' (ibid.: I, IV, xxii).

Having rejected any suggestion of an innate endowment of knowledge, Locke sets out to show how its 'fountain' is experience. It is in experience that 'all our knowledge is founded; and from which it ultimately derives itself' (ibid.: II, I, ii). On account of statements like this, Locke has been characterized as an empiricist. (Indeed, his place in the history of philosophy has often been seen as the founder of the so-called school of British Empiricism, a school of which BERKELEY (chapter 30), HUME (chapter 31) and, later, MILL (chapter 35), are supposed to be members.)

But it is important to see that he does not hold that knowledge is immediately 'made out to us by our senses' (Locke 1990: 75) by themselves. What is immediately derived from experience are 'ideas', and ideas in themselves are not knowledge. They are, rather, 'the materials of knowledge' (Locke 1975: II, I, ii). Besides having SENSES (pp. 000–00) which give them ideas from experience, humans have reason and understanding too, and it is by their means that knowledge is *ultimately*, as Locke carefully says, *derived from* ideas: 'reason . . . by a right tracing of those ideas which it hath received from sense or sensation may come to . . . knowledge . . . which our senses could never have discovered' (Locke 1990: 75). The frequent classification of Locke as an empiricist must not be allowed to hide that he clearly holds that reason too is essentially involved in the ultimate derivation of knowledge.

What the classification as an empiricist does correctly capture is Locke's view that, prior to experience, the human mind is 'white paper, void of all characters, without any *ideas*' (Locke 1975: II, I, ii), and that 'all those sublime thoughts which tower above the clouds, and reach as high as heaven itself, take their rise and footing' (ibid.: II, I, xxiv) in experience. But how is our knowledge derived from this experiential material and how does our reason come to knowledge on its basis?

Locke takes knowledge to be 'the perception of the connexion and agreement, or disagreement and repugnancy of any of our ideas' (ibid.: IV, I, ii). His thought is that some ideas have necessary connections with others. Knowledge of the truths about these connections consists in the 'perception', the recognition by our understanding, of the connections. So, our knowledge that a triangle's three angles are equal to two right angles consists in our intellectual 'perception' of the connection between the idea of this equality and the idea of the triangle's three angles. We intellectually 'see' that 'that equality to two right ones, does necessarily agree to, and is inseparable from the three angles of a triangle' (ibid.: IV, I, ii).

Such connections are sometimes direct and immediate, sometimes indirect and mediated by connections with other ideas. When 'the mind perceives the agreement or disagreement of two ideas immediately by themselves, without the intervention of any *other*', we have *intuitive* knowledge, as when we 'perceive' directly 'that *three* are more than *two*, and equal to *one* and *two*' (ibid.: IV, II, i). When the connection is indirect, we have *demonstrative knowledge*, as when we cannot know that the angles of a triangle are equal to two right angles 'by an immediate view and comparing them', but need instead to 'find out some other angles, to which the three angles of a triangle have an equality; and finding those equal to two right ones, comes to know their equality to two right ones' (ibid.: IV, II, ii).

Besides *intuitive* and *demonstrative* knowledge Locke recognizes *sensitive* knowledge: knowledge of 'the existence of particular extended objects, by that perception and consciousness we have of the actual entrance of ideas from them' (ibid.: IV, II, xiv), that is, knowledge by our senses of what is now going on before our eyes. Sensitive knowledge seems not to fit Locke's official definition of knowledge: it does not pertain to some connection between two ideas, but to the present existence of something in the world corresponding to our present sensory perceptions or ideas.

These three 'degrees' of knowledge cut across a classification Locke proposes of the agreement or connection between ideas, the perception of which constitutes knowledge, into four 'sorts': '*Identity*, or *diversity*'; '*relation*'; '*co-existence*, or *necessary connection*'; and '*real existence*' (ibid.: IV, I, iii). These four sorts of connection give rise, respectively and roughly, to intuitively known propositions such as that '*white* is *white*' or that '*three* is more than *two*'; to intuitively or demonstratively known propositions such as those about geometrical figures; to propositions about the properties of substances such as gold; and to the propositions that make up sensitive knowledge.

It is plausible to think that our knowledge of the properties of triangles is based on our grasp, by means of our understanding, of connections between ideas. But what of our knowledge of the properties of silver (that it dissolves in nitric acid, for example), or of gold (that it does not so dissolve)? Here, as Locke freely says, there is no connection, discoverable by and intelligible to our understanding, between our ideas; here, he acknowledges, we are 'left only to observation and experiment' (ibid.: IV, III, xxviii). His position on this is, simply, that these are *not* cases of knowledge. They are cases of what he calls 'belief' or 'opinion' (ibid.: IV, XV, iii).

Knowledge and Belief

Locke's notion of KNOWLEDGE (chapter 1) as he defines it is related to the more recent one of *a priori* or 'conceptual knowledge'. His statement that 'in some of our ideas there are certain relations, habitudes, and connexions, so visibly included in the nature of the ideas themselves, that we cannot conceive them separable from them, by any power whatsoever' (ibid.: IV, III, xxix) parallels what has sometimes been said in this century about the *a priori* knowledge such as that which we have in mathematics. Similarly, his notion of 'belief', which is based on 'observation and experiment' because of 'a want of a discoverable connection between those ideas which we have' (ibid.: IV, III, xxviii), can be related to the notion of the *a posteriori* knowledge of the kind which we have, in a systematic form, in the empirical sciences. Yet just as Locke would call such empirical knowledge not 'knowledge' as such but rather 'belief', so he would not call an organized body of it, as in chemistry, 'a science'. Geometry and arithmetic are sciences for him, and (so he says) MORALITY (chapter 6) could become one, but 'natural philosophy is not capable of being made a science' (ibid.: IV, II, x).

Locke's view is, then, quite clearly, that there is a horizon and limit to our knowledge. Moreover, the question we might ask of him – namely, why this is so, why it is that in some cases there are intelligible and graspable connections between our ideas, and in other cases there are not – is one to which he gives a structured answer. Along the way to uncovering that structure we will review some other, but related, aspects of his philosophy too.

As a help to supporting his claim that all our ideas, all the materials of knowledge, stem from experience, Locke makes an appeal to a distinction between simple and complex ideas – an appeal which had been made earlier by Gassendi (1592–1655) and was to be made by some later philosophers, including Hume. So, for example, the ideas of a centaur, of God and of infinity (ideas of whose objects we can hardly have had experience) are *complex* ideas, whose component simples or parts must (perhaps as parts of other complexes) have come from experience. At the same time he divides complex ideas into various categories, of which *substances* and *modes* are two.

'Substances', says Locke, are ideas of 'things subsisting by themselves' (ibid.: II, XII, vi); they are, as is plain from his examples, ideas of naturally occurring kinds of material thing – just the kind of thing, in fact, about whose properties we form beliefs on the basis of experience and observation.

Locke distinguishes these properties that make up our idea of gold into 'primary and original', and 'secondary'. This famous distinction, which he shared with other early modern philosophers and scientists, such as Galileo (1564–1642), DESCARTES (chapter 26) and Boyle, is made against the background of corpuscularianism – a theory common in the seventeenth century, but one derived from the classical Greek atomists, Democritus (*c*.460–*c*.370 BC) and Epicurus (341–270 BC), who held that matter is composed of tiny, imperceptible particles. Primary qualities are qualities that belong not only to substances such as gold, but also to the insensible corpuscles which make them up. Thus, a piece of gold is solid, has extension and shape, and can be moved; and, according to the corpuscular theory, its corpuscles have these qualities too. Secondary qualities, such as colour and taste, belong to a piece of gold but not to its component corpuscles. It is because these secondary qualities were supposed to arise from the arrangement of the solid, shaped and movable corpuscles which constitute gold, that is, from the primary or 'original' (originating) qualities of the parts, that they were not to be attributed to the corpuscles themselves.

A further point to be noted, and one which has led to continuing controversy, is that Locke says about our complex ideas of substances that their main component of the complex is 'the supposed, or confused idea of substance', something which he also calls 'substratum' or 'pure substance in general' (ibid.: II, XXIII, ii). Locke is sometimes taken to be saying here that material things are more than 'bundles of coexisting properties' (as Bertrand RUSSELL (chapter 37) later held), but have, in addition to their properties, a propertyless 'substratum' which 'supports' their properties. According to another interpretation, however, Locke is not interested in abstract questions about the difference between 'things' and 'properties' or in the ontology underlying the distinction between SUBJECT AND PREDICATE (pp. 93–6). Rather, his talk of a 'substratum' supporting properties is a reference not to some featureless I-know-not-what, but to matter as understood by the corpuscular theory, and in terms of which the properties of a substance are to be explained.

Our complex idea of gold, which we have derived from experience, comes to be that for which the word 'gold' stands – Locke speaks of it as 'nothing but that abstract idea to which the name is annexed' (ibid.: III, VI, ii), and, as such, he refers to it as a 'nominal essence'. But this nominal essence of gold, composed as it is from various qualities which experience and observation have shown us go together in the material stuff we call 'gold', is different from what Locke calls its 'real essence'. This latter is that 'upon which depends this nominal essence, and all the properties of that sort' (ibid.: III, VI, ii); it is that 'on which all the properties of the species depend, and from which alone they all flow' (ibid.: III, V, xiv). In the case of substances it is, in short, that arrangement of primary-qualitied imperceptible corpuscles on which depend the primary and secondary qualities of the substance as we experience it. Different material substances have different observable qualities because there are differences in the shape, size, arrangement and motion of the 'insensible corpuscules' (ibid.: IV, III, xxv) which make up their real essences or real constitutions.

This account of a substance's real essence in terms of the corpuscular theory of matter is one of the anti-Aristotelian features of the *Essay* which were mentioned earlier. 'Concerning the real essences of corporeal substances', he says, 'there are . . . two opinions'. His, the 'more rational', takes it that substances 'have a real, but unknown constitution of the insensible parts, from which flow those sensible qualities, which serve us to distinguish them one from another'. The other belongs to the hylomorphic theory of the Aristotelians according to which a material substance is a composite of 'form' (*morphe*) and 'matter' (*hyle*). Accordingly, it supposes 'a certain number of forms or moulds, wherein all natural things, that exist, are cast, and do equally partake' (ibid.: III, III, xvii). Like Robert Boyle, the Royal Society chemist – who made the point in his book *The Origin of Forms and Qualities* (published 1666) – Locke and other 'modern' philosophers of the seventeenth century felt that this account of real essences had 'very much perplexed the knowledge of natural things' (Locke 1975: III, III, xvii). Material substances were better understood, they thought, in terms of another classical Greek theory, that of atomism.

Now the reason why natural philosophy, the study of substances such as gold or lead, is 'incapable of being made a science' is simply that the nominal essence of those substances, our ideas of them, are not ideas of their real essences; even supposing that the corpuscular theory is true, we do not know the actual details of the corpuscular constitution of any substance. As a consequence, our ideas or nominal essences of the various substances relate instead to some collection of the properties which are supposed to flow from and depend on their real essences. Now though, it may be supposed, gold's malleability is necessarily connected with its real, atomic constitution; because our idea of gold is not of that constitution, there is no necessary connection between gold's malleability and *our* idea of gold. Natural philosophy is not capable of being made a science because we do not have the right ideas; we do not have knowledge of the corpuscular details of the real essences of the substances which it studies.

The case with GEOMETRY (chapter 11) and the modes it studies is much the same, but different in at least one very important respect. Like substances, geometrical figures, such as the triangle, have a real essence too, a real essence on which their properties depend. Of course, since the triangle is not a material thing but rather a shape, or a way in which material things may be arranged, its real essence is not a corpuscular constitution or arrangement of atomic particles. However, just as gold *is*, in its real essence, atomic particles arranged in a certain way (the details of which are unknown to us), a triangle *is*, quite obviously, 'a figure of three lines enclosing a space'. This is, as Locke says, 'not only the abstract idea to which the general name is annexed' (ibid.: III, III, xviii), not only the nominal essence of triangularity and what a triangle is to us, but also the real essence, what a triangle really is: it is 'the very *essentia*, or being, of the thing it self, that foundation from which all its properties flow, and to which they are all inseparably annexed' (ibid.: III, III, xviii).

So the properties of a triangle, such as its having external angles equal to its internal opposites, flow from, and so are necessarily connected with, its real essence, and our idea of the triangle is an idea of its real essence. It follows that there *is* a necessary connection, in this case, between our idea of a triangle and its various properties. The following passage points up this contrast between the way our knowledge is limited in natural philosophy, due to a want of the relevant ideas, and the way it is not limited in this way in geometry:

> Substances afford matter of very little general knowledge; and the bare contemplation of their abstract ideas, will carry us but a very little way in the search of truth and certainty . . . Experience here must teach me, what reason cannot: and it is by trying alone, that I can certainly know, what other qualities co-exist with those of my complex idea, *v.g.* whether that yellow, heavy, fusible, body, I call gold, be malleable, or no; which experience . . . makes me not certain, that it is so, in all or any other yellow, heavy, fusible bodies, but that which I have tried . . . Because the other properties of such bodies, depending not on these, but on that unknown real essence, on which these also depend, we cannot by them discover the rest. (Ibid.: IV, XII, ix)

Our knowledge in natural philosophy is, therefore, severely limited by the nature of our ideas, by the fact that they are not ideas of the relevant real essences. But geometry and mathematics are not the only areas where it is not subject to similar limits. On the grounds that the ideas of morality are, like those of mathematics, modes, whose real essences we might come to know, Locke suggests the possibility of 'plac[ing] morality amongst the sciences capable of demonstration: wherein I doubt not, but from self-evident propositions, by necessary consequences, as incontestable as those in mathematics, the measures of right and wrong might be made out' (ibid.: IV, III, xviii).

The 'moral science' Locke envisages would have as one of its bases the idea of God, 'infinite in power, goodness, and wisdom' (ibid.: IV, III, xviii), whose dictates are 'the only true touchstone of moral rectitude' (ibid.: II, XXVII, viii). It would have as another the idea of ourselves as dependent creatures of God who have sufficient understanding and rationality to understand his will: from this we 'as certainly know that man is to honour, fear and obey God, as . . . that three, four, and seven, are less than fifteen' (ibid.: IV, XIII, iii). Though not supposing this systematic moral science to be more than a possibility yet to be realized, Locke nevertheless thought that we had already reasoned our way to some items of moral knowledge. He makes clear, however, particularly in the *Reasonableness of Christianity*, that what he calls reason's 'great and proper business of morality' (Locke 1873: 140) is not an easy one. So those who are immersed in the necessities of everyday life, and have neither the time nor ability to uncover moral truths by reason can find it in the gospels. The 'law which God has set to the actions of men . . . [is] promulgated to them by the light of nature [reason], or the voice of Revelation [the gospels]' (Locke 1975: II, XXVIII, viii).

But even though morality can be shown to us by REVELATION (pp. 622–4) and without recourse to reason, the voice of revelation is still answerable to the light of nature. For one thing, we need to be assured that the voice is genuine, and reason must be the judge of this. Moreover, we cannot be as certain of this as we are of knowledge which is based directly on the use of our own reason. 'The knowledge, we have, that this revelation came at first from God, can never be so sure, as the knowledge we have from the clear and distinct perception of the agreement, or disagreement of our own ideas' (ibid.: IV, XVIII, iv).

As we have seen, it is a God-given duty carefully to examine any proposition before autonomously giving or withholding our individual assent: it 'would be to subvert the principles, and foundations of all knowledge . . . [if] what we certainly know, give way to what we may possibly be mistaken in' (ibid.: IV, XVIII, v).

Reason is superior over revelation in another way too. Though some things are discoverable only by revelation, any knowledge that is necessary for salvation can be reached by our natural faculties. God has 'given all mankind so sufficient a light of reason, that they to whom this written word [the Bible] never came, could not (whenever they set themselves to search) either doubt of the being of a God, or of the obedience due to Him' (ibid.: III, IX, xxiii).

Personal Identity

In the course of reaching conclusions about the origin and limits of knowledge, Locke had occasion to concern himself with topics which are of philosophical interest in themselves. One of these is the question of identity, which includes, more specifically, the question of personal identity: what are the criteria by which a person at one time is numerically the *same person* as a person at another time? Here he makes the point, taken up by later writers, that there is a relativity about identity. When we point and ask whether 'this' is what was here before, it matters what kind of thing 'this' is meant to be. If 'this' is meant as a mass of matter then it is what was before so long as it consists of the same material particles; but if it is meant as a living body then its consisting of the same particles does not matter and the case is different. 'A colt grown up to a horse, sometimes fat, sometimes lean, is all the while the same horse: though . . . there may be a manifest change of the parts' (ibid.: II, XXVII, iii). So, when we think about personal identity, we need to be clear about a distinction between two things which 'the ordinary way of speaking runs together' – the idea of 'man', and the idea of 'person'. As with any other animal, the identity of a man consists 'in nothing but a participation of the same continued life, by constantly fleeting particles of matter, in succession vitally united to the same organized body' (ibid.: II, XXVII, vi). But the idea of a person is not that of a living body of a certain kind. A person is a 'thinking, intelligent being, that has reason and reflection' (ibid.: II, XXVII, ix) and such a being 'will be the same self as far as the same consciousness can extend to actions past or to come' (ibid.: II, XXVII, x). Locke is at pains to argue that this continuity of self-consciousness does not necessarily involve the continuity of some immaterial substance, in the way that Descartes had held. For all we know, says Locke, consciousness and thought may be powers which can be possessed by 'systems of matter fitly disposed' (ibid.: IV, III, vi); and even if this is not so the question of the identity of person is not the same as the question of the identity of *an immaterial substance*. For just as the identity of a horse can be preserved through changes of matter, and depends not on the identity of a continued material substance but on 'the unity of one continued life' (ibid.: IV, XXVII, x), so the identity of a person does not depend on the continuity of an immaterial substance. The unity of one continued consciousness does not depend on its being 'annexed only to one individual substance, [and not] . . . continued in a succession of several substances' (ibid.: II, XXVII, x). For Locke, then, personal identity consists in an identity of consciousness, and not in the identity of some substance whose essence it is to be conscious.

2 Locke's Political Philosophy

Locke's anonymous *Treatises of Government*, which contain his political philosophy, were published in the same year as his *Essay*, and two years after the Glorious Revolution in which William of Orange replaced James II on the English throne. But their composition dates from some ten years earlier, and to the time of the Exclusion crisis during which Lord Shaftesbury, Locke's patron, sought, with others, to exclude James from succession to the throne. The *Treatises* supported their arguments for government by consent, and for the right to religious dissent.

The *First Treatise* contains criticism of theories of absolute monarchy, and of the divine right of kings, theories for which Robert Filmer (*c.*1588–1653) had argued in his *Patriarchia* (published 1680). Locke found quite unworkable the theory that Adam had been given absolute and total political authority by God, authority which was then passed on to his heirs. The theory cannot show of any particular ruler that he is a genuine heir to Adam's original authority, and so it is incapable of justifying any actual political authority.

In the *Second Treatise* Locke sought some other, and more workable, foundation for political authority. Subjects do have a duty to God to obey their ruler, he did not deny. But rulers themselves correspondingly have duties to their subjects. Rulers are not absolute, and if their commands do not deserve obedience then resistance to them might be justified.

Locke began with the idea of families and informal groups of people living in a STATE OF NATURE (p. 574). In such a natural state there are no political authorities and people's duties stem directly from God; they are duties not to 'harm another in his life . . . liberty . . . or goods' (Locke 1960: II, §6). But what makes the 'goods', to which a person has a right, *his* goods in the first place? How, in the state of nature, can it come about that a person has a *right* to the land he cultivates? According to Filmer, just as absolute political authority is passed down from Adam to his heirs, so is possession of the earth and its fruits. According to Locke's labour theory of property, by contrast, just as all men were made free and equal in God's eyes, with no one directly set in power over them, so God gave the earth and its fruits to all men equally. Clearly it follows from this that Adam and his heirs could not be alone in having private property, but this is not because *no one* has private property and because there is worldwide communal ownership. The land someone cultivates, and its fruits and crops, are his, Locke explains, because each individual has a God-given right to his own life and labour, and consequently, an individual right to what he 'mixes' that labour with and produces by it. 'Whatsoever then, he removes out of the state that nature hath provided, and left it in, he hath mixed his labour with, and joined to it something that is his own, and thereby makes it his property' (ibid.: II, §27).

The rights and duties, concerning life, liberty and possessions, which people have in the state of nature, may not necessarily be respected and obeyed. People may lack the power to defend their rights, or go too far in their defence. They therefore agree to come out of the state of nature and to form POLITICAL SOCIETY (chapter 8). They agree to unite, and to 'enter into society to make one people, one body politic, under one supreme government' (ibid.: II, §89). They agree to empower an authority over them; they 'set up a judge on earth with authority to determine all the controversies and redress the injuries that may happen to any member of the commonwealth' (ibid.: II, §89). But this authority into whose hands people put power is not, in Locke's analysis of civil society, absolute. He is answerable to 'the will and determination of the majority' (ibid.: II, §96). The views and wishes of the majority are a court of appeal against the decisions of the ruling authority. Lockean political society is not only begun by 'the consent of any number of freemen capable of a majority' (ibid.: II, §99), it is continued and sustained by it too. People under an absolute authority (whether divinely established as in Filmer's view, or set up, as in the equally absolutist account of HOBBES (chapter 28) by the people) are, for Locke, not in a civil society; they are effectively still in a state of nature.

Of course, unlike those who for some time have been in a state of nature, most people are simply born into an already existing civil society. It is not by any choice of theirs that they come under its laws and authority; they entered into no agreement to unite and set up the authority. But just as continuing consent is what underwrites an authority as well as what created it, so Locke distinguishes between tacit and explicit consent. A person may not choose where to be born, and so whose authority to be subject to; but by remaining there he gives his tacit consent.

From the idea that it is the 'will and determination of the majority' (ibid.: II, §96) that is the ultimate basis of political authority, there follows the possibility of legitimate resistance to that authority, a possibility which does not follow from Filmer's divine right theory: 'The community perpetually retains a supreme power of saving themselves from . . . their legislators, whenever they shall be so foolish, or so wicked, as to lay and carry on designs against [their] liberties and properties' (ibid.: II, §149). Just as it is in the will of the people that power resides, so it is that 'the People shall be Judge' (ibid.: II, §240) of when that power should be used.

Further Reading

James Gibson's *Locke's Theory of Knowledge* (1917) and R. I. Aaron's *John Locke* (1937) are two valuable classic accounts of Locke's epistemological thought. There are more recent general accounts by Dunn (1984), Mabbot (1973), Woolhouse (1983) and Yolton (1985). More detailed and specialized (whether historically or philosophically) treatments can be found in Ayers (1992), Bennett (1971), Mackie (1976), Woolhouse (1971) and Yolton (1970). Ashcraft (1987) and Dunn (1969) deal specifically with Locke's political philosophy, Colman (1983) with his moral philosophy, and Ashcraft (1969) and Cragg (1950) with his philosophy of religion. The last full-length biography of Locke is that of Cranston (1957). An exhaustive list of books and articles on Locke is provided by Hall and Woolhouse (1983).

References

Locke

Locke, John 1873 [1695]: *The Reasonableness of Christianity*. Vol. 7 of *The Works of John Locke*. London.

——1960 [1690]: *Two Treatises of Government* (edited by Peter Laslett). Cambridge: Cambridge University Press.

——1975 [1690]: *Essay Concerning Human Understanding* (edited by P. H. Nidditch). Oxford: Clarendon Press.

——1990 [1671]: *Draft A of An Essay Concerning Human Understanding* (edited by Peter H. Nidditch and G. A. J. Rogers). Oxford: Clarendon Press.

Other writers

Aaron, R. I. 1937: *John Locke*. Oxford: Clarendon Press.

Alexander, P. 1985: *Ideas, Qualities and Corpuscles: Locke and Boyle on the External World*. Cambridge: Cambridge University Press.

Ashcraft, R. 1969: Faith and Knowledge in Locke's Philosophy. In J. W. Yolton (ed.) *John Locke: Problems and Perspectives*. Cambridge: Cambridge University Press.

——1987: *Locke's Two Treatises of Government*. London: Allen and Unwin.

Ayers, M. 1992: *Locke*, 2 vols. London: Routledge and Kegan Paul.

Bennett, J. 1971: *Locke, Berkeley, Hume: Central Themes*. Oxford: Oxford University Press.

Chappell, V. 1994: *The Cambridge Companion to Locke*. Cambridge: Cambridge University Press.

Colman, J. 1983: *John Locke's Moral Philosophy*. Edinburgh: Edinburgh University Press.

Cragg, G. R. 1950: The Religious Significance of John Locke. In G. R. Cragg (ed.) *From Puritanism to the Age of Reason*. Cambridge: Cambridge University Press.

Cranston, M. 1957: *John Locke: A Biography*. London: Longmans.

Dunn, J. 1969: *The Political Thought of John Locke*. Cambridge: Cambridge University Press.

——1984: *Locke*. Oxford: Oxford University Press.

Gibson, J. 1917: *Locke's Theory of Knowledge and its Historical Relations*. Cambridge: Cambridge University Press.

Hall, R. and Woolhouse, R. 1983: *80 Years of Locke Scholarship: A Bibliographical Guide*. Edinburgh: Edinburgh University Press.

Mabbot, J. D. 1973: *John Locke*. London: Macmillan.

Mackie, J. L. 1976: *Problems from Locke*. Oxford: Clarendon Press.

Martin, C. B. and Armstrong, D. M. (eds) 1968: *Locke and Berkeley: A Collection of Critical Essays*. London: Macmillan.

Tipton, I. (ed.) 1977: *Locke on Human Understanding: Selected Essays*. Oxford: Oxford University Press.

Woolhouse, R. S. 1971: *Locke's Philosophy of Science and Knowledge*. Oxford: Blackwell.

——1983: *Locke*. Brighton: Harvester.

Yolton, J. W. 1970: *Locke and the Compass of Human Understanding*. Cambridge: Cambridge University Press.

——1985: *Locke: An Introduction*. Oxford: Blackwell.

Discussion Questions

1 Did the mechanical philosophy and the experimental philosophy of the seventeenth century improve upon Aristotelian philosophy?

2 Was Locke's method well suited to his project of surveying our understanding?

3 If our knowledge has limits, how can we determine what they are?

4 Is our knowledge best understood as answering theoretical demands or as answering the practical needs of everyday life?

5 How is knowledge related to experience?

6 To what extent was Locke an 'empiricist'?

7 What does Locke mean by 'idea'?

8 Must senses, reason and understanding all be involved in our explanation of human knowledge?

9   Prior to experience, is the mind a 'white paper, void of all characters, without any ideas'?

10   How adequate is an account of knowledge in terms of perceiving the connection or disagreement of ideas?

11   Was Locke justified in thinking that empirical science cannot yield knowledge?

12   How can we tell when an idea is simple?

13   Should we accept the distinction between primary and secondary qualities?

14   Was Locke correct in claiming that our ideas of physical things are not ideas of their real essences?

15   What, for Locke, is the role of real essences in geometrical knowledge?

16   Can morality be a science?

17   Is reason superior to revelation?

18   Are questions of identity relative to the kinds to which the things asked about belong? What are the implications of your answer for questions of personal identity?

19   What problems might arise for the claim that personal identity consists in the continuity of consciousness? What other views are worth considering?

20   Would being an heir to original legitimate authority justify one in holding current political authority?

21   What role does the 'state of nature' play in Locke's political thought? Would it matter if a rival view of the state of nature turned out to be more accurate? Or if there never was a state of nature?

22   How can something be the property of a person?

23   What is civil society? What is the ultimate basis of authority in such a society? What limits the authority of its rulers?

24   Is 'tacit consent' consent at all?

30

Berkeley

HOWARD ROBINSON

As a critic of Locke and a precursor of Hume, Berkeley offered a profoundly original perspective on central questions in epistemology and metaphysics. This chapter, informed by recent critical discussion of Berkeley's idealism, focuses on his immaterialism: his claim that the physical world and its contents cannot be understood as existing independent of the mind. Berkeley's discussion of abstract ideas, which is intimately related to his immaterialism, is examined along with other important supporting arguments. The chapter ends with an exploration of two features completing the Berkelian system, namely his doctrine of spirits and the role he assigned God in explaining our experience.

In sections 1–4 of this chapter I consider two groups of arguments that Berkeley (1685–1753) used in his attempt to prove idealism.

With regard to the first group, after investigating Berkeley's attack on abstract ideas, I conclude that a revised version of the argument shows that we can have no positive conception of matter. This is strengthened by a proof that no sensible quality – nor, probably, anything analogous to a sensible quality – could be mind-independent. As mind-independent matter would have to be more than an empty structure, and as only something like a sensible quality could fill such a structure, the concept of mind-independent matter is defective.

With regard to the second group, Berkeley's overstrong implication that, because my thought is in my mind, so is its object, can be reformed to the weaker claim that, because all our conceiving of objects is of them as they are from viewpoints, it follows that we conceive of them, not as they are 'in themselves' but as they are to a potential perceiver. I raise doubts about whether this is correct, but augment it with Berkeley's argument that size is perception-dependent, for bodies cannot be mind-independent if their dimensions are not. In section 5 I briefly discuss Berkeley's use of his doctrine of spirit and his invocation of God to explain experience in the absence of a mind-independent world.

1 Introduction: Berkeley, Common Sense and the 'New Philosophy'

Common sense is usually thought to affirm the following two principles:

(CS1)   In normal visual and tactile experience we are directly aware of physical objects.

(CS2) The existence of physical objects does not depend on, nor consist in, their being perceived: they are mind-independent.

The 'new philosophy' of the seventeenth century was taken by many philosophers and scientists as refuting the first of these principles: the objects of our awareness are not objects in the external world. This had to be so because objects in the external world do not themselves possess secondary qualities in the form in which those qualities are perceived. The external physical world is colourless, odourless and silent; secondary qualities in the form we know them are *ideas in the mind*. All we are aware of are our ideas; the physical world, which is a great machine composed of insensible atoms, lies concealed behind the veil of perception that is constituted by those ideas.

Berkeley accepted the arguments that were supposed to show that we could not be directly aware of a mind-independent physical world. Instead of concluding, like his more conventional contemporaries, that we are not directly aware of the physical world, he concluded that the physical world is not mind-independent: he chose, that is, to save CS1 rather than CS2. He had two motives for this preference. Firstly, he thought that putting the physical world behind the 'veil of perception' opened the way to SCEPTICAL DOUBT (p. 50) about its existence; secondly, he feared that the mechanistic conception of the world behind the veil favoured by the new science, smacked of a materialist and, therefore, an atheist metaphysic (Berkeley 1713).

Berkeley's idealistic theory of the physical world is expressed in the maxim that *esse est percipi* – to be is to be perceived. This famous maxim is equivalent to the affirmation of CS1 without CS2, for it is the affirmation that the physical world is that of which we are directly aware, together with the denial that it is mind-independent. By making the physical world directly accessible to experience, this strategy seems to avoid the threat of scepticism, and by making the world mental it avoids materialism. Of course, if CS1 and CS2 are both parts of common sense, Berkeley, in rejecting CS2, sets himself against common sense. According to Berkeley, however, the claim that the physical is mind-independent is not truly a part of common sense, for he believes that it rests on a confusion between the truth that the physical world is more than the experience of any given individual and hence independent of any given mind, and the falsehood that it transcends all the experiences that might be had of it by all minds taken together (Berkeley 1713: III, 230–1). According to Berkeley, this latter kind of mind-independence is not merely *not* common sense, it is strictly unintelligible. So it is not just that when faced with an exclusive choice between accepting the direct perceivability of the physical world and accepting its mind-independence, he prefers the former; rather, he denies the intelligibility of a fully mind-independent physical existence.

Berkeley has a variety of arguments against the possibility of mind-independent or unperceived objects. My strategy in this chapter is to examine these arguments sympathetically, which involves development as well as exposition. I shall organize Berkeley's more or less independent arguments so that they form two groups, each group constituting an extended line of argument. One line of argument starts from Berkeley's attack on abstract ideas. By reforming that attack, and augmenting it with a cluster of arguments centring on the maxim that 'nothing can be like an idea but an idea', we can find in Berkeley a plausible case for believing that we can form no contentful conception of MATTER (pp. 647–8). The other group of arguments starts from the claim that we cannot conceive of unperceived objects; by buttressing this with his arguments about the sense-dependence of size, we can develop reasons for thinking that all the supposedly objective properties of the external world are really perception-relative.

2   Abstract Ideas, Relative Ideas and Immaterialism

HUME (chapter 31) remarked that Berkeley's dismissal of abstract ideas was 'one of the greatest and most valuable discoveries that has been made of late years in the republic of letters' (Hume 1739: Bk I, VII). Berkeley himself regarded his attack on abstract ideas as a vital component in the argument for immaterialism, for '[i]f we thoroughly examine [the belief in unperceived objects] it will, perhaps, be found at bottom to depend on the doctrine of abstract ideas' (Berkeley 1710: §5). But many philosophers have been puzzled as to the exact connection between abstraction and matter, and tend to leave it on the sidelines when expounding Berkeley's arguments for idealism. It will be helpful, therefore, to look carefully at what the attack on abstraction is about.

Berkeley's argument has an immediate target and a remote target. The immediate target is LOCKE's (chapter 29) account of the ideas of determinable or generic things, such as red as opposed to any particular shade of red, for example, or triangle as opposed to an isosceles triangle or a right-angled triangle. The remote target is any doctrine of concepts that allows that they are, in some sense, intrinsically universal: he is, that is, trying to carry to completion the idea that *everything*, whether outside the mind or within it, is particular, and thereby to free his philosophy of the perennial problem of universals, which, in some form or other, had been the heart of most scholastic metaphysics. According to this ambitious theory, not only are there no forms, species or universals in the world itself, but even concepts are, in themselves, purely particular. Locke, too, believed in particularism, but, according to Berkeley, he adopted an incoherent form of it. The particularist programme faces a dilemma, expressed by Locke and quoted by Berkeley: 'Since all things that exist are only particulars, how come we by general terms?' (Locke 1689: III, III, vi; quoted in Berkeley 1710: §11). How can a concept, for example the concept of red, which by definition is something that covers many things, simply be a particular, rather than being universal? Even if one can manage to avoid realism about universals in things, surely one must be a conceptualist, that is, a realist about universality in the mind, in the concepts through which we think? Locke gives the answer: 'Words become general by being made the signs of general ideas'. Locke grouped all mental contents, including concepts, together as *ideas* and treated ideas as mental images (see Yolton 1984 and Ayers 1991: I, 60–9 for, respectively, an attack on this imagist interpretation and a defence of it). Taken in a literal way as a kind of mental picture, a mental image is pretty clearly a particular, but how can it have as its content a generic or determinable concept such as *red* or *triangle*? According to Berkeley, Locke's answer is to say that this kind of image has an indefiniteness to it:

> does it not require some pains and skill to form the general idea of a triangle . . . for it must be neither oblique nor rectangle, neither equilateral, equicrural, nor scalenon, but *all and none* of these at once. In effect, it is something imperfect that cannot exist, an idea wherein

some parts of several different and *inconsistent* ideas are put together. (Locke 1689: IV, VII, ix; quoted in Berkeley 1710: §13)

So there is an indefiniteness which is expressed in two different ways. On the one hand the image is triangular without being scalene or equilateral; on the other hand it is all of these incompatible properties at once, because it includes them all. In this way one has a particular object – the image – which both leaves out all specific forms, and is a superimposition of the specific forms: in these ways it is deemed to encompass just the right generality of things. Berkeley's objection is that one can have neither indeterminate particulars, lacking a specific form, nor contradictory ones, containing incompatible forms. Locke's attempt to combine imagism with intrinsic generality, therefore, fails.

Many commentators have argued that Berkeley misinterprets Locke's account of abstraction, but the exegetical question is not very important. The theory of generality ascribed to Locke by those who think Berkeley misinterprets him is the theory Berkeley himself adopts; and, although some philosophers allow that images can be genuinely vague to some extent, it is generally agreed that they cannot be vague to the extent and in the way that the theory attributed to Locke requires. So everyone agrees that the view Berkeley attacks is false: they also agree that the account he wishes to replace it with is the only other one available to the imagist. The real issue, therefore, is whether Berkeley's own theory is adequate.

Berkeley's theory of generality has two parts. The central claim is that 'an idea, which considered in itself is particular, becomes general, by being made to represent or stand for all other particular ideas of the same sort' (Berkeley 1710: §12). So an entirely particular image of a triangle, for example, is taken as standing for triangles as a whole. This account explains the meaning of an idea in terms external to it – that is, by making it consist in the idea's relations to other ideas. But the meaning of the ideas we think is something we experience in our thinking – we know that in a certain act of thinking we mean 'triangle'. This subjective element in general ideas Berkeley explains by the second part of his account, which is the doctrine of *selective attention* or *partial consideration*:

> a man may consider a figure merely as triangular, without attending to the particular qualities of the angles or relations of the sides . . . In like manner we may consider Peter so far forth as man, or so far forth as animal, without framing the forementioned abstract idea, either of man or of animal, in as much as that all that is perceived is not considered. (Berkeley 1710: §16)

So the significance of a particular idea consists in the way it represents other particulars and in the way a feature of it can be grasped while neglecting the rest.

The connection between this account of thought and idealism is quite straightforward and can be stated in a simple argument.

1 Ideas are images. Therefore,
2 abstract ideas would be abstract images.
3 There are no abstract images. Therefore,

4   there are no abstract ideas.
5   If there were an idea of matter – or of unperceived existence or mind-independent existence – it would be an abstract idea. Therefore,
6   there is no idea of matter – nor of unperceived existence nor mind-independence.

(1) asserts Berkeley's imagism; (2) follows by simple logic; (3) is the core of the argument against Locke's supposed position; (4) follows from (2) and (3) by simple logic (namely, *modus tollens*). The crucial claim is in (5). We have seen that, for Berkeley, a non-abstract idea is one that can be identified with an image or an aspect of an image. It is difficult to see how the ideas of matter, unperceivedness or mind-independence could be actual, realized features of images. Images can occur in dreams and hallucinations, so they cannot actually possess the properties of materiality, unperceivedness or mind-independence, for such images are purely mental objects of awareness. (6) follows from (4) and (5), also by *modus tollens*.

Objections to Berkeley's Imagism

The argument is valid but unsound because Berkeley's account of generality – explained above and enshrined in (1) – is subject to two massive objections. Firstly, he presents no account of what he means by 'representing' or 'standing for'. This is not merely a gap in the argument; it suggests a complete failure to understand the problem. The problem of universals, classically referred to as the problem of the 'one over the many', is essentially about what is involved in something comprehending or standing for many instances. To invoke as an unexplained notion the idea of *standing for* is, therefore, to name the problem, not to propose a solution to it. The second feature of Berkeley's theory is open to an additional objection. What, within Berkeley's particularist ONTOLOGY (chapter 2), is it to attend to an aspect of an idea? Attending might seem to be a purely sensory thing, analogous to focusing a camera, but, because the focusing is on an *aspect*, not a *region*, of the image, the focusing is a conceptual one. One cannot focus on the triangularity of a triangle – as opposed to its colour or size, for example – except by deploying the concept 'triangle'. Selective attention is of no help in explaining how the concept could be no more than the image, for the selection in question is no more than bringing a certain concept to bear on the image. If one is seeking an account of concepts, the notion of *selective attention* will not help, any more than will the notion of 'standing for'.

Given the inadequacy of Berkeley's imagism, can anything be saved of the argument for immaterialism that rests upon it? To see that something can, we must consider the distinction between positive and relative ideas, which Berkeley adopted from Locke (Locke 1689: II, XXIII, iii; Berkeley 1710: §80; and for a full contemporary discussion see Flage 1987: 134–42). To have a positive idea of something is to know what it is like in itself – to know its intrinsic nature. To have a relative idea of something is not to know its intrinsic nature, but only that it stands in some specific relation to something of which we have a positive idea. Divested of imagism and of the misconceived attempts to solve the problem of universals by giving a particularist analysis of concepts, Berkeley's arguments can be used to show that we do not have a positive idea of matter or of unperceived or mind-independent existence. This would be done by replacing the hopeless theory that ideas are images with the more plausible claim that the contents of positive ideas can be represented in images. This is not a theory about what ideas or concepts are in themselves, but a far more modest theory about the conditions under which we can know what *that of which it is a concept or idea* is like in itself. The claim is that, as far as aspects of the empirical world are concerned, we can only know what they are like in themselves if they can feature as aspects of sensory ideas. This is the complement of the claim often expressed by saying that our theoretical or purely scientific knowledge of the world is *topic-neutral*, meaning that it tells us about the structural, relational and causal properties of things, but not about their intrinsic or qualitative natures: only direct sensory contact will give you the latter (Lockwood 1989). This then generates a new argument:

7   Any feature of the physical world of which we can have a positive idea can be specifically represented in a sensory idea; that is, in an image. Therefore,

8   if we have a positive idea of matter – or unperceived existence or mind-independence – then it can be specifically represented in an image.

9   Matter – or unperceived existence or mind-independence – cannot be specifically represented in an image. Therefore,

10   we do not have a positive idea of matter – or unperceived existence or mind-independence.

I have already suggested the plausibility of (7), and (8) is merely an instantiation of (7). The arguments for (9) are the same as those for (5), for there is no feature of an image which just is, or is dedicated to the representation of, materiality or unperceivedness or extra-mentality: any feature of an image must be a sensible feature of it and so must represent something more specific and sensible than materiality, unperceivedness or extra-mentality.

There are in fact two different questions in the air here. Firstly, what sort of properties is mind-independent matter supposed to possess? Secondly, what kinds of ideas (if they are real ideas at all) are the ideas of *materiality, unperceived existence* and *mind-independence*? I have argued that we cannot have a positive idea of these latter, because we cannot experience or image the properties in question. Berkeley considers the suggestion that we have a relative idea of materiality – that is, of that component in matter which is more than its qualities.

We may note that the question of the intelligibility of mind-independence and of unperceived existence is more complicated than the question of matter. Hume in his *tour de force* 'On scepticism with regard to the senses' (Hume 1739: I, IV, ii) showed how we come, through a series of mistakes, to attach sense to the former two, which is consistent with deriving all our ideas from sense. This is why the Berkelian needs a separate argument against the possibility of there being external qualities.

Returning to the main argument, we can see that to have a relative idea of one related thing (*relatum*), one must have a positive idea of both the other *relatum* and the relation itself. In the case of matter we cannot form a proper conception of the relation it is supposed to stand in to that of which we have the positive idea. The example Berkeley considers is that matter is the SUBSTRATUM (p. 686) for the quality of extension, which he explains as meaning that matter supports extension. Thus we have a relation Rxy, with y being identical to the quality of which we know the nature directly (that is, some instance of extension), R being the relation of supporting, and x, matter, being known only as that which stands in the *supporting* relation to the extended quality. Berkeley challenges this by denying that we have a clear idea of the relation in question. Pillars support roofs and bridges, but it is not in that sense that matter supports qualities. It is doubtful whether a property-less substratum can be said to do anything: nor is it clear that it makes sense to say that an unextended substratum stands under and supports the quality of extension. This shows that it is hard to see how one could have a relative idea of materiality (Berkeley 1713: I, 197ff.).

There are complications here, however. Berkeley is discussing the possibility of a relative idea of matter according to which there is no more to matter than the bare property of being a support. He is discussing, that is, the idea of materiality as such. This is not the same as discussing the question of the nature of matter. Locke has usually been taken as claiming that matter consists of substratum and primary qualities. Berkeley shows that we cannot make much sense of the substratum element, but one might try to get by on the qualities alone. This brings us to another battery of famous Berkelian arguments which are intended to show that there cannot be extra-mental qualities. These can best be approached through the claim that an idea can be like nothing but an idea; which means that nothing external could be like a feature of a mental image; which means in turn that we could have no positive idea of any external quality.

3   Qualities, Ideas and Sensations

The claim that an idea could be like nothing but an idea has been given fairly short shrift on the grounds that it is simply question-begging against representationalism (Berkeley 1710: §8). What is more, any force that it seems to possess comes from the confusion arising from Locke's extension of the ordinary notion of 'idea'. When 'idea' means something like 'concept' or 'thought' then it does seem to be a category mistake to have replicas of them in the physical world, but once *idea* is extended to include sense-contents, the issue seems quite different. But the argument can be expanded and made quite plausible, as follows:

1   A sensation could be like nothing but a sensation; most especially, nothing extra-mental could be like a sensation.
2   There is no distinction in kind between sensations and ideas. Therefore,
3   An idea could be like nothing but an idea; most especially, nothing extra-mental could be like an idea.

The first premise is entirely intuitive: the idea of an extra-mental pain or itch seems to make no sense and, hence, the suggestion that there could be such could plausibly be regarded as a category mistake. The second premise is what Berkeley is defending when he argues that the feeling of heat and a certain kind of pain are continuous, so that the latter is nothing more than an intense version of the former (Berkeley 1713: I, 176ff.).

Two kinds of objection are made to this argument's second premise. One is to affirm that we can distinguish the perception of heat from the feeling of pain, even when they occur together, so that they are not merely differences of degree. The other accepts that Berkeley's argument is true for the senses that operate by contact, but denies that it applies to vision. Firstly, I shall provide a clarification of the argument. Berkeley does not need to deny that the painful aspect of a sensation is distinguishable from its hot aspect; he needs only to affirm that they are aspects of the same thing, such that one cannot exist in a different way from the other. The timbre and pitch of sounds, or the brightness and hue of colours, would be examples of this. It is not necessary, therefore, to claim that they differ *only* in degree, and Berkeley can allow that the pain is an extra feature of the heat phenomenon it acquires through intensity. The issue then concerns whether the painfulness – or any similar sensational feature that can accompany tactile experience – is experienced as *caused by but separable from* some other feature of the experience, or as just another aspect of it. It seems to me to be highly plausible to claim that (1) the purely sensational element in tactile experience and (2) those parts of tactile experience thought to be candidates for being the direct perception of something external are not separable.

In fact, this point is best brought out by considering a visual case (Berkeley (1709) is largely devoted to showing that vision, in itself, does not present externality). If I look at an unpleasantly dazzling light, three things are true: (1) the light, including its dazzlingness, seems to be outside me; (2) I experience the unpleasantness as a kind of sensation, that is, as something internal to me, a feature of how I am affected; (3) the unpleasantness of the experience is not separable from the dazzling quality of the light. The paradox is that the unpleasant sensational quality is both an external feature of the world and a sensational feature of my experience. It is more clear phenomeno- logically than in the case of heat and pain that light, brightness and unpleasant dazzle are only a matter of degree, for there is not a recognizable separate sensation of pain, distinct from the dazzle.

Someone might try arguing that there is a difference between the datum of extreme brightness and the feeling of its unpleasantness and that the latter is merely caused by the former, not an aspect of it. That this is not plausible is brought out by the follow- ing thought experiment. Imagine that someone blind from birth were given a dazzling- light experience by direct stimulation of the cortex: do you think (1) that they would experience the light as putatively external or merely as a sensation no less internal to themselves than a bodily sensation? Assuming the answer to (1) is that they would not experience the light as external, (2) do you think that they would experience the unpleasantness as other than a feature of the brightness? The answer seems to me to be plain, and it is that they would think of them both as integral features of the sen- sation; this strongly suggests a Berkelian interpretation. This interpretation is that whether or not something is experienced as external is a matter not of its intrinsic phenomenology but of how it is interpreted into one's picture of the world. Such interpretation does, in one sense, alter the *phenomenology*, but it does not alter the *ontological standing* of the content: learning to see colours *as if* external does not make them external.

This seems to me to be a strong argument for the assimilation of ideas to sensations and, therefore, for saying that nothing extra-mental could be like them. In reply it might be argued that it only shows that the ideas of secondary qualities are assimilable to sensations, not that those of primary qualities are. But even if this is so it does not subvert the argument. One Berkelian response would be to point out that there is no idea of, say, shape independent of the secondary qualities of a given sense (Berkeley 1710: §10). So visual shape is inseparable from colour and tactile shape from felt sensation, hence the associated primary quality cannot be extra-mental. Even if shapes could exist independently of these secondary qualities, it is generally agreed that such primary qualities alone could not constitute a world because they are too formal – merely shapes without any filling. Something analogous to a secondary quality is necessary to give body to this conception. Although the argument has only shown that our actual secondary qualities are assimilable to sensations, it strongly suggests that any intensive quality of a kind like that of our secondary qualities *would be* of that kind *by being* a mode of experience and that, therefore, the idea of something like a secondary quality, yet extra-mental, is of dubious intelligibility (Foster 1982: 84–107). So all ideas are essentially modes of sensation, and the argument is sound; nothing extra-mental could be like an idea. This discredits the suggestion that an external world could possess or consist of anything like, or be analogous to, the qualities we experience.

We started by looking at Berkeley's attack on abstract ideas, both to understand it in itself and to see how it related to his immaterialism. We discovered that Berkeley's anti-abstractionism as he conceives of it is a tissue of confusions, but it is closely associated with arguments that are very powerful. If the imagist theory of thought is transformed into an imagist criterion for positive empirical content and combined with arguments that suggest that all monadic qualities are sensational ('an idea can be like nothing but an idea'), then Berkeley's arguments show that it is doubtful whether mind-independent matter could possess any intrinsic properties at all and, hence, whether such a thing could exist.

There are standard conceptions of matter according to which it does not possess any intrinsic monadic properties, but only relational and dispositional ones. The idea that it consists solely of powers, forces or fields is such a conception. So is a Lockean view that matter is just impenetrability distributed in space. There is no room to consider this here, but readers might wish to look at recent discussions (Foster 1982: 67–72; Robinson 1982: 108–23).

4   Conceivability, Perceivability and Intrinsic Properties

Berkeley's Master Argument

In what has been called his 'master argument' Berkeley claims that we cannot conceive of unperceived things.

But say you, surely there is nothing easier than to imagine trees, for instance, in a park, or books existing in a closet, and nobody by to perceive them. I answer, you may [say] so, there is no difficulty in it. But what is all this, I beseech you, more than framing in your mind certain ideas which you call *books* and *trees*, and at the same time omitting to frame the idea of anyone that may perceive them? But do you not yourself perceive or think of them all the while? This therefore is nothing to the purpose. It only shows that you have the power of imagining or forming ideas in your mind; but it does not show that you can conceive it possible, the objects of your thought may exist without the mind. To make out this, it is necessary that you conceive them existing unconceived or unthought of, which is a manifest repugnancy. When we do our utmost to conceive the existence of external bodies, we are all the while only contemplating our own ideas. (Berkeley 1710: §23)

There must be something wrong with this argument because, by parity of reasoning, one could prove the impossibility of conceiving of ideas in *other people's* minds or of ideas had at other times: one could prove, that is, solipsism of the present moment. The argument moves from the premise that whatever I think of, the thought is in my mind, to the conclusion that what I think of is in my mind. By parity of reasoning, when I form the idea of an idea in someone else's mind, this thought is in my mind: and if I form the thought of an idea in my own mind at some other time, this thought is in my mind now: so these thoughts can only be about objects that are now in my mind. This pattern of argument rests on denying that ideas are intrinsically intentional – that is, on denying that they make essential reference beyond themselves. This follows from treating them simply as images, for an image is only a pattern of sensible qualities and such qualities are not about anything but themselves.

Suppose that we accept the intentionality of thought, does this remove all force from the argument? It does not, if one accepts some connection between what we can CONCEIVE (pp. 726–33) and what we can imagine. Whenever we imagine an object, we imagine what it would be like perceived from a certain viewpoint: we do not imagine what it is like in itself, in abstraction from some possible perception. Any attempt to conceive of the object as it is independently of some possible perceptual perspective would have to be more abstract than a concrete imagination. As a physical object is an empirical object, with empirical properties, it might seem that there was something peculiar about the idea that it possesses a mode of existence that could not be represented imagistically, that is, in a form in which those empirical properties are actualized.

The natural reply to this is that a good perspective on an object enables one to form a conception of the object as it is in itself. This is most simply represented by a clear view of a flat surface, which enables one to see it not merely *from* a perspective but *as it is* in its own plane. Our visual perception comes to be structured in three dimensions, so its having a perspective does not force us into having a merely abstract conception of the object in its own space, as it would do if vision were two dimensional and distance was only inferred.

Another of Berkeley's arguments can be deployed here. The conception of *how the object is in itself*, independent of any perceptual perspective, includes the idea of what size it is in itself. Berkeley argues that there is no such notion of size: to a mite everything is larger than to a human, which is to say that, ultimately, size is not separable from the proportion of a sensory field that an object occupies (Berkeley 1713: I, 188). It is, of course, no answer to this to say that there are objective units of measurement – the foot, the inch, the metre – for what kind of content is ultimately given to these except by their connection with perception? The obvious answer is that size is purely relative. Once one understands the *comparative* size of something an inch long when constrasted with something a foot long, and one has these set in a context relating them to the size of human beings, cats, mountains, the distance to the Sun, and so on, then there is nothing more to know about size. It is, after all, generally accepted that it makes no sense to think of everything doubling in size, and this could only be because there is nothing more to size than what can be analysed relationally. This answer, though plausible, is not, I think, adequate. SPACE (p. 729) is not purely relational, in the sense that it is not simply a relation of numerical magnitudes; an intuitive notion of space or extendedness is also required to give these formal relations an empirical interpretation (Foster 1982: 73–88). Things would look larger to an intelligent mite than to a human being, even though they agreed in all their relational judgements. The mite and the human disagree precisely in respect of the intuitive element that is essential for the empirical interpretation of space. They are, therefore, disagreeing about something that is essential to the nature of experienced space.

This disagreement could be defused only if the intuitive element could be wholly projected on to and absorbed by the relational physical structure, so that the only way of characterizing the size of the intuitive, phenomenal component in spatial experience was in terms of the physical measurements that are essentially relational. That this is not so follows from the fact that objects 'look huge' to the mite. The situation is as follows. Physical size can be treated as purely relational but only at the cost of not being realist about it. Any real space must include the intuitive element as well as the relation of magnitudes, and the intuitive element is not separable from how it seems to a certain kind of subject, this not being collapsible into the relational.

It would be wrong to think that Einstein's relativity theory can be invoked against Berkeley here. Einstein is concerned with the variability of size in different frames of reference, which means frames of reference that are in motion in relation to each other. In a sense, the Berkelian point is an extension of Einstein's, for it adds a further frame of reference to the determinants of size, namely the phenomenal field of the subject; though it is not a determinant of physical size, which is an abstraction from the phenomenal.

5   From Phenomenalism to Theism

Rather than trying in this chapter to give a guided tour around the whole of Berkeley's system, I have concentrated on showing to their best effect his arguments for denying the existence of mind-independent matter, for it is this feature of his system that is of most fundamental interest and to which there is most natural resistance. My approach so far, therefore, emphasizes the negative thrust of his system and thereby ignores the things that mainly distinguish it from the sceptical PHENOMENALISM (pp. 53–4) of Hume. To rectify this imbalance I shall end by sketching the rationale for moving from immaterialism to theism.

This move has two elements, both of which distinguish Berkeley from Hume. Firstly, there is the notion of spirit which is essential for Berkeley's conceptions of the SELF (pp. 650–2) and of GOD (chapter 15); secondly, there are his reasons for claiming that our experience is caused by God. Although he had originally toyed with conceiving of the self as merely a collection of ideas, thus anticipating Hume, by the time of writing the *Principles* he had decided that we are aware of ourselves as active as well as being aware of the objects on to which our activities are directed. Because ideas are passive and the self is active we cannot have an idea of spirit. We can, however, understand it because we are conscious of ourselves in our activities, though not as an *object* of them; he calls this having a *notion*, rather than an idea, of ourselves: 'I say . . . that I have a notion of spirit, though I have not, strictly speaking, an idea of it. I do not perceive it as an idea or by means of an idea, but know it by reflexion' (Berkeley 1713: III, 233).

In response, Hylas, a main character in Berkeley's *Three Dialogues*, immediately suggests that if spirit can be let in without a corresponding idea, so can matter. But the asymmetry with material substance is preserved; we cannot have a notion of matter because that is not directly available to consciousness, even in the form of reflection. So the association between meaningfulness and conscious acquaintance is not lost.

Having established the ontology of spirits and ideas, all that is needed is to show that God is responsible for those ideas that are not the products of our imagination – that is, for those that constitute the physical world. We can conceive of God because God is spirit in the same sense as we are, with all the limitations and imperfections thought away.

It is natural to believe – and Berkeley believes – that our experience has some kind of systematic cause. The simplest hypothesis is that it is caused by mind-independent physical objects, but this explanation has been ruled out by the arguments for immaterialism. This leaves us with a choice between postulating some kind of immaterial cause or of abandoning the natural belief that there is a cause. The latter is Hume's sceptical phenomenalism. Berkeley chooses the former. Because we do not seem to be the causes of our own experiences, either as single individuals or as a species, we are forced to postulate some other immaterial agent and Berkeley naturally casts God in this role. One could, in principle, opt for a pagan Berkelianism, as did W. B. Yeats, and postulate a whole tribe of gods and demons, but Berkeley's Irishness was of a more rationalistic kind than Yeats's and he stuck to the orthodox picture. The real rival to Berkelian theism comes, once idealism has been established, from the double Humean challenge: firstly, that experience in general requires no explanation; and, secondly, that nothing could constitute such an explanation even if it were required. For Hume, something requires an explanation only if its occurrence without an explanation is improbable, and something is improbable only if experience suggests that it would not naturally happen. Consequently, how an aeroplane can fly requires an explanation. That experience (seemingly of a physical world) continues to flow in its normal course, however, is the standard run of events and needs of no explanation: that is just the way the world is. The opinion that *the way the world is* needs explanation cannot be based on experience, for experience cannot show how things in fact usually are to be improbable. For such things to be judged improbable, one must employ a standard of *a priori* PROBABILITY (pp. 308–10), and Hume did not believe that there was any such standard for empirical matters. Furthermore, asking for an explanation in this context is asking what *brought about* the world of experience. This involves a concept of causation as real power or force, which Hume rejects. For Hume, a causal explanation of the world merely involves marshalling phenomena into constantly conjoined pairings so that one can have the satisfaction of seeing the world as an ordered structure. All this is no more than the regimenting of actual and possible experiences and has nothing of a general kind to say about what brings experience about; it is wholly internal to the world of phenomena.

Berkeley's position is more commonsensical than Hume's and is expressed in sections 25–6 of the *Principles*:

> 25 All our ideas, sensations or the things which we perceive, by whatsoever names they may be distinguished, are visibly inactive, there is nothing of power or agency included in them . . .
>
> 26 We perceive a continual succession of ideas, some are anew excited, others are changed or totally disappear. There is therefore some cause of these ideas whereon they depend, and which produces and changes them. That this cause cannot be any quality or idea or combination of ideas, is clear from the preceding section. It must therefore be a substance; but it has been shewn that there is no corporeal or material substance: it remains therefore that the cause of ideas is an incorporeal active substance or spirit. (Berkeley 1710: §§25–6; see also Berkeley 1713: III)

There is nothing in Berkeley to suggest that he was aware of the possibility of scepticism about *a priori* probabilities. He treats it as obvious that experience must come from somewhere. He had entertained Humean-style scepticism about causal efficacy and held to such a view concerning causation in the realm of ideas and, hence, the physical world as he understood it. But he believed that reflection made us aware of the real causal efficacy of the will. By such efficacy, he held, God's will produces in our minds the ideas which constitute the external world.

Further Reading

Urmson's (1982) excellent book on Berkeley in the Past Masters series is an elegant and brief introduction. Tipton (1974), Pitcher (1977), Dancy (1987), Grayling (1986) and Winkler (1989) are more detailed and more concerned to argue their own theses, but all can be used as general guides. Bennett (1971) relates Berkeley to Locke and Hume in a philosophically stimulating way, though rather too much to Berkeley's disadvantage and, some think, with too little regard to the historical context.

Contemporary defences of roughly Berkelian forms of idealism can be found in John Foster's contribution to Robinson (1993), which is a much simpler version of the difficult Foster (1982): there are defences also in Robinson's contribution to Foster and Robinson (1985) and in the final chapter of Robinson (1982). An idealism that owes much to Berkeley, but which finally takes a Hegelian form, is defended by Sprigge (1983).

References

Berkeley

The standard edition is:

Berkeley 1948–55: *Works of George Berkeley, Bishop of Cloyne*, 7 vols (edited by A. A. Luce and T. E. Jessop). London: Nelson.

Easily available one-volume paperback editions, containing at least the *Principles* and the *Three Dialogues* include:

Berkeley 1962: *The Principles of Human Knowledge with other writings* (edited and with an introduction by G. J. Warnock). Glasgow: Fontana.

—— 1988: *Principles of Human Knowledge/Three Dialogues* (edited and with an introduction by R. Woolhouse). Harmondsworth: Penguin Books.

—— 1993: *Philosophical Works: including the works on vision* (edited and with an introduction by M. R. Ayers). London: Everyman, Dent.

—— 1995: *Principles of Human Knowledge and Three Dialogues* (edited and with an introduction by H. Robinson). Oxford: Oxford University Press.

With one exception, my references to Berkeley's texts are either to *The Principles of Human Knowledge* (1710) or to *Three Dialogues between Hylas and Philonous* (1713). References to the former give the section number alone, for the sections are generally shorter than a page and this facilitates the use of any edition. There is no such short-cut with the *Dialogues*, and here I cite the number of the dialogue and the page reference in volume two of Luce and Jessop's standard edition of Berkeley's works. There is one reference to *An Essay Towards a New Theory of Vision* (1709). Locke, *An Essay Concerning Human Understanding* (1689) and Hume, *A Treatise of Human Nature* (1739) are also mentioned.

Other writers

Ayers, M. 1991: *Locke*, 2 vols. London: Routledge and Kegan Paul.

Bennett, J. 1971: *Locke, Berkeley, Hume: Central Themes*. Oxford: Oxford University Press.

Dancy, J. 1987: *Berkeley: An Introduction*. Oxford: Blackwell.

Flage, D. E. 1987: *Berkeley's Doctrine of Notions*. Beckenham: Croom Helm.

Foster, J. 1982: *The Case for Idealism*. London: Routledge and Kegan Paul.

Foster, J. and Robinson, H. (eds) 1985: *Essays on Berkeley*. Oxford: Oxford University Press.

Grayling, A. C. 1986: *Berkeley: The Central Arguments*. London: Duckworth.

Lockwood, M. 1989: *Mind, Brain and the Quantum: The Compound 'I'*. Oxford: Blackwell.

Martin, C. B. and Armstrong, D. M. (eds) 1968: *Locke and Berkeley*. London: Macmillan.

Pitcher, G. 1977: *Berkeley*. London: Routledge and Kegan Paul.

Robinson, H. 1982: *Matter and Sense*. Cambridge: Cambridge University Press.

—— 1993: *Objections to Physicalism*. Oxford: Oxford University Press.

Sosa, E. (ed.) 1987: *Essays on the Philosophy of George Berkeley*. Dordrecht: D. Reidel.

Sprigge, T. 1983: *The Vindication of Absolute Idealism*. Edinburgh: Edinburgh University Press.

Tipton, I. C. 1974: *Berkeley: The Philosophy of Immaterialism*. London: Methuen.

Turbayne, C. (ed.) 1982: *Berkeley: Critical and Interpretive Essays*. Manchester: Manchester University Press.

Urmson, J. O. 1982: *Berkeley*. Oxford: Oxford University Press.

Warnock, G. J. 1953: *Berkeley*. Harmondsworth: Penguin Books.

Winkler, K. P. 1989: *Berkeley: An Interpretation*. Oxford: Oxford University Press.

Yolton, J. W. 1984: *Perceptual Acquaintance from Descartes to Reid*. Oxford: Blackwell.

Discussion Questions

1   How is Berkeley's attack on abstract ideas related to his arguments for immaterialism?

2   What are the advantages and disadvantages of Berkeley's own account of the generality of ideas?

3   Does representative realism of the kind found in Locke really open the way to scepticism about the existence either of the external world or of God?

4   Is the doctrine that 'an idea can be like nothing but an idea' better than question-begging as an objection to representative realism?

5   In what sense, if any, is the physical world mind-independent?

6   Should we agree that 'to be is to be perceived'?

7   Is it true that a painful heat and a pleasant heat differ not in kind, but only in degree? How can one set about trying to answer questions of this kind?

8   Does the fact that we cannot image an instance of a primary quality without a secondary quality show that it is – or might be – impossible for a primary quality to exist without a secondary one?

9   Would someone who had gained sight after being blind from birth be in a position to recognize particular shapes visually on the strength of having previously felt them? If not, would it mean that visual and tactile shapes are different qualities?

10   Does the fact that whenever we imagine a physical object we imagine it as it would appear from a particular perspective mean that we cannot form a proper conception of how anything is in itself?

11   Must there be an intuitive element in any adequate account of real space?

12   How can we determine whether experience as a whole requires explanation?

13   To what extent are Berkeley's doctrines matters of common sense?

14   Is it possible to have a notion of spirit if we cannot have an idea of it? Is the case different for matter?

15   If God is directly responsible for my experience, do I have any reason to think that there are any other agents – human minds, for example – connected with the things that I experience?

16   How does an idealist account of the physical world affect natural theology?

31

Hume

PETER JONES

David Hume (1711–76) is without doubt one of the greatest philosophers to write in English. His elegant style complemented the depth and originality of his philosophical thought. The range of his work is wide, but he is best known today for his views on causation, induction, perception, personal identity and on the nature of morality. He agreed with his predecessors that understanding how and why things change is the only way to explain the past and to plan for the future, and that only a knowledge of causes can help to dispel our most natural fears. He believed, however, that many had misunderstood the precise nature of such knowledge, and had thus failed to benefit from it. He also held that it was not enough to examine the natural world; as the investigator, human beings set out to know, but often in ignorance of their own contributions to a task. Philosophy should begin, therefore, with an investigation into the nature of humanity, for this would also enable us to understand the nature and limits of our knowledge. Hume argued that we are all governed much less by reason than has often been claimed, and are motivated essentially by our passions. Moreover, in everyday life we must learn to live with probabilities rather than certainties. The public, and intensely practical, benefits which could result from such an understanding are profound.

1 Biography

David Hume was born in Edinburgh in 1711. He enrolled at the University of Edinburgh at the age of 11, and studied there for three, or possibly four, years. As was usual at the time, he left without graduating. After a brief study of the law, he embarked on a long and private study of philosophy. From 1734 until 1737 he lived in France and wrote *A Treatise of Human Nature* (Hume 1978a), which was published anonymously in 1739–40. In 1740, to boost disappointing sales of the book, Hume published an anonymous summary of its main theses. The document, now simply called the *Abstract* (Hume 1978b), emphasized precisely those tenets he chose to discuss when he later rewrote parts of the *Treatise*.

Hume was over 40 years of age before he obtained his first full-time job. He had twice failed to become a professor of philosophy, in Edinburgh in 1745, and Glasgow in 1752.

In 1741 and 1742 he had published two volumes of essays, under the title *Essays, Moral, Political, and Literary* (Hume 1985a), and thereafter rewrote parts of the first and third books of the *Treatise*; these appeared in 1748 and 1751 and are now known as the *Enquiry Concerning Human Understanding* (Hume 1975b), and the *Enquiry Concerning the Principles of Morals* (Hume 1975c). In 1752 he published, under his own name, a very successful set of essays on political and economic topics, under the title *Political Discourses* (Hume 1985b). In the same year, he was appointed Keeper of the Advocates' Library in Edinburgh. Using their magnificent collection, which later became the National Library of Scotland, he published between 1754 and 1762 the six volumes of his *History of England* (Hume 1985c), which were also immensely successful.

From 1763 until 1766 Hume served in Paris, first as Secretary and then as Chargé d'affaires at the British Embassy. He became friendly with almost all the great philosophers and writers of the day, such as Diderot (1713–84), D'Alembert (1717–83) and Rousseau (1712–78), but to their mutual regret he never met Voltaire (1694–1778).

On returning to London Hume became Under Secretary of State, handling diplomacy with foreign powers to the north of France, including the Russia of Catherine the Great. He was also in charge of home affairs for Scotland, and official patron of the Scottish Church.

In 1769 Hume retired to Edinburgh, renewed old friendships, particularly with Adam Smith (1723–90), and played host to all the important visitors to the city, such as Benjamin Franklin (1706–90). In retirement Hume continually revised new editions of his *History*, and worked on his *Dialogues Concerning Natural Religion*, modelled on Cicero (106–43 BC) and published posthumously in 1779.

2 Philosophy

Great philosophers very often are not the first people to express the ideas for which they themselves become famous; their distinction lies in the routes they take in what they see as the context of their thought, in the syntheses they offer, and above all in the precise arguments they offer for their conclusions. Moreover, all philosophers write in the first place for their contemporaries, and are influenced by other thinkers whose work may be unknown to later generations. Hume himself was profoundly influenced by the Roman politician Marcus Tullius Cicero, and by the seventeenth-century French philosopher Nicholas Malebranche (1638–1715). Moreover, the historical context in which he lived was very different from our own. For example, when he was writing, nothing was known about latent heat or the composition of air and water, about any powers other than light and heat, about animal generation or evolution, about the age of the Earth or the size of the universe; and such commonplace terms as 'police', 'magistrate', 'government', 'agriculture', 'art' and 'city' carried different meanings from today. If concepts like these irradiate our thought today, then we need to identify what we must unthink in order to understand Hume's thought. It must be remembered, therefore, that although many contemporary problems have a Humean ancestry, in a very obvious sense Hume was not discussing twentieth-century issues.

2.1   Causation

Hume was interested in the processes by which we acquire KNOWLEDGE (chapter 1); the processes of perceiving and thinking, of feeling and reasoning. He recognized that much of what we claim to know derives from other people secondhand, thirdhand or worse; moreover, our perceptions and JUDGEMENTS (pp. 726–9) can be distorted by many factors – by what we are studying, as well as by the very act of study itself. The main reason, however, behind his emphasis on 'probabilities and those other measures of evidence on which life and action entirely depend' (Hume 1978b) is this:

> it is evident that all reasonings concerning *matter of fact* are founded on the relation of cause and effect, and that we can never infer the existence of one object from another unless they are connected together, either mediately or immediately. (Ibid.)

When we apparently observe a whole sequence, say of one ball hitting another, what exactly do we observe? And in the much commoner cases, when we wonder about the *unobserved* causes or effects of the events we observe, what precisely are we doing?

Questions about Causality

In considering causality Hume separated importantly different issues:

1   Questions about the causal *relation*: what exactly is it for one event to be the cause of another? What is the evidence of causal relations between events?
2   A question about the causal *inference*: what entitles us to *infer* from the occurrence of one event that another event is its cause or its effect?
3   Questions about the causal *principle*: why do we insist that every event has a cause, and what entitles us to do so?
4   Three extra questions about *necessity*: (4a) why do we insist that what distinguishes a genuine causal relation from a merely casual relation is the *necessity* of that particular pair of events occurring together? (4b) what entitles us to *infer* that if one event is the cause or effect of another, then it *must* have occurred with it, or immediately before or after it? (4c) why do we insist that *every* event *must* have a cause?

Hume recognized that a notion of 'must' or necessity is a peculiar feature of causal relations, inferences and principles, and challenges us to explain and justify the notion. He argued that there is no observable feature of events, nothing like a physical bond, which can be properly labelled the 'necessary connection' between a given cause and its effect; events simply *are*, they merely *occur*, and there is no 'must' or 'ought' about them. However, repeated experience of pairs of events sets up the habit of expectation in us, such that when one of the pair occurs we inescapably expect the other. This expectation makes us *infer* the *unobserved* cause or unobserved effect of the observed event, and we mistakenly project this mental inference on to the events themselves. There is no necessity observable in causal relations; all that can be observed is regular sequence: there is necessity in causal inferences, but because inferences are what observers do, we can say that this necessity is only in the mind. Once we realize that causation is a RELATION (p. 800) between pairs of events, we also realize that often we are not present for the whole sequence which we want to divide into 'cause' and 'effect'. Our understanding of the causal relation is thus intimately linked with the role of the causal inference, because only causal inference entitles us to 'go beyond what is immediately present to the senses' (Hume 1978a: I, III, ii). But now two very important assumptions emerge behind the causal inference: the assumption that 'like causes, in like circumstances, will always produce like effects', and the assumption that 'the course of nature will continue uniformly the same' – or, briefly, that the future will resemble the past (Hume 1978b). Unfortunately, this last assumption lacks either empirical or *a priori* proof; that is, it can be conclusively established neither by experience nor by thought alone.

Hume frequently endorsed a standard seventeenth-century view that all our ideas are ultimately traceable, by analysis, to sensory impressions of an internal or external kind. Accordingly, he claimed that all his theses are based on EXPERIENCE (p. 52), understood as sensory awareness together with memory, since only experience establishes matters of fact. But is our belief that the future will resemble the past properly construed as a belief concerning only a matter of fact? As Bertrand Russell remarked, earlier this century, the real problem that Hume raises is whether future futures will resemble future pasts, in the way that past futures really did resemble past pasts. Hume declares that 'if . . . the past may be no rule for the future, all experience becomes useless and can give rise to no inference or conclusion' (Hume 1975b: IV). And yet, he held, the supposition cannot stem from innate ideas, since there are no innate ideas in his view, nor can it stem from any abstract formal reasoning. For one thing, the future can surprise us, and no formal reasoning seems able to embrace such contingencies; for another, even animals and unthinking people conduct their lives as if they assume the future resembles the past: dogs return for buried bones, children avoid a painful fire, and so on. Hume is not deploring the fact that we have to conduct our lives on the basis of PROBABILITIES (pp. 308–10); and he is not saying that inductive reasoning could or should be avoided or rejected. Rather, he accepted inductive reasoning but tried to show that whereas formal reasoning of the kind associated with mathematics cannot establish or prove matters of fact, factual or inductive reasoning lacks the 'necessity' and 'certainty' associated with mathematics. His position, therefore, is clear: because 'every effect is a distinct event from its cause', only investigation can settle whether any two particular events are causally related; causal inferences cannot be drawn with the force of logical necessity familiar to us from *a priori* reasoning, but, although they lack such force, they should not be discarded. In the context of causation, inductive inferences are inescapable and invaluable. What, then, makes 'past experience' 'the standard of our future judgment'? The answer is *custom*: it is a brute psychological fact, without which even animal life of a simple kind would be more or less impossible. 'We are determined by custom alone to suppose the future conformable to the past' (Hume 1978b); nevertheless, whenever we need to calculate likely events we must supplement and correct such custom by self-conscious reasoning.

2.2   Some implications: free will, history and the uniformity of nature

Hume was well aware of the potential impact of his analysis, and he began his explanation of its implications by trying to reconcile the arguments of those who hold that all our actions are determined, and those who hold that we are genuinely free to do what we choose. The determinists are right, he said, to insist that every event has a cause, but mistaken in the view they take of necessity, failing to see that it belongs only to an inference in the mind; advocates of free will, on the other hand, are right to say that responsibility makes sense only if we are truly the agents of our actions, but mistaken in holding that 'free' in this sense means 'uncaused'. Hume's view is that our ACTIONS (compare pp. 733–6), like all other events, have causes, namely, the choices and decisions that immediately precede our actions, and for which we accept responsibility. However, although these mental happenings function as the MOTIVES (p. 673) of our actions, they themselves have causes, of which we are normally unaware and for which we are not held responsible. His point in discussing the free-will issue is to show that human actions can be understood, and are properly understandable, in terms of what he has said about causation in general – we notice patterns of behaviour, we infer motives precisely in order to offer 'interpretations' of actions:

> were there no uniformity in human actions, and were every experiment which we could form of this kind irregular and anomalous, it were impossible to collect any general observations concerning mankind, and no experience, however accurately digested by reflection, would ever serve to any purpose. (Hume 1975b: VIII)

Such thoughts were important when he came to reflect on the nature of HISTORY (chapter 14). Here, however, two features of the discussion should be noticed. Firstly, human behaviour is capable of causal explanation, and therefore also of prediction, he was saying, albeit not yet with the same degree of precision or certainty that we expect in the natural sciences. The second feature is related to this. So important is our belief that similar causes produce similar effects, that we hold to it even when we cannot find the required uniformities; and when we find something puzzling or inexplicable we neither suppose that the laws of nature have changed, nor that we have encountered a causeless event. *Absence of adequate evidence* for a cause is not taken as adequate evidence for the *absence of a cause*.

External Objects

In 'Of scepticism with regard to the senses', Hume (1978a: I, IV, ii) discussed problems that have particularly interested twentieth-century philosophers, namely, those concerning our knowledge of external objects and personal identity. Hume regarded both external objects and the self, in an important sense, as imaginative CONSTRUCTIONS (p. 000). The texts, together with their various modern commentaries, are unusually complex and reward close examination.

Everyone assumes that the world goes on around us, whether we are awake or asleep, unconscious or dead. But this view is troublesome to philosophers who held that we are only really conscious of our internal perceptions, and that ultimately sensory experience consists of unconnected atomic instants (for instance, Hume 1978a: I, IV, vi). Hume asked 'whether it be the *senses, reason* or the *imagination,* that produces the opinion of a continu'd or of a *distinct* existence' of objects (ibid.: I, IV, ii). He argued that immediate sense experiences cannot generate any notion of unsensed objects, and 'never give us the least intimation of any thing beyond' themselves (ibid.: I, IV, ii). The solution to such problems lies in the power of the imagination to disguise the disjointed and interrupted character of sensory experience, by uniting or bonding our ideas of it in the mind (ibid.: I, IV, vi). 'The opinion of the continu'd existence of body depends on the *coherence* and *constancy*' (ibid.: I, IV, ii) of some of our impressions, namely those which our memory assures us preserve some degree of resemblance and repetition over time; this feature of our perceptions is then projected on to the external world. When we do 'infer the continu'd existence of objects of sense from their coherence' it is 'in order to bestow on the objects a greater regularity than what is observ'd in our mere perceptions' (ibid.: I, IV, ii). Philosophers since Hume have made much of the theoretical and practical advantages of projecting on to the objects we sense a greater coherence than seems to be strictly warranted by the sensory evidence itself.

2.3   Personal identity

Hume anchored his discussion of external objects in reflections on identity, or sameness and change: he told us that his aim was 'to prove, that all objects, to which we ascribe identity, without observing their invariableness and uninterruptedness, are such as consist of a succession of related objects' (ibid.: I, IV, vi). It is hardly surprising, then, that he stated: 'the identity, which we ascribe to the mind of man, is only a fictitious one, and of a like kind with that which we ascribe to vegetables and animal bodies' (ibid.: I, IV, vi). (Fiction, it must be noted, meant 'hypothesis' or 'invention', in Hume's day.) In fact, however, Hume asked different questions about personal identity, and consequently said different things about it. He asked: 'how far we are *ourselves* the objects of our senses'? What is 'the nature of the uniting principle, which constitutes a person' (ibid.: I, IV, ii)? What 'impression gives rise to the idea of self' (ibid.: I, IV, vi)? He held that 'what we call a *mind*, is nothing but a heap or collection of different perceptions, united together by certain relations, and suppos'd tho falsely, to be endow'd with perfect simplicity and identity' (ibid.: I, IV, ii; see also I, IV, vi). He likened the mind to a 'republic or commonwealth' (ibid.: I, IV, vi) but also to a 'theatre, where several perceptions successively make their appearance'; the identity 'is nothing really belonging to these different perceptions, and uniting them together; but is merely a quality, which we attribute to them, because of the union of their ideas in imagination' (ibid.: I, IV, vi) – and the capacity of the memory which is said to 'not so much *produce* as *discover* [that is, reveal] personal identity' (ibid.: I, IV, vi). Commentators have pointed out that Hume confined his mainly first-person account to mental phenomena, and in these contexts did not consider the roles of physical criteria or social behaviour in our idea of the self. His reflections in other passages, however, on moral, social and political structures and behaviour, considerably enriched his formal consideration of persons. Nevertheless, his discussions of identity, especially his reflections on 'numerical and specific identity' (ibid.: I, IV, vi), need radical revision and supplementation.

2.4   Miracles and religion

The cases that most clearly conflict with what Hume has said about causation are those of alleged miracles. His own discussion was eventually published in the 1748 *Enquiry*

(Hume 1975b), but it is not primarily about whether miracles occur – he rather brusquely defines them as impossible; rather, it is about the nature and reliability of evidence for factual claims of any kind whatsoever. The recurrent term in his discussion is 'testimony', that is, reports of evidence.

Hume readily concedes that all of us have to rely on reports from other people; knowledge is a social phenomenon in the sense that agreement about what happened is important in defining what we count as knowledge. Moreover, none of us has enough first-hand experience of our own to make very extensive claims. Hume holds that, as a general rule, testimony is reliable, and he does so for two reasons: our memories are moderately reliable, and humans have a natural inclination, strongly re-enforced by social sanctions, to tell the truth, and to feel shame if detected in falsehood. These general assurances, however, cannot help us in particular cases of doubt, so Hume suggests that in weighing the probability of evidence the content and the context of what a witness says must both be examined. We need to consider not only the type and quantity of evidence, but also the manner and motive in giving it. In the end we must rely on 'experience and observation'. But surely we must be told whose experience is to count, and why and how the tests of evidence are to be performed. *Ex hypothesi*, we cannot appeal to our own experience in order to test reports by others of experiences unlike our own; and in weighing what people say we neither appeal indiscriminately to anyone, nor require the assent of everyone. Hume relies on a notion of experts, or qualified observers, to whom we can appeal for help. Typically we learn who count as the experts while learning the procedures for making reports of the kind in question; the learning may be quite informal, even unconscious, and the experts range from the sublime to the ridiculous – at its lowest, anyone might count as an expert who seems to know more than oneself. Parents and teachers are the first experts children encounter, but their own friends also play this role for children on many occasions. Hume uses the notion of experts and agreement to secure both the social dimension of our judgements, and their objectivity – although that term was not used in the eighteenth century.

Hume takes stories of miracles to be reports of unique events, the cause of which is allegedly known by inference, not by experience, even though none of the conditions for establishing an inferred cause is satisfied. We are entitled to infer a cause, he holds, with a greater or lesser degree of probability, when the event to be explained resembles others which we have directly experienced in conjunction with their causes. Many questions arise here. How much resemblance is needed to warrant such an inference? What properties or characteristics is one entitled to assign to such an inferred cause? Hume's extended reflections on such issues were published posthumously in 1779 in his brilliant *Dialogues Concerning Natural Religion* (Hume 1947).

Protestant theologians in Hume's day were eager to embrace what little they understood of Newtonian science and its methods, and they popularized an ancient argument known as the argument from design. This was supposed to establish the nature of God by means of inferences from the observable world around us – in Hume's words, it was 'an argument drawn from effects to causes' (Hume 1975b: XI). Schematically it ran like this: it is impossible to describe all the diverse phenomena in the known universe without implying some overall plan behind it, which causally explains the nature of the phenomena and their interconnections; such a plan, however, would need to be of such complexity itself, that it could be attributed only to some being with capacities far exceeding human capacities – in brief, it could belong only to God. Sophisticated versions of this argument are still popular, but Hume maintained that they inherently lack a determinate base in experience, that they are untestable, unrevisable and claim a dogmatic finality and uniqueness inimical to genuine scientific enquiry. The necessary reliance on inductive arguments in such enquiry, after all, means that in any given case we could turn out to be mistaken. No event, considered by itself, points beyond itself to its causes or effects; these have to be discovered by experience, and what is more, *no* features of a cause need resemble any of the effect – they could be 'totally different' (ibid.: IV). Factual inferences rest on the assumption of similarity of cases, and can be assigned various degrees of probability. In the absence of direct experience we are allowed only to postulate what is *sufficient* to bring about the alleged effects. Hume is quick to see that this fails to satisfy his own definition of what a causal relation is, and of how we can know one, since the crucial notion of necessity is lacking. He concludes that allegedly 'unique' causes cannot legitimately be inferred from, or used to explain, allegedly 'unique' effects. When uniqueness is claimed for an event, we can never know whether we have adequately identified or circumscribed it. In addition, if we have no experience of a thing's attributes we cannot pick it out from among other things, and if we cannot do this even vaguely, we have no means to confirm that it exists. It is useless to postulate a cause whose attributes, by definition, are unknown. Finally, there is too much pain, suffering and chaos in the world as we know it, to justify any inference to a fully competent cause of it all.

2.5   Moral philosophy

Hume regarded his own moral views as those of a common-sense man, albeit with a strictly secular outlook. He held that a human being cannot be adequately defined or understood as an essentially rational animal, as ARISTOTLE (chapter 23) and so many other philosophers and theologians had proclaimed. Indeed, pure thought, or abstract reasoning of the kind associated with pure mathematics, is itself inert, and cannot motivate anyone to do anything; all that such thought can do is enable us to recognize relations between things. This recognition can somehow influence what does motivate us, namely, our sentiments, which are forms of the most basic desires to avoid pain and attain pleasure. In the *Treatise* Hume dramatically summarized his view that thought plays only a subordinate role in the moral life by declaring that 'reason is, and ought only to be, the slave of the passions' (Hume 1978a: II, III, iii). It helps in the formulation of our goals, but not in our motivation towards them. When he came to rewrite this passage in 1751, however, he toned it down: 'no doubt *reason* and *sentiment* concur in almost all moral determinations and conclusions . . . [but] it is probable . . . that this final sentence depends on some internal sense or feeling, which nature has made universal in the whole species' (Hume 1975c: I). For such views, Hume drew inspiration from Shaftesbury and from Francis Hutcheson, Professor of Moral Philosophy in Glasgow until his death in 1746. One of the features which most distinguished the philosophers of the Scottish Enlightenment from their successors in the French and German Enlightenment, is an emphasis on the essential part played in our lives by the passions; their influence is a brute psychological fact, to be neither condemned nor condoned, but a fact nevertheless that theories of humanity and morality ignore at their peril. Very often, as it happened, the French and German writers regretted the fact, thought it to be avoidable, and proclaimed the sovereignty of reason.

In deciding what to do, we all weigh the possible consequences, but the merit of an action, Hume holds, derives from the motive behind it. It is worth recording that Hume's language is sometimes confusing: he uses the term 'sentiment' to mean both feeling and thought, and this makes his claim that passions or sentiments are the sole causes of action more plausible than it might otherwise appear. He draws a distinction between 'artificial' and 'natural' virtues. 'Artificial' virtues are those which we might nowadays describe as sociologically conditioned, in the sense that they are procedures we adopt, as individuals or groups, and often unselfconsciously, to help things run smoothly and to temper our self-seeking and divisive tendencies. For example, our sense of JUSTICE (chapter 8) arises 'artificially, though necessarily, from education and human convention'; indeed, at one place, Hume states that 'public utility is the *sole* origin of justice' (Hume 1975c: III). 'Natural' virtues, by contrast, are said to be grounded in our universal tendency to share, quite literally, the feelings of others. Such 'sympathy' (and the notion is not equivalent to the modern idea of compassion) ultimately explains even the artificial virtues. Both artificial and natural virtues, then, are understood as qualities which human beings find useful or agreeable both in their own case, as owners of those qualities, and in other people whom they observe as spectators. Hume's notion of 'sympathy' proved fruitful, and was taken up and developed by Adam Smith, as was the idea of learning to judge ourselves impartially.

2.6   Art, taste and aesthetic judgement

Hume's brief account of AESTHETIC JUDGEMENTS (chapter 7) builds on what he says about moral goodness and moral judgement. By talking about the thing that currently pleases or displeases someone, we can change that person's response to it; that is, we can change how they perceive it, think of it, or react to it, and in this way induce them to feel differently about it. Such emphasis on feeling, however, should not be taken to imply that our discussions are incurably personal or subjective. On the contrary, Hume tries to show that agreement is possible, and of a kind that is quite strong enough to satisfy our deepest yearning for so-called objectivity. Three conditions must be met: firstly, the conventions of language must be observed by all disputants and, if necessary, clarified in the particular context; secondly, it must be possible to establish publicly shareable viewpoints and referents; and finally, we must assume a shared psychological make-up among the disputants. Personal idiosyncrasies due to age or background should be recognized as idiosyncrasies and discounted. And the old saying that there can be no disputing in matters of taste should be seen as being harmlessly, because only trivially, true. If the exercise of taste involves no judgement, then, indeed, there can be no dispute or discussion; but if it does involve judgement, as most people think, then discussion is not only possible but desirable. Moreover, judgement, understood as public discourse, is always capable of reaching a pragmatic, if not a formal, resolution of difficulties.

Hume's remarks on art mostly occur when he is discussing features of our social life. That is why he considers art from the standpoint of human actions: the artist is trying to get something done, and spectators are trying to establish the why and the wherefore of what the artist does. Works of art, in this way, are pleasurable means of communication, and their acceptance depends on their making sense to spectators who can agree in their responses. Hume held that as an historical phenomenon, art occurs only when a person has time to turn aside from the brute necessities of living. Nevertheless, in the more leisurely context of Hume's own epoch, the arts could be held to refine the temper and make people more sociable, because an artist trying to please spectators had to consider their needs and interests. This point has an important consequence for criticism of the arts: because art is a human activity, one of the general criteria for understanding any human action applies to it – namely, knowledge of how the agent viewed the context and appropriateness of what he or she was doing. So we should consider works of art in terms of the audience for which they were intended, as well as in terms of their internal character, their genre, style and tradition. Hume held that one can achieve the 'proper sentiment' towards most, and certainly towards the best, works of art. There are two elements in his claim. To be causally affected by a work's properties, we must adopt the right frame of mind or viewpoint, as well as the right physical standpoint. The second element is even more important. What distinguishes a *proper response* from a merely *passive reaction*, as when we enjoy basking in the hot sun, is the active contribution of the spectator. This involves an INTERPRETATION (pp. 247–50) of the work's meaning and value, over and above identification of the aspects we find affecting; meaning, after all, cannot be detected by the five senses alone, any more than necessity. Interpretation involves the exercise of the mind.

Hume's views on art and criticism receive their most sustained treatment in a single essay, 'Of the Standard of Taste', published in 1757, and they belong to a period when the modern notion of aesthetics was receiving only its first tentative formulation. Public concerts were beginning to take place, easel painting was becoming popular, and the first novels were appearing; except for those who travelled to Europe, however, most people saw very few paintings, had access to no museums, had little knowledge of Greek – as opposed to Roman – sculpture and architecture, and knew nothing of the art of other cultures.

2.7   Views on history and politics

Hume's view of the nature of historical writing and understanding, which brings together his thoughts on evidence and human testimony, as well as on agency and motivation, rests on two fundamental tenets: firstly, agents act with certain intentions, but are necessarily ignorant, when they set out, of the outcome; secondly, observers know the outcome, but are doomed merely to conjecture the intentions necessary for understanding it. The unbridgeable gap between foresight and hindsight of the 'actor' and 'spectator', as Hume called them, can baffle the most diligent enquirer. One important point here is the tension between the agent's passions, which alone can motivate him or her, and the spectator's reason, which functions in his or her understanding: 'Mens' views of things are the result of their understanding alone: Their conduct is regulated by their understanding, their temper, and their passions' (Hume 1985c: LIII). Spectators do have access, however, to data logically unavailable to the agent: in particular, to the longer-term consequences of the agent's acts and to the varying significance ascribed to them from different perspectives, and in relation to different sets of issues. The judgements of hindsight are transient, nevertheless, because the possibility of reinterpretation is ever present in the light of succeeding events.

A central theme of Hume's historical reflections concerns the unavoidable struggle between LIBERTY (pp. 258–61) and authority. He is primarily concerned with liberty under the LAW (chapter 13) and with constraints upon it exercised by various kinds of authority; to a lesser degree he considers limits on personal liberty imposed by habit or education. For Hume, a discussion of liberty is not ultimately separable from a discussion of virtue, and thus of how to live as a social being; the real threat to society stems from faction. On one point Hume was adamant: 'violent innovations no individual is entitled to make' (Hume 1975b: 'On the Original Contract'). And precisely because the consequences of excess cannot be foreseen, there is never a case for instigating a revolution or resisting the law. The stability and very structure of society depend on the upholding of law, and society faces its greatest peril when resistance to law is itself proclaimed as 'lawful or commendable'. Gradual change should be sought, in the recognition also, that the complexity of political questions means that 'there scarcely ever occurs, in any deliberation, a choice, which is either purely good, or purely ill. Consequences, mixed and varied, may be foreseen to flow from every measure: and many consequences, unforeseen, do always, in fact, result from every one' (ibid.: 'On the Protestant Succession', published 1752).

Throughout his writings, Hume observes that personal inclinations, political interests, religious zeal, are constant threats to society. It is 'not enough for liberty to remain on the defensive', not least because, however carefully framed, no laws could 'possibly provide against every contingency' (Hume 1985c: XLVIII, XLVII). Hume held that TOLERATION (p. 690) developed historically not as a result of positive policy, but from a slow recognition that attempts at repression merely stiffened resistance. He did not think, however, that toleration always wins through. In this context, Hume faced a deep recurring conflict in his philosophy between upholding moderation and stabilizing the unavoidable tension between liberty and authority. Since there is no criterion of moderation in advance of a particular context with clear boundaries (for moderation is definable only by reference to limits), there can be no fully intelligible principle of moderation independent of cases: but how are such cases to be identified? Moreover, it is unclear how an attitude of moderation could, in practice, motivate anyone to displace deeply engrained habits, on the one hand, or fanaticism, on the other.

The aim of government, in Hume's view, is to establish and then to preserve just laws. But the laws must not suppose that human nature can be very much changed. The law-makers, in other words, whether in the sphere of government or morality, must first seek to understand HUMAN NATURE (pp. 672–3). They must also grasp that threats to liberty stem from various sources. On the economic front Hume saw the national debt, with its attendant taxation levies, together with the prospect of nationalization of property, as especially dangerous. He considers that low interest rates, controlled labour costs, and competitive pricing are all essential to ensure both successful foreign trade, and a buoyant home economy which motivates the labour force. He attacked all isolationism in politics or economics, and recognized that diversification would be necessary for an economy resting on a few staple products, because such an economy is always vulnerable to decreasing demand, and to lower pricing by successful competitors. It might be added that he disapproved of state ownership on the grounds that a state can always secure itself against enquiry and accountability. The Scotland of Hume's day was poor, sparsely populated and entirely agrarian; how far his reflections are adaptable to modern, urban, industrial society, and for populations of immensely greater size, is hotly debated.

2.8 Scepticism

Hume was by no means ashamed of his sceptical stance and his sceptical arguments, although his opponents, using the same label, regarded it extremely unfavourably. As a general term of abuse, 'sceptic' covered all those who challenged orthodox views, asked difficult questions (even when no one else claimed to know the answer), omitted mention of God or canvassed views that left little or no room for a God, denied the existence of things for which words nevertheless existed, or merely confessed ignorance. On all these grounds Hume qualifies for the label. At different times he explicitly denies that we have innate ideas; that the causal relation is observably anything other than constant conjunction; that there are observable necessary connections anywhere; that there is either an empirical or demonstrative proof for the assumptions that the future will resemble the past, and that every event has a cause; that there is an irresolvable dispute between advocates of free will and determinism; that formal reasoning is crucially involved in everyday life; that there is a case for believing reports of miracles; that there is explanatory force to the design argument; that extreme scepticism is coherent; and that he can find the experiential source of our ideas of self, substance or God.

In spite of this list, which can easily be supplemented, Hume thought of his own position as one of only moderate scepticism. In this, he was carrying forward the scientific temperament of the seventeenth century and also following his mentor Cicero, who urged that, even if we lack a foolproof test for distinguishing truth from falsehood, in practical life probability is enough; things have to get done, and we do not need the last ounce of evidence in order to do them. Hume was frequently misunderstood, however, as denying the truth of certain claims, when he was asking how we know them to be true.

2.9 Influence and disputed questions

However much we may think that his contemporaries misunderstood Hume's views, there is no doubt that they reacted strongly to them. Adam Smith derived many of his notions in moral, economic and political philosophy from Hume, extending them where need be – as in the case of 'sympathy' and 'the impartial spectator'. Adam Ferguson (1723–1816), likewise, developed his conception of civil society against the background of Hume's reflections. In America, James Madison (1751–1836) and Alexander Hamilton (1755–1804) studied Hume's political writings and History with great care while formulating their views on the future structure and direction of their nation. In France, too, Hume's political, economic and historical writings were widely admired and discussed by the leading intellectuals before the Revolution. In Scotland,

Thomas Reid (1710–96) devoted a great deal of time to rebutting Hume's views on the nature of both knowledge and morality. One of the most troublesome notions for many of Hume's contemporaries, however, was that of causation: in Germany, Immanuel KANT (1724–1804) (chapter 32), having credited Hume with waking him from a dogmatic slumber, devoted a considerable portion of his philosophy to formulating a cogent alternative to Hume's position. A great deal of Western philosophy since the end of the eighteenth century can be associated with the rival views of Hume and Kant.

In terms of sales the most popular of Hume's works was the *History*. It went through 150 editions within a century of publication, whereas the *Treatise* had to wait nearly as long for a second printing. In the nineteenth century a few philosophers claimed Hume as their mentor, such as August Comte (1798–1857) in France, and J. S. MILL (chapter 35) and T. H. Huxley (1825–95) in England; William JAMES (chapter 36), in America, drew much inspiration from him. There has been an astonishing resurgence of interest in Hume's work since the 1960s, although in the earlier part of this century his name had been kept alive in Scotland. In the first place, dispute has centred on the appropriate contexts for understanding Hume's work and the due weight to be given to his various claims, which were made over a 40-year span in works of different kinds. Hume was trying to displace many of his readers' views on the nature of humanity and society, and his own knowledge of their beliefs profoundly influenced the style, content and emphasis of his approach. In this context there is dispute over Hume's conception of philosophy and its roles, and over the nature and scope of his scepticism.

On more particular topics, there is considerable disagreement about the need for, or the possibility of, modifying his account of causation to cope with developments in modern science, especially at the level of very small or very large phenomena. Do appeals to statistical frequencies avoid the sceptical elements in Hume's position? Are his own views on inductive argument and the weighing of probabilities fundamentally sound? If our sensory experience is a seamless continuum, as some people maintain, does it make sense to divide it up into events with beginnings and ends? If we cannot explain how we identify, separate and classify events, can we talk of separate causes and effects at all? Hume emphasized the importance of resemblance or similarity in this theory of causation: similar causes are assumed to produce similar effects. Things are similar, however, only in certain respects. How do we decide on the relevance and existence of similarities?

His views on the nature of the self provoke lengthy argument in legal and medical spheres, as well as among philosophers; and his views on freedom and determinism, the roles of reason and sentiment, and the nature of justice, are much debated. His economic views are now closely compared with those of Adam Smith. Studies of seventeenth-century and eighteenth-century Scottish legal thought, and the precise theological issues of the day, together with attempts to establish the nature of Hume's rather slight scientific knowledge, are likely to lead to revised interpretations of his work. One sign of a great thinker is that later readers deem it a cultural duty to define their position in relation to that thinker, and to treat him or her, however anachronistically, as a contemporary. With the attention now being given to the whole range of his works, including the *Essays* and the *History*, it is unlikely that his views will soon suffer neglect.

Further Reading

There is no standard or uniform edition of Hume's works, but most of them are available in paperback. Convenient editions of Hume's *Essays* and also of his *History* are published in the Liberty Classics series (Hume 1985a and 1985c respectively). There are many editions of *An Enquiry Concerning Human Understanding* and *An Enquiry Concerning the Principles of Morals*, and they are printed together in the Clarendon Press edition edited by Nidditch (1975a). Nidditch (1978a) has also edited *A Treatise of Human Nature*, which is published along with the *Abstract*. The best edition of the *Dialogues Concerning Natural Religion* (1779) is edited by N. Kemp Smith, who also provided a long introduction.

Mossner (1980) has become the standard biography, with the Scottish Enlightenment and other contexts explored in Daiches, Jones and Jones (1986), Jones (1989, 1982) and Sher (1985).

Classic studies of Hume include Church (1934), Laird (1932), Passmore (1952), Price (1940) and Smith (1941). Of recent general studies of Hume's philosophy, I can mention Capaldi (1974), Norton (1982), Noxon (1973), Penelhum (1975), Stroud (1977) and Wright (1983). Bennett (1971) explores major themes in Locke, Berkeley and Hume.

Ardal (1966), Baier (1991), Fogelin (1985), Flew (1961) and Pears (1991) examine different aspects of the *Treatise*. Beauchamp and Rosenberg (1981) and Strawson (1989) consider Hume's account of causation, which is also a central concern of Mackie (1974). Stove (1973) discusses Hume on induction.

Hume's philosophy of religion is discussed by Gaskin (1978), Hurlbutt (1965), Jeffner (1966), and Tweyman (1986), and his politics is discussed by Millar (1981).

References

Hume

Hume, D. 1947 [1779]: *Dialogues Concerning Natural Religion* (edited by N. Kemp Smith). London: Nelson.

——1975a [1748–51]: *Enquiries Concerning Human Understanding and Concerning the Principles of Morals*, 3rd edn (edited by P. H. Nidditch). Oxford: Clarendon Press.

——1975b [1748]: *Enquiry Concerning Human Understanding*. In Hume (1975a).

——1975c [1751]: *Enquiry Concerning the Principles of Morals*. In Hume (1975a).

——1978a [1739–40]: *A Treatise of Human Nature*, 2nd edn (edited by P. H. Nidditch). Oxford: Clarendon Press.

——1978b [1740]: *An Abstract of a Treatise of Human Nature*. Reprinted in Hume (1978a).

——1985a [1741–2]: *Essays, Moral, Political, and Literary*. Indianapolis, IN: Liberty Fund. Published with *Political Discourses* (Hume 1985b).

——1985b [1752]: *Political Discourses*. Indianapolis, IN: Liberty Fund. Published with *Essays, Moral, Political, and Literary* (Hume 1985a).

——1985c [1754–62]: *History of England*, 6 vols. Indianapolis, IN: Liberty Fund.

Other writers

Ardal, P. S. 1966: *Passion and Value in Hume's Treatise*. Edinburgh: Edinburgh University Press.

Baier, A. C. 1991: *A Progress of Sentiments: Reflections on Hume's Treatise*. Cambridge, MA: Harvard University Press.

Beauchamp, T. L. and Rosenberg, A. 1981: *Hume and the Problem of Causation*. Oxford: Oxford University Press.

Bennett, J. F. 1971: *Locke, Berkeley, Hume: Central Themes*. Oxford: Oxford University Press.

Capaldi, N. 1974: *David Hume: The Newtonian Philosopher*. Boston: Twayne.

Church, R. W. 1934: *Hume's Theory of the Understanding*. London: Allen and Unwin.

Daiches, D., Jones, E. J. and Jones, P. 1986: *A Hotbed of Genius*. Edinburgh: Edinburgh University Press.

Flew, A. 1961: *Hume's Philosophy of Belief*. London: Routledge.

Fogelin, R. J. 1985: *Hume's Scepticism in the Treatise of Human Nature*. London: Routledge.

Gaskin, J. C. A. 1978: *Hume's Philosophy of Religion*. London: Macmillan.

Hall, R. 1978: *Fifty Years of Hume Scholarship*. Edinburgh: Edinburgh University Press.

Hendel, C. W. 1963: *Studies in the Philosophy of David Hume*. Indianapolis, IN: Garland.

Hurlbutt, R. H. 1965: *Hume, Newton and the Design Argument*. Lincoln: University of Nebraska Press.

Jeffner, A. 1966: *Butler and Hume on Religion*. Stockholm: Diakonistyrelsens bokforlag.

Jones, P. 1982: *Hume's Sentiments: Their Ciceronian and French Context*. Edinburgh: Edinburgh University Press.

——(ed.) 1989: *The Science of Man in the Scottish Enlightenment: Hume, Reid and Other Contemporaries*. Edinburgh: Edinburgh University Press.

Laird, J. 1932: *Hume's Philosophy of Human Nature*. London: Methuen.

Livingston, D. W. 1984: *Hume's Philosophy of Common Life*. Chicago: University of Chicago Press.

Livingston, D. W. and King, J. T. 1976: *Hume: A Re-evaluation*. New York: Fordham University Press.

Mackie, J. L. 1974: *The Cement of the Universe*. Oxford: Clarendon Press.

——1980: *Hume's Moral Theory*. London: Routledge.

Michaud, Y. 1983: *Hume et la fin de la philosophie*. Paris: Presses Universitaires de France.

Millar, D. 1981: *Philosophy and Ideology in Hume's Political Thought*. Oxford: Clarendon Press.

Mossner, E. C. 1980: *The Life of David Hume*, 2nd edn. Oxford: Clarendon Press.

Norton, D. F. 1982: *David Hume: Common Sense Moralist, Sceptical Metaphysician*. Princeton, NJ: Princeton University Press.

——(ed.) 1993: *The Cambridge Companion to Hume*. Cambridge: Cambridge University Press.

Norton, D. F., Capaldi, N. and Robison, W. L. (eds) 1979: *McGill Hume Studies*. San Diego, CA: Austin Hill Press.

Noxon, J. 1973: *Hume's Philosophical Development*. Oxford: Clarendon Press.

Passmore, J. 1952: *Hume's Intentions*. Cambridge: Cambridge University Press.

Pears, D. 1991: *Hume's System*. Oxford: Oxford University Press.

Penelhum, T. 1975: *Hume*. London: Macmillan.

Price, H. H. 1940: *Hume's Theory of the External World*. Oxford: Clarendon Press.

Sher, R. B. 1985: *Church and University in the Scottish Enlightenment*. Edinburgh: Edinburgh University Press.

Smith, N. K. 1941: *The Philosophy of David Hume*. London: Macmillan.

Stove, D. C. 1973: *Probability and Hume's Inductive Scepticism*. Oxford: Oxford University Press.

Strawson, G. 1989: *The Secret Connexion: Causation, Realism and David Hume*. Oxford: Clarendon Press.

Stroud, B. 1977: *Hume*. London: Routledge.

Tweyman, S. 1986: *Scepticism and Belief in Hume's Dialogues Concerning Natural Religion*. The Haig: Martinus Nijhoff.

Wright, J. P. 1983: *The Sceptical Realism of David Hume*. Manchester: Manchester University Press.

Discussion Questions

1 Are there causal relations between events? What grounds are there for believing so?

2   If necessity cannot be observed, how can causality involve necessity?

3   Why should we believe the claim that every event has a cause?

4   Will the future resemble the past? Can we prove it? Are we justified in believing it?

5   What are ideas? Do they all have their origin in impressions?

6   Does experience provide a sufficient basis for knowledge of matters of fact? What else might be needed?

7   Does custom justify inductive inference or explain why we make such inferences even though they are not justified?

8   Do we act freely even if all our actions are caused?

9   Could we ever be justified in supposing that the laws of nature had changed or that we have encountered an event without a cause?

10   Does each of our perceptions exist independent of any other perception?

11   Are we justified in believing that there are physical objects?

12   Why did Hume come to believe that his account of personal identity was unsatisfactory? If there is a deficiency, can it be remedied?

13   Should our account of personal identity differ from our account of the identity of physical objects?

14   What is the role of agreement in our account of knowledge? Is knowledge possible where experts disagree?

15   What philosophical problems arise from reports of miracles? How can these philosophical problems be resolved?

16   Can the complexity and order of the world tell us anything about the existence of God? Can they tell us anything about the nature of God?

17   Does Hume's naturalism answer his scepticism?

18   What role does reason have in explaining actions?

19   What makes a quality a virtue?

20   How is it possible to judge oneself impartially?

21   Can aesthetic judgements be objective? Can aesthetic disputes be resolved?

22   Must the intention of the artist or relevance to an audience enter into judging a work of art?

23   In historical knowledge, how can we combine the knowledge of the actor and that of the spectator?

24   How is there room for reinterpretation in historical knowledge?

25   Can liberty and authority be reconciled?

26   Is there ever a right to resist the law? Is there a right to instigate a revolution?

27   What are the main threats to liberty?

28   Is Hume's thought concerning law, government and society applicable today?

32

Kant

DAVID BELL

There is hardly an area of philosophy to which Immanuel Kant (1724–1804) did not make massive and profound contributions, including metaphysics, philosophy of mind, epistemology, philosophical logic, the foundations of mathematics, ethics, aesthetics, philosophy of science and political philosophy. There are, however, two centres of Kant's philosophical thought, which comprise the foundation for the whole. On the one hand, there is the 'critical' or 'transcendental' metaphysics outlined in his Critique of Pure Reason (first published in 1781), and on the other hand, there is the ethical theory that he published in a number of works after 1784. In the former he developed an account of the mind and its place in nature that was designed to overcome the limitations inherent in the thought of his rationalist and empiricist predecessors. In his works on ethics he formulated a compelling vision of how moral law, autonomy, rationality, freedom, duty and virtue are related to one another in moral life. The following chapter concentrates on these two central areas of Kant's thought.

1 Life

Immanuel Kant was born in Königsberg, a flourishing Prussian port on the Baltic Sea. He went to the local grammar school, by all accounts an unwholesome place, where the pietist religious atmosphere was enforced by the 'pedantic and gloomy discipline of fanatics', but where he nevertheless succeeded in supplementing his limited means with his winnings from billiards and cards. At the age of 16 he began his studies at Königsberg University. During the next decade he studied, among other disciplines, mathematics, theology, physics and philosophy.

In 1755 Kant gained the qualifications necessary for him to become a *Privatdozent* (an independent teacher) at the university. As a Privatdozent he was not entitled to a salary, but instead received a small fee from each student he taught. In order to survive financially Kant was forced to lecture for up to 36 hours per week, on subjects as diverse as logic, metaphysics, geography, ethics, physics, pedagogics, arithmetic, geometry, trigonometry, natural theology, astronomy, meteorology and anthropology; and in 1764 he was offered, but declined, the post of Professor of Poetry. In spite of this 'monstrous academic workload', Kant was anything but a recluse. One contemporary recalled that Kant 'spent almost every midday and evening outside his house in social activities, frequently taking part also in a card party, and only getting home around midnight'. During this 'pre-critical' period Kant published a number of minor works on a variety of subjects. (Though important for a full understanding of Kant's thought, these pre-critical writings (Kant 1968) will not be examined in the present chapter.)

Kant became Professor of Logic and Metaphysics in Königsberg in 1770, but it was not until some eleven years later, at the age of 57, that he produced the first in the series of incomparably great and massively influential works that was to embody his so-called Critical Philosophy: the first edition of the *Critique of Pure Reason* appeared in 1781. It was followed, with remarkable rapidity, by the *Prolegomena* (published in 1783), the *Foundations of the Metaphysics of Morals* (published in 1785), the *Metaphysical Foundations of Natural Science* (published in 1786), the second, substantially revised edition of the *Critique of Pure Reason* (published in 1787), the *Critique of Practical Reason* (published in 1788), and the *Critique of Judgement* (published in 1790).

Two months before his eightieth birthday Kant died in Königsberg. His funeral was attended by many thousands of mourners, and it is clear that he was universally revered as much for his humanity and moral integrity as for his philosophical genius. On his tombstone was inscribed, appropriately, a motto taken from the passage with which he had concluded the *Critique of Practical Reason*: 'Two things fill the mind with ever new and increasing admiration and awe, the oftener and more steadily we reflect on them: the starry heavens above me, and the moral law within me'.

As this last sentence hints, the two great issues to which Kant's critical philosophy is addressed are, firstly, the nature of our understanding of the universe and, secondly, the nature of our moral life. These issues are the topics, respectively, of the following two sections.

2   The Metaphysics of Experience

How can we understand the universe and the things it contains? How is this even possible? As this is a huge, and hugely complex problem, we might begin by breaking it down into more manageable parts. We might ask: in what ways *do* we, as a matter of fact, understand the world and the things it contains? And for an initial, very rough answer, we might say something like this. On the one hand, our understanding of *the world* is couched very largely in terms of objects – objects that possess properties, participate in events, occupy space, persist through time, interact causally with one another, are substantial and obey the laws of logic, arithmetic, geometry and physics. We might call these the *object-related* aspects of the problem. On the other hand, our *understanding* of the world is based on our observations and perceptions, our concepts, thoughts, judgements and inferences. We might call these, in contrast, the *subject-related* aspects of the problem.

The object-related aspects can be made more explicit in a number of METAPHYSICAL (chapter 2) questions. For example: what is an OBJECT (p. 713)? What is a PROPERTY (pp. 96–7)? What is an event? What are TIME (pp. 82–5) and SPACE (pp. 358–9)? What is CAUSALITY (chapter 9)? How is logic, or mathematics or natural science, possible?

Correspondingly, the subject-related aspects yield a number of questions that belong, broadly speaking, to EPISTEMOLOGY (chapter 1) and the PHILOSOPHY OF MIND (chapter 5): what is it to perceive something? What is a concept? What is a JUDGEMENT (p. 797)? How are concepts related to judgements? How are concepts related to perceptual experiences? How are perceptual experiences related to sensations? The questions mentioned in this paragraph are among the most important that Kant addresses in the *Critique of Pure Reason*, and they are questions to which, indeed, he there provides specific and often provocative answers.

There is, however, a very general, overarching philosophical problem which can itself be characterized intrinsically as neither object-related nor subject-related; for it is, precisely, the general problem of how things that are object-related can possibly fit together with those that are subject-related. Again, this problem can be spelled out in a number of more specific questions. For example, how do our concepts refer to items in reality? How do our subjective sensations and experiences give us objective knowledge of the material universe? How can our inner thoughts and judgements be objectively true of the external world?

Kant's critical philosophy makes this overarching metaphysical problem its most fundamental concern; and that philosophy as a whole is characterized, above all else, by his insistence that in any acceptable solution to the metaphysical problem, object-related and subject-related phenomena must be taken to be mutually dependent and, ultimately, inseparable. In other words, no coherent theory of either one is possible that is not, already, a theory of the other. In particular, Kant claimed, no coherent theory of (objective) properties, objects, events, causal relations, substance, time or space can be provided that is not already also an account of our (subjective) perceptions, concepts and judgements concerning such things. In the last analysis, that is, the nature of the reality we know is inseparable from the nature of the mind that knows it. This is how Kant famously expressed this doctrine in the preface to the second edition of the *Critique of Pure Reason*:

> Hitherto it has been assumed that all our knowledge must conform to objects. But all attempts [for instance, to account for the possibility of objective knowledge] have, on this assumption, ended in failure. We must therefore make trial whether we may not have more success in the tasks of metaphysics, if we suppose that objects conform to our knowledge. (Kant 1929: B xvi)

Kant called this change in metaphysical perspective his 'Copernican revolution'. The resulting theory is a form of transcendental idealism.

The Copernican Revolution

Copernicus, a sixteenth-century astronomer, pointed out that the apparent motion of the Sun and stars had hitherto been assumed to be real motion: it was claimed that the reason the Sun appears to rise in the east, travel across the sky, and set in the west, is simply that it really is moving round a stationary Earth. Copernicus, however, argued that precisely the same appearances would result if, instead, the Sun were in fact stationary and the Earth were spinning on its axis. Copernicus replaced the naive theory, which took the apparent motion of the Sun to be real motion, with a theory according to which the apparent motion of the Sun is in effect a product of the real motion of the observer: it is because we are spinning that the Sun seems to move across the sky. Kant's so-called Copernican revolution is analogous. It had hitherto been assumed that there appear to be spatio-temporal objects that exist independently of us because there really are such things. Kant replaced this naive realism with a theory according to which the apparent nature and independence of the objective world is a product of our perceptions, concepts and judgements; in the last analysis, it is because we perceive and think as we do that the world seems to be as it is.

Kant's idealism is motivated by a number of considerations, one of which is as follows. There are certain very basic principles and judgements which form the foundation of our understanding of the universe. These principles and judgements include, for example, the truths of arithmetic, the truths of geometry, the principle that every event has a cause, the judgement that objects never simply go out of existence, and likewise the judgement that objects never simply come into existence, out of nowhere and out of nothing. According to Kant such claims as these have a number of interesting and problematic characteristics:

1   They are necessarily true, and cannot be either justified or falsified by appeal to contingent facts or perceptual experience (that is, they are *a priori*).
2   They are not merely logical truths, or truths by definition (that is, they are *synthetic*).
3   They are essential to our understanding of reality.

Kant called the knowledge we have of truths of this kind 'synthetic *a priori* knowledge', and his idealism is motivated by a combination of two beliefs: (1) that without synthetic *a priori* knowledge, no knowledge, or understanding, or meaningful experience would be possible at all; and (2) synthetic *a priori* knowledge is not knowledge we can possibly receive 'from without', as a result of our experience of the world. On the contrary, synthetic *a priori* knowledge is only possible if it encodes the judgements and principles we adopt in making sense of our experience. The Copernican revolution in philosophy is necessary, in other words, because without it we cannot make intelligible the possibility of synthetic *a priori* knowledge – and in the absence of that possibility, Kant believed, the very possibility of any knowledge or understanding whatsoever would become unintelligible.

Synthetic Knowledge a priori

'Analytic' is short for 'analytically true', and a judgement is analytic if its truth is solely a consequence of the concepts it contains. So, for example, the truths of logic are analytic, as are such conceptual truths as, for instance, the fact that all bachelors are unmarried, or that red is a colour. 'Synthetic' simply means 'not analytic'. The term *a posteriori* is short for 'acquired *a posteriori*', and something is known *a posteriori* if the knowledge is acquired on the basis of sensory experience, that is, if it is in principle falsifiable by experience. The term *a priori* simply means 'not *a posteriori*'. So synthetic *a priori* knowledge is knowledge that is necessarily true, which cannot be falsified by experience, but which is not merely trivially, logically or analytically true.

In conformity with this idealist perspective, the *Critique of Pure Reason* analyses both the object-related and the subject-related elements of knowledge with the aim of showing that all *a priori* elements must ultimately be explained by appeal to our essential subjective constitution – the ways in which we necessarily perceive, conceptualize and think – and cannot be explained by appeal to the way the world is independently of any access we may have to it. It is not because reality, in and of itself, is spatial, temporal or causal that we experience it as such. Rather, the explanation runs in the opposite direction: it is because of the essential nature and structure of our minds that our experience is, precisely, of a spatial, temporal, causal reality. Kant puts it bluntly: 'we can know *a priori* of things only what we ourselves put into them' (Kant 1929: B xviii).

The overall structure of Kant's critical philosophy – and, as we will see, the organization of the *Critique of Pure Reason* itself – depends upon his distinction between three fundamental, irreducible powers of the mind. Firstly, we have the capacity to receive or register sensory items such as sensations, impressions, sense-data, percepts and the like. Kant's term for such sensory items is 'intuitions', and he calls the capacity to register them 'sensibility'. Secondly, we have capacities of an essentially intellectual kind, involving the power to conceptualize, to think and to judge. Kant assigns such abilities to what he calls 'the understanding', a faculty which is responsible for our ability to use concepts. Thirdly, we are able to infer logically, to draw valid conclusions – that is, to reason. Sensibility, according to Kant, is largely passive: sensations and intuitions are things we undergo or that happen to us. Understanding, however, and reason are essentially active: concepts are things we use, and of course thinking and reasoning are things we do.

Kant is adamant about two claims. The first is that sensibility and understanding are quite distinct. They have their own operations, principles and functions. The second is that in all knowledge whatsoever that is available to us, both sensibility and understanding – both intuitions and concepts – must be involved. Kant categorically denies, in other words, that we can have any knowledge that is purely sensory, or, equally, that we can have any knowledge that is exclusively conceptual; for 'thoughts without content are empty, intuitions without concepts are blind' (ibid.: B 75).

The organization of the *Critique of Pure Reason* is complex, and can indeed be baffling. The distinction between sensibility, understanding and reason can, however, help us to make some sense of it. Figure 32.1 (which is not exhaustive) represents some of the most important divisions within the structure of Kant's text.

The following remarks may be of some help in navigating this maze. The main division of the *Critique of Pure Reason* into the Transcendental Aesthetic and the Transcendental Logic corresponds to Kant's distinction between sensibility, on the one hand, and understanding and reason on the other. The Transcendental Aesthetic is so-called – from the Greek word *aisthesis*, meaning perception or sensation – because it deals with the *a priori* elements that are to be found in sensory, perceptual experience (so this part of the text in fact has nothing to do with 'aesthetics' as that word is used now). One of Kant's main objectives in this part of the *Critique* is to demonstrate that space and time are *a priori* forms of sensory experience. In other words, as a transcendental idealist, he aims to show that it is because (1) our intuitions have *a priori* spatial and temporal forms that (2) empirical objects in the external world are spatio-temporal.

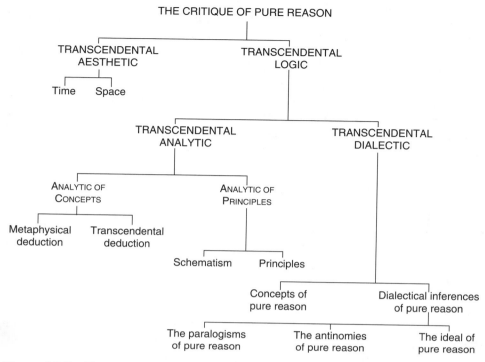

Figure 32.1   The main divisions of Kant's *Critique of Pure Reason*.

He believes no attempt to explain (1) in terms of (2) can be coherent. The Transcendental Logic is so-called – from *logos*, the Greek word for proposition or meaning – because it deals with the *a priori* elements that are present in our conceptual, intellectual make-up (so this section is only partially and indirectly related to 'logic' as the term is used today). Within the Transcendental Logic itself, the Transcendental Analytic concerns itself primarily with the nature of our understanding, that is, with the necessary features on which our entire ability to judge and apply concepts ultimately rests. Here Kant argues, among other things, that if we did not possess and apply certain fundamental, primitive, *a priori* concepts (he calls them the 'categories'), then no understanding or thought would be possible. The categories include such basic, *a priori* concepts as those which we typically express, for example, with the words 'all', 'one', 'not', 'is', 'maybe', 'exists' and 'causes'. (Kant respectively labels these categories Totality, Unity, Negation, Reality, Possibility, Existence and Causality.) In the Transcendental Dialectic, on the other hand, Kant addresses the philosophical problems associated with our capacity to use – and, more importantly, with our tendency to abuse and misuse – our powers of reason. (Kant calls reasoning 'dialectical' when it is invalid or fallacious.) The overall aim of the Transcendental Dialectic is to show that pure reason alone, when divorced from any input from, or application to, sensory experience, can provide us with no genuine knowledge whatsoever. That, in essence, is Kant's criticism or 'critique' of pure reason. Within the Transcendental Dialectic, the section entitled the Paralogisms of Pure Reason aims to show that any attempt to deduce facts about the mind or self, on purely rational grounds and independently of all reference to sensory experience, is doomed to failure. (A paralogism is a certain sort of invalid argument.) In the Antinomies of Pure Reason, Kant attempts to demonstrate the impossibility of purely conceptual, sense-independent knowledge of the material world. (An antinomy is a paradox or contradiction.) And in the Ideal of Pure Reason, he attempts to prove that pure reason alone can yield no knowledge of God.

A Transcendental Enquiry

As Kant typically uses it, the term 'transcendental' is intended to contrast sharply with two other terms, namely 'immanent' and 'transcendent'. Something is immanent with respect to certain bounds or limits if it lies within them. Something is 'transcendent' if it lies beyond those bounds or limits. Something is 'transcendental', however, if it lies neither within nor without those limits, but is, rather, a matter of the essential nature of those very limits themselves. Kant was concerned to establish the essential, *a priori* limits of human knowledge. Now nothing can possibly provide information about what is transcendent, that is, whatever by definition lies beyond the limits of knowledge. Science and common sense provide us with information about what lies within the limits of the knowable. But a special, non-scientific, peculiarly metaphysical investigation is required if we are to acquire any knowledge of the very limits of the knowable themselves. Kant calls such an investigation 'transcendental': 'I entitle transcendental all knowledge which is occupied, not so much with objects, as with the mode of our knowledge of objects in so far as this mode of knowledge is to be possible *a priori*. A system of such concepts might be entitled transcendental philosophy' (Kant 1929: B 25).

The heart of Kant's metaphysics is contained in the Transcendental Analytic, for it is here that he provides his analysis not only of how the mind must work if understanding or knowledge are to be possible, but also of how the world must be if it is to be capable of being known or understood. The remainder of this section is devoted to an examination of Kant's account in the Transcendental Analytic.

Our senses present us with a multiplicity of different sensations or, in Kant's terminology, with a manifold of intuitions. These intuitions are extended in time, and some of them have spatial properties, but their intrinsic nature guarantees them no permanence, stability, determinacy, objectivity or conceptual articulation. A manifold of intuitions is what HUME (chapter 31) had in mind when he wrote of consciousness as containing sensory contents 'which succeed each other with an inconceivable rapidity, and are in a perpetual flux and movement'. Now if our awareness is ever to be, say, an awareness of an intelligible, predictable world, containing determinate, stable objects that persist through their changes and interact causally with one another, then we must be capable of unifying and interpreting this manifold of intuitions. That is, we must have the ability to find our way about within the diversity of our ever-changing sensory experience. And we do this by construing those sensory states as experiences of objects in the external world.

Kant takes it as axiomatic that 'the combination of a manifold in general can never come to us through the senses', and he concludes that 'all combination, be we conscious of it or not . . . is an act of understanding'. He then adds: 'To this act the

731

general title of "synthesis" may be assigned' (ibid.: B 130). In short, if we are to be able to make any sense of the diversity of sensations we undergo, we must be able to combine or unite those sensations so that they come to represent to us aspects of objects in the world. For instance, I may take a manifold comprising certain particular tactile sensations, sensations of shape, colour and movement, sensations of sound, smell and the like, as belonging together, by taking them to be various forms of awareness of one and the same object – my motorbike, say. To take a variety of disparate sensory intuitions as belonging together, in virtue of their being different experiences of one and the same thing, just is to synthesize those intuitions. To unify one's sensory states is to understand them to be representations of objects and properties in the external world. So, in the absence of such synthesizing activities, Kant claims, we could have no awareness of an external world, and indeed no experience that would make any sense to us.

Synthesis cannot, of course, be a merely random or arbitrary process, but must proceed in conformity with rules. Moreover, the most fundamental rules governing synthesis cannot be learned or acquired on the basis of experience, for they are precisely the rules which must already be in place if there is to be any knowledge or coherent experience. Kant therefore concludes that the basic rules governing synthesis are *a priori* rules – and the most fundamental of all are the *a priori* rules which enable a number of different sensory states to be referred to one and the same object. Now according to Kant, concepts are nothing but rules for synthesis, and the categories are the most basic, *a priori* such rules. So the categories together specify the rules to which human understanding must conform if we are to be able to take our various sensory states as representing objects in the world. In Kant's own terminology, the categories together comprise 'the concept of an object in general'. Kant writes that the categories 'serve as the antecedent conditions under which alone anything can be . . . thought as object in general' (ibid.: B 125).

In the Metaphysical Deduction Kant attempts to identify just those concepts which are categories. (There are twelve of them: Unity, Plurality, Totality, Reality, Negation, Limitation, Substance, Causality, Community, Possibility, Existence and Necessity.) In the section called the Transcendental Deduction of the Categories, Kant offers a complex set of arguments aimed at proving the claim that in the absence of synthesis in conformity to *a priori* rules (the categories), no objective, intelligible experience would be possible at all.

One central train of thought that runs through the Transcendental Deduction is, in briefest outline, as follows. There is an inescapable condition that must be met by any plurality of mental states and mental contents if they are all to belong to one, single, unified consciousness – if, for example, they are all to be my states and contents of consciousness. The necessary condition, according to Kant, is that the consciousness or mind in question should possess self-consciousness: I must not merely have the capacity to be in an arbitrary mental state, S, I must also be able to *know* that I am in that state. And this requires, in turn, that I have the ability to ascribe state S to myself, roughly speaking by being able to make the judgement, '*I am aware of S*'. Kant writes: 'It must be possible for the "I think" [or "I am aware"] to accompany all my representations' (ibid.: B 131); 'for the manifold of representations . . . would not be one and all *my* representations, if they did not all belong to one self-consciousness' (ibid.: B 132).

In other words, the unity of consciousness requires self-consciousness, and self-consciousness in turn requires the ability to ascribe one's mental states to oneself. The principle which governs the unity of consciousness Kant calls the transcendental unity of apperception.

The Transcendental Unity of Apperception

This term does not stand for an object or entity of any sort, and in particular it is not the name as anything like an ego, self, soul or mind. Rather, it is the name of the formal principle which is responsible for the unity of consciousness. 'Apperception' is any form of consciousness that involves self-consciousness; and the unity of apperception is 'transcendental' because it is an *a priori* condition for the possibility of intelligible experience. So the transcendental unity of apperception is a condition that consciousness must meet if it is to comprise a coherent, integrated unity or whole – the condition, namely, that it be a form of self-consciousness. Kant expresses the condition thus: 'It must be possible for the "I think" to accompany all my representations'. If this condition were to fail, he claims, then self-consciousness would be impossible, in which case the unity of consciousness would be impossible, in which case one could have no intelligible experience of any kind.

In the final stage in the Transcendental Deduction Kant examines in more detail the conditions that must obtain if the ascription of different experiences to oneself is to be possible: what exactly must I be able to do, if I am to have the capacity to be self-conscious? P. F. Strawson writes: 'Kant's answer must be admitted to have a certain sublimity. What is required for a series of experiences to belong to a single consciousness is that they should possess precisely that rule-governed connectedness which is also required for them collectively to constitute [the] experience of a single objective world' (Strawson 1966: 92–3). In other words, the unity of my consciousness requires me to synthesize my different sensory experiences in conformity with the rules embodied in the categories. But for me to synthesize my various experiences in this way just is for me to experience a single objective world – a world made up of stable, material objects that possess properties, persist through time and interact causally with one another.

On the basis of this argument Kant feels justified in concluding that knowledge, intelligible experience, even the unity of consciousness itself, would be impossible if we did not possess and apply the *a priori* categories in ways that provide us with experience of an objective, external world. 'In other words', as Kant himself says, 'the consciousness of my existence is at the same time an immediate consciousness of the existence of other things outside me' (Kant 1929: B 276).

3 Autonomy and the Moral Law

Kant's major contributions to ETHICS (chapter 6) are contained in two works: *The Foundations of the Metaphysics of Morals* (1785) (whose original title, *Grundlegung zur Metaphysik der Sitten*, is variously translated into English, not only as *The Grounding, The Groundwork, The Foundations* or as *The Fundamental Principles of the Metaphysics of Morals*, but also under the title The Moral Law), and the second Critique, entitled *Critique of Practical Reason* (1956). The first of these works is beyond doubt one of the most profound and influential works of moral philosophy ever written. The first section opens resoundingly with the famous words: 'It is impossible to conceive of anything in the world, or indeed anything beyond the world, which can be considered good without qualification, except a *good will*.' And, as Kant himself puts it, 'the sole aim' of the book is to 'seek out and establish *the supreme principle of morality*'. Kant's aim, in other words, is to identify and defend the most basic moral principle or law which directly determines the ETHICAL VALUE (p. 203) possessed by acts of WILL (p. 219), and which, as a consequence, indirectly determines all other moral values without exception. He calls this supreme principle of morality the Categorical Imperative.

The underlying picture, in terms of which we can begin to make sense of Kant's moral theory, is as follows. Like all animals, human beings are governed to a great extent by their desires: much of our behaviour is intelligible when it is seen as directed towards ends that are determined by our wishes, passions, appetites, desires and the like. In this respect, as Hume said, 'reason is and ought to be the slave of the passions'. Here the role of practical reason is merely to supply rational, efficient means for the attainment of the things we want. On the other hand, and unlike many animals, we are capable in certain circumstances of acting on principle, and of following the dictates of reason – even when this in fact goes against our appetites and desires. We do this when, for instance, we keep a promise at significant cost or inconvenience to ourselves, when we volunteer for some unpleasant task purely out of a sense of duty, or when we decide we must 'do the right thing' in spite of a strong inclination to do otherwise. When we act in this way, Kant says, the moral worth of our action does not reside 'in the purpose to be attained by it, but in the maxim in accordance with which it is decided upon'.

A maxim is a general rule or principle which a person can use as a guide to action: 'Always tell the truth'; 'If you think it will rain, carry an umbrella'; 'Don't always take the biggest piece of cake'; 'Never eat trout on a Thursday', and so on. As these examples show, however, not every maxim is a moral one; for there are maxims that express principles of prudence, say, or etiquette, or even whim and superstition. For an action to be a purely moral one, Kant demands that three conditions must be met:

1 The maxim governing the action must be a genuinely moral maxim (and not one of mere prudence, say, or etiquette).

2 The action itself must not merely *conform to* the maxim, but rather must be done *for the sake of* the moral principle that the maxim embodies. A purely moral action, in other words, is one motivated exclusively by a desire to implement a moral principle. It is one that is performed, as Kant says, 'exclusively from a sense of duty' and 'for the sake of duty'.

3 The action must be performed freely, by an autonomous agent.

Autonomy

Kant believed that mature, adult human beings are autonomous, and that it is for this reason that they possess moral dignity, deserve moral respect, and ought never to be treated as mere means to an end, but always as ends in themselves. Possession of genuine autonomy depends upon the presence of three things. Firstly, an autonomous agent must be free, that is, capable of acts of will that are not causally determined, either by inner forces like inclinations, desires and passions, or by external forces in the outer world. Secondly, autonomy requires that agents can exercise rational self-control over their decisions and their actions. And, thirdly, autonomy requires that the rational principles governing such self-control are the sole responsibility of the individual agent: no genuinely autonomous agent can relinquish responsibility for the principles on which he or she acts to any external authority – whether it be the church, the state, the law, society, family, teachers or friends. On the contrary, all such principles must be chosen and imposed by the agent alone. And the supreme principle of rational, moral autonomy is the Categorical Imperative.

At this point we need to ask: when does a maxim embody an intrinsically moral principle? How, that is, are we to tell a genuinely moral maxim from one that has no intrinsic moral content or relevance? The answer to this question is stated below, at the beginning of the following paragraph. Before providing the answer, however, some preliminary scene-setting is required. We can predict, in advance, that the answer will be highly abstract and general – after all, we are asking for nothing less than a principle which will enable us to identify all and only those maxims that are morally good, irrespective of where, when and by whom they are formulated, and regardless of the particular acts, or goals, or agents they are intended to govern. We can also predict that the principle will be both synthetic and *a priori*. It must be *a priori*, for in so far as it is to determine the moral value of any possible act, performed by any possible rational agent, in any possible circumstance, it must clearly be independent of all that is merely contingently the case. In particular, it must be independent of whatever contingent desires and inclinations an agent might possess, and of whatever contingent consequences an action might have in particular circumstances. The principle must also be synthetic because a merely trivial, analytic answer to our question would be incapable of providing the substantive knowledge we seek. And finally, the answer to our question will itself be a moral principle, albeit a very general, abstract one. What we require at this point is not a descriptive assertion specifying what is the case and the ways in which we do in fact act, but rather a normative rule which will specify what *should be* the case and how we *ought* to act. Moral principles, that is, have the primary function of regulating and evaluating behaviour, and as such, Kant believed, they have imperative force. So what we seek, in answer to our question, is a (second-level) moral imperative that specifies which maxims (first-level imperatives) we *ought* to adopt as reasons for action.

A maxim comprises a morally good basis for action when it conforms to the Categorical Imperative; and the Categorical Imperative is precisely a second-level, universally applicable, abstract, normative, *a priori*, synthetic rule for the evaluation of first-level maxims. In its most famous formulation the Categorical Imperative reads: 'Act only on that maxim through which you can at the same time will that it should become a universal law.'

The Categorical Imperative

An imperative is a command, instruction or rule governing how one should act. An imperative is 'categorical' when it is exceptionless, that is, when it is binding on all rational agents, in all circumstances, at all times. Kant believed that what he called 'the supreme principle of morality' was just such a categorical imperative, and he provided a number of different formulations of it. The most important are:

1   Act only on that maxim through which you can at the same time will that it should become a universal law.
2   So act as to use humanity, both in your own person and in the person of every other, always at the same time as an end, never simply as a means.
3   So act as if you were always through your maxims a law-making member of a kingdom of ends.

The Categorical Imperative is, for Kant, an *a priori*, abstract law which governs the moral value of the maxims on which we act – maxims which, in turn, determine the moral value of those acts themselves. So an act is morally good if it is performed for the sake of a morally good maxim; and a maxim is morally good if it conforms to the Categorical Imperative.

The relation of Kant's moral theory to his metaphysics of experience is complex and obscure. One thing, however, is clear. In the *Critique of Pure Reason* Kant had attempted to establish the limits of genuine knowledge, that is, to discover the *a priori* conditions that must obtain if knowledge is to be possible. One of his conclusions was that, for us, there can be no knowledge of any super-sensible, non-empirical reality. In other words, a necessary condition of the possibility of human knowledge is that it involve not only intellectual concepts, but also sensory intuitions. For Kant, therefore, there could be no *knowledge* of God, the immortality of the soul, or the freedom of the will. To such matters as these, he maintained, concepts like observation, discovery, evidence, truth, science, explanation and the like must remain forever inapplicable. But about such matters we can nevertheless have *faith*. Faith in God, commitment to the moral law, respect for other persons, appreciation of the dignity that autonomy bestows – these were for Kant among the highest ideals that his philosophy, as a whole, was intended to protect. And in particular, his metaphysics of experience and his account of the limits of knowledge were intended to show that no empirical, naturalistic or scientific treatment of these transcendent matters could possibly be intelligible. As he says in the preface to the second edition of the *Critique of Pure Reason*: 'I have therefore found it necessary to limit knowledge, in order to make room for faith' (Kant 1929: B xxx).

Further Reading

For those who are new to Kant, a number of general, introductory works are available which cover all or most of the major aspects of Kantian thought. Copleston (1964) presents a conscientious, accessible and detailed, though rather unexciting, overview. Scruton (1982) is briefer and more spirited. Kemp (1968) and Körner (1955) are both reliable introductions, though they are slightly less elementary than those mentioned above. Walker (1978) is another excellent, though non-elementary, introduction to Kant's thought as a whole.

Among introductory works that concentrate specifically on themes from the *Critique of Pure Reason* the following are noteworthy. Broad (1978) presents a thorough, helpful discussion of the first *Critique*. Wilkerson (1976) is sometimes helpful as an introduction, though it is too often unsympathetic and impatient. Walsh (1975) writes with exemplary clarity and sophistication, as does Bird (1962), a good introduction to Kantian epistemology. For rather more advanced readers, Bennett (1966 and 1974) are idiosyncratic and iconoclastic, but can assist not only in understanding Kant's thought, but also in finding it philosophically exciting. Schwyzer (1990) provides a sympathetic and accessible treatment of some of the most central concerns of the first *Critique*. Allison (1983) is clear, scholarly and insightful. Although Strawson (1966) has been hugely influential, it is perhaps most suitable for advanced readers. Paul Guyer's (1987) exhaustive study, though doubtless important, is too dense and too long to be recommended to any but the most determined reader.

On individual philosophical topics, important and helpful material can often be found in collections of articles (though this material is rarely of an elementary or introductory nature). Among the most accessible and useful of such anthologies are Walker (1982), Wolff (1967), Guyer (1992) and Schaper and Vossenkuhl (1989).

For those seeking help in understanding particular sections, passages, or even words and phrases in the *Critique of Pure Reason*, a number of commentaries are available which provide detailed textual clarification. Among the most important are Kemp Smith (1923), Paton (1936) and Ewing (1938).

An introduction to the overall philosophical context of Kant's moral philosophy can be obtained from Singer (1961) and Broad (1930). Sympathetic, scholarly and clear treatments of Kantian ethics are to be found in Allison (1990), Sullivan (1989), Paton (1947) and Acton (1970). There are, in addition, a number of excellent commentaries on Kant's ethical writings. Among the best are Beck (1960), Ross (1954) and Wolff (1973).

References

Kant

Kant, I. 1783: *Prolegomena to Any Future Metaphysics*. In various translations: translated by L. W. Beck, Indianapolis, IN: Bobbs-Merrill (1950); translated by P. G. Lucas, Manchester: Manchester University Press (1953); translated by J. Ellington, Indianapolis, IN: Hackett (1985).

—— 1785: *The Groundwork of the Metaphysics of Morals*. In various translations: translated by H. J. Paton, London: Hutchinson (1949); translated by L. W. Beck (as *The Foundations of the Metaphysics of Morals*), Indianapolis, IN: Bobbs-Merrill (1959).

—— 1790: *Critique of Judgement*. In various translations: translated by J. Meredith, Oxford: Clarendon Press (1952); translated by J. H. Bernard, New York: Haffner (1968); translated by W. S. Pluhar, Indianapolis, IN: Hackett (1987).

—— 1929 [1781, 1787]: *Critique of Pure Reason* (1st edn (A), 1781, 2nd edn (B), 1787) (translated by N. Kemp Smith). London: Macmillan.

—— 1956 [1788]: *Critique of Practical Reason* (translated by L. W. Beck). Indianapolis, IN: Bobbs-Merrill.

—— 1968: *Selected Pre-Critical Writings and Correspondence with Beck* (translated by G. B. Kerford and D. E. Walford). Manchester: Manchester University Press.

Cambridge University Press is currently preparing new English translations of all Kant's published works, under the series title The Cambridge Edition of the Works of Immanuel Kant. Its general editors are Paul Guyer and Allen W. Wood.

Kant's life and historical background

Beck, L. W. 1969: *Early German Philosophy: Kant and His Predecessors*. Cambridge, MA: Harvard University Press.

Cassirer, E. 1951: *The Philosophy of the Enlightenment* (translated by F. C. A. Koelln and J. P. Pettegrove). Princeton, NJ: Princeton University Press.

—— 1981: *Kant's Life and Thought* (translated by J. Haden). New Haven, CT: Yale University Press.

Gulyga, A. 1987: *Immanuel Kant: His Life and Thought* (translated by M. Despalatovic). Boston: Birkauser.

General surveys of Kant's thought

Beck, L. W. 1965: *Studies in the Philosophy of Kant*. Indianapolis, IN: Bobbs-Merrill.

Copleston, F. 1964: *A History of Philosophy*, vol. 6, parts I and II. New York: Image Books.

Guyer, P. (ed.) 1992: *The Cambridge Companion to Kant*. Cambridge: Cambridge University Press.

Kemp, J. 1968: *The Philosophy of Kant*. Oxford: Oxford University Press.

Körner, S. 1955: *Kant*. Harmondsworth: Penguin Books.

Scruton, R. 1982: *Kant*. Oxford: Oxford University Press.

Walker, R. C. S. 1978: *Kant*. London: Routledge and Kegan Paul.

Wolff, R. P. (ed.) 1967: *Kant: A Collection of Critical Essays*. London: Macmillan.

Metaphysics and epistemology

Allison, H. E. 1983: *Kant's Transcendental Idealism*. New Haven, CT: Yale University Press.

Ameriks, K. 1982: *Kant's Theory of Mind: An Analysis of the Paralogisms of Pure Reason*. Oxford: Clarendon Press.

Aquila, R. E. 1983: *Representational Mind: A Study of Kant's Theory of Knowledge*. Bloomington: Indiana University Press.

Bennett, J. 1966: *Kant's Analytic*. Cambridge: Cambridge University Press.

—— 1974: *Kant's Dialectic*. Cambridge: Cambridge University Press.

Bird, G. 1962: *Kant's Theory of Knowledge*. London: Routledge and Kegan Paul.

Broad, C. D. 1978: *Kant: An Introduction*. Cambridge: Cambridge University Press.

Ewing, A. C. 1938: *A Short Commentary on Kant's Critique of Pure Reason*. Chicago: University of Chicago Press.

Friedman, M. 1992: *Kant and the Exact Sciences*. Cambridge, MA: Harvard University Press.

Guyer, P. 1987: *Kant and the Claims of Knowledge*. Cambridge: Cambridge University Press.

Kemp Smith, N. 1923: *A Commentary to Kant's 'Critique of Pure Reason'*. London: Macmillan.

Kitcher, P. 1990: *Kant's Transcendental Psychology*. Oxford: Oxford University Press.

Paton, H. J. 1936: *Kant's Metaphysic of Experience: A Commentary on the First Half of the Kritik der reinen Vernunft*. London: George Allen and Unwin.

Pippin, R. B. 1982: *Kant's Theory of Form: An Essay on the Critique of Pure Reason*. New Haven, CT: Yale University Press.

Schaper, E. and Vossenkuhl, W. (eds) 1989: *Reading Kant: New Perspectives on Transcendental Arguments and Critical Philosophy*. Oxford: Blackwell.

Schwyzer, H. 1990: *The Unity of Understanding: A Study in Kantian Problems*. Oxford: Clarendon Press.

Strawson, P. F. 1966: *The Bounds of Sense*. London: Methuen.

Walker, R. C. S. (ed.) 1982: *Kant on Pure Reason*. Oxford: Oxford University Press.

Walsh, W. H. 1975: *Kant's Criticism of Metaphysics*. Edinburgh: Edinburgh University Press.

Wilkerson, T. E. 1976: *Kant's Critique of Pure Reason: A Commentary for Students*. Oxford: Oxford University Press.

Wolff, R. P. 1963: *Kant's Theory of Mental Activity: A Commentary on the Transcendental Analytic of the Critique of Pure Reason*. Cambridge, MA: Harvard University Press.

Moral philosophy

Acton, H. B. 1970: *Kant's Moral Philosophy*. London: Macmillan.

Allison, H. E. 1990: *Kant's Theory of Freedom*. Cambridge: Cambridge University Press.

Beck, L. W. 1960: *Commentary on Kant's Critique of Practical Reason*. Chicago: University of Chicago Press.

Broad, C. D. 1930: *Five Types of Ethical Theory*. London: Routledge and Kegan Paul.

O'Neill, O. 1989: *Constructions of Reason: Explorations of Kant's Moral Philosophy*. Cambridge: Cambridge University Press.

Paton, H. J. 1947: *The Categorical Imperative: A Study in Kant's Moral Philosophy*. London: Hutchinson.

Ross, D. 1954: *Kant's Ethical Theory: A Commentary on the Groundwork of the Metaphysics of Morals*. Oxford: Clarendon Press.

Singer, M. 1961: *Generalization in Ethics*. New York: Alfred A. Knopf.

Sullivan, R. J. 1989: *Immanuel Kant's Moral Theory*. Cambridge: Cambridge University Press.

Williams, T. C. 1968: *The Concept of the Categorical Imperative*. Oxford: Clarendon Press.

Wolff, R. P. 1973: *The Autonomy of Reason: A Commentary on Kant's Groundwork of the Metaphysics of Morals*. New York: Harper and Row.

Discussion Questions

1   How, if at all, does Kant reconcile the claims (1) that all our actions are causally determined, and (2) that as moral agents we can act freely?

2   Which of Kant's various formulations of the Categorical Imperative is ethically the most defensible?

3   'Thoughts without content are empty, intuitions without concepts are blind.' What does this mean? Is it true?

4   How convincing are Kant's central arguments in the Transcendental Deduction?

5   Does Kant's treatment of the Transcendental Unity of Apperception comprise a solution to Hume's problems concerning the self?

6   Did Kant show that there could be no 'ontological proof' of God's existence?

7   How adequate an account of causality does Kant provide in the Second Analogy?

8   What are Kant's aims in the Schematism chapter of the second *Critique*? How successfully does he realize those aims?

9   Is time a necessary form of all sensory experience? If so, does this give us any grounds for claiming that time is transcendentally ideal?

10   How good is the case that Kant makes for the claim that we have knowledge that is both synthetic and *a priori*?

11   What is the relation, if any, between morality and rationality?

12   Are there any necessary limits to what can be known, and if so, how could we establish what they are?

13   Which is more morally significant: the motives from which a given action is performed, or the consequences that that action has?

14 Can one consistently be a transcendental idealist and at the same time an empirical realist?

15 Are there any *a priori* concepts? If so, how did we acquire them?

16 Are the truths of geometry (or arithmetic) synthetic and *a priori*?

17 Can an object simply come into existence, out of nowhere and out of nothing?

18 If we cannot perceive identity (or necessity; or substance; or causality), how can we have any empirical knowledge of it?

19 Could a moral agent lack autonomy?

20 What is metaphysics?

33

Hegel

MICHAEL INWOOD

Hegel created a great and deeply influential system of philosophy, ranging over metaphysics, epistemology and logic; ethics, political, social and legal philosophy; and aesthetics, religion and the nature of philosophy itself. He was fundamentally concerned with rationality, freedom and self-consciousness, but saw them as historical phenomena, developing through an intelligible succession of forms, moved by 'spirit' and structured by 'dialectic'. Hegel's response to Kant provides an initial basis for understanding his difficult texts. His work illuminates the thought of his contemporaries Fichte and Schelling and later idealists as well as features of Marx's writings. Many English-speaking philosophers turned away from Hegelianism after criticism by Russell and Moore at the beginning of the twentieth century, but the last twenty years has seen a strong revival of interest in many aspects of Hegel's thought.

1 Introduction

Georg Wilhelm Friedrich Hegel (1770–1831) was born in Stuttgart, Germany, in 1770. He trained as a theologian at the Tübingen theological seminary, where his room-mates were Hölderlin (1770–1843) and Schelling (1775–1854), and throughout his life he remained a devout Lutheran. After a period as a house-tutor in Bern (1793–7) and Frankfurt (1797–1800), he began to lecture, in 1801, at the University of Jena, where Schelling was already professor of philosophy; here he published his first book, on the *Difference between Fichte's and Schelling's System of Philosophy* (Hegel 1977a), and co-edited with Schelling *The Critical Journal of Philosophy* (published 1802–4). Napoleon's victory at Jena in 1806 interrupted Hegel's career and in 1807 he became editor of a Napoleonic newspaper in Bamberg in Bavaria. His first major work, the *Phenomenology of Spirit* (Hegel 1977b), was completed in 1806 and published in 1807. In 1808 he became rector of a high school in Nuremberg, where he married Marie von Tucher in 1811 and published the *Science of Logic* (Hegel 1969) in three parts between 1812 and 1816. In 1816 he became a professor at Heidelberg and in 1817 published his *Encyclopaedia of the Philosophical Sciences* (Hegel 1991a), which was originally intended as a bare outline to accompany his lectures but was greatly expanded in further editions in 1827 and 1830. From 1818 until his death (of cholera) in 1831 he was professor of philosophy at Berlin, where he published *The Philosophy of Right* (Hegel 1991b) in 1821. He was buried in Berlin next to Fichte, his predecessor as professor of philosophy at Berlin. His friends and pupils edited his works posthumously, including his lectures on aesthetics, history, the philosophy of religion and the history of philosophy.

Hegel's first significant writings, produced between 1793 and 1801 but not published until 1907, dealt with religious questions such as 'How did Christianity degenerate from a religion of love into a "positive" religion of rules and dogmas?' and 'Can the complexity and fluidity of the world as religion conceives it be adequately captured in philosophical and conceptual terms?' At this stage he tended to disfavour the methodical rigour of the conceptual understanding. The world is to be conceived in terms of 'life' and 'love', notions which, he held, cannot be captured in philosophical concepts; he preferred the natural simplicity of early Christianity, or of the Greek city-state, to the complex order of modern bourgeois society and its religion. But on moving to Jena he began to develop a philosophy adequate for the conceptualization of the world as a whole, and especially of the modern world. This task occupied him for the rest of his life.

Hegel's Response to Kant

Hegel's knowledge of the philosophy of the past, especially GREEK PHILOSOPHY (chapters 22 and 23), was both wide and deep. But the immediate context of his philosophical activity was the thought of KANT (chapter 32) and the philosophers inspired by it, notably Fichte and Schelling. Like them, Hegel was dissatisfied with Kant's view that we cannot know 'things-in-themselves': Kant's attempt to assign limits to our knowledge is self-defeating, since to be aware of a limit is to transcend it. Hegel often spoke of Kant as a 'subjective idealist' and argued that the categories or thoughts that structure our experience are not, as Kant held, simply imposed by us on our sensory intuitions, but are embedded in the nature of things. He felt that Kant's thought was insufficiently systematic, and that this was largely due to Kant's failure to examine our categories, and their systematic interconnections, in sufficient depth. The categories are not, as Kant supposed, the same for all people at all times; they develop over HISTORY (chapter 14), not haphazardly, but in a way that broadly reflects their logical order. While Kant focused on mathematics and the natural sciences as the primary forms of our categorial knowledge, Hegel regarded every specifically human enterprise – morality, social institutions, political life, art, religion and philosophy – as a way in which we come to understand our world and ourselves; the enterprises are not all of equal status – philosophy, for example, is superior to art – but they all help to domesticate the initially alien world and to make us at home in it. In general, Kant, as Hegel viewed him, accepted the stark oppositions of the understanding: between thought and reality, concept and intuition, duty and inclination and between 'is' and 'ought'; Hegel attempts to overcome these oppositions in a higher synthesis of 'speculative reason'.

2 Phenomenology of Spirit

Hegel developed these ideas reflecting his response to Kant in his lectures at Jena, but he first gave them public, if somewhat chaotic, expression in the *Phenomenology of Spirit* (Hegel 1977b). The work begins with an EPISTEMOLOGICAL (chapter 1) problem stemming from Kant: if we regard cognition as an instrument that we apply to the object, or else as a medium by which the 'ray' from the object is transmitted to us, we cannot be sure that the object is not distorted by cognition and that access to 'the absolute' (that is, things as they are in themselves) is not forever closed to us.

Hegel proposed to meet this difficulty by examining not objects directly, but the 'forms' of our consciousness of objects, since we cannot coherently suppose that our knowledge of the form of our consciousness is distorted in the same way as our knowledge of objects may be. In this way we can, he believed, survey the rise of knowledge or 'science', since a form of consciousness develops into another, higher form as a result of its internal defects. Thus we begin with 'sense certainty', which attempts to pick out individual items in its experience by means of such terms as 'this', 'here' and 'now'. It finds that it is unable to do this, since such terms are 'universal': anything whatsoever, for example, can be referred to as 'this'. Sense certainty is thus transformed into 'perception', which deals in explicitly universal terms, regarding things as bearers of universal properties. Plagued by its inability to give a coherent account of the relation between a thing and its properties, perception gives way to 'understanding', which views the surface qualities of things as the manifestation of inner forces and the laws that govern them.

The forms of consciousness considered so far are situated in no particular social or historical context. But from now on – beginning with the account of 'self-consciousness', in which two people fight to secure recognition from each other and thus to confirm or realize their self-consciousness – the work becomes a review of human cultural development, examining phases of our history (such as medieval Christianity and the French Revolution) which are nevertheless of general significance. Hegel believed that knowledge is not wholly separate from our religious, moral and political practices; he believed that it is a social, interpersonal enterprise – the work of 'spirit' or of the 'I that is a we and the we that is an I', rather than of a lone individual – and that it changes in an intelligible way from one epoch to another. Since Hegel's own system was the latest phase of this evolution, the *Phenomenology* attempted to record the historical preconditions of its emergence. At the same time it was intended as an introduction to this system. The reader is led by successive stages to the 'absolute knowledge' with which the work concludes. Absolute knowledge is what Hegel himself had; it enabled him to review, in a way that no earlier form of consciousness could, all the forms by which it was reached and to distil the logic that underlay their development.

3   Hegelian Logic

The *Phenomenology* was originally conceived as the first part of Hegel's system, to be followed by logic and the 'sciences' of nature and spirit. He did not fulfil this plan, and the logics that he eventually produced, the *Science of Logic* (Hegel 1969) and the first volume of the *Encyclopaedia* (Hegel 1991a), were conceived independently of the *Phenomenology*. (*The Encyclopaedia Logic* is preceded by an alternative Introduction, including a critique of previous German philosophy; a philosophical system cannot dispense with an introduction – however simple and apparently self-evident our starting-point may be, we need to explain why we are able to adopt that starting-point and what is the point of doing so, and this explanation forms an integral part of the system.) Logic is an examination of the abstract thought-determinations or categories that constitute the core of the human mind and are involved (with varying degrees of explicitness) in our ordinary experience and discourse, in our practical activities and institutions, in our systematic ways of understanding the world – such as religion, the sciences and philosophy – and in the very structure of the world itself. The first section of the *Logic*, the 'Doctrine of Being', examines the categories involved in the surface features of things: it begins with pure being (the obvious starting-point, since it is an all but empty concept, little more than the blank space of our thinking), which 'passes into' nothing, and thus gives rise to 'determinate being', the determinate quality that makes something 'other' than something else. From there it proceeds to 'quantity'. The quantitative features of something, such as the *size* of a field, are initially seen as independent of its quality, of the fact that it is a field, but in the third phase of this section, 'measure', quality and quantity are interdependent: if, for example, a field increases in size sufficiently it becomes a plain or prairie rather than a field, and the measurement of 'intensive' quantities, such as temperature, presupposes abrupt qualitative changes (such as that of water into ice) at certain nodal points on a continuous scale.

The second section, the 'Doctrine of Essence', considers the paired concepts in terms of which scientists and traditional METAPHYSICIANS (chapter 2) have understood the relation between the outer surface of things and their inner nature: these paired concepts include essence and appearance, thing and properties, substance and accident, cause and effect and the reciprocal interaction of substances.

The final section, the 'Doctrine of the Concept', begins with the 'concept', in part as a response to the difficulty of explaining, for example, the growth of a plant in causal terms, without reference to the concept encoded in the seed. But it expands into an account of the forms of 'subjective' logic: universal (such as 'coloured'), particular (such as 'red') and individual concepts; the types of judgement; and the types of inference or syllogism. (Hegel tended to regard these too as forms not only of our thinking, but also of objective entities such as the solar system and the state.)

Next, Hegel turned to 'objectivity' and considered three increasingly sophisticated ways in which objects are conceived: mechanism, chemism and teleology or purposiveness. Finally, he comes to the 'idea', the unification of subjectivity and objectivity. The most primitive version of such unity is 'life'. But from there he proceeds to our attempts to achieve unity on a higher plane, in cognition of 'the true' and in realization of 'the good'. The climax of the *Logic* is the 'absolute idea', which represents the ultimate unification of subject and object, and serves several purposes in Hegel's system: it represents, for example, the enterprise of logic itself, in which the thinker is not distinct from the thoughts that he or she thinks about – like the *Phenomenology*, the *Logic* concludes with a survey of the steps by which the conclusion was reached. Past logics (such as ARISTOTLE's (chapter 23) or Kant's) were 'finite': they failed to accommodate their own thoughts about the thoughts that they described. But Hegel's logic is 'infinite': the absolute idea contains all the thoughts required to think adequately about itself.

4 Nature and Spirit

The absolute idea also represents the relationship between the pure thoughts with which logic deals and the concrete worlds of nature and spirit. It is to these that Hegel turned in the second and third parts of his *Encyclopaedia* (Hegel 1970, 1971). Nature, in Hegel's view, does not develop over time: its changes are cyclical and repetitive. It does, however, have a complex hierarchical structure, the successive phases of which embody successively higher categories: space, for example, with which the *Philosophy of Nature* (Hegel 1970) begins, approximates closely to pure being, while the animal organism, with which it concludes, can only be explained in conceptual terms. Hegel did not attempt to deduce the details of nature from logic, but tried to supply from the natural sciences the empirical 'content' of the relatively abstract framework certified by logic. He was not loath, however, to criticize the theories of the day and distinctly preferred the more qualitative theories of Kepler and Goethe to Newtonianism and atomism.

The third main section of the *Encyclopaedia*, the *Philosophy of Mind* (Hegel 1971), is, like the other sections, subdivided into three parts, dealing respectively with 'subjective spirit' – the INDIVIDUAL MIND (chapter 5); 'objective spirit' – the interpersonal SOCIAL STRUCTURES (chapter 12) that humans create; and 'absolute spirit' – ART (chapter 7), RELIGION (chapter 15) and philosophy. The *Philosophy of Right* (Hegel 1991b) gives a fuller account of objective spirit or 'right'. Right has three main phases: 'abstract right', in which we become persons in virtue of owning PROPERTY (pp. 261–4) and are governed by LAWS (chapter 13) protecting our persons and property and sanctioned by PUNISHMENT (p. 760) (which is justified not by deterrent or UTILITARIAN (chapter 35) considerations, but solely by the occurrence of an infringement of right); 'MORALITY' (chapter 6), primarily the individual (Kantian) morality of conscience, according to which, for example, one is responsible only for the intended consequences of one's acts; and 'ethics' or 'SOCIAL MORALITY' (chapter 8) (*Sittlichkeit*), the institutions and norms that confer objective rights and duties on us and mould us into fully fledged human beings. Ethics in turn involves three phases: the family, whose members are united by love; 'civil society', the field of economic competition between individuals, whose acquisitive drives are nevertheless moderated by laws, policing and 'estates' (classes) and 'corporations' (trade guilds); and the STATE (pp. 261–4), which restores humans to unity on a higher level and makes them citizens rather than simply economic agents.

Spirit and the State

Hegel's state is a fairly liberal (but not very democratic) constitutional monarchy, designed to reconcile the rights secured by the French Revolution with social stability. It accords its citizens *both* 'objective' freedom, which involves a conformity between the rationality of the social order and the rationality that constitutes the deepest level of their selfhood, and a degree of 'subjective' freedom, which involves the freedom to make personal and moral choices, and which was unknown in the Greek city-state. A state is essentially one of a system of states and it must engage in warfare to maintain its unity by drawing the citizens together out of their private INTERESTS (p. 761). States which fail to do this fall into decay. A people or nation forming a state has a 'spirit' of its own, a way of thinking and acting that pervades its social and political life. The successive rise and fall of states constitutes 'world history', a history that is not haphazard, but rational, each national spirit being intelligibly related to its predecessors. Hegel marks this by viewing history as the work of a single spirit, the 'world-spirit', which circuitously realizes its final goal, the freedom and self-consciousness of humanity, by exploiting the passions of human agents who are only dimly aware of the purposes they serve. The spirit of a people informs not only its historic deeds, but also its art, religion and philosophy, though at higher levels these tend to become less marked by national peculiarities. They are the main ways by which a person gains insight into the world and into himself or herself; in art a person does so in a sensory form, in religion in the form of imagination or *Vorstellung*, and in philosophy by pure thought.

5   Dialectic and System

Hegel's system is knit together by dialectic, and dialectic also operates in the natural and spiritual realms in virtue of the thoughts embodied in them. 'Dialectic' derives from the Greek for the 'art of conversation, dialogue'. Hegel's dialectic does not, however, involve a dialogue between philosophers or between the philosopher and his or her subject matter. The dialectical 'movement' is intrinsic to the subject matter, such as forms of consciousness or categories, and the philosopher simply watches their development. Often, if not invariably, this involves the resolution of two opposites in a higher unity: for example, the simple unity of the family proves to be inadequate (or 'contradictory') on its own and thus gives rise to its opposite or 'negation', civil society, which is characterized by the individualism that enables its members to develop their own personalities and interests; but this in turn proves defective, and requires for its completion the higher unity of the state, the 'negation of the negation' which 'sublates', or at once destroys, preserves and elevates, the two opposites. Historical processes also exemplify this dialectic: for example, the unified city-state of antiquity gives way to the individualism of modernity, but Hegel's proposed state reconciles the two, giving free play to individualism while containing it within the differentiated unity of the state.

Another feature of dialectic is that Spirit essentially reflects on itself: for instance, logic is thinking about thoughts, the philosopher reflects on past philosophies and the historian reflects on historical events. But in reflecting on itself, Spirit changes itself: to think about a thought we need more complex thoughts; in thinking about other philosophies, we develop a new philosophy; historical writing raises humans to a new level of awareness and thus changes the patterns of their thought and conduct. Thus Spirit advances by continually reflecting on itself. This way of proceeding is often combined with the resolution of oppositions: for example, Hegel, in reflecting on apparently opposed philosophies (such as Spinoza's monism (chapter 27) and Leibniz's pluralism (chapter 27)), attempts to sublate them in an overarching unity.

This feature of Hegel's thought raises a difficulty. Do reflection and the resolution of oppositions come to an end or proceed to infinity? For example, are his logic and his philosophy complete in the sense that further reflection on them will generate no new categories not already contained in them, and that logic and philosophy are thus at an end? Has history come to an end in his own time or is there more to come (perhaps, as he occasionally suggests, in Russia or America), even if we cannot predict what it will be? On such questions as these Hegel was ineradicably ambiguous.

Human beings think not only about themselves and their thoughts, but about what is, initially at least, other than thought, namely, 'nature'. Thoughts are implicit in nature, but only gradually do humans make them explicit by their theoretical and practical activities, domesticating nature and coming to see it as a projection or extension of themselves. This is why Hegel regarded himself as an idealist: he believed not only that mind (or minds) exist, but, firstly, that the thoughts that constitute the core of the human mind are also implicitly embedded in things, and, secondly, that nature is progressively sublated or 'idealized' by the spiritual activities of human beings. We thereby achieve freedom, since freedom consists in self-determination, in not being determined by an 'other', and nature is now seen as being no longer starkly other than ourselves. Freedom is also enhanced by a person's self-understanding, which advances along with his or her understanding of nature. The workings of history and of the societies we inhabit, as well as the logical structures that underlie them, become increasingly perspicuous to us. Thus the growth of our self-consciousness accompanies that of our freedom.

Hegel held that his philosophical system expresses in the form of thought the essential 'content' of Trinitarian Christianity. In religious imagery, God the Father 'alienates' or externalizes himself by producing a natural world (the 'son') as the object of his 'consciousness', and becomes self-conscious in the spiritual reclamation that people make of nature and of themselves (the 'holy spirit'). In conceptual terms, the 'logical idea', the system of concepts studied by logic, 'freely releases itself' into nature which is then spiritualized by human beings. The question whether this amounts to atheism or not is another of those ambiguities (along with his attitudes to the political status quo and to the future course of history) that are intrinsic to his thought. Not surprisingly his followers divided into 'right', 'left' and 'centre' Hegelians, according to whether they were conservatives, radicals or moderate reformers in religious and political matters. Hegel's immense influence – in Germany (on D. F. Strauss, Feuerbach and Marx), Britain (on Bradley, Bosanquet and McTaggart), Italy (on Gentile and Croce) and in France (on Kojève, Sartre and Derrida) – depends in large measure on the comprehensive richness of his thought and its accompanying ambiguity.

Further Reading

For a reliable and interesting account of Hegel's life and works, Kaufmann (1965) is still unsurpassed. The best brief general studies of Hegel's thought are Mure (1965) and Soll (1969). The philosophical background to his thought is lucidly presented by Copleston (1965), and the essays in Priest (1987) explore in more detail his relationship to Kant. The complexities of Hegel's terminology are unravelled in Inwood (1992). Longer general studies include Findlay (1958), Taylor (1975) and Inwood (1983). On particular aspects of Hegel's thought, O'Brien (1975), Wood (1990), Pinkard (1994) and Forster (1998) are to be recommended. Essays on various aspects of his thought and its influence are to be found in Inwood (1985), Beiser (1993) and Stern (1993).

References

Hegel

Hegel, G. W. F. 1892–6: *Lectures on the History of Philosophy*, 3 vols (translated by E. S. Haldane and F. H. Simson). London: Kegan Paul. Also translated by T. M. Knox and A. V. Miller, *Introduction to the Lectures on the History of Philosophy*. Oxford: Clarendon Press, 1985.

——1948 [1793–1800]: *Early Theological Writings* (translated by T. M. Knox). Chicago: University of Chicago Press.

——1969 [1812–16]: *Science of Logic* (revd edn 1832) (translated by A. V. Miller). London: Allen and Unwin.

——1970 [1817]: *Philosophy of Nature* (Pt 2 of the *Encyclopaedia*) (translated by A. V. Miller). Oxford: Clarendon Press. Also translated by M. J. Petry, 3 vols. London: Allen and Unwin.

——1971 [1817]: *Philosophy of Mind* (Pt 3 of the *Encyclopaedia*) (1830 edn translated by W. Wallace and A. V. Miller). Oxford: Clarendon Press.

——1975a [1835]: *Aesthetics: Lectures on Fine Art* (revd edn 1842), 2 vols (translated by T. M. Knox). Oxford: Clarendon Press. Also translated by B. Bosanquet, edited by M. Inwood, as *Introductory Lectures on Aesthetics*. Harmondsworth: Penguin Books, 1993.

——1975b [1837, 1840]: *Lectures on the Philosophy of World History: Introduction: Reason in History* (translated by H. B. Nisbet). Cambridge: Cambridge University Press. Also translated by L. Rauch from a less recently edited text, as *Introduction to the Philosophy of History*. Indianapolis, IN: Hackett, 1988.

——1977a [1801]: *Difference Between Fichte's and Schelling's System of Philosophy* (translated by H. S. Harris and W. Cert). New York: State University of New York Press.

——1977b [1807]: *Phenomenology of Spirit* (translated by A. V. Miller). Oxford: Clarendon Press.

——1983 [1805–6]: *Hegel and the Human Spirit: A Translation of the Jena Lectures on the Philosophy of Spirit (1805–6) with Commentary* (translated by L. Rauch). Detroit, MI: Wayne State University Press.

——1984–6 [1832, 1840]: *Lectures on the Philosophy of Religion* (translated by P. Hodgson, R. F. Brown and J. M. Stewart). Berkeley: University of California Press. Also translated by E. B. Speirs and J. B. Sanderson, 3 vols, from a less recently edited text, London: Kegan Paul, 1895.

——1986 [1804–5]: *The Jena System 1804–5: Logic and Metaphysics* (translated by J. S. Burbidge and G. di Giovanni). Montreal: McGill-Queen's University Press.

——1991a [1817]: *The Encyclopaedia Logic* (Pt 1 of the *Encyclopaedia of the Philosophical Sciences*) (revd edns 1827, 1830, with posthumous edns 1840–5) (translated by T. F. Geraets, H. S. Harris and W. A. Suchting). Indianapolis, IN: Hackett. Also translated by W. Wallace as *Hegel's Logic*. Oxford: Clarendon Press, 1975.

——1991b [1821]: *The Philosophy of Right* (translated by H. B. Nisbet, edited by A. W. Wood). Cambridge: Cambridge University Press. Also translated by T. M. Knox, Oxford: Clarendon Press, 1942.

Other writers

Beiser, F. (ed.) 1993: *The Cambridge Companion to Hegel*. Cambridge: Cambridge University Press.

Copleston, F. 1965: *A History of Philosophy, vol. 7, Part I: Fichte to Hegel*. New York: Doubleday.

Findlay, J. N. 1958: *Hegel: A Re-examination*. London: Allen and Unwin.

Forster, M. 1998: *Hegel's Idea of a Phenomenology of Spirit*. Chicago: University of Chicago Press.

Inwood, M. 1983: *Hegel*. London: Routledge and Kegan Paul.

——(ed.) 1985: *Hegel*. Oxford: Oxford University Press.

——1992: *A Hegel Dictionary*. Oxford: Blackwell.

Kaufmann, W. 1965: *Hegel: Reinterpretation, Texts and Commentary*. London: Weidenfeld and Nicolson.

Mure, G. R. G. 1965: *The Philosophy of Hegel*. London: Oxford University Press.

O'Brien, G. D. 1975: *Hegel on Reason and History*. Chicago: University of Chicago Press.

Pinkard, T. 1994: *Hegel's Phenomenolgy: The Sociality of Reason*. Cambridge: Cambridge University Press.

Priest, S. (ed.) 1987: *Hegel's Critique of Kant*. Oxford: Clarendon Press.

Soll, I. 1969: *An Introduction to Hegel's Metaphysics*. Chicago: University of Chicago Press.

Stern, R. (ed.) 1993: *G. W. F. Hegel: Critical Assessments.* London: Routledge.

Taylor, C. 1975: *Hegel.* Cambridge: Cambridge University Press.

Wood, A. W. 1990: *Hegel's Ethical Thought.* Cambridge: Cambridge University Press.

Discussion Questions

1   Does Hegel refute Kant's view that things-in-themselves are unknowable?

2   In what sense, if any, is Hegel an idealist?

3   Does the *Phenomenology of Spirit* have a coherent plan?

4   Can we have self-consciousness without conflict?

5   What is dialectic?

6   Is Hegel's 'logic' really logic?

7   Does Hegel have any good reason for believing that philosophy must be systematic?

8   Can Hegel give a coherent account of the transition from logic to nature?

9   What use does Hegel make of the notion of infinity?

10   What is spirit?

11   Do we need objective freedom as well as subjective freedom?

12   Is history rational?

13   Is Hegel committed to the view that history has come to an end?

14   Was Hegel an atheist?

15   Is it plausible to suppose that art, religion and philosophy have the same 'content'?

34

Marx

RICHARD NORMAN

The writings of Karl Marx span many disciplines besides philosophy, such as history, economics, and political and social theory. This chapter reviews recent work on the philosophical aspects of his theory of history, and on his view of ethics, in order to suggest that the connections between those two themes are essential to an understanding of Marx's philosophical significance.

1 Introduction

For a period of about twenty years after the 1939–45 war, Marx's ideas were given little serious academic attention. There were exceptions, such as Popper's influential book *The Open Society and its Enemies* (1945), but on the whole Marx was ignored by philosophy as he was by other intellectual disciplines. Since then, there has been a veritable explosion of serious interest in him, beginning in the late 1960s with the period of political radicalism in the universities of Western Europe and North America. A huge amount has been written on all aspects of his thought – far more than I can do justice to in this chapter. I shall concentrate on just two themes which have been prominent in recent philosophical discussions of Marx: his theory of HISTORY (chapter 14) and his view of ETHICS (chapter 6).

The revival of serious interest in Marx's philosophy initially took a form which threw new light on his ethics. This was the discovery of his early writings, unpublished in his lifetime and for many years thereafter. In particular his *Economic and Philosophical Manuscripts*, written in 1844, first published in 1932 and first translated into English in 1959, reveal a whole new dimension of his thought. A key concept here is that of 'alienation', a term which Marx took over from HEGEL (chapter 33) and used to describe the relation of workers to their product and to their productive activity within a capitalist system of production. The workers' own labour, and the products of that labour, come to dominate and enslave them. Because their work is imposed on them by others and its products are appropriated by others, work lacks all meaning for the workers themselves. Instead of being a source of fulfilment through the employment of mental and physical energy, it 'mortifies his body and ruins his mind'. It thereby alienates the worker from his or her very humanity.

Marx's theory of alienation confirms the view that, at least in his early writings, Marx condemns capitalism not just for its historical obsolescence but because of its effects on the lives of those who live and work within such a system. The concept of alienation also serves as a moral tool with which to criticize more than just the workings of a capitalist economy. Economic alienation is only one aspect of alienation. Other forms of it are religious alienation, which involves a human being's self-abasement before beings that are the product of his or her own imagination, and political alienation, which involves the domination of human beings by the state which is created and sustained through their own activity. One obvious reason why Marx's early writings received so much attention when they were discovered is that they showed very clearly the moral distance between Marx's own ideas and the character of self-proclaimed 'Marxist' regimes such as that in the Soviet Union.

The philosophical interest of the early writings was also that they revealed a distinctive and positive ethical theory lying behind the concept of alienation. It is a theory in the same tradition as ARISTOTLE's (chapter 23) account of *eudaimonia* and MILL's (chapter 35) account of the 'higher pleasures': the view that the good life for human beings consists in the full actualization of their distinctively human capacities. For Marx, however, these capacities are not just intellectual and theoretical; they are, above all, practical – the capacity for free creative work which transforms the external world and gives it a human significance. A human being 'duplicates himself not only intellectually, in his mind, but also actively in reality and thus can look at his image in a world he has created' (Marx 1977: 82). Alienated labour thwarts these capacities for self-objectification and self-realization. It de-humanizes human beings and the world they have created.

The discovery of these early writings generated controversy about their relation to Marx's later work. Some commentators saw an essential continuity. They could point to the passages in *Capital* (1867) and other economic writings where Marx describes how, 'within the capitalist system . . . all means for the development of production transform themselves into means of domination over, and exploitation of, the producers', and 'mutilate the labourer into a fragment of a man' (Marx 1977: 482). Other commentators, however, regarded the theory of alienation and Marx's later theory of history as incompatible. The foremost advocate of this view was the French philosopher Louis Althusser, whose 'structuralist Marxism' posited a decisive 'epistemological break' between Marx's early 'humanism' and the later 'scientific' writings. Althusserian Marxism was for a time the height of intellectual fashion. I do not intend to discuss it here, and do not find much of value in it, but it did serve as a reminder that the core of Marx's work is to be found in his mature social and historical theory, and that any philosophical engagement with Marx must come to terms with that work.

2   Marx and Analytical Marxism

A landmark in the study of Marx's mature work was the publication in 1978 of Cohen's book *Karl Marx's Theory of History: A Defence*. Cohen drew explicitly on the techniques and style of analytical philosophy in the attempt to introduce a new clarity and rigour into the exposition and defence of Marx's theory. The three main achievements of

Cohen's book are: firstly, the provision of a clear and precise conceptual apparatus for Marx's theory; secondly, a general exposition and defence of the thesis of 'the primacy of productive forces'; and thirdly, the claim that the kind of explanation employed in Marxian theory is 'functional explanation'.

Cohen takes as a definitive text Marx's 1859 preface to his *Critique of Political Economy*. The theory sketched there identifies three levels of social life: (1) the 'productive forces' (tools and materials, skills and techniques), to which there correspond (2) 'relations of production' which constitute the 'economic structure' and which give rise to (3) 'a legal and political superstructure' and 'forms of social consciousness'. Earlier critics of Marx, such as Acton and Plamenatz, had argued that the theory was incoherent because these three levels were not in fact distinct. Cohen therefore provides clear definitions of these concepts in order to show that the three levels can in fact be distinguished and that it is possible for Marx to make precise and definite claims about the explanatory relations between them. The essential claims are that the character of non-economic institutions is largely explained by the nature of the economic structure, and that the nature of the economic structure (that is, the set of relations of production) is largely explained by the level of development of the productive forces. Cohen refers to the second claim as 'the primacy of the productive forces', and, after providing textual evidence that Marx made this claim, he proceeds to offer his own general defence of it.

The first stage is the defence of a preliminary claim which Cohen calls the Development Thesis: that the productive forces tend to develop throughout history. He then suggests that the stronger Primacy Thesis can be defended on the basis of the Development Thesis together with a further fact: that a given level of productive power is compatible only with certain types of economic structure. For example, a society based on computer technology could not be a slave society. Therefore, though productive forces can develop within a given set of production relations, that development is liable to reach a point at which it is no longer compatible with those production relations. When this happens, it is to be expected that the incompatibility will be resolved by the alteration of the production relations, since otherwise further development of the productive forces would be impossible, and this is denied by the Development Thesis.

Cohen does not offer any similar general argument for the claim that the economic structure in turn largely explains the character of non-economic institutions, and I shall come back later to this omission, but I turn now to his third important contribution: his account of the kind of explanation employed by Marx's theory.

Marx and Functional Explanation

Marx's explanations, Cohen argues, are functional explanations. These are explanations of the form 'F occurs because it brings about E'. Such explanations appear to be employed in other fields, for example in biology, in statements such as 'Birds have hollow bones because hollow bones facilitate flight'. Such statements have a complex structure. The initial explanatory claim is that F brings about E, but the wider explanatory claim is then that F itself occurs *because* it brings about E. Attributing to Marx the use of functional explanations has the attraction of removing a puzzle in Marxian theory. Marx is clearly committed to the claims that production relations facilitate the growth of productive forces, and similarly that superstructural institutions help to sustain the economic structure. This seems to suggest that the relations explain the forces, and that superstructures explain economic structures, which seems to run directly counter to the central claims of the theory. Those claims are, however, that the relations of production obtain *because* they facilitate the growth of productive forces, and that the superstructural institutions have the particular character that they have *because* they thereby help to sustain the economic structure.

The use of functional explanations is, however, contentious, and their value is strongly contested by Elster, another philosopher associated with ANALYTICAL MARXISM (pp. 273–4). The mere fact that something has beneficial consequences is not, according to Elster (1985), sufficient to explain it. Consider as an example the crude explanations offered by some Marxists for the existence of racism: it divides the working class, and thereby serves the interests of the ruling class. Elster would say of this example that, though it may be true that racism serves the interests of the ruling class, this does not in itself provide any grounds for asserting that that is *why* racism exists. No explanation has been given unless we can cite a *mechanism*, an account of how racism is explained by its tendency to promote the interests of the ruling class. Such a mechanism might be identified by, for instance, a 'conspiracy theory' which claimed that racism was deliberately fostered by members of the ruling class in order to promote their interests. But evidence for this would have to be cited, and in the absence of such evidence no explanation has been given. Elster does not think that the misuse of functional explanation is confined to crude versions of Marxism. Marx's own work, he suggests, is flawed by the reliance on unsupported functional explanations. Marx offers no account of how the need to promote the development of productive forces explains the emergence of new production relations. The mechanism is supposed to be found in the operation of class conflict, but Marx would have to explain how the existing constraints on the growth of productive forces motivate the members of a class to change the relations of production, and this he fails to do. More seriously still, Marx's theory of history relies not just on unsupported functional explanations that invoke beneficial consequences for groups of human beings, but also on vague speculative explanations of social change and social institutions that promote the goals of supposed impersonal agents such as 'History' or 'Capital'.

Cohen would agree with Elster on the desirability of specifying a mechanism in order to back up a functional explanation. The real disagreement between them is that Elster thinks that functional explanations are worthless without such backing, whereas Cohen thinks that even if we cannot specify a mechanism, functional explanations may still explain, though they would explain more fully if they could be elaborated. What Cohen does recognize is that, though functional explanations may lack an elaboration, they do, like ordinary causal explanations, have to be backed by a *generalization*. The mere fact that F has a functional effect E in a particular case does not constitute an explanation of F; but it becomes a relevant explanation if it can be backed by a generalization of the form 'Whenever F would bring about a functional effect E, F occurs'.

3   Explaining Superstructure and Ideology

I think it is fair to say that Cohen does not specify in any detail the kinds of generalization that would back the functional explanations in Marx's theory of history, and that Cohen's own defence of that theory does not appeal to such generalizations. That defence, as outlined above, concentrates primarily on the role of productive forces in explaining the relations of production, but I want now to look briefly at the second level of Marxian explanation, the role of the economic structure in explaining legal and political institutions (the 'superstructure') and forms of consciousness ('ideology'). It is here that the question of what kind of generalization we are looking for intersects with another important problem: the question of the *scope* of Marx's 'economic determinism'.

Marx sometimes appears to claim that *all* legal and political institutions and all forms of consciousness can be explained by reference to the economic structure. This claim is wildly implausible. I shall not argue the point here; I shall simply assume that the claim has to be qualified in some way. The problem is then that the theory is in danger of becoming vague or vacuous. From Engels onwards, Marxists have taken refuge in such phrases as that the economic structure is determinant 'ultimately' or 'in the last instance', and it is notoriously difficult to pin down what such claims mean or how they could be assessed. Cohen has tackled the problem in his more recent writing, and has distinguished between 'inclusive' and 'restricted' construals of historical materialism. Whatever the appropriate general formulation, I take it that the explanatory power of historical materialism must be looked for in its capacity to explain *specific* superstructural and ideological phenomena: this particular institution, this particular theory or belief, are as they are because they help to sustain a particular structure of relations of production.

This now returns us to the question of the kind of generalization that could back such a claim. The claim would be, for instance, that liberal-democratic political institutions, or liberal-individualist theories of political freedom, prevail because they help to legitimate and support market economies, and this would be backed by the generalization that such institutions, or such theories, emerge and become dominant precisely when they can help to sustain market economies. There is a certain plausibility in this. In the case of my two examples, it may well be possible to show that liberal-democratic institutions and liberal theories of freedom are particularly well suited to market economies, and it is then a striking general fact that those institutions and theories come to the fore in just those historical circumstances where they can serve that function. This, however, does not settle the question of explanatory primacy. An alternative 'idealist' account would be that these institutions or these theories have been adopted because human beings have good *reasons* for adopting them, because they are in some appropriate sense 'good' institutions or theories; if they also happen to support certain kinds of economic structures, it is not surprising that they have done so, but that is not why they have been adopted. To support the functional explanation, then, something more than the generalization is needed. We have to be able to claim that the institution or the theory would not have been adopted unless it served to sustain the economic structure. The problem of how we can support counterfactual historical statements of this form is a notoriously difficult one, but I want to suggest that in such a context a plausible candidate to support it would be some kind of *normative* judgement: the institution or theory can be shown to be flawed or defective in some way, and *that* is why we are inclined to say that it would not have been adopted unless it served this function in relation to the economic structure.

4 Marxist Ethics

It is in the light of this suggestion that I want to return finally to the question of Marx's view of ethics, a topic that has been the subject of voluminous debate in the past twenty years. Marx regularly spoke of morality as a typical example of ideology, implying that all moral beliefs are by their very nature a product of class interests and class standpoints, that they are relative to particular social and historical conditions and that they can have no independent rational validity. However, Marx himself also seemed to be committed to his own moral judgements about the oppressive and exploitative character of class societies, and in particular about the degrading and dehumanizing conditions of work in the capitalist societies of his own day. As Lukes puts it, we then seem driven to the conclusion that 'Marxism's attitude to morality is paradoxical' (Lukes 1985: 1).

The most promising way of attempting to resolve the paradox is to distinguish between different forms of morality. Lukes proposes a distinction between the morality of *Recht*, that is of JUSTICE AND RIGHTS (chapter 8) and the morality of *emancipation*, and suggests that 'the paradox in Marxism's attitude to morality is resolved once we see that it is the morality of *Recht* that it condemns as ideological and anachronistic, and the morality of emancipation that it adopts as its own' (ibid.: 29). This distinction, however, has to be qualified in various ways. On the one side, it is not clear that Marx would regard his own use of the language of 'emancipation' as an appeal to *morality*. Not all condemnation of aspects of human life counts as 'moral' condemnation, and Marx may have been quite consistent in maintaining that moral forms of condemnation are intrinsically ideological while other forms of condemnation are not. What is obviously needed here is some more precise account of the difference between 'the moral point of view' and other forms of evaluation.

The other qualification needed to Lukes's distinction is that, as he recognizes, Marx's attitude to the morality of *Recht* is not simple. Wood (1981) and others have argued that Marx did not regard capitalism as unjust. For Marx, the concept of justice is essentially a *juridical* concept. As such, it is a component in a set of rules by which a particular mode of production is regulated. Each historical mode of production has its own appropriate set of JURIDICAL INSTITUTIONS (chapter 13) and concepts. Therefore, from the standpoint of the juridical framework appropriate to the capitalist mode of production, particular acts may be unjust but capitalism itself cannot be. Other commentators, however, have pointed to passages in which Marx did appear to criticize injustice from a standpoint which transcends that of capitalism. Lukes suggests that 'Marx's view of capitalism's justice was both internally complex and hierarchically organized' (Lukes 1985: 58). Marx did identify a conception of justice which is internal to the capitalist mode of production, but he also criticized it from an external standpoint. This is the standpoint of 'the first phase of communist society', as Marx called it in his *Critique of the Gotha Programme* (1875). It is the standpoint defined by the principle that each individual should be rewarded in proportion to the labour he or she has contributed. That standpoint, however, will itself be transcended in the 'higher phase of communist society', embodying the principle, 'To each according to his needs'. The latter is not itself a principle of *justice*; it is the expression of a society of abundance in which juridical principles regulating the social allocation of goods are no longer necessary. Lukes goes on to criticize Marx's assumption that principles of justice can eventually be dispensed with. This assumption, he thinks, has diverted the Marxist tradition from the necessary search for an adequate account of justice and rights, and has left the way open for the appalling injustices and violations of human rights committed by 'Marxist' political movements and regimes.

Marx's ethical theory, then, is complex and contentious. I doubt whether it is possible to arrive at any definitive conclusion about it. His remarks on the subject are too brief, scattered and contradictory for there to be such a thing as 'what Marx really thought' about ethics. My own concluding suggestion is simply a view about what is philosophically fruitful in Marx's approach to ethics, and it is a view which links it with my comments about his theory of history. That theory, I have indicated, is neither plausible nor helpful when formulated as a general theory which purports to explain *all* political and legal institutions and all forms of consciousness as products of an economic structure. I also suggested that, when interpreted as a more selective theory which explains *specific* institutions and forms of consciousness, it depends for its plausibility on being also a *critical* theory. Particular institutions, beliefs or theories are criticized as being flawed or defective in ways that can be explained when it is seen how they serve to sustain a particular economic structure and the power of a particular class. The same judgement now has to be made of Marx's ethical theory. Whatever Marx himself may have said, his theory is self-defeating if it is understood as the claim that *all* values are socially and historically relative and are the expression of specific class interests and positions. It is most fruitful when understood as a critical account of how particular values and ethical beliefs come to be distorted by reflecting a limited class standpoint and class interests. And there is of course a particular reason why Marx's ethical theory needs to be interpreted as being selective, not as all-inclusive; for if what Marx offers is a critical theory, it must itself appeal to values, and cannot therefore treat all values as the ideological by-products of economic structures. Marx's theory needs its own values.

Further Reading

No one work by Marx encapsulates his contributions to philosophy, and the use of an anthology is essential. A useful collection is the one edited by McLellan (Marx 1977). A good brief general introduction to Marx's thought is that by Singer (1980). When completed, the best scholarly resource in English for advanced work will be Marx and Engels's *Collected Works* (1975–).

Popper's influential criticisms of Marx, and in particular of Marx's historicism, can be found in volume 2 of *The Open Society and its Enemies* (1945). Other important critical discussions of Marx's theory of history are those by Acton (1955) and Plamenatz (1954, 1963). Cohen (1978) is strongly recommended. Some of Cohen's more recent work, both amplifying and modifying his earlier discussion, is collected in his *History, Labour, and Freedom* (1988). Elster's interpretation and assessment of Marx is set out at length in his *Making Sense of Marx* (1985), and much more briefly and readably in his *An Introduction to Karl Marx* (1986). There is good material on the theory of history in McMurtry (1978), Shaw (1978) and Wood (1981); Wood is also the most convenient general guide to Marx from a philosophical point of view. The best introduction to the debate on Marx and ethics is Lukes (1985). Essays on the subject are collected in Cohen, Nagel and Scanlon (1980), in Nielsen and Patten (1981) and in Ware and Nielsen (1989). Nielsen (1988) is another useful guide. Wood's position is set out in an article in the collection by Cohen, Nagel and Scanlon (1980) and in Wood (1981). On Marx's concept of alienation, see Plamenatz (1975), Ollman (1971) and Meszaros (1972).

References

Marx

Dates given in square brackets are dates of final composition, except for *Capital*, vol. 1, which was completed in 1865–6 and published in 1867.

Marx, K. [1844]: *Economic and Philosophical Manuscripts*. In Marx (1977).

——[1859]: Preface to *A Critique of Political Economy*. In Marx (1977).

——[1864]: *Capital*, vol. 3 (translated by E. Untermann). London: Lawrence and Wishart.

——[1867]: *Capital*, vol. 1 (translated by S. Moore and E. Aveling). London: Lawrence and Wishart.

——[1875]: *Critique of the Gotha Programme*. In Marx (1977).

——1971 [1857–8]: *Grundrisse* (translated by M. Nicolaus). Harmondsworth: Penguin Books.

——1977: *Selected Writings* (edited by D. McLellan). Oxford: Oxford University Press.

Marx, K. and Engels, F. (1975–): *Collected Works*, 58 vols. London: Lawrence and Wishart.

Other writers

Acton, H. B. 1955: *The Illusion of the Epoch*. London: Cohen and West. Reprinted in 1972 by Routledge and Kegan Paul.

Cohen, G. A. 1978: *Karl Marx's Theory of History: A Defence*. Oxford: Oxford University Press.

——1988: *History, Labour, and Freedom*. Oxford: Oxford University Press.

Cohen, M., Nagel, T. and Scanlon, T. (eds) 1980: *Marx, Justice, and History*. Princeton, NJ: Princeton University Press.

Elster, J. 1985: *Making Sense of Marx*. Cambridge: Cambridge University Press.

——1986: *An Introduction to Karl Marx*. Cambridge: Cambridge University Press.

Lukes, S. 1985: *Marxism and Morality*. Oxford: Oxford University Press.

McMurtry, J. 1978: *The Structure of Marx's World-View*. Princeton, NJ: Princeton University Press.

Meszaros, I. 1972: *Marx's Theory of Alienation*. London: Merlin Press.

Nielsen, K. 1988: *Marxism and the Moral Point of View*. Boulder, CO: Westview Press.

Nielsen, K. and Patten, S. C. (eds) 1981: Marx and Morality. *Canadian Journal of Philosophy*, supplementary volume 7. Guelph: Canadian Association for Publishing in Philosophy.

Ollman, B. 1971: *Alienation*. New York: Cambridge University Press.

Plamenatz, J. 1954: *German Marxism and Russian Communism*. London: Longman.

——1963: *Man and Society*, vol. 2. London: Longman.

——1975: *Karl Marx's Philosophy of Man*. Oxford: Oxford University Press.

Popper, K. R. 1945: *The Open Society and its Enemies*, vol. 2. London: Routledge and Kegan Paul.

Shaw, W. 1978: *Marx's Theory of History*. Stanford, CA: Stanford University Press.

Singer, P. 1980: *Marx*. Oxford: Oxford University Press.

Ware, R. and Nielsen, K. (eds) 1989: Analyzing Marxism. *Canadian Journal of Philosophy*, supplementary volume 15. Calgary: University of Calgary Press.

Wood, A. 1981: *Karl Marx*. London: Routledge and Kegan Paul.

Discussion Questions

1   What is alienation? Does Marx's account succeed in explaining why people, in some societies at least, are alienated?

2   Are intellectual capacities or practical capacities more important for realizing the good life for human beings?

3   Can the style and techniques of analytical philosophy help us to understand and assess Marx's historical materialism?

4   Should we accept the primacy of productive forces in explaining social phenomena?

5   If there are levels of social life, how can we determine which aspects of society belong to each level?

6   How can we assess the claim that the economic structure is determinant 'in the last instance'?

7   If historical materialism cannot explain all the main features of society, can it explain any of them?

8   Can features of the legal and political superstructure and ideology of a society be explained by the nature of its economic structure? What other hypotheses are worth considering?

9   What are functional explanations? Can we interpret Marx's explanations as functional explanations?

10   Are functional explanations justified only for institutions or theories that are flawed or defective in some way?

11   Was Marx's attitude toward morality paradoxical? If so, can the paradox be overcome?

12   Can we eventually dispense with principles of justice and rights?

13   If Marx's theory needs its own values, can it treat all values as the ideological by-products of economic structures?

35

Bentham, Mill and Sidgwick

ROSS HARRISON

Jeremy Bentham (1748–1832), John Stuart Mill (1806–73) and Henry Sidgwick (1838–1900) are the leading representative thinkers of the British utilitarian tradition. Bentham declared at the start of his first work, A Fragment on Government (published in 1776), that the 'fundamental axiom' is that 'it is the greatest happiness of the greatest number that is the measure of right and wrong'. Happiness (or, as Bentham otherwise called it, utility) is hence taken as the unique measure of value.

Bentham was chiefly concerned with the applications of this fundamental principle. He was a practical thinker, centrally interested in making improvements in the real world. With J. S. Mill we get a more nuanced statement of the central principle aided by a more subtle surrounding psychology. His chief work in this area was his Utilitarianism (which appeared as a sequence of articles in 1861 and as a book in 1863). Finally, Sidgwick in his Methods of Ethics (1874) criticized Mill but also added a more complete epistemological base for utilitarianism.

Recent work on these three has been much more on Bentham and Mill than on Sidgwick, and this balance will be followed here. In particular, in the last thirty years there has been a sustained revisionary interpretation of Mill, which has removed him from the criticisms of previous standard commentators. Since the central focus of attention in this chapter is with this recent work, the order of exposition will not be chronological. Instead, it moves between the original texts and recent commentators, and also back and forward between Bentham and Mill.

1   The Central Idea

It is simplest to take the central idea of utilitarianism from Bentham. In the first chapter of his major work, *An Introduction to the Principles of Morals and Legislation* (1968–), Bentham says that 'by utility is meant that property in any object, whereby it tends to produce benefit, advantage, pleasure, good, or happiness (all this in the present case comes to the same thing) or (what comes again to the same thing) to prevent the happening of mischief, pain, evil, or unhappiness'. The key point is that there is a single source of VALUE (p. 203), which can be indifferently called utility, happiness or pleasure. This is to be maximized.

Utilitarianism, Bentham's ethic, is a consequentialist ethic. Things are to be measured and evaluated by their actual and possible consequences. Right action is justified by future states of affairs rather than by past events. For example, Bentham's account of the justification of punishment is a deterrent account. PUNISHMENT (p. 645) is justified if it deters people from committing undesirable actions. It is justified, that is, by the prevention of future harms rather than by retribution for past wicked acts. More precisely, for Bentham, the proper aim of punishment, as of anything else, is to produce pleasure and to prevent pain. Yet all punishment is in itself unpleasant, a pain. It can therefore only be justified if this particular pain is the cause of a greater reduction in pain elsewhere. So if people are deterred by a punishment from doing things which would otherwise produce more pain (such as, for example, rape, theft or murder), then that punishment will be justified. If there are two alternative punishments, each of which would produce less pain than the actions they would deter, then the least painful option is the appropriate one. Reduction of pain, and success in deterring pain-causing behaviour, are all that count. No other questions about the appropriateness of a particular penalty are relevant.

Similarly, Bentham's account of the justification of obedience to the state looks to actual and possible future consequences rather than to past actions or events. An example of a contrasting justification which looks to the past is that of the original contract, which supposes that obedience is justified by an (actual or tacit) agreement to obey the state. Such a device was used by the leading contemporary defender of British law in Bentham's day, William Blackstone (1723–80). Bentham attacks Blackstone vehemently in his *Fragment on Government* (1968–) and ridicules this kind of justification. For Bentham, justification of obedience to government depends upon the calculation of consequences. As he puts it in the *Fragment*, it depends upon calculation of whether the 'probable mischiefs of obedience are less than the probable mischiefs of resistance'. Again, the justification is not based on a past act (a past promise), but on the avoidance of possible future harms.

These examples should suffice to give the central idea of utilitarianism, at least as it was expounded by Bentham. It can, of course, be criticized on many accounts; and there has been continuous criticism since Bentham's own day. Both J. S. Mill and Sidgwick, although they continued the utilitarian tradition, were also critics of Bentham. However, before Mill's criticism and extension of Benthamism is examined, more should be said about the use which Bentham himself makes of utilitarianism.

2   Bentham's Use of Utility

It is not accidental that the two examples given of utilitarianism in the previous section concerned the relations between an individual and the state. Bentham was uninterested in private ethics. Instead he was interested, as he puts it in the *Introduction*, in 'that system, the object of which is to rear the fabric of felicity by the hands of reason and of law'. The end is felicity (happiness); the utilitarian end. The means to be used, however, are reason and LAW (chapter 13): reason, because the method deployed will not be appeal to history, prejudice or custom; and law, because the project is a POLITICAL (chapter 8) project. It is the project of designing a perfect system of law and government.

Such a project needs two kinds of fundamental assumptions: assumptions about what ought to be the case and assumptions about what is the case. The former set the evaluative ends, the latter describe the actual materials which have to be worked with in order to achieve these ends. The former is the VALUE THEORY (p. 212), and for Bentham this is clearly utilitarianism. The latter is a psychology, explaining how people actually act. Unless this is known, then it cannot be known what should be done to people to produce the desired end. The psychology which Bentham deploys is that people act in their own INTERESTS (p. 205). For Bentham, this is also understood in terms of pleasure and pain. People are taken to be seekers after pleasure and avoiders of pain.

It is of utmost importance in understanding Bentham that these two principles are not confused. The statement about what ought to happen (that the general happiness ought to be maximized) is quite separate from the statement about what people actually do (attempting to maximize their own happiness). They are clearly distinguished by Bentham and, indeed, no sense can be made of the overall project unless they are distinguished. For this depends upon taking people as they are (seekers after their own pleasure) and so constructing a system of law and government that they, acting in this way, will also do what they ought (promote the general pleasure).

One example of a Benthamite solution is the account of punishment given in the previous section. People moved by their own interest (the desire of avoiding the pain of punishment) are led to do what they ought by a correct system of threatened punishments. They are, that is, led by such SELF-INTEREST (p. 261) to consider also the interests of others and act in a manner which promotes the general happiness. The same principle can be applied to the design of institutions and was applied by Bentham to everything from the design of governments down to the designs of prisons. The key principle, in his words, was the 'duty and interest junction principle'. Things had to be cunningly arranged so that duty and interest coincided.

This is the kind of project for which J. S. Mill worked as a young man when he was an unreconstructed Benthamite. Later he became more detached. If we now move on to investigate this, and the criticism of Bentham that it supplies, we should remember that Benthamism was never intended to be anything other than a system of politics and government.

3   Traditional Interpretation: Mill

Although Mill took himself to be a utilitarian, he wanted to be a utilitarian with a difference. He himself was one of Bentham's critics, and in criticizing Bentham it is arguable that he criticized the central core of utilitarianism itself. Such, at least, is part of the substance of the traditional interpretation of Mill; and it is this traditional interpretation which will be examined next, concentrating on *Utilitarianism* (1963–), which is the text that everybody reads and which Mill himself took to be a defence of the doctrine.

The first point of criticism concerns chapter 2, which is entitled 'What Utilitarianism Is'. Mill here began by saying:

> The creed which accepts as the foundations of morals, Utility, or the Greatest Happiness
> Principle, holds that actions are right in proportion as they tend to promote happiness,

wrong as they tend to produce the reverse of happiness. By happiness is intended pleasure, and the absence of pain; by unhappiness, pain, and the privation of pleasure.

This is exactly like Bentham's remarks quoted above: there is the same use of the word 'tend' and the same promiscuous movement between 'utility', 'happiness' and 'pleasure'.

However, Mill shortly afterwards claimed that 'it is quite compatible with the principle of utility to recognize the fact, that some *kinds* of pleasure are more desirable and more valuable than others'. Here, at least on the traditional interpretation, the trouble starts. For the central point of utilitarianism is its claim that there is a single source of value (which may be called by different names). If this is so, then it would seem that distinctions in this value can only be quantitative rather than qualitative. Yet Mill explicitly wants qualitative distinctions. He famously says that 'it is better to be a human being dissatisfied than a pig satisfied; better to be Socrates dissatisfied than a fool satisfied'. This may well be true; but the traditional objection holds that this is because Mill has introduced values in addition to satisfaction (or happiness or utility). The human being and Socrates, that is, are only better because they have more of these other values, compensating for their lesser satisfaction.

In 1859, just before Mill wrote *Utilitarianism*, he wrote a famous defence of political liberty, *On Liberty* (1963–). This contains a strong support of the value of such things as truth, individuality and autonomy. Its object is, as Mill says, 'to assert one very simple principle'; which is 'that the sole end for which mankind are warranted, individually or collectively, in interfering with the liberty of action of any of their number, is self-protection'. Mill holds, that is, that there should be a purely private area beyond the control of law or public opinion. He says specifically that someone's 'own good' is 'not a sufficient warrant for interference'. These may all be admirable sentiments, but the question is, again, whether Mill's assertion of them is compatible with utilitarianism.

Mill himself says that it is. Shortly after the assertion of his 'simple principle' he says that he regards 'utility as the ultimate appeal on all ethical questions'. However, the standard interpretations, starting with the nineteenth-century attack by J. F. Stephen (1829–94), again hold that Mill can only defend liberty by relying on other independent values; and so again by breaking with utilitarianism's single value. Conversely, if maximizing utility is the sole permitted goal, then paternalist interference with others would sometimes be permitted; for it would be permitted precisely on those occasions on which such interference increased their utility. Utilitarianism is concerned with maximizing the good, irrespective of whose good it is. Hence, contrary to what Mill asserts, someone's good would be a sufficient warrant for interference.

Here are two versions of the objection that, by trying to include more in the idea of happiness than Bentham does, Mill in fact breaks with the central spirit of utilitarianism.

The greatest negative energy of the commentators has been reserved not for chapter 2 but for chapter 4 of *Utilitarianism*. This short chapter, entitled 'Of What Sort of Proof the Principle of Utility is Susceptible', has produced an enormous amount of critical commentary. Most commentators since F. H. Bradley (1846–1924) and Sidgwick have held that Mill here made elementary and embarrassing errors; so that it has been suggested (Berger 1984: 45) that Mill's current reputation would be very much higher if this short chapter had not been written.

It seems that the chapter intends to provide a proof of the utility principle. The supposed fallacies are hence fallacies of inference. The two most famous ones occur in the third paragraph. Here Mill starts by suggesting an analogy with proving that something is visible. 'The only proof capable of being given that an object is visible', he writes, 'is that people actually see it.' Similarly for something being audible: the proof is that people hear it. 'In a like manner', he continues, 'the sole evidence that it is possible to produce that anything is desirable, is that people do actually desire it.' The standard criticism of Mill is that he here derives the desirable (what ought to be the case) from the desired (what is the case). That is, he confuses ought and is; or in the terminology of G. E. MOORE (1873–1958) (chapter 38) he commits the naturalistic fallacy.

Nor is this the end of the infamous howlers that have been found in this short paragraph. For after showing, as he thought, that each person's happiness was 'a good to that person', Mill concluded that 'the general happiness' was 'therefore, a good to the aggregate of all persons'. Here by sleight of hand he seems to move from egoism to altruism; from the claim that everyone is interested in their own happiness to the claim that they are therefore interested in everyone else's happiness.

4 Reinterpretation (1): The Art of Life

This catalogue of apparent disasters might be thought to spell the end of Mill as a serious thinker; and so also the end of his revised version of utilitarianism. On the other hand, Mill's own criticisms of Bentham might be held to spell the end of the original utilitarian project. However, Mill has recently been subject to a sustained process of reinterpretation and defence. A 'new Mill' has emerged to whom it is harder to attach the traditional criticisms; and perhaps that reinterpretation can provide sustenance for a revised form of utilitarianism.

It was noted in section 3 that much of the criticism has been devoted to a single paragraph in a short chapter of a single one of Mill's works. One way that Mill has been reinterpreted is by getting a broader view. So, in *Utilitarianism* itself, consideration has been given to chapters not so far mentioned, particularly chapter 5 on JUSTICE (chapter 8). But it has also been noted that *Utilitarianism* is a relatively small part of Mill's total output. Mill's largest works – whether this is measured by bulk, by contemporary esteem, or by the amount of description he himself accords them in his *Autobiography* (1963–), which describes his intellectual development – are works of logic and metaphysics.

Mill made his name among his contemporaries with his *System of Logic* (1963–), which was published in 1843, and towards the end of his life he wrote his massive metaphysical work *An Examination of Sir William Hamilton's Philosophy* (1963–), which was published in 1865. It is therefore completely appropriate that John Skorupski's (1989) large study and reinterpretation of Mill pays much more attention to the logic than anything else. This balance will not be followed in the present chapter, since students read *Utilitarianism* and *On Liberty* much more than Mill's other books. However, it does suggest that a better view can be gained of these familiar texts if they are placed in the context of Mill's overall thought, and hence of the *Logic*.

The part of the *Logic* that is most relevant for the understanding of Mill's ethical and political thought is the last chapter, which is about 'morality and policy'. In it, Mill says that 'a proposition of which the predicate is expressed by the words *ought* or *should be*, is generically different from one which is expressed by *is* or *will be*'. In other words, Mill here very clearly distinguishes between is and ought. Furthermore, he says that every art has its leading principle. The leading principle of architecture, for example, is that it is desirable to have buildings. Standing above all these particular arts is the Art of Life itself. Its leading principle is that what is 'conducive to happiness' is desirable. Mill divides the art of life into 'three departments, Morality, Prudence or Policy, and Aesthetics; the Right, the Expedient, and the Beautiful or Noble'.

From this it can be extracted that Mill not only clearly distinguishes between is and ought, but that he also distinguishes between what is good and what it is right to do. Otherwise put, he only takes morality as part of what the principle of utility would promote. If, with this clue, we now return to *Utilitarianism*, but to the less familiar chapter on justice, we find there Mill saying that 'we do not call anything wrong, unless we mean to imply that a person ought to be punished in some way or other for doing it; if not by law, by the opinion of his fellow creatures; if not by opinion, by the reproaches of his own conscience'. So morality seems to concern only those parts of life in which there ought to be sanctions deterring specific kinds of conduct. For the rest of life, even though there may be principles of expediency, or matters of aesthetic taste, there is not in the same way obligations about what ought to be done.

The importance of this is that the root idea of utilitarianism as a personal ethic seemed to be that everyone ought all the time to be doing what produced the greatest utility; an impossibly strenuous obligation. In so far as Bentham avoids private ethics, he also avoids this problem of strenuousness. But Mill, unlike Bentham, is concerned with private ethics. Furthermore, the statements of the 'creed' quoted in section 3 above ('actions are right in proportion as they tend to promote happiness, wrong as they tend to produce the reverse of happiness', currently dubbed the 'proportionality criterion') does seem to advise such a strenuous performance. It says that, in proportion as utility can be increased, so something ought to be done. However, if we consider instead the statement just quoted from chapter 5 (currently dubbed 'the punishment criterion'), then this strenuousness can be avoided. Mill can be taken to hold that only certain very central human interests need protection by the imposition of such sanctions. Only these count as morality; and hence morality need not become overstrenuous.

Assuming that autonomy and security are among these vital human interests, we now see how we can get a coherent account of morality and law, as well as of Mill's proposals in *On Liberty*. For when such vital interests are concerned, they have to be protected either by law (using the threat of legal punishment) or else by morality (using the threat of public disapproval). Otherwise, in particular with the exercise of matters that are purely private, there should be no such sanctions.

The account here is like Bentham's theory of punishment. Certain kinds of conduct are subject to sanctions, either legal or moral. The reason people do not perform these actions (in the main) is because of their desire to avoid these sanctions. So, the connection between action and utility is indirect. Therefore, if Mill is still a utilitarian on this interpretation, it is of the indirect rather than the direct kind.

5   Reinterpretation (2): Happiness and Indirect Utilitarianism

The idea of a moral sanction did not originate with Mill. Bentham also talked of a 'moral' sanction. In chapter 3 of his *Introduction* he describes four sanctions: physical, political, moral and religious. He thinks that people can be deterred by the simple idea of pain (which might be caused physically, legally, socially or by God). Mill is also interested in how people can be made by sanctions to do desirable things. But what Mill adds to Bentham is a richer psychology, involving use of the association of ideas.

When Mill describes in his *Autobiography* his separation from the original utilitarian creed he says: 'I never, indeed, wavered in the conviction that happiness is the test of all rules of conduct, and the end of life. But I now thought that this end was only to be attained by not making it the direct end.' As he puts it, 'the only chance is to treat, not happiness, but some end external to it, as the purpose of life'. This describes individual motivation. Yet the same points apply as with morality. In both cases, happiness is the ultimate end. But in both cases the approach is indirect. The immediate or apparent end of action may be not happiness but something else. And it is only this other thing that is explained or justified by happiness.

Mill's main concern in the infamous fourth chapter of *Utilitarianism* was not to show that happiness is an end of action (which he passes over quickly in the much-discussed paragraph) but, rather, to show that it is the only such end. For this he needs his fuller account of happiness in which the theory of the association of ideas is pressed into explanatory service. As he says there, something which becomes associated with something as a means to an end naturally 'comes to be desired for itself'. So, for example, virtue can start as a means to happiness, and then become an apparently self-sufficient end of action. The explanation of action by happiness is, again, indirect.

There is, therefore, considerable current support for the interpretation of Mill as an indirect utilitarian. This might seem to determine also an older interpretative issue, the question of whether Mill is a rule utilitarian. This was proposed by J. O. Urmson in 1953 (see Schneewind 1968: 179–89). However, the main weight of the subsequent debate has run against this interpretation; and the more recent interpreters of Mill as an indirect utilitarian also do not usually think that this makes Mill a rule utilitarian.

Mill, Rules and Conduct

On any interpretation, Mill clearly gives a special position to rules. Morality is not only defined as 'the rules and precepts for human conduct'; Mill also emphasized the special position of 'secondary' principles. He thought that the past experience of humankind has shown us which kinds of action promote happiness and which do not. 'During all that time', he said, 'mankind have been learning by experience the tendencies of actions.'

All this is, however, compatible with Mill not meaning rules to apply in more than a shorthand manner. The rules, that is, can be held to be practical rules, giving knowledge about the tendencies of actions when no better information is available. Although it is practical to use such rules, this does not in itself mean that the action is only justified by the rule; and hence it is not rule utilitarianism in the narrow, or strict, sense. Furthermore, once the art of life conception is taken seriously, more is justified by utility than morality. Even if, that is, morality consists only of rules there are also the other parts of the art of life, such as prudence and aesthetics. They escape the analogy with law and punishment; and so escape whatever pressure this analogy may assert towards a rule utilitarian interpretation.

The proposed interpretation of Mill as an indirect utilitarian is sometimes made by contrast with Bentham. But Bentham can also be made out to be an indirect utilitarian. He was centrally concerned with the creation of the right system of law. Therefore, why someone acts in such a right system can also be interpreted as being indirectly connected with utility. They act directly because it is the law; or because they are afraid of the punishment. But the law is the right law because it promotes utility. Bentham also lays down secondary ends or goals, which are particularly prominent in his writings on civil law. The four secondary ends he lists in his *Civil Code* (1843b) are subsistence, abundance, equality and security. These are what a good system of law should promote. They again, as in Mill, stand in the position of being intermediate principles of justification. Again, as in Mill, they can be justified by reference to the past, or to the general, experience of humankind because they are ends that promote the fundamental principle of maximizing utility.

6 Mill's Metaphysics and Logic

It was noted above that recent work on Mill has stressed the breadth of his project and has revealed that its centre of gravity is more in the writings on logic than in the more familiar ethics and politics. No proper consideration can be given here of the logic and metaphysics; but it will be useful to have a glance at Mill's overall project before returning finally to his supposed proof of utility.

In both morals and metaphysics Mill can be seen as working in the central tradition of Bentham. They both thought that there are basically two kinds of philosophical position, which can be distinguished by the methods they use. On the one hand is the method of relying on INTUITIVE (pp. 726–33) or *a priori* knowledge. On the other is the empiricist method of relying on experience. Mill aligns himself with the latter. This method holds that moral and metaphysical conclusions, and hence political ends, are not to be established by some innate intuitive faculty, or moral sense; they are to be established according to the effects of varying courses of possible action on demonstrable and unmysterious experience, namely the happiness they produce.

This distinction not only explains Mill's position in moral and political philosophy but also his wider intellectual project. It gives the central purpose of his *Logic* as well as his *Examination of Hamilton*. The chief object of the *Logic* is to show how there can be right reasoning and discovery of truth when no basis is used except for experience. Mill here attempts to show that all candidates for truths known intuitively and independent of experience (such as MATHEMATICAL TRUTHS (chapter 11) or the belief that every event has a cause) are in fact founded on experience. The *Logic* also deals with MEANING (chapter 3) and with DEDUCTIVE ARGUMENT (p. 287) (where he holds that the real inference in a syllogism is the establishment of the major premise and is therefore inductive). However, its central focus is to produce an empiricist PHILOSOPHY OF SCIENCE (chapter 9), showing how knowledge may be acquired from experience.

Mill's experiential treatment of logic and mathematics is in stark opposition to the prevailing tone of this century's philosophy of logic. However, as recent work has brought out, it has similarities with the work of QUINE (b. 1908) (chapter 4). Neither Mill nor Quine ultimately hold logic or mathematics to be special. In the end, they too are subject to the tribunal of experience. So Mill's can also be seen as a naturalizing project; giving natural explanation rather than *a priori* justification. Things thought to be necessary are explained as the product of the natural effects of the environment on the mind. This applies for logic and mathematics with their supposed intuitive, or necessary, truths. It also applies for morality, analogously supposed by many to be intuitive or necessary.

Both Skorupski (1989) and Scarre (1989), who bring out this analogy with Quine, find a tension between this naturalism and Mill's own metaphysics (which is chiefly found in his long *Examination of Hamilton*). In the *Examination* Mill presents an account of reality in which all items are constructed from the basic atoms of experience. Such constructions are a person's own MIND (chapter 5), OTHER MINDS (p. 692), as well as OBJECTS IN THE EXTERNAL WORLD (pp. 726–33) (which are famously classified as 'permanent possibilities of sensation').

The *Examination* is currently not much read or studied, but one interest of it is that it contains (in chapter 12) the first appearance of the argument by analogy for the nature of other people's minds, the attack on which has done so much to shape current, post-Wittgensteinian philosophy of mind. The basis of Skorupski and Scarre's attack is that the philosophy of science demands a realist attitude to the world, which is undercut by the PHENOMENALISM (pp. 53–4) of the METAPHYSICS (chapter 2).

7   Proof of the Principle of Utility

It has been noted that Mill's defence of the use of experience against the use of *a priori* intuition extends also to his writings in ethics. The chief object of *Utilitarianism* is to demonstrate that ethical principles do not need to rest on *sui generis* ethical intuitions. Hence the point of the long chapter on justice. Justice is shown not to be a separate intuition, but to be founded on the observable utility of the actions that justice recommends.

Hence also the point of the so-called proof. It is not intended as a deductive proof of utility. It is not intended to show that utility is an intuitive or *a priori* principle. Rather, it is intended to reveal its empirical support; to show how the principle connects with observations of what actually happens. It appeals not to moral sense, or moral intuitions, but, rather, to actual, observable, desires.

It is quite clear from the text itself that Mill never intended it as a deduction. Earlier in the work (in chapter 1) he says that 'questions of ultimate ends are not amenable to direct proof'; the infamous chapter itself is entitled 'Of what sort of proof . . . '; and it starts with Mill repeating his claim that 'questions of ultimate ends do not admit of proof'. So instead of proof we have suggestions; not a deduction, but experience.

Something exactly similar had happened previously in Bentham, who also claims that the first principle, being a first principle, cannot be proved by something more ultimate. So Bentham provides, instead of a proof, something which may lead the reader to 'relish' the principle. Mill, similarly, provides something which may lead the reader to look on the principle more favourably.

As an empirical task, the claim is that, to see what might best serve as an ultimate end of conduct, some control can be got by seeing what, as a matter of fact, people actually do treat as ends. The desirable is not taken to be the same in meaning as what is desired. Rather, by observing what people actually desire, we get some kind of empirical control, or test, about what it is possible to desire. And, by seeing what it is possible to desire, we get an analogous empirical control, or test, on what should be desired. It is a necessary condition, not a sufficient one: there is no point in an ethics that proposes something as desirable when, as a matter of empirical fact, it is not possible to desire it.

What Mill is trying to show is that, as a matter of fact, happiness is the only thing that is actually desired (as an end); hence that it is reasonable to suppose that it is the only thing that it is possible to desire (as an end); hence that it is the only proper object of morality, prudence and life. The initial empirical observation here may be held to be highly dubious; although it is obviously helped by Mill's enlarged sense of happiness, which was discussed above. Following from this enlarged sense, it will not be a refutation that people take themselves to be aiming at something quite other than happiness (as long as, that is, happiness has to enter the explanation of this).

8   Bentham on Clarification

It has been seen how Mill wished to connect significant thought with experience. Bentham also took experience as a guide, but was more prepared than Mill to talk about this giving meaning. Without the principle of utility, he said, we have 'sounds instead of sense'; and his constant aim is to extirpate nonsense. The connection of both the central evaluative principle and the central psychological principle with pains and pleasures – that is, with the raw data of experience – endows both these central principles with meaning.

Bentham's practical project of producing the perfect system of law led him into an investigation of the nature of law. Law, he thought, had to be clarified and understood (so that, once understood, it could be reformed). Understanding the law means understanding rights and duties. Understanding is gained by placing things in contact with experience. Yet, since rights and duties seem to be neither observable entities, nor complexes of observable entities, this would not seem to be possible. However, Bentham solved this problem by inventing a technique he called 'paraphrasis', which anticipates twentieth-century techniques of analysis.

The idea is not to understand problematic words in isolation but, rather, 'some whole sentence of which it forms a part is translated into another sentence'. So in the analysis of what Bentham called 'fictional entities' (such as 'right', 'duty', 'property', 'obligation', 'immunity' and 'privilege': the whole language of the law), he uses his technique of paraphrasis to place these terms in sentences for which he then gives substitute sentences not containing the offending term. For example, sentences about rights are explained by Bentham in terms of sentences about duties. A particular right is for him the benefit that is conferred on someone by the imposition of duties on others. With duties we still, of course, have fictional entities. But these, in turn, can be placed in sentences that are translated into sentences about the threat of punishment. Punishment is, for Bentham, the threat of the imposition of pain. So here, at last, we reach what Bentham calls real entities; that is, things that can be directly understood by perception. We reach pain and pleasure, which are the ultimate clarifiers both of how the law is and also of how the law ought to be.

Natural Rights and Nonsense

Bentham was opposed to the existence of natural rights. They formed part of the opposing rhetoric to utility and were thought by him to be nonsense. At first sight it might be thought that they could be saved by the same technique. However, comparing a natural right with a legal right exposes the difference. Both can be analysed in terms of corresponding duties. Yet, as we saw above, Bentham analyses a legal duty in terms of the law (or threat of punishment) which creates it. There is no corresponding law, he holds, with respect to supposed natural duties. Hence he holds that natural rights are just imaginary rights.

Bentham's most famous slogan expressing this view is that talk of natural rights is 'nonsense on stilts'. This comes in a work normally called *Anarchical Fallacies* (1843a), which is a critical analysis of the French Declaration of Rights, which was issued in 1791. Bentham thinks that the French are not really declaring existing rights but, rather, giving reasons why there ought to be rights. Yet, as he puts it, 'a reason for wishing that a certain right were established, is not that right; want is not supply; hunger is not bread'. So to suppose that such rights actually exist is nonsense. Furthermore, to suppose that they are unalterable – that is, to suppose in advance of experiment, that they are right for all time – is even worse than normal nonsense. It is nonsense on stilts.

9 Sidgwick

Finally, a coda on Sidgwick. Bentham's *Civil Code* was one of Sidgwick's favourite books and he started his intellectual life as a follower of Mill. However, just like Mill, be broke with and criticized his mentors. He was still prepared to say that he was a utilitarian, but, again, the utilitarianism is worn with a difference. Sidgwick produces so fundamentally different a base for utilitarianism that, again, it might be thought that he removes its central point.

It has been seen how both Bentham and Mill took themselves to be opposing schools of thought (or political movements) that relied upon direct intuition of the right answer. Against this they both posed observation and experience. Yet although Sidgwick argued for utilitarianism, he did so precisely on an intuitionist base. He saw himself as healing the split in the previous generation: the war between the utilitarians and the intuitionists. Sidgwick was both.

Healing splits, or understanding different points of view, was very much Sidgwick's personal and philosophical temperament. His central work is called *The Methods of*

Ethics (1874). This is, as the title says, a study not just of one but of several methods. Intuitionism, utilitarianism, common sense and egoism are all examined. The history of the subject is fully deployed. The problem is how, being completely impartial in the face of all this material, to find the rational basis for action.

The *Methods* is hence a study of good reasons. The maxims of common-sense morality, he thinks, do not meet the criteria he lays down for something being an intuitively good reason for action. However, these criteria are met by certain 'absolute practical principles' of a more abstract nature, such as that future good is as important as present good. Another such principle is that, as Sidgwick puts it, 'the good of any one individual is of no more importance, from the point of view (if I may say so) of the Universe, than the good of any other'. This involves utilitarianism; hence Sidgwick provided utilitarianism with an intuitionist foundation.

However, Sidgwick thinks that egoism is also an intuitive principle of action. So we are caught, he thinks, in a 'dualism of practical reason' with two independent principles that are both rationally compelling: an egoistic principle telling me to mind my own happiness and an altruistic principle telling me to mind the general happiness. This split was threatened in Mill and Bentham, but eluded (for Bentham, by making the egoistic principle a psychological principle rather than an evaluative one; for Mill, by allowing them both to be evaluative but giving them different spheres). For Sidgwick, however, the problem of collision is harsh. It would only be avoided, he thinks, if God (working as a sort of divine Benthamite legislator) kept the two in step. However, Sidgwick, who had considerable religious doubts, was reluctant to introduce God for this purpose. The famous last words of the first edition of the *Methods* state that 'the prolonged effort of the human intellect to frame a perfect ideal of rational conduct is seen to have been foredoomed to inevitable failure'. (Sidgwick himself said that he wanted to write a book in which the first word was 'ethics' and the last word 'failure'; in this, at least, he succeeded.)

Mill waged war on contemporary Cambridge professors, like Whewell, who used intuition. Mill, like Bentham, fought from outside the academy. They both proposed a secular ethic, in competition with the church-supported English universities and establishment. Sidgwick, by contrast, was a Cambridge professor. Like his predecessor, Whewell, he uses intuition, albeit with different results. He tries to dispense with God; but this gives him problems. However, writing as a professor, he succeeds in giving a thoroughly professional treatment of the subject, recognizable as such in this century. After all, it was Sidgwick who produced the critique that G. E. Moore (a later Cambridge professor) used to the effect that Mill confused the desired with the desirable and so confused is and ought. From this critique, much twentieth-century ethical thought follows.

Further Reading

Readers might reasonably begin with Bentham, *A Fragment on Government* and *An Introduction to the Principles of Morals and Legislation*; with Mill, *Utilitarianism* and *On Liberty*; and with Sidgwick, *The Methods of Ethics*, before turning to secondary sources.

Dinwiddy (1989) provides a good brief introduction to Bentham, with a more comprehensive examination in Harrison (1983). Hart (1982) offers engaging essays which have set the tone of contemporary Bentham studies. Bentham's theories of justice, government, law and democracy are (respectively) considered by Kelly (1990), Lyons (1991), Postema (1986) and Rosen (1983).

Ryan (1974) gives an excellent and clear introduction to Mill, but some readers will want to move quickly to the more demanding recent studies by Scarre (1989) and Skorupski (1989). Schneewind (1968) and Thomas (1985) are also valuable and Skorupski (1998) is an authoritative survey of all aspects of Mill's thought. Gray (1983), Ten (1980) and Riley (1998) provide different perspectives on Mill's account of liberty. Robson (1968) explores Mill's social and political thought, while aspects of his ethical and political thinking are discussed by Berger (1984) and Semmel (1984). Crisp (1997) is a guidebook specifically devoted to Mill's *Utilitarianism*.

Schneewind (1977) places Sidgwick in historical context, and Schultz (1992) reflects a recent renewal of interest in Sidgwick's philosophy.

References

Bentham

Bentham, J. 1776: *A Fragment on Government*. In Bentham (1968–).
——1789: *An Introduction to the Principles of Morals and Legislation*. In Bentham (1968–).
——1843a: *Anarchical Fallacies*. In Bentham (1962), vol. 2.
——1843b: *Principles of the Civil Code*. In Bentham (1962), vol. 2.
——1962 [1838–43]: *The Works of Jeremy Bentham*, 11 vols (edited by Sir J. Bowring). New York: Russell and Russell.
——1968– : *Collected Works* (edited by J. H. Burns). London: Athlone Press.

Writers on Bentham

Dinwiddy, J. 1989: *Bentham*. Oxford: Oxford University Press.
Harrison, R. 1983: *Bentham*. London: Routledge.
Hart, H. L. A. 1982: *Essays on Bentham*. Oxford: Oxford University Press.
Kelly, P. J. 1990: *Utilitarianism and Distributive Justice*. Oxford: Oxford University Press.
Lyons, D. 1991: *In the Interest of the Governed*. Oxford: Oxford University Press.
Postema, G. J. 1986: *Bentham and the Common Law Tradition*. Oxford: Oxford University Press.
Rosen, F. 1983: *Jeremy Bentham and Representative Democracy*. Oxford: Oxford University Press.

Mill

Mill, J. S. 1843: *A System of Logic*. In Mill (1963–), vols 7–8.
——1859: *On Liberty*. In Mill (1963–), vol. 18.
——1863: *Utilitarianism*. In Mill (1963–), vol. 10.
——1865: *An Examination of Sir William Hamilton's Philosophy*. In Mill (1963–), vol. 9.
——1873: *Autobiography*. In Mill (1963–), vol. 1.
——1963: *Collected Works*, 33 vols (general editor J. M. Robson). London: University of Toronto Press and Routledge and Kegan Paul.

Writers on Mill

Berger, F. R. 1984: *Happiness, Justice and Freedom*. Berkeley: University of California Press.
Crisp, R. 1997: *Mill on Utilitarianism*. London: Routledge.
Gray, J. 1983: *Mill on Liberty: A Defence*. London: Routledge.
Riley, J. 1998: *Mill on Liberty*. London: Routledge.
Robson, J. M. 1968: *The Improvement of Mankind: The Social and Political Thought of John Stuart Mill*. Toronto: Toronto University Press.
Ryan, A. 1974: *J. S. Mill*. London: Routledge.
Scarre, G. 1989: *Logic and Reality in the Philosophy of John Stuart Mill*. Dordrecht: Kluwer.

Schneewind, J. B. (ed.) 1968: *Mill*. London: Macmillan.

Semmel, B. 1984: *John Stuart Mill and the Pursuit of Virtue*. New Haven, CT: Yale University Press.

Skorupski, J. 1989: *John Stuart Mill*. London: Routledge.

Skorupski, J. (ed.) 1998: *The Cambridge Companion to Mill*. Cambridge: Cambridge University Press.

Stephen, J. F. 1967: *Liberty, Equality, Fraternity*, new edn (edited by R. J. White). Cambridge: Cambridge University Press.

Ten, C. L. 1980: *Mill on Liberty*. Oxford: Oxford University Press.

Thomas, W. 1985: *Mill*. Oxford: Oxford University Press.

Sidgwick

Sidgwick, H. 1874: *The Methods of Ethics*. London: Macmillan.

Writers on Sidgwick

Schneewind, J. B. 1977: *Sidgwick's Ethics and Victorian Moral Philosophy*. Oxford: Oxford University Press.

Schultz, B. 1992: *Essays on Henry Sidgwick*. Cambridge: Cambridge University Press.

Discussion Questions

1   Are there good reasons to believe that happiness is the unique measure of value?

2   Could the utilitarian principle be accepted even if people did not act to maximize their own utility?

3   Should we equate utility, pleasure and happiness?

4   Should our actions and institutions be evaluated by their actual and possible consequences? What other way might we have of assessing them?

5   What justifies punishment?

6   Is utilitarianism equally suited to designing public institutions and to guiding private ethics?

7   Was Bentham justified in rejecting a role for history, prejudice and custom in his design of a system of law and government?

8   Is it reasonable to attempt to design a perfect system of public institutions?

9   Can institutions be arranged to reconcile duty and interest?

10   Does utilitarianism fail if some kinds of pleasure are 'more desirable and more valuable than others'?

11   On what grounds are we justified in interfering with the liberty of another person?

12   Does Bentham or Mill provide a more acceptable account of happiness?

13   What sort of proof, if any, can be given for the utility principle?

14   Should we accept Mill's claim 'that the sole evidence that it is possible to produce that anything is desirable, is that people do actually desire it'?

15   Does the 'punishment criterion' protect utilitarianism from making impossible demands on our actions?

16   Is it more helpful to consider Mill as a rule utilitarian or as an indirect utilitarian? Was Bentham an indirect utilitarian?

17   What follows from the claim that the art of life includes prudence and aesthetics as well as morality?

18   Should we seek a natural explanation wherever an *a priori* justification is offered?

19   In what sense, if any, might one's own mind, the minds of other people, and objects in the external world be said to be constructed?

20   Is Mill's phenomenalism compatible with the requirements of the philosophy of science?

21   Is the fact that people often take themselves to be aiming at something other than happiness an empirical refutation of the claim that happiness is the only thing that is actually desired?

22   How successful was Bentham in showing us how to recognize and avoid nonsense?

23   If rights and duties are fictional entities, how can they be understood?

24   Are 'natural rights' imaginary?

25   How should we assess Sidgwick's project of providing an intuitionist base for utilitarianism?

26   If there are absolute practical principles, how can we determine what they are?

36

Pragmatism

SUSAN HAACK

Pragmatism, a style of philosophy initiated by Charles Sanders Peirce and William James, is best characterized by the method expressed in the pragmatic maxim, according to which the meaning of a concept is determined by the experiential or practical consequences of its application. Peirce's aspiration to a reformed, scientific philosophy free of metaphysical excesses is sustained by the realist elements of his view of perception and of natural laws; muted by nominalist leanings in James and Hegelian leanings in Dewey, pragmatism is transformed by Schiller into a revolutionary relativism – and, in our own time, by Richard Rorty into a conception of philosophy as, not a form of inquiry, but only 'carrying on the conversation' of Western culture.

1 Introduction: From Reformist to Revolutionary Pragmatism

'It has probably never happened', Peirce wrote in 1905, 'that a philosopher has attempted to give a general name to his own doctrine without that name's soon acquiring in common philosophical usage, a signification much broader than was originally intended.' His 'pragmatism', he continued, had by then acquired a signification so much broader than his original intention that it was 'time to kiss his child good-by' and 'to announce the birth of the word "pragmaticism," which is ugly enough to be safe from kidnappers' (Peirce 1931–58: 5.412: subsequent references are to volume and paragraph number).

Not unexpectedly, therefore, it is scarcely possible to give an accurate brief statement of the philosophical tendencies characteristic of pragmatism. The need to acknowledge, for instance, the significance for his conception of pragmatism of Peirce's shift from early nominalist sympathies to his mature realism, or of the influence on James's conception of pragmatism of his doctrine of the Will to Believe, makes it hard enough to specify what important philosophical ideas were shared by Peirce and James, the founders of pragmatism. And it is harder yet to find a characterization that would also comfortably accommodate Dewey, Schiller and Mead, let alone to extend it to include more recent pragmatists, neo-pragmatists and sympathizers as diverse as Ramsey, Lewis, Sellars, Quine, Putnam, Rescher, Rorty and so on.

Schiller's observation that there are as many pragmatisms as pragmatists, shrewd as it is, suggests at worst only a formidable diversity; but the fact is that there are not merely different, but radically opposed, pragmatisms. The scientific philosophy envisaged by Peirce's pragmatism calls for 'inquiry into the truth for truth's sake', and maintains that 'in order to reason well it is absolutely necessary to possess . . . a real love of truth', and that the truth 'is SO, whether you or I or anybody thinks it is so or not' (Peirce 1.44, 2.82, 2.135). The literary post-philosophy envisaged by Rorty's pragmatism, in starkest contrast, aspires only to 'carrying on the conversation', and declares that 'true' means nothing more than 'what you can defend against all comers', and 'rationality' nothing more than 'respect for the opinions of those around one' (Rorty 1979: 377–8; 1991a: 32, 37).

As a preliminary to understanding how pragmatism came to be so startlingly transmuted, it will be useful to distinguish two broad styles: the reformist and the revolutionary (a distinction adapted from Migotti 1988). These have in common the aspiration to free philosophy of metaphysical excesses and, more specifically, of the artificial confines of the CARTESIAN THEORY OF KNOWLEDGE (chapter 26). Relinquishing the requirement of absolute certainty in knowledge, more inclined to NATURALISM (p. 767) than to apriorism, emphasizing the social aspects of inquiry, pragmatism of a reformist stripe acknowledges the legitimacy of traditional questions about the truth-relatedness of our cognitive practices, and sustains a conception of truth objective enough to give those questions bite. Pragmatism of a revolutionary stripe, by contrast, relinquishing the objectivity and denying the value of truth, can acknowledge no legitimate epistemological questions not strictly internal to the cognitive practices of this or that community. And, since it is a tautology that inquiry aims at the truth, the very possibility of bona fide inquiry, and *a fortiori* the conception of philosophy as a kind of inquiry, is thereby undermined.

That this distinction of reformist versus revolutionary does not map perfectly on to the list of pragmatists, neo-pragmatists and sympathizers, so far from detracting from its usefulness, precisely fits it to serve as a framework for understanding the transformation – or, one might better say, the vulgarization – of pragmatism. The diagnosis will be that the delicate balance of objectivity and fallibilism attempted in Peirce's reformist pragmatism, somewhat disturbed by James's nominalistic tendencies and by revolutionary, or revolutionary-sounding, Hegelisms in Dewey, is destroyed when Schiller (mis)interprets James as relativizing truth, and Rorty (mis)interprets Dewey as repudiating the theory of knowledge and as aspiring, not to the reconstruction, but the deconstruction, of philosophy.

2   C. S. Peirce (1839–1914)

At the heart of Peirce's pragmatism lies the pragmatic maxim: 'if one can define accurately all the conceivable experimental phenomena which the affirmation or denial of a concept could imply, one will have a complete definition of the concept, and there is *absolutely nothing more* in it' (Peirce 5.412). Meaning is a matter of the conceivable experimental, experiential consequences of a concept's applying; *pragmatisch*, in the Kantian sense. The pragmatic meaning of 'x is F' is given by a list of conditionals; as the mature Peirce overcame youthful nominalist leanings, he insisted on the subjunctive formulation: 'if you were to do A_1, experiential consequence E_1 would result', 'if you were to do A_2, experiential consequence E_2 would result', and so on. Thus, a diamond really *is* hard if it *would* scratch other substances if it *were* rubbed against them – even if it never is rubbed. And Peirce stresses that the list of meaning-specifying conditionals is open-ended; meaning grows, as he puts it, as our knowledge grows.

Pragmaticism is, as Peirce acknowledges, a kind of positivism; one role of the pragmatic maxim is to reveal that 'almost every proposition of ontological metaphysics . . . is gibberish' (Peirce 5.423). But the maxim is not intended to rule out METAPHYSICS (chapter 2) altogether, but rather to discriminate the illegitimate, the pragmatically meaningless, from 'scientific' metaphysics, which uses the method of science, observation and reasoning, and which is undertaken with the scientific attitude, that is, from the desire to find out how things really are – and not, as happens when philosophy is in the hands of theologians, from the desire to make a case for some doctrine which is already immovably believed. Scientific philosophy, as Peirce conceives it, is an observational science, differing from the other sciences not in its method but in its reliance on aspects of experience so familiar, so ubiquitous, that the difficulty is to become distinctly aware of them. (So it would be a misunderstanding to think of Peirce's aspiration to make philosophy scientific as in any way scientistic; Peirce expressly denies that philosophical issues could be resolved within, and certainly never suggests that philosophy ought to be replaced by, the natural sciences.)

It is as scientific metaphysics that Peirce presents his own metaphysical theories. For example, Peirce offers a theory of categories – firstness, potentiality; secondness, particular existence, reaction; and thirdness, generality, connection, law – based both phenomenologically and, like Kant's categories, on logic, but on Peirce's more adequate logic, capable, unlike Aristotle's, of expressing relations. Among his other important contributions to metaphysics are his tychism (there is chance, objective indeterminacy, as well as law, in the universe); his synechism (the ubiquity of continuity); agapism (the gradual evolution of the world from chaos towards order, 'concrete reasonableness'); and his scholastic realism (the reality of 'generals', natural kinds and laws).

But Peirce's conception of a reformed, scientific philosophy is perhaps most directly seen in his thoroughgoing critique of Cartesian epistemology, and in the more naturalistic theory of inquiry with which he proposes to replace it.

With Descartes, philosophy 'put off childish things, and began to be a conceited young man' (Peirce 4.71). Descartes's method, according to Peirce, is a sham, a matter of feigned, 'paper' doubts which inevitably led to the eventual reinstatement of the beliefs supposedly doubted. There is no such faculty as the intuition on which Descartes's criterion of clearness and distinctness relies, and no such intuitive self-consciousness as his reliance on the *cogito* as the indubitable starting-point for the reconstruction of knowledge requires. Descartes's aspiration to certainty is misplaced, his subjective criterion of truth viciously individualistic.

Unlike Descartes, and in strikingly Darwinian spirit, Peirce sees human belief as continuous with animal expectation, human inquiry as continuous with animals' explorations of their environment. Following Alexander Bain, Peirce conceives of belief as a habit of action, a disposition to behave, and of doubt as the unsettled state resulting from the interruption of a belief-habit by recalcitrance on the part of experience. Real doubt – unlike Descartes's paper doubt – is thus involuntary and unpleasant. The primitive basis of the most sophisticated human cognitive activity, scientific inquiry, is a homeostatic process by which the organism strives to return to equilibrium, a process halted when a new habit, a revised belief, is reached.

This homeostatic process is its primitive basis, but it is not yet scientific inquiry. The beliefs thus 'settled' are likely only temporarily fixed; so the most sophisticated inquirers, realizing that, unless a belief is true, though it may be temporarily settled, it cannot be permanently so, and aspiring to indefeasibly settled belief, will always be motivated to further inquiry, never fully satisfied with what they presently incline to think. The primitive homeostatic process is thus transmuted into scientific inquiry.

Among possible methods for the 'fixation of belief', the SCIENTIFIC METHOD (chapter 9), Peirce holds, is distinguished by its appropriateness to the end of inquiry. Unlike the *a priori* method traditionally favoured by metaphysics, the scientific method, if it were sufficiently persisted in, would enable inquiry to come to rest with beliefs which are indefeasibly stable, permanently safe from recalcitrance. The scientific method, according to Peirce, is the method of OBSERVATION (pp. 295–7) and reasoning: more precisely, it is the method of accommodating the perceptual judgements forced upon one by experience into an explanatory framework, by means of reasoning of three types: abduction, the postulation of hypotheses to explain some puzzling phenomenon; deduction of consequences from such abductive hypotheses; and the inductive testing of such hypotheses. As Peirce puts it, we wish our beliefs to conform to hard facts; and it is in the brute compulsiveness of experience that the hardness of fact consists.

Even MATHEMATICS (chapter 11), according to Peirce, is an observational science. Though mathematical truths are necessary, mathematical knowledge depends on experience, but on inner experience, the construction, manipulation and observation of imagined 'icons' or diagrams.

The desire to learn the truth requires an acknowledgement that one does not satisfactorily know already. The scientific inquirer is therefore a 'contrite fallibilist' who is ready to 'drop the whole cartload of his beliefs, the moment experience is against them' (Peirce 1.14, 1.55). In the critical common-sensism of Peirce's mature philosophy – an attempted synthesis, as the phrase suggests, of KANT's (chapter 32) and Reid's responses to HUME (chapter 31) – the scientific inquirer is seen as submitting the instinctive beliefs of common sense to criticism, refinement and revision. A scientific doubt, as Peirce puts it, 'can never get completely set to rest until, at last, the very truth about that question gets established' (Peirce 7.77).

It could with some justice be protested that the critical common-sensist's policy of deliberate critical scrutiny and attempted falsification of the beliefs with which he initially finds himself bears a more than passing resemblance to Descartes's method of doubt. And in any case Peirce's objections to the critical phase of Descartes's project seem largely to miss their mark. However, his critique of Descartes's assumption that any knowledge worthy of the name must be absolutely certain, of the subjectivity of his criterion of truth, and of his first-person, strictly individualistic approach, is more sustainable – and not only compatible, but intimately connected, with the key themes of Peirce's own theory of inquiry.

That theory is fallibilistic and, in a sense, thoroughly social: in the sense that Peirce thinks of the scientific inquirer as just one contributor to a vast enterprise extending both within and across generations. Scientific inquiry may be undertaken by individuals; but the individual inquirer will make his work freely available to others and, even if he fails, his will be one of the carcasses over which future generations of inquirers climb as they finally storm the fortress of knowledge. Fallible and imperfect as scientific inquiry is, if it were to continue long enough – Peirce is aware that there is no guarantee that it will – eventually a final, indefeasible 'ultimate opinion' would be agreed.

What supports Peirce's confidence that, if inquiry continued long enough, eventually consensus would be reached? The idea that evolutionary adaptation has given human beings an instinct for guessing right which enables them to come up with successful abductions, and the thesis that induction tends to be self-corrective, both play obvious roles here. Less obvious, but no less important, is the role of the unusual combination of the direct and the interpretative in Peirce's theory of perception; and, less obvious again, the role of the metaphysical doctrine Peirce sometimes calls 'extreme scholastic realism'.

Peirce distinguishes the percept, the perceptual event or presentation, from the perceptual judgement, the belief prompted by the experience. The perceptual judgement, he maintains, is thoroughly interpretative – indeed, but for its compulsive character, it is analogous to the conclusion of an abduction – and hence, though incorrigible, thoroughly fallible. But Peirce's acknowledgement of the interpretativeness of the perceptual judgement is combined with an insistence that the percept is not a REPRESENTATION (p. 732) but a presentation, and that we directly perceive, not images or mental representations, but real, external objects. Hallucinations and illusions may be indistinguishable phenomenologically from genuine perception; they may share its quality of insistency, of bruteness; they may even be experienced by more than one individual; but they are distinguishable by the fact that the behaviour of the real, external objects of genuine perception is predictable on the basis of our knowledge of the LAWS OF NATURE (pp. 305–6).

Peirce's 'extreme scholastic realism' is the thesis that there are real generals; that is, that there are natural kinds and laws which are independent of how we think them to be. (Peirce distinguishes his scholastic realism not only from nominalism, which maintains that generals are not real but figments, but also from PLATONISM (chapter 23) – which he dubs 'nominalistic platonism' because it maintains that generals exist; existence being for Peirce the characteristic mode of being of seconds, not thirds. And he distinguishes it from Scotistic realism, its closest ancestor, because, unlike Scotus, he holds that *which* generals are real, *which* general terms represent real kinds, is a matter for scientific inquiry to discover.) Scholastic realism is intended by Peirce as a hypothesis of scientific metaphysics. If there were no real generals, he argues, scientific inquiry would be impossible; for the very possibility of PREDICTION (pp. 289–90), induction and explanation depends on the reality of kinds and laws. There is a pattern of generals, of natural kinds and laws, underlying the particular objects and events we perceive, which is 'independent of how you or I or any number of men think'. And so it can be expected that the 'arbitrary, accidental element' in inquiry introduced by the peculiar circumstances and idiosyncrasies of individual inquirers would eventually be overcome as inquiry proceeds, and consensus eventually reached (Peirce 8.13).

Peirce contrasts scholastic realism not only with nominalism and nominalistic platonism, but also with what one might call 'noumenalism', the idea that the really real is in principle inaccessible to human cognition. This is a characteristically pragmatist attitude, for the pragmatic maxim disqualifies as meaningless any hypothesis devoid of all possible experiential consequences, any question which would resist settlement no matter how long scientific inquiry were to continue.

The thesis that the goal of inquiry is permanently settled belief, and the thesis that the scientific attitude is a disinterested desire for truth, are united by Peirce's definition of 'true'. He does not think it false to say that truth is correspondence to reality, but shallow – a merely nominal definition, giving no insight into the concept. His pragmatic definition identifies the truth with the hypothetical ideal theory which would be the final upshot of scientific inquiry were it to continue indefinitely. 'Truth is that concordance of . . . [a] statement with the ideal limit towards which endless investigation would tend to bring scientific beliefs'; 'any truth more perfect than this destined conclusion, any reality more absolute than what is thought in it, is a fiction of metaphysics' (Peirce 5.565, 8.13). These quotations reveal something both of the subtlety, and of the potential for tension, within Peirce's philosophy. His account of reality aims at a delicate compromise between the undesirable extremes of transcendentalism and idealism, his account of truth at a delicate compromise between the twin desiderata of objectivity and (in-principle) accessibility.

3   William James (1842–1910)

'There can *be* no difference anywhere that doesn't make a difference elsewhere' (James 1907: 30): his version of the pragmatic maxim lies at the heart of James's pragmatism too. Unlike Peirce, however, James thought that philosophy would do well to go round Kant, rather than through him; and this is reflected in his interpretation of the maxim, which stresses praxis, the practical consequences of a concept's applying. The point is not that Peirce does not, like James, hold that meaning is purposive, that the meaning of a concept lies in its application; it is rather that the mature, realist Peirce, unlike James, regards this kind of formulation as unfortunate if it encourages 'subordinat[ing] the *conception* to the *act*, knowing to doing' (Peirce 1900: 332). This difference of emphasis is magnified by James's readiness to construe 'the consequences of a belief' in a way that includes not only the consequences of the *truth of the proposition believed*, but also the consequences of *the person's believing it*.

It is not surprising, in view of this, that readers of James, and even James himself, sometimes have difficulty disentangling his pragmatism from his doctrine of the Will to Believe, his 'defence of our right to adopt a believing attitude in religious matters, in spite of the fact that our merely logical intellect may not have been coerced' (James 1897: 1–2). When a hypothesis by its nature cannot be decided on the basis of evidence; when it is live for us, that is, it appeals to us as a real possibility; when the choice between believing it and disbelieving it is forced, that is, unavoidable, and momentous for our lives – then '*our passional nature . . . lawfully may . . . decide*' (ibid.: 11). RELIGIOUS BELIEFS (chapter 15) which in principle cannot be verified or falsified may be legitimated by their salutary effect on the believer's life.

Peirce – to whom *The Will to Believe* is dedicated – the following year is found describing the scientific attitude as the 'Will to Learn', and observing that, for himself, he 'would not adopt a hypothesis, and would not even take it on probation, simply because the idea was pleasing' to him; that to do so would be 'a crime against the integrity of the reason that God has lent' him (Peirce 5.583, 5.598). He puts it, one might think, if anything too mildly; for by the standards of the pragmatic maxim as he interprets it, any hypothesis which is in principle incapable of settlement by observation and reasoning, would be no genuine hypothesis at all.

Also associated with James's pragmatism is his mature 'radical empiricism', by means of which he hopes to escape the dualism of Cartesian metaphysics and the subjectivity of Cartesian epistemology. What James calls 'pure experience' is, he holds, of itself neither mental nor physical; the separation into consciousness and content, knower and OBJECT (p. 794) known, is a matter of relations among different bits of 'pure experience'. (How can one and the same thing be both in space and in the mind? James answers, as one and the same point may be on two lines, if situated at their intersection.) The knowing relation, James suggests, is 'successful leading'; one counts as knowing a thing if one's idea of it enables one to act successfully towards it.

One might reasonably feel that the 'cash value' of radical empiricism scarcely matches that of Peirce's reconciliation of the direct and the interpretative elements in perception, and that James's talk of 'leading' is at best a promissory note. Its importance for the present argument lies, however, in its clear connection with James's account of the true as 'the satisfactory in the way of belief'.

Radical empiricism is monistic; it was, indeed, influential in the development of RUSSELL's (chapter 37) neutral monism. Nevertheless, it is compatible with the ideas of James's Hibbert lectures, entitled 'A Pluralistic Universe'. For radical empiricism, as James puts it, 'lays the explanatory stress upon the part, the element, the individual'; it is a 'mosaic' philosophy (James 1912: 24). There is only one kind of stuff, but many portions or individual bits of it. This reveals James's marked predilection for the particular, the concrete.

Like Peirce, James thinks it not exactly false but inadequate to say that truth is correspondence with reality. Again much like Peirce, he characterizes 'truth absolute' as 'an ideal set of formulations towards which all opinions may be expected in the long run to converge' (James 1909: 143). The difference between true beliefs and false ones is that they are verifiable, they lead us successfully. The true, James says, is the satisfactory, the useful, the expedient in the way of belief. True beliefs work. Critics like Moore and Russell were scandalized by what they saw as a crass identification of truth and utility – a criticism James describes as a 'slander' (ibid.: 147); for, though indeed he had written that '*the true . . . is only the expedient in the way of belief*', he had gone on to explain, 'expedient in the long run and on the whole of course; for what meets expediently all the experience in sight won't necessarily meet all further experience equally satisfactorily. Experience . . . has ways of *boiling over*, and making us correct our present formulas' (James 1907: 106).

Distinguishing his 'radical' empiricism from earlier variants, James disassociates himself from the disconnectedness of earlier empiricisms; and, specifically, from the theses that similars have nothing really in common, and that the causal tie is nothing but habitual conjunction. But, unlike Peirce, he does not appeal to the reality of kinds and laws to explain why, in the long run of experience, opinions can be expected to converge. Rather, his predilection for the particular leads him to a preoccupation with specific truths rather than truth as such. He manifests some discomfort with the notion of verifi*ability*, preferring to concentrate on particular truths actually verified. This leads to apparent inconsistencies, as James seems sometimes to allow that beliefs which are verified are thereby shown to have been true all along, sometimes to suggest that beliefs become true when they are verified. Consistency can be restored by means of a distinction James sometimes makes, but does not always mark, between 'abstract' or 'absolute' Truth and 'concrete' or 'relative' truths, identifying abstract Truth with the verifiable, and concrete truths with the verified. Of course, what James calls 'concrete truths' are not really *truths* at all; his distinction is really between a belief's being true and its being shown to be true – or, more accurately, since he allows that what is at one time 'verified' may later turn out to be false, between a belief's being true and its being confirmed. James's stress on the particular – which the mature Peirce would no doubt have felt betrays nominalist leanings – manifests itself in his tendency to downplay abstract Truth and to emphasize concrete truths. And his use of 'concrete truth' for 'proposition now confirmed' encourages the idea that *truth* (and not merely 'concrete truths') is made by us, and changes over time.

4   John Dewey (1859–1952)

Dewey describes one of Peirce's best-known characterizations – '[t]he opinion which is fated to be agreed by all who investigate' (Peirce 5.407) – as 'the best definition of truth' (Dewey 1938: 345n.). Like James, however, he tends to stress the concrete over the abstract, actual verification over potential verifiability, truths over Truth. In much of what he writes one hears a certain ambivalence about just how radical he means to be. The intellectualist's horror of acknowledging that verification is, as etymology suggests, a matter of *making* a belief true, he declares, is 'largely sentimental'; but he goes on to explain that to make an idea true 'is to modify and transform it' (that is, presumably, to change the proposition concerned) until it is able to survive testing (Dewey 1910: 139). A belief that is verified, he says, is thereby shown to have been true all along, but he goes on to explain that this means only that it was going to be verified (ibid.: 142–4). The pragmatist does not deny, Dewey insists, that truth is correspondence of thought to existence, though he does deny that it is correspondence of thought to unknowable things-in-themselves; but he goes on to explain that this correspondence means *co-respondence*, a matter of 'interadjustment' of our ideas to problematic situations (ibid.: 158–9).

Not surprisingly, perhaps – given that concrete truth is not really truth at all – Dewey is also drawn to the idea that it might be as well to stop using the word 'true', and to work instead with the concept of warranted assertibility.

Like Peirce and James, Dewey repudiates the 'quest for certainty'. Unlike them, he goes on to offer a psycho-sociological diagnosis of the motivation for that quest: it arose, he suggests, from the sharp dichotomy of theory versus practice, and the distaste for the practical, the changeable, the uncertain, embodied in the slave-owning culture of ancient Greece. The most HEGELIAN (chapter 33) of the pragmatists, Dewey is suspicious of traditional philosophical dualisms; and this is reflected in his epistemological writings, which are critical of the whole tradition from Plato through Descartes to his own contemporaries, because of its reliance on the dichotomies of object–subject, fact–value, mind–body, theory–practice. 'Special theories of knowledge differ enormously from one another. Their quarrels . . . fill the air. The din thus created makes us deaf to the way in which they all say one thing in common . . . They all hold that the operation of inquiry excludes any element of practical activity that enters into the construction of the object known' (Dewey 1929: 22).

Dewey, by contrast, insists that knowing is not isolated from practice, but is itself a kind of practice – to be judged, like other practices, by its purposive success rather than by some supposed standard of accuracy of reflection of its objects. The object of knowledge is not an immutable, independent reality, but is changed, and is in part constituted by, our cognitive interactions with it; for inquiry transforms a problematic, indeterminate situation into a determinate one.

Like Peirce, Dewey conceives of logic broadly. It is the theory of inquiry, of which FORMAL DEDUCTIVE LOGIC (chapter 4) – logic in the usual modern sense – is only a part. Peirce was an important contributor to the development of modern formal logic, discovering quantifiers and the logic of relations independently of FREGE (chapter 37), anticipating *Principia Mathematica*'s definition of number by more than thirty years, and devising truth-tables and venturing into three-valued logic more than a decade before Post and Łukasiewicz. Dewey's logical work is not formal, but this is not why Peirce is critical of it; Peirce's objection is that it is too purely descriptive, amounting only to a 'natural history' of inquiry, not a normative methodology. But by the time of *Logic, The Theory of Inquiry*, at any rate, Dewey is clearly acknowledging that logic is normative – stressing, however, that its recommendations about how inquiry should proceed can only be based on scientific study of what procedures have proven themselves to work.

The cumulative effect of the shifts of emphasis from Peirce through James to Dewey is, it might be fair to say, from an essentially reformist attitude to the philosophical tradition to a potentially revolutionary one. Peirce's theory of inquiry is behaviouristic, naturalistic and fallibilist; it is thoroughly anti-Cartesian, but clearly reformist in its approach. So too is James's, but his stress on the so-far-satisfactory in the way of belief, especially given the misleading terminology of 'concrete truths', hints at something more revolutionary. Dewey is perhaps least misleadingly described as half-straddling the reformist–revolutionary distinction. For side by side with reformist elements – his distinction of state and content senses of 'belief', his insistence on a conception of experience much richer than the old sensationalist one, and, especially, his aspiration to transcend the old dichotomy of rationalism versus empiricism and to acknowledge the interlocking of experience and reason – are revolutionary, or at least revolutionary-sounding, suggestions about the making of truth, the modification of the objects of knowledge through inquiry, and the replacement of the traditional theory of knowledge by a critical scrutiny, internal to science, of the methods of inquiry science employs.

5 F. C. S. Schiller (1864–1937)

Schiller is uncompromisingly revolutionary. In his writings one finds a straightforward identification of truth with verification, and an unequivocal commitment to the making, and the mutability, of truth. James acknowledges that his account of concrete truths could not stand alone: 'to admit, as we pragmatists do, that we are liable to correction . . . involves the use on our part of an ideal standard' (James 1909: 142). But Schiller offers a theory of concrete truths *as a complete theory of truth*. He denies outright that truth is correspondence with reality, an idea which he describes as not only worthless as a criterion but absurd in itself. Truth is practical working. 'True', he says, means 'valued by us'. A proposition is true if it 'forwards our ends'. Truth is mutable, since propositions become true only when successfully applied; 'a truth which will not . . . submit to verification, is not yet a truth at all' (Schiller 1907: 8). Reality is also mutable, growing as truth grows. Truth is dependent on us, relative to our purposes. And so is reality; facts are not discovered but selected, even made, by us. In a spirit, no doubt, of deliberate provocation, Schiller likens his views to those of PROTAGORAS (chapter 22). Certainly his revolutionary, relativistic humanism could scarcely be further removed from Peirce's realistic pragmaticism.

'The apostle of Humanism', Peirce wrote of Schiller in 1905, 'says that professional philosophists "have rendered philosophy like unto themselves, abstruse, arid, abstract and abhorrent." But I conceive that some branches of sciences are not in a healthy state if they are not abstruse, arid and abstract'; and in 1908: '[i]t seems to me a pity that [Mr Schiller and the pragmatists of today] should allow a philosophy so instinct with life to become infected with the seeds of death in such notions as . . . the mutability of truth' (Peirce 5.537, 6.485).

These observations are not only poignant but prophetic. Peirce's warnings of the dangers of Schiller's humanistic pragmatism bring to mind Russell's dismissal of pragmatism as an 'engineers' philosophy', bound to lead to cosmic impiety, or at least to fascism; Schiller's disdain for the mummified pedantry of the philosophical tradition brings to mind Rorty's unkind words about the logic-chopping of analytic philosophy.

6 Recent and Contemporary Pragmatisms

Rorty, most radical of contemporary self-styled neo-pragmatists, and the closest to Schiller, uses 'pragmatist' as the contrast to 'realist'. He tells us that truth is not the kind of thing one should expect to have a philosophically interesting theory about, that to call a proposition true is just to give it a rhetorical pat on the back (Rorty 1982: xxi, xiii). He transmutes inquiry into 'carrying on the conversation' of Western culture (Rorty 1979: 377–8) and experiential falsification into 'conversational objections' (Rorty 1982: 165–6); and refers to those who describe themselves as seeking the truth as 'old-fashioned prigs' (Rorty 1991b: 86).

The affinity of Rorty's and Schiller's conceptions of pragmatism, it should be said, is not the result of Schiller's influence on Rorty; perhaps it is, in part, the result rather of Rorty's (mis)reading James much as Schiller did. Neither, it should also be said, is Rorty prepared, as Schiller is, to admit to relativism.

Indeed, it is not quite unambiguously clear that Rorty *is* properly construed as a relativist; but only because he seems to shift, as occasion demands, between a con-textualist, and hence relativist, conception of epistemic justification (A is justified-relative-to-community-C in believing that *p* just in case he can defend the belief that p against the objections of members of C), and a tribalist one (A is justified in believing that p just in case he can defend the belief that p against the objections of *our* community). But, either way, Rorty's position is thoroughly anti-epistemological; for he is unambiguously committed to the thesis that criteria of evidence are not objectively grounded in their relation to the truth, but entirely a matter of conventional, conversational constraints. Indeed, as Rorty cheerfully acknowledges, this is not only thoroughly anti-epistemological, but anti-philosophical, undermining the traditional conception of philosophy as a form of inquiry. Still, he thinks there is a future for the ex-philosopher, but it is to be 'hermeneutic' rather than epistemological, 'edifying' rather than systematic, literary rather than scientific, a matter of 'carrying on the conversation of Western culture' rather than of inquiring into how things are.

Rorty appeals to Dewey's repudiation of the epistemological tradition. But the appeal is strained, for Dewey looks to the 'naturalization of intelligence', to a scientific approach to replace the 'spectator theory of knowledge' (Dewey 1929: 195, 196), while Rorty declares that epistemology needs no successor-subject, and, far from welcoming a shift towards science, anticipates the future of post-philosophy as a genre of literature or of literary criticism. True, James writes of the affinity of some moral philosophy with 'novels and dramas of the deeper sort' (James 1897: 210). This is best construed, however, not as denying that moral philosophy is a form of inquiry, but as suggesting the role that imaginative empathy might play in such inquiry; and, so construed, need not conflict with Dewey's vision of a normative ethics in which scientific inquiry into the nature of true human flourishing would play an important role.

Peirce writes, with characteristic verve, of the need 'to rescue the good ship Philosophy for the service of Science from the hands of the lawless rovers of the sea of literature'; '[a]s for that phrase, "studying in a literary spirit"', he remarks, 'it is impossible to express how nauseating it is to any scientific man' (Peirce 5.449, 1.33). Perhaps it is no wonder, then, that Rorty refers so dismissively to Peirce's 'undeserved apotheosis', and tells us that Peirce's only contribution to pragmatism was to give it a name (Rorty 1982: 160–1). But it would be a mistake to read Peirce's harsh remarks about literary philosophy as scientistic, or as hostile to literature; they express, rather, his insistence that philosophy, like science, is a form of inquiry, of truth-seeking, and that, in this pursuit, testability is paramount, and clarity and precision of language must take priority over euphony or elegance of style.

This point is doubly important because the revolutionary wing of contemporary pragmatism also shelters, besides Rorty and other admirers of literary philosophy, others of a notably scientistic stripe. Paul Churchland argues, from the non-propositional workings of the ganglia of the sea-slug and the successes of connectionist artificial intelligence in training up a computer to distinguish a mine from a rock on the ocean floor, that cognitive processing is not propositional, and truth not the goal of inquiry. Another contemporary proponent of vulgar pragmatism, Stich, maintains that the goal of inquiry is, not truth, but beliefs that conduce to whatever it is the subject values; ironically enough, he rests his case in part on a denial that truth is instrumentally valuable – and cites, as justification for calling this 'pragmatism', a passage in which James is arguing the utility of true beliefs.

Other contemporaries have sought habitable ground between the reformist and the revolutionary wings of the pragmatist tradition. An important theme here is the hope of some kind of *rapprochement* of the 'analytic' and CONTINENTAL (chapters 41 and 42) camps. The hope is reasonable enough: the pragmatist tradition, after all, antedates the split; both Peirce and James make significant contributions to phenomenology (or, as Peirce sometimes calls it, 'phaneroscopy'); and Dewey's stress on the historical, the social, and on *praxis* have led some to see him as America's (thoroughly democratic) answer to Marx. Margolis, for example, believes it possible to develop a 'pragmatism without foundations' in which the plausible elements of realism can be reconciled with the plausible elements of relativism. Bernstein wants, instead, to move beyond the supposed opposition of realism and relativism by overcoming what he calls the 'Cartesian Anxiety', the quest for fixed constraints.

Pragmatists of a plainer reformist stripe would respond – perhaps after protesting the implication that their philosophy is driven by the neurotic need suggested by the term 'anxiety' – that it is not necessary to move beyond objectivity, or to reconcile it with relativism, provided it is tempered by a sufficiently thoroughgoing fallibilism. And it is to my mind within the tradition of reformist pragmatism that the most enduring contributions are to be found: Mead's theory of the social construction of the self, inspired by Peirce's critique of the intuitive self-consciousness assumed by Descartes; Lewis's pragmatic account of the *a priori*, itself an inspiration for Quine's call for 'a more thorough pragmatism'; Ramsey's BEHAVIOURISTIC (pp. 65–7) approach to belief, and Quine's, also, to meaning (Quine cites Dewey: 'meaning is . . . a property of behavior'); Quine's association of natural kinds, induction and evolutionary epistemology; Reichenbach's 'pragmatic vindication' of induction; Hanson's defence of the idea of an abductive logic of scientific discovery, Sellar's appeal to the notion of explanatory coherence, and Harman's to inference to the best explanation; Putnam's explorations of conceptions of truth intermediate between metaphysical realism and relativism; Apel's of the need for an account of the pragmatic dimensions to supplement Tarski's semantic theory of truth; Rescher's investigations of criteria of success and improvement of cognitive methods, Jardine's of scientific progress; and many more. In my own work, such key ideas as explanatory integration (central to the articulated quasi-holism of my account of evidential support), the distinction of the state and the content senses of 'belief', and the combination of direct and interpretative elements in perception (both central elements of my account of the role of experience in justification), were mined, as I can testify, from the same vein.

This list illustrates the formidable diversity as well as the richness of the reformist tradition in pragmatism. This diversity is unified by what one might call the ongoing project of reformist pragmatism: the aspiration to find a middle ground between dogmatism and scepticism; a conception of truth as accessible enough to be realistically aspired to, yet objective enough to be worthy of the name; an articulation of the interplay between the world's contribution to knowledge, and ours. This is the essential spirit of reformist pragmatism, succinctly summed up by James: 'Please observe . . . that when . . . we give up the doctrine of objective certitude, we do not thereby give up the quest or hope of truth itself' (James 1897: 17). So conceived, the tradition of reformist pragmatism still flourishes; and, though very far as yet from the 'catholic consent' Peirce saw (Peirce 8.13) as the end of inquiry, it is, indeed, 'instinct with life'.

Further Reading

Dewey writes on 'The Development of American Pragmatism' in his *Philosophy and Civilization*, New York: Minton, Balch, 1931. Useful selections of the writings of the classical pragmatists are H. S. Thayer, ed., *Pragmatism: The Classic Writings* (details under Lewis in References), and A. Rorty, ed., *Pragmatic Philosophy*, Garden City, NJ: Doubleday Anchor, 1966 (the former includes an interview with William James published in the *New York Times* in 1907, entitled 'Pragmatism – What It Is'; the latter includes excerpts from criticisms of pragmatism by contemporaries such as Russell and Moore, and Reichenbach's 'pragmatic vindication of induction'). For a bibliography of primary materials, see *Pragmatism: An Annotated Bibliography 1898–1940*, ed. John R. Shook, Amsterdam: Rodopi, 1998. Thayer has a fine article on pragmatism in the *Encyclopedia of Philosophy*, ed. P. Edwards, New York: MacMillan, 1967 (updated by Haack in the new edition, published in 1996); see also Thayer's *Meaning and Action: A Critical History of Pragmatism*, Indianapolis, IN: Bobbs-Merrill, 1968. I. Scheffler, *Four Pragmatists*, London: Routledge and Kegan Paul and New York: Humanities Press, 1974, is a clear introduction to Peirce, James, Mead and Dewey. A. J. Ayer, *The Origins of Pragmatism*, San Francisco: Freeman, Cooper, 1968, is illuminating on the relation of pragmatism and Ayer's own, logical positivist, approach. The *Transactions of the Charles S. Peirce Society* is a quarterly journal of American philosophy, which carries articles on every aspect of pragmatism as well as reviews of significant books in the area.

T. Goudge, *The Thought of C. S.Peirce*, Toronto: Toronto University Press, 1950, and New York: Dover, 1966, and C. Hookway, *Peirce*, London: Routledge and Kegan Paul, 1985, are useful introductions to Peirce's work. M. Murphey, *The Development of Peirce's Philosophy*, Cambridge, MA: Harvard University Press, 1961, and Indianapolis, IN: Hackett, 1993, has become a classic. Two collections of papers that have stood the test of time are *Studies in the Philosophy of Charles Sanders Peirce*, first series, ed. P. P. Wiener and F. Young, and second series, ed. E. C. Moore and R. S. Robin, Amherst: University of Massachusetts Press, 1952 and 1964. On Peirce's logic, Putnam, 'Peirce the Logician', *Historia Mathematica*, 9 (1982) 290–301, is a good starting-point. See K. L. Ketner, *A Comprehensive Bibliography of the Published Works of Charles Sanders Peirce with a Bibliography of Secondary Sources*, Bowling Green, OH: Philosophy Documentation Center, 1986, for a bibliography of work on Peirce up to that date. A new, chronological edition of (selected) works of Peirce, *Writings of Charles S. Peirce*, is being published by Indiana University Press, under the editorship of Max Fisch et al., the first five volumes (up to 1886) being available at the time of this writing. Also with Indiana University Press are two volumes of *The Essential Peirce* (papers from 1867–93, published in 1992; and papers from 1893–1913, published in 1998).

James's *Works* are published by Harvard University Press under the editorship of F. Burkhardt and F. Bowers. *William James: Selected Writings*, ed. G. Bird, Everyman, London: Dent, Dutton, and Vermont: Charles E. Tuttle, is compact and handy. Ralph Barton Perry, ed., *The Thought and Character of William James*, 2 vols, Boston: Little, Brown, 1936, and (abridged, one volume) Cambridge, MA: Harvard University Press, 1948, is unparalleled as an intellectual portrait of the man and his work. See also G. Myers, *William James, His Life and Thought*, New Haven, CT: Yale University Press, 1986, and his bibliography; W. R. Corti, ed., *The Philosophy of William James*, Hamburg: Felix Meiner, 1976; E. Fontanell, *God, Self and Immortality: A Jamesian Investigation*, Philadelphia, PA: Temple University Press, 1986; T. L. S. Sprigge, *James and Bradley: American Truth and British Reality*, La Salle, IL: Open Court, 1993.

S. Hook, *John Dewey: An Intellectual Portrait*, New York: John Day, 1939, is a fine brief introduction. J. Tiles, *Dewey*, New York: Routledge and Kegan Paul, 1988, will also be found useful. *John Dewey: The Man and his Philosophy*, Cambridge, MA: Harvard University Press, 1930, includes an essay by G. H. Mead. There is a volume in the Library of Living Philosophers devoted to Dewey's work (*The Philosophy of John Dewey*, ed. P. A. Schilpp, Evanston, IL: Northwestern University Press, 1939); this includes a bibliography of Dewey's writings. R. W. Sleeper, *The*

Necessity of Pragmatism, New Haven, CT: Yale University Press, 1986, a study of Dewey's logic, also includes critical bibliographies. See J. Boydston and K. Poolos, eds, *A Guide to the Works of John Dewey*, Carbondale, IL: Southern Illinois University Press, 1970, and *Checklist of Writings About John Dewey, 1887–1977*, Carbondale, IL: Southern Illinois University Press, 1978, for further references. Dewey's complete works are published in 17 volumes by Southern Illinois University Press under the editorship of Jo Ann Boydston. Two volumes of *The Essential Dewey*, the first on pragmatism, education and democracy, the second on ethics, logic and psychology, edited by L. Hickman and T. Alexander, were published by Indiana University Press in 1998.

On Schiller, see R. Abel, *Humanistic Pragmatism*, New York: Free Press, and London: Collier-MacMillan, 1966, and *The Pragmatic Humanism of F. C. S. Schiller*, New York: King's Cross Press, Columbia University Press, 1955.

On Mead, see A. J. Reck, ed., *Selected Writings*, Indianapolis, IN: Bobbs-Merrill, 1964, and W. R. Corti, ed., *The Philosophy of George Herbert Mead*, Winterthur, Switzerland: Amriswiler Bucherei, 1973, both of which include bibliographies of Mead's writings.

There is a volume in the Library of Living Philosophers on the work of C. I. Lewis (*The Philosophy of C. I. Lewis*, ed. P. A. Schilpp, La Salle, IL: Open Court, 1968); this includes a bibliography of Lewis's writings. See also S. Rosenthal, *The Pragmatic A Priori*, St Louis, MO: Warren H. Green, 1976.

Nicholas Rescher's three-volume *A System of Pragmatic Idealism* was published by Princeton University Press (Princeton, NJ: 1992–4). Hilary Putnam's *Pragmatism: An Open Question* was published by Blackwell (Oxford: 1995).

J. J. McDermott, R. W. Sleeper and A. Edel, in a symposium published in *Transactions of the C. S. Peirce Society*, 21, 1 (1985), 1–38, argue that Rorty misrepresents Dewey. Haack, 'Philosophy/philosophy, an Untenable Dualism', *Transactions of the C. S. Peirce Society*, 29, 3 (1993), 411–26, argues that Rorty misrepresents Peirce. Haack's ' "We Pragmatists . . ."; Peirce and Rorty in Conversation', *Partisan Review*, 1/1997, 91–107, is a dialogue compiled from Peirce's and Rorty's own words; her 'As for that phrase "studying in a literary spirit" . . .', *Proceedings of the American Philosophical Association*, 70, 2, November 1996, 57–75, contrasts Peirce's and Rorty's accounts of the relation of philosophy to science and to literature (both are reprinted in Haack, *Manifesto of a Passionate Moderate: Unfashionable Essays*, Chicago: University of Chicago Press, 1998).

H. O. Mounce, *The Two Pragmatisms: From Peirce to Rorty*, London: Routledge, 1997, presents pragmatism as sharply divided into two wings ever since Peirce and James.

Some recent collections reflect the growing influence of revolutionary pragmatism. R. Goodman, *Pragmatism: A Contemporary Reader*, New York: Routledge, 1995, includes papers on pragmatism and literature; L. Menand, *Pragmatism: A Reader*, New York: Vintage Books, 1997, presenting the pragmatist tradition as culminating in Rorty, includes papers by contemporary literary, historical and legal writers sympathetic to revolutionary neo-pragmatism (but see also Haack's critical notice, 'Vulgar Rortyism', *The New Criterion*, November 1997, 67–70).

References

Apel, K.-O. 1983: C. S. Peirce and Post-Tarskian Truth. In *The Relevance of Charles Peirce*, ed. E. Freeman. La Salle, IL: Hegeler Institute, Monist Library of Philosophy.

Bernstein, R. J. 1983: *Beyond Objectivity and Relativism*. Philadelphia: University of Pennsylvania Press.

Churchland, P. M. 1989: *A Neurocomputational Perspective: The Nature of Mind and the Structure of Science*. Cambridge, MA: Bradford Books, MIT Press.

Dewey, J. 1910: *The Influence of Darwin on Philosophy*. New York: Henry Holt.

—— 1925: *Experience and Nature*. La Salle, IL: Open Court, 1958.

——1929: *The Quest for Certainty*. New York: Putnam, 1960.

——1938: *Logic, the Theory of Inquiry*. New York: Henry Holt.

Haack, S. 1993: *Evidence and Inquiry: Towards Reconstruction in Epistemology*. Oxford: Blackwell.

Hanson, N. R. 1958: *Patterns of Discovery*. Cambridge: Cambridge University Press.

Harman, G. 1965: The Inference to the Best Explanation. *Philosophical Review*, 71, 86–95.

James, W. 1897: *The Will to Believe and Other Essays in Popular Philosophy*. New York: Dover, 1956.

——1907: *Pragmatism*, ed. F. Burkhardt and F. Bowers. Cambridge, MA: Harvard University Press, 1975.

——1909: *The Meaning of Truth*, ed. F. Burkhardt and F. Bowers. Cambridge, MA: Harvard University Press, 1975.

——1912 and 1909: *Essays in Radical Empiricism* (1912) and *A Pluralistic Universe* (1909), ed. R. J. Bernstein. New York: Dutton, 1971.

Jardine, B. 1986: *The Fortunes of Inquiry*. Oxford: Clarendon Press.

Lewis, C. I. 1923: A Pragmatic Conception of the A Priori, *Journal of Philosophy*, 20, 169–77; reprinted in H. S. Thayer (ed.) *Pragmatism: The Classic Writings*. New York: Mentor, 1970, and Indianapolis, IN: Hackett, 1983.

Margolis, J. 1986: *Pragmatism Without Foundations*. Oxford: Blackwell.

Mead, G. H. 1934: *Mind, Self and Society*, ed. C. W. Morris. Chicago: University of Chicago Press.

Migotti, M. 1988: Recent Work in Pragmatism: Revolution or Reform in the Theory of Knowledge? *Philosophical Books*, 29, 65–73.

Peirce, C. S. 1900: Review of Clark University, 1889–1899: Decennial Celebration. *Science*, 620–2; reprinted in P. P. Wiener (ed.) 1958: *Charles S. Peirce: Selected Writings*. New York: Doubleday.

——1931–58 *Collected Papers*, ed. C. Hartshorne, P. Weiss and A. Burks. Cambridge, MA: Harvard University Press (references by volume and paragraph number).

Putnam, H. 1978: *Meaning and the Moral Sciences*. London: Routledge and Kegan Paul.

Quine, W. V. 1953: Two Dogmas of Empiricism. In *From a Logical Point of View*. Cambridge, MA: Harper Torchbooks.

——1969: *Ontological Relativity and Other Essays*. New York: Columbia University Press.

Ramsey, F. P. 1931: Belief and Propositions. In *The Foundations of Mathematics*, ed. R. B. Braithwaite. London: Routledge and Kegan Paul.

Reichenbach, H. 1951: *The Rise of Scientific Philosophy*. Berkeley: University of California Press.

Rescher, N. 1977: *Methodological Pragmatism*. Oxford: Blackwell.

Rorty, R. 1979: *Philosophy and the Mirror of Nature*. Princeton, NJ: Princeton University Press.

——1982: *Consequences of Pragmatism*. Brighton: Harvester Press.

——1991a: *Objectivity, Relativism and Truth*. Cambridge: Cambridge University Press.

——1991b: *Essays on Heidegger and Others*. Cambridge: Cambridge University Press.

Russell, B. 1910: Pragmatism; and William James's Conception of Truth. In *Philosophical Essays*. New York: Longman's, Green.

Schiller, F. C. S. 1907: *Studies in Humanism*. London: Macmillan.

Sellars, W. 1973: Giveness and Explanatory Coherence. *Journal of Philosophy*, 61.

——1979: More on Giveness and Explanatory Coherence. In *Justification and Knowledge*, ed. G. Pappas. Dordrecht: Reidel.

Stich, S. P. 1990: *The Fragmentation of Reason: Preface to a Pragmatic Theory of Cognitive Evaluation*. Cambridge, MA: Bradford Books, MIT Press.

Discussion Questions

1 Explain Peirce's version of the Pragmatic Maxim, and the role it plays in his attitude to metaphysics.

2   What does Peirce mean by saying that 'pragmaticism could hardly have entered a head that was not already convinced there were real generals' (Peirce 5.503)? Was he right about this?

3   Explain Peirce's definition of truth as the 'Ultimate Opinion'. Do you think it is a defensible account of the concept of truth?

4   What does Peirce mean by saying that philosophy should be undertaken with 'the scientific attitude'?

5   'Our passional nature . . . lawfully may . . . decide an option between propositions, whenever it is a genuine option that cannot by its nature be decided on intellectual grounds' (James 1897: 11). Do you agree?

6   What are the main themes of James's 'radical empiricism'? How does it differ from the empiricism of Locke or Hume?

7   ' "[T]he true" . . . is only the expedient in the way of belief.' What did James mean by this? Is it plausible?

8   Critically compare James's observation that 'books upon ethics . . . so far as they truly touch the moral life, must more and more ally themselves with . . . novels and dramas of the deeper sort' (James 1897: 210), with Dewey's that '[e]xperimental empiricism in the field of ideas of good and bad is demanded' (Dewey 1929: 258).

9   Critically discuss Dewey's attitude to the idea that, when we verify a proposition, we discover it to have been true all along.

10   Explain and discuss the merits of Dewey's critique of 'the Spectator Theory of Knowledge'.

11   What does Schiller mean by saying that truth is relative to our purposes? Is he right?

12   Critically discuss Mead's theory of the 'social construction of the self'.

13   Explain Lewis's doctrine of the pragmatic *a priori*; is it a plausible approach to the question of alternative logics?

14   'Pragmatists think that the history of attempts to isolate the True, or the Good, or to define the word "true" or "good," supports their suspicion that there is no interesting work to be done in this area' (Rorty 1982: xiv). Is that what pragmatists think?

15   'According to the pragmatists, to say "it is true that other people exist" means "it is useful to believe that other people exist" . . . Now if pragmatists only affirmed that utility is a *criterion* of truth, there would be much less to be said against their view' (Russell 1910: 119–20). Is this a fair comment on James's account of truth?

37

Frege and Russell

R. M. SAINSBURY

Gottlob Frege (1848–1925) and Bertrand Russell (1872–1970) both came to philosophy through mathematics. They both contributed to a doctrine known as logicism, according to which mathematics is a part of logic, and so is as unquestionable as logic. In pursuit of this aim, each developed the basis of what we now think of as modern logic. Each regarded his logical language as better able to represent thought than ordinary language. This view generated the notion of 'logical form', which has been crucial in the development of philosophy for the last century. Each was led into fundamental discussions about meaning. In the areas in which their work overlapped, they agreed about which problems were central, but disagreed in many cases about how to solve them. All current work in logic, the philosophy of mathematics and the philosophy of language either takes for granted something owed to one or both of them, or else takes their views as the most important ones to defend or attack. This chapter will focus on the notion of meaning as it occurs in the works of these two philosophers and will expound two central ideas from each: Frege's notion of a concept, and his distinction between sense (Sinn) and reference (Bedeutung); and Russell's account of names and his theory of descriptions. In both cases, and especially Russell's, whose work ranged more widely than Frege's, this is a very small proportion of the ideas for which they are famous.

1   Introduction

Frege was born in 1848, and spent most of his adult life in the mathematics department of the University of Jena. His first major work, the *Begriffsschrift* or 'concept-script', in which he set out his formal language, was published in 1879, when Russell was a child of seven. In his *Grundlagen* (Groundwork of Arithmetic) of 1884 he gave an informal exposition of his logicist position, defining numbers in terms of extensions of concepts, which he took to be a purely logical notion. The two works were brought together in his *Grundgesetze* (Basic Laws of Arithmetic, 1893), in which the formal devices of the *Begriffsschrift* were applied to the logicist programme set out in the *Grundlagen*. Close to this time, he wrote the two articles upon which this chapter focuses: 'Function und Begriff' of 1891 ('Function and Concept', 1984) and '*Uber Sinn und Bedeutung*' ('On Sense and Meaning', 1892).

Russell's first exposition of logicism, and one of his earliest works, was in his *Principles of Mathematics* (1903). At a late stage in its preparation, he discovered that apparently true assumptions led to a contradiction concerning classes, a discovery known as Russell's paradox. He wrote to Frege in 1903, showing that Frege's logical system in the *Grundgesetze* permitted a proof of the contradiction. The blow had a paralysing effect upon Frege. An appendix to volume 2 of the *Grundgesetze* (which was added in 1903) suggested a weakening of the axiom (Basic Law V) which he regarded as the root of the trouble, but he came to see that this would prevent derivations which were needed for the logicist programme, and Dummett has suggested that it is likely that, by 1906, Frege had despaired of carrying through his logicism (Dummett 1981: 21–2).

Russell's own final response to the contradiction, taking the form of a theory of types, was published in 1908, and the full statement of his logicism, incorporating type theory, is his monumental *Principia Mathematica* (1910–13), written jointly with A. N. Whitehead.

The first decade or so of the twentieth century was a very fruitful period for Russell, and the two articles I shall mainly focus on date from then. They are 'On Denoting' (1905) and 'On Knowledge by Acquaintance and Knowledge by Description', which was published in 1911 and which is reprinted almost unchanged in his *Problems of Philosophy* (1912). This represents only a fragment of Russell's philosophy, omitting not only his work in the PHILOSOPHY OF MATHEMATICS (chapter 11), but also his logical atomism (see especially Russell 1918–19), his theories of mind (see especially Russell 1921) and his late works (which include *Inquiry into Meaning and Truth*, 1941, and *Human Knowledge*, 1956).

In addition to work in philosophy, Russell had wide-ranging interests, and never held an established university post. He wrote a number of popular books (for example, *Marriage and Morals*, 1929), won the Nobel Prize for literature in 1950, was a civil rights activist in the 1950s and 1960s, and became a well-known public figure, especially as a member of the Campaign for Nuclear Disarmament (he was arrested for participating in one of their protest demonstrations). His *Autobiography* caused a stir by its selective frankness, and by the rather unattractive picture it conveyed of the great man's tardy yet intense emotional development. He died in 1970, outliving Frege by 45 years.

2   Frege on Function, Concept and Object

Many sentences say something true or false about the world. What makes this possible? Perhaps, as Russell thought, a crucial point is that the words of the sentence stand for parts or features of the world. Perhaps, in 'London is beautiful', 'London' stands for London, and 'beautiful' for beauty. Even if this is the right start, it cannot be the end of the story, for nothing has been said to distinguish the sentence from the mere list 'London, beauty': the words in the list also stand for parts or features of the world. As Russell put it, the process of analysis, itemizing what the parts of a sentence stand for, seems to dissolve the *unity of the proposition*: the features that make a proposition, unlike a mere list, something that represents the world as being thus-and-so, and something that can be affirmed or denied.

Russell himself never gave any detailed solution to this problem. However, one of the cornerstones of Frege's approach, set out in detail in his 'Function and Concept' (Frege 1891), suggests a way of approaching it.

In standard arithmetical notation, an expression like 'x^2' is said to stand for a function. If we replace 'x' by '3' we have an expression which stands for 9. The function for which 'x^2' stands yields 9 as its *value* when 3 is its *argument*; in general, this function yields as value the square of the argument. An expression like '$x^2 = 9$' is in some ways similar, in having the undetermined part 'x'. Can we view such an expression as also standing for a function? If we replace 'x' by '3' we get a sentence which is true; if we replace it by an expression for any other positive number, we get a sentence which is false. Frege suggested that this reveals how we can think of '$x^2 = 9$' as standing for a function: it stands for a function which yields the value *true* for the argument 3, and the value *false* for any other positive number as argument. This involves supposing that there are abstract objects, the True and the False, and equating being true with being appropriately related to the True, and similarly for being false.

A function is incomplete. Just as an expression for a function contains an undetermined part, say 'x', calling for completion by a determinate expression, say '3', so this feature is mirrored in the nature of the function itself. It needs an object as argument to yield a value.

A concept is a function of a special kind: one whose value, for every argument, is a truth value. If a concept-word is completed by inserting a word for an object, which Frege calls a proper name, into the blank space, the result is a sentence. The concept expressed by '( ) is beautiful' has an incompleteness which mirrors that of the expression: there is an undetermined part, here marked by '( )'. If we insert a proper name, say 'London', into the space, the result is the sentence 'London is beautiful'. Although he did stress the predicative nature of concepts (see, for example, Frege 1892a: 187), Frege himself did not explicitly use this account to address the problem of the unity of the proposition. However, one can see in the account at least the beginning of a solution. It is one thing to devise a list, listing say an object and a concept; it is another to insert the object into the slot which constitutes the incompleteness of the concept. Frege thus has room for the difference with which Russell was concerned. Frege's immediate use of the analysis of sentences in terms of concepts and objects was to introduce his theory of generality in terms of quantifier and variable. 'All men are mortal' is to be understood as in effect claiming that the value of the function 'if x is a man then x is mortal' is the True whatever object is argument. His theory of quantification is one of his greatest achievements, and, while it has been refined, and alternatives developed, it is in no danger of being supplanted. Russell produced a similar theory (Russell 1905). He claimed that, although he had read Frege's *Begriffsschrift* in the 1890s, he had not understood it. The poor quality of Russell's first presentation compared to Frege's supports his claim to have rediscovered the theory for himself (Russell 1967–9: 68). Russell's later accounts of the theory (particularly Russell 1908, 1918–19; Russell and Whitehead 1910–13), though so much later than Frege's account, were probably more widely read and influential.

3   *Sinn* (Sense) and *Bedeutung* (Reference)

Compare a truth of the form '*a* is (identical to) *b*' with one of the form '*a* is (identical to) *a*'. We are to imagine '*a*' and '*b*' replaced by proper names, for example by 'Hesperus' and 'Phosphorus' respectively. These were names supposedly given by the ancients to Venus: 'Hesperus' was used for a planet which was first to be seen in the evening at certain times of the year; 'Phosphorus' was used for a planet which was last to fade in the morning at certain other times of the year. They did not realize that both appearances were of the same heavenly body. Each proper name stands for (*bedeutet*) Venus; Venus is the *Bedeutung* of both names. In ordinary contexts *Bedeutung* is best translated as 'meaning'. However, it has been common to mark Frege's somewhat technical use of the word by a different translation, most popularly 'reference', and I shall follow this precedent. That *a* is *b* can be a valuable extension of our knowledge: under appropriate circumstances, coming to know this has 'cognitive value'. However, that *a* is *a* seems trivial and uninformative, and of little or no cognitive value. This contrast, which it is natural to treat as involving two distinct items of knowledge, cannot be explained in terms of reference, since the two sentences coincide point-by-point in reference.

Frege correctly inferred that a complete account of a name must allude to other properties than its reference. For all that has been said, these further properties could be idiosyncratic (varying from person to person), or could be SYNTACTIC (pp. 158–60) (for example, residing merely in the fact that in the one case two different names are involved). However, Frege's hypothesis was that the difference is one of sense (*Sinn*), where this is connected with what must be grasped in coming to learn how to use a name, and with how something is presented or thought of. Sense is thus neither idiosyncratic, since it is implicated in coming to learn the proper public use of a word, nor merely syntactic, since it is implicated in how things are thought of. The sense of an expression is an abstract object, not a mere idea, and is in principle available to anyone. Whether a sentence expresses something of cognitive value to us will, on this theory, depend not only upon the reference of each of its names but also upon their sense. If we think that coming to know that *a* is *b* can extend our knowledge in a way that coming to know that *a* is *a* cannot (supposing we can so much as make sense of 'coming' to know the latter), then we are counting the things we know, objects of knowledge, as objects individuated by sense.

Whereas a brief, and in my view decisive, argument leads to the conclusion that there is more to a name than its reference, we should not think of Frege as offering any direct argument for the conclusion that this something is sense, regarded as public and semantic; rather, the merit of the view is supposed to emerge as it is elaborated, extended to expressions other than names, and applied to various problems.

The distinction between sense and reference was first introduced for proper names like 'Hesperus'. Do these notions also apply to whole sentences? Frege affirmed that an assertoric sentence expresses a thought, and argues that this should be taken as the sentence's sense and not as its reference. He held it to be obvious that, for example, 'Hesperus is Hesperus' expresses a different thought from 'Hesperus is Phosphorus'. Since names in the sentences agree in their reference, it would seem that we cannot identify the thoughts the sentences themselves express with their reference. So, if the thought a sentence expresses is either its sense or its reference, it must be its sense. This does not give Frege what he needs unless the antecedent of the conditional can be established. Given that sense was originally introduced to explain a difference between names which affects what is known, and to individuate OBJECTS OF KNOWLEDGE (p. 782), and given that thoughts are possible objects of knowledge, it is plausible to stipulate that the sense of a sentence is the thought it expresses.

Can an assertoric sentence as a whole be credited with a reference? Reference was introduced in terms of the seemingly transparent relation holding between a name and its bearer. If we think of reference as wholly determined by this relation, then it would seem that the reference of a complete sentence like 'Hesperus is a planet' would simply be Hesperus. However, Frege invited us to consider another feature of the reference of 'Hesperus': it exhausts the word's contribution to the determination of the truth or falsehood of typical sentences in which the word occurs. In 'Hesperus is a planet', all that 'Hesperus' contributes to whether the sentence expresses something true or something false is to introduce Hesperus as its reference. So far as truth and falsity go (as opposed to cognitive value) only reference seems to matter.

To establish this connection between the reference of the parts of a sentence, and whether the whole sentence is true or false, Frege invited us to think of a special case: fiction. In the sentence 'Odysseus was put ashore at Ithaca while sound asleep' we have a sentence containing a proper name, 'Odysseus', which lacks reference (Frege 1892b: 162). The sentence as a whole is neither true nor false. So it looks as if when a part lacks reference, the whole sentence lacks the property of being true and the property of being false.

Frege's suggestion was that we should see whole non-fictional sentences as having one or other of the truth values as their reference. We saw that almost this view was suggested to him by his treatment of concepts as kinds of functions. If the concept expressed by 'is a planet' takes the value True for argument Hesperus, then the sentence 'Hesperus is a planet' must be related in some special way to this value. Having the value as its reference seems just the right relation. The application of the notions of sense and reference to parts of speech other than proper names was guided by compositionality principles. Frege in effect stipulated that the sense and reference of a sentence are determined by the sense and reference of its parts in at least the following sense: substitutions of parts which agree in sense (reference) leave the sense (reference) of the whole unchanged. Given this, that the proper names 'Hesperus' and 'Phosphorus' differ in sense but are alike in reference establishes that the sentences 'Hesperus is Hesperus' and 'Hesperus is Phosphorus' differ in sense (express different thoughts) but are alike in reference (have the same truth value).

4 Identity Statements and Bearerless Names: Russell's View of Names as Associated with Descriptions

Frege's first characterization of sense is 'the mode of presentation of the thing designated'. The idea is that the same object can be presented in more than one way (as Venus is presented in one way in connection with uses of 'Hesperus' and another in connection with uses of 'Phosphorus'). Sense 'determines' reference in that expressions that agree in sense agree also in reference. However, Frege seemed to allow that sense without reference is possible: 'The expression "the least rapidly convergent series" has a sense but demonstrably nothing is its reference' (Frege 1892b: 159). Though this is the orthodox interpretation of Frege, it has been challenged by Gareth Evans (1982), who points out that Frege very often used the case of fiction when discussing the possibility of sense without reference. His remarks about fiction, Evans suggests, could be interpreted as claiming that in fiction we pretend that there is a sense (and also that there is a reference). One does not have to suppose that there really is a sense. Evans's view receives support from such remarks of Frege's as: 'A sentence containing a proper name lacking reference is neither true nor false; if it expresses a thought at all, then that thought belongs to fiction' (Frege 1979: 194). In other words, if a sentence contains a name without reference, then it lacks sense (except for the pretend thoughts of fiction); which can only be explained by the fact that a name lacking reference lacks sense. Not all the evidence supports Evans's view, as the sentence quoted above makes plain. If we return to the orthodox interpretation, we should not hold that, for Frege, sense 'determines' reference, if this is understood to entail that each sense is associated with a reference.

Frege says that an expression expresses its sense and designates its reference (we should presumably add 'if any'). Russell, using 'meaning' for sense and 'denoting' for reference, argued that a theory of this kind leads to 'an inextricable tangle' (Russell 1905: 50). The exegesis of Russell's argument is no easy matter, and commentators disagree both on how it should be understood and on whether it is of any significance for Frege's views (see Hochberg 1976; Blackburn and Code 1978; Pakuluk 1993). What cannot be disputed is that Russell's own account of the workings of thought and language used a single notion, which he usually calls meaning, in place of Frege's two notions of sense and reference. According to this single notion, simple expressions like 'this' have meaning by standing for something. Complex expressions are capable of being understood so long as they are composed of simple expressions having meaning. To remind us of the distinction between how the account treats simple and complex expressions, Russell said of the latter that they have no meaning on their own account. One way to form a conception of the adequacy of Frege's two-notion theory is to compare it with Russell's contrasting single-notion one.

How could Russell have allowed that it is one thing to believe that Hesperus is Hesperus, and another to believe that Hesperus is Phosphorus, without allowing something like Frege's distinction between sense and reference? The answer, according to Russell, was that names like 'Hesperus' and 'Phosphorus' cannot be used to give the best account of what is going on in a thinker. Rather, 'the thought in the mind of a person using a proper name correctly can generally only be expressed explicitly if we replace the proper name by a description' (Russell 1967–9: 29). By 'description', in this context, Russell means a definite description, that is, a phrase of the form 'the so-and-so'. Perhaps someone associates 'Hesperus' with 'the Evening Star' and 'Phosphorus' with 'the Morning Star'. Does not the original problem arise again? Since 'the Evening Star' and 'the Morning Star' stand for the same thing – or, in Frege's terminology, have the same reference – yet 'the Morning Star is the Morning Star' differs in cognitive value from 'the Morning Star is the Evening Star', must one not recognize something over and above what expressions stand for? Russell's answer is that one need not, for in such cases, where the phrase is complex, one can explain the difference in terms of the different parts of the complexes. One can explain the differences between 'the Evening Star' and 'the Morning Star' in terms of the fact that one phrase contains a word which stands for the morning and not the evening, and the other contains a word which stands for the evening and not the morning. There is no need to appeal to anything corresponding to Fregean sense. (For more details on how Russell developed this view, see section 6 below.)

Some names have no bearers, and yet have a systematic role in language (such as 'Santa Claus' or 'Vulcan' – the planet postulated, needlessly as it turned out, to explain the orbit of Mercury). On the conventional interpretation of Frege adopted here, he can account for this simply as a case of sense without reference. How could a single-notion theory like Russell's cope with such cases? Russell again appealed to the link between names (of the kind in question) and descriptions. We associate 'Santa Claus' with, for example, 'the bearded man from Lapland who brings Christmas presents', and 'Vulcan' with 'the planet lying between Mercury and the Sun'. Each component of these descriptions can, on Russell's single-notion view, be regarded as having meaning by standing for something; and this accounts, at one remove, for the intelligibility of the names without their having to stand for anything. Such names and their associated descriptions have no meaning on their own account, unlike genuinely simple expressions.

5 Names and Communication

How should we compare these theories? One way is to ask to what extent each provides the resources for a correct account of the working of language.

Frege's notion of sense is firmly connected to language: 'the sense of a proper name is grasped by everybody who is sufficiently familiar with the language' (Frege 1892b: 158). He stressed that we must not confuse the sense of an expression, which is objective and in principle available to all, with the ideas in the minds of people when they use it, which, being psychological, are subjective and confined to a single person. He held that, unlike the public sense of an expression, 'every idea has only one owner; no two men have the same idea' (Frege 1918: 361). One intuition is that Frege's insistence is correct: languages like English or German, or the formal languages which were Frege's main concern, are indeed public, and a correct account must be in public terms like sense, rather than idiosyncratic ones like ideas. We communicate in a public language, and the straightforward Fregean account of this is that we do so by sharing thoughts: for a speaker to succeed in communicating is for him to arouse in the mind of the hearer the thought that he or she expresses.

Russell's account as so far described, applied to names like 'Hesperus', is based on possibly idiosyncratic features of various speakers. We are to find the descriptions in the mind of someone who uses such a name, and Russell was explicit that 'the description required to express the thought will vary for different people, or for the same person at different times' (Russell 1967–9: 29). On the face of it, this seems ill-adapted to provide a good account of the functioning of a public language.

Before investigating this, it is important to stress that Russell's theory connecting names and descriptions was not advanced primarily as a theory of a public language, but rather as an account of thought or JUDGEMENT (pp. 726–9). It was thus not advanced under the constraint of publicity which Frege took upon himself. However, in a brief passage, Russell showed how his ideas could be developed to provide an account of communication in a public language. The account is of interest because it moves away from the Fregean model of communication as thought-sharing.

Let us consider the two philosophers' reactions to a problem about names. When trying to say what the sense of a name like 'Aristotle' or 'Dr Lauben' is, Frege found it natural to produce a definite description. However, he observed that

> in the case of an actual proper name such as 'Aristotle' opinions as to the sense may differ. It might, for instance, be taken to be the following: the pupil of Plato and teacher of Alexander the Great. Anybody who does this will attach another sense to the sentence 'Aristotle was born in Stagira' than will a man who takes as the sense of the name: the teacher of Alexander the Great who was born in Stagira. (Frege 1892b: 158)

Frege put this variability down to imperfections of ordinary language, and claimed that it ought not to occur in a perfect language. This is, in effect, an admission that sense, though appropriate to an account of a public language in virtue of the general feature of being public, fits uneasily with the fact that names are associated with definite descriptions in a variable, and to that extent non-public, way. The variability of associated descriptions, the apparently unequivocal character of our use of names, and the supposition that descriptions are often constitutive of sense, should have led Frege to deny that proper names in ordinary language have sense; but this would have undermined the explanation of the cognitive value of 'Hesperus is Phosphorus'.

Russell steered through this difficulty by saying that the feature of a name like 'Hesperus' that matters in communication, and the feature that fixes the name's contribution to whether what is said is true or false, is not the description associated with it by this or that user, but rather what the name stands for, where this is determined by the various associated descriptions. Suppose a speaker, S, utters the words 'Bismarck was astute'. In so doing, he will, on Russell's theory, think a thought more explicitly expressible as, perhaps, 'The first Chancellor of Germany was astute'. S communicates successfully with his interlocutor, H, just on condition that, for some description, perhaps 'the ugliest man in Europe', which also denotes Bismarck, H realizes that S has said something about the ugliest man in Europe which is true if and only if he is astute. It is not necessary that S and H should share a thought. All that is required is that the possibly various descriptions they associate with the name 'Bismarck' should stand for the same thing; for this is what it means to say that the name 'Bismarck' has a (public) reference in the language community to which S and H belong (Sainsbury 1993).

The upshot is that if an account of names is to be couched in terms of definite descriptions, one does better to view the relationship in Russell's way than to view the descriptions as specifications of Fregean sense. Although Frege offered definite descriptions as examples of a name's sense, he was not committed to the view that the sense of a proper name can typically be given by a description, and a Fregean does best to deny this (see McDowell 1977; Kripke 1972).

6 Russell's Theory of Descriptions

We have seen that Russell provided an account of the intelligibility of definite descriptions without supposing they had to stand for anything; it is enough that their parts be intelligible, which is typically a matter of the parts standing for something. The notion of 'standing for', or as Russell often says 'meaning', is thus the single notion which is supposed to give a better account than Frege's twin notions of sense and reference.

In more detail, Russell thought genuinely simple singular and general terms had meaning by standing for something: a particular in the case of singular terms like 'this', a universal in the case of general terms like 'red'. Understanding such expressions involves acquaintance with what they stand for. There is just one other source of meaning, and that derives from the logical constants, like 'and', 'not', 'is identical to' and 'all'. Russell never gave a satisfactory account of how such expressions had meaning, but it is obvious that they contribute to the intelligibility of complex expressions.

Russell admitted a very narrow class of 'logically proper names', singular terms which a logician, as opposed to an ordinary person or a grammarian, should count as proper names. These are genuinely SIMPLE (pp. 813–18) singular terms, and understanding them involves acquaintance with what they stand for. Russell supposed that if two such terms, say '*a*' and '*b*', stood for the same thing, anyone who understood both would be aware of the truth of '*a* is *b*'. Since most of what we ordinarily call proper names, such as 'Hesperus' and 'Aristotle', do not satisfy this requirement, he excluded them from the category of logically proper names, and explained their functioning in terms of associated descriptions, in the fashion already described. The only logically proper names in ordinary English, according to Russell, are 'this' and 'that'.

Definite Descriptions

Russell is famous for his theory of definite descriptions. He said that a phrase of the form 'the moon' is a quantifier phrase, like 'no moons' and 'all moons', and should not be likened to a logically proper name like 'this'. In particular, 'the' is the uniqueness quantifier, so 'the moon is cold' is true if, and only if, there is exactly one moon and it is cold, and 'the moon exists' is true if, and only if, there is exactly one moon. This enabled Russell to explain how a sentence like 'the golden mountain does not exist' can be true: it is true if, and only if, either nothing or more than one thing is both golden and a mountain. If the intelligibility of the phrase 'the golden mountain' required that it stand for something then, unless there are things which do not exist, the sentence 'the golden mountain does not exist' could not be true: if 'the golden mountain' stood for something, the sentence would be false, and if 'the golden mountain' did not stand for anything, the sentence would be unintelligible. Russell explained the intelligibility of the phrase in terms of the intelligibility of its parts: 'the' is in effect a logical constant like 'all' (since it is defined in terms of such expressions) and so has meaning in whatever way logical constants do; 'golden' and 'mountain' can have meaning by standing for the universals of goldenness and mountainhood.

Frege thought that even though there is certainly a concept corresponding to an expression like 'square root of −1', one should not without care permit oneself to use the expression 'the square root of −1': one would need to assure oneself that the expression had a reference before admitting it into a perfect language. If by any chance one does find oneself with expressions without reference, one can introduce the special stipulation that the unruly expression is to have the number 0 as its reference. As Russell said, this is an 'artificial' and unsatisfactory suggestion, and one out of keeping with other Fregean theses. To provide a reference by *ad hoc* stipulation is to forget that, for Frege, an expression's sense determines its reference (if any), and the sense of an expression is determined by that of its parts. Frege's view on this matter is not easy to understand, since it is very hard to see how a perfect language adequate for mathematics could fail to have the resources to permit such phrases as 'the prime number between 5 and 7'. Frege does indeed explain how the sentence 'there is no such thing as the prime number between 5 and 7' can be true, without attributing a reference to 'the prime number between 5 and 7'. Similarly to Russell, he would have us regard the sentence as saying that no object uniquely falls under the concept of being a prime number between 5 and 7. What is hard to see is how Frege could suppose that the syntax for a language could properly discriminate between concept-words which may, and those which may not, be prefixed by 'the'.

7   Indirect Discourse

Frege's doctrine of sense and reference has a complication we have not yet mentioned. He thought it obvious that in indirect speech, for example when we say that the ancient astronomers did not realize that Hesperus was Phosphorus, 'it is quite clear that in this way of speaking words do not have their customary reference but designate what is usually their sense' (Frege 1892b: 159). In short, in indirect speech, words have an 'indirect' reference: it is their customary sense.

Rather than taking this as obvious, Frege could have used his compositional principles to prove it. If we replace one occurrence of 'Hesperus' by 'Phosphorus' in

The ancients believed that Hesperus is Hesperus

we turn truth into falsehood. Since, by compositionality, replacing a part by an expression with the same reference cannot affect the reference of the whole sentence, that is, its truth value, this shows that 'Hesperus', as it occurs in the displayed sentence, does not have Hesperus (that is, Phosphorus) as its reference.

The hypothesis that, in an indirect context, 'Hesperus' has as its reference the sense it has in ordinary contexts is suggested by the fact that, in an indirect context, we are trying to identify someone's thought, and a thought is a sense. It would be confirmed if we found that exchanging expressions in such contexts by ones having the same customary sense was guaranteed to leave the reference of the whole sentence unchanged. It would be refuted if we could find expressions with the same sense, and a sentence whose truth value was changed just by replacing one of them by the other. Perhaps 'pail' and 'bucket' have the same sense, yet replacing one by the other in 'John said that a pail is a bucket' alters the truth value (Wiggins 1976). This observation might instead be used to show that on Frege's technical conception of sense, 'pail' and 'bucket' differ in sense. This puts pressure upon us to examine Frege's conception more carefully.

The indirect reference of a name is its customary sense; but what is its indirect sense? Frege himself said that 'we distinguish . . . customary sense from . . . indirect sense'. But he makes no more of the point, and Dummett has argued, convincingly in my view, that he would have done better to identify customary and indirect sense. In other words, he would have done better to deny any distinction between sense and reference in indirect contexts. This conclusion would follow from Frege's compositionality principles, if we could take as a premise that the conditions that govern SUBSTITUTIVITY *SALVA VERITATE* (p. 95) in the displayed sentence above coincide with the conditions governing it in a sentence like:

> Some philosophers dispute that the ancients did not realize that Hesperus is Phosphorus.

Frege's distinction between sense and reference arguably helps us understand indirect speech. The shift in reference as between ordinary and indirect contexts mirrors the fact that in ordinary contexts, truth is a matter of how things are, whereas in indirect contexts truth is typically affected by how things are thought to be. Given that Russell made no distinction like that between sense and reference, how can he deal with such contexts?

Russell's theory does not explicitly deal with the different substitutivity principles required by indirect contexts. His goal is to give an account of sentences like

> Othello believes that Desdemona loves Cassio

which does not require any single entity corresponding to a Fregean thought. Russell held that, although one might allow that there are such things as truths, one could not allow that there are such things as falsehoods; hence one could not analyse a sentence like the one just displayed as a relation between Othello and some single object (Russell 1967–9: 72). To understand why he held this, one needs to appreciate what one might call his 'non-conceptualism' (Sainsbury 1986). On pain of idealism, he believed that the mind had to stand in direct relations to the world, not relations mediated by ideas or other representations. A true proposition could be thought of as a fact; but a false proposition would be some kind of false representation, and, for Russell, there are no such things as representations. It is a pity that Russell never considered Frege's view of representations (thoughts) as abstract rather than mental.

Russell's analysis of the sentence 'Othello believes that Desdemona loves Cassio' is that it expresses a four-term relation of belief holding between Othello, Desdemona, love and Cassio. Using the standard conventions of first-order logic, we might write this as

> Believes (Othello, Desdemona, love, Cassio).

Suppose 'N' is some other name for Cassio; suppose Othello has encountered the use of this name, but wrongly believes that it designates someone else. Then we could not infer that Othello believes that Desdemona loves N. Yet on Russell's account, it would follow that such an inference is valid. In other words, Russell's theory fails to do justice to the substitution principles appropriate to indirect contexts.

Russell would accept this consequence, provided that the names in question are logically proper. For these, he held, unqualified substitution *salva veritate* is permissible. What makes us find the substitutions unacceptable is that we are thinking of these names not as logically proper ones, but as ones for which a correct account is of the kind, already sketched in section 6 above, that involves associated descriptions. Perhaps Othello associates 'Cassio' with one description, say 'the F' and 'N' with another, say 'the G'. The analysis of sentences ascribing belief would have to be complicated to deal with this, and Russell gives no hint about how to proceed in this direction. However, there is no question of problems for substitution principles, for these require for their premises identity statements. According to Russell, expressions of the form 'the F is the G' are not identity statements, for the expressions flanking the identity sign are not really referring expressions. The logical form of such a sentence is simply: something is uniquely F and is uniquely G. This does not even look as if it would licence substitution *salva veritate*. (Russell allowed that in certain contexts we can treat something like 'the F is the G' as if it were an identity: see *Principia Mathematica* 14.16 and the related discussion.)

8 Conclusion

How should we compare Frege's and Russell's contributions? Frege has sole claim to the theory that concepts are functions, and to the use of this in explaining quantifiers and variables. He was also the first to introduce the sense–reference distinction. Russell attacked him for this, and invented distinctive theories of names, communication and definite descriptions to explain phenomena which Frege explained in terms of sense and reference.

Suppose one added Russell's theory of descriptions to Frege's view. One could then imagine Frege insisting that every simple expression has a sense which consists in the mode of presentation of an object, where this could be understood in such a way as to ensure the existence of the object presented. The sense and reference of the simple expressions would then determine the sense, and reference if any, of the complexes they compose, and there would be nothing imperfect about sense without reference. The question would then remain: do we need sense as well as reference to explain the working of the simple expressions? It is essential to anything like Frege's view that the answer should be affirmative, and to anything like Russell's view that it should be negative.

Further Reading

The first thing is to read Russell and Frege. I suggest the following four articles to begin with: Frege (1891, 1892b) and Russell (1905) (or perhaps better, in the first instance, the later and clearer discussion in chapter 16 of Russell 1919), and Russell (1967–9, esp. ch. 4).

A good commentary involving both philosophers is Salmon (1986). He criticizes Frege's distinction between sense and reference from a Russellian perspective. On Frege, the best starting-point is Kenny (1995) or Beaney (1996). For further study, Dummett's writings are essential:

Dummett (1973) supplemented by Dummett (1981). For an indication of the current state of thought about Frege on sense and reference, see the Frege issue of *Mind*, vol. 101, 1992. On Russell, you might try Sainsbury (1979). Recent collections include Wade Savage and Anderson (1989) and Irvine and Wedekind (1993).

References

Frege and Russell

Frege, G. 1972 [1879]: *Begriffsschrift*. Translated by T. W. Bynum, *Conceptual Notation and Related Articles*. Oxford: Clarendon Press.

—— 1884: *Die Grundlagen der Arithmetik*. Breslau: W. Koebner. Translated by J. L. Austin, *The Foundations of Arithmetic*. Oxford: Blackwell and Mott, 1950.

—— 1891: Function and Concept. In B. McGuinness (ed.) *Collected Papers on Mathematics, Logic and Philosophy*. Oxford: Blackwell, 1984.

—— 1892a: On Concept and Object. *Vierteljahrsschrift für wissenschaftliche Philosophie*, 16, 192–205. Translation in B. McGuinness (ed.) *Collected Papers on Mathematics, Logic and Philosophy*. Oxford: Blackwell, 1984.

—— 1892b: On Sense and Meaning. *Zeitschrift für Philosophie und philosophische Kritik*. Translation in B. McGuinness (ed.) *Collected Papers on Mathematics, Logic and Philosophy*. Oxford: Blackwell, 1984.

—— 1893: *Grundgesetze der Arithmetik, begriffsschriftlich abgeleitet. Band I*. Jena: Hermann Pohle. Parts translated by M. Furth, *The Basic Laws of Arithmetic: Exposition of the System*. Los Angeles: University of California Press, 1964.

—— 1918: Logical Investigations: Thoughts (translated by P. Geach and R. H. Stoothoff). In B. McGuinness (ed.) *Collected Papers on Mathematics, Logic and Philosophy*. Oxford: Blackwell, 1984.

—— 1979: *Posthumous Writings*. Oxford: Blackwell.

Russell, B. 1903: *The Principles of Mathematics*. Cambridge: Cambridge University Press.

—— 1905: On Denoting. *Mind*, 14, 479–93. Reprinted in R. C. Marsh (ed.) *Logic and Knowledge*. London: Routledge and Kegan Paul.

—— 1908: Mathematical Logic as Based on the Theory of Types. *American Journal of Mathematics*, 30, 222–62. Reprinted in R. C. Marsh (ed.) *Logic and Knowledge*. London: Routledge and Kegan Paul.

—— 1912: *Problems of Philosophy*. Oxford: Oxford University Press.

—— 1918–19: Lectures on the Philosophy of Logical Atomism. *Monist*, 28, 29. Reprinted in R. C. Marsh (ed.) *Logic and Knowledge*. London: Routledge and Kegan Paul.

—— 1919: *Introduction to Mathematical Philosophy*. London: George Allen and Unwin.

—— 1921: *The Analysis of Mind*. London: George Allen and Unwin.

—— 1929: *Marriage and Morals*. London: George Allen and Unwin.

—— 1940: *Inquiry into Meaning and Truth*. London: George Allen and Unwin.

—— 1948: *Human Knowledge*. London: George Allen and Unwin.

—— 1967–9: *Autobiography*. London: George Allen and Unwin.

Russell, B. and Whitehead, A. N. 1910–13: *Principia Mathematica*. Cambridge: Cambridge University Press.

Other writers

Beaney, M. 1996: *Frege Making Sense*. London: Duckworth.

Blackburn, S. and Code, A. 1978: The Power of Russell's Criticism of Frege: 'On Denoting'. *Analysis*, 38, 65–77.

Dummett, M. 1973: *Frege: Philosophy of Language*. London: Duckworth.

———1981: *The Interpretation of Frege's Philosophy*. London: Duckworth.

Evans, G. 1982: *The Varieties of Reference*. Oxford: Clarendon Press.

Hochberg, H. 1976: Russell's Attack on Frege's Theory of Meaning. *Philosophica*, 18, 2. Reprinted in his *Logic, Ontology and Language*. Munich: Philosophia Verlag.

Irvine, A. and Wedekind, G. (eds) 1993: *Russell and Analytic Philosophy*. Vancouver: University of British Columbia Press.

Kenny, A. 1995: *Frege*. Harmondsworth: Penguin Books.

Kripke, S. 1972: *Naming and Necessity*. Oxford: Blackwell.

McDowell, J. 1977: On the Sense and Reference of a Proper Name. *Mind*, 86, 159–85.

Pakuluk, M. 1993: The Interpretation of Russell's Gray's Elegy Argument. In A. Irvine and G. Wedekind (eds) *Russell and Analytic Philosophy*. Vancouver: University of British Columbia Press.

Sainsbury, R. M. 1979: *Russell*. London: Routledge and Kegan Paul.

———1986: Russell on Acquaintance. In G. Vesey (ed.) *Philosophers Ancient and Modern*. Cambridge: Cambridge University Press.

———1993: Russell on Names and Communication. In A. Irvine and G. Wedekind (eds) *Russell and Analytic Philosophy*. Vancouver: University of British Columbia Press.

Salmon, N. 1986: *Frege's Puzzle*. Cambridge, MA: MIT Press.

Wade Savage, C. and Anderson, A. (eds) 1989: *Rereading Russell: Essays in Bertrand Russell's Metaphysics and Epistemology*. Minnesota Studies in the Philosophy of Science. Minneapolis: University of Minnesota Press.

Wiggins, D. 1976: Frege's Problem of the Morning Star and the Evening Star. In M. Schirn (ed.) *Studies on Frege*. Stuttgart: Freidrich Frommann Verlag.

Discussion Questions

1   What features make a proposition something other than a mere list?

2   Discuss the following objection to the claim that Frege's notion of a concept can be used to explain the unity of the proposition:

> There is no account of incompleteness except in terms of the unity of the proposition: incompleteness is just what generates the unity. So it cannot explain the unity.

3   Can expressions other than names have sense and reference?

4   Why does sense matter for cognitive value and reference matter for truth and falsity?

5   If a part of a sentence lacks reference, does the whole sentence lack truth and falsity?

6   Frege held that fictional sentences were neither true nor false. Russell, by contrast, held that fictional sentences were false. A third view is that some fictional sentences are true (like 'Hamlet was a prince') and others false (like 'Hamlet was decisive'). What reasons are there to choose between these views?

7   How do we explain why there is point to saying 'Hesperus is Phosphorus', but no point in saying 'Hesperus is Hesperus'?

8   Show that Frege's compositionality principle for reference entails a version of Leibniz's law of the indiscernibility of identicals (if $x = y$, anything true of x is true of y).

9   Discuss the following argument: Frege's theory uses two basic notions (sense and reference), Russell's only one (standing for); so Russell's theory should be preferred.

10   According to Russell, ordinary names are intelligible through their association with descriptions. This view involves regarding an expression like 'Vulcan' as not genuinely simple, because it is associated with a description, which is complex. So you cannot tell by looking whether an expression is simple or not. What test for genuine simplicity can Russell use?

11   Are there any logically proper names? Would it matter if there were none?

12   Discuss the following objection to the argument that Frege should deny that proper names in ordinary language have sense because they are associated with variable and, hence, non-public definite descriptions:

> To be public is one thing, to be invariant across a whole community is another. Frege could well hold that sense varies from person to person, without prejudice to the publicity of sense, provided he holds that such an idiosyncratic sense is public in the sense of being in principle graspable by anyone (even all those other people who in fact do not grasp it). By contrast, an idea of mine is private in that it cannot even in principle be had by you.

13   Can we distinguish between thoughts that are objective logical entities and ideas that are subjective psychological entities?

14   What are the philosophical consequences of adopting Russell's theory of definite descriptions?

15   How do logical constants have meaning?

16   What can be substituted *salva veritate* in indirect contexts? What are the philosophical implications of your answer?

17   Can Frege respond adequately to the objection that on his theory, one who reports a belief refers to things other than those that the belief itself refers to? (You need first to amplify the objection.)

38

Moore

THOMAS BALDWIN

G. E. Moore (1873–1958) was one of the most influential British philosophers of the twentieth century. At an early stage in his career he established his reputation by his critical rejection of the idealist philosophy that was dominant in Britain at the end of the nineteenth century. He also rejected the empiricist philosophy that appeared to be the alternative to idealism, maintaining that its application in ethics leads to a fallacy – the 'naturalistic fallacy'. In place of both idealism and empiricism Moore advanced an extreme form of realism which centred on the hypothesis of a domain of 'propositions' as both objects of thought and possible states of affairs. In his later years Moore refined his techniques of 'philosophical analysis', combining them with a sustained defence of 'the common sense view of the world' against the assaults of sceptical and critical philosophers. He spent most of his career in Cambridge, where he was a friend and colleague of RUSSELL *(chapter 37) and* WITTGENSTEIN *(chapter 39).*

1 Ethical Theory

Moore's first writings concerned the foundations of ETHICS (chapter 6), in particular, KANT's (chapter 32) ethical theory. Moore argued that Kant (1724–1804) was wrong to suppose that the fundamental principles of ethics have any special connection with human reason or the WILL (p. 734). Instead, they concern questions of value which are as objective and mind-independent as any ordinary matter of fact. Generalizing from this rejection of an idealist foundation for ethics, Moore is equally critical of empiricist theories which suggest that questions of value can be resolved by reference to 'nature', including HUMAN NATURE (chapter 35). In opposition to both idealism and empiricism, therefore, Moore proposed in his famous ethical treatise *Principia Ethica* (Moore 1903) that the fundamental truths of ethics have a status comparable to the truths of arithmetic: they are abstract necessary truths concerning the intrinsic value of states of affairs. In support of this thesis, he maintained that there is a fallacy, the 'naturalistic fallacy', in all theories which seek to resolve questions of value by defining values in terms of further facts, such as facts concerning human nature. His main argument for this charge was that any supposed definition of goodness, which he took to be the fundamental value, can be seen to be incorrect when we see that it incorporates a substantive ethical thesis. For example, suppose one were to define goodness as that which we desire to desire: then, Moore argues, we would have to accept that whatever one desires to desire is *ipso facto* good. Yet we cannot but observe that it is a substantial question whether this is the case, and thus that the proposed definition is incorrect.

This argument is in many ways problematic. Moore appears to assume that definitions must be obvious, if true; yet this is not itself obvious, as Moore recognized in his later writings. Furthermore, because Moore's argument is only an appeal to the way in which we think about questions of value, it is vulnerable to sceptics who offer an alternative set of ethical concepts without claiming that their new concepts capture the whole content of our ordinary ones. For they can argue that even if our ordinary concepts involve some purely abstract conception of value, then so much the worse for them; we would be better off without them. Hence Moore's position needs to be embedded in a broader METAPHYSICS (chapter 2) which elucidates ethical concepts and explains why they are indefinable. Moore himself offers a PLATONIST (chapter 23) metaphysics of goodness as a simple, non-natural, property whose *a priori* relationships to the natural properties of things we are able to discern through reflective intuitions. But this has little persuasive power for those not antecedently favourable to it, and many of those who accepted his claim that values are not definable in non-evaluative terms sought to justify it by arguing that the distinctive content of ethical statements arises from the fact that these statements have a special role as expressions of emotion, or as recommendations and prescriptions. From this latter perspective, Moore seemed right in thinking that ethical concepts are not definable in terms of non-ethical ones, but mistaken in concluding that ethical values constitute a *sui generis* domain of being.

This 'linguistic' reformulation of Moore's critique of ethical naturalism no longer finds much favour, because the implied conception of ethical thought as just a special type of non-descriptive discourse appears rather shallow. At the same time, versions of ethical naturalism which link human values to human nature have returned to favour. Such positions conflict with Moore's theory, but because Moore does not consider the hypothesis that goodness is both indefinable and natural, his discussion does not apply to naturalistic theories that do not offer a reductive definition of value. Since theories of this kind imply that ethical values have an irreducible role within human psychology as reasons for action, the debate about Moore's treatment of ethical naturalism connects with debates in current PHILOSOPHY OF MIND (chapter 5) concerning reductionism and naturalism in psychology.

Moore's ethical theory is now studied primarily because of his discussion of naturalism; but it is also famous as a version of ideal utilitarianism, according to which the ideal end of action is the maximization, not of pleasure, but of goodness – where goodness, though indefinable, is said to be found especially in the enjoyment of Art and Love. Moore's straightforward commendation of these values, which are celebrated without any of the weighty metaphysical hypotheses concerning their significance that are characteristic of Romantic thought, found a ready audience among his younger friends. In particular, the members of the 'Bloomsbury Group' (J. Maynard Keynes, Leonard Woolf, Clive Bell, Lytton Strachey and others) acknowledged their intellectual debt to Moore, taking from him the thesis that it is only certain refined states of consciousness that have positive intrinsic value.

2   The Rejection of Idealism

Just as Moore developed his ethical value in the light of his criticisms of idealist theory, in other early papers he developed his conception of a 'proposition', as the object of thought, in the course of his criticisms of idealist metaphysics. To begin with, Moore argues against BERKELEY (chapter 30) that it is a mistake to treat the 'object' of perception as if it were merely a subjective 'content' or 'idea'; instead, he argues, experience is essentially awareness of things whose existence is independent of us. He then generalizes this point to apply to thought as well as perception, arguing that even the truth of *a priori* propositions depends upon us no more than does the existence of the objects of experience. Since he takes it that true propositions coincide with the states of affairs that obtain just where a proposition is true, he takes it that propositions, the objects of thought, are structures of objects and properties whose existence is independent both of their truth and of our thought of them. The resulting THEORY OF JUDGEMENT (p. 796) is manifestly incompatible with idealist metaphysics; and, just like Moore's ethical theory, it is equally incompatible with an empiricist theory of judgement. Yet fairly soon he came to feel that this extreme realist theory was simply not credible. In his writings from 1911 onwards, he abandoned belief in the existence of propositions because he could no longer accept that reality included false propositions as well as true ones. He likewise abandoned his unquestioning realism concerning the objects of experience, and inclined towards the view that the objects of sense experience, which he called 'sense data', are non-physical representations of the physical world. Finally, in the light of this last point, he acknowledged that it is a good deal more difficult to find fault with traditional sceptical arguments concerning knowledge of the external world than he had earlier supposed.

3   Defending Common Sense

These problems largely set the agenda of Moore's later writings. In order to handle SCEPTICAL ARGUMENTS (pp. 45–6) Moore introduced his appeal to common sense. This appeal concerns the status of philosophical arguments. Moore maintained that the general principles which philosophers employ are answerable to our common-sense judgements concerning particular matters of fact. Hence sceptical philosophers undermine the reasons one might have for accepting their general principles if they dispute our common-sense judgements. We are more certain that we know such things as that 'This is a pencil' than we can be of the premises of any sceptical argument that casts doubt on such knowledge. Moore's critics may well want to urge that this is too simple, in that sceptical arguments typically exploit tensions already inherent in our ordinary cognitive practices and Moore himself came to recognize that more had to be said. In his famous lecture of 1939, 'Proof of an External World' (Moore 1959), he argued that, contrary to idealist claims, one could prove the existence of an external world simply by demonstrating the existence of one's hands. But Moore at this time explicitly denied that one could similarly prove the existence of knowledge of an external world; in order to effect such a proof, he maintained, one had to refute sceptical arguments, which one could not accomplish by waving one's hands at them. Moore then attempted this task of refutation, but had to acknowledge by the end of it that he was unsuccessful. One reason for this, I think, is that he lacked the confidence to rethink the full implications for EPISTEMOLOGY (chapter 1) of his appeal to common sense. It was therefore left to WITTGENSTEIN (chapter 39) to take over this task, where Moore had left off, in his notes *On Certainty* (Wittgenstein 1969) which arose out of reflections prompted by Moore's writings.

4 Philosophical Analysis

Moore's discussions of his problems concerning the objects of thought (propositions) and the objects of experience (sense data) make essential use of his other characteristic philosophical method – philosophical analysis. As we saw, Moore's early theory of judgement involved the hypothesis of propositions as complex structures involving objects and properties which coincide with actual state of affairs when a proposition is true. Since the philosophical analysis of a proposition was supposed to reveal the structure of its constituent objects and properties, it followed that philosophical analysis had an important METAPHYSICAL (chapter 2) role. This role was, however, greatly enhanced as Moore appreciated the significance of RUSSELL's (chapter 37) work in LOGICAL THEORY (chapter 4). For he saw that Russell's conception of a logical fiction enables one to talk as if there were entities of a certain type, while presenting an analysis of the meaning of what is thereby said in which there is no reference to such entities. Moore used this idea in his discussions of propositions. For although he standardly represented himself as concerned with the truth of 'propositions', he did not want this talk to be taken as carrying with it a commitment to the existence of propositions as genuine entities to which reference is made in the analysis of what is meant by sentences in which we attribute thoughts to each other. Whether his position on this matter was altogether consistent can be doubted.

Moore's Paradox

There is something very odd about the sentence 'It is raining, but I do not believe that it is'. There is no explicit contradiction here; and indeed, when uttered in a suitable context, the sentence might well be true. Yet if we imagine ourselves hearing someone utter it, we would immediately feel that their utterance was absurd. The same situation arises for any sentence of the form '*p but I do not believe that p*' and it is characteristic of Moore's analytic acumen that he should have identified this puzzle, which Wittgenstein called 'Moore's Paradox'.

Moore proposed that the sense of absurdity here arises from a conflict between what speakers *assert* by their utterance, and what they *imply* by it. When Jones utters 'It is raining' he asserts that it is raining and thereby implies that he believes that it is raining; when he then goes on to say 'but I do not believe that it is' he asserts that he does not believe that it is raining. So what he implies by the first part of his utterance contradicts what he asserts in the second part. The truth or falsity of his utterance depends only on what he asserts; so his utterance might be true. But the conflict between what he implies and what he asserts none the less renders the utterance absurd.

Moore's explanation appears largely correct, although it remains disputed just what account should be given of the *implications* of the utterance. Wittgenstein's discussions of Moore's Paradox, which occur in his later writings, derived from his sensitivity there to wide-ranging differences between first-person and third-person discourse and thought, and connect with his earlier views about the METAPHYSICAL SUBJECT (p. 816).

Moore also applied his conception of philosophical analysis to his discussions of perception and its objects: he held that although we all know for certain such propositions as 'This is a hand', their *analysis* is deeply puzzling. He took it that the demonstrative 'This' refers here to a sense datum, typically an object of visual experience, and that the really difficult question concerns the relationship between such a sense datum and one's hand. Moore discussed several alternatives here, though in the end, I think, it was a PHENOMENALIST (pp. 53–4) position that he was most inclined to favour. Indeed one can best appreciate the role of analysis in Moore's philosophy from the fact that he favoured a phenomenalist analysis of propositions such as 'This is a hand' at the very time that he was advancing his proof of an external world by demonstrating the existence of his hands to his audience. For this shows that the appeal to common sense does not tell us much about the propositions of whose truth it assures us; we also require an analysis of these propositions, and this analysis can be as disconcerting as one likes, as long as the truth-values of our common-sense judgements are respected. Thus Moore's use of analysis undermines the apparent conservatism of his defence of common sense.

Moore is today regarded as a paradigm of an 'analytic philosopher'. Indeed, his early theory of judgement played a crucial part in the development of analytic philosophy, since it implied that the analysis of propositions is of direct philosophical significance. But because Moore remained detached from the all-encompassing doctrines of logical atomism and logical positivism, his use of philosophical analysis was always piecemeal and idiosyncratic. None the less, particularly because his work combines sophisticated techniques of logical analysis with the defence of common sense, it provides a classic example of 'analytic philosophy'.

Further Reading

Moore (1993) is a selection of writings drawn from all stages of Moore's philosophical career. Schilpp (1942) is a classic collection of papers concerned with Moore's philosophy, which also contains Moore's autobiography and his reply to his critics. Regan (1986) attempts to set the development of Moore's ethical theory in the context of the Bloomsbury Group. Baldwin (1990) is a critical study of all aspects of Moore's philosophy.

References

Moore
G. E. Moore 1903: *Principia Ethica*. Cambridge: Cambridge University Press. Revised edition edited by T. R. Baldwin. Cambridge: Cambridge University Press, 1993.
——1912: *Ethics*. London: Williams and Norgate. Revised edition, Oxford: Oxford University Press, 1966.

——1922: *Philosophical Studies*. London: Routledge.

——1953: *Some Main Problems of Philosophy*. London: George Allen and Unwin.

——1959: *Philosophical Papers*. London: George Allen and Unwin.

——1986: *Early Papers* (edited by T. Regan). Philadelphia, PA: Temple University Press. (This volume contains Moore's papers from the period 1898–1903.)

——1993: *Selected Writings* (edited by T. R. Baldwin). London: Routledge. (This volume contains some of Moore's early papers, selections from Moore 1922, 1953, 1959 and further late writings.)

Other writers

Baldwin, T. R. 1990: *G. E. Moore*. London: Routledge.

Keynes, J. M. 1949. My Early Beliefs. In *Two Memoirs*. London: Hart-Davies. Reprinted in J. M. Keynes, *Collected Papers*, vol. 10. London: Macmillan.

Regan, T. 1986: *Bloomsbury's Prophet*. Philadelphia, PA: Temple University Press.

Schilpp, P. A. (ed.) 1942: *The Philosophy of G. E. Moore*. Evanston, IL: Northwestern University Press. Third edition, La Salle: Open Court, 1968.

Stroud, B. 1984: *The Significance of Philosophical Scepticism*. Oxford: Clarendon Press.

Wittgenstein, L. 1969: *On Certainty*. Oxford: Blackwell.

Discussion Questions

1   Should the definition of a familiar word appear to us as obvious if it is correct?

2   Is it a mistake in principle to suppose that ethical values can be defined – for example, by reference to religious beliefs?

3   Must 'ethical naturalism' include a commitment to the thesis that ethical values can be defined?

4   Can one refute idealism by demonstrating the existence of a pair of hands?

5   Can one refute scepticism by demonstrating the existence of a pair of hands?

6   What could you do to vindicate your knowledge that you have two hands in the face of sceptical doubt to the contrary?

7   Is thought a relationship with a special kind of object – a 'proposition'? If so, what are false propositions? If not, what account should one give of the contents of thought?

8   When Macbeth has a vision as of a dagger, does he see anything? If so, what?

9   Does the term 'sense datum' have any worthwhile use in philosophy?

10   Is analysis the method of philosophy?

39

Wittgenstein

DAVID PEARS

Wittgenstein has been a dominant figure in twentieth-century philosophy, his thought altering the terms of philosophical debate and challenging traditional conceptions of philosophy. His early work, culminating in the Tractatus Logico-Philosophicus, dealt with questions raised by FREGE AND RUSSELL (chapter 37) but also pursued his own distinctive agenda concerning logic, language and their implications for philosophy. A transition period began with dissatisfaction over the Tractatus and led to his second major work, the posthumous Philosophical Investigations. Both the Tractatus and the Investigations have fascinated readers by their unusual, but differing styles as well as by their philosophical content. This chapter concentrates on Wittgenstein's early discussions of logical necessity and factual propositions, his transitional accounts of meaning and the self, and his later examinations of the possibility of a private language, the nature of rules and the foundations of mathematics. It also considers the development of his views on philosophical method. Readers might wish to read chapters on PHILOSOPHY OF LOGIC (chapter 4), PHILOSOPHY OF LANGUAGE (chapter 3), PHILOSOPHY OF MATHEMATICS (chapter 11), DESCARTES AND MALEBRANCHE (chapter 26), SPINOZA AND LEIBNIZ (chapter 27), KANT (chapter 32), FREGE AND RUSSELL (chapter 37) and MOORE (chapter 38).

1 Life

Ludwig Wittgenstein was born in Vienna in 1889 and died in Cambridge in 1951. He studied engineering, first in Berlin and then in Manchester, and he soon began to ask himself philosophical questions about the foundations of mathematics. What are numbers? What sort of truth does a mathematical equation possess? What is the force of proof in pure mathematics? In order to find the answers to such questions, he went to Cambridge in 1911 to work with RUSSELL (chapter 37), who had just produced in collaboration with A. N. Whitehead (1861–1947) *Principia Mathematica* (1910–13), a monumental treatise which bases mathematics on logic. But on what is logic based? Wittgenstein's attempt to answer this question convinced Russell that he was a genius. During the 1914–18 war he served in the Austrian army and in spare moments continued the work on the foundations of logic which he had begun in 1912. His war-time journal, *Notebooks 1914–16* (1961), reveals the development of his ideas more clearly than the final version, *Tractatus Logico-Philosophicus*, which he published in the early 1920s.

He then abandoned philosophy for a life of a very different kind. He taught in a village school in Austria and after that worked in the garden of a monastery. He returned to philosophy in the late 1920s, drawn back into it by discussions with some of the members of the Vienna Circle and with the Cambridge philosopher Frank Ramsey (1903–30). They wanted him to explain the *Tractatus*, but their request for elucidations soon produced second thoughts. When he returned to Cambridge, he developed a different philosophy which made its first public appearance in 1953 in his posthumous book, *Philosophical Investigations*. Before its publication, direct acquaintance with his new ideas had been confined to those who attended his lectures and seminars in Cambridge.

In the second period of his philosophy, as in the first, his notes are the key to his published work. Written continuously from 1929 until his death, they would occupy many metres of shelves if they were all edited and published as books. Philosophers usually intend what they write to be read by others, but these notes are a kind of thinking on paper. It is true that some of the sets are evidently being steered towards publication, but in most of them Wittgenstein is facing problems alone. Since his death many books have been extracted from this material.

2   The General Character of Wittgenstein's Philosophy

Wittgenstein's philosophy is difficult to place in the history of ideas largely because it is anti-theoretical. It is true that in his early work he did produce a theory of LOGIC (chapter 4) and LANGUAGE (chapter 3), but it was a theory which demonstrated its own meaninglessness. That was a paradox which he presented, appropriately enough, in a metaphor borrowed from the Greek sceptic, Sextus Empiricus (*c*.150–*c*.225): 'Anyone who understands me eventually recognizes [my propositions] as nonsensical, when he has used them – as steps – to climb up beyond them. (He must, so to speak, throw away the ladder after he has climbed up it)' (Wittgenstein 1922: 6.54). After 1929 he completely avoided theorizing. The task of philosophy, as he now saw it, was never to explain but only to describe. Since Western philosophy had mainly been conceived as a search for explanations at a very high level of generality, his work stood to one side of the tradition.

Wittgenstein was not a SCEPTIC (pp. 46–56). The reason why he rejected philosophical theorizing was not that he thought it too risky and liable to error, but because he believed that it was the wrong way for philosophers to work. Philosophy could not, and should not try to, emulate science. That is a point of affinity with KANT (chapter 32), but while Kant's critique resulted in a system in which each of the many forms of human experience found a place, Wittgenstein attempted no such thing. His method was to lead any philosophical theory back to the point where it originated, which might be some very simple routine, observable even in the life of animals but rendered unintelligible by the demand for an intellectual justification. Or it might start from the 'crossing of two pictures' – for example, we construe SENSATIONS (pp. 700–2) as objects that are not essentially dependent on their links with the physical world, and so we attribute to them a basic independence modelled on the basic independence of physical objects. His aim was to cure this kind of illusion by a therapy that would gradually lead the sufferer to recognize, and almost to recreate its origin, and so to escape from its domination.

Philosophers are expected to be able to abstract the general from the particular, but Wittgenstein's gift was the opposite – a rare ability to see the particular in the general. He could demolish a theory with a few appropriate counter-examples. His method was to describe an everyday situation which brings a philosophical speculation down to earth. When he used imagery, it was carefully chosen to reveal the structure of the problem under examination. All this helps to explain why his later philosophical writings have been read and appreciated by people with very little philosophical training. However, the explanation of the wide appeal of his later work is not just stylistic. He is evidently taking apart a philosophical tradition that goes back to antiquity. That is a way of treating the past which can be found in many other disciplines today, and even when the scene that he is dismantling has not been precisely identified he can still be read with sympathy and with intuitive understanding.

3   Wittgenstein's Early Philosophy

In spite of the wider appeal of his later work, Wittgenstein was without a doubt a philosopher's philosopher. In the *Tractatus* he developed a theory of language that was designed to explain something that Russell had left unexplained in *Principia Mathematica*, the nature of logical necessity. The marginal status of theories in his early philosophy did not deflect this theory from its main goal, which was to show that logically necessary propositions are a kind of by-product of the ordinary use of propositions to state facts. A factual proposition, according to Wittgenstein, is true or false with no third alternative. For he agreed with Russell's theory of definite descriptions: failure of a complex reference simply makes a proposition false. So if two propositions are combined to form a third, compound, proposition, its truth or falsity will simply depend on the truth or falsity of its two components. Now suppose that we want to find out if it really is a contingent, factual proposition, like its two components. What we have to do is to take the two components and run through all their combinations of truth and falsity, and we will find that there are three possible outcomes to this test. The compound proposition may be true for some combinations of the truth-values of its components but false for others, in which case it is a contingent factual proposition. Or it may come out false for all combinations, in which case it is a contradiction. Or, finally, it may be a tautology, true for all combinations.

Contradictions and tautologies say nothing. However, they achieve this distinction in two opposite ways, the former by excluding, and the latter by allowing, every state of affairs. So propositions whose truth or falsity are guaranteed by logical necessity are limiting cases, extreme developments of the essential nature of factual propositions.

This explanation of logical necessity answered a question that the axiomatization of logic by Frege and Russell had left unanswered: why should we accept the axioms and rules of inference with which such calculi start? In fact, if every proposition can be tested independently for logical necessity, there does not seem to be any need to promote some of them as axioms and to deduce the others from them. Schopenhauer (1788–1860) had taken the same view of the axiomatization of geometry, which seemed to him to be rendered superfluous by spatial intuition.

Wittgenstein's early account of the foundations of logic relies on semantic insight. If a formula is logically necessary, we can see that it is. There is no need to prove its status from axioms, because a truth-functional analysis will reveal it. If one factual proposition follows from another, we can see that it does, and there is no need to demonstrate that it does by a proof that starts from a logically necessary formula. The two propositions will simply show that their senses are connected in a way that validates our inference. This treatment of logic leaves proof without any obvious utility – a problem that Wittgenstein took up later in his philosophy of mathematics.

Propositions as Pictures

Wittgenstein's early theory of language was also developed in another direction. If it threw light on the foundations of logic, it ought also to throw light on the structure of ordinary factual discourse. In order to understand this development, we have to go back one step and ask why he thought that factual propositions must be true or false with no third alternative. His reason was that he took them to be a kind of picture. If the points on the canvas of a landscape-painter were not correlated with points in space, no picture that he painted would succeed in saying anything. Similarly, if the words in a factual proposition were not correlated with things, no sentence constructed out of them would say anything. In both cases alike the constructions would lack sense. But, given the necessary correlations, the painting and the proposition have sense and what they say can only be true or false.

Now this runs up against an obvious objection. Many words designate complex things, which do not have to exist in order that the propositions containing them should make sense, and this casts doubt on the analogy between points on a canvas and words. The obvious response would be to claim that such words are complex and that the simpler words out of which they are compounded do have to designate things. Wittgenstein went further and argued that it must be possible to continue this kind of analysis to a point at which no more subdivision would be possible. His argument for this extreme version of logical atomism had nothing to do with empiricism. What he argued was that, if analysis stopped short of that terminus, the sense of a proposition containing a word which designated something complex would depend on the truth of a further proposition. This further proposition would say that things had been combined to form the complex but it would not be part of the sense of the original proposition. That, he argued, was an unacceptable result both for pictures and propositions. Their senses must be complete, self-contained and independent of one another.

The pictorial character of propositions is a theme with many developments in the *Tractatus*. Not only is it used to explain the foundations of logic and the internal structure of factual language; it also has implications for SCIENTIFIC THEORIES (chapter 9), it yields a treatment of the self which carries the ideas of HUME (chapter 31), Kant and Schopenhauer one stage further, and it allows Wittgenstein to demonstrate that factual language has definite limits.

Wittgenstein believed that ETHICAL (chapter 6), AESTHETIC (chapter 7) and RELIGIOUS (chapter 15) discourse lie beyond those limits. This has started a long-running controversy about the implications of his placing of the 'softer' kinds of discourse. Was he a positivist, as the philosophers of the Vienna Circle later assume? Or could the opposite conclusion be drawn from what he said about the *Tractatus* in a letter to L. Ficker: 'The book's point is an ethical one . . . My work consists of two parts: the one presented here plus all that I have *not* written. And it is precisely this second part that is the important one. My book draws limits to the sphere of the ethical from the inside, as it were' – that is, from inside factual language. If this epigram is taken literally, it appears to put a low value on his solutions to the problems of language and logic. However, nearly all his later work is concerned with the same problems, and there is really no need to subject the *Tractatus* to such a simple dilemma. Its point is Kantian: ethics (and the whole softer side of discourse, including philosophy itself) must not be assimilated to science.

4 Transition

The first modification of the system of the *Tractatus* appeared in 1929 in Wittgenstein's article, 'Some Remarks on Logical Form' (the only other piece of work that he published – everything else is posthumous). He no longer believed in the extreme version of logical atomism for which he had argued in 1922. The requirement, that elementary propositions be logically independent of one another, now struck him as excessive. The reason for his change of mind was simple: singular factual propositions always contain predicates belonging to ranges of contraries. So colour-predicates are incompatible with one another and there is no hope of analysing them into simpler predicates that would not be incompatible with one another. Position, length, velocity and, in general, all measurable properties, show the same recalcitrance to the analysis required by the *Tractatus*. He therefore dropped the requirement.

There are two things that make this change of mind important. Firstly, though the *Tractatus* contains an atomistic theory of language, there are passages that reveal an underlying holism. For example, he says: 'A proposition can determine only one place in logical space: nevertheless the whole of logical space must already be given with it' (Wittgenstein 1922: 3.42). But the new view of elementary propositions is an open move towards holism. What is now said to be 'laid against reality like a ruler' (ibid.: 2.1512) is not a single, independent, elementary proposition, but, rather, a set of logically incompatible elementary propositions. For when one predicate in a group of contraries is ascribed to a thing, the others are necessarily withheld. It is plausible to regard this holism as the natural tendency of Wittgenstein's mind, and the atomism as something that he took over from Russell and eventually repudiated.

The change of mind also has a more general importance. The atomism of the *Tractatus* was offered not as a theory that was supposed to fit the observable surface of factual language, but as a theoretical deduction about its deep structure. Indeed, Wittgenstein was so confident of the validity of the deduction that he was not worried by his inability to produce a single example of a logically independent elementary proposition. This dogmatism evaporated when it occurred to him that the logical structure of language might be visible on its surface and might actually be gathered from the ordinary uses that we make of words in ordinary situations. This was the point of departure of his later philosophy.

5   His Later Philosophy: The Blue Book

The most accessible exposition of the leading ideas of Wittgenstein's later philosophy is to be found in the *Blue Book* (1958), a set of lecture-notes that he dictated to his Cambridge pupils in 1933–4. What he then did was so far out of line with the tradition that we may at first feel inclined to question whether it really is philosophy. His answer was that it might be called 'one of the heirs of the subject which used to be called "philosophy"'. The conspicuous novelty is the absolute refusal to force all the multifarious variety of thought and language into the mould of a single theory. He criticized the 'contempt for the particular case' that any such attempt would involve, and he systematically repressed the craving for generality that has characterized Western philosophy since Socrates first instigated the search for the essences of things. We may, of course, ask such questions as 'What is knowledge?', but we must not expect to find the answer wrapped up in the neat package of a definition. There will be many different cases, and though they will show a family resemblance to one another, they will not be linked by the possession of a single set of common properties. Socrates asked for a conjunction of properties, but we must be content with a disjunction.

That is an accurate placing of Wittgenstein's new philosophy in the history of ideas, but it leaves an important question unanswered. Why should a catalogue of examples be regarded as a solution to a philosophical problem? Is it not just a collection of the kind of material that poses the problem? The point of these questions is that 'the heir to philosophy' needs to be something more than well-documented negative advice not to theorize: it ought to teach us to see philosophical problems from the inside and to find a more positive way of laying them to rest.

There are, in fact, two discussions in the *Blue Book* that demonstrate that Wittgenstein's later work was a positive continuation of the philosophy of the past. One is the long investigation of MEANING (chapter 3) and the other is the treatment of the SELF (pp. 732–3). Both are very illuminating.

The discussion of meaning is a development of a point made in the *Tractatus*: 'In order to recognize a symbol by its sign, we must observe how it is used with a sense' (Wittgenstein 1922: 3.326). This remark consorts uneasily with the picture theory of propositions, which derives meaning from the original act of correlating name with object. The theory implies that meaning is rigid, because it is based on a single, self-contained connection which, once made, remains authoritative, without any need for interpretation or any possibility of revision. The remark points the way to a more flexible account of meaning which will accommodate all the different uses that we make of words and leaves room for plasticity. This is the difference between treating language as a fossil and treating it as a living organism.

The discussion of meaning in the *Blue Book* develops the isolated remark in the *Tractatus* and criticizes the rigidity of the theory offered elsewhere in the book.

Ostensive definition, which was supposed to attach a word to its object, is shown up as a very inscrutable performance, compatible with many different interpretations of a word's meaning: the underlying assimilation of all descriptive words to names designating objects is rejected; and so too is the assumption that the meaning of a word is something that belongs to it intrinsically, and, therefore, independently of its use. This last point proved to be important. For if meaning never belongs to a word intrinsically, it will never be possible to explain the regularity of a person's use of a word by citing the rule that he or she is following. For the meanings of the words in which the rule is expressed will themselves need to be interpreted. This line of thought is developed in *Philosophical Investigations* (1953).

The treatment of the self in the *Blue Book* is very clear and strongly argued. As in the *Notebooks* and the *Tractatus*, it is presented as part of an examination of solipsism, but it is much easier to discern the structure of the later version of the argument. The central point is that the solipsist's claim, 'Only what I see exists', is not what it seems to be. The solipsist seems to be referring to himself as a person, but really he or she is using the pronoun 'I' to refer to something entirely abstract which is introduced merely as 'the subject which is living this mental life' or 'the subject which is having these visual impressions'. But if the subject is not given any independent criterion of identity, there is no point from which the reference to 'these impressions' can be made. The solipsist constructs something which looks like a clock, except that he pins the hand to the dial, so that they both go round together. Saying what exists, like telling the time, must be a discriminating performance. The idea that the subject is a vanishing point, which was developed by Hume, Kant and Schopenhauer, is here put to a new use.

6 Philosophical Investigations: The Private Language Argument

The so-called 'private language argument' of *Philosophical Investigations* is closely related to the rejection of a solipsism which is based on an ego without a criterion of identity. What the two critiques have in common is a requirement which was later expressed very concisely by W. V. O. Quine, 'No entity without identity'. The solipsist's ego lacks any criterion of personal identity, and similarly, if the quality of a sensory experience were completely disconnected from everything in the physical world – not only from any stimulus but also from any response – it would lack any criterion of TYPE IDENTITY (p. 178). The parallelism of the two critiques is very close in the lecture-notes in which Wittgenstein first developed the so-called 'private language argument'. Against the solipsist who says, 'But I *am* in a favoured position. I am the centre of the world', he objects, 'suppose I saw myself in a mirror saying this and pointing to myself, would it still be all right?' (Notes for lectures on 'Private Experience' and 'Sense-data', 1968: 299). Against the PHENOMENALIST (pp. 53–4) who argues for detached sensation-types and says, 'But it seems as if you are neglecting something', he objects, 'What more can I do than distinguish the case of saying "I have tooth-ache" when I really have toothache, and the case of saying the words without having tooth-ache? I am also (further) ready to talk of any *x* behind my words so long as it keeps its identity' (ibid.: 297).

The interpretation of this important line of thought in his later work is difficult. The parallelism between the two critiques is always a helpful clue, a thread which we must never relinquish in the labyrinth of confusing indications.

One source of confusion is hardly Wittgenstein's fault. He himself never used the phrase 'private language argument'. It is his commentators who use it and, by doing so, they have created the illusion that a single, formal argument ought to be extractable from the text of *Philosophical Investigations*. But that is not the structure of his critique. He argued dialectically, and when his adversary tries to introduce the 'neglected *x*' behind the words reporting a sensation, he always tries to show his adversary that, if this *x* is not covered by ordinary criteria of identity based on the physical world, it will not have any criterion of identity at all.

At this point it is a good idea to ask who his adversary is. Evidently, his adversary is a philosopher who supports some kind of sense-datum theory. But what kind? One suggestion that has been made is that it is the sense-datum theory which he himself adopted in the *Tractatus* (not very openly). Since he extended his critique to include other mental entities besides sensations, this suggestion has been generalized, and he has been taken to be criticizing the 'mentalistic theory of meaning of the *Tractatus*' (Malcolm 1986: ch. 4). But a brief review of the development of his philosophy of mind will show that these suggestions are mistaken.

Anyone who compares what Wittgenstein said about simple objects in the *Notebooks* and in the *Tractatus* will see immediately that he was uncertain of their category in the former and in the latter was convinced that his uncertainty did not endanger his logical atomism. Maybe they were material particles or perhaps they were Russellian sense data. He did not care, because his argument for their existence did not depend on their category and he did not think that it needed verification by the actual discovery of examples. However, the possibility that they were sense data was worth exploring, especially after his abandonment in 1929 of the extreme version of logical atomism. So when he returned to these problems after the long interval that followed the publication of the *Tractatus*, he worked out the consequences of identifying them with sense data. This fitted in very well with the programme of the Vienna Circle philosophers. They were interested in the philosophy of science and predisposed to accept a simple stratification of language, with the phenomenal vocabulary on the basic level and the physical vocabulary on the upper level and complete inter-translatability between the two levels.

It is notorious that this kind of phenomenalism looks impregnable until we examine the route that led us into it. That is what Wittgenstein did, and he found an obstacle which seemed to him to make the route impassable. The original position from which it started was supposed to be one in which people spoke a phenomenal language with a vocabulary completely disconnected from the physical world. It is obvious that such a language would be necessarily unteachable, and since Wittgenstein used the word 'private' to mean 'necessarily unteachable', it would be a private language. What is not so obvious is how he thought that he could show that such a language would be impossible.

The primary target of his critique of private language is the sense-datum language that phenomalists claimed that each of us could set up independently of anything in the physical world and, therefore, in isolation from one another. But the scope of his attack is much wider, because it would show that no mental entity of any kind could ever be reported in such a language. However, neither in its narrow nor in its wide scope is it directed against anything in the *Tractatus*. For just as there was no commitment to phenomenalism in the early work, so too there was no commitment to the thesis that the meaning of a sentence is derived from the meaning of the thought behind it. If the critique of private language is related to anything in the *Tractatus*, it is to the critique of ego-based solipsism, but positively, as a further application of the same general demand for a criterion of identity.

It is necessary to distinguish two moves that Wittgenstein made in his dialectical critique of a necessarily unteachable sensation-language. The phenomenalist believes that we can set up this language and use it to report our sense data in complete independence from anything in the physical world. Against this, Wittgenstein's first move was the one that has already been described: he asked for the criterion of identity of the supposedly independent sensation-types. That is a purely destructive demand. His second move was to point out that a report of a sensation will usually contain an *expression* of the sensory type and seldom a *description* of it. This move was the beginning of a reconstruction of the situation, designed to lead to a better account of sensation-language.

The destructive move is made most perspicuously in *Philosophical Investigations*. Suppose that a word for a sensation-type had no links with anything in the physical world and, therefore, no criteria that would allow me to teach anyone else its meaning. Even so, I might think that, when I applied it to one of my own sensations, I would know that I was using it correctly. But, according to Wittgenstein, that would be an illusion, because in such an isolated situation I would have no way of distinguishing between knowing that my use of the word was correct and merely thinking that I knew that it was correct. Notice that he did not say that my claim would be wrong: his point is more radical – there would be no right or wrong in this case (Wittgenstein 1953: §258).

The common objection to this criticism is that it simply fails to allow for the ability to recognize recurring types of things. This, it is said, is a purely intellectual ability on which we all rely in the physical world. So what is there to stop a single person relying on it in the inner world of his mind? Perhaps Carnap was right when he chose 'remembered similarity' as the foundation of his *Logical Structure of the World* (1967).

Here Wittgenstein's second move is needed. If the ability to recognize types really were purely intellectual, it might be used in the way in which Carnap and others have used it, and it might be possible to dismiss Wittgenstein's objection by saying, 'We have to stop somewhere and we have to treat something as fundamental – so why not our ability to recognize sensation-types?' But against this Wittgenstein argues that what looks like a purely intellectual ability is really based on natural sequences of predicament, behaviour and achievement in the physical world. Pain may seem to be a clear example of a sensation-type which is independently recognizable, but the word is really only a substitute for the cry which is a natural expression of the sensation (Wittgenstein 1953: §§244–6). Or, to take another example, our ability to recognize locations in our visual fields is connected with the success of our movements in physical space. Our discriminations in the inner world of the mind are, and must be, answerable to the exigencies of the physical world.

At this point we might begin to regret Wittgenstein's refusal to theorize. If he had offered a more systematic account of the dependence of our sensory language on the physical world, the so-called 'private language argument' might have carried more conviction. In fact, many philosophers have been convinced by it, but there is a large opposition, containing few doubters and consisting almost entirely of philosophers who feel sure that the argument is invalid. The dialectical character of Wittgenstein's argument has contributed to this result.

7 Philosophical Investigations: Meaning and Rules

Another, similar-sounding, but in fact very different, question is discussed in *Philosophical Investigations*. Could a person speak a language that was never used for communication with anyone else? Such a language would be private in the ordinary sense of that word, because it would be unshared; but it would not be necessarily unteachable, because it would be a language for describing the physical world, and so it would not be private in Wittgenstein's sense. The question is important, but we have to go back to the theory of meaning of the *Tractatus* in order to see why it is important.

A rough, but useful, distinction can be drawn between two kinds of theory of meaning, the rigid and the plastic. The theory offered in the *Tractatus* is rigid. Once names have been attached to objects everything proceeds on fixed lines. The application of the names is settled once and for all, and propositions and truth-functional combinations of propositions, including the two limiting cases, namely tautology and contradiction, all unfold without any more help from us. The theory does not actually treat the meaning of a name as something intrinsic to it, because we do have to correlate the name with an object. If we want an example of a theory that does take the further step and treats meaning as an intrinsic feature of a symbol, there is the theory that a mental image automatically stands for things that it resembles. That illustrates the extreme degree of rigidity: we would have no options.

A plastic theory of meaning would reject the analogy between a descriptive word and a name, and it would deny that the meaning of a descriptive word can be fixed once and for all by ostensive definition. Both these moves are made in *Philosophical Investigations*. It is, of course, not denied that our use of a descriptive word will exhibit a regularity: what is denied is that it is a regularity that is answerable to an independent authority. We do have options. We may say, if we like, that we are following a rule, but that will not be an *explanation* of the regularity of our practice, because it is our practice that shows how we are interpreting the words in which the rule is expressed. Are there, then, no constraints? Is the use of descriptive language pure improvisation? Evidently, there must be some limit to plasticity, and one obvious possibility is that it is imposed by the need to keep in step with other people. That is how the question 'Does language require exchanges between members of a community of speakers?' comes to be important in *Philosophical Investigations*. When we trace the line of development from Wittgenstein's early to his late theory of meaning, we need to know how far he moved in the direction of plasticity.

His first two steps were taken soon after his return to philosophy in 1929. The meaning of a symbol can never be one of its intrinsic features, and even an ostensive definition cannot saddle it with a single, definite meaning, because an ostensive definition is always compatible with many different sequels. Meaning, then, must depend on what we do next with a word – on our use of it.

The Authority of Rules

Wittgenstein's next step in the development of his theory of meaning was to argue by *reductio ad absurdum*. Given that the meaning of a word is never contained in the word itself, either intrinsically or after an ostensive definition, it must be a mistake to hold that someone who follows a linguistic rule is obeying an independent, external authority. For any basis that we might propose for the so-called 'authority' will always leave it open what the speaker should do next, and, what is more, open between many different alternatives. If we try to remedy this situation by offering a more explicit statement of the rule that he is supposed to be following, he will still be able to interpret that statement in many different ways. So when we try to fix the right use of a word purely by precept and past applications, we fail, because we end by abolishing the distinction between right and wrong. We feel that the distinction requires a rigid external authority and so we eliminate all plasticity, but, when we do that, we find we have lost the distinction.

It would be absurd to suggest that the meaning of a *particular* instruction is determined by what a person does when he tries to obey it. If the instruction did not already stand there complete with its meaning, there would be no question of obedience. But when the same suggestion is made about a *general* instruction, or rule, it is not absurd but only paradoxical. In order to understand Wittgenstein's argument, we have to elucidate the paradox.

It shocks us, because in daily life there is no doubt about what counts as obeying the instruction 'Always take the next left turn'. However, there is an important grain of truth in the paradox. For the reason why there is never any doubt about what counts as obeying this instruction is that in the ordinary course of our lives nobody ever does take it to mean anything bizarre, like 'Always take the opposite turn to the one you took last'. But if someone did understand it in this eccentric way, a verbal explanation of what it really meant might well fail to put him right. For he might give our verbal explanation an equally eccentric interpretation. Now because this sort of thing never happens in real life, we find Wittgenstein's argument paradoxical. It simply does not fit our picture of the independent authority of a rule. However, his point is that it *could* happen, and that indicates something important. It indicates that our use of language to give general instructions and state rules depends on our shared tendency to find the same responses natural. We have to agree in our practice *before* rules can have any independent authority. The independent authority is limited by the requirement that makes it possible. Wittgenstein's argument is not concerned with the real possibility of linguistic crankiness but with the logical structure of the situation.

It appears, then, that the intellectual performance of following a linguistic rule is based on something outside the realm of the intellect. Its basis is the fact that we, like other animals, find it natural to divide and classify things in the same way as other members of our species. This line of thought runs parallel to the line that Wittgenstein took about sensation-language. For there too the intellectual achievement of reporting sensations was based on pre-established natural responses and behaviour of a more primitive kind.

What limit to plasticity did Wittgenstein recognize? Did he treat agreement with the responses of other people as an absolute constraint? And did he recognize any other absolute constraints? It is difficult to extract definite answers to these questions from his later writings. Both in *Philosophical Investigations* and in *Remarks on the Foundations of Mathematics* (1978) he says that agreement in judgements is required if people are going to communicate with one another. But that does not rule out the possibility that a wolf-child might develop a language solely for his own use. It would, of course, be a language of written signs with which he would communicate with himself across intervals of time. But it would not require the co-operation of other people. So it looks as if Wittgenstein went no further than maintaining that, if there are other people around and if the language-user is going to communicate with them, the plasticity of his language will be limited by the exigencies of agreement with them. This squares with the fact that in several of his texts dating from the 1930s he allows that a person might set up a system of signs solely for his own use. However, though Wittgenstein does not deny this in *Philosophical Investigations* or in *Remarks on the Foundations of Mathematics*, he does not reassert it either. There seems to be some ambivalence.

In any case, there is another, more important constraint on plasticity which really is absolute. If we are going to discover regularities in nature, our language must exercise a certain self-discipline: it must follow routines which allow us to collect evidence, to make predictions and, later, to understand them. Sheer improvisation will not put us in a position to do these things. This obvious constraint is overlooked by those who attribute to Wittgenstein a 'community theory of language'. It is hardly likely that he overlooked it.

8 Wittgenstein's Philosophy of Mathematics

Wittgenstein's PHILOSOPHY OF MATHEMATICS (chapter 11) is another development of the same general idea. For here too our most elaborate intellectual constructions are said to be founded on basic routines that cannot be justified intellectually. When we count, we feel that we are using footholds already carved for us in a rock-like reality.

> But counting . . . is a technique that is employed daily in the most various operations of our lives. And that is why we learn to count as we do with endless practice, and merciless exactitude . . . 'But is this counting only a *use*, then? Isn't there also some truth corresponding to this sequence?' . . . it can't be said of the series of natural numbers – that it is true, but that it is useful, and, above all, it is used. (Wittgenstein 1978: I, 4)

The application of this idea to the philosophy of mathematics has proved less fruitful than its application to the philosophy of language. The reason for this may only be the greater distance between the superstructure and the proposed basis in this case. Or some would argue that mathematics is really not amenable to this treatment. It is, for example, questionable whether it can yield a convincing account of proof in mathematics.

9 Conclusion

Inevitably people ask what message can be extracted from Wittgenstein's philosophy. If a message is a theory, then, as we have seen, the message is that there is no message.

Like any other philosopher, he pushed the quest for understanding beyond the point at which the ordinary criteria for understanding are satisfied. However, unlike others, he believed that philosophical understanding is more like the experience of a journey than the attainment of a destination. He regarded philosophy as an activity that is like Freudian therapy. You relive all the temptations to misunderstand and your cure recapitulates the stages by which it was achieved.

So it is not the restoration of a state of unreflective health. In fact, rather than aiming to reestablish any kind of state, philosophy is concerned with the process.

If there is a single structure discernible in his philosophy, it is his rejection of all illusory, independent support for our modes of thought. Rigid theories of meaning treat linguistic rules as independent authorities to which we who follow them are supposed to be wholly subservient. But he argues that this is an illusion, because the system of instruction and obedience involves a contribution from each individual and presupposes a basic like-mindedness. Similarly, the necessity of mathematics is something which we project from our practice and then mistakenly hail as the foundation of our practice. Evidently, he was rejecting realism, but his treatment of rules shows that he was not recommending conventionalism in its place. Certainly, his investigations have a structure, but it is not the structure of traditional philosophy.

Further Reading

There are several ways in which Wittgenstein's writings may be approached for the first time. Someone unfamiliar with philosophy might read *Culture and Value* (1977). This is a collection of remarks that are not direct contributions to philosophy; they are about art, religion, Wittgenstein's own life and especially about what it is like to be a philosopher.

A closer approach would be to read his *Cambridge Lectures 1930–1932* or the *Blue Book* (1958), which was written in 1933–4. In the former he explains the leading ideas of the *Tractatus* to an audience of Cambridge students; the latter deals with the nature of his later philosophy and with two specific philosophical problems: meaning and the self. Both are easier to follow than his other works, because they are written in the continuous, consequential way in which treaties are usually written, unlike the major part of his *oeuvre*, which consists of independent remarks, which are carefully, but not always perspicuously, arranged.

In the preface to *Philosophical Investigations* he compares his remarks to sketches made by an artist on many different journeys, crossing and re-crossing the same terrain. This work can be appreciated only by someone who travels on the same routes, following in his footsteps – that is, only by someone who can read his remarks as contributions of the philosophical problems with which they are concerned. Reading a book of this kind is not like ordinary reading. It is, of course, partly a matter of taking in what he writes, but it is also much more than that. You have to stop and think after reading a remark, and sometimes you have to follow up a long train of thought before going on to his next remark. But how can you get into a position to read Wittgenstein's texts in this way? That is the problem.

One solution is to use *A Wittgenstein Workbook* (compiled by Coope, Geach, Potts and White; Oxford: Blackwell, 1970). This helpful companion takes 18 topics of central importance in Wittgenstein's thought, and for each of them gives references to his writings and to related discussions by other philosophers, and a list of questions to which the reader can work out answers.

Another solution is to use one of the many books about Wittgenstein's philosophy in a similar way. Instead of reading it through from beginning to end, take a chapter dealing with a particular topic, read it and then look up all the references to Wittgenstein's work in the footnotes. The chapter will help you to understand Wittgenstein's remarks and, in the reverse direction, the remarks will serve as a check on the accuracy of the interpretation offered in the chapter.

In general, his earlier philosophy is more difficult to penetrate than his later philosophy, because it is directly and immediately related to the work of Frege and Russell. But though it is easier to find points of entry into the dialectical discussions of *Philosophical Investigations*, a full understanding of them requires familiarity with the theories under criticism, whether they are those of other philosophers or of Wittgenstein's earlier persona.

References

Wittgenstein: general
Wittgenstein, L. 1977: *Culture and Value* (edited by G. H. von Wright and H. Nyman, translated by P. Winch). Oxford: Blackwell.

Wittgenstein's early period
Wittgenstein, L. 1922: *Tractatus Logico-Philosophicus* (translated by C. K. Ogden). London: Routledge. Also translated by D. F. Pears and B. McGuinness, London: Routledge, 1961.
——1961: *Notebooks 1914–1916* (edited by G. H. von Wright and G. E. M. Anscombe, translated by G. E. M. Anscombe). Oxford: Blackwell.

Wittgenstein's transitional period
Wittgenstein, L. 1966: Some Remarks on Logical Form. *Proceedings of the Aristotelian Society*, supplementary vol. 9. Reprinted in R. Beard and I. Copi (eds) *Essays on Wittgenstein's Tractatus*. London: Routledge and Kegan Paul, 1966.
——1975a: *Philosophical Remarks* (edited by R. Rhees, translated by R. Hargreaves and R. White). Oxford: Blackwell.
——1979: *Ludwig Wittgenstein and the Vienna Circle: Conversations Recorded by Friedrich Waismann* (edited by B. McGuinness, translated by J. Schulte and B. McGuinness). London: Blackwell.
——1980: *Wittgenstein's Lectures, Cambridge, 1930–1932* (edited by D. Lee). Oxford: Blackwell.

Wittgenstein's later period
Wittgenstein, L. 1953: *Philosophical Investigations* (translated by G. E. M. Anscombe). Oxford: Blackwell.
——1958: *The Blue and Brown Books* (edited by R. Rhees). Oxford: Blackwell.
——1967: *Zettel* (edited by G. E. M. Anscombe and G. H. von Wright, translated by G. E. M. Anscombe). Oxford: Blackwell.
——1968: Notes for Lectures on 'Private Experience' and 'Sense-data'. *Philosophical Review*, 77. The notes taken on these lectures by R. Rhees are published in the journal *Philosophical Investigations*, 7, January 1984.
——1969: *On Certainty* (edited by G. E. M. Anscombe and G. H. von Wright, translated by D. Paul and G. E. M. Anscombe). Oxford: Blackwell.
——1975b: *Wittgenstein's Lectures on the Foundations of Mathematics* (edited by C. Diamond). Hassocks: Harvester Press.
——1978: *Remarks on the Foundations of Mathematics* (edited by G. H. von Wright, R. Rhees and G. E. M. Anscombe, translated by G. E. M. Anscombe). Oxford: Blackwell.

Other writers
Baker, G. and Hacker, P. M. S. 1984: *Scepticism, Rules and Meaning*. Oxford: Blackwell.
Bolton, D. E. 1979: *An Approach to Wittgenstein's Philosophy*. London: Macmillan.

Budd, M. 1989: *Wittgenstein's Philosophy of Mind*. London: Routledge.

Carnap, R. 1967 [1928]: *Logical Structure of the World* (translated by R. A. George). London: Routledge.

Coope, C., Geach, P., Potts, T. and White, R. 1970: *A Wittgenstein Workbook*. Oxford: Blackwell.

Kenny, A. 1973: *Wittgenstein*. Harmondsworth: Penguin Books.

Kripke, S. A. 1982: *Wittgenstein on Rules and Private Language: An Elementary Exposition*. Oxford: Blackwell.

McGuinness, B. 1988: *Wittgenstein: A Life: Young Ludwig 1889–1921*. London: Duckworth.

Malcolm, N. 1986: *Nothing is Hidden*. Oxford: Blackwell.

Monk, R. 1990: *Ludwig Wittgenstein: The Duty of Genius*. London: Jonathan Cape.

Pears, D. F. 1987–8: *The False Prison: A Study of the Development of Wittgenstein's Philosophy* (vol. 1, 1987; vol. 2, 1988). Oxford: Clarendon Press.

Wright, C. 1980: *Wittgenstein on the Foundations of Mathematics*. London: Duckworth.

Discussion Questions

1   Does logic have a basis?

2   What kind of theory is philosophical theory? Is theorizing the wrong way for philosophers to work?

3   How can 'crossing two pictures' lead to philosophical illusions?

4   Can we accept a therapeutic method of dealing with philosophical problems?

5   What is the nature of logical necessity? How are logically necessary propositions related to factual propositions?

6   Must a proposition be a kind of picture in order to have sense? What kind of picture is in question?

7   Must elementary propositions be complete, self-contained and independent of one another? Can there be such propositions?

8   Is Wittgenstein's logical atomism compatible with an empiricist interpretation? Are other interpretations available?

9   What are the implications of placing ethical, aesthetic and religious discourse beyond the limits of factual language?

10   How does Wittgenstein's thought display holism? Discuss in relation to at least two stages of his development.

11   Should the logical structure of language be a deep structure or visible on the surface?

12   Is Wittgenstein's thought a continuation of philosophy or its heir?

13   Why should a catalogue of examples linked by family resemblance be regarded as a solution to a philosophical problem?

14   How is ostensive definition possible? What does your answer indicate about the nature of language?

15   How is the meaning of a word related to its use?

16   Is there anything wrong with the solipsist's use of 'I'? What are the implications of your answer for our account of the self?

17   What constraints does the need for a criterion of identity place on our account of sensory experience? What sort of identity is involved?

18   What are the consequences if there is no way of distinguishing between knowing that my use of a word is correct and merely thinking that I knew that it was correct?

19   If we must treat something as fundamental, why not treat our ability to recognize sensation-types as fundamental?

20   Are what look like purely intellectual abilities really based on natural involvements in the physical world?

21   Does the 'private language argument' succeed?

22   Is the meaning of a word contained in the word itself?

23   Can the meaning of a descriptive word be understood on analogy with the meaning of a name?

24   Is following a linguistic rule obeying an independent, external authority?

25   How can the authority of a linguistic rule depend on agreement in the practice of obeying it?

26   Can Wittgenstein's approach to mathematics account for proof?

40

Nietzsche

DAVID E. COOPER

Within a few years of his death in 1900, Friedrich Nietzsche was widely recognized as a thinker and writer of genius, a devastating critic of religion, an acute diagnostician of the cultural ills of Europe, and a master of German prose. It was later – first among continental European philosophers, then among English-language philosophers – that the originality of Nietzsche's treatments of perennial questions in METAPHYSICS *(chapter 2),* EPISTEMOLOGY *(chapter 1),* PHILOSOPHICAL PSYCHOLOGY *(p. 19) and* ETHICS *(chapter 6) was appreciated. By the end of the millennium, it was clear that no other nineteenth-century thinker had so decisively shaped the contours of contemporary philosophical discussion. This 'professional' appreciation did not eclipse the earlier reputation, for much of the excitement in reading Nietzsche owes to an interplay between philosophical speculation and diagnosis of the parlous modern condition of humanity. Nietzsche is sometimes treated as a 'playful', unsystematic thinker revelling in 'masks' and contradictions. In this chapter, a different view is taken. Although not written in a systematic style, the works of Nietzsche's mature years articulate a cohesive general position, one which, arguably, flows from convictions expressed in his very early essays. While this chapter will focus on Nietzsche's contributions to philosophy, to the relative exclusion, therefore, of more 'empirical' ones to psychology, sociology and history, no sharp distinction is intended here. Nietzsche himself certainly denied such a distinction.*

1 Life and Writings

Another sharp distinction Nietzsche denied was that between someone's philosophy and their life. 'Every great philosophy', he wrote, has been 'the personal confession of its author' (BGE 6). Since any great philosophy will 'command and legislate', will 'make and create' concepts, not just 'accept [them] as gifts' (WP 409), its author must be something of an outsider – an eagle rather than a starling (WP 989) – uncomfortable with the intellectual habits of his times. Certainly Nietzsche's life was, in the main, closer to that of the eagle than the starling.

Friedrich Wilhelm Nietzsche (1844–1900) was the son of a Lutheran pastor who died when Friedrich was only four. Educated at Germany's best-known school, the Schulpforta, and at the universities of Bonn and Leipzig, the precocious Nietzsche became a Professor of Classics in Basel at the age of 25. The years at Basel were marked by intoxication with the writings of Schopenhauer and with both the music and personality of Wagner – influences which accelerated Nietzsche's disillusionment with academic scholarship. Illness and the hostile reception of his first book, *The Birth of Tragedy*, further induced him to abdicate from university life. For 12 years the pattern of Nietzsche's life was one of lonely wandering – from hotel to hotel, in the Swiss mountains or Northern Italy – occasionally punctuated by intense, usually difficult meetings with friends. (He ended relations with Wagner in 1876, appalled by the philistine atmosphere at the Bayreuth festival and by the gushing religiosity of Wagner's last opera.) In 1888 Nietzsche's health and mind collapsed, the result of excessive work and perhaps of syphilis either inherited or contracted through, possibly, his sole sexual encounter. For the remainder of his life, Nietzsche was a vegetable, a childlike man nursed by his mother and sister.

It is familiar to divide Nietzsche's writings into 'early', 'middle' and 'late' periods. The most substantial 'early' works are his reappraisal, imbued with a Schopenhauerian vision of a blind cosmic 'will', of Greek thought and art, *The Birth of Tragedy*, and a number of *Untimely Meditations* critical of contemporary culture and education. Attention, however, is now deservedly paid to some unpublished sketches of the 1870s in which Nietzsche develops a distinctive, radical account of the relation between thought or LANGUAGE (chapter 3) and the world. During the 'middle' or 'positivist' period, in works such as *Human, All Too Human*, Nietzsche's primary concern is the more 'scientific' one of exposing, often with wit and venom, the facts of human psychology which, he believed, would both explain and discredit the pretensions of RELIGION (chapter 15), metaphysics and ART (chapter 7) to reveal an 'eternal' realm of 'absolute truth'.

The 'late' period, during which Nietzsche develops such famous notions as 'eternal recurrence', 'will to power', 'perspectival knowing' and 'the Overman (*Übermensch*)', begins with the later sections of *The Gay Science* and *Thus Spoke Zarathustra*. While that latter work – a philosophical fantasy woven around the life of an imaginary wandering sage – may be Nietzsche's literary masterpiece, its main themes are made clearer by the two great works which shortly followed, in 1886–7, *Beyond Good and Evil* and *On the Genealogy of Morals*. The writings of the final year of lucidity, such as *The Antichrist* and *Ecce Homo*, while full of perceptive material, are marred by shrillness and excess, symptoms of Nietzsche's impending descent into madness.

Throughout his career, Nietzsche wrote notes and plans for books which did not materialize (his *Nachlass*). Commentators differ on the weight to be put upon these writings, especially those from the 1880s subsequently assembled by Nietzsche's sister under the title *The Will to Power*. In this chapter, and in opposition to some recent commentaries, the immensely interesting material found in those notes is freely drawn upon. Where there are tensions with the published works, I do not pre-emptively settle the issue in favour of the latter.

2 'Catastrophe'

Like other nineteenth-century thinkers, including MARX (chapter 34), Nietzsche thought that Western civilization was at a critical juncture, indeed that it was facing a 'catastrophe' which he called 'the advent of nihilism' (WP preface). The symptoms of the crisis were various, even anomalous: political anarchism, revolutionary socialism, world-weary apathy, undiscriminating tolerance, vulgar hedonism, religious hypocrisy, and so on. All these, for Nietzsche, were symptomatic of the erosion of beliefs which had, for centuries, given 'meaning' to civilized life. In a famous passage he wrote that 'God is dead . . . we have killed him' (GS 125. cf. Z Prologue 2). Enlightenment rationalism, the natural sciences and modern psychology, with their 'cultivation of "truthfulness"' (WP 3), had made it increasingly difficult to maintain religious belief and, therefore, to subscribe to moral values which presupposed the existence of God.

By 'the death of God', however, Nietzsche has much more in mind than the erosion of specifically religious beliefs and values. God is only an especially vivid instance of a being imagined to exist in a 'true world' set against an 'apparent' world of everyday sense-experience. Other instances would be PLATO's 'forms' (chapter 23) and KANT's 'things in themselves' (chapter 32). 'The advent of nihilism' spells the loss of belief in any such 'higher' or 'true world' and, consequently, in the 'ascetic ideal' which has grounded our hitherto 'highest values' on the nature of that world – on the will of God, say, or 'the Form of the Good'.

Despite the catastrophic upheavals it occasions, Nietzsche largely welcomes this 'war on . . . a true world' (WP 583), since it is one waged by 'truthfulness' on illusion. He welcomes it, moreover, despite his appreciation of just how radical it must be. To begin with, it is a war which must eventually be waged against many of those – including scientists – who are busily dispelling the old illusions. This is because they too are guilty of setting up a 'true world' – of natural laws, particles and so on – set against, and allegedly underlying, an 'apparent' world of 'becoming'. Indeed, it must be waged against all those 'articles of faith' – including 'bodies, lines, planes, causes and effects, motion and rest' – without which all of us, and not just scientists and philosophers, must find it hard to 'endure life', so engrained are they in our familiar ways of thinking and speaking (GS 121). For Nietzsche, these 'articles of faith' are as much 'fictions' as God or platonic 'forms'. Further, the war cannot be ended by hitting upon new beliefs even remotely analogous to the discredited ones. If nihilism is to be overcome, and life reaffirmed and invested with meaning, this will be because human beings are able to dispense with ideals of the kind hitherto embraced. Whether they can do this and still 'endure life' is uncertain. So, therefore, is our future history.

To understand how Nietzsche arrives at his perception of the modern 'catastrophe', we need, first, to grasp both why he concurs in the 'assassination' of the illusion of 'the true world' (section 3), and how he explains our proneness to this illusion (section 4). Second, we need to appreciate why Nietzsche thinks that science, despite – or because of – its urge to 'truthfulness', falls victim to the same illusion, and to understand how he tries to exonerate his own 'truths' from such a criticism (section 5). Special attention must be paid, third, to religion and morality (section 6): for it is here that the illusion has both its origin and most damaging impact. We will then be in a position to revisit Nietzsche's vision of the modern condition and the prospects for 'overcoming' it (section 7).

3   Concepts, World and Life

The confluence of two lines of thought resulted in Nietzsche's total rejection of 'the true world' – of any structured, 'OBJECTIVE' REALITY (pp. 726–33) deemed to exist independently of human concerns, judgements and valuations. The first of these is already visible in his earliest essays, where he argues that any account we can give of the world is indelibly 'anthropomorphic'. There can be no reason to suppose that the concepts and judgements employed to describe the world capture its antecedent, objective layout, since these are the outcome of various humanly wrought 'transferences' or 'metaphors'. In particular, it is we, not Nature, who divide the flux of sensory experience into classes or species, such as leaves or dogs – something we do by imposing a 'sameness' among the data which they do not themselves possess. 'Every concept arises from the equation of unequal things' (PT, p. 83). That these, but not those, objects fall under a certain concept, is due to us, not to the pre-given structure of reality. This 'nominalist' or 'constructivist' view inspires Nietzsche's much-quoted remark that 'truths are illusions which we have forgotten . . . metaphors that have become worn out' (PT, p. 84). So habitual have our concepts become that we imagine them, and the judgements which employ them, to record the objective layout of the world. That is an illusion, and none of those judgements is true, therefore, in the traditional sense of corresponding to the way things objectively are.

The formation and use of concepts is not, then, due to the demands of the world. It owes, rather, to practical human interests – in organizing the relative chaos of experience, in predicting and controlling the course of experience. For the young Nietzsche, these claims were compatible with the postulation of 'things in themselves': it's just that, as Kant rightly emphasized, we can have no knowledge of what these are like. In a second line of thought, however, the mature Nietzsche comes to reject the very intelligibility of things in themselves, of a domain of reality inaccessible to human beings. 'The "true world" finally became a fable', he writes, with the move from the Kantian view of it as 'unattainable' to the recognition that it is 'superfluous' – that, indeed, the very contrast between a 'true' world and a merely 'apparent' one must be abolished (TI IV). If the 'apparent' world of leaves, dogs and people contrasts with anything, this is the 'chaos of sensations' which we have brought to order, to something we can cope with, in that 'apparent' world. It cannot contrast with some more 'real, truly existing' order of things, for no sense can be made of such an order. This is because the very meaning of terms like 'real' and 'exist' is tied to what 'concerns us', what has 'efficacy' for us, what engages with our life and experience (KGW VIII 1.5.19). The question earlier allowed, 'what of the world would still be there' if the 'human head' through which it is viewed were 'cut off' (HAH 1, 9), is now proscribed.

As these remarks suggest, Nietzsche's first line of thought did not expire. He continues to emphasize the manner in which our concepts are actively 'constructed' or moulded by us in keeping with our interests and practical concerns. For example, the concept of punishment is really a 'whole synthesis of "meanings"' in which has 'crystallized' a whole 'history of [the] employment [of punishment] for the most various purposes' (GM II 13). To suppose that concepts could mirror an independent reality is to ignore their subjection to 'form-giving forces' at work in our 'fundamental . . . activity' (GM II 12), their role in a 'general economy of life' which Nietzsche comes to equate with 'will to power' (BGE 23, WP 675).

Nietzsche's 'abolition' of 'the true world' means that he is, in recent parlance, a robust 'anti-realist', who denies that there is a way the world anyway is independent of human interests, perspectives and judgements. Some commentators (for example, Clark 1990, 1998) suggest that, in his late works, Nietzsche retracted this position and embraced a 'commonsense realism' which rules out only a 'metaphysical realism', according to which there may exist a reality closed to 'any possible knower'. This suggestion, however, requires one to ignore many late remarks in the unpublished notes, such as 'we can comprehend only a world that we ourselves have made' (WP 495). It also requires one to suppose that his prolonged criticisms of realistic conceptions of TRUTH (pp. 74–5) and KNOWLEDGE (chapter 1) – ones of which, incidentally, he thinks 'common sense' is guilty – were levelled against a position which, arguably, almost no one has ever held (see Poellner 1995). If 'commonsense realism' is the view that there are true statements which correspond to a reality independent of human perspectives, it is one which Nietzsche consistently rejected.

Nietzsche's rejection of 'the true world' indeed raises the question of the status as 'truths' both of perfectly acceptable everyday statements, such as 'It's raining', and of the philosophical claims which he himself advances. Nietzsche does not want to deny the availability of truth and knowledge in some sense of those terms. His relatively sketchy remarks on this question will be considered in section 5. One reason his remarks are sketchy is that he is less interested in this question and, hence, in the analysis of truth, than in the question of why people value truth (see Pippin 1998). Why, especially, have they needed the illusion of a 'true world' for their beliefs to correspond to? To understand Nietzsche's answer to that question, we turn to his philosophical psychology.

4   Psychology and 'Genealogy'

Nietzsche's account of human psychology is doubly important. First, it mounts a robust attack, often prescient of WITTGENSTEIN's (chapter 39), on a traditional, entrenched conception of mind. Second, it plays a key role in explaining the illusion of 'the true world'. Attack and explanatory role are closely connected, since it is Nietzsche's view that the conception he rejects is itself a model instance of 'the true world' illusion. Hence, understanding why people are so attracted to the mistaken conception of mind will aid in understanding people's proneness to the broader illusion. If, in particular, we can account for belief in a substantial mental 'subject', we will have done much to explain the view that reality consists of substantial objects distinct from 'the medley of sensations', since 'it is only after the model of the subject that we have invented [that] reality' (WP 552).

The mental subject is, in fact, Nietzsche's central critical target. Whether referred to as a subject, self, ego, I, mind or soul, it is 'a fable, a fiction', the product of a 'crude fetishism' which postulates some entity as the hidden cause of thoughts, feelings and actions (TI VI 3, III 5). To suppose that there must be a doer 'behind' the deed, a thinker 'behind' the thought, is like supposing that the lightning is something distinct from its flashing. These wrong suppositions, Nietzsche remarks, are encouraged by verbal forms like 'I did/thought/felt X' or 'The lightning flashed', which tempt us to postulate a substantial subject corresponding to the grammatical subject.

Nietzsche's rejection of the self, subject or ego as 'only a word' (TI III 5) registers his 'NOMINALIST' (pp. 628–9) hostility, akin to HUME's (chapter 31), to thinking that there must be some entity in common to, or causing, the diverse thoughts, feelings and actions attributed to a person. More importantly, he thinks that the notion of self or subject has become irretrievably invested with wrong-headed conceptions of what human beings are like. It is not only philosophers like DESCARTES (chapter 26), but educated common sense, that conceive of a person as being, essentially, a rational, conscious (and self-conscious), self-directing agent possessed of free will, only contingently connected to a body. Nietzsche rejects this whole conception. People hardly ever act rationally, in the sense of acting for reasons – these being, typically, 'rationalizations' after the event which 'cause nothing'. Neither reason nor conscious thought plays anything like as large a role in bringing about behaviour as does 'the nervous system' (WP 529, 476, 526). More generally, there is no 'helmsman' serving as the 'directing force' behind our behaviour (GS 360). As for self-consciousness, far from being an essential property of human beings, it is something which 'developed only under the pressure of the need for communication' (GS 354). Self-reflective concern owes to the practical need to let others know of one's condition, and hence presupposes the development of language. Freedom of the will, to which our notion of self or subject is especially in hock, is another fable or fiction (TI VI 3), incompatible with an honest recognition – itself at odds with the traditional conception – of the inseparability of mental and bodily life. 'Body am I entirely', proclaims Zarathustra, and 'soul is only a word for something about the body' (Z I 4).

Nietzsche does allow for the possibility of certain individuals achieving what deserve to be called freedom, self-direction and, hence, selfhood. Precisely because this would be an achievement, however – a rare and difficult one, at that – it is wrong to depict the actual lives of ordinary human beings as those of free, self-directing selves. Why, then, is this depiction so entrenched? Nietzsche will use the resources of the philosophical psychology he pits against the traditional one to supply an answer.

The psychology or, as he sometimes prefers, 'physio-psychology' which Nietzsche recommends is a 'minimalist' one which seeks to understand all 'doing and willing', believing and valuing, in terms of a single 'universal and basic instinct' (WP 675). At one level, a person is a 'multiplicity' or 'social structure' of various drives, instincts and affects, but all of these may be subsumed under the 'universal instinct' for 'life' which Nietzsche calls 'will to power' (BGE 12, 23) – an 'instinct' manifested in growth and expansion, in overcoming obstacles, in adaptation to circumstances, and so on. All judgements and evaluations are 'in the service of' and 'expression(s)' of will to power (WP 675).

Nietzsche's 'physio-psychology' is at the centre of his 'genealogical' account of the illusion of 'the true world'. For while genealogy – 'the attempt to show us how we have become what we are, so that we may see what we might yet become' (Ridley 1998: 8) – also incorporates reflection on the roles of, say, historical processes in bringing about beliefs, it is clear that, for Nietzsche, these roles are not autonomous. The historical developments to which he alludes, such as 'the slave revolt' in morality, are themselves explicable in terms of 'physio-psychology'.

Nietzsche's genealogy is intended, not only to explain beliefs and evaluations, but to break people's attachment to them. It can do this, despite the fact that 'the question of [their] origin . . . is not at all equivalent to their critique' (WP 254). From *Human, All Too Human* on, a prominent theme is that implicit in many beliefs and evaluations is a further belief about their origins. Especially in the case of our 'highest concepts' – moral and religious ones, say – the implicit conviction is that 'the higher may not grow out of the lower' (TI V 4). To demonstrate that such concepts are not the products of reason or intuition, but develop out of something as humble or 'shameful' as natural needs, is therefore bound to discredit them.

The ultimate target of Nietzsche's genealogy or 'physio-psychology' is the whole illusion of 'the true world'. Since, as we have seen, the entities with which people populate that world – God, atoms, Forms and so on – are modelled on the substantial self or subject, debunking the latter will strike a major blow at the larger illusion. So what is the genealogical explanation of belief in the self or subject? For Nietzsche, it is no accident that the properties with which the self is invested are ones of moral significance – free will, self-direction and the like. Freedom of the will – that 'foulest of all theologians' artifices' – is concocted so that 'men . . . might be judged and punished' (TI VI 7). The image of ourselves as rational 'helmsmen', by separating us from mere animals, is integral to moral esteem (GS 360). The traditional philosophical psychology Nietzsche attacks is, in short, a requirement of morality. Hence we can only understand Nietzsche's explanation of the illusion of 'the true world', including the illusion of the self or subject, by attending to his genealogy of morality (section 6). It is there that his 'physio-psychology' of drives, affects and will to power does its corrosive work.

5 Science, Perspective and Power

The term 'physio-psychology' may suggest that, for Nietzsche, the proper antidote to 'true world' metaphysics is a natural scientific account of the world. Certainly, he admires conscientious scientists for their respect for the evidence of the senses and their commitment to 'truthfulness'. 'Hurray for physics!', that it teaches us to observe, he proclaims in *The Gay Science* (340). Four sections later, however, he writes that people with 'faith in science' in fact 'affirm . . . another world than that of life, nature, and history', and thereby 'deny . . . this world, our world' (GS 344). Science, it emerges, is the latest form of the illusion of 'the true world', of 'faith in the ascetic ideal itself' (GM III 24). The scientist, no less than the theist, is incapable of accepting 'our world' of 'chaos' and 'becoming' as the only one and opposes to it a more 'real' world of Being – one populated, not by gods, but by forces, substances, laws of nature and so on.

Nietzsche is an 'instrumentalist' with respect to such theoretical entities. They 'simply don't exist' (GS 112), being at best 'regulative fictions' required for certain purposes, such as predicting the course of experience, but in no way explanatory of experience. Physics is 'only an interpretation . . . of the world (to suit us . . .) and not a world-explanation' (BGE 14). If it were recognized as such, there would be no objection: indeed, it is an 'interpretation' which may be 'imperative for . . . machinists and bridge-builders' (ibid.). Not only, however, does the ascetic ideal impel people to think that science is explanatory of experience, they privilege scientific descriptions over all others. That is a terrible 'prejudice' whose effect is to reduce the world to something 'essentially meaningless'. Music, for instance, gets reduced to what can be 'counted, calculated, put into [the] formulas' of mathematical physics (GS 373).

Since faith in science, like belief in the self and free will, is a product of the ascetic ideal, with its relegation of 'our world', explanation of it belongs, ultimately, to the genealogy of morality. With the scientific 'will to truth', we 'stand on moral ground' (GS 344), since this is the breeding-ground for the ascetic ideal and the illusion of 'the true world'. Before turning to that, however, we need to discuss the problems which Nietzsche's attitude to science poses for his own claims about the world and human beings. Related problems loomed in section 3 as a result of Nietzsche's denial of the existence of truth in the traditional sense of correspondence with 'objective' facts. Those problems become more acute when he writes that 'there is . . . only a perspective "knowing"' (GM III 12) and that 'facts are precisely what there is not, only interpretations' (WP 481). Everyone, not just physicists and theists, is advancing only interpretations from a certain perspective.

For some critics, the claim that there are only perspectives or interpretations is plain paradoxical. If true, it is either false or no better warranted than any other claim – since it itself expresses just one more perspective or interpretation. This criticism misses its mark. When Nietzsche calls a judgement perspectival, he does not mean that it is mistaken, but that it is not true in the sense of corresponding to reality. And that a theory or judgement is an interpretation does not preclude there being reasons to prefer it, in certain contexts at least, over a rival one (see Nehamas 1985). The physicist's interpretation, recall, may be 'imperative' for 'bridge-builders'.

If it is wrong to charge perspectivism with paradox, so it is, at an opposite extreme, to construe it as the uncontentious epistemological claim that knowledge presupposes some standpoint, that knowers must have some cognitive interests. For Nietzsche, the standpoints and interests which it is impossible to transcend are practical, 'all too human' and 'biological' ones. That these are presupposed by all enquiry is far from truistic. Moreover, Nietzsche persistently connects his perspectivism with metaphysical assertions to the effect that any structured world – any facts – of which sense can be made is one 'invented' or 'made'. Perspectivism is of a piece with his anti-realism.

Nietzsche is often understood to regard his own claims as perspectival interpretations which are true in the sense of being superior on PRAGMATIC (chapter 36) grounds to rival ones. Many of his remarks support this reading. He says of his doctrine of will to power, 'supposing that this also is only interpretation . . . well, so much the better' (BGE 22). And there are many passages in *The Will to Power* where he urges that it is 'value for life' which is the 'final determinant' of truth in the only viable sense which remains once the traditional notion is abandoned (WP 493). Even in the case of logical and mathematical propositions, 'their utility alone is their "truth"' (WP 514).

If this is Nietzsche's position, it is not an obviously incoherent one. But his perspectival account of the sciences still poses a real problem. This is because his own 'physio-psychology' looks like a scientific theory. Now, science (psychology and biology included) inquires into the relatively ordered empirical world which, for Nietzsche, is the 'product' of the drives, affects, etc., subsumed under our will to power. The problem is, how can one explain the very existence of an ordered world on the basis of phenomena which belong within it? Nietzsche is aware that one cannot: it is absurd to propose that 'the external world is the work of our organs', of anything investigated by physiology or biology, for then our organs, as 'part of this external world . . . would be – the work of our organs!' (BGE 15).

If coherence is to be maintained then, as HEIDEGGER (1987: 46) (chapter 41) urges, Nietzsche cannot be 'thinking biologically' about our drives, instincts and 'life'. That these are not the processes studied by the biological sciences is supported by descriptions of them as, *inter alia*, 'interpreting' and 'having perspectives' (WP 643, 581). The 'ruling drives' which comprise our will to power are not natural processes, but belong, as Heidegger (1987: 72) puts it, to 'the praxis of life'. They are the basic, purposive activities without which intelligent thought and action are impossible – those which 'impose upon chaos', through schematizing, simplifying, ordering, 'subduing' data and the like, the 'regularity and form' required by the 'practical needs' of all but the crudest kind of human existence (WP 515). It is the impositional, ordering character of this praxis which invites the label 'will to power'. The drives etc. subsequently investigated by biology and physiology belong, not to this 'form-giving' praxis, but to the natural order which is its 'product'.

A snag with this interpretation is that while Nietzsche sometimes equates will to power with 'life', in other places he speaks of it as present 'in all events' (GM II 12), as the 'innermost essence' of the world at large (WP 693). (In so doing, he partly resurrects the position, inspired by Schopenhauer, of *The Birth of Tragedy*.) A possible way to explain this proclamation of a 'cosmic' will to power is the following. 'The total character of the world', he writes, is one of 'chaos', in that it lacks, 'in itself', the 'arrangement' into objects, species, causal processes and so on which are a 'human contribution' (GS 109). Still, the 'chaos' is a relative one, for the world must display that degree of 'direction' and 'organization' (WP 561) which makes it possible for the concepts and schemas we impose to gain any purchase (see Schacht 1983: 194–9). If we are to characterize, however inadequately and metaphorically, this quasi-chaotic organization of 'forces', it can only be by 'employ[ing] man as an analogy' (WP 619), by invoking the terminology of power – of will, subjection and indeed force itself.

If this is right, then Nietzsche's own metaphysics is 'only interpretation' or 'only perspectival' in a special way. It is not a rival, on the same level, to perspectives he rejects, such as the religious and 'mechanistic' interpretations of the world. Unlike these, it is not guilty of the illusion of a structured, 'true world' of 'Being'. On the other hand, Nietzsche recognizes that the metaphors which the characterization of the world as will to power invokes might 'eventually seem unsuitable' and 'too human' (BGE 22). Nietzsche's characterization is 'only interpretation' to the degree that he does not exclude the possibility of more fitting and resonating metaphors.

6 Morality and Religion

The domain to which Nietzsche most resolutely applies his 'physio-psychology' of will to power is religious morality. This is partly because, as noted, the various metaphysical illusions he exposes, such as the self or 'faith in science', turned out to 'stand on moral ground'. It is also because, in Nietzsche's view, it is Judaeo-Christian morality whose emergence was the decisive event of Western culture and whose atrophy is the primary reason for 'the advent of nihilism'.

A genealogy of morality is made imperative by the impossibility of concurring in people's own estimate of their moral judgements as statements of moral fact. '[T]here are altogether no moral facts', only a 'moral interpretation' of phenomena (TI VII 1). The need, then, is to explain how, from a 'pre-moral' condition of life, properly moral interpretations emerge. 'Properly' needs emphasizing, since Nietzsche distinguishes between a broad, thin notion of morality as, roughly, 'obedience to . . . law or custom' (HAH 1, 96), and the narrower, richer notion now suggested by the term 'moral'. Morality, in the latter sense, comprises several components missing from the thinner notion: a concern for the motives of actions more than for the actions themselves; an emphasis on conscience and a sense of guilt; a determination to hold responsible, blame and punish; a premium on 'disinterested', altruistic actions; the idea that moral demands are universal, binding on all human beings as such; and the aim of minimizing suffering.

Nietzsche has his objections to each of these components. For example, the universal prescription 'This is how everyone should act' ignores both the the 'rank-order' of human beings and the unique context of each action (GS 335). Again, moral blame presupposes the untenable concept of free will. Crucially, however, he also has a central criticism of the whole package – of morality itself. It is 'against life' (GM III 13), 'directed against . . . the instincts of life' (TI V 4), 'the morbid softening . . . through which . . . "man" finally learns to be ashamed of all his instincts' (GM II 7). In explaining how morality proper emerges from morality *qua* custom or mores, genealogy must also explain, therefore, the apparent paradox of 'life [turning] against life', of an institution which, like everything human, is in thrall to 'basic instincts' coming to be directed against them.

Nietzsche's genealogy takes the form of an historical reconstruction in which the decisive event is 'the slave revolt in morality' against the ethical codes of the 'masters' or 'warrior-nobles' who have hitherto dominated the 'slaves'. The revolutionary result was that 'pre-moral' conceptions of good, right and duty were hijacked and transformed by the 'weak' in accordance with an 'ascetic ideal' successfully promoted by those friends and exploiters of the weak, the 'ascetic priests'. After the revolt, for example, the pre-moral term 'bad', which the warrior-nobles had earlier applied to those 'inferior in nature', is given the moral meaning of 'evil' and applied by the slaves to their erstwhile masters (GM I 11).

One motive for the slave revolt is obvious: resentment against masters whose natural aggression, especially when external enemies were lacking, turned towards the slaves themselves. The slave's advantage in persuading his oppressors to subscribe to such virtues as humility and charity is apparent. This, however, can hardly explain the success of the revolt – the masters' self-emasculation – and anyway, Nietzsche argues, ignores a deeper dimension of the slaves' *ressentiment*. This is their rancour towards themselves, the result in part of directing inwards an impotent resentment 'denied the true reaction, that of deeds' (GM I 10), and in part of self-loathing. The latter is due to a sense of inferiority with respect, especially, to the power exercised by the nobles of 'creation and imposition of forms', of determining how things should be called and actions valued (GM II 17).

The genius of that 'repulsive caterpillar', the ascetic priest, is to convert this corrosive, inner resentment into something 'joyful'. He does so by inventing and successfully marketing two related dualisms: between the mundane world and the 'true world' of God, and between material existence and that of the immortal soul. The first distinction is elaborated so as to 'devaluate' and deny serious point to 'our earthly reality' (EH IV 8), and to construe suffering as something deserved, through 'original sin'. This strategy, it might seem, could hardly alleviate the slaves' suffering, but in a virtuoso display of speculative psychology, Nietzsche argues that it does. For people ascetically fixed on an ideal, divine realm, the tribulations of an earthly life now perceived as a 'mistake' become trivial. Moreover, it was never 'suffering as such but the senselessness of suffering' which was unbearable, and it is precisely the idea that there is 'any such thing as senseless suffering' which Christianity has 'abolished' (GM II 7).

The second dualism, with the promise it affords of the soul's immortal beatitude, reinforces the ascetic ideal's devaluation of the earthly, and serves in two further ways to bolster the weak. First, the identification of the person with an inner self or soul facilitates a doctrine of equality, since overt differences in strength and beauty between masters and slaves may now be dismissed as superficial. The way is open for principles of equal human rights, of Kantian 'respect for persons' as such. Second, the soul is made the locus of a freedom of the will which is deployed, not only for the purpose of holding the masters culpably responsible for their deeds but, more subtly, to erase the slaves' sense of inferiority. If they behave meekly and unaggressively, this is not because they are weak, but because they have chosen so to behave. It is as if, Nietzsche observes, lambs were to convince themselves that their difference from birds of prey consists in electing not to predate (GM I 13).

Nietzsche's story of the emergence of morality proper via the dualisms, illusions and ideals promoted by ascetic priests is of a complexity that no brief account can accommodate. It is, in sum, the story of 'life turned against life'. In this, for Nietzsche, there is no paradox. All human life is will to power, whose 'natural' expression is creative control of, 'form-giving' imposition on, the world. Among 'botched and bungled' people denied such expression, the will must be 'sublimated' into other strategies, ones which 'devaluate' the kinds of expression of which such people are incapable. If, *in toto*, the religious morality of the ascetic priests and their clientèle, the weak, represents a net 'diminution of life', it has nevertheless been an expression of life – of their life.

7 Overcoming Nihilism

That final point indicates a certain ambivalence of Nietzsche's towards the erosion of religious morality, for he recognizes the genuine benefits it has brought to 'the herd' –

indeed, to all of us, since its civilizing effects have been responsible for 'the superiority . . . of men over other animals' (GM I 6). Certainly he does not advocate a return to the mores of the warrior-nobles who, for all their courage and absence of rancour, were 'stupid' and 'barbaric'.

On balance, nevertheless, Nietzsche welcomes the demise of religious morality, 'the end of its tyranny' over those capable of rising above the herd (WP 361) and the abolition of the 'true world' illusion which has sustained it. This is despite the upheavals this demise must cause, the entrenchment of the 'true world' illusion in new forms (notably 'faith in science'), and Nietzsche's prediction, in darker moods, that nihilism will last for the foreseeable future. This will not be the 'active', and transitory, nihilism of bomb-chucking revolutionaries, but something more enduring and depressing – the 'passive', 'decadent', 'sickly' nihilism of people without ideals and purpose, indeed without will. At least the 'active' nihilist willed something, if only something negative and destructive, and it is better that 'man will nothingness than not will' at all (GM III 28). The truly 'nau-seating' spectre is that of the 'maggot-men', 'little men' or 'last men' of Zarathustra's Prologue, with their easy-going hedonism, liberal tolerance of all opinions and tastes, 'thickly padded humanity' (TI IX 37), and lack of commitment to any 'decisive and hard' Yes or No – men for whom the only sin, perhaps, is to think anything a sin.

This remarkable anticipation of a 'postmodern' climate of thought is sometimes countered, or accompanied, by Nietzsche's confidence in the emergence, if only as the occasional 'lucky hit' (GM I 12), of a 'redeeming' kind of person in whom nihilism and decadence are overcome. Like the 'last man', and unlike the ascetic priest, this redeem-ing type will be without 'articles of faith', liberated as he is from the illusion of a 'true world' of values there to be discovered. But like the ascetic priest, and unlike the 'last man', he will be committed to values and ideals, albeit ones which are 'moraline-free' and 'created'. As such, this 'Overman', as Nietzsche sometimes calls the redeeming type, will indeed be 'new, unique, incomparable', for never previously have people attempted, let alone successfully managed, to live with commitment to ideals of which they recognize themselves to be the sole source. Where faith in a 'transcendental' source has atrophied, so, as with the 'last man', has any sense of meaningful purpose.

Nietzsche nowhere paints a detailed portrait of the Overman (or his near-relatives – the 'higher type', 'sovereign individual', 'free spirit' and so on). After all, 'there has never been an Overman' (Z II 4), and since the Overman creates his own values, indeed 'creates himself', no blueprint of his life can be prepared in advance. Nevertheless, we are told of some of the qualities the Overman must have if he is to be the 'supreme type' of human being through maximally embodying will to power. To begin with, he must, as the name suggests, overcome, for in 'the degree of resistance . . . continually over-come' is a measure of 'freedom understood . . . as will to power' (WP 770). Unlike the ascetic priest, what the Overman overcomes are not our instincts and 'ruling drives', but the ascetic ideal itself and other obstacles to the expression of those drives. Second, his attitude to life as a whole must be that of the 'Yea-sayer', of unqualified affirma-tion, to the point indeed of celebrating the thought of 'eternal recurrence', of life – one's own included – 'return[ing] to you, all in the same . . . sequence' innumerable times (GS 341; cf. Z III 2). This is because the ultimate exercise of power is control of the past, 'to recreate all "it was" into a "thus I willed it"' (Z II 20), which, given eternal recurrence, is something one can indirectly do in the sense of willing past events to reoccur. (Whether Nietzsche regarded eternal recurrence as a plausible cosmological hypothesis, and not simply as a thought experiment for testing people's strength of affirmation, is much contested. See, for example, Danto 1965.)

Finally, the redeeming human type must possess the 'great and rare art of "giving style" to one's character', in the specific sense of incorporating everything in his or her life – drives, affects, values, ideals – into an 'artistic plan' (GS 290). To be weak is to be disintegrated, torn apart, without a centre. To be powerful is to achieve, like Goethe, 'totality', an integration of 'reason, senses, feeling, and will'. It is because Goethe 'disciplined himself to wholeness' that he can be said to have 'created himself' and to have approximated, at least, to the Overman (TI IX 49). In effect, the Overman, an 'artist of his life', combines the two great 'art drives of nature', Dionysian and Apollonian, vividly depicted in Nietzsche's first book (BT 1). Like the Apollonian artist, the Overman gives form and structure to his life, but like the Dionysians, with their insight into the 'primal oneness' of the world, this is done in full recognition that 'all is redeemed and affirmed in the whole' (TI IX 49), that forms are imposed by the 'form-giver'. This is why 'style', hence power, hence the redeeming type of human being, are possible only in the wake of the deaths of God and the illusions of an already structured 'true world'. Whether such types will be a few 'lucky hits' in a world dominated by 'last men', or whether they can be 'bred' in sufficient number to bring about the demise of nihilism too – this is an issue Nietzsche leaves to the future to decide.

Further Reading

Until very recently, the only reliable translations of Nietzsche's main works were those by Kaufmann and Hollingdale, listed below. Currently, however, no less than three university presses – Oxford, Cambridge and Stanford – are publishing good, well-edited translations of these works.

For brief surveys of Nietzsche's life and writings, see Hollingdale (1999) and Tanner (1994). The best more detailed and general account of his thought remains Schacht (1983), though the pioneering works by Kaufmann (1974) and Danto (1965) are still worth consulting. Books on particular areas of Nietzsche's philosophy have mushroomed in recent years. For contrasting accounts of his epistemology, metaphysics and theory of truth, see Clark (1990) and Poellner (1995). (The present chapter is closer in approach to the latter's.) For illuminating discussions of his moral philosophy and genealogy, see Ridley (1998) and May (1999). Three advanced and original interpretations of Nietzsche's philosophy are Nehamas (1985), Staten (1990) and Mueller-Lauter (1999). On Nietzsche's complicated relationship to Schopenhauer, see Janaway (1998); on his views on art, Young (1992) is helpful; on his views on politics and education, see Ansell-Pearson (1994) and Cooper (1991), respectively. Craig (1987) and Pippin (1998), though not solely dedicated to Nietzsche's philosophy, contain useful chapters on it.

Among 'continental' contributions to Nietzsche scholarship, Deleuze (1983) and Kofman (1993) have their admirers. Heidegger (1987) – one of four volumes translated from his lectures on Nietzsche – is in a class of its own: one great thinker's ruminations on another.

References

Nietzsche

References in the text are to section numbers of Nietzsche's works, not page numbers, unless otherwise specified. Titles of the works have been indicated by acronyms which are explained in the following list of works cited.

F. W. Nietzsche 1960: *The Portable Nietzsche* (translated by W. Kaufmann). New York: Viking. Includes: *Thus Spoke Zarathustra* [Z] (1883–5), *Twilight of the Idols* [TI] (1889), *The Antichrist* [A] (1889).

——1967–84: *Kritische Gesamtausgabe: Werke* [KGW], ed. G. Colli and M. Montinari. Berlin: de Gruyter.

——1968a: *Basic Writings of Nietzsche* (translated by W. Kaufmann). New York: Modern Library. Includes: *The Birth of Tragedy* [BT] (1872), *Beyond Good and Evil* [BGE] (1886), *On the Genealogy of Morals* [GM] (1887)

——1968b: *The Will to Power* [WP] (1880s) (translated by W. Kaufmann and R. J. Hollingdale). New York: Vintage.

——1974: *The Gay Science* [GS] (1882; Part V, 1887) (translated by W. Kaufmann). New York: Vintage.

——1986: *Human, All Too Human* [HAH] (1878) (translated by R. J. Hollingdale). Cambridge: Cambridge University Press.

——1993: *Philosophy and Truth: Selections from Nietzsche's Notebooks of the Early 1870s* [PT] (translated by D. Breazeale). Atlantic Highlands, NJ: Humanities Press.

Other writers

Ansell-Pearson, K. 1994: *An Introduction to Nietzsche as a Political Thinker.* Cambridge: Cambridge University Press.

Clark, M. 1990: *Nietzsche on Truth and Philosophy.* Cambridge: Cambridge University Press.

——1998: Nietzsche, Friedrich. In *The Routledge Encyclopedia of Philosophy*, ed. E. Craig. London: Routledge.

Cooper, D. E. 1991 [1980]: *Authenticity and Learning: Nietzsche's Educational Philosophy.* Aldershot: Gregg.

Craig, E. J. 1987: *The Mind of God and the Works of Man.* Oxford: Clarendon Press.

Danto, A. C. 1965: *Nietzsche as Philosopher.* New York: Macmillan.

Deleuze, G. 1983 [1962]: *Nietzsche and Philosophy* (translated by H. Tomlinson). New York: Columbia University Press.

Heidegger, M. 1987 [1961]: *Nietzsche, Vol. 3: The Will to Power as Knowledge and as Metaphysics* (translated by J. Stambaugh, D. F. Krell and F. A. Capuzzi). San Francisco: Harper and Row.

Hollingdale, R. J. 1999: *Nietzsche: The Man and His Philosophy.* Cambridge: Cambridge University Press.

Janaway, C. (ed.) 1998: *Willing and Nothingness: Schopenhauer as Nietzsche's Educator.* Oxford: Clarendon Press.

Kaufmann, W. 1974 [1950]: *Nietzsche: Philosopher, Psychologist, Antichrist*, 4th edn. Princeton, NJ: Princeton University Press.

Kofman, S. 1993 [1972]: *Nietzsche and Metaphor* (translated by D. Large). London: Athlone Press.

May, S. 1999: *Nietzsche's Ethics and His War on Morality.* Oxford: Clarendon Press.

Mueller-Lauter, W. 1999 [1971]: *Nietzsche: His Philosophy of Contradictions and the Contradictions of His Philosophy* (translated by D. Parent). Urbana: University of Illinois Press.

Nehamas, A. 1985: *Nietzsche: Life as Literature.* Cambridge, MA: Harvard University Press.

Pippin, R. B. 1998: *Idealism as Modernism: Hegelian Variations.* Cambridge: Cambridge University Press.

Poellner, P. 1995: *Nietzsche and Metaphysics.* Oxford: Clarendon Press.

Ridley, A. 1998: *Nietzsche's Conscience: Six Character Studies from the 'Genealogy'.* Ithaca, NY: Cornell University Press.

Schacht, R. 1983: *Nietzsche.* London: Routledge and Kegan Paul.

Staten, H. 1990: *Nietzsche's Voice.* Ithaca, NY: Cornell University Press.

Tanner, M. 1994: *Nietzsche*. Oxford: Oxford University Press.

Young, J. 1992: *Nietzsche's Philosophy of Art*. Cambridge: Cambridge University Press.

Discussion Questions

1   Is Nietzsche right to see a close connection between a person's life and their philosophy?

2   What does Nietzsche mean by 'nihilism' and how does he explain its 'advent'?

3   What are Nietzsche's objections to the ideas of a 'true world' and 'things in themselves'?

4   Why does Nietzsche hold that all truths are 'metaphors'?

5   On what grounds does Nietzsche regard the self or subject as a 'fiction'?

6   What is Nietzschean 'genealogy'? How can it be used to discredit people's beliefs and values?

7   What, for Nietzsche, is the status of natural science?

8   What is Nietzsche's 'perspectivism'? Is it a paradoxical doctrine?

9   How should one understand Nietzsche's claim that everything is 'will to power'?

10   How does Nietzsche explain the transition from custom and mores to morality 'proper'?

11   What roles do the 'ascetic priest' and his 'ascetic ideal' play in the 'slave revolt in morality'?

12   In what ways, according to Nietzsche, is the notion of freedom of the will crucial to morality?

13   What are the main features possessed by Nietzsche's 'redeeming' type of person, the Overman?

14   What role in Nietzsche's philosophy is played by the thought of 'eternal recurrence'?

41

Husserl and Heidegger

TAYLOR CARMAN

Edmund Husserl (1859–1938) was the founder of phenomenology, a philosophical movement that exerted enormous influence on European thought, especially during the first half of the twentieth century. His assistant, Martin Heidegger (1889–1976), now widely recognized as one of the most important philosophers in recent history, radically redirected phenomenology by applying it to the question of the meaning of being and the structure of human existence. It was Husserl's descriptive approach to the problem of intentionality, avoiding theoretical construction and metaphysical specula-tion as much as possible, that initially inspired the young Heidegger. Yet their approaches to philosophy soon proved to be deeply at odds, in both style and substance. For whereas Husserl identified intentionality with 'pure' consciousness, or transcendental subjectiv-ity, Heidegger traced it back instead to the pragmatic context and the temporal struc-ture of our everyday 'being-in-the-world', which he thought preceded any distinction between subjectivity and objectivity. In his later writings Heidegger moved beyond anything Husserl would have recognized as genuine phenomenological inquiry, reflect-ing on the nature of art, poetry, science, technology, and the nihilism he came to regard as inherent in all metaphysical thinking.

1 Husserl

Edmund Husserl was born in 1859 in Prossnits, Moravia (now Prostejov, Czech Republic). He studied in Leipzig, then in Berlin, where he worked with the mathemati-cian Karl Weierstrass. After receiving his Ph.D. in mathematics in 1881, he attended Franz Brentano's lectures in philosophy and psychology in Vienna from 1884 to 1886 and thereupon chose to devote himself entirely to philosophy. He taught at Halle (1887–1901), Göttingen (1901–16), and finally Freiburg (1916–28), where he was succeeded by his apparent protégé, Martin Heidegger. In retirement, Husserl, who was Jewish, suffered the effects of anti-Semitic legislation for a brief period when the Nazis rose to power in 1933. He grew increasingly isolated, both professionally and personally, until his death in 1938.

1.1   Psychologism, intentionality and categorial intuition

In his book, *Philosophy of Arithmetic* (published 1891), Husserl tried to work out an empiricist theory of arithmetical concepts by tracing them back to their psychological origins. The concept of multiplicity, he argued, is rooted in our concrete intuition of aggregates, or clusters of things. When we intuit aggregates, we group objects together in an act of 'collective combination'. It is this mental act of combining that underlies our concept of the cardinal numbers, regardless of what sorts of objects we combine; whether they are real or imaginary, abstract or concrete. Our intuitions of concrete ensembles are the most basic, however, and from them we acquire a notion of abstract wholes and the purely formal concepts *something* and *one*, as well as *multiplicity* and *number*. We understand the number 3, for example, as a determinate multiplicity of collectively combined 1s: 'something and something and something,' or 'one and one and one' (Husserl 1970a: 335). The concept of number, Husserl concludes, is derived from a reflection on the mental act of combining particulars.

Late in 1894 Husserl was still working on the projected second volume of *Philosophy of Arithmetic*, but by 1896 he had abandoned the project and renounced the psychologism on which his theory rested. His change of heart was very likely prompted, at least in part, by a review Gottlob FREGE (chapter 37) wrote of the first volume in 1894. Frege objected strenuously to any blurring of the lines between LOGIC (chapter 4) and psychology, between objective concepts and mere subjective 'ideas' (*Vorstellungen*). In psychologistic theories like Husserl's, Frege complains, 'everything is turned into ideas' (Frege 1984: 197).

By 1896 Husserl began work on his first properly phenomenological treatise, *Logical Investigations* (published 1900–1). The entire first volume of the *Investigations*, the 'Prolegomena to Pure Logic', is an extended refutation of psychologism. Although Husserl did not at the time mention any direct influence, he later acknowledged that 'Frege's significance was decisive' (quoted in Føllesdal 1982: 55), and that 'Frege's criticism . . . hit the nail on the head' (Spiegelberg 1972: 66). All Husserl says in the foreword to the *Investigations* is that he began to have 'doubts of principle, as to how to reconcile the objectivity of mathematics . . . with a psychological foundation for logic', and that these doubts forced him to rethink the relation 'between the subjectivity of knowing and the objectivity of the content known' (Husserl 1970b: 42). Like Frege, Husserl would now insist that the normativity of logic cannot have its theoretical foundations in psychology. For logical laws are exact, while psychological laws are inexact. Moreover, whereas logical laws are knowable *a priori* and purely by insight, psychological theory is necessarily empirical and inductive. And logic affords certainty, while knowledge in psychology is always merely probable. Finally, the laws of logic yield norms governing our reasoning, while the laws of psychology are mere descriptions of causal regularities. (For Husserl's explicit repudiation of his earlier theory of number, see ibid.: 784.)

This distinction between the objective contents of logic and MATHEMATICS (chapter 11) and the subjective stuff of experience, between matters of *essence* and matters of *fact*, would figure prominently in all of Husserl's subsequent work. Most importantly, it informs his theory of intentionality, which is the centrepiece of his mature phenomenology. 'Intentionality', a technical term that Brentano imported into modern philosophy from the scholastic tradition, refers to the directedness of consciousness. Consciousness always has an accusative; it is always *of* (or rather *as if* of) an object. We do not just see or remember; we see or remember *something*. Intentionality, then, is the 'of-ness' or 'about-ness' of our mental states. Drawing a sharp distinction between the *ideal* contents of experience and the *real* (temporally extended) experiences themselves, Husserl now attributes the intentionality of an attitude to its ideal content, or what he calls its 'act-matter', relegating its psychological character to its 'act-quality' (ibid.: 586–90). Each of these two components of an intentional state can vary to some degree independently of the other: perceptions all have the same act-quality *qua* perceptions, for example, though they may intend different objects (or indeed one and the same object) by means of different act-matters; so too, acts of anticipation, perception and memory all have different act-qualities, though they may be directed toward one and the same thing in virtue of the same act-matter.

Even more significant is the distinction Husserl draws between the internal contents and the external objects of intentional acts, for philosophers have perpetuated a number of long-standing problems about the ontological status of intentional objects by conflating the latter with the former. If all consciousness is consciousness *of* something, for example, what should we say about dreams, hallucinations, false memories and expectations, and non-veridical acts generally? Do we in those cases stand in relation to 'non-existent objects', as Alexius Meinong (1853–1920), who was also a student of Brentano's, proposed? Traditional epistemology tended to obscure the phenomenon of intentionality altogether by describing mental life not as a directedness toward external objects, but as an immediate possession of, or inner confrontation with, ideas, from which we would then have to infer the existence of the external world and other minds.

Husserl's theory undermines the indirect representative picture, for he distinguishes the ideal content that organizes our awareness from the objects to which we are putatively related in virtue of that content. Intentionality is not a real external relation between the mind and objects, Husserl argues, but a mental directedness that obtains and has content whether or not the objects of our attitudes themselves exist, hence whether or not we stand in any real relation to them. It has been noted (see Føllesdal 1969) that Husserl's distinction between content and object bears a striking resemblance to Frege's notions of the sense (*Sinn*) and reference (*Bedeutung*) of linguistic expressions. In this case, however, it was almost certainly not Frege who inspired Husserl, but rather earlier figures such as Bernard Bolzano (1781–1848) and J. S. MILL (1806–73) (chapter 35), who had drawn very similar distinctions.

In the Sixth Investigation Husserl argues for a notion of intellectual or 'categorial' intuition, over and beyond sense perception. Perceptual consciousness involves two distinct, sometimes coinciding, intentional acts: an empty intending or signifying act, and an intuitive or fulfilling act. Perception is not wholly passive, then, since we experience our sensuous intuitions as satisfying (or failing to satisfy) prior signifying acts, or anticipations. Not everything anticipated in our signifying acts, however, can be given in sense perception. An act that merely signifies or intends *white paper*, say, may be fulfilled in a sensuous intuition of white paper, but one does not literally see its *being* white. The copula 'is' in the proposition 'The paper is white' does not itself correspond to anything given sensuously, as the expressions 'white' and 'paper' do. Nevertheless,

Husserl maintains, an intention whose signifying content is that the paper *is* white can be adequately fulfilled in a non-sensuous, categorial intuition. Categorial intuitions fulfil acts whose contents include the meanings of purely formal terms like 'is' and 'not', the logical connectives 'and' and 'or', and quantifiers like 'all', 'some' and 'none'. Contrary to empiricists like LOCKE (chapter 29) and HUME (chapter 31), Husserl insists that our understanding of states of affairs as satisfying propositional attitudes cannot be based on a mere abstraction from our perception of sensuous particulars answering to individual ideas or linguistic terms. A higher-level intuition, he insists, affords us direct insight into the structured states of affairs in the world that make our beliefs true or false.

1.2   Pure phenomenology and transcendental subjectivity

Husserl would elaborate and modify his theories of intentionality and intuition in his middle period, which began around 1905 and culminated in his *magnum opus*, the First Book of *Ideas Pertaining to a Pure Phenomenology and Phenomenological Philosophy* (published 1913). Husserl now no longer referred to his project as 'descriptive psychology', an expression he inherited from Brentano, but as 'pure phenomenology', which he says is an 'eidetic' science, a science of essences. Phenomenology thus promises to elevate philosophy beyond the mere expression of a world view (*Weltanschauung*) to the level of a rigorous science, whose watchword is, as Husserl often put it, 'To the things themselves!' (see Husserl 1965: 96ff.). By the late 1920s Husserl had moved so far from his earlier, more strictly psychological approach to intentionality that he came to characterize phenomenology itself as a form of 'transcendental idealism' (Husserl 1931: 18–19; 1960: 83–6). He regretted this terminological choice within a few years, however, complaining in 1934 that 'No ordinary "realist" has ever been as realistic and as concrete as I, the phenomenological "idealist" (a word which, by the way, I no longer use)' (letter to Abbé Baudin, quoted in Kern 1964: 276n.).

This TRANSCENDENTAL (pp. 731–3) phase of Husserl's development is marked by two philosophical innovations: the 'phenomenological reduction', a methodological notion he devised in the summer of 1905; and the new conception of intentional content he formulated by 1907, which he would now call the *noema*, in contrast to the real mental act, or *noesis*. These notions specify what Husserl regards as the privileged site for any inquiry into intentionality, namely 'transcendental subjectivity', or 'pure' consciousness, abstracted from all real psychological determinations. Husserl frequently emphasizes the radical break between our ordinary 'natural attitude' common to everyday life and empirical science, prior to the reduction and the reflection on pure consciousness, and the phenomenological attitude, which reveals transcendental subjectivity, which Husserl calls 'the wonder of all wonders' (Husserl 1980: 64).

This methodological gap between natural (and naturalistic) cognition and phenomenological reflection mirrors what Husserl insists is an essential discontinuity between consciousness and reality. 'Insofar as their respective senses are concerned', he writes, 'a veritable abyss yawns between consciousness and reality' (Husserl 1983: 111); he even goes so far as to say that although consciousness 'would indeed be necessarily modified by an annihilation of the world of physical things its own existence would not be touched' (ibid.: 110). Passages such as these have generated controversy concerning Husserl's metaphysical and epistemological commitments. In any event,

845

although he rejects substance dualism (Husserl 1970c: 212), Husserl himself is frequently at pains to stress the spirit of CARTESIANISM (chapter 26) animating his philosophical orientation at large.

The Phenomenological Reductions and the Noema

Husserl describes a number of different 'reductions', but two in particular are central to his conception of phenomenological method: the *eidetic* reduction and *transcendental* reduction. Taken together, Husserl suggests, the two serve to identify the pure intentional content of consciousness as such, or what he calls the *noema*.

The eidetic reduction consists in ignoring real (temporal) particulars and focusing instead on general and ideal (atemporal) features of things. So, for example, one can abstract from all the other contingent properties of roses and fire trucks and grasp the redness instantiated in both. Husserl calls such general properties 'essences' – hence 'eidetic' from the Greek *eidos* (Plato's 'form'). So too, phenomenological reflection on consciousness abstracts from the real features of concrete psychological episodes occurring in time and concentrates instead on their ideal structures and contents (Husserl 1983: xx).

The transcendental reduction, which Husserl also calls the *epochē* (a term borrowed from ancient scepticism), consists in setting aside, or 'bracketing' out, all objects transcendent to consciousness, focusing instead on the intentional contents immanent within it (ibid.: §§31–4, 56–64). An object is 'transcendent', in Husserl's sense, if only one side or aspect of it can be immediately present to us at any one time; such things are necessarily given perspectivally, or in 'adumbrations'. An object is 'immanent' if it is given to consciousness all at once, transparently, so that no perspectival variation mediates our apprehension of it. Physical bodies and states of affairs are transcendent objects, for example, and so too are the abstract entities of mathematics and formal ontology. The contents of consciousness are immanent, by contrast, since we each have immediate, transparent access to our own thoughts and experiences.

The inward reflection of the *epochē*, then, first presents a mental state as a concrete particular, or *noesis* – including sensation, which Husserl calls *hylē* – and the eidetic reduction then sets aside its concrete psychological features in favour of the ideal intentional structures and contents it instantiates. Those ideal structures and contents constitute the *noema* of the mental state, which includes a 'core' of representational content, or 'sense' (*Sinn*), as well as the ideal 'positing character' in which that sense is put forward in one's mind as either (say) perceived, judged, remembered, anticipated, imagined or wished for. The transcendental and eidetic reductions together purport to isolate the sphere of 'pure' phenomenological inquiry, namely transcendental subjectivity. An analogy between the core or 'sense' component of the *noema* and Frege's notion of linguistic sense (*Sinn*) finds support in Husserl's remark that 'the noema in general is nothing other than the generalization of the idea of [linguistic] meaning (*Bedeutung*) to all act-domains' (Husserl 1980: 76).

Another major shift in Husserl's thought during this period concerns his account of the phenomenological status of the self. In *Logical Investigations* he defends a version of Hume's 'bundle theory', rejecting Kantian appeals to a pure ego, supposedly needed to unify our various intentional acts. 'I must frankly confess', he writes in the Fifth Investigation, echoing Hume, 'that I am quite unable to find this ego, this primitive, necessary centre of relations' (Husserl 1970b: 549). In the second edition, published in 1913, however, he retracts the denial in a footnote, writing simply, 'I have since managed to find it' (ibid.: note). While still repudiating what he calls 'corrupt forms of ego-metaphysic', Husserl now considers it phenomenologically evident that pure consciousness exhibits a structure of ownership, centred around a pure, transcendental 'I', which is 'essentially *necessary*' and remains 'absolutely identical' through the whole of one's experience (Husserl 1983: 132), but which 'is not a piece of the world' (Husserl 1960: 25).

Husserl's doctrine of the transcendental ego later drew criticism, first from Heidegger, then from Jean-Paul SARTRE (1905–80) (chapter 42) and Maurice Merleau-Ponty (1908–61), all of whom felt that it violated phenomenology's commitment to a description of experience as we actually live it, prior to all theoretical embellishment. Their common complaint is that Husserl's notion of a pure or transcendental self constantly inhabiting all our thoughts and actions amounts to a reflective distortion of our concrete engagement with the world. When I am actively absorbed in what I am doing, no such abiding centralized ego manifests itself in my awareness. Husserl's position is also vulnerable to Wittgenstein's critique of solipsism in *Tractatus Logico-Philosophicus*, in the *Blue Book*, and in the celebrated 'private language argument' in *Philosophical Investigations*. Like Husserl, WITTGENSTEIN (chapter 39) distinguishes the embodied person from the purely formal 'subject' of experience; he even denies that the latter is an object *in* the world. But whereas Wittgenstein conceives of the subject as nothing more than an ideal limit or vanishing point, borrowing Schopenhauer's metaphor of the eye that does not appear in its own field of vision, Husserl regards the pure ego 'as something absolutely identical' across all one's experience (Husserl 1983: 132). My transcendental ego, then, turns out to be a kind of enduring private object, after all, internal to my consciousness. But if it remains identical across time, what are the criteria of its identity? Apparently there are none, at least none I can specify, even in principle, in which case one can hardly assert its temporal persistence, as Husserl does.

1.3   Intersubjectivity and the lifeworld

Whether or not one can speak of a third distinct phase in Husserl's thought, his later work at least places new emphasis on practical as opposed to theoretical attitudes, on intersubjectivity, the body, and the cultural and social constitution of what he calls the 'lifeworld' (*Lebenswelt*). At the same time, in his last works Husserl continues to revisit and elaborate the basic methodological principles of phenomenology.

Cartesian Meditations (based on the 'Paris Lectures' he delivered at the Sorbonne in 1929 and first published in French translation in 1931), for example, bears the subtitle 'An Introduction to Phenomenology'. The book is far from a mere reiteration of Husserl's previous work, however, for in the Fifth Meditation he sketches an original account of intersubjectivity, partly in order to quell suspicions that his transcendental method entails solipsism. Husserl introduces a new reduction, a reduction to my sphere of 'ownness', that is, an abstraction from everything referring overtly or covertly to other selves. I then discover, in a primordial 'here', my own body as the unique locus of my own will and sensations. Other outwardly similar bodies occur 'there' in my perceptual environment, but I neither control their movements nor locate my sensations in them.

Thanks to a kind of 'pairing' association of those other bodies with my own body, I recognize them as linked to transcendental ego spheres of their own, which cannot in principle be given directly to me in intuition. I thus perceive them as other egos, not just objects, and I see our respective subjectivities as constituting an intersubjectivity.

Husserl is not attempting to reconstruct our actual psychological acquisition of our concept of OTHER MINDS (pp. 817–20), but instead what he takes to be the structure of our mature consciousness of others *qua* other. He also insists that the 'pairing' association supposedly underlying my recognition of others is not an inference, but an apperception. That is, just as I neither directly intuit nor merely infer the back sides of physical objects, but instead see them as *whole* objects *with* back sides, so too I neither intuit the inner contents of the consciousness of others nor merely infer them from a single case, my own. Does Husserl adequately describe our intentional relation to others? Is a systematic reduction to a sphere of ownness itself a plausible notion? Here too, as with the doctrine of the pure ego, the existential phenomenologists remained dissatisfied with Husserl's account.

In 1934 Husserl began writing the text eventually published in its entirety twenty years later as *The Crisis of European Sciences and Transcendental Phenomenology*, also subtitled 'An Introduction to Phenomenological Philosophy'. Though the term occurs in his manuscripts as early as 1917, Husserl's concept of the 'lifeworld' makes its first appearance in print in *Crisis* (the first two parts of which were published in the journal *Philosophia* in 1936). The term is roughly equivalent to 'natural concept of the world', a phrase Husserl had borrowed in his lectures of 1910–11 from Richard Avenarius (1843–96), which in turn recalls the distinction he had drawn in 1907 between the natural and the phenomenological attitudes. The lifeworld is not just a collection of physical objects, but includes such things as cultural and historical artefacts and social institutions. Husserl equivocates about whether there are many lifeworlds, or only one, and about whether the term refers to the immanent subjective content of our consciousness *of* the world or to the cultural world itself in its transcendence.

Husserl sometimes draws a contrast between the lifeworld and the world as described by the sciences, particularly in the wake of the Galilean 'mathematization of nature' (Husserl 1970c: 23). It is therefore tempting to assimilate Husserl's point to the distinction Wilfrid Sellars (1912–89) draws between the 'manifest image' of common-sense belief and the 'scientific image' of advanced theory. But whereas, for Sellars, the scientific image is the only true image, and so may in principle supplant our common-sense beliefs altogether, Husserl insists on the primacy of the lifeworld, to which science itself belongs (ibid.: 380), and to which it is forever beholden. For Husserl, that is, scientific theories acquire meaning and justification only by referring back to the world as it is given to us in ordinary experience. All 'theoretical results have the character of validities for the life-world', Husserl writes. 'The concrete life-world, then, is the grounding soil of the "scientifically true" world' (ibid.: 131).

2 Heidegger

Martin Heidegger was born in 1889 in the town of Messkirch in Baden. He attended the Bertholdgymnasium and the Theological Seminary at the University of Freiburg, intending eventually to enter the priesthood. Having discovered the work of Brentano and Husserl, however, he chose instead to study logic, mathematics and philosophy. He wrote a dissertation on psychologism and the theory of judgement under Heinrich Rickert (1863–1936), a Neo-Kantian, and began lecturing in Freiburg. His 1915 *Habilitationsschrift*, 'The Doctrine of Categories and Meaning in Duns Scotus', is a study of a scholastic text since shown to have been written by Thomas of Erfurt. In 1916 Husserl succeeded Rickert at the University of Freiburg, and Heidegger became his most promising assistant. By 1919 Heidegger had abandoned his Catholicism and begun lecturing on phenomenology. He was appointed professor at Marburg University in 1923, where he worked on the manuscript that would become his *magnum opus*, *Being and Time* (published 1927).

In 1928 Heidegger took over Husserl's chair at Freiburg, and in 1933 he joined the Nazi Party and assumed the position of rector of the university. Contrary to a popular rumour, Heidegger did not ban Husserl from use of the university library. Husserl's temporary suspension was instead the result of legislation enacted before Heidegger took office and subsequently revoked during his term. Still, after his arrival in Freiburg, Heidegger cut off almost all personal contact with Husserl and in 1941 acceded to his publisher's demand that he remove the dedication to Husserl from the fifth edition of *Being and Time*. He resigned as rector in 1934, after less than a year in office, but never explicitly renounced National Socialism. After the war he was barred from teaching in Germany until 1951, though he was lecturing again privately by 1949, to great acclaim. He died in 1976.

2.1   The analytic of Dasein and the question of being

Heidegger was deeply impressed by the aim of phenomenology to forgo abstract theoretical constructs and get back to a concrete account of 'the things themselves', as Husserl had urged. Husserl, for his part, saw in Heidegger a protégé worthy of taking over and continuing his work and reportedly often said to Heidegger, 'You and I are phenomenology' (Cairns 1976: 9). Years later Husserl would come to realize, to his chagrin, that their respective approaches to philosophy had in fact always been profoundly at odds.

First, perhaps above all, Heidegger criticizes Husserl's strict distinction between immanence and transcedence, between the inner and the outer: 'there is no outside', Heidegger says, 'for which reason it is also absurd to talk about an inside' (Heidegger 1982: 66). Repudiating what he calls the 'worldless subject' of Descartes and Husserl, Heidegger (1962: 254) insists that human existence is essentially 'being-in-the-world'. Intentionality is necessarily tied to its worldly context, and the idea of isolating a sphere of pure transcendental subjectivity from all worldly objects and states of affairs by means of an *epochē* must be fundamentally misconceived.

Second, Heidegger objects to what he calls 'the ontologically unclarified separation of the Real and the ideal' (ibid.: 259), on which the substance and method of Husserl's phenomenology both depend. Although he reports that the doctrine of categorial intuition in *Logical Investigations* inspired some of his early reflections on the question of the meaning of being (Heidegger 1972: 78), Heidegger explicitly rejects Husserl's theory, along with its later incarnation in the concept of eidetic insight. By maintaining instead that all forms of perception and insight are parasitic on a background of common-sense understanding, Heidegger declares, 'we have deprived pure intuition of its priority . . . Even the phenomenological "intuition of essences" is grounded in existential understanding' (Heidegger 1962: 187). Heidegger consequently abandons Husserl's ideal of a pure theoretical description of intentional phenomena and, adopting the hermeneutical stance of Wilhelm DILTHEY (1833–1911) (pp. 384–5), declares, 'the meaning of phenomenological description as a method lies in *interpretation*' (Heidegger 1962: 61). Far from resting on pure categorial intuition or eidetic insight, Heidegger writes, 'The phenomenology of Dasein is a *hermeneutic*' (ibid.: 62).

Third, whereas Husserl draws a sharp distinction between phenomenology and ontology, Heidegger insists that the two are inseparable: all phenomenology has its ontological presuppositions, and '*Only as phenomenology, is ontology possible*' (ibid.: 60). Indeed, Heidegger's original conception of phenomenology cannot be understood apart from his deeper commitment to a question that remained foreign to Husserl, and indeed to much of the history of Western philosophy, according to Heidegger: the question concerning the meaning (*Sinn*) of being (*Sein*). Whereas traditional ontology concerns itself with entities, or what is (*das Seiende*), Heidegger asks what it *means* for anything to be. He sets out to shed light on the question by investigating phenomenologically our *understanding* of being, which is constitutive of human beings, which Heidegger calls 'Dasein' (literally *being-there*). The question of being, then, boils down to the question 'what do we understand when we understand *that* and *what* entities *are*, including ourselves?'

Modelling *Being and Time* loosely on Kant's Transcendental Analytic in the *Critique of Pure Reason*, then, Heidegger calls his own project an 'analytic' of Dasein, which will constitute a 'fundamental ontology'. Fundamental ontology is fundamental relative to ordinary thought and traditional ontology, both of which systematically obscure and distort our pre-theoretical understanding of existence. For the metaphysical tradition and common sense both tend to construe all entities as objects or substances occurring in a present moment, the horizon of the now. Heidegger, by contrast, bases his interpretation of being-in-the-world on the phenomenon of purposive, future-directed practical understanding. We understand ourselves, that is, in light of the possibilities into which we *project*, the already constituted world in which we find ourselves situated, or *thrown*, and the enduring present in which we encounter other entities. Dasein's being-in-the-world thus has a temporal structure Heidegger describes as 'thrown projection'. The entities we encounter, by contrast, show up for us in the horizon of the present, either as inconspicuously 'available' (or 'ready-to-hand') in our practical activity or as 'occurrent' (or 'present-at-hand') as objects.

The 'Availability' of Equipment and the 'Worldliness' of the World

In an effort to get back to 'the things themselves', as Husserl insisted it was the task of phenomenology to do, Heidegger deliberately focuses his analytic of Dasein not on the kind of reflective cognitive attitude that philosophers so often take as their paradigm, but on our background immersion in mundane activity.

When we see Dasein in its 'average everydayness', Heidegger suggests, we see that what situates us in a world most fundamentally is not our subjective experiences or mental states, but our externally situated skills and practices. So too, the entities we typically encounter and concern ourselves with in our everyday practical activity present themselves not as 'occurrent' (*vorhanden*) objects, but as transparently 'available' (*zuhanden*) equipment, which we rely on and take for granted in carrying out our tasks. When I grasp a doorknob or wield a hammer, I am neither perceiving nor thinking about it as an object with properties, but availing myself of it unthinkingly, skilfully treating it as an element in the overall purposive structure of the situation. Moreover, individual pieces of equipment do not just occur alongside one another in objective space and time, but instead form an organized equipmental totality, which holistically assigns the particular items their respective practical meanings.

That equipmental totality is in turn implicated in a broader intelligible network of pragmatic relations assigning tools to contexts, to tasks, to goals, and to the ultimate underlying point of what we are doing, which Heidegger calls our 'for-the-sake-of-which'. He describes these practical relations as 'signifying' (*be-deuten*), and calls the entire intelligible network of signifying relations 'significance' (*Bedeutsamkeit*). The pragmatic structure of significance is a condition of the possibility of linguistic meaning and mental content, both of which occur only against a background of practical understanding. More generally, it is our primordial familiarity with the structure of significance that constitutes our being-in-the-world. For 'being-in' consists not in entertaining cognitive attitudes, but in being competently oriented and involved in intelligible situations; similarly, what Heidegger calls the 'worldliness' of the world is not just a sum total of objects, properties and relations, but a meaningfully structured domain of practices and institutions.

In spite of their methodological and stylistic differences, Heidegger's account of significance in *Being and Time* warrants comparison with Wittgenstein's idea in the *Blue Book* and *Philosophical Investigations* that linguistic meaning is tied essentially to our use of words, and with his claim in *On Certainty* that all knowledge is embedded in a particular 'form of life'. As Heidegger puts it, knowledge or cognition (*Erkennen*) is always only 'a founded mode of being-in' (Heidegger 1962: 86).

The central thesis of *Being and Time* is that being is intelligible always only in terms of time, and that traditional ontology from Plato to Kant (and including Husserl) has interpreted the being of all entities as occurrentness because of its fixation on the temporal present. Since Dasein's temporality has the form not of presence but of thrown-projection, however, we cannot make sense of ourselves in terms of the metaphysical CATEGORIES (pp. 594–8) that structure our knowledge of objects. Heidegger therefore introduces a number of fundamental concepts, or 'existentials', that define Dasein's unique temporal existence.

Heidegger also maintains that our understanding of entities is mediated by an anonymous social normativity, which he calls 'the one' (*das Man*), a term alluding to everyday locutions describing and prescribing what is proper, that is, what 'one does'. Heidegger maintains that *das Man* is a primitive existential structure of being-in-the-world, but he also associates it with Dasein's tendency to lapse into an 'inauthentic' or disowned (*uneigentlich*) mode of existence, in which we fail to come to grips with the concrete particularity and finitude of our individual existence. To exist authentically, by contrast, is to recognize the 'groundlessness' of one's being and to anticipate one's eventual death in a mood of anxiety (*Angst*), but with an attitude of openness and resolve (*Entschlossenheit*).

2.2   The work of art and the scientific image of the world

According to Heidegger's original plan, *Being and Time* was to consist of two parts, each comprising three divisions (see 1962, p. 64). Of the total six divisions, Heidegger wrote only the first two, at which point he abandoned the project of fundamental ontology, apparently because he came to doubt that an analytic of Dasein could in principle open the way to a more general inquiry into the meaning of being. It is also plausible to suppose, however, that he abandoned the assumption that being has a unified ahistorical meaning at all, and so turned instead to a genealogical account of the successive understandings of being that have informed different epochs in the history of Western thought.

It has thus become customary to contrast the hermeneutical phenomenology of the 'early' Heidegger during the period of *Being and Time* with the reflections on poetry, science, technology and the history of metaphysics which one finds in the 'later' Heidegger, much as one distinguishes early and later stages in the work of Ludwig WITTGENSTEIN (1889–1951) (chapter 39). The transition from the early to the later Heidegger is often referred to simply as 'the turn' (*die Kehre*), and its precise motives remain a subject of speculation and debate among scholars. At any rate, for whatever reason, by the early 1930s Heidegger had renounced the ahistorical system-building approach to philosophy that he inherited from KANT (chapter 32) and the neo-Kantian tradition. No longer composing ambitious treatises in the grand style, he now wrote essays and lectures, collected in volumes bearing homely titles like 'Forest Trails' (*Holzwege*) and 'Pathmarks' (*Wegmarken*). The substance and style of Heidegger's thinking had now broken away completely from Husserl's conception of phenomenology as a 'rigorous science'.

In 1935, in what is probably his most influential essay, 'The Origin of the Work of Art', Heidegger (1971a) supplements the two-fold distinction he had drawn in *Being and Time* between occurrent objects and available equipment, arguing that works of art can no more be understood as practical equipment with supervening aesthetic properties than equipment can be understood as so many bare objects with utility predicates added on. Consequently, alongside his earlier concept of 'world', he introduces a complementary notion, what he calls 'earth'. Whereas transparently useful things make up the purposive structure of a world, an earth always harbours something recalcitrant and anomalous, something ordinarily hidden in everyday life, but which we constantly rely on, and which works of art bring to the fore. In instituting an open battle or 'strife' between earth and world, the work of art emerges as a cultural paradigm that inaugurates the history of a people. Heidegger's examples include an ancient Greek temple, a Gothic cathedral, and (somewhat problematically) Van Gogh's painting of a pair of shoes. Like the founding of a state, the presence of God, and genuine philosophical thinking, Heidegger says, works of art let truth 'happen' in their own way by disclosing the grounds and limits of intelligibility in an historical world.

Heidegger appeals here, as he does in *Being and Time* (§44), to what he takes to be the archaic meaning of the Greek word for truth, *alethēia*. In the essay 'Plato's Doctrine of Truth' (written 1931–2) he argues that whereas the word orginally meant 'what has been wrested from hiddennness' (Heidegger 1998: 171), in the cave allegory of the *Republic* it takes on the additional, by now customary, sense of 'correctness of apprehending and asserting' (ibid.: 177) and thereafter remains ambiguous, even in Aristotle. Heidegger would later acknowledge the historical incorrectness of this interpretation, though he continued to insist that correspondence in fact presupposes 'the opening of presence' (Heidegger 1972: 70).

In the 1930s Heidegger also lectured extensively on the philosophy of Friedrich Nietzsche (1844–1900) (chapter 40) and on the poetry of Friedrich Hölderlin (1770–1843). In Heidegger's eyes, Hölderlin is the poet *par excellence* of the present age, whose work embodies a reflection on the nature and significance of poetry itself, and who stands as a witness to the cultural spirit and mission that Heidegger believes the German people have inherited from the Greeks. Heidegger's readings of Hölderlin's poems and fragments, like his interpretations of canonical philosophical texts, are often idiosyncratic, at times plainly untenable. Nonetheless, his lectures on Hölderlin remain essential to an understanding of his thought, not least of all because Hölderlin's poetry turns out to be the source of the concrete examples and the terminology that Heidegger invokes throughout his later work, particularly in the 'Work of Art' essay. The origin of the Work of Art (p. 231), Heidegger concludes, is not the artist but art itself, which he says is essentially poetry, and it is Hölderlin's poetry above all that speaks to us of the nature of poetry, and so of the meaning and prospects of art in a technological age.

In his two-volume *Nietzsche* (published in 1961, but drawing largely on his lectures of the 1930s and 1940s), Heidegger presents Nietzsche as the last great thinker of the Western metaphysical tradition, whose doctrines of the will to power and the eternal return reiterate the concepts of *essentia* and *existentia*, that is, the *what* and the *that* of entities in general. For Nietzsche, will to power is *what* everything is, while *to be* at all is to recur eternally. Moreover, Heidegger argues, Nietzsche's thought belongs essentially to the subjectivism of modern metaphysics, though his nihilism also anticipates the 'technological' understanding of being that holds sway in the present age. Heidegger's interpretation of Nietzsche, too, is as controversial as it is original, in this case owing in part to his reliance on the miscellaneous collection of notes published posthumously, and misleadingly, as Nietzsche's *magnum opus*, under the title *The Will to Power*. Yet Heidegger always denied that his interpretations were intended as contributions to scholarly research. Rather, his readings of philosophers and poets of the past amount to productive, if inevitably 'violent', confrontations and conversations with fellow thinkers. His aim, he insists, is not to ascertain objective historical facts, but to open up new paths of thinking.

Unlike art, religion and philosophy, Heidegger contends, 'science is not an original happening of truth, but always the cultivation of a domain of truth already opened' (Heidegger 1971a: 62). Anticipating the social conception of science advanced decades later by Thomas Kuhn (1922–96), Heidegger argues in his 1938 essay, 'The Age of the World Picture', that the modern scientific image of the world is a product of rigorous research, which rests on the projection of an underlying 'ground plan' (Heidegger 1977: 118). The ground plan provides a kind of *a priori* schema or normative framework for the procedural, industrious character of scientific practice. Consequently, not only is our modern 'world picture' peculiar to us, but the very idea of a world picture is a uniquely modern phenomenon, a construct of the research sketched out in advance and prescribed by an underlying plan. Strictly speaking, then, previous ages did not have world pictures different from ours, since they did not conceive of the world itself as a representation present to, indeed constructed by, an autonomous subject at all.

2.3   Technology and the forgetfulness of being

Modern science thus rests on an understanding of being that differs radically from understandings operative in the ancient and medieval worlds. For example, the ancient Greeks understood being as *phusis*, which was translated into Latin as *natura* and became our word 'nature', but which Heidegger interprets to mean 'self-blossoming emergence' and 'opening up, unfolding' (Heidegger 1959: 14). The Christian middle ages, by contrast, conceived of the world as *ens creatum*, a made thing separated by a chasm from its maker, God (ibid.: 106). The metaphysics of the modern period, by contrast, as we have seen, moves us to regard the world as an objective picture or representation standing over against a thinking subject.

In his 1955 lecture, 'The Question Concerning Technology', Heidegger argues that we are now in the grip of a 'technological' understanding of being, defined in terms of efficient ordering, or 'Enframing' (*Ge-stell*), and that we tend to treat entities in general, including ourselves, as resource material, or 'standing-reserve' (*Bestand*). The technological age differs fundamentally from the modern age, the age of the world picture, for 'Whatever stands by in the sense of standing-reserve no longer stands over against us as object' (Heidegger 1977: 17). The hydroelectric plant on the Rhine is Heidegger's favourite example of the nearly total but inconspicuous technological manipulation of entities, which at once flattens the world out and obscures meaningful differences. Other manifestations of our current technological understanding of being include high-speed transportation and information technology, above all television, all of which abolish distances and corrode our sense of things being near or far, noble or base, important or trivial. Works of art, by contrast, disclose historical worlds and mark differences, while mundane artefacts such as a windmill, a wooden bridge or a jug let ordinary things *be* what they are by revealing them in their local worlds, as opposed to fitting them into more and more efficient, totalizing, homogeneous orderings.

Like every historically realized understanding of being, Heidegger says, 'Technology is a way of revealing' (ibid.: 12). Indeed, 'So long as we represent technology as an instrument, we remain held fast in the will to master it' (ibid.: 32), and so fail to understand its essence as a way for entities as a whole to show up as intelligible. Unlike earlier modes of revealing, then, technology tends to conceal the fact that it is one; moreover it conceals that very concealing. As a result, our current technological world is systematically resistant to the kind of meditative questioning that Heidegger calls 'the piety of thought' (ibid.: 35). Indeed, the technological understanding of being represents the culmination of the nihilistic 'forgetfulness of being' (*Seinsvergessenheit*) that he thinks has fuelled the metaphysical tradition since the Presocratics (Heidegger 1959: 18). What he envisions in its place, however, is neither a renunciation of our technical devices and habits nor a regression to an earlier understanding of being, but an appreciation of technology as the way things show up for us and a recognition that we are not the masters of our mode of revealing, but its witnesses. Heidegger therefore concludes the 'Technology' essay with Hölderlin's gnomic declaration, 'where danger is, grows / The saving power also'. For Heidegger, 'precisely the essence of technology must harbour in itself the growth of the saving power' (Heidegger 1977: 28). The saving power is what Heidegger calls the 'freeing claim' (ibid.: 26) that technology will make on us when we come to understand its essence as a way of disclosing entities, that is, as a mode of truth, or unhiddenness (*alētheia*).

Further Reading

The best way to approach Husserl initially is to read the first few *Cartesian Meditations* and the essay 'Philosophy as Rigorous Science'. It has been said that Husserl is harder to read than to understand, and the lifelessness of his writing, especially in translation, makes a serious study of *Ideas I* a somewhat forbidding task. Fortunately, there are two particularly useful collections of critical essays. Dreyfus and Hall (1982) contains classic articles by Aron Gurwitsch and Dagfinn Føllesdal (see especially Føllesdal's 1969 'Husserl's Notion of *Noema*'); essays by J. N. Mohanty, David Woodruff Smith, Ronald McIntyre and Izchak Miller relating Husserl's views to recent developments in philosophy of mind, language and logic; and finally two papers, which make no mention of Husserl, by contemporary theorists of intentionality, John Searle and Jerry Fodor. The other valuable collection, covering a wide range of topics, is Smith and Smith (1995). An excellent presentation of the Føllesdal interpretation, and an illuminating account of Husserl's theory of time conciousness, can be found in Miller (1984). Bernet, Kern and Marbach (1993) is also a valuable guide, and Spiegelberg (1982) provides a useful historical catalogue of personalities and ideas. Finally, for a brilliant close reading, and to see how Husserl's work has influenced contemporary French thought, see Jacques Derrida's early essays in Derrida (1989, 1973).

There are two English translations of *Being and Time*. Macquarrie and Robinson's (1962) classic is generally excellent. Stambaugh's (1996) version is truer stylistically to Heidegger's peculiar blend of colloquial language and neologism, but is not as accurate or reliable. The best available secondary source is Dreyfus (1991), which concentrates almost exclusively on Division I of *Being and Time*. The most thorough treatment of Heidegger's conception of temporality in Division II, but which also offers a superb account of the first half of the book, is Blattner (1999). There are two excellent volumes of critical essays: Dreyfus and Hall (1992) and Guignon (1993). Mulhall (1996) is a good introduction, and Guignon (1983) and Richardson (1986) are helpful in analysing *Being and Time* as a critique of Cartesianism. Kisiel (1993) provides a painstaking record of Heidegger's very early development, while Okrent (1988) offers a provocative interpretation of Heidegger as a verificationist. Lafont (2000) offers an interpretation and a critique of Heidegger's conception of language, relating it both to the hermeneutic tradition in Germany and to contemporary analytic philosophy. Finally, further elaboration and analysis of many of the themes I have discussed in this chapter can be found in Carman (forthcoming). Three particularly good studies of Heidegger's later thought are Schürmann (1987), Haar (1993) and Young (2001). Ott (1993) and Safranksi (1998) are both admirable biographies. The best discussions of the philosophical significance of Heidegger's Nazism, however, can be found in Sluga (1993) and Young (1997).

References

Husserl

Husserl, E. 1931: Author's preface to the English edition. *Ideas: General Introduction to Pure Phenomenology* (translated by W. R. Boyce Gibson). New York: Humanities Press.

—— 1960 [1931]: *Cartesian Meditations: An Introduction to Phenomenology* (translated by D. Cairns). The Hague: Martinus Nijhoff.

—— 1965 [1911]: Philosophy as Rigorous Science. In *Phenomenology and the Crisis of Philosophy* (translated by Q. Lauer). New York: Harper and Row.

—— 1970a [1891]: *Philosophie der Arithmetik* (edited by L. Eley). The Hague: Martinus Nijhoff.

—— 1970b [1900–1]: *Logical Investigations*, 2 vols (translated by J. N. Findlay). New York: Humanities Press.

—— 1970c [1954]: *The Crisis of European Sciences and Transcendental Phenomenology: An Introduction to Phenomenological Philosophy* (translated by D. Carr). Evanston, IL: Northwestern University Press.

—— 1980 [1952]: *Ideas Pertaining to a Pure Phenomenology and Phenomenological Philosophy. Third Book. Phenomenology and the Foundations of the Sciences* (translated by T. E. Klein and W. E. Pohl). The Hague: Martinus Nijhoff.

—— 1983 [1913]: *Ideas Pertaining to a Pure Phenomenology and to a Phenomenological Philosophy. First Book* (translated by F. Kersten). The Hague: Martinus Nijhoff.

—— 1989 [1952]: *Ideas Pertaining to a Pure Phenomenology and to a Phenomenological Philosophy. Second Book* (translated by R. Rojcewicz and A. Schuwer). Dordrecht: Kluwer Academic.

—— 1999: *The Essential Husserl: Basic Writings in Transcendental Phenomenology* (edited by D. Welton). Bloomington: Indiana University Press.

Writers on Husserl

Bernet, R., Kern, I. and Marbach, E. 1993: *An Introduction to Husserlian Phenomenology*. Evanston, IL: Northwestern University Press.

Cairns, D. 1976: *Conversations with Husserl and Fink* (edited by R. M. Zaner). The Hague: Martinus Nijhoff.

Derrida, J. 1973 [1967]: *Speech and Phenomena, And Other Essays on Husserl's Theory of Signs* (translated by D. B. Allison). Evanston, IL: Northwestern University Press.

—— 1989 [1962]: *Edmund Husserl's 'Origin of Geometry': An Introduction* (translated by J. P. Leavey, Jr.). Lincoln: University of Nebraska Press.

Dreyfus, H. L. and Hall, H. (eds) 1982: *Husserl, Intentionality, and Cognitive Science*. Cambridge, MA: MIT Press.

Føllesdal, D. 1969: Husserl's Notion of *Noema*. *Journal of Philosophy*, 66, 20, 680–7. Reprinted in H. L. Dreyfus and H. Hall (eds) 1982: *Husserl, Intentionality, and Cognitive Science*. Cambridge, MA: MIT Press.

—— 1982: Husserl's Conversion from Psychologism and the *Vorstellung*–Meaning–Reference Distinction: Two Separate Issues. In H. L. Dreyfus and H. Hall (eds) 1982: *Husserl, Intentionality, and Cognitive Science*. Cambridge, MA: MIT Press.

Frege, G. 1984 [1894]: Review of E. G. Husserl, *Philosophie der Arithmetik* I. *Collected Papers on Mathematics, Logic, and Philosophy* (edited by B. McGuinness). Oxford: Blackwell.

Kern, I. 1964: *Husserl und Kant: Eine Untersuchung über Husserls Verhältnis zu Kant und zum Neukantianismus (Phenomenologica 16)*. The Hague: Martinus Nijhoff.

Miller, I. 1984: *Husserl, Perception, and Temporal Awareness*. Cambridge: MIT Press.

Smith, D. W. and McIntyre, R. 1982: *Husserl and Intentionality: A Study of Mind, Meaning, and Language*. Dordrecht: D. Reidel.

Smith, D. W. and Smith, B. (eds) 1995: *The Cambridge Companion to Husserl*. Cambridge: Cambridge University Press.

Spiegelberg, H. (ed.) 1972: From Husserl to Heidegger: Excerpts from a 1928 Freiburg Diary by W. R. Boyce Gibson. *Journal of the British Society for Phenomenology*, 2, 1.

—— 1982: *The Phenomenological Movement: A Historical Introduction*, 3rd revd edn. The Hague: Martinus Nijhoff.

Heidegger

Heidegger, M. 1959 [1954]: *An Introduction to Metaphysics* (translated by R. Manheim). New Haven, CT: Yale University Press.

—— 1962 [1927]: *Being and Time* (translated by J. Macquarrie and E. Robinson). New York: Harper and Row. Also translated by J. Stambaugh. Albany: State University of New York Press, 1996.

—— 1968 [1954]: *What Is Called Thinking?* (translated by J. G. Gray). New York: Harper and Row.

—— 1971a: *Poetry, Language, Thought* (translated by A. Hofstadter). New York: Harper and Row.

—— 1971b [1959]: *On the Way to Language* (translated by P. D. Hertz). New York: Harper and Row.

—— 1972 [1969]: *On Time and Being* (translated by J. Stambaugh). New York: Harper and Row.

—— 1977: *The Question Concerning Technology and Other Essays* (translated by W. Lovitt). New York: Harper and Row.

—— 1979–82 [1961]: *Nietzsche*, 4 vols (edited by D. F. Krell). San Francisco: Harper and Row.

—— 1982: *The Basic Problems of Phenomenology* (translated by A. Hofstadter). Bloomington: Indiana University Press.

—— 1988 [1975]: *The Basic Problems of Phenomenology*, revd edn, Lectures, 1927 (translated by A. Hofstadter). Bloomington: Indiana University Press.

—— 1993: *Basic Writings*, revd edn (edited by D. F. Krell). San Francisco: Harper and Row.

—— 1994 [1984]: *Basic Questions of Philosophy: Selected 'Problems' of 'Logic'*. Lectures, 1937–8 (translated by R. Rojcewica and A. Schuwer). Bloomington: Indiana University Press.

—— 1998 [1967]: *Pathmarks* (edited by W. McNeill). Cambridge: Cambridge University Press.

Writers on Heidegger

Blattner, W. 1999: *Heidegger's Temporal Idealism*. Cambridge: Cambridge University Press.

Carman, T. forthcoming: *Heidegger's Analytic: Interpretation, Discourse, and Authenticity in 'Being and Time.'* Cambridge: Cambridge University Press.

Dreyfus, H. L. 1991: *Being-in-the-World: A Commentary on Heidegger's 'Being and Time', Division I.* Cambridge: MIT Press.

Dreyfus, H. L. and Hall, H. (eds) 1992: *Heidegger: A Critical Reader*. Oxford: Blackwell.

Guignon, C. B. 1983: *Heidegger and the Problem of Knowledge*. Indianapolis, IN: Hackett.

—— (ed.) 1993: *The Cambridge Companion to Heidegger*. Cambridge: Cambridge University Press.

Haar, M. 1993 [1990]: *Heidegger and the Essence of Man* (translated by W. McNeill). Albany: State University of New York Press.

Kisiel, T. 1993: *The Genesis of 'Being and Time'*. Berkeley: University of California Press.

Lafont, C. 2000: *Heidegger, Language, and World-Disclosure* (translated by G. Harman). Cambridge: Cambridge University Press.

Mulhall, S. 1996: *Routledge Guidebook to Heidegger and 'Being and Time'*. London: Routledge.

Okrent, M. 1988: *Heidegger's Pragmatism: Understanding, Being, and the Critqiue of Metaphysics*. Ithaca, NY: Cornell University Press.

Ott, H. 1993 [1988]: *Martin Heidegger: A Political Life* (translated by A. Blunden). New York: Basic Books.

Pöggeler, O. 1987 [1963]: *Martin Heidegger's Path of Thinking* (translated by D. Magurshak and S. Barber). Atlantic Highlands, NJ: Humanities Press.

Richardon, J. 1986: *Existential Epistemology: A Heideggerian Critique of the Cartesian Project*. Oxford: Clarendon Press.

Safranski, R. 1998 [1994]: *Martin Heidegger: Between Good and Evil.* Cambridge, MA: Harvard University Press.

Schürmann, R. 1987 [1982]: *Heidegger on Being and Acting: From Principles to Anarchy* (translated by C.-M. Gros). Bloomington: Indiana University Press.

Sluga, H. 1993: *Heidegger's Crisis: Philosophy and Politics in Nazi Germany.* Cambridge, MA: Harvard University Press.

Young, J. 1997: *Heidegger, Philosophy, Nazism.* Cambridge: Cambridge University Press.

——2001: *Heidegger's Philosophy of Art.* Cambridge: Cambridge University Press.

Discussion Questions

1   What is the relation between our mathematical concept of number, on the one hand, and our perception of aggregates, on the other? Husserl observes that most people can differentiate only up to about a dozen particulars at a time without resorting to counting. Is this fact relevant to arithmetic?

2   What is the relation between logic and psychology? Do both disciplines study the way we think? Do they both describe 'laws' of thought? Do logical norms stand in need of theoretical foundations at all, whether in psychology or in some other purely theoretical discipline?

3   What is 'intentionality'? If all consciousness is consciousness *of* something, what should we say about dreams, hallucinations, and false memories and expectations? Are such attitudes not intentional after all, though they seem to be? Are all our attitudes directed toward mental tokens internal to our minds?

4   Why does Husserl insist that a merely psychological theory of mental acts will always fail to capture the intentional content of thought and perception? Why does he distinguish the intentional content, or 'act matter', of a mental state from its pyschological mode, or 'act quality'? Do the two components vary completely independently of one another?

5   Why does Husserl distinguish between the content and the object of an intentional state? How does that distinction undercut potential problems about our access to the external world and about the ontological status of so-called 'intentional objects'?

6   What is 'categorial intuition'? Is it necessary to suppose that we can intuit anything fulfilling the signifying sense of terms like 'is', 'not', 'and', 'or', 'all', 'some' and 'none'?

7   What is the 'eidetic reduction'? What is the *epochē*, or 'transcendental reduction'? How do the two reductions purport to reveal pure consciousness, or transcendental subjectivity? What is the *noema*?

8   Is all of our experience centred around a transcendental ego? What motivated Husserl's initial denial that reflection reveals any such pure ego? What then motivated his later admission that all consciousness must be owned by an 'I'?

9   How does Husserl describe our consciousness of other subjective selves? How do we come to understand our subjectivity as constituting an intersubjectivity? Is his account plausible?

10   What is the 'lifeworld'? How are we to understand the sense and justification of scientific theories that depict a world radically different from the world given to us in ordinary experience? Can our ordinary experience ever be partly wrong about the way the world is? Can it be wholly mistaken?

11   What are the principal differences between Heidegger's phenomenology and Husserl's? Is Heidegger right to reject the distinctions between immanence and transcendence, between the real and the ideal, and between phenomenology and ontology? What does it mean to say, 'The phenomenology of Dasein is a *hermeneutic*'?

12   How does the temporality of Dasein's being-in-the-world differ from that of the available equipment and occurrent objects we encounter in our everyday experience? Why does Heidegger maintain that the availability of useful artefacts and tools cannot be analysed in terms of their occurrent properties and relations?

13   How does an anxious, resolute anticipation of death allow one to 'own up' to one's existence authentically? Is authenticity a good thing? Why?

14   What is a work of art? What does a work of art accomplish? Is Heidegger's notion of 'art' consistent with our ordinary use of the word?

15   How, according to Heidegger, is the modern conception of the world as a 'picture' rooted in the projection of a systematic groundplan for rigorous scientific research? How does the normative structure of scientific practice presuppose the givenness of the world as a representation to an autonomous subject?

16   What is the 'technological' understanding of being? How does the technological age differ from the age of the 'world picture'? What does it mean to treat everything as resource material, or 'standing-reserve'? Is it wrong to do so? Is it possible to be open to technology as an understanding of being, as a way of revealing entities, while continuing to make use of technological devices?

42

Sartre, Foucault and Derrida

GARY GUTTING

During the second half of the twentieth century, French philosophy was dominated by Jean-Paul Sartre, Michel Foucault and Jacques Derrida. Sartre was the leading figure of existential phenomenology, an approach that, with important debts to the Germans HUSSERL AND HEIDEGGER *(chapter 41), tried to develop a comprehensive philosophical vision of human beings and their place in the world through the careful description of our concrete experience. Foucault and Derrida represent, in different ways, what has come to be called the poststructuralist reaction against phenomenology.*

1 Sartre

Sartre was important not only as a philosopher but also as a literary figure and a political activist. Our discussion will be restricted to his philosophy and, within philosophy, to what is by far his most important and most influential achievement, *Being and Nothingness*.

Sartre's position derives from his two fundamental claims about consciousness: that it is always *of something*, but that it itself is *not something*. CONSCIOUSNESS (pp. 185–7) is always of something in the sense that for me to be conscious implies that there is some object – typically something real, though in some cases something imaginary or illusory – that I am conscious of. Consciousness is, in the language of Husserl's phenomenology, essentially *intentional* – directed toward something else. Intentionality is a relation, but it cannot be understood on analogy with ordinary relations between things in the world; for example, the relation whereby a box is on top of a table or a fish is in a stream. This is because consciousness is not a thing, not a material thing but also not an immaterial thing such as a soul or a spiritual substance. It is not a thing because its entire existence is exhausted by its relation to its objects. It has no content or structure of its own. Nor does it take on content or structure by somehow incorporating its objects. Our ordinary talk of what we experience or think about 'being in the mind' is misleading. In typical cases (for example, sense perception, non-deceptive memory) the object experienced exists outside the mind in the real world. But even when, as in imagination or illusions, there is no real object, the object is not literally in the mind.

Consciousness is a totally 'transparent' intending of its objects and nothing more. In view of this, Sartre is prepared to say that consciousness is *nothing*.

Consciousness is also transparent in another sense. It is always aware, directly and immediately, of itself as consciousness. As Sartre puts it, to be conscious is to be self-conscious. But here we need to be careful. Self-consciousness might seem to mean consciousness of self, where 'self' refers to consciousness as an object of awareness like any other. But then consciousness would also be a thing like any other, and this of course Sartre firmly denies.

Because consciousness is always self-aware, Sartre says that it has *being-for-itself*: its very existence involves an internal relation to itself. The objects of consciousness are not self-aware (even when we are aware of other people, they are not conscious precisely as objects of our awareness). On the other hand, unlike consciousness, objects of consciousness are things, with the presence and solidity of intrinsic content; they have, in Sartre's terminology, *being-in-itself*, which consciousness of course lacks.

Sartre's account seems to ignore an obvious feature of our experience: the person (or psychological self) as the subject of the properties (habits, character traits, beliefs, inclinations) that define us as individuals. In fact, Sartre does not ignore this obvious reality, but he displaces it. Rather than identifying it with (or situating it within) consciousness, he maintains that the self exists only as an object of consciousness, that it is a part of the world, like any other thing.

We need, finally, to say a bit more about the relation of being-in-itself to being-for-itself. Our ordinary experience is of objects that have a basic intelligibility; for example, patterned or functional behaviour in nature, a purpose in our lives that give them a meaning. In Sartre's view, however, this intelligibility does not belong to the object in virtue of its most basic reality as being-in-itself. On the fundamental level it is a brute, unstructured given, merely existing with no intrinsic meaning. On this level we should not, in fact, speak of different things, since the structure necessary for differentiation is not present. There is just sheer indistinct being-in-itself. In the literary phenomenology of his novel *Nausea*, Sartre characterizes the unintelligibility of being-in-itself in terms of *superfluity*, *absurdity* and *contingency*. Being-in-itself is meaningful (and divided into discrete, intelligible objects) only in so far as it is the object of consciousness. Consciousness is, therefore, the ultimate source not of the reality of being-in-itself but of its meaning.

Sartre understands the relation of being-for-itself (consciousness) to being-in-itself in terms of negativity (nothingness). Consider a paradigm case he discusses in *Being and Nothingness*: I enter a café, late for an appointment with Pierre, who is meticulously punctual. I at first seem to encounter a fullness of being; everywhere I look there are objects or activities. But, since I am looking for Pierre and worried that he may have already left, every element of this scene falls back, as soon as it begins to present itself, because I see it as not-Pierre.

Nothingness

Sartre introduces the neologism 'nihilation' (*néantisation*) to denote the process whereby negation is introduced on the concrete level of immediate perception (as opposed to the reflective level of intellectual judgement). Correspondingly, *nothingness* is his term for the ontological reality of negation that is introduced by nihilation. The fact that my experience of the Pierreless café involves nihilation – of both the absent Pierre and of the café that lacks him – shows that negation exists as a concrete reality and that therefore nothingness is required as a distinct ontological category, in addition to being-in-itself and being-for-itself. Nothingness must, therefore, exist like 'a worm in the heart of being'. But how does it arise? Certainly not from itself, through some incoherent self-nihilation, nor from being-in-itself, which is entirely enclosed in its inert givenness. Nothingness must therefore be somehow derived from consciousness (and hence from being-for-itself), a conclusion supported, moreover, by our experience of negations as arising in the face of our expectations and fears. But consciousness is always of being-in-itself and so it must give rise to nothingness by negating being-in-itself.

This negation is not, of course, a matter of literally destroying (annihilating) being-in-itself. Rather, consciousness negates by *withdrawing* from being. Sartre identifies this withdrawal of consciousness from being with *freedom*, since freedom is a transcending of the determinism of causal laws and these laws exist only as structures of being-in-itself. FREEDOM (pp. 206–8) exists as consciousness's ability to withdraw from (revise or even reject) the self. Because I am free, I can deny what I am (that is, what I have been up to now) and constitute at any moment a new meaning for my existence as a self. Negation enters the world in virtue of consciousness's choice to make its self *this* and not *that* in relation to the rest of the world. Another way to put Sartre's point is to say that consciousness is entirely free in the sense that it is the ultimate source of all meaning. Freedom is not a matter of determining what happens but of determining the meaning of what happens. Consciousness obviously has no control over the causes that, say, cripple me or destroy a town by a flood. But it does, Sartre thinks, absolutely determine the meaning of such events.

We are likely to respond to Sartre that we do not typically think of ourselves as possessing such radical freedom. Surely much of what the world means for me is beyond my control! But this, he would reply, results from our efforts to flee from the truth, to pretend to ourselves that we are not really free, despite our implicit awareness of our freedom. This flight from freedom expresses the widespread behaviour of *bad faith* (*mauvaise foi*, sometimes translated as 'self-deception'). Sartre does not maintain that bad faith is inevitable, but he clearly does regard it as very common, at least in our current social situation, and takes elaborate pains to describe the many varieties and subtleties of its manifestations. His overriding point, however, is that bad faith is based on the distinction of being-for-itself and being-in-itself and the essential relation of the former to the latter. Bad faith is possible because being-for-itself is characterized by a funda-mental duality whereby it is both separated from and identified with being-in-itself.

Sartre's radical understanding of the freedom from which bad faith flees is at the heart of his existentialism. He accepts the traditional idea that freedom requires freedom *from* a standard set of evils: the lies and values of popular materialistic culture (in Sartre's terms bad faith and bourgeois morality). But he rejects the traditional view that freedom must also be regarded as freedom *for* some objective *summum bonum* (truth, happiness, virtue and so on). Although accounts of the *summum bonum* have differed considerably, they all see freedom as directed toward an objective, pregiven order (Platonic Forms, human nature, scientific laws, divine providence). By contrast,

Sartre denies that there is any objective order of things that is normative for human freedom. Accordingly, the central positive features of the traditional conception of freedom (freedom for) become negative features (freedom from) for Sartre. Specifically, Sartrean freedom requires freedom from God (anti-theism) and freedom from objective ethical values (anti-moralism).

For Sartre, the anti-theistic dimension is axiomatic. He simply finds the very idea of a God entirely incredible. He occasionally suggests arguments for his atheism. But he places little weight on argument and mostly treats his atheism as simply a basic starting-point. At the most, we might say that Sartre starts with a fundamental experience of human beings as so radically free that the idea of their being created by a God makes no sense. Given atheism, Sartre thinks that anti-morality follows logically because of the Dostoyevskian premise: if God does not exist, everything is permitted.

Sartre further maintains that human actions are entirely free in the sense that there is nothing outside my choice that constrains it. This does not, however, mean that freedom has no limits, only that any limits freedom has are themselves the result of free choices. More fully, the idea is that any obstacle to or constraint on my free act is such only as a result of my decision to act. For example, a mountain is an obstacle only once I have decided to climb it. My decision makes an obstacle of what would otherwise be merely, say, an object of my curiosity, indifference or aesthetic sensibility. (So the mountain is no obstacle to the tourist who is merely interested in admiring its grandeur.)

We might accept this point about things outside the mind, but what about internal, psychological causes of behaviour? Surely such things as an overpowering feeling, an obsessive desire, a deeply ingrained character trait determine me to act in certain ways? I may, for example, really want to keep climbing the mountain, but my feeling of fatigue may be so great that I simply cannot go on. Sartre, however, suggests that whether or not the feeling is 'so great' as to stop me depends on whether or not I really want to go on no matter what. In fact, I could keep pushing myself to the point of collapse or even death. The fatigue is an obstacle only if I allow it to be.

As radical as Sartre's freedom is, it would seem to have no significance for us if it is not deployed for some purpose. But as we have seen, Sartre excludes all traditional goals for human life. How, then, can he see our existence as meaningful? The answer, put briefly, is that he excludes all external goals for freedom but takes freedom itself as its own goal. In other words, freedom ceases to be a means to something else (freedom for) and becomes an absolute end in itself. As a result, Sartre's fundamental ethical category becomes authenticity, that is, acceptance of one's status as radically free. Authenticity is opposed to bad faith (self-deception), which involves the effort to deny or flee from one's freedom.

Sartre's existential phenomenology (and related views developed by his associates, Simone de Beauvoir and Maurice Merleau-Ponty) dominated French thought from the end of the Second World War until about 1960. After that, there was a sharp reaction against his views, led by thinkers often labelled as structuralists or poststructuralists. Structuralism was a short-lived, mostly French phenomenon of the 1960s that claimed to give various social scientific and humanistic disciplines a scientific basis by offering rigorous accounts of the objective structures underlying their domains. It rejected the essentially subjective viewpoint of phenomenology by focusing on structures that lie outside the scope of conscious awareness. Poststructuralism retains the structuralist *style* of objective, technical, and even formal discourse about the human world, but rejects the structuralist *claim* that there is any deep or final truth that such discourse can uncover. Since the latter claim is characteristic not only of structuralism but of the historical mainstream of Western philosophy, poststructuralism has a much wider significance than its name suggests.

As poststructuralists, Foucault and Derrida both reject the traditional project of philosophy, although they also propose alternative employments for its intellectual legacy. They seek, we might say, not a continuation of philosophy by other means but a continuation of philosophy's means for other ends. But Foucault's work is centrifugal in relation to philosophy, moving away from its traditional aporiae toward successor projects ('archeologies' and 'genealogies' of knowledge). Derrida's work, by contrast, is centripetal, relentlessly coming back to dissect the body of failed philosophical knowledge.

2 Foucault

Foucault rejects the standard philosophical project of discovering necessary or essential truths about ourselves and our world in favour of the inverse project of discovering cases in which what are presented as necessary truths about our condition are in fact only contingent products of our historical situation. His writings, therefore, do not offer a coherent vision of what we must be, but rather a series of histories designed to show how we might be different. We will look briefly at the books in which he develops his four major histories: *The History of Madness in the Classical Age*, *The Order of Things*, *Discipline and Punish* and *The History of Sexuality*.

Foucault sees the history of madness in Europe as characterized by two major 'breaks': one in the mid-seventeenth century which sharply separates classical views of madness from those of the middle ages and Renaissance; another at the end of the eighteenth century that inaugurates the modern view of madness. His treatment of pre-classical (medieval and Renaissance) madness is cursory. But he does make one claim crucial for his argument: prior to the classical age, madness was seen as an integrally human phenomenon. Madness was opposed to reason, but as an alternative mode of human existence, not a simple rejection of it.

In contrast to the medieval and Renaissance views, the classical age saw madness as merely the negation of the essential human attribute of reason. It was regarded as unreason (*déraison*), a plunge into an animality that had no human significance. There was, accordingly, a *conceptual exclusion* of the mad from human society. Here Foucault cites as a prime example DESCARTES's (chapter 26) rejection in the *First Meditation* of the possibility of his own madness as a grounds of doubt. Correlative to this conceptual exclusion, there was a physical exclusion of the mad effected by their confinement in institutions that isolated them from ordinary human life.

The conceptual and physical exclusion of the mad reflected a moral condemnation of them. The moral fault, however, was not the ordinary sort, whereby a member of the human community violates one of its basic norms. Rather, madness corresponded to a radical choice that rejected humanity and the human community *in toto* in favour of a life of sheer (non-human) animality. On the classical view, the animality of the mad was expressed in their domination by passions, a domination that led them to a delirium in which they mistook the unreal for the real. Passionate delirium thus resulted in a fundamental blindness that cut the mad off from the light of reason. So construed, classical madness is an affliction of the mind–body composite, not something specifically psychological or somatic. In particular, it is not conceived as a 'mental illness'.

With the modern age (roughly, from the nineteenth century on), the mad are once again regarded as within the human community (not as animals beyond the pale of humanity). But, within the human community, they are now seen as moral offenders, violators of specific social norms, who should feel guilt at their condition and who need reform of their attitudes and behaviour. Corresponding to this new conception of madness is the characteristic modern mode of treating the mad: not merely isolating them but making them the objects of a moral therapy that would subject them to social norms. This is the move from the merely custodial confinement of the classical age to the therapeutic asylum of the modern period, founded by the Tukes in England and by Pinel in France.

Although the therapeutic asylum is widely regarded as an unquestionable advance in humanitarianism, Foucault sees it as merely a more subtle and thorough method for controlling the mad. Rather than a true liberation of the mad, it is a 'gigantic moral imprisonment'.

We readily see that, for Foucault, the identification of madness as mental illness is not primarily an objective scientific discovery. Rather, it was introduced as a means of legitimating the authority of physicians in the asylum once the idea of a distinctively moral therapy was abandoned. More fully, the fact that physicians came to be in charge of asylums initially had little to do with their medical expertise. The moral treatment recommended by Tuke and Pinel was not essentially medical and could be carried out by any person with moral authority. However, as the nineteenth century developed, medicine became dominated by the ideal of objective, value-free knowledge, which left no room for value-laden moral therapies. The idea of a distinctively mental sort of illness was introduced primarily to justify the continuing authority of doctors over the mad, not because of its scientific truth or curative success.

The Order of Things covers roughly the same chronological periods as *The History of Madness*: the Renaissance, the classical age and the modern age. For each period, Foucault sketches the general epistemic structure (the *epistemé*) underlying its thought and then shows how the disciplines that are the counterparts of today's human sciences can be understood in terms of this basic epistemic structure. This, he maintains, shows that these earlier disciplines are not halting anticipations of the modern human sciences but autonomous alternatives for construing human reality. From this he will argue for the contingency and replaceability of the HUMAN SCIENCES (chapter 12).

Foucault's Archeology

Methodologically, *The Order of Things* is the full fruition of the archeological method toward which Foucault was groping in *The History of Madness* (and also *The Birth of the Clinic*). Archeology emerges as a method of analysis that reveals the intellectual structures that underlie and make possible the entire range of diverse (and often conflicting) concepts, methods and theories characterizing the thought of a given period.

The level of concepts, methods and theories corresponds to the conscious life of individual subjects. By reading texts to discover not the intentions of their authors but the deep structure of the language itself, Foucault's archeology goes beneath conscious life to reveal the epistemic 'unconscious' that defines and makes possible the knowledge of individuals. As Foucault explains in his subsequent methodological treatise, *The Archaeology of Knowledge*, archeology is similar to logic and grammar in that it discovers rules governing our discursive behaviour of which we may well not be aware. Grammar formulates the rules defining the domain of sheer meaningfulness and logic the rules of sheer consistency. But it is obvious that there are many grammatically and logically acceptable statements that are never uttered in a given domain of discourse. We may be inclined to attribute this simply to the fact that no individuals happen to want to make these statements. But Foucault maintains that, in addition to the rules of grammar and logic, there are further underlying rules limiting the range of permissible statements. (For example, the rules of classical discourse about madness did not permit the statement: 'Madness is simply a disease of the mind'.) Foucault's archeology, the archeology of knowledge, is the historical method that uncovers such rules.

With *Discipline and Punish* Foucault's work returns to the explicitly ethical motivations of *The History of Madness*, but now with a firm sense of how to incorporate causal accounts of changes in knowledge systems. His particular focus is the emergence of the modern discipline of criminology and other related social scientific disciplines. With a bow to Nietzsche (chapter 40), he characterizes his new approach as genealogical. The general idea is hardly original: that shifts in the power structures of a society produce changes in epistemic formations. What is new is his understanding of the nature of power and of the precise way in which power and knowledge are related. I will here comment briefly on the latter point, but defer the former to our discussion of Foucault's history of sexuality.

Genealogy deals with the connection between non-discursive practices and systems of discourse (bodies of knowledge). In this regard, Foucault's central claim is that there is an inextricable interrelation of knowledge (discourse) and power (expressed in non-discursive practices, in particular, the control of bodies). This is why an understanding of his genealogical approach requires an understanding of his view of the relation of knowledge and power.

Negatively, Foucault does not have in mind the standard Baconian (chapter 25) idea, which sees knowledge as first existing as an autonomous achievement, which is then used as an instrument of action (for example, pure science vs. technology). He maintains that knowledge simply does not exist in complete independence of power, that the deployment of knowledge and the deployment of power are simultaneous from the beginning.

On the other hand, Foucault does not go so far as to identify knowledge with power; for example, to make knowledge nothing more than an expression of social or political control. As he himself noted, if he thought there was no difference between knowledge and power, he would not have had to take such pains to discover the precise ways in which they are related to one another. His positive view is that systems of knowledge, although expressing objective (and perhaps even universally valid) truth in their own right, are nonetheless always more or less closely tied to the regimes of power that exist within a given society. Conversely, regimes of power necessarily give rise to bodies of knowledge about the objects they control (but this knowledge may – in its objectivity – go beyond and even ultimately threaten the project of domination from which it arises). Foucault pretty clearly intends this interconnection of knowledge/power as a general thesis, but he defends it and is specifically committed to it only with respect to particular modern disciplines.

In *Discipline and Punish* Foucault deals with knowledge/power with respect to the connection between the disciplinary practices used to control human bodies in the modern period and modern social scientific disciplines. His primary example is the practice of imprisonment as a way of punishing criminals in its relation to criminology and other social scientific disciplines relevant to crime and punishment (social psychology and so on). But he develops his discussion of imprisonment in the context of a discussion of modern disciplinary practices in general (as employed, for example, in schools, factories and the military); and he shows how the prison served as a model and centre of diffusion for this whole range of disciplinary practices.

As always, Foucault begins by contrasting the modern age with the classical age immediately preceding. He notes that the most striking (and essential) difference between the two periods was the violent and flamboyantly public nature of the punishment of criminals of the premodern period in contrast to the physically much milder and 'low profile' modern punishment of imprisonment. Whereas standard accounts have attributed this difference primarily to a more humane, compassionate modern attitude (based on new philosophical ideas and a scientific understanding of criminality), Foucault's power/knowledge hypothesis suggests that there is something else going on (although he agrees humaneness may be a secondary factor). Specifically, he explores the idea that punishment becomes milder not simply for the sake of mildness but for the sake of new, more effective and more extensive forms of control. As he puts it, the point was not so much to punish less as to punish better.

Although modern disciplinary practices originated in isolated, enclosed institutions such as prisons and asylums, they rapidly spread throughout society, to schools, factories, medical clinics, welfare agencies, and so on. In this expansion, these practices became positive as well as negative, not just preventing disapproved behaviour but increasing production and knowledge. Detached from particular institutions, the practices also fell under the control of the national state and exerted their influence on society as a whole. The general result was the transformation of society from one of spectacle to one of surveillance.

In the first volume of his *History of Sexuality* Foucault shows how modern control of sexuality parallels modern control of criminality by making sex, like crime, an object of allegedly scientific disciplines, which simultaneously offer knowledge and domination of their objects. However, it becomes apparent that there is a further dimension in the power associated with the sciences of sexuality. Not only is there control exercised via others' knowledge of individuals; there is also control via individuals' knowledge of themselves. Individuals internalize the norms laid down by the sciences of sexuality and monitor themselves in an effort to conform to these norms. Thus, they are controlled not only as *objects* of disciplines but also as self-scrutinizing and self-forming *subjects*.

This is the reason Foucault sees our apparently liberating focus on our sexuality as just a reinforcement of the mechanisms of social control. In trying to discover our deep sexual nature through self-scrutiny and to express this nature by overcoming various hang-ups and neuroses, we are merely shaping ourselves according to the norms and values implicit in modern sciences of sexuality. We may break with certain social conventions and constraints, but we do so only by putting ourselves just as firmly in the control of another system of constraints.

The second volume of Foucault's history of sexuality was projected as a study of the origins of the modern notion of a subject in practices of Christian confession. Foucault wrote such a study (*The Confessions of the Flesh*) but did not publish it because he decided that a proper understanding of the Christian development required a comparison with ancient conceptions of the ethical self. This led to two volumes on Greek and Roman sexuality: *The Use of Pleasure* (1984) and *The Care of the Self* (1984). These final writings make explicit the ethical project that in fact informs all of Foucault's work: the liberation of human beings from contingent conceptual constraints masked as unsurpassable *a priori* limits and the adumbration of alternative forms of existence.

3   Derrida

Although Derrida disavows traditional philosophy, he remains its most assiduous reader. And he is, indeed, above all a remarkable reader with a distinctive talent for close, subtle and imaginative scrutiny of texts. Why should a philosopher, particularly one at Derrida's historical site, be so obsessed with what others have written? Because, as Derrida sees it, writing reveals the essential peculiarities and limitations of human thought. A written text will always escape total clarification. There will always be textual ambivalences that remain unresolvable and prevent us from understanding fully 'what the author really means'. We may think, as Plato sometimes suggests, that the problem is due simply to the medium of writing. If we could directly speak to the author, our perception of intonations and gestural nuances – along with the possibility of follow-up questions – would eliminate all ambivalence, all undecidability. But of course even face-to-face speaking will not convey a message perfectly. The inevitable differences (in past experience, in expectations, in idiolect) between speaker and hearer maintain permanent possibilities of misunderstanding. Suppose, then, that to eliminate these differences, I consider just the case of my own internal formulation of my thoughts. But even here, Derrida maintains, the linguistic formulation will not be totally adequate. The generality of any linguistic expression will make it a less than perfect expression of the precise details of my thought or the exact nuances of my feelings. It would seem that perfect adequacy is achieved only in the immediate, pre-linguistic presence of my thought to itself. But Derrida argues that there is no such pure presence of thoughts to the self. All thought is mediated through language and can never attain the total clarity of pure presence to the self. There is always a difference between what is thought (or experienced or said or written) and the ideal of pure, self-identical meaning.

The above line of argument is a prototype of Derrida's repeated demonstrations, in different contexts and terms, that the apparently contingent and remediable defects of writing are in fact inevitable features of all thought, all expression, all reality. Derrida's philosophical project is an unending extrapolation of the reader's inability to master a text.

Despite our relentless failure to attain perfect meaning and truth, all our thought and language is based on the assumption of and drive for such meaning and truth. This assumption and drive can be formulated by three principles that are central in the Western philosophical tradition. (Derrida himself never formulates the principles in these terms, but they catch what he has in mind by 'logocentric' thinking.) First, the basic elements of thought and language are pairs of opposing concepts, such as presence/absence, truth/falsity, being/nothingness, same/other, one/many, male/female, hot/cold. This we can call the Principle of Opposition. Next, the opposing pairs are regarded as exclusive logical alternatives, governed by the principles of identity $(A = A)$ and non-contradiction (nothing is both A and not-A). This we can call the Principle of Logical Exclusion. For example, being present excludes being absent; the present is simply what it is (present) and is in no way what it is not (absent). Finally, each fundamental pair is asymmetrical in the sense that one term has in some crucial sense priority over the other (for example, is more fundamental, more real, morally better than the other). This is the Principle of Priority.

Deconstruction

A typical Derridian reading will reveal the extent to which a given text does not fit the model of a logical system as defined by the Principles of Opposition, Logical Exclusion and Priority. Specifically, it will show that the binary oppositions on which the text is based are not sustained, that the alleged relations of logical exclusion and priority cannot be coherently formulated and are implicitly denied by the very text that formulates them. Derrida calls this technique *deconstruction*. Deconstruction is thus a method of showing how texts based on binary oppositions themselves violate both the Principle of Exclusion and the Principle of Priority. Thus, a deconstructive reading of a text reveals points at which it introduces one of the opposing terms into the definition of the other or reverses the order of priority between the two terms.

Derrida characterizes in various ways the views put into question by deconstructive analysis. The general project of deconstructing the fundamental dichotomies built into thought yields a critique of *logocentrism*. The dominant terms of the standard polar oppositions always correspond to some sort of presence, a reality that is positive, complete, simple, independent and fundamental (Plato's Forms, Aristotle's substances, Aquinas's God, Hegel's Absolute). This presence is always understood as the polar opposite of something that is negative, incomplete, complex, dependent and derivative (matter, creatures, appearance and so on). Derrida's deconstructive analyses show, however, that the purity and priority of presence is never sustained in the texts of the great metaphysicians. For example, Plato discovers that the Forms participate in non-being, or Christians think of God as somehow humanly incarnate. The result is a critique of *metaphysical presence*.

Derrida's deconstructive readings are complemented by a more positive and, in some ways, even systematic philosophical project. This is carried out through his repeated efforts to introduce vocabularies that attempt to adumbrate the ontological level at which dichotomies dissolve and their oppositions reverse and slide into one another. This project is systematic both in the comprehensive applicability of each of the vocabularies and in the complex interconnections that bind together terms from different vocabularies. As an example, we will discuss the vocabulary of *différance*, the one Derrida has most developed and most often deploys.

'Differance', a transliteration of the French neologism *différance*, is meant to evoke the instability of the binary oppositions fundamental to logical systems. Derrida designed the term to have two basic connotations: difference and deferral. (The French verb from which it derives, *différer*, means both *to differ* and *to defer*.) The first connotation corresponds to the way in which any pair of binary opposites always fails to match exactly the domain to which it is supposed to apply. There are always irreducible *differences* between the structure of the actual phenomenon (a historical event, a text, a personality) and the binary divisions required by a logical system. For example, Rousseau's actual use of the concepts *speech* and *writing* does not correspond to the sharp division he claims to make between them.

Further, efforts to impose the sharp distinction required by binary oppositions must always be 'put off' (deferred) in the face of the recalcitrance of the phenomenon. For example, when we see that Plato has violated the speech/writing dichotomy by defining the thought expressed by speech as a writing in the soul, we may try to fall back to a distinction between 'good writing' – which is like speech – and 'bad writing'. The idea is that, even if the distinction fails at one level, it can be revived at another level (we merely 'defer' drawing it). But, Derrida maintains, further analysis will show that even the 'fall-back' distinction can be undermined and that a truly sharp distinction will remain elusive, will have to be indefinitely deferred.

We see, then, Derrida's point in forming a noun from *différer*. But why does he introduce the 'misspelling' *différance* instead of the standard *différence*? First, although he wants his term to recall the standard one, he also wants to emphasize the difference between his use of the term and that of other thinkers (Hegel, Saussure, Heidegger). Further, the *a* in the final syllable follows the pattern in French for forming verbal nouns (gerunds), so that *différance* maintains a pointed ambivalence between an action (a making different) and the state resulting from this action (a difference). In this way, Derrida's term suggests a reality not caught by such standard metaphysical dichotomies as active/passive, event/state, action/passion. Finally, the fact that there is a *written* but no *spoken* difference between *différance* and *différence* evokes Derrida's discussion of the speech/writing dichotomy, and gives a priority to writing (which alone can express Derrida's meaning) that subverts the force of the standard distinction.

The above way of talking about differance is neither incoherent nor merely cute. It reflects rather Derrida's conviction that, despite the intrinsic limitations of the standard dichotomies – signalled by their 'production' by a differance that eludes them – we have no way of thinking apart from them. There is no standpoint outside of the dichotomies from which we can overlook and master them. Differance is not, like Hegel's Absolute, a synthesis of all opposites into a fully intelligible whole. It is itself caught in the endless play of differences, neither controlling nor controlled, always generating new paradoxes. We can use 'differance' to indicate the limitations of our concepts and language but not to overcome them. Derrida's questioning of the distinctions on which thinking is based is not in the name of a new set of definitive answers (that is, a new set of dichotomized concepts), but in the name of the perpetual need to be aware of the limits of any answers.

Up until about 1980 Derrida had little to say about specifically ethical issues; and, in contrast to Sartre and Foucault, for example, he did not tie his philosophical reflections to political activity. But subsequently he has made ethics (and religion) a major theme. Some attention to this theme will give us a sense of Derrida's more recent writings.

Derrida's view of ethics is best developed through his treatment of the central ethical concept of justice. Here he begins from an essential tension: justice is in one sense nothing other than the rule of law; but in fact the mere, literal application of the law is generally unjust. The point is not merely the traditional one that there is a distinction between any positive law (legislated by some particular human society) and the absolute standards defined by, say, divine command, the Form of Justice, or human nature. Derrida's claim is much stronger, that any system of laws – human, natural, divine – will never be able in itself to specify adequately the conduct that is just in a given situation.

Accordingly, any system of laws is subject to deconstruction. No matter how stable, consistent and coherent it may be in its own terms, there will be points of application where it becomes incoherent. At such critical points of application, we see the tension between law and justice.

Derrida does not, however, mean to suggest that we have access to justice through anything other than law. There is, as always, no question of some special access through a privileged experience or insight to what lies beyond the law. Just as we can never get beyond our concepts, we cannot get beyond our laws, which are just conceptualizations of ethical obligations. Rather, we move toward justice simply by remaining ever sensitive to possible limitations of laws, by being always ready to deconstruct laws that are working against justice. This is one reason that Derrida can suggest that 'deconstruction is justice'.

This deconstruction is not a sceptical rejection of the law but a clearing of the ground for a new judgement of how we should behave. This new judgement (decision) does not itself draw authority from any system of law – how could it, when it presupposes a deconstruction of previous systems? But neither does it draw authority from some privileged insight beyond the law (say a Platonic intuition of Justice). The judgement is a leap, a taking of a stand when there is no adequate justification for taking a stand. In this regard, Derrida cites Kierkegaard: 'The instant of decision is a madness' – the movement of the individual as such beyond the universal. But this leap does not take us beyond the realm of law as such. It moves beyond previous formulations of law but must in turn justify itself by constructing a new, more adequate system of law that will, of course, itself be subject to deconstruction. In contrast to dangerous irrationalisms (for example, fascism, religious fanaticism) that leave reason behind in a flood of mere will or emotion, Derrida's deconstructive approach always subjects our 'leaps' beyond one system of rational thought to the constraint of constructing a new system of rational thought. In this way, he balances reason and a sense of its limitations against one another in a constant play of tensions.

Further Reading

The primary text for Sartre's existentialism is, of course, *Being and Nothingness*. His famous popular lecture 'Existentialism Is a Humanism' remains, despite his own disavowal, the best single introduction to the difficult ideas of *Being and Nothingness*. His early critique of Husserl, *The Transcendence of the Ego*, gives a good view of Sartre's distinctive notion of consciousness. Sartre's later philosophical thought is primarily developed in *The Critique of Dialectical Reason*, a large and difficult work devoted to synthesizing existentialism and Marxism. A fascinating portrait of both Sartre's thought and personality emerges in the extensive interviews with Simone de Beauvoir printed in her *Adieux* (which also includes her account of the last days of Sartre's life).

Foucault's *History of Madness* is only partially available in English: *Madness and Civilization* translates a little over half the original text. *The Order of Things* (the French title is *Les Mots et les choses*), *Discipline and Punish* (*Surveiller et Punir*) and the three volumes of *The History of Sexuality* (I: *Introduction*, II: *The Use of Pleasure*, III: *The Care of the Self*) are all fully translated. A superb selection of Foucault's essays, lectures and interviews (based on the comprehensive French collection *Dits et rits*) has been published in three volumes as *Essential Works of Foucault, 1954–1984*, edited by Paul Rabinow.

Perhaps the most accessible introduction to Derrida's thought is through the three interviews published under the title *Positions*. The essays collected in *Writing and Difference* and *Margins of Philosophy* give a good sense of his interests and methods. For his more recent work on ethics and religion, see *The Gift of Death*.

As to secondary literature, the best brief discussion of the whole of Sartre's work is Caws (1979), while Danto (1975) provides a very accessible guide to Sartre's existentialism. The best biography is Cohan-Solal (1987). On Foucault, a good general survey is McNay (1994), and the best biography is Macey (1993). For more detailed analysis of Foucault's earlier works (through *The Order of Things* and *The Archaeology of Knowledge*), see Gutting (1989).

Two good and accessible introductions to Derrida are Norris (1987) and Howells (1998). On Derrida's later work, Caputo and Derrida (1997) is invaluable – both the opening discussion with Derrida and Caputo's following analysis.

References

Sartre

Sartre, J.-P. 1946: *Existentialism Is a Humanism*. Paris: Nagel.
—— 1957a [1943]: *Being and Nothingness: An Essay on Phenomenological Ontology* (translated by H. Barnes). London: Methuen.
—— 1957b: *The Transcendence of the Ego: An Existentialist Theory of Consciousness*. New York: Noonday Press.
—— 1976: *The Critique of Dialectical Reason I*. London: New Left Books.

Writers on Sartre

de Beauvoir, S. 1984: *Adieux: A Farewell to Sartre*. London: André Deutsch; Weidenfeld and Nicolson.
Caws, P. 1979: *Sartre*. London: Routledge and Kegan Paul.
Cohan-Solal, A. 1987: *Sartre: A Life*. New York: Pantheon Books.
Danto, A.1975: *Jean-Paul Sartre*. New York: Viking Press.

Foucault

Foucault, M. 1967 [1961]: *Madness and Civilization: A History of Insanity in the Age of Reason* (translated by R. Howard). London: Tavistock.
—— 1970 [1966]: *The Order of Things: An Archaeology of the Human Sciences*. London: Tavistock.
—— 1977: *Discipline and Punish: The Birth of the Prison*. London: Allen Lane.

—— 1981–: *The History of Sexuality*. Harmondsworth: Penguin Books.

—— 1988–: *Essential Works of Foucault, 1954–1984*, 3 vols (edited by Paul Rabinow). London: Allen Lane.

Writers on Foucault

Gutting, G. 1989: *Michel Foucault's Archaeology of Scientific Reason*. Cambridge: Cambridge University Press.

Macey, D. 1993: *The Lives of Michel Foucault*. London: Hutchinson.

McNay, L. 1994: *Foucault: A Critical Introduction*. Cambridge: Polity Press.

Derrida

Derrida, J. 1978 [1967]: *Writing and Difference* (translated by A. Bass). London: Routledge and Kegan Paul.

—— 1981 [1972]: *Positions* (translated by A. Bass). Chicago: University of Chicago Press.

—— 1982 [1972]: *Margins of Philosophy* (translated by A. Bass). Chicago: University of Chicago Press.

—— 1995: *The Gift of Death*. Chicago: University of Chicago Press.

Writers on Derrida

Caputo, J. and Derrida, J. 1997: *Deconstruction in a Nutshell: A Conversation with Jacques Derrida*. New York: Fordham University Press.

Howells, C. 1998: *Derrida: Deconstruction from Phenomenology to Ethics*. Cambridge: Polity Press.

Norris, C. 1987: *Derrida*. London: Fontana.

Discussion Questions

1　Is consciousness *nothing*?

2　Is to be conscious always to be self-conscious?

3　If consciousness is not an object, how can the self be part of the world like any other thing?

4　Can we accept Sartre's account of how being-in-itself and being-for-itself are related?

5　Do we need an ontological category of nothingness as well as a logical concept of negation?

6　Is freedom a matter of determining what happens or of determining the meaning of what happens?

7　How is self-deception or *bad faith* possible?

8　Can freedom itself, rather than any external end, be the goal of freedom?

9　Are what appear to be necessary truths about our condition only contingent products of our historical situation?

10　Does the existence of different historically located epistemic structures show that the human sciences are contingent and replaceable?

11　What are the implications for philosophy of Foucault's archeological method?

12　Does a genealogical account of the relations between knowledge and power limit the claims of scientific knowledge in modern society?

13　Is Foucault's genealogy an improvement on his archeology as a method in the human sciences?

14   How should we assess the claim that the spread of modern disciplinary practices resulted in the transformation of society from one of spectacle to one of surveillance?

15   Does a liberating focus on our sexuality merely place modern human beings in the control of another system of constraints?

16   Should we reject the idea of a perfectly clear text, thought, expression and reality? What are the implications of this rejection for Derrida's conception of philosophy?

17   Does the method of deconstruction yield insights about philosophy?

18   What are the consequences of Derrida's account of differance for the employment of basic dichotomies in philosophy?

19   What are the consequences for ethics if applying any system of law will produce injustice?

20   Can we live with paradox?

Glossary

a priori–a posteriori   An epistemological distinction. *A priori* propositions, unlike *a posteriori* propositions, do not require experience to establish their truth. We derive or justify *a priori* concepts, unlike *a posteriori* concepts, independent of experience.

abstract ideas   Locke's attempt, rejected by Berkeley, to explain how an idea can stand for individuals of a given kind, even though the individuals vary in their properties. Locke held that abstraction from the different properties would produce a general idea covering the right individuals.

abstract objects   Objects, such as numbers or universals, that do not exist as spatio-temporal particulars. Philosophers disagree about whether there can be such objects or, if they do exist, how they are related to concrete physical objects.

ad hominem argument   A fallacious argument attacking the holder of a view rather than the position itself, or a sound argument showing an inconsistency between a view held by a person and a consequence of that view. The person pointing out the inconsistency need not hold the initial view.

akrasia   The Greek term for weakness of will. In *akrasia* one does not do what one knows to be best or does what one knows not to be best. Socrates and Aristotle initiated attempts to determine whether *akrasia* is possible.

alienation/estrangement   Hegelian concept, also used by Marx and later European philosophers, to stand for a state of being cut off from something of importance, such as oneself, others, nature or the product of one's labour. The analysis and interpretation of alienation varies according to the philosopher.

altruism   The view that the well-being of others should have as much importance for us as the well-being of ourselves. Some argue that altruism, even if it is desirable, is not possible, and that our ethics must be based on egoism.

analysis   The central method of analytical philosophy, shaped by the development of modern logic and found in the work of Frege, Russell, Moore and Wittgenstein, according to which philosophical problems can be overcome through replacing the apparent structure of statements by their real logical structure. Many philosophers, while still considering themselves analytical philosophers, have altered or even abandoned this programme.

analytic–synthetic   According to Kant's formulation of the distinction, in an analytic proposition the concept of the predicate is contained in the concept of the subject, and we can tell that the proposition is true by analysis. In a synthetic proposition, the concept of the predicate adds something new to the concept of the subject, and the truth or falsity of the proposition cannot be determined by analysis. There has been much dispute over the adequacy of this account, but there is general agreement that synthetic propositions tell us something about the world.

Together with the metaphysical distinction between necessary and contingent propositions and the epistemological distinction between *a priori* and *a posteriori* propositions, this logical distinction sets the framework for much modern philosophy. Kant famously argued that some *a priori* necessary propositions are synthetic. Contemporary discussion has developed from Quine's criticism of the distinction as a dogma of empiricism.

anthropocentrism   Literally, 'human-centred'. Hence in ethics, for example, the view that human actions and human welfare are the sole proper focus of moral concern.

aporia   A puzzle or perplexity. In the early Platonic dialogues Socrates raised problems without offering solutions to them and showed that those he questioned could not offer an acceptable solution either. This aporetic method led to the development of the dialectical method, by which Socrates elicited truth through questioning. The term aporia ('no way through') was introduced by Aristotle for puzzles concerning incompatibilities that arise among views we hold without prompting or among reputable beliefs adopted commonly or by the wise. His approach was to seek the minimal adjustments needed to reconcile these conflicting views.

archeology   Foucault's method for determining the deep structure or form of the conditions of the possibility of knowledge in a particular historical period.

argument from design   The argument for the existence of God, disputed by Hume, according to which the complex and intricate order of the world can only be explained (or can best be explained) by positing an intelligent and powerful creator.

artificial intelligence (AI)   The use of programs to enable machines to perform tasks which humans perform using their intelligence. Early AI avoided human psychological models, but this orientation has been altered by the development of connectionism, which is based on theories of how the brain works. In connectionism, complex functions, including learning, involve the transmission of information along pathways formed among large arrays of simple elements. AI raises questions about the conditions, if any, in which we would be justified in ascribing mental attributes to purely physical systems.

A-series and B-series of time   McTaggart's terms for the temporal ordering of events according to whether they are past, present or future (A-series) or earlier or later than one another (B-series).

association of ideas   A view, especially important in Hume, explaining the patterned occurrence of our ideas according to laws of association. Philosophers today generally seek to maintain what is important in Hume while rejecting this mechanism.

autonomy   An autonomous being is one that has the power of self-direction, possessing the ability to act as it decides, independent of the will of others and of other internal or external factors.

axioms   Propositions selected as the foundations of a field – classically geometry – which, together with methods of proof, allow other propositions to be proved in an ordered way. The axiomatic method has powerfully influenced philosophy, although each feature of the method has been criticized as inappropriate for philosophy.

being   According to Plato, only Forms have being. For Aristotle, who distinguished different senses of being, being *qua* being is the central concern of metaphysics. In contemporary phenomenology, Heidegger considered the meaning of Being and characterized human Being as Dasein ('being there') and being-in-the-world. Sartre distinguished the being-for-itself of consciousness from the being-in-itself of objects.

Categorical Imperative   The fundamental formal demand (or set of demands) which Kant placed on our choice of principles on which to act. It is contrasted with hypothetical imperatives, which have force only if we have certain desires or inclinations. Formulations of the Categorical Imperative seem to be radically different from one another, and some critics argue that the Categorical Imperative produces an empty formalism. Sympathetic commentators believe that both of these problems can be overcome. The formulations test the principles on which we act according to whether they can be universal laws or laws of nature, whether we treat humanity in ourselves and others never simply as means but also as ends, whether we treat every rational being as a will-making universal law, and whether we treat our shared moral life as taking place within a kingdom of ends. None of the principal notions used in expressing the Categorical Imperative is easy to understand.

categories   The basic general concepts of thought, language or reality, sometimes claimed to have an origin or justification differing from those of ordinary concepts. Aristotle and Kant provide the classical discussions of categories, although categories play different roles in their thought.

category mistake   An ascription of something to one category when it belongs to another. For Ryle, who introduced the term, discriminations among categories were not confined to the grand Aristotelian or Kantian categories, but worked their way with great subtlety through the whole of our language. The interesting mistakes are those with philosophical consequences.

causal theory of reference   The view of Kripke and others that names, and perhaps some other terms, gain meaning from an initial act of naming and then preserve meaning through suitable causal links.

causation   In causal relations between events, if an event of the first kind occurs, an event of the second kind will or must occur, and the first event will explain the occurrence of the second event. Possibly items other than events can enter into causal relations. Since Hume, we have been puzzled about whether causal relations are real or are just matters of our imposing our habits upon the world and over the nature of causal necessity.

certainty   Descartes sought to build knowledge on the basis of certainty, with no room for doubt. Although the project as a whole, as well as its detail, has been contested, certainty remains an ideal for many philosophers.

chaos theory   The theory of non-linear functions, such that small differences in the input of the function can result in large and unpredictable differences in the output.

class   A collection of entities satisfying a condition for membership in the class. To avoid problems arising if classes get too large, or belong to other classes, or are not completed, set theory distinguishes classes from sets.

clearness and distinctness   Descartes's criteria of indubitable truth derived from his reflection on the impossibility of doubting his own existence (see *cogito ergo sum*). Clear perceptions are 'present and accessible'. Distinct perceptions are 'sharply separated' from other perceptions and contain only what is clear. We can hope to specify clearness and distinctness in an illuminating way, but this might involve replacing perceptual characterizations by conceptual ones.

cogito ergo sum   Descartes's crucial claim 'I think therefore I am' provides a standard of certainty for the rest of his philosophy and leads on to the claim that what he is is a thinking thing.

concept   'Concept' can be taken psychologically or logically for what we grasp in understanding an expression, but since Frege the logical side has had primary importance. For Frege, there was a crucial distinction between objects (referred to by names or subjects) and concepts (referred to by predicates). Different accounts of logical form might challenge this claim. If concepts are thought of as components of propositions, scepticism about propositions can produce scepticism about concepts as well.

consciousness   A philosophical explanation of what consciousness is or how it might be explained eludes us. If we stick to what it is like to be a conscious human being, we have no explanation; if we try to explain consciousness in terms of what goes on in our brains, the sheer feel of consciousness itself is left aside.

consent   From Locke, the liberal theory of government has required the consent of the governed for political rule to be legitimate. Because explicit consent is not always available, Locke introduced a notion of tacit consent, but it is not always easy to distinguish tacit consent from non-consent to determine whether tacit consent is consent.

consequentialism   The view that the value of an action is determined by the value of its consequences rather than by the principle on which the action is performed or the virtue it expresses. Utilitarianism is a consequentialist theory, where the relevant value is individual happiness or well-being.

conservative   In politics, a loosely defined term indicating adherence to one or more of a family of attitudes, including respect for tradition and authority and resistance to wholesale or sudden changes.

consistency   Propositions are consistent if they can all be true. A system of propositions can be shown to be inconsistent if it contains a contradiction (a proposition and its negation). Consistency and completeness are two key concerns of modern logic.

constructivism   In the philosophy of mathematics, a broad position (encompassing both intuitionism and formalism but also going beyond them) which holds that mathematical entities exist only if they can be constructed and that proof and truth in mathematics are co-extensive. Constructivists oppose the realist (or Platonist) view that mathematical objects or truth exist independently of human procedures. This has the consequence that certain classical results whose proofs rely on Platonic assumptions are not constructively valid.

contents of consciousness   Mental states, like statements and other linguistic items, have contents, but it is a philosophical problem how this can be so. Furthermore, there are disputes over the extent to which internal factors and external environmental factors respectively contribute to determining the contents of mental states.

contingent–necessary   Contingent propositions happen to be true or false but could be otherwise. Necessary propositions must be true. It is not clear that there are any necessary propositions or, if there are, that they are restricted to analytic propositions or other propositions true because of their logical form. A contingent event is one that does not necessarily take place. If there are necessary events, natural rather than logical necessity is involved.

continuum   A collection of points, such that between any two points there are distinct points. Classical examples of a continuum are a line, plane or space.

continuum hypothesis   The claim that there are only two classes into which any thinkable collection of infinitely many distinct real numbers may fall.

contradiction   A conjunction of a proposition and its negation, which, according to the principle of non-contradiction, cannot be true. Aristotle pointed out the dangers of accepting contradictions. Except in some specially designed logics, anything can follow from a contradiction.

conventionalism   The view that human conventions rather than independent realities or necessities shape our basic concepts of the world, scientific theories, ethical principles and the like. On this view, we could have chosen other conventions, which would have been as satisfactory as the conventions entrenched in our actual account of the world or morality. Some conventionalist positions allow for a contribution by reality as well as by conventions, but it is difficult to distinguish these contributions.

counterfactual conditional   A conditional (if p, then q) in which the 'if clause' is contrary to fact; for example, 'if the water had been boiling, you would have been scalded'. There is no generally satisfactory analysis of counterfactual conditionals, although some philosophers believe that we need them to deal with many important philosophical problems.

criterion   A test or standard by which truth, existence, identity or meaning can be determined. Questions arise over the choice of criteria and over the relation between criteria and that for which they are criteria.

critique   Kant introduced the term for the critical examination of reason by itself. Later European philosophers have pursued a method of critique, but some have relinquished Kant's commitment to reason as the key element of their reflective method.

Darwinism Originally referring to the views of the naturalist Charles Darwin concerning his theory of species change and development through the filter of natural selection. Now commonly more loosely (and perhaps misleadingly) used as a synonym for evolutionary theory in general.

das Man For Heidegger, a basic structure of anonymous social normativity that is associated with our tendency to lapse into inauthenticity.

Dasein In Heidegger's pursuit of what he considered to be the central question in philosophy – that is, the question of the meaning of Being – he spoke of our Being as human beings as Dasein ('being there'). In talking of ourselves in this way, he meant Dasein to break with the whole history of ontology, including the inherited Cartesian conception of the self, and to replace it with a new orientation.

deconstruction Derrida's method aiming to overcome crucial metaphysical dichotomies. By showing that one term of an opposition is unjustifiably privileged with respect to the other, deconstruction allows us to use the pair of terms freed from metaphysical distortion. His approach to deconstruction employs sophisticated and surprising responses to language, culture and society derived from Freud and others.

defeasible The standard criteria for the correct application of a defeasible concept allow for that application to be retracted in the light of further evidence. Verification of claims using defeasible concepts is never conclusive, in principle being always open to revision. For example, in epistemology, a defeasible knowledge claim is one made confidently, but in recognition of the possibility (no matter how apparently unlikely) that further evidence could give reason for the claim to be withdrawn.

definite description A description picking out something as the sole individual having a certain property. Russell's theory of definite descriptions analyses sentences containing definite descriptions to remove the burden of finding objects to which these expressions seem to refer.

deontology An ethics based on acting according to duty or doing what is right, rather than on achieving virtue or on bringing about good consequences. It is too crude to make sharp divisions or to deny a place for more than one approach to ethics. Kant is the most important deontological theorist.

dialectic The Socratic method of discovering truth through questioning and debate, altered and developed by his Greek successors, and still a model of overwhelming importance in philosophy. Kantian dialectic expressed reason's capacity to reach contradictory conclusions from apparently sound premises. Hegel's dialectic drove the necessary unfolding and development of concepts in history. Marx's dialectic explained the historical development of society through class conflict and the relations between the forces and relations of production and the base and superstructure.

didactic Offered with an intention of instructing or teaching.

différance Derrida's term meaning both 'to differ' (related to spatiality and the basis of all conceptual oppositions) and 'to defer' (related to temporality and the perception of change in the relationship determining meaning).

dualism The view that each person is two entities, a mind with mental attributes and a body with physical attributes, instead of a single entity with attributes of both sorts.

egoism The view that we are always motivated by self-interest or that we always should be so motivated. Contemporary rational choice theorists attempt to understand how actual social institutions can be based on the choices of individuals acting according to egoist principles. The prisoner's dilemma and other problem cases show difficulties with this approach.

elenchus The Socratic method of seeking truth by cross-examining people to show conflicts in their beliefs.

eliminative materialism The view that our mental concepts, such as belief and desire, are inappropriate for a serious scientific account of human beings and should, or will be, eliminated.

empiricism   The claim that all knowledge or all meaningful discourse about the world is related to sensory experience or observation. Logical empiricism (or logical positivism) combined modern logical analysis with the demands of empiricism and was most famous for its verificationist theory of meaning.

Enlightenment   A broad intellectual movement in eighteenth-century Europe, particularly Britain, France and Germany, characterized by a rejection of superstition and mystery and an optimism concerning the power of human reasoning and scientific endeavour (hence its alternative name: the Age of Reason).

entailment   The intuitive notion of strict logical implication, such that necessarily if p, then q (that is, it is impossible that p and not q).

epochē   A term used by the sceptics for the suspension of belief or judgement and by Husserl for 'bracketing out' all objects that transcend consciousness.

essence   For Aristotle, that which remains the nature of a thing throughout its change from potentiality to actuality. More generally, the necessary defining characteristic of a thing, such that without that characteristic the thing would not be the thing it is.

eternal recurrence   Nietzsche's term for the infinite cyclical process of the will to power which provides meaning without teleology by moving from the simple to the complex and the complex to the simple.

ethical intuition   The immediate awareness of an ethical property or an ethical truth, but for Rawls intuitionism is the claim that there is an irreducible body of first principles which cannot be ordered in terms of priority.

ethical naturalism   The view, criticized by G. E. Moore, that ethical properties like goodness can be defined in terms of the natural properties that justify their use. Moore's alternative account in terms of non-natural intuition of goodness has seemed implausible, but new ways of conceiving relations among properties have also been important in the revival of ethical naturalism.

eudaimonia   'Flourishing' or 'well-being', the central aim of Aristotelian ethics, the realization of which is a complete and self-sufficient combination of virtue and its rewards in happiness. It is important to realize the complexity of the notion and not to reduce it to one of its components.

event   We can think of events as changes in objects or in relations among objects, so that the basic entities in our account of the world are objects and relations rather than events. However, some philosophers see advantages in recognizing events as basic, although events might have to take on some of the character of objects for this to be acceptable.

evolution (theory of)   Darwin's theory of evolution accounts for the changes in species of living things, according to which all organisms are derived from common ancestors through natural selection. For modern biologists, evolution is identified with changes in the genetic composition of populations.

evolutionary epistemology   An approach to the development of human knowledge in evolutionary terms, either as an integral part of natural selection or as an independent process modelled on biological natural selection. Evolutionary epistemology is part of a broader programme of naturalized epistemology. Rather than seeking to secure our knowledge claims against sceptical doubts, naturalized epistemology tries to explain major features of our knowledge as necessary or inevitable features of ourselves as natural beings.

expert system   A computer with 'built-in' expertise, which, used by a non-expert in a particular subject area, can evaluate or make other decisions concerning that subject.

explanation   An account characteristically telling us why something exists or happens, or must exist or happen. The covering law model of explanation proposed by Hempel has been widely influential, but has many critics. There are controversies over the nature of functional or teleological explanation, over the legitimacy of inferring to the best explanation, and over Dilthey's contrast between scientific explanation and historical understanding.

fallibilism   Peirce's view that none of our beliefs, even the apparently most fundamental, is certain and that any of our beliefs can be revised. Peirce believed that, rightly understood, relinquishing certainty does not open the way to sceptical doubt.

family resemblance   Wittgenstein's term in his later philosophy for the way in which expressions apply to things or kinds of things not sharing a common defining property, but instead sharing some of an interwoven complex of likenesses, as in the facial features of family members. He made the same point regarding the overlapping features of games.

fictional entities   Not all expressions pick out things which exist. Non-existing or fictional entities can play havoc with our account of language and reality. If they do not exist, we are tempted to enrich our ontology with an existence-like status to allow reference to them. Analysis, in one form or another, might avoid such temptations by showing that we can mean what we need to mean without committing ourselves to odd ontological items. Problems remain for real as opposed to notional fictions. We can say what is true or false about Anna Karenina or Sherlock Holmes, yet we cannot be certain how to understand our ability to do so.

first philosophy   In Aristotle, the study of the general characteristics of all types of existence or the principles of being. More generally, especially since Descartes, the position that there is an essential role for philosophy, prior to any science. Such a claim is challenged by scientistic views, which reverse the priority.

form of life   What Wittgenstein takes to be fundamental in his later account of understanding language as variously embedded in shared human activity. The crucial notion of 'form' shifts from logical form in his early writing to form of life. What is fundamental in understanding the possibility of language shifts from objects to language games and forms of life.

formal   In general, formal considerations have to do with the abstract structure, or pattern, of a subject, rather than with its content. Hence formal logic, for example, is concerned not with the content of particular sentences in an argument, but only with their structure of truth values.

Forms   According to Plato's theory of Forms, objectively existing immaterial entities that are the proper object of knowledge. Ordinary things exist by participating in Forms. Forms are also held to be necessary for the objectivity of ethics and aesthetics and the meaning of language.

foundationalism   The view that knowledge is possible only if some items serve as a certain foundation for the rest. Special attention is drawn to the alleged certainty of the proposed foundations and to the relation between the foundations and the rest of knowledge.

free will and determinism   There are threats to freedom involving the apparent determination of human action independent of our will. These include divine foreknowledge and in modern philosophy the possibility that our actions are determined by causal laws. One way out would be to argue that freedom and a particular form of determinism are compatible by showing that determinism has weaker implications than at first seems the case. One could also argue that what one values in freedom is not risked by determinism and is not aided by indeterminism. Nevertheless, some philosophers still claim that, on a proper understanding of freedom and foreknowledge or freedom and causal laws, we cannot have both.

function   A function is a relation between the value of variables and the value of the function as a whole. Giving a definite value to the variables yields a definite value to the whole function.

functional explanation   Also teleological explanation, in which an item is explained by the role or function it has in producing something which promotes or preserves the entity or kind of entity of which it is a part. Functional explanation is prominent in biology and in some of the social sciences. There is disagreement whether functional explanation is a rival to causal explanation or a form of causal explanation.

genealogy   Nietzsche's attempt to explain our basic beliefs and evaluations and to break our attachment to them. For Foucault, the exploration of the multiple interrelations between knowledge and power.

good Many approaches to ethics are centred on achieving what is good, although others are based on doing what is right. Priority to one goal need not exclude the other, but might shape the contents or limit how we pursue the other. We can ask about the relationship between human goodness and the goodness of other things, such as a knife that cuts well. On some views, goodness is reduced to one quality, like happiness or pleasure or satisfying desire, but others think of goodness as inherently complex. In either case, goodness has a place in moral psychology, motivating our actions and explaining our emotions.

happiness According to different ethical views, happiness might be one goal in life, the only possible goal, or a fortunate by-product of the pursuit of other goals. Happiness might concern one's aggregate of pleasure or require a complex balance involving virtue, pleasure, achievement and good fortune.

hedonism The belief that pleasure is the greatest good and highest aspiration of humankind. In early utilitarian thinking, this belief provided the interpretation of 'utility' or 'good'.

hermeneutics A method of interpretation, initially of biblical texts but later extended to other texts and with Dilthey to whole cultures. Characteristically, the method improves our understanding of what is obscure, corrupt or incomplete by placing it in the context of a whole. The hermeneutic circle is a problem which classically arises because the understanding of an item in a text depends on our understanding of the whole text, while the understanding of the whole text depends on our understanding of that and other items. This interdependence of interpretation, however, need not be vicious, although it might call for modesty rather than dogmatism in advancing any interpretation.

historicism The view that concepts, beliefs, truths and even standards of truth can be understood only in relation to the whole moral, intellectual, religious and aesthetic cultures of the historical periods in which they arise or flourish. This position is linked to demands for a hermeneutic method to achieve appropriate understanding. The term is also used by Popper for the view that history is governed by necessary laws of development.

holism The view that wholes have some priority over the elements, members, individuals or parts composing them. Social holism claims that individuals can be understood only in terms of the practices or institutions in which they take part and is a rival to some aspects of individualism. Methodological holism and methodological individualism propose different methodological constraints on the study of phenomena without pronouncing on their real constitution, while metaphysical holism claims that wholes are distinct entities, whose existence cannot be reduced to that of the items composing them. Holistic views in the philosophy of science and the philosophy of language propose that the meaning and truth of our claims cannot be assessed one by one, but must be assessed as part of theories, bodies of theory, or all we believe about the world.

humanism An intellectual movement of Renaissance Italy which argued that the Greek and Latin classics contained all the wisdom needed to lead a moral and effective life. Such a view contributed to the development of a rigorous kind of classical scholarship, which attempted to correct, and better understand, the ancient texts. A corollary of this view was an increasing intellectual confidence in the power of humankind to discover truth and falsehood.

iconographic Derived from the Greek word for 'image': hence, an artefact of some kind (such as a painting) that visually resembles the object it represents.

idealism The view that the existence of objects depends wholly or in part on the minds of those perceiving them or that reality is composed of minds and their states. There are many varieties of idealism, ranging from Plato's doctrine of independently existing ideas or forms to Berkeley's subjective idealism and Hegel's absolute idealism. Kant attempted to combine empirical realism with transcendental idealism.

ideas For Plato, an alternative term for Forms, the unchanging independently existing bases of the perceived world and thought about the world, and in seventeenth- and eighteenth-century philosophy, the vehicles of sensory representation of external objects and of thought. Locke and

Leibniz initiated disputes whether ideas could be innate, in us independent of sensory experience. Berkeley rejected Locke's distinction between the ideas of primary qualities (which resemble the qualities that produce them) and the ideas of secondary qualities (which are produced by qualities that they do not resemble). Hume argued that ideas originated in impressions, but still retained sensory and intellectual functions for ideas. Kant separated these functions (and used the term 'idea' for other purposes).

identity In order to use a concept we must be able to individuate different entities falling under that concept and to identify these individual entities over time. It is unclear whether or not individuating and identifying entities must refer to the kind concepts under which they fall. A special case of identity, discussed by Locke, Hume and many contemporary philosophers, is personal identity. Both the memory and bodily criteria for personal identity have encountered difficulties, leading Parfit to question the importance of personal identity. The identity theory of mind, according to which mental states are identical with states of the central nervous system, led to much discussion, although other forms of materialism have supplanted it in current controversy. Kripke's rejection of the notion of contingent identity in favour of necessary identity helped to renew discussion of the nature of the identity relation itself.

idol For Francis Bacon, an illusion or false appearance that hinders the acquisition of knowledge through prejudice or false ways of thinking.

illocutionary act In J. L. Austin's theory of speech acts, what one does in uttering what one utters. A perlocutionary act is what one does by uttering what one utters.

imagination The ability to represent objects or states of affairs which cannot exist, which do not exist or which do not exist here and now. Imagination is both condemned for its link with falsity and prized for its role in artistic creativity and human understanding. In Kant's account, imagination performs indispensable roles in perception as an intermediary between our sensibility and understanding which allows us to have knowledge of a unified world.

immaterial substance Berkeley argued that the notion of material substance could not be sustained, but that immaterial substances, human minds and God, were crucial to our account of reality.

immutable Literally, not able to change.

individualism An approach to ethics, social science and political and social philosophy which emphasizes the importance of human individuals in contrast to the social wholes, such as families, classes or societies, to which they belong. In different contexts, individualism is contrasted to holism and collectivism. Metaphysical individualism claims that social objects like societies can be reduced to individuals. Methodological individualism does not make metaphysical claims, but rather constrains the ways we explain social action.

induction A process of reasoning contrasted with deduction in which conclusions are drawn that all individuals of a kind have a certain character on the basis that some individuals of the kind have that character.

inference The process of reasoning whereby one statement (the conclusion) is derived from one or more other statements (the premises).

infinite regress An infinite regress in a series of propositions arises if the truth of proposition P_1 requires the support of proposition P_2, and for any proposition in the series P_n, the truth of P_n requires the support of the truth of P_{n+1}. There would never be adequate support for P_1, because the infinite series needed to provide such support could not be completed.

intensionality A feature characterizing sentences about mental states, according to which the truth value of the sentence may be altered by replacing expressions in the sentence by other expressions referring to the same objects. In extensional contexts, unlike intensional contexts, such substitutions do not affect the truth value of the sentence.

intentionality A characteristic feature of mental and linguistic acts or states according to which they have an object or content and are thus about something. An intentional object or content is that which a mental or linguistic state or act is about. Problems arise because intentional objects need not exist and mental contents need not be true.

intersubjectivity For Husserl, the structure allowing us to see others as egos rather than as objects and thus to escape the solipsistic implications that some critics derive from his account of oneself as a transcendental ego.

introspection Popularly, any 'inward-looking' at one's own mental states, easily lampooned as an inadequate source of evidence. More specifically, in the history of psychology, a technique developed to a sophisticated experimental level at the end of the nineteenth century.

irreducible To reduce X's to Y's would be to show how X's were, in reality, only Y's or in a linguistic guise to show that X-talk could be systematically eliminated in favour of Y-talk in a way involving no loss of content. Properties are said to be irreducible then, if they resist such reductions.

Leibniz's Law If A = B, for any true statement about A there will be a corresponding true statement about B, and vice versa. There are disputes over the way to deal with statements for which this law does not seem to hold.

lifeworld Our natural conception of the world, including such things as physical objects, cultural and historical artefacts and social institutions. For Husserl, the lifeworld has priority over the scientific account of the world that is grounded in it.

logical atomism The view held for a time by Russell and Wittgenstein that for language to have meaning it must be analysable into mutually independent propositions, the atomic elements of which correspond to elements in states of affairs. For Wittgenstein at this stage, propositions had meaning by logically picturing possible states of affairs. Russell's logical atomism, unlike Wittgenstein's, was tied to an empirical interpretation.

logical positivism A general philosophical position, also called logical empiricism, developed by members of the Vienna Circle on the basis of traditional empirical thought and the development of modern logic. Logical positivism confined knowledge to science and used verificationism to reject metaphysics not as false but as meaningless. The importance of science led leading logical positivists to study scientific method and to explore the logic of confirmation theory.

logomachy A controversy of no real substance, depending on a merely verbal dispute.

material biconditional The biconditional if and only if ('iff') is a relation between two statements p and q, such that p implies q and q implies p. The biconditional is material if the implications are contingent and strict if the implications are necessary.

materialism The doctrine that all items in the world are composed of matter. Because not all physical entities are material, the related doctrine of physicalism, claiming that all items in the world are physical entities, has tended to replace materialism.

matter and form Aristotle's metaphysical distinction used to explain the properties of objects. Matter, form and the composite of matter and form are Aristotle's candidates for the status of substance.

mauvaise foi For Sartre, self-deception in which one attempts to evade one's freedom by denying one's being-for-itself in favour of the being-in-itself of an object. His account raises the general question of how self-deception is possible.

maxim A statement expressing a general truth or rule of conduct.

method Philosophical methods are combinations of rules, procedures and examples determining the scope and limits of philosophy and establishing acceptable ways of working within those limits. The question of philosophical method is itself a matter for philosophy and constitutes a major feature of philosophy's reflective nature. Philosophers disagree about what is an appropriate philosophical method and about the relationship between philosophical method and the methods of other disciplines, especially scientific method.

methodological Concerning the study of method, particularly scientific method. Questions asked in contemporary methodology concern not only the characterization of scientific method, but also whether a single such characterization is necessary, or can do justice to the multitude of approaches and devices actually used.

minimalism In philosophy of language, the view that meaning has no substantial nature and so there is nothing substantive for a theory about meaning to say.

model In science, a representation such that knowledge concerning the model offers insight about the entity modelled. Whether models are heuristic devices or essential features of scientific explanation is a matter of debate. Mathematical models are interpretations of a formal system assigning truth values to the formulae of the system, thus testing the system for consistency.

modern For philosophical purposes, the period of philosophy and general intellectual life following Descartes and his contemporaries. The broad characteristics of the period are often taken to include an emphasis on individualism, the intellect, the universality of judgement, and the consequence of adopting these features as starting-points.

modus ponens and modus tollens *Modus ponens*, or affirming the antecedent (the if clause in an if-then proposition), is an argument of the valid form, 'If *p*, then *q*; *p*; therefore *q*'. *Modus tollens*, or denying the consequent (the then clause in an if-then proposition), is an argument of the valid form, 'If *p*, then *q*; not *q*; therefore not *p*.'

natural kind A naturally existing species of thing, such as cats, or an element, such as gold. There is philosophical dispute over how natural kind terms are related to natural kinds.

natural selection A central thesis of the biologist Charles Darwin which suggests that within every population of living organisms there are random variations which have different survival value. Those which aid survival (or enhance reproductive capacity) are 'selected' by being genetically transmitted to succeeding generations.

necessary *See* contingent–necessary.

neo-Platonist Any movement which seeks to reinstate Plato's doctrines as a central philosophical framework. More narrowly the term refers to the school initiated by Plotinus in third-century Greece, and to a later Renaissance form whose leading members were Nicholas Cusanus, Marsilio Ficino and Pico della Mirandola.

neutral monism A position according to which the difference between minds and bodies derives from different arrangements of the same neutral entities. The entities are neutral because they themselves are neither mental nor physical. This position proposed a solution to the mind–body problem, but there are difficulties with the neutral status of that which constitutes minds and bodies and with how arrangements of what is neutral can issue in minds and bodies. If experiences are proposed as the neutral entities, it is not clear whether neutral monism clarifies or obscures the nature of experience.

nihilism For Nietzsche, the loss of belief in a higher world and in the ideals and values grounded in such a world.

noema and noesis That which is thought about and the act of thinking. For Husserl, the material and the formal aspects of intentional experience.

nominalism The view that the only feature that particulars falling under the same general term have in common is that they are covered by the same term. Nominalism is opposed to realism, for which universals are required to explain how general terms apply to different particulars. For nominalism, language, rather than independent reality, underlies perceived likeness. Many philosophers are attracted to the ontological austerity of nominalism, but problems remain concerning how language, especially predication, works on nominalist principles.

nomothetic Literally, 'constituting the law', but generally used to refer to the philosophical aspects of law or to scientific theories constituted by laws.

non-Euclidean geometry Euclid's Fifth 'Parallels' Postulate (or Axiom XI) is rendered informally as: 'through a given point P not on a line L, there is one and only one line in the plane of P and L that does not meet L'. Non-Euclidean geometries explore systems in which two different denials of this postulate are used: Lobachevskyan geometry contains an infinite number of parallels through P; Reimannian geometry contains no parallels through P. Reimannian geometry has played a crucial role in the development of the general theory of relativity.

non-monotonic logics   In logic, deductive validity is cumulative, or monotonic, in that no matter what further premises are added to an originally valid argument, the argument remains valid. Non-monotonic logics, used in artificial-intelligence research, explore logical systems in which monotonicity does not hold.

nothingness   For Sartre, the ontological reality of negation that is derived from consciousness's negation of being-in-itself.

occasionalism   Malebranche's account of causation according to which rather than one event causing another, God wills the second event *on the occasion of* the first event.

Ockham's razor   The principle enunciated by the medieval nominalist William of Ockham that entities are not to be multiplied beyond necessity. Applied to systems of ontology or bodies of scientific theory, the principle encourages us to ask whether any proposed kind of entity is necessary. This principle of metaphysical economy retains influence in contemporary philosophy, although in judging rival systems it is not always clear which best meets the requirements of Ockham's razor.

omnipotence and omniscience   Attributes of being all-powerful and all-knowing, traditionally ascribed to God. The two combined with divine goodness give rise to the problems of explaining how there can be evil in the world. Puzzles about omnipotence have led to explanations that it is constrained by logical and metaphysical possibility. Divine omniscience, including foreknowledge, has been seen as a threat to human free will, and other philosophers have been concerned about what an omniscient being without a body in space and time could know.

ontology   The study of the broadest categories of existence, which also asks questions about the existence of particular kinds of objects, such as numbers or moral facts.

operator   An expression which alters the logical properties of other expressions to which it is applied. A sentential operator can be applied to sentences to yield new sentences.

Overman   For Nietzsche, persons of a new type who recognize that they are the sole source of the values and ideals by which they live.

paradox   An argument which seems to justify a self-contradictory conclusion by using valid deductions from acceptable premises.

perception   Our awareness of the world and its contents through sensory experience. The analysis of perception and the attempt to deal with sceptical arguments about perceptual knowledge are central philosophical topics. Perception involves both our capacity to be sensorily affected by external objects and our ability to bring these objects under concepts, although other capacities might also have a role to play. What we perceive and how these objects of perception are related to us and to physical objects are matters of continuing concern.

perspectivalism   The view that there can be no non-perspectival knowledge and that all knowledge is from a perspective.

phenomenological reduction   For Husserl, the method of ignoring real temporal particulars and focusing instead on the general and ideal atemporal features of things (the eidetic reduction) and setting aside all objects transcendent to consciousness to focus on the intentional contents immanent within consciousness (the *epochē* or transcendental reduction).

phenomenology   For Hegel, the study of the dialectical development of Spirit through stages towards rational, self-conscious freedom; for Husserl, a philosophical method based on the reflective and descriptive study of consciousness focused on the intentionality of mental states. The structure of consciousness revealed, which includes an ego that exists absolutely, aimed to provide a sure foundation for knowledge. In response to Frege's early criticism, Husserl attempted to draw a sharp boundary between phenomenology and psychology. In his later writing, Husserl altered many features of his notion of phenomenology, and other writers, especially Heidegger, used the term in radically different ways.

phronesis   For Aristotle, the intellectual virtue of practical wisdom, a kind of moral knowledge guiding us to what is appropriate in conjunction with moral virtue.

picture theory of meaning   Wittgenstein's view in the *Tractatus Logico-Philosophicus* that a proposition has meaning in virtue of sharing a form with an actual or possible state of affairs. The proposition provides a logical picture of the state of affairs, and is true if its elements stand in the same relation as the objects in the state of affairs. Philosophers disagree over the extent to which Wittgenstein moved away from this theory in his later writings.

pluralism   In metaphysics, the belief that there is more than one kind of fundamental reality or of fundamental existents. Hence, pluralism stands in contrast to monism (one kind of fundamental reality or existent) and dualism (two kinds of fundamental reality or existent). In ethics, the belief that there is more than one kind of fundamental good or supreme ethical value.

polis   The Greek term for city-state, from which the term 'politics' is derived. The character of the *polis* was examined in ancient times, and many later thinkers yearned for its re-establishment as an ideal of political life.

possible world   The analysis of statements in terms of 'possible worlds' comes from the semantic treatment of modal logic – the logic of possibility and necessity. A possible world is a way the world might have been. A necessary statement is one that is true in all possible worlds; a contingent statement is one that is true in at least one possible world.

postmodernism   If Descartes is seen as the father of modernism, then postmodernism is a variety of cultural positions which reject major features of Cartesian (or allegedly Cartesian) modern thought. Hence, views which, for example, stress the priority of the social to the individual; which reject the universalizing tendencies of philosophy; which prize irony over knowledge; and which give the irrational equal footing with the rational in our decision procedures all fall under the postmodern umbrella.

prescriptive statement   A statement, for example in ethics, which says how things should be, as opposed to a descriptive statement, which says how things are.

presupposition   A generally implicit assumption (though it can be made explicit) underlying a claim or a process of inference.

primary and secondary qualities   Seventeenth-century scientists and philosophers attempted to distinguish qualities like size and shape, which produce in us ideas (ideas of primary qualities) that resemble the qualities themselves, from qualities that produce in us ideas (ideas of secondary qualities), like colour and taste, which do not resemble the qualities themselves. The former ideas, unlike the latter, offered something that could be measured, and were thus considered a suitable basis for scientific explanation. Berkeley argued against the distinction.

principle of non-contradiction   The logical principle rejecting the possibility that propositions of the form '*p* and not *p*' are true, that a subject can be and not be, or that we can ascribe and deny the same attribute to the same subject.

proposition   That which is characteristically stated by a declarative sentence and can be true or false. Understanding the nature and structure of propositions is often seen as the central task of the philosophical examination of logic. Philosophers consider the apparently different functions of components of propositions (names, predicates and logical constants) and how they are unified into something capable of having a truth value. They ask about how the form, meaning and use of propositions are related and how different propositions have logical relations. They ask how linguistic or psychological states can have propositional contents. The existence of propositions, as opposed to sentences, is challenged by those suspicious of their abstract nature.

psychologism   A programme, criticized by Frege and then by Husserl, to explain logic in terms of human psychology.

quantifier Modern predicate logic uses quantifier expressions some ($\mid$) and all ($\ldots$) in sentences with variables (x, y, $\ldots$), predicates (F, G, $\ldots$), relations (R, $\ldots$), identity and logical constants (and, or, not, if-then). ($\mid x$) ($\mid y$) (if Fx and Gy, then $x = y$) reads 'For some x and for some y, if x is F and y is G, then x is identical with y'. The individual or multiple use of the universal quantifier 'all' and the existential quantifier 'there exists' to bind variables in sentences has been seen as the key to the development of a powerful and flexible system of modern predicate logic.

quantum mechanics A modern physical theory (much developed and refined since Neils Bohr's ground-breaking work in 1913) which deals with the structure and behaviour of subatomic particles. It has given rise to philosophical problems of its own (some quantum phenomena seem to require a non-classical logic) and has also been used by both sides in the philosophical dispute between realist and instrumentalist construals of scientific theories.

rational number Any number of the form x/y, where x can be any positive or negative integer or 0, and y is a positive integer. An irrational number is any real number which is not rational.

real number A real number is any number which can be represented as a non-terminating decimal.

realism A variety of doctrines in different areas of philosophy holding that entities or facts of contested sorts exist. There are, of course, different arguments concerning the reality of numbers in mathematics, the reality of moral facts in ethics, and the reality of time in physics or metaphysics. The kind of reality ascribed to universals differs from the kind of reality seen as belonging to common-sense material objects or to theoretical entities in science. Various realisms are hence opposed by nominalism, idealism, instrumentalism, reductionism, eliminativism, conventionalism, constructivism, relativism and anti-realism. Kant argued for both empirical realism and transcendental idealism. In recent years many philosophers have discussed Michael Dummett's argument for anti-realism, in which he rejects the claim that every proposition must be either true or false and argues that realism must be false because it implies this claim.

reason An ability to move from the truth of some beliefs to the truth of others. Some philosophers have seen this capacity as more or less sufficient to determine one correct systematic account of reality, while others have argued that such an account, if possible at all, must be based primarily upon experience. Kant, following Aristotle, saw reason divided between theoretical and practical reason, the latter issuing in actions rather than beliefs, but held that at a deep level the two capacities were the same. Hegel saw reason and much else altering at different stages of historical development. Hume restricted practical reason to finding means to obtain ends set out by the passions; others have rejected the means–ends account. Reason enters the account of institutions through models of the interaction of the choices of individuals and through the direct assessment of practices and societies.

recursive function A function for which the value of the function for any argument X_{n+1} is a function of the value of the function for the argument X_n.

reductionism The view that the concepts or theories of all sciences can be reduced to physics.

reflective equilibrium A term used by Nelson Goodman and John Rawls for a two-way reconciliation between judgements and principles. Judgements about individual cases are guided by principles, but principles can be modified in light of judgements. Equilibrium is reached when principles and judgements fit one another without further alteration. An equilibrium is always liable to be upset by new cases, but that is also true, although less transparently so, if one tries to determine principles by other procedures.

relativity (theory of) The special theory of relativity is a modern physical theory due to Einstein, giving an account in which neither space nor time has an independent absolute value or existence but is each relative to the other. Thus the classical view of space and time is replaced with one in which the two are aspects of the same underlying reality: space-time. The general theory of relativity extended the special (from considering frameworks in uniform relative motion to considering frameworks in arbitrary relative motion to one another) and is the currently accepted basis for our theory of gravitation.

rights   Legal or moral capacities, often correlated with duties, which may be exercised without interference by others, including the state, or in some cases with the assistance of others. Rights can regard such matters as belief, actions, relationships, property, or the safety and integrity of oneself. Some rights involve limiting the rights of others or the creation of duties. Rights can be considered one by one or from the standpoint of a system of rights and duties. Philosophers discuss the status of rights in morality, in particular whether rights can provide the basis of moral or political philosophy or must be understood within the context of other notions, such as principles, virtues, utility or a social contract, from which their legitimacy might derive. Philosophers have discussed the claim that rights 'trump' other considerations, the claim that there are collective as well as individual rights, and the claim that animals have rights. Exploring this last question can help to see what one must be like in order to hold rights. Philosophers have also considered the relationship between legal and moral rights and, in the face of Bentham's attack on natural rights, have examined the notion of natural, universal or human rights.

rigid designator   A subject term designating the same object in all different possible situations (or possible worlds) in which the object exists, so long as the meaning of the term is held constant. A non-rigid designator with constant meaning can designate different objects in different possible situations (or possible worlds).

Rorschach test   A personality test, bearing the name of its Swiss inventor, in which a set of ink-blots is shown to a patient, who has to describe what they resemble or suggest.

rule   A principle guiding action. For Kant, concepts are rules, the understanding is the faculty of rules, and our use of rules is central to our account of objectivity. Much of Wittgenstein's discussion of following a rule runs parallel to the Kantian insight that rules do not determine their own application. The question of what gives a rule authority and holds it and its application in place led to the rejection of the possibility of a private language and Wittgenstein's emphasis on practices and forms of life. Interrelations among rules, roles and practices are central concerns in the philosophy of social science. Discussions of what constitutes a legal rule and how such rules have normative force are main features of the philosophy of law.

rule utilitarianism   A version of utilitarianism in which general rules rather than acts are assessed for utility, thus shifting concern from individuals to practices and institutions. Acts are endorsed not in their own right, but because they accord with practices or institutions which meet the test of maximizing utility.

Russell's paradox   A paradox based on the notion of class membership discovered by Bertrand Russell and undermining the crucial notion of class or set in Frege's foundations of mathematics. The paradox led to important changes in set theory and in the notion of a set, in part also to prevent further paradoxes from arising. The paradox arises from asking whether the class of all classes that are not members of themselves is a member of itself.

sanctions   Negative and positive sanctions are punishments or rewards for behaviour that transgresses or is in accord with a rule.

scope   In logic, the shortest propositional function in which a logical operator occurs. Scope ambiguities are common in ordinary language but are eliminable during formalization.

semantics   In the study of language, semantics is concerned with the meaning of words, expressions and sentences, often in relation to reference and truth. Semantics is contrasted with syntax (the study of logical or grammatical form) and pragmatics (the study of the contribution of contextual factors to the meaning of what language users say). Meta-semantic theories study key semantic notions such as meaning and truth and how these notions are related.

sense data   In empiricist theories of perception, which were popular early in the twentieth century, that which is given by the senses. Questions arise concerning whether anything is purely given in perception, what might be given, and how what is given might be related to the external objects of common sense.

set   A set is a collection of definite distinguishable entities. Set theory, however, allows for the null set: the set that has no members.

social contract   An actual or hypothetical contract providing the legitimate basis of sovereignty and civil society and of the rights and duties constituting the role of citizen. The contract can be agreed between people and a proposed sovereign or among the people themselves.

solipsism   The view confining reality to oneself and one's experiences.

sub specie aeternitatis   Literally, 'from the aspect of eternity', hence a claim for an absolutely non-perspectival account of knowledge.

subjective–objective   The subject contributes what is subjective to such things as perceptual, moral and aesthetic judgement and experience; the objects of such judgements and experience contribute what is objective. The subjective seems prone to variation among subjects, while the objective appears to provide a basis for universal agreement. There is disagreement over the contribution of the subject and the object to such judgements. Different notions of objectivity might be suitable in different domains. Historical judgements, for example, might be objective if the historian making them is unbiased rather than through having a favoured relation to relevant objects.

sublation   A change which both cancels and preserves an entity or concept by raising it to a higher level. The full complex meaning of this term (*aufheben* in German) was established by Hegel.

substance   Something which can exist by itself, is the substrate underlying the existence of other things, and is the subject of which other things are predicated. In his *Metaphysics* Aristotle considered what can be substance: matter, form, or a combination of matter and form. According to various criteria he used, different answers seemed plausible, although he finally preferred form. Seventeenth-century philosophers, including Descartes, Spinoza and Leibniz, came to strikingly different solutions to the problem of what qualifies as being substance. Locke's account seems to suggest an unknowable substratum which falls out of any account of knowledge, but it can also be seen to offer a corpuscular substrate linked to his doctrine of primary qualities and their explanatory role in science.

sui generis   Literally, 'of its own kind', or unique.

supervenience   A property F supervenes on a property G, firstly, if anything which has property F has it in virtue of having property G and, secondly, if something has property F in virtue of having property G, then anything else having property G would also have to possess property F. Supervenience is intended to allow for non-reductive relations among hierarchies of properties.

syllogism   An argument according to Aristotle's logical theory involving a major premise, a minor premise, and a conclusion.

teleology   The explanation of a thing or feature of a thing in terms of its function or goal.

theodicy   Often refers only to Leibniz's text of the same name, but can refer to any philosophical position which seeks to prove the existence of God, or to justify a belief in such existence in the face of the problem of evil.

things-in-themselves   Kant distinguished appearances (phenomena) from things-in-themselves (noumena). Things-in-themselves are meant to exist independently of how we experience them, in particular independently of space, time and the categories.

third man argument   Plato's argument, endorsed by Aristotle, that the relation between a Form and the group of things having that Form in common leads to an infinite regress.

thought   For Frege, a thought is the sense of a sentence which can be used to make an assertion or to ask a question that is answerable by either 'yes' or 'no'. The contents of thoughts can be true or false. Thoughts in this sense are logical or conceptual rather than a matter of individual psychology. Different individuals may share the same thought, although they cannot share the same act of thinking.

thought experiment   An attempt to conceive the consequences of an intervention in the world without actually intervening. In some cases, an actual experiment would be preferable but is impossible in practice or perhaps even in theory.

three-valued logic   Classical logic allows 'true' and 'false' as the only values for propositions, as expressed by the law of excluded middle (which states that every proposition is either true or false). Three-valued logic can reject this law by adding an additional value like 'indeterminate' or can replace the two initial values with three other values like 'necessarily true', 'necessarily false' and 'contingent'.

Torricelli   The early seventeenth-century natural philosopher who was the first person to create a sustained vacuum, thus apparently threatening Descartes's claim that there could be no vacuum in nature.

transcendental   For Kant, 'transcendental' is contrasted with 'transcendent'. Something transcendent goes beyond the limits of experience, while something transcendental relates to the conditions of the possibility of experience.

truth   Propositions, statements, sentences, assertions and beliefs have been offered as appropriate bearers of truth or falsity. Understanding truth is filled with difficulty. Philosophers have explored the possibility that truth is: a correspondence between what we say and how things are; a matter of coherence between statements and a background of settled beliefs; an ideal limit which enquiry will approach; a feature of assertions which function well in enquiry or in life more generally; a matter of giving a truth definition for a language; a redundancy, because 'It is true that p' is equivalent to 'p'; or disclosedness of being. Some of these theories are compatible and might be integrated in a more comprehensive theory. On some accounts, each proposition is true or false on its own, while others adopt a holistic view. The relation between meaning and truth is of central philosophical concern.

truth function   The truth value of a combination of propositions which depends only on the truth values of the constituent propositions and the logical constants (and, if-then, or, not) by which they are combined. Truth functions can be set out in truth tables:

p	q	p or q
T	F	T
T	T	T
F	F	F
F	T	T

Not all propositions are truth functions of their constituents. For example, the truth value of 'I believe that it will rain' is not determined by the truth value of 'It will rain'.

understanding   The capacity to use concepts and to bring individuals under them. Kant distinguished sensibility, understanding and reason as fundamental to our capacity for experience and knowledge. He understood concepts as rules and saw the understanding as the faculty of rules, including both empirical concepts and the categories as pure concepts of the understanding. In the social sciences and history, Dilthey and Weber have contrasted understanding (*verstehen*) and explanation, with explanation providing the causal accounts of science and understanding offering insight into such things as human lives, culture and historical periods. Hermeneutics has been proposed as the method appropriate to understanding. Philosophers have disagreed over the claimed difference between explanation and understanding, about the character of understanding, and about the methodological implications of recognizing understanding as a distinctive mode of knowledge.

universals Abstract objects intended to explain how general terms have meaning and how they apply to individuals. There were medieval disputes over universals involving realism, which accepted their existence, and nominalism, which denied it. Some philosophers see problems in embracing any abstract object, especially in this case because their relation to individuals seems opaque, yet it is also difficult to see how an account of how names have meaning and refer to individuals will explain the contribution of predicates and relations to the meaning and truth or falsity of sentences or propositions. Explaining these roles might not require classic universals, derived from independently existing Platonic Forms, but there are other possibilities short of nominalism.

verification principle A central doctrine of logical positivism according to which the meaning of a proposition is its method of verification. Claims without a method of verification, such as those of religion and metaphysics, are meaningless. Verificationism thus offered a criterion of meaningfulness.

verisimilitude Literally and as used in aesthetic criticism, the appearance of being true or real. In philosophy, a surrogate for the truth of scientific theories offered by Karl Popper as part of his vision of the nature of scientific progress.

vicious regress An attempt to solve a problem which reintroduced the same problem in the proposed solution. If one continues along the same lines, the initial problem will recur infinitely and will never be solved. Not all regresses, however, are vicious.

Vienna Circle An intellectual (mostly philosophical) group, led by Moritz Schlick, which met from 1924–36, though its influence continued for much longer. Their general position, pro-science and hostile to speculative metaphysics, gave rise to the doctrines of logical positivism.

virtue An excellence of moral or intellectual character. Plato, Aristotle and many subsequent philosophers explored the nature of the virtues, their relations among themselves and to non-virtuous states, their place in our psychology and their role in achieving happiness. Virtues offer a basis for ethical life rivalling those provided by Kantian principles or a utilitarian calculation of happiness, although an account of ethics might reasonably include principles, consequences and virtues. A recent revival of virtue ethics has been motivated in part by dissatisfaction with the abstract universal nature of the main alternative views. The emphasis on cultivating virtues in concrete human individuals could correct this, but it is not clear that a perfectionist concern for individual excellence is satisfactory to ground ethics.

vitalism Any position which holds that life is a non-reducible, non-physical attribute of living things. Specific forms of vitalism have arisen in the history of philosophy as reactions to a perceived overemphasis on determinist and materialist metaphysics.

will to power For Nietzsche, the basic human drive to attain a higher and more perfect state, manifested in form-giving practical activity that explains the world and the nature of reality.

Appendix

Many of the authors discussed in this Companion are listed below in chronological order with some of their main works. The list is not comprehensive, but it should be a helpful guide to the diversity of philosophical questions and to the complex history of philosophical thinking.

Plato 427–347 BC
Protagoras; Gorgias; Meno; Timaeus; Philebus; Phaedrus; Symposium; Phaedo; Republic; Theaetetus; Sophist; Parmenides; Cratylus; Laws

Aristotle 384–322 BC
Metaphysics; Nicomachean Ethics; Politics; Categories; De Interpretatione; Prior and Posterior Analytic; Topics; Physics; De Anima; Rhetoric; Art of Poetry

Marcus Tullius Cicero 106–43 BC
On the State; On the Laws; On Duties

Plotinus AD 204–70
Enneads

Porphyry the Phoenician *c.* 232–304
Introduction to Aristotle's Categories

St Augustine of Hippo 354–430
Confessions (397–400); *City of God* (413–26)

Pseudo-Dionysus the Areopagite, fifth century
On the Divine Names and the Mystical Theology

Boethius *c.* 480–524
Consolation of Philosophy

John Eriugena *c.* 810–75
De Praedestinatione; De Divisione Naturae

Avicenna of Baghdad (Ibn Sina) 980–1037
Healing; The Directives and Remarks; Deliverance

St Anselm of Canterbury 1033–1109
Monologion; Proslogion

Peter Abelard 1079–1142
Dialectica

Averroes of Cordoba (Ibn Rushd) 1126–98
The Incoherence of the Incoherence

Moses Maimonides *c.* 1135–1204
The Guide for the Perplexed

Robert Grosseteste *c.* 1170–1253
De Luce; De Motu Corporali et Luce; Hexameron

Albert the Great *c.* 1200–80
Opera Omnia

Roger Bacon *c.* 1214–92
Opus Maius

St Thomas Aquinas 1224–74
Summa Theologiae

John Duns Scotus *c.* 1265–1308
Ordinatio; Quaestiones Quodlibetales

William of Ockham *c.* 1285–1349
Summa Logicae

Joseph Albo *c.* 1360–1444
The Book of Principle (1425)

Nicolaus Copernicus 1473–1543
On the Revolutions of the Heavenly Orbs (1543)

Jean Calvin 1509–64
Institutes of the Christian Religion (1536)

Michel Eyquem de Montaigne 1533–92
Essays

Francisco Suárez 1548–1617
Disputationes Metaphysicae (1597)

Francis Bacon 1561–1626
Novum Organum (1620)

Galilei Galileo 1564–1642
Dialogue Concerning the Two Chief World Systems (1632); *Dialogues Concerning Two New Sciences* (1638)

Hugo Grotius 1583–1645
On the Law of War and Peace (1625)

Thomas Hobbes 1588–1679
De Cive (1642); *Leviathan* (1651); *De Corpore* (1656); *De Homine* (1658)

René Descartes 1596–1650
Discourse on Method (1637); *Meditations on First Philosophy* (1641); *Replies to Objections to the Meditations* (1641–2); *Principles of Philosophy* (1644); *Passions of the Soul* (1649)

Blaise Pascal 1623–62
Pensées (1670)

Robert Boyle 1627–91
The Origin of Forms and Qualities according to the Corpuscular Philosophy (1666); *A Disquisition about the Final Causes of Natural Things* (1688)

Benedict de Spinoza 1632–77
The Principles of Descartes's Philosophy (1663); *Treatise on the Improvement of the Intellect*; *Short Treatise on God, Man and his Well Being*; *Tractatus Theologico-Politicus* (1670); *Ethics* (1677)

John Locke 1632–1704
Essay Concerning Human Understanding (1690); *Two Treatises on Government* (1689); *A Letter Concerning Toleration* (1689)

Nicolas Malebranche 1638–1715
The Search after Truth (1674–5); *Dialogues on Metaphysics and Religion* (1688)

Isaac Newton 1642–1727
Philosophiae Naturalis Principia Mathematica (1687)

Gottfried Wilhelm Leibniz 1646–1716
Discourse of Metaphysics (1686); *New Essays on Human Understanding* (1704); *Theodicy* (1710); *Monadology* (1714); *Leibniz–Clarke Correspondence* (1717); *Correspondence with Arnauld* (1846)

George Berkeley 1685–1753
Essay towards a New Theory of Vision (1709); *A Treatise Concerning the Principles of Human Knowledge* (1710); *Three Dialogues between Hylas and Philonous* (1713)

Francis Hutcheson 1694–1746
Inquiry into the Origins of Our Ideas of Beauty and Virtue (1725)

Thomas Bayes 1702–61
An Essay towards Solving a Problem in the Doctrine of Chances (1763)

Thomas Reid 1710–96
Essays on the Intellectual Powers of Man (1785); *Essays on the Active Power of Man* (1788)

David Hume 1711–76
A Treatise of Human Nature (1739); *Enquiry Concerning Human Understanding* (1748); *Dialogues Concerning Natural Religion* (1799)

Jean Jacques Rousseau 1712–78
Discourse on Inequality (1755); *The New Héloïse* (1761); *Émile* (1762); *The Social Contract* (1762); *Confessions* (1782–9)

William Blackstone 1723–80
Commentaries on the Laws of England, 8th edn (1778)

Adam Smith 1723–90
Theory of Moral Sentiments (1759); *The Wealth of Nations* (1776)

Adam Ferguson 1723–1816
Essay on the History of Civil Society (1767)

Immanuel Kant 1724–1804
Critique of Pure Reason (1781, 2nd edn 1787); *Groundwork of the Metaphysics of Morals* (1785); *Metaphysical Foundations of Natural Science (1786); Critique of Practical Reason* (1788); *Critique of Judgement* (1790); *religion within the Limits of Reason Alone* (1793); *Metaphysics of Morals* (1797); *Opus Postumum*

Marquis de Condorcet 1734–94
Essay on the Application of Analysis to the Probability of Majority Decisions (1785); *The Sketch for a Historical Picture of the Progress of the Human Mind* (1795)

Johann Gottfried Herder 1744–1803
Outlines of a Philosophy of the History of Man (1784–91)

Jeremy Bentham 1748–1832
A Fragment on Government (1776); *An Introduction to the Principles of Morals and Legislation* (1789)

Mary Wollstonecraft 1759–97
A Vindication of the Rights of Men (1790); *Vindication of the Rights of Women* (1792)

Friedrich Schiller 1759–1805
Letters on the Aesthetic Education of Mankind (1794–5)

Johann Gottlieb Fichte 1762–1814
The Science of Knowledge (1794 and later revised editions); *The Science of Ethics as Based on the Science of Knowledge* (1796); *The Vocation of Man* (1800); *The Characteristics of the Present Age* (1806)

George Wilhelm Friedrich Hegel 1770–1831
The Jena System 1804–5: Logic and Metaphysics (1804–5); *The Phenomenology of Spirit* (1807); *Science of Logic* (1812–16); *Encyclopaedia of the Philosophical Sciences* (1817); *The Philosophy of Right* (1821); *Aesthetics* (1835); *Lectures on the Philosophy of Religion* (1832, 1840); *Lectures on the Philosophy of World History* (1837, 1840); *Lectures on the History of Philosophy* (1892–6)

Friedrich von Schelling 1775–1854
Ideas for a Philosophy of Nature (1797); *The System of Transcendental Idealism* (1800); *On the Essence of Human Freedom* (1809)

Bernard Bolzano 1781–1848
Wissenschaftslehre, 4 vols (1837)

William Hamilton 1788–1856
Lectures of Metaphysics and Logic (1859–60)

Arthur Schopenhauer 1788–1860
On the Fourfold Root of the Principle of Sufficient Reason (1813); *The World as Will and Idea* (1818)

John Austin 1790–1859
The Province of Jurisprudence Determined (1832)

Auguste Comte 1798–1857
Cours de philosophie positive, 6 vols (1830–42)

John Stuart Mill 1806–73
Bentham (1838); *Coleridge* (1840); *System of Logic*, 2 vols (1843); *Principles of Political Economy*, 2 vols (1848); *On Liberty* (1859); *Utilitarianism* (1861); *an Examination of Sir William Hamilton's Philosophy* (1865); *Subjection of Women* (1869); *Autobiography* (1873)

Charles Darwin 1809–82
The Origin of Species by Means of Natural Selection (1859); *The Descent of Man* (1871)

Søren Kierkegaard 1813–55
On the Concept of Irony (1841); *Either/Or* (1843); *Fear and Trembling* (1843); *Philosophical Fragments* (1844); *The Concept of Dread* (1844); *Stages on Life's Way*; *Concluding Unscientific Postscript* (1846); *The Sickness Unto Death* (1849)

Karl Marx 1818–83
Economic and Philosophical Manuscripts (1844); *The Communist Manifesto* (with Engels, 1848); *Grundrisse* (1857–8); *Preface to A Critique of Political Economy* (1859); *Capital* (1867–94)

Eduard Hanslick 1825–1904
On the Musically Beautiful (1854)

Wilhelm Dilthey 1833–1911
Introduction to the Human Sciences (1883); *Formation of the Historical World in the Human Sciences* (1910)

Franz Brentano 1838–1917
Psychology from an Empirical Standpoint (1874), augmented in 2nd edn (1911) and 3rd edn (1925); *The Origin of Our Knowledge of Right and Wrong* (1889); *Truth and Evidence* (1930)

Henry Sidgwick 1838–1900
The Methods of Ethics (1874)

Ernst Mach 1838–1916
The Analysis of Sensations (1914)

Charles Sanders Peirce 1839–1914
Collected Papers (8 vols, 1931–58)

William James 1842–1910
The Principles of Psychology, 2 vols (1890); *The Varieties of Religious Experience* (1902); *Pragmatism* (1907); *The Meaning of Truth* (1909); *Essays in Radical Empiricism* (1912)

Friedrich Nietzsche 1844–1900
The Birth of Tragedy (1872); *Daybreak* (1881); *The Gay Science* (1882); *Thus Spoke Zarathustra* (1883–5); *Beyond Good and Evil* (1886); *On the Genealogy of Morals* (1887); *The Twilight of the Idols* (1889); *Ecce Homo* (1908)

Francis Herbert Bradley 1846–1924
Appearance and Reality (1893)

Gottlob Frege 1848–1925
Begriffsschrift (Concept–Script) (1879); *The Foundations of Arithmetic* (1884); *The Basic Laws of Arithmetic* (1893); 'The Thought' in Strawson, ed., *Philosophical Logic* (1967); *Translations from the Philosophical Writings of Gottlob Frege* (1980)

Ferdinand de Saussure 1857–1913
Course in General Linguistics (1916)

Émile Durkheim 1858–1917
The Rules of Sociological Method (1895); *Suicide* (1897); *The Elementary Forms of Religious Life* (1912)

John Dewey 1859–1952
Experience and Nature (1925); *The Quest for Certainty* (1929); *Art as Experience* (1933); *Liberalism and Social Action* (1935)

Edmund Husserl 1859–1938
Logical Investigations, 2 vols (1900–1); *Ideas: General Introduction to Pure Phenomenology* (1913); *The Phenomenology of Internal Time Consciousness* (1928); Cartesian Meditations (1931); *The Crisis of European Sciences and Transcendental Phenomenology* (1954)

David Hilbert 1862–1943
Foundations of Geometry (1899)

Max Weber 1864–1920
The Protestant Ethic and the Spirit of Capitalism (1904–5); *Economy and Society* (1922)

Ferdinand Canning Scott Schiller 1864–1937
Humanism: Philosophical Essays (1903)

Benedetto Croce 1866–1953
Aesthetics as the Science of Expression and General Linguistics (1902)

John McTaggart 1866–1925
Nature of Existence, 2 vols (1921–7)

Bertrand Russell 1872–1970
Principles of Mathematics (1903); *Principia Mathematica* (with Whitehead, 1910–13); *Problems of Philosophy* (1912); *The Theory of Knowledge* (1913); *Our Knowledge of the External World* (1914); *The Philosophy of Logical Atomism* (1918); *Introduction to Mathematical Philosophy* (1919); *The Analysis of Mind* (1921); *The Analysis of Matter* (1927); *An Inquiry into Meaning and Truth* (1940); *Human Knowledge* (1948)

George Edward Moore 1873–1958
Principia Ethics (1903); *Philosophical Studies* (1922); *Some Main Problems of Philosophy* (1953); *Philosophical Papers* (1959)

Albert Einstein 1879–1955
The Meaning of Relativity (1921); *Collected Papers*, 2 vols (1987–9)

Luitzen Egbertus Jan Brouwer 1881–1966
Collected Works (1975–6)

Hans Kelsen 1881–1973
General Theory of Law and State (1949); *Principles of International Law* (1967); *Pure Theory of Law* (1967); *General Theory of Norms* (1991)

Clarence Irving Lewis 1883–1964
An Analysis of Knowledge and Valuation (1946); *The Ground and Nature of the Right* (1955)

Karl Barth 1886–1968
The Epistles to the Romans (1919); *Church Dogmatics* (1932)

Robin George Collingwood 1889–1943
The Principles of Art (1938); *An Essay on Metaphysics* (1940); *The Idea of History* (1946)

Martin Heidegger 1889–1976
Being and Time (1927); *The Basic Problems of Phenomenology* (1927); *Kant and the Problem of Metaphysics* (1929); *Basic Questions of Philosophy: Selected 'Problems' of 'Logic.'* Lectures (1937–8); *An Introduction to Metaphysics* (1954); *What is Called Thinking?* (1954); *The Principle of Reason* (1957); *On the Way to Language* (1959); *Nietzsche*, 4 vols (1961); *Pathmarks* (1967); *On Time and Being* (1969); *Poetry, Language, Thought* (1971); *The Question Concerning Technology and Other Essays* (1977)

Ludwig Wittgenstein 1889–1951
Tractatus Logico-Philosophicus (1922); *The Blue and Brown Books* (1933–5); *Philosophical Investigations* (1953); *Notebooks 1914–16* (1961); *Remarks on the Foundations of Mathematics* (1966); *Zettel* (1967); *On Certainty* (1969); *Philosophical Remarks* (1975); *Culture and Value* (1980)

Rudolph Carnap 1891–1970
The Logical Structure of the World and Pseudoproblems in Philosophy (1928); *The Logical Syntax of Language* (1934); *Meaning and Necessity* (1947); *Logical Foundations of Probability* (1950)

Friedrich August von Hayek 1899–1992
The Road to Serfdom (1944); *The Constitution of Liberty* (1960); *Law, Legislation and Liberty*, 3 vols (1973–9)

Gilbert Ryle 1900–76
The Concept of Mind (1949); *Dilemmas* (1954); *Collected Papers*, 2 vols (1971)

Hans-Georg Gadamer 1900–2002
Truth and Method (1960)

Michael Oakeshott 1901–92
Experience and Its Modes (1933); *Rationalism in Politics* (1963); *On Human Conduct* (1975); *On History* (1983)

Frank Plumpton Ramsey 1902–30
The Foundations of Mathematics and Other Logical Essays (1931)

Lon Fuller 1902–78
The Morality of Law (1969)

Karl Popper 1902–94
The Open Society and Its Enemies, 2 vols (1945); *The Logic of Scientific Discovery* (1959); *Conjectures and Refutations* (1963); *Objective Knowledge* (1972)

Alfred Tarski 1902–83
Logic, Semantics, and Metamathematics (1956)

Theodore Adorno 1903–69
Dialectic of the Enlightenment (with Horkheimer, 1947); *Negative Dialectics* (1966)

Alonzo Church 1903–95
Introduction to Mathematical Logic (1956)

Emmanuel Levinas 1905–96
Totality and Infinity (1961); *Otherwise than Being or Beyond Essence* (1974); *Ethics and Infinity* (1982)

Carl Hempel 1905–97
Aspects of Scientific Explanation (1970)

Jean-Paul Sartre 1905–80
Sketch for a Theory of the Emotions (1939); *The Psychology of Imagination* (1940); *Being and Nothingness* (1943); *Critique of Dialectical Reason*, 2 vols (1960, 1985)

Kurt Gödel 1906–78
Collected Works (1986–)

Nelson Goodman 1906–98
The Structure of Appearance (1951); *Fact, Fiction and Forecast* (1954); *The Languages of Art* (1968); *Ways of World-Making* (1978)

Leopold Senghor 1906–2001
Liberté (1964)

Herbert Lionel Adolphus Hart 1907–92
Causation in the Law (with Honoré, 1959); *The Concept of Law* (1961); *Essays on Bentham: Studies in Jurisprudence and Political Theory* (1982)

Simone de Beauvoir 1908–86
The Second Sex (1949)

Claude Lévi-Strauss 1908–
Structural Anthropology (1958); *The Savage Mind* (1962)

Maurice Merleau-Ponty 1908–61
Phenomenology of Perception (1945); *The Adventures of the Dialectic* (1955); *Signs* (1960); *The Visible and the Invisible* (1964)

Willard Van Orman Quine 1908–2000
From A Logical Point of View (1953); *Word and Object* (1960); *Set Theory and its Logic* (1963); *The Ways of Paradox* (1966); *Ontological Relativity* (1969); *The Roots of Reference* (1974); *Theories and Things* (1981)

Isaiah Berlin 1909–97
Four Essays on Liberty (1969); *Vico and Herder: Two Essays in the History of Ideas* (1976); *Against the Current* (1980); *The Crooked Timber of Humanity: Chapters in the History of Human Ideas* (1991)

Alfred Jules Ayer 1910–89
Language, Truth and Logic (1936); *Foundations of Empirical Knowledge* (1940); *The Problem of Knowledge* (1954); *The Central Questions of Philosophy* (1973)

John Langshaw Austin 1911–60
How to Do Things with Words (1961); *Philosophical Papers* (1961); *Sense and Sensibilia* (1962)

Alan Turing 1912–54
Collected Works of A. M. Turing (1990)

Wilfred Sellars 1912–89
Science, Perception and Reality (1963); *Science and Metaphysics: Variations on Kantian Themes* (1968); *Naturalism and Ontology* (1980)

Herbert Paul Grice 1913–90
Studies in the Ways of Words (1989)

William Herbert Walsh 1913–96
An Introduction to Philosophy of History (1967)

Monroe Beardsley 1915–85
The Aesthetic Point of View (1982)

Donald Davidson 1917–
Essays on Actions and Events (1980); *Inquiries into Truth and Interpretation* (1984)

Louis Althusser 1918–90
For Marx (1965)

Gertrude Elizabeth Margaret Anscombe 1919–2001
Intention (1957); *An Introduction to Wittgenstein's Tractatus* (1959); *Collected Philosophical Papers*, 3 vols (1981)

Richard Mervyn Hare 1919–2002
The Language of Morals (1952); *Freedom and Reason* (1963); *Moral Thinking* (1981)

Peter Frederick Strawson 1919–
Introduction to Logical Theory (1952); *Individuals* (1959); *The Bounds of Sense* (1966); *Logico-Linguistic Papers* (1971); *Freedom and Resentment* (1974); *Subject and Predicate in Logic and Grammar* (1974); *Skepticism and Naturalism: Some Varieties* (1985); *Analysis and Metaphysics* (1992)

Philippa Foot 1920–
Virtues and Vices (1978)

John Jamieson Carswell Smart 1920–
Philosophy and Scientific Realism (1963); *Essays Metaphysical and Moral* (1987); *Our Place in the Universe* (1989)

William Alston 1921–
Divine Nature and Human Language (1989); *Epistemic Justification* (1989); *Perceiving God* (1991)

William Dray 1921–
Laws and Explanation in History (1957); *Perspectives on History* (1980)

John Rawls 1921–
A Theory of Justice (1971); *Political Liberalism* (1993); *The Law of Peoples* (1999); *Collected Papers* (1999)

Thomas Kuhn 1922–97
The Copernican Revolution (1957); *The Structure of Scientific Revolutions* (1962); *The Essential Tension* (1977)

John Hick 1922–
Faith and Knowledge (1957); *Evil and the God of Love* (1966); *Philosophy of Religion* (1966)

Paul Feyerabend 1924–94
Against Method (1974); *Philosophical Papers*, 2 vols (1981)

Arthur Danto 1924–
Analytic Philosophy of History (1965); *Analytic Philosophy of Action* (1973); *The Transfiguration of the Commonplace* (1981)

Michael Dummett 1925–
Frege: Philosophy of Language (1973); *Truth and Other Enigmas* (1978); *The Logical Basis of Metaphysics* (1991); *Origins of Analytic Philosophy* (1993)

Michel Foucault 1926–84
Madness and Civilisation (1961); *The Order of Things: An Archaeology of the Human Sciences* (1966); *The Archaeology of Knowledge* (1969); *Discipline and Punish* (1975); *The History of Sexuality I–III* (1976–84)

David Armstrong 1926–
A Materialist Theory of Mind (1968); *Universals and Scientific Realism* (1978)

Hilary Putnam 1926–
Mathematics, Matter and Method (1975); *Mind, Language and Reality* (1975); *Realism and Reason* (1983); *Representation and Reality* (1988)

Noam Chomsky 1928–
Syntactic Structures (1957); *Cartesian Linguistics* (1966); *Knowledge of Language* (1986); *Deterring Democracy* (1992); *Language and Thought* (1993), *The Minimalist Program* (1995)

Jürgen Habermas 1929–
Knowledge and Human Interests (1968); *The Theory of Communicative Action*, 2 vols (1981); *The Philosophical Discourse of Modernity* (1985)

Alasdair MacIntyre 1929–
A Short History of Ethics (1966); *After Virtue* (1981); *Whose Justice? Which Rationality?* (1988); *Three Rival Versions of Moral Enquiry* (1990)

Bernard Williams 1929–
Problems of the Self (1973); *Descartes: The Project of Pure Enquiry* (1978); *Moral Luck* (1981); *Ethics and the Limits of Philosophy* (1985); *Shame and Necessity* (1993); *Making Sense of Humanity* (1995)

Jacques Derrida 1930–
Speech and Phenomena (1967); *Of Grammatology* (1967); *Writing and Difference* (1967); *Margins of Philosophy* (1972); *Positions* (1972); *The Gift of Death* (1995)

Ronald Dworkin 1931–
Taking Rights Seriously (1977); *A Matter of Principle* (1985); *Law's Empire* (1986)

Richard Rorty 1931–
Philosophy and the Mirror of Nature (1979); *Consequences of Pragmatism* (1982); *Contingency, Irony, and Solidarity* (1989); *Objectivity, Relativism, and Truth* (1991)

Charles Taylor 1931–
The Explanation of Behaviour (1964); *Hegel* (1975); *Philosophical Papers*, 2 vols (1985); *Sources of the Self* (1989); *The Ethics of Authenticity* (1991); *Multiculturalism and the Politics of Recognition* (1992)

Luce Irigaray 1932–
Speculum of the Other Woman (1974); *Je, Tu, Nous: Towards a Culture of Difference* (1990)

Alvin Plantinga 1932–
God and Other Minds (1967); *The Nature of Necessity* (1974)

John Searle 1932–
Speech Acts (1969); *Intentionality* (1983); *The Rediscovery of the Mind* (1992); *The Construction of Social Reality* (1995)

Richard Wollheim 1932–
Art and Its Objects (1968); *The Thread of Life* (1984); *The Mind and its Depths* (1993)

Jerry Fodor 1935–
The Language of Thought (1975); *The Modularity of Mind* (1983); *Psychosemantics* (1987); *A Theory of Content and Other Essays* (1990); *Holism: A Shopper's Guide* (with Lapore, 1992)

Michael Walzer 1935–
Spheres of Justice (1983)

Thomas Nagel 1937–
The Possibility of Altruism (1970); *Mortal Questions* (1979); *The View from Nowhere* (1986)

Robert Nozick 1938–2002
Anarchy, State and Utopia (1974); *Philosophical Explanations* (1981); *The Nature of Rationality* (1993); *Invariance: The Structure of the Objective World* (2001)

Joseph Raz 1939–
Practical Reason and Norms (1975); *The Authority of Law* (1979); *The Concept of a Legal System* (1980); *The Morality of Freedom* (1986)

Saul Kripke 1940–
Naming and Necessity (1980); *Wittgenstein on Rules and Private Language* (1982)

David Lewis 1941–2002
Convention (1969); *Counterfactuals* (1973); *Philosophical Papers* (1983–7); *On the Plurality of Worlds* (1986)

Gerald Alan Cohen 1941–
Karl Marx's Theory of History: A Defense (1978); *History, Labour and Freedom: Themes from Marx* (1988)

Daniel Dennett 1942–
Content and Consciousness (1969); *Brainstorms* (1978); *The Intentional Stance* (1987); *Consciousness Explained* (1991)

Gareth Evans 1946–80
The Varieties of Reference (1982); *Collected Papers* (1985)

Peter Singer 1946–
Animal Liberation (1975); *Practical Ethics* (1979); *Rethinking Life and Death* (1995)

Michele le Doeuff 1948–
Hipparchia's Choice: Essays Concerning Women and Philosophy (1990)

Index